Substance Use Disorders

A Biopsychosocial Perspective

CW00959207

This textbook surveys the current knowledge on substance use disorders (SUD), summarizing scientific evidence from numerous fields. It uses a biopsychosocial framework to integrate the many factors that contribute to addictions, from genetic predispositions, neurological responses caused by drugs, co-occurring psychiatric disorders, personality traits, and developmental conditions to cultural influences. Real-life vignettes and first-person accounts build understanding of the lived experience of addiction. The currently accepted practices for diagnosis and treatment are presented, including the role of 12-step programs and other mutual-assistance groups. The text also investigates the research methods that form the foundation of evidence-based knowledge. The main body text is augmented by study guideposts, such as learning objectives, review exercises, highlighted key terms, and chapter summaries, which enable more efficient comprehension and retention of the book's material.

Perry M. Duncan is Emeritus Professor in the Department of Psychology at Old Dominion University, USA. There, he has taught courses in behavioral neuroscience, psychopharmacology, and substance use disorders to undergraduate and graduate students for forty years.

Substance Use Disorders

A Biopsychosocial Perspective

Perry M. Duncan

Old Dominion University

CAMBRIDGE
UNIVERSITY PRESS

University Printing House, Cambridge CB2 8BS, United Kingdom

One Liberty Plaza, 20th Floor, New York, NY 10006, USA

477 Williamstown Road, Port Melbourne, VIC 3207, Australia

314–321, 3rd Floor, Plot 3, Splendor Forum, Jasola District Centre, New Delhi – 110025, India

79 Anson Road, #06–04/06, Singapore 079906

Cambridge University Press is part of the University of Cambridge.

It furthers the University's mission by disseminating knowledge in the pursuit of education, learning, and research at the highest international levels of excellence.

www.cambridge.org
Information on this title: www.cambridge.org/9780521877770
DOI: 10.1017/9781139025515

© Perry M. Duncan 2021

This publication is in copyright. Subject to statutory exception and to the provisions of relevant collective licensing agreements, no reproduction of any part may take place without the written permission of Cambridge University Press.

First published 2021

Printed in the United Kingdom by TJ International Ltd, Padstow Cornwall 2021

A catalogue record for this publication is available from the British Library.

Library of Congress Cataloging-in-Publication Data
Names: Duncan, Perry Marshall, 1939– author.
Title: Substance use disorders : a biopsychosocial perspective / Perry Marshall Duncan, Old Dominion University, Virginia.
Description: Cambridge, United Kingdom ; New York, NY : Cambridge University Press, 2021. | Includes bibliographical references and index.
Identifiers: LCCN 2020010907 (print) | LCCN 2020010908 (ebook) | ISBN 9780521877770 (hardback) | ISBN 9781139025515 (ebook)
Subjects: LCSH: Substance abuse – Textbooks. | Drug addiction – Textbooks.
Classification: LCC RC564 .D87 2021 (print) | LCC RC564 (ebook) | DDC 362.29–dc23
LC record available at https://lccn.loc.gov/2020010907
LC ebook record available at https://lccn.loc.gov/2020010908

ISBN 978-0-521-87777-0 Hardback
ISBN 978-1-108-81909-1 Paperback

Cambridge University Press has no responsibility for the persistence or accuracy of URLs for external or third-party internet websites referred to in this publication and does not guarantee that any content on such websites is, or will remain, accurate or appropriate.

To Nancy, my life partner and colleague, with much love

Brief Contents

Contents

x   Contents

Figures

Tables

Boxes

Preface

Substance use disorders (SUD) are a serious problem for public health and safety and one of the most prevalent psychiatric disorders. Opioid overdose ended the lives of 47,600 individuals in the United States in 2017. However, 88,000 died from alcohol-related causes, and the leading preventable cause of death was tobacco use – which contributed to 480,000 fatalities, including 41,000 from passive exposure to "secondhand smoke." Opioid overdose causes death within minutes or hours, but the delayed effects of chronic alcohol and tobacco use result in many more fatalities. With the exception of tobacco and illicit opioids, only a minority of those who use addictive substances develop a use disorder (an SUD), but many individuals who are not addicted experience adverse consequences from drug use.

A large amount of information exists about the origins, the course of development, and outcomes of drug abuse and addiction – based on years of extensive scientific investigation, clinical reports, and first-person accounts of problematic drug use. In my years of teaching courses on psychopharmacology and SUD, I found that many students appreciate receiving evidence-based knowledge about drug effects, the misuse of drugs, and addiction, especially when so much information of doubtful validity is prevalent in the popular culture.

This book presents a summary of current knowledge about substance use disorders that will be useful for anyone interested in learning about this important subject. The information will be especially valuable to students intending to pursue a career in scientific investigation or treatment of SUD.

Education about addiction – especially concerning the risk factors for, origins of, and consequences of the disorder – is often neglected in the training of counselors, social workers, clinical psychologists, and even medical doctors (including psychiatrists). Therefore, information provided in this book can be of use to individuals currently providing these services. Although only two chapters deal directly with clinical topics (diagnosis, treatment), information in all chapters will also be helpful to health care professionals. Most people with SUD never enter treatment for their harmful drug use but often seek assistance from medical or mental health professionals for related issues, such as anxiety or other problems. Knowledge of SUD will also be of value to many other individuals who will come into contact – perhaps at a personal level – with these widespread disorders.

SUDs arise from combinations of several sources: genetic and neurological factors, early-life and later experiences, psychiatric syndromes, and cultural influences – all interacting with the pharmacological actions of psychoactive drugs.

Because of the multiple causes, the behavioral disorders of substance abuse and addiction are best described as *biopsychosocial* in nature.

A disease theory of SUD is widely accepted and is supported primarily by the biological (genetic and neurological) aspects of addiction. Although there are definite limitations to the generality of a disease-based theory of SUD, this explanation of the self-destructive behavior has value for the treatment and recovery of afflicted individuals.

In this book, I describe how a cognitive behavioral explanation – although often rejected by proponents of conventional disease theory – is actually compatible with most parts of disease theory when SUDs are seen as biopsychosocial in nature. Cognitive processes, including learning and conditioning, are of special importance for the less severe, but more prevalent, forms of the disorder. I also explain how 12-step tactics for maintaining recovery (a major part of the many Minnesota-Model addiction treatment programs) share some features with cognitive behavioral treatment procedures – although the similarity is rarely acknowledged.

Three important topics of research on addictive disorders that sometimes receive little attention in discussions of SUD are given extensive coverage here: tobacco use and nicotine addiction; the role of craving in addiction and relapse; and the significant influence of co-occurring psychiatric disorders that so often accompany addiction. I summarize much of the large body of research-based information related to these aspects of SUD.

Harmful and compulsive use of alcohol and other addictive drugs has plagued humanity for many centuries, and scientific investigations of the problem began in the twentieth century. I include a very brief account of recent history of the use and misuse of each addictive substance. Some lessons have been learned – although several seem to have been forgotten. I also describe some important recent SUD-related discoveries, especially from the areas of genetics, brain function, and the biological basis of drug effects and addiction. The current state of knowledge is better appreciated with some understanding of the gradual process of scientific advancement.

Each chapter starts with a fictional vignette, previewing and illustrating some basic features of SUD discussed in that chapter.

Acknowledgments

My wife, Dr. Nancy Duncan, greatly contributed to all stages of creation of this book. She helped clarify my thinking and writing on many aspects of substance use disorders and identified points that I had omitted or not adequately explained. Having another professor of biological psychology as an in-house editor and a major contributor was a definite advantage. Thank you, Nancy, for years of commitment to this long-term project!

I also benefited from discussions with students in my classes on psychopharmacology and substance use disorders, especially those in the Professional Psychology Consortium Program of Old Dominion University, Eastern Virginia Medical School, and William and Mary University. These graduate students in a clinical doctoral program read and commented on early versions of several chapters. Other students at Old Dominion University, including some in recovery from SUD, also shared their relevant experience, which informed my writing of this book.

I appreciate the support, guidance, and patience of several editors and other personnel at Cambridge University Press.

Organization of the Book

Chapter 1 introduces the biopsychosocial concept of substance use disorders and describes research methods used to investigate substance use disorders (SUD).

Chapter 2 describes the diagnosis of SUD, including use of diagnostic criteria listed in the *Diagnostic and Statistical Manual of Mental Disorders* published by the American Psychiatric Association.

Chapter 3 presents the disease theory of addiction, including the benefits and limitations of this explanation of the disorder.

Chapters 4 and 5 present basic information from neuroscience relevant to SUD. Chapter 4 summarizes psychopharmacological principles of how psychoactive drugs affect brain function. Chapter 5 describes current theories of how drug-produced changes in brain function contribute to addiction.

Chapters 6, 7, and 8 present findings about the causes of and risk factors related to SUD. These origins of the disorder include abnormal brain function, genetic factors, psychiatric and developmental factors, and processes, such as reinforcement, learning, and inhibition, that control behavior in general and also give rise to compulsive drug use. Chapters 5 through 8 identify the essential components of a biopsychosocial explanation of SUD.

Chapter 9 describes the harmful effects of alcohol, a drug with widespread use in many cultures. Although alcohol has moderate addictive potential, its heavy use damages and shortens the lives of many who are not addicted.

Chapters 10 through 15 describe SUD for specific drugs of abuse, including risk factors, the course of the disorder, and adverse consequences.

Chapter 16 describes how many individuals suffering from SUD stop compulsive and destructive drug use, either with or without the assistance of health care professionals.

PART I
Identifying the Causes and Consequences of Disordered Substance Use

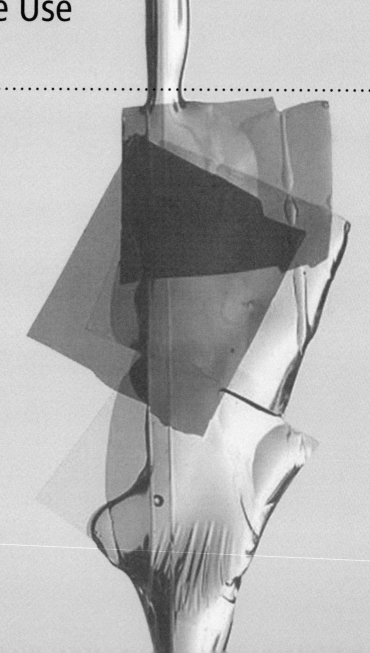

PART I

Identifying the Causes and Consequences of Disordered Substance Use

1

The Biopsychosocial Perspective and Research Methods for Investigation of Substance Use Disorders

LEARNING OBJECTIVES

1. Describe the incentives for and the hazards of using psychoactive drugs.
2. Describe how substance use disorders are identified in the DSM diagnostic system.
3. Describe the characteristics of and problems resulting from the addictive lifestyle.
4. Explain why it is difficult to identify the causes of substance use disorders (SUD).
5. Explain why simple observation is an unsatisfactory method of studying SUD.
6. List and describe each of the scientific methods of studying SUD.
7. Describe the biopsychosocial explanation of SUD.

Introductory Vignette: Losing a Good Team Member

Billy, a key player on the university basketball team, overdosed on heroin in late summer, before preseason practice and urine screens started. Prompt injection of Narcan saved his life, but he is off the team and suspended from the university. The team captain is trying to establish how this shocking event could have happened. He talks with two senior team members:

TEAM CAPTAIN: Billy's heroin overdose was a surprise – at least for me and the coach. The coach asked me if the team knew that Billy was using heroin – addicted, I guess – and if anybody knows why.

FIRST TEAM MEMBER: I realize now that I missed some things about Billy, but at the time I didn't suspect anything like using drugs. We used to be real close, but he didn't talk much anymore – seemed sort of down and mostly stayed away from all of us. Sometimes, though, he did have what you might call mood swings. I think he was worried about keeping his grades up this year, even with all the help we get for our classes. He was drinking hard too, sometimes getting into fights for no good reason. He managed to keep that stuff hidden from most of us. I knew more than the others, but sometimes he lied even to me. I couldn't understand why he did that.

SECOND TEAM MEMBER: I know he had a rough time when he was a kid. His dad drank a lot, and his mother pretty much abandoned him and his brother. He got into running with a low-life crowd, until he started playing basketball in high school. I thought he had come out of a bad situation pretty well. Then this summer he went back to his hometown in the mountains. I know there's a lot of oxycodone, heroin, and fentanyl on the streets there. I'm pretty sure his brother is a heroin addict.

TEAM CAPTAIN: I didn't know most of these things about Billy. I did notice that his playing wasn't as good in the last couple of games last year. And – I knew the doc gave him some pain pills after he got hurt, but I thought he had recovered okay. Several of us – including me – took oxycodone for a few days after an injury. As far as I know, none of us had trouble stopping taking it when we were ready to play again. Billy had a lot of potential, but it looks like there were some things that messed up his head, and then he made some really bad moves about using smack. I sure wish we could have seen how much trouble he was in and could have helped him.

Use and Misuse of Psychoactive Drugs

Psychoactive drug use presents a major worldwide threat to public health and safety (Degenhart and Hall 2012, World Health Organization 2008). Drug use is not always harmful, but for many individuals, use disorders of psychoactive drugs disrupt normal life activities and cause or contribute to health or living problems.

   Two prominent addiction researchers, William Miller and Kathleen Carroll, acknowledge the breadth and complexity of drug use, including its origins and adverse consequences:

> It became obvious that the behavior of drug use is not isolated, but is intimately intertwined with a range of common, long-standing human issues and societal problems.... In some ways, the central issues of this field represent a microcosm of classic human dilemmas: why we persist in patterns of behavior that clearly lead to devastating consequences. (Miller and Carroll 2006, p. 12)

Some with difficulties related to drug use seek assistance from general medical practitioners or mental health providers. However, because **harmful consequences** of drug use are commonly entangled with other life problems, there is often an inability or refusal to recognize a major source of the medical problem or life difficulty. As a highly visible example, the singer Amy Winehouse experienced a combination of emotional and behavioral problems – including extreme abuse of drugs – before she succumbed to a fatal alcohol overdose at age twenty-seven. The drug-related problems of entertainers and other celebrities are often widely publicized. However, for most people, the tragic consequences of drug use are known only to close friends or relatives. In 2017, more than 70,000 Americans died as a result of unintentional drug overdose (Scholl et al. 2019).

Because alcohol, nicotine, cocaine, opioids, and other psychoactive drugs provide desirable effects, their use is widespread and frequent in many nations and cultures. In the United States, the National Survey on Drug Use and Health (NSDUH) for the year 2017 indicated that 51.7 percent of people age twelve or older drank alcohol, 22.4 percent used a tobacco product, and 11.2 percent used an illicit drug within the month before the survey (Substance Abuse and Mental Health Services Administration 2018). The prevalence of use varies with the age of the respondents, with young adults (ages eighteen to twenty-five) reporting the highest use rates. Illicit drug use includes cannabis and other drugs as well as nonmedical use of stimulants and opioid pain relievers.

Incentives for Use of Psychoactive Drugs

Psychoactive drugs – which alter subjective experience and behavior – have been used for various purposes since ancient times. Drug effects seen as beneficial and desirable include those that (1) are utilitarian, (2) are medical (distress relieving), (3) produce altered states of consciousness, or (4) are simply pleasurable. Utilitarian effects include increased concentration and vigilance or facilitation of relaxation and sleep, as produced by caffeine and alcohol. The use of opioid drugs for relief of pain and the accompanying emotional distress are perhaps the clearest example of the medical use of psychoactive drugs. Utilitarian, medical, and pleasurable effects of drugs are the most frequent incentives for regular drug use, which in some individuals can lead to heavy **compulsive use** and dangerous consequences. These motivations for drug use are discussed in the subsequent drug-specific chapters.

Many individuals – especially adolescents and other young people – enjoy experiencing novel altered states of consciousness, an effect provided by psychoactive drugs as well as by some other experiences not related to drug use. The attraction to new and different states of thinking, feeling, and perceiving the world can encourage experimentation with drugs, which in some cases is followed by regular, excessive, and harmful drug use. Although such tentative use of drugs does present some risk of eventual drug use problems, most who sample the novel effects of psychoactive drugs do not progress into persistent and dangerous substance use.

Psychoactive drug effects are often experienced as pleasurable because they increase enjoyment of other human activities, such as recreation and play, consumption of food, appreciation of music and art, spiritual experiences, and especially social interaction (including intimacy and sex) (Figure 1.1). Pleasurable effects also often accompany other incentives for drug use. For example, opioid drugs might produce pleasure as well as relieving pain. A stimulant (amphetamine or caffeine) can promote a positive mood change as well as enabling sustained work performance.

Figure 1.1 Alcohol can enhance the pleasure of good times with friends. Photo: SolStock / E+ / Getty Images.

However, drugs can also produce pleasurable feelings different from or more profound than most other enjoyable human experiences. Such drug effects can be very intense with initial use – such as the "rush" produced by injection or inhalation of stimulant or opioid drugs (e.g., cocaine or heroin). This brief, intensely rewarding feeling is sometimes described as similar to sexual orgasm – but without the intimate human contact that can be a part of sexual activity. The vivid euphoria of injected or inhaled drugs can be especially alluring and dangerous, often gaining control of behavior and promoting compulsive drug use. Positive reinforcement produced by addictive drugs is discussed extensively in Chapters 4 and 7.

Hazards of Psychoactive Drug Use

As with many other useful and pleasurable activities ranging from consumption of food through contact athletic sports to driving automobiles, psychoactive drug use can result in harmful consequences. Hazards include personal losses leading to a greatly diminished life, biological toxicity, and premature death – due to fatal overdose or other causes related to drug use. Painful or dangerous consequences typically result from overindulgence (frequent or high-dose drug use) and use in inappropriate situations – such as consuming alcohol or cannabis prior to driving. Unfortunately, for many individuals, patterns of chronic dangerous high-dose use emerge and become quite resistant to change.

Substance Use Disorders

Persistent drug use that significantly damages or threatens a safe and healthy life is designated as a **substance use disorder (SUD),** the causes and consequences of which are the subject of this book (Figure 1.2). Not all users of psychoactive drugs suffer harm from drug use, but the NSDUH indicated that in the United States, 5.3 percent of the adolescent and adult population (14.5 million individuals) had an alcohol use disorder in 2017, and 2.8 percent (7.5 million individuals) had a use disorder for illicit drugs or therapeutic psychoactive drugs. Alcohol use disorder was about twice as prevalent as disordered use of illicit drugs, although 2.3 million individuals had both types of substance use disorder. Many additional individuals experience drug-related problems that are less severe than a diagnosable SUD but make their lives more difficult. Table 1.1 presents NSDUH estimates of the extent of drug and drug-containing substance use and misuse and substance use disorders in the United States. Demographics of drug use and SUD are described in the

Figure 1.2 Heavy and persistent alcohol use can cause isolation and depression. Photo: Rafael Ben-Ari / Photodisc / Getty Images.

subsequent drug-specific chapters. However, age and gender are the most predic-tive demographic variables for drug use and misuse, with prevalence consistently highest for men of ages eighteen to twenty-five.

Table 1.1 Use, misuse, and use disorders of addictive psychoactive drugs: Percentage of adult and adolescent population in the United States

Drug or substance	Current users[a]	SUD[b]
Licit substances		
Alcohol	51.7%	5.3%
Tobacco	22.4%[c]	12.1%
Illicit substances		
Cannabis[d]	9.6%	1.5%
Cocaine	0.8%	0.4%
Methamphetamine	0.3%	0.4%[e]
Heroin/fentanyl	0.2%	0.2%[e]
Misuse of therapeutic psychoactive drugs used in medical practice[f]		
Opioid Analgesics	1.2%	0.6%
Stimulants	0.7%	0.2%
Tranquilizers	0.7%	0.3%
Sedatives	0.1%	–

Note. Estimates are for percentage of US population of age twelve years or older as reported by the NSDUH (Substance Abuse and Mental Health Services Administration 2018).

[a] Current use indicates use during the month of the survey. [b] SUD prevalence indicates occurrence of the disorder during the twelve months prior to the survey. [c] Seventy-eight percent of current tobacco users smoke cigarettes. [d] Cannabis use is prohibited by federal law, although medical and recreational use is not prohibited by the statutes of several states. [e] Some individuals with SUD for methamphetamine or heroin did not use the drug in the month of the survey. Use prevalence for all drugs during previous year was higher than current use level. [f] Current use entries for therapeutic drugs indicate misuse prevalence (use not prescribed by a medical professional). Pharmaceutical stimulants include d-amphetamine (Adderall) and methylphenidate (Ritalin). Tranquilizers include benzodiazepines (Valium and similar drugs). Opioid analgesics include hydrocodone (Vicodin), oxycodone (OxyContin), and similar drugs. Survey results did not include SUD prevalence for sedative drugs (barbiturates or similar drugs).

Identification and Diagnoses

The American Psychiatric Association publishes the *Diagnostic and Statistical Manual of Mental Disorders* (referred to as the DSM), a widely accepted system for identifying substance use disorders (SUD). Since its origin in 1952, the DSM has been revised five times, with the latest revision (DSM-5) published in 2013. The large amount of clinical information collected prior to 2013 and reported in scientific journals used DSM-IV or earlier terminology. In both versions of the DSM, the presence of **diagnostic criteria** – damaging consequences of drug use, and difficulty of controlling that use – determine the diagnosis of SUD.

Mild cases of SUD involve various harmful consequences of drug use – such as relationship problems, reckless driving or accidents, and poor work or academic performance – that often resemble antisocial behavior or other problems not directly related to intoxication. As a result, these less intense levels of the disorder may be difficult to identify as a psychiatric syndrome. In the DSM-IV, such less severe cases were designated as **substance abuse**.

At moderate and severe levels of SUD (designated as **substance dependence** in the DSM-IV), damaging consequences worsen and are more frequent and persistent, but despite these harmful outcomes, drug use continues and becomes compulsive. The priorities of afflicted individuals often narrow to obtaining and using the drug, with neglect of other interests and obligations. An emotional relationship with the drug makes stopping or even reducing its use very difficult or seemingly impossible without outside intervention.

Although the terminology and specific diagnostic criteria for SUD listed in DSM-5 are somewhat different from those of the DSM-IV, the behavior and symptoms of substance use disorders are essentially the same as in earlier years. The number of DSM-5 diagnostic criteria seen in an individual indicates whether the SUD is mild, moderate, or severe.

The terms *abuse* and *dependence* are no longer official designations of SUD in the DSM-5. Severe cases of the disorder are unofficially but widely referred to as addiction. DSM-5 designation of SUD is further discussed in Chapter 2, and treatment and recovery are discussed in Chapter 16.

Physiological or Psychological?

A question often arises regarding whether an addiction is "physiological" or merely "psychological" – implying that there are two distinct disorders, which is an invalid assumption. This supposed difference in addictions typically refers to the presence or nature of a withdrawal syndrome – which for opioid drugs includes overt symptoms of vomiting and diarrhea and for alcohol can produce life-threatening seizures. A "merely psychological" addiction is often incorrectly seen as less serious – similar to a bad habit and perhaps not even qualifying as an actual psychiatric disorder. However, an overt withdrawal syndrome is not a critical feature of addiction and is neither necessary nor sufficient for diagnosis of a severe SUD. As discussed in Chapter 2, compulsive (addictive) drug use can occur without an overt withdrawal syndrome. Furthermore, with medical use of opioid drugs, withdrawal symptoms are common – often in the absence of addictive behavior.

The **process addictions** – compulsive behaviors that do not involve drug use but are extremely difficult to control – provide further evidence that an overt physiological withdrawal syndrome is not a critical component of addictive behavior. The DSM-5 lists a gambling disorder and the eating disorder bulimia nervosa as compulsive addictions. Other behaviors, including sexual activity, shopping, and internet use can also become excessive and compulsive, causing heavy losses and life disruption. The inability to control these behaviors, coupled with the harmful consequences, differentiates these disorders from the "bad habits" previously mentioned. As with SUD, such deviant behavior comes from both psychological and physiological factors – as discussed at length in Chapters 5 and 7.

Addictive Lifestyles

Some with severe addiction live chaotic lives, with little or no attempt to hide or explain their extreme behavior, except to avoid attracting the attention of law enforcement officials when drug use is illicit. Such individuals are likely to exist in a subculture of heavy drug users, as described in Nic Sheff's *Tweak: Growing Up on Methamphetamines* (Sheff 2008). However, many addicts carefully maintain the facade of a normal life, expending extraordinary effort to conceal their heavy drug use and to provide acceptable explanations for the resultant behaviors that cannot be hidden. This addictive lifestyle eventually exerts heavy demands on energy, self-esteem, and relationships. These demands are mingled with the direct effects of frequent intoxication, making the addict's life very stressful, and eventually – in the terminology of twelve-step (e.g., Alcoholics Anonymous and Narcotics Anonymous) groups – life becomes unmanageable.

For some, heavy drug use results in arguments, fights, and other dangerous or embarrassing actions. Other adverse consequences include paranoia, depression, and anxiety, which can develop during or as a delayed effect of intoxication. These effects may be obvious only to those near the drug user, including family members and close friends. Inconsistent behavior, failure to meet obligations, unexplained absences, mood swings, and emotional volatility are also characteristic of heavy drug users and often require explanations to coworkers, supervisors, and others.

Many addicts have much practice – and so become very proficient – at concealing their drug use and evading responsibility for erratic behavior. Such evasion typically requires ongoing dishonesty. In David Carr's account of his cocaine addiction, *Night of the Gun*, he describes the "montage of deceit" he used to prevent others from getting too close and seeing the hidden parts of his life (Carr 2008). Caroline Knapp, in her autobiographical *Drinking: A Love Story*, tells a similar story of continued deception of coworkers and family. Knapp recounts a "double life" of heavy alcohol use each evening and during the day, followed by severe hangovers – while with great effort maintaining the appearance of a normal life by continuing to work as a journalist. Although she came to her office daily, poor work performance and social withdrawal required the fabrication of many elaborate excuses (Knapp 1996).

Secrecy and deception can be effective in hiding heavy drug use and disguising its consequences, and as addiction progresses, use of the drug becomes increasingly important and dominant, as do the methods of concealment. Unfortunately, for many addicts, these tactics of isolation and dishonesty generalize to life in general – even to matters not closely related to excessive and harmful drug use (Kinney 2009).

An addictive lifestyle commonly results in loss of close, supportive relationships. Family members and close friends may witness disturbing bouts of drug use and withdraw from contact with the addict. Even those who cannot actually leave, or who choose to remain near the addict for various reasons (children, parents, partners, longtime friends, etc.), are likely to become emotionally distant. Secrecy, obvious or suspected falsehoods, and erratic behavior may also harm relations with those who do not actually see the drug use. The damage to relationships can also come from perceiving the priorities of the addict – as the addict places greater value on drug use than on close, drug-free interaction with a partner, child, or close friend. Perhaps even more damaging to close relationships is the repeated use of a friend or family member to evade responsibility for drug-related difficulty. The friend may be asked to corroborate bogus excuses for work absences. Worse yet, a spouse or partner may be falsely blamed or manipulated into taking responsibility for the problem. The lack of openness (secrecy), the dishonesty, and the manipulation are very corrosive to relationships – causing isolation and a loss of support that promotes the progression of addiction (further described in Chapter 7).

In summary, addicts typically attempt to hide their drug use and its consequences by being secretive and dishonest – often blaming others for their shortcomings and problem behaviors. As others withdraw support and avoid contact, the addict becomes isolated. Disordered drug use greatly reduces the pleasures originally enhanced by drugs – especially enjoyable and close social contact. Addictive behavior interferes with all aspects of an individual's life, including physical and mental health, emotional well-being, relationships, education, and employment.

Dishonesty and manipulation of others often emerge in individuals with severe SUD, including those who, prior to heavy drug use, did not display these undesirable characteristics. Such behavior typically improves with recovery from the disorder. For those with antisocial personality disorder, the negative characteristics precede SUD and may persist even after recovery from addiction. Manipulation, dishonesty, and disregard of other people's welfare are primary characteristics of antisocial personality disorder, a behavior pattern that is a definite risk factor for SUD (Chapter 8).

Addiction to drugs that do not cause intoxication, and whose behavioral effects are subtle, is unlikely to result in the addictive lifestyle described here. Nicotine is the best example of a highly addictive licit drug with fewer disturbing behavioral effects that must be hidden or excused – although the current reduction in cultural acceptance of tobacco use can cause some difficulties for nicotine-dependent users. A somewhat similar example is the legitimate medical management of opioid addiction by means of methadone or buprenorphine maintenance. These opioids can produce intoxication and addiction, but when the medications are used appropriately, behavioral effects are minimal. Although still drug dependent, the individual need not adopt the problematic addictive lifestyle.

Identifying Causes and Consequences of Substance Use Disorders

Some individuals are especially vulnerable to developing SUD. With most addictive drugs, use disorders develop in only a minority of those who choose to consume the substance. Tobacco use seems to be an exception to this generalization in that at least half of regular users become addicted to nicotine (Chapter 11). However, some users of even highly addictive tobacco do not become nicotine dependent. Cocaine, heroin, and some other addictive drugs are not generally available other than from illicit sources – a factor that limits the prevalence of their use. If such drugs were legal commodities, as are tobacco and alcoholic beverages, their addictive use would be much more prevalent. However, even if their purchase were safe, convenient, and legal, many users would not become addicted to these dangerous illicit drugs. Identification of the factors underlying these differences in vulnerability is essential to understanding the causes of addiction and of less severe forms of SUD.

In addition to identifying the causes of SUD, determining the consequences of drug use is important. Potential threats to public health and safety are concurrent with even the generally acceptable and often beneficial uses of psychoactive drugs. A definite threat is the possibility of addiction or a less severe form of disordered drug use. Another possible outcome is death, as with fatal opioid or alcohol overdose, in which the immediate consequence is obvious or confirmed by postmortem medical examination. However, with less extreme consequences – such as domestic arguments, academic failure, or criminal activity – drug use might be suspected as a possible cause among many other contributing factors. Both the causes and the consequences of disordered drug use are intermingled with the complex array of influences and events that are part of all lives.

Certain identification of the causes, as well as some of the consequences, of SUD is hampered by at least three features of the disorder. The first and perhaps foremost problem comprises the **multiple causes** – ranging from biological/genetic through developmental to social/cultural – that contribute to excessive drug use. This multivariate nature of SUD etiology is also characteristic of most psychiatric disorders and many other behavioral problems, as well as of influences on the course of life in general.

Substance use disorders vary in intensity, a second feature that adds to the difficulty of identifying causal factors. Less severe cases of SUD often resemble nonpathological – if ill considered – use of addictive drugs. Such cases present a challenge for SUD diagnosis and for establishing causes for intermittent, moderately hazardous drug use. Causal factors for less extreme misuse of drugs may be indistinguishable from those that promote a wide range of life problems.

A third complicating feature comprises the many possible manifestations of SUD, both among users of different drugs (nicotine addiction, compared to alcohol use disorder), and among users of the same drug (individuals from all cultures and socioeconomic classes addicted to alcohol). This factor of differences among those with SUD resulted in a very inclusive list of diagnostic criteria found in the DSM-5 (as well as in earlier versions of the DSM). The wide range of symptoms indicating SUD is discussed further in Chapter 2.

Methods of Learning about Drug Effects and Substance Use Disorders

Knowledge about causes and consequences of SUD is gained by several different methods. Each of these methods has advantages as well as limitations or disadvantages.

Personal Experiences and Anecdotal Accounts

The most common method of learning about the consequences of psychoactive drug use is simple (nonscientific), everyday observation of drug-using individuals. When drug use is prevalent, there are unfortunately many opportunities to use this simple method. **Anecdotal information** about drug effects also accumulates, as accounts of the actions of intoxicated or addicted individuals become part of the "common knowledge" of a culture. Box 1.1 presents an anecdotal account (by a friend of the author) of the powerful control exerted by an addictive drug.

BOX 1.1 A story from the federal prison for addicts

Vernon was a former graduate student who became my friend, as well as a source of first-person stories about heroin addiction. A middle-aged jazz musician, he had been opioid-free for years after being addicted to heroin at an earlier time in his life. He had spent time as a patient/inmate in the federal prison/hospital that operated from the 1930s until the 1970s in Lexington, Kentucky (Musto 1999). Some residents of the facility were volunteers, but two-thirds were either convicted of drug use crimes or committed to the hospital as an alternative to imprisonment for drug-related offenses. Vernon sardonically referred to the Lexington facility as the "dope fiend prison." In addition to treatment regimens, the facility also conducted studies on the effects of opioid drugs. Many of the early studies involved administering drugs to prisoners, in some cases for extended periods, in order to observe withdrawal syndromes (Kosten and Gorelick 2002).

According to Vernon, subjects were recruited for these studies by offering prisoners a choice of incentives for their participation. They could choose to be released earlier – in some cases as much as a year – or as an alternative reward they could be given extended access to morphine when the study was concluded. Most prisoners (all of whom had histories of opioid use) initially opted for the earlier release. However, during the course of the research, these subjects were administered morphine, apparently rekindling their addictive attraction to the drug. At the conclusion of the study, many subjects changed from their earlier preference of early release – to the reward of receiving additional morphine. The shift in choice could be seen as an example of preference for immediate, compared to a delayed reward. However, it also demonstrates the power of an addictive drug to control behavior.

The Lexington prison/hospital is described more completely in Chapter 14.

Many accounts of addiction, such as Christopher Lawford's *Moments of Clarity*, feature dramatic, often poignant stories of devastated lives (Lawford 2009). Lawford also describes how addicts recover from severe SUD. Subjective descriptions, often presented as autobiographical accounts, of the course and consequences of addiction are widely available in books, magazines, and other forms of mass distribution, including the Internet and other media sources. Some of these stories are cited in the current chapter and excerpts are included in subsequent chapters to convey a sense of the first-person experience of excessive and disordered drug use. They provide often-harrowing accounts of addiction's progression as harmful consequences develop and worsen – as experienced by a specific individual. Although the stories may not be common to all those with addiction problems, they often have a "ring of truth" (face validity). These vivid descriptions of heavy drug use are often of limited value for identifying the initial *causes* of addiction – in part because of their subjective nature.

The harm inflicted by heavy drug use also gives rise to emotion-based biases for explaining the nature of the disorder – "alcoholics/addicts are bad, weak, dishonest people." Even though limited by doubtful validity and uncertain generality, assumptions about SUD based on direct observation are often very convincing to those who witness the problems associated with excessive substance use.

Law enforcement personnel, medical professionals (especially those working in emergency rooms), social workers, school counselors, and others who work to provide public health and safety routinely see and deal with criminal or dangerous behavior in drug-using, sometimes intoxicated individuals. However, most drug users do not encounter extreme difficulties or exhibit antisocial behavior. Mental illness, domestic violence, poor academic performance, and other conditions, situations, or events quite often accompany or precede the problems of distressed, endangered, or sometimes dangerous individuals. Drug use may contribute to, be a consequence of, or merely be correlated with the problematic behavior. Mental illness frequently co-occurs with heavy drug use, and the role of SUD in other psychiatric disorders is discussed in Chapter 8.

Simple observation of disordered substance use is even less satisfactory for determining the causes of SUD than for identifying the consequences of drug use. Similar complexities and variability – many possible causes and differences among individual cases – present difficulties for understanding how persistent and destructive drug use develops. The suspected causes are often not easily observable, and their actual influence is uncertain. Is the SUD a result of "bad character," a genetic predisposition, a difficult childhood, peer pressure, the rewarding effects of initial drug use, a brain abnormality – or a combination of these or other factors?

Direct observation of apparent consequences of drug use can be very convincing to the nonscientist and in many instances requires neither special effort nor expense. However, the *validity* and *generality* of the supposed drug effect are often in doubt. Simple observation also helps little with finding the *contributing causes* of an SUD. Systematic and controlled scientific observations are more certain indicators of the consequences of drug use and of how addiction develops, and they can provide evidence of causes contributing to the disorder.

Controlled Observations of Psychoactive Drug Effects

Controlled observations (experiments) are the optimal method for establishing cause–effect relations. For the science of psychopharmacology, the tentative cause is typically administration of a drug, and the observed effect is a difference in behavior, cognition, or, in some cases, subjective experience. Controlled experiments are very effective for determining drug effects when the conditions that might influence the outcome can be manipulated, held constant, or otherwise accounted for. Designs and procedures for controlled experiments can be simple or rather complex, but the overall strategy is isolation of the drug effect from other possible causal factors. Experimental designs typically include a placebo group to control for subjects' expectations of drug effects. Random assignment of subjects to drug or control conditions minimizes group differences not related to drug effects. Most psychopharmacology experiments are conducted in a laboratory setting, providing control of environmental factors. Investigations are sometimes conducted in a controlled setting intended to appear less artificial and more like the natural world. For example, in studies of alcohol effects, the subjects might consume alcoholic or placebo drinks in a room resembling a bar.

An example of an experiment on drug effects is a study in which nonsmokers were administered nicotine via a transdermal patch. The drug had mixed effects on cognitive performance, impairing tasks requiring attention and vigilance, but improving performance on other measures of cognition (Wignall and de Wit 2011). Another investigation demonstrated the effect of two variables on the behavior of social drinkers. Both experimental conditions – a moderate dose of alcohol and alcohol-related stimuli (pictures of beer cans or bottles) – resulted in decreased inhibition of inappropriate responses on a behavioral test. The disinhibition effect was greatest when the two factors were combined (Weafer and Fillmore 2015).

The subjective feelings resulting from drug use are of special interest for the study of addictive behavior, and standardized instruments (rating scales) have been developed to measure the experiential nature of drug effects. The Profile of Mood States (POMS) scale is often employed for this purpose (McNair et al. 1971). POMS scale responses indicate feelings of vigor, elation, friendliness, or other pleasant feelings or unpleasant states, including anxiety, fatigue, or confusion. Ilse Schrieks and colleagues conducted an investigation of the effects of alcohol consumption in conjunction with a meal served in a pleasant, compared to an unpleasant, ambiance on the mood of social drinkers (Schrieks et al. 2014). POMS scale responses indicated that a moderate dose of alcohol improved mood in the unpleasant environment but not in the pleasant ambiance – an outcome apparently related to the difference in baseline mood states. More recently developed measures of subjective states include the Drug Effects Questionnaire (Wignall and de Wit 2011).

During recent decades, very many controlled psychopharmacology studies have been conducted. Consequently, there are at least two methods of summarizing and integrating the large amount of research-based information. Systematic reviews summarize the results of many investigations of the effects of a drug, such as the influence of cannabis use on driving performance (Bondallaz et al. 2016). Another approach to integrating many similar studies is meta-analysis, a method of statistically combining the studies' results to determine the presence or size of a specific drug effect.

Controlled experiments are the most certain way to determine the behavioral effects of drugs, including how these effects change as drug dose increases. However, drug effects on some types of behavior cannot be investigated in a controlled setting. Intimate social interactions (including sexual activity and aggression) are examples of such behaviors, although researchers have made creative attempts to study how drugs influence similar behaviors, such as verbal or simulated aggression (Duke et al. 2013, Gallagher and Parrott 2011). Drug effects on complex behaviors – such as the influence of cannabis on automobile driving – can be safely assessed in simulators, but the impairment is thought to be more pronounced in a noncontrolled natural environment (Neavyn et al. 2014).

Special **ethical considerations** are required for controlled investigations that involve administration of addictive drugs to human subjects. Alcohol and tobacco are licit and culturally accepted substances with addictive potential, and controlled studies of their effects from limited administration at moderate doses are permitted when conducted with reasonable precautions for the safety and health of human subjects. Similar concerns for the well-being of subjects apply for study of other psychoactive drugs approved for use in medical (mainly psychiatric) treatments. Investigations involving administration of other addictive drugs require more stringent control and approval by government agencies, primarily for protection of subjects.

In 1968, Andrew Weil and colleagues at Harvard University conducted the first well-designed controlled studies of cannabis behavioral effects in healthy (non-addicted) human subjects (Weil et al. 1968). At that time, such research was controversial, but controlled investigation with cannabis and other illicit drugs is now acceptable with medical supervision of subject care and required licensure of investigators. For example, low doses of cocaine can be administered for observation of certain acute effects. Such studies include those investigating cocaine's effect on brain activity as revealed by imaging instruments (described below) and the drug's interaction with hormonal levels (e.g., Reed et al. 2011).

Scientific journals, including *Psychopharmacology, Experimental and Clinical Psychopharmacology*, and similar publications, disseminate the results of peer-reviewed controlled experiments investigating behavioral and physiological drug effects. Other journals, including *Drug and Alcohol Dependence* and *Psychology of Addictive Behaviors*, focus more specifically on the use and effects of addictive drugs. Reports of drug effects as demonstrated by controlled investigations are cited throughout the drug-specific chapters of this text.

Quasi-experimental Studies

Ethical restraints prevent the conduct of controlled studies with human subjects for investigation of the effects of repeated administration of large doses of addictive drugs. Extended administration of these drugs in addiction-producing doses, as in the early research protocols carried out at the Lexington prison/hospital, is no longer permissible. Results from controlled experiments with animal subjects yield much useful information about the toxic and behavioral effects of alcohol, nicotine, and illicit drugs when administered at high doses for extended periods. However, some harmful consequences – both toxic and behavioral – occur or are evident only in humans. Many drug effects on cognition and behavior in animal subjects appear to be similar to such actions in humans. However, the consequences of heavy drug use on higher levels of cognition, use of language, complex social interactions, mood states, self-esteem, and the addictive lifestyle are among the aspects of human behavior that cannot be studied by means of fully controlled experimental observations – in either animals or human subjects.

Unfortunately, no shortage exists of people who self-administer addictive drugs frequently and at high doses. Systematic studies of addicted individuals make up much of the large amount of research on SUD. In many studies, typically those conducted in a clinical setting, the drug-using subjects had been diagnosed as suffering from an SUD. Very few studies involve administration of addictive drugs to subjects with SUD. Many include tests of cognition or behavior – such as memory and inhibition. Performance of individuals with current or previous heavy drug use is compared to that of a group without a history of drug use. The design of such experiments is designated as **quasi-experimental**, indicating incomplete control of possibly causal factors.

Not surprisingly, addicted individuals often differ from subjects with no history of heavy drug use in performance on many psychological and behavioral tests. Differences related to alcohol use disorder (as described in Chapter 10) are perhaps the most investigated consequences of heavy drug use. However, the implication that these differences are entirely due to the effects of previous drug use is uncertain in that the subjects were not randomly assigned to the drug use group. Several other factors in addition to drug use often differ between those with and without an SUD. Some of these factors may cause or contribute to the behavioral or physiological differences or might even have promoted the heavy drug use. Because the drug was self-administered, a similar unknown factor is the actual amount of drug use. When the investigator does not control drug use and other factors, observed differences are often referred to as being *associated* with drug use. The term *comparison group* (rather than *control group*) indicates lack of full control of relevant causal factors.

Potential subjects in psychopharmacology studies are often screened to eliminate identifiable differences that could complicate interpretation of test results. For example, cannabis-dependent subjects demonstrated greater impulsivity as indicated by scores on the Barratt Impulsivity Scale than did a comparison group (Gruber et al. 2011). During recruitment of subjects for this study, individuals with certain characteristics were not selected to participate. Those with a history of head trauma, a non-drug-related psychiatric disorder, or a diagnosis of SUD other than for cannabis or tobacco were not included in the study. Participants were also selected so that variables like age, educational level, and IQ scores were similar between the cannabis-using group and the comparison group.

Longitudinal Studies
Longitudinal studies – in which subjects are observed or tested more than once over a period of time – can implicate causes for SUD when they reveal that a suspected risk factor preceded rather than followed disordered drug use. SUD are more prevalent in individuals with another concurrent psychiatric disorder (Chapter 8). The co-occurrence of the two general types of psychiatric problem is a prime

example of a situation in which two possible causal variables are present and the nature of a causal relation (if any) cannot be determined from simple observation. Does heavy drug use cause or contribute to the other psychiatric condition, or vice versa? In a large-scale survey of drug use and psychiatric disorders, Lazareck and colleagues initially assessed the presence of mood disorders (clinical depression or bipolar disorder) and SUD and repeated the observations three years later (Lazareck et al. 2012). These investigations indicated that individuals with a mood disorder (but no SUD) at the initial assessment and who self-medicated with (either or both) illicit and pharmaceutical drugs during the intervening years had an increased prevalence of SUD at the time of the second survey. For these survey respondents, the preexisting mood disorder appeared to promote a drug use disorder.

Multivariate Statistical Analysis

Multivariate statistical analysis is another widely used technique for investigating the consequences of drug use and, to some extent, the causes of SUD. Many conditions or events that are often concurrent with drug use could potentially contribute to the occurrence of harmful outcomes. The increased risk of severe birth defects or developmental differences in infants born to women who consume alcohol or cocaine during pregnancy is an example of a medical problem whose cause is not easily identifiable. In addition to drug use during pregnancy, many of these women also experience unhealthy living conditions, tobacco use, poor diet, inadequate prenatal medical care, disease, and other conditions that can threaten infant health. Controlled research with animal subjects (discussed below) confirms the toxic effects of alcohol and cocaine administration on prenatal development. However, the closely controlled animal studies do not duplicate the complexity of human behavior and living conditions. Multivariate statistical methods can provide estimates of the amount of variability accounted for by each of the identified possible causal factors. Investigations using multivariate analyses indicate that heavy drug use by women during pregnancy contributes to birth and development abnormalities, effects potentiated by the other adverse prenatal conditions (Arria et al. 2006, Thomas et al. 2010).

Because in the Arria, Thomas, and similar studies, the contributing factors (e.g., poor diet, drug use) were identified but not controlled, and other causal factors might remain unknown, determination of the cause–effect relation is not as certain as in a fully controlled experimental investigation. However, multivariate techniques provide valuable information about drug effects when many factors contribute to or influence the behavior of interest.

When the potential causes can be identified, multivariate techniques offer a method of determining the strength of association of each risk factor. Multivariate procedures were used to determine that genetic predisposition accounts for about 60 percent of the variation among individuals in the susceptibility for developing an addictive disorder (Chapter 5).

Epidemiological Surveys

Controlled experiments and clinical studies of individuals in treatment for SUD provide useful information about effects of addictive drugs and factors contributing to the development of the disorder. However, drug effects in a laboratory setting often differ from those occurring in natural environments, and patients in treatment may not accurately represent the much larger and more varied population of individuals with addiction or less severe forms of SUD. Epidemiological surveys provide information about drug use and related conditions by means of a method not influenced by the somewhat artificial and ethically limited nature of the controlled laboratory environment.

Epidemiological surveys collect information from individuals randomly selected from the general population with no attempt to control or manipulate conditions. These surveys include respondents representing a wide variety of personal characteristics and living conditions, including age, geographical location, socioeconomic status, and other variables. Respondents' confidentiality is assured, a precaution especially important in the surveys that feature extensive diagnostic interviews, as in the National Epidemiological Survey on Alcohol and Related Conditions (NESARC) (Grant and Dawson 2006). These more detailed indicators of drug use under natural conditions supplement the information produced from controlled investigations conducted with carefully screened subjects and from interviews with patients in treatment for SUD.

Epidemiological surveys provide population estimates of the prevalence of drug use, SUD, and accompanying conditions identified as **risk factors** for hazardous drug use. Some surveys are conducted annually, providing information about population trends in drug use. Large sample sizes increase the reliability of the estimates. The NESARC survey, first conducted by the National Institute of Alcohol Abuse and Alcoholism in 2001 and 2002, included 41,093 respondents in its first wave. The initial NESARC study was followed at successive three-year intervals by further surveys of selected individuals, providing longitudinal observations. The National Survey on Drug Use and Health (NSDUH) has been conducted annually since 2002 by the Substance Abuse and Mental Health Services Administration. In 2017 the NSDUH included 68,032 respondents (Substance Abuse and Mental Health Services Administration 2018). Monitoring the Future, a survey conducted annually by the University of Michigan under the sponsorship of the National Institute on Drug Abuse, provides estimates of drug use prevalence and attitudes about drug use among high school and middle school students in the United States. In 2014, this survey collected information from 41,600 respondents (Johnston et al. 2015). Results of these large-scale surveys are further discussed in drug-specific chapters of this text.

Large-scale epidemiological surveys provide critical information about the incidence of hazardous drug use, including addiction and less severe forms of

SUD in the general population. Such knowledge is of special importance in that a large majority of individuals with disordered substance use neither seek treatment nor attend mutual-support group meetings (Alcoholics Anonymous or Narcotics Anonymous). This finding – a result of the NESARC and other epidemiological surveys – indicates that those in treatment for SUD are not representative of all individuals suffering from the consequences of heavy use of alcohol or medically prescribed or illicit addictive drugs. The differences between individuals in treatment for SUD and those who have substance use problems but do not seek treatment are further discussed in Chapter 16.

Because epidemiological surveys assess the prevalence of drug use, as well as drug use disorders, they can provide realistic estimates of the addictive potential of drugs, information especially useful for drugs not used by a majority of the population. The National Comorbidity Study, conducted in the early 1990s, indicated that 15–16 percent of cocaine users became addicted within ten years of initial use of the drug, whereas for cannabis, the proportion of addicted users was about 8 percent (Wagner and Anthony 2002). The estimate of addiction potential for cannabis is similar in the second decade of the twenty-first century (Chapter 12).

Correlations between SUD and certain events and conditions can be identified by the results of surveys and, in some cases, indicate causes contributing to SUD. Multivariate statistical analysis can indicate the strength of association between SUD and multiple risk factors like family history of addiction, stressful events, and co-occurring psychiatric disorders. For example, Katherine Keyes and colleagues review the abundant epidemiological evidence linking stress (resulting from several different sources) to disordered alcohol use (Keyes et al. 2012). In some cases, the causal relation between stressful events and SUD might be uncertain in that heavy drug use can cause, as well as be a consequence of, stress. However, many epidemiological studies indicate that childhood maltreatment – a potent source of stress unlikely to be a result of drug use by the respondent – predicts emergence of SUD later in life. Maltreatment of children is more prevalent in adults with an SUD, so the greater incidence of eventual drug use problems in mistreated children could be a result of family history (genetic predisposition for addiction) as well as abuse by the parents. Multivariate analysis of an epidemiological study revealed that childhood abuse was significantly associated with adult SUD, even after accounting for the factor of family history of addiction (Young-Wolff et al. 2011). In other words, the increased vulnerability for addiction presented by childhood abuse was also seen in the absence of a biological predisposition for the disorder.

Investigations of Brain Structure and Activity

During recent decades, much has been learned about the biological processes involved in drug effects, including those related to addiction. Imaging of brain structure and functioning have advanced the understanding of brain activity during the phases of addictive behavior – craving for drugs, intoxication, and withdrawal (Koob 2013). **Neuroimaging technology** has identified brain structures and circuits involved in overvaluing of drug reinforcement, undervaluing of alternative reinforcement, and deficits in inhibitory control. Magnetic resonance imaging (MRI) reveals brain structure, and activity in specific brain areas is measured by functional MRI and positron emission tomography (PET) imaging.

MRI procedures reveal abnormalities in cortical and subcortical areas of addicted individuals (Figure 1.3). Some of these differences are in brain structures related to emotional regulation, inhibitory control, and decision-making (Parvaz et al. 2011). In most cases, the addiction-related significance of a specific brain abnormality is uncertain in that it could have preceded – and so contributed to – the disorder, or it could be a result of extensive drug use. Shirley Hill and colleagues conducted MRI studies that detected smaller amygdalae (subcortical structures that regulate emotional responses) in many addicted individuals. In further studies, these investigators found similar differences in amygdala size in young children who were at risk for SUD based on family history of addiction (Hill et al. 2001). Because these young subjects had consumed little or no alcohol or other addictive drugs, the brain abnormality was not a result of drug use but is a risk factor indicating greater vulnerability to development of an SUD.

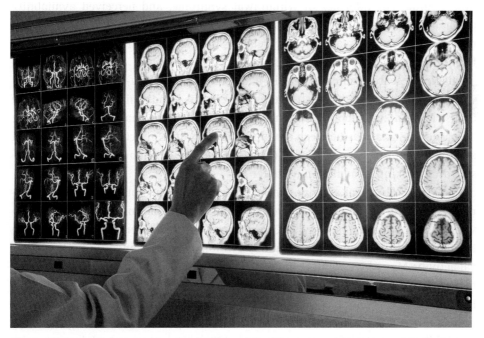

Figure 1.3 Magnetic resonance imaging (MRI) reveals brain structures and interconnections. Photo: iStock / Getty Images Plus.

PET imaging reveals the distribution of radioactively tagged drugs and the activity of relevant neurotransmitters in the brain. A major finding from PET studies was confirmation of the important role of the neurotransmitter dopamine in the acute and chronic actions of cocaine and other addictive drugs (Parvaz et al. 2011). These effects were initially indicated by research with animal subjects, and the minimally invasive PET scans reveal how dopamine function is altered in humans with a history of heavy drug use. Addictive drugs initially increase dopamine activity, but with continued heavy use, the number of dopamine receptors decreases. These actions are thought to contribute to the euphoria of early drug use as well as negative mood states that emerge after extensive use of the drug (Chapter 4).

PET imaging also reveals differences between brain activity in response to drugs in addicted relative to nonaddicted subjects. Using PET imaging, Yoder and colleagues found that alcohol administration produced greater dopamine release in the ventral striatum (a component of the brain's positive reinforcement circuit) of alcohol-dependent subjects as compared to social drinkers (Yoder et al. 2016).

Functional MRI indicates the rate of metabolic activity in specific brain areas and provides a more detailed picture of brain function than PET imaging. Stimuli associated with drug use reliably elicit craving – the state of aroused anticipation or memory of addictive drug effects – in addicted individuals. The neurological correlates of craving have been extensively investigated by means of fMRI procedures. Drug-cue reactivity as indicated by brain activity increases with duration of drug use, intensity of withdrawal syndrome, and perceived availability of the addictive drug (Jasinska et al. 2014). In addicted individuals, neurological responses are much greater to drug-related stimuli than to neutral stimuli, a difference not seen in healthy subjects.

Imaging research indicates that in addicted subjects, drug-related stimuli activate many of the same brain structures and circuits as administration of addictive drugs. This finding supports current theories of addiction that give a critical role to learned associations between stimuli predicting drug effects and the rewarding actions of the drugs, a connection that underlies the development of the compulsive drug-seeking of addiction (Chapter 5).

The brain's electrical activity can be detected by means of **electroencephalography (EEG)**, a noninvasive research method considerably older than those providing images of brain activity. EEG recording provides better temporal resolution than fMRI or PET imaging, allowing observation of rapid changes in brain electrical activity. Many investigators have reported differences indicated by EEG related to heavy use of addictive drugs. In a series of studies Henri Begleiter and colleagues detected abnormal EEG activity characteristic of many alcohol-addicted individuals, a difference thought to be related to impaired information processing and inhibitory control (Rangaswamy et al. 2007). Tests of young adolescents with a family history of alcohol use disorders demonstrated that the EEG differences preceded drug use and are markers of vulnerability for SUD.

Investigations of Genetic Vulnerability to SUD

Epidemiological studies show clearly that a family history of SUD increases the probability that the disorder will develop. Further evidence is provided by many investigations that, using some of the research methods described previously, indicate differences – metabolic, neurological, psychiatric, emotional, and behavioral – mediating the genetic predisposition for SUD. Chapter 6 summarizes results from several areas of research directed toward understanding the nature of the inherited biological risk factor for addiction.

Investigations of how the vulnerability is transmitted by means of variations in the DNA of the human genome employ complex and highly technical methods of molecular biology as well as specialized procedures for statistical analysis. For these investigations, information is collected from thousands of individuals, as in the Collaborative Study for the Genetics of Alcoholism (Begleiter et al. 1995). The genetic variations that underlie the vulnerability to SUD are not easily identified. There is neither one nor even several "addiction" genes, but the effect apparently comes from combinations of subtle differences in many (perhaps hundreds) of the approximately 25,000 genes and other parts of the DNA molecules.

Research with Nonhuman Animal Subjects

Research conducted with nonhuman animal subjects is an important part of behavioral neuroscience, the study of how the brain controls behavior. Brain circuitry and neurotransmitter function are similar among all vertebrate animals, including humans. Neurological actions of psychoactive drugs in humans and other animals are also very similar, as are many behavioral effects of addictive drugs. Rodents and primates are the most used animal subjects for investigations of behavioral pharmacology, an important area of brain-behavior research (McKim and Hancock 2013). Much of the recent progress in understanding the biological mechanisms of addiction has come from animal models of the disorder.

In comparison to studies with humans, investigation of drug effects in animal subjects allows for much greater control of relevant conditions. Genetic background, diet, environment, and similar factors that influence the behavioral effects of drugs can be held constant or manipulated. Fewer ethical restraints limit research with animals, allowing the use of invasive and possibly harmful procedures, such as extensive administration of large drug doses. However, investigators are required to follow ethical guidelines for conduct of research as provided by several professional organizations, including the Society for Neuroscience and the American Psychological Association. These regulations are intended to protect animal subjects as much as possible – without undue limitation of the investigative effort – by minimizing the use of aversive procedures and requiring clear justification for the use of such procedures.

Behavioral and **neurological effects** of addictive drugs can be studied in animal subjects, including some closely related to addictive behavior in humans.

Of special importance is positive reinforcement, a rewarding action of addictive drugs. This drug effect is demonstrated in animal subjects by means of operant behavior (performance of specific actions to access drugs or receive drug injections). Another method is conditioned place preference (exhibiting preference for a distinctive location associated with the drugged state). Brain structures and neurotransmitters involved in positive reinforcement have been identified and are quite similar for primates and humans (Haber and Knutson 2010). Of similar importance is an animal analogue of addictive relapse in humans. Conditions known to trigger relapse in human addicts – stress, drug-linked stimuli, and administration of the addictive drug – also reliably cause a return to drug-seeking in experimental animals previously trained to self-administer an addictive drug (Koob 2013).

The neurological basis of other addiction-related drug effects can also be effectively studied in animal subjects. These effects include decreased behavioral inhibition, cognitive impairment, stimulus properties of drugs (perception of drug effects), and withdrawal syndromes. Animal studies also reveal drug-specific toxicity, made possible by control of factors such as the use of multiple drugs often seen in humans with histories of heavy drug use. Another valuable area of research is controlled investigation of drug effects in immature animals, studies obviously unethical with human infants, children, or adolescents.

Animal models of addiction do not fully emulate the human condition of substance use disorders. Several features of complex human lives relevant to the disorder cannot be duplicated in the much simpler behavioral realm of animal subjects. An obvious limitation is the absence of shame, social disapproval, and the many other adverse consequences that make an SUD so devastating to many human drug users. Nonetheless, the **animal analogues** have advanced our understanding of the biological causes and consequences of compulsive drug use.

The Biopsychosocial Explanation of Substance Use Disorders

Deviant and harmful use of drugs – including SUD – is influenced by multiple causes. Evidence gained from the varied methods of learning about SUD indicates three very general types of conditions, events, or situations that are associated with the development of the disorders: brain function and genetics, psychopathology and personality, and environmental and social conditions (including early-life development and experiences).

Based on the broad range of probable causes, a basic premise of this text is that a *biopsychosocial* (BPS) explanation is most appropriate for the behavioral disorders of addiction and other forms of dangerous drug use. Wallace (1993) outlines some of the history of the BPS approach to understanding addiction and other SUDs. Wallace cites some of the earliest scholarly presentations of a multifactor etiology of SUDs, including those by Ewing (1983) and Tarter (1983). George Vaillant and Robert West added support to the concept that multiple factors promote SUD (Vaillant 2003, West 2006). Many other scientists and scholars who investigate SUD also present evidence that both biological and nonbiological factors influence addictive behavior (e.g., Donovan 2005, Shurtleff et al. 2009, Washton and Zweben 2006). The BPS view of disordered substance use is now widely accepted.

A BPS explanation of SUD development starts with identification of *risk factors* for the harmful use of drugs. Risk factors are conditions, events, behavioral tendencies, neurological abnormalities, and family history associated with SUD. Most risk factors are known – or suspected – to precede and contribute to the development of SUD. Others are early indicators that predict SUD, and yet others may be consequences of heavy drug use. Risk factors include genetic makeup, neurological abnormalities, certain parenting styles, and early-childhood experiences. Expectation of beneficial drug effects, exposure to rewarding experiences from drug use, certain cognitive processes, and cultural acceptance of drug use and intoxication are also risk factors. Sexual trauma or frequent drug use during childhood or adolescence are especially strong risk factors, as are several psychiatric disorders. Figure 1.4 illustrates the many risk factors associated with disordered drug use. Consideration of these risk factors for SUD is a main theme of subsequent chapters.

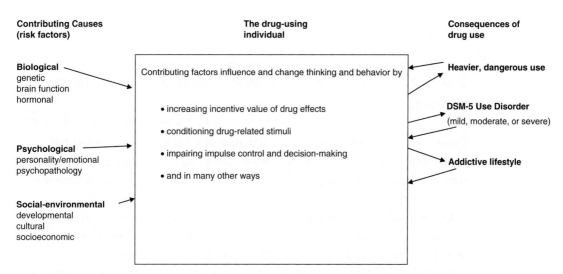

Figure 1.4 A biopsychosocial explanation of SUD emphasizes the multiple risk factors that contribute to the dangerous and compulsive use of psychoactive substances. Heavy drug use and the addictive lifestyle can feed back to and worsen the effects of contributing causes – such as emotional distress or altered brain function. Owing to the many interacting causes, there are numerous pathways into the dangerous use of psychoactive drugs

Risk factors often interact, rather than independently influencing drug use and related behavior. A single factor might not cause excessive drug use but would contribute to the emergence of SUD when combined with other risk factors. Owing to the many interacting causes, there are numerous pathways into the dangerous use of psychoactive drugs. Some pathways might be relatively direct, such as a genetic predisposition for risk acceptance and sensation seeking. Other routes involve several factors, such as an abnormality in certain brain functions in conjunction with childhood sexual abuse and, eventually, extensive opportunities for cocaine use. The probability, earlier emergence, and severity of SUD increase with a greater number of risk factors (Babor and Cateano 2006, Dick and Kendler 2012). However, some of these pathways to SUD – especially for less severe cases – may not include detectible genetic predispositions or neurological abnormalities.

Development of a comprehensive theory to explain the complex, multiple, and interacting causes of human behavior is not only a challenge for understanding addictive disorders but is also one encountered in most areas of psychology. Scientists and scholars in specialized areas of behavioral science typically develop less general theoretical approaches, often attempting to explain the dynamics of only a particular aspect of behavior, such as social conformity, decision-making, or memory. Box 1.2 lists some of the specialized areas of psychology and related disciplines whose investigators have attempted to explain SUD. Each of these approaches contributes useful knowledge regarding the nature and causes of the behavioral disorders of drug use. However, a complete and general biopsychosocial theory has not yet been developed.

BOX 1.2 Specialized areas of research related to substance use disorders

Current knowledge of the origins and nature of substance use disorders has been advanced by research in these areas. Some basic findings are briefly stated here. Investigators working in each area seek to determine specifically how the many relevant variables contribute to drug use, drug effects, and SUD.

Behavioral neuroscience. Abnormal function of certain neurotransmitters (dopamine, glutamate, endogenous opioids) and brain circuits (subcortical, prefrontal cortex) underlies some forms of compulsive drug use.

Behavioral genetics. Vulnerability for SUD is partially determined by genetic predisposition (biological family history).

Behavioral (classic Skinnerian). Consequences of actions (reinforcement and punishment) and drug-linked stimuli are important determinants of drug use.

Social-cognitive. Social factors (such as modeling of drug use by family and peers) and cognitive mediation (such as expectation of positive drug effects) influence drug use.

Developmental. Parental actions (beneficial or harmful) and stressful childhood experience influence later drug use.

Personality. Impulsivity and negative emotionality predispose early drug use and SUD.

Psychopathology. Both less common (schizophrenia, bipolar disorder) and more prevalent (anxiety, depression) psychiatric disorders are associated with greater vulnerability for SUD.

Cultural anthropology. Drug use, disordered use, and addiction are more likely in cultures that are tolerant of intoxication and provide easy access to psychoactive drugs.

Chapter Summary

Psychoactive drugs can produce pleasure, reduce boredom and pain, and bring about other useful effects, resulting in their widespread and pervasive use. Tobacco, alcohol, cannabis, stimulants, opioid analgesics, and other drugs or substances containing drugs present threats to public health and safety when used improperly and excessively. A substance use disorder occurs when adverse consequences of drug use become clinically significant – as happens with many users. With addiction – the most severe form of the disorder – compulsive drug use continues even as the afflicted individual endures and tolerates the harmful results.

The secrecy, dishonesty, and antisocial behavior typical of addiction disrupt close, supportive relations. The addictive lifestyle results in isolation, anger, and depression, perpetuating the disorder as the addict becomes fixated on drug use, giving the destructive behavior highest priority.

The breadth and complexity of disordered drug use present a difficult challenge for learning about the origins and outcomes of SUD. Simple observation of an apparent cause or consequence of SUD is inadequate and can lead to conclusions that are erroneous or with limited generality. However, several methods of research have increased our understanding of compulsive and harmful drug use.

Experiments are controlled observations that can reveal behavioral effects of drugs with a high degree of certainty. Even so, questions often remain regarding the degree to which experiments accurately represent drug effects and motivations for drug use in the natural world outside the laboratory. Many important variables relevant to SUD cannot be controlled.

Studies of addicted individuals provide valuable information about the consequences of heavy drug use relative to nonaddicted comparison groups. Although some factors in these quasi-experimental investigations are not controlled, associations between addiction and behavioral or neurological abnormalities can be determined.

Multivariate analysis determines the strength of association between the numerous conditions or events that often accompany or precede SUD and might contribute to the disorder. Most such factors (e.g., genetic inheritance, childhood stress) cannot be manipulated as in a controlled investigation, but these analytical procedures provide a form of statistical control (or isolation) of identifiable possible causes.

Epidemiological studies indicate the extent of addictive drug use and its consequences in the natural world by surveying individuals randomly selected from the general population. Such information, in conjunction with multivariate statistical analyses, also allows identification of probable causes (risk factors) of SUD – including other (non-SUD) psychiatric disorders and a genetically determined predisposition for disordered drug use.

Research with animal analogues (models) of addiction has revealed much about brain circuitry and neurotransmitters – the biological basis of compulsive drug-seeking thought to be very similar to that of humans. Animal studies also contribute to the understanding of genetic factors that influence addiction. These methods of highly controlled research are of great value, even though not completely replicating SUD in the more complex human situation.

A biopsychosocial explanation of SUD posits that multiple causes – biological (genetic and neurological), psychological, and environmental (including social and developmental) – contribute to the compulsive and damaging use of psychoactive drugs. Risk factors are specific biological and nonbiological conditions or events associated with development of the disorder. Effects of these many risk factors interact, and their combinations often lead to SUD via several possible pathways.

Review Exercises

1. Why are less severe cases of SUD difficult to identify?
2. As reported in Table 1.1, what drugs are associated with the highest incidence of SUD, and what is their legal status?
3. How is the severity of an SUD indicated by the DSM-IV? The DSM-5?

4. Describe the key features of the addictive lifestyle.
5. Describe three features of SUD that make it difficult to identify the causes of this disorder.
6. What are the limitations of simple observation, anecdotal accounts, and autobiographical accounts of addiction?
7. What are the advantages and disadvantages of the use of experiments for establishing the behavioral effects of psychoactive drugs?
8. Describe the types of research methods that are used to investigate SUD in addicted individuals.
9. What are epidemiological studies, and what is their value in determining the effects of drug use?
10. Brain-imaging techniques have revealed much information about the effects of drugs on the brain. Describe three of these techniques and what they have revealed.
11. What is the basic premise of the biopsychosocial explanation of SUD?
12. Name and describe at least three specialized areas of research that provide information about the causes and consequences of SUD.

Key Terms

anecdotal information (14)
animal analogues (26)
compulsive use (6)
diagnostic criteria (10)
electroencephalography
 (EEG) (24)
ethical considerations (18)

harmful consequences (5)
multiple causes (13)
neuroimaging technology
 (23)
neurological effects (25)
process addictions (10)
quasi-experimental (19)

risk factors (21)
substance abuse (10)
substance dependence (10)
substance use disorder (SUD)
 (8)

2 Diagnosis of Substance Use Disorders

LEARNING OBJECTIVES

1. Describe the essential features of SUD.
2. Describe the nomenclature and diagnostic criteria of DSM-IV and DSM-5.
3. Describe the requirements for a DSM-5 diagnosis of SUD.
4. Describe the heterogeneity of SUD.
5. Describe the common routes of entry into a diagnostic evaluation for possible SUD.
6. Describe tests used to screen for SUD and their limitations.
7. Describe supplementary information used in SUD diagnosis.

Introductory Vignette: Martin's Diagnosis

Martin and David have been close friends since their military service during Operation Desert Storm. Recently, their shared activities have narrowed to heavy drinking and frequent marijuana use. Martin has asked David to meet him at a coffee shop. Martin is already seated at a table as David enters.

DAVID: Hi, Martin – so how come we are meeting at Starbuck's and not at the Thirsty Camel? Do they have a happy hour here? Might increase their business!

MARTIN: I wanted a more private place to talk to you about an important problem I have. The bar always has too many loud guys getting loaded – not good for a serious discussion.

DAVID: So, what's going on? I did notice you seem pretty quiet lately. Something bad happen?

MARTIN: Well, yeah, but maybe not all bad. Remember I told you about my trouble sleeping, not being able to stay focused at work, bad arguments with the wife and kids? I thought maybe I was depressed or something. I went to see Dr. Johnson, my GP. He sent me to a counselor – actually, she is a clinical psychologist. At first, I didn't want to see a shrink, but Dr. Johnson was pretty insistent. Now I think he was right about the kind of help I needed.

This psychologist is good! I found myself laying out everything about my situation to her. She is easy to talk to – not at all critical of me – but, at the same time, doesn't pull any punches about what I need to do.

By the end of the first session – I've been to see her twice now – I had told her a lot about my drinking and smoking weed. She listened carefully to all that has been happening to me lately. But she kept coming back to my drinking and smoking, and with most people, I would not have been so honest as I was with her. But like I said, she is *good* at what she does, getting people to talk about their problems. There is quite a bit I haven't even told you – about all the bad stuff going down in my life these days. I've been in a pretty bad place. The weird thing is, I thought that drinking and getting stoned were helping me get by, to cope with the crap coming down on me. But she thinks that the booze and weed are actually causing most of the trouble!

DAVID: Man, I am sorry you are having such a hard time and feeling so bad. But I doubt that the problem is drinking and smoking weed – why, you don't drink or smoke any more than I do! (*Laughs nervously*)

MARTIN: She was pretty convincing – but she didn't argue with me – just sort of repeated back to me what I had told her. She helped me see that there are some pretty serious consequences from my heavy drinking, and it seems that I can't keep from drinking, and drinking too much. I sure didn't like hearing that, but I couldn't say she was wrong.

DAVID: Did she say you were an alcoholic? Or an addict?

MARTIN: She said medical professionals don't use those terms much anymore – but her diagnosis is that I have a severe alcohol use disorder and a moderate marijuana use disorder. She did say that for my drinking problems, the diagnosis is about the same thing as what used to be called alcohol dependence. That was hard for me to hear – and I'm still not completely buying it. But, I suspect she may be right. She was optimistic and encouraging, though – says that many people have this problem and with help and treatment have gotten their better lives back. I am starting group therapy with her and some other people with problems like mine. We'll meet twice a week, in the evening.

I wanted to tell you about this right away. I probably won't be coming to the Camel to party, at least until I figure out what is really going on with me. I want to avoid that hard-drinking crowd, but you and I have been friends for a long time. Over the years we have spent a lot of time together drunk and stoned, but it seems to me that we are more than just drinking buddies.

DAVID: That's for sure. We don't have to drink or smoke weed when we get together. I'm still not convinced you're an alcoholic – or alcohol dependent or whatever they call it now. But I am glad that you are getting help with your problems.

Introduction

How do you identify an individual as an alcoholic or a drug addict? Is it some-one who drinks too much or uses drugs a lot (at least, more than you do)? Extreme cases may be unmistakable, as with an individual who has lost his home, family, and livelihood due to excessive drinking or drug use. Sometimes, however, the losses are more subtle and their relation to drug use uncertain. Informal and subjective methods are often used by the general public to label individuals as suffering from a substance use disorder (SUD). Most medical and mental health professionals who work with those having use disorders, and scientists who study the disorder, use more **objective methods** to determine the presence of an SUD. Although objectivity is an important requirement for iden-tifying problematic drug use, achievement of complete objectivity in diagnosis can be difficult.

One's interactions with an individual who drinks alcohol or uses other drugs can prevent objectivity. A positive personal relationship with the individual can result in denial of and protection against a derogatory label. Conversely, harm done by the drug-using individual can cause unjustified use of a pejorative term, such as *alcoholic* or *addict*. A family member or a work associate who drinks heavily and is also abusive, disagreeable, or disliked for some other reason may be seen as having an SUD even when drinking is not the source of the difficulty.

Drinking alcoholic beverages and the recreational use of other drugs are often seen as hedonistic and self-indulgent. Irresponsible drug use may cause a wide variety of personal and public harms, ranging from birth defects to traffic fatal-ities. It is understandable that people are frequently quite judgmental regarding individuals who use alcohol and other drugs excessively or with bad consequences. However, the meanings of such terms as *excessive use* and *harmful consequences* vary greatly and are hardly objective.

The Language and Labels of Disordered Substance Use

The previous question ("How do you identify ...") includes terms (*alcoholic*, *addict*) that are in wide public use, as well as by participants in Alcoholics Anonymous (AA), Narcotics Anonymous (NA), and other twelve-step programs. However, these terms or labels are not included in professional diagnostic systems. Diagnostic systems provide objective and relatively nonjudgmental methods for identifying individuals with SUD by using terms more specific and with less implied disapproval than the words *alcoholic* and *addict*.

Within the twelve-step fellowships of AA or NA, use of these terms is common but not intended to criticize or judge those with SUD. Rather, their use is a reminder of the destructive effects of the drugs when the disorder is active and not dealt with by "working the steps" of the recovery programs. For members of these support groups, the labels of alcoholic and addict are meant to prevent complacency and denial of the ongoing vulnerability to relapse.

Substance use disorder (SUD) is currently the term most used by medical and other professionals to designate problematic drug or alcohol use. In this book, the more familiar terms **abuse** and *addiction* are also sometimes used. *Abuse* will refer to the overall harmful use of substances, and *addiction* indicates a severe form of the disorder. Additionally, the term *drug* includes the drug alcohol, so *drug abuse* or *drug addiction* can refer to the harmful use of alcohol.

Formal (Professional) and Informal Diagnoses of Substance Use Disorders

For both clinical and scientific purposes, it is important that SUD be objectively identified and diagnosed by means of a valid and reliable diagnostic system. A common language (use of terms whose meanings are generally accepted) is critical for communication among clinicians and is even more important for those conducting research on the basic nature of, causes of, and treatments for SUD (Widiger 2005). The DSM-5 (the fifth edition of the *Diagnostic and Statistical Manual of Mental Disorders*) is the most used diagnostic system in the United States (American Psychiatric Association 2013).

Treatment of SUD requires time and effort of health care professionals and is often expensive. Diagnostic evaluations are the primary basis for determining who should receive treatment. Diagnoses, which may include prognosis and prediction of treatment outcomes, can also influence other professional decisions, such as child custody and the disposition of criminal cases.

Standard, generally accepted criteria for behavior indicative of SUD are also necessary for the many types of scientific studies of addictive disorders. These investigations include epidemiological surveys, which provide estimates of SUD prevalence in large populations. In genetic research, attempts to determine patterns of harmful drug use within families or to establish that certain genotypes are associated with SUD depend heavily on common identification systems that confirm the presence of the disorder. The search for neurological abnormalities that might underlie drug use disorders can be successful only if these disorders are identified by valid and objective diagnostic standards.

Identification is recognition of the presence of a disorder, and diagnosis is an attempt to further classify or assign the disorder to an established category or type – often including a level of severity. A clinician may collect information about possible causes as she works toward arriving at a diagnosis, but finding the source of an SUD is not the purpose of a diagnostic system. The diagnostic systems described in this chapter are based on observable or self-reported behavior and symptoms and not on conditions that may have produced the harmful substance use. Put simply, the process of identification answers only the question "Does this behavior constitute a substance use disorder?" Identification and diagnosis do not address causes for the disorder.

Methods other than formal diagnostic systems are often used to identify SUD. Some are quite simple, such as the descriptive phrase used by twelve-step programs: "A desire to stop drinking (or using drugs)." If an individual feels that these words describe his or her situation, then according to AA and NA principles, the individual belongs in the group, of which all members have a similar problem.

There is often a trade-off between ease of use and the value of the information collected by a test or method of detecting the presence of SUD. Use of diagnostic procedures, such as the Addiction Severity Index (McLellan et al. 1992), requires much time and effort for collection of extensive amounts of information. Some are intended to guide a diagnostic interview conducted by a trained clinician (Miller et al. 1995). Lengthy questionnaires are often used in research projects. These instruments provide much information useful for investigating SUD but may not be suitable for clinical use (Hasin 2003). Screening tests, further described below, may consist of only a few brief and simple questions and by themselves are not adequate for reliable diagnosis.

The Three Cs

A simple, informal method for identifying SUD is referred to as the "three Cs" test. Three brief questions address the **consequences** of drug use, the **compulsive** nature of drug use, and problems with **controlling** this behavior. These questions succinctly capture the two essential features of SUD: the (1) harmful consequences of drug use and (2) inability or difficulty in stopping (compulsion) or limiting (controlling) such destructive use. The three Cs test can be useful, especially as a self-evaluation of whether an individual has a substance use disorder. However, a formal diagnosis is usually required for admission to treatment. In particular, reimbursement from an insurance company for treatment expenses requires a more complete and professional diagnosis.

Although SUD as broadly defined includes at least one of the two essential features just mentioned (harmful consequences and control problems) wide differences are seen among individual cases of SUD. Differences among patterns and consequences of harmful drug use give rise to confusion (as well as denial) about the presence of SUD in those who suffer from the disorder. The natural tendency to compare one's own situation with that of another individual (typically one with more severe problems) facilitates the defense "I'm not as bad as she is – she is a *real* addict!" However, even with marked differences among patterns of problematic drug use, some generalizations are possible. These commonalties are the basis of diagnostic systems.

Essential Features of Substance Use Disorders

All useful methods or systems for identification or diagnosis of SUD assess the two characteristics of disordered drug use (Goodman 1990). Even the simplest recognition test ("a desire to stop drinking/using") implies that the drug use is **causing harm**, and **stopping use** *seems to be difficult or impossible.* Impaired control of drug use may not be obvious in less severe forms of the disorder, in which harmful consequences are the most prominent feature. In the more severe form of SUD (addiction), control of drug-using behavior is impaired, resulting in a continuation of the destructive consequences.

In other words, at one level of SUD, drug use has adverse effects. At a further level of involvement, the individual persists in the maladaptive behavior, seemingly unable to prevent the destructive drug use.

Harmful Consequences

When used frequently, at high doses, or in inappropriate situations, drugs with abuse potential often cause a variety of consequences that are at least uncomfortable, and sometimes life-threatening. Aversive consequences differ, depending on the specific drug taken. These consequences include biological toxicity (e.g., cancer, liver damage) and disturbing or dangerous behavior (e.g., embarrassing actions, arguments, physical violence). Although most addictive drugs can be consumed infrequently and at low doses without harm, patterns of chronic heavy drug intake typically emerge as an SUD develops. Chapters 9 through 15 of this book describe the various adverse effects of addiction to specific drugs of abuse – including medications intended for relief of pain or anxiety.

Some harmful consequences of SUD are indirect – such as the addictive lifestyle summarized in Chapter 1 – and are often dependent on the social context or the overall cultural environment. Deceit, secretive behavior, guilt, shame, and isolation from close friends and associates are typical unless heavy drug use and intoxication are tolerated or encouraged. For example, if all of a young man's friends indulge in binge drinking, there may be little guilt or shame associated with his excessive alcohol use.

Drugs with abuse potential can make an individual feel better – that is, less anxious, depressed, or bored – and more engaged with other people and with life in general. These pleasurable and comforting effects usually occur sooner and more reliably than any aversive consequences. However, most of those who use alcohol, cannabis, cocaine, MDMA, or other drugs in a "social/recreational" manner have also experienced negative consequences of this activity. Perhaps the most common example is hangover – the delayed effect of alcohol. Many who use addictive drugs but do not develop a use disorder learn to avoid bad consequences (most of the time) by limiting the amount of and occasions for drug use.

Less severe forms of SUD are often similar to social-recreational and largely benign drug use, which sometimes does cause problems. Consequently, a mild form of the disorder can be difficult to identify and diagnose. Although professional diagnosis is intended to be objective and reliable, less severe cases often present a diagnostic challenge and may be influenced by the assessor's experience or personal values. Adverse experiences that often accompany or follow drug use may not be recognized – especially by the drug-using person – as consequences of taking the drug. Relationship difficulties, career failure, or medical problems are not invariably the result of drug use, even in individuals who drink alcohol or use drugs to excess. A diagnosis of alcohol use disorder is likely after repeated arrests for intoxicated driving. Evaluation of a different case, such as one involving relationship problems in a user of cannabis, is more difficult – and diagnosis could vary among clinicians.

Less severe forms of the disorder – which are much more common than the extreme cases (Kessler et al. 2005) – can be quite dangerous. Many consequences of drug use are fatal (vehicle crashes) or life altering (divorce, incarceration). Excessive and inappropriate drug use is a serious public health and safety problem with huge socioeconomic costs to society.

Impulsive risk taking, faulty decision processes, the immediate benefits of drug use, and other risk factors discussed in Chapters 7 and 8 apparently underlie persistent hazardous drug use. Finding definitive answers to questions about volitional control of behavior is difficult. However, a consensus among many scientists and clinicians who investigate and treat SUD is that those with a less severe SUD (designated as substance abuse in the older DSM-IV diagnostic system) voluntarily choose to use drugs, albeit in a dangerous manner (e.g., Erickson 2007, Gitlow 2007, Washton and Zweben 2006).

Impaired Control of Behavior

In more severe forms of SUD, problems with *compulsion* and impaired *control* (the other two Cs of the informal method of diagnosis) become more prominent. The term *addiction* is not a diagnostic classification in DSM-5, although it is in common usage in many countries to designate severe problems related to compulsive use of drugs (American Psychiatric Association 2013). With severe SUD – addiction – the drug user experiences adverse consequences that are worse and more persistent than with less intense SUD but seems unable to interrupt the compulsive, self-destructive behavior. It is sometimes said that the addiction "takes on a life of its own," implying that the behavior is not under voluntary control. Both impulsive and compulsive behaviors are characteristic of SUD, and both are examples of poorly controlled actions (Koob 2009). Some cases of dangerous drug use are essentially impulsive actions, done with little forethought. Compulsive behavior, often driven by anxiety, persists in the face of adverse consequences and is frequently more difficult to restrain than impulsive actions.

Volitional control of behavior and its converse, absence of self-regulation, vary in degree, and neither operates under binary, either–or conditions (Martin et al. 2006). With nonaddictive drug abuse, the possibility of harmful consequences may be ignored or minimized, but the choice of drug use appears to be, at least to some extent, voluntary. However, in advanced cases of the disorder, the individual's life is dominated by drug use. The addicted person has developed an **emotional connection** with the drug, sometimes described as "overwhelming pathological involvement" (Fals-Stewart 2005, p. 303). "There is often evidence of an automatic, stereotyped, compulsive pattern of drug use that is occurring without the person's full volitional control" (Washton and Zweben 2006, p. 38).

Answering the question of who is actually in charge (of the addicted individual's actions) presents philosophical difficulties. Skog (2000) and Heyman (2009) present the argument that even in extreme cases of drug **dependence**, volitional control is impaired but not completely absent. Chapter 3 of this text also summarizes evidence against the concept that addictive behavior cannot be controlled. However, the inadequacy of "willpower" in those with SUD is often mentioned in testimonials of twelve-step group participants as they recount their struggles with compulsive drug use. The evidence of neurological dysfunction and genetic predisposition for SUD is much stronger for the more severe forms of the disorder, of which **impairment of volitional control** is an important diagnostic feature.

In early stages of SUD, before adverse consequences become severe and disruptive, drug users are typically reluctant to admit their inability to limit their excessive use. Justification of their actions might include statements like "I enjoy drinking. If I spend too much money, have a bad hangover, or get into some kind of trouble, the fun I have makes up for the downside. So – I go for it." An emotional relationship with the drug, based on the pleasure and comfort of its effects, often prevents acknowledgment of self-control difficulties. In later stages, when aversive consequences become more serious and unmistakable, the impaired control eventually becomes apparent, even to individuals most emotionally invested with drug use.

The progression of SUD from the less severe level of abuse into the more extreme state of addiction is further described in Chapter 7. Such progression is frequent, but not inevitable, in that abusers do not invariably become addicts. The relationship between lesser and greater severity of the disorder is of much interest to investigators of SUD and is discussed further in a subsequent section of this chapter.

Diagnostic Systems

The complex behavior and the multiple signs and symptoms of disordered substance use are described and listed for purposes of diagnosis by means of two widely used systems: the DSM system of the American Psychiatric Association and the International Classification of Diseases and Related Health Problems (ICD) system of the World Health Organization.

The DSM System of the American Psychiatric Association

The *Diagnostic and Statistical Manual of Mental Disorders*, published by the American Psychiatric Association and used extensively by mental health professionals, has been revised several times since its creation in 1952. These revisions were made by experts who evaluate ongoing research and feedback from clinicians who diagnose psychiatric disorders. The fourth revision, DSM-IV, was published in 1994 and then expanded in 2000 as DSM-IV-TR (American Psychiatric Association 2000). The most recent revision (DSM-5) was completed in 2013. However, both of the two most recent revisions are described here because a very large number of investigations of SUD were carried out during the nineteen years over which the DSM-IV guided the diagnosis of the disorder. The National Epidemiological Survey of Alcoholism and Related Conditions (NESARC) (Grant et al. 2004) – cited and discussed frequently in this book – is a prominent example of research that provided a large, extremely valuable database of SUD cases as defined by the DSM-IV diagnostic system. Both DSM-IV and DSM-5 facilitate objective diagnosis, but clinical judgment is still required. Identification of a disorder requires the presence of a *pattern of maladaptive use*, but the number of occurrences that qualify as a pattern is not specified (Box 2.1).

BOX 2.1 Nomenclature of substance use disorders

The publication of DSM-5 in 2013 resulted in changes in the official nomenclature used to designate substance use disorders. The older terminology of DSM-IV appears in many reports about harmful drug use published prior to

BOX 2.1 Continued

2013. Following is a summary of the terms used in the two systems and other terms related to harmful substance use.

DSM-IV Terminology

Substance abuse is a less severe use disorder.
Substance dependence is a more severe disorder.

DSM-5 Terminology

Substance use disorders are designated as **mild**, **moderate**, or **severe** – depending on the number of diagnostic criteria satisfied.
Addiction is not an official term but is commonly used in reference to substance dependence or a severe substance use disorder. Impaired control of substance use, in addition to harmful consequences of such use, is typical of addiction.
Physiological dependence, discussed in Box 2.3, has a special meaning related to certain types of withdrawal syndrome.

All of these terms are used in this book.

DSM-IV

The "Substance-Related Disorders" chapter of DSM-IV-TR defined two *substance use disorders* (*abuse* and *dependence*). The diagnostic criteria for these use disorders were general in that they can apply to any of several types of drugs with potential for disordered use.

The *abuse* diagnosis required the presence of a pattern of maladaptive use that resulted in various difficulties – social, legal, or medical. Compulsive or uncontrollable use, as well as tolerance and withdrawal, were not criteria for the less severe disorder. Some cases of abuse occurred in younger individuals with shorter histories of maladaptive substance use. Some, but not all, with an abuse diagnosis will progress into the more severe level of substance dependence (Hasin 2003).

Many investigators and clinical practitioners noted problems with the abuse diagnosis. For individuals evaluated as substance abusers, the diagnosis proved less reliable and stable than for those diagnosed with a more severe disorder (e.g., Babor and Caetano 2008, Martin et al. 2008). These and other investigators maintained that the abuse criteria of DSM-IV described unwise, risky, and irresponsible behavior but did not meet a reasonable definition of a psychiatric syndrome (mental disorder). One of four diagnostic criteria was required for a diagnosis of substance abuse.

The abuse category was a useful (if imperfect) indicator of a less severe form of SUD in epidemiological studies (Hasin and Beseler 2009). As an example, the NESARC study (Grant et al. 2004) cataloged the alcohol use patterns of 43,000 respondents, chosen as representative of the adult population of the United States. These respondents were interviewed to determine the presence of DSM-IV alcohol abuse and dependence criteria. The NESARC study found that in 2002, among the 26,642 respondents who drank alcohol, the occurrence of alcohol abuse during the twelve months before the survey was 7.1 percent, and the prevalence of alcohol dependence was 5.8 percent (Moss et al. 2012). Actual abuse rates may be even greater than the NESARC estimate in that abuse is difficult to differentiate from the varied harmful effects of heavy alcohol use that do not qualify as indicating a use disorder (Willenbring 2013).

A diagnosis of abuse was unusual for individuals evaluated in SUD treatment centers (Gitlow 2007). Patients or clients in these clinical settings were much more likely to receive a diagnosis of substance dependence, partly due to some redundancy between the diagnostic criteria for the two disorders. However, perhaps the most important reason for the difference between clinical and epidemiological measures of the prevalence of substance abuse is that the less severe disorder had not caused individuals to seek treatment.

DSM-IV-TR *substance dependence* indicated a more severe use disorder, often informally referred to as addiction. Dependence was defined as three or more of seven diagnostic criteria occurring at any time in the same twelve-month period. These criteria include problems with control of drug use, tolerance, and withdrawal syndromes. Although no longer the official designation for a severe substance use disorder, the word *dependence* is used frequently throughout this book because the term referred to SUD for the nearly two decades that the DSM-IV was the standard diagnostic system. A major professional journal that publishes the work of prominent scientists is entitled *Drug and Alcohol Dependence*.

DSM-5

The most important revision in DSM-5 is the elimination of the two categories of disorder (abuse and dependence) of DSM-IV. Only one diagnosis – *substance use disorder* – is possible with the DSM-5 system (Box 2.2). Whereas the abuse category of the older system was intended to capture less severe cases of problematic drug use, the number of diagnostic criteria satisfied with DSM-5 now indicates the severity of the disorder. As previously mentioned, a severe SUD – as indicated by the occurrence of six or more symptoms – is often informally described as addiction. The dependence diagnosis was also eliminated, partly due to the occurrence of physiological dependence (tolerance and withdrawal symptoms) in the absence of a drug use disorder – not unusual in patients medicated for chronic pain (Box 2.3; see also Chapter 14).

The DSM-IV-TR was a **categorical** conceptualization of psychopathology, guiding attempts to determine whether individuals have or do not have SUD. The DSM-5 reflects the alternative to the dichotomous (either–or) view of psychiatric disorders. With the **dimensional** concept, normality and abnormality differ incrementally along a continuum of severity.

Most investigators (e.g., Hasin and Beseler 2009, Martin et al. 2008) view SUD as dimensional in nature. Several types of mental or emotional disorders, such as depression and anxiety, vary incrementally from mild to severe and are more intense manifestations of nonpathological states (Maddux and Winstead 2005). These disorders then are dimensional in nature, as are SUD. A dimensional-based diagnosis provides a better indication of the severity of the disorder than does a diagnosis resulting from a categorical system. Such information regarding severity is valuable for scientific investigation of the causes of the disorder.

Several investigations have compared diagnostic outcomes between DSM-IV and DSM-5 by means of evaluating individuals with both systems. Most such studies (e.g., Compton et al. 2013, Peer et al. 2013) indicate adequate concordance (similar SUD prevalence) between the systems for identification of opioids, cannabis, cocaine, and alcohol use disorders.

In DSM-5, diagnostic criteria are listed separately for use disorders of nine substances or drug types: alcohol, cannabis, phencyclidine, other hallucinogens, inhalants, opioids, sedative/anxiolytics, stimulants, and nicotine. An additional listing identifies disordered use of an unknown intoxicating substance. Diagnostic criteria are similar for all these substances, with the exception of phencyclidine and other hallucinogens, for which the presence of a withdrawal syndrome has not been established. The criteria for alcohol use disorder are presented in Box 2.2.

BOX 2.2 DSM-5 diagnostic criteria for alcohol use disorder

A. A problematic pattern of alcohol use leading to clinically significant impairment or distress, as manifested by at least two of the following, occurring within a twelve-month period:
   1. Alcohol is often taken in larger amounts or over a longer period than was intended.
   2. There is a persistent desire or unsuccessful efforts to cut down or control alcohol use.

3. A great deal of time is spent in activities necessary to obtain alcohol, use alcohol, or recover from its effects.
4. Craving, or a strong desire, to use alcohol.
5. Recurrent alcohol use resulting in failure to fulfill major role obligations of work, school, or home.
6. Continued alcohol use despite having persistent or recurrent social or interpersonal problems caused or exacerbated by alcohol effects.
7. Important social, occupational, or recreational activities are given up or reduced because of alcohol use.
8. Recurrent alcohol use in situations in which it is physically hazardous.
9. Alcohol use is continued despite knowledge of having a persistent or recurrent physical or psychological problem that is likely to have been caused or exacerbated by the alcohol.
10. Tolerance, as defined by either of the following:
    a. A need for markedly increased amounts of alcohol to achieve intoxication or the desired effect.
    b. A markedly diminished effect with continued use of the same amount of alcohol.
11. Withdrawal, as manifested by either of the following:
    a. The characteristic alcohol withdrawal syndrome.
    b. Alcohol (or a closely related substance) is taken to relieve or avoid withdrawal symptoms.

The presence of two to three symptoms indicates a mild disorder, four to five indicate a moderate disorder, and six or more indicate a severe disorder.

The substances that can produce a use disorder: alcohol, cannabis, phencyclidine, other hallucinogens, inhalants, opioids, sedative/anxiolytics, stimulants, nicotine.

Reprinted with permission from the *Diagnostic and Statistical Manual of Mental Disorders*, Fifth Edition (Copyright © 2013). American Psychiatric Association. All rights reserved.

DSM-5 Diagnostic Criteria

A DSM-5 SUD diagnosis is intended to capture a wide range of the disorder, from a mild to a severe state of chronically relapsing, compulsive drug-taking (American Psychiatric Association 2013). Cognitive, behavioral, and physiological symptoms indicate that the individual continues use of the substance despite significant problems related to that use. The disorder is defined as two or more of the eleven diagnostic criteria occurring at any time within a twelve-month period, with additional symptoms indicating a more severe disorder (Box 2.2). The list of symptoms is essentially a combination of those from DSM-IV that indicated dependence or abuse – with the exclusion of the abuse criterion *recurrent substance-related legal problems*. As with the earlier diagnostic system, the array of DSM-5 diagnostic criteria reflects the multiple ways in which drug use disrupts normal function:

Impaired control of drug use (criteria 1 and 2). These criteria describe the compulsive nature of the disorder. The failed attempts to abstain from drug use or to limit the amount and frequency of use are often quite disturbing to both the afflicted individual and others. Problems with self-regulation, as discussed previously, are central to a moderate or severe addictive disorder. Various aspects of impaired control are also considered further in subsequent chapters. The neurological basis of impaired behavioral control is discussed in Chapter 4, its critical role in classic disease theory of addiction in Chapter 3, the intense desire for the addictive substance (craving) in Chapter 7, and the personality trait of impulsivity in Chapter 8.

Impact on normal activities (criteria 3 through 7). These characteristics indicate that the individual's personal autonomy is seriously compromised by substance use and that many important activities are impaired or interrupted. In an addictive lifestyle, much time, effort, and money are spent using alcohol or other drugs. Intoxication and its aftermath interfere with work and family-related responsibilities. Relationships with nonusing friends suffer. Some individuals recovering from SUD describe the condition as "losing myself" to the overwhelming involvement with the addictive substance.

Persisting in self-destructive behavior (criteria 8 and 9). These features of the disorder indicate the extreme importance of drug use to the individual. Addicted individuals often maintain their destructive behavior, even though they foresee, at least to some extent, the damage that follows.

Tolerance and withdrawal syndrome (criteria 10 and 11). These criteria indicate the brain's adaptation to the drug's effect. Tolerance is indicated by a marked increase in the amount of drug required to produce a desired effect, such as intoxication or relief from an aversive state. A high degree of tolerance ordinarily indicates a history of heavy substance use.

When heavy, prolonged use of addictive drugs is interrupted, especially if the intake stops abruptly, a physiological withdrawal syndrome often occurs (Box 2.3). For alcohol and other central nervous system depressants (e.g., barbiturates), the withdrawal syndrome can be fatal. For all addictive drugs, physiological withdrawal syndromes are usually aversive and uncomfortable, even if not medically dangerous. Most addicted individuals have had some experience with aversive withdrawal. Their knowledge that taking the drug can alleviate the discomfort results in an often intense desire (craving) for the drug.

In earlier diagnostic systems, these indicators of the brain's adaptation to the drug effect – physiological dependence – were critical identifying features of dependence/addiction. In the DSM-5 (as well as the DSM-IV), tolerance and withdrawal syndrome satisfy two use disorder criteria. However, their presence is neither necessary nor in many cases sufficient for such a diagnosis (Box 2.3). Motivational and behavioral factors have replaced these more overtly physiological factors as the critical components of an SUD. Since withdrawal from some drugs presents a medically important risk, the formal diagnosis must include a notation specifying these criteria, if present.

BOX 2.3 Physiological withdrawal syndrome and the SUD diagnosis

A physiological withdrawal syndrome is not a critical (necessary) symptom of a substance use disorder in current diagnostic systems for three primary reasons. The first reason is that some addictive drugs, even when their heavy use is abruptly halted, produce a withdrawal syndrome less dramatic than that of alcohol or opioid drugs (e.g., heroin). Drugs with definite addiction potential, such as THC (from marijuana), nicotine, and cocaine, were previously not considered as addictive because the withdrawal syndromes consist primarily of depression, irritability, sleep disturbances, and an intense desire for the drug. These effects are caused by the brain's adaptation to chronic drug use, as are the more visible withdrawal syndromes. These withdrawal symptoms are just as "physiological" as the tremor and convulsions from alcohol withdrawal or the diarrhea and vomiting of opioid withdrawal. Although they are less obvious to an untrained observer, these dysphoric effects can be quite serious. The dysphoria and depression of withdrawal are subjective and emotional states that may drive an individual back to drug use or, in extreme cases, promote suicide.

The second reason is that some patterns of disordered drug use are quite harmful and satisfy other criteria for a diagnosis of SUD but do not result in a serious withdrawal syndrome. For example, frequent binge drinking can be diagnosed as an alcohol use disorder, even though not causing the harrowing alcohol withdrawal syndrome that can include extreme anxiety, hallucinations, and fatal convulsions.

The time-limited nature of acute withdrawal syndromes is a third reason that this condition is not required for a diagnosis of even a severe use disorder. Although the overt syndrome eventually abates with the passage of time after stopping drug use, the compulsion to use the drug often lasts much longer. Many addicts recount their experience of resuming heroin, cocaine, or alcohol

BOX 2.3 Continued

use immediately after release from a lengthy time in prison. These individuals underwent severe and painful withdrawal symptoms while incarcerated, but that experience typically ran its course within days after their initial confinement. Similar stories come from individuals who resume addictive drug use soon after discharge from treatment in an environment allowing no access to drugs. Relapse, quite frequently occurring long after the initial withdrawal syndrome subsides, is not unusual in the long time course of this persistent disorder. Changes in brain function apparently endure for lengthy periods of time, influencing thinking and behavior (Chapter 4). If addiction were driven only by the temporary state of acute withdrawal, elimination of compulsive drug use would require only an enforced period of abstinence. For most cases of SUD, such a period of drug-free time is important, but not sufficient for long-term recovery.

A final consideration regarding physiological withdrawal symptoms and addictive dependence is related to the extended use of analgesic drugs (opioids) and antianxiety drugs (including benzodiazepines such as Xanax). These drugs can be addictive, but they also have important and effective medical applications for management of chronic pain and certain anxiety disorders. Extended use produces tolerance, and discontinuation often results in a definite withdrawal syndrome. Although the patients may be physiologically dependent, appropriate use under medical supervision is not an SUD. The presence of tolerance and the occurrence of a physiological withdrawal syndrome are not sufficient for a diagnosis of addiction – a moderate or severe SUD requiring the presence of at least four diagnostic criteria. The issue of the appropriate medical use of drugs with addiction potential is discussed in Chapters 14 and 15.

DSM Diagnoses and Long-Term Studies of SUD

Substance use disorders can persist for many years. Long-term studies are invaluable for determining the natural history of the disorder, for monitoring demographic changes in SUD prevalence, and evaluating treatment effectiveness. The diagnostic categories and criterion sets for SUD in the DSM system have undergone several revisions, and the process will continue based on better understanding of the disorders. Cultural changes may also contribute to the revision process. Although the diagnostic systems have changed to some extent, the critical identifying features of SUD remain essentially the same. This continuity allows ongoing use of information (research results) collected under earlier versions of the DSM. An example of current analysis of results of a long-term study, originally conducted with

DSM-III criteria, is the Collaborative Study on the Genetics of Alcoholism (COGA), and investigation of alcohol dependence described in Chapter 5. A huge amount of information has resulted from research conducted since the DSM-IV revision became available in 1994. These results, based in part on DSM-IV definitions of SUD, will be of great value for many years, even though the DSM-5 revision now guides the conduct and analysis of addiction research.

The ICD System of the World Health Organization

The International Classification of Diseases and Related Health Problems (ICD) is a diagnostic system created by the World Health Organization (WHO), an agency of the United Nations with 193 member countries. Diagnostic criteria for SUD of the ICD-10 and DSM-IV are quite similar, especially regarding the dependence classification (Martin 2009, Widiger 2005).

The DSM system is primarily concerned with clinical management (mainly diagnosis and classification) of psychiatric disorders in the United States, the United Kingdom, and other countries with similar cultures. The ICD system has a broader orientation, relating to public health issues in many countries. The parts of the ICD-10 relevant to substance use disorders are intended to help the member countries reduce the disease burden of mental disorders and certain unhealthy behaviors. Its focus is somewhat wider than that of the DSM system in that some patterns of substance misuse are public health hazards at the collective and individual levels but do not qualify as psychiatric disorders. The toxic effect of passive exposure to tobacco toxins ("secondhand smoke") is an example of this type of concern.

Diagnostic Systems and the Disease Theory of SUD

Identification and diagnosis of SUD are essentially atheoretical – diagnostic systems do not address causes of the disorder. However, both of the widely used diagnostic systems have certain features implying that drug use disorders are disease based. The DSM is a product of the American Psychiatric Association, and psychiatry is a medical specialty. The complete title of the ICD is the International Statistical Classification of Diseases, Injuries, and Causes of Death (World Health Organization 1992), which of course includes the term *disease*. Additionally, with the exception of DSM-5, these recent or current diagnostic systems are categorical in nature. Categorical classification usually implies a disease entity rather than a behavioral disorder (Epstein 2001).

Establishing Thresholds for Identification of Psychopathology

Amounts of drug use and adverse consequences vary incrementally among individuals on a continuum of intensity or severity. A basic requirement of a diagnostic system is to establish thresholds or cutoff points that mark the transition between use that is not dysfunctional and disordered or pathological use (Maddux and Winstead 2005, Martin et al. 2008). The clinician whose task is to assess an individual's drug use must then determine whether this specific case meets or exceeds the defined threshold for diagnosis of an SUD.

The amount of drug use (dose and frequency) and the type of drug used (legal and culturally accepted or prohibited and seen as deviant) are in most cases not major determining factors in identifying SUD. The adverse consequences, rather than the amount of drug use, are the more important features of the disorder. Some individuals might often drink large amounts with no apparent bad outcomes, while others suffer quite harmful results from considerably less alcohol intake. Similar differences also occur among users of other addictive drugs.

Although use levels alone generally indicate neither safe use nor SUD, there are exceptions to this principle. Heavy drug use increases the probability of harmful effects. Binge drinking (considered to be a hazardous use of alcohol) is defined by the National Institute on Alcohol Abuse and Alcoholism as consumption of five (for men) or four (for women) or more standard drinks within a two-hour period. Conversely, the low-risk level of drinking for adult men younger than sixty-five years of age is no more than four standard drinks per day and no more than four-teen drinks per week. The maximum low-risk level of drinking for women is three per day and seven per week. These lower levels of use rarely cause behavioral or medical problems in healthy individuals. Specific amounts designated as safe are lower for those over age sixty-five (http://niaaa.nih.gov).

In the DSM-5, the threshold for a diagnosis of an SUD depends on the occurrence of a minimum number of diagnostic criteria (Box 2.2). There are several of these markers (characteristic features) for the disorder because of the many ways in which drug use can cause problems in an individual's life. Reliable and objective evaluations are the intended purpose of both the diagnostic systems and the training of health care professionals who make use of these systems. However, the diagnostic criteria leave considerable latitude for their interpretation (West 2006). For example, how strong must the (unsuccessful) desire to stop drug use be to satisfy that criterion? What about the occurrence of low-intensity withdrawal-like symptoms? Different clinicians may not reach identical diagnoses of a given individual, especially in borderline cases.

Diagnosis of a psychopathological syndrome usually requires the presence of a significant state of *distress* (a painful symptom, such as anxiety or sadness) or *disability* (impairment in an important area of functioning) (APA 2000). The distress or disability should not come from the normal problems of living but should indicate some underlying psychological dysfunction (Wakefield 1999, Widiger 2005). Making that distinction regarding the source of the problems is often difficult and somewhat subjective (Maddux and Winstead 2005). For diagnosis of SUD, the distress or disability should be associated with drug use.

Cultural and Social Influences on Diagnosis

Objectivity is an important goal for diagnosis of SUD, but attainment of complete objectivity is difficult. Conceptions of psychopathology in general, including specific disorders, such as drug use, are social constructs in that they are determined by **cultural contexts**. The definitions and meanings of psychopathology are negotiated among the people and institutions of a culture that reflect the values and power structure of that culture at a given time (Maddux and Winstead 2005). The results of such negotiations regarding the diagnosis of SUD are reflected in the successive changes in the DSM and ICD systems made since the mid-twentieth century.

An example of a culturally determined view of addiction comes from changes in attitude over the years of both the public and the medical profession in the United States concerning the habitual use of tobacco. Health hazards and the difficulty in stopping tobacco use were recognized for many years, but the addictive nature of nicotine dependence was acknowledged by government authorities only during the 1980s. The addictive potential of nicotine is now fully recognized, and compulsive tobacco use is defined as an SUD (Chassin et al. 2007). The change reflects a cultural difference (promoted by scientific evidence) in consideration of tobacco use.

Social contexts and cultural concepts of addiction can influence the diagnosis of SUD to some extent (Hasin 2003, Willenbring 2010). A typical stereotype of addiction probably includes unemployment, isolation, or association only with other addicts, physical and mental health problems, and perhaps criminal activity or homelessness. Unfortunately, such extreme adverse consequences of SUD do occur. However, both clinical and epidemiological studies reveal that a majority of those with drug or alcohol addiction are not in such desperate situations. Individuals with the disorder can maintain the outward appearance of an intact life for years, even while they struggle with compulsive drug use and its consequences (Dawson et al. 2006). Much of the pain and loss is often carefully hidden, and as previously mentioned, not all life difficulties are due to drug use – making it possible to conceal the actual maladaptive nature of the heavy drug use. Clinicians specializing in SUD often see cases in which the addicted individual tenaciously maintains the facade of a normal life. The stubbornly defended markers that supposedly demonstrate an absence of a serious problem often include maintaining employment (particularly in a prestigious or highly paid profession), and for parents, maintaining an intact family. Such outwardly normal lives may be characteristic of the so-called **high-functioning** addict, whose life is actually diminished by distress and unhappiness. These individuals are at risk for progressing to even greater difficulties and losses if the SUD is not recognized and arrested. Most of those suffering from SUD are functional, if at some reduced level.

The SUD of many (relatively) high-functioning individuals may go undetected, especially in a general hospital, an office-based psychiatry or clinical psychology practice not specializing in addictive disorders (Blume and Zilberman 2005). Many who seek help from a mental health professional for a non-drug-related issue also have a disorder of alcohol or other drug use that underlies or at least contributes to their distress. After establishing trust with the client, a skilled clinician can often uncover such unacknowledged SUD. However, an engaging, cooperative client who presents himself well and is successful in a prestigious profession or occupation is less likely seen as having an SUD (Hasin et al. 2007). Such clients with a mild or moderate level of SUD are more likely to seek evaluation and therapy at the office of a general mental health professional than at a treatment center specializing in addictive disorders. For further discussion of treatment choices as influenced by level of disorder severity, see Chapter 16 (treatment of SUD).

The clinical staff of a drug abuse treatment center is less likely to be influenced by client characteristics such as an apparently high level of general functioning. Clinicians with much experience in dealing with SUD recognize that addictive disorders can be present in individuals who have not yet experienced grievous losses. However, clinicians specializing in SUD sometimes incorrectly diagnose addiction in a client if there is any admission or indication of illicit drug use, particularly in adolescents. Adolescent patterns of alcohol use may also result in false-positive evaluation (overdiagnosis) of SUD (Chung and Martin 2005). In such cases the "cultural climate" of the SUD treatment facility (basically an assumption that all individuals who appear for evaluation have a serious drug use problem) may contribute to erroneous evaluation of the severity, or even the presence, of an SUD (Denning et al. 2004, Fletcher 2013, Wakefield and First 2003).

Heterogeneity of Substance Use Disorders

Individuals with SUD vary considerably in patterns of drug use and the adverse consequences of such use. The individual diagnostic criteria presented in Box 2.2 appear in different combinations among individuals suffering from the general disorder (Hasin and Beseler 2009). With the DSM-5, six of the eleven diagnostic criteria are required for a diagnosis of a severe SUD, and the presence of fewer symptoms indicates a moderate or mild disorder. Therefore, two individuals diagnosed with an SUD might share none of the same symptoms. This variability in combinations of diagnostic symptoms and behaviors indicates the heterogeneous nature of the disorder. Even if the common features are more important than the differences, there may be several distinct types of SUD, and the characteristic **heterogeneity** can influence diagnosis as well as treatment outcomes (Basu et al. 2004).

Consider the following individuals who might appear for diagnostic evaluation, all of whom have actual or potential problems possibly related to drug use: (1) male, age sixty-eight, retired salesman, heavy drinker of alcohol, has experienced seizures and hallucinations during withdrawal from alcohol, also suffers from clinical depression; (2) female, age forty-three, attorney, smokes two packs of cigarettes daily, is diabetic, hypertensive, and at risk for cardiac failure; (3) female, age eighteen, university student, uses cannabis daily, at risk of not completing her engineering degree due to poor academic performance, diagnosed as having borderline personality disorder; (4) male, age thirty-one, construction worker, frequent user of cocaine and heroin, on parole after serving a prison term for burglary, at risk of returning to prison if he fails a urine screen.

A diagnosis of having an SUD would seem likely for each of these individuals. However, the marked differences among them in drugs used; the nature of adverse consequences; concurrent psychiatric or other medical problems; and age, gender, and occupation are characteristic of the heterogeneity of the disorder, or general class of disorders. These factors affect the prognosis and treatment as well as the diagnosis of SUD.

The adverse consequences of individuals addicted to nicotine differ from those with a use disorder of alcohol or heroin. DSM-5 includes separate diagnostic criteria lists for these and other SUDs, although the criteria are similar for most addictive drugs. Differences among the problems encountered with heavy use of different drugs are also reflected in the multiple signs or symptoms included in each criterion list.

Use patterns and adverse consequences also differ among individuals using a specific drug or drug type. Variations are especially evident in use disorders of alcohol and opioid drugs. The differences in the vulnerability of individuals and the course of these subtypes of disorders are summarized in Chapters 10 and 14.

Characteristics of Individuals with SUD

Diagnosis of SUD can be influenced by personal characteristics, especially gender and co-occurring psychiatric disorders.

Co-occurring Psychiatric Disorders

Many individuals with SUD also suffer from an additional emotional, cognitive, or behavioral disorder. A primary difficulty for the diagnostic process is that acute and chronic drug effects, withdrawal syndromes, and indirect effects of the addictive lifestyle can closely resemble many psychiatric syndromes. Depression, mania, anxiety, thought disorder, and difficult interpersonal relationships are but some of the problems common to both SUD and non-drug-related psychiatric disorders. Psychiatric syndromes that frequently accompany heavy drug use include major disorders (depression, anxiety) and problematic personality types (primarily antisocial and borderline personality disorders). These disorders have a complex relationship with SUD, and the presence of one typically worsens the intensity of the other. The co-occurrence presents a challenge for valid diagnosis and effective treatment. The co-occurrence of SUD and other psychiatric syndromes is discussed further in Chapter 8.

Gender Differences in SUD

There are many gender-related differences in SUD (Blume and Zilberman 2005, Zilberman 2009). Perhaps the gender-related difference most important for diagnosis comes from the higher rate of co-occurring psychiatric disorders in women suffering from SUD (Zilberman et al. 2003). Women with any form of SUD frequently seek medical care for relief of distress from depression and anxiety as well as for other ailments of a less obviously psychological nature. In general medical settings, their SUD may escape detection. The failure to recognize the harmful use of alcohol or other drugs can come in part from the presence of an accompanying psychiatric disorder as well as from medical professionals' generally lower expectation that a female client might have an SUD.

Women with SUD are sometimes seen as sexually vulnerable and promiscuous and are at definite risk of losing custody of children. Threat of these adverse consequences of SUD related to sexuality and parenthood facilitates greater denial, guilt, and shame for harmful and compulsive use of drugs. Therefore, women with SUD may be less forthcoming and candid with the physician or counselor concerning their drug or alcohol use. Finally, because addictive behavior in women is often more secretive and less obtrusive, family members or work associates may be less likely to insist on appropriate medical or other assistance to deal with the disorder. All these factors can decrease the probability of detection and diagnosis of SUD in women.

Other Personal Differences Relevant to Diagnosis

In addition to the important factors of co-occurring psychiatric disorders and gender, other personal differences can influence diagnosis of SUD. These sources of heterogeneity include age, socioeconomic status and occupation, degree of insight into problematic drug use, and readiness to change (Greenfield and Hennessy 2004). Most diagnostic information is obtained by means of a conversation between the clinician and the individual being evaluated. An experienced clinician will modify the evaluative interview to determine the presence of adverse consequences and difficulties of controlling drug use. For example, an interview of an adolescent regarding his marijuana use would be different from that of an elderly widow whose alcohol use has increased after the death of her husband. Differences in overall level of functioning, occupation, and socioeconomic status are also important.

Instruments and Procedures for Screening and Diagnosis

Several possible events can result in an individual's substance use being evaluated by a medical or mental health professional (Box 2.4). In some cases, state licensing boards require evaluation for possible SUD in medical or other professional personnel after the occurrence of erratic or dangerous behavior. The court system can order evaluation of individuals involved in criminal behavior. In yet other situations, family members or employers request the evaluation after an intervention prompted by apparent drug-related impairment.

Individuals sometimes request evaluation for possible SUD with no coercion or external motivation, although such self-referrals are not typical. It is not unusual for a client's problematic drug or alcohol use to be identified during the course of treatment or therapy for some ostensibly non-drug-related issue, such as depression or anxiety (Washton and Zweben 2006). Primary care physicians (general practitioners or gynecologists) may also suspect excessive drug use and refer patients for SUD evaluation.

BOX 2.4 Routes of entry into diagnosis of substance use disorder

Self-referral
Referral by mental health professional (psychologist, counselor, social worker, psychiatrist)
Referral by general practitioner MD (primary care physician)
Formal planned intervention arranged by concerned family or friends
Results of SUD screening test (e.g., AUDIT, RAPS4)
Evaluation mandated by court system, military, or professional licensure board

---

The process of detecting and diagnosing SUD can involve several separate stages or steps. The sequence may include (1) screening tests or other preliminary evaluations, (2) collecting additional information about drug use and its consequences, and (3) an interview with a clinician. Screening and diagnostic instruments (standard protocols) are available for each stage of this process.

Screening for Hazardous Substance Use and SUD

Individuals may not realize that their substance use is excessive and harmful. Many users of drugs with abuse potential do not experience clinically significant adverse effects, so some that do have an SUD may not recognize that in their own situation, substance use is a major source of their distress and impairment. Such lack of recognition is most likely when a drug or substance is in wide general use, such as with alcohol or cannabis. However, the harm resulting from use of even more addictive drugs such as cocaine or opioids may not be fully appreciated if use is common among peers.

Screening refers to the application of a test to members of a selected population (e.g., college students with disciplinary violations) to estimate their probability of having an SUD. A screening test requires brief answers to a few predetermined questions relevant to substance use. Screening is not the same as diagnostic testing, which is more extensive and serves to establish a definite diagnosis of the disorder. Complete diagnostic evaluation of large numbers of individuals is impractical due to the time, effort and expense required, and the reluctance of many to cooperate. Screening is much quicker, less intrusive, and intended to identify individuals who are likely to have the disorder. Those who have positive scores on a screening test are often advised to undergo a more detailed evaluation to confirm or rule out an SUD. If the individual will not agree to further diagnostic testing, she may be warned that her substance use is hazardous and advised to stop or decrease this behavior (Stewart and Conners 2004). Nonjudgmental suggestions for specific methods to decrease drug use are termed *brief interventions* (Chapter 16).

Populations Appropriate for Screening

Screening tests are most appropriate for populations with a high incidence of heavy drug or alcohol use or for which substance use is especially hazardous. Settings or situations where SUD screening is useful include medical practices, college campuses, and law enforcement. Individuals in certain occupations relevant to public safety, such as bus drivers or commercial airline pilots, may also be subjected to screening tests. In some cases, the results of these self-report tests are supplemented by urine screen tests. However, analysis of body fluids (urine or blood) indicates only recent substance *use* rather than adverse consequences, including behavioral impairment resulting from illicit drugs, prescribed medications, or alcohol. These biological assays can be quite expensive, limiting their use for screening large populations.

Many visits to primary care physicians, and especially to hospital emergency departments, involve medical problems caused or exacerbated by heavy use of alcohol or other drugs (Saitz 2005). Screening for alcohol problems revealed positive results in as many as 30 percent of emergency department visits, with a 50 percent positive rate for severe trauma patients (D'Onofrio and Degutis 2002). Screening tests for pregnant women or those who intend to become pregnant can be appropriate to obtain information about use of alcohol or other drugs.

Screening tests can be effective in identifying college students at risk for problematic drug and alcohol use. Many students "mature out" of heavy substance use and reduce their consumption when they assume responsibilities of work and family, but the college years are clearly a high-risk time for hazardous use and SUD (O'Malley and Johnston 2002). Colleges often administer screening tests to students at counseling centers and campus health care centers or to those involved in judicial or grievance proceedings (Larmier et al. 2004).

Specific Tests for Special Purposes

Many different screening tests have been developed (Maisto and Krenek 2009). All these instruments consist of a series of questions about patterns, amounts, and/or consequences of drug use. Most tests are self-administered, either by computer or by paper and pencil. Certain tests were designed or have been shown effective for specific populations. Some examples of these specialized tests are the Adolescent Drug Involvement Scale (ADIS), the Young Adult Alcohol Problems Screening Test (YAAPST) used for college students, the TWEAK (tolerance, worried, eye-opener, amnesia) test for women, and the T-ACE test for prenatal screening.

Tests are available to screen for disorders or hazardous use of specific drugs or substances, such as cannabis (Piontek et al. 2008). At least one scale, the Alcohol, Smoking, and Substance Involvement Screening Test (ASSIST), is used to screen for problematic use of several substances with abuse potential (Humeniuk et al. 2008). However, by far the greatest number of screening instruments are those used to detect alcohol use disorders.

The CAGE test consists of only four questions, and its brevity and ease of use contribute to its popularity and wide use in screening for alcohol use problems. However, its frequent use has been criticized since the answers may indicate lifetime (rather than current or recent) alcohol use problems, and it does not assess levels of drinking, including binge drinking (Cooney et al. 2005).

Longer tests, such as the twenty-five-question Michigan Alcoholism Screening Test (MAST) and the ten-question version of the Alcohol Use Disorders Test (AUDIT), include questions about alcohol consumption and its consequences. Most questions on these tests require graded answers, indicating frequency of use or adverse consequences rather than the simple yes–no answers of the briefer tests. The AUDIT test (Saunders et al. 1993) was developed as a cross-cultural screening instrument intended to detect problem drinkers and those in early stages of more severe alcohol use disorders. Three of its ten questions are about levels of alcohol consumption. The remaining questions relate to dependence symptoms and other alcohol-related problems.

A brief test, the Rapid Alcohol Problems Screen (RAPS) (Cherpitel 1995), was developed after analysis of the psychometric properties of CAGE, MAST, AUDIT, and other standard screening instruments. The most discriminating items from each of these tests were included in the RAPS test. A four-item version of the RAPS test was shown to be highly sensitive to alcohol dependence across populations of different ethnicity and gender and of acceptable sensitivity to hazardous drinking. The RAPS4 outperformed the standard screening tests in detecting alcohol use disorders in emergency room patients (Cherpitel 2000). The RAPS4 test items are shown in Box 2.5.

BOX 2.5 The RAPS4 test

Note. Words in parentheses refer to actions or consequences and are not part of the test item.

1. During the last year, have you had a feeling of guilt or remorse after drinking? (remorse)
2. During the last year, has a friend or family member ever told you about things you said or did while you were drinking that you could not remember? (amnesia, blackout)
3. During the last year, have you failed to do what was normally expected of you because of drinking? (perform)
4. Do you sometimes take a drink in the morning when you first get up? (starter, "eye-opener")

Validity of Screening Tests

A valid screening test should identify those at greater risk for problematic substance use, differentiating them from those with less risk. Test results are interpreted as positive, suggesting the presence of a disorder, or negative, suggesting that no disorder is present. These results can be correct or incorrect, with two possibilities for incorrect results. A false-negative result occurs when the test fails to identify a person with a probable SUD, and a false-positive result indicates a probable disorder when none is actually present (Stewart 2009).

The validity of a screening test is indicated primarily by two psychometric measures – **sensitivity** and **specificity**. *Sensitivity* refers to the ability of a test to correctly identify those people in a population who actually have the disorder. A highly sensitive test would have fewer false negatives and so be effective at ruling out the presence of a disorder. If an individual's score on a sensitive test is negative, he is quite unlikely to have an SUD. Conversely, a highly *specific* test would have few false positives, so if a score is positive, the individual is quite likely actually to have an SUD. It should be obvious that highly sensitive tests are more susceptible to false-positive errors and that very specific tests are more likely to yield false negatives.

Screening tests can be made more sensitive by lowering the cutoff score used to define a positive result (indication of an SUD). Raising the cutoff score decreases sensitivity but increases specificity. Higher cutoff points are selected when screening is intended to indicate a more severe disorder relative to a lesser problem, such as hazardous use.

The consequences of a false-negative or a false-positive error are considered in the selection of a cutoff score. For some screening purposes, such as testing of school bus drivers, a high cutoff score (a less sensitive test) could produce false-negative errors with possibly tragic consequences. Sensitivity is often valued more than specificity, because a positive result on a screening test is not a certain indicator of hazardous use or an SUD. A definitive diagnosis can result only from further evaluation. However, complete diagnostic assessment is expensive, so a large number of false-positive errors, associated with a low cutoff score and a less specific test, is also undesirable.

The validity of all self-report screening tests depends on the honesty of the tested individuals in giving accurate answers to the questions about their substance use. For many years there has been particular interest in developing instruments that accurately detect SUD regardless of the respondents' dishonesty or denial (Miller 1976). In some cases, test validity has been determined by means of additional, more objective information obtained from other sources to verify the results of the screening process (Del Boca and Darkes 2003). Not surprisingly, the problem of withholding critical information is greater in populations that have reasons to conceal their problematic use of alcohol or other drugs. College students often prefer to avoid identification as drug users or heavy drinkers (Tarter 2005). Individuals in the criminal justice system also have reasons to give socially desirable answers. Substance-using adolescents, whose use of alcohol or any drug is illegal and prohibited, are also unlikely to give truthful responses in many test settings (Tevyaw and Monti 2004). Deception is less problematic when anonymity is assured, such as in surveys of hazardous use prevalence.

Most screening tests consist of direct questions about the respondent's substance use. For example, a question from the AUDIT asks, "How often during the last year have you found that you were not able to stop drinking once you had started?" A socially acceptable answer, even if dishonest, is obvious. A few tests include indirect questions that do not seem related to substance use or its consequences, so a "correct" answer is not apparent. As an example, an indirect test question might inquire, "Are you ever at a loss for words?" Other types of indirect questions relate to impulse-control difficulties, social deviance, poor judgment, sensation seeking, and overall emotional distress, features characteristic of many with SUD. Interpretation of indirect test results of an individual involves comparison of his answers with those collected from a large number of individuals with diagnosed substance use problems. A pattern of responses similar to that of the population known to suffer from SUD is considered an indication of a probable disorder.

The Substance Abuse Subtle Screening Inventory (SASSI-3) is intended for use with adults, the SASSI-A2 for adolescents (Miller and Lasowiski 1999, 2001). These tests include both direct and indirect questions and are marketed specifically for their purported ability to detect SUDs regardless of the respondent's honesty or motivation. However, the SASSI tests lack specificity in that they result in a high rate of false positives and generally are not more accurate than the direct screening tests described previously. Positive results on the SASSI tests apparently indicate global distress and social deviance, which are only moderately correlated with SUD (Feldstein and Miller 2007). The false-positive errors are especially problematic in that the SASSI tests are sometimes used as diagnostic instruments rather than as screening tests administered prior to more complete diagnostic interviews. Additionally, the SASSI tests consist of more than 100 items, sacrificing the brevity that is an important advantage of most screening instruments.

Use of Additional Information in Diagnosis

Although in most cases the primary information useful for diagnosis comes from the diagnostic interview (self-report of the individual under evaluation), often other types of evidence are available to support a diagnosis of SUD. The additional information is seldom sufficient for a conclusive diagnosis but can provide a more complete picture of the person's life, and possibly the effects of substance use and the attachment to such use.

History of Deviant or Antisocial Behavior

Some of this information may come from the circumstances of referral (Box 2.4). It may also include records of school or college performance (especially expulsions and disciplinary actions), military service, involvement with police or the court system, child welfare services, and so on. Problems seen in any of these records do not necessarily indicate heavy drug use but can reflect a history of antisocial behavior or other difficulties. Such behavior often, but not invariably, accompanies SUD.

Personality Inventories and Psychiatric Evaluation

Personality inventory questionnaires (discussed further in Chapter 8) can reveal behavioral traits (impulsivity, risk taking, anger, anxiety) that are positively correlated to a moderate degree with heavy and destructive substance use. Older tests include the specialized questionnaires derived from the MMPI, such as the MAC test (Feldstein and Miller 2007). More recently developed inventories assess the factors postulated by various theories of personality. As with the records of deviant behavior, these results are neither necessary nor sufficient for clinical diagnosis. Personality profiles, based on the aggregate results of large numbers of research subjects, are of little use for evaluating specific individuals. Other written tests, such as depression or anxiety scales, can provide useful information. See the risk factors for SUD in a subsequent section.

Toxicology Tests and Medical Examinations

Toxicology tests of blood, urine, or hair are useful in treatment programs for monitoring abstinence from substance use. Such results are of limited value for initial diagnosis. Positive test results indicate only recent use, but not a use disorder. Conversely, an individual who suffers from SUD could show negative results from urine or blood tests if she had not used the drug within the last few days. Cannabis use is an exception to this brief period of urine test sensitivity, and hair tests can detect less recent use of most addictive drugs (Warner 2003).

In most branches of medicine, tests of blood and urine, imagery (X-rays, ultrasound, functional MRIs, etc.), and tests of organ function (e.g., EKG) provide much diagnostic information for the clinician. These results are used in addition to those obtained from physical examination and symptoms reported by the patient. Currently such tests are of limited definitive diagnostic value to the mental health professional. Malfunction of certain organs (e.g., liver pathology) can suggest heavy alcohol or other drug use, but even these abnormalities can result from causes other than substance use. Conversely, organ damage is not apparent in many with SUD. Absence of physiological abnormality is especially likely in younger individuals with a shorter history of addictive substance use, or in the use of relatively less toxic substances, such as benzodiazepines (antianxiety drugs).

Brain Imaging: MRI and PET Scans

Brain imagery has advanced our understanding of addictive behavior and ultimately may bridge the gap between neurology and psychiatry (Koob et al. 2014). However, the current state of knowledge provided by such investigations is similar to that described previously for personality inventories. Differences can be seen when the records of the brain activity of many individuals with SUD are combined and compared with similar results of healthy research subjects. This information is invaluable for understanding of the neurological aspects of SUD, but so far cannot be used for diagnosis of the disorder in individuals. Despite enthusiasm for its potential diagnostic value, as of yet there is no evidence that brain imagery information can provide independent "blind" identification of SUD.

Presence of Risk Factors for SUD

Diagnosis of SUD does not directly involve determining the complex and often-uncertain causes of the disorder. Diagnosis consists primarily of evaluating the consequences of substance use and the attachment of the individual to this maladaptive behavior. However, another type of ancillary information sometimes considered in the diagnosis is the presence of risk factors for the disorder (Hasin 2003). Subsequent chapters of this text discuss risk factors – conditions, situations, or behaviors often associated with SUD. A concurrent or preexisting psychiatric syndrome (in addition to the SUD) is a very important risk factor. Some risk factors, such as family history of SUD, probably contribute to the development of the disorder by means of genetic predisposition and/or early-childhood experience. Other risks, such as regular alcohol, tobacco, or other drug use during early adolescence, can predict an eventual use disorder.

Similar to the other sources of information that are indirectly relevant to SUD, the risk factors alone are not sufficient for diagnosis of the disorder. Many individuals with these risk factors never experience problematic substance use, and others who do have an SUD were exposed to none of these often-correlated conditions. However, the presence of these risk factors may increase confidence in a positive diagnosis and could be considered in the evaluation of borderline cases.

The Diagnostic Interview

The primary basis for diagnosis of SUD is an extensive conversation between an individual and a health care professional trained for evaluation of the disorder. The interview is conducted with the intent of determining whether the client's actions, symptoms, and the consequences of drug use meet the diagnostic criteria for an SUD. Validated assessment instruments are available to guide the diagnostic interview. Some guides, such as the Structured Clinical Interview for DSM (SCID) system (Spitzer et al. 1992), allow for some flexibility by the interviewer. However, more structured interviews increase diagnostic reliability and may be more suitable for interviewers with less training and experience (Stewart 2009).

Although human behavior is complex and SUDs are heterogeneous, an effective diagnostic interview can provide an objective evaluation of drug use and its impact on the client. Well-trained professionals should make the same diagnosis of an individual most of the time, given the same symptoms and history of substance use (Yalisove 2004).

In most cases, at the time of the interview, the clinician will already have some knowledge that suggests the presence of a substance use problem. This information can come from a screening test, a more complete drug use inventory, or the results of medical tests. The events or entities that initiate a diagnosis (Box 2.4) may also provide useful information.

Several instruments are available for collection of detailed information about an individual's substance use and consequent problems (Maisto and Krenek 2009). Two such instruments often used in clinical settings in the United States are the Addiction Severity Index for adults (McLellan et al. 1992) and for adolescents (Kaminer et al. 1991). These instruments are much longer than the brief screening tests, and some require administration by personnel trained in their use. They can provide detailed information beyond that required for basic diagnosis of SUD. This information is often of use in treatment planning, including determining the need for medically supervised detoxification. These questionnaires are administered at a time different from the diagnostic interview to facilitate a more comfortable and therapeutic conversation between the clinician and the client during the initial contact.

When given the opportunity, many individuals with drug use problems will downplay their level of use, the adverse consequences, and the overall importance of drugs in their lives. This minimization of involvement with drugs may indicate denial or other defense mechanisms (unconscious distortion of reality) but more often is a deliberate evasion of revealing their actual situation. However, "it is a grave mistake for clinicians to presume that all people with alcohol and drug problems are liars, manipulators, and sociopaths" (Washton and Zweben 2006, p. 124). Inaccurate reporting about substance use often results from the threat of real or imagined consequences of full and honest disclosure and from shame or embarrassment concerning the true extent of their drug use. The problem is similar to that mentioned previously regarding the validity of screening tests, but in the diagnostic interview, full disclosure can be promoted by the **clinical skills** of the interviewer (Figure 2.1).

Figure 2.1 A skilled therapist establishes trust during the diagnostic interview. Photo: Tom M Johnson / Getty Images.

Conducting an accurate assessment for SUD requires expertise in clinical inquiry similar to that required for any other type of mental health problem. Conveying empathy, nonjudgmental acceptance, and a warm, caring attitude yields much better results than aggressive confrontation. It is also important that the clinician clearly convey the impression that she does not view the problems as indicating personal inadequacy or wrongdoing (Gitlin 2007). Factors shown effective in promoting the collection of accurate information are listed in Box 2.6.

Although the diagnostic interview provides information critical for diagnosis of SUD and treatment planning, this initial contact is also the first step in the treatment process. The same clinical skills that promote honest disclosure of drug use and its consequences are also important in establishing the therapeutic alliance between the clinician and client. Many clinicians feel that the trust that can begin in the first session is critical for the long-term effectiveness of the treatment.

BOX 2.6 Factors facilitating accurate self-report of substance use

For diagnosis of SUD, clinicians and clinical researchers rely heavily on self-reports of alcohol and other drug use and the consequences of that use. Reliability and validity of self-reports are greatest when the individual is

- Not under the acute effects of alcohol or another drug
- Not showing major psychiatric symptoms (including acute substance withdrawal)
- Assessed with structured or standardized methods
- Aware that the assessor may attempt to corroborate his self-report by use of biomarkers or reports of significant others
- Has good rapport with the assessor
- Does not have an incentive to distort or deceive
- Is assured of and trusts that his or her self-report will remain confidential within specified boundaries
- Does not perceive that the assessor is judging him or her based on the reported behavior

From Maisto and Krenek (2009)

Chapter Summary

Consistent, valid diagnostic standards are important for both the treatment and scientific study of substance use disorders. The importance for treatment is obvious, but if subjects in research projects are incorrectly identified as suffering from SUD, hypotheses about the nature of the disorder cannot be properly tested.

Currently most diagnoses of SUDs are guided by the DSM-5 of the American Psychiatric Association, which in 2013 replaced the DSM-IV. With DSM-IV, two SUDs could be diagnosed – substance abuse (a less severe use disorder) and substance dependence (more severe, often informally referred to as addiction). In

DSM-5, disorder severity is determined by the number of eleven diagnostic criteria satisfied – resulting in a diagnosis of mild, moderate, or severe SUD.

The DSM-5 provides lists of diagnostic criteria that identify the critical components of SUD for nine types of psychoactive drugs. These criteria include the varied adverse consequences of substance use – failure to meet important responsibilities, interpersonal difficulties, antisocial behavior, problems with mental or physical health, and continued use despite these harmful effects. Compulsive use or impaired control of use indicates overwhelming involvement with the addictive drug characteristic of a severe use disorder.

In severe cases, the disability and distress resulting from drug use are unmistakable. However, less severe patterns of disordered use may be difficult to differentiate from behavior that, although disturbing and irresponsible, does not indicate the presence of a psychiatric syndrome.

Many differences occur among patterns of harmful substance use and the consequences of such use. The heterogeneity presents a challenge for diagnosis and is a primary reason why the diagnostic systems include several criteria, encompassing the many variations of SUD. The frequent presence of an additional psychiatric disorder further complicates the diagnosis of SUD.

In earlier diagnostic systems, the presence of tolerance and an observable physiological withdrawal syndrome (as with opiate drugs or alcohol) were critical for identifying addiction. In DSM-5, compulsive behavior and adverse outcomes, rather than a dramatic withdrawal syndrome, are the essential features of SUD. The change in diagnostic criteria resulted partially from the increased use of cocaine and the recognition that nicotine is highly addictive – both occurring in the latter decades of the twentieth century.

Many with SUD do not match common stereotypes of addicts as desperate individuals whose lives are in complete disarray. In early stages, and in less extreme cases, a facade of a normal life may be maintained in high-functioning addicts. Harmful use of alcohol or other drugs by women is also less reliably detected than is SUD in men, in part because women often withhold full accounting of such problems due to greater guilt and shame.

Screening tests are brief, self-administered questionnaires that, when answered truthfully, can reveal dangerous levels of drug or alcohol use and adverse consequences. These tests are most often used in populations with a high incidence of individuals at risk for SUD. A screening test suggesting the presence of an SUD should be followed by a complete diagnostic evaluation.

Diagnosis is based largely on an extensive interview with an individual who may suffer from SUD. Reluctance to disclose full information about the extent of, attachment to, and consequences of heavy drug use is common in individuals with the disorder. Experienced clinicians can often counteract the denial and defensiveness by warmth and nonjudgmental acceptance. The diagnostic interview is often considered as the first step in treatment for SUD, so establishing a close relationship with the patient is very important.

In addition to the patient's subjective account, several other sources of information are useful for the evaluation. A history of antisocial behavior or of psychiatric or other medical problems can provide insight but is not definitive for diagnosis. Consideration of risk factors for SUD, such as a family history of the disorder or early-adolescent drug use, can also assist in the evaluation.

Review Exercises

1. What are the main differences, including terms used, in how SUD are identified by mental health professionals relative to nonprofessionals?
2. What are the essential features of SUD?
3. Why is it possible for an individual to use drugs in a manner that causes harm, yet not be diagnosed as having an SUD?
4. Describe the nomenclature and diagnostic criteria of DSM-IV and DSM-5.
5. What consequences of drug use must be present in an individual for a diagnosis of SUD?
6. Why are typical stereotypes of addiction invalid for diagnosis of SUD?
7. Why is the presence of objectively detectible "physiological" withdrawal symptoms not required for a diagnosis of SUD?
8. Why, in many cases, is the amount of drug use not a critical factor in identifying SUD?
9. Why are there eleven DSM-5 criteria for use disorders of most addictive substances?
10. What populations are most likely to be administered SUD screening tests?
11. How can a mental health professional facilitate honesty in a client's description of her drug use and its consequences?

Key Terms

abuse (36)
categorical (44)
causing harm (38)
compulsive (37)
consequences (37)
controlling (37)
cultural contexts (51)
dependence (40)

dimensional (44)
emotional connection (40)
heterogeneity (52)
high-functioning (51)
impairment of volitional control (40)

less severe forms of the disorder (39)
objective methods (35)
sensitivity (58)
specificity (58)
stopping use (38)

3 | The Disease Concept

CHAPTER OUTLINE

LEARNING OBJECTIVES

1. Understand the central features of a disease-based explanation of SUD.
2. Understand what is meant by the behavioral manifestation of a disease.
3. Describe how Alcoholics Anonymous facilitated public acceptance of addiction as a disease.
4. Describe the scope of consequences produced by the acceptance of disease theory.
5. Explain the limitations of the disease theory of addiction.
6. Explain the reasons why harmful drug use and some forms of SUD can occur without an underlying brain disease.
7. Describe the limits of each of the five basic tenets of the disease concept of addiction.

Introductory Vignette: A Good Person with a Bad Disease?

Stephanie is a case manager and counselor in an addiction treatment center. Angie is a nurse practitioner whose diversion and illicit personal use of fentanyl (a powerful opioid drug used in surgery) was discovered, resulting in loss of her job as an anesthetist and suspension of her nursing license.

STEPHANIE: Angie, this is your third week in our treatment program for impaired medical professionals. Like most of our patients, you told me that you were feeling very low when you first came in – emotionally devastated by your addiction and the trouble it brought you. So how are you feeling today?

ANGIE: Not as bad as last week, but most of the time I can't get past the shame for what I have done. I am a nurse anesthetist with years of training and experience. Sick and injured people entrust their lives to me when they are at their most vulnerable. I administer drugs that help these patients through the painful and frightening experience of surgery. I took advantage of my access to these drugs and used them to relieve my own work-related stress. I always saw myself as an intelligent woman, a competent nurse, but then I –

STEPHANIE: And of course you really *are* smart, competent, compassionate, and a *great* nurse. You also suffer from a terrible and insidious disease – the disease of addiction. You are a good person with a bad disease.

ANGIE, *after a moment of reflection*: I have heard that, or something similar, repeatedly from you and from others in group sessions since entering treatment here. Maybe I'm starting to believe it, at least at an intellectual level. I was so ashamed and guilty for so long. I knew I had a problem, that what I was doing was wrong and against my professional ethical standards, but my guilt and shame kept me from admitting what was happening, even to myself – for a long time.

STEPHANIE: I see from the record of your intake interview that your grandfather was a heavy smoker and died from lung cancer. Your father was an active alcoholic until his liver disease eventually killed him. You were at high genetic risk for an addictive disorder from the moment you were conceived. You had no choice in your genetic makeup. Is that a source of shame?

ANGIE: No, of course not. You make a convincing argument. I think it will take a while before I let go of the guilt and shame, but if I can do that – can free myself to make some changes and learn to manage the disease – maybe I can recover and again become of some value to myself and others.

STEPHANIE: Many others in your situation have done just that. Stay with it, because it is worth the effort. Shame and guilt are toxic, and recovery will go much better if you keep in mind that your problems were due to a treatable and manageable disease, not to a moral failing or weakness on your part.

Introduction

Many individuals cause great harm to themselves (and others) by their use of alcohol, cocaine, opioids, or other addictive drugs. Since ancient times, those who use drugs in this manner have often been seen as weak or immoral and have sometimes been punished severely or shunned for their destructive, apparently irresponsible behavior. A different view that has gained acceptance over the years is that such drug use is the result of a disease. In the United States and some other parts of the Western world, this concept of harmful drug use as a disease is often a preferred alternative to the earlier premise of immorality or personal weakness (Thombs and Osborn 2019).

Evidence of the influence of neurological abnormalities and genetic predisposition on addictive behavior – summarized in subsequent chapters – provides support for a disease-based explanation of addiction. However, there are objections to and criticisms of the disease theory of substance use disorders, which in its simplest form is not universally accepted (Hammer et al. 2013, Heyman 2009, Lewis 2017, White 2000).

A scientifically based alternative to a straightforward disease explanation of compulsive and destructive drug use is the *biopsychosocial* approach, favored by many psychologists and others with a more behavioral perspective on addictive disorders (e.g., Snoek and Matthews 2017, Stewart 2009, Thombs and Osborn 2019). The biopsychosocial concept (Chapters 1, 7, and 8) of SUD acknowledges that addictive behavior can result partially from a neurological disorder, but also gives much emphasis to nonbiological factors.

An important aim of this text is to show that the behavioral/biopsychosocial approach is actually not a challenge to an appropriately updated disease-based explanation. Both concepts have matured to the point that they are different, but not incompatible, ways to understand the complex etiology of addictive disorders (Berridge 2017, White 2001).

The Disease Concept of Substance Use Disorders

The current scientific literature does not appear to include a specific, comprehensive, and generally accepted theoretical account or systematic explanation of how addictive behavior is the result of a disease. Perhaps the closest approximations to an actual theory are those presented by Leshner (2003) and by Koob and Le Moal (2006). Leshner discusses how older concepts of a separation of brain and mind must be abandoned to accept the concept that drug-modified brain function can result in compulsive behavior. Koob and Le Moal, in the first chapter of *Neurobiology of Addiction*, describe a theoretical framework to explain how biological factors contribute to addiction. However, both Leshner and Koob acknowledge that addiction is also influenced by motivational, psychodynamic, psychological, social, and cultural factors.

These and most other current versions of disease theory are based primarily on changes in brain function that result from exposure to addictive drugs. The amount of drug use required to produce the neurological changes varies among individuals and is an important determinant of vulnerability to developing a substance use disorder. The **amount of drug exposure** factor is important to disease theory but is also a basic feature of the biopsychosocial explanation of SUD.

This chapter summarizes both the strengths and the limitations of a disease-based explanation of addiction and other SUDs. It also briefly traces how disease theory emerged and became prominent in the United States.

Basic Tenets of a Disease-Based View of SUD

The researchers, clinicians, scholars, and others who advocate for a disease theory of addiction differ somewhat in their accounts and explanations of addictive disorders. These differences in emphasis may be related to the authors' training and experience as biologists, psychologists, physicians, psychiatrists, or in other professions and possibly to their own personal experiences with drugs (Thombs and Osborn 2013). Some authors prefer to use the term *brain disease model of addiction* when discussing this view of SUD (e.g., Lewis 2017, Snoek and Matthews 2017).

The American Society of Addiction Medicine's public policy website defines addiction as a disease:

> Addiction is a primary chronic disease of brain reward, motivation, memory and
> related circuitry.... Like other chronic diseases, addiction often involves cycles of
> relapse and remission. Without treatment or engagement in recovery activities,
> addiction is progressive and can result in disability or premature death. (www.asam.org/
> for-the-public/definition-of-addiction)

Box 3.1 lists the essential features (tenets) of the disease-based concept of addiction as extracted from the fifth edition of the American Society of Addiction Medicine's *Principles of Addiction Medicine* (Reis et al. 2014).

BOX 3.1 Essential features of addiction according to the American Society of Addiction Medicine

1. Addiction is a primary disorder and not a reaction to some other medical or emotional disorder (such as an anxiety or mood disorder).
2. The disorder is chronic and progressive in that it persists and becomes more severe if not arrested.
3. Distortions of reality, mainly denial, are typical.
4. Impaired control of behavior results in compulsive drug use.
5. Genetic, psychosocial, and environmental factors contribute to the development and manifestations of this neurobiologic disease.

From Reis et al. (2014)

Note that this description of addiction differs from the diagnostic criteria for SUD (as in the DSM-IV and DSM-5). These tenets refer to the nature of the disorder but also mention underlying causes that are not directly observable. A diagnosis identifies the disorder based on observation of objective signs and reported symptoms.

Behavioral Manifestation of a Disease

The exact definition of the term *disease* varies to some extent depending on the source and length of the definition and the context or intended use of the term. However, the entry found in a medical dictionary is representative of most such definitions: "A pathological condition of a body part, an organ, or a system resulting from various causes such as infection, a genetic defect, or environmental stress and characterized by an identifiable group of signs or symptoms" (American Heritage 2004). The DSM-5 and other diagnostic systems clearly indicate that the problem of concern is the destructive *use* of abusable drugs, so the disorder is one of *behavior*. The question then becomes, is it appropriate and valid to consider this behavioral disorder as resulting from a disease?

Behavior is produced by the activity of the nervous system (including the brain), and some brain diseases, such as epilepsy and Tourette's syndrome, do cause aberrant behavior. Additionally, brain malfunction contributes to certain psychiatric disorders (e.g., schizophrenia, bipolar disorder) that have obvious behavioral as well as cognitive and emotional manifestations. In a similar manner, brain pathology could be a cause of disorders of substance use. If the disordered use of drugs results from brain pathology, then SUD is the behavioral manifestation of a disease. However, abnormal brain function is neither necessary nor sufficient for all forms of SUD.

The case for SUD as a disease is strongest for the most severe form of the disorder – addiction. Addiction most closely matches the disease definition primarily because of the characteristic compulsion and impaired behavioral control. The question of voluntary versus uncontrollable and compulsive behavior is discussed later in this chapter. However, many examples of harmful drug use are rather obvious results of **ignorance, irresponsibility, or poor judgment**. In such cases, it is quite inappropriate to attribute this behavior to an underlying disease. The combination of acute drug effects (intoxication) and common features of human behavior – such as the powerful incentive of an immediate reward – makes identifying underlying causes difficult.

Although there is much support for viewing severe SUD (addiction) as a brain disease, the malady is more than a result of neurological malfunction. Brain activity and changes caused by drugs are often an integral part of the disorder. However, the behavior of SUD occurs in a social milieu. When the social context is included, the brain disease definition becomes unsatisfactory. Addiction can be seen as a chronic **hybrid behavioral disorder** that cannot be fully understood without consideration of both biological processes and environmental (mostly social) factors (Hammer et al. 2013).

We now have a moderate degree of understanding of how genetic factors and drug-altered brain function can contribute to the development of some types of SUD (Chapters 5 and 6). However, as discussed later in this chapter, neither neurological nor genetically influenced differences in behavior invariably indicate the presence of a disease.

Even with some ongoing disagreement and controversy regarding the disease concept of addiction, it is apparent that the disease label for SUD is in wide use. An entry of "addictive disease" into an internet search engine yields many thousands of URLs that include this phrase. Many of these internet sites are neither scientific nor medical; however, this huge collection of internet addresses also includes links to credible sources, such as the *Journal of Addictive Diseases*, a professional medical journal published by the American Society of Addiction Medicine.

Not all cases of harmful and irresponsible drug use are caused by a disease state, but there is little doubt that the various forms of SUD are a significant **public health problem**. Persons with these disorders are likely to require medical care for the biological or behavioral toxicity caused by the drugs. Heavy use of most drugs can damage the body, as described in the drug-specific chapters of this book. The hazards of drug misuse are somewhat similar to those presented by other environmental chemicals or conditions (e.g., lead-based paint, asbestos, interpersonal violence, industrial accidents), which also cause disease or other physical trauma.

Historical Perspective of the Disease Concept

Patterns of psychoactive drug use in any culture, and especially the society's response to both the useful and harmful consequences of such drug use, are quite complex. These issues interface with many aspects of public life, including medicine, public health, law enforcement, and government policies. Many historians and other scholars (e.g., White 1998, 2001; Tracy 2005) have written extensively about the history of harmful alcohol use in the United States. In Western cultures, alcohol is the most widely used psychoactive drug with addiction potential and other harmful effects. Because of the widespread use and misuse of alcohol, attitudes and policies regarding alcohol have greatly influenced the current views concerning SUD in general.

Basic reasons for society's ambivalence and reluctance to consider many cases of harmful drug use as a disease are numerous. A primary cause is the harm to individuals and society resulting from drug use. Since the choice to consume alcohol or other social drugs is commonly seen as a voluntary action, the drug user is then held responsible for any untoward consequences. Additionally, the excessive and harmful use of drugs is often interwoven with other types of irresponsible, **antisocial behavior**. One example is given in a review of studies of psychosocial characteristics of intoxicated drivers by Miller and Windle (1990). They report that men who had been arrested repeatedly for driving while intoxicated were also more likely to have arrest records for non-drug-related traffic offenses and other criminal activities. Therefore, the behavior of many with drug use difficulties is often viewed as a moral failure, not as the result of a disease.

Sarah Tracy, in *Alcoholism in America*, summarizes and comments on the history of societal responses to harmful alcohol use in the United States during the last two centuries (Tracy 2005). In her informative and well-documented book, Tracy describes the emergence of the disease concept of alcoholism. She describes attempts by prominent figures, such as the colonial physician and statesman Benjamin Rush in 1784, to promote the idea that "chronic inebriety" was actually a medical problem and a disease rather than a moral weakness. During the nineteenth century, there were more organized attempts to "medicalize inebriety." Such attempts to promote the acceptance of habitual intoxication as a disease did achieve some success. However, with the advent of prohibition in 1920, governmental and public attitudes markedly shifted back toward the "immorality and sin" viewpoint.

The Influence of Alcoholics Anonymous

The formation of Alcoholics Anonymous (AA) in 1935 eventually had important influence on public opinion toward the acceptance of disease theory, even though the basic doctrines of AA emphasize spiritual deficits and character faults rather than biological abnormalities (White 2000). AA's success in supporting the recovery of many persons who successfully quit drinking is well known. These success stories gave credence to the AA philosophy, which came to include an explanation that the underlying problem was the "disease" of alcoholism. Many AA members felt that the "disease" was actually an affliction of the human spirit, but much of the nonalcoholic public assumed that the disease was physical, or perhaps mental, in nature.

E. M. Jellinek and his collaborator Howard Haggard at the Yale University Center for Alcohol Studies conducted systematic studies of the then-current literature on alcohol misuse and collected personal accounts of harmful drinking from AA members. The publication of *Alcohol Explored* (Haggard and Jellinek 1942) and *The Disease Concept of Alcoholism* (Jellinek 1960) were important early attempts to bring scientific rigor and objectivity to the study of harmful alcohol use. Although Jellinek was an early advocate of the disease concept, he considered only some types of alcohol dependence to be a disease (Leggio et al. 2009).

An excerpt from a scholarly article by Dwight Anderson (Anderson 1942), reprinted in the AA publication *The Grapevine*, stated that "the compulsive drinker, or alcoholic, is a sick man, exceptionally reactive to alcohol; that he can be helped, that he is worth helping, and that the problem is therefore the responsibility of the healing professions." This statement was presented in many publications and speeches in an attempt to remove the stigma of the alcoholic as an immoral person. This and similar statements influenced the gradual change in the public's attitude regarding alcohol and drug addiction. Not surprisingly, however, many remained unconvinced that compulsive drug usage was a disease and that addicts were not basically immoral individuals.

Acceptance by the Medical Profession

The development of the role of the medical profession in dealing with SUD occurred in at least two phases. During the 1950s, organizations like the World Health Organization (1951) and the American Medical Association (1956) issued statements declaring that alcoholism was a disease, or at least that the consequences of heavy drinking were suitable for treatment by hospitals. However, at this time, the compulsive use of drugs was seen by most physicians as a reaction to other problems, probably of a psychiatric nature. Not included in this view was an important basic tenet of disease theory – that addiction is a primary disorder and not a secondary result of some other medical or life-adjustment problem.

In 1990 the American Medical Association recognized addiction medicine as a designated specialty. This event probably indicated the essential acceptance by the medical establishment that compulsive drug use is a primary disorder in its own right. The endorsement of the medical profession was a major and critical step for acceptance of the disease concept because after important advances (such as the introduction of effective antibiotics) earlier in the twentieth century, medicine now had a much more powerful influence on society's attitudes than it did in Benjamin Rush's colonial America.

Thom (2001) outlines the history of views about harmful alcohol use in the United Kingdom and other European countries over the past two centuries. Some of the events occurring in the United States were paralleled in these other parts of the Western world. For example, Thomas Trotter, in late eighteenth-century England, influenced public opinion to some extent with a disease-based account of alcoholism that was similar to that of Benjamin Rush. The twentieth-century advances in biology and medicine helped advance the disease concept in several Western countries, as did the influence of Jellinek's work (Figure 3.1).

During the last thirty years of the twentieth century, "there was a sea change in the way alcoholism was regarded throughout American society" (Tracy 2005, p. 286). An indicator of this trend was the rise of a "**treatment industry**" for SUD. In the 1950s, there were only a few dozen alcoholism treatment programs, but by 1977, the number had reached 2,400; by 1987, 6,800; and by 1991, 9,000 (White 1998). During this growth period, most treatment centers also accepted persons addicted to other drugs as well as those with alcohol use problems. Another indication of the lessened stigma of suffering from an SUD was the public admission of the disorder by many celebrities, including some family members of more than one US president. In 2003, the number of substance abuse facilities exceeded 13,000 (statista.com 2019).

Figure 3.1 Substance use disorder is often seen as a disease, appropriate for treatment by a physician. Photo: SDI Productions / E+ / Getty Images.

Formation of the NIAAA and NIDA

In 1970, the National Institute for Alcohol Abuse and Alcoholism (NIAAA) was established, initially as a part of the National Institutes of Mental Health. In 1974, NIAAA became a separate institute of the National Institutes of Health. The establishment of NIAAA was essentially a "bottom-up" movement, initiated by groups such as the National Council on Alcoholism and enabled by sympathetic senators and congressional representatives, some of whom were themselves recovering alcoholics.

Although there is much similarity in compulsive use of all psychoactive drugs, SUD for alcohol has traditionally been viewed somewhat differently from SUD of illicit drugs like heroin, cocaine, and marijuana. This difference in cultural attitudes still exists to some extent and is exemplified in the United States by the existence of two separate entities of the National Institutes of Health intended to address SUD.

The National Institute of Drug Abuse (NIDA) was established in 1974. The formation of NIDA emerged from the ongoing "war on drugs." Like NIAAA, NIDA's mission is to promote a better scientific understanding of the causes and treatment of abuse and addiction, although for drugs other than the legal and socially accepted drug alcohol.

Much of our current knowledge of the actions of drugs of abuse on brain function has come from research sponsored and funded by NIDA and NIAAA. In the years prior to the formation of these federal agencies, there was very little scientific evidence that neurological malfunction contributes to some forms of SUD.

Continuing Cultural Ambivalence Regarding SUD

Although the view of drug abuse and addiction as immoral behavior is supposedly outmoded in our modern era, much of this judgmental attitude persists due to the very real damage resulting from use of substances like tobacco, alcohol, stimulants, opiates, and other psychoactive drugs of abuse (Thombs and Osborn 2019). Studies were conducted in the United States (Link et al. 1999), the United Kingdom (Crisp et al. 2000), and Germany (Schomerus et al. 2006, Beck et al. 2003) to assess public attitudes toward drug addicts, including alcoholics. All of these studies revealed that even though many people do consider addiction to be a disease (or perhaps an illness), they nevertheless felt that the illness was self-inflicted, that the addicts were responsible for their drug-produced problems, and that these respondents preferred to avoid much contact with addicted persons. Fals-Stewart (2005) refers to the "disease-moral model of addictive behavior," meaning that in the United States, the disease and moral approaches coexist, often uneasily. He states, "At the social policy level, much energy is expended in veering between these two models" (p. 306).

Disease Concept of Addiction in the Early Twenty-First Century

In the United States, many – perhaps most – health care professionals who diagnose, treat, and provide care for SUD-afflicted persons fully accept a disease concept of SUDs. Clinical psychologists and counselors with a cognitive behavioral orientation often disagree with the widespread view that SUD is a disease (Fletcher 2013, McLellan and Meyers 2004, Szalavitz 2016, Willenbring 2013). However, this view of drug abuse and addiction is also typical of the recovery community, which includes those who are or have been active in twelve-step groups and the families of these recovering persons.

The material presented in Chapters 5 and 6 shows the deep involvement of the neuroscience community in further determining the neurological basis for the compulsive use of drugs. However, in a recent issue of the professional journal *Neuroethics*, many scientists, including several who investigate neurological aspects of SUD, question the validity and generality of the brain disease model of addiction (Lewis 2017, Snoek and Matthews 2017). Many of the points made in these articles are similar to those made subsequently in this book.

Individuals in the legal and criminal justice professions are often reluctant to accept the disease explanation of addiction. Many academically based behavioral and social scientists as well as other scholars (e.g., philosophers) are also skeptical of a disease-based account of addiction (Hammer et al. 2013). However, much of American society does accept the premise that many – and probably most – instances of SUD are manifestations of a disease.

NIDA and NIAAA, the federal agencies whose primary mission is the study of destructive drug and alcohol use, have broadened their scope of interest to some extent in recent years. These agencies' research efforts now include the more widespread but less severe forms of substance misuse (Tracy 2005, Heather 2001). For example, in 2005, an issue of *Alcohol Research and Health* (24[4]), a scientific journal of NIAAA, was entitled "Focus on Young Adult Drinking" (as opposed to specific consideration of alcohol use disorders). This change in emphasis is similar to that seen in other countries and reflects the growing realization that much harm is done by drug and alcohol use at levels that would not meet diagnostic criteria for a use disorder. Most would agree that these less intense forms of drug misuse are less appropriately viewed as disease based, even though many such substance users will eventually escalate their use levels until they do meet the DSM-5 criteria for substance use disorders. Therefore, the concerns of the government and scientific establishment are less selectively focused on the "disease of addiction," also including other relevant topics, especially prevention of SUD.

Consequences of Accepting a Disease-Based Explanation of SUD

General acceptance of the disease concept of addiction made possible increased **availability of medical care** and other forms of assistance for afflicted individuals. Medical Insurance coverage often includes some costs of treatment, which can be quite expensive. Many employee assistance programs provide a limited amount of free counseling and referral services for drug-related problems, which are seen as similar to other medical issues. Greater participation in treatment programs has also resulted in many individuals becoming active in twelve-step groups, which provide recovery assistance for extended periods with no financial expense.

Society's acceptance of disease theory and the subsequent justification for treatment of SUD also had economic consequences. The medical profession and the chemical-dependency treatment industry benefited from the shift toward medicalization of addiction treatment, as did pharmaceutical companies (Kushner 2010, Thombs and Osborn 2019).

Lessened Shame and Stigma

Persons suffering from an SUD, especially in Western cultures, in which self-control and personal responsibility are highly valued, typically experience much shame and guilt. When a person who suffers from an SUD accepts the explanation that her destructive actions are not indicative of personal weakness or irresponsibility but are caused by a disease, her shame and guilt are greatly decreased – and entry into treatment is encouraged. Shame and guilt play an important role in maintaining the maladaptive behavior and are major barriers to recovery from addiction. Obviously, recovery from addiction requires more than a basic acceptance that a disease underlies the harrowing compulsion to persist in the self-destructive activity, but for many addicts, such a belief is a major step toward recovery. As George Vaillant comments, "alcoholics who label themselves as ill – and not bad – will be less helpless; they will have higher self-esteem; and most important they, like diabetics, and in contrast to pickpockets, will try harder to change and to let others help them to change" (Vaillant 1995, p. 378).

Although rejection of the depiction of addicts as immoral reduces one type of stigma, the "diseased" label can also convey a different stigma, possibly creating a marginalized population (see previous discussion of cultural ambivalence). As an example, whether schizophrenia is the fault of the mentally ill person counts little toward diminishing society's negative connotation of the condition (Hammer et al. 2013, Heather 2017). Additionally, some may see a brain disease of addiction as a "secular possession" – similar to the seventeenth-century theological belief in demonic possession as a cause for antisocial behavior (Reinarman 2005, Room 2004). This comparison might seem unwarranted, but in twelve-step groups, it is not unusual to hear a recovering addict declare, "My disease was talking to me – urging me to drink again."

Objections to and Limitations of the Disease Concept

The "Substance Use Disorders" chapter of the DSM-5 of the American Psychiatric Association includes standardized criteria used extensively for identification of SUD. These diagnostic criteria make very clear the fact that the disorders are identified primarily by means of *behavioral* indicators. The two nonbehavioral criteria, tolerance and physiological withdrawal syndrome, are by themselves neither necessary nor sufficient for a diagnosis of an SUD (Chapter 2). Although the object of a lengthy and intense search, there is still no reliable biological (genetic or neurological) marker for *addiction*. Biological damage that is the result of drug use is sometimes mistakenly identified as the cause of the many toxic consequences of heavy drug use.

Many health care professionals assume that a disease underlies the (mostly behavioral) DSM-5 criteria for SUD, even though the behavioral diagnostic criteria do not necessarily imply the presence of an underlying biological disorder (Hammer et al. 2013). The DSM-5 is atheoretical regarding causes and makes no mention of substance use disorders as being a disease. However, the American

Psychiatric Association publishes the DSM-5 (as well as the earlier versions of the DSM), and addiction psychiatry is a board-certifiable medical specialty of the American Medical Association. The close association of the DSM system with the medical profession lends support to the common assumption that the disorders described and classified are disease based.

The case for SUD as a disease is strongest for the more severe form of the disorder primarily because of the impaired control and compulsive behavior characteristic of addiction (Fenton and Wiers 2017). Using DSM-IV terminology, substance *dependence* is more likely to result from a disease (brain disorder) than is substance *abuse*. Epidemiological studies, such as the NESARC survey described in subsequent chapters, clearly indicate that the less severe forms of SUD are *more prevalent* than addiction – the most severe manifestation of the disorder.

Three important criticisms of a simplistic disease theory are as follows: (1) harmful drug use can often be explained without appealing to an underlying disease process; (2) the simplest form of disease theory (as typically presented in SUD treatment) essentially ignores or deemphasizes the many nonbiological factors which contribute to addictive behavior; and (3) there is doubt about the validity or the generality of some of the basic tenets of disease theory.

SUD without an Underlying Brain Disease

Deviant and destructive behavior, including the heavy drug use of SUDs, is studied and researched by psychologists, sociologists, and criminologists. Some sociologists (e.g., Schneider 2003), criminologists (e.g., Wilbanks 1989), and psychologists (Heyman 2009, 2011, Kushner 2010, Peele et al. 1992, Snoek and Matthews 2017) raise objections to the explanation of irresponsible and harmful use of drugs as being caused by a disease. A complex array of social and other environmental influences causes most other types of deviant behavior, ranging from violent crime through allegiance to various cults. Therefore, many social and behavioral scientists maintain that primarily nonbiological factors are also largely responsible for many cases of SUD. The environmental or developmental causes include inadequate parenting, poor living conditions, influence of deviant role models, and many other adverse conditions.

Most problems of dealing with relationships, work demands, chronic medical conditions, and other sources of stress and difficulties are viewed and treated as behavioral, emotional, or cognitive disorders rather than as diseases. Of course, some cases of deviant behavior are due to observable neurological malfunction, underlying schizophrenia, bipolar disorder, and some other psychiatric conditions. However, with the obvious exception of these syndromes, psychiatrists and clinical psychologists do not rely heavily on disease-based explanations to account for clients' distress. These clinicians often prefer to consider the effect of developmental, experiential, or other less overtly biological influences. Even the therapeutic use of medication – for treatment of addiction or another psychiatric disorder – does not necessarily imply the presence of a disease state. The possible neurological bases of many psychiatric disorders is under intense research scrutiny, as described for SUD in Chapters 5 and 6.

Genetic evidence identifies a biological risk factor for many cases of maladaptive drug use – and is often given as the primary rationale for classifying SUD as a disease. However, the genetic loading is a predisposition rather than a certain predictor of the emergence of SUD. Although they are at increased risk, most children of alcohol-addicted individuals do not develop the disorder (Chapter 6). Approximately half of the incidence of drug use problems cannot be accounted for by inherited biological factors. The genome directly controls the production of proteins but only indirectly influences behavior, which is affected by many other conditions and events.

The presence of a genetic risk factor for development of SUD does not require that the disorder be defined as a disease. Many genetically influenced human traits, both desirable and less desirable – including level of intelligence, athletic ability, and a tendency for chronic anxiety – are not considered to be diseases (Heyman 2009, Thombs and Osborn 2013). As a specific example, a genetic loading similar to that for the occurrence of SUD also influences the occurrence of antisocial personality disorder (ASPD). Much of the genetic predisposition for SUD may be expressed as a tendency for antisocial behavior. Not surprisingly, the two disorders (SUD and ASPD) co-occur quite frequently (Chapters 6 and 8). Mental health care providers classify ASPD as a psychiatric disorder. However, even given the proven genetic predisposition that influences the occurrence of the disorder, the legal establishment, law enforcement officials, and society in general are quite unlikely to consider extreme antisocial behavior as a disease.

Modern medicine acknowledges the importance of behavior, especially habitual activities often termed "lifestyle," in the etiology of several diseases. Diet and exercise influence the occurrence of obesity and diabetes, as does exposure to carcinogens (e.g., tobacco smoke) the likelihood of developing lung and other types of cancer. George Vaillant, in *The Natural History of Alcoholism Revisited* (Vaillant 1995), comments extensively on the often complex interaction between behavior and a disease state. His example is of coronary heart disease and the influence of certain behaviors, such as insufficient exercise, diet, smoking, and poor stress management. These behaviors, in combination with a biological predisposition, can result in atherosclerosis and coronary heart disease (CHD). Vaillant (1995, p. 18) compares the behavioral factors partially responsible for the biological pathology of CHD to the example of alcoholism, which also has multiple causal factors. Although behavioral and biological causes may interact in both cases (heart disease and alcoholism), behavior has an additional and different role in the drug use disorder. For CHD the main expression of (evidence for) the disease is atherosclerosis and the subsequent malfunction of the heart. In one case (CHD) the behavior contributes to (is a cause of) the disorder but does not identify or characterize the disease. In the other case (addiction) the behavior and its consequences are the primary diagnostic signs (results) of the disorder. Although extensive drug use can cause organ damage, there is currently no biological indicator necessary and sufficient to identify the behavioral disorder of addiction.

Neurological Dysfunction and Compulsive Drug Use

The case for a disease-based explanation for SUD – resulting from altered brain function – becomes much stronger when limited to certain cases, usually those involving compulsive drug use, an important hallmark of addiction (Berridge 2017, Fenton and Wiers 2017). However, critics of disease theory often argue against designating even the compulsion seen in severe drug dependence as definite evidence of a disease. They point out that many other examples of compulsive behavior, including some forms of gambling, overworking, and preoccupation with physical exercise, are seldom seen as a disease. Although such extremes of behavior are thought to have at least a partial biological basis, there is currently little evidence that these individuals have neurological abnormalities similar to those linked to drug use as described in the subsequent chapters. At some point an explanation of excessive behavior as a disease (watching television? playing video games? social networking on the Internet? hoarding?) becomes untenable and, if accepted, would erode our basic concept of the meaning of the term (Heyman 2009, Peele 2000, Vrecko 2010). The compulsive nature of addictive behavior is further discussed in Chapter 7 and in a subsequent section of the current chapter.

A compromise between extreme positions (disease/biological vs. environmental/social/learning accounts of SUD) is offered by Marc Lewis: "Neuroscience doesn't have to cast addiction as a disease. Rather it can offer a way out of the **disease-choice dichotomy** by identifying the biological processes that connect reward to decision-making in-the-moment and goal-seeking habits over time" (Lewis 2011, p. 150). As Rachel Hammer states, "we are embodied beings. Biologically, that addiction rests on a neurochemical platform is evident and useful. However, it is not necessary to frame addiction as a disease to access the benefits from biological addiction research" (Hammer 2013, p. 31).

Marc Lewis further develops a learning/developmental alternative to the brain disease model of addiction in his book *The Biology of Desire: Why Addiction Is Not a Disease* (Lewis 2015). Lewis, a developmental neuroscientist, acknowledges that certain changes in brain function accompany addiction but emphasizes that a primary characteristic of the brain is modification in response to environmental demands. Conditions like adversity and emotional turmoil in early development can make drug effects especially rewarding and comforting, promoting deep learning and "enduring footprints in neural tissue" (Lewis 2017, p. 15). These neurological changes are not a disease but a developmental consequence of experiences, including use of addictive drugs. Lewis points out that many with such altered brain function eventually learn new ways to think and act, as their brains change further during recovery from addiction. Lewis's view, and the views of others with similar criticisms of a brain disease model of addiction, is in general agreement with the biopsychosocial concept of SUD.

Disease-Based Explanations Often Discount Nonbiological Factors

Proponents of a disease theory of alcoholism and addiction to other drugs acknowledge that the disorder's etiology is complex and involves nonbiological factors (White 2001). Jellinek stated, "The usefulness of the idea that alcoholism is a medical and public health problem depends, to a large extent, upon the recognition of social and economic factors in the etiology of all species of alcoholism" (Jellinek 1960, p. 158). Mark Keller wrote in the *Journal of Alcohol Studies* that alcoholism quite possibly "comes into being as an interactive effect of sufficient alcohol with constitutional, personality, psychological and social co-factors" (Keller 1976, p. 1714). Vaillant maintained that "there is no other so-called disease in which both etiology and cure are more profoundly dependent upon social, economic and cultural variables" (Vaillant 1995, p. 17). More recent discussions of the biology of addiction also mention the importance of additional causes to that of altered brain function (Leshner 2003, Koob and Le Moal 2006). All these important theorists view the disease concept as the appropriate way to understand addiction. However, their realistic assessments of the complexity of the causes of the behavioral disorder are similar to the biopsychosocial approach currently favored by most psychologists and many other scholars and scientists.

Unfortunately, such realistic complexity is rarely acknowledged in information presented to the general public or in much "self-help" literature. **One-dimensional accounts** of the basis of addiction are typical of many books and internet-based sources of information intended for general audiences. These sources typically put much emphasis on the neurological aspects of the disorder, and some largely dismiss psychological and cultural influences. For example, *Beyond the Influence: Understanding and Defeating Alcoholism* (Ketcham and Asbury 2000), a book intended for general readership, contains useful information but gives little or no credence to nonbiological factors in the etiology of alcohol use disorders. The authors' simplistic explanation includes the statement that

> *physiology, not psychology, determines whether one drinker will become addicted to alcohol and another will not.* This is not theory but fact, based on thousands of research studies detailing the nature, causes, and progression of this ancient yet perpetually misunderstood disease. (p. 4, italics original)

This statement is, of course, incorrect in that neither physiology nor "psychology" alone determines the fate of any individual consumer of alcohol or another addictive drug. The etiology of addiction is multivariate because both factors are involved. An invalid exclusion of psychological and behavioral influences on addiction may come from a common perception that in comparison to matters of psychology, physiological factors are more "real" (Hammer et al. 2013).

Acceptance of a simple version of the disease concept tends to relieve shame and guilt and so can be beneficial for promoting recovery. However, another possible objection to the needed inclusion of **psychological factors** is that such considerations might be seen as dangerously close to some type of "mental disorder," again bringing shame and stigma. Presenting the disorder as a strictly biological disease and excluding the role of social, behavioral, and psychological factors may also be an attempt to avoid a return to an earlier view of addiction as "willful misbehavior" and the designation of addicts as immoral individuals.

The presentation of a simple version of a complex problem to a nonscientific audience is understandable, and the supposed relative simplicity is often mentioned as an advantage of a disease-based explanation. Indeed, simplicity may be beneficial for the educational component of treatment programs serving persons suffering from an SUD. One of the useful slogans often given as advice in twelve-step programs is "Keep it simple," which warns against undue complications that might render a recovery plan unworkable. However, the influence of such treatment considerations obscures the true complexity of the basis of SUD, including a lack of understanding of the role of psychological factors in the causes of the disorders. Chapter 16 describes the benefits for treatment of addiction in acknowledging the behavioral causes of the disorder – which can be modified and so are very different from the permanent genetic predisposition for addiction.

Limits to the Generality of the Basic Tenets of a Disease-Based Explanation

The basic tenets of the current disease-based explanations of addiction were derived from clinical experience with drug-abusing persons, and evidence of the involvement of genetic predisposition and drug-related neurological adaptations in SUD. The following considerations and criticisms of these basic tenets are based on two general points: (1) these principles are valid for only a subset of persons suffering from SUD and (2) some features of addictive behavior are taken to be disease based when an alternative nondisease behavioral explanation seems to be equally valid.

First Tenet: Substance Abuse and Addiction Are Primary Disorders

This basic principle clearly differentiates current disease concepts from the older view that SUD was "reactive" to a psychiatric disorder or some other life-adjustment problem. This important tenet of a disease explanation is valid in many cases, in that SUD is not invariably a reaction to some other (non-drug-related) source of emotional pain or discomfort. In 1995 George Vaillant emphasized that in two cohorts of men that were monitored from adolescence through middle age, those who exhibited alcohol-related problems were not different in premorbid psychological stability from those without such problems (Vaillant 1995). Vaillant's observations were consistent with a disease theory view that for many cases of SUD, the accompanying psychological distress such as anxiety and depression are *consequences*, rather than *causes* of excessive drug use.

However, there is now abundant evidence that many environmental, early-experience, and psychological factors (including personality and psychiatric disorders) increase the probability of SUD and therefore are risk factors for the disorder. The complex relationship between lifetime experiences (especially those that cause difficulty during childhood and adolescence), psychiatric disorders and SUD is discussed at length in Chapter 8. Heavy drug or alcohol use does cause and worsen several types of distress, but the presence of these many risk factors (some which precede drug use) supports the view that SUDs often have a **reactive component**. Women appear to be even more vulnerable than men to experiential and environmental risk factors (Blume and Zilberman 2004).

Vaillant's (1995) treatise on the development of alcoholism in men deemphasized the likelihood of reactive addiction. However, he later acknowledged that some cases of addiction "result in part from efforts at self-medication due to premorbid psychiatric co-morbidity – of which heroin and polydrug abuse are examples" (Vaillant 2003, p. 3). He bases this distinction in part on heroin's very effective antianxiety properties, which produce powerful reward value in vulnerable individuals – including those with chronic anxiety.

SUD can occur in the absence of identifiable environmental or developmental risk factors, so not all abuse or addiction is reactive. In such cases, the designation of SUD as a primary disorder is appropriate. Even when the disorder is to some extent reactive, once compulsive drug use has become established, it typically does take on a "life of its own." At this time, the disorder is no longer driven solely by or dependent on an underlying condition like depression or anxiety. In most cases, intervention and treatment of the addictive behavior per se should be addressed first, or at least simultaneously with the accompanying psychiatric disorder. Effective treatment of anxiety or depression is unlikely if heavy drug use continues. After the client is drug-free, improvement of these other problems can reduce the probability of relapse.

Second Tenet: Addiction Is a Progressive Disorder
Diseases often follow a progressive course, in that the underlying pathology and the resulting symptoms become more pronounced with the passage of time.

Increasing severity of addictive behavior is often a prominent feature of SUD. However, progression is not inevitable, and when the disorder does worsen, there are reasonable explanations that are not disease based.

Many individuals who seek (or are forced to accept) treatment for SUD exhibit the escalation of drug-related problems referred to as progression. Most who suffer from SUD experienced few (if any) bad consequences from their initial use of addictive drugs (including, of course, alcohol). Eventually, the problems listed as DSM diagnostic criteria for the disorder emerged and, for many individuals, became worse as drug use continued. Jellinek (1960) and other more recent investigators describe progression as an ever-worsening sequence of adverse consequences, culminating in a greatly diminished life and eventual premature death if the drug use continues. Although such progression does occur, especially in those who seek treatment for SUD, Jellinek's information came from self-reports of selected individuals in Alcoholics Anonymous (AA) groups (Jellinek 1946). These respondents were not representative of the entire population of individuals with alcohol use disorders.

Longitudinal studies demonstrate that the pattern of predictable, invariable progression is atypical, rather than a universal characteristic of SUD. Erratic patterns of alcohol use and its consequences over a period of years are typical of long-term follow-up studies of effectiveness of treatment for SUD (Chapter 16). William White, in a discussion of a disease concept for the twenty-first century, describes a variety of recovery experiences, indicating the many ways in which people resolve alcohol- or drug-related problems (White 2001).

Epidemiological studies of abuse and addiction (not based on clinical populations) also reveal a complex picture of the long-term course of addiction, often different from the traditional view of inevitable progression. The National Epidemiological Survey of Alcohol and Related Conditions (NESARC), a population study of 43,000 respondents (of whom 4,422 were or had been alcohol dependent based on DSM-IV diagnosis) was conducted under the sponsorship of NIAAA (Dawson et al. 2006). Respondents who were currently or previously addicted to alcohol described their alcohol use and associated problems, which for some spanned a period of twenty years. About three-fourths of these respondents had never sought treatment nor participated in AA.

Long-term patterns of alcohol use in these NESARC respondents included abstinence, safe levels of alcohol use, and dangerous levels of drinking and continued alcohol abuse and dependence. Thirty-three percent of these never-treated individuals had stopped drinking or had reduced their alcohol intake to safe levels. It appears that although ever-worsening progression of harmful alcohol use does occur, it is not an invariable characteristic of alcohol addiction.

Other epidemiological surveys indicate similar prevalence of untreated remission of SUD (Chapter 16). These results demonstrate that for many individuals,

SUD does not appear to be a chronic, progressive disease but a behavioral disorder that often lessens or disappears, apparently in response to changed life circumstances or other unknown factors rather than because of medical treatment. As with many aspects of SUD research, much more information is available concerning long-term use patterns in alcohol use disorders than for problematic use of other addictive drugs.

The progression sometimes seen in addiction could result from a worsening disease process. Neurological changes often require repeated drug exposure to fully develop and so could be seen as a subtle but worsening abnormality of a biological system (the brain). Alternatively, rather than progressive brain damage, escalation of maladaptive behavior could result from a drug-produced reduction in sources of reward and ways in which to cope with difficult life situations. This nonbiological account of progression, further described in Chapter 7, is an important part of the cognitive behavioral alternative to a simple disease theory account of addiction.

Third Tenet: Denial and Other Defense Mechanisms Are Disease Symptoms

The concept of *denial*, introduced in Freud's psychoanalytic theory, is prominent in the simple version of the disease explanation of addiction typically presented to individuals receiving treatment for SUDs. This term refers to one of several defense mechanisms often employed to avoid awareness of a painful, unpleasant reality. The current ASAM description of addiction refers to "diminished recognition of significant problems with one's behavior and interpersonal relationships." For addicts, the presence of a destructive relationship with the drug is often not acknowledged and sometimes not even recognized. Rationalization is another defense mechanism in which reality is interpreted in a manner more acceptable to the person with an SUD.

Denial is probably overused to explain addictive behavior (Doweiko 2006, Heyman 2009). The defense mechanism is often inappropriately invoked to account for an individual's refusal or reluctance to enter treatment or to agree with a counselor's interpretation of her situation. There are instances when simple disagreement, ignorance, or inability to perform some recovery-related activity may be mistaken for denial or another defense mechanism. Even if an individual is quite aware that her drug use is addictive, she may simply refuse to admit that realization because she is not willing to change her behavior.

Individuals suffering from SUD often have distorted perceptions of their own behavior and their relationship with an addictive drug. It is accurate to say that denial is a frequent characteristic of drug abuse and addiction. However, there seems to be little justification to regard denial as indicating the presence of a disease state. As Thombs and Osborn (2013) maintain, "instead of narrowly defining it (denial) as a symptom of a disease, it is useful to take a broader view and consider how other forces, in combination, foster its use. For instance, the general social stigma attached to addiction is responsible in part for the emergence of the defense" (p. 51). Defense mechanisms, including denial, are widely used, both by addicted individuals and by those without an SUD. Denial and rationalization are likely to occur when one must deal with unpleasant, painful situations, especially when there is no ready solution to the problem.

It is somewhat ironic that denial is relied on so heavily in most disease-based explanations of addiction, given the psychoanalytic origin of the concept of defense mechanisms. Current (as well as classical) psychoanalytic explanations of addiction typically describe compulsive use of drugs as a reaction to or symptom of some underlying psychological disorder (Leeds and Morgenstern 1996). As stated previously (Box 3.1), one of the main tenets of a disease theory of addiction maintains that the addiction per se is the primary disorder, rather than a reaction to some other source of discomfort.

Fourth Tenet: Addictive Behavior Is Uncontrollable

Loss of control is an important principle of classic disease theory often used to account for the compulsive and destructive behavior characteristic of severe SUD. The impaired-control explanation of disease theory often helps to relieve the heavy burden of guilt and shame of addicted individuals. Some investigators (e.g., Walters 1999) maintain that the concept of losing volitional control is poorly conceived, not clearly defined, and should be replaced by more specific references to controlling factors, such as craving or situational influences. Intense craving, often experienced during withdrawal, can drive drug use, even though the addicted individual has conflicted feelings and motivation about taking the drug. However, much addictive drug use occurs in the absence of craving (Chapter 7).

A primary problem for a general "loss of control" explanation is that deliberate intent often precedes addictive drug use. In some situations (such as when the drug is not conveniently available) drug procurement and use requires careful planning and extensive effort, and is obviously under complete volitional control. The professed impairment of control might then be offered later, after the fact, to justify what turned out to be a very bad course of action. In many instances, the "uncontrollable" behavior (drug use) could result from voluntary risk taking and/or poor judgment (Martin et al. 2008). Heyman (2009) maintains that even self-destructive behavior is often chosen voluntarily. "Poor judgment" can result from a number of factors, and although not a very satisfactory explanation, does result in many types of problematic behavior ranging from overeating to the commission of crimes. Loss of volitional control is rarely accepted as a justifiable reason for such actions (Leeman et al. 2009, Morse 2007).

Another reason to doubt loss of volition is that in certain circumstances (such as the presence of others that might disapprove of or prevent the drug use) the action can be halted or modified – that is, controlled (Heyman 2009, Lyvers 2000). A similar example is that most alcohol-addicted individuals can reliably resist consuming alcohol when they have taken the therapeutic drug Antabuse and are aware that drinking would result in certain, immediate, and severe discomfort.

Addictive drug use does sometimes occur in the apparent absence of purposeful, volitional control of behavior. Addictive behaviors can become automatic and stereotyped, with no consideration of possible outcomes. Dangerous drug use can also be a form of impulsive behavior involving little forethought. Although impulsivity often plays an important role in SUD, it can be argued that even impulsive behavior involves a choice of sorts (Goldman 2002, Heyman 2009). Impulsivity in addictive behavior is further discussed in Chapter 7.

O. J. Skog points out that motivation, in addicts as well as in healthy individuals, is often quite changeable. "In short, a person's actions must be understood in terms of his preference at the moment of choice. The fact that preferences change over time does not suggest that he has lost the capacity for volition" (Skog 2000, p. 1310). It can also be argued that the self-destructive behavior of addiction is controlled, but by urges and incentives that are not in the addicted individual's long-term best interests (Ainslie 2001, Lewis 2011). The question of the underlying reasons for self-destructive behavior is addressed more completely in Chapter 7 under the discussion of the progression of addiction.

Apparent loss of control in SUD also occurs when an individual fails to limit the amount of drug taken. Recreational drugs, such as alcohol and stimulants (cocaine, amphetamine), can impair judgment even at moderate doses, often leading to further drug intake and dangerously high levels of intoxication. These acute effects are not seen only in those with SUD but can occur in almost anyone who uses the drug. Most individuals who drink alcohol socially learn to overcome this disinhibitory effect. They usually avoid high levels of intoxication, except when they deliberately seek that state. Many who suffer from SUD are especially vulnerable to and often unable to overcome this acute drug effect of **impaired judgment**. Jellinek described this inability to limit drinking as characteristic of his gamma subtype of alcohol dependence. The impairment of control is caused by the drug's action on brain circuits that initiate and control behavior, although some of the disinhibitory effect also comes from expectation of such diminished control (Goldman 2002, Lyvers 2000). In such cases, the anticipated loss of control becomes an excuse for extreme behavior, including overindulgence in drug consumption.

Another type of apparent failure of volitional control occurs when an addicted individual relapses to drinking or drug use after a period of abstinence. In such cases the person starts drug use in the sober state, so an acute drug effect cannot be responsible. The relapse is especially disturbing to the individual who maintains that he "did not really want to take the drug, but did so anyway." Several factors can promote a return to drug use in this situation, including the neurological basis of "wanting, but not liking," as discussed in Chapter 5, and cognitive, behavioral, and cultural influences covered in subsequent chapters.

There are also limitations of a philosophical nature to the "loss of control" concept that involve questions about the nature of free will, rational choice, and "disordered appetites" in individuals suffering from SUD (Anslie 2001, Elster 1999, Morse 2007, Skog 2000). However, these considerations about free will and volitional behavior can have little relevance to the subjective experience of an addicted person. To the addict, and to those close to him, "out of control" can often seem an accurate, frightening description of addictive behavior.

William White, a scholar-historian of addiction disease theory, suggests that addictive behavior is best portrayed not as completely uncontrolled but in terms of degrees of diminished voluntary control and impaired judgment (White 2001). Although volitional control is rarely completely "lost," acute and chronic drug effects, drug aftereffects (withdrawal), other psychiatric disorders, and the addictive lifestyle certainly interfere with judgment and control. Even with the limitations mentioned here, it is evident that many individuals suffering from the most severe form of SUD – addiction – frequently suffer from impaired volitional control of their behavior in their use of addictive drugs.

Fifth Tenet: Genetic, Psychosocial, and Environmental Factors Contribute to Substance Use Disorders

This tenet of a disease-based account of addiction is entirely valid and is the basic premise of the biopsychosocial explanation of SUD. The neurological and genetic evidence discussed in the subsequent chapters is obviously relevant to compulsive behavior, which to the afflicted person seems to be driven and often uncontrollable. The inclusion of nonbiological influences in this one-sentence summary of the etiology of SUD is critical for a realistic explanation of these behavioral disorders. These nonbiological risk factors are discussed in the following chapters.

Concluding Comment

The wide – if not universal – acceptance of the brain disease model of addiction has resulted in more humane and effective approaches to the treatment and management of SUD. However, many considerations limit the generality of the disease concept as an explanation for all forms of SUD. In this book, SUDs are viewed as *behavioral disorders,* often influenced but never entirely determined by the genetic and neurological factors emphasized in disease-based explanations of addiction.

Chapter Summary

A disease-based explanation of substance use disorders is now dominant in the United States and many Western countries, especially in treatment settings. Scientific evidence that genetic and neurological factors contribute to addictive disorders as well as the public relations efforts of Alcoholics Anonymous promoted the general acceptance of a disease concept of SUD. The highly influential medical care establishment and the pharmaceutical industry have also benefited greatly from this cultural change.

Much drug misuse and many instances of less severe SUD use result from factors other than a disease process and are better explained as behavioral disorders. Even addiction – the most extremely disordered use of drugs – is influenced by developmental, experiential, and societal factors.

A basic tenet of disease theory is that SUD is a primary disorder rather than a reaction to adversity or an underlying psychological disorder. The presence of nonbiological risk factors that often precede SUD and the absence of identifiable genetic predisposition in many addicted individuals indicate a multivariate etiology and limit the generality of the disease theory principle of a primary disorder.

Additional tenets are that the progression seen in SUD and the common defense mechanism of denial indicate the presence of a disease process. However, neither of these features of SUD necessarily results from a disease because behavioral explanations can account for progression, and many individuals without problematic drug use employ defense mechanisms.

Another important tenet is that addictive behavior is uncontrolled, indicating a neurological malfunction. Critics concede that compulsive behavior and poor impulse control are common in SUD and that drug effects can impair decision-making. However, many instances of drug use by addicted individuals require deliberation and apparent full control, especially when the behavior occurs in a nondrugged state. Judgment is often impaired by addiction, but behavior is rarely actually uncontrolled.

Most of these criticisms of disease theory are addressed in the *biopsychosocial* approach to the disorders. For severe cases, the biopsychosocial explanation retains most features of classic disease theory but also includes nonbiological factors in a more behavioral (but also more complex) account of the etiology of SUD.

An important advantage of a disease concept of SUD is the reduction of shame and guilt for suffering individuals, a definite benefit for treatment of the disorder. Some resistance to complete acceptance of a disease-based explanation is due to a reluctance to abandon a punitive response for misbehavior, given the damage done by the misuse of addictive drugs.

All forms of SUD constitute threats to public health and safety. In many Western nations, and in Australia, societal concern has shifted to some extent from exclusive attention to the most severe form of SUD (addiction) toward including the more prevalent but less extreme forms of drug abuse and misuse.

Review Exercises

1. Define the disease theory of SUD.
2. What are the essential features of addiction as proposed by the American Society of Addiction Medicine?
3. What is meant by behavioral manifestations of a disease, and explain how this question relates to the disease theory of SUD?
4. Relative to the disease theory, what are the strengths of the biopsychosocial approach to understanding drug addiction?
5. How did Alcoholics Anonymous and the medical profession promote the acceptance of the disease theory of addiction?
6. What consequences resulted from the acceptance of the concept that addiction is a disease? Name at least two types of consequences.
7. SUD occur in various forms and severities. Which of these are most compatible with the disease explanation?
8. Give examples of how harmful drug use and SUD can occur in the absence of an underlying brain disease.
9. Describe the limits of each of the five basic tenets of the disease concept of addiction.

Key Terms

amount of drug exposure (70)
antisocial behavior (73)
availability of medical care (78)
disease–choice dichotomy (82)
hybrid behavioral disorder (72)
ignorance, irresponsibility, or poor judgment (72)
impaired judgment (89)
loss of control (88)
one-dimensional accounts (83)
psychological factors (84)
public health problem (73)
reactive component (85)
treatment industry (75)

PART II
The Neuroscience of Substance Use Disorders

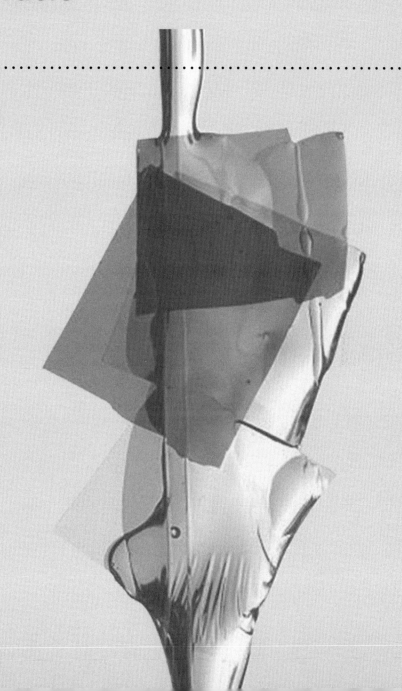

PART II

The Neuroscience of Substance
Use Disorders

4

Psychopharmacology
Drug Effects on Brain Function

CHAPTER OUTLINE

LEARNING OBJECTIVES

1. Identify and describe the basic parts of the neuron and their functions.
2. Identify the neurotransmitters whose actions are influenced by addictive drugs, producing drug effects that contribute to SUD.
3. Describe the steps in synaptic transmission of information between neurons.
4. Describe the two primary types of neuronal receptors and their role in synaptic transmission.
5. Define agonist and antagonist mechanisms of drug action and give examples of each.
6. Describe the biological mechanisms underlying pharmacodynamic and metabolic tolerance and withdrawal symptoms after chronic drug use.
7. Describe the pharmacokinetics of routes of drug administration and the blood–brain barrier.
8. Describe how psychoactive drugs and their metabolites are removed from the body.
9. Define and explain behavioral tolerance.

Introductory Vignette: "I Want a New Drug"

HUEY: The lyrics in an old song – from the 1980s – "I want a new drug, one that won't hurt my head – one that won't make my mouth too dry or make my eyes too red! One that won't make me nervous, wondering what to do – one that makes me feel like I feel when I'm with you!" So, how do drugs work? What happens in your head when drugs change the way you think, feel, and act?

LEWIS: That's a good question. Pharmacologists have learned a lot about the changes in brain function caused by psychoactive drugs. They can't completely explain yet how the altered neurological activity produces the different thoughts and feelings, but it's a good start.

Introduction

Psychoactive drugs can produce many varied effects on thinking, feelings, and behavior. These effects can be useful and desirable as well as uncomfortable, annoying, or dangerous. We understand much about the neurological basis of many drug actions, including those that produce rewarding effects that lead to addiction, and the aversive consequences often experienced by individuals with an addictive disorder.

This chapter is a brief general summary of the current knowledge about how drugs influence neuron activity. Coverage is limited to drug actions most closely related to substance use disorders, and the information presented here is obviously not a full account of psychopharmacology and brain function. More complete and detailed information about these important topics is available elsewhere (e.g., Meyer and Quenzer 2018, Stahl 2008).

Neurons, Neurotransmitters, and Receptors

Emotions, thoughts, and actions result from the activity and interaction of neurons – the information-processing components (cells) of the brain. Neuroscience research has yielded much information about the activity of individual neurons and the circuits formed by complex interconnections among the estimated 100 billion neurons of the human brain.

Early in the twentieth century, it was discovered that neurons communicate by means of neurotransmitters – chemical messengers discharged from sending neurons to receptors on receiving neurons. Neurotransmitters connecting with receptors can produce brief **excitation** or **inhibition** in the receiving neuron – termed an **ionotropic** action. Neurotransmitter activation of other receptors can trigger a **metabotropic** action, resulting in a longer-lasting effect by means of changes mediated in the nucleus of the receiving neuron.

Most neurons receive information (signals) from, as well as send signals to, other neurons (Figure 4.1). Throughout the past century, a great deal of knowledge concerning this **chemical transmission process** has accumulated, including the role of the many neurotransmitters involved in the production of behavior and cognition.

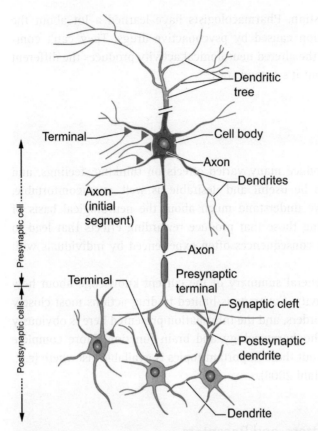

Figure 4.1 Neurotransmitters are released from presynaptic terminals located at the ends of axons. The synaptic cleft is the small space between adjacent neurons. Receptors are located on postsynaptic dendrites and cell bodies. Most neurons send signals to and receive information from other neurons by means of neurotransmitter activity. Information travels among neurons interconnected in complex networks. Reprinted from *Cognitive Neuroscience* (Banich and Compton 2018) with permission of Cambridge University Press. Reproduced with permission of the Licensor through PLSclear.

Neurotransmitters

Innumerable complex chemical processes occur in the brain, including the synthesis and eventual breakdown (metabolism) of the chemicals identified as neurotransmitters. Stahl (2008) lists eighty "known or suspected" neurotransmitters (including hormones having a similar communication function), divided into several categories or classifications based on chemical structure.

Most psychoactive drugs influence subjective experience and behavior because they mimic, facilitate, or interfere with the activity of one or more neurotransmitters. Some neurotransmitters were discovered or identified during pharmacologists' attempts to understand how certain psychoactive drugs influence neuron function. A well-known example of such neurotransmitter discovery is that of the opioid peptide neurotransmitters following from investigation of the action of morphine. In a similar manner, the discovery of the endocannabinoids came from research on the actions of tetrahydrocannabinol (THC, a primary psychoactive ingredient of cannabis).

A few of the many **identified neurotransmitters** are critically involved with the actions of addictive drugs and with the alterations in brain function that underlie substance use disorders (SUD). Abnormalities of some of these neurotransmitters are also implicated in the occurrence of certain psychiatric disorders not specifically related to SUD. Following are brief descriptions of neurotransmitters most clearly related to the actions of addictive drugs. Subsequent chapters include further information concerning these neurotransmitters' involvement in SUD.

Dopamine, Noradrenaline, and Serotonin

These neurotransmitters are of the monoamine chemical classification. Because of the similarity of their chemical structure, some drugs, such as monoamine oxidase inhibitors (an older type of antidepressant medication), act on all three in a similar manner. Of these monoamine brain chemicals, *dopamine* is most clearly implicated in positive reinforcement (Chapter 5). Dopamine also performs other important functions, including directing attention and initiation of movement. Most addictive drugs activate dopamine circuits, which are critically involved in the development of compulsive drug use. Some theorists maintain that dopamine-mediated reinforcement is a "final common pathway" for brain activity that drives essentially all types of addictive behavior (Blum et al. 2014, 2015). Consequently, researchers investigating a genetic basis for drug dependence intensively study abnormalities in dopamine neurons and in genes related to dopamine function.

Noradrenaline circuits are activated in states of arousal and modulate emotional memories. High arousal states (e.g., excitement, anxiety) are associated with relapse to drug use in persons recovering from drug dependence. Noradrenaline and other stress-related brain chemicals are implicated in the development of addiction as well as relapse to compulsive drug use after a period of abstinence (Chapter 5).

Serotonin, the third monoamine neurotransmitter, is involved in several brain and body processes, including sleep, control of mood states and emotions, and temperature regulation. Abnormalities in serotonin function may contribute to some types of depressive disorders, although the presumed differences in serotonergic circuits have not been identified. The effectiveness of antidepressant drugs (e.g., duloxetine/Cymbalta), whose actions include effects on serotonin, implicate this neurotransmitter in the affective (mood) disorders.

Amphetamine and cocaine, stimulant drugs with addictive potential, increase activity in both dopamine and noradrenaline brain circuits. Cocaine also increases serotonergic function, in addition to its primary effects on the other monoamine neurotransmitters. The abused and sometimes addictive drug MDMA ("ecstasy," "molly") also increases all monoamine activity, although its primary actions facilitate serotonin function.

GABA and Glutamate

Circuits of neurons whose neurotransmitters are *GABA* or *glutamic acid* (glutamate) are found throughout the brain and contain the majority of the brain's neurons. These amino acid neurotransmitters have important inhibitory (GABA) and excitatory (glutamate) functions in the brain. High doses of drugs that activate these circuits can cause death, either by inhibiting such basic processes as breathing (GABA enhancement) or by inducing seizure activity (glutamate activation). Most addictive central nervous system (CNS) depressant drugs, including alcohol and barbiturates, and the anxiolytic benzodiazepines (e.g., alprazolam/Xanax) facilitate GABA activity. Drugs that directly activate glutamate circuitry are rarely abused and do not produce addiction, but abnormal glutamate function contributes to drug craving in humans and drug-seeking in laboratory animals. The drug Campral (acamprosate), which stabilizes glutamatergic neurons, is moderately effective in preventing relapse in recovering alcoholics, presumably due to its amelioration of craving (see Chapter 10).

Opioid Neurotransmitters and Hormones

The opioid neuropeptide class of neurotransmitters and psychoactive hormones includes at least four similar brain chemicals. The function of some are still not well understood, but the action of *beta-endorphin* in dampening the emotional component of pain is well established. The opioid drugs, such as morphine and codeine, exert their beneficial analgesic effects on brain function by imitating these neurotransmitters. Opioid drugs, including heroin, are sometimes considered the prototypical addictive drugs. Naltrexone, which blocks the actions of these neurotransmitters and also prevents the action of the opiate drugs, can be quite effective for management of opioid addiction (Chapter 14).

Acetylcholine

Acetylcholine was the first neurotransmitter whose role in controlling a bodily function (cardiac muscle of the heart) was definitely established. We now know that acetylcholine has several important functions in cognition and behavior, including the formation of memory and the initiation of REM sleep. The addictive drug nicotine directly influences acetylcholine circuits, although its reinforcing effects are due to indirect action on dopamine circuits.

Cannabinoids

Anandamide and *2-AG*, contrary to other neurotransmitters, transmit information between neurons in a retrograde manner – providing feedback from receiving to sending neurons to modulate and fine-tune neurological activity. These lipid (fat-like) neurotransmitters are involved in motivation for food, and perception of pain and other types of sensory input. Tetrahydrocannabinol, a psychoactive chemical found in cannabis, changes the activity of neurons that respond to anandamide as it produces altered states of consciousness and perception.

Synaptic Transmission

Information transmission between neurons occurs by means of a sequence of events common to all neurons, with the exception of those synthesizing the endo-cannabinoid neurotransmitters. Figure 4.2 illustrates synaptic events that provide communication between neurons. Most psychoactive drugs affect brain function by altering one or more steps in this process of neural transmission:

1. *Neurotransmitter synthesis.* Amino acids (from digested protein) and glucose (from carbohydrates) are extracted from food and conveyed to the neurons via the brain's blood supply. Inside the neuron, neurotransmitters are produced from these precursor molecules. Neurotransmitter synthesis is controlled via enzymes and gene expression, which in turn can be influenced by drug action. Many neurons synthesize and release two different neurotransmitters.
2. *Neurotransmitter release into the synapse.* Neurons have several different structural configurations, but all have a tubular extension (an axon) – often with many branches – from which neurotransmitter is released. Such release normally occurs when the neuron sends an electrical action potential (a wave of depolarization) down the axon. So, when the neuron sends an electrical pulse down its axon, millions of neurotransmitter molecules are released into the synaptic space outside the neuron at the end of each axon branch.
3. *Neurotransmitter binds with postsynaptic receptors.* These receptors are located on the outer surface (the cell membrane) of other neurons or, in some cases, on the surface of the same neuron that released the neurotransmitter. The synaptic gap (the synapse) is an extremely minute space between the axon of the presynaptic sending neuron and the cell membrane of the postsynaptic target neuron. The action of neurotransmitter that crosses this narrow synaptic gap is a main route of communication between neurons. However, some neurotransmitter activation of receptors can also occur in neurons located some distance away from the point of neurotransmitter release. Receptor binding, activation, and the consequences of this critical aspect of neurotransmitter (and drug) action are further discussed in a subsequent section.
4. *Neurotransmitter is removed from the synapse or is inactivated.* Neurons can send information ("fire" or send an action potential down the axon) at high frequencies, some having firing rates of 1,000 per second. Two processes can quickly erase the previous message of a neuron's firing (neurotransmitter

release) from the synapse. Some neurotransmitters, including peptides such as endorphin, are broken down into inactive components by enzymes found in the extracellular synaptic space. Other types of neurotransmitters, including the monoamines, are taken back into the presynaptic neuron for eventual reuse in a "recycling" process (*reuptake*). Several interesting drugs, including some with addiction potential – cocaine – or use for treatment of psychological disorders – Prozac (fluoxetine) – influence neuron function by interfering with the reuptake process.

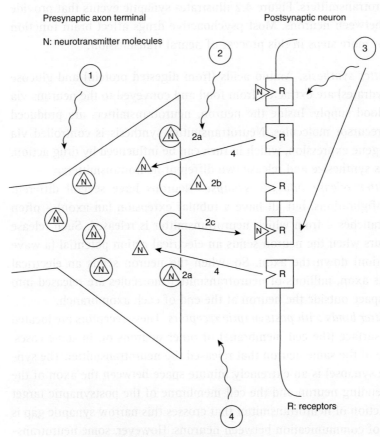

1. Neurotransmitter stored in presynaptic neuron
2. 2a, 2b, 2c Neurotransmitter molecules released into synaptic gap
3. Neurotransmitter binds with receptors
4. Neurotransmitter inactivated or reabsorbed into presynaptic neuron

Figure 4.2 Sequence of steps in synaptic transmission. With each action potential, the neuron releases thousands of neurotransmitter molecules from the axon into the synaptic gap. In the postsynaptic neuron membrane, many molecules bind with receptors before being inactivated by enzymes or reabsorbed into the axon. Enzyme inactivation, another step 4 process, is not shown here.

Regulatory processes maintaining the level of activity within a normal range control each step of this sequence of events. Drug effects often activate these homeostatic regulatory processes that counteract the drug action – producing tolerance.

Neurotransmitter Function in Behavior and Cognition

A considerable amount of our knowledge about the brain's control of behavior and subjective experience comes from identification of specific neurotransmitter involvement in these functions. Much of this understanding about neurotransmitters and behavior has come from the use of drugs as probes or tools to manipulate (reduce, or increase) neurotransmitter action, in conjunction with observing the behavioral result of administering the drug. For example acetylcholine, the earliest neurotransmitter to be identified, is critically involved in processes of storing and retrieving information (learning and remembering). Drugs which interfere with this neurotransmitter (such as scopolamine) can cause amnesia, whereas drugs which facilitate the action of acetylcholine (e.g., donepezil/Aricept) are among those administered in an attempt to counteract the effects of declining memory function during the early stages of Alzheimer's disease.

However, most mental or behavioral functions depend on the action of more than one neurotransmitter. In the case of memory processes, the availability of the neurotransmitter glutamate seems to be necessary in addition to that of acetylcholine. Conversely, any given neurotransmitter seems to be involved in more than one aspect or type of behavior. Perhaps the best example of a specific neurotransmitter's multiple roles in behavior is that of serotonin, which is involved in the regulation of sexual arousal and responses, mood states, sleep, and body temperature. Some of this diversity in neurotransmitter function is due to variations in types of receptor sites, as described subsequently.

Receptors

Receptors are large protein molecules located in the outer surface (membrane) of neurons. Neurotransmitter, released into the synaptic gap by a presynaptic neuron, influences the activity of a postsynaptic neuron by fitting into (binding with) receptors. This binding action, and subsequent effects on the target neuron, depends on the spatial configuration (shape) of both the neurotransmitter and the receptor. Information flows between neurons in a chemical process analogous to the action of a key (the neurotransmitter molecule) fitting into a lock (the receptor).

The diversity and complex nature of brain function in even relatively simple organisms is made possible partly because of the myriad types of receptors. There are specific receptor types for each neurotransmitter, but another level of differences comes from subtypes within a neurotransmitter category (Table 4.1). These subtypes make possible the involvement of a given neurotransmitter in more than one aspect of behavior or cognition as mentioned earlier.

The existence of **subtypes of receptors** for a specific neurotransmitter was originally indicated by the effects of two or more drugs that blocked or facilitated the action of a particular neurotransmitter, yet had quite different behavioral effects. The drug curare produces paralysis by preventing activation of a certain type of acetylcholine receptor found in muscle cells. The drug scopolamine also blocks acetylcholine, but at a different type of acetylcholine receptor. Therefore, instead of paralysis, this drug causes amnesia. Using current research instrumentation and techniques, the molecular structure of such differing types of receptors can often be determined.

The actions of several abused or addicting drugs occur by means of interactions with specific receptor subtypes. Opioid drugs (e.g., heroin, morphine) exert their analgesic and euphoric effects because they activate the *mu* subtype of endorphin receptor. The activation of *kappa* endorphin receptors (a different subtype) produces unpleasant feelings of dysphoria, and these receptors are not sensitive to the addictive opioid drugs. The hallucinogenic effects of LSD apparently result from its relatively specific activation of serotonin 5HT2 receptors, a subtype of the large family of serotonin receptors.

Fast-Acting and Slower-Acting Receptors

Receptors can also be classified at a more general level into two categories: fast acting or slower acting. Activation of some fast-acting receptors causes a very brief tendency for the target neuron to initiate an action potential (to fire) and is termed an *excitatory effect*. An opposite action, also very brief, tends to prevent the neuron from firing; it is termed an *inhibitory effect* and results from activation of a different subtype of fast-acting receptor. Activation of either of these two types of receptors (excitatory and inhibitory) very quickly produces a short-lived action on the neuron by means of opening or closing ion channels in the neuron membrane. Such *ionotropic* actions originate in the neuron membrane and are distant from and do not immediately involve the cell's nucleus. These fast effects are relatively simple in comparison with the function of the other general type of receptor site. Ionotropic effects underlie behaviors like quick responses to sensory input, as might be required in operating an automobile or in athletic activity.

Activation of the slower-acting types of receptor sites has a more complex result of longer duration. A **cascade of chemical reactions** is initiated inside the neuron, and this action can alter various aspects of neuron metabolic activity including function of genes (located in the cell nucleus) as they control the structure and activity of the neuron. These receptors, and the results of their activation, are termed *metabotropic*, and many psychoactive drugs, including abused and addictive drugs, influence these processes. Metabotropic effects are often neither directly excitatory nor inhibitory, but bias the neuron's response to subsequent excitatory or inhibitory input. These actions mediate slower changing states, such as moods and motivation for food or sexual activity.

Receptors and Tolerance to Drugs

Although the total number of neurons in a brain is relatively stable, the population of receptors in an individual neuron is dynamic. When brain function is modified, as by the effects of drug administration, the number of receptors can increase or decrease to counteract the change. The process at least partially restores normal neural activity. This adaptive response promotes tolerance to the drug effect, as further described subsequently.

Autoreceptors

Autoreceptors are located in the outer membrane of presynaptic neurons. These receptors are activated by the neurotransmitter released by the neuron and provide inhibitory regulatory feedback that can change the rate of firing. Neuron firing rate can also be decreased when autoreceptors are activated by some psychoactive drugs.

Table 4.1 Neurotransmitters and receptors

Neurotransmitter	Receptor type	Subtypes
Dopamine	metabotropic	5 (divided into two families)
Noradrenaline	metabotropic	4 (alpha 1,2; beta 1,2)
Serotonin	ionotropic	1 ($5HT_3$)
	metabotropic	13 (divided into 5 families)
Acetylcholine	ionotropic	1 (nicotinic)
	metabotropic	1 (muscarinic)
Glutamate	ionotropic	3
	metabotropic	8
GABA	ionotropic	1 ($GABA_A$)
	metabotropic	1 ($GABA_B$)
Endocannabinoids (anandamide, 2-AG)	metabotropic	2 (CB1, CB2)
Endogenous opioids (endorphins, enkephalin)	metabotropic	4 (mu, delta, kappa, NOP-R)

Note. The wide variety of receptor types and subtypes indicates the complexity of neurotransmitter activity in the central nervous system. Receptor subtypes influence different aspects of brain function producing cognition, motivation, memory formation, and behavior. Drugs that bind to specific receptors may block or facilitate certain actions of the relevant neurotransmitter. Receptors discovered earlier were named for these drugs, but more recently discovered receptors are designated by Greek letters or numerical subscripts. Opioid and cannabinoid neurotransmitters were discovered after receptors for opium- and cannabis-derived drugs were identified. The *endo-* prefix indicates that these are druglike chemicals that occur naturally in the brain and other locations in the body.

Source. Meyer and Quenzer (2018).

Drug Interaction with Brain and Body Function

Psychoactive drugs influence mental activity and behavior mainly because they change the process of neural transmission of information. Depending on the neurotransmitters, receptors, and brain areas affected, the drugs will change mood, cognition, sensations, and perception – and most addictive drugs activate brain circuits that produce feelings of pleasure or reduce neural activity underlying pain or anxiety. The actions of drugs on brain function are referred to as *pharmacodynamics*. After a drug enters the body, it may reach the bloodstream and, eventually, the brain. Eventually, the drug is degraded and eliminated. The extent and duration of a drug's entry into or presence in various systems of the body are referred to as *pharmacokinetics*.

Pharmacodynamics

Psychoactive drugs affect brain activity by altering several processes of neural function. A drug can enhance, or boost the activity of a neurotransmitter as it exerts an **agonist effect**. Conversely, a drug may interfere with the function of a neurotransmitter in an **antagonist effect**. Either of these actions can occur by means of changing the availability (amount and duration) of neurotransmitter in the synapse, or by an action on the receptors. The specific manner in which either neurotransmitter function or receptor activation is altered is termed the drug's **mechanism of action**. Several mechanisms of action for both agonist and antagonist effects are relatively well understood (Table 4.2, Figure 4.3). The positive

Table 4.2 Drug mechanisms of action

Agonist mechanisms	Antagonist mechanisms
Increases NT synthesis	Interferes with NT synthesis
Promotes NT release into the synapse	Prevents release into the synapse
Binds to and activates postsynaptic receptors	Blocks postsynaptic receptors
Blocks presynaptic autoreceptors	Binds to and activates presynaptic autoreceptors
Blocks reuptake or prevents breakdown of NT in the synapse	

Note. Drugs can facilitate the actions of a neurotransmitter – an agonist effect – or interfere with the neurotransmitter's action – an antagonist effect. Most such drug actions occur by influencing the availability of neurotransmitters or by interaction with receptors. Drug actions on receptors often produce more specific effects than actions influencing neurotransmitters. Most drugs with abuse potential are agonists for one or more neurotransmitters. Certain drugs (e.g., nicotine, buprenorphine) have complex actions that cannot be described simply as purely agonist or antagonist.

reinforcement (rewarding) action of most drugs results from agonist effects on one or more neurotransmitters. However, at least one abusable drug, the hallucinogen phencyclidine ("angel dust" is a common street name), exerts its primary effect as an antagonist for a type of glutamate function.

Neurotransmitter Availability in the Synapse

One way in which agonist actions occur is by increasing neurotransmitter availability in the synapse. The drug amphetamine increases release of dopamine from presynaptic neurons. Larger amounts of dopamine in the synapse result in more binding to and activation of receptors, resulting in an agonist effect. MDMA ("ecstasy") has a similar agonist mechanism of action on serotonin.

Cocaine produces another dopamine-agonist mechanism of action as it inhibits the reuptake process, increasing neurotransmitter availability in the synapse. As cocaine retards this step in the sequence of synaptic events, the longer duration of dopamine molecules in the synapse increases their binding with receptors and results in an agonist effect on dopamine function.

With these mechanisms of drug action, the drug does not bind with receptors on the target neuron, but the agonist action comes from the "natural" neurotransmitter, whose presence in the synapse is increased or prolonged by the drug. It then follows that since all neurotransmitter subtypes are activated by the neurotransmitter, drugs with these actions generally have less specific effects than those that interact directly with the receptors.

Antagonist mechanisms of action can also occur by influencing (decreasing) neurotransmitter availability, usually as they prevent the synthesis of neurotransmitter within the neuron, or its release into the synapse. Several interesting drugs work via the latter mechanism of action, including the toxin of the botulism bacteria (and the commercial cosmetic treatment Botox) as it prevents release of acetylcholine. However, few if any drugs of abuse work primarily by this type of antagonist mechanism of action.

Direct Interactions with Receptors

In more direct and specific mechanisms of action, drugs bind with receptors, either in the receiving (postsynaptic) neuron, or in some cases with autoreceptors located in the sending (presynaptic) neuron. Morphine binds with and activates opioid receptor sites. In this agonist action, the drug "mimics" the endogenous opioid neurotransmitter, so the sequence of events in the receiving neuron is identical to those produced by the natural neurotransmitter. The narcotic antagonist naloxone has an opposite effect as it binds with, but does not activate these receptors. The blocking action prevents normal binding and activation of the receptor by the natural neurotransmitter, and so exerts an antagonist effect.

Drugs vary in specificity of the types of receptors with which they bind and thereby activate or block. Alcohol is a very nonspecific drug in that it has indirect agonist effects on dopamine, serotonin, GABA, and endorphin function. Morphine binds primarily to endorphin-type receptors, and is relatively specific in its activation of the *mu* receptor subtype. The hallucinogen phencyclidine's primary mechanism of action is the blocking of a subtype of glutamate receptor.

Medications for treatment of psychiatric disorders vary widely in specificity of receptor interaction. Thorazine (an older antipsychotic medication) blocks dopamine receptors, decreasing the intensity of some signs and symptoms of psychosis. However, this drug is relatively nonspecific in its binding action, and its blockade of receptors for several other neurotransmitters in addition to dopamine produces undesirable side effects, such as reduced salivation. Haldol, another antipsychotic drug, has a more specific action as it blocks primarily one subtype of dopamine receptor. An ongoing purpose of psychopharmacology research is the development of medicines with more precise actions on targeted receptors, with the intent of reducing drug side effects.

Many drugs' actions on receptors are completely agonist (activating) or antagonist (blocking). However, the actions of other drugs lie on a continuum between these two endpoints, producing mixed or partial effects of drugs that cannot be designated as simply agonist or antagonist (Stahl 2008). Buprenorphine is an example of a partial agonist, in that it activates endorphin receptors to some extent, although to a lesser degree than does a complete agonist such as morphine. As a result, the drug produces some but not all effects of the pure agonist drug. This partial agonist for the endorphin system is useful in recovery from opiate dependence as it can relieve the withdrawal syndrome without producing addictive euphoria (Chapter 14). Additionally, some drugs are *inverse agonists* as they have an effect on receptors opposite to that of the natural neurotransmitter, and so can reverse some neurotransmitter action. Some effects of inverse agonists are similar to that of antagonists for a given neurotransmitter, but in addition to blocking the action of a neurotransmitter, the inverse agonist has an opposite effect on neural function.

Dose Effects

A psychoactive drug can produce a range of different effects on brain function and behavior. The effects that occur depend primarily on the dose of the drug. Lower-dose effects often include desirable results, such as lessened fatigue from caffeine or decreased anxiety from medications like Xanax (alprazolam). Larger doses may increase the desired effect but can also result in undesirable effects, such as anxiety in the case of caffeine and memory impairment for alprazolam. Most drugs can produce disruptive, dangerous, and even lethal effects at sufficiently high doses, often by means of suppressing vital bodily functions (such as respiration) or by inducing seizures.

Adaptation to the Action of Drugs: Tolerance

The preceding discussion described the actions of drugs on neurons, including modifying the release of neurotransmitter, and binding with receptors to facilitate or impede neurotransmitter function. However, the central nervous system has the ability to adapt to and counteract some externally caused alterations in its function. **Compensatory processes** of *homeostasis* limit the duration and degree of departure from a baseline level in order to maintain a relatively steady state of activity. Other examples of homeostatic controls on bodily functions include those that regulate body temperature and blood pressure.

Neuroadaptive processes that counteract drug action occur in both presynaptic and postsynaptic neurons. **Autoreceptors** in presynaptic neurons are activated by the neuron's own neurotransmitter after release into the synapse. If an agonist drug causes abnormally large amounts of neurotransmitter release, the increased activation of these autoreceptors provides feedback to the neuron and decreases subsequent neurotransmitter release. This inhibitory feedback is often compared to the function of a thermostat as it monitors room temperature and turns off a furnace to prevent overheating.

Consideration of the nervous system's ability to adapt to drug-induced changes is required to understand basic aspects of drug effects, as well as dependence and addiction. **Neuroadaptation**, involved in the development of *tolerance* to drugs, is responsible for withdrawal syndromes, and is an integral feature of current theories of addiction discussed in Chapter 5. In pharmacology, the term *tolerance* refers to the decrease in physiological and behavioral effects of a drug that is most evident when the drug is repeatedly administered. Not all psychoactive drug actions diminish with repeated use, but neuroadaptation does occur for several effects of most drugs of abuse.

Unfortunately, for several drugs of abuse, tolerance occurs more rapidly and completely for the (typically desirable) euphoric effects than for the undesirable and dangerous effects of high drug doses. This difference in the development of tolerance is partially responsible for a dangerous but common pattern of addictive drug use. An addicted individual takes increasingly larger amounts of drugs in an attempt to reproduce the euphoric effects experienced previously from lower drug doses – but then is at increased risk of possibly fatal overdose because a similar degree of tolerance has not developed for the lethal effects.

Some drug effects – such as the paranoia-inducing actions of amphetamine or cocaine – can become sensitized, as these effects emerge at *lower* doses after extensive usage (Chapter 5). Although sensitization in some respects resembles a reversal of tolerance, it does not result from the adaptive processes that underlie normal tolerance and the reduction of drug effects.

An important neuroadaptive process occurs as drug effects initiate changes in **receptor density**. When an agonist drug excessively activates receptors on the postsynaptic neuron, the neuron may respond by decreasing the density of receptors (number of receptors per unit of surface area) in a process termed **down-regulation**. If an antagonist drug decreases receptor activation (by blocking the receptors or reducing the amount of neurotransmitter), the neuron may adapt by **up-regulation**, which is an increase in receptor density. These changes in the number of receptors then counteract the agonist or antagonist effect of a drug, and so contribute to the development of tolerance.

The overall development of tolerance to drug effects results from the summation of three processes (Table 4.3). The neuroadaptive process described here results in **pharmacodynamic tolerance**. Two additional tolerance-producing processes are described in subsequent sections.

Table 4.3 Three types of tolerance

Type of tolerance	Produced by	Results in
Pharmacodynamic	Changes in receptor density (up- or down-regulation)	**Reduction in drug effect on neural activity, withdrawal syndrome when drug intake stops**
Metabolic	Increased efficiency of drug metabolism by the liver	Reduction in duration and peak levels of drug in the bloodstream and brain
Behavioral	Practice in overcoming drug behavioral effect, Pavlovian (classical) conditioning of compensatory drug responses	Reduction in drug-produced behavioral impairment

Withdrawal Syndrome

Up- or down-regulation counteracts and limits drug-produced changes in neural activity. These adaptive responses require some time to develop fully, so the adaptation becomes increasingly effective if the drug is administered repeatedly. As the resulting tolerance emerges, the drug's effect at the same dose decreases with subsequent administration. When drug intake stops, a similar time lag occurs for the abatement of the compensatory activity, although the changes in receptor density eventually diminish or disappear. During this period when there is no drug effect to be counteracted, the adjusted neural activity results in effects generally opposite to that of the primary drug action. This opposite effect on neurotransmitter function is then responsible for the withdrawal syndrome, as in the hyperexcitability of the nervous system until it readapts to the absence of alcohol after a prolonged period of alcohol-induced CNS depression.

Pharmacokinetics

For a drug to influence brain function, it must come into direct contact with receptors and/or enter neurons. Several interrelated bodily processes control **bioavailability,** a term that refers to a drug's access to the brain. After a single administration of a drug, the concentration of drug molecules in brain tissue rises from zero, reaches a maximum level, and eventually returns to zero. The amount of the drug (number of molecules) having access to neurons primarily determines the dose-related effects of a drug discussed previously. The rates of increase, as well as the rate of subsequent decrease of this molecular concentration also play important roles in drug effects, including those involved in dependence and addiction. The interaction among various bodily process and organ systems in the determination of bioavailability of a drug is indicated in Figure 4.3.

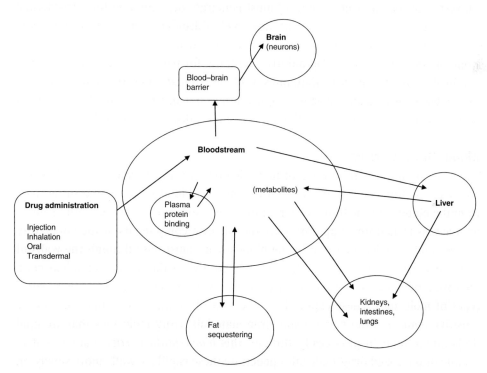

Figure 4.3 Pharmacokinetics and drug bioavailability. Routes of administration can produce rapid (inhalation, injection) or slower (oral, transdermal) drug entry into the bloodstream. Psychoactive drugs penetrating the blood–brain barrier enter the brain and alter neuron function. Some drugs are temporarily bound to proteins in the bloodstream, or sequestered in fat deposits. The liver metabolizes some drugs, facilitating removal from the bloodstream by the kidneys. Drugs or their metabolites are excreted in urine, feces, perspiration, or exhaled breath.

Routes of Administration

Drugs gain entry to the brain via blood circulation, which is copious and relatively constant for the central nervous system (CNS). The brain requires an uninterrupted supply of oxygen and glucose, supplied by the bloodstream. Another important blood-dependent process is the synthesis of neurotransmitters from nutrients supplied to neurons.

Drugs can be introduced into the body by various routes of administration, which differ in the rate at which the drug enters the blood circulation. The most rapid bloodstream entry results from inhaling a drug in vapor, gas or airborne particulate form (smoke) into the lungs (Meyer and Quenzer 2013). Nicotine (from tobacco) and cocaine (from cocaine base, "crack") are ready examples of drugs which, when administered by inhalation, enter the brain within a few seconds. Intravenous injection is also a very rapid-entry route of drug administration. The slowest entry occurs when the drug must penetrate the skin, and this transdermal route is used to produce a constant, low level of drug concentration in the blood. The "patch" is used for transdermal delivery of such drugs as nicotine to aid in stopping smoking, and the opioid drug fentanyl for pain management. Routes of administration with intermediate rates of blood circulation entry include injection (into muscle, or beneath the skin), application to mucous membrane (mouth, nasal passages), and intragastric (swallowing capsules, pills, or beverages).

Blood–Brain Barrier

The route of administration is a primary determinant of the rate of entry into the blood circulation. However, after entry into the bloodstream, some drugs pass from the blood into the brain very rapidly, some more slowly, and yet others never gain access to neurons. Capillaries are the smallest components of the circulatory system, and chemicals carried in the bloodstream must pass through the walls of these tiny vessels in order to alter neural activity. In the brain and spinal cord, the capillaries have structural features that prevent or retard the passage of some types of molecules. These capillaries serve as a filtration system that protects the sensitive neurons from some bloodborne materials. Drug molecules that are lipid (fat)-soluble tend to pass easily through this *blood–brain barrier*. Larger, water-soluble or polarized drug molecules penetrate these capillary walls more slowly or, in some cases, cannot pass through so do not gain access to neurons.

Drugs that do not penetrate the blood–brain barrier cannot directly influence brain function and so are not psychoactive. Such drugs may have actions outside the CNS at the neuromuscular junction or on the autonomic nervous system, causing paralysis, cardiovascular changes, or reduced salivation. Drugs with addiction potential are obviously psychoactive and penetrate this filtration barrier to gain access to neural tissue. There are, however, differences among psychoactive drugs regarding the ease in which they penetrate the blood–brain barrier.

Morphine and heroin have very similar actions in activating endorphin receptors. However, heroin passes through the blood–brain barrier much more rapidly than does morphine, resulting in heroin's greater potency in comparison to morphine when administered by injection.

These two factors – route of administration and ease of passage from the bloodstream into neural tissue – are primary determinants of the rate of increase of concentration of drug molecules at the neuron level. Psychoactive drugs produce changes in behavior and subjective experience, and some of these effects are heavily influenced by this rate of increase of drug concentration in brain tissue. A subjective experience of importance to SUD is the "euphoric rush" experienced by many persons who inhale cocaine or methamphetamine vapor, or who intravenously inject heroin or cocaine. This quick onset of pleasurable feeling is only one example of the importance of a rapid increase of drug levels in the brain, although it may be the most vivid demonstration of this effect. In general, drug-produced reward is greater when drug levels in the brain rise rapidly.

The impermeability of the blood–brain barrier to large molecules provides a rationale for attempts to develop vaccines to immunize against the effects of cocaine or other drugs. For cocaine, the experimental vaccine consists of a cocaine analog linked to an inactive adenovirus that, when administered, stimulates the immune system to produce large-molecule antibodies. When cocaine enters the bloodstream, the antibodies attach to the drug molecules, preventing their penetration of the blood–brain barrier and entry into the brain (Evans et al. 2016, Hicks et al. 2014). Most immunotherapy research is conducted with animal subjects, and several major problems remain to be solved before a safe and effective vaccine that prevents the rewarding effects of an addictive drug becomes available.

Elimination of the Drug from the Body

After a drug enters the bloodstream it is eventually removed from the body, and this elimination is dependent on the drug or its metabolites (breakdown products) being carried by body fluids (urine, perspiration), feces, or exhaled air. Many drugs are eliminated primarily by the kidneys as these organs extract various chemicals from the blood in the production of urine. The liver serves an important function in drug elimination as it converts fat-soluble drugs into water-soluble metabolites, which are much more efficiently filtered from the blood by the kidneys. Most drugs are removed from the body by means of this combination of liver and kidney function.

As the liver is exposed to some drugs, its production of enzymes that perform the metabolism of the drug may be stimulated. The resultant increase in the liver's efficiency in breaking down the drug is responsible for **metabolic tolerance**, which is a second process contributing to the overall development of tolerance. Metabolic tolerance primarily decreases the duration of a drug's effect, as the liver more rapidly converts the psychoactive drug into (usually) less active and more easily eliminated breakdown products. In the case of a few drugs, the liver-converted metabolites are also psychoactive, but consideration of such complexities of liver function and drug elimination are beyond the scope of the present discussion.

In addition to influencing the intensity of drug effects, the pharmacokinetics of drug elimination play an important role in another aspect of drug dependence, the withdrawal syndrome. Drugs that are rapidly eliminated from the body result in more intense withdrawal effects due to the lingering neuroadaptation processes of pharmacodynamic tolerance, as discussed previously – that produce a drug-opposite action. The antianxiety drugs Xanax (alprozalam) and Valium (diazepam) have similar mechanisms of action in that both are $GABA_A$ agonists. For these drugs, the rebound withdrawal syndrome is increased anxiety. Diazepam's much more gradual rate of elimination from the body gives it a longer time course of action and also results in a less intense (if more protracted) withdrawal syndrome as compared to the rapidly metabolized and eliminated alprazolam.

Although elimination processes most obviously control the duration of a drug's action, they also influence the strength or degree of drug effects, especially for the routes of administration that result in more gradual bloodstream entry. Some attenuation of the maximum drug effect occurs because the processes of removal (metabolism and elimination) commence immediately upon the drug's entry into the blood circulation. So it could be said that entry into the brain competes with the processes of elimination. The oppositional nature of the processes of brain entry versus metabolism is also illustrated by the *first-pass effect*, a pharmacokinetic feature that applies only to the oral route of administration. When administered via the digestive tract, most drugs are absorbed into the blood circulation from the small intestine. Blood vessels from the small intestine first deliver the blood to the liver, so much of the drug may be metabolized by liver enzymes before any of the drug can enter the CNS.

The pharmacokinetics of a drug are greatly influenced by the degree to which drug molecules become attached (bound) to large protein molecules after they enter the bloodstream. Such **protein binding** essentially increases the duration of a drug's effect, reduces the strength of its action, and prolongs but attenuates the withdrawal syndrome. For many drugs, a certain percentage of the molecules in the bloodstream bind to protein molecules (such as albumin), but the remaining molecules remain in the free or unbound state. Only these unbound molecules can penetrate the blood–brain barrier to influence neuron function, so the extent of protein binding influences the strength of behavioral/subjective drug effects. Although the protein-bound drug molecules cannot enter the brain, they are also protected from metabolism by the liver and excretion by the kidneys. Only a certain percentage of the total number of drug molecules bind with protein – a basic principle of pharmacology. Some become unbound as the free drug molecules are metabolized and eliminated. By this process all of the drug eventually becomes unbound, may penetrate the blood–brain barrier, and finally eliminated from the body. A high degree of protein binding thus prolongs the duration of a drug's effect, decreasing the rate of entry into the brain and increasing the time required to eliminate the drug. Approximately 90 percent of Valium (diazepam) becomes bound to albumin, and this protein binding is largely responsible for the decreased rate of elimination and the subsequently lessened intensity of withdrawal syndrome for this drug as compared to Xanax (alprazolam).

A somewhat similar effect is seen when drugs become sequestered in fatty tissue, as occurs for THC, a psychoactive component of cannabis. However, fat-sequestered drugs are released into the bloodstream even more slowly than for most cases of protein binding. This slow rate of release results in THC metabolites being detectable in the urine of a heavy user of marijuana for weeks after the last use of this drug. It is also a factor in the relatively mild withdrawal syndrome after cessation of marijuana use.

Behavioral Tolerance

As previously mentioned, the overall phenomenon of tolerance involves three separate mechanisms of adaptation to drug effects (Table 4.3). Pharmacodynamic tolerance results from neuroadaptation and produces withdrawal syndromes, and metabolic tolerance influences the rate of drug elimination. **Behavioral tolerance** is the third process that lessens drug effects, especially impairment of behavior. The development of behavioral tolerance does not depend on changes in either pharmacodynamics or pharmacokinetics – but is essentially a learning process.

Behavioral tolerance occurs as a drug user learns to compensate for an unwanted behavioral effect produced by a drug. A similar adaptation is seen as an individual experiencing motor impairment after a stroke caused by an interruption of blood supply to the brain. Stroke victims can often regain some degree of functioning by means of intensive physical therapy, which includes extensive and directed practice in walking or the execution of other bodily movements. Brain tissue typically does not regenerate after stroke trauma, and the behavioral improvement is largely due to deliberate effort and learning to compensate for the impaired neural function.

Extensive research on behavioral tolerance has been done with both animal and human subjects (e.g., Gauvin et al. 2000, Vogel-Sprott 1997). In these and similar experiments the subjects received repeated administration of drugs (often alcohol or another CNS depressant), and the initial and subsequent effects were monitored as tolerance developed to the behavioral or cognitive impairment. Comparison to control groups revealed the effects of pharmacodynamic and metabolic tolerance as only the experimental group practiced a drug-impaired task while intoxicated. Greater performance improvement in the intoxicated practice group indicated behavioral tolerance. Although behavioral tolerance can partially compensate for drug effects, some impairment often persists at high drug doses.

In the case of drug abuse and addiction (in the natural environment, not in a controlled study), individuals often attempt to proceed with various activities while they are under the drug's influence, so behavioral tolerance is definitely a relevant consideration. Unfortunately, one of the most common instances in which intoxicated practice occurs is in the case of automobile driving under the influence of alcohol.

Another process by which the brain develops resistance to drug effects is also a type of behavioral tolerance. If distinctive stimuli reliably precede or accompany the onset of drug action, the pharmacodynamic compensatory responses described previously may be elicited as these stimuli become classically conditioned.

Such conditioned oppositional responses are responsible for the many examples of context-specific tolerance to drug effects (Siegel et al. 2000), including certain cases of fatal drug overdose when opioid drugs are administered in a novel environment (Siegel 2001). In this situation, the familiar drug-related environment acts as a conditioned stimulus, producing adaptive responses that counteract the primary drug effect. When the drug is administered in an unfamiliar environment (in the absence of the conditioned stimuli), the drug has a stronger, sometimes lethal effect. Conditioned tolerance is further discussed in Chapters 5 and 7.

Influence of Expectation and Environment

All drugs of abuse cause changes in behavior and subjective experience by altering neuron function. Brain activity that produces behavior and consciousness is heavily influenced by an individual's personal history and current situation. At high doses, drugs can produce sleep, coma, or convulsions and so eliminate consciousness and purposeful behavior. However, at lower drug doses, the drug-produced alteration of behavior and consciousness combines with the influence of memory, perception of the current environment, and anticipation of future events. The overall effect of a drug, then, is partially determined by expectation and environment, sometimes referred to as "set and setting."

These **nonpharmacological influences** on drug effects can be of special importance in the development and maintenance of addiction. The role of environmental/expectancy factors in SUD is seen with the use of addictive drugs in the management of certain medical conditions. Examples include opioid drugs for pain suppression, benzodiazepine drugs for anxiety disorders, and dopamine-agonist stimulants prescribed for attention-deficit hyperactivity disorder (ADHD). Most patients who take these drugs as medications for the relevant disorders do not become addicted. The generally benign use of these abusable drugs is partly due to physician (and pharmacist) control of drug access, but patients' attitudes and expectations also limit misuse of these effective therapeutic agents. Most often, patients are seeking relief from pain, debilitating anxiety or problems with focusing attention, and less interested in any other rewarding drug effect. The abuse potential of these drugs will be further discussed in subsequent chapters, as will be the general topic of the effects of expectancy on the overall actions of drugs.

Concluding Comments

We have identified the neurotransmitters whose functions are altered by addictive drugs. Since we understand the mechanisms by which most of these drugs of abuse exert their effects, it might be expected that other drugs could be developed that would block or prevent the attractive but ultimately dangerous consequences of taking the abused drugs – that is, the abused drugs' rewarding and reinforcing actions. The pharmacological treatment or management of addiction is a very active area of research and has had limited success in some areas – primarily for dependence on opioids and alcohol (Nielsen et al. 2014, 2015). With few exceptions (e.g., narcotic antagonists; see Chapter 14), we cannot yet effectively block or otherwise prevent the primary rewarding effects of addictive drugs – at least not in a clinically useful manner. The fact that addictive drugs exert their effects via brain circuits that produce critical functions – including reward, motivation, and memory formation – is a major obstacle for the development of drugs intended to alleviate addiction.

Psychopharmacology does not offer a complete explanation of drug addiction, but it does provide a great deal of information concerning how drugs influence brain function. This knowledge is a starting point for understanding the overall phenomenon of compulsive and destructive use of drugs.

Chapter Summary

Psychoactive drugs alter behavior and consciousness by changing the function of the central nervous system – specifically, communication among neurons. The effects that produce reward as well as addiction and other aversive consequences occur as the drugs interfere with or facilitate the action of neurotransmitters. At least eighty different brain chemicals are identified as neurotransmitters, but only a few are known to be closely involved in the development of compulsive drug use. Altered function of the neurotransmitters dopamine and glutamate may underlie all forms of addiction. Other neurotransmitters – acetylcholine, anandamide, endorphins – are also implicated in addiction to certain drugs (nicotine, THC, opioids).

Communication among neurons occurs as neurotransmitters released from pre-synaptic axons activate postsynaptic receptors. Drugs can influence the release of neurotransmitter or bind with receptors. Agonist or antagonist effects on neuron function can occur at either site of drug action. Drugs differ in the specificity of their actions on receptors – some have general effects on several types of receptors, while others bind with only one receptor type. Unwanted side effects may occur when a drug acts on several neurotransmitters.

Neurons adapt to and counteract some drug actions by increasing or decreasing neurotransmitter release and by changing the density of postsynaptic receptors. This neuroadaptation (pharmacodynamic tolerance) contributes to the overall development of tolerance and is responsible for withdrawal effects that are opposite to the initial drug action. Withdrawal syndromes occur when drug use stops, during the time before the adaptive changes dissipate.

Several factors influence the rate of drug entry into the brain, which partially determines the intensity of the resulting behavioral and experiential effects. Lipid-soluble drugs and drugs administered via inhalation or intravenous injection (e.g., heroin, cocaine) rapidly enter the brain and produce stronger effects than more water-soluble drugs or those administered by other routes, such as by oral ingestion. The kidneys eliminate most drugs after metabolism by the liver. Drugs with a longer duration of action because of slower elimination by the liver and kidneys result in less intense but more prolonged withdrawal after drug intake stops. After repeated drug exposure, these elimination processes can become more efficient (metabolic tolerance) and reduce the duration of drug effects.

In addition to pharmacodynamic and metabolic tolerance, behavioral tolerance contributes to overcoming (at least partially) drug-produced impairment of behavior and cognition. Learning that occurs during practice of a specific task during an intoxicated state can counteract the drug effect and improve performance. Tolerance can also result if a distinctive environment predicts and becomes conditioned to the onset of drug action. These stimuli then elicit compensatory conditioned responses that counteract the drug effect. Such conditioned tolerance occurs when drugs are repeatedly administered in a specific location – and promotes dangerously high drug doses in addicts that can be lethal when drugs are taken in a different environment.

Nonpharmacological factors – which do not come from a drug's biological action on brain function – also greatly influence the overall behavioral and subjective consequences of drug use. The influences of expectation and environment are important in the development of addiction as well as in benign uses of psychoactive drugs. These factors – especially motivations for drug effects – allow the relatively safe use of addictive drugs for medical purposes with most patients.

Review Exercises

1. Describe the basic parts of the neuron (axon, cell body, dendrites) as well as the synaptic cleft and be able to identify them in a drawing.
2. What are the functions of the basic parts of the neuron, the presynaptic terminals, presynaptic and postsynaptic receptors, and neurotransmitters?
3. Identify the functions (positive reinforcement, arousal, etc.) of the neurotransmitters involved in drug effects and addiction.
4. Describe the steps in synaptic transmission of information between neurons.
5. Describe ionotropic and metabotropic receptors as well as autoreceptors and their roles in synaptic transmission.
6. What are receptor subtypes, and why are they important?
7. Describe pharmacodynamics, pharmacokinetics, and mechanism of action, and explain why they are important features of drug effects.
8. Define agonist and antagonist mechanism of drug action, and describe how each affects the availability of neurotransmitter at the synapse.
9. Describe the biological basis of pharmacodynamic and metabolic tolerance and of the withdrawal syndrome.
10. Describe the pharmacokinetics of routes of drug administration and the blood–brain barrier.
11. What is behavioral tolerance, and why is it important?

Key Terms

agonist effect (106)

antagonist effect (106)

autoreceptors (109)

behavioral tolerance (115)

bioavailability (111)

cascade of chemical reactions (104)

chemical transmission process (97)

compensatory processes (109)

down-regulation (110)

excitation (97)

identified neurotransmitters (99)

inhibition (97)

ionotropic (97)

mechanism of action (106)

metabolic tolerance (113)

metabotropic (97)

neuroadaptation (109)

nonpharmacological influences (116)

pharmacodynamic tolerance (110)

protein binding (114)

receptor density (109)

subtypes of receptors (104)

up-regulation (110)

CHAPTER OUTLINE

LEARNING OBJECTIVES

1. Explain the importance of identifying the biological basis of addiction.
2. Describe the essential features of the four stages of addiction.
3. Identify the brain circuits and neurotransmitters involved in positive reinforcement, the most important feature of Stage 1.
4. Describe the neurological substrates of the shift from reinforcing to aversive drug effects, the essential feature of Stage 2.
5. Describe the brain processes that underlie the immediate and the protracted withdrawal syndromes.
6. Explain the biological and psychological processes that produce compulsive drug-seeking, the essential feature of Stage 3 of addiction.
7. Define lingering vulnerability to relapse (Stage 4) and describe the events or conditions that cause relapse.
8. Explain the role of long-term memory and gene expression in addiction.

Introductory Vignette: Sally Quits Using Cocaine … Until She Starts Again

Sally was on her way to the party at Jennifer's beach house. Sally had been feeling down and bad recently, and she didn't understand why she was in such a bummed-out state. It surely couldn't still be from the cocaine – the last run had sort of gotten out of control, lasting for two days: no sleep, just snorting coke, all night and through the next day. She did feel really horrible for almost a week after that, but she had laid off the coke for a month, and now she no longer felt *that* bad – but still not so great. Maybe this party would cheer her up.

As she drove toward the beach, she thought about how much she had liked snorting cocaine when she first started using. Confident, energetic, optimistic, sexy – it was all good, and the aftereffects were not too hard to handle. However, during recent months, she had noticed that coke didn't quite do that much for her – maybe the product wasn't as good as what she was able to score last year.

The thought of using some crystal meth, probably smoking it with a pipe, had crossed her mind – but she knew that was probably a really bad idea. It was strange, but the thought of going to the pipe, even though it made her anxious, actually made her think *more* about doing some coke!

She told herself that since her last coke run had ended badly, this time she would not do any – at all. She would just talk to people who weren't using, drink some wine, and dance.

As she walked up on the porch, she heard music, laughter, and a babble of excited voices. The first person she saw when she entered the room was Sam. Sam always had plenty of good coke to share, or at least sell at a decent price, and sure enough, he was laying out lines, right on the bar. In a part of her mind, Sally was surprised that suddenly she was very intent on getting in on the action, especially after her last bad experience. She knew she would not like it much – and would probably regret doing coke again – but now her previous intent to stay away from coke tonight seemed overly cautious. She knew all the moves to make – didn't even have to think about it.

"Hey, Sam – what's up?"

Introduction

A prominent neuroscience researcher emphasized the importance of understanding the neurological basis of addictive disorders:

> Despite the importance of numerous psychosocial factors, at its core, drug addiction involves a biological process: the ability of repeated exposure to a drug of abuse to induce changes in a vulnerable brain that drive the compulsive seeking and taking of drugs, and loss of control over drug use that define a state of addiction. Until we learn how to counteract the biological disturbances, treatment of addiction will remain handicapped and less than optimally effective. (Nestler 2013, p. 431)

As presented in the previous chapter, we have much knowledge of how addictive drugs influence neuron function at the level of neurotransmitters and receptors. A more complete understanding of the biological basis of substance use disorders (SUD) will depend on our learning how these neurological drug actions result in the compulsive behavior of addiction. Some basic aspects of behavior and its control, such as pleasure and reinforcement, motivation and emotion, anxiety and stress, behavioral inhibition, and memory, are clearly involved in addiction. In recent decades, neuroscientists have learned much about the brain activity underlying these behavioral components of addiction. Several investigators have made use of this increased understanding of brain function to develop theoretical accounts of how addictive drugs cause the characteristic compulsive behavior (e.g., Berridge and Robinson 2016, Johnston et al. 2016, Kalivas 2009, Koob et al. 2014, Koob and Volkow 2010, Nestler 2013). These theories, and the work of other investigators, represent the current state of understanding of the biological basis of addiction.

Biological Factors and SUD

Information gained from research with both human and animal subjects has enabled the current level of understanding of addiction-related brain function and behavior. Some of the progress has come from brain-imaging studies utilizing human subjects. Changes in brain activity caused by drug administration or drug-related stimuli are detected by these methods, as is abnormal brain function in addicted individuals. Some of the abnormalities endure for long periods and result from altered brain circuitry or from differences in the expression of genes. The cellular or synaptic basis of these changes cannot be determined by studies of human subjects but must be ascertained from research with animal subjects. To have much explanatory value, the results of the laboratory studies must be consistent with the behavior and experiences of those suffering from SUD and the observations of the clinicians who work with these addicted individuals. This chapter includes examples illustrating the clinical relevance of neuroscience research.

Brain Malfunction and Disease Theory of SUD

Evidence that addictive behavior is a result of abnormal brain function caused by drug use provides support for the argument that SUD should be viewed as a disease. This "brain disease" concept is generally accepted by many in positions of leadership in the scientific community. Some brain abnormalities may precede drug use (Chapter 6), and much evidence shows that addictive use of drugs causes malfunction in a vulnerable brain. However, there are limitations to the generality of the disease explanation for these disorders (Chapter 3). Chapters 1 and 7 present the biopsychosocial approach to the basis of SUD, a behavioral explanation of addiction that does include the role of altered brain function but is less dependent on the concept of disease.

Overview of How Addictive Drugs Alter Brain Function

Addictive drugs very effectively engage the natural **reward-sensing and behavior-directing system** of the brain. A nontechnical but descriptive term for this aspect of brain function is the "go" system. Several investigators (e.g., Childress 2006) use the framework of "go" and "stop" systems to describe the actions of addictive drugs on the basic behavioral functions of approach and of avoidance/inhibition. Intense drug-produced engagement of the "go" system, plus the brain's compensatory response to that action, can produce changes in brain circuitry, neuron excitability, and gene expression and result in compulsive drug use. This behavior may persist for long periods because the changes in the brain are maintained by processes similar to those responsible for long-term memory. The exaggerated and persistent engagement of these neural circuits is sometimes described as "hijacking" the brain's survival systems (Kauer and Malenka 2007).

A second and equally important drug-produced alteration in brain function is an impairment of the brain's "stop" system. When functioning normally, these **brain structures and circuits inhibit or suppress behaviors** likely to result in discomfort or harm. Drug-produced dysfunction of these two systems then results in the compulsive drug-taking characteristic of addiction.

Stages and Essential Features of Addiction

The "Substance-Related and Addiction Disorders" chapter of the DSM-5 is many pages in length, reflecting the complexity of identifying these disorders. However, there are characteristic features that appear at **successive stages** in the development of addiction, the most severe form of SUD. These basic stages and essential features are as follows:

1. With early use, addictive drugs produce positive or negative reinforcement. In most cases, pleasure or euphoria, or alleviation of aversive states, accompanies the reinforcement.
2. There is a shift from the initially pleasurable and desirable effects toward lessened euphoria and eventual development of aversive dysphoric states, including withdrawal syndromes.
3. There is the appearance of compulsive drug-seeking and the acceptance of aversive consequences of continued drug use.
4. Vulnerability to recurrence of compulsive drug-seeking persists, even after a period of drug abstinence.

The first two stages of this sequence are not unique to addiction but occur in anyone using addictive drugs at high doses for an extended period. In vulnerable individuals, adaptation and other responses of the nervous system to drug effects contributes to the emergence of addictive behavior in the third stage.

George Koob and Michel Le Moal describe the compulsive behavior and experiences of addiction as a **repetitive cycle** of (1) anticipation and preoccupation, (2) bingeing and intoxication, and (3) dysphoria/negative affect leading back to the start of the cycle (Koob and Le Moal 1997, 2006). If the cycle of compulsive drug-seeking (Stage 3) is interrupted, the individual remains vulnerable to recurrence of active addiction even during an extended period of drug abstinence (Stage 4).

The current knowledge of neurological activity during the four stages of addiction is summarized in this chapter. Other, less overtly biological factors and events also influence the development of addiction (Chapters 7 and 8). The drug-related behavior and subjective experiences of addiction described here do not include all of the DSM-5 criteria for clinical assessment and diagnosis of SUD – specifically the adverse social, psychological, and biological consequences of destructive drug use.

Stage 1: Reinforcing Effects of Addictive Drugs

Reinforcing events often (but not always) produce subjective feelings of pleasure or relief from an unpleasant state. However, the defining characteristic of reinforcement is not subjective experience but the strengthening of behavior that brings about the reinforcing event. Essentially, if a stimulus that follows a particular behavior causes that behavior to be repeated, then that stimulus is *positively reinforcing.* This objective definition does not depend on whether the stimulus "feels good." McKim and Hancock (2013, p. 109) describe the brain's reinforcement circuitry as "a do-it-again system, not a pleasure system." Advanced stages of drug addiction often provide examples of behavior (drug-seeking) maintained (reinforced) by an event (drug administration), although little or no hedonistic benefit occurs.

Negative reinforcement occurs when behavior is increased or strengthened by the lessening or termination of an aversive condition. Relief from pain or anxiety usually produces negative reinforcement. Chapters 14 and 15 discuss addiction to drugs that relieve pain and anxiety for which negative reinforcement has a more obvious role during the initial stages of the disorder. However, current theories implicate positive reinforcement as being critical for the development of addiction in most instances (Koob and Volkow 2010, Kalivas and O'Brien 2008).

Subjective accounts of addictive drug effects typically describe some type of pleasure, or relief from an aversive state such as anxiety. These effects, sometimes erroneously considered equivalent to positive and negative reinforcement, are obviously not unique features of addiction since they can also occur in those who are not (and do not become) addicted. Although the occurrence of drug-produced reinforcement is not sufficient to identify addiction, positive reinforcement appears to be critical, at least in the early stages of the disorder. The most dramatic accounts may come from persons who have intravenously injected opiates or stimulants, and these descriptions often allude to sexual feelings (e.g., "a full-body orgasm, lasting for several minutes!"). However, the pleasurable feelings produced by some addictive drugs, including nicotine, alcohol, and cannabis, are much more subtle than are the intense effects resulting from heroin or cocaine injection.

The behavior-promoting and -directing effect of reinforcing events, important in the biopsychosocial view of addiction, are discussed further in Chapter 7.

Neurological Substrates of Positive Reinforcement and Pleasure

In the early 1950s Olds and Milner (1954) discovered that electrical stimulation of specific parts of the rat brain reliably and dramatically reinforced behavior. In an operant-response apparatus (a "Skinner box"), rats readily self-administered electrical brain stimulation through implanted electrodes by pressing a response lever. After identification of the relevant midbrain structures in rats that produced positive reinforcement, similar reinforcement effects were found in all mammalian species so tested, including humans. In humans, the effects of electrical stimulation of these brain areas were determined during surgical procedures intended to relieve neurological disorders, such as epilepsy. Patients reported that electrical stimulation of these brain areas was indeed very pleasurable. These accounts demonstrated that the function of these brain circuits is similar for humans and rodents and that this type of stimulation pleasure does accompany positive reinforcement.

The anatomy (structure and interconnections) of these reinforcement-related circuits and the neurotransmitters and receptors functioning in the neurons of these brain areas have been extensively described and identified (Wise 1998, Fields et al. 2007). The rewarding actions of brain stimulation involve areas throughout the brain, but the **mesolimbic pathway** is an important and heavily researched circuit that arises in the ventral tegmentum (VTA) area of the midbrain and sends axons to the nucleus accumbens (NAc). The VTA also interconnects with other structures, including the amygdala and prefrontal areas of the cerebral cortex (Figure 5.1). The monoamine dopamine is a critical neurotransmitter for the reinforcement function of these circuits.

Although rat and human brains (Figure 5.1) are different, they also have many similarities. Both consist of billions of neurons (nerve cells), which are massively interconnected via axons. Basic neuron functions, including synaptic transmission by means of neurotransmitters, are very similar. The cerebral cortex, the outermost layers of neurons, is larger and more complex in humans. However, in both rat and human brains, specific areas of the cerebral cortex are connected to various subcortical structures.

Earlier views of dopamine function in the mesolimbic structures focused on production of pleasure and the behavior-energizing effect of positive reinforcement. Although dopamine activation does strengthen (reinforce) behavior, more recent research indicates an added role for dopamine: directing behavior toward rewarding stimuli. Some investigators (Di Chara 1999, Joseph et al. 2003) describe activation of the mesolimbic dopamine circuits as signaling the occurrence of any stimulus that is of importance and so being critically involved in associative learning. This more complex view of dopamine function in selecting, initiating, and invigorating learned appetitive behaviors (Fields et al. 2007, Koob et al. 2014) is featured in current theories of addictive behavior, described further below.

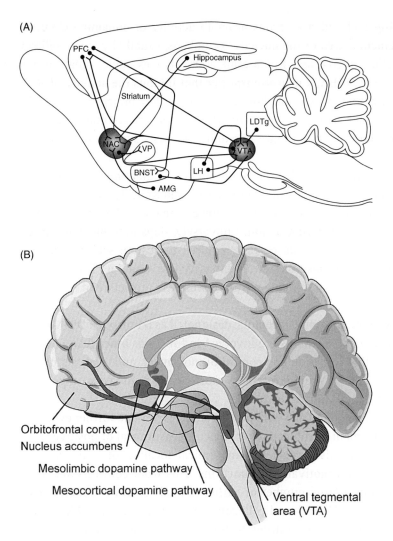

(A)

PFC

Hippocampus

Striatum

LDTg

NAC

VP

VTA

BNST

LH

AMG

(B)

Orbitofrontal cortex

Nucleus accumbens

Mesolimbic dopamine pathway

Mesocortical dopamine pathway

Ventral tegmental area (VTA)

Figure 5.1 Mesolimbic dopamine system circuitry. These diagrams of the (A) rat brain and (B) human brain illustrate the connections among brain areas that compose the mesolimbic dopamine system. Addictive drugs activate this circuit, resulting in positive reinforcement and the strengthening of behavior that produced the activation. Abbreviations for brain structures in (A) relevant to addictive drugs: VTA, ventral tegmental area; NAc, nucleus accumbens; PFC, prefrontal cortex; AMG, amygdala; BNST, bed nucleus of the stria terminalis. Dopamine is the neurotransmitter for most of these connections, but glutamate and other transmitters are also involved in this circuit. Figure 5.1A reprinted from "Synaptic Plasticity and Addiction" with permission from Macmillan Publishers Ltd. *Nature Reviews Neuroscience* (Kauer and Malenka 2007). Figure 5.1B reprinted from *The Neuroscience of Addiction* (Filbey 2019) with permission from Cambridge University Press. © Francesca Mapua Filbey 2019. Reproduced with permission of the Licensor through PLSclear.

The normal function of the brain's reward circuitry is to strengthen behavior promoting survival of the individual (food, water intake) or of the species (sexual behavior, parenting activity). Dopamine-agonist drugs that activate this system are those most readily self-administered by animals. These drugs (e.g., cocaine, amphetamine) also have very high addiction potential in humans.

Other reinforcing and addictive drugs promote activity of dopamine circuitry in the ventral tegmental area or the nucleus accumbens, usually by some indirect mechanism of action (Pierce and Kumaresan 2006). For example, opiate drugs decrease the release of GABA, a neurotransmitter that inhibits the activity of VTA neurons. Nicotine, cannabis, and alcohol also promote dopaminergic activity in the NAc, although their indirect or dose-limited agonist effects may not be as reinforcing as are those of the primary dopamine agonists such as cocaine and amphetamine.

Dopamine-agonist drugs sensitize the brain circuits originating in the VTA to the reinforcing effect of electrical stimulation (Kreek and Koob 1998). This greater sensitivity is indicated by a decrease in the lowest amount of electric current required to produce the rewarding action. Conversely, dopamine-blocking drugs cause an increase in the minimum current required to sustain self-stimulation, indicating that these drugs make the reward circuitry less sensitive. The extent to which a drug sensitizes the mesolimbic reward circuitry is predictive of the drug's addictive potential.

There are five types of dopamine receptors, designated as D1 through D5 (Missale et al. 1998). Some dopamine circuits are involved in functions other than positive reinforcement, including initiation and control of movement, and other actions as discussed below. D1 and D2 are the receptors most clearly involved with positive reinforcement (Pierce and Kumaresan 2006).

Brain-imaging studies conducted with human subjects provide further evidence of dopamine's involvement in subjective feelings of pleasure and of positive reinforcement. These studies also reveal the anatomical location of brain activity related to these important motivational functions. This work confirms and supplements the results of a large number of earlier animal studies conducted over a period of decades. Nora Volkow and colleagues (Volkow et al. 2002, 2003) used PET scans and radioactive-labeled drugs to investigate dopamine D2 and reuptake transporter receptor function in humans administered cocaine and methylphenidate (Ritalin, a dopamine agonist). After drug administration, extracellular dopamine concentrations increased in the ventral striatum, a brain area that includes the nucleus accumbens. Pleasurable feelings ("high," "rush," "euphoria") as indicated by subjects' responses on the POMS scale (Chapter 1) were positively correlated with the degree of dopamine release. These feelings commenced with the initial occupation of D2 receptors and then diminished with time. In a description of the implications of their imaging studies, Volkow and her colleagues state that "the neurotransmitter dopamine is highly concentrated in the striatum, which forms part of the brain's reward system. Dopamine ebb and flow in these areas is a main determinant of how much pleasure we derive from our experiences; it also helps us focus our attention on what is important" (Fowler et al. 2007, p. 10).

Dopamine activity is often involved with pleasurable feeling and positive reinforcement in humans and laboratory animals. However, there are limits to dopamine's importance in these processes (Koob et al. 2014, Nutt et al. 2015). Other neurotransmitters, most notably endorphins, glutamate, serotonin, noradrenaline, and cannabinoids, are also involved in positive reinforcement, especially in the overall experience of pleasure (see Box 5.1). Dopamine-agonist actions are most obviously critical in the reinforcing effects of stimulants such as cocaine. The opiates, alcohol, nicotine, and cannabis exert reinforcing effects via their activation of dopamine circuitry, but these drugs can also produce positive reinforcement via nondopaminergic actions (Pierce and Kumaresan 2006).

BOX 5.1 Positive reinforcement, pleasure, and brain activity

Which brain structures activated by addictive drugs produce pleasurable effects? Reward circuitry of the brain (structures and interconnections) revealed by brain imaging in humans and brain stimulation in animals includes the ventral striatum, the prefrontal cerebral cortex, and other brain areas (Haber and Knutson 2010). Addictive drugs activate these reward circuits and produce positive reinforcement, which when produced by nondrug rewards increases survival-promoting behavior. This activation can also result in the subjective experience of pleasure, as reported by humans and implied by certain responses in nonhuman animals.

Addictive drugs change the activity of many brain structures – but not all the areas activated by drugs are responsible for the subjective experience of pleasure. Some activity seems to indicate the *occurrence* of pleasure but does not actually *produce* the experience. For humans, activity of the orbital frontal area of the prefrontal cortex most closely indicates the intensity of pleasure. Human subjects' ratings of pleasurable stimuli (e.g., sweet tasting liquids) correlate with the level of activity in this brain area. However, in both humans and experimental animals, pleasurable feelings appear to arise from the activity of subcortical brain areas. For humans, the procedure of prefrontal lobotomy severed connections of the orbital frontal area to and from other brain structures but did not eliminate the experience of pleasure in psychiatric patients who underwent this (no longer used) surgical procedure.

Evidence from animal studies indicates that the production of pleasure is due to the activity of rather small "hedonic hot spots" located within subcortical brain areas, including the nucleus accumbens and the ventral palladium (both in the ventral striatum) (Berridge and Kringelbach 2013). Activation of opioid

BOX 5.1 Continued

or cannabinoid – but not dopamine – receptors in these structures produces responses indicating pleasure. The activity of dopaminergic neurons is intimately involved with positive reinforcement and pleasure, especially that produced by stimulant drugs like cocaine. However, dopaminergic activity does not appear to be the final step in the sequence of neural events that result in pleasure. Neural activity triggered by dopamine in other parts of the reward circuitry is hypothesized to release opioid and cannabinoid neurotransmitters in these small areas, activating neurons that produce the experience of pleasure.

Stage 2: Shift from Pleasurable to Dysphoric Drug Effects

Addictive drugs initially produce pleasure and positive reinforcement in most users. However, with chronic heavy use, the desirable effects diminish as larger amounts of the drug are required to produce a feeling of rewarding euphoria. Not only does tolerance develop for drug-produced reward but also aversive effects eventually emerge. At high doses and with extended use, all addictive drugs have delayed aversive effects, a well-known feature of addiction. These feelings of anxiety, depression, and dysphoria (unpleasant mood state) often limit heavy drug use in nonaddicted individuals (Chapter 7). These effects most often appear only after the initial pleasurable feelings subside, but at high drug doses, aversive effects may not be long delayed. Examples of these early-onset effects are subjective feelings of depression resulting from alcohol and anxiety and paranoia caused by cocaine or amphetamine. Individuals who become addicted persist in drug use despite these harmful consequences, for reasons outlined in a subsequent section.

Neurological Substrates of Acute and Protracted Withdrawal Syndromes

As previously discussed in Chapter 4, brain function changes as it adapts to and compensates for drug effects. Pharmacodynamic tolerance is very important in addiction because it not only decreases the pleasurable effect of addictive drugs but also is responsible for withdrawal syndromes. Withdrawal syndromes can range from irritability (from nicotine use) through potentially fatal convulsions (from alcohol use).

Neuroadaptations that underlie pharmacodynamic tolerance and withdrawal syndromes include down-regulation of receptors so fewer (a lower density of) receptors are available for activation by neurotransmitters. Decreased neurotransmitter release, often resulting from activation of autoreceptors, is another adaptive process. A lessening of receptor sensitivity is a third compensatory mechanism (Kreek and Koob 1998).

The occurrence of a withdrawal syndrome is neither necessary nor sufficient for a diagnosis of addiction (Chapter 2), although when present, the syndrome can be a powerful incentive to maintain drug use. When drug use stops, homeostatic processes eventually adapt to the absence of the drug and the aversive withdrawal effects diminish, at least to some extent. Even after acute withdrawal subsides, some degree of dysphoria usually lingers, often promoting resumption of drug use.

Drug-produced changes in the dopamine circuitry of the mesolimbic reinforcement system also contribute to the less intense but protracted dysphoria. Evidence comes from electrical brain stimulation and drug self-administration studies with rats and monkeys and from brain-imaging studies done with addicted human subjects.

A basic feature of a system controlled by homeostasis is a **set-point**, which is a level of activation that the system attempts to maintain as it responds to departures from this baseline state. By analogy, the temperature setting on a thermostat would be a set-point for heating or cooling of a room or building. According to George Koob and colleagues, the activation level of the mesolimbic dopamine system controls affective feelings (Koob and Le Moal 2006). A baseline level of neural activity in this system is the set-point for the hedonic state (mood and emotion). An increased level of neural activity in this brain circuit is associated with a positive hedonic state (some type of pleasurable feeling), but low activity levels would indicate dysphoria. Various positive and negative experiences (e.g., food consumption, pain) cause temporary changes in hedonic state, but over time a neutral emotional state is maintained by homeostatic regulation of this system. In rats (as previously described), dopamine-agonist drugs initially increase the sensitivity of this reinforcement circuit to rewarding electrical stimulation. This sensitization presumably reflects a positive hedonic state, objectively indicated by the decreased brain-stimulation threshold. Similar brain changes in humans are thought to be a biological process producing the euphoric feelings that occur after taking an addictive drug.

Koob's theory is a modification of an opponent process concept originated by Solomon and Corbit (1974). The older theory was developed to account for delayed, opposite "rebound" effects that often occur after either pleasurable or aversive experiences. The theory was later used to explain some aspects of drug addiction by Siegel (1975) and Poulos and Cappell (1991). Koob's theory is similar to these earlier explanations, but he also presents evidence that drugs cause the initial and then the delayed effects on the reward system because they alter the neural activity in specific brain areas.

Koob and his colleagues found that in a delayed effect after bouts of cocaine self-administration, the mesolimbic reward system becomes *less* sensitive, as

indicated by the increased level of current required to support electrical self-stimulation (Koob et al. 2004). Similar changes also occur after repeated administration of alcohol (Schulteis and Liu 2006) or morphine (Liu and Schulteis 2004).
Koop concluded that after extended intake of these drugs, the state of the hedonic
system is no longer neutral, but has changed to one producing dysphoria. The
dysphoric state results from overcompensation of the adaptive processes, which
decreases the neural activity in these circuits, and produces the aversive subjective
component of the acute withdrawal syndrome.

Koob's theory features the concept of **allostasis,** which refers to the flexibility
of some homeostatic systems in which the set-point can change (Schulkin 2003).
Altered set-points usually result from frequent extreme changes imposed on a
homeostatically regulated system (Figure 5.2). The mesolimbic reward system

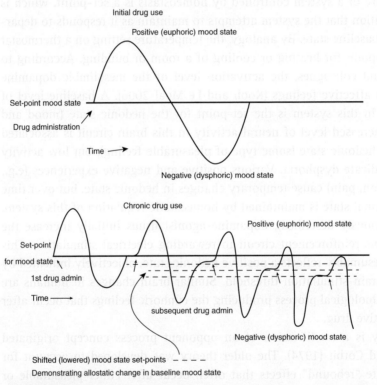

Figure 5.2 Homeostasis, allostasis, and the hedonic state set-point. (A) Immediate positive (euphoric)
and the subsequent negative (dysphoric) change in hedonic (mood) state as caused by the initial use
of addictive drugs. The delayed dysphoric state results from homeostatic overcompensation, but mood
eventually returns to a neutral baseline set-point. (B) Illustration of how repeated drug use causes an
allostatic change as the set-points drop to deeper and enduring levels of dysphoria. Subsequent drug use
still lessens negative mood but eventually no longer produces positive levels of euphoria. Reprinted and
adapted from "Drug Addiction, Dysregulation of Reward, and Allostasis" with permission from Macmillan
Publishers Ltd. *Neuropsychopharmacology* (Koob and Le Moal 2001).

remains desensitized and less active for extended periods, far longer than other behavioral indicators of withdrawal. The enduring change in brain-stimulation threshold indicates that the set-point is driven downward by the actions of the compensatory processes activated by drug administration. The lowered set-point (decreased baseline) for activity in the reward system causes a persistent state of dysphoria, which is often described by detoxified addicts as a protracted, if less intense, withdrawal. Such a consequence is consistent with the subjective accounts of many addicted persons who describe that "taking a drug to feel good" eventually shifted to "taking a drug to feel less bad (and more nearly normal)."

Several groups of investigators using PET scan imaging have detected a lower density of D2 receptors in detoxified human subjects. These differences in the dopamine system were seen in individuals with histories of dependence on alcohol (Heinz et al. 2005), cocaine (Martinez et al. 2004), methamphetamine (Volkow et al. 2001), or heroin (Wang et al. 1997). Comparisons were made between individuals having no history of addictive drug use and subjects who had been abstinent from drugs for lengths of time varying from a few weeks to several months.

In these studies of drug-dependent humans, the brain scans were recorded only after their addictive drug use. Since **D2 receptor density** prior to drug exposure was not known, the abnormality could have preceded, and thus contributed to (at least partially caused) their SUD. However, brain-imaging studies with primates have allowed determination of D2 receptor levels before, as well as after extended cocaine self-administration. Dopamine receptor density showed persistent decreases from predrug baseline, indicating that cocaine does cause abnormalities in dopaminergic circuits (Morgan et al. 2002, Nader et al. 2006). The down-regulation of dopamine receptors in these areas indicates adaptations similar to those seen in the brain-stimulation studies with rat subjects.

The changes in brain-stimulation threshold and availability of dopamine receptors indicate neurological adaptations thought to underlie the aversive aftereffects of drug use, including acute withdrawal and lingering dysphoria. As drug use continues and addiction advances, negative reinforcement (relief from dysphoria) replaces the positive reinforcement (euphoria) characteristic of initial drug use. Koob and colleagues describe this change in the nature of reinforcement as contributing to a shift from impulsive drug use during the early phase of drug abuse, to compulsive drug use in full-blown addiction (Koob et al. 2014). Such a change would explain how although decreased dopamine function causes dysphoric feelings, an addictive drug such as cocaine could maintain a reinforcing effect, eventually producing less euphoric pleasure – but temporarily relieving a dysphoric state.

Among nonaddicted humans, individuals with lower densities of D2 receptors report that dopamine-agonist drugs are more rewarding, than do those with higher receptor density (Volkow et al. 2002b). Some scientists maintain that a deficit in dopamine receptors reduces the pleasure from ordinary activities not related to drug use. Individuals in this state might be highly susceptible to the pleasurable effects (even if of lesser intensity) produced by a dopamine-agonist drug (Fowler et al. 2007). The reward deficiency hypothesis, discussed in Chapter 6, is related to this possibility of increased vulnerability to addiction.

Extensive use of addictive drugs initiates a complex array of stress responses in the brain (Koob et al. 2004). These stress responses include activation of parts of the amygdala as well as the hypothalamic–pituitary axis and the subsequent production of corticotropin releasing factor (CRF). In Koob's theory of addiction, repeated **activation of stress responses** contributes to the shift in hedonic set-point (which results in long-term dysphoria). Much evidence, based on human clinical studies as well as animal research, implicates stress responses as a common element associated with the aversive effects of chronic use of addictive drugs (Johnston et al. 2016).

Hormonal stress responses become overactive (sensitized) during withdrawal from opiate drugs or alcohol and are activated by the initial effects of cocaine and similar stimulant drugs. Heavy users of cocaine or methamphetamine often attempt to counteract the drug-produced anxiety by simultaneous use of their preferred drug (the stimulant) with antianxiety drugs (benzodiazepines) or depressants (such as alcohol).

Aversive Effects of High Drug Doses

A basic principle of pharmacology also contributes to the development of the unpleasant, possibly harmful consequences of addiction. The nature of a drug's effect depends largely on the dose administered. This *dose-effect* relationship means that extremely high doses of addictive drugs produce unwanted, aversive results. Examples include impaired motor coordination and amnesia ("blackout") from alcohol, anxiety and paranoia from cocaine or amphetamine, and death from opioid overdose. High-frequency drug-taking – typical of addiction – produces tolerance and so reduces the rewarding effects of these drugs. Such tolerance for the pleasurable effects develops more rapidly and completely than does tolerance to the unwanted effects of high doses. Koob (2006) suggests that the hedonic system is regulated such that its ability to produce an intense, prolonged pleasurable state is limited, especially when abnormally stimulated by dopamine-agonist drugs. Futile attempts to regain the initially pleasurable effects by increasing the drug dose then produce the unpleasant, often dangerous or toxic effects.

BOX 5.2 Neurological changes resulting from chronic drug use

- Pleasurable effects of addictive drugs become weaker with frequent use.
- Homeostatic adaptation to drug effects produces tolerance and the acute withdrawal syndrome.
- Decreased density of dopamine receptors lowers activity of reward circuits, resulting in persistent dysphoria of the protracted withdrawal syndrome.
- Stress caused by drugs or acute withdrawal also contributes to the lowered hedonic set-point and the persistent low mood state.
- Higher doses of addictive drugs taken in attempts to regain initial pleasurable responses cause toxic and aversive effects.

Stage 3: Compulsive Drug-Seeking

Most individuals who frequently take large amounts of addictive drugs experience the first two essential features of addiction: initially pleasurable/positive reinforcement effects from the drug, and emergence of aversive effects (Box 5.2). Addiction, however, includes the additional and critical feature of *compulsive drug-seeking* – which perpetuates the binge/intoxication – dysphoria/negative affect – anticipation/preoccupation cycle of drug use.

Compulsive behavior is strongly motivated (often self-described as "driven"), and persists even when little benefit is gained and aversive consequences are highly probable. Therefore, two factors involved in compulsive behavior are *motivation*, and *control*. Addictive drugs can compromise the function of both the "go" and the "stop" systems that promote – or inhibit – approach to potential reinforcements that might also be harmful. Understanding of the neurological basis of compulsion is very important for a satisfactory biological theory of addiction, and current theories include consideration of the pathology of both motivation and control.

Koob's theory of chronically depressed activity of hedonic regulation circuits in the brain accounts for some aspects of addiction, especially for behavior driven by negative reinforcement (relief from persistent dysphoria). Other researchers have developed a theory of addiction in which drug-related stimuli drive the compulsive behavior by their abnormal activation of the positive reinforcement system (Kalivas and O'Brien 2008, Berridge and Robinson 2016). This theory is not contradictory to Koob's explanation but rather is complementary because the theories address somewhat different aspects or phases of addictive behavior. Johnston and colleagues present a theory of addiction that includes interaction of stress and dopamine function throughout the addictive cycle, combining these two important components of addictive drug effects (Johnston et al. 2016).

Motivation for Drugs

Addicts often describe an intense desire for the drug, even long after aversive withdrawal has diminished or disappeared. Stimuli (e.g., people, places and things) linked to the drug can elicit these desires, often referred to as craving. Treatment professionals as well as those recovering from SUD generally consider craving to be a serious problem and a definite risk for relapse. Craving is widely researched and is discussed further in Chapter 7. Not all addicts report craving, and this subjective state of aroused anticipation is not a DSM-IV criterion for dependence or abuse – although it was added to the DSM-5 criteria for SUD. Memory of the initially pleasurable experience is sometimes a part of craving. However, a typical comment from addicted individuals experiencing craving is that they realize quite clearly that taking the drug will not produce much pleasure or (especially with stimulants) relief, yet they still "want it." This disturbing and seemingly paradoxical dilemma (desiring something that one knows will not be good) may be one reason that the AA "Big Book" describes alcohol addiction as "cunning and baffling." Persistent drug-seeking behavior in experimental animals is considered to be similar (analogous) to craving for drugs in addicted human subjects.

The intriguing dissociation of "wanting" from "liking" has been addressed by several theorists (e.g., Berridge and Robinson 2016, Gardner 1999, Robinson and Berridge 2000, Volkow and Fowler 2000). These two components of reward, although normally closely connected, have somewhat different neurological substrates. Brain circuits for "wanting" (and identifying and approaching rewards) are more widespread and chemically diverse than are those for "liking" (experiencing pleasure) (Berridge et al. 2009). Addictive drugs can separate and differently influence these related aspects of seeking and obtaining rewarding experiences.

Chronic use results in tolerance for many drug effects – including reward value, as discussed above. However, under certain conditions some drug effects can become stronger with repeated administration. This strengthening of drug effects is termed *sensitization,* and is not as well understood as is tolerance, which causes drug effects to become weaker. Behavioral sensitization, the increase in certain behavioral effects of drugs, is considered to be an animal model of some aspects of drug addiction (Kauer and Malenka 2007, Steketee and Kalivas 2011). Behavioral sensitization occurs most readily with repeated administration of cocaine or amphetamine to rats in a specific location. The presence of stimuli that reliably predict the onset of drug action increases the drug effect of behavioral activation. This facilitation of the drug effect (sensitization) indicates that classical conditioning contributes to sensitization, although the behavioral sensitization does not depend entirely on associative (memory) processes (Badiani and Robinson 2004).

Early studies of behavioral sensitization investigated cocaine-produced increases in rat motor activity. Research that is more recent has demonstrated sensitization with other drugs, including ethanol, and in behaviors more clearly related to the incentive (reward) value of the drug. Most research on sensitization is done with animal subjects, but sensitization-like effects with amphetamine administration to human subjects have been reported (Strakowski and Sax 1998, Evans et al. 2006). Sensitization of certain aspects of addictive drugs' reinforcement effect is thought to contribute to the development of addictive compulsion.

According to a theory introduced by Robinson and Berridge, **incentive sensitization** underlies the increased motivation for addictive drugs often seen with repeated use of the drug, even though the actual reward produced by the drug has diminished. Because goal-directed behavior is guided by sensory input, stimuli leading to (predicting) a reinforcing event become a powerful motivational force. This ability to guide and energize behavior is termed the incentive value of the stimulus. A high-incentive stimulus is attractive and commands attention. Incentive value may depend on the state of the subject. As an example, the sight and smell of a pizza is very attractive and interesting to a hungry person, but less so to someone who has recently eaten. Drug-related stimuli are thought to acquire an exaggerated, high incentive value by means of the sensitization process. Incentive sensitization then results in these stimuli gaining powerful control over behavior. Such sensitization would then account for the often reported "wanting" even though not "liking" the drug experience – at least not liking it enough to warrant the strong motivation for the drug (Robinson and Berridge 2008). Drug-produced behavioral sensitization endures for extended periods, as does the compulsive behavior of addiction.

The neurological changes that underlie incentive sensitization are not completely understood, but evidence implicates drug-produced alterations in dopaminergic and glutamatergic receptors and circuits (Scofield et al. 2016, Steketee and Kalivas 2011). Addictive drugs – and especially the dopamine agonists cocaine and amphetamine – intensely activate the reward system, increasing dopaminergic input from the ventral tegmental area into the nucleus accumbens. This abnormal dopamine activation also promotes changes in other brain circuits and structures, including the amygdala and the prefrontal cortex. A major excitatory neurotransmitter in these other structures is glutamate, and axons of glutamatergic neurons extend from the prefrontal cortex and the amygdala back to the mesolimbic reward system (Koob and Volkow 2010).

The amygdala, hippocampus, and certain areas of the cerebral cortex function to make and remember associations between emotionally significant events and stimuli predicting such events. These associations are a result of changes in neural circuits thought to be the basis of memory formation. The burst of intense dopaminergic stimulation produced by an addictive drug very effectively promotes formation of these altered neural connections and the resultant strong associations between the drug-produced reward and stimuli predicting that drug action. Glutamate input from the prefrontal cortical areas into the subcortical components of the reward circuit modulates motivation for drugs, and in particular that triggered by drug-associated stimuli.

Glutamatergic activity is altered by the extreme drug-produced activity of the reward system, disrupting normal glutamate function (Kalivas 2009, Scofield et al. 2016). These changes in dopamine and glutamate circuits apparently underlie the increased motivation for drugs, and especially craving elicited by drug-paired stimuli in addicted humans as well as drug-seeking behavior in experimental animals. Even after the processes producing tolerance have reduced the initial rewarding action of the drug, the incentive value of the drug persists and increases, motivating and guiding the addictive behavior.

When drug-addicted humans are presented with stimuli closely related to drug effects (such as videos of people insufflating cocaine, as in Figure 5.3), neuronal activity increases greatly in certain prefrontal cortical areas, and in the amygdala. The orbitofrontal cortex is a critical part of the interconnection between the mesolimbic system and the prefrontal areas. The increased metabolic activity in these areas, detected by PET scans and functional MRI, is correlated with the intensity of drug craving (e.g., Kalivas and O'Brien 2008, Childress et al. 1999). Drug-related stimuli do not cause such increased metabolic activity in subjects with no history of addictive drug use.

Figure 5.3 Exposing addicts to images of cocaine use triggers craving for the drug. Photo: Massimo Merlini / E+ / Getty Images.

Alterations in receptors, neurotransmitter release, or dendrite structure underlie changes in neuron function. Detection of such specific changes responsible for behavioral sensitization or addiction requires the use of invasive procedures, so these studies are conducted with animal subjects. Drugs that block neurotransmitters or that activate particular receptors are injected into specific areas of the rat brain. In vitro investigations of isolated slices of brain tissue (after removal from the animal) also provide detailed information about synaptic activity at the molecular level. Many of these studies reveal drug-produced changes in dopamine and glutamate function consistent with the theory outlined above (Kalivas 2009, Kalivas and O'Brien 2008, Kauer and Malenka 2007).

The therapeutic drug acamprosate alters glutamate transmission and reduces craving in some patients with alcohol use disorder (Chapter 10). Additional drugs that modify glutamatergic function are in development for possible clinical use in treating addiction (Spencer et al. 2016).

In experimental animals, self-administration of addictive drugs and active drug-seeking behavior, rather than passive receipt of the drug as administered by an experimenter, seems to be a critical requirement for development of the addiction-relevant changes in dopamine and glutamate function (Dumont et al. 2005). Stress-producing periods of extinction, during which the operant behavior is not reinforced by a drug injection, also contribute to alteration in brain function, especially in the amygdala (Kalivas and O'Brien 2008). Hormonal and neurological changes related to stress are important components of Koob's theory that long-duration changes in the reward system are responsible for compulsive drug use.

Koob's theory, emphasizing relief from lingering dysphoria (negative reinforcement), is a well-supported explanation for vulnerability to relapse during early recovery from active addiction. Long-term vulnerability to relapse is perhaps better explained by the theories emphasizing engagement of the positive reinforcement "go-system" when activated by drug-related stimuli.

Impaired Cognitive Control

Compulsive behavior, in addition to being driven toward an object or activity, is very resistant to *inhibition* or *control*. Most of the evidence of drug-produced changes in mesolimbic dopamine and glutamate function comes from research with animal subjects. These abnormalities primarily influence the positive reinforcement functions that drive drug-seeking (the "go-system"), which has cortical as well as subcortical components. The neurotransmitters and brain structures relevant to compulsive drug use in addicted humans have similar functions in drug self-administration by laboratory animals (Haber and Knutson 2010, Koob et al. 2014). However, healthy (nonaddicted) humans ordinarily have much cognitive control over their behavior, often inhibiting and avoiding risky, potentially harmful behavior by means of anticipating outcomes (the "stop-system"). An important characteristic of human addiction is impairment of normal cognitive control of destructive behavior (Garavan and Hester 2007, Yucel and Lubman 2007).

Heavy use of addictive drugs by humans can cause aversive delayed effects like dysphoria and anxiety due to physiological processes previously described. For humans, such drug use often leads to additional adverse outcomes that are less certain and immediate and largely depend on social and cultural factors. Obvious examples include damage to or loss of interpersonal relations (e.g., family), financial security (employment), or personal freedom (prison). The ability to make rational choices, including those based on consideration of long-term outcomes, is termed **executive function** by cognitive psychologists and neuropsychologists who study decision-making and brain function. Antoine Bechara refers to the ability to restrain stimulus-driven impulsive behavior as a function of the *reflective system* (Bechara 2005). This term refers to the previously identified (inhibitory) stop-system, which in humans often influences behavior by means of deliberate evaluation of probable consequences. Both Bechara and Stephen Stahl (Stahl 2008) also use the term *willpower* in their descriptions of the reflective system's function. Chapter 7, biopsychosocial approaches to addiction theory, further discusses the interesting question of willpower and rationality in behavioral choices related to addiction.

A large number of controlled laboratory studies indicate **impaired behavioral inhibition** in individuals with histories of SUD (Chapter 8). The inhibition deficits occur in heavy users of alcohol (e.g., Bechara et al. 2001), cocaine (e.g., Fillmore and Rush 2002), cannabis (Bolla et al. 2005), heroin (Verdejo-Garcia and Perez-Garcia 2007), or a variety of addictive drugs (Yucel et al. 2007). This impairment of executive function occurs during intoxication (acute drug effects) and, although diminished, persists much longer than overt intoxication. A preexisting impairment of executive function may contribute to (be a partial cause of) addiction (Dalley et al. 2011, Goldstein et al. 2009, Kirisci et al. 2004). However, much evidence indicates that most addictive drugs also cause or exacerbate the impairment. In either case (cause or result of excessive drug use) the impaired cognitive control obviously plays a critical role in the maladaptive behavior and destructive consequences of addiction.

The brain structures critical to executive control of behavior have been identified, and their function is relatively well understood (Figure 5.4). The prefrontal areas of the cerebral cortex provide behavioral inhibition in many situations. Walle Nauta, a renowned neuroanatomist, referred to the frontal and prefrontal lobes as the "neocortex of the limbic system." Nauta's description of prefrontal function is based on the extensive reciprocal connections between these areas of the cerebral cortex and subcortical structures involved in emotion and motivation (Nauta 1971). Many clinical studies implicate damage to or dysfunction of

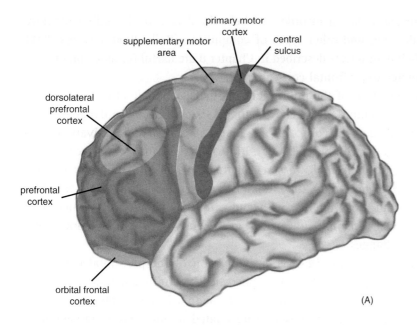

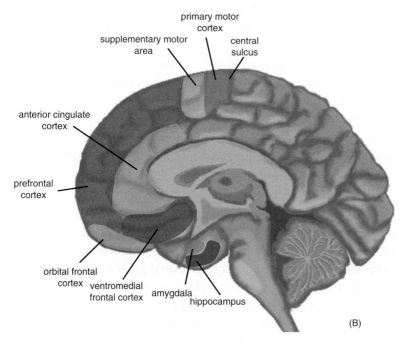

Figure 5.4 Areas of the prefrontal cortex involved in regulation of behavior, including impulses resulting from activity of subcortical structures. In addiction, these impulses are often driven by stimuli related to the drug or memory of the drug's pleasurable effects. A simplified description of these areas' function: the orbitofrontal cortex receives impulses toward action from subcortical structures; the dorsolateral prefrontal cortex evaluates the possible outcomes of actions; the ventromedial prefrontal cortex integrates the input of the other two areas. Other nearby cortical areas that influence prefrontal activity include the anterior cingulate cortex (involved in regulation of emotional states) and the insula (not shown in this illustration; responds to interoceptive information from peripheral areas of the body). Reprinted from *Stahl's Essential Psychopharmacology,* Third Edition with permission from Cambridge University Press (Stahl 2008). Copyright © Stephen M. Stahl.

prefrontal cortical areas in disorders of behavioral control, including obsessive compulsive disorder and other types of compulsion (Rolls 2000, Lyvvers 2000). Most of the behavioral tests described in Chapter 8 are useful for assessment of the effects of damage to prefrontal cortical areas.

The overall function of the prefrontal area makes possible effective executive control, including inhibition of behavior that is likely to result in dangerous consequences. This area of the cortex also regulates emotional and motivational processes as it exerts control over behavior. Brain-imaging studies and the effects of damage to specific prefrontal areas reveal their related but somewhat different functions (Alvarez and Emory 2006, Chambers et al. 2009, Kringelbach and Rolls 2004). These brain areas interact with and often counteract the actions of the previously described, mainly subcortical go-system, which is also vulnerable to drug-produced changes.

The orbitofrontal cortex (OFC) is a subdivision of the prefrontal cortex that receives dopaminergic input from the subcortical ventral tegmental area as well as other structures, such as the amygdala. In addicted individuals, the OFC displays increased activity in response to drug-related stimuli, indicating heightened attention to these stimuli, and the altered behavior-directing function of the positive reinforcement system. Increased activity in the OFC correlates with subjective ratings of drug-produced pleasure as well as craving for drugs and is thought to generally promote drug use and drug-seeking behavior.

The dorsolateral prefrontal cortex (DLPC) provides evaluation of situations based on memory and prediction of probable outcomes, which can inhibit the drug-seeking behavior. The ventromedial prefrontal cortex (VMPC) integrates the activity of the OFC and the DLPC and essentially determines whether the behavior will be initiated or inhibited (Bechara and Van Der Linden 2005). Other brain areas and structures in or near the prefrontal area, such as the anterior cingulate gyrus and the insula, also send input about emotional states and bodily conditions to the VMPC (Craig 2009). This account of prefrontal function is somewhat simplified but describes in general how these brain areas provide executive control of behavior, often overriding impulsive actions promoted by activity of subcortical structures.

MRI studies have detected structural damage to several prefrontal areas in heavy users of cocaine and of other addictive drugs (Matochick et al. 2003, Schlaepfer 2006). There is also ample evidence from fMRI and PET scans of a general reduction of metabolism and blood flow in prefrontal cortical areas in individuals who are heavy users of cocaine, opiates, or alcohol (Volkow et al. 2012, Goldstein and Volkow 2002). The decreased metabolic activity in prefrontal areas persisted after four weeks of abstinence from cocaine.

Brain-imaging techniques also provide measurement of activity levels in prefrontal areas during behavioral tests of inhibitory control. Decreased levels of metabolic activity, along with lower behavioral scores, occurred during these tests in active cocaine users (Hester and Garavan 2004, Kaufmann et al. 2003). These subjects were cocaine-free at the time of testing. Bolla and colleagues found similar differences in abstinent, but previously chronic users of large amounts of marijuana (Bolla et al. 2005). In some of these studies the severity of impaired behavioral control and of the abnormality of brain function were positively correlated.

The impaired function of these brain areas, indicating reduced effectiveness of the behavioral stop-system, apparently contributes to the addict's inability to regulate drug use. Bolla and colleagues (Bolla et al. 2003) reported a significant positive correlation between the degree of abnormality of metabolic brain activity and the self-reported amount of cocaine consumed by the subjects. This correlation suggests (but does not prove) that the brain abnormality was a result, rather than a preexisting cause, of the cocaine use. It is not yet known whether the impaired prefrontal function is secondary to the drug action on dopamine circuits at the subcortical level or results more directly from drug effects on the cortical structures (Koob and Volkow 2010).

The impairment of behavioral inhibition seen in addicted individuals may not be as pervasive or severe as what is seen in patients with prefrontal damage resulting from brain trauma. For some with SUD the inability to withhold responses might be apparent only in drug-related situations. Bechara (2005) compared Iowa Gambling Task performance by addicts with that of subjects with VMPC damage caused by vascular events (strokes) or physical trauma. Sixty-three percent of addicts performed within the range of VMPC patients, as compared to 27 percent of normal control subjects. As a group, these addicted individuals were apparently less impaired in behavioral regulation than the VMPC patients but were still significantly impaired in comparison to healthy control subjects. Even a relatively low level of executive impairment, coupled with the exaggerated response of a subcortical go-system sensitized to drug-related stimuli, could easily result in disinhibited, compulsive behavior. In other words, an addicted individual might not show noticeably impaired executive control until an opportunity for drug use is encountered.

As addiction progresses, drug-seeking and drug use behavior often become more habitual and automatic, and (at least sometimes) apparently less deliberate and voluntary. Several investigators now believe that the transition from flexible and voluntary behavior to more stimulus-driven, compulsive, and ingrained behavior is due to a change in brain areas controlling drug-seeking. As prefrontal cortical structures become less able to inhibit behavior, subcortical brain circuits assume greater control (Belin et al. 2013, Koob and Volkow 2010, Pierce and Vanderschuren 2010).

> ### BOX 5.3 Neurological processes underlying compulsive drug use
>
> - Addictive drugs can compromise the function of the brain's "go-system" (approach) and the "stop-system" (inhibition).
> - Drug effects on dopamine and glutamate function are thought to cause incentive sensitization.
> - Incentive sensitization increases the craving ("wanting") stimulated by drug-associated stimuli even after the pleasurable effects ("liking") of the drug are decreased due to tolerance.
> - Activity in the prefrontal cortex and other brain areas exerts executive control to inhibit the approach behavior (drug use) initiated by subcortical brain structures.
> - Neurological activity in prefrontal areas is deficient in many addicted individuals – possibly even prior to drug use.
> - Addictive drugs further impair the inhibitory function and behavioral regulation of the prefrontal brain areas.
> - The combination of sensitization of the brain's "go-circuits" and the deficient executive inhibitory control result in craving for and compulsive use of addictive drugs.

Stage 4: Lingering Vulnerability – the Recurrence of Compulsive Drug Use

We have partial understanding of how addictive drugs can alter brain function to cause compulsive drug use (Box 5.3). Although brain activity gradually returns toward normal when drug intake stops, vulnerability to relapse persists during long periods of abstinence. Prevention of relapse to active addiction is a primary purpose of effective treatment programs (Chapter 16).

The conditions most likely to cause a resumption of drug use are well known, and they apply to both humans suffering from SUD and to rats and primates trained to self-administer addictive drugs in research paradigms intended to model human addiction. Clinical studies, anecdotal accounts of addicts, and controlled experiments with animals all indicate that (1) reexposure to the addictive drug, (2) stimuli (locations, visual and olfactory cues) related to drug usage, and (3) stress-inducing conditions or procedures often lead to resumption of compulsive drug use. This knowledge guides investigators as they attempt to understand the brain activity and other biological processes that underlie relapse.

There are obvious practical and ethical limitations on laboratory studies of how drug reexposure, drug-related stimuli, and stress cause relapse to addictive behavior in humans. Some controlled research is done with human subjects with histories of SUD, mainly to study the effects of drug-linked stimuli on craving for drugs and brain activity as revealed by brain imaging. However, investigations of specific brain areas and neurotransmitter involvement in relapse-like behavior often require the use of invasive procedures, so are primarily conducted with animal subjects.

Recurrence of Drug-Seeking in Experimental Animals

Animal models of drug self-administration are analogous to human addiction, with definite similarities between animals and humans concerning the resumption of drug-seeking behavior after a period of no drug intake. Animal subjects trained to self-administer drugs intravenously eventually stop the operant behavior (usually lever-pressing) when, under extinction conditions, the action no longer produces a drug injection. In the **reinstatement (RI) paradigm**, animals with drug reinforcement histories reliably attempt to resume drug self-administration when subjected to stress-producing procedures, drug-related stimuli, or when given priming injections of the self-administered drug (Shaham et al. 2003, Shalev et al. 2002). Injection of receptor activating or blocking agents into specific brain structures indicates how neurotransmitter circuits are involved in the renewed drug-seeking behavior.

The RI paradigm is used extensively to investigate the neurological basis of drug-seeking behavior in laboratory animals (Scofield et al. 2016). RI testing starts only after an extensive drug-free period intended to avoid the effects of an acute withdrawal syndrome. The operant behavior during the RI test does not result in drug injection, preventing renewed reinforcement of the drug-seeking behavior. Rats are the subjects in most RI experiments.

Although the RI model has much similarity to addictive relapse in humans, there are some obvious differences between these two situations. With human addicts, drug-taking usually stops due to restricted access (e.g., resulting from entry into a treatment program, or incarceration) or because the aversive effects of the drug become intolerable. In the animal model (the RI paradigm), the operant behavior stops because it no longer produces the rewarding drug, a situation rarely encountered by human addicts. So long as an addicted individual inhales tobacco smoke, injects heroin, or ingests another addictive drug, brain function is affected and compulsive drug use is likely to continue. Another difference between the RI model and addiction relapse in humans is that when an addict resumes drug use after a period of abstinence, the drug effects (including reinforcement of the drug-taking behavior) are restored. In the animal paradigm, no such restoration of reinforcement occurs – the operant responses produce no drug injection. However, both clinicians and behavioral neuroscientists agree that the RI model has sufficient validity to be useful in addiction research, in particular for the development of therapeutic drugs intended to aid in relapse prevention (see review articles by Epstein and Preston 2003, Epstein et al. 2006).

RI studies show that the same brain areas whose functions underlie the initial self-administration of addictive drugs are also involved in relapse to drug-seeking behavior. These structures include the subcortical mesolimbic circuitry (primarily the ventral tegmental area and the nucleus accumbens), the amygdala and related structures, and prefrontal cortical areas. However, since the brain is changed by the extensive drug self-administration, it is not surprising that neurotransmitter function is now somewhat different than in drug-naive animals (Scofield et al. 2016, Shaham et al. 2003). Dopamine function in the subcortical structures is still important, but glutamate now plays a major role. Injection of glutamate antagonists directly into these specific areas (in particular the ventromedial prefrontal cortex) reveals that this neurotransmitter is critically involved in resumption of drug-seeking as initiated by all three of the conditions that trigger RI (Kalivas and O'Brien 2008).

Cocaine is the most studied drug in RI investigations, and the neurological structures and processes involved appear similar (although not identical) to those found with heroin, alcohol, nicotine, and cannabinoids. The large number of these investigations has provided a wealth of information about RI for these drugs as promoted by each of the three procedures that trigger renewed drug-seeking behavior. Summaries of these results are provided by Koob et al. (2014), Robbins et al. (2007), and Scofield et al. (2016).

Reexposure to the Addictive Drug

A single exposure to the drug can reactivate addictive behavior patterns. In humans with a history of SUD, limited and controlled drug use does not invariably result in resumption of addictive behavior. Medically supervised use of pain or anxiety medication for individuals recovering from SUD can be appropriate and relatively safe in many cases (Chapters 14 and 15). However, reexposure to an addictive drug presents a definite risk for relapse.

In the RI paradigm with animal subjects, a "priming" injection of the previously self-administered drug is a reliable method for reinstatement of drug-seeking behavior. The priming drug treatment is not self-administered by the animal, but is injected (intravenously or by another peripheral route of administration) by the experimenter independently of the animal's behavior. Injection of dopamine or glutamate receptor antagonists directly into the ventral tegmental area, the nucleus accumbens or the ventromedial prefrontal cortex blocks RI as caused by a priming administration of the drug. These results demonstrate the overall importance of dopamine and glutamate activity in RI as produced by reexposure to all classes of addictive drugs.

In the case of RI after self-administration of heroin or alcohol, drug-seeking caused by a priming dose of the drug is blocked by injections – administered peripherally, not into the brain – of agents that block the mu subtype of endorphin receptors. These injections do not influence RI after cocaine self-administration. This involvement of the endorphin system demonstrates that for opiates and alcohol, neurotransmitters, in addition to glutamate and dopamine, are involved in relapse to relapse-like drug-seeking behavior.

Drug-Related Stimuli

Stimuli or situations associated with drug use and drug effects are the second factor implicated in relapse to addictive drug use (in humans) and in recurrence of drug-seeking behavior (in animals). Stimuli predicting rewarding or aversive experiences motivate and guide behavior, and stimulus control of behavior is an essential feature of current theories of drug addiction. The risk of relapse resulting from exposure to drug-related stimuli is indicated by many clinical case studies, as well as by twelve-step lore, which warns against contact with "people, places and things" related to addictive drug use.

Drug-related stimuli can activate motivational or emotion-producing brain activity by means of Pavlovian conditioning and incentive sensitization, as previously described. These conditioned stimuli, such as the odor of alcoholic beverages or tobacco smoke, usually elicit druglike conditioned responses although in some cases the conditioned response is compensatory to the primary drug effect.

Controlled investigations of some risk factors for relapse (especially that of drug reexposure) with addicted human subjects are limited by ethical considerations. However, the effects of drug-related stimuli can be studied in these subjects with relative safety. Subjective responses are indicated by instruments such as the Profile of Mood States (McNair et al. 1992) or the Cocaine Craving Questionnaire (Tiffany et al. 1993). Autonomic responses and changes in brain activity that accompany the subjective states indicate neurological correlates of craving or other stimulus-produced feelings. Craving cannot be directly investigated in animal subjects, but vigorous drug-seeking behavior (as in the RI paradigm) is assumed to indicate a somewhat similar motivational state.

Exposure to stimuli associated with addictive drugs activates dopamine release in the striatum, a subcortical area containing some of the mesolimbic circuits of the positive reinforcement "go-system." In a PET scan study, Volkow et al. (2006) investigated the effects on cocaine addicts of viewing videos of cocaine use. These visual stimuli elicited dopamine release in the dorsal striatum, concurrent with craving for cocaine. The degree of dopamine release was positively correlated with the severity of the craving state, and subjects with the most severe levels of addiction also had the greatest increase in dopamine activity.

Many other imaging studies also reveal increased activity in several cortical and subcortical brain areas in response to stimuli conditioned to the effects of all types of addictive drugs. In addicted individuals, these brain areas include those initially activated by the drugs (Figure 5.1A, Box 5.4), as well as the hippocampus, the dorsal striatum and other circuits. Several factors appear to influence the degree of stimulus-elicited activity in these areas – including whether the subject is undergoing stress, and the expectation of actually receiving the drug. Both of these conditions cause greater activity increase. The intensity of addiction (indicated by clinical diagnostic criteria) also predicts the amount of brain activity increase. The correlation between stimulus-elicited brain activity and addiction severity could indicate that the increased neural response partially causes addictive behavior. However, the higher level of brain activity could be a result of heavier drug use – and the causal relation between neural response and behavior may be reciprocal (Jasinska et al. 2014).

RI studies, mainly done with rat subjects trained to self-administer cocaine, indicate that a part of the amygdala has a critical role in stimulus-elicited drug-seeking. The amygdala is a limbic system structure whose function is required for learning about emotion-producing events, and especially in making associations between such important events and stimuli which predict their occurrence. Injections of dopamine D1-receptor blocking drugs into the basolateral area of the amygdala prevent RI of cocaine-seeking behavior as caused by exposure to drug-related stimuli (Kalivas and O'Brien 2008). The amygdala sends information to the prefrontal cortex, and blocking glutamate transmission in this cortical area has similar effects of interrupting stimulus-induced drug-seeking.

Brain-imaging studies conducted with humans also indicate that drug cues activate the amygdala, although these studies do not provide the detailed anatomical or neurotransmitter-specific information gained from the RI studies with animals. However, the research with both animal and human subjects reveals that the amygdala is activated by drug-related stimuli. This brain activity is thought to trigger drug-seeking behavior and craving for cocaine and other addictive drugs.

Research with animal subjects, as well as studies of addicted humans, show that stimuli associated with drug effects often elicit neural activity similar to that caused by drug administration. However, some conditioned responses to drug-related stimuli can be in the direction opposite to that of the primary drug effect. Such drug-oppositional responses counteract and compensate for some drug effects, and they often resemble the withdrawal syndrome (Siegel and Ramos 2002).

Compensatory conditioning occurs most often for stimuli predicting the effects of CNS depressants, or of opioids. Alcohol decreases body temperature, but the conditioned response is a rise in temperature. A similar conditioned compensatory effect occurs as stimuli conditioned to morphine's analgesic action elicit the opposite effect of increased pain sensitivity (Siegel et al. 2000). Duncan and colleagues found that although alcohol injections decreased motor activity in rats, placebo injections in the distinctive alcohol-paired location elicited activity increases, an apparent opposite-direction conditioned response (Duncan et al. 2000). Such conditioned oppositional responses seem to be responsible for the many examples of context-specific tolerance to drug effects (Siegel et al. 2000) as discussed in Chapter 4.

None of the brain-imaging studies described previously indicated a compensatory (drug-opposite) brain response to drug-associated stimuli – perhaps because the conditioned (or sensitized) incentive value of these stimuli is not diminished by the adaptive processes that produce tolerance for the drug's effect on reward circuitry.

Robbins et al. (1997, 2000) found that in response to cocaine-related cues, some abstinent human cocaine addict subjects reported druglike subjective feelings of "high," others reported feelings of withdrawal, and feelings of craving could accompany either of these subjective states. Most subjects in this experiment exhibited increased physiological reactivity (decreases in skin temperature and electrical resistance) in response to videos depicting cocaine use or preparation, but these physiological responses (indicative of arousal) did not differentiate between feeling of druglike high, or withdrawal. These studies indicate that conditioned cocaine effects are complex and variable regarding their "druglike" or "drug-opposite" nature.

Either type of conditioned response (druglike or drug-oppositional) could facilitate a return to drug usage. A druglike conditioned response could promote relapse by having effects similar to a priming drug administration, and a drug-opposite conditioned response could motivate a return to drug use due to anticipation of relief from effects similar to the withdrawal syndrome.

Kreek and Koob (1998) suggest that conditioned withdrawal responses are more likely to cause relapse in humans in early withdrawal, whereas druglike conditioned responses may be more conducive to relapse after a protracted period of abstinence. The possible role of conditioned withdrawal responses in relapse by human addicts is considered further in Chapter 7, biopsychosocial approaches to understanding SUD.

Stress

Stress is the third factor that promotes addictive relapse in humans (Johnston et al. 2016, Koob and Le Moal 2006, Sinha 2001) and resumption of drug-seeking in animal subjects (Shaham et al. 2000, Heilig and Koob 2007). Stress is also implicated in initial vulnerability to addiction (Kreek et al. 2005, Sinha 2007). Stress, and especially emotional and physiological responses to a stressor, are the subject of a very large amount of psychological and medical research. "Stress" is a general term, and for the present discussion refers to the physiological response to an unpleasant, noxious stimulus or event. For humans, stress can also come from negative mood states and thoughts. The folk-wisdom of Alcoholics Anonymous includes several slogans and acronyms that are widely used by those in twelve-step programs for prevention of relapse. HALT is an example of one of these "quick access" acronyms. These letters stand for the conditions of hunger, anger, loneliness, and fatigue (Tired), which are to be avoided because they are risk factors for relapse. These conditions are considered to be moderate stressors, perhaps more likely to be encountered by a typical recovering addict than an extreme stressor such as physical pain.

Stressors and the stress response differ in several ways from the other two primary relapse-risk factors. Stress effects may be more powerful than drug reexposure

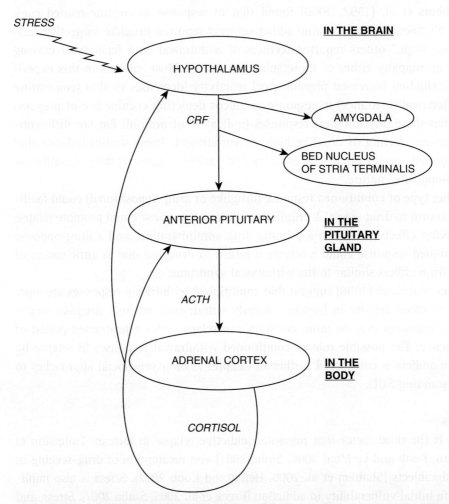

Figure 5.5 The hypothalamic–pituitary–adrenal axis and the hormonal response to stressors. Stress causes the release of corticotropin releasing factor (CRF) from the hypothalamus. CRF stimulates the anterior pituitary gland to secrete adrenocorticotropic hormone (ACTH), which then causes the adrenal gland cortex to secrete glucocorticoids. In the brain, CRF triggers drug-seeking as it activates receptors in the bed nucleus of the stria terminalis and in the amygdala. The diagram also illustrates regulatory feedback as cortisol, released into the bloodstream, inhibits the secretions of the hypothalamus and anterior pituitary.

or drug-linked stimuli (Johnston et al. 2016, Shaham et al. 2000), and it could be argued that stressors are more difficult to avoid by a recovering addict than these other relapse-promoting situations. Stress responses contribute to the persistent changes in brain function that occur after chronic use of addictive drugs (Shaham et al. 2003, Koob et al. 2004). Abnormal (exaggerated) responses to stressors may also be a component of the genetic vulnerability for the initial development of addiction (Chapter 5). Additionally, different brain structures and neurotransmitter function appear to be critical for stress-produced relapse, than for the risk factors of exposure to drugs or drug-related stimuli.

Both hormones and neural activity are involved in the complex response of the brain and body to stressors. Figure 5.5 illustrates the interaction among brain structures and endocrine glands that make up the **HPA axis** (hypothalamus, pituitary, adrenal gland). Hormonal and neural activation of the adrenal glands causes secretion of adrenaline, noradrenaline, and in humans, cortisol (in rats the adrenal cortex secretes a similar hormone, corticosterone). The adrenal hormones contribute to the activation of the sympathetic nervous system and other stress responses in the body. In addition to its activation of the pituitary gland, the hormone CRF also stimulates receptors in the *extended amygdala* and other brain areas whose activity mediates behavioral and cognitive responses to stressors. The extended amygdala consists of several limbic system structures, including the nucleus accumbens, the bed nucleus of the stria terminalis (BNST) (Figure 5.1A), and other brain areas as well as the central nucleus of the amygdala. These structures, along with the hormones (mainly CRF) that activate them in response to stressful events, are sometimes referred to as the brain's "alarm system" (Heilig and Koob 2007).

Extensive research reveals the immediate and prolonged effects of chronic drug use on the neurological and hormonal response to stressors (Belujon and Grace 2015, Kreek and Koob 1998). Heroin addicts incarcerated in the federal prison in Lexington, Kentucky in the 1950s were subjects for early clinical studies. More recent clinical information comes from studies of cocaine, alcohol, and nicotine addiction. Abstinent human addicts often demonstrate long-lasting exaggerated stress reaction as indicated by hormonal and behavioral responses (Kreek 1987). This hyperactive stress response may result from the repeated activation of the HPA axis during active addiction. Stress, and the accompanying HPA activation, is a secondary (withdrawal) effect of most drugs, but especially alcohol and opiate use. Stress responses are also a primary (initial) result of alcohol, cocaine, amphetamine and nicotine use.

Because a heightened stress response may increase vulnerability to the initial development of addiction, the greater stress reactivity seen in human addicts could precede, rather than being caused by excessive drug use. However, animal studies have demonstrated that physiological dependence on alcohol (Heilig and Koob 2007) and cocaine (Wang 2005) does produce long-term increases in anxiety, as measured by standard laboratory tests of stressors. Up-regulation of receptors for CRF and glutamate in the extended amygdala occurs and apparently contributes to the increased anxiety.

Hyperreactivity of the HPA axis in human addicts is most evident during the weeks of early withdrawal from addictive drugs, and persists to some extent after months of abstinence. Therefore, the increased reactivity to stress that accompanies heavy drug use is also a lingering risk factor for relapse to active addiction. Kreek and Koob suggest that the anxiety accompanying the abnormal stress-produced activation of the HPA system is similar to that of early withdrawal, a dysphoric state that could promote a return to drug use.

Intermittent electrical footshock reliably reinstates drug-seeking in the RI paradigm with rat subjects. The critical component of hormonal responses to stress for reinstatement appears to be the action of CRF as it activates receptors in brain structures of the extended amygdala, and in particular the bed nucleus of the stria terminalis. Infusion of CRF directly into these brain areas triggers resumed drug-seeking, and drugs that block CRF receptors prevent shock-induced return to this behavior.

Stress-produced RI is mediated by brain structures and neurotransmitter or hormonal receptors different from those critical for the actions of the other two relapse-inducing procedures (Shaham et al. 2003, Heilig and Koob 2007). Blocking of dopamine or mu-opioid receptors in the extended amygdala or other parts of the mesolimbic reinforcement system does not prevent RI produced by stressors. Conversely, resumed drug-seeking resulting from drug reexposure or drug-linked stimuli is not prevented by CRF blockers. All these RI-promoting procedures are, however, effective only with normal function of the prefrontal cortical area. The general effect of inactivating the prefrontal area demonstrates its critical function as a common final pathway for the resumption of drug-seeking (Kalivas and O'Brien 2008).

Moderate degrees of food deprivation produce stress responses in animals, and can promote resumed drug-seeking in the RI paradigm. However, CRF activity is apparently less involved in the neural and hormonal basis of RI caused by food deprivation. Evidence suggests that the hormone leptin, involved in hunger and satiation, is more important in the effect of hunger on drug-seeking (Shaham et al. 2003).

The neurotransmitter noradrenaline increases arousal level in response to stressors, and drugs that decrease the firing of noradrenergic neurons interfere with shock-induced drug-seeking. The central nucleus of the amygdala has neural connection with the bed nucleus of the stria terminalis, and suppression of noradrenergic activity in these specific areas prevents RI caused by footshock.

> ## BOX 5.4 Lingering vulnerability to resumption of addictive drug use
>
> - Reexposure to the addictive drug, stimuli associated with drug effects, and stress can trigger resumption of compulsive drug use, even after long periods of abstinence.
> - Tests with the reinstatement paradigm show that the same factors that trigger addictive relapse in humans also trigger resumption of drug-seeking behavior in experimental animals.
> - The function of the prefrontal cortical areas and the neurotransmitter glutamate are critical for reinstatement as produced by all three relapse-inducing procedures.
> - Dopamine activity in subcortical areas, including the mesolimbic reinforcement circuit and the extended amygdala, also underlies resumed drug-seeking.
> - The effects of stress differ from those of the other two factors due to the importance of the hormone CRF and the neurotransmitter noradrenaline.
> - Stressors are often the most powerful and pervasive of the three factors that cause relapse to active addiction.
> - Addictive drug use causes long-term sensitization of stress responses.

Long-Term Memory, Gene Expression, and Addiction

Addictive drugs alter brain function in many ways. Some of these disturbances of normal function eventually dissipate after drug intake stops, but other effects linger, perhaps indefinitely. The enduring nature of some drug-produced behavioral changes strongly suggests that they result from alterations of neural circuits, probably involving the microstructure of synapses. Drug action also modifies neurotransmitter and hormonal function but these changes are more transient than those of neuron structure. Much is known about changes in brain structure and activity caused by addictive drugs, but important questions remain. Research efforts are directed toward identifying synaptic modifications that endure long enough to cause the persistent behavioral changes, and determining the mechanisms producing such changes.

Investigators working to understand the vulnerability to the recurrence of addictive behavior view these enduring effects as a form of long-term memory (Nestler 2002, 2013, Hyman et al. 2006). The general problem of determining the biological basis of information storage and retrieval (memory) has been intensively investigated since the time of Karl Lashley and Ivan Pavlov in the early twentieth century. This question is so important that it might be considered as the "holy grail" of behavioral neuroscience. While considerable progress has been made in determining how the brain stores information for extended time periods, the physiological processes underlying memory are far from completely understood (Carlson 2014).

Learning and memory are so complex that simpler "memory-like" processes in experimental animals are studied in attempts to understand their biological basis and discover how the brain stores information. Two such research paradigms relevant to addiction are sensitization, and long-term potentiation. Sensitization, in which drug effects on behavior become stronger with repeated exposure to the drug, was discussed earlier in this chapter. Some evidence indicates that changes in glutamate receptors in the nucleus accumbens seen after repeated cocaine treatment are critical for the development of behavioral sensitization (Boudreau and Wolf 2005, Scofield et al. 2016).

Long-term potentiation alters the electrical and chemical activity of the hippocampus and related structures in rats. Neurons are electrically stimulated, and the aftereffects of the stimulation indicate changes in neural circuits. The synaptic events (changes in receptors and ion channels) involved in this simple form of learning are partially understood. Long-term potentiation is most likely responsible for behavioral sensitization and so is relevant to addiction (Kauer and Malenka 2007). These examples illustrate the ongoing investigation of memory processes at the molecular and cellular levels, which may eventually explain the endurance of addiction vulnerability.

Memory of emotional and motivation-relevant events (e.g., avoiding physical harm, and accessing food and sexual activity) are important for survival, and the brain efficiently stores such information. Since addictive drugs engage these same brain circuits that evolved to insure survival, the rapid creation of enduring drug-related memories is not surprising. Many human addicts would readily agree that enduring memory of drug-produced euphoria and relief of anxiety or other types of discomfort plays a critical role in years-long vulnerability to relapse.

Memory can take several different forms, and memories relevant to addictive drug use are expressed in more than one manner. Conscious recall of rewarding drug effects is an obvious example of memory. Craving for drugs often involves memory of relief from boredom, depression or anxiety. As previously discussed, stimuli associated with drugs or drug availability can also elicit addictive behavior patterns that are automatic and often do not involve conscious deliberation. Processes underlying such "behavioral memory" apparently mediate the enduring influence of addictive drugs (Nestler 2013). Memory processes are necessary for both the conscious recall (as in craving), as well as for reflexive behavioral responses.

Addictive Drugs Influence Gene Expression

The nucleus of each neuron contains the genes that regulate the production of proteins critical for the neuron's function. These proteins control receptor formation, neurotransmitter synthesis, changes in dendrite structure, and many other neuron functions. Production of these proteins is not constant, but often depends on the activation (*expression*) of the gene. Although the molecular structure of the DNA, which makes up the genes is not ordinarily changed by external events (mutations – permanent alterations in DNA – are unusual exceptions), genes can be expressed by the influence of a variety of environmental factors. Illumination changes, diet, exercise, stress, and many types of drugs are examples of factors that can promote gene expression. Neuron function and structural changes can occur when a gene is expressed. Therefore, although genes exert much control of neuron activity, their control is in turn influenced by events outside the neuron. Chemical modifications that occur within the genome without changing the DNA sequence – enduring gene expression effects – are referred to as *epigenetic* alterations. Epigenetic effects are of much interest to researchers investigating the biological bases of addiction (Blum et al. 2015, Starkman et al. 2014). Gene expression, as influenced by all addictive drugs, is implicated in the long-term vulnerability to addictive relapse. Gene expression is also a critical step in the formation of long-term memory (Nestler 2011). Gene expression and genetic control of behavior is discussed further in Chapter 6.

Neurons respond to various influences, including drugs, hormones, and neurotransmitters released by other neurons. When neurotransmitters bind with ionotropic receptors, the effects (ion movements) in the target neuron are very brief. Activation of a neuron's metabotropic receptors produces a more complex and longer-lasting response. Gene expression can result from the metabotropic initiation of a sequence of chemical reactions and transformations. These signaling pathways eventually convey information to the nucleus, activating transcription factors – proteins that bind to regulatory regions of genes and enable the genes to control production of neuron-regulating proteins (Box 5.5, Figure 5.6).

Two transcription factors relevant to addictive drug effects are CREB (cAMP response element binding protein) and delta FosB. Both these factors cause expression of many genes by means of epigenetic processes that can have long-lasting influences on the genes' activity. As a result, the structure and function of dopaminergic and glutamatergic neurons in the hippocampus, nucleus accumbens, amygdala and other components of the mesolimbic reward circuit are modified (Nestler 2013).

CREB is activated by opioid and stimulant drugs. The genes expressed by CREB cause increased levels of *dynorphin* (an endogenous opioid producing dysphoria) and CRF (corticotropin releasing factor). Therefore, CREB is involved in the stressful and aversive effects of these drugs that result from chronic use.

Delta FosB is activated by all addictive drugs, including alcohol and nicotine. This transcription factor is of special interest regarding addiction in that it potentiates the reward value of subsequent drug use, has an especially long duration and accumulates in the nucleus accumbens. The induction of delta FosB by addictive drugs is greatest in adolescent animals during the developmental stage of highest addiction vulnerability (Ehrlich et al. 2002). It also mediates the increase in cocaine effects following exposure to nicotine, possibly contributing to the increased vulnerability to subsequent addiction after early-adolescent tobacco use in humans (Levine et al. 2011).

Changes in Synaptic Microstructure

One result of gene expression is the production of **brain-derived neurotrophic factor (BDNF)**, a chemical that maintains, nourishes, and promotes structural changes in neurons. BDNF produces enduring potentiation of information transmission in dopamine neurons in the ventral tegmental area and is implicated in neuronal changes underlying memory formation (Kalivas and O'Brien 2008). BDNF promotes the formation of dendritic spines that increase the surface area of dendrites (Box 5.5, Figure 5.6) (Bramham and Messaoudi 2005). This change in

---

BOX 5.5 Initiation and result of gene expression (as triggered by natural events or by drugs, including dopamine agonists)

Figure 5.6 indicates location of occurrence in a neuron of these individual steps leading to gene expression.

Steps in overall sequence	Specific example(s)
1. Neurotransmitter binds to	Dopamine
2. Receptor in neuron membrane which activates first step in	Dopamine D1 receptor (G-protein)
3. Signaling pathway (receptor to nucleus)	Complex chain of molecular events
4. Transcription factor which causes expression of	Delta FosB, CREB
5. Gene	Many possible genes
6. Gene product which promotes	Brain-derived neurotrophic factor
7. Structural change resulting in changed synaptic function	Growth of dendritic spines (Figure 5.7)

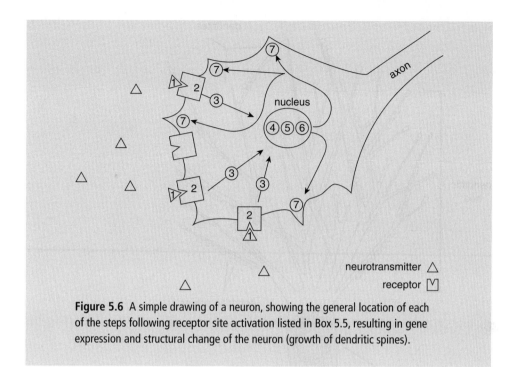

Figure 5.6 A simple drawing of a neuron, showing the general location of each of the steps following receptor site activation listed in Box 5.5, resulting in gene expression and structural change of the neuron (growth of dendritic spines).

the microstructure of neurons increases the efficiency of information transmission at the synapses and is a prime candidate for the mechanism producing **synaptic structural changes** underlying both memory formation and addiction (Mulholland and Chandler 2007). Increased density of dendritic spines in the nucleus accumbens of experimental animals after cocaine self-administration is mediated by delta FosB activation (Robison et al. 2013).

Although drug-produced gene expression may be temporary, the structural changes (such as increased density of dendritic spines; Figure 5.7) resulting from these alterations in gene function are more durable. However, dendritic spines grow and shrink, appear and disappear, as their formation and duration are influenced by many factors (Alvarez and Sabatini 2007). Neuroscientists refer to changes in neural circuits as *synaptic plasticity*, and further elucidation of the mechanisms by which experiences (such as drug usage) bring about long-term alterations in brain function are a subject of current research (Pizzimenti and Lattal 2015).

The complex sequences of chemical events leading up to and following gene expression are sites of action at which therapeutic drugs might interrupt addictive behavior. The development of such drugs awaits advances in understanding how gene expression produces long-term compulsive drug-seeking.

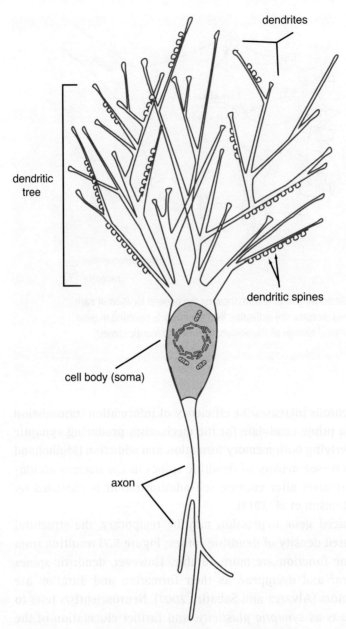

Figure 5.7 Location of neuron dendritic spines, small protrusions that form on dendrites, increasing their surface area and providing space for additional receptors. Addictive drug use, as well as many natural processes, can cause changes in dendritic spine density, resulting in alteration of synaptic transmission. Reprinted from *Stahl's Essential Psychopharmacology*, Third Edition with permission from Cambridge University Press (Stahl 2008). Copyright © Stephen M. Stahl.

Chapter Summary

Drugs with addictive potential activate dopamine circuits in the brain that produce subjective feelings of pleasure by stimulating neurons in subcortical "hedonic hot spots." More importantly, activation of dopamine circuits promotes repetition of the behavior that caused the activation and marks an important event to be remembered. This positive reinforcement occurs when ventral tegmental area neurons release dopamine at synapses in the nucleus accumbens. Other neurotransmitters (endorphins, endocannabinoids, glutamate, serotonin, and noradrenaline) and additional brain structures (the extended amygdala and the prefrontal cortex) are also involved in the neurological basis of positive reinforcement.

Repeated activation of these circuits produces tolerance, a neuroadaptation that lessens the euphoric drug effects and results in withdrawal syndrome. The hedonic regulation system is disrupted, causing a lingering, unpleasant dysphoria. These delayed aversive effects result from a decrease in density of dopamine receptors and from repeated activation of stress responses. Persistent and compulsive drug-seeking behavior then emerges as reinforcement shifts from predominately positive and pleasurable to the negative reinforcement of relief from dysphoria.

Drug-seeking behavior is also strengthened because intense dopamine activation results in the formation of associations between the drug effects and stimuli predicting these effects. Glutamate activity is also increased and is involved in the development of incentive sensitization thought to underlie the strong response to drug-related stimuli. These stimuli then drive the "approach and repeat" function of the reinforcement circuitry, even after the initial rewarding drug effect is greatly reduced – producing the "wanting, but not liking" disassociation often seen in addiction.

Most human behavior is controlled by the opposing actions of the "approach–engage" influence of the reinforcement system and the "stop–wait" inhibitory control exerted by the prefrontal areas of the cerebral cortex. This inhibitory control is often deficient in addicted individuals, a result of heavy drug use or due to a preexisting condition.

The dysfunction in these systems by which the brain controls behavior eventually dissipates to some extent if drug intake stops. However, the brain remains vulnerable for an extended period. Relapse to compulsive drug use may occur if stress, reexposure to the drug, or exposure to stimuli related to the drug is encountered. Dopaminergic and glutamatergic activation in the reinforcement circuits is critical for relapse as triggered by drug reexposure and drug-associated stimuli. Stressors are especially potent in promoting relapse, with the stress hormone CRF having a critical role in this action.

Drug-produced changes in the expression of genes contribute to the extended vulnerability of brain function to these relapse-triggering events. Resultant changes in synaptic efficiency cause functional alterations in neural circuits, thought to be the basis of both long-term memory and tendencies to relapse to active addictive behavior.

We have much evidence giving us a moderate degree of understanding of the role of brain function in the development of some types of SUD. The compulsive drug use of addiction arises from functions of the brain that are important for survival, coupled with homeostatic neuroadaptation processes. The nervous system is flexible in its adaptation to changing events, and in most instances, this adaptation is useful. However, when exposed to addictive drugs, these normally beneficial processes sometimes promote maladaptive, compulsive, and destructive drug intake.

Two basic and evolutionarily ancient features of brain function are responsible for addiction and its persistence. The positive reinforcement/approach system underlies behavior essential for survival of the species and the individual, and this system is co-opted by addictive drugs. The information storage and retrieval function ensures that these critical behaviors are remembered by making enduring changes in the brain, which result in long-term vulnerability to relapse.

A primary and important feature of SUD is that not all individuals who are exposed to addictive drugs develop destructive usage patterns. The search for the critical distinctive characteristics, including preexisting differences in brain function and in the genotype of this vulnerable subset of drug users, is a basic theme of the next chapter, which considers the genetic basis of addictive disorders.

Review Exercises

1. Briefly describe some human and animal research techniques used to identify changes in brain function in addicted individuals.
2. State the simplified explanation of how drug-produced changes in the "go" and "stop" systems result in addictive behavior.
3. Describe the essential features of the four stages of addiction.
4. Define and give an example of drug-produced positive and negative reinforcement.
5. What is the mesolimbic dopamine system, and what role does it play in positive reinforcement?
6. Define and explain Koob's concepts of a hedonic system, hedonic set-point, and allostasis.
7. How does tolerance increase the probability of taking higher doses of a drug, and why is this result important for the development of addiction?
8. Describe the cycle of compulsive behavior and related feelings postulated by Koob and Le Moal. Why is it an essential feature of addiction stage 3?

9. What are hypothesized to be the neural substrates of craving?

10. Explain the role of impaired cognitive control in producing compulsive behavior.

11. Describe the neurological processes underlying the "wanting, but not liking" characteristic of compulsive drug use.

12. Describe the three factors that can reactivate compulsive drug use.

13. What is the RI animal research procedure, and what does it indicate about the lingering vulnerability to relapse in addicted individuals?

14. What is gene expression, and why is it a possible cause of long-term susceptibility to relapse?

Key Terms

activation of stress
  responses (134)
allostasis (132)
brain-derived neu-
  rotrophic factor
  (BDNF) (156)
brain structures and
  circuits inhibit or
  suppress behaviors
  (124)

D2 receptor density
  (133)
executive function (140)
impaired behavioral
  inhibition (140)
incentive sensitization
  (137)
mesolimbic pathway
  (126)

reinstatement (RI)
  paradigm (145)
repetitive cycle (124)
reward-sensing and
  behavior-directing
  system (123)
set-point (131)
successive stages (124)
synaptic structural
  changes (157)

PART III
Biopsychosocial Risk Factors

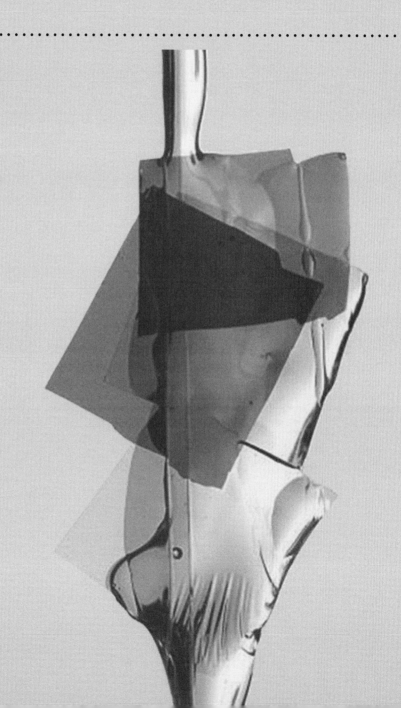

PART III

Biopsychosocial Risk Factors

Genetic Influence on Substance Use Disorders

LEARNING OBJECTIVES

1. Explain the role of heredity as a cause of SUD, especially addiction.
2. Describe the procedures used in epidemiological studies of genetic inheritance of addiction and the findings of this research.
3. Describe the ways in which genetically based personality characteristics increase vulnerability to SUD.
4. Describe the differences in brain function found in addicted adults and children with a positive history of family drug abuse.
5. Provide a brief introduction to behavioral genetics.
6. Explain the difficulties in identifying the genes involved in SUD.
7. Describe the importance and consequences of drug-produced gene expression.
8. Identify some specific genes that are related to SUD.

Introductory Vignette: Russell Cons His Mother – Again

"That's right, Mom, I need this cash for a book about how to pass the test to get my GED. Then I can get a good job, maybe enroll at the community college! It will be different this time. You'll see – I won't let you down." Russell left the house, quite pleased with how he had hustled a hundred dollars from his mother. He could get really loaded tonight, party good and hard – maybe even score some crystal meth. He found his sister's Honda key – supposedly hidden, but he could always find it – and unlocked the car to "borrow" three packs of her Marlboros. Liz would be mad at him when she missed them, but he could lay low until she cooled off. She smoked a couple of packs a day and always got very angry when Russell got into her stash. If she did run out, she could get some of Mom's – who smoked almost as much as Liz did. In the car, he saw that Liz had Dad's old Zippo lighter. The reminder of his father brought up feelings of contempt – what a loser! Drank hard and bad since he was a kid – straightened out long enough to marry Mom and learn a trade. He drifted back into heavy boozing and started smoking crack, missing work, and getting into all kinds of trouble. Finally lost his job at the shipyard but still managed to steal some expensive tools from the work site and is now doing four years in the state prison. Oh, well, he would be a lot smarter than the old man.

Maybe he would head on down to the Blue Moon right away – he could get an early start on some serious drinking.

Introduction

Many individuals who use addictive drugs do not experience adverse consequences, and even fewer develop compulsive patterns of drug-taking (addiction). Approximately two-thirds of adults in the United States drink alcohol at least occasionally. Of those who do use alcohol, about 10 percent report the occurrence of an alcohol use disorder at some time in their life (Dawson et al. 2006, Substance Abuse and Mental Health Services Administration 2018). Of those who use tobacco beyond the very tentative "experimental" stage, about one-third become nicotine dependent (Grucza and Bierut 2006). Even the most addictive drugs (nicotine, cocaine, and heroin) do not produce addiction in all who are exposed to the drug – and many use the drug only occasionally (Center for Behavioral Health Statistics and Quality 2016).

Individual differences in susceptibility to harmful drug use play a major role in the investigation of causes of substance use disorders (SUD). The basic question is "how are these persons with SUD different from those who use alcohol or other drugs safely?" Part of the answer comes from in the addicted person's life experiences, including family, social and cultural conditions (Figure 6.1). Like all complex human behavior, addiction is determined by a combination of many causes. However, a large amount of evidence implicates biological heredity (i.e., genetics) as a predisposing risk factor for SUD.

For many years, it has been apparent that alcohol use disorders are seen more often in some families than in others. The clustering of alcohol use disorders in specific families suggests that biological inheritance plays a role in the development of alcoholism, and similar family patterns of SUD incidence occur for other drugs of abuse. When parents rear their own biological offspring the effects of nature (genetics) are obviously combined with the effects of nurture (e.g., home environment, including child-rearing practices), and this confound complicates determination of the impact of each type of influence.

Several lines of investigation initiated during the latter half of the twentieth century provide evidence that genetic factors do play an important role in the development of at least some types of SUD. During the 1970s and 1980s studies of adopted children indicated that the correlation of parental and offspring alcoholism was partly due to genetic inheritance rather than resulting completely from the experience of living with an alcoholic parent. Since the 1980s studies of identical and fraternal twins have provided further evidence of genetic factors in the occurrence of SUD for alcohol as well as nicotine and of several other drugs of abuse.

Figure 6.1 Patterns of alcohol consumption are likely to be similar among adult family members, as is the prevalence of alcohol and substance use disorders. Photo: Chris Ryan / OJO Images / Getty Images.

The adoption and twin studies established that SUD are to some extent heritable, and recent technical advances have made possible the study of the biological nature of the inherited predisposition. Investigations are under way to examine brain structure and function in individuals with a family history of SUD in attempts to detect genetically determined differences that may be markers for the vulnerability.

Identification of specific genes and detection of variations in components of genes has enabled investigations of genetic transmission of SUD vulnerability at the molecular level. Selective breeding, and more recently the production of specific mutations in the genetic makeup of laboratory animals, has also shed light on the genetic basis of abnormal responses to addictive drugs. Gene expression, the study of how genes are activated by drug exposure or other environmental events, is another current area of intense investigation.

Genetic influence on SUD is probabilistic, rather than deterministic, which means that genetic factors never predict with certainty or completely control the complex behavior of compulsive drug use (Kendler 2005). Typical estimates of the heritability (the degree of genetic determination in relation to environmental factors) of most types of SUD are between 40 and 60 percent. Such numerical values might be interpreted as meaning that the genetic and environmental effects simply combine in an additive manner to influence behavior. However, the relationship is complex and interactive in that some genetic factors influence behavior only in certain environments. Some investigations indicate that environmental conditions apparently prevented the occurrence of SUD although a genetic predisposition was present (e.g., Jacob et al. 2003).

Although genetic factors contribute to the vulnerability for drug use disorders, SUD can develop in the absence of known family history or detectible genetic predisposition of the disorder (Walters 2002). The heterogeneity of causes for SUD was considered in Chapter 3 (the disease concept) and will be discussed further in Chapter 7 (behavioral, cognitive, and social factors).

The genetic basis of alcohol abuse and addiction has been the subject of much more research than has the genetics of other types of SUD (Prescott et al. 2006). In part, this difference reflects the fact that in most cultures, alcohol use occurs among a much larger proportion of the population than the use of all other abusable drugs. Although only a fraction of all alcohol users suffer from abuse or dependence, this subset provides large numbers of subjects for clinical or epidemiological studies. In addition, the prevalence of alcohol use and abuse is relatively stable over decades and generations, making possible studies of the family transmission of alcohol use disorders. Although cultural factors and historical changes influence alcohol use, these effects are much greater for the use of other drugs such as cannabis, cocaine/amphetamine, and opiates such as heroin and fentanyl. Opportunities to use certain drugs (e.g., Quaaludes, which were widely available for only a few years in the 1970s and 1980s in the United States) may wax and wane. Such rapidly changing cultural influences on prevalence of drug usage usually make the detection of SUD-related genetic factors more difficult (Anthenelli and Schuckit 1991).

Several important questions may eventually be answered concerning the genetics of addiction vulnerability. A very basic question is, What is inherited that predisposes an individual toward SUD? Related questions involve how genetic factors influence experimental drug use, and the transition from regular use into harmful usage patterns. Also of interest is whether genetic predispositions are specific for certain types of drugs, and how various psychiatric disorders are related to these genetic vulnerabilities. Yet another question would address whether genetic factors influence the marked differences in treatment effectiveness which are seen in persons who enter treatment programs for recovery from SUD. Finally, the nature of protective factors which reduce or override the effects of genetic predisposition is a question of definite importance.

Epidemiological Studies

Merikangas and Risch (2003) point out that for persons with first-degree relatives diagnosed with substance dependence, the risk of substance dependence is four to eight times that of a person with no substance-dependent relatives. The family-associated increased risk of an SUD is greater than for the psychiatric disorder of unipolar depression, but less than that for schizophrenia. As mentioned previously, this aggregation of SUD within families could result from either genetic or environmental influences, and most probably comes from a combination of both factors. Studies of unusual and **genetically informative relationships,** that is of adoptions and of twins, are used in attempts to disentangle the relative effects of biological heritability from that of nonbiological family environment. Although these investigations study special populations (twins and adoptees), most are classified as epidemiological, rather than clinical, studies in that they survey groups of subjects not specifically selected for SUD. Such investigations determine the prevalence of the disorder in the samples studied. Differences in the type of information derived from clinical, as compared to epidemiological, investigations are discussed in Chapter 1.

Adoption Studies

Convincing evidence of the heritability of alcohol use disorders was first provided by studies of the biological children of alcoholics who were adopted by nonalcoholic families. Adoption studies offer the most direct method of separating genetic and environmental risk factors (McGue 1999). As Prescott (2002) states, "Adoption studies allow researchers to separate the effects of genetic and environmental factors because adoptees receive their genetic heritage from one set of parents and their rearing environments from another set. Given some assumptions ... the degree to which adoptees resemble their biological relatives is a direct measure of genetic influence" (Prescott 2002, p. 265).

Three groups of investigators are among those who have conducted such investigations. Goodwin and colleagues (Goodwin et al. 1973) in a study done in Denmark, found that sons of alcoholic parents (mostly fathers) adopted by families without alcohol problems were four times more likely to develop alcohol dependence or abuse in comparison to those adopted from nonalcoholic parents. Subsequent studies conducted in the United States (Cadoret et al. 1987) and in Sweden (Cloninger et al. 1981, Sigvardsson et al. 1996) also found similarly increased risk of alcohol use disorder in male adoptees, apparently due to genetic rather than nonbiological family influence (Figure 6.2). These studies were conducted in different countries and used somewhat different diagnostic standards for identifying alcohol use disorders, so their consistent agreement of the moderate to strong degree of genetic influence of alcoholism in males is impressive.

Figure 6.2 Even if reared by an adoptive father with no drinking problem, the biological son of an alcoholic man is at increased risk of developing an alcohol use disorder. Photo: RgStudio / E+ / Getty Images.

One of these adoption studies (Cadoret et al. 1985) showed evidence of a genetic predisposition for alcohol use disorder in women. However, the other studies cited here did not indicate such significant genetic effects for daughters of alcoholic parents. Prescott (2002) and McGue (1999) suggest that the relatively low incidence of alcoholism in women resulted in a lack of statistical significance in some adoption studies. Twin studies, described below, provide better evidence for the heritability of SUD in women, but some gender-related differences may exist in transmission of alcoholism risk among family members.

Results of adoption studies also gave the first indication that heritability may differ among different types or levels of alcohol use disorders. This research also provided early evidence of a connection between the genetics of alcoholism and the occurrence of other behavioral patterns or psychiatric disorders. Cloninger and his colleagues (Cloninger et al. 1981, Sigvardsson et al. 1996) found that heritability was much greater for men with early-onset alcohol problems who also had antisocial personality characteristics, including criminal records. Heritability estimates for such men was 90 percent, whereas for less antisocial men with later occurring, less severe alcohol use problems, the heritability estimate was less than 40 percent.

Cloninger developed a classification system for male alcoholism, in which the more heritable, early-occurring disorder was designated as Type 2, with Type 1 being the less heritable and later-occurring form of the disorder. Cloninger's work and similar studies of clinical variation in the types of alcohol use disorders (Chapter 10) indicate that there are at least two forms of alcoholism which are differently influenced by genetic risk factors. In general, the evidence for the heritability of more extreme cases of SUD is stronger than for that of milder forms of these disorders (Ball et al. 2007).

Goodwin et al. (1977) found an increased incidence of depression (but not alcoholism) in biological daughters of alcoholics. This observation, along with Cloninger's finding of the greater incidence of antisocial personality in some types of male alcoholics, were early indicators of the complex relationship between genetic risk for SUD and other psychiatric disorders or personality characteristics.

In summary, the adoption studies indicate that a genetic predisposition increases the probability of some types of alcoholism in men, and possibly also in women. However, most children of alcoholic parents did not become alcoholic, and some adoptees with no history of alcohol use disorder in their biological family did exhibit such problems. This pattern of differences demonstrates the probabilistic effects of a genetic heritage for alcoholism and implies the importance of environmental factors.

Twin Studies

The second type of epidemiological study of genetically informative populations compares the incidence of SUD in identical, relative to fraternal, twins. Both individuals of a pair of monozygotic (identical) twins have the same genotype – that is, the genetic makeup of each twin is identical to that of the other twin (Figure 6.3). With dizygotic (fraternal) twins, the individuals have an average of 50 percent of shared genes. These studies provide estimates of the strength of genetic factors as well as that of shared and specific environmental effects. More simply put, the degree to which identical twins are more similar regarding SUD than are fraternal twins indicates the degree of genetic determination of the disorders.

Figure 6.3 Monozygotic twins have identical genotypes at birth. Photo: James Woodson / DigitalVision / Getty Images.

Alcohol Use Disorders

McGue (1999), Prescott (2002), and Yalisove (2004) summarize the results of the many twin studies done since the 1980s to investigate the genetic influence on alcohol SUD. Consistent with the adoption studies, almost all of these investigations have indicated that for males, the heritability (genetic influence) for alcohol use disorders is between 50 and 60 percent. More recent investigations, with larger sample sizes, found similar degrees of heritability for alcohol use disorders for both men and women (Kendler and Prescott 2006). These studies were done in several different countries. A partial listing includes the United Kingdom (Gurling et al. 1984), the United States (Kendler et al. 1992), Sweden (Kendler et al. 1997), and Australia (Heath et al. 1997). Somewhat different diagnostic systems were used in these investigations to identify alcohol abuse and dependence. As with the adoption studies, the results are largely consistent across cultures and varying definitions of alcohol use disorders. McGue (1999, p. 377) states: "The converging evidence from adoption and twin studies ... provides support for the existence of genetic influences on alcoholism risk in men that is as strong as the evidence supporting the existence of a genetic influence on any behavioral disorder."

Twin studies provide support for some aspects of Cloninger's concept of differential heritability of certain types of alcohol use disorders. McGue and colleagues (McGue et al. 1992) found much greater heritability in male twins whose alcohol use problems occurred prior to age twenty as compared to those with a later-appearing use disorder. This age-related difference in heritability was less apparent in some more recent studies, especially those including women. Prescott (2002) suggests that the greater the number of either/both environmental as well as genetic risk factors, the earlier the age at which alcohol misuse problems will appear.

Nicotine Use and Dependence

Genetic influences on various aspects of smoking behavior and on nicotine addiction have been intensively investigated by means of twin studies. These studies, done in several different countries, all indicate that nicotine addiction is at least as strongly influenced by genetic factors as is alcohol addiction. Sullivan and Kendler (1999) reviewed and summarized the results of several twin studies to that date, and reported an aggregate heritability value for nicotine addiction of 67 percent. More recent twin studies conducted in the United States, the Netherlands, and in Australia indicated similar degrees of nicotine addiction heritability (Maes et al. 2004, Vink et al. 2005, Pergadia et al. 2006).

Most of these investigations also determined the extent of genetic influence on smoking initiation as well as on smoking persistence and nicotine dependence/ addiction. A general finding is that heritability of becoming a regular smoker (smoking persistence) is similar to, but often somewhat lower than for nicotine addiction. The heritability of nicotine addiction appears to be closely related to genetic influences on the nature and intensity of the nicotine withdrawal syndrome, which is discussed further in Chapter 11.

Use of and SUD for Other Drugs

Several twin studies have provided estimates of the heritability of use and use disorders of illicit (or medical drugs with abuse potential) addictive drugs – stimulants, opioids, cannabis, sedatives and hallucinogens. These estimates are generally within the range of 50–70 percent for abuse/dependence, with no significant differences seen among types of drugs (Prescott et al. 2006). As is the case with nicotine, heritability estimates for use of these drugs are in general lower than such estimates for abuse and addiction (Agrawal et al. 2006, Kendler et al. 2012).

Two large-scale twin studies examined the specificity of genetic and environmental influence on the use and abuse/dependence of several classes of drugs. Both these surveys made extensive use of multivariate statistical analysis procedures to reveal whether the genetic influences on use and SUD were common to all classes of drugs studied, or if there were genetic effects specific to certain drug classes. Both studies also attempted to partition genetic factors into those that influence drug use, and those involved with abuse and dependence.

Tsuang et al. (1999) interviewed more than 3,200 male twin pairs from the Viet Nam Era Twin Registry to determine their use and abuse of five classes of drugs: cannabis, stimulants, opioids, hallucinogens, and sedatives. A **common genetic factor** was found to influence use and use disorders of all the drug classes, although there were some differences among genetic predispositions for the various drugs. Heroin use showed the greatest amount of unique genetic influence not shared by the use of the other drugs, although the common genetic factor also influenced the use of this opiate drug. Genetic factors appeared to influence transitions of drug usage from experimental to regular use and then on to abuse and dependence.

Kendler and colleagues studied female and male twin pairs from the Virginia Twin Registry (Karkoski et al. 2000, Kendler et al. 2003a). Both of these surveys (which together included more than 5,600 individuals) indicated the presence of a genetic factor common to several classes of drugs that influenced initial drug use as well as abuse and addiction. These investigators found no drug-specific effects for abuse and addiction. The initial use factors also probably promote early deviant and abusive use of alcohol (e.g., binge drinking by adolescents). However, the genetic factor promoting initial drug use is not as strong as is the inherited vulnerability for progression into an addictive disorder.

These studies of twins indicate that genetic factors significantly influence the use of and especially dependence on, illicit drugs. Much (perhaps most) of this genetic propensity to develop SUD is common to all addictive drugs, including alcohol and nicotine, but there appears to be a genetic factor specific for the opiate drugs such as heroin. Although a common factor promotes both initial use of several types of drugs as well as the transition into drug abuse and addiction, there is also evidence that specific and separate genetic factors influence these two levels of drug use and SUD (Agrawal et al. 2005).

Many studies show frequent co-occurrence of use disorders for more than one type of drug – including alcohol, nicotine and illicit drugs – within individuals (e.g., Wagner et al. 2002, Kendler et al. 2003a, Rhee et al. 2006). The SUD is more heritable (the genetic predisposition is more evident) in such cases of multiple addiction than when addiction involves only one substance (Dick and Agrawal 2008).

BOX 6.1 Epidemiological evidence of SUD heritability

- Studies of adoptions, and of twins, firmly establish that genetic factors account for at least half of the vulnerability among individuals for SUD.
- Environmental conditions interact with genetic factors, so the biological inheritance is a predisposition rather than a certain predictor of SUD.
- Even with a family history of SUD, most users of alcohol or other addictive drugs do not develop SUD – although the genetic factor does increase the incidence of the disorder.
- The degree of genetically influenced vulnerability is similar for all addictive substances, including nicotine and illicit drugs.
- The inherited vulnerability is greater for the more severe and earlier-occurring forms of the disorder.
- The genetic predisposition is greater in individuals with addiction to more than one substance.
- Genetic factors also promote the initial use of tobacco and illicit addictive drugs, although the initial use effect is not as great as the genetic influence on SUD.

What Is Inherited to Increase SUD Vulnerability?

After the basic determination that the vulnerability to SUD is in part inherited, the question "What is inherited?" then arises. There are three general approaches or types of research intended to reveal the nature of the biological predisposition. The first is consideration of whether genetically influenced personality characteristics or psychopathology might cause or contribute to the development of SUD. A second approach is to search for abnormal brain function in persons exhibiting SUD, and perhaps more importantly, those at risk for the disorder. Yet a third approach involves examination of the genome to determine the molecular basis of the genetic influence on SUD.

Genetic makeup influences many aspects of behavior, and this influence could occur by means of variations of brain, hormonal, or other bodily function. In the case of SUD, the influence could be due to a general effect on personality or behavior, or via a more specific influence on the response to the addictive drug, including possible differences in activation of the brain's reward pathways. A combination of these mechanisms is probably involved in genetic transmission of vulnerability to SUD (Kendler and Prescott 2006, Uhl et al. 2008).

Personality Characteristics and Psychopathology

Much of the genetic influence for development of SUD is common to use disorders for all addictive drugs. One explanation for how a common genetic influence could promote destructive use of several types of drugs involves certain behavioral tendencies and psychopathological conditions known to be associated with most SUD. Many investigators and theorists maintain that these personality characteristics and/or conditions such as mood, conduct and anxiety disorders can mediate maladaptive use of drugs. The term *mediate* as used here describes the effect of a variable in the causal pathway between a genetic influence and its manifestation as an SUD. In a mediated relationship the drug use would start, or escalate into abusive levels, because of high levels of sensation seeking, impulsivity, anxiety, or some other personality trait or psychiatric disorder.

Certain behavioral tendencies or personality characteristics might seem to promote dependence on specific drugs. Opiates and benzodiazepines are likely to be highly rewarding to individuals with greater anxiety. Cocaine and binge drinking might be more reinforcing to those with a tendency for thrill-seeking and risk taking. However, at present there is little evidence that genetically determined behavioral tendencies are differentially predictive of SUD for specific drugs.

Initial Drug Use

The personality characteristics most closely associated with SUD include impulsivity, risk taking, sensation and novelty seeking, behavioral undercontrol, and negative affect. The occurrence of all these is influenced by genetic factors and in some cases the genetic influence is at least partially in common with that promoting initial drug usage or SUD (Plomin et al. 2008). The case for a common genetic factor promoting both a personality characteristic and deviant drug or alcohol use is particularly strong for antisocial personality disorder (ASPD). Individuals with ASPD typically exhibit some of the behavioral traits mentioned previously (impulsivity, risk taking, behavioral undercontrol).

The databases of both large-scale twin studies (the Viet Nam Era, and the Virginia Twin registries) were studied to determine the incidence and genetic influences on personality and psychopathology, and how these factors relate to SUD (Fu et al. 2002, Kendler et al. 2003b). The relationship between SUD and behavioral disorders was also investigated in the Minnesota Twin Family Study (Hicks et al. 2004). All these investigators found much heritability for ASPD, and this heritability accounted for at least half of the genetic effect for alcohol use disorder. The Hicks study also indicated a similar shared heritability between ASPD and cannabis dependence.

Although ASPD is a good predictor of the development of SUD, this personality type does not always precede or accompany maladaptive drug use, and the same holds for other personality and behavioral correlates of SUD. According to Schuckit (2002) although almost two-thirds of people with ASPD are alcoholics, only about 20 percent of alcoholic men fulfill criteria for this disorder. There is no "addictive personality," which is necessary and sufficient to result in abuse of or dependence on drugs, including nicotine and alcohol.

Apparently at least some of the risk for initiating illicit drug use, early use and binge drinking of alcohol, and developing an SUD is intimately involved with, and perhaps mediated by a tendency to take risks, to act impulsively, and to seek new and exciting experiences. Such a cause–effect relationship could at least partly account for the common genetic influence on maladaptive use of several types of addictive drugs.

Kendler and Prescott (2006, p. 217) make an interesting comparison between genetic influence on initial cannabis use, and the genetic effect on SUD associated with this substance. The study also estimated the strength of the genetic influence on novelty seeking (closely related to sensation seeking). For initial use of cannabis, 70 percent of the overall genetic influence was shared with the genetic effect for novelty seeking. However, for cannabis abuse or dependence, only 26 percent of the genetic influence was shared with that for novelty seeking. These results are consistent with the view of other investigators such as Mary Jane Kreek and Robert Cloninger who maintain that these personality factors (impulsivity, novelty seeking, behavioral undercontrol, and ASPD) are more important as risk factors for the initiation of drug use, and relatively less important for the transition into an SUD (Cloninger 2004, Kreek et al. 2005). Cloninger also states that these personality factors are most clearly involved in the development of the early-onset (Type II) form of alcohol use disorder, in which antisocial behavior typically accompanies alcohol use. The relationship between SUD and personality factors and disorders is further discussed in Chapter 8.

Transition to SUD

Some of the same genetic factors that promote initial drug use also contribute to the harmful use that is characteristic of SUD. However, there is considerable evidence of additional genetic factors connected specifically to the maladaptive use of drugs (Kendler et al. 2012). In addition to certain personality traits or disorders, heavy use of drugs is also closely linked to a variety of other psychiatric problems. These co-occurring and genetically influenced psychological disorders are possible mediators for the transition from lower levels of drug use into SUD.

Disorders of mood (depression and bipolar disorder) and anxiety are the most frequent accompaniments of SUD (Grant et al. 2004) but other and often more severe disorders such as schizophrenia also co-occur. The possible role of genetically influenced psychopathology in the development of SUD is briefly considered here, and a more complete discussion of this co-occurrence is presented in Chapter 8.

There are several possible reasons for the co-occurrence of the two types of disorders (Neale and Kendler 1995). It is well known that heavy use of drugs can exacerbate several types of psychiatric disorders (Meuser et al. 2006), so additional mental health problems may be at least partially caused by an SUD. Conversely, most addictive drugs can temporarily relieve emotional distress, such as anxiety or depression. This self-medication explanation of SUD is widely accepted by the public. A third possibility is that both types of disorder are caused by yet another factor, such as a common genetic influence. There is some evidence for each of these three possible relationships, and there is much controversy and little general agreement among theoretical explanations. These multiple pathways into SUD could account for some of the inconsistent evidence supporting these different views of how psychopathology relates to SUD.

The self-medication explanation of how SUD is related to psychological disorders could involve genetic factors. There is much evidence that mood and anxiety disorders are partially genetically determined (Sullivan et al. 2000, Smoller et al. 2000), and some of this genetic influence predisposes for both depression and alcohol dependency (Kendler and Prescott 2006). Many cases of SUD are not preceded by identifiable non-drug-related mental health problems, so there is little support for a self-medication explanation for all drug use disorders. However, this lack of consistent evidence (a reliable correlation) might partially result from the fact that feelings of depression or anxiety can be subclinical, so though not diagnosed as meeting DSM criteria for a psychiatric disorder, could still promote maladaptive drug use.

Although addictive drugs can initially relieve stress and dysphoria, their delayed effects are usually aversive, and intensify any preexisting anxiety or depression. The escalating spiral of drug-produced dysphoria and continuing drug use is discussed further in Chapter 7.

Another explanation for the co-occurrence of SUD and other types of psychological disorders is designated as the **correlated liability** model by Kendler and Prescott (2006, p. 204). According to this theoretical model, the SUD would not necessarily be mediated by the psychiatric condition, although the same or a similar genetic influence might cause both problems. Kendler and colleagues found such a relationship in both male and female twins. These investigators observed a considerable amount of common or overlapping genetic vulnerability for alcohol dependence and major depression, although they did not see evidence that the alcoholism resulted from the depression. In other words, even if depression did not occur in an individual with this genetic vulnerability, there was still elevated risk for the development of alcohol dependence.

Limitations of Correlational Studies

Much has been learned about the relationship between SUD and other psychological disorders by use of correlational studies and multivariate statistical analysis. However, the important question of the causal relationship between these disorders cannot be satisfactorily answered by such studies, especially when the data are collected at only one time. Another useful approach is prospective (longitudinal) studies, in which the same subjects are followed and observed for a number of years to determine the sequence of occurrence of drug use, deviant behavior, and psychological disorders. Yalisove (2004) reviews some of these longitudinal studies of alcohol use problems. These research efforts are by nature time-consuming and expensive and therefore are not often conducted. However, most of these investigations indicate that behavior problems (related to ASPD or conduct disorder) as well as other psychological disorders typically emerge prior to the development of alcohol use problems. This sequence of events is consistent with the self-medication of nondrug problems as contributing to the SUD. However, as demonstrated by the Kendler results mentioned above, the SUD could still result directly from a genetic factor, rather than indirectly from the earlier-occurring psychological disorder. Longitudinal studies and developmental (childhood and adolescence) influences are discussed further in Chapter 8.

Other genetic influences, including those affecting brain activity and responses not clearly related to personality or psychopathology are also apparently involved in the development of SUD.

BOX 6.2 Personality, psychopathology, and genetic influence

- Initial use of tobacco or illicit addictive drugs as well as early and deviant use of alcohol are associated with genetically influenced personality characteristics.
- These personality characteristics include antisocial personality disorder, impulsive risk taking, and tendencies for anxiety and depression.
- Although these personality factors are also associated with SUD, there is no "addictive personality" that is necessary and sufficient to identify addictive use of drugs.
- SUD for all addictive drugs is also associated with the genetically influenced psychological disorders of anxiety, depression, and bipolar disorder.
- Self-medication of these disorders can promote addictive drug use.
- The genetic influences on SUD and depression or other psychological disorders are correlated but not always causally connected – either disorder can occur in the absence of the other.
- As with the personality factors, the correlation between psychological disorders and SUD is strong but not complete. All individuals with SUD do not have an additional disorder of anxiety or mood.
- Genetic influence on SUD can be mediated via more than one pathway.

Differences in Brain Function

The brain of an addicted person functions somewhat differently than that of a nonaddicted individual. Some abnormalities in brain structure and function of addicted individuals are a consequence of frequent high-dose intake of the addictive drug, but differences might also be of genetic origin, present before drug use commences.

Alcohol, as well as other addictive drugs, can produce neurotoxic effects, as established by a very large body of clinical and experimental evidence. Some long-term drug effects on brain function, previously described in Chapter 5, contribute to the development of compulsive drug use. These addiction-implicated drug effects include incentive sensitization, changes in baseline hedonic tone and abnormalities of prefrontal cortical function. The fact that extensive use of addictive drugs alters and sometimes permanently impairs brain function presents a major difficulty in identifying structural or functional differences that might predate drug use and increase vulnerability to addiction. This question (cause, or consequence?) regarding brain abnormalities seen in addicts is also encountered in other areas of addiction research, including the study of co-occurring psychiatric disorders.

Several investigators have attempted to avoid this problem by studying individuals known to be at risk for alcohol use problems (based on their family history of the disorder), but who have not used alcohol or other drugs excessively at the time of testing. These subjects are assumed to have some degree of genetic predisposition which might result in detectable brain or other biological differences, possibly useful as markers to predict the development of SUD. Identification of such abnormalities might also help understand the causes of the SUD. Interesting and potentially useful results have been obtained from four types of research with "family history positive" (FHP) subjects. These research areas are (1) electrical activity of the brain, (2) the intensity of response to acute administration of alcohol, (3) the response of the brain and the adrenal glands to stress, and (4) structure and function of certain brain areas as revealed by brain imaging.

EEG Abnormalities

Starting in the early 1970s Henri Begleiter and his colleagues studied the electrical activity of the brain of alcohol-dependent subjects. These investigators extensively described characteristic electroencephalographic (EEG) patterns that occur in many individuals with histories of chronic alcohol abuse. The heritability of some types of alcoholism enabled Begleiter to identify young people at high risk for alcohol use disorders. EEG activity recorded from these "prealcoholics" (with no history of personal alcohol use) revealed patterns quite similar to those seen in mature alcoholic individuals (Begleiter et al. 1984, Polich et al. 1994). These differences obviously could not be caused by alcohol use. Although some alcohol-produced electrophysiological abnormalities tend to normalize after a period of extended abstinence from alcohol, these EEG activity patterns persist without much diminution, which also suggests that these differences might be a marker for vulnerability to alcoholism, and predict the occurrence of the disorder.

These characteristic EEG activity patterns are seen in both response to novel stimuli and in spontaneous, ongoing electrical activity of the brain. The response to unfamiliar stimuli (such as a flashing light) includes the **P300 potential**, which is an indicator of the brain's processing of novel information. The P300 component is smaller in the subjects with alcohol-dependent fathers, suggesting less efficient use of available information and less proficiency in evaluating unfamiliar stimuli. Memory and attention deficits seem to be related to these differences in EEG activity (Porjesz and Begleiter 2003). Subtle differences in ongoing brain electrical activity (not triggered by a discrete stimulus) are also characteristic of alcoholic subjects, as well as those at risk (FHP) for alcohol use disorders. These differences are in the theta and beta frequencies of EEG in both resting and active (as during mental calculation tasks) states of brain activity and suggest an underlying tendency toward disinhibition of brain activity (Rangaswamy et al. 2004).

Additional EEG abnormalities in delta and theta oscillations in response to unexpected stimuli presented during a visual monitoring task were detected in the adolescent offspring of alcoholics (Rangaswamy et al. 2007). This electrophysiological marker of SUD vulnerability is similar to, but even more definitive than, the original finding of differences in the P300 response.

Overall, these differences in EEG activity indicate an imbalance between inhibition and excitation in brain function that may be involved in a predisposition toward alcoholism (Begleiter and Porjesz 1999). These investigators suggest that this underlying hyperexcitability of the central nervous system also contributes to other disorders of impulse control, such as ADHD and antisocial personality disorder, which co-occur with drug use disorders.

Smaller P300 amplitude is also associated with several externalizing psychiatric disorders (e.g., ADHD, conduct disorder) characterized by behavioral disinhibition (Iacono et al. 2002, Patrick et al. 2006). This characteristic EEG activity also occurs more often in those with cocaine or opiate dependence (Bauer 2001), nicotine dependence (Anokhin et al. 2000), or antisocial behavior (Bauer and Hesselbrock 2003). In a large study of male twins, Hicks et al. (2007) found that the reduced P300 amplitude was partly determined by genetics, with a heritability of 0.64. These investigators also determined that the externalizing disorders and the electrophysiological marker shared a modest (but significant) amount of genetic influence.

The association of the genetically influenced EEG marker with SUD for several types of drugs is consistent with the results previously described from the twin studies which indicate a general genetic influence on maladaptive use of addictive drugs.

Lower Response to Alcohol

There is much evidence (Chapter 5) that after repeated exposure, the brain of an addicted person responds differently to the addictive drug. Does a vulnerable brain respond in an abnormal manner to drug administration even before the appearance of addictive behavior? Marc Schuckit and his colleagues employed the strategy of studying the response to alcohol in sons and daughters of alcoholic men at a relatively young age, prior to the emergence of any alcohol use disorders. Schuckit found that these young subjects' response to alcohol was markedly *less* intense than the responses of similar subjects who did not have a family history of alcohol abuse. Initial results of this longitudinal study were published in 1980 (Schuckit 1980), and an extensive amount of related research followed. Much of this research is summarized and reviewed by Newlin and Thompson (1990) and Schuckit and Smith (2006).

With few exceptions these studies demonstrate that vulnerable (FHP) subjects exhibit a lower level of response to a moderate dose of alcohol as indicated by self-report of degree of intoxication, physical movement (increased body sway), and hormonal response. The subjective effects are usually judged as less intense by these subjects for both the positive (euphoric) as well as for the negative (e.g., nausea) aspects of alcohol intoxication. Follow-up studies conducted ten, fifteen, and twenty years after the initial experiments revealed that the incidence of alcohol use disorders developing later in life was positively correlated with the low level of response to alcohol as originally measured by Schuckit's team (Schuckit et al. 2004). The low response to alcohol is one of the most investigated predictors of alcohol use disorders, with four longitudinal studies reporting a relationship between the lessened response and an increased risk for alcohol-related problems (Heath et al. 1999, Rodriguez et al. 1993, Volavka et al. 1996, Schuckit and Smith 2000).

Two twin studies have shown that 40 to 60 percent of the variability among persons for this characteristic lower alcohol response can be attributed to genetic factors (Heath et al. 1999, Viken et al. 2003). Schuckit (2002) suggests that this inherited tendency to respond less intensely to a moderate amount of alcohol promotes the consumption of larger amounts of alcoholic beverages and association with heavier-drinking peers, both of which could contribute to the development of alcohol use disorders. Although this lesser response to alcohol does significantly predict later alcohol use disorders, Schuckit points out that this characteristic does not seem to predict SUD for other drugs, and does not seem to be correlated with the P300 EEG characteristic described previously. This somewhat surprising absence of correlations apparently indicates the multiplicity of genetic factors that can promote SUD, as well as the heterogeneity of the disorders.

Neither the characteristic EEG activity (described above), nor the low response to acute alcohol administration are certain predictors of eventual drug or alcohol use disorders. However, their increased incidence in high-risk persons is sufficient for their use as markers to aid in the search for specific genes that might contribute to the development of SUD (Porjesz et al. 2005, Schuckit and Smith 2006). The use of these **endophenotypes** (which are not diagnostic criteria for the disorder, but biological or behavioral characteristics related to SUD) to investigate the genetics of addiction is discussed below.

Greater Response to Psychological Stress

The responses of the brain and endocrine system to stressful situations are involved in the development of SUD, although the specific role of possibly abnormal stress responses in the disorder is not yet understood (Uhart and Wand 2009). Koob and Le Moal (2006, p. 400) emphasize that stress responses facilitate both the start of compulsive drug use as well as relapse after a period of abstinence. Chapter 5 describes how stress responses promote self-administration of addictive drugs in experimental animals. Stressful conditions or events, either in childhood or in mature individuals, are risk factors for SUD (Chapter 8).

Responses initiated by harmful or distressing events are very complex and involve many brain structures, several neurotransmitters and the endocrine system. One component in this array of stress-induced activity is the response sequence of the **hypothalamic–pituitary–adrenal (HPA) axis** (see Figure 5.5 in Chapter 5). The hypothalamus secretes the hormone corticotropin releasing factor (CRF) which stimulates the pituitary gland to release adrenocorticotropic hormone (ACTH) and beta-endorphin. ACTH increases arousal level and stimulates the adrenal cortex to secrete glucocorticoids (in humans, cortisol). Beta-endorphin has several actions, including reduction of emotional and physical pain.

Levels of ACTH and glucocorticoids indicate the degree of activation of the HPA axis both in human and animal subjects in stressful situations. For example, human experimental subjects are required to deliver a self-disclosing verbal report on short notice, or to compete against other subjects in the solution of mathematical problems. These social stress tests reliably increase blood concentrations of ACTH and cortisol.

The level of activation of the HPA axis in response to psychological stressors is influenced strongly by genetic factors (Federenko et al. 2004). This genetic influence has led several investigators to compare the HPA responses of subjects with a family history of alcohol use problems (FHP) with those of subjects without such family history (FHN). There is much evidence that family history of alcohol use disorders predicts the degree of stress responses.

Zimmerman et al. (2004) found that both ACTH and cortisol responses were greater in FHP than in FHN subjects after a social stress test, and similar results were reported by Uhart et al. (2006). Both these groups of investigators also recorded subjective self-ratings of stress-related discomfort. In both studies, the

FHN group (no family history of alcohol use) reported a significant positive correlation between the degree of hormonal response and their self-rating of stress level. However, the FHP groups' hormone responses were not correlated with the subjective ratings of stress.

These results of the Zimmerman and Uhart studies suggest that individuals with a family history of alcohol use disorder have an exaggerated hormonal response to a social stressor, but are less aware of their physiological response to the stressful situation. Earlier studies provide similar evidence of this greater reactivity to stress in FHP individuals (e.g., Finn et al. 1990). The increased stress responses, even if not subjectively recognized, could contribute to drug-produced changes in brain function that potentiate compulsive drug use.

Injections of narcotic antagonists also stimulate hormonal stress responses by counteracting the action of endorphins that attenuate the secretion of ACTH and cortisol. In a series of experiments, Wand and colleagues found that the narcotic antagonist naloxone stimulated a much greater increase of the stress hormones in FHP, relative to FHN subjects (Wand et al. 2001). These results also indicate a presumably genetically determined difference in the hormonal stress response in persons with a family history of alcohol use disorders.

Brain Imaging

Brain-imaging methods, including positron emission tomography (PET), magnetic resonance imaging (MRI), functional MRI and similar methods have become important in the investigation of the biological basis of addiction (e.g., Fowler et al. 2007, Volkow et al. 2014). These noninvasive techniques produce images which allow visualization of brain structures and their activity in living organisms. The brain's response to drugs or drug-related stimuli can be determined in humans or in experimental animals. In humans, brain activity accompanying subjective states associated with drugs, such as anxiety, euphoria or drug craving can also be visualized.

In most addiction-related brain-imaging research with human subjects, brain structure and function in drug-dependent individuals are compared to that of subjects who do not suffer from SUD. In addicted subjects, several differences are seen in both the "go" and "stop" systems whose malfunctions are implicated in compulsive drug use (Childress 2006, Goldstein et al. 2009). Understanding the possible role of these brain abnormalities in genetic vulnerability to SUD is complicated by the same problem of cause versus consequence as described above for other types of brain differences seen in addicts. The research tactic of observing at-risk individuals who are essentially drug-naive, but with positive family history for SUD, has been employed to some extent in brain-imaging studies, but such investigations are not as plentiful as for the previously discussed research areas (EEG, degree of response to alcohol, stress responses). Chapter 5 includes a more complete discussion of SUD-related differences in brain structure and function as revealed by brain-imaging research. The following discussion is focused on how such investigations have contributed to understanding genetic influences on SUD.

Magnetic resonance imaging (MRI) reveals size (volume) of specific brain structures. Many such studies have established the neurotoxic effects of long-term use of alcohol, and of stimulants such as methamphetamine (Chapters 10 and 13). These studies supplement the evidence obtained from direct examination of brain tissue during autopsies. Only a few brain-imaging studies have examined brain structures in at-risk offspring of alcohol-dependent parents. Shirley Hill and her colleagues conducted a long-term developmental study of such high-risk subjects, including MRI determination of differences in relevant brain structures. These investigators found that the right **amygdala** of FHP subjects (mean age of seventeen years) was significantly smaller as compared with matched (age, gender) FHN subjects. Amygdala volume was also correlated with the size of the P300 EEG response, the brain electrophysiological characteristic previously shown to be related to SUD vulnerability. Subjects with smaller amygdalas had correspondingly smaller P300 responses (Hill et al. 2001). Hill interprets the brain structure abnormalities as indicating a delay in brain maturation.

Benegal et al. (2007) conducted a similar MRI study in India, studying subjects with a mean age of fifteen years. Their results were largely consistent with those of Hill in that the amygdalas of FHP subjects were smaller than those of the FHN group. Benegal et al. observed reduced volume in both the left and right amygdala of these at-risk, but alcohol-naive, subjects, and also found an inverse correlation between amygdala size and externalizing behaviors. Individuals with smaller amygdalas also had records of more frequent behavior problems, including oppositional defiant disorder and ADHD.

These findings of reduced amygdala volume in FHP subjects is of interest in that this subcortical limbic system structure partly determines emotional responses, and is also thought to be involved in both drug-related reward and stress-induced drug consumption. The relationship between the size of the amygdala and neurological and behavioral characteristics often seen in persons with SUD also suggests that this anatomical feature is relevant to the genetic vulnerability of FHP individuals.

As with imaging of brain structure, the function or activity of specific brain areas has received intensive attention from researchers using brain-scanning techniques to search for indications of genetically influenced vulnerability to SUD. PET images require the injection of radioactively tagged chemicals – either glucose to reveal energy consumption, or a chemical which becomes incorporated into a neurotransmitter system. For example, the radiotracer [^{11}C]raclopride binds to specific types of dopamine receptors, and information such as the density or availability of these receptors can then be determined. The small amount of radioactive chemicals introduced into the brain, while not harmful to adults, does preclude the conduct of PET research with child or adolescent subjects.

The most interesting results have come from PET studies indicating abnormalities of dopamine function in drug-dependent persons. The neurotransmitter dopamine plays an important role in the development of SUD, especially in the early stages of the disorder as drug-produced rewards become strongly associated with stimuli predicting these rewards (Chapter 5). Several PET studies of drug-dependent persons reveal reduced density of **dopamine D2 receptors** in the ventral striatum area of the brain. This area contains the limbic system structures, described in Chapter 4, implicated in the development of compulsive drug use. There are five subtypes of dopamine receptors, but the D2 receptor is the type most clearly involved with drug-produced reward and SUD.

The lower density of (fewer) D2 receptors has been observed in detoxified subjects with histories of dependence on alcohol (Heinz et al. 2005), cocaine (Martinez et al. 2004), methamphetamine (Volkow et al. 2001), or heroin (Wang et al. 1997). In the Heinz studies, D2 density was inversely correlated with craving for alcohol, in that subjects with fewer D2 receptors reported more intense craving for alcohol when presented with alcohol-related stimuli. In the Volkow et al. study, decreased D2 density was associated with lower rates of metabolism in the orbitofrontal cortex, an inhibitory brain area critical for normal function of the brain's "stop-system." The subjects in the investigations cited here had been abstinent from drugs for varying lengths of time, ranging from a few weeks to several months, when the PET images were recorded.

These brain abnormalities, reliably observed in individuals dependent on any of three types of drugs (alcohol, stimulants, opiates), could obviously be either a cause, or a consequence of extensive drug usage. All these drugs of abuse increase dopamine activation of receptor sites, and prolonged increases in dopamine activity are known to cause receptor down-regulation, resulting in decreased density of D2 receptors (Chapter 4).

The decreased density of dopamine receptors lessens the activity of the meso-limbic reward circuitry in experimental animals (Chapter 5), and in humans is thought to result in a lower, dysphoric mood state. Although some drug effects are decreased by the development of tolerance, even a small increase in dopamine activity then results in negative reinforcement due to temporary relief from the depressed state.

Dopamine receptor levels vary among individuals even before exposure to drugs, and low D2 density in the ventral striatum may be a risk factor for development of SUD, as well as a result of drug action on the brain. The density of dopamine receptors, including that of the D2 subtypes, is partly determined by genetic factors (Jonsson et al. 1999). Several investigators have suggested that a genetically determined deficit in D2 density results in increased vulnerability to drug use disorders (Childress 2006, Kalivas and O'Brien 2008, Nader and Czoty 2005).

Blum and colleagues (Blum et al. 2014, 2017, Comings and Blum 2000) proposed a **reward deficiency syndrome**, which predisposes individuals toward abuse of or dependence on addictive drugs. According to this theory, inadequate dopamine function results in reduced sensitivity to natural (nondrug) rewards. Such an abnormality of the brain's dopamine circuitry could then underlie the increased vulnerability to development of compulsive drug use since most drugs of abuse are very effective dopamine agonists. Proponents of the theory maintain that an allele (a variation) of a gene which regulates production of the D2 receptor is associated with the reward deficiency syndrome. The evidence for a role of this specific genetic difference in the occurrence of SUD is discussed in a subsequent section of this chapter.

Most addictive drugs can produce subjectively pleasant effects in many individuals, including those not dependent on these drugs. The nature and degree of the subjective effects depends on the drug dose and even at a given dose may vary considerably among individuals. Sometimes these effects are not pleasant or are even aversive. However, accounts by addicts typically describe initial drug effects as extremely pleasurable. Investigation of factors influencing the varying subjective responses to drugs in nonaddicted persons may provide insight regarding the more reliably pleasurable effects experienced by persons who eventually develop SUD.

PET scan studies have shown that the density of dopamine D2 receptors in the striatum is associated with (and possibly influencing) the type and intensity of response to an addictive drug in nonaddicted subjects. Volkow et al. (2002) found that subjects with lower levels of D2 receptors reported more pleasurable subjective effects from an intravenous injection of methylphenidate (Ritalin) than did those with higher levels of these receptors. Several of the subjects with higher D2 levels described the effect of this dopamine-agonist stimulant as unpleasant. This investigation indicates a neurological difference that seems likely to increase drug-taking.

Yoder et al. (2005) gave intravenous alcohol injections to subjects who were not alcohol dependent. PET images revealed that at equal blood alcohol levels subjects with lower density of D2 receptors rated themselves as less intoxicated as compared to those with higher D2 density. These results suggest that compared to subjects with higher D2 levels, those with lower D2 density would need to drink more alcohol to achieve similar levels of the intoxication. This relative insensitivity to alcohol's subjective effects is reminiscent of Schuckit's findings of less sensitivity to this drug in the subjects whose fathers were alcoholic. These investigations (by Volkow, and Yoder) demonstrate that D2 density levels are associated with variations in the subjective effects of alcohol and dopamine-agonist stimulants, differences which seem likely to increase drug-taking.

Nutt and colleagues point out that the evidence for differences in dopamine receptor density associated with alcohol effects is less compelling than for the actions of cocaine and similar stimulants (Nutt et al. 2015). Blum, in a review of the role of dopamine in addiction, maintains that dopamine function is more complex than as described in earlier theories. Although various addictive drugs may interact with the dopamine system in slightly different ways, the overall importance of the neurotransmitter and its receptors in addiction is well established (Blum et al. 2015).

Many studies with animal subjects demonstrate that the reinforcement value of addictive drugs is influenced by availability of D2 receptors (e.g., Thanos et al. 2001). The use of PET imaging in longitudinal studies with animal subjects allows more certain understanding of how drug self-administration interacts with dopamine function in the striatum. Morgan et al. (2002) measured D2 levels in cynomolgus monkeys before and after the animals were moved from individual housing into groups of four – resulting in the establishment of dominance hierarchies. D2 densities increased by 20 percent in monkeys that became dominant, but did not change in subordinate animals. When given access to cocaine via operant responding, the subordinate animals readily self-administered cocaine, but the drug was not reinforcing to the dominant monkeys during the initial phase of this experiment. Eventually even the dominant animals did self-administer cocaine. Czoty et al. (2004) found that after months of cocaine self-administration D2 levels had decreased in both these groups and were similar between dominant and submissive monkeys.

Nader et al. (2006) investigated the D2 availability in rhesus monkeys by means of PET imaging during and after cocaine self-administration. Baseline D2 density correlated negatively with response rates for cocaine (animals with lower D2 levels responded more readily for cocaine reward), replicating the predictive relationship originally reported by Morgan and colleagues. D2 receptor availability decreased 20 percent within one week of cocaine access. This reduction persisted during one year of drug self-administration and persisted in some animals after a year of abstinence from cocaine.

Dalley et al. (2007, 2011) determined impulsivity in rats, a behavioral trait previously established as predicting a readiness in these animals to self-administer cocaine or amphetamine. The inability to suppress inappropriate responses is considered a risk factor for SUD in humans (see the sections on externalizing disorders, and for the P300 EEG response, discussed earlier in this chapter). Premature responses for food in response to a light stimulus indicated the degree of impulsivity in this rodent model of impulse control. Higher levels of performance correlated positively with PET-indicated D2 receptor density. Rats with lower D2 levels responded incorrectly and prematurely for food, and subsequently responded at higher rates for cocaine injections and self-administered more of the drug.

These studies show that in primates and rodents, lower density of dopamine D2 receptors predicts a greater reward value of cocaine. The primate studies also demonstrate that repeated cocaine intake results in a further decrease in D2 density. These findings are consistent with the apparent relationship between drug effects and dopamine function in humans, and probably have relevance for both the causes and consequences of SUD for most addictive drugs. Lower D2 density may be a risk factor for addiction, although chronic drug use further decreases dopamine receptor levels and results in dysphoria that is temporarily relieved by ongoing drug intake.

In addition to the evidence (cited previously) that genetic factors influence the availability of dopamine receptors, the primate studies also indicate that D2 density can be altered by environmental conditions, including social interactions as well as the intake of dopamine-agonist drugs. The lowered levels of D2 receptors reliably seen in drug-dependent individuals are likely to be a result of an interaction among genetically determined baseline receptor levels, environmental conditions (such as stress) and the effects of the addictive drugs on the dopamine system (Volkow et al. 2006).

BOX 6.3 SUD and genetically determined differences in brain function

- Brain differences detected in addicted individuals can result from heavy drug use or predate and possibly contribute to SUD.
- Brain differences observed in adolescents at genetic risk for SUD (FHP) but with no history of drug use indicate possible neurological sources of the disorder.
- FHP subjects show differences in specific EEG activity patterns and increased hormonal response to psychological stress – suggesting deficiencies in inhibition and impulse control.
- FHP subjects show lower subjective and behavioral responses to moderate doses of alcohol – possibly promoting heavier alcohol use.
- Genetically determined lower density of dopamine D2 receptors is associated with greater reward value of addictive drugs in both human and nonhuman animal subjects – although D2 density is also influenced by environmental events, including addictive drug use.

SUD Vulnerability and the Genome

Danielle Dick, a prominent investigator of the genetic basis of addiction, comments: "We have made tremendous progress in understanding the genetic epidemiology of substance use problems. We understand a good deal about the genetic architecture of substance use disorders with respect to other psychiatric conditions, and how genetic influences change across development and as a function of environment. We are further behind in identifying specific genes involved in substance use disorders" (Dick 2016, p. 673).

We now know that some substance use disorders are partially determined by biological inheritance, and we have some understanding of the genetically determined differences in brain function that precede or accompany these disorders. Acquiring this large amount of useful knowledge about "genetic effects" did not require the study of genes, or understanding of the actual mechanism of how genetic influence is transmitted.

Impressive progress has been made in determining the molecular basis of several genetically based medical conditions. Accordingly, intensive research efforts are under way to understand how differences in the genotype transmit the vulnerability for behavioral abnormalities, including SUD. It is now apparent that a (single) "gene for addiction" does not exist, and initial anticipation of rapid progress in understanding the gene-SUD relationship was overly optimistic (Kendler 2005). However, knowledge of the molecular mechanisms of genetic vulnerability for addictive disorders is steadily, if slowly, accumulating (Hancock et al. 2019, Palmer et al. 2014, Levey et al. 2014).

Behavioral Genetics and DNA

Twenty-three pairs of long threadlike molecules of **deoxyribonucleic acid (DNA)** determine the structure and influence the function of the body, including the brain. Each of these is a chromosome and consists of hundreds of millions of nucleotide base pairs, which are "steps" along the double helix structure of DNA. In humans these twenty-three chromosome pairs, found in the nucleus of most cells in the body, contain 20,000–25,000 genes, which are locations on the DNA structure (Collins et al. 2004). Each gene is a segment of DNA consisting of many (from a few thousand to several million) base pairs (Plomin et al. 2008, p. 44). These DNA areas encode or direct the production of RNA, and eventually chains of amino acids that combine to form proteins. In the brain, these proteins determine the structure and are critical in the activity of neural circuits regulating behavioral functions such as motivation, memory, cognition and decision-making. Some examples of gene-encoded protein molecules are receptor sites, and enzymes involved in the synthesis or breakdown of neurotransmitters. Although 99.5 percent of the DNA sequence is identical among individual humans, about 0.5 percent of the approximately 3 billion base pairs can vary in their specific molecular structure. These variations are termed polymorphisms, or **alleles**. Variations among alleles contribute to differences in behavioral traits and disease vulnerability as well as determining certain physical characteristics. The **genotype** is the combination of genes, including the allele variations, which with the exception of identical twins and cloned animals, is unique for each individual (Figure 6.4).

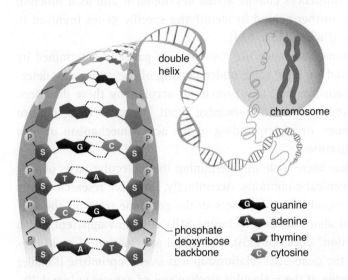

double helix

chromosome

P

S   G   C   S

P

S   T   A   S

P

S   C   G   S

P

S   A   T   S

P

G   guanine
A   adenine
T   thymine
C   cytosine

phosphate
deoxyribose
backbone

Figure 6.4 A representation of a chromosome, a portion of a DNA double helix molecule, and the base-pair steps that compose the many genes in each chromosome. Photo: jack0m / Digital Vision Vectors / Getty Images.

The **phenotype** is the configuration of the body, which for some physical features such as eye color or blood type is completely determined by the genotype. In the case of behavioral genetics, phenotypes are certain behavior patterns (e.g., emotional reactivity) or variations in cognitive abilities (e.g., intelligence). Substance use disorders are behavioral phenotypes, and like other genetically influenced behaviors, their relation to the genome (the twenty-three pairs of chromosomes) is indirect and complex.

The early years of the twenty-first century saw much progress toward the goal of understanding the biological basis of human diseases and psychiatric disorders, exemplified by the completion of the human genome project (Venter and Celera Genomics 2001, Collins et al. 2004) and similar gene-mapping endeavors.

The complexity of the human genome and of the brain's structure and function present formidable obstacles to progress in understanding how differences in DNA promote SUD vulnerability. The very large base of information resulting from the mapping of the genome suggests many possible locations of SUD-relevant genomic differences – genes related to brain structures and neurotransmitters implicated in the development of the disorders (Chapter 5). However, knowledge of how DNA structure determines the function of these brain structures or chemicals is far from complete, as is the understanding of how these genetic differences promote addictive drug use.

Psychiatric disorders (including SUD) are expressed as abnormal behaviors, cognition or emotion. The genetic basis of these disorders is much more complicated than for a monogenetic disorder such as Huntington's disease (Lachman 2006, Uhl et al. 2008). The complex probabilistic, rather than a simpler deterministic, influence of gene variation for these disorders results from (1) involvement of several or many genes, (2) the influence of environmental factors, and (3) variations in how the disorders are identified and diagnosed.

Involvement of Multiple Genes

Some physical characteristics (blood type, eye color, and others) are determined by the status of one pair of genes. The appearance of these characteristics follows inheritance patterns based on Mendel's classical principles which involve recessive and dominance relations between the paired genes. Some rare brain abnormalities which underlie such disorders as Huntington's disease are also determined by the status of a single gene. Furthermore, environment has essentially no influence on such diseases. An individual with the critical allele will eventually succumb to the disorder and such factors as diet, stress or early-childhood experience cannot prevent or promote its occurrence. Additionally, most of these characteristics or disorders are qualitative rather than quantitative in nature, meaning that they are all-or-none, and do not occur in greater or lesser degrees or intensities.

Genetic researchers have gathered much evidence that combined effects of many genes influence complex behavior such as SUD. An **odds ratio** indicates the degree of risk seen with any associated factor, including the presence of a particular allele. As an example of an environmental risk factor for a nonpsychiatric disease, the odds ratio of a heavy smoker developing lung cancer, compared to a nonsmoker, is approximately twenty (20:1; Khuder 2001). Odds ratios for the influence of single genes on the incidence of psychiatric or behavioral disorders are very low, such as 1.43 for schizophrenia and 1.30 for ADHD (Kendler 2005, Plomin et al. 2008). These small effects of single genes are typical of genetic influence on most psychiatric disorders. The allelic status of many genes contributes to the overall genetic effect on the incidence and severity of these disorders. Schizophrenia is linked to gene differences on seven different chromosomes, and similar multiple-gene involvement occurs for bipolar disorder (Lachman 2006). The discovery of a single gene whose variations would yield a high odds ratio for the risk of psychiatric disorders such as SUD is very unlikely.

Finding the correlation between a certain combination of genetic variations and SUD is made even more difficult because there are probably different causal pathways into the development of compulsive drug use. Such diverse factors as abnormal stress reactions, a tendency for risk taking and sensation seeking, subtle differences in EEG activity, or a lower density of dopamine receptors may contribute to the vulnerability for developing an SUD. Although all of these predispositions might be related to a common set of genetic variations, it seems more likely that different combinations of alleles underlie these varied risk factors (Dick and Foroud 2003, Uhl et al. 2008).

Several genes can be involved in the production of even the individual components of neurological circuits. As an example, at least twelve genes, located on three different chromosomes, determine the production of GABA$_A$ receptors (Dick and Bierut 2006). Genes related to this receptor for an important inhibitory neurotransmitter are among those which can produce a detectable risk for alcohol dependence (Edenberg and Foroud 2006, Agrawal and Bierut 2012). For variations in these genes as well as in others related to SUD, the effect of a single allele is small (Hancock et al. 2019). The involvement of many genes in this very specific aspect of brain function (production of GABA receptors) further illustrates how the effects of combinations of genes underlie increased vulnerability to SUD.

Interaction with Environmental Influences

The second basic difficulty of identifying genes influencing the occurrence of SUD is that the effects of these genes interact with many environmental factors as they promote compulsive use of drugs. Most genetic effects on SUD are conditional in that they influence behavior only in the presence of certain situations or events, with access to the addictive drug being a prime example of such a condition. A huge amount of clinical and epidemiological research has addressed environmental influences on SUD, ranging from early-childhood experience to the broadest cultural factors. These risk factors can also cause some forms of SUD even in the absence of identifiable genetic predisposition (Hill 1998). Environmental-experiential influences are discussed in subsequent chapters, and brief consideration of genetic-environmental interaction is given later in this chapter.

The strong effects of nongenetic factors are the main reason why the genetic influence is probabilistic rather than a certain determinant of SUD. Life experiences can moderate or exacerbate the occurrence of other genetically influenced psychiatric disorders. Prolonged traumatic stress can trigger unipolar depression in some individuals, but not others. This difference is presumably an example of the interaction of life events and genetic predisposition.

Ball et al. (2007) suggest that a gene-environmental interaction often seen in the etiology of some types of cancer might also apply to SUD. In this interaction, a genetic predisposition is apparent only at intermediate levels of exposure to an environmental risk factor. For lung cancer, tobacco smoke is the risk factor. For SUD the risk would be drug usage. Minimal exposure would not result in dependence even in those with genetic vulnerability, and with heavy exposure (drug intake), dependence could occur even without the genetic influence. Moderate drug use would be likely to result in SUD only in those with the genetic predisposition.

Expression of Genes

All genes are not active at all times or in all parts of the body. The genotype is fixed at conception and ordinarily does not change throughout the life of an individual. Genes control the functions of the body by the production of RNA which in turn directs the synthesis of proteins. However, genes become active and initiate protein production only when **expressed**, or "turned on." Gene expression is controlled by a variety of factors, including the actions of DNA sequences located between or within genes. The noncoding areas (some are termed **introns**) govern the activation of the protein-encoding DNA areas (**exons**). Many environmental conditions or events activate gene-control mechanisms. Some examples of such conditions that influence gene expression include illumination changes (day-night cycles), stressful experiences, and the introduction of psychoactive drugs into the brain. Most behavior that results in ongoing changes in sensory input affects gene expression. Gene expression is then a special case of interaction between genes and the individual's environment, and is the mechanism for the reciprocal relationship between the genotype and behavior. While genes do influence behavior, the consequences of behavior – including consumption of alcohol or other drugs – often feed back to change the expression of genes (Hoffman et al. 2003, Ponomarev 2013). Such changes in gene activation may be brief, or of longer duration and result in altered brain activity.

The conditional expression of genes (meaning that some genes are active only at certain times or after certain events) underlies the complex and dynamic relationship between genes and behavior. When a gene is expressed, brain function is altered by means of the protein product of the RNA as encoded by that gene. Gene expression in the brain is detected by instruments and procedures that identify either the RNA or the protein produced by the activated gene. Information gained by these procedures is quite valuable in understanding behavioral genetics, but their use does require samples of brain tissue. Consequently they are used with animal subjects, or with human tissue obtained after death. Blood samples can indicate some gene expression that is not specific to the brain.

The term **epigenetics** designates the study of gene expression via function of noncoding areas of chromosomes (Cecil et al. 2016).

Albertson et al. (2006) studied gene expression in deceased heroin and cocaine addicts. These researchers found that the specific patterns of gene expression in the nucleus accumbens (a brain structure involved in drug-produced reward) varied with the type of drug used. Both drugs altered gene activation in this critical brain structure, but these effects were different between the two groups of drug users.

Endophenotypes

Diagnostic systems (e.g., the DSM-IV and DSM-5) were developed for clinical purposes, and often present difficulties when used to identify associations between genotype and psychiatric disorders. One difficulty occurs because of the rather wide range of behaviors that can contribute to an overall assessment of a substance use disorder (Chapter 2). For a DSM-5 diagnosis of a moderate cannabis use disorder, four (of a list of eleven possible) criteria are required, and for a mild disorder only two are required. Similar guidelines apply to other addictive substances in both DSM-IV, and the DSM-5 systems. Consequently, it is quite possible that two individuals with somewhat (or even completely) different symptoms could receive the same diagnosis of SUD. A second, equally important, problem is that some of these diagnostic indicators, especially those relating to negative consequences of using the drug, are only indirectly related to the drug's biological action. Since genes influence behavior by directing the synthesis of proteins, this basic genetic action may be rather far-removed (distal) from the behavioral consequence.

One important approach to dealing with the complications presented by the variability of behavior that characterizes SUD diagnosis involves the use of endophenotypes to investigate the genetic basis of these disorders. Endophenotypes are components of addictive behavior or biological characteristics associated with SUD (Hines et al. 2005). These biological, behavioral or cognitive characteristics by themselves would not result in a clinical diagnosis of the disorder. However, they are more proximal to (directly influenced by) genetic differences (and less affected by nongenetic factors) than are the more encompassing and clinically useful diagnostic clusters of signs and symptoms.

Endophenotypes have proven useful in identifying genetic risk for alcoholism (e.g., Dick et al. 2006a, Kapoor et al. 2013). They supplement, but have not completely replaced, investigations using clinical diagnostic systems for identification of SUD. Examples of these endophenotypes for alcohol use disorders are: EEG activity patterns (including differences in the P300 response), less intense subjective and behavioral responses to alcohol, a history of alcohol-produced amnesia ("blackouts"), age at first intoxication, and the maximum number of drinks ever consumed in a twenty-four-hour period. The first two of this list were discussed previously as heritable characteristics seen at higher incidence in offspring of alcoholic parents. Only endophenotypes proven heritable are used in genetic research. Another advantage of the use of endophenotypes is that most are quantitative in nature, in that they can be weak or strong as opposed to the "either–or" categories of some clinical diagnostic systems (including the DSM-IV and DSM-5).

The use of endophenotypes to investigate the genetics of addictive behavior is somewhat similar to behavioral studies of addictive drug effects in animal subjects. Human SUD cannot be completely modeled in experimental animals, but much has been learned by studying specific drug-related behaviors in animal subjects (Belin et al. 2016). Some examples of the behaviors studied in animals include sensitivity to aversive and rewarding drug effects, development of tolerance, and the occurrence of withdrawal-related seizures. These components of addictive behavior are quite similar to some endophenotypes used to investigate the behavioral genetics of addiction in humans. Since research with animal subjects permits such procedures as the production of specific genetic mutations (discussed below), the parallels between human and animal response to addictive drugs provide useful information about genetic influence on SUD.

Identification of Specific SUD-Related Genes

Several potential benefits might follow if specific genotypes associated with SUD can be identified. Genetic screening could inform an individual's choice regarding use of addictive drugs, in that such information could predict the development of addiction, or vulnerability to organ damage (e.g., cancer and cardiac disease related to tobacco usage). The effectiveness of medications or other clinical treatments for SUD may depend partially on genetic differences. Eventually, information about a dependent person's genotype could be useful in treatment planning (Nielsen et al. 2014). Finally, determining how variations in DNA structure promote SUD occurrence would greatly aid the basic understanding of the biological basis of addictive disorder, and in particular the differences in vulnerability seen among those who are exposed to these drugs.

All people, other than identical twins, have unique genotypes. Obviously, all genomic differences among individuals are not related to the occurrence of SUD. *Stratification* refers to the presence of the many addiction-irrelevant differences. Such differences are often considered as **noise** that obscures the detection of the **signal** of the differences among SUD-relevant alleles. Stratification is greatest for comparisons between members of different racial groups, and least problematic for within-family comparisons (Plomin et al. 2008). The confounding effects of stratification are thought to be responsible for many false-positive results, when initially promising findings of SUD-relevant alleles cannot be duplicated in subsequent studies. Consistent findings from several investigations based on different populations are usually required before researchers accept the validity of reported genetic effects (Merikangas and Risch 2003, Lachman 2006).

The availability of detailed information about the genome has enabled progress in identifying alleles that contribute to SUD vulnerability. Variations in individual base pairs of the DNA sequence – **single-nucleotide polymorphisms (SNPs)** – can be detected, permitting analysis of differences at the molecular level. In 1989 the

NIAAA initiated the **Collaborative Study of the Genetics of Alcoholism (COGA)**, a large-scale family study to investigate the genetics of alcohol dependence and related disorders (Begleiter et al. 1995). Groups of investigators at several different institutions collected information from more than 3,500 subjects. Extensive interviews, clinical diagnoses, blood samples (to obtain genotypes), and EEG recordings were taken from selected individuals. Patients in treatment programs for alcohol dependence were selected as subjects for the study if their families displayed a high density of alcohol use disorders. Additional subjects were selected from families without a high density of alcohol use disorders. In the "alcoholic families," at least three first-degree relatives suffered from an alcohol use disorder. An extensive pedigree (ancestry) was obtained for alcoholic subjects, as were the genotypes of both parents. The large number of subjects increased the sensitivity of the statistical tests, and the within-family comparisons reduced stratification.

A primary aim of the COGA project was identification of genotypes associated with relevant endophenotypes as well as those related to clinical diagnoses of SUD. The incidence of characteristic EEG patterns was given special attention, including the P300 response, and event-related oscillations (ERO). The results of several COGA investigations are included in the following discussion.

Candidate-Gene Association Studies

Association studies are intended to identify differences in individual genes (allelic variations) between behavioral phenotypes. The behavioral phenotypes are typically the presence (or absence) of overt SUD, or the incidence of a related endophenotype. These studies require the selection of a **candidate gene**, often based on information derived from nongenetic research, such as investigations of an addictive drug's mechanism of action. One problem of selecting a candidate gene for study is the polygenic regulation of even specific components of neurotransmitter systems. As mentioned above, several genes are involved in the production of any one subtype of neurotransmitter receptor. Given the correct selection of a candidate gene, this method can be very powerful for detecting effects of small genetic differences. Association studies are the oldest and most straightforward method of investigating gene-SUD relations.

The Dopamine System and the DRD2 Gene

Genes regulating three types of dopamine receptors, the reuptake transporter, and an enzyme for dopamine synthesis are implicated in SUD by some studies. Dopamine function is a critical part of current theories of reinforcement and addiction (Chapter 5), and much research evidence suggests that abnormalities of dopamine receptor density promote compulsive drug use. In 1990 Kenneth Blum and his colleagues reported a higher incidence of a dopamine-related allele (*DRD2 A1*) in deceased alcoholics (Blum et al. 1990). This allele is near the TAQI A location, associated with the DNA area regulating production of the dopamine D2 receptor subtype. The reward deficiency theory of SUD includes the premise that this allele promotes addiction and similar compulsive behavior disorders because it alters the sensitivity of the positive reinforcement function of the mesolimbic dopamine system (Blum et al. 2014, 2015, 2017).

Many investigators have determined the occurrence of the *DRD2 A1* allele in various populations of subjects with SUD for alcohol and other addictive drugs. The prevalence of this allele has also been examined in relation to the occurrence of obesity, gambling and other behavioral and psychiatric disorders. Inconsistent findings, due to failures of replication, are a common feature of association studies, and this problem definitely applies to *DRD2* research.

Some of the inconsistencies in the research findings may be due to inadequately screened control groups that sometimes included nicotine-dependent individuals (addictions to nicotine and alcohol may have some common genetic basis) (Noble 2003). Significant differences are reported more often in studies of severely addicted subjects, relative to those of individuals with less severe SUD. Young et al. (2004) conducted a meta-analysis of sixty-four of these studies and found an overall significant association between presence of the allele and severe SUD.

Lachman (2006) concluded that after fifteen years of intensive research, the role of this *DRD2* allele in SUD was still unclear. However, there is evidence of its involvement in several kinds of compulsive behavior (Blum et al. 2015). This variation in the *DRD2* gene is implicated in the occurrence of SUD for several drugs in addition to alcohol, with the evidence perhaps being strongest for nicotine dependence (Munafo et al. 2004).

Research has also been directed toward determining the involvement of other dopamine system genes in addition to the *DRD2* allele in SUD or related behaviors. A meta-analysis conducted by Li et al. (2006) indicated that alleles of genes regulating dopamine D4 receptors were associated with ADHD. Other investigations of D4 gene alleles found associations with a behavioral measure of impulsivity (Eisenberg et al. 2007), and with craving for alcohol (MacKillop et al. 2007). A more recent study, using whole-genome association testing (described below), also found correlations between variations in genes of the dopamine system and craving for alcohol in DSM-IV alcohol-dependent individuals (Agrawal et al. 2013).

GABA and Acetylcholine

Much evidence from research with both human as well as animal subjects indicates the importance of the major inhibitory neurotransmitter GABA, and in particular the GABA$_A$ subtype, in the response to alcohol (Dick and Foroud 2003). Genes responsible for production of GABA receptors are located in clusters on several chromosomes. COGA investigations have confirmed the connections between GABA genes on chromosomes 4 and 5, and alcohol dependence or related endophenotypes. The Gene *GABRA2* on chromosome 4p was found to contain thirty-one SNPs related to alcohol dependence (clinical diagnosis) and twenty-five SNPs associated with the characteristic ERO EEG endophenotype (Edenberg et al. 2004). Dick et al. (2006a) conducted further analysis on COGA families and found that the *GABRA2* allelic variations were also associated with childhood conduct disorder as well as with the type of alcohol dependence that develops during early adulthood (Chapter 10). They also found significant association of this genotype with SUD for illicit drugs.

The alleles in the GABA genes identified as related to SUD are introns that regulate the expression of the exons that produce messenger RNA, and eventually, GABA receptors. Fewer GABA receptors could result in decreased neural inhibition, causing the increased electrical excitability indicated by the EEG differences (Nurnberger and Bierut 2007). The hyperexcitable nervous system would then promote poor impulse control and increased likelihood of SUD.

There is a considerable amount of evidence that in addition to SNPs in or near the *GABRA2* gene, other GABA-controlling genes are associated with alcohol dependence (Dick and Bierut 2006). Dick et al. (2006b) investigated several SNPs located in the *GABRA1* gene located on chromosome 5q. They found associations with these alcohol-related endophenotypes: history of blackouts, age at first intoxication, and the level of response to alcohol.

The neurotransmitter acetylcholine is involved in a variety of critical brain functions, including movement, cognition, memory, the balance of excitation and inhibition, and control of mood. There is now good evidence of influence on SUD of variations in the gene *CHRM2*, located on chromosome 7q, which encodes the production of the muscarinic subtype of acetylcholine receptors. In a COGA study, Wang et al. (2004) found several SNPs in or near this gene which were associated with alcohol dependence, depression, and the characteristic ERO EEG endophenotype. Luo et al. (2005) independently confirmed these findings and also found SNPs in this gene associated with dependence on illicit drugs. The close association between alleles related to depression and to alcohol use disorders suggests that in some cases these two co-occurring disorders may have a common genetic basis. The twin studies, described in a previous section, also suggest an at least partially shared genetic vulnerability for the two types of disorders.

Approximately half of the alcohol-dependent subjects in the COGA investigations also had a use disorder of at least one additional drug. Approximately 72 percent were dependent on marijuana, 59 percent were dependent on cocaine, and smaller (but sizable) percentages were dependent on opiates or sedatives. Dick et al. (2007) conducted further analysis of the results of the Wang et al. (2004) study (*CHRM2* gene) to investigate how the subjects addicted to both alcohol and an illicit drug might differ from those addicted only to alcohol. Agrawal et al. (2006) conducted a similar reanalysis of the results of the Edenberg et al. (2004) *GABRA2* gene study. In both these investigations, the genome differences were much more apparent in the subjects with co-occurring SUD than in the alcohol-dependent-only subjects. The alcohol-plus-drug-dependent subjects also displayed more severe alcohol addiction, had a higher incidence of depression, and a fivefold increase in the occurrence of externalizing disorders (ASPD and conduct disorder). They were also significantly more likely to be habitual smokers and started regular drinking at a significantly younger age. These results indicate that alleles of GABA and acetylcholine genes are risk factors for an especially heritable vulnerability for extreme dependence on more than one type of drug, including alcohol.

Genes That Control Alcohol Metabolism

Alleles of genes regulating the activity of the dopamine, GABA, acetylcholine and other neurotransmitter systems probably influence SUD vulnerability by altering the brain's excitability or its response to addictive drugs. Another group of genes, whose effects on alcohol use disorders are relatively well understood, are those controlling the production of enzymes that metabolize alcohol. Alcohol is converted by a two-stage process into chemicals that are eventually excreted in urine. Two classes of enzymes produced by the liver enable this metabolic sequence. The first metabolic product, acetaldehyde is produced as the enzyme alcohol dehydrogenase (ADH) mediates the initial breakdown of alcohol. A second enzyme, aldehyde dehydrogenase (ALDH) then catalyzes the oxidation of the first metabolic product. High levels of acetaldehyde cause extremely aversive effects such as facial flushing, headache, nausea and tachycardia. The drug disulfram, sometimes used to discourage drinking in alcoholics, inhibits the action of ALDH and its use results in this toxic reaction when alcohol is consumed.

Protective effects for alcohol use disorders occur when drinking results in high levels of acetaldehyde, limiting the amount of alcohol that can be consumed without extreme discomfort. This protective effect can come either from an increased rate of ADH activity, which promotes the first stage of the metabolic process, or from decreased rates of ALDH activity which slow the elimination of acetaldehyde. Alleles of genes controlling both of these alcohol-metabolizing enzymes have been identified, and these gene variations influence vulnerability to SUD for alcohol. The incidence of these genetic variations varies markedly among racial groups, with the highest frequencies seen in East Asian populations.

Seven genes located on chromosome 4q regulate the production of ADH. Alleles of the *ADH1B* gene can cause an eightfold increase in the rate of conversion of alcohol to acetaldehyde. A rather high incidence of these alleles, or variations in other ADH genes occurs in East Asian populations, and they are associated with a definite protective effect (Edenberg 2007). Whitfield (2002) found that these alleles do occur, although at a much lower incidence, in populations of European-descent, and they have a protective effect against alcohol abuse in these individuals. This protective effect seems weaker in Caucasians that do carry the alleles, perhaps because of the greater acceptance of alcohol use in Western societies, a cultural factor that could interact with the genetic effect.

Two genes, located on chromosomes 9q and 12q, regulate the production of ALDH, and so control the rate of elimination of the toxic intermediate product of alcohol metabolism, acetaldehyde. An allele of the gene *ALDH2*, rather common in the East Asian population, results in the production of a form of ALDH which is very inefficient in the breakdown of acetaldehyde, and its presence is associated with a robust protective effect against alcohol use disorders (Crabb et al. 1989). This allele is quite rare in European-descent populations.

Nicotine Dependence

Nicotine influences brain function by means of its action on one type of acetyl-choline receptor site, and the subsequent activation of dopaminergic neurons. The indirect activation of dopamine circuits then mediates nicotine's positive reinforcement effect. Genes related to dopamine and acetylcholine function are implicated in nicotine addiction by several association studies (Li 2006, Munafo et al. 2004, Palmer et al. 2014).

Studies of nicotine dependence indicate an overall pattern of genetic involvement similar in complexity to that for alcohol dependence because areas on several chromosomes are implicated. The contribution toward nicotine dependence from individual SNPs in these genes is small. Some of these SNPs are also implicated in dependence on alcohol and in compulsive use of multiple drugs by individuals. Although genes related to acetylcholine are associated with polydrug abuse, some genes related to this neurotransmitter are specific to nicotine dependence (Kendler et al. 2012).

Use Disorders with Illicit Drugs

There is much co-occurrence of SUD for stimulants, cannabis or opioids as well as for alcohol and nicotine, with some degree of common genetic predisposition. In the case of opioids, a more specific genetic factor apparently also contributes to the liability for addiction (Dick et al. 2007, Mistry et al. 2014, Ozburn et al. 2015). The neurotransmitters by which the opioids and stimulants influence brain function are well known, and this knowledge suggests candidate genes whose variations might contribute to heritability for the relevant SUD. Many association studies have implicated various alleles of several genes in the SUD vulnerability (Kreek et al. 2005, Nielsen and Kreek 2012). However, as with candidate-gene association studies for other types of SUD, consistent replication of many of these initial positive results has proven to be difficult.

Some of these inconsistent results are probably due to stratification, which was minimized in the COGA studies by comparing allelic variations among several members of families with a high density of SUD. This tactic for reducing stratification is much more difficult to use in the investigation of SUD for illicit drugs. Identification and recruitment of "complete families" including both parents and two or more siblings, is rarely accomplished in studies of SUD with heroin or cocaine-type drugs. Some of this problem apparently results from the destructive effect of the use of these illicit drugs on intact family structure, as well as other cultural aspects of these SUD (Lachman 2006, Gelernter et al. 2007). The difficulty in using the powerful approach of association studies within families has slowed the progress of research on the genetics of SUD with these drugs.

Whole-Genome Association Tests

The requirement of a hypothesis about the specific genes that might be involved with an SUD is a limitation of candidate-gene association studies. Some genes with no known connection to drug effects, or DNA sequences interspersed between genes, might be important factors in SUD vulnerability.

Two major technological advances enabled the use of **whole-genome association tests** to detect alleles located throughout the genome that may be associated with diagnosed SUD or endophenotypes related to addiction. DNA markers are locations on the genome for which the sequence of base pairs in these areas is known, providing landmarks on the chromosome. Many thousands of DNA markers, most of which are single-nucleotide polymorphisms (SNPs), were identified by the International HapMap project (International HapMap Consortium 2005). Subsequently, microarrays have become commercially available that provide hundreds of thousands of DNA sequences (markers) mounted on a glass slide the size of a postage stamp, providing a standardized method for detection of a large number of SNPs (Plomin and Schalkwyk 2007). The effort and expense of comparing hundreds of points located across the genome was greatly reduced by these innovations. Because the presence of thousands of alleles can be detected, no starting hypothesis (candidate gene) is required to search for addiction-related differences. Many whole-genome association (WGA) tests have been conducted to determine the genetic basis of SUD, as well as for diseases including Parkinson's and Type II diabetes.

Whole-genome association studies of alcohol and nicotine dependence have confirmed the association of some, but not all of the alleles implicated in these disorders by earlier candidate-gene association tests (Agrawal and Bierut 2012, Olfson and Bierut 2012, Hancock et al. 2019). Five SNPs located in the *GABRA2* gene were shown to have a modest, but significant relationship with alcohol dependence, with odds ratios between 1.11 and 1.16 (Bierut et al. 2010). The protective effect against alcohol dependence associated with alleles of the alcohol-metabolizing genes is also confirmed by the newer studies of the entire genome. Additionally, WGA studies indicate that certain SNPs are correlated with endophenotypes related to alcohol dependence (maximum drinks per day, craving for alcohol) (Agrawal et al. 2013, Kapoor et al. 2013).

The results of tests for statistical significance of observed differences, which indicate whether a correlation or a difference is "real," or due to chance, depends on the size of the difference but also on the number of comparisons made during one investigation. In WGA studies many alleles may be detected and a great number of differences tested, requiring a smaller alpha level (a more stringent requirement) and a bigger difference for a correlation to be deemed as statistically significant (not due to chance). However, this correction procedure may decrease the detection of the small differences typical of polygenic effects. The sensitivity of statistical tests becomes greater with the use of larger numbers of subjects, but the problem of detection of small differences when many comparisons are made is a basic feature of WGA studies.

A WGA study of cannabis dependence illustrates the difficulty of establishing the reliability of many small observed differences (Agrawal et al. 2011). This study of 3,054 subjects taken from the SAGE (Study of Addiction: Genetics and Environment) data set involved comparison of many SNPs. Four SNPs in or near the gene *ANKFN1* were much more frequent in cannabis-dependent subjects than in nondependent controls, but due to the stringent requirements resulting from the many comparisons, none of these suspect SNPs reached genome-wide statistical significance. The *ANKFN1* gene mediates protein interaction and has been implicated in a general vulnerability to SUD, but its possible specific role in cannabis dependence is not known.

The "genetic architecture" of addiction vulnerability may eventually be revealed by the results of WGA studies, followed by additional candidate-gene studies. The more specific association tests of alleles implicated by the broader-scope studies are expected to detect the small effects contributed by many polymorphisms occurring throughout the genome.

The complex patterns resulting from various combinations of subtle effects are likely to differ among individuals who are vulnerable to SUD (Hancock et al. 2019, Levey et al. 2014). Some SUD vulnerability is associated with alleles in genes related to neurotransmitters and other obviously drug-relevant brain function. Other genes implicated have less immediately apparent involvement with drug effects, such as several that influence the formation of connections among neurons during brain development (Uhl et al. 2008).

Research with Nonhuman Animal Subjects

Compulsive drug use in humans consists of an array of behaviors that cannot be completely duplicated in animal subjects. However, experimental animals show differences in drug effects such as arousal level changes, tolerance, withdrawal syndromes, and preference for voluntary drug intake. These drug effects are components of addictive behavior, similar to some endophenotypes related to addiction in humans. Genetic differences in rodents in response to alcohol were first observed in the mid-twentieth century, and animal models have been a major influence on alcoholism research since that time (Crabbe et al. 2013).

Animal genotype is indirectly manipulated by use of the classical method of selective breeding, as well as directly changed by the much newer and specific techniques of induced mutations. The greater control available in research with animals should eventually facilitate a better understanding of genetic influence on SUD in humans (Barkley-Levenson and Crabbe 2012). Most SUD-relevant behavioral genetic research is conducted with rodent subjects, with alcohol the most studied drug. Estimates of similarity or identity between the mouse and human genome are 80–85 percent (Copeland et al. 1993, Plomin et al. 2008).

Selective Breeding of Experimental Animals

Selective breeding has long been used to shape and enhance physical and behavioral characteristics of domestic animals. The wide range of variations in size, body configuration, temperament and behavioral traits of dogs is but one example of how selective breeding can dramatically change animal appearance and behavior. Selective breeding of rats and mice, facilitated by the short gestation and maturation times of these rodents, has produced strains exhibiting marked differences in sensitivity to addictive drugs, and especially for responses to alcohol (Graham 2000).

Selective breeding of more than fifty generations of rats has produced two strains with distinctly different patterns of voluntary alcohol consumption. Alcohol-preferring (P) rats are also more anxiety-prone and have a greater attraction for novel places and stimuli than alcohol-nonpreferring (NP) rats. These characteristics are genetically transmitted to successive generations, and interbreeding rats with highest, and lowest, alcohol preference resulted in the development of these different strains (McBride and Li 1998). P rats quickly develop tolerance to the behaviorally impairing effects of high doses of alcohol, and this tolerance endures longer than in NP rats. This difference in response to alcohol suggests similarity to the low alcohol-response characteristic of sons and daughters of alcoholics as studied by Schuckit and colleagues.

Inbred Mice and Quantitative Trait Loci (QTL)

Inbreeding of mice (mating of siblings) has resulted in the development of mouse strains with exaggerated differences in responses to drugs, with most research again focused on sensitivity to rewarding or aversive effects of alcohol. This endeavor is similar to the selective breeding of rats, but the extensive inbreeding produces mice that within a specific strain are "near clones" in that there is almost no genetic variability among individuals. Crossbreeding of different strains of inbred mice then results in relatively limited genetic differences that can be correlated with behavioral and brain differences. Most of these behaviors, such as preference for voluntary alcohol drinking, vary in degree and so are not "either–or" responses. They are thus termed quantitative traits, and the locations on specific chromosomes of differences related to these behaviors are termed **quantitative trait loci (QTL)**.

The rapid development of DNA markers facilitated the study of the specialized genomes of inbred mice. More than thirty QTL for drug (mostly alcohol) effects have been identified in mice, including areas related to loss of righting reflex, extreme ataxia, hypothermia, and severity of withdrawal syndrome, as well as the rewarding and aversive effects (Crabbe 2002). In many respects, QTL-related behaviors resemble the previously described behavioral endophenotypes used in genetic investigations of human SUD.

QTL information was a major improvement in determining the specific areas of chromosomes related to various drug responses. Individual genes rarely have much influence on behavioral traits, so investigations are initially focused on identifying the locations of multiple genes, whose effects in combination may determine responses to addictive drugs. Some of these QTL are in areas that regulate the production of receptors mediating drug effects. For example, GABA-regulating genes are related to the severity of alcohol withdrawal. Areas near the *DRD2* gene are implicated in preference for alcohol, as are several areas on other chromosomes. This diversity of relevant chromosomal involvement is characteristic of drug-related genetic effects.

Mutant Mice: Specific Manipulation of the Genome

Further evidence of genetic involvement in drug effects comes from direct manipulation of the genome by inducing mutations of specific genes. Genes are altered in early-stage mouse embryos, resulting in the absence of, or a different form of specific genes. Deletion of a gene produces a mutated **knockout (KO)** mouse strain, and insertion of a foreign gene results in a **transgenic (TG)** strain (Barkley-Levenson and Crabbe 2012). Another form of mutation (the **knockdown**) results in minimizing the expression of a specific gene. The behavioral effect of removal of a specific gene (such as the *DRD2* gene) is often similar to that of a specific antagonist drug, and some genetic manipulation research confirms the results of earlier pharmacological studies. However, the advantages of studying KO mice include the complete and permanent absence of the activation of these receptors.

Nearly 100 genes have been studied for their role in alcohol effects, mainly those indicating reward or aversion, seen in KO and TG mice. In these investigations, a specific type of receptor for the relevant neurotransmitter is deleted or modified, and the resultant effect on voluntary ethanol drinking preference (relative to water) is measured. Conditioned place preference (CPP) is also often measured as another indicator of the rewarding or aversive effect of alcohol. About one-fourth of the genes manipulated cause modest increases, and about one-third result in decreases, in alcohol's reward value. Not suprisingly, the dopamine, opioid, serotonin, neuropeptide Y, cannabinoid, and CRF neurotransmitter systems are implicated by the results of these studies (Crabbe et al. 2006). None of these mutations result in either complete avoidance of alcohol, or in addiction-like drinking, but alcohol preference and intake is significantly changed, sometimes depending on other conditions as described below.

Deletion of the D2, as well as the D1 dopamine receptors, causes decreased alcohol drinking and diminution of conditioned reward as indicated by CPP. A similar decrease in alcohol-produced reward occurs in mu-opioid receptor KO mice. These effects on voluntary alcohol drinking and CPP demonstrate that specific dopamine and opioid receptors are involved in alcohol-produced positive reinforcement, but of course do not prove that abnormalities of these neurotransmitter systems are responsible for addiction. One difficulty for a clear interpretation of the result of deleting dopamine-related genes is that these mutations may also cause changes in overall motor activity, motivation and response tendencies (Crabbe et al. 2006). Researchers attempt to control for these less relevant behavioral differences.

The GABA system is of particular interest for the effects of alcohol, mainly related to its sedative and ataxic (impairment of locomotion) actions. Several lines of mutant mice are available with different types of GABA-gene manipulations. Most of these mutations are deletions of specific subunits of the $GABA_A$ receptor (Chapter 15). Some of these GABA receptor mutations decrease alcohol intake slightly, and decrease alcohol-produced ataxia and withdrawal-produced convulsions.

Manipulation of the mouse genome by targeted mutations has much potential for understanding genetic control of brain function, which in turn determines behavioral responses to addictive drugs. However, there are problems involved in conducting and interpreting the results of this type of research. The primary concern is that a KO or TG mouse develops from the early embryonic stage with a modified genotype, and genes are involved in the formation and maturation of the brain. Crabbe mentions the possibility of compensation during brain development in response to the altered genotype. Therefore, a KO mouse may have subtly altered brain structure or function in addition to the absence of the targeted gene. Differences in response to a drug might be due to these other, unknown abnormalities. Some of the effects described here depend on the behavior and drug responses of the inbred strain in the absence of the mutation, and among inbred mice these strain differences can be dramatic. Another consideration is that we assume that many interacting genes contribute to addiction vulnerability, so the knowledge gained by altering individual genes may be limited. Finally, genetic variations involved in addiction are probably more subtle than the partial or complete absence of a gene as in a KO strain, so more precise manipulation of genetic structure may be required to produce a convincing model of addiction in animals.

BOX 6.4 Genomic differences and SUD

- Most genomic differences among individuals are unrelated to SUD, presenting a challenge for the identification of SUD-relevant alleles.
- Endophenotypes are behavioral or physiological components of SUD, often more useful for genetic research than clinical diagnoses of the disorder.
- The influence of a single gene on the occurrence of SUD is very small.
- Genes act in combination with many other genes to influence behavioral effects, including SUD.
- Genetic effects occur after the gene is expressed, often by environmental conditions or events.
- Early investigations identified differences in genes (alleles) related to dopamine receptors in individuals addicted to alcohol or nicotine.
- The COGA studies identified alleles of genes controlling production of GABA and acetylcholine receptors in members of families with a high density of alcoholism.
- Genes have been identified that control alcohol metabolic processes, providing a protective effect against alcohol use disorders in individuals with certain genotypes.
- Whole-genome association studies enable the identification of SUD-related differences in specific SNPs in genes throughout the genome, with no requirement to select a candidate gene prior to the investigation.
- Studies of nonhuman animal subjects using selective breeding or induced mutations provide information about genetic influence on effects of addictive drugs.

Interaction of Genetic and Environmental Factors

As frequently mentioned in this chapter, environmental conditions and events very often interact with genetic influences on SUD. Such an interaction was seen in the marked decline of tobacco smoking (and nicotine dependence) during the late twentieth century in the United States. The decrease in tobacco use was primarily due to increased public awareness of the related health hazards – rather than a lessening of genetic predisposition for nicotine addiction. Another possible example is the lessened protective effect for alcohol dependence provided by alleles influencing alcohol metabolism in European, as compared to Asian populations. This difference may be due to the widespread consumption and cultural acceptance of alcoholic beverages in European countries. These examples demonstrate how cultural influence moderates genetic influences on drug use and SUD.

In some cases, socioeconomic disparities apparently interact with genetic risk factors, as in the much greater incidence of opioid addiction in geographical areas of the United States with high rates of poverty and unemployment (National Institute of Drug Abuse 2017).

Researchers have begun to investigate some of these gene-environment interactions in a more deliberate manner, which may clarify the role of genetic variation in compulsive use of addictive drugs (Dick and Kendler 2012). In a twin study of adolescent smoking behavior in Finland, Dick et al. (2007) found that at high levels of parental monitoring, genetic influences were less important than environmental factors on the initiation of smoking. These investigators found that with low levels of parental monitoring, genetic influences had a threefold greater effect on smoking, presumably due to creation of an environment that allowed greater opportunity for expression of genetic predisposition – by means of exposure to tobacco.

Similar studies conducted with female twins in Australia found moderating influences of religious upbringing on the genetic vulnerability for development of alcohol dependence (Koopmans et al. 1999). Women with the genetic risk, raised in a religious tradition, had no greater incidence of alcohol dependence than women with no genetic vulnerability. Another study of twin Australian women found a similar protective effect of marriage on incidence of alcohol dependence (Heath et al. 1998).

Several additional investigations present evidence of protective, or facilitating, environmental conditions for the occurrence of SUD. The amplifying effect of genetic influence on SUD caused by dysfunctional parenting is discussed in Chapter 8. Most nongenetic risk factors that increase SUD vulnerability can interact with the genetic risk, as discussed in subsequent chapters.

Chapter Summary

Adoption studies indicate that children of alcohol-addicted fathers are about four times more likely to suffer from the disorder than are children of healthy fathers, even when reared by nonalcoholic adoptive parents. However, many of these children did not become alcoholic, demonstrating that although it is a definite risk factor, biological heritage does not completely determine the occurrence of drug use disorders. The adoption studies also indicated that early-onset alcohol problems, typically accompanied by antisocial tendencies, are especially heritable.

Studies of twins indicate that heritability for SUD of alcohol, nicotine, and most addictive drugs accounts for at least 50 percent of variability in the disorder among individuals. Rather than being drug-specific, genetic predisposition increases vulnerability to SUD for all addictive drugs.

Some personality or behavioral characteristics (e.g., ASPD, behavioral undercontrol) and psychiatric disorders (e.g., depression) are much more prevalent in persons at risk for, and in those actually exhibiting, SUD. Some genetic factors apparently influence both SUD and the related personality and psychiatric differences. The causal relation between SUD and the psychiatric disorders/personality types is not clear and probably differs among individuals. In some cases, these conditions promote the development of SUD in that the drug use escalates in response to dysphoria or anxiety. In other cases, genetic factors more directly, but independently, cause both types of disorder. SUD can also occur in the absence of a psychiatric disorder or personality characteristics often related to addiction. ASPD is a definite risk factor for some types of SUD, but many persons with drug use disorders do not exhibit ASPD. The differences among individuals related to these co-occurring psychiatric conditions illustrate the heterogeneity of the causes for SUD.

Many individuals with SUD exhibit abnormal brain activity. To identify brain differences that might promote – rather than result from – addictive drug use, much research has involved young subjects with little or no previous drug use but with family histories of SUD. Many of these genetically predisposed individuals exhibit differences in brain electrical activity, lessened subjective and behavioral response to alcohol, and greater hormonal response to stressful situations. These heritable characteristics are thought to partially account for the vulnerability to compulsive drug use. The abnormal EEG responses indicate decreased inhibitory function and greater electrical excitability of the brain. Lower subjective and behavioral effects of a moderate dose of alcohol predict the eventual occurrence of alcohol use problems. Individuals with lesser effects from alcohol may drink larger amounts of alcoholic beverages and associate with heavier-drinking peers.

Some studies indicate that lower density of dopamine receptors in certain brain areas is associated with greater subjective (pleasurable) response to addictive drugs. Studies with animal subjects also implicate lower levels of dopamine receptor density in impulsive behavior and in readiness to self-administer cocaine. Dopamine receptor density is partially governed by genetics, and abnormal dopamine function is an integral part of the reward deficiency theory of compulsive behavior. The relation between dopamine function and addictive behavior is an ongoing area of investigation of the genetics of SUD.

Advances in molecular biology and techniques for DNA analysis have resulted in the gradual accumulation of knowledge regarding how specific variations in the genome are associated with the incidence of SUD. Several alleles (variations in one or a few DNA base pairs) located in genes governing the dopamine, GABA, and acetylcholine neurotransmitter systems are implicated in SUD for alcohol, tobacco, and simultaneous use disorders of multiple drugs. Areas associated with SUD for other drugs, including stimulants (e.g., cocaine) and opioids (e.g., heroin), have been identified on several chromosomes. Each of these areas can include many genes, and association studies have implicated many alleles related to several aspects of brain function.

It is clear that for all types of SUD, no single gene has more than a modest effect. Genetic influences on brain function and behavior apparently come from varying combinations of many allelic differences. Some of these combinations also influence the occurrence of the personality characteristics and psychiatric disorders that co-occur with SUD. Whole-genome association tests, providing a wider view of allelic differences, will eventually provide a more complete picture of the overall genetic architecture of addiction vulnerability.

Some DSM-IV and DSM-5 clinical diagnostic criteria are only indirectly related to biological causes of addictive disorders and so result in much genomic heterogeneity among individuals classified as drug dependent. Endophenotypes are specific behaviors or responses closely related to SUD that are more useful in establishing correlations between genotypes and behavioral or neurological phenotypes. The EEG abnormalities in particular represent an endophenotype closely correlated with specific alleles.

Selective breeding of experimental animals and the production of specifically targeted genomic alterations (mutations) in mice provide an alternate, well-controlled method of studying genetic influence on responses to addictive drugs. Investigation of gene expression in brain structures after drug administration is an important area of addiction research. Such studies are usually limited to experiments using animal subjects or postmortem studies of human brains.

Some environmental conditions can facilitate – or prevent – the effects of genetic predisposition on the occurrence of SUD. The influence of parental monitoring, religious involvement, and marital status can counteract a genetic predisposition and so decrease the incidence of some types of SUD.

Review Exercises

1. The role of genetics on SUD is probabilistic rather than deterministic. Explain what this means and why it is important for understanding the causes of addiction.
2. Explain the nature of the relationship between genetics and the environment (additive, interactive, or some other combination that increases the probability of SUD).

3. Describe the rationale of the epidemiological studies using adoptees and twins to determine the genetic influence on development of SUD.

4. Summarize what the epidemiological evidence on the heritability of SUD has revealed.

5. Define *gene*, *genotype*, and *phenotype*.

6. Describe the ways in which genetically based personality characteristics increase vulnerability to SUD.

7. There are several possible reasons why there is a correlation between psychological problems like anxiety and depression and SUD. Describe each reason and how genetics could be involved in each.

8. Describe the differences in brain function found in addicted adults relative to children with a positive family of history of drug abuse.

9. What is meant by *expression of genes* and how gene expression interacts with behavior (such as behaviors involved in the development of SUD).

10. Explain and give examples of genetic protective effects for alcohol use disorders.

11. Define endophenotypes, and state how they have been used to identify the genetic risk for alcoholism. Include a few examples of endophenotypes in your answer.

12. When an allele is determined to be associated with SUD, how large is the effect of that specific altered gene?

13. What is the advantage of whole-gene association analysis of genomic differences over candidate-gene analysis?

Key Terms

alleles (192)

amygdala (186)

association studies (198)

candidate gene (198)

Collaborative Study
    of the Genetics of
    Alcoholism (COGA)
    (198)

common genetic factor
    (175)

correlated liability (179)

deoxyribonucleic acid
    (DNA) (191)

dopamine D2 receptors
    (187)

endophenotypes (184)

epigenetics (195)

exons (195)

expressed (195)

genetically informative
    relationships (170)

genotype (192)

hypothalamic–
    pituitary–adrenal
    (HPA) axis (184)

introns (195)

knockdown (206)

knockout (KO) (206)

noise (197)

odds ratio (193)

P300 potential (182)

phenotype (192)

quantitative trait loci
    (QTL) (206)

reward deficiency
    syndrome (188)

signal (197)

single-nucleotide
    polymorphisms
    (SNPs) (197)

transgenic (TG) (206)

whole-genome
    association tests
    (203)

7 Behavioral, Cognitive, and Social Factors Promoting SUD

CHAPTER OUTLINE

LEARNING OBJECTIVES

1. Understand why there is more than one pathway into addiction.
2. Be able to identify the basic principles that are critical in behavioral explanations of both benign drug use and SUD.
3. Understand why it is important to recognize the nonbiological factors that influence addictive drug use.
4. Be able to identify conditions that decrease the behavioral control exerted by any one source of positive reinforcement.
5. Understand why harmful consequences of drug use often do not stop individuals from taking drugs.
6. Be able to explain how conditioned stimuli can maintain addictive drug use.
7. Understand how cognitive mediation can promote harmful and addictive drug use.
8. Be able to explain how expectations of a drug's effect can encourage drug use and influence the drug's subjective effect.
9. Be able to describe theoretical views of craving in addiction.
10. Understand the role of cultural factors in promoting drug use, including the heavy drug use that can lead to SUD.

Introductory Vignette: The Power of an Immediate Reward

Nick wanted a cigarette. It was early morning, no coffee or breakfast yet – he remembered how good the first smoke tasted when he was a heavy smoker. Catching up and having a few beers with an old friend last night was good. However, he did smoke several Marlboros, which was disappointing because he had been off cigarettes for almost three weeks! The urge to smoke wasn't too strong this morning. He wouldn't even call it "craving," like what he had felt when he first stopped his pack-a-day consumption. However, he did need to work on the presentation he was preparing, and the distraction of wanting a smoke made it harder to concentrate.

He thought about his involvement with tobacco over the years – at first it was mostly an attempt to be like his Uncle Charlie. A surfer, a biker, a great guy – and a heavy smoker. When Nick first started smoking, he liked the image of himself as a bit daring and edgy. Eventually he started savoring and enjoying the taste, smell, and feel of the smoke in his mouth and throat. He liked the small rituals of smoking too, and the whole process became so automatic and easy that he didn't think about it much. Nick took it hard when Uncle Charlie died of a heart attack at age forty-four. He knew that smoking was unhealthy, but hey – life has many dangers, some smokers live to be old men, and maybe Charlie had some other medical problem.

Nick was surprised how much he craved a cigarette when he ran out during that backpacking trip last year. The irritability, depression, and just plain wanting a smoke had been really intense. That was when he started thinking about quitting, and he made several attempts with limited success. He knew the triggers quite well – being in a bad mood, or anxious, angry, or just seeing a cigarette pack. A strong trigger was a situation that made it easy to smoke, like being in a bar with a friend who had cigarettes. The triggers were not so hard to resist when the withdrawal became less intense – but they could still get you, as happened last night!

Nick now had a new and better reason to stay off tobacco. On Instagram, Jennifer stated clearly that she would not date anyone who smoked. He was really attracted to her, and things went well both times they had gotten together. He had declared himself to be a former smoker, and (he thought) she was impressed that he had kicked the "disgusting habit." He was quite sure if he smelled like smoke, or she learned that he was back on cigarettes, he would not see her again. Losing out with an attractive girl wasn't as bad as cancer or a heart attack. However, it was sooner and a more certain consequence of smoking.

Introduction

In Chapters 5 and 6 we saw that neurological abnormalities and genetic factors are often associated with use of addictive drugs. However, disorders of substance use are heterogeneous, and some types of SUD have no detectable underlying genetic or preexisting neurological basis. Even when these biological causes can be identified, additional factors are also critical in all forms of SUD.

Genetic factors influence the occurrence of SUD, accounting for at most about 60 percent of the factors influencing addiction (and even less for milder forms of SUD). Biological inheritance of certain differences in brain or hormonal function increases the probability of SUD but does not completely determine its occurrence. Obviously, there remains a sizable effect from nongenetic influences. The genetic effects interact with a broad range of environmental conditions ranging from prenatal to cultural. Currently no genetic screening test reliably predicts the occurrence of SUD.

Neurological abnormalities, such as diminished P300 EEG response, often precede addiction. Other differences in brain function, such as amygdala activation by drug-related stimuli, also often occur in addicted persons. These neurological markers, however, do not identify or define the behavioral disorder of SUD, which is diagnosed by patterns of drug *use*. Behavior, emotions, and cognitive processes (perception, memory, etc.) that influence behavior originate from brain activity. However, events and conditions in the environment are also important determinants of behavior.

Some neurological disorders, such as Tourette's syndrome, Parkinson's disease, multiple sclerosis, Alzheimer's disease, Huntington's disease, epilepsy, and schizophrenia, produce disorders of movement, memory, or cognition and emotion. However, a different type of altered brain function influences addiction. When addictive behavior arises from an underlying neurological abnormality, the behavioral effect is expressed via problems with motivation and inhibition, resulting in compulsive drug-seeking. Unlike movement disorders or some other neurological impairment, the altered motivation and inhibition of addictive behavior are likely to be affected by developmental, cognitive, and other less overtly "biological" influences. In short, when addictive behavior results from drug-produced brain dysfunction, environmental conditions and cognitive processes, including learning, can also influence the altered behavior.

The Biopsychosocial Explanation of SUD

Recognizing the role of the many determinants of human behavior, including biological, environmental, and developmental factors, is the underlying principle of the **biopsychosocial** (BPS) approach to understanding SUD, as introduced in Chapter 1.

Cultural and other social and environmental factors are important determinants of the socially acceptable use of alcohol and other drugs. Deviant and harmful use of drugs – including SUD – is also influenced by multiple causes including those not directly linked to abnormal brain function.

Robert West maintains that there are three basic types of causes that underlie addiction: those related to such states as anxiety and depression, those related to rewarding drug effects such as incentive sensitization, and those resulting from environmental causes such as social relations or other distressing circumstances (West 2006). Many other scientists and scholars who investigate SUD also present evidence that nonbiological factors influence addictive behavior (e.g., Donovan 2005, Heilig et al. 2016, Shurtleff et al. 2009, Vaillant 2003, Washton and Zweben 2006).

For many years, there was animosity between disease theory and cognitive behavioral explanations of addiction. To advocates of disease theory, the assertion of behavioral theorists that general principles of behavioral control and learning produce the destructive behavior seemed uncomfortably close to earlier explanations that SUD was essentially immoral and willful misbehavior. A wider acceptance of a biopsychosocial explanation of SUD has removed much of the theoretical disagreement between older versions of disease and behavioral theories. The newer BPS approach gives importance to altered neurological function in conjunction with the role of learning and developmental and environmental factors.

Owing to the many interacting causes, there are **numerous pathways** into the dangerous use of psychoactive drugs. Some pathways might be relatively direct, such as a genetic predisposition for risk acceptance and sensation seeking. Other routes involve several factors, such as a genetically determined deficit in dopamine receptors in conjunction with childhood sexual abuse and, eventually, extensive opportunities for cocaine use. Some of these pathways – especially for less severe cases of SUD – do not include detectable genetic predisposition or neurological abnormalities.

Most of the varied pathways into addiction eventually converge into a common final link of altered brain function. However, the characteristic neurological changes often become a critical feature of the developing addiction only after extensive drug use, late in the progression of the disorder. This "late appearance" of persistent brain changes is more characteristic of the mid-life occurring type of alcohol use disorder, and less descriptive of addiction to crack cocaine. In the first disorder, years of nonpathological alcohol use can precede the eventually compulsive use pattern. In the second case, compulsive cocaine use often emerges within days or weeks of the initial drug experience – due in part to the intensely rewarding action of inhaled cocaine vapor.

The biological components are impressive and intriguing in part because they are not obvious or easily seen, detectable only by high-tech research methods like brain imaging and genomic mapping. The altered brain function directly controls behavior and is often a final common pathway for compulsive addiction. However, the components or factors that are less overtly biological often promote initial heavy drug use, which is also a critical link in the chain of events that eventually result in SUD.

In this chapter, we will discuss the contributions of two important and related areas of psychology that are essential to the biopsychosocial concept of SUD. These areas are classical **behavioral theory**, and cognitive-social learning theory. Cultural factors, as related to the social influences on drug use, are also briefly considered.

Behavioral Theory of SUD

Behavioral approaches to understanding SUD, as well as cognitive and social learning theories, view drug use as behavior governed by the same principles that determine behavior in general. A basic premise of these theories is that most human behavior is learned as a result of experience. Becoming proficient at skiing, memorizing a computer password, acquiring acceptable table manners, and starting a pattern of repetitive cocaine use are all examples of how learning can bring about a change in behavior. Human behavior is quite flexible and adaptable, mainly because so much of it is learned. This adaptability, which usually promotes survival in changing environments, also gives rise to behavioral instability and the potential for development of maladaptive behavioral patterns (West 2006). Disordered use of drugs results from this behavioral flexibility.

Two types of associative learning relate to the voluntary use of psychoactive drugs. In **instrumental conditioning** specific behavior is associated with a drug effect, and with **respondent (classical) conditioning** the action of a drug becomes associated with a specific stimulus. Both forms of learning involve connecting survival-promoting events with relevant stimuli or behavior. These two types of learning underlie behavioral change in many situations, including harmful, as well as benign, use of psychoactive drugs.

Early twentieth-century versions of classical learning theories, such as those developed by Pavlov, Thorndike, and Skinner, did not include much consideration of the biological processes underlying behavior. This lack of interest in brain function was in large part due to ignorance of how neural activity might underlie behavior change resulting from experience (learning). In recent decades, neuroscience research has revealed much about the brain structures and neurotransmitters that are involved in learning and memory.

Behavioral principles, such as motivation, reinforcement, and stimulus control of behavior, are of critical importance in current bio-behavioral explanations of drug addiction as described in Chapter 5. Additionally, experimental procedures and instruments, such as the Skinner box, developed to investigate operant (a type of instrumental) conditioning, are used extensively in behavioral neuroscience research. An example of an operant procedure that is quite useful for studying the biological basis of SUD is the use of **drug self-administration** to investigate relapse-like behavior in rodents and primates.

Genetic predisposition and neurological abnormalities are involved in many cases of SUD. In addiction, brain function is markedly altered, resulting in compulsive drug use. However, preexisting biological influences are rarely amenable to change and in many cases, medications are not very effective in interrupting addictive behavior. Recovery from SUD relies heavily on changing the thought processes (cognitions) and environmental situations that, in addition to the biological factors, promote destructive drug use. Application of learning and behavioral principles is critical to the success of most therapeutic interventions (including twelve-step and other mutual-assistance programs) in attaining and maintaining a drug-free life.

A basic principle of behavioral theory is that the **consequences of behavior** are very important in influencing subsequent behavior. Behavior can be strengthened by positive or negative reinforcement. The basic principles of reinforcement are simple but critical concepts for explaining the maladaptive behavior of SUD as well as drug use in general. Behavioral research, in which environmental conditions and behavioral contingencies are carefully controlled, reveals the basic features of reinforced behavior. These principles are also valid in the more complicated world outside the behavioral laboratory, but this complexity results in less certain prediction and control of behavior. Behavioral pharmacology research investigates how drug effects interact with the behavior of animal and human subjects. The nature and consequences of drug-produced reinforcement is a major research area of behavioral pharmacology.

Positive Reinforcement

Subjective feelings of pleasure often accompany positive reinforcement. However, the defining feature of reinforcement is not the feeling of pleasure, but the strengthening of the behavior that produces the reinforcing event (Figure 7.1). Nicotine is an example of a drug with potent reinforcing properties that usually provides relatively little pleasure during the early stages of use. Eventually tobacco use in addicted individuals is maintained by relief from aversive withdrawal syndrome, an example of negative reinforcement (discussed subsequently). However, for most addictive drugs the positive reinforcing actions initially include either subjective pleasure, or other effects perceived as beneficial – such as peer-approval.

Figure 7.1 These young people's athletic performance is positively reinforced by verbal praise and medals. The rewards of winning will strengthen their performance in future competitions. Photo: Alistair Berg / DigitalVision / Getty Images.

The basic principles of positive reinforcement were identified before much was known about the function of the mesolimbic dopaminergic system. The biological basis of this effect, which energizes, directs, and generally strengthens behavior was discussed at some length in Chapter 5, as was its overall importance in current theories of addiction. The theories of Volkow, Kalivas, Koob, Robinson and Berridge attribute alterations in positive reinforcement processes as a basic change in brain function that contributes to development of the compulsive behavior of addiction.

Detecting and Measuring Positive Reinforcement

Most drugs that are addictive for humans are also positively reinforcing to animal subjects, as demonstrated by their avid self-administration of stimulants, opioids, and other drugs. Operant reinforcement procedures are used in most self-administration studies with animal subjects. In operant paradigms, drugs are administered, most often via intravenous catheters, when the subject presses a lever or performs some other behavioral response. Less often, the reinforcing drug is delivered for oral consumption, as in some research with alcohol. Increased rates of responding indicate the occurrence of positive reinforcement. Human subjects in behavioral pharmacology research may receive drugs (typically via the oral route of administration) contingent upon performing some task, such as pedaling a stationary exercise bicycle.

There are differences among individuals in the strength of drug-produced reinforcement. Self-reports of pleasure and other subjective effects produced by reinforcing drugs in humans can be obtained with rating scales, such as the **Profile of Mood States** (McNair et al. 1971) or the Drug Effects Questionnaire (Evans et al. 1996). Differences in reinforcement are more objectively measured by operant conditioning procedures with animal or human subjects. One such method is to establish the number of operant responses the subject will make in order to receive the drug. If a rat presses a lever 100 times to receive one morphine injection, the drug has greater reinforcement value than for a rat who will press the operant lever only forty times for the same injection. Similar tests of effort expended for drug delivery can measure reinforcement value of drugs in human subjects.

Genetically determined sensitivity to the reinforcing effect of drugs can influence addictive use, especially for drugs that have limited addictive liability for the general population. Most individuals who consume alcoholic beverages do so responsibly (much of the time), and although many adolescents experiment with smoking cigarettes, most of these tentative users do not become regular smokers. The reward deficiency theory – with intuitive appeal and some scientific support – maintains that those most vulnerable to addiction are more strongly rewarded (their behavior is more strongly reinforced) by their initial use of the drug than are less vulnerable individuals. Due to ethical and other limitations, the basic proposition of the theory is difficult to test empirically in humans. There is, however, evidence of different reward-sensitivity for some drugs in selectively bred animals. Differences in the reinforcement value of alcohol and other addictive drugs are genetically transmitted in strains of alcohol-preferring rats and in inbred mice (Chapter 6).

Delay Time and Reinforcement Strength

The effect of positive reinforcement is much stronger if the reward comes very soon after the preceding behavior. The importance of time delay between the behavior and the reinforcement is obvious in the training of animals and young children. A reward of food or verbal praise given immediately strengthens the behavior much more than if the reward is delayed for a even a few minutes. Time delay may be somewhat less critical for older children and adults, in that reinforcements such as allowances and paychecks are not delivered immediately and constantly, but at intervals of weeks. However, the investigation of delay discounting (Box 7.1) demonstrates that even in adult humans, a reward delayed is often a reward whose value is weakened. Delay discounting can be demonstrated in controlled studies for various incentives including drugs as well as money, both real and hypothetical (de Wit and Richards 2004).

Elevated rates of delay discounting are indicative of a type of impulsivity (Winstanley et al. 2004). Several investigators have reported high rates of delay discounting in heavy users of cocaine, alcohol, and nicotine (e.g., Towe et al. 2015, Moallem and Ray 2012). Some evidence suggests that both a genetic predisposition, as well as current use of addictive drugs, is associated with greater levels of delay discounting (Hamilton et al. 2012).

The strong behavior-controlling effect of immediate reinforcement is clearly seen in addictive use of drugs. Intravenous and inhalation routes of administration provide the most rapid entry of the drug into the brain. The short time lag between drug administration and the subjective feeling of pleasure contributes to the powerful control over behavior that often comes with smoking of tobacco, inhalation of cocaine or methamphetamine, and intravenous injection of opiate or stimulant drugs. Beneficial results of not using the drug – better health, good family relations, financial security – typically occur much later, and so often exert less influence over behavior.

BOX 7.1 Delay discounting

Delay discounting (DD) refers to the decreased incentive value of a reward when not presented immediately. In a behavioral test of delay discounting, subjects are given a choice between a fixed cash reward, such as $10, that would be given immediately and a greater amount of money to be given after a certain time period, such as 30 or 180 days.

	Amount of immediate reward	Perceived equivalent delayed reward	
		30 days	180 days
Lower degree of DD	$10	$12	$15
Higher degree of DD	$10	$16	$23

Note. Varied delay intervals and amounts offered are presented to determine how the increasing delay period results in greater devaluation of the incentive. In this hypothetical example (similar to many actual studies), an individual with less DD would choose a 30-day reward only if greater than $12 and a 180-day reward greater than $15. For smaller delayed amounts, the immediate $10 is preferred. The individual with a higher level of DD would require greater amounts to choose the delayed reward.

Subjective Pleasure and Positive Reinforcement

Subjective experience, including that produced by addictive drugs, cannot be directly observed, but verbal reports of humans indirectly provide some insight into neurological processes underlying drug-produced pleasurable feeling and positive reinforcement. The routes of administration just mentioned produce a very rapid rise of drug concentration in the brain, which correlates with reports of pleasure in some subjects (Volkow et al. 2003, Volkow and Swanson 2003). The rapid change in affective state is sometimes described as a "rush." One effect of this quick onset of a euphoric state is extreme reinforcement due to the sense of power that comes from the immediate (if temporary) control of one's own feeling state (Metzner 2005).

Although the experience of subjective pleasure does not define, or even reliably accompany positive reinforcement, an increase in positive affect is quite often characteristic of reinforcing events. Intense euphoric states (a nondrug example is sexual orgasm) are of brief duration, possibly due to inherent compensatory properties of the reward-reinforcement circuitry of the brain (Koob 2006). The rapid onset and brief duration of an intense pleasurable effect (as from inhaled cocaine vapor) or even a much weaker effect (as from inhaled nicotine) are very effective in promoting repetitive, compulsive drug use.

Direct and Indirect Sources of Positive Reinforcement

Some drug-produced reinforcement effects come directly from the drug's action on neurotransmitter function in the brain. Most addictive drugs are agonists for dopamine, or they increase dopamine function by means of acting on another neurotransmitter. These reinforcing effects are designated here as "direct" because they do not depend on environmental conditions for their behavior-strengthening action. The euphoric rush from injection or inhalation of opiates, cocaine or amphetamine are examples of such direct reinforcement effects. Positive reinforcement from self-administered drugs in animal subjects is often relatively independent of environmental conditions. If the drug administration causes increased dopamine levels in the nucleus accumbens, the behavior that preceded the effect on dopamine is strengthened. Metzner (2005) suggests that in the case of humans, such direct, context-independent reinforcing drug actions narrow the focus and restrict the attention of the drug user to the drug experience. This narrowed focus on the drug effect is often characteristic of advanced stages of addiction. The restricted attention and behavioral direction occurs most readily with intravenous and inhalation routes of administration, but can also emerge with oral intake of alcohol and other addictive drugs.

Some positive reinforcement effects of drugs can depend on the environmental context of the drug user. These indirectly reinforcing effects are often seen in human drug use. For many who drink alcoholic beverages, positive reinforcement occurs primarily in certain social situations, such as when drinking in the company of friends. The reinforcement is then a product of a drug's facilitation of social interactions, which provides much of the pleasurable result. Other examples include performance demands, such as vigilance and concentration that can be improved by caffeine intake and steroid and stimulant use to enhance athletic performance. In these cases, the drug's effect on biological function is important, but the positive reinforcement effect does not come solely from that neurotransmitter or hormonal action. Further examples of situation-dependent drug reinforcement are given in the drug-specific chapters.

In yet a third type of positive reinforcement associated with drug use, the biological effect on neurotransmitter function is not even required for the behavior-strengthening action. Perhaps the best example is peer pressure, in which the act of participating in drug use gives social acceptance or a feeling of courageous risk taking. Although effects on brain function need not be present for reinforcement resulting from social or self-image considerations, taking an addictive drug for such reasons could eventually bring about the brain alterations that result in compulsive drug use.

In the complex world outside of the behavioral laboratory, direct and indirect drug effects typically occur in the context of other reinforcement sources not associated with drug use. These multiple sources of reinforcement often influence the behavior-controlling effect of any one type of reinforcement, including drug-produced reward. An individual with several opportunities for interesting and pleasurable activities is less likely to be greatly attracted to use and abuse of a recreational drug than is one for whom the drug effects are a sole or major source of reward. Alterations of drug reinforcement by the availability of other activities or incentives have been demonstrated in controlled behavioral research with human (Higgins et al. 2004, Correia 2005, Sigmon 2007) and animal subjects (Alexander et al. 1981).

The interaction among reinforcement sources means that drug use can be markedly increased *or* decreased by the availability of nondrug reinforcements. Perhaps use of tobacco as well as contraband drugs by prisoners illustrates this principle. Most traditional sources of comfort or pleasure (family, entertainment, work) are scarce during incarceration in a jail or penitentiary. Consequently, there is great temptation to use any available psychoactive substance for pleasure or to reduce boredom, even in those not previously dependent on nicotine or other drugs. This principle of the power of alternative reinforcements is important in a behavioral explanation of the progression of addiction (in a subsequent section of the current chapter) and in treatment of addiction and prevention of relapse (Chapter 16).

Intermittent Reinforcement

Reinforcement drives behavior in many situations, but often a rewarding event does not follow every time such behavior occurs. The benefits of intermittent reinforcement's effectiveness in maintaining behavior seem obvious. Foraging for food or attempts at mating are necessary for survival and, even though not consistently reinforced, need only to produce rewarding consequences occasionally.

Evolutionary pressure (adaptive significance) would hardly favor an organism that "gave up" too quickly if reinforcement were not forthcoming after each behavioral response.

Of course, if a response is not reinforced for an extended period of time, or after many responses, that behavior eventually stops under these conditions of extinction. However, if a behavior has been reinforced intermittently, the behavior will persist much longer during an extinction period than will a behavior that was rewarded upon each occurrence. The results of intermittent reinforcement can be seen in many cases of SUD, and especially in addiction. As drug dose and frequency of use increase, direct positive reinforcement effects may diminish due to tolerance. As drug dose increases, aversive effects often emerge. Even more important, some indirect reinforcement effects may become inconsistent and occur only on rare occasions. For example, as a person more often becomes extremely intoxicated when drinking, pleasurable social interactions become less reliable – perhaps she is often seen as an "offensive, argumentative drunk." Unfortunately, even rarely occurring pleasant drinking experiences may continue to motivate drug use long after such rewards have become unreliable – for example, "*sometimes* getting drunk is still fun."

Negative Reinforcement: Relief from Discomfort or Pain

Reinforcement also occurs when a specific behavior relieves an unpleasant, aversive condition – in which case it is referred to as negative reinforcement. Initial drug use is often promoted mainly by positive reinforcement, but both positive and negative reinforcement are featured in the biological theories of addiction described in Chapter 5.

Negative reinforcement is most evident in SUD when continued drug use is motivated by relief from aversive withdrawal syndromes, ranging from the harrowing anxiety occurring after heavy use of alcohol through the irritability of nicotine withdrawal. The prompt negative reinforcement from resumption of drug intake is powerful in maintaining compulsive drug use. Dysphoric states resulting from extensive drug use can persist much longer than the more severe (and overtly physical) symptoms of acute withdrawal. Owing to the slow recovery of the mesolimbic dopamine system and the hedonic set-point, negative reinforcement can promote resumption of drug use even after a long period of abstinence (Koob and Le Moal 2006).

Humans are subject to many adverse conditions and emotional states that can be temporarily relieved by alcohol or other addictive drugs and so produce negative reinforcement. Several risk factors for SUD enable such negative reinforcement. These risk factors include boredom, depression and anxiety, extreme poverty, and other undesirable conditions, such as difficult work situations (Boardman et al. 2001, Sutin et al. 2013).

The incidence of several types of psychiatric disorders is relatively high in individuals who are heavy users of alcohol, nicotine, or illicit drugs. Some cases of SUD originate with self-medication of the pain and distress of psychiatric disorders. However, heavy use of addictive drugs can exacerbate anxiety, depression, and thought disorder and generally increase the difficulty of many life problems. The high co-occurrence rate of psychiatric disorders and SUD is an important feature of addictive disorders (Chapter 8).

Aversive Consequences: Drug-Produced Punishment

Aversive consequences (e.g., embarrassment, pain, various types of loss) can be very effective in preventing repetition of the behavior that produced them, especially if their occurrence is swift and certain and their connection to that behavior is unmistakable. In behavior theory terminology, response-suppressing events are designated as punishing consequences.

For many types of behavior that include an element of risk, the inherent possibility of a dangerous outcome can be attractive and so provide powerful positive reinforcement – so long as the harmful outcome is not certain. In addition to use of addictive drugs, other examples include gambling, contact athletic sports, and some occupations, such as the military and law enforcement. There is much variability among individuals regarding their attraction to hazardous activity and acceptance of the risks involved. Personality researchers have developed concepts of *harm avoidance* and *sensation seeking* as they study these characteristics. The relationship of personality variables to SUD is discussed in Chapter 8.

The use of psychoactive drugs, especially those with addictive potential, obviously involves some risk of harmful outcomes. Behavioral toxicity (accidents, arguments) often occurs during states of intoxication. Biological toxicity (liver damage, cancer) is a probable result of heavy alcohol or other drug use. Aversive consequences can result from drug use by any individual, not just by those with an SUD. However, addicted individuals typically suffer multiple types of damaging consequences, but their relationship (emotional connection) with the drug makes harm prevention very difficult.

The threat or the actual occurrence of punishing effects of drugs, taken in large doses or at inopportune times, prevents or at least discourages repetition of such risky behavior in many individuals. Behavioral theory and biopsychosocial explanations of SUD emphasize that compulsive, dangerous use of drugs is governed primarily by principles that determine behavior in general. An important question, then, for behavioral theory is, **why do many individuals persist in heavy drug use despite the frequent adverse outcomes?** In other words, **why do addicts bring so much pain and trouble onto themselves?**

The first answer to this question is that for many who use drugs compulsively or in an abusive manner, harmful results actually can inhibit further use, at least temporarily, when the consequences become severe. Epidemiological and clinical studies show that patterns of SUD are often erratic and episodic, with periods of abstinence or reduced usage that often follow a particularly damaging or threatening drug-related event (Hanninen and Koski-Jannes 1999, Dawson et al. 2006). Addicts sometimes seek treatment or attend self-help groups when their overall life situation becomes intolerable. This "bottoming out" state is a result of the direct and indirect damaging effects of heavy drug use. One of the unfortunate aspects of addiction is that by the time these adverse effects force an attempt to escape the addictive lifestyle, some of the losses may not be recoverable.

Behavioral principles can explain why the harmful outcomes are often ineffective, at least until much damage is done. The punishing consequences of drug use are typically **delayed aftereffects**, occurring only much later than the more immediate reinforcing consequences. For example, the "hangover" of excessive alcohol intake does not occur until the alcohol is metabolized, typically a few hours after drinking stops. One might imagine the effect on the high-dose consumption of alcoholic beverages if the sequence of consequences was reversed. This reversal would result in the lethargy, headache, nausea, and general dysphoria appearing very soon after drinking, with the pleasant feelings and enhanced social interactions emerging only hours later, possibly on the following morning! Because they are delayed, usually much longer than the reinforcing effects, punishing consequences of drug use often have less control over the preceding behavior.

Another reason that aversive consequences often fail to suppress drug-taking is that their actual occurrence is not certain. Hangovers are not inevitable – in most instances, occurring only after heavy drinking. Social drinkers who sometimes drive in a state of moderate intoxication may never be arrested or cause an accident. Most biologically toxic effects (e.g., lung cancer) are of uncertain probability, as well as being far from an immediate concern. The threat of various bad outcomes does prevent excessive and hazardous drug use in many who occasionally indulge. However, as is evident with most cases of SUD, the possibility of a delayed, dangerous result – that may not even actually happen – frequently has less control of behavior than does anticipation of an imminent, highly probable, pleasurable event.

Not only are aversive outcomes of drug use typically delayed and their occurrence uncertain but some individuals experience almost none of these punishing effects until their addiction reaches an advanced stage. Marc Schuckit's extensive research (Chapter 6) shows that relative insensitivity to the immediate and short-term effects (pleasurable as well as aversive) of alcohol is a significant predictor of future alcohol use disorder. Schuckit's findings may underlie the well-known risk factor for alcohol use problems presented by immunity to hangovers. Some protection from adverse effects may come from genetically determined biological factors. Environmental conditions, such as a social context permissive of heavy drug use and intoxication, may decrease the chance of social disapproval. Although abuse and addiction usually produce eventual harmful results, their absence during initial and intermediate stages of increasing drug use are definite risk factors for the development of SUD.

Most addicted individuals eventually suffer much damage from their heavy drug use and an addictive lifestyle. These losses and bad outcomes are difficult to ignore, although they may not be recognized or acknowledged as consequences of drug use. The ability to arrive at alternative (and more acceptable) interpretations of harmful results of drug use is discussed later in this chapter in the section on cognitive theory.

BOX 7.2 Consequences of drug use – reward, relief, and punishment

- Positive reinforcement – often experienced as a pleasurable drug effect – increases drug-using behavior most effectively when it closely follows drug intake.
- Previously reinforced behavior persists longer when reinforcement stops (extinction conditions) if the behavior was reinforced intermittently.
- Negative reinforcement – relief from a distressing state – often becomes a greater incentive for drug use as SUD develops.
- The behavioral control of drug-produced positive and negative reinforcement depends on the availability of other (nondrug) sources of reward or relief.
- Adverse effects of drug use – punishment – can reduce or stop drug use, but the behavioral control is weakened by delay or uncertainty of the harmful consequence.

Stimulus Control of SUD

In addition to learned connections between drug-taking and its consequences, associations are also formed between the drug stimulus and other stimuli related to the drug. These associations between stimuli, a result of classical conditioning, are a critical part of a drug's behavioral control, which becomes quite powerful in addiction. In the natural world the associations between behavioral actions and drug effects, and the associations between drug-related stimuli often develop simultaneously and influence each other. In other words, instrumental (operant) and classical conditioning usually develop simultaneously (Bolles 1972, Rescorla 1987). However, these two types of conditioning can be separated conceptually, and they are also studied separately in the laboratory.

Stimuli gain control of behavior by signaling the availability or predicting the occurrence of pleasurable or punishing events. These stimuli energize and direct behavior as they become associated with survival-related benefits or threats. In SUD, the environmental context (conditioned stimuli) preceding the drug's positive reinforcement effect activates dopamine and glutamate circuitry and so engages the brain's "go-system." Drug-associated stimuli are necessary for incentive sensitization, implicated in the development of compulsive drug use (Chapter 5). Stimulus control of behavior also often triggers relapse to addictive behavior after a period of abstinence.

In classical conditioning of drug effects, a previously neutral stimulus, such as a distinctive location, sound, odor or object, reliably precedes drug administration. Much of the early classical conditioning research emphasized passive, reflexive responses such as salivation elicited by food in dog subjects, or eye-blink responses elicited by an air-puff in humans. Reflexive responses to drug-related stimuli are also studied in current investigations, which may utilize either human or animal subjects. These conditioned responses, typically not under direct voluntary control, include autonomic activity (e.g., cardiac responses), hormonal responses, and brain metabolic activity as indicated by fMRI or PET scan imaging. One important type of investigation with human subjects is the study of emotional and craving responses triggered by drug-linked stimuli.

In addition to conditioned stimuli, other features of the environment can become discriminative or contextual stimuli related to drug use. Certain locations, people, or even time of day (e.g., late-afternoon "happy hour") may indicate drug availability and the opportunity for drug use. These distal stimuli are less consistently and directly related to drug effects, but they can also facilitate drug use (Conklin et al. 2008).

Exposure to videos of drug use or paraphernalia elicit craving for the drug, autonomic responses and distinctive changes in brain activity of addicted subjects. Images of a person smoking a cigarette, or a crack pipe or an injection syringe can produce these conditioned responses. Several investigators have observed such conditioned responses in individuals with SUD for cocaine (Childress et al. 2002, Volkow et al. 2006), amphetamine (Boileau et al. 2007), nicotine (Franklin et al. 2007), alcohol (Heinz et al. 2004) and heroin (Langleben et al. 2008). These studies are among the many conducted during recent years to investigate conditioned responses, including craving, and the activation of certain brain areas (Jasinska et al. 2014). The brain areas activated by these conditioned stimuli are primarily those implicated in the development and maintenance of compulsive drug use: the mesolimbic circuits, including the extended amygdala, and prefrontal cortical areas (Chapter 5). In many of these studies, the degree of activation of the brain areas correlated positively with the intensity of craving.

Conditioned Compensatory Responses

Drug-conditioned stimuli can produce responses in autonomic activity and brain metabolism similar to the initial effects of drug administration. However, for some drugs a conditioned arousal response resembles the brain's compensatory response to the drug effect. This drug-oppositional conditioned response is especially evident for opiates and depressant drugs such as alcohol. Shepard Siegel and his colleagues have studied the conditioning of the drug-oppositional response in a research program initiated in the 1970s (Siegel 1975). When the conditioned stimulus becomes associated with the drug-compensatory response, the conditioned response often resembles the withdrawal syndrome.

The compensatory response is an important part of the overall result of drug use, and is especially relevant to the development of addiction. This adaptive response to the drug is responsible for pharmacodynamic tolerance and the withdrawal syndrome. It is also thought to bring about the decreased sensitivity of the reward-sensing brain circuits in Koob's theory of lowered hedonic set-point (Chapter 5).

Tolerance to several effects of addictive drugs, including opiates and alcohol, is context dependent (Siegel and Ramos 2002, Siegel et al. 2000). When animal subjects are repeatedly administered morphine injections in a distinctive location, this location becomes a conditioned stimulus that elicits a drug-compensatory conditioned response and so diminishes the overall drug effect. If the context is changed, much of the tolerance is lost due to the absence of the conditioned drug-oppositional effect (Siegel 2001). The protective nature of tolerance resulting from this conditioned compensatory response was demonstrated in an experiment in which mice were administered increasingly large doses of alcohol in one location. After this location had become a conditioned stimulus (producing conditional tolerance), the mice were given the same large alcohol dose in a different location. The absence of conditional tolerance in the new location resulted in a much greater alcohol effect, causing the death of many of the mice (Melchoir 1990). When heroin addicts inject the drug in an unfamiliar place, overdoses are much more likely to occur (Gutierrez-Cebollada et al. 1994), again presumably due to a decrease in context-dependent tolerance.

A common characteristic of conditioned responses elicited by drug-linked stimuli is an increase in arousal level. The increased arousal, as indicated by autonomic or other behavioral responses, occurs whether the conditioned response is similar to the initial effect of the drug, or similar to the drug-compensatory effect and so resembles the withdrawal syndrome. In humans, the increased arousal and changes in brain metabolism (indicated by blood flow or dopamine release) are often accompanied by craving. Craving, further discussed in a subsequent section, can include emotional discomfort as well as anticipation of the drug effect.

So, although the drug-conditioned responses are essentially passive reflexive changes in physiological processes, they are also intimately related to deliberate behavioral actions, including active seeking of the drug. The active drug-seeking promoted by drug-linked stimuli is clearly shown by the behavior of animal subjects in the reinstatement paradigm studies (Chapter 5) (Shaham et al. 2003). In that procedure, behavior previously rewarded by injections of addictive drugs – but later extinguished – is reactivated by stimuli associated with drug administration. A similar effect of drug-related stimuli (craving) is also often part of human addicts' self-reports of events driving their compulsive drug use.

When a conditioned response resembles the withdrawal syndrome, it is easy to understand why craving for the drug often is a part of the response to the drug-linked stimulus. However, since the conditioned response, especially with stimulant drugs such as cocaine and nicotine, is often "druglike," it may be less obvious why the conditioned effect includes craving. It might seem more logical that the conditioned dopamine release would produce a pleasurable effect, rather than the sometimes-aversive craving state. This harder-to-understand result is related to the concept of incentive sensitization, described in Chapter 5. Incentive sensitization is thought to be responsible for the fact that although dopamine activation is involved in positive reinforcement, the action of this neurotransmitter eventually also becomes one of energizing and directing behavior. Therefore, the drug-paired stimulus elicits dopamine release and aroused anticipation of the drug effect, which is experienced as craving.

Another possibility regarding the nature of subjective responses elicited by drug-conditioned stimuli is suggested by Risinger et al. (2005). These investigators comment that for subjects asked to describe responses to repeated injections of cocaine, the "high" state and the "craving" state sometimes become intertwined, and difficult to disentangle for purposes of subjective report. In other words, because cocaine injection often causes craving for more of the drug – as well as euphoria – a druglike conditioned response might also be experienced as desire for more of the drug.

Conditioned Responses to Subliminal Stimuli

The influence of conditioned drug responses is often obvious, as in most cases of craving for the drug. Addicts often describe how the sight or smell of a cigarette or an alcoholic beverage is a vivid reminder of the drug effect, usually invoking memory of pleasure or relief from tension, and desire for the smoke or drink. However, even drug-related stimuli not consciously perceived can elicit brain activity related to emotional responses, likely causing actual craving for the drug (Childress et al. 2008, Young et al. 2014). Childress, Young and colleagues presented pictures of cocaine use to cocaine-dependent individuals in a manner in which these subjects did not consciously perceive these stimuli. The pictures were presented very briefly (thirty-three milliseconds) which prevented their **conscious recognition**. Even though not "seen," fMRI scans showed that these stimuli produced activation of brain areas related to emotional arousal and drug-produced reinforcement. The degree of this activation predicted affective responses – craving – to the stimuli when visibly presented at a later time. Another investigation yielded similar results when subliminal images were presented to cannabis-dependent subjects (Wetherill et al. 2014). These results indicate that the brain of a person with a history of SUD is exquisitely sensitive to drug-related cues, and suggest that these conditioned stimuli, even if outside the realm of conscious awareness, could influence drug-taking behavior.

Cognition and SUD

The basic principles of learning and behavioral control can account for human behavior in a variety of situations, ranging from phobias and anxiety disorders to learning in a schoolroom. Early behavioral theories did not mention cognitive processes (including any reference to consciousness). The early behaviorists preferred to rely on the associations among (conditioning of) stimuli, and the consequences of behavior (reinforcement) for their explanations. These early behavioral theories were useful in explaining how behavior can be controlled in both humans (behavior modification) and animals (training procedures used since the original domestication of dogs and horses). However, their exclusion of cognitive processes (reflection, deliberation and planning, etc.), so important in human behavior, were unsatisfactory to many psychologists. In the 1980s theorists such as Albert Bandura extended the basic principles of behavioral theory to include cognitive factors.

The question presented previously can be modified to ask, "How can rational, thinking and planning humans behave in such a manner as to bring the pain and suffering that often comes with drug abuse and addiction?" **Cognitive theory** was not developed specifically to explain SUD, but certain cognitive principles offer some explanation for the self-destructive use of drugs.

Bandura (1977) referred to his work as Social Learning Theory, primarily because his approach emphasized both the social nature of human behavior, as well as importance of behavioral flexibility based on learning from experience. This approach to understanding behavior was further developed by many others, including those who have applied the theory to addictive behavior (Marlatt and Gordon 1985, Abrams and Niaura 1987). Cognitive theory's origins in, and its influence by, behavioral principles are reflected in its current designation as *cognitive behavioral theory* (CBT).

Three principles of cognitive behavioral theory are of special relevance to SUD (Rotgers 2003). These principles are (1) cognitive mediation, providing flexibility in response to a complex and changing environment, (2) self-efficacy and the ability to cope with difficult situations, and (3) the powerful influence of social interactions and learning by observation (modeling).

The human sense of self often includes the perception that one is not merely a passive target of environmental forces (rewards, punishments, and stimuli predicting these events). Most individuals have a sense of self-regulation, in that much of the time they can actively avoid behavior that leads to bad consequences. Coping, the ability to deal actively with demanding situations, is an important aspect of cognitive behavioral theory. Of equal importance is a person's confidence in his coping ability, which is a main component of self-efficacy.

Cognitive Mediation

Cognitive mediation consists of several internal processes including evaluation of the complexities and uncertainties of human life. Most people live in an environment with many potential reinforcements and hazards. Long-term behavioral consequences may be anticipated, even when their actual occurrence is only probable rather than certain. Important events are often influenced by multiple factors, leaving their actual cause and significance open to interpretation. Selective attention allows some events to be ignored or minimized, while others are emphasized. The sense of self-efficacy is another example of cognitive mediation, in which the individual predicts his ability to cope with difficult situations.

These cognitive processes provide the adaptability required for survival in a complex social environment. However, according to cognitive behavioral theory, cognitive mediation can lead to erroneous conclusions, enable maladaptive behavior and contribute to the development of SUD (Rotgers 2003). Regarding the sense of self-efficacy, excessive drug use sometimes results from a real or perceived inability to cope with difficult situations by methods not involving drugs. In other cases, the self-perceived ability to cope with the possible consequences of risky drug use is unwarranted. DiClemente (2003) points out that even in advanced addiction the drug-using individual may have a false sense that "I can handle it," which allows the continuation of hazardous behavior. Finally, the flexibility inherent in cognitive mediation permits the reduction of cognitive dissonance, which can also prevent **realistic assessment** of the hazards of ongoing drug use.

The complexity of most lives, and the fact that the causes of distressing events may not be simple or obvious, often results in more than one reasonable (or at least possible) explanation of the basis of those events. Carlo DiClemente, in a book chapter titled "The Well-Maintained Addiction," describes how addicts are protective of their drug use, by not making the connection between their addictive behavior and the damaging consequences (DiClemente 2003). Cognitive dissonance (and its reduction) may be responsible for the reluctance to acknowledge that harm results from drug use (Miller and Rollnick 2002). Reduction of cognitive dissonance occurs in many situations, including those not related to addiction or drug use, when an individual searches for and finds an alternate, more acceptable, reason for harmful behavior. This cognitive explanation does not rely on unconscious processes, but is otherwise similar to the defense mechanism of rationalization.

An account typical of those heard many times by clinicians is that of a man who will not admit that his frequent intoxication is a threat to his marriage. His interpretation of the problem would include any number of factors other than his drinking, such as some personal inadequacy of his wife. Since not all relationship difficulties result from excessive alcohol use, he may view his explanation as credible – and certainly more acceptable (to himself) than to recognize the role of his own heavy drinking.

The failure to see what is obvious to an objective observer is explained by psychodynamic theorists as resulting from unconscious defense mechanisms (Leeds and Morgenstern 2003). In addition to rationalization, another defense mechanism is denial, the failure to perceive that a problem exists. Many counselors in SUD treatment programs assume that these supposedly unconscious ego-protective processes underlie much addictive behavior. Rationalization, denial and other defense mechanisms may be overused in these explanations of addictive thinking and behavior (Thombs and Osborn 2013; see also Chapter 3). However, the reluctance or inability to perceive the primary reason for their many problems is often a prominent feature of those with SUD.

Another, perhaps simpler, way in which cognitive mediation fails or is inadequate occurs when deliberate conscious thought processes are not employed, and control of behavior becomes primarily automatic and reflexive. As described in Chapter 5, there is some brain-imaging evidence indicating that stress can cause this shift from cortical to subcortical or cerebellar control of behavior. Heavy use of addictive drugs is stressful, and can also cause a similar change in behavioral control.

Cognitive behavioral therapy, as currently used in many SUD treatment programs, is based on the premise that these maladaptive cognitive processes can be corrected, and so promote abstinence and recovery (Marlatt and Donovan 2005). Although seldom recognized as cognitive behavioral concepts, these principles are also of great importance in twelve-step programs. As an example, members with years of stable abstinence are models of successful recovery for emulation by recently abstinent individuals (Chapter 16).

Cognitive Mediation and Drug Effects

Psychoactive drug effects can influence cognitive mediation – including the evaluation of and anticipation of the consequences of drug use. At high doses, addictive drugs severely disrupt ongoing purposive behavior as they produce extremely low or high states of arousal such as sedation, coma, anxiety or seizure. However, at low to moderate doses more subtle cognitive and behavioral effects can promote continued drug intake. These effects include altered judgment, often due to decreased expectation of hazardous effects of higher drug doses. Because alcohol interferes with cognition and can reduce anxiety (Carrigan et al. 2008), the effect of the first three margaritas lessens the concern about the results of ordering a fourth. Similar effects often occur with cocaine in that the drug increases confidence and optimism at low doses (de Wit 2005), making it more likely that the downside of insufflating a few more lines will be ignored.

Disinhibition of behavior is a frequent result of low to moderate alcohol doses in both humans (Reynolds et al. 2006, Dougherty et al. 2008) and animal subjects (Evenden and Ryan 1999, McKim and Hancock 2013). Other addictive drugs can also facilitate disinhibition. Disinhibition of behavior by alcohol in humans has been described as resulting from a myopic effect (Julien et al. 2008, Steele and Josephs 1990; see also Chapter 9). This term refers to the direction of attention toward the immediate situation, such as enjoyable social interactions, and away from more distant, but possibly dangerous result of intoxication. In that respect, the drug strengthens the greater behavioral control exerted by immediate (as opposed to delayed) consequences, a difference often seen even in the nondrugged condition.

The **impairment of cognitive evaluation** by moderate intoxication, resulting in heavier and often dangerous drug intake, can occur in the absence of SUD. Many social drinkers are familiar with the disinhibition effect of low doses of alcohol. However, this effect of alcohol and other addictive drugs is an important factor in the consistent failure of many individuals with SUD to avoid extreme intoxication once drug use has commenced.

Expectancy Effects in SUD

Prediction of future events, especially the consequences of one's own behavior, is a cognitive function critical for survival. The anticipation or expectation of behavioral outcomes is an important component of cognitive behavioral theory.

A drug's overall effect on cognition, emotion, and behavior is partially determined by the expectation of the consequences of taking the drug. In other words, what happens when you take a psychoactive drug depends partly on what you think will happen. Conversely, what you expect to happen when you take a drug has a big effect on your choice to take that drug. So, expectancies of a drug's effect partly determine drug use, as well as the consequence of that use including SUD. Expectancy effects are one of the two types of nonpharmacological influences on drug action, the other being the environmental context in which the drug is taken (Figure 7.2).

Figure 7.2 Expectation of a drug's effect influences the experience of drug use.
Photo: Richard Theis / EyeEm / Getty Images.

Many correlational survey studies reveal how drug effect expectancies are related to drug use, as have a smaller number of controlled experiments. Most of this research has dealt with expected effects of alcohol, although some investigations have surveyed expectations of cannabis or cocaine effects. In many of these investigations, SUD was studied only indirectly in that subjects were not selected for high or low levels of drinking or drug use. Alcohol consumption was assessed, and subjects indicating high levels of drinking undoubtedly included some with current or potential alcohol use problems (Montes et al. 2017, Sher et al. 2005).

Alcohol outcome expectancies are measured by means of such instruments as the **Alcohol Expectancy Questionnaire (AEQ)** (Brown et al. 1987), or similar self-report questionnaires. Not surprisingly, many studies have shown that subjects who drink alcohol have more positive expectations of alcohol effects than do abstainers. The decision to drink is associated with (and seems to be driven partly by) the belief that alcohol consumption will result in certain desirable consequences, such as tension relief, mood improvement or the facilitation of social interaction (Leigh and Stacy 2004, Treloar et al. 2015).

Outcome expectancies can be positive or negative. Examples of positive expectancy statements, as found on alcohol expectancy questionnaires: "If I were to drink alcohol, I would have a good time (or be more energetic, or feel more relaxed)." Examples of negative expectancy statements: "If I were to drink alcohol, I might do things I wouldn't do otherwise (or feel sad or depressed, or become clumsy or uncoordinated)" (Leigh and Stacy 2004).

The anticipated result of taking a drug arises from both vicariously gained information and from direct experience. The vicarious learning comes from observing the effects of the drug on others, both in real life and in the many accounts of actual or dramatized drug use in electronic media, television, movies and literature. Outcome expectancies for the effects of alcohol and other drugs are predictive of future use of these substances, and often antedate their actual use by young people.

Prospective longitudinal studies have obtained self-reports from subjects repeatedly over extended periods. Stacy and colleagues measured outcome expectancies for and use levels of alcohol and cannabis twice over a nine-year period (Stacy et al. 1991). The subjects were initially surveyed at mean age of eighteen, and then again at age twenty-seven. Positive expectancies for effects of alcohol and marijuana predicted use and abuse of these drugs at the time of the second measurement, and this prediction was not dependent on use levels at age eighteen. Other prospective studies have shown similar prediction of later alcohol use, based on positive outcome expectancies measured at the time of the initial data collection (Montes et al. 2017, Smith et al. 1995, Sher et al. 1996).

After alcohol or cannabis use commences, direct experience has influence on outcome expectancies (Leigh and Stacy 2004, Skenderian et al. 2008). Although expectations generally become more positive during middle adolescence, they tend to become more moderate in early adulthood (during college years) (Sher et al. 2005). These changes apparently indicate a growing awareness that alcohol and cannabis use can be problematic as well as pleasurable, and presumably result from direct experience with the drugs.

Certain expectations are associated with hazardous patterns of alcohol consumption (e.g., Bot et al. 2005, Leigh and Stacy 2005). The expectancy factors of social and sexual enhancement and tension reduction (as measured by the AEQ) are those most closely related to higher levels of alcohol use (Sher et al. 2005). Heavy drinking seems to be associated with expectance of increased arousal, as contrasted with expectance of sedating effects of alcohol in lighter-drinking subjects (Rather et al. 1992).

Expectancy factors associated with problem drinking are partially dependent on gender. Women college students with drinking problems had greater expectations of becoming more socially aggressive after drinking alcohol than did women without such problems. For problem-drinking men, the distinguishing expectation factor was physical and social pleasure (Thombs 1993). These expectations suggest primary incentives for alcohol use in heavy-drinking college students.

Positive expectations for the effects of alcohol not only predict earlier and more hazardous levels of drinking, but even more importantly, these expectancies are thought to mediate the effects of some known risk factors for heavy, problematic use of alcohol. Risk factors such as sensation seeking and antisocial personality may promote heavy alcohol use because individuals with these behavioral characteristics expect certain desired outcomes from drinking alcohol (Finn et al. 2000, Darkes et al. 2004). These expectations, often for the excitement resulting from alcohol use, provide a cognitive pathway by which the personality variable promotes high levels of alcohol consumption. Alcohol use was higher in sensation (or excitement)-seeking individuals who also had positive expectations for drinking as compared to those with the sensation-seeking trait who did not have such beliefs about the effects of alcohol. As the prospective longitudinal studies demonstrate, positive expectancy effects precede – and so could partially cause rather than merely reflect – the increased levels of drinking.

Failure to anticipate possible dangers (negative outcomes) of intoxication also seem to promote some of the vulnerability for SUD related to risk taking and antisocial behavior. Hartzler and Fromme (2003) measured outcome expectancies in college students who displayed personality traits associated with Type 2 alcoholism – a severe, more genetically loaded form of the disorder seen most often in young men. These students drank heavily and took behavioral risks while intoxicated. A lack of negative outcome expectations, combined with strong expectations of positive outcomes of alcohol consumption apparently mediated the dangerous behaviors.

Outcome expectancies also apparently mediate protective factors that decrease the likelihood of heavy alcohol use. Darkes et al. (2004) found that the protective factor of religious involvement was closely associated with the absence of positive expectancies for alcohol effects. Subjects with high levels of religiosity expected none of the positive effects often attributed to alcohol, including social facilitation and tension reduction. Most of these subjects abstained completely from alcohol use.

Craving

Most addicted individuals frequently experience a desire to use the drug. When the feeling is intense, the urge to use is often described as a state of **craving**, a special type of drug-related expectancy. The DSM-5 lists craving as one of the eleven diagnostic criteria for SUD. Anticipation of a drug effect often includes expectation of relief from an unpleasant withdrawal syndrome, as when nicotine-dependent individuals crave a cigarette soon after awakening from a night's sleep due to the hours of nicotine deprivation. Although craving is often a part of a withdrawal syndrome, it also occurs during states of negative affect, such as anger, anxiety, or sadness, not caused by drug withdrawal (Sinha and Li 2007). **Memory and anticipation** of a pleasant drug effect can also trigger a state of craving even in the absence of emotional distress. Whether it involves anticipation of pleasure (reward craving) or expectation of relief from an unpleasant state (relief craving), an intense desire for the drug is the characteristic feature of craving (Anton 1999, Heinz et al. 2003).

Measurement of Craving

Many investigators have attempted to quantify the craving experience. Monitoring of autonomic responses (such as sweating, or body temperature changes) that often accompany craving provide some useful information. However, these physiological responses are less sensitive and specific than is verbal self-report (Sayette et al. 2000). Heart rate, respiration or other autonomic responses may change due to any arousing stimulus or thought and might not be indicative of drug-related craving.

Self-report questionnaires provide measurement of the subjective experience of craving for most addictive drugs. Examples of these instruments include those for alcohol (Bohn et al. 1995), cocaine (Weiss et al. 2003), opiates (Franken et al. 2002), tobacco/nicotine (Cox et al. 2001), and cannabis (Heishman et al. 2001). States of craving for these various drugs share several common features (Carter and Tiffany 1999), although they are not identical.

Craving is sometimes measured simply as a level of intensity, as by means of the question "on a scale of 1 (none) through 10 (extremely high), how strong is your desire for the drug?" However, the complexity of the subjective experience is better captured by questions that are more specific. Carter and colleagues presented subjects with twenty-two statements related to craving for smoking tobacco. These statements referred to domains of affect ("I am irritated"), cognition ("I am having trouble concentrating"), and physiological states ("I am short of breath"). They also included direct questions about desiring a cigarette ("Nothing would be better than smoking a cigarette right now") (Carter et al. 2008). The chapter on tobacco use disorders includes further discussion of addictive craving.

Craving's Role in Addiction

Craving is often a prominent feature of addicted individuals' accounts of their compulsive drug use. As a result, many clinicians and researchers have long considered craving as a critical component of addiction, especially important in relapse to drug use after a period of abstinence (Drummond 2001). However, not all investigators support the view of craving as a simple, direct cause of drug use in addiction (Lowman et al. 2000, Tiffany et al. 2009). Studies of causes of relapse have not shown consistently that craving predicts recurrence of drug use after treatment (Heyman 2009, Litt et al. 2000). Some addicted individuals profess that craving does not precede their compulsive drug intake. Conversely, some who remain abstinent report that they do crave the drug, but are able to resist these strong urges.

Stephen Tiffany and colleagues introduced a cognitive view of compulsive drug use which gives craving a limited, rather than a general, role in the maintenance and recurrence of addiction (Tiffany 1990, Tiffany and Conklin 2000). Tiffany maintains that addictive drug use is most often a highly practiced behavior, which eventually becomes largely automatic and stereotyped. The drug use requires little cognitive effort or conscious deliberation unless interrupted or prevented. When the behavior is disrupted, the aversive craving state occurs along with attempts to acquire the drug.

Although some theories do not view craving as critical for the maintenance of addiction, the role of craving should not be minimized in the explanation of compulsive drug use. "To do so would clearly be contrary to the experience of addicts and clinicians. Rather, it poses a challenge for research to define the conditions under which craving occurs and in which it is related to drug-taking behavior" (Drummond 2001, p. 35).

Tiffany (2009) suggests that inadequate detection of craving by investigators may contribute to its unreliability for prediction of relapse. A related problem is the dynamic, transient nature of some subjective experiences. Craving states may be general and pervasive, especially when due to withdrawal (drug abstinence), but may "spike" sharply when drug-related stimuli are encountered. Another factor decreasing the value of craving for relapse prediction comes from the wide variability among individuals in their ability to tolerate discomfort (Abrantes et al. 2008).

Conditions Producing Craving

Controlled investigations, reports from clinicians treating SUD, and subjective accounts from addicted individuals consistently indicate that craving most often occurs during (1) withdrawal from heavy drug use, (2) exposure to drug-related stimuli, (3) the availability of drugs, and (4) stress and negative emotional states (Figure 7.3). Positive emotional states can also produce craving, but apparently not as reliably as do anxiety, sadness, loneliness, boredom, and other unpleasant subjective states.

A desire for relief from dysphoric withdrawal is frequently experienced as craving, especially when the drug has often provided such relief during the course of addiction and previous bouts of withdrawal. However, even the aversive nature of acute withdrawal produces craving only when the distress is interpreted as being due to a need for the drug. In most cases of addiction, the prospect of gaining relief by taking the drug is quite apparent to the person in distress. However, when withdrawal occurs in nonaddicted individuals, typically after medical use of opiate drugs for management of acute pain, the discomfort often does not cause a strong desire for the drug. This difference in response to the withdrawal syndrome (little or no drug craving) is an important characteristic of nonaddictive dependence (Chapter 14).

Figure 7.3 Drug-related stimuli, as well as an immediate opportunity to use the drug, stimulate craving for the drug effect in heavy users. Photo: Westend61 / Getty Images.

The altered brain function produced by heavy and persistent drug use eventually normalizes, at least partially, after drug use stops. Craving in the addicted individual lessens as the withdrawal syndrome subsides, but it can reappear under certain circumstances even in the absence of subjective feelings of withdrawal.

Stimuli predicting drug effects or situations related to drug use reliably produce craving (Brody et al. 2007, Jasinska et al. 2014). Because drug-related stimuli can be presented in a controlled environment, cue-reactivity has made possible a large amount of laboratory research on craving (Sayette 2016). Craving as a conditioned response in drug-dependent humans was discussed earlier in this chapter and in Chapter 5.

Stimuli associated with drugs can produce especially strong craving when the addicted individual perceives that the drug is immediately available – that is, not only can she see the drug (or people or paraphernalia related to drug use), but also believes that she can soon have access to the drug (Wertz and Sayette 2001, Wilson et al. 2013). Addicts often describe such instances of craving to clinicians or in support group meetings. Being in a bar, or in the presence of others who are injecting heroin or using cocaine apparently causes extreme craving in drug-dependent individuals. Opiate addicts report similar intense craving states when attempting to receive morphine injections by feigning painful symptoms in hospital emergency rooms. Researchers have often speculated about this "drug availability" effect (e.g., Ehrman et al. 1992), but actually providing drugs to addicted persons in a research setting presents a definite ethical problem. This limitation on research procedures is less restrictive in the case of nicotine addiction. Tobacco is not illicit, does not produce noticeable intoxication, and its use is still often culturally accepted. Tiffany and colleagues reported robust craving produced when cigarettes were made available in research conducted with nicotine-dependent subjects (Tiffany et al. 2009).

Memory of positive drug experiences (sometimes referred to as **euphoric recall**) can trigger craving even in the absence of specific conditioned stimuli, as can emotional states of anxiety, anger and depression (Fox et al. 2008, Sinha and Li 2007, Niaura 2000). States of negative affect are probably more common, and more closely related to craving, than are thoughts of pleasurable intoxication. Negative affective states are characteristic of acute withdrawal, but these emotions can also cause craving and recurrence of drug use even in the absence of an acute withdrawal syndrome, long after the cessation of drug use (Sayette 2016).

Craving and Cognition

Thoughts of taking a drug, whether triggered by memory, stress, or drug-conditioned stimuli, are often disruptive of cognitive processes not related to drug use. Working memory is a cognitive function necessary for most deliberative thinking, including concentration, planning, written or oral communication and other common mental activities. Brain areas active during stimulus-elicited drug craving are also active during working memory tasks (Hester and Garavan 2009, Garavan et al. 2007). Because the capacity of working memory is limited, thoughts of drug use, or even cognitive efforts to avoid drug use, impede simultaneous cognitive function. The demands on working memory resulting from craving are probably responsible for impaired performance on concurrent cognitive tasks. Such **cognitive performance deficits** occur in cocaine- or alcohol-dependent subjects when exposed to drug-relevant stimuli (Tiffany 1990, Hester et al. 2006).

An addicted individual might minimize craving and the resultant loss of focus on other cognitive demands by diverting attention away from drug-associated stimuli. However, these stimuli typically become very demanding of attention and so are difficult to ignore (Ryan 2002, Garavan and Hester 2007). The "distraction" aspect of craving might not be as distressing as the frank desire for the drug. However, even this annoying result of craving could promote a return to drug use – especially for stimulant drugs, including nicotine.

Brain-Imaging Investigation of Craving

Since the 1990s, many brain-imaging studies have revealed patterns of neurological activity resulting from administration of addictive drugs, as well as anticipation of these drug effects (Wilson and Sayette 2014). Functional MRI and PET scan images indicate levels of blood flow and glucose metabolism in specific brain structures. PET scans can also detect dopamine activity in brain structures and circuits. Imaging studies of brain activity during craving states typically involve presenting drug-related stimuli to subjects who have a history of heavy use of an addictive drug. Most brain-imaging investigations determined responses of cocaine-dependent subjects, but nicotine dependence has also received much attention in recent studies. Although craving as elicited by drug-related stimuli is especially robust with cocaine and nicotine addiction, similar studies of craving states have been done with subjects dependent on other drugs, including alcohol, opiates, and cannabis (Jansiska et al. 2014, Koob and LeMoal 2006, Volkow et al. 2006).

As described previously, craving is not a simple, one-dimensional feeling but is usually a complex experience. The state includes emotional and motivational components, cognitions such as memories of the drug effect, as well as possible intentions to acquire and take the drug or to avoid such use. The presence or intensity of a withdrawal syndrome also influences the neural activation that accompanies (and presumably produces) the craving experience (Jasinska et al. 2014).

Despite the multiple dimensions of the craving experience, and differences in craving among drug-dependent individuals, much consistency is seen among subjects in patterns of brain activity accompanying craving states elicited by drug-related stimuli (Garavan et al. 2007). Brain activation patterns are also similar, although not identical, during craving states in heavy users of various types of addictive drugs, ranging from cocaine through nicotine, alcohol, and opioids (Koob and LeMoal 2006). The arousal component common to most craving states appears to be largely responsible for the similarity of brain activity seen during these states.

Most of the brain structures and circuits – both cortical as well as subcortical – that become more active during craving are those also implicated in the overall development of compulsive drug use (Chapter 5). The close similarity between brain activity during craving and actual drug use is not surprising in that craving typically includes remembering, imagining, and anticipating the effects and feelings of drug use (Garavan and Hester 2007). The insular cortex is also involved in some craving states. The function of this subdivision of the cerebral cortex is critical for the awareness of bodily states, which are a component of some types of craving, in particular the craving related to nicotine dependence (Naqvi and Bechara 2009, Verdejo-Garcia and Bechara 2009).

Brody and colleagues instructed nicotine-dependent subjects to attempt to suppress or resist stimulus-elicited craving. These investigators found that most brain structures activated during "passive craving," when the subjects were not trying to suppress craving, became even more active during the attempts to resist the desire for a cigarette. These results were interpreted as being due to greater mental effort required for the suppression attempts. In this case, simple acceptance of the feelings may be easier than attempting to ignore the experience and avoid thoughts of smoking (Brody et al. 2007). See also the use of mindfulness therapy (Chapter 16) for treatment of SUD.

Research with animal subjects has fewer ethical limitations and greater control of relevant conditions. It is not known whether an animal analog of human drug craving influences the behavior of animal subjects in the reinstatement tests after extensive self-administration of addictive drugs (Chapter 5). However, such investigations have contributed much to the understanding of addiction-like behavior, even including indirect insights into the nature of craving in humans (Vann and Wolfgang 1999). A large amount of evidence, much derived from animal-based research, indicates that the onset of addiction occurs in part because drug-related stimuli become powerful incentives, initiating automatic motivational processes that drive drug use.

Management and Prevention of Craving

Although craving may be neither necessary nor sufficient to cause relapse to addictive use after a period of abstinence, this aroused state of discomfort and desire does often promote a return to compulsive use. Both pharmacological and nonpharmacological approaches are used to prevent, lessen, or to deal with the craving state and avoid relapse. Pharmacological treatments, such as the use of Campral, are discussed in subsequent chapters. Campral (acamprosate) is a drug that stabilizes the glutamate hyperactivity thought to underlie craving in cases of alcohol dependence. Drugs can also be effective in decreasing craving in other addictions, such as Chantix (varenicline) for nicotine dependence and Baclofen, sometimes used to treat addiction to a variety of addictive drugs (Tyacke et al. 2010).

Cognitive behavioral therapy approaches, also discussed further in Chapter 16, emphasize avoidance of stimuli and situations likely to produce craving. This nondrug therapy also guides recovering addicts in reinterpreting feelings of and thoughts related to craving. Management of urges to return to drug use is based partially on strengthening a client's self-efficacy. Tactics for managing craving are also important in twelve-step programs. Although spirituality is emphasized in twelve-step programs, some tactics of AA and NA for dealing with craving are quite similar to those used in cognitive behavioral therapy.

BOX 7.3 Drug use outcome expectancies and craving

- Expectation of drug effects influences decisions to use drugs as well as the overall experience of drug use.
- Light to moderate consumers of alcohol most often expect effects of relaxation and social facilitation from drinking.
- Heavy users of alcohol are likely to expect increased arousal and excitement from drinking.
- Craving for drugs often occurs in individuals with a history of heavy drug use, especially when access is interrupted.
- Craving is one of eleven DSM-5 diagnostic criteria for SUD, and some individuals with SUD apparently do not experience craving.
- Craving often includes anxiety or depression and cognitive disruption due to intrusive drug-related thoughts.
- Craving can occur in addicted individuals during withdrawal, stress, or other negative mood states; during pleasant memories of drug effects; and in the presence of drugs or drug-associated stimuli.
- Brain-imaging studies show that brain activity during craving is similar to that produced by drug administration.
- Cognitive behavioral therapy as well as twelve-step tactics for preventing relapse help addicts manage craving and avoid situations that trigger craving.

Social and Cultural Influences on SUD

Cognitive behavioral theory emphasizes the powerful influence of social interactions and learning by observation (modeling). The social aspects of human behavior are of critical importance because humans must deal with a variety of other individuals in complex situations that may change frequently. Some theorists even suggest that the development of a sense of self as a separate entity (self-awareness) evolved due to the adaptive advantage of accurate prediction of the behavior of others. This ability is obviously very useful in social environments, ranging from that of the immediate family, to the more complex interactions of adult life.

Albert Bandura recognized that modeling of behavior is a very efficient form of learning new behavior patterns by observing the actions of others. Modeling of complex social behavior is especially adaptive because good or bad consequences can be anticipated, without personally encountering the results of unfamiliar actions by means of trial and error. Unfortunately, vicarious learning via modeling can promote dangerous drug use by young people, as seen in the effects of peer pressure, or the influence of older siblings or parents with SUD. Such modeling can occur when the pleasurable effects are more immediate and visible than the delayed and less certain harmful consequences of heavy drug use – which often is the case in early stages of SUD.

Cultural Influences

The term *culture* refers to the sum total of a group's life ways, including its worldview, social organization, symbols, diet, ceremonial events, use of free time and disposable income, technology, and other aspects of living. Cultural influences are important environmental determinants of drug availability and use, abuse and addiction (Westermeyer 2004). Many studies have been conducted concerning the cultural anthropology of drug use. Only matters relating to cultural risk factors for excessive and harmful use of psychoactive drugs are mentioned here.

Drug use and attitudes about this practice vary widely among the numerous subcultures that exist within most countries. Ethnicity, socioeconomic status, religion, occupation, age, and geographical location (urban, suburban, rural) are factors which may identify different subcultures.

Availability of Addictive Drugs

Variability among subcultures notwithstanding, certain general conditions pervasive in most industrialized societies promote moderate to extensive drug use. These risk factors include ready access to generally accepted legal drugs or substances with definite addiction potential, primarily alcohol and tobacco, and somewhat less convenient access to illicit drugs, such as cannabis (currently illegal for recreational use in most of the United States), opiates and cocaine-amphetamine type stimulants. Medical use of opioid analgesics and antianxiety drugs is also common, although legal restraints provide some (if not completely effective) limits on addictive use and other forms of misuse of these drugs. Concentrated preparations of most drugs are available (distilled alcoholic beverages, high-potency cannabis, crack cocaine, heroin and fentanyl). Some of these high-potency substances can be taken by inhalation or intravenous injection – routes of administration that rapidly produce high blood levels of the drug and increase the addictive potential. Modern transportation facilitates delivery of drugs to locations far from the source of the plant product or manufactured drug. Cocaine and heroin are examples of drugs distributed through such illegal and widespread delivery systems.

Cultural Acceptance of Intoxication

In addition to availability of addictive substances, positive attitudes about drug use and tolerance for intoxication are cultural risk factors for SUD. Most cultures accept some use of alcohol for celebrations and rites of passage. Champagne toasts at weddings and other important life events are an example in which the symbolic, rather than the pharmacological drug effect is often the primary reason for alcohol consumption. In general, limitation of alcohol use (and other drug use in some countries) to rituals and celebrations minimizes misuse and SUD. Tolerance of obvious intoxication on such occasions varies greatly among subcultures. Flagrant alcohol intoxication during St. Patrick's Day or Mardi Gras celebrations are examples of special days when heavy drinking by many individuals is more likely seen as acceptable behavior – or at least tolerated.

In most industrialized countries alcohol use extends far beyond ritual and celebratory occasions. When drug-containing substances, mainly alcoholic beverages and tobacco (and recently in some states – cannabis), become **marketable commodities**, their use often increases, as does SUD (Room 2014). Advertising intends to instill a favorable image of drug products in the general population, and such positive attitudes encourage greater use and misuse. Drugs that are commodities are often used on a routine basis for utilitarian purposes, such as for relaxation, to ease informal social interactions, or to increase concentration and work performance.

Music, comedy, dramatic presentations and celebrity appearances in motion pictures and television convey current attitudes and fashions sometimes referred to as the "popular culture." These sources of entertainment and information present a cultural risk factor when intoxication and illicit drug use are portrayed as amusing, daring and exciting. Comedy and drama often deal with matters that are arousing and somewhat offensive and dangerous, with elements of risk and conflict. Such subjects are perhaps an integral part of a dynamic society that is relatively free of strict regulation by religious or governmental authority. Most people accept and welcome such realistic entertainment, but drug use and intoxication depicted as a humorous and interesting – if somewhat dangerous – activity promotes positive attitudes about consciousness-altering substances.

Interaction with Other SUD Risk Factors

Availability of drugs and tolerance of intoxication obviously encourage heavy drug use and acceptance of the harmful consequences of drug abuse. When drug use is not seen as deviant, individuals with fewer risk factors (such as those without multiple social and family problems) are more likely to become heavily involved with drugs (McKeganey et al. 2007). These cultural risk factors also promote the development of addiction by means of facilitating drug use in vulnerable individuals. SUD often results from genetic predisposition and the consequent long-term alteration of brain activity by the addictive drug. However, these neurological changes develop only after some initial drug use, which can be promoted by cultural conditions.

In the mid-1960s almost half of the adult population of the United States used tobacco on a regular basis, and most of these frequent smokers were nicotine dependent. Tobacco was heavily advertised, free cigarettes were given to college students as a marketing ploy, and there were few locations where smoking was prohibited. During the latter years of the twentieth century, the toxicity of tobacco became increasingly evident and acceptance of tobacco and widespread smoking declined markedly. In 2017 only about 22 percent of adult Americans used tobacco. The genetic component that contributes to vulnerability for nicotine dependence has not changed during this fifty-year period. However, during this time cultural attitudes about smoking in the United States shifted. The decreased tolerance of smoking allowed increased governmental restrictions on tobacco use and resulted in a significant reduction in the addictive use of this substance. This example illustrates how a change in cultural acceptance and attitude produced a decrease in drug dependence – even though nicotine addiction is heavily influenced by genetic predisposition.

Religion and General Societal Stress

In some countries and in certain subcultures religious influence can prevent drug use by most individuals, as in the proscription of alcohol in many predominately Islamic nations. Similar protection against alcohol and other drug use is provided by some religions in the United States. Children born into fundamentalist Christian families are unlikely to use any addictive drugs so long as they remain in that subculture. However, when young adults move away from their family of origin they often become less connected to the protective influences. They may then be even more affected by the larger culture and at definite risk for drug use and SUD (Westermeyer 2004).

When the population of a country suffers widespread hardship, causing prolonged stress such as from social upheaval or severe economic problems, drug use and SUD are likely to increase, especially if heavy drug use and intoxication were already prevalent (Carlson 2006). The increase in alcohol and nicotine abuse and addiction that occurred in Russia during the decade after the fall of the Soviet Union is an example of such a consequence of nationwide stress.

Progression of Addictive Behavior

The most disturbing and damaging patterns of addictive drug use typically emerge after some initial period of relatively benign experience with the drug. Progression – increasing severity of addictive drug use – is often characteristic of the disorder, and this delayed onset of adverse effects makes early detection of the disorder difficult. Harmful drug use does not always escalate to produce ever-worsening consequences and increasing dominance of the victim's life. However, such progression often does occur, and such advanced cases of addiction are those most likely to be studied by researchers, treated by clinicians, or come to a tragic end.

Progression of SUD can be seen in the disordered use of most addictive drugs, and it occurs in all of the many different types of individuals who develop patterns of compulsive drug use (Chapter 2). Consider the example of a college student who initially used cannabis only infrequently at parties, at which listening to music, dancing and socializing were the main activities. This student's life involved study and class attendance, part-time work, and varied recreational activities, typically including much social interaction with friends. With her initial limited use, the drug caused no obvious problems and was part of an exciting social scene. However, her drug use gradually escalated, until eventually she used the substance every day, frequently becoming intoxicated by mid-morning and consuming large amounts of potent cannabis throughout the day. In this advanced state of addiction her academic work was neglected, she was terminated from her job, and became isolated from her friends. She became quite depressed, and her dark mood was relieved only by cannabis use even though the drug sometimes made her feel paranoid. She also suffered frequent bouts of respiratory distress due to the constant exposure to smoke, and sometimes drove her car while quite intoxicated. Such increasing dominance of drug use in the life of an individual with SUD is typical of the progression of the disorder.

Toxic drug effects are often cumulative, so repeated high-dose exposure can eventually cause biological harm, which could include impaired brain function. However, abstinence and recovery typically result in marked improvement in many negative aspects of addictive lifestyle. Since most of the behavioral changes are reversible, it seems likely that factors other than progressive biological damage are responsible for the severely diminished life often seen in advanced addiction. The altered brain function seen in addiction (described in Chapter 5) can contribute to the overall behavioral deterioration and narrowed focus on drug use. However, the complexity of human behavior and the personal and social consequences of heavy drug use are also involved in its escalation to increasingly disruptive and disturbing levels.

The basic principles of behavioral pharmacology, behavioral and cognitive behavioral theory offer convincing explanations of the progressive nature of addiction – including acceptance of the adverse consequences of late-stage SUD. During the initial phase drug use is maintained by the behavioral principles of (mainly) positive, and (perhaps to a lesser extent) negative reinforcement. Modeling of other individuals' behavior can also promote drug use. Immediate aversive consequences are avoided by limiting drug use to moderate amounts, taken infrequently and only on certain occasions. Potential problems related to drug use rarely occur, and when they are encountered usually appear only some time later than the initial reinforcing effects. The *relative ease* by which some reinforcing effects can be gained (e.g., pleasant feelings, relief of boredom, acceptance by peers) can lead to *neglect of other ways of achieving these effects, with increasing reliance on the drug.* Situations and people connected to the drug may promote usage, which as of yet causes few bad effects.

Frequent use of the drug produces tolerance – especially for pleasurable effects – leading to greater amounts and even higher frequency of use. As doses and frequency gradually increase, *adverse consequences often occur,* but drug-produced disinhibition *may prevent regulation of the greater amounts consumed.* Exposure to drug-conditioned stimuli causes craving for the drug, further undermining attempts to limit its use. As drug use becomes more prevalent, *frequent intoxication and its aftermath often cause problems with several life activities,* including required duties (work), and personal interaction (family, friends). These difficulties require some form of coping, which may be accomplished (but typically not very well) by use of even *more of the drug.* At this point, for most individuals the drug use is largely maintained by the negative reinforcement produced by *relief from serious emotional states* such as anxiety, anger, and depression. *Alternate (nondrug) ways of coping* with these problems are *often unavailable,* especially if the individual is alienated from others who might give advice or support (Heilig et al. 2016). *This vicious cycle of drug use to deal with drug-produced difficulties results in increasing amounts of distress, but even greater involvement with the drug.*

At this point, the drug is often seen as the only remaining source of reinforcement – relief and comfort – even though its continued use results in a worsening situation. The addicted individual now has developed an emotional relationship with the drug. Addicts typically describe a *"love–hate" relationship,* believing that even though the drug causes much pain and suffering they *could not bear to do without its very marginal benefits.* Realistic evaluation of the drug's effects – positive as well as aversive – is frequently distorted by reduction of cognitive dissonance or even further removed from awareness by defense mechanisms. In advanced cases of addiction, even faulty cognitive mediation rarely occurs because behavior has become automatic and reflexive, falling back on well-learned habitual patterns of continued drug use.

To summarize, in a cognitive behavioral account of addiction progression negative reinforcement gradually replaces the original positively reinforcing drug effects. Adverse drug effects cause a loss of nondrug coping abilities and reinforcement sources, and a resultant narrowing of activities to those closely related to drug use. Impaired cognitive mediation then prevents recognition of the true nature of the situation and a loss of confidence in the ability to break out of the destructive pattern of behavior. An explanation for this progression to end-state seen in many cases of addiction can thus be derived from a few basic principles of behavior, coupled with the distortion of some cognitive processes and the disinhibitory effects of most addictive drugs. This explanation is at least a partial answer to the critical question: **"How do these unfortunate individuals come to self-inflict so much pain and suffering?"**

The predisposing genetic factors and the abnormal brain function described in previous chapters are the scientific basis for the disease concept of SUD. The biopsychosocial account of addiction presented here is compatible with such an "altered brain" explanation of the disorder, but this behavioral explanation also includes the complexity of the human condition, its social nature, and its capacity to change in negative as well as positive directions.

SUD Risk Factors

Any use of addictive drugs presents some risk of eventual harmful and compulsive drug use. Essentially all users are somewhat vulnerable because these drugs engage some of our most basic behavioral tendencies and cognitive capabilities, which can lead to SUD. The general risk is greatest in cultures or social groups that place few limits on drug use and intoxication. However, some individuals are at even greater risk for drug-related behavioral disorders. Genetic predisposition, discussed in Chapter 6, is a major risk factor. Increased risk of SUD also comes from various psychiatric disorders, characteristics of personality, or stressful events – especially during childhood. These additional risk factors are the subject of the following chapter, which is a continuation of the biopsychosocial approach to accounting for the occurrence of SUD.

Chapter Summary

The multivariate biopsychosocial approach to understanding the etiology of SUD combines biological factors and cognitive behavioral principles. This approach also includes developmental and cultural influences. The biopsychosocial explanation identifies risk factors, which are conditions or behaviors associated with SUD. A risk factor may contribute to the cause of SUD, but like all complex human activity, many factors are involved in the overall determination of maladaptive drug use.

Behavioral theory explains the harmful and compulsive use of drugs in terms of basic principles known to control behavior in many situations. Two general controlling factors are the consequences of behavior (reinforcement and punishment) and stimuli associated with positive or negative incentives. Cognitive theory includes behavioral principles but also incorporates the influence of the social context and the human capacity for thought and self-awareness. Human cognition features the ability to arrive at alternative interpretations of ambiguous situations. The resultant cognitive and behavioral flexibility enable adaptation to environmental changes, but can also promote disordered and hazardous use of addictive drugs.

Cognitive and behavioral principles, in combination with some basic actions of addictive drugs, offer a convincing explanation of drug abuse and addiction. These principles are compatible with and complementary to the biological explanations of SUD. They are particularly useful in cases where genetic predisposition and the associated neurological abnormalities are not evident.

The consequences of drug use are basic to a behavioral explanation of both nondeviant, benign use of drugs as well as to SUD. Positive reinforcement, often experienced as pleasure, exerts strong control when it immediately follows a given behavior. Addictive drugs often produce such rapidly occurring rewarding effects. Any aversive (punishing) consequences usually appear much later, and this delay lessens their power to suppress behavior.

Negative reinforcement, resulting from the relief of an aversive or uncomfortable state, is also powerful in strengthening and controlling behavior. Discomfort or dysphoria accompanies many human conditions, ranging from boredom to the pain of a chronic medical problem. Addictive drugs can temporarily relieve most, if not all, of these unpleasant states. One such source of discomfort is withdrawal syndrome or other aftereffects of drug use. Another is the shame and guilt that often result from addictive behavior.

Not suprisingly, individuals who expect a good result when they take drugs are more likely to do so. Relaxation and social facilitation are pleasant effects frequently sought and anticipated. Heavy users of alcohol, including those with alcohol-related problems, often expect excitement and arousal from the drug.

Many addicted individuals experience craving, an aroused state of desire for the drug. Craving often occurs during the withdrawal syndrome or when elicited by a drug-associated stimulus. Memory of the drug experience as well as stress from a variety of sources can trigger intense desire for the drug. Craving has been associated with addiction since ancient times but is not always a critical feature of drug dependence. Some addicts do not experience craving, especially if their drug use is routine and ordinarily does not require much effort.

Cultural factors, which are pervasive social-environmental influences, can encourage and facilitate drug use and misuse. When drugs are easily available and intoxication is tolerated in a society, heavy use is more prevalent, abuse is enabled, and dependence can develop in those with fewer risk factors. Some religions and family traditions can provide protection against harmful drug use so long as the individual remains within that subculture.

SUD typically develops gradually – progresses – after drug use commences. Heavy drug use often results in eventual loss of nondrug rewards and ways of dealing with difficult situations. In advanced SUD, the drug may be the sole remaining source of reward and the only accessible coping tactic. Continued drug use brings additional unpleasant consequences but now has even greater control over behavior, mainly because of the absence of other reinforcements. The drug still provides some comfort, and the desperate state typical of advanced addiction gives much power to even a poor source of temporary relief. The changes that occur during progression contribute to the self-imposition of further pain and suffering – from ongoing drug use – by many in advanced stages of addiction.

Review Exercises

1. What is the difference between positive reinforcement and pleasure?
2. Give an example of delay discounting.
3. How does negative reinforcement differ from punishment?
4. How does the nature of drug-produced reinforcement typically change as SUD progresses from early drug use into an advanced state of addiction?
5. Explain how the effects of some addictive drugs can increase the effect of delay discounting.
6. How do expectations about the effects of alcohol differ between light and heavy drinkers?
7. What conditions produce craving in addicted individuals?
8. How would a therapist trained in mindfulness therapy advise a recovering-addict client to deal with craving for a drug?
9. What cultural factors increase the prevalence of SUD?
10. Give an example of how cultural acceptance of use of a toxic addictive substance changed over a period of a few decades.
11. Summarize the behavioral explanation of the progression of addiction.

Key Terms

Alcohol Expectancy
    Questionnaire (AEQ)
    (236)
behavioral principles
    (218)
behavioral theory (218)
biopsychosocial (216)
cognitive performance
    deficits (242)
cognitive theory (232)
conscious recognition
    (232)

consequences of
    behavior (219)
craving (238)
delayed aftereffects
    (227)
drug self-administration
    (219)
euphoric recall (242)
impairment of cognitive
    evaluation (235)
instrumental
    conditioning (218)

marketable commodities
    (247)
memory and
    anticipation (238)
numerous pathways
    (217)
Profile of Mood States
    (221)
realistic assessment
    (233)
respondent (classical)
    conditioning (218)

8

Psychiatric Disorders, Personality, and Developmental Factors

CHAPTER OUTLINE

LEARNING OBJECTIVES

1. Describe the importance and the incidence of co-occurrence of SUD and psychological disorders.

2. Describe the three major types of relationships between SUD and psychopathology.

3. Describe the research that demonstrates that psychological disorders are a risk factor for SUD.

4. Describe the evidence suggesting that self-medication of certain psychiatric disorders often leads to SUD.

5. Define addictive personality and its limitations as an explanation for SUD.

6. Describe the relationship between personality disorders and SUD.

7. Describe how research guided by three theories of personality assesses the behavior and thinking of addicted individuals.

8. Describe the personality factors and traits that are more prevalent in heavy users of addictive drugs.

9. Describe the incidence of drug use in adolescents.

10. Explain how patterns of recreational drug use in adolescents are different from drug use in most adults.

11. Identify some early developmental indicators and risk factors for SUD.

Introductory Vignette: Preparing for the Job Interview

Libby sat in her car in the insurance company's parking lot. She looked at the entrance to the human resources office as she sipped her decaf latte. It was half an hour before her 10:00 AM appointment with the personnel director – just enough time to take care of the anxiety she could feel building up. Her heart was pounding, her stomach queasy, tension running all through her body. She took the one-ounce ("airline-sized") vodka bottle from her purse, twisted the cap off, and poured the contents into the coffee. Libby scanned the nearby cars furtively. She was well aware that drinking in your car in the morning, dressed in conservative but stylish business attire, was a little strange. However, she had her reasons. She knew she was good with all kinds of computer use: software installation, website maintenance, data mining, network security – you name it, she could handle it. However, working with people was a challenge that often made her very anxious. People could be so unpredictable, and the position of network administrator demanded both high-tech savvy and dealing with all sorts of people – many of whom were either stupid or just plain jerks. Once she landed the job, her technical expertise would compensate for her anxiety problems in working with people she didn't know well – or with some that she knew too well! However, first she had to get through this interview with human resources. She fully realized that she did not present herself well in job interviews. She always became very anxious, often spoke awkwardly, and sometimes could not even think clearly. She quickly finished the "latte plus," her private term for the quick fix for anxiety, and she already felt the tension subsiding a bit.

Sometimes she worried about her use of alcohol to loosen up for job interviews. At least she wasn't nearly as bad as her cousin, who was obviously getting into heavy use of booze, marijuana, and maybe even some harder drugs since he had returned from his second tour in Afghanistan and separated from the army. The VA counselor said it was PTSD – and she could believe that, because he certainly was in a bad place emotionally – nightmares, anger, obsessive reliving of the trauma, extreme fear of any situation remotely related to his combat experience. She knew he was using drugs too much, but when she tried to warn him, he said that getting loaded or stoned made him feel better for a while.

Okay, enough of those unpleasant thoughts. Her immediate challenge was to impress this person conducting the interview – stay calm, keep it together. She felt less tense now, but she was thinking about the second little bottle stashed under the seat.

Introduction

The incidence of psychiatric syndromes, including depression, anxiety and certain personality disorders, is much higher in individuals suffering from SUD than in the general population (Hasin et al. 2011, Hasin and Grant 2015, Lister et al. 2015). The

National Survey for Drug Use and Health (NSDUH) estimated that in the United States, 3.4 percent of adults – 8.5 million individuals – suffered from both mental illness and an SUD (Substance Abuse and Mental Health Services Administration 2018).

The co-occurrence of SUD and an additional psychiatric disorder typically increases the severity and complicates the diagnosis and treatment of both conditions. This frequent **comorbidity** is a prominent feature of SUD and must be considered in any explanation of maladaptive drug use. There are several possible reasons for the frequent close linkage of the disorders, so the underlying basis of the co-occurrence is difficult to determine (Lai et al. 2015, Martins et al. 2009).

Two assumptions are often made concerning persons suffering from SUD: (1) these individuals have an "addictive personality" and (2) they use drugs excessively to relieve an underlying distressing condition, such as anxiety, depression, or some other source of emotional pain. These commonly held notions have partial validity for some individuals with SUD. However, neither the concept of addictive personality nor that of self-medication is accepted as a general description or sole explanation of compulsive and destructive use of alcohol, nicotine, and illicit drugs. The multiple underlying causes make the etiology of substance use disorders much more complex.

The NSDUH survey indicates that in 2017 nearly half (45.5 percent) – but not all – individuals with SUD also have a disorder of depression, anxiety or another psychiatric syndrome. The frequent but inconsistent relationship between SUD and other psychiatric disorders is convincing evidence of the **multiple causal factors** and different pathways that can lead into compulsive and destructive use of drugs.

Certain experiences during childhood and adolescence predict the occurrence of SUD, so the investigation of developmental factors is an important area of addiction research. The presence or strength of certain personality factors in individuals (even in those without a personality disorder) is also correlated with problematic drug use. In addition to the co-occurrence of SUD and other psychiatric syndromes, these relevant areas of research are also discussed in this chapter.

Interaction between SUD and Other Psychiatric Disorders

Clinical populations (those in treatment for SUD), show very high rates of co-occurrence of an additional psychiatric disorder. Estimates of the incidence of a second disorder in those in treatment for SUD range from 60 to 80 percent (Mueser et al. 2006). Epidemiological surveys, based on large, randomly chosen samples of adults and adolescents, also show much co-occurrence of SUD and other psychiatric disorders in the general population (Grant et al. 2004a, 2004b,

Lai et al. 2015, Roberts et al. 2007, Substance Abuse and Mental Health Services Administration 2018). The community (nonclinical) samples show a lower incidence of co-occurrence than do the clinical samples. The difference between co-occurrence rate in clinical, compared to community populations is likely due to the greater distress and coping difficulty in those with two (or more) identifiable disorders, increasing their need for professional intervention (Mueser et al. 2006).

The degree of co-occurrence is often expressed as an **odds ratio (OR)**. To determine an odds ratio the incidence of a second condition, such as depression, in those with SUD is compared to the incidence of that disorder in those without the substance use disorder. For example, an epidemiological survey found that the odds ratio for bipolar disorder in those dependent on a drug other than alcohol or nicotine is 13.9, meaning that this mood disorder is nearly fourteen times more probable in those addicted to a drug than in those with no SUD. A comparable odds ratio for antisocial personality disorder (ASPD) in those dependent on an illicit drug is 18.5 (Grant et al. 2004a, 2004b). Odds ratios for the occurrence of a psychiatric disorder in those with problematic substance use are generally higher (1) for clinical compared to **community samples**, (2) for drug than for alcohol use disorders, (3) for more severe disorders than for less severe, and (4) for women than for men (Compton et al. 2005, Conway et al. 2006, Fink et al. 2015, Lai et al. 2015).

In those who exhibit both an SUD and another psychiatric disorder, does that disorder somehow give rise to, or at least contribute to the SUD? Conversely, does the problematic drug use cause the other type of disorder? These questions have no general, unqualified answers because the causal relationship between the two types of disorders varies for different psychiatric conditions and even among individuals exhibiting the same disorder (Martins et al. 2009). There are, however, at least three ways in which one disorder is related to the occurrence and course of the other condition. The possible relationships are summarized in Box 8.1.

BOX 8.1 Possible relations between SUD and other psychopathologies

Some evidence exists for each of these types of relationships between the two disorders, although no simple cause–effect relation underlies all cases of co-occurrence. One condition often influences, rather than directly producing, the other disorder, and a bidirectional cause–effect interaction often occurs (Martins et al. 2009). Like most human behavior, SUD is determined by many causes, and psychiatric disorders are one element in this complex multivariate matrix of causes and consequences.

> ## BOX 8.1 Continued
>
> ### The Secondary Psychopathology Model: Drug Use Causes or Worsens Psychiatric Symptoms
> Individuals using alcohol or other drugs heavily have a high incidence of distress characteristic of several types of psychopathology, including depression, anxiety, and other disorders. In this model the initial or delayed (withdrawal) effects of the drug cause emotional or cognitive problems. The addictive lifestyle (discussed in Chapter 1) could also contribute to these and other difficulties, especially in relationships with other people.
>
> ### The Secondary Substance Use Disorder Model: Psychiatric Syndrome Is a Cause of SUD
> Psychiatric disorders including schizophrenia, bipolar, and unipolar depression; anxiety disorders; antisocial personality (ASPD); and borderline personality are major risk factors for SUD. This model proposes that the drug abuse or addiction is a direct or indirect consequence of the co-occurring (often preexisting) nondrug disorder. The risk-taking behavior of ASPD, the mania of bipolar disorder, and the impaired judgment of schizophrenia are examples of direct causes of excessive drug use. Self-medication with alcohol or another drug to relieve the distress of social anxiety or posttraumatic stress disorder is an example of an indirect cause of substance abuse.
>
> ### The Common Factor Model: The Two Disorders Are Caused by a Third Factor
> This model attributes the source of both SUD and other psychiatric problems to a third factor (variable), such as a **genetic predisposition**, and/or environmental or developmental influences. Childhood trauma, parental behavior, and peer influences are life experiences that promote both types of psychopathology.

Secondary Psychopathology

Many individuals with SUD experience frequent periods of anxiety and depressed mood, which may closely resemble psychiatric disorders unrelated to drug use. These bouts of anxiety and depression, not unusual in those with addictive disorders, cause distress and dysphoria and in extreme cases present increased risk of suicide, or other hazards. Even so, these conditions are often not "true" co-existing psychiatric disorders, but instead are drug-induced states that mimic other disorders.

These distressing states often result from heavy drug use or withdrawal syndromes (Schuckit 1996). Alcohol intoxication can cause depressed mood, and alcohol withdrawal (including hangover) reliably causes anxiety. Anxiety and depression also accompany heavy cocaine use, but in comparison to alcohol intoxication, the sequence of dysphoric mood and anxiety states is often reversed. Cocaine can produce initial anxiety, but depression is typical of cocaine withdrawal. The role of drug use in causing the dysphoric feelings is evident if they subside or disappear after some days or weeks of abstinence. Improved mood and lessened anxiety often follow termination of drug use.

Addictive drug or alcohol use is rarely the sole cause of a lingering (postabstinence) anxiety or depressive disorder. However, when an SUD develops in individuals suffering from these **co-occurring disorders**, the heavy drug or alcohol use often exacerbates the preexisting condition. Although the initial effect of the drug can temporarily relieve some distress of the other condition, the delayed or withdrawal effects typically intensify the depression or anxiety. Unfortunately, the presence of a mood or anxiety disorder is a risk factor for both development of SUD and for relapse to active addiction after a period of abstinence. A true co-occurring disorder typically persists after drug use stops, making treatment of and recovery from SUD more difficult.

Use of addictive drugs can also mimic or increase the severity of other psychiatric disorders in addition to those of depression and anxiety. These effects, such as paranoia or thought disorder, occur most often with heavy use of cocaine, amphetamine, cannabis, or alcohol withdrawal. These drug-induced syndromes are discussed in the drug-specific chapters.

Secondary Substance Use Disorder

The occurrence of major mental illness often predates the onset of SUD in both adults (Swendsen et al. 2010) and in adolescents (Lazereck et al. 2012). The first-occurring disorder may predispose the maladaptive drug use by means of an overall impairment in judgment and life management ability. Heavy substance use may also be driven by attempts to self-medicate – to reduce anxiety, depression, or other dysphoric states.

Self-Medication of Emotional Distress

A theory of self-medication of distressing psychiatric disorders by drug or alcohol use as contributing to SUD has considerable appeal to many, including some clinicians or theorists with a psychoanalytic orientation (e.g., Khantzian 1997). Cognitive behavioral theories of SUD also feature an important role for negative reinforcement, which could come from self-medication. During psychotherapy sessions, individuals with SUD often maintain that their heavy drug or alcohol use is an attempt to relieve depression or anxiety, and similar accounts are frequently given in self-help groups.

A strictly defined **self-medication theory** holds that specific addictive drugs are chosen to alleviate symptoms of a particular psychiatric disorder. The evidence for such selective self-medication of all psychiatric disorders as an important factor in promoting SUD is inconsistent (Mueser et al. 2006). However, temporary relief of sadness and similar distressing states apparently promotes addictive drug and alcohol use in some populations, such as adolescents with mood disorders (Deas and Thomas 2002, Fink et al. 2015). Even though the drug use is often ineffective in alleviating dysphoria, the emotional discomfort could well encourage even futile attempts to find a way to feel better.

Several epidemiological studies indicate that both depression and anxiety often precede (and predict) the emergence of heavy use of alcohol, illicit drugs, and nonmedical use of pharmaceutical opioids (Edlund et al. 2015, Lai et al. 2015, Lazareck et al. 2012, Swendsen et al. 2010). The Edlund study analyzed results from 112,600 adolescent respondents in the 2013 National Survey on Drug Use and Health survey. The Swendsen study was based on interviews with 5,001 respondents participating in the National Comorbidity Survey, initially in 1991 and again in 2001. Lai and colleagues combined the results of twenty-two epidemiological surveys conducted in several countries in a meta-analysis. All these investigators conclude that in a majority of cases of co-occurrence, self-medication appears to have precipitated the emergence of an SUD.

The case for self-medication as a mediator of SUD is relatively strong for some types of anxiety disorders, especially for those of social anxiety, posttraumatic stress disorder, and panic disorder with agoraphobia (Logrip et al. 2012, Zimmerman et al. 2003). Alcohol is generally seen (at least culturally accepted) as an effective antianxiety agent, and in some situations does have a tranquilizing effect (Sayette 1999). Sedatives, such as barbiturates, and benzodiazepines such as Xanax/alprozalam and Valium/diazepam, can be quite effective for temporary relief of anxiety. In a similar manner, opiates such as morphine, Fentanyl, and heroin are useful for management of pain and pain-related anxiety. The rapid and effective relief of anxiety by alcohol, analgesic opiates, and antianxiety drugs no doubt underlies their abuse and addiction potential for some users with anxiety disorders.

Schizophrenia and Bipolar Disorder

Schizophrenia and bipolar mood disorder are two of the most severe and disruptive psychiatric disorders. Epidemiological studies (e.g., Lai et al. 2015, Regier et al. 1990) indicate that approximately half of those with either of these disorders also exhibit a concurrent SUD, so these conditions are major risk factors for maladaptive substance use. However, because only about 1 percent of the general population suffers from schizophrenia, and the incidence of the most severe form of bipolar disorder is similar, these disorders co-occur in only a relatively small fraction of those with SUD. In the NESARC study, only 5 percent of respondents with SUD also suffered from bipolar disorder (Grant et al. 2004a). The prevalence of schizophrenia in SUD populations is similar (Regier et al. 1990).

Although relatively small in number, individuals with this co-occurrence require much attention and effort from the staff in clinical settings, and their treatment presents a difficult challenge. Not only are these severe mental illnesses major risk factors for SUD, excessive alcohol or drug use usually intensifies the negative aspects of the concurrent disorder. Alcohol, cannabis and cocaine are the drugs most often used by those with these co-occurring disorders. Nicotine dependence is also quite frequent among the population with severe mental illness. The incentive for nicotine use in these individuals may be somewhat different than for other addictive drugs. Co-occurrence of nicotine addiction and psychiatric disorders is discussed in Box 8.2.

Many of these severely impaired individuals do not reside in protected clinical environments, but live in conditions that are dangerous as well as being conducive to drug use. Homelessness is an extreme example of an unstable, hazardous lifestyle. The co-occurrence of SUD and a major psychiatric disorder in the population of homeless individuals is estimated at 30 percent (Kertesz et al. 2006). Homeless individuals with both disorders are especially vulnerable to many hazards such as disease (including those transmitted by sexual activity), accidents, homicide and suicide (Mueser et al. 2003). Unfortunately, a lifestyle of homelessness often includes increased exposure to addictive drugs and excessive alcohol use.

Although drug or alcohol use is likely to intensify the symptoms of schizophrenia or bipolar disorder, such use is often a futile attempt to lessen the disturbing effects of these conditions. Heavy use of alcohol or other drugs can also be an expression of the extreme risk-taking behavior seen in the manic phase of bipolar disorder.

Some evidence suggests that those with co-occurrence of SUD and major mental illness (especially schizophrenia) are highly sensitive to the negative effects of addictive drugs, such as worsening of disordered thinking. As a result of this increased vulnerability to pharmacological effects, these individuals suffer extensive adverse consequences from relatively small amounts of drugs (Mueser et al. 2003).

BOX 8.2 Nicotine addiction and psychiatric disorders

Nicotine addiction frequently co-occurs with major psychiatric disorders, including depression, anxiety, schizophrenia, and bipolar disorder. Self-medication for relief of some symptoms of these disorders by means of tobacco smoking is a partial explanation of the co-occurrence (Ziedonis et al. 2008). Individuals with certain symptoms of depression are much less successful than are healthier people in attempts to quit smoking (Leventhal et al. 2009). There is also evidence of a bidirectional relationship in that nicotine use can

BOX 8.2 Continued

intensify some psychiatric disorders. Nicotine also interacts with antipsychotic medications, sometimes decreasing their side effects or altering sensitivity to these drugs (Chambers et al. 2001). The increased prevalence of addiction to this highly toxic drug in psychiatric populations is an important public health problem – a complex topic discussed further in Chapter 11.

Disorders of Depression and Anxiety

The disorders of anxiety and unipolar depression present definite risks (increased vulnerability) for the occurrence of SUD. These disorders are much more prevalent in the general population than are schizophrenia and bipolar disorders, and co-occur frequently in those exhibiting problematic drug or alcohol use (Figure 8.1).

Figure 8.1 Unipolar depression is a common mood disorder. Photo: Michael Heim / EyeEm / Getty Images.

In 2001–2002 the NIAAA conducted the first wave of the National Epidemiological Survey on Alcohol and Related Conditions (NESARC). In this survey, information was collected about the drug and alcohol use of 43,000 respondents of age eighteen or older. Interviews also determined the incidence of several psychiatric disorders in these respondents (Grant and Dawson 2006, Grant et al. 2004a, 2004b). NESARC was the first major national survey to base data collection interviews on DSM-IV criteria. This survey provided a wealth of information on the co-occurrence of SUD and other psychiatric disorders in the general population. The investigators identified and accounted for drug-induced effects of anxiety and depression, thereby increasing the accuracy of information concerning the co-occurring psychiatric disorders not directly caused by drug use. The NESARC results include the two categories of SUD (abuse and dependence) as designated by the DSM-IV (Chapter 2).

The NESARC survey revealed the greater prevalence of mood and anxiety disorders in respondents with problematic drug or alcohol use. The incidence of major depressive disorder (excluding bipolar disorder) for respondents without reported substance use problems was 6 percent, but the incidence of depression for those addicted to alcohol or another drug was 20 percent. The incidence of any type of anxiety disorder in respondents with no SUD was 10 percent, as contrasted with an incidence of 25 percent for those with substance addiction. The NESARC survey determined the occurrence of these disorders in the previous year only, so the incidence values are lower than those for lifetime occurrence (Grant et al. 2004a).

Table 8.1 Co-occurrence of SUD with disorders of depression or anxiety

	Any SUD	Any substance dependence (addiction)	Alcohol dependence	Drug dependence
All respondents	9.35	4.07	3.8	.63
Major depression (7% of all respondents)	19.20	12.59	11.03	3.54
Any anxiety disorder (11% of all respondents)	14.9	9.02	8.06	2.43
Panic disorder with agoraphobia	17.3	14.80	12.42	5.94
Social phobia	16.5	10.12	8.64	2.94
Generalized anxiety disorder	19.8	13.30	10.52	5.24

Note. Values are given as a percentage of NESARC respondents exhibiting the disorder within the twelve-month period prior to the conduct of the survey. Entries in the top row show the incidence of substance use disorders in all respondents. Entries in the subsequent rows show the incidence of SUD in respondents who also exhibit depression or an anxiety disorder. The larger values in these rows demonstrate the increased risk of SUD for those with an additional psychiatric disorder. In DSM-IV terminology, abuse and dependence are categories of substance use disorder, with dependence being the more severe form of problematic substance use. The "any SUD" classification included respondents with either dependence on or abuse of alcohol or another addictive substance. Some respondents were dependent on (addicted to) both alcohol and another drug. Drug dependence designates respondents dependent on (addicted to) opioids, amphetamine, cocaine, cannabis, sedatives, antianxiety agents, or solvents/inhalants. Of these drug use disorders (excluding alcohol), the prevalence of cannabis abuse (1.13%) and dependence (0.32%) were highest, and solvent/inhalant abuse (0.02%) was lowest. Solvent/inhalant dependence was virtually nonexistent in this survey of 43,000 respondents.

Source. Grant et al. (2004a).

The NESARC survey also provided estimated risk for problematic substance use associated with disorders of depression or anxiety by comparing the incidence of SUD in those with these disorders to SUD prevalence in all respondents (Table 8.1). These data indicate that the presence of a major unipolar (nonbipolar) depressive disorder doubles the probability of a substance use disorder (abuse or addiction), and triples the risk of drug or alcohol dependence (addiction). Anxiety disorders present varying amounts of increased risk, with three (included in Table 8.1) showing a high co-occurrence with SUD. The incidence of drug or alcohol dependence increases by at least a factor of two for respondents with any of these disorders of anxiety. In the DSM-IV diagnostic system, substance dependence was a more severe form of the disorder than substance abuse. Compulsive drug use characterized substance dependence (Chapter 2).

Hasin and Grant (2015) review and summarize the more than 850 research reports of NESARC waves one and two. The second wave, conducted in 2004–2005, confirmed the significant association between SUD and other psychiatric and personality disorders indicated by the original survey. Wave two also indicated that the association between SUD and other psychiatric disorders was stronger for externalizing disorders (e.g., antisocial personality) in men, but stronger for internalizing disorders (e.g., depression) in women.

In 2012–2013 NESARC wave three assessed psychiatric disorders including SUD as defined by DSM-5 criteria. Results of this survey concerning alcohol use disorders again indicated much comorbidity between alcohol use disorders and additional mental health problems (Grant et al. 2015). Survey results also revealed comorbidity at all levels of SUD severity for most psychiatric disorders including PTSD, not assessed in previous NESARC surveys.

There is much interest in understanding why those with disorders of anxiety or depression are more vulnerable to SUD. Several investigators have listed numerous explanations for the association between SUD and these relatively common psychiatric disorders (Kendler and Prescott 2006, Martins et al. 2009, Mueser et al. 2003, 2006, Neale and Kendler 1995). Most of these explanations fit into one of the three general theories summarized in Box 8.1.

Support for each theory depends to some extent on the type of psychiatric condition and addictive drug. Some explanations have intrinsic appeal, but finding objective evidence of their validity is often difficult. The search for general explanations is hampered by the variability among types of anxiety, mood, and substance use disorders. The causal relationships apparently differ among individuals (Martins et al. 2009).

As mentioned previously, self-medication of dysphoria or anxiety could promote heavy alcohol or drug use, leading to an SUD. Several epidemiological surveys indicate that the mood or anxiety disorder preceded development of disordered substance use.

Lazareck and colleagues found that NESARC respondents who reported self-medication of depression with drugs were seven times more likely to develop SUD than those who did not use drugs to relieve emotional distress (Lazareck et al. 2012).

In addition to self-medication, another common feature of unipolar depression could also encourage SUD. Heavy use of addictive drugs is quite hazardous, and the prospect of a dangerous outcome prevents or minimizes such use, at least in most people without a co-occurring mood disorder. Depressed individuals may have high levels of guilt and shame, and are often self-destructive, perhaps feeling that they deserve the adverse consequences of excessive substance use. The pessimism so characteristic of depression could also sabotage attempts to stop maladaptive drug use if the prospect of gaining a better life through abstinence and recovery is incomprehensible to the afflicted individual (Busch et al. 2005).

Posttraumatic Stress Disorder

Posttraumatic stress disorder (PTSD) – listed in the DSM-5 as a trauma- and stressor-related disorder – is a consequence of an extremely threatening, fearful experience. A complex array of symptoms, including both anxiety and depression, characterize PTSD. A DSM-5 diagnostic criterion of "a persistent negative emotional state" (including fear) indicates the prominence of anxiety in PTSD. Alcohol use disorders are quite prevalent in individuals suffering from PTSD resulting from a wide variety of traumatic events (Kachadourian et al. 2014, Stewart 1996), and such trauma can also increase vulnerability to cannabis use disorders (Hyman and Sinha 2009). SUD is three to five times more prevalent among PTSD patients than in the general population (Mills et al. 2006). The incidence of PTSD in alcohol-dependent individuals was found to be 26 percent for women and 10 percent for men (Driessen et al. 2008, Kessler et al. 1997).

Two common sources of trauma that precede PTSD are military combat or other incidents of extreme physical danger, and emotional and sexual abuse – especially that occurring during childhood or adolescence. These sources are to some extent gender-specific, in that men are more likely to experience battle trauma and women are somewhat more vulnerable to sexual assault. However, women are sometimes exposed to physical threats or attack, and boys can be sexually and emotionally abused, with resultant PTSD emerging after both types of trauma (Walker et al. 2004). The vulnerability to SUD associated with childhood sexual abuse is especially evident in women, who show a threefold greater incidence of alcohol use disorders when compared to those without such abuse during childhood (Keyser-Marcus et al. 2015). Like most other psychiatric disorders, PTSD increases the severity of SUD and makes treatment and recovery more difficult (Hyman and Sinha 2009).

The strong association between PTSD and SUD indicates that stressful life experiences can promote heavy use of alcohol and other addictive drugs. PTSD is a diagnosable psychiatric disorder, but less intense and disruptive levels of depression and anxiety often result from more prolonged and less obviously traumatic experiences and living conditions. The role of negative reinforcement by drug use in the development of SUD was discussed in the previous chapter. Alcohol and other drugs are often used to alleviate moderate levels of dysphoria that do not satisfy DSM diagnostic criteria for psychiatric disorders. Epidemiological studies have found significant association between SUD and subclinical conditions such as low self-esteem (Costello et al. 2003). The direction of causality between drug misuse and various sources of unhappiness may not be apparent in many cases, since SUD itself causes much life disruption. However, many studies show that stressful life experiences frequently precede the onset of SUD, suggesting a causal relation between less dramatic events and harmful drug use – similar to that resulting from the more intense consequences of PTSD (Shankman et al. 2008).

Psychiatric disorders that co-occur with problematic drug use are most often experienced before the appearance of the SUD (Costello et al. 2003, Martins et al. 2009, Swendsen 2010). This sequence of occurrence is consistent with a version of the **secondary substance use disorder** theory of co-occurrence. The SUD could be a direct result of the nondrug psychopathology, as in the reckless behavior of mania, or an indirect consequence from self-medication, as with PTSD. However, in some cases the sequence of appearance of the disorders is also consistent with the explanation that a **third (common) factor** causes both the SUD as well as the additional psychopathology.

Common Factor Model of Co-occurrence

Genetic predisposition is often proposed as a common factor that sometimes promotes the occurrence of both disorders. Genetic predispositions are causal factors in both SUD and other psychiatric disorders, and the heavily researched area of behavioral genetics is discussed at length in Chapter 5. Some genetically transmitted characteristics, such as an abnormality in brain electrical activity (the smaller P300 response), are risk factors for both SUD and certain types of psychiatric disorders (Patrick et al. 2006).

Based on their extensive nonclinical population-based twin studies, Kendler and Prescott (2006) found a moderate degree of correlation between genetic predisposition for unipolar depression and alcohol dependence. The twin studies support the correlated liability model, in which the genetic influences on the two disorders are not identical, but tend to occur together. Although an individual with genetic predisposition for alcohol dependence is also likely to have a similar genetically based tendency for depression, the SUD can occur in the absence of the mood disorder (Neale and Kendler 1995).

Other conditions and life experiences are thought to increase the incidence of both an SUD and a nondrug psychiatric disorder. Such predisposing events and conditions include poverty, cognitive impairment, inadequate or abusive parenting, and other stressful situations (Anthony and Chen 2004, Copeland et al. 2007, Fink et al. 2015, Heilig et al. 2016, Mulia et al. 2008). This explanation is somewhat similar to the "relief of general dysphoria or unhappiness" suggestion for SUD as described previously. Many sociological studies indicate that several psychiatric disorders – including SUD – are associated with these generally aversive life experiences (e.g., Swendsen et al. 2009). Few systematic attempts have been made to rigorously test the effects of these conditions on psychiatric disorders (Mueser et al. 2006).

BOX 8.3   SUD and other psychiatric disorders

- SUD frequently co-occurs with other psychiatric syndromes, including schizophrenia and mood and anxiety disorders.
- Co-occurrence is most likely in cases of severe SUD (addiction), in hospitalized psychiatric patients, and in women – although it is not limited to these populations.
- SUD can contribute to or worsen depression, anxiety, or thought disorder.
- Psychiatric syndromes not directly related to drug use are risk factors for SUD.
- Both types of disorder can also be caused by a third factor, including genetic predisposition or stressful life events.
- Schizophrenia and bipolar disorder are major risk factors for SUD, with co-occurrence rates of about 50 percent in individuals suffering from these mood or thought disorders.
- Unipolar depression and some anxiety disorders double or triple the prevalence of SUD – with the greatest increase in the occurrence of severe SUD.
- The risk for SUD often comes from self-medication by drugs of distressing emotional states – especially as in PTSD and anxiety disorders.

Personality Types and Disorders

The concept of *personality* refers to "enduring patterns of perceiving, relating to, and thinking about the environment and oneself that are exhibited in a wide range of social and personal contexts" (American Psychiatric Association 2000, p. 686). Personality consists of behavioral cognitive traits that are characteristic of an individual, are relatively stable over time, and have motivational and adaptive significance (Watson et al. 1994).

Personality disorders listed in the DSM-5, such as antisocial, borderline, or narcissistic personality, are long-standing patterns of characteristic thought, emotion, and behavior, which are often quite resistant to change. With certain exceptions (e.g., borderline personality disorder), individuals may not be much distressed by problems related to their personality, and less likely to seek treatment than those suffering from depression, anxiety, or other psychiatric disorders. Personality disorders are often concurrent with other psychiatric and behavioral problems in addition to their close relation to SUD.

An Addictive Personality Type?

During the middle years of the twentieth century the concept of "addictive personality" as an explanation for harmful and compulsive drug use was promoted by many psychologists and psychiatrists, mainly those with a psychoanalytic (Freudian) orientation (Mulder 2002). The basic notion was that those with substance abuse or addiction had characteristic ways of thinking and behaving which were responsible for their compulsive, harmful use of alcohol or other drugs. The concept of a specific personality type, *reliably and uniquely associated with SUD*, was eventually found to be invalid, and of little use for understanding and predicting addictive behavior (Keller 1976).

Although with very limited scientific credibility, the basic concept of "addictive personality" is still in wide use among recovering individuals, and is emphasized in some treatment programs (Gendel 2006). Members of self-help support groups sometimes describe themselves as having an addictive personality. Often this term means little more than the recognition of a tendency for excessive use of alcohol or other drugs. A typical self-description and justification might be: "How do I know that I have an addictive personality? Simple – because I used a lot of drugs." Perhaps this terminology comes partly from the frequent mention in twelve-step literature of an important role for "character defects" in addictive behavior. "Character defects" apparently refer to certain pervasive and maladaptive patterns of thought and behavior (e.g., perfectionism, narcissism), so the term has some resemblance to a scientific definition of personality.

Two questions are relevant to this traditional concept of addictive personality. The first question is: Do all, or even most addicts have similar personalities? The second question is: If there is a common personality type, is this unique combination of behavioral traits responsible for addictive behavior?

Regarding the first question, certain behavioral features, such as poor impulse control and negative emotionality, are often seen in individuals with problematic drug use. However, such tendencies for behavior and emotional responses also occur in some without SUD, and they are not seen in all those who do suffer from the disorder (Sher et al. 2005).

The answer to the second question is also not simple. Some characteristic behaviors apparently promote addictive behavior, but may also be a result of heavy drug use or the addictive lifestyle. Both these questions are considered more fully in the following discussion.

The study of personality in relation to addiction is currently an active area of research, although considerably modified from the earlier simple and broad concept of an addictive personality type (Birkley and Smith 2011, Kopetz et al. 2013, Müller et al. 2017, Sher et al. 2005). A primary goal of SUD-related personality research is to identify patterns of thought and behavior that predict the eventual development of the disorder. Another purpose is to characterize the behavior and thinking of those who abuse or are addicted to drugs, but to be of much value the investigations must go beyond a basic description of excessive drug use. These research efforts often supplement information gained from genetic, brain-imaging, and behavioral investigations.

Investigators who study personality attempt to describe and understand normal, as well as deviant or distressing patterns of thought, feeling, and behavior. The two basic approaches used to describe personality types and traits are the **categorical personality models** and the **dimensional personality models** (Kring et al. 2007). In the categorical model, individuals are seen as exhibiting combinations of behavioral characteristics common to most individuals with that specific *personality type*. This approach is perhaps most useful in clinical applications for classifying disorders of personality.

Dimensional models are more complex, usually involving several *factors* that consist of combinations of specific *traits*. These personality dimensions and their components may vary independently of each other. This approach (discussed further in the next section) is currently used in scientific investigations of personality structure of individuals in general populations – and is not limited to clinical studies.

Personality Disorders Associated with SUD

The DSM-5 lists ten personality disorders that are viewed as distinct clinical syndromes, each defined by a list of characteristic features. A syndrome is assigned to one of three clusters, with the disorders in each cluster sharing some common features. The disorders that make up Cluster B, often referred to as the dramatic/impulsive disorder cluster, are those most reliably associated with SUD (Sher et al. 2005). Cluster B consists of antisocial, borderline, histrionic, and narcissistic personality disorders. Antisocial (ASPD) and borderline (BLPD) disorders are much more likely to co-occur with SUD than are the other two Cluster B personality disorders.

Previous versions of the DSM classified SUD as a personality disorder, rather than the current designation as a distinct and separate clinical syndrome. The earlier view of problematic drug or alcohol use as a type of personality disorder may have been partly due to the frequent close association between SUD and Cluster B disorders. These personality disorders (especially ASPD and BLPD) co-occur with SUD even more often than do the previously discussed disorders of mood and anxiety (Hasin et al. 2011). Not all individuals with SUD suffer from a co-occurring personality disorder. However, when both disorders do co-occur, they are intimately interconnected and in such cases the SUD is invariably more severe and resistant to treatment (Bogdanowicz et al. 2015). Personality disorders may show some improvement during abstinence from maladaptive substance use, but these disorders are less likely to show substantial remission during recovery than are those of anxiety and depression (Verheul et al. 2000).

As with the co-occurrence of SUD and other psychiatric disorders, the causal relationship between SUD and personality disorders is complex, often bidirectional, and probably differs among individuals, as well as among specific types of disorders. The genetic predisposition for ASPD is strongly correlated with that for some types of SUD, and at least some of the genetic influence for the two disorders is thought to be identical (Chapter 5).

Antisocial Personality Disorder

The defining characteristics of ASPD include persistent impulsivity, deceitfulness (lying or conning others), reckless disregard for safety of self and others, irritability and aggressiveness, and consistent irresponsibility. These behaviors identify an ongoing disregard of and violation of the rights of others (American Psychiatric Association 2013).

Antisocial personality disorder is highly correlated with SUD. The co-occurrence has been reported in many clinical studies as well as in epidemiological surveys (Compton et al. 2005, Grant et al. 2004b, Hasin and Grant 2015). The incidence of ASPD is greater in men (5.5 percent) than in women (1.9 percent), with the total incidence of 3.6 percent of the adult population as indicated by the NESARC survey. The relative incidence of SUD in all NESARC respondents, as compared to those with ASPD indicates that the personality disorder is associated with a fivefold increased risk for alcohol dependence and a tenfold increased risk for dependence on drugs other than alcohol (Table 8.2).

Although ASPD is probably the closest match for an "addictive personality" type, not all those with problematic substance use fit this behavioral profile. However, when the two disorders do co-occur, the SUD develops at an earlier age, is more resistant to treatment, and results in more harm to the individual and to society (Holdcraft et al. 1998).

Although an individual must be at least age eighteen for a DSM-5 diagnosis of ASPD, the related syndrome of conduct disorder (diagnosable in younger adolescents and children) is also associated with and predictive of eventual SUD

Table 8.2 Co-occurrence of SUD and antisocial personality disorder

	All alcohol use disorders	Alcohol dependence	All drug use disorders	Drug dependence
All respondents	8.5	3.8	2.0	0.6
Respondents with ASPD (3.6%)	28.7	19.2	15.2	6.8

Note. Values are given as a percentage of NESARC respondents exhibiting the disorder within the twelve-month period prior to the conduct of the survey.

(Roberts et al. 2007). ASPD is most common among young males, but women that do exhibit this personality disorder are at even greater risk for SUD than are men with this behavioral profile (Kessler et al. 1997).

Most of the behavioral characteristics of ASPD are clearly related to (consequences or probable causes of) disordered patterns of alcohol and other drug use as described in Chapter 2. Impulsivity is thought to be the trait most likely to promote hazardous drug use (Iacono et al. 2008). The important role of this behavioral characteristic is further discussed in a later section of the present chapter. The characteristics of deceitfulness, irresponsibility, and reckless disregard for the safety of self and others are those of an addictive lifestyle, including concealing substance use and evading responsibility for harmful consequences. These features of ASPD encourage risky substance use, including use of illegal drugs as well as hazardous use of alcohol (e.g., intoxicated driving).

Borderline Personality Disorder

Borderline personality disorder (BLPD) is a severe clinical syndrome characterized by disturbed interpersonal relationships, uncontrolled anger, intense and frequent mood changes, impulsive acts, and a high risk of suicide (Bornovalova et al. 2005, Linehan et al. 1993). BLPD frequently co-occurs with other DSM-5 disorders including those of mood and anxiety as well as SUD. Individuals with BLPD frequently seek assistance from mental health providers, and often utilize general emergency medical care (Grant et al. 2008). Although the incidence of BLPD in the overall population is estimated at 2–4 percent, prevalence of the disorder is much higher among individuals in outpatient therapy (10 percent), and among psychiatric inpatients (20 percent) (Trull et al. 2000). Individuals with this personality profile often experience significant distress and impairment, especially as a consequence of their turbulent interpersonal relations.

Borderline personality disorder frequently co-occurs with hazardous and compulsive alcohol or drug use. Clinical studies indicate that approximately 60 percent of patients in treatment for BLPD also suffered from SUD (e.g., Walter et al. 2009, Zanarini et al. 2004). Community surveys also indicate a substantial degree of co-occurrence of the two disorders in nonclinical populations (Hasin et al. 2011, Hasin and Grant 2015, Trull et al. 2000).

Borderline personality disorder also frequently co-occurs with antisocial personality disorder. In addition to their common association with SUD, there are other similarities between the two Cluster B personality disorders. Both are seen most frequently in older adolescents and young adults, and tend to moderate (become less severe and persistent) with age in some individuals. Poor impulse control is a central component of both syndromes, as are frequent anger, irritability and problematic interpersonal relations (Zanarini 1993).

The two personality disorders differ in regard to the levels of distress experienced associated with each syndrome. Individuals – especially women – with BLPD are typically quite unhappy and distressed, and often seek help from mental health professionals (Daigre et al. 2015). In contrast, both men and women with ASPD are less often distressed by their own reckless irresponsibility and violation of the rights of others, and are much less likely to voluntarily seek treatment for relief of their personal problems. The high incidence of suicide in those with BLPD, relative to ASPD, is indicative of the different levels of subjective distress and dysphoria characteristic of the two syndromes.

Behavioral tendencies and ways of thinking common to BLPD are also typical of those seen with SUD. As with ASPD, the impulsive behavior characteristic of this disorder promotes hazardous substance use. The volatile mood, intense dysphoria, anger, and unstable interpersonal relationships could be either a cause, a consequence of, or have a bidirectional relationship with frequent intoxication, hangover and withdrawal, or an addictive lifestyle.

SUD and Other Personality Disorders

Co-occurrence of SUD and other personality disorders has received relatively little attention from investigators. Narcissistic and histrionic personality profiles are also included in the Cluster B category of personality disorders. However, individuals with these disorders are not especially vulnerable to SUD. The absence of the critical trait of impulsivity in the narcissistic and histrionic disorders may result in this contrast with the high prevalence of SUD among those with antisocial or borderline personality disorders.

The classic literature of Alcoholics Anonymous emphasizes the role of "false pride" in addiction, a term that apparently refers to narcissism. It seems likely that rather than being a primary cause of SUD, some features of narcissism may occur in those who are especially resistant to the suggestions of a twelve-step program for recovery from addiction. These narcissistic characteristics include a grandiose sense of self-importance, expectation of special treatment and self-perceived infallibility. These tendencies, along with unrealistic fantasies of great power, are incompatible with the twelve-step emphasis on humility and acknowledgment that addiction cannot be controlled by the individual without assistance from a higher power.

Certain features of certain personality disorders and SUD may underlie the few reports of their co-occurrence. Morgenstern et al. (1997) found that 18 percent of a clinical population suffering from SUD also exhibited avoidant personality disorder, and 21 percent were diagnosed with paranoid personality disorder. Those with the avoidant disorder are also likely to have a social anxiety disorder, which often co-occurs with alcohol use disorders (American Psychiatric Association 2000). Suspicion and mistrust of others characterize paranoid personality disorder, which could be related to the interpersonal difficulties that are a prominent feature of substance abuse or dependence (Chapter 2).

BOX 8.4 SUD and personality disorders

- Antisocial personality disorder and borderline personality disorder present a greatly increased risk for SUD.
- The impulsiveness characteristic of both these disorders promotes heavy drug use.
- Heavy drug use can worsen the reckless disregard for harm done to others characteristic of ASPD and the anger and turbulent interpersonal relations seen in BLPD.
- The presence of these personality disorders increases the severity of SUD and decreases the probability of abstinence and lasting recovery.
- ASPD and BLPD are the closest matches to the hypothetical "addictive personality," a concept not part of the current scientific view of SUD.
- No particular personality type or disorder is specific to or universally seen in individuals with an SUD.
- Many who are diagnosed with SUD do not display the characteristic features of ASPD or BLPD.

Personality Theory: Factors, Traits, and SUD

Classification of personality disorders, as in the DSM system, is useful to clinicians in their work with psychiatric patients or clients. However, scientists that study personality investigate the relatively consistent patterns of behavior and thinking of individuals in the general population. These patterns of thought, emotional response and behavior are determined by combinations of traits. The term *trait* refers to a specific dimension or characteristic – such as trust, self-discipline, assertiveness, or hostility. Most **personality traits** are present to some extent in everyone, but they vary in strength or intensity among individuals. Personality disorders occur in those in whom some of these traits are exaggerated, as in impulsiveness and disregard for others (antisocial disorder), and the negative emotions of anger and depression (borderline disorder).

Personality theorists combine specific, but related traits into more general groups, usually referred to as factors. Some of the most well-known systems or theories of personality are based on either three, or five of these general factors. The theories differ to some extent, but some common behavioral tendencies or dimensions of temperament (e.g., anxiety, extraversion, ambition) are either factors or components of factors in most of these theories (Sher et al. 1999).

Only three of the many theories of personality are discussed here. McCrae and Costa, Tellegen, and Cloninger are among those who have developed theories or systems of personality, and each has advanced our understanding of how personality and SUD are related. These personality theories, and the questionnaires developed for use with a particular theory, were not originally intended to explain or investigate hazardous or compulsive drug use. Few items (individual questions) inquire about the respondent's use of alcohol, nicotine, or other drugs. However, **personality questionnaires** have been used in a large amount of SUD-related research. This extensive research literature is reviewed elsewhere (Mulder 2002, Sher et al. 2005).

In personality research, questionnaires are most often administered to large nonclinical populations, providing information about the behavioral tendencies and temperamental characteristics of a wide range of individuals. The respondents include individuals with SUD as well as those with nonproblematic patterns of drug use. The relevance of these research efforts to the study of SUD depends on whether personality profiles, based on the measurement of traits, can differentiate the respondents with harmful patterns of drug use from those without such problematic behavior. Another important intended use of these questionnaires is prediction of eventual drug use and SUD in adolescent populations. Personality research has had some success in both these endeavors. Identification of traits that precede problematic alcohol or drug use can indicate risk factors for SUD, and to some extent separate possible causes of heavy drug use from its consequences.

Because control and manipulation of personality factors is either impossible or unethical, investigation of the relationship between these factors and SUD is necessarily limited to identifying correlations among behavioral and temperamental predispositions, and substance use disorders. Advanced methods of statistical analysis, such as structural equation modeling, allow estimates of the contribution made (variance accounted for) by several variables. These variables include family background, previous exposure to drugs, and the traits and behavioral tendencies that compose personality (Schuckit et al. 2006). However, the causal role of personality factors associated with SUD is often difficult to determine, a situation similar to that seen with various forms of psychopathology.

McCrae and Costa Five-Factor Theory

The personality theory of McCrae and Costa features five factors (McCrae and Costa 1990). These factors, and an example of a questionnaire item assessing each factor are: Neuroticism (I often feel tense and jittery), Extraversion/Introversion (I really like most people I meet), Openness to Experience (I have a very active imagination), Agreeableness/Antagonism (I tend to be cynical and skeptical of others' intentions), and Conscientiousness (I always try to be prepared for a test). These personality factors appear to be moderately heritable (Jang et al. 2002). The five factors of this theory are each subdivided into six "facets" or traits, which are assessed by the **Revised NEO Personality Inventory (NEO-PI)** (Costa and McCrae 1992).

Terracciano and colleagues administered the NEO-PI to 1,102 subjects, mean age fifty-seven, including users of heroin, cocaine, and marijuana, as well as individuals who had never used any drug (Terracciano et al. 2008). Profiles (strength of the five factors) were determined for high-frequency users of cocaine or heroin, many of whom were probably addicted. In comparison to respondents who never used drugs, the cocaine and heroin users' profiles showed significantly higher scores on the Neuroticism and lower scores on the Conscientiousness factors. Significant facets making up the Neuroticism factor included anxiety, angry hostility, depression, and impulsivity. Significant facets of the Conscientiousness factor included competence, dutifulness, and self-discipline.

The NEO-PI also shows elevated scores on the Neuroticism factor in respondents diagnosed with alcohol use disorder (Martin and Sher 1994) and in heavily drinking college students (Grekin et al. 2006). A similar high Neuroticism score was associated with frequent alcohol intoxication in women (Musgrave-Marquart et al. 1997).

Cloninger's Tridimensional Theory

Robert Cloninger developed a three-factor theory that has stimulated and influenced a large amount of research investigating personality factors characteristic of alcoholism and other forms of SUD (Cloninger 1987, Cloninger et al. 1993). Cloninger's work is of special importance in that it addressed the marked variability seen among those with drug use disorders (Chapter 2). The original version of Cloninger's tridimensional personality theory included three main factors of temperament: novelty seeking, harm avoidance, and reward dependence.

According to Cloninger's three-factor personality theory, those with a high level of *novelty seeking* are impulsive, fickle, quick-tempered, extravagant and disorderly, whereas individuals with a lower level of this factor tend to be reflective, rigid, loyal, orderly and persistent. A high level of *harm avoidance* is associated with caution, tension, inhibition, shyness, and fear. In contrast, those with low levels of this factor tend to be confident, relaxed, optimistic, disinhibited, and carefree. High levels of the *reward dependence* factor are associated with ambition and persistence. Detachment and a tendency to be irresolute (vacillating) characterize low levels of this component.

Many studies featured the Tridimensional Personality Questionnaire (TPQ), designed to assess the traits and factors of Cloninger's theory (e.g., Howard et al. 1997). High levels of novelty seeking were positively correlated with tobacco use and early-onset alcohol use disorders. The factors of harm avoidance and reward dependence were not consistently related to heavy drug use or SUD.

Sher and colleagues utilized Cloninger's TPQ in a prospective study of SUD in 457 college students (Sher et al. 2000). These students were given a diagnostic interview to identify SUD and were also administered the TPQ initially, and again after a period of seven years. High scores on the novelty-seeking factor were associated with problematic use of alcohol, nicotine, and other drugs at the time of the initial testing, and predicted further involvement at the follow-up assessment.

Cloninger's theory represents an early attempt to understand the heterogeneity seen among those with SUD. Research related to this theory has provided much evidence of high levels of the novelty-seeking factor, which includes personality traits most prominent in those with the early-onset, antisocial form of drug use disorders. The trait of impulsiveness is a component of Cloninger's novelty-seeking factor, and additional research (discussed below) reveals a high level of impulsiveness in many with SUD.

Tellegen's Three-Factor Theory

Tellegen developed a three-factor system somewhat similar to the earlier personality theory of Eysenck (Tellegen 1985). The three personality factors of this theory are positive emotionality, negative emotionality, and constraint. *Positive emotionality* refers to the tendency to view life as an essentially pleasurable experience, and consists of traits of social potency, achievement, social closeness and a feeling of well-being. *Negative emotionality* indicates a propensity to experience psychological distress and negative mood states, and consists of the traits of intense stress response, alienation, and aggression. *Constraint* indicates a tendency to endorse traditional values and act in a cautious and restrained manner, and consists of the traits of reflective and cautious control, avoidance of danger, and endorsement of high moral standards.

The relationship between the personality factors of Tellegen's system and the hazardous use of alcohol, tobacco, and illicit drugs (predominately marijuana) was investigated in a three-year prospective study of adolescence and young adulthood (Elkins et al. 2006). These investigators administered the Multidimensional

Personality Questionnaire (MPQ), developed by Tellegen and Waller (2001), to 1,000 seventeen-year-old respondents. Clinical assessments of SUD were conducted at the time of the personality assessment, and again at the end of the three-year period. The association between drug use disorder and personality factors was determined for both early and later appearance of problematic drug use.

Respondents with low scores on the Constraint factor were more likely to have a preexisting SUD (as determined at the start of the three-year period), and were also more likely to have developed a new use disorder by the time of the follow-up interview. These individuals were generally impulsive risk-takers. The Negative Emotionality factor was also associated with SUD at both the first and the second assessment times. Respondents with high scores on Negative Emotionality (who often experienced distress or anger) were also likely to develop a new SUD during the three-year period.

A personality profile of low Constraint, and high Negative Emotionality (often occurring in the same individuals) also predicted emergence of SUD in those with no drug use problems at the time of the first assessment. Most traits making up the Positive Emotionality factor were not related to the presence or the emergence of SUD.

Although SUD for all three types of drugs were much more likely in male respondents, the personality profiles associated with SUD were similar for males and females. SUD for each of the three drug types was associated with these personality factors, but the relationship was especially strong for nicotine addiction. One standard deviation of difference for higher Negative Emotionality, or for lower Constraint increased the odds of emergence of nicotine dependence during the three-year period by 50 and 89 percent, respectively.

Generally similar associations of MPQ-measured personality traits with SUD were reported by Krueger in a study of late adolescents conducted in New Zealand (Krueger 1999), and in investigations of adults in the United States (Elkins et al. 2004, McGue et al. 1999). These previous studies demonstrated a strong association between Negative Emotionality and alcohol use disorder.

Multiple-Drug Use and Drug-Specific Personality Factors

The similarity of personality profiles among users of different types of drugs may be partly due to the high incidence of multiple-drug use, especially in those with more extreme levels of SUD. Conway et al. (2003) tested patients in treatment for SUD by means of the NEO-PI Five-Factor Inventory as well as additional personality questionnaires. The number of drugs used, but not the specific drug of choice, was associated with more extreme scores that indicated greater behavioral disinhibition and lower conscientiousness. The hazardous use of several addictive drugs may prevent the identification of personality factors associated with a specific drug.

Impulsivity and Negative Emotionality

Two general personality factors are associated with the hazardous use of alcohol, nicotine, and illicit drugs. The factors of poor impulse control and a propensity for negative emotional states are implicated in the occurrence of SUD by investigations guided by the theories of Costa and McCrae, Tellegen, and Cloninger. As summarized in Table 8.3, these factors, featured in all three theories, contribute to a personality profile often seen in respondents with SUD. These personality factors are not drug-specific, but are associated with a general tendency for SUD, including simultaneous use of multiple drugs. Aggregate results from large-scale surveys reveal that these characteristics are more prevalent in respondents suffering from SUD.

These behavioral tendencies – especially that of greater impulsivity – are partially determined by genetic predisposition (Chapter 5) and so contribute to biologically inherited vulnerability for SUD.

The factor of negative emotionality consists of a high incidence of anger, hostility, anxiety, depression, and other forms of distress. Prospective studies with adolescents show that this factor can predict the development of SUD. Distressing emotions often abate with abstinence and recovery from an addictive lifestyle, suggesting that negative emotionality is a consequence, as well as a possible cause of SUD.

Table 8.3 Personality factors and traits associated with substance use disorders

Relevant personality factors for each theory and differences associated with SUD	Specific traits for each factor
Costa and McCrae five-factor theory	
Neuroticism (higher)	Anxiety, angry hostility, depression, impulsivity
Conscientiousness (lower)	Low self-discipline, irresponsible, low sense of duty, undependable
Agreeableness/antagonism (lower)	Cynical, skeptical of others
Cloninger tridimensional theory	
Novelty seeking (higher)	Impulsivity, quick-tempered, extravagant, disorderly
Tellegen three-factor theory	
Negative emotionality (higher)	Emotional distress, aggression, anger
Constraint (lower)	Impulsive, risk taking

Note. Personality factors consist of several related traits, which are characteristic ways of thinking and acting. Questionnaires, designed specifically for a particular system or theory, provide personality profiles that indicate the strength of each factor in various groups tested. Certain factors are stronger in many adults with substance use disorders. Similar profiles are also typical of adolescents who eventually develop SUD. The factors listed here do not include all those featured in each theory. Only the factors shown to be different in those with SUD by at least two groups of investigators are included. Results summarized here are based on investigations of SUD or heavy use of alcohol, nicotine, cannabis, heroin, or cocaine.

Impulsivity indicates inability to restrain behavior, a low degree of self-discipline, and a tendency for risk taking. Impulsivity and related behavioral tendencies appear to be precursors of problematic use of drugs as well as associated with other forms of externalizing behavior disorders. This important topic is discussed further in the following section.

Impulsivity and SUD

The previous discussion of personality disorders, traits and theories clearly implicates *impulsivity*, as evaluated by clinicians and/or as measured by personality questionnaires, as an important part of SUD. The study of impulsivity includes several lines of research: neurological, developmental, genetic, behavioral and personality (Dalley et al. 2011, Iacono et al. 2008, Perry and Carrol 2008, Verdejo-Garcia et al. 2008, Li and Sinha 2008). Impulsivity, broadly defined, refers to a deficiency in regulation of behavior – especially inappropriate or maladaptive actions. Substance use disorders are a prime example of failure to restrain harmful behavior.

The tendency to "go for it" in response to an opportunity for a desirable experience, while disregarding the probable hazards of such action, may be the most basic form of impulsivity, with obvious relevance to SUD. *Urgency*, or the very strong impulse to act, can underlie disinhibited behavior, as can impairment in processes that normally restrain inappropriate responses (de Wit and Richards 2004, Dick et al. 2010).

To illustrate both sides of the motivational conflict typical of some drug use opportunities, an adolescent might strongly desire the excitement, peer acceptance, and pleasurable intoxication of binge drinking. Embarrassing behavior, nausea and vomiting, accidents, and sexual exploitation would be possible adverse outcomes of such intoxication. Failure to contemplate or disregard of these hazards would then result in a choice to participate in the alluring, if risky, behavior.

Several factors contribute to the control of behavior, and especially to the failure of behavioral restraint (Evenden 1999). One form of impulsivity is a tendency to act quickly without much forethought, reflection, or consideration of consequences (Figure 8.2). A related but separate tendency is a preference for immediate small incentives at the expense of greater but delayed rewards. Risk acceptance and susceptibility to boredom (short attention span) can also influence the balance between approach to rewards and restraint of behavior.

The role of sensation seeking as a behavioral trait facilitating drug use and possible SUD was advanced by Zuckerman (1994). An attraction for new and exciting experiences, susceptibility to boredom, and inability to maintain concentration are sometimes interrelated, and all are associated with drug use at an early age (Gullo

Figure 8.2 Impulsive acts often occur without much forethought. Photo: Mint Images / Mint Images RF / Getty Images.

and Dawe 2008, Iacono et al. 2008). However, there are differences among these behavioral tendencies and all do not necessarily imply impulse-control difficulties. Eysenck (1993) describes a trait of *venturesomeness*, which is a willingness to take risks, such as in contact sports or other exciting but hazardous activities. Such behavior need not be impulsive, in that it might require careful planning and execution (e.g., skydiving, mountain-climbing). Such a risk-tolerating tendency could promote initial drug use, and perhaps further progression toward abuse and addiction.

Impulsivity can be measured by at least three general methods. The personality test instruments (self-report questionnaires) discussed previously include items intended to detect impulsiveness (Whiteside and Lynam 2001). Self-report questionnaires have also been developed specifically to assess certain aspects of impulsiveness (e.g., the Barratt Impulsiveness Scale; Patton et al. 1995). Although the self-report measures that are in wide use have been well validated, these questionnaire test results are probably influenced to some extent by social desirability (i.e., biased toward "socially acceptable" responses).

Behavioral tests, most of which are less influenced by the factor just mentioned, are a second method of measuring impulsiveness. These tests are conducted in behavioral laboratories under controlled conditions. Ratings of behavior by trained observers are a third indicator of impulsiveness often used in studies of children.

Some investigators maintain that impulsiveness is most important during the early tentative phases of drug use (e.g., Kreek et al. 2005, Cloninger 2004). However, according to most scientists who study addiction, impulsive tendencies facilitate SUD at all stages of its development (e.g., Perry and Carrol 2008, Verdejo-Garcia et al. 2008, de Wit 2009, de Wit and Richards 2004).

Compulsive use of drugs is a primary characteristic of addiction – the most severe form of SUD. The relationship between compulsivity and impulsivity is complex, and not completely understood. It is generally thought that impulsive behavior is driven mainly by positive reinforcement and compulsive behavior by negative reinforcement (Koob and Le Moal 2006). However, impulsive and compulsive behavior are sometimes considered as being different points on a single continuum of disturbances of behavioral control (Belin et al. 2008).

Neurological Factors and Impulse-Control Deficit

Abnormalities of neurological function (described in Chapter 5) underlie increased urgency or reward-sensitivity as well as the impaired behavioral inhibition characteristic of SUD. A lower density of dopamine receptors, seen in many heavy users of addictive drugs, are thought to contribute to malfunction of both the basic behavior-controlling brain systems (the "go-system" and the "stop-system"). The neurological abnormalities may precede drug usage, but studies with animal subjects show that chronic administration of addictive drugs produces persistent changes in dopamine function. Heavy drug use probably increases malfunction of specific brain systems in vulnerable individuals (Gullo and Potenza 2014).

Stress impairs executive control of behavior (decision-making) and increases impulsivity (Garavan and Hester 2007, Li and Sinha 2008). In individuals with SUD, stress also increases craving for drugs (Chapter 7).

Deficient control of impulsive behavior, as well as difficulties with sustaining attention and concentration are prominent features of attention-deficit hyperactivity disorder (ADHD). Elkins and colleagues found that a diagnosis of ADHD predicted use of tobacco, alcohol and illicit drugs by age fourteen and SUD by age eighteen (Elkins et al. 2007). ADHD in children and adolescents is a definite risk factor for development of SUD (Iacono et al. 2008, Groman et al. 2009).

As with other correlates of SUD (e.g., anxiety) impulsiveness seems to be a consequence as well as a predictor of excessive drug use. Most addictive drugs, and especially alcohol and stimulants (cocaine, amphetamine, and methamphetamine), can disinhibit behavior during a state of intoxication. This acute drug effect has often been demonstrated in controlled laboratory tests of human subjects (e.g., for alcohol, Dougherty et al. 2008, 2015). These effects are usually situation-specific, and do not occur in all drug users. However, this loosening of restraint can exacerbate bouts of heavy drug use, increasing SUD severity. However, SUD-related impulsivity is not entirely a result of overt intoxication. Personality questionnaires and behavioral tests reveal poor impulse control in many respondents with SUD who are presumably drug-free at the time of data collection. The greater impulsivity often precedes the SUD, and can also be a lingering effect of heavy drug use (Koob and Le Moal 2006).

Behavioral Tests of Impulse Control

Several behavioral tests, administered in laboratory settings, are used to investigate response inhibition in both healthy subjects and in heavy users of addictive drugs. These tests can also assist neuropsychologists in their assessment of the behavioral effects of brain damage. Tests of cognitive impulsivity, such as the Matching Familiar Figures Test (Kagan 1966), require information processing before a correct response can be made. Other instruments, including the Stroop Test (MacLeod 1991) and the Stop Signal Task (Logan et al. 1984) require little deliberation, and simply measure the ability to withhold a prepotent response. In the Iowa Gambling Task (Bechara et al. 2000) and similar tests, subjects can choose between small, certain gains and larger but more risky options.

An extensive research literature indicates that groups of drug-addicted subjects show significant performance deficits on all these behavioral tests of response inhibition (reviewed by Perry and Carrol 2008, Verdejo-Garcia et al. 2008). As with the personality inventories, the behavioral tests of subjects with SUD are typically conducted in the nondrugged condition. The differences mentioned here do not result from acute drug effects.

Impulsive Choice and Delay Discounting

In addition to its effect on the commission of a particular action, impulsivity also influences response choice. Choices among several possible behaviors, with each having a different consequence, are part of everyone's daily life. Delayed consequences, either beneficial or harmful, often have less controlling influence on behavior than do immediate consequences. *Delay discounting* (discussed in Chapter 7) is a basic principle of reinforcement and behavior control.

Use of recreational drugs with abuse potential usually provides some type of immediate pleasure, or relief from conditions such as boredom or anxiety. The many possible adverse consequences, ranging from the mini-withdrawal of alcohol hangover through life-disrupting addiction or lung cancer are delayed for hours or years. The lengthy time delay, plus the uncertainty of such outcomes, considerably reduces their influence on impulsive choice to use the drug.

Although delayed incentives are generally less valued than immediate payoffs of equal value, the strength of this time-dependent difference varies among individuals and is an indicator of impulsiveness. Many studies demonstrate greater delay discounting in subjects with SUD as compared to healthy subjects, meaning that individuals with problematic substance use are even more likely than control subjects to choose smaller, sooner incentives over larger, later rewards (Perry and Carrol 2008, Reynolds 2006, Verdejo-Garcia et al. 2008, de Wit and Richards 2004). These differences are seen in individuals with use disorders of alcohol, nicotine, heroin and cocaine. There is also some evidence of greater delay discounting in those with marijuana use problems (Bobova et al. 2009, Kollins 2003).

As with many other correlates of SUD, establishing the direction of causality between delay discounting and heavy drug use is difficult. In comparison to subjects with no history of alcohol use problems, Petry and colleagues found a greater degree of discounting in actively drinking alcoholic subjects (Petry et al. 2001). Smaller differences were seen in thirty-day abstinent subjects, suggesting that the heavy alcohol use contributed to the greater delay discounting, which is to some extent reversible. Because these subjects were designated by their drug use histories rather than by random assignment to experimental groups, preexisting differences in delay discounting could be responsible for the results. A moderate degree of delay discounting might well facilitate abstinence, and a greater degree of the behavioral tendency would supposedly make abstinence more difficult. Results similar to those of the Petry investigation were observed after cessation of tobacco smoking, and with abstinence from other addictive drugs (Heil et al. 2006, Kirby and Petry 2004).

A preexisting tendency toward greater discounting of delayed consequences seems a likely risk factor for early use of tobacco, alcohol and other drugs, and several studies suggest such an association. Adolescents with higher levels of delay discounting are more likely to use tobacco (Reynolds et al. 2007), alcohol (Field et al. 2007), and other drugs in an abusive manner (Kollins 2003). Most of these studies did not assess delay discounting prior to drug use. However, the relatively brief drug use history of these subjects suggests that the tendency for impulsive choices did predate, and so may have facilitated the early involvement with drugs.

A greater degree of delay discounting is predictive of relapse after a period of abstinence from addictive drug use (Perry and Carrol 2008, Yoon et al. 2007). An important goal of a drug treatment program is to instill appreciation for the benefits of a drug-free life. Some rewards of long-term sobriety are delayed, especially as compared to the immediate incentive of a drink, a smoke, or a drug. Discounting of delayed rewards is an intrinsic feature of human behavior, and can be quite difficult to overcome, especially after a long history of heavy drug use.

Conclusions about Impulsivity and SUD

Impulsivity, clearly related to SUD, is present to some extent in all people, but is often exaggerated in those with problematic use of addictive drugs. Although acute or chronic drug effects can increase some types of impulsivity, poor impulse control often precedes and so promotes SUD. The increased risk of dangerous drug use in impulsive individuals may be most critical in early stages of SUD, but the lessened behavioral control facilitates problematic drug use at all stages of its development. Difficulty in restraining behavior also decreases the probability of long-term abstinence and recovery from SUD.

Difficulty in withholding responses cannot account for all addictive behaviors. Disordered drug use can result in confrontation by family or employers, or arrest by police. Addicted individuals often circumvent such sanctions by devious behavior that is not at all impulsive.

Evenden (1999) points out that the "feeding and hiding" of SUD often requires much nonimpulsive behavior. Locating and acquiring illicit drugs may require much deliberate effort and "foraging" (searching in many places until a source is located), and in such instances cannot be a rash, poorly planned action. Many individuals addicted to a culturally accepted drug such as alcohol often take elaborate measures to conceal their compulsive excessive use, and the resulting secretive dishonesty typically becomes part of the addictive lifestyle. As with the procurement of illegal drugs, such deception involves careful control and self-monitoring of behavior in attempts to prevent others from detecting their problematic drug use. Such behavior is not impulsive, and is often a prominent feature of SUD.

Some investigators of addictive behavior point out that even impulsive behavior is actually a choice, and not an uncontrollable reflexive action (e.g., Goldman 2002, Heyman 2009, Skog 2000, Somers and Satel 2005). However, in SUD the choice of drug use is often made without thoughtful deliberation and with a sense of loss of control (West 2006). "Loss of control" presents an interesting philosophical question, and the concept is important to a traditional disease theory account of addiction (Chapter 3). Addicted individuals often maintain that they are unable to control their drug intake. However, West makes the observation that even though drug addiction may eventually be fatal, an addicted individual is quite unlikely to take a drug if he believes that action will immediately cause death. Drug-dependent persons are rarely faced with such a certain outcome. A quote attributed to the late William F. Buckley Jr., who suffered fatal emphysema after many years of nicotine addiction: "Yes, smoking may eventually kill me, but I am not convinced that this particular cigarette will do so!."

A final consideration about impulsivity relates to its role in the ongoing, nondeviant behavior of human beings. Unplanned actions are not always dangerous, and risky choices may have beneficial outcomes. Many behaviors are spontaneous, including creative and artistic endeavors and a great deal of pleasurable, recreational activity. Risk taking is usually intrinsic to entrepreneurial actions, which when successful receive rewards and approval. The same holds for exploration, innovation and much activity in a dynamic society. Spontaneity, closely related to impulsiveness, is a valued attribute of youth and adolescence. Learning to enjoy (as well as to moderate) these tendencies is important in acquiring a productive and satisfying level of maturity (Gullo and Dawe 2008). However, the impulsivity of adolescence does contribute to experimentation with and dangerous use of drugs with definite addiction potential.

Drug Use and SUD in Adolescence

Monitoring the future is a large-scale survey of self-reported use of alcohol, tobacco, and other addictive drugs by approximately 45,000 US students in the eighth, tenth, and twelfth grades. Survey results also assess student perceptions of drug availability and hazards of drug use. Each year since 1975, the University of Michigan has conducted this survey, sponsored by the National Institute on Drug Abuse. Table 8.4 presents a summary of the survey results for 2018. The percentage of students with drug use experience is smaller for the tenth- and eighth-grade students, but still represents a considerable proportion of respondents. Representative of this age difference, 23 percent of eighth graders reported having consumed alcohol at least once, and 9 percent had experienced alcohol intoxication (National Institute of Drug Abuse 2018).

The **Monitoring the Future survey** reveals that the rate of cannabis use by high school students in the United States has been relatively stable for several years and that in 2018 only about 27 percent of seniors thought that regular cannabis use offers risk of great harm.

Regular use of illicit drugs – other than cannabis – or unsupervised use of pharmaceutical drugs has decreased slightly over previous years.

Alcohol consumption and intoxication in twelfth-grade students has decreased significantly over the past five years, and self-reported binge drinking (five or

Table 8.4 Use of addictive drugs by high school seniors

Use frequency	At least once	Previous month	Daily
Alcohol	58.5	30.2	1.2
Cannabis	43.6	22.2	5.8
Tobacco	23.8	7.6	3.6
Nicotine vaping	–	20.9	–
Any vaping	42.9	26.7	–
Cocaine	3.9	1.1	–
Any prescription drug	15.5	4.2	–
Heroin	0.8	0.2	–

Note. Entries are estimates for percentage of twelfth-grade respondents self-reporting drug or substance use for each use level, as indicated by the Monitoring the Future survey for 2018. Nicotine vaping refers to inhalation of nicotine vapor by means of an electronic delivery device. Any vaping refers to inhalation of vapor from nicotine, cannabis extract, or non–drug flavored solutions. See text for further information on vaping of nicotine and cannabis extracts. Entries for "any prescription drug" indicate that stimulants, tranquilizers, sedatives, or opioids were taken without a prescription or other medical authorization. No information was provided by NIDA for daily use of some drugs or substances.

Source. National Institute of Drug Abuse (2020).

more drinks on one drinking occasion) has also become less frequent. At its peak in 1998, 31.5 percent seniors reported binge drinking in the previous two weeks. In 2017 the prevalence of binge drinking was 16.6 percent, with a further significant reduction to 13.8 percent in 2018.

In 2018 regular tobacco use was at its lowest point since in the history of the survey. However "vaping" – the inhalation of flavored vapor by means of an electronic delivery device has increased markedly in eighth-, tenth-, and twelfth-grade students in only one year. Although some respondents report that they inhale only vapor from nondrug solutions, rates for previous-month vaping of nicotine by senior students almost doubled from 11 percent 2017 to 20.9 percent in 2018. As further discussed in Chapter 11, vaping of nicotine is considered to be a risk for the transition to tobacco cigarettes. Prevalence of past-year cannabis vaping by seniors also increased – from 9.5 percent in 2017 to 13.1 percent in 2018.

The prevalence of drug use by older adolescents is similar to that seen in adults, in that a majority drink alcohol at least occasionally and a much smaller percentage use tobacco or illicit drugs (Figure 8.3). Most adolescent drug users (with the exception of those consuming tobacco) are not addicted, but use disorders in some individuals emerge during adolescence (Substance Abuse and Mental Health Services Administration 2018). The highest prevalence of SUD occurs between late

Figure 8.3 A majority of older adolescents drink alcohol at least occasionally. Photo: sturti / E+ / Getty Images.

adolescence (approximately age eighteen) and early adulthood (mid-twenties), so many adolescents whose drug use has not yet progressed to diagnosable SUD are in the early stages of the disorder.

One of the most robust findings in alcohol research is the association between early initiation of alcohol use and risk of eventual alcohol addiction (McGue and Iacono 2008). Several studies show that individuals who commence more than experimental alcohol use prior to age fifteen are four times as likely to eventually have a diagnosis of alcohol addiction in comparison to those who first drink after age twenty (Grant and Dawson 1997, Hingson et al. 2006, Keyes et al. 2007). A similar increased risk for development of alcohol use disorder is seen in adolescents who start regular tobacco use (smoking) at a very early age (Grucza and Bierut 2006).

Even with the increased risk of SUD that accompanies early drug use, most adolescent drug users (again with the exception of tobacco) do not become addicted. Frequent users typically adopt more responsible use levels when faced with the demands of adult life, including full-time employment, marriage, becoming a parent, or (with some obvious exceptions) attending college (Lee and Sher 2018). The college environment increases and extends the opportunity for irresponsible alcohol use, including binge drinking (Merrill and Carey 2016, O'Malley 2004). Although attendance at a college is in some respects a time of prolonged adolescence for some students, most of those who drink heavily in college moderate their use when they assume adult responsibilities.

Regular use of tobacco, especially when combined with regular alcohol use, is the most probable initial step toward further serious drug use (Grucza and Bierut 2006, Vega and Gil 2005). Few adolescents who never or only rarely use tobacco become heavy users of addictive drugs, including alcohol or marijuana (Orlando et al. 2005, Myers and Kelly 2006). This "gateway effect" of tobacco use might be due to a specific action of nicotine on the brain, as suggested by animal studies (McMillen et al. 2005). Smoking by young adolescents might also be an early expression of genetically determined general addictive vulnerability that promotes eventual addictive use of other drugs (Kendler and Prescott 2006, McGue and Iacono 2005, 2008, Vanyukov et al. 2012). Exposure to tobacco-using peers also appears to encourage use of other drugs, so the social environment is also a risk factor (Ferguson et al. 2002, Kirisci et al. 2007).

Tobacco use by adolescents has dropped to historically low levels in recent years. However, even if the prevalence of adolescent tobacco use continues to decline, addiction to other drugs will still be an important public health problem. Several years of observation will be required before it can be determined whether

Figure 8.4 Inhalation of vapor containing nicotine is more prevalent among teenagers than is tobacco smoking. Photo: sestovic / E+ / Getty Images.

the recent increase in nicotine vaping by adolescents incurs a risk of addiction for all drugs similar to that of smoking tobacco (Figure 8.4).

Hazards of Adolescent Drug Use

Although most adolescent drug users do not become addicted to alcohol, cannabis or other drugs, drug use still presents special risks for teenagers. Adolescence is a critical developmental stage and a time of challenging personal and social choices. Societal concern about drug use by adolescents is indicated by ongoing and expensive efforts to monitor this behavior as in the NIDA project described above. Misuse of drugs is but one of the many ways in which a young person can self-inflict long-term damage during this vulnerable stage of life.

Adolescents often display high levels of impulsiveness, feelings of invulnerability, and have less regard for possibly bad outcomes of dangerous activities. Alcohol is a leading contributor to injury, and is a major cause of death for people under the age of twenty-one (Patrick and Azar 2018). Simple ignorance of some dangers of drug use, such as death from extreme alcohol overdose, may accompany these impulsive tendencies. During the process of becoming an adult many new situations are encountered and new skills required, ranging from complex social interactions to driving an automobile. These demands and risks have been referred to as the "minefield of adolescence." When addictive drugs are used, adverse consequences become more probable.

Adolescents tend to use drugs to produce extreme levels of intoxication, increasing the hazards of this behavior. A similar pattern of alcohol and other drug use by adolescents is common in many European countries as well as in the United States and Canada (Hibell et al. 2004). Some adults, especially those with SUD, may drink or use drugs in this manner, but for many adolescents, even those who only use drugs "recreationally" extreme intoxication is frequently the desired effect. Two examples are the use of inhalants, and binge drinking – "drinking to get drunk."

Inhalation of various solvents, as contained in glue or paint, gasoline, and several types of gases, can produce an extreme altered state of consciousness sought by some adolescents. Very young individuals who might not have access to alcohol or other drugs can easily obtain these chemicals. The Monitoring the Future survey indicates that inhalant abuse, although not common, is more frequent in eighth-grade than in tenth or twelfth-grade students. In 2018, the percentage of respondents who had used these substances recently for intoxication was 1.8, 1.0, and 0.7 percent for these three age levels, respectively. Even though inhalant use is relatively rare, the practice is extremely dangerous in that brain or other organ damage is possible, and deaths due to asphyxiation sometimes occur.

Binge drinking, defined as consuming five or more standard alcoholic drinks on any one occasion, is much more prevalent among adolescents than is use of solvents or gases for intoxication. In the United States this manner of drinking alcohol by adolescents has declined markedly from the highest incidence in the late 1990s. In 2018, 16 percent of high school seniors reported binge drinking within the two previous weeks, and 5.3 percent of adolescents ages twelve to seventeen binge drank in the month previous to the NSDUH survey (National Institute of Drug Abuse 2018, Substance Abuse and Mental Health Services Administration 2018). Binge drinking can have dangerous consequences for adolescents, including consumption of even larger amounts of alcohol (Jones et al. 2018, Patrick and Azar 2018). However, binge drinking per se does not satisfy diagnostic criteria for an alcohol use disorder.

In contrast to heavily drinking adults, many alcohol-abusing adolescents have not had sufficient alcohol exposure to cause major bodily physical damage. However, the immature brain may be particularly vulnerable to some long-term effects caused by alcohol (Chambers et al. 2003, Spear 2018, Thatcher and Clark 2008). Structural abnormalities have been found in adolescents with alcohol use disorders. Differences in size of the hippocampus and in microstructure of white matter brain tissue are more pronounced in individuals who commence heavy drinking in early adolescence, as compared to those who start drinking later and consume less alcohol (De Billis et al. 2000, Jones et al. 2018). Because brain structure is rarely examined before alcohol consumption begins, the abnormalities could precede and possibly contribute to the disordered alcohol use.

In addition to the possibility of actual tissue damage, alcohol affects the immature brain somewhat differently, and in ways that can promote abuse, addiction and dangerous behavior. In teenage drinkers, high levels of alcohol intoxication readily promote arousal and excitement, with less intense delayed aversive effects. These different responses to alcohol are well documented for immature animals. The aversive aftereffects of alcohol (hangover) which to some extent discourage heavy drinking in adults are less pronounced in immature animals. Young animals also show relatively greater arousal and less sedating and motor-impairment effects from alcohol as compared to mature animals (Shnitko et al. 2016, Spear and Swartzwelder 2014). Clinical observations suggest that similar differences occur in adolescent humans.

Alcohol's greater arousing effects in adolescents often results in highly rewarding subjective feelings during intoxication, increased chance of reckless behavior, and a lesser degree of distressing physical aftereffects. With unfortunate consequences for their health and safety, adolescents apparently enjoy getting drunk more, and pay less of a "price" in the form of a hangover, than do most adults. As discussed in Chapter 7, expectation of more arousing and less sedating alcohol effects are associated with heavier drinking patterns.

One relatively subtle effect of heavy drug use during adolescence is interference with the process of emotional maturation (Hesselbrock and Hesselbrock 2006). The quick and easy, if temporary, relief from boredom, depression or anxiety promotes reliance on drugs for this purpose. Self-medication by drugs can promote SUD, and this practice can become habitual during a difficult adolescence. Heavy substance use could decrease practice of self-control, and impair connection with supportive relationships that enhance self-regulation without the use of drugs (Willis et al. 2006).

Early Indicators and Risk Factors for SUD

Many investigators consider events and conditions during the early years of life as critical for the eventual occurrence of SUD. "In fact, alcohol abuse and dependence are probably best characterized as developmental disorders, with sequelae that play out throughout the life span" (Faden and Goldman 2004, p. 107). A number of long-term longitudinal studies identify early indicators and risk factors for early drug use and subsequent occurrence of SUD (Costello 2007). Some, such as temperament and behavioral characteristics (restlessness, distractibility, impulsiveness) appear in preschool children as early as three years of age (Caspi et al. 1996). Obviously not all children with these common characteristics develop SUD, but they are early predictors of higher probability of a wide range of problem behaviors, including early alcohol and tobacco use (Iacono et al. 2008). Genetic predisposition influences these early temperamental characteristics, which also interact with environmental conditions in the determination of behavior during subsequent stages of life (Hessselbrock and Hesselbrock 2006, Kendler and Prescott 2006, Szalavitz 2016, Thatcher and Clark 2008).

Conduct Disorder and Other Psychopathologies

One of the most reliable childhood and adolescent indicators of later problematic drug use is conduct disorder (e.g., Cohen et al. 2007, Fergusson et al. 2007). Conduct disorder is a psychiatric syndrome listed in the DSM-5, and is often considered to be essentially a childhood or adolescent version of adult antisocial personality disorder. Conduct disorder can be diagnosed in children at least seven years of age who consistently disregard the rights of others and persist in such behavior as lying, truancy, vandalism, and aggression.

Conduct disorder is often a component of various forms of child and adolescent psychopathology that are risk factors for either concurrent or later-occurring SUD (McGue and Iacono 2005, Roberts et al. 2007). Conduct disorder, evaluated at age thirteen, predicted the development of abuse and dependence of alcohol, marijuana and other drugs over a period of thirty years in a community sample of 680 participants (Cohen et al. 2007).

Attention-deficit hyperactivity disorder (ADHD) is also a definite risk factor for SUD (Iacono et al. 2008, Groman et al. 2009).

Neurobehavior Disinhibition

The behavioral and emotional difficulties that constitute risks for SUD in adolescence and adulthood indicate a generalized tendency of neurobehavior disinhibition (Tarter et al. 2004), which is sometimes designated as childhood psychological dysregulation (Thatcher and Clark 2008). Three distinct but related components (behavioral, emotional, and cognitive) contribute to this deficiency of self-regulation and inhibitory control. Several measures of behavior, combined with tests and evaluations of cognition and emotional responses, were used to derive the construct of neurobehavior disinhibition.

The neurological abnormalities discussed in Chapters 5 and 6 that are often found in individuals with SUD are thought to underlie the lack of inhibitory control. Two of these differences in brain activity are the diminished P300 EEG response, and less effective function of prefrontal areas of the cerebral cortex (Yancey et al. 2013).

According to Tarter and colleagues, the *cognitive* component of neurobehavior disinhibition includes difficulty with executive functions such as control of attention, abstracting, strategic problem solving, self-monitoring, and goal-directed motivation, These abilities are deficient in children who are at high risk for SUD (Giancola and Tarter 1999). The *behavioral undercontrol* of impulsivity was discussed earlier as an important aspect of SUD in both adolescents and adults. The *emotional* component includes sudden unpredictable mood changes, irritability, anger rumination, and overreaction to provocation. In younger children, there is also a lack of "soothability," including inability to calm oneself or to be comforted by others after emotional arousal. These emotional tendencies are sometimes referred to as a difficult temperament.

Male children of parents with SUD had significantly higher neurobehavior disinhibition scores than those of parents without the diagnosis of SUD (Tarter et al. 2003, 2004). These scores in turn predicted SUD for alcohol and marijuana that developed between ages twelve and nineteen. In addition to composing a risk factor for adolescent SUD, high levels of neurobehavior disinhibition also manifest as conduct disorder in childhood and antisocial and borderline personality disorders in adulthood (Thatcher and Clark 2008). The deficiency of psychological self-regulation has genetic origins, but also may be promoted by parenting practices that are more prevalent in adults suffering from SUD (Beaver et al. 2008). This nonbiological parental influence is further discussed below.

The relationship of behavioral and emotional self-control to the use of alcohol, tobacco and marijuana was investigated by analysis of the self-report questionnaires of 1,000 middle and high school students (Willis et al. 2006). Students reporting better self-control of emotions and behavior were less likely to use the substances. Those with less emotional and behavioral self-control were more likely to use drugs or alcohol, and were also prone to associate with deviant peers. Coping with negative emotions was often given by these students as a reason for drinking or smoking tobacco or marijuana.

Peer Association and Influences

Association with deviant peers, including those who use drugs at an early age, is a definite adolescent risk factor for substance use and SUD (Bray et al. 2003, Cornelius et al. 2007). The influence of drug-using friends and peers on the development of SUD is an environmental risk factor, rather than a biological or temperamental tendency to initiate and continue drug use. However, there is much evidence that personal characteristics, including a low level of Neurobehavioral Inhibition, play a role in the selection of friends and associates during adolescence (Cornelius et al. 2007, Kirisci et al. 2007, 2009). A tendency toward deviance and poor self-regulation often encourages association with those of similar attitudes and behaviors (Gifford-Smith et al. 2005). Kirisci and colleagues maintain that the selection of deviant and behaviorally dysregulated friends by an adolescent with these characteristics is a principal pathway for mediation between neurobehavior disinhibition and the development of SUD. Therefore, contact with peers who use drugs at an early age seems to be both a result of, as well as a cause, of such use by adolescents.

Attitudes and Expectations

Andrews and colleagues tracked attitudes about the use of alcohol and tobacco, and actual use of these substances in 712 elementary school students (second through fifth grade) over a period of seven years (Andrews et al. 2008). These respondents also indicated their view (social image) of individuals who used these substances, and their estimates of how many of their friends and acquaintances smoked tobacco or drank alcohol. These investigators found that children's early cognitions about alcohol or tobacco use predicted their actual use in later years of the study. The perceived social images of those that smoked or drank and their estimates of the extent of use by their peers changed in a positive direction during the seven-year period. However, these attitudes and estimates also predicted actual use of the substances. In other words, children and young adolescents that believed more of their peers drank or smoked were also more approving of drug use, and were more likely to eventually engage in such activity. Attitudes and other cognitions associated with adolescent drug use are initially formed very early in life.

Parenting Practices and Childhood Stress

Certain parenting practices are linked to early use of drugs, including tobacco and alcohol. Like most risk factors, these events during early childhood and adolescence are probabilistic, rather than certain determinants of SUD. One of these factors is a low level of parental monitoring of children and adolescents. Several studies have shown that inadequate supervision of adolescents increases the likelihood of alcohol or drug use, and subsequent SUD (e.g., Clark et al. 2005). In addition to basic awareness of children's activity, ongoing positive parental engagement with adolescents also promotes mature levels of socialization and is associated with low levels of disruptive behavior and SUD. Even in adolescents with neurobehavioral disinhibition, supportive interaction with parents encourages the development of self-regulation and so reduces behavioral undercontrol (Tarter et al. 2004). Low levels of parental involvement and inadequate monitoring of children's activity are sometimes considered as less severe forms of child neglect.

Severe neglect, maltreatment and abuse of children are major risk factors for several psychiatric disorders, including SUD (Dunne et al. 2002, Moran et al. 2004). The prevalence of adolescent and adult alcohol problems increases with the severity of childhood maltreatment and the number of childhood adversities (Bulik et al. 2001, Dube et al. 2002, Hasin and Grant 2015).

Kaufman and colleagues compared the alcohol and tobacco use of a group of children who suffered from various types of maltreatment with that of a demographically matched comparison group (Kaufman et al. 2007). The maltreatment was determined by protective-service records, case-workers, parents and the accounts given by the children. Maltreatment involved physical and sexual abuse, severe neglect, emotional abuse and exposure to domestic violence. Posttraumatic stress disorder was diagnosed in 50 percent of the maltreated children. Other psychiatric disorders including oppositional defiant disorder and childhood conduct disorder were also significantly more frequent in the maltreated group. Those in the maltreated group first drank alcohol at a mean age of 11.2 years, as compared to the mean age of 13.5 for the comparison group. At a two-year follow-up, the maltreated group adolescents were seven times more likely to drink alcohol weekly, and were twice as likely to be regular tobacco users. Parental SUD was more prevalent in the maltreatment group, but the degree of maltreatment predicted early and problematic alcohol and tobacco use even after adjustment for the factor of parental drug use.

Low socioeconomic status is a moderate environmental risk factor for SUD, the risk being mediated by such factors as delinquent friends and economically disadvantaged neighborhoods (Collins et al. 2016, Hansen and Chen 2007, Swendsen et al. 2009). Severe child neglect and other types of child maltreatment are more prevalent in low-income populations (Dunn et al. 2002, Heilig et al. 2016, National Institute of Drug Abuse 2017).

Systematic surveys, observations of mental health professionals and social workers, and other sources of evidence clearly indicate that SUD "runs in families." Children of parents with SUD are often at greatly increased risk for developing problematic drug or alcohol use. As discussed in Chapter 6 of this text, biological inheritance (genetic predisposition) contributes approximately 60 percent of the multivariate influence on the occurrence of SUD. A dysfunctional, disrupted family, with neglectful or abusive parents amplifies the genetic risk, including that of neurobehavioral disinhibition.

Dysfunctional parenting can result from many sources, such as difficult living conditions or medical problems and psychiatric disorders. SUD is a frequent source of parental dysfunction, and often results in children's modeling of heavy substance use in addition to other inadequate or stress-producing parenting actions. Neglect and maltreatment of children is more prevalent in parents with active SUD. However, some of the familial risk is reduced when parents are in stable recovery or whose drug use does not impair their parenting practices (Dunn et al. 2002, Tarter et al. 2004).

Conclusions about Childhood, Adolescence, and SUD

Most individuals who use alcohol, tobacco, or marijuana first do so during their adolescent years. A majority of high school seniors has had some experience with alcohol, nearly half have tried cannabis, and a smaller number inhale nicotine vapor or are regular users of tobacco. Regular alcohol or tobacco use before age fifteen is associated with a fourfold increase in probability of eventual alcohol use disorder.

Teenage tendencies for risk taking are often increased by intoxication, and alcohol is more arousing, less sedating, and causes fewer unpleasant delayed effects for young users. "Social drinking" or use of other drugs in groups of adolescents often involves high levels of intoxication that can lead to injury – or death from overdose.

In many cases SUD appears to be a developmental (childhood and adolescent) disorder that has lifelong ramifications. A number of conditions or events during childhood or adolescence are associated with SUD. These risk factors include family history of addiction (genetic predisposition); active SUD in parents; child neglect, maltreatment or traumatic abuse and low socioeconomic status (Box 8.5).

Early indicators are behavioral or temperamental characteristics that further increase the probability of problematic drug use, and so are risk factors in themselves. These early indicators/risk factors include conduct disorder, other behavioral/psychiatric disorders such as ADHD, borderline and other personality disorders, and poor self-control and neurobehavioral disinhibition. The temperamental or behavioral early indicators promote exposure to additional environmental or experiential risk factors. These partly self-determined risk factors are early alcohol or tobacco use, contact with deviant and drug-using peers, and positive expectations and attitudes about drugs and drug users.

Problematic substance use can develop in the absence of known risk factors. However, SUD becomes increasingly probable, and at a younger age, in the presence of multiple factors.

BOX 8.5 Childhood and adolescent risk factors and early indicators of SUD

Risk Factors Not Involving the Individual's Behavior

Family history of SUD (genetic predisposition)
Active SUD or heavy substance use by parents or older siblings
Inadequate parental monitoring of child/adolescent activity
Low level of parental involvement with children
Severe child neglect, abuse, maltreatment (including sexual trauma)
Trauma not involving parents (natural disasters, war, accidents, illness)
Low socioeconomic status or extreme poverty (including the ongoing stress of homelessness)

BOX 8.5 Continued

Early Indicators of SUD Tendency or Vulnerability
Note. Most involve temperamental or behavioral characteristics and are risk
factors as well as early indicators.

  Childhood psychological dysregulation (neurobehavior disinhibition)
  Frequent use of alcohol, tobacco, or illicit drugs before age fifteen
  Conduct disorder
  Difficult temperament, borderline personality disorder
  Other childhood psychiatric disorders (anxiety, depression, ADHD)
  Deviant, drug-using friends and associates
  Positive expectations for drug effects

Conclusions about the Etiology of Substance Use Disorders

Many conditions, events, and behavioral characteristics are associated with the
development of harmful drug use. Some are consequences of heavy drug use, but
several have been identified as risk factors that precede and are thought to cause
or contribute to the occurrence of SUD. Some risk factors may not cause SUD, but
are early indicators of increased vulnerability to the disorder. The specific nature
of interactions among these risk factors probably differs among individual cases
of the disorder. The biopsychosocial view of SUD acknowledges this complex etiology of interrelated vulnerabilities and causes.

Risk factors, as described in previous chapters, include genetic differences, drug
effects on brain function, events occurring during childhood and adolescence,
certain temperamental and personality traits, cognitive processes, and social and
cultural influences. Psychiatric disorders including psychosis, depression, anxiety,
and personality disorders also increase vulnerability to SUD.

Anyone who uses addictive drugs is at some degree of risk for SUD. For many
drug users a considerable amount of exposure (drug-taking) is required for SUD to
develop, and this exposure to the drug actions must also occur under conditions
that maximize the drug's behavioral control (reinforcing effects). In the absence of
additional risk factors, drug use may never escalate to a level of abuse or addiction. Other biological, psychological or social risk factors can promote increased
drug usage or make the individual more vulnerable to SUD with relatively less
drug exposure.

The wide array of risk factors demonstrates that there are different pathways
leading into compulsive and harmful use of psychoactive drugs. Individuals seldom

recognize the critical choice points in these routes into an SUD as they proceed toward a bad outcome of drug use. Robert West maintains that most of our behaviors, including those of addiction, are not often perceived as requiring deliberate choices: "Choice involves conscious consideration of alternatives, by definition. Yet in the flow of behavior, we usually do not consider alternatives – instead, we react to stimuli or execute plans we have made. It is unrealistic to assume that each time an alcohol addict takes a drink s/he is weighing up the costs and benefits. We need to recognize that there is a flow to behavior in which one thing leads to another, and the extent to which we deliberate over it is highly variable" (West 2006, pp. 130–131). Although the flow of behavior is rarely determined by reflective deliberation, some consequences of drug use are dramatic and tragic, such as loss of life due to suicide or accidental overdose. Other losses can result in a life diminished by an accumulation of many less obvious but still destructive consequences. Perhaps "weighing up the costs and benefits" (if recognized) can promote better choices concerning drug use.

Chapter Summary

Previous chapters of this text emphasize that mentally healthy individuals, whose lives are in good order, often initially use addictive drugs for a pleasurable effect. Those with no obvious personality disorder or emotional or mental distress are at some risk for development of SUD. However, the strong association between psychiatric disorders and SUD demonstrates that distressed, unhappy individuals who are dealing with difficult life situations – including emotional or mental disorders – are at even greater risk for dangerous use of addictive drugs.

Approximately half of the individuals diagnosed with schizophrenia or bipolar affective disorder exhibit some form of SUD. The more common disorders of unipolar depression and anxiety are also associated with a greater incidence of SUD – double or triple that seen in the general population. Self-medication is rarely effective for safe, long-term management of emotion or mood states but often drives chronic drug use – and, for some individuals, does so to levels of abuse and addiction.

Personality disorders also frequently co-occur with SUD. Two of these disorders, antisocial and borderline personality, are the closest approximations to an "addictive personality," although this term no longer has much scientific credibility. Individuals with either antisocial or borderline personality disorder are quite likely to use drugs heavily and with harmful consequences. However, many with SUD do not display these troublesome extremes of emotion and behavior.

Impulsivity can facilitate initial drug use, and then promote progression into heavier usage, abuse, and addiction. Behavioral tests and self-report questionnaires reveal that impulsivity is greater in heavy drug users, addicted individuals, and adolescents who eventually develop SUD.

Although poor impulse control is often seen in those with SUD, some addictive behaviors cannot be explained by inability to restrain behavior. Addicted individuals often devise elaborate procedures to acquire drugs and conceal their use. In such cases, behavior is quite well controlled and not at all impulsive.

Adolescence and childhood are of special relevance to the etiology and development of SUD. The most evident adolescent risk factor for SUD is regular use of an addictive drug before age fifteen. Such drug use is an early indicator of addictive vulnerability and is associated with a fourfold increase in the probability of eventual SUD. Other adolescent risk factors include deviant and drug-using friends, expectations of positive drug effects, and impaired self-regulation of behavior, emotions and cognition.

Low levels of parental monitoring of child and adolescent activities are also associated with earlier alcohol and drug use and the concomitant vulnerability to SUD. Extreme neglect or actual maltreatment of children are additional risk factors. A severely dysfunctional family or emotional or sexual abuse increase the risk of a wide range of psychopathologies, including problematic drug use and PTSD.

Most risk factors for SUD described in this chapter involve conditions or situations that make life difficult. Subtle as well as obvious sources of unhappiness constitute a major type of risk factor for SUD. The rapid, often dramatic (if only temporary) drug-produced relief from dysphoric states promotes progression from infrequent drug use into abuse and addiction.

Review Exercises

1. Which psychiatric disorders present the greatest risk for SUD, and why?
2. What personal characteristics are most strongly associated with the co-occurrence of psychiatric care and SUD?
3. Which psychiatric disorders are most likely to be self-medicated with addictive drugs?
4. What characteristics of bipolar disorder and schizophrenia can promote SUD?
5. What are possible common factors that can promote both psychiatric disorders and SUD?
6. Define addictive personality and its limitations as an explanation for SUD.
7. How does impulsivity promote dangerous drug use?
8. What evidence establishes an association between antisocial personality disorder and SUD for alcohol and other addictive drugs?

9. How do the characteristics of borderline personality disorder resemble some features of SUD?
10. What is one important difference between the characteristics of antisocial compared to borderline personality disorder?
11. Describe the incidence and nature of drug use in adolescents.
12. What is a recent major change in recreational use of an addictive drug by adolescents?
13. The text states that "drug use presents special risks for teenagers." Explain this statement.
14. What are some characteristics of conduct disorder and neurobehavior disinhibition that increase the likelihood of SUD for young children?
15. What parental practices during childhood and adolescence predict early use of recreational drugs and increased prevalence of SUD?

Key Terms

categorical personality models (271)

community samples (259)

comorbidity (258)

co-occurring disorders (261)

dimensional personality models (271)

genetic predisposition (260)

Monitoring the Future survey (287)

multiple causal factors (258)

odds ratio (OR) (259)

personality questionnaires (276)

personality traits (276)

posttraumatic stress disorder (PTSD) (267)

Revised NEO Personality Inventory (NEO-PI) (277)

secondary substance use disorder (268)

self-medication theory (261)

third (common) factor (268)

PART IV
Use Disorders with Specific Drugs

PART IV

Use Disorders with Specific Drugs

9

Alcohol
A Dangerous Drug

CHAPTER OUTLINE

LEARNING OBJECTIVES

1. Describe the prevalence of alcohol consumption by age in the United States.
2. Describe the factors that affect the bioavailability of alcohol.
3. Describe the multiple effects of alcohol on the brain and the neurotransmitters involved.
4. Explain how high doses of alcohol produce neurological and hormonal stress responses.
5. Describe the subjective, cognitive, and behavioral effects of alcohol as a function of blood alcohol concentration.
6. Describe the positive and negative reinforcing effects of alcohol.
7. Describe alcohol's undesirable and dangerous effects.
8. Explain how the context and expectancy can affect both experience of and use of drugs.
9. Describe the reasons for and patterns of concurrent use of alcohol and other addictive drugs.

Introductory Vignette: Selling the Proposal

Ken woke up feeling nauseous, shaky, and with a terrific headache. He felt even worse when he checked his phone and saw that it was almost 11:00 AM. He was scheduled to present the advertising agency's proposal to an important potential client in two hours, and he had not yet completed the preparation, including deciding on the specific points he would emphasize. Ken rarely drank heavily, but last night this same client – whom he was entertaining – put away several Long Island iced teas, and Ken had tried to keep up with him. To make matters worse, Ken could not recall what they'd discussed during the later hours of their extended drinking session. They probably talked about the contract he was proposing. He might have even mentioned the problems about the product that the company would be required to deal with to create an effective commercial. That part of the sales pitch required a careful explanation of how Ken and his colleagues could make the product look good and divert attention away from the less attractive features – and he might have blown it by bringing up the matter while rather intoxicated. In the next two hours, he had to finalize his presentation – with a bad hangover – and then deliver it without knowing what he had said last night. His immediate supervisor, as well as a company vice president, would also be present. Ken knew that not only was the contract on the line but so was his next promotion. He needed something to help him finish his preparation in time and give him some self-confidence for making the presentation. Coffee would help him focus now, and Xanax might take the edge off his anxiety when he had to make the pitch this afternoon. A bloody mary could also relieve some hangover discomfort, but since alcohol got him into this mess, vodka was probably not the best way to manage things.

Introduction

Ethyl alcohol, the psychoactive ingredient in alcoholic beverages, is quite possibly the world's favorite, in addition to being the most dangerous, intoxicating drug (Heather 2001). It is difficult to make meaningful comparisons among different cultures and drug types for the purpose of determining the most used or the most destructive psychoactive drug or substance. It is certain, however, that alcoholic beverages (referred to here, simply as alcohol) are widely used by people of many different cultures, a practice that is thought to have commenced during prehistoric times. Moderate use apparently has some health benefits, thought to result from positive effects on cholesterol levels (Holahan et al. 2012, Dawson 2000). Alcohol can also cause many destructive consequences, and its misuse is a major worldwide public health problem.

Alcohol can provide euphoric (or more subtle) pleasure as well as relief from emotional pain. Benjamin Franklin is quoted as saying "Beer is proof that God loves us and wants us to be happy," reflecting a long-standing pervasive cultural attitude about these pleasurable effects of alcohol – sociability, laughter and less attention to life's difficulties. Such positive expectations about alcohol effects encourage its use and influence the experience of drinking beverages containing the drug (Sher et al. 2005).

Alcohol is an important commodity in that its production and sale are highly profitable, provide a livelihood for many, and are sources of tax revenue. Advertisements promote sale of alcoholic beverages and convey a favorable image of drinking. The creative and alluring beer commercials featured in the television broadcasts of professional football games are but one example of the positive presentation of alcohol. However, cultural attitudes about alcohol use are varied and ambivalent. Realistic negative and sometimes moralistic views coexist with the approval and encouragement of drinking.

Alcohol Consumption

In the United States, a majority of the adult population drinks alcohol at least occasionally. A World Health Organization survey indicated that in 2010, 68.9 percent of US citizens older than age fifteen had consumed alcohol at least once in the previous year (World Health Organization 2014). Such estimates of the prevalence of drinking alcohol have not changed much since the 1940s. However, the amount of alcohol consumed per capita decreased from a high of about 2.7 gallons in 1980 to 2.3 gallons in 2014. The 2014 level of mean individual (per capita) annual consumption for the entire adult population is equivalent to about 590 twelve-ounce servings of domestic beer. Mean individual consumption for the two-thirds of the population who sometimes drink alcohol is about 3.5 gallons – equivalent to 900 servings of beer. The alcohol consumption quantities are based on the alcohol contained in all forms of alcoholic beverages (Haughwout et al. 2016).

Gender and age influence use of alcohol. Surveys consistently show that men are more likely to be drinkers (nonabstainers), and to drink alcohol more often and in larger amounts than do women. About 10 percent of twelve-year-olds have consumed at least one drink, and the prevalence of at least low levels of drinking increases sharply throughout adolescence (Masten et al. 2009). Prevalence of alcohol consumption is consistently highest in young adults of ages 18–25 (Figure 9.1).

Figure 9.1 Young men are the most prevalent consumers of alcoholic beverages. Photo: Image Source / DigitalVision / Getty Images.

Frequency, patterns and amounts of drinking vary greatly among individuals. Some drink only on special occasions such as birthdays or holidays. Others drink much more frequently, and many do so on most days. A small percentage of heavy drinkers consume relatively large amounts of alcohol. A representative survey of consumption patterns indicated that 25 percent of those who drink account for 87 percent of total alcohol consumption (Greenfield and Rogers 1999). The National Institute on Alcohol Abuse and Alcoholism (NIAAA) defines **binge drinking** for men as consuming at least five standard alcoholic drinks on one drinking occasion, and at least four drinks for women. The NIAAA definition of **heavy drinking** is binge drinking on at least five days in a month (http://niaaa.nih.gov).

The National Survey on Drug Use and Health (NSDUH) collects information annually on alcohol use of approximately 68,000 respondents. Estimates for current use (consumption during the month before the survey) for 2017 are presented in Table 9.1.

Table 9.1 Prevalence of alcohol consumption

Age range	Any use	Binge drinking	Heavy drinking
12 or older	51.7%	24.5%	6.1%
12–17	9.9%	5.3%	.7%
18–25	56.3%	36.9%	9.6%
26 or older	55.8%	24.7%	6.2%

Note. Estimates are based on self-reports of drinking alcohol during the month before the 2017 NSDUH survey (Substance Abuse and Mental Health Services Administration 2018). See text for definitions of binge and heavy drinking.

Problematic Alcohol Use

Alcohol use is clearly associated with various antisocial activities, including crime and violence. An amendment to the US Constitution made alcohol consumption illegal during the 1920s. However, an increase in illegal alcohol trafficking and organized crime, which was a consequence of prohibition, eventually led to another amendment repealing the ill-fated attempt to suppress alcohol consumption. The federal government's recognition of the public health hazard of excessive alcohol consumption resulted in the establishment of the National Institute on Alcohol Abuse and Alcoholism in the early 1970s (Warren and Hewitt 2010).

Attempts to deal with the damaging effects of alcohol also arose from the concerns of individuals who had suffered harm from their alcohol use, or from that of others whose drinking presented a danger. Alcoholics Anonymous, originating in the 1930s, provides support for recovery from alcohol use problems and has influenced cultural awareness of the pervasive nature of the disorder (Chapter 3). Other "grassroots" organizations that reflect concern about harmful effects of alcohol use are Mothers Against Drunk Driving (MADD) and Adult Children of Alcoholics (ACOA). All these actions and events demonstrate public and governmental concern regarding alcohol use in the United States.

An estimated 5.3 percent of the adolescent and adult population of the United States (14.5 million individuals) suffers from an alcohol use disorder (Substance Abuse and Mental Health Services Administration 2018). There is no clearly established difference between heavy use of alcohol and a mild alcohol use disorder (Vaillant 2003, Willenbring 2010). A consistent pattern of irresponsible or harmful alcohol consumption is required for diagnosis of the disorder.

In addition to the harm caused by individuals with diagnosable alcohol use disorders, much damage results from nonpathological alcohol use (Gmel and Rehm 2003). One example of such harm is the many alcohol-related traffic injuries and deaths involving individuals who, on most occasions, drink alcohol in a responsible manner. The current chapter summarizes the large amount of information about these harmful effects of alcohol misuse that can occur in any individual who drinks heavily – but may not suffer from an alcohol use disorder. Alcohol use disorders are discussed in the following chapter.

Alcohol in the Brain and Body

Alcoholic beverages vary widely in alcohol concentration. Alcohol concentration in beer is usually between 3 and 6 percent (sometimes higher for craft brews), in wine about 12 to 15 percent, and for liquor 40 to 50 percent. For purposes of scientific or legal discourse concerning the effects of alcohol consumption, the alcohol content of the three types of beverages are roughly equalized by the definition of a standard "drink." A standard drink is 12 ounces of 5 percent beer, 8 ounces of 7 percent malt liquor, 5 ounces of 12 percent wine, or 1.5 ounces of 40 percent liquor. Each of these amounts of an alcoholic beverage contains 0.6 ounces of pure alcohol, the Centers for Disease Control definition of a standard drink in the United States (www.cdc.gov/alcohol/faqs.htm). The volumes and alcohol concentrations designating a standard drink correspond to those of a typical serving of an alcoholic beverage.

Ethyl alcohol is unique among drugs in that in addition to its psychoactive properties (ability to alter brain function) it is also a source of calories. The alcohol content of a standard drink contains about seventy-five calories. Most beverages, other than vodka, contain other ingredients such as sugar that provide calories in addition to those from the alcohol. Alcoholic beverages are often consumed as part of a meal, and connoisseurs of wine and beer emphasize how these beverages enhance the experience of dining. Before the discovery of bacteria and recognition of the importance of sanitation in food preparation and storage, beer and wine were often safer beverages than water, which was sometimes of doubtful purity. Beer and wine are less hospitable environments for disease germs due to their alcohol content.

Compared to most psychoactive drugs, alcohol is of relatively low potency, so larger amounts must be ingested to produce behavioral effects (Koob and Le Moal 2006). Of course, the low potency does not imply that the drug cannot have major physiological actions – it only means that more must be consumed to produce such effects. Individuals readily ingest amounts of alcohol that produce behavioral effects ranging from subtle to dramatic in nature. Although chronic heavy drinking has many toxic effects, the lower potency makes it relatively difficult to consume a lethal amount of alcohol during a single drinking session. Drugs with similar effects, such as sodium pentobarbital and other barbiturates, are much more potent than alcohol. Ingestion of *2 grams* of a barbiturate drug can result in death (Keltner 2003), but for alcohol a lethal dose is about *250 grams* (based on eighteen standard drinks consumed within one hour) for an adult male. The use of barbiturates presents a much greater risk of death due to accidental or deliberate overdose than does alcohol.

Pharmacokinetics: Bioavailability

Alcohol is a volatile substance. When blood containing alcohol passes through the lungs, a small amount of alcohol is vaporized and expired along with air and can be detected and measured, giving an accurate indication of blood alcohol content. The concentration of alcohol in expired breath is 1/2,100 of that in the blood. **Blood alcohol concentration (BAC)** can also be measured directly by analysis of blood samples, but the analysis of breath is a more convenient method of determining alcohol content of blood. Alcohol can be detected in urine, but such tests do not provide an accurate measure of BAC. BAC values are often used to describe dose-related effects of alcohol (Table 9.2).

Table 9.2 Blood alcohol concentration and behavioral effects

BAC	Effects
0.01%–0.02%	feeling of well-being and relaxation
0.03%–0.04%	slight exhilaration, lessened anxiety, slightly lowered inhibition
0.05%–0.06%	emotional changes more noticeable, greater disinhibition, judgment impaired, decreased coordination of movement
0.07%–0.09%	increased reaction time, greater impairment of judgment (0.08% is minimum BAC for legal definition of intoxication in the United States)
0.10%	greater increases in reaction time and decreased motor coordination
0.15%	possible impairment of speech, perception, balance, and movement

Table 9.2 (cont.)	
BAC	Effects
0.20%	slurred speech, tendency to sleep, major reduction in sensory and motor capabilities, difficulty in walking and standing, partial or total amnesia
0.30%	confusion and stupor, possible loss of consciousness, less comprehension of surroundings and events
0.40%	unconscious, cannot be awakened (comatose), 50% probability of death (respiration stops)
0.50%	probability of death greater than 50%

Note. In highly tolerant individuals, these effects are less intense at each BAC level or seen only at a higher level of alcohol concentration. BAC, percentage of alcohol in the bloodstream.

When the stomach contains little or no food, the absorption of alcohol is most rapid, and BAC rises within a few minutes after drinking commences. Peak levels are reached within thirty minutes after drinking stops.

After absorption into the bloodstream, alcohol is distributed to essentially all tissues and fluids of the body but is less concentrated in fatty areas. It readily penetrates the blood–brain barrier and the placental barrier (Chapter 4). Several factors determine the maximum concentration of alcohol in the bloodstream (e.g., rate of drinking, contents of the GI tract), but body weight is of major importance. A given amount of alcohol will produce a lower BAC in a person of heavier body weight than in a smaller individual. Gender is also a factor because women generally have a greater proportion of fat than men, which results in a greater concentration of alcohol in the blood. Men also have higher levels than women of the primary metabolic enzyme that breaks down alcohol in the GI tract, further increasing the relative difference in BAC.

Alcohol metabolism commences immediately by the action of enzymes in the GI tract and continues in the liver after entry into the bloodstream. Unlike many other drugs, alcohol does not bind to proteins and is not stored in fat cells. Alcohol is metabolized at a constant mean rate of about 0.35 ounces per hour, although the rate of metabolism varies among individuals. At the mean metabolic rate the amount of alcohol contained in a standard drink (0.6 ounces) is eliminated in somewhat less than two hours (Jones 1993). Most alcohol is metabolized by the enzyme alcohol dehydrogenase, found in both the stomach and the liver, which converts alcohol to acetaldehyde. This toxic metabolite is then further broken down by another enzyme and eventually converted to carbon dioxide and water.

A second pathway for alcohol elimination is the microsomal ethanol oxidizing system of the liver in which alcohol is catalyzed by the enzyme P450E1-CYP2E1. The efficiency of this metabolic system is increased by chronic alcohol consumption, an effect primarily responsible for metabolic (drug-dispositional) tolerance to alcohol (Chapter 4). Although this pathway metabolizes less alcohol than does the alcohol dehydrogenase system, its increased efficiency after heavy drinking can appreciably increase the rate of elimination of alcohol from the body. Metabolites of alcohol are highly toxic and may contribute to liver damage from alcohol (Lieber 1997).

The processes of absorption and metabolism result in an initial increase, eventually followed by a decrease in BAC. As previously mentioned, several factors, including body weight, gender, rate of drinking, and tolerance-produced differences in metabolic rate determine the level of alcohol in the blood. Approximate peak BAC can be predicted for a given combination of these controlling factors. For example, one standard drink (defined previously) consumed during a one-hour period by a 160-pound man will produce a BAC of 0.02 percent (the percentage, by weight, of alcohol in the blood). For a 120-pound woman, the single standard drink will result in a BAC of 0.04 percent. An individual with a BAC of 0.08 percent or higher can be charged with driving under the influence of alcohol. Approximately 3.5 drinks consumed within one hour will produce a BAC of 0.08 percent for the larger man just described, and two drinks during the same time period produce this BAC in the smaller woman. Behavioral effects of BAC levels are further discussed below.

Pharmacodynamics: Effects on Neurotransmitters and Brain Function

Alcohol has complex and multiple actions on brain function that are detectable in neurotransmitter-specific circuits, individual neurons, and at the molecular level of ion channels and receptors (Koob and Le Moal 2006). Some of these actions occur with a single administration of the drug in all who drink alcohol. Other effects may be greater in those who develop an alcohol use disorder and some are seen only after chronic alcohol intake. Alcohol is a central nervous system depressant in that it suppresses brain activity at high doses. At low to moderate doses, alcohol has varied behavioral and cognitive effects as subsequently described. Higher doses cause sleep, coma, and death.

Unlike many other psychoactive drugs that mimic or block specific neurotransmitters, alcohol is a small molecule that does not resemble any neurotransmitter. It does however, alter the function of several different neurotransmitter circuits. Most behavioral effects of alcohol can be linked to actions on specific neurotransmitters. Drugs used to treat alcohol use disorders act on neurotransmitters whose function is altered by alcohol (Chapter 10).

Amino Acid Neurotransmitters

Alcohol does not directly block or activate receptors, but changes the function of certain receptors for two important amino acid neurotransmitters, GABA and glutamic acid. The ionotropic receptors for these neurotransmitters are chemically gated ion channels (Chapter 4), and alcohol alters the flow of ions through these channels. For GABA$_A$ receptors the ion flow is facilitated, so alcohol is an indirect agonist for the inhibitory action of GABA (Mehta and Ticku 1988). In NMDA receptors for glutamate (glutamic acid) the ion flow is decreased, so alcohol is an antagonist for this excitatory neurotransmitter (Hoffman et al. 1989).

The neurotransmitter GABA provides the major inhibitory action in the brain, so its facilitation by alcohol has wide-ranging effects on brain activity and behavior. A large amount of research, including studies of animal subjects, indicates that GABA-agonist actions are critical in alcohol's anxiety reduction, anticonvulsant effects, amnesia, and impaired coordination of movement (Lingford-Hughes and Nutt 2001). The mechanism of action for these effects is similar to that of the benzodiazepine drugs such as diazepam (Valium), which act at a subunit of the GABA$_A$ receptor complex. Both alcohol and the benzodiazepine drugs facilitate the flow of chloride ions into the neuron when GABA occupies the receptor site. GABA$_A$ receptor sites differ in sensitivity to alcohol, with those located in certain brain areas such as the cerebellum and part of the amygdala being the most vulnerable to the drug effect (Criswell and Breese 2005). These brain areas are critical for motor coordination and emotional responses. Their inhibition, when facilitated by alcohol, causes ataxia and decreases anxiety.

The antianxiety effect provides negative reinforcement for alcohol consumption. At low to moderate doses, the reduced anxiety results in marked disinhibition of behavior, further reinforcing alcohol intake in some individuals. The initial effect on GABA also indirectly increases dopamine activity, producing positive reinforcement (Koob and Le Moal 2006). These behavioral effects and the underlying GABA facilitation are greatest with acute alcohol intake, and become weaker with chronic heavy intake as tolerance develops. Withdrawal from alcohol after chronic use results in increased anxiety and vulnerability to convulsions, partially caused by reduction of GABA activity below that of normal levels.

In addition to the facilitation of GABA, the depressant effect of alcohol is also produced by the antagonism of the excitatory amino acid neurotransmitter glutamate. As with most neurotransmitters, there are several types of receptors for glutamate. Most research has been directed toward alcohol effects on the NMDA glutamate receptor. For these receptors, alcohol interferes with the influx of calcium ions (Ca^{++}) that normally follows their activation. The glutamate-related depressant effect contributes to the cognitive impairment and severe amnesia ("blackout") caused by high levels of alcohol intoxication (Diamond and Gordon 1997).

With chronic alcohol intake, the NMDA receptors are up-regulated (increased) and glutamate levels increased by the adaptive homeostatic processes of the nervous system. These changes cause the glutamate circuits to be overactive and promote seizure activity upon alcohol withdrawal (Roberto et al. 2004). Glutamate hyperactivity is also implicated in the neurotoxic effects of heavy alcohol use. The brain-damaging effects are at least partially due to repeated bouts of alcohol withdrawal that cause toxic levels of glutamate (Heinz 2006).

Other Neurotransmitters

In addition to the effects on the ion channel receptors for amino acid neurotransmitters, alcohol also changes activity in other brain circuits. Alcohol directly alters the function of some neurotransmitters, whereas other effects are indirect and due to the drug's facilitation of GABA or interference with glutamate-responsive neurons (Stahl 2008). Brain circuits are heavily interconnected, so a drug effect on a specific brain area is likely to have indirect influence on other areas.

Acute administration of alcohol increases **dopamine** activity in brain areas that produce positive reinforcement, including the ventral tegmental area and the nucleus accumbens (Boileau et al. 2003, Brodie et al. 1999, Urban et al. 2010). Most, if not all, addictive drugs also facilitate dopamine function in these mesolimbic circuits. Alcohol's enhancement of dopamine is less direct, more variable among individuals, and perhaps less effective than that of other addictive drugs such as cocaine (Bradberry 2002, Nutt et al. 2015). However, the rewarding effect of alcohol is sufficient to promote its prevalent use as well as the development of use disorders. The dopamine activation diminishes with chronic use as tolerance develops (Diana et al. 2003). Long-term decreases in dopamine function persist after cessation of extended heavy use and are thought to underlie the dysphoria that lingers beyond the initial effects of alcohol withdrawal (Bailey et al. 2000; see also Chapter 5).

Alcohol is an indirect agonist for **serotonin** at the ionotropic $5HT_3$ receptor (Lovinger and White 1991), which has some structural similarity to receptors for GABA and glutamate. This action, or another of the several indirect influences of alcohol on serotonin function, then facilitates dopamine activity (Campbell and McBride 1995).

Research with animal subjects shows that serotonin function interacts with behavioral effects of alcohol. Differences in alcohol intake and behavioral effects of alcohol are found in mice with altered serotonin function due to transgenic or "knockout" mutations (Bowers 2000; see also Chapter 6). Additionally, drugs that block or activate various serotonin receptors alter alcohol-produced behavioral effects in experimental animals.

For many years, serotonin function has been of interest to investigators searching for neurological abnormalities in humans that might contribute to the occurrence of alcohol use disorders. There is some evidence that specific serotonin abnormalities are associated with the early-onset type of alcohol use disorder (Johnson et al. 2011; see also Chapter 10). However, no evidence specifically links serotonin deficiency with alcohol use disorders in general.

The neurotransmitter enkephalin and the hormone endorphin are termed **endogenous opioids** because opiate drugs such as heroin and morphine bind to and activate the receptors for these peptides. Among other functions, the endogenous opioids suppress the emotional component of pain.

Acute alcohol administration in rats causes release of enkephalin from neurons in the mesolimbic reward circuits, release of endorphin from the pituitary gland, and increases expression of genes controlling these opioids (Froehlich 1997, Jarjour et al. 2009). These brain chemicals contribute to the rewarding effects of alcohol by facilitating dopamine release and by direct action on opioid receptors (Trigo et al. 2010).

Alcohol has a greater effect on expression of opioid-relevant genes in inbred, alcohol-preferring rats, relative to animals not bred for high alcohol preference. Alcohol also increases endogenous opioid levels in humans, and some evidence suggests that abnormalities in the opioid neurotransmitters and hormones are associated with increased vulnerability to alcohol use disorders (Trigo et al. 2010, Uhart and Wand 2009).

The drug naltrexone (Vivatrol) blocks the mu subtype of receptors for the endogenous opioids. Naltrexone reduces or eliminates the reinforcement effects of opiate drugs such as heroin and morphine and can be quite effective in managing addiction to these drugs.

This narcotic antagonist drug decreases alcohol drinking in rats (Davidson and Amit 1997), and is used to treat recovering alcoholics – with some success in certain cases (O'Malley et al. 2002, Zindel and Kranzler 2014). The use of naltrexone in SUD treatment is discussed further in Chapter 10.

The **endocannabinoids** are yet another class of neurochemicals implicated in the mediation of alcohol's rewarding effects (Caille et al. 2007, Cheer et al. 2007). Anandamide is an endocannabinoid neurotransmitter thought to function in the motivation for food consumption and other rewarding activities (Stahl 2008). Delta-9-THC and other chemicals contained in cannabis activate the receptors (designated as CB) for this neurotransmitter system. Distribution of CB receptors overlaps extensively with that of some opioid receptors, and there is bidirectional interaction between these two neurotransmitter systems (Maldodano et al. 2006).

Antagonists for the CB1 receptor (the most studied CB receptor type) reduce alcohol intake in mice and rats mutated or bred for alcohol preference (Colombo et al. 1998).

Agonists for these receptors increase alcohol intake in these experimental animals (Malinen and Hyytia 2008). The drug rimonabant (Acomplia) is a CB1 antagonist approved for treatment of addiction and eating disorders in some European and South American countries. However, there is concern that while the drug reduces the pleasurable effects of alcohol and other addictive drugs, it may also cause depression and suicidal ideation.

In addition to the actions on multiple neurotransmitter systems described here, alcohol has other effects on brain activity. At high doses, alcohol disrupts ion movements through the neuron membrane (not only at receptors), degrading the activity of all neurotransmitter systems. Alcohol also influences gene expression by altering internal communication in the neuron between receptor activity and the cell nucleus.

Since alcohol affects so many aspects of brain function, it is difficult to identify which system is most critical in transition from nondestructive "social drinking" to compulsive alcohol use. Consequences of adaptation to alcohol effects in the neurotransmitter systems involved in both positive and negative reinforcement (dopamine, opioids, endocannabinoids, and GABA) seem most likely to underlie the development of alcohol use disorders (Vengeliene et al. 2008).

Neuroadaptation and Hormonal Stress Responses

Chronic use of alcohol produces pharmacodynamic tolerance that decreases the behavioral effects unless the dose is increased. The rewarding effects can be maintained to some extent in heavy drinkers by consumption of larger amounts of alcohol, although the initial level of euphoria may never be fully regained. The neurological adaptation to alcohol causes depression and anxiety that emerge as the alcohol is metabolized and the initial effects dissipate. Both hangover and withdrawal syndrome (described in Chapter 10) are results of the homeostatic adaptation to alcohol's action on several neurotransmitters and other neurological functions.

Alcohol consumption, especially chronic use at high doses, causes severe dysregulation of the complex neurological and hormonal stress-response system (Koob and Le Moal 2006). Alcohol disrupts the function of two major stress-related hormones, *corticotropin releasing factor* (CRF) and *neuropeptide Y* (NP-Y). Alcohol administration recruits the CRF system, which initiates stress responses in the brain. The activation is also increased by withdrawal from alcohol. In normal function, NP-Y attenuates the stress-initiated cascade of neurological and hormonal responses, so this peptide is essentially an "antistress" hormone. Chronic alcohol use decreases NP-Y levels, an effect that continues during withdrawal and further intensifies stress responses.

The nervous system's response to the stress-producing actions of alcohol is therefore somewhat different from that of the adaptive regulatory responses of the GABA, dopamine, and endogenous opioid neurotransmitter systems. These systems are initially activated by alcohol, and then suppressed by homeostatic compensation that becomes most evident during withdrawal. Alcohol initially activates the stress system to some extent, but stress responses are even greater during withdrawal. These sensitized stress responses persist beyond the acute stage of alcohol withdrawal, and promote the resumption of drinking (relapse) characteristic of alcohol use disorders (Johnston et al. 2016, Kreek and Koob 1998).

Behavioral and Cognitive Effects

Alcohol has several characteristic effects on thought processes, emotion, movement and behavior. Some acute effects are studied in controlled laboratory settings (Sher et al. 2005). However, some of the most interesting, as well as dangerous effects of alcohol, such as its influence on intimate relationships and physical aggression, cannot be easily studied in the laboratory because of practical or ethical limitations. Information about alcohol effects on such behavior comes primarily from naturalistic observations and surveys (often self-reports) of the consequences of alcohol use. The harmful results of alcohol consumption can occur in "social drinkers," that is in the absence of an alcohol use disorder.

Ethical restraints also prevent controlled investigations of chronic alcohol effects in humans. Clinical and epidemiological studies of alcohol use disorders reveal many of the harmful consequences of prolonged moderate or heavy drinking. Some behavioral and cognitive effects of chronic alcohol administration are also determined by controlled studies of animal subjects.

Although certain effects of alcohol are typical (especially at high doses), not all episodes of drinking result in the same behaviors. One of the most certain statements about alcohol is that its effects depend on a number of interacting factors (Sher et al. 2005). Consider the behavior that might occur in two drinking situations. In the first setting, members of a "biker gang" (mostly antisocial men, including some with female companions) drink large amounts of malt liquor in a remote location. In the second scenario, members of a garden club (mostly women, but including a few men who share the group's interest in horticulture) attend a reception where wine is served. The first group's behavior would probably become more boisterous after drinking, with displays of risk taking, verbal or physical aggression and similar machismo activity. In the second group, more animated, less inhibited conversations and greater consumption of tempting food are likely to follow wine drinking. The behavioral consequences of drinking alcohol would be quite different for the two groups. This fictional but realistic example illustrates some of the many factors that determine the varied consequences of drinking.

The factors that influence alcohol's behavioral effects include dose (amount consumed), rate of consumption, tolerance (acute and chronic) and concurrent use of other drugs. Additional and very important factors are the expectation of alcohol effects, and the situation in which drinking occurs. Consequences of drinking also depend on personal characteristics and behavioral tendencies of the individual in the sober state (Sher and Wood 2005). Although alcohol effects can differ among individuals, at a given dose some general behavioral actions are predictable.

Dose, Blood Alcohol Concentration, and Tolerance

The biological and behavioral consequences of drinking alcohol depend heavily on the amount consumed. Drug dose is the amount of drug per unit of body weight, which for medical use or scientific investigations is expressed as grams (or milligrams) per kilogram. For alcohol, dose may also be informally (if less accurately) described simply as number of standard drinks consumed. As mentioned previously, alcohol concentration in the blood can be measured directly, or indirectly indicated by breath analysis. Amount and rate of alcohol consumption, as well as body weight, determine the blood alcohol concentration (BAC). BAC levels are often used to describe typical dose-related alcohol effects as presented in Table 9.2.

Alcohol typically produces the effects listed in Table 9.2, which indicate the importance of dose, a primary determinant of BAC. However, previous exposure to alcohol produces tolerance, which diminishes the effects of alcohol. Overall tolerance is a result of three separate types of adaptation to alcohol effects (Chapter 4). Metabolic (drug-dispositional) tolerance results in more rapid elimination of alcohol from the body, lowering the blood alcohol level resulting from drinking a certain amount of alcohol, but not changing the behavior typical at a given BAC. Behavioral and pharmacodynamic tolerance processes lessen the behavioral, cognitive and emotional responses to alcohol at each BAC. In a person with a high level of tolerance the effects described in Table 9.1 can still occur, but are most evident at a higher BAC.

Some effects of alcohol consumption occur earlier, and others predominate later in the course of a drinking session. As the BAC rises when alcohol is first consumed, arousal level may increase and feelings of euphoria are more likely than later, as BAC falls. When metabolic processes decrease the amount of alcohol in the bloodstream (and the brain), sedation and negative feelings often occur. These different effects, associated with the same BAC but whose nature depends on whether BAC is rising or falling, are the results of acute tolerance (Martin et al. 1993). This aspect of tolerance is thought to be an immediate or rapid expression of the adaptive responses underlying pharmacodynamic tolerance, one of the processes that produce overall chronic tolerance.

Rewarding Effects of Alcohol

The widespread and well-established cultural beliefs about the pleasures and comforts of alcohol are touted in an old song – "roll out the barrel, we'll have a barrel of fun! Roll out the barrel, we'll have the blues on the run!" Many other examples – including song lyrics, stories, and personal accounts could also be used to illustrate the allure of drinking. These beliefs, based on real (if somewhat unreliable) effects of alcohol are obvious incentives for drinking. The positive and negative reinforcement actions promote drinking, and in vulnerable individuals contribute to development of alcohol use disorders. However, as with all addictions, the pleasurable effects eventually decrease and the aversive consequences become much greater.

The pleasurable effects are most noticeable as alcohol levels in the blood increase, which may account for an informal description of intoxication – "*Getting* drunk is more fun than *being* drunk." This sometimes realistic expectation of alcohol effects often encourages prolonged drinking and results in greater levels of intoxication – which can be dysphoric. Most individuals who drink responsibly learn to resist the futile attempt to maintain the initial euphoric and arousing effect of alcohol. Pleasurable consequences are time and dose-limited in that sedation and sleep eventually occur if drinking continues.

Not all individuals who drink alcohol experience much increase in arousal. Informal observations of alcohol consumption as well as laboratory studies (Holdstock and de Wit 1998) indicate that some individuals predominately experience relaxation, lessened anxiety and sedation, even as BAC rises.

Alcohol produces anxiolytic (anxiety-reducing) effects in experimental animals, seen most clearly in behavioral tests of conflict (approach vs. avoidance) (Fromme and D'Amico 1999). Alcohol's effects on cognition and attentional processes, described below, at least partially mediate its anxiolytic action (Kassel et al. 2010). Anxiety often inhibits behavior in both humans and laboratory animals so the anxiolytic effect can contribute to the alcohol-produced increase in some types of activity. In humans, social interaction often becomes easier and less inhibited. Decreased caution about the amount of drinking sometimes results in levels of intoxication greater than originally intended.

The negative reinforcement of anxiety reduction is a definite incentive for alcohol consumption. However, the anxiolytic effects are not as general and reliable as commonly assumed, but are heavily influenced by both the context in which drinking occurs (Sayette 1999), and by the expectation of relaxation and decreased anxiety (Sher et al. 2005). Alcohol does have a reliable, if temporary, effect of relieving the anxiety experienced during alcohol withdrawal (McCarthy et al. 2010).

Current theories of SUD for most addictive drugs, including alcohol, emphasize the role of positive reinforcement in early stages of drug use, with negative reinforcement becoming more prominent as dependence progresses (Chapters 4 and 7). However, anxiety is a critical component of some psychiatric disorders (e.g., posttraumatic stress disorder, social anxiety disorder) that are risk factors for SUD (Chapter 8). When these disorders are concurrent with SUD, negative reinforcement from anxiety relief appears to be a factor even in the initial development of alcohol dependence.

Alcohol-Produced Myopia

Many scientific observations support the common cultural belief that alcohol lessens the restraint on several types of behavior (Fillmore 2003, Lyvers 2000). Several theories provide explanations for the behavioral disinhibition that can result in dangerous or maladaptive activity. One of the most concise and well-accepted theories of this general effect of alcohol is that of **alcohol myopia** (Steele and Josephs 1990). This theory maintains that alcohol reduces attentional capacity because of its impairment of cognitive processing. The "near-sighted" (myopic) effect results from the narrowing of attention so that only immediate and salient environmental cues are fully noticed and considered. Obviously, this effect is not absolute – less immediate factors (the associated risks or adverse consequences) are not completely ignored, but their control over behavior is reduced. Predictions of the alcohol myopia model are well supported by many naturalistic observations and laboratory studies of disinhibited behavior, including aggression, risky sex, and unrestrained eating (Giancola et al. 2010).

However, the alcohol myopia theory can also account for what may be alcohol's most benign and positive effect – its enhancement of pleasant social interaction, including casual relaxation with friends as well as parties and celebrations of special occasions. In the presence of friends or other nonthreatening individuals, it is usually desirable for one's attention to be more focused on the immediate environment. Decreased attention to more distant concerns, whether related to work, health, relationships or other potential problems is likely to reduce anxiety. The enhancement of pleasant social interaction brings about both positive and negative reinforcement. Most people would concur that it feels good to talk freely with friends, and to be less occupied with negative thoughts. These rewarding consequences of low-level intoxication obviously depend on the context of drinking, further discussed below.

Effects on Sexual Activity

Alcohol effects on sexual feelings (arousal and interest) and behavior have long-standing and pervasive cultural assumptions and expectations. This folklore, based on the experiences of many with attempted or actual sex during a state of intoxication, reflects the complexity and paradoxical nature of these effects. Alcohol often increases interest in sex and promotes sexual overtures, but high doses can interfere with the physiological responses (in particular, erection in men) required for satisfactory sexual activity. Overall, however, the assumption is that alcohol encourages sexual activity.

Sexual behavior is difficult to study by means of scientific investigation, although sexual arousal in response to erotic stimuli can be measured objectively, and alcohol effects on these physiological responses have been determined. Alcohol impairs erection in men (Bridell and Wilson 1976) and lessens the increased vaginal blood flow that accompanies sexual arousal in women (Wilson and Lawson 1976). These classic studies of alcohol and the human sexual response have been confirmed by more recent research (George et al. 2006, 2011). The interference with physiological indicators of sexual arousal usually occurs at higher BAC (above 0.05 percent) and become greater as concentrations of blood alcohol increase. In men, subjective ratings of arousal correspond with the erectile dysfunction (less arousal is reported at high alcohol doses), but women may report increased feelings of arousal even as the physiological response declines. In young, healthy individuals, sexual activity is still possible and quite often occurs at moderate to high levels of intoxication, even though physiological arousal might be somewhat impaired.

At low to moderate doses, drinking often promotes sexual overtures and activity in certain contexts, mainly those involving the presence and availability of prospective sexual partners (Abbey et al. 2000). Decreasing standards for acceptance of sexual partners as intoxication progresses often occurs – and is sometimes a topic of humor in the popular culture. This change in acceptability appears to be an example of impaired cognitive processing.

Although alcohol is not an aphrodisiac in all situations (such as when drinking alone, or when heterosexuals drink in the company of same-sex individuals), alcohol myopia decreases the concern related to possible delayed negative consequences of sexual activity. This effect of reduced caution no doubt increases the probability of sexual activity. Context and expectations, further discussed below, obviously have a strong influence on how alcohol promotes sexual behavior.

Undesirable and Dangerous Effects

At low to moderate doses, alcohol effects are often rewarding and mostly harmless. However, mild intoxication can easily lead to more drinking, and there is no distinct boundary between the low-dose effects and the unpleasant, dangerous consequences of higher doses as listed in Table 9.2. Higher levels of intoxication result in greater cognitive dysfunction, which impairs driving and similar tasks that require vigilance and quick responses. Negative emotional states, such as anger and depression, may occur. Walking and speaking become difficult, and nausea and dizziness are common, with eventual loss of consciousness probable after prolonged drinking. Death from a high dose of alcohol is a possibility, but unlikely, unless other drugs are also taken.

Most people who enjoy drinking responsibly avoid consuming alcohol in amounts that produce extreme effects, which are often uncomfortable, embarrassing or frightening. Dionysus, the ancient Greek god of wine, madness and ecstasy, is sometimes associated with unrestrained intoxicated revelry. For some who consume alcohol irresponsibly, the **Dionysian aspect** of drunkenness can be appealing (Babor 1996). Adolescents, who often experience relatively more arousal and less sedation from alcohol (see Chapter 8), sometimes drink with the deliberate intent of attaining a novel, amusing and exciting altered state of consciousness (Maggs and Schulenberg 2004/2005, Windle 2016). Binge drinking, consumption of five or more drinks during a single drinking session, usually results in such high levels of intoxication. In certain contexts (e.g., spring break parties, St. Patrick's Day celebrations) some young adults may also seek the reckless abandon of extreme intoxication. The risk of unexpected, possibly dangerous, outcomes involved in this style of drinking is often attractive to certain special populations (e.g., antisocial male thrill-seekers) (Carpenter and Hasin 2001).

In the United States, more than half of the roughly 88,000 annual alcohol-related deaths stem from binge drinking (Kanny et al. 2015). Binge drinking also accounts for 77 percent of the heavy annual economic cost of alcohol misuse (Sacks et al. 2015).

Impaired Cognition and Dangerous Behavior

Impaired cognition can facilitate several types of dangerous, often harmful behavior. Moderate to extreme intoxication is associated with a variety of devastating outcomes, including violent aggression (Zerhouni et al. 2013), **traffic fatalities** (National Highway Traffic Safety Administration 2018) and the transmission of HIV and other diseases from unprotected sexual activity (Barta et al. 2008).

Unwanted sexual advances, including rape, are also associated with drinking and intoxication. Drinking, and in particular binge drinking, by eighteen- to twenty-four-year-old men and women is related to increased incidence of date rape and acquaintance-rape as well as other forms of **sexual assault** (Howard et al. 2008, White and Hingson 2014, Wilhite et al. 2018). Undergraduate college women's recognition of risks for date rape decrease after consuming alcohol (0.04 BAC) (Loiselle and Fuqua 2007, Melkonian and Ham 2018). These studies indicate that for women even moderate amounts of alcohol can increase the probability of sexual assault.

Police officers, social workers, and emergency department personnel of hospitals often see victims or perpetrators of crime or violence related to alcohol use (Sumner et al. 2015). Surveys of both victims and offenders yield estimates that at least 40 percent of the perpetrators of crime or violence had been using alcohol at the time of the offense (Greenfield 1998). Professionals working in the areas of public safety or criminal justice give even higher estimates of the degree of association between alcohol and **criminal violence** (Graham and West 2001, Yalisove 2004).

Mere association or correlation does not prove a causal relation between drinking and dangerous behaviors. In some cases, both the drinking and the harmful behavior could be a result of a third factor. Impulsive, antisocial behavioral tendencies can promote alcohol intoxication as well as violence or criminal activity (Moeller and Dougherty 2001). The alcohol use could also be a result of the associated **traumatic experience**. For example, in some instances of domestic violence, drinking and intoxication might result from being a victim, rather than a perpetrator of violence.

Although physical aggression cannot be studied in the laboratory, some forms of aggression can be observed under controlled conditions (Taylor 1993). Many such studies (e.g., Leonard 1989) have demonstrated that under some conditions alcohol does facilitate aggression.

Controlled scientific investigations have also found that males have an increased intent to engage in unsafe sex after alcohol consumption (MacDonald et al. 2000), as well as increased acceptance of intoxicated driving (MacDonald et al. 1995). In addition, the evidence from driving simulation studies clearly shows that alcohol impairs operation of an automobile (e.g., Calhoun et al. 2004). These studies indicate a causal link between alcohol use and dangerous behavior, as suggested by a large amount of naturalistic observation.

The effect of alcohol to restrict attentional capacity and impair cognition promotes many instances of aggressive behavior. Alcohol does not always produce aggression, but aggressive response to provocation (an immediate stimulus) is more likely after alcohol consumption, a result predicted by the alcohol myopia theory (Giancola et al. 2010). This theory about lessened inhibitions can also account for the other types of dangerous behavior associated with alcohol use. However, cultural expectations about alcohol effects, as well as reduced caution and impaired judgment, may also promote potential hazardous sexual activity after drinking alcohol (George et al. 2009). The manner in which expectation of alcohol's effects influences behavior is discussed in a subsequent section.

Partial or Total Memory Impairment

Alcohol impairs memory in a dose-related manner. At low to moderate blood alcohol concentrations (BAC), details of events that occurred during the state of intoxication may not be recalled when sober (Ryback 1971, White 2003). Inability to recall exactly what was said during a conversation is an example of such a memory deficit. The impairment is much greater for the acquisition of new information (memory formation) than for recall (while intoxicated) of previously learned material (Lister et al. 1991). This deficit might be annoying or embarrassing but typically is not a serious or disturbing consequence of drinking, especially in relaxed social settings.

However, complete amnesia for events that occurred during the intoxicated state is a particularly striking, sometimes dramatic and frightening consequence of high levels of alcohol consumption (Lee et al. 2009). This profound absence of episodic memory (the time, place, and actual occurrence of events) for a period while intoxicated is referred to as a "blackout." The amnesia results from impaired transfer of information from a short-term representation in the brain into a more permanent long-term memory (White 2003). Investigations with animal subjects implicate alcohol's antagonist effect on glutamate activity as underlying the memory impairment (Swartzwelder et al. 1995). Since short-term memory is largely unaffected, this amnesic effect on the formation of long-term memory is similar to that seen after damage to the hippocampus (Silvers et al. 2003, White et al. 2000).

Amnesia can occur when BAC reaches approximately 0.15–0.20 percent. The memory impairment is most likely if the blood alcohol level rises rapidly, usually due to consuming large amounts of alcohol when the stomach is empty (Goodwin 1995, Goodwin et al. 1969). In these scientific investigations, alcohol-dependent individuals drank large amounts of alcohol to produce the high BAC levels. Useful information was gained from these studies. However, such procedures would not be approved under current ethical standards for conduct of research with human subjects. Many individuals are obviously intoxicated at these high BAC levels, although they are not unconscious. In some individuals with a higher tolerance for alcohol, behavioral signs of intoxication may not be evident, and conversation and other activities (such as driving an automobile) not noticeably impaired during the amnesic state (Lee et al. 2009, White 2003).

Blackouts were traditionally considered an important hallmark of alcoholism (Lee et al. 2009). Amnesic episodes were prominent in Jellinek's description of alcoholism, based on his survey of members of Alcoholics Anonymous (Jellinek 1946). Although many individuals with alcohol use disorders experience frequent blackouts, episodes of complete amnesia can also occur in people without chronic alcohol use problems. White and colleagues found in a survey of college undergraduates that 40 percent of those who drank alcohol had experienced a blackout during the previous year. Approximately equal numbers of men and women reported blackouts, but the women respondents apparently experienced the memory impairment after relatively fewer drinks than did the men (White et al. 2002). In other surveys, 33–35 percent of medical students indicated that they had experienced at least one amnesic episode after drinking (Goodwin 1995, Knight et al. 1999). Additional studies (e.g., Hartzler and Fromme 2003) indicate a similar prevalence of alcohol-produced blackouts. Epidemiological surveys estimate the incidence of alcohol use disorders in the general adult population at less than 10 percent (Grant et al. 2004). Presumably, most of the respondents that experienced blackouts did not suffer from an alcohol use disorder. Complete amnesia is a possibility for almost anyone who rapidly consumes a large amount of alcohol, although there are individual differences in vulnerability to blackouts.

Many of the respondents in White's study said that the amnesic experience was frightening and motivated them to moderate their alcohol consumption. Mundane, as well as hazardous events, transpired during the blackout period. Dangerous or undesirable activities that could not be recalled (but were described by friends or other observers) included spending money, driving an automobile, vandalism, and unprotected sexual intercourse. A greater number of women, relative to male respondents expressed concern about the blackout experience (White et al. 2002). A history of alcohol-related blackouts was associated with sexual assault victimization in college women (Wilhite et al. 2018).

In addition to total amnesia (referred to as *en bloc* blackouts), heavy drinkers may also experience partial (fragmentary) blackouts. In this less severe amnesia, only some parts of events during the intoxicated state seem to be forgotten, although they may be recalled if reminder cues are given. Such prompted memory recall does not occur for the complete, permanent amnesia of an *en bloc* blackout. Some investigators suggest that these fragmentary blackouts may contribute to the failure to restrict drinking as an alcohol use disorder develops. The earlier, more pleasurable parts of a drinking session might be vividly recalled, with less memory retained for the aversive consequences, occurring later during more extreme intoxication (Hartzler and Fromme 2003, Lee et al. 2009). For some drinkers, memory of unpleasant drinking experiences on previous occasions helps to limit alcohol consumption. Faulty memory of such consequences of heavy drinking could well counteract this moderating influence.

Enduring Cognitive Effects of "Social" Drinking

Impairment of memory and other cognitive functions during and within a few hours after a drinking session occurs at moderate and high levels of alcohol-produced intoxication. Some dose-related detrimental effects of alcohol on cognition endure for longer periods – at least days or weeks – given persistent drinking. Although the subjects for most investigations of alcohol-related brain damage and cognitive impairment are alcoholics in treatment (Chapter 10), some studies have assessed cognitive performance in social drinkers. **Social drinking** is an imprecise term that can refer to a wide range of amounts and patterns of alcohol consumption – and identifies individuals who drink, but do not meet DSM criteria for an alcohol use disorder. Controlled experiments featuring extended consumption of varying doses of alcohol are not feasible for obvious ethical and practical reasons. However, self-reports of the drinking habits of research participants allow inferences about the effects of light, medium or heavy drinking.

Studies of social drinkers strongly suggest a continuum of cognitive impairment that roughly correlates to the daily/weekly amount of alcohol consumed. After reviewing seventeen studies, Parsons and Nixon made the following conclusions: In subjects who drink fewer than sixteen standard drinks per week, no cognitive impairments are reliably detected. With consumption of thirty-five to forty-two drinks per week for an extended period, certain cognitive functions become less efficient in some individuals. At fifty to sixty-five drinks per week, **mild cognitive deficits** are often present, and at seventy or more drinks per week, cognitive deficits equivalent to those found in diagnosed alcoholics are typical (Parsons 1998, Parsons and Nixon 1998). The tests used in these investigations measured learning and memory, abstracting, problem solving, perceptual analysis and synthesis, and speed and efficiency of information processing.

In another investigation, the cognitive performance of social drinkers in their late fifties was tested with a newer and less extensive assessment instrument, the Repeatable Battery for the Assessment of Neuropsychological Status (RBANS) (Randolph et al. 1998). The cognitive performance of moderate to heavy drinkers (twenty-one to forty-nine drinks per week, mean of twenty-six) was significantly lower than that of light drinkers (three to six drinks per week). The impairment at a lower mean level of drinking than in earlier studies may have been due to use of a different test instrument, or to the age of these participants, who were somewhat older than those in most previous investigations (Green et al. 2010).

The results of these tests of social drinkers' cognitive performance indicate that based on group means no reliable impairment is apparent from consumption of as much as two to three drinks each day. Low degrees of cognitive impairment are unlikely to interfere with most daily activities. NIAAA guidelines for safe alcohol use advise no more than two drinks per day for healthy adult men younger than age sixty-five, and one drink per day for women and older people (www.niaaa.nih.gov).

At higher rates of alcohol consumption, cognitive impairment is increasingly more frequent and more pronounced. Vulnerability to these adverse effects of alcohol varies greatly among moderate drinkers, probably due to genetic differences and other factors.

Negative Emotions and Suicide

In addition to the pleasurable consequences of drinking, alcohol intoxication can promote negative emotional states, such as depression, sadness, and anger (Figure 9.2). These aversive states are most likely to occur as BAC declines after a high level of intoxication.

Figure 9.2 Alcohol consumption can promote sadness, depression, and other negative emotional states. Photo: D-Keine / E+ / Getty Images.

Alcohol has a clearly established (but poorly understood) role in producing psychological distress (Lang et al. 1999). In some individuals and under certain circumstances, the negative emotions emerge, contributing to the variability and inconsistency of alcohol's effects.

Intoxication is also associated with **suicidal behavior** in both adults (Hufford 2001) and adolescents (Bagge and Sher 2008). Alcohol use, including acute intoxication, increases the risk of suicide in those not addicted to alcohol as well as in alcohol-dependent individuals (Pompili et al. 2010). Although acute intoxication is a risk factor for suicide in individuals who are not alcohol dependent, the probability of suicide among those with alcohol use disorders is very high. In a meta-analysis, Darvishi and colleagues found significant associations between alcohol use disorder and suicidal ideation, attempts, and completed suicides (odds ratio, relative to no SUD, 2.59) (Darvishi et al. 2015).

The increased risk of suicide in alcohol-dependent individuals may be mediated by depression, which often co-occurs with alcohol use disorders (Chapter 8). Clinical depression (unipolar and bipolar mood disorders) is a definite risk factor for both alcohol use disorders and for suicide. Those who suffer from both depression and alcohol abuse or dependence have an especially high risk of suicide (Hufford 2001).

Suicide is the third leading cause of death among adolescents (Caine 2013). Alcohol involvement by adolescents (ages fourteen to eighteen) is consistently associated with suicide attempts as well as suicidal deaths (Mehlenbeck et al. 2003). Alcohol involvement refers to both alcohol use and the consequences of drinking in adolescents, and is not limited to individuals with an alcohol use disorder (Windle 2016). It is uncertain to what extent involvement with drinking or acute intoxication are immediate causes of suicide attempts by adolescents, in that impulsive behavior can lead to suicide attempts as well as promoting drinking. Depressive disorders in adolescents are also associated with both heavy underage drinking and in suicide attempts (Bagge and Sher 2008).

Investigations into the complex and multiple causes of suicidal behavior are inevitably retrospective and correlational in nature, so isolating the role of a particular factor, such as alcohol use, can be quite difficult. However, four characteristics of alcohol intoxication would seem to promote attempts at self-destruction (Bagge and Sher 2008, Hufford 2001). First, intoxication is often expected to diminish pain, including that of self-inflicted death. Second, high levels of intoxication can increase psychological distress. Third, drinking can increase aggressiveness, and suicide is often considered as a form of self-aggression. Finally, the diminished cognitive processing can reduce consideration of possible alternative courses of action that are less immediately available than suicide. This last factor is an aspect of alcohol-produced myopia.

Lethal Overdose

In the absence of medical intervention, about half of nontolerant individuals who drink enough alcohol to reach a BAC of 0.4 percent will die due to respiratory failure (Oehmichen et al. 2005). Higher concentrations of alcohol in the blood make death even more likely. Tolerance (as seen in heavy drinkers) increases the **lethal alcohol dose** (and BAC), but some individuals are more sensitive to the respiratory depressant effect and will die at lower BAC levels. The often-lethal concentration of alcohol in the blood is reached only after drinking large amounts and in a 160 pound man would result from consuming about eighteen standard drinks within an hour. In a larger person, or at a slower rate of drinking, even more drinks would be required to reach this lethal amount of alcohol in the blood and brain.

Even when intending to become extremely intoxicated, most drinkers lose consciousness (and therefore stop drinking) long before consuming a lethal dose of alcohol. Beverages with a high alcohol concentration (e.g., distilled liquor) can irritate the GI tract and drinking large amounts can cause vomiting, which prevents further absorption of alcohol into the bloodstream. Unfortunately, vomiting while unconscious can also interfere with respiration and cause death. When BAC rises rapidly to a high level – as with extreme binge drinking – the vomit reflex of the central nervous system can be depressed, allowing ingestion of a lethal amount of alcohol before loss of consciousness. Unintentional lethal overdoses (as well as suicide by deliberate overdrinking) are relatively rare, due to vomiting or loss of consciousness.

In the United States during the years 2010–2012, an annual mean of 2,221 individuals died from alcohol overdose – a death rate of 6 per day (Centers for Disease Control and Prevention 2015). Some unintentional alcohol-overdose deaths occur among young, relatively inexperienced drinkers. However, most of the deceased individuals (76 percent) were age thirty-five to sixty-four, and many were alcohol dependent. The fatalities of middle-aged or older people are typically less publicized than those of college students or other young people who consume lethal amounts of alcohol.

Although relatively few deaths occur from accidental overdose when alcohol is the only drug taken, combining even moderate amounts of alcohol with other drugs results in many fatalities. "Alcohol in combination with ... (another drug)" is a leading cause of deaths as reported by the **Drug Abuse Warning Network (DAWN)** system (Martin 2008). Certain drugs, legally available only by means of prescription, present special dangers when combined with alcohol. Heroin, fentanyl, Oxycodone (OxyContin), hydrocodone (Vicodin) and other opioid analgesic drugs are sometimes taken concurrently with or after drinking alcohol. These drugs depress respiration, and their depressant effect is added to that produced by alcohol, causing many overdose deaths incorrectly attributed to the sole actions of the analgesic drug (Hickman et al. 2008). Similar additive or synergistic effects result when alcohol is combined with benzodiazepine drugs such as alprazolam (Xanax) (Bachhuber et al. 2016). Although a high dose of the opioid drugs can be fatal, the antianxiety drugs have very little lethal potential when taken under medical supervision, and not in combination with alcohol.

Cocaine and other addictive stimulants also present increased hazards when combined with alcohol. The stimulant effect of cocaine taken during a drinking session may prevent the loss of consciousness that would normally accompany extreme intoxication, thereby allowing consumption of a lethal amount of alcohol. Similar dangerous effects can result from the consumption of large amounts of caffeinated malt liquor beverages.

Hangover

Moderate or high levels of alcohol intoxication typically have a delayed aversive consequence that many social drinkers experience at least occasionally. Anxiety, irritability, fatigue, dysphoria, and other unpleasant effects (headache, gastric distress) are symptoms of hangover. Hangover is considered a briefer and much less intense version of withdrawal from alcohol, resulting from homeostatic rebound from the initial – typically pleasurable – effects of alcohol. The unpleasant aftereffects of drinking often provide a restraining influence on the consumption of alcohol. The amount and rate of alcohol consumed is the main determinant of the intensity of the hangover state, and many who drink responsibly learn to limit their drinking to avoid the discomfort of hangover. However, the disinhibitory actions of alcohol previously described coupled with the pleasant feeling as the BAC rises often promote an amount of drinking sufficient to result in a hangover. In a sample of college students, 87 percent of those who drank reported at least one hangover symptom during the past year (Slutske et al. 2003).

Some evidence suggests that hangover acts as a deterrent to the development of alcohol use disorder, so a relative absence of hangovers after drinking may be a risk factor for alcohol use problems (Piasecki et al. 2010). However, determination of how hangover influences the development of alcohol use disorders is complicated by evidence that hangover is more frequent in individuals with a family history of alcoholism. Hangover discomfort can be at least temporarily relieved by a resumption of drinking (the "hair of the dog" effect). The negative reinforcement of this practice might underlie the increased risk for alcohol use disorder as related to more frequent and severe hangovers (Piasecki et al. 2005). Put simply, frequent hangovers might counteract the development of problematic alcohol use, unless the aversive aftereffects of drinking are often alleviated by more drinking.

Effects of Context and Expectancy

Changes in the function of neurotransmitters and neural circuits can account for some basic behavioral consequences of alcohol use. Effects of alcohol, such as positive reinforcement, behavioral disinhibition, memory impairment, and decreased arousal level, can be demonstrated in experimental animals as well as in humans. However, the effects of alcohol on some of the more interesting aspects of human behavior are more complex and less mechanistic and predictable than are agonist or antagonist actions of the drug on neurotransmitters.

As with all psychoactive drugs, the situation or context in which alcohol intake occurs and expectations of the consequences of drinking are important determinants of alcohol effects (Chapter 4). Because alcohol is consumed in a wide range of situations or settings, and individuals can differ in their expectations of alcohol effects, its influence on much human behavior is also quite variable (Sher et al. 2005). These factors of environment and expectation are important in both non-problematic social alcohol use and alcohol use disorders.

The **social context** is probably the most important determinant of alcohol's effect on mood and emotion. Drinking with others, especially those who are friends and/or enjoyable company, is widely seen as more pleasurable than drinking alone. To quote from a Joni Mitchell song, "drinkin' alone is a shame, it's a cryin' shame." Laboratory studies provide support for the cultural assumption that mood improves when alcohol is consumed in the company of others, and mood may worsen when an individual drinks alone. Doty and de Wit (1995) found that over a range of alcohol doses, subjects reported higher levels of positive mood, elation and friendliness in a social drinking condition. Subjects who drank in a solitary condition reported mostly opposite changes in mood. Other researchers have reported similar findings concerning the mood-altering effects of drinking alone or in social settings (Giancola et al. 2010).

As well as influencing mood and emotion, the social context is also critical in the initiation of behaviors sometimes facilitated by alcohol, especially those of aggression and sexual activity.

The situation (context) of drinking also influences the amount of alcohol consumed on a specific occasion. As an example, much less drinking is likely when a supervisor's birthday is celebrated with a champagne toast in the workplace, relative to the amount of alcohol consumed by a group of friends watching a football game in a sports bar. Naturalistic observations suggest that individuals tend to adjust their rate and amount of alcohol consumption to match that of their friends in the context of social drinking (Figure 9.3). Such modeling behavior is also demonstrated by controlled studies, conducted in laboratory environments that resemble a typical drinking environment (Heather 2001, Sher et al. 2005). The modeling effect also occurs in adolescents, who more often drink to excess in the presence of heavy-drinking peers (Chung et al. 2018). Several investigations indicate the importance of social interaction in heavy-drinking college students (e.g., Lange et al. 2011).

Figure 9.3 The amount of alcohol consumed by an individual is influenced by the drinking behavior of her companions. Photo: Jim Arbogast / DigitalVision / Getty Images.

Because alcohol is so widely used and has a major cultural presence, most people have expectations about the consequences of drinking. Not surprisingly, individuals who drink heavily have mostly positive expectations of alcohol effects. Those who drink frequently and in larger amounts tend to expect arousing, rather than sedating effects from alcohol. Lighter-drinking respondents more frequently expect sedating actions. The anticipated pleasurable effects of the heavier drinkers also include tension reduction, social facilitation and enhancement of sexual activity (Sher et al. 2005; see also Chapter 7). Those who drink more heavily also expect fewer negative consequences from alcohol use.

Expectations can influence the consequences of drinking as well, encouraging (or discouraging) alcohol consumption. An example of the power of expectancy is shown by alcohol's effect in reducing anxiety. A general and reliable anxiety-reducing effect of alcohol is a firmly established cultural assumption. Controlled investigations of alcohol's anxiolytic action show that the effect can occur, but is less reliable than commonly assumed. Some of alcohol's ability to decrease anxiety is due to the anticipation that it will produce that often-sought effect (Sayette 1999, Sher et al. 2005).

Investigations with placebo beverages, thought by subjects to contain alcohol, have shown that the pervasive expectation of sexual arousal from alcohol is a major part – stronger than the pharmacological action – of alcohol's overall effect on sexual responses and behavior (George et al. 2000, 2006).

Concurrent Use of Alcohol and Other Addictive Drugs

Those who use other psychoactive drugs that have addiction potential (including nicotine) are also likely to drink alcohol. The prevalence of drinking in the United States has not changed much since World War II. However, the illicit use of some other addictive drugs has increased since the mid-1960s whereas tobacco use has declined markedly during the same period. Although many individuals who consume alcohol do not use tobacco or illicit drugs, a large majority of those who do use these other addictive substances also drink alcohol (Harrison and McKee 2008, Midanik et al. 2007, Substance Abuse and Mental Health Services Administration 2018).

Why are individuals who use tobacco or illicit drugs also likely to drink alcohol? Perhaps the most frequent incentive for the concurrent intake of two or more addictive drugs is to increase the pleasurable effects of intoxication. The simultaneous use of alcohol and cannabis (the most frequent combination of alcohol and an illicit drug) apparently serves this purpose. Another reason for using two drugs often involves counteraction of an aversive effect of one of the drugs. Cocaine or amphetamine are often used to reduce the sedative action of alcohol, enabling a prolonged drinking session. Conversely, alcohol, or benzodiazepines such as Xanax can relieve the anxiety produced by high doses of stimulants (Martin 2008).

Sometimes two drugs are used sequentially, rather than simultaneously, in an attempt to relieve the aversive aftereffects of the initial drug use (McCabe et al. 2006). Alleviation of alcohol hangover by benzodiazepines is an obvious example of such sequential use. Another type of sequential use of different drugs is substitution of benzodiazepines or sedatives for alcohol in situations where alcohol consumption is inconvenient or prohibited.

In addition to the incentive of increased (or reduced) pharmacological actions resulting from combinations of drugs, some concurrent use is facilitated by lifestyle, cultural or other environmental factors. For adolescents, alcohol consumption is a clandestine behavior, as is the use of illicit drugs. Consequently, both drinking and drug use usually require finding suitable locations where the activity is concealed from public view. Contact with peers who encourage and facilitate use of illicit drugs as well as alcohol is likely in such locations. A similar cultural influence affects the concurrent use of tobacco (primarily smoking) and alcohol in adults (Figure 9.4). Bars and other places (e.g., parties in a private home) in which drinking is a primary activity are one of few remaining places where smoking is sometimes permitted in a culture that increasingly restricts public use of tobacco.

Figure 9.4 Heavy-drinking individuals are more likely to be nicotine dependent than are moderate drinkers, light drinkers, and especially those who are lifetime abstainers from alcohol use. Photo: Rainer Fuhrmann / EyeEm / Getty Images.

Regardless of the motivation, concurrent use of alcohol and another drug has even greater potential for hazardous consequences than does the use of only one addictive substance. The most immediate risk is due to the increased toxicity, including death, from combinations of alcohol with opioid drugs, sedatives, and (to a lesser extent) antianxiety medications.

Acute behavioral toxicity (dangerous intoxicated behavior) is also an increased hazard when alcohol is combined with illicit drugs. Along with the often-sought increased pleasure from combining drugs comes greater cognitive impairment and lessened behavioral control (Martin 2008). Because alcohol consumption impairs judgment, the use of additional "recreational" drugs, at higher doses, is more likely than in a nondrinking individual.

Among the special hazards of concurrent use of alcohol and other drugs, including nicotine, is an increased probability of addiction to these substances. As alcohol decreases an immediate or delayed aversive effect of amphetamine or cocaine, it negates some of the consequences that can prevent or retard development of dependence on the stimulant. If alcohol increases the pleasurable intoxication from cannabis, it promotes use of and dependence on the illicit drug. The alcohol myopia effect also probably facilitates tobacco usage – by diverting attention and concern away from the eventual toxic consequences of smoking. The myopic effect of alcohol can also facilitate continued use of other highly addictive drugs.

The prevalence of **nicotine addiction** is much greater in individuals with an alcohol use disorder. Based on NESARC evidence (expressed in DSM-IV terminology), nicotine dependence occurred in only about 3 percent of alcohol-abstaining individuals (not including former drinkers), but approximately 46 percent of alcohol-dependent respondents were also addicted to nicotine (Falk et al. 2006). Prevalence of nicotine addiction is also positively correlated with the levels of alcohol use not diagnosable as an SUD (Table 9.3). Even light drinkers of alcohol are at least three times more likely to be addicted smokers, and the probability of nicotine addiction rises as alcohol consumption increases, with a dramatic tenfold (or greater) increase in those addicted to alcohol.

Table 9.3 Association of levels of alcohol use with use disorders of nicotine and illicit addictive drugs

	Nicotine dependence						
Alcohol use[a]	LA	FD	L	M	H	AA	AD
Men	3.8	13.0	11.7	12.3	17.5	24.8	44.6
Women	2.9	11.2	12.3	13.8	17.1	27.2	47.3
	Illicit drug use disorder						
Alcohol use[b]	LA	FD	L	M	H	AA	AD
Men	.6	1.0	1.2	1.5	3.0	7.5	21.9
Women	.3	.4	.8	1.9	1.6	5.1	18.2

Note. Drugs of abuse/dependence (listed in descending order of disorder prevalence) were cannabis, opioids, sedatives, cocaine, hallucinogens, tranquilizer, amphetamine, solvents. LA, lifetime abstainer; FD, former drinker; L, light drinker (three or fewer drinks per week); M, moderate drinker (men, four to fourteen drinks per week; women, four to seven drinks); H, heavy drinker (men, more than fourteen drinks per week; women, more than seven drinks per week); AA, alcohol abuse; AD, alcohol dependence.

[a]Entries are percentage of NESARC respondents with nicotine dependence. [b]Entries are percentage of NESARC respondents with drug abuse or dependence during the previous twelve months.

Source. Based on information presented in Falk et al. (2006, 2008).

A similar association between frequency of drinking and the prevalence of SUD for other addictive drugs is also indicated in Table 9.3 (Falk et al. 2008). The use of illicit drugs assessed in this survey includes cannabis, opioids, cocaine, and amphetamine. Hallucinogens and solvents are also included, although a very small proportion of the population uses these drugs. The use of sedatives, tranquilizers, and other psychoactive drugs that have legitimate medical use are also included as illicit drug use when these medications were taken without a prescription. Similar results indicating a high co-occurrence between use disorders of alcohol and other addictive drugs were indicated by the third wave of the NESARC survey (Saha et al. 2018).

The increased risk for use disorders of nicotine or illicit drugs related to alcohol use disorders is quite clear. The previous discussion suggested possible ways in which heavy alcohol use can facilitate a second SUD. However, as with many risk factors, the cause–effect relationship is often uncertain. In some cases, the drug use could promote heavy drinking and alcohol dependence, so the drinking could be a result rather than a cause contributing to the drug use disorder or nicotine dependence. Another possibility is that some other factor, such as a co-occurring psychiatric disorder, drives heavy use of both addictive substances. In addition, investigators are increasingly convinced that a common genetic factor predisposes destructive use of several types of addictive drugs, especially in severe cases of polysubstance dependence (Dick and Agrawal 2008; see also Chapter 6).

Chapter Summary

Alcohol is a major cultural presence in societies throughout the world. The harmful effects of alcohol promoted prohibition of its use in the United States in the 1920s, but the restrictive law was eventually repealed, in part due to the general acceptance and popularity of alcohol consumption.

Alcohol is a central nervous system depressant, and large doses can suppress respiration and cause death. Low to moderate doses have less extreme biological and behavioral effects, many of which can be associated with actions on specific neurotransmitter systems. The amino acid neurotransmitters GABA and glutamic acid are those most directly influenced by alcohol, but the drug also alters the functions of dopamine, serotonin, opioids, and cannabinoids.

Chronic alcohol consumption produces tolerance that lessens some of the subjective and behavioral effects of drinking. The adaptive processes producing tolerance cause a rebound effect after alcohol is metabolized, resulting in dysphoric hangover. These processes also cause withdrawal syndrome when drinking stops after prolonged heavy alcohol consumption.

Positive consequences of drinking include pleasurable feelings and facilitation of social interactions. Alcohol may decrease anxiety, although this effect is not as reliable as is commonly assumed. Both the easing of social interaction and some of the anxiolytic effect may come from alcohol-produced "myopia," in which the immediate events and surroundings become more salient than remote or distant concerns. Disinhibition, the lessening of restraint on behavior, is often part of the rewarding effect of low to moderate amounts of alcohol. However, larger amounts and greater degrees of disinhibition can lead to embarrassing or dangerous behavior.

When consumed in large amounts or in certain situations, alcohol causes many harmful consequences. Most of these destructive outcomes can occur even in individuals who do not have a diagnosable alcohol use disorder. At high levels of intoxication, the disinhibition and alcohol myopia produce marked cognitive impairment, often resulting in faulty judgment and dangerous behavior. Aggression, violence, and other types of criminal behavior are associated with alcohol use. Intoxication also increases the probability of risky sexual activity and date rape. Driving while intoxicated causes many traffic accidents, and alcohol impairs other behaviors requiring coordination, concentration, or vigilance.

Although alcohol use is widely regarded as producing good feelings (e.g., the term *happy hour* to designate reduced drink prices), negative emotions sometimes emerge during intoxication. Alcohol-produced depressive states are not uncommon, and suicide is a definite risk, especially for individuals suffering from preexisting clinical depression.

The context in which drinking occurs and the expected results of drinking greatly influence alcohol effects and consumption. Alcohol use is common in many cultures, and this cultural presence establishes drinking patterns and expectations of what alcohol may do for the drinker. Although alcohol at high doses impairs physiological sexual arousal, folklore generally assigns an aphrodisiac effect to drinking, and the expectation of that result contributes to the overall effect of alcohol on sexual activity.

Although most drinkers do not use tobacco or illicit drugs, consuming alcohol is a risk factor for their use. Individuals with alcohol use disorder are at especially high risk for use disorders of nicotine and other addictive drugs.

Many individuals who drink develop alcohol use disorders, presenting a very important public health concern. Because about two-thirds of the adult population in the United States consumes alcohol, even the small percentage with an alcohol use disorder comprises an estimated 14.5 million individuals. This prevalent type of SUD is the topic of the next chapter.

Review Exercises

1. How does age influence the amount and prevalence of alcohol consumption in the United States?
2. What factors affect the bioavailability of alcohol?
3. Why is alcohol content in the breath an accurate indication of blood alcohol level?

4. What are the multiple effects of alcohol neurotransmitters in the brain?
5. Describe the subjective, cognitive, and behavioral effects of alcohol as a function of blood alcohol concentration.
6. What are the positive and negative reinforcing effects of alcohol?
7. What is alcohol myopia, and how does it affect human behavior?
8. Of the harmful effects of alcohol, which ones do you consider to be the most harmful? Justify your answer with research results cited in the text.
9. Explain how the context of use and expectancy can affect both experience of alcohol and alcohol consumption.
10. What are the reasons why individuals combine alcohol with other addictive drugs?
11. Describe in words the relationship of levels of alcohol use to nicotine dependence found in Table 9.3. Do the same for alcohol and illicit drug use.

Key Terms

alcohol myopia (321)
amnesia (314)
binge drinking (309)
blackout (314)
blood alcohol concentration (BAC) (311)
criminal violence (323)
Dionysian aspect (322)
dopamine (315)

Drug Abuse Warning Network (DAWN) (329)
endocannabinoids (316)
endogenous opioids (316)
GABA (313)
glutamic acid (314)
heavy drinking (309)
lethal alcohol dose (329)

mild cognitive deficits (326)
nicotine addiction (335)
serotonin (315)
sexual assault (323)
social context (331)
social drinking (326)
suicidal behavior (328)
traffic fatalities (323)
traumatic experience (323)

10 Alcohol Use Disorders

LEARNING OBJECTIVES

1. Explain the limitations of the use of the terms *alcoholism* and *alcoholic*.
2. Describe the incidence of alcohol users who drink safely and those with an alcohol use disorder.
3. Identify the risk factors for development of an alcohol use disorder.
4. Describe typical psychological consequences of alcohol addiction as well as the causes of the negative emotional states.
5. Describe the varied nature of the life-span course of alcohol use disorders as revealed by longitudinal studies.
6. Describe types of alcohol use disorders based on the studies of Jellinek, Babor, and Cloninger.
7. Delineate the patterns, risk factors, and consequences of alcohol use disorders for women.
8. Describe the medical problems that result from extensive and heavy use of alcohol.
9. Identify the medications used to reduce or eliminate problematic use of alcohol.

Introductory Vignette: The AA Meeting

Henry, who is recovering from a years-long alcohol use disorder, is attending a meeting of Alcoholics Anonymous. Henry has not drunk alcohol for two months and is becoming more comfortable with sharing his experiences of drinking and recovery.

Jim is the group leader.

JIM: Good evening. My name is Jim, and I am an alcoholic. Tonight I am asking for volunteers to tell us briefly about the damage done and losses you suffered while your alcohol addiction was active. In these rooms, we mostly talk about recovery, but sometimes it is worthwhile to reflect on how bad it was.

SUSAN: During the first few years that I was drinking I liked what alcohol did for me. But in later years, drinking took so much from me – even the full understanding of how much I had lost.

(*Several group members then relate how their drinking had disrupted their lives, causing them to lose jobs, good health, career opportunities, the trust of their families, and self-respect. Finally, it was Henry's turn to speak.*)

HENRY: Because of my drinking, I hurt my family, damaged my health, and lost friends – but eventually I lost something even more important. *I lost myself*!

Introduction

Many who use alcohol drink too much, too often, or at inappropriate times or places – all of which can have immediate or eventual adverse outcomes. The many harmful consequences include addiction/dependence, the costs of an addictive lifestyle, and toxic effects of chronic high dose use (Figure 10.1). Isolation, loneliness, and negative emotional states often predominate in alcohol use disorders and are expressed in popular culture in many ways – such as in Kris Kristofferson's song "Sunday Morning Comin' Down": "There ain't nothing short of dyin', that's half as lonesome as the sound – of the sleepin' city sidewalks, and Sunday morning comin' down."

Although an alcohol use disorder (often referred to as alcoholism) is still sometimes viewed as a moral failing (as discussed in Chapter 3), individuals with this disorder ("alcoholics") are generally less ostracized and less likely to face criminal charges than are those dependent on illicit drugs ("drug addicts"). This difference in social disapproval and legal sanctions between an SUD with a licit versus an illicit drug gives a relative advantage to the conduct of alcohol studies, primarily in the availability of research subjects. Finding representative subjects for

Figure 10.1 Alcohol use disorders often bring isolation and sadness. Photo: CHBD / E+ / Getty Images.

investigations of cocaine, heroin, or cannabis addiction has often presented greater difficulties due to the illicit status of these drugs. Much of our current knowledge about SUD in general (for most addictive drugs) has come from clinical observations and scientific investigations of alcohol use disorders. Examples of large-scale research efforts are the Collaborative Study of the Genetics of Alcoholism (COGA) (Begleiter et al. 1995), the **National Epidemiologic Survey on Alcohol and Related Conditions (NESARC)** (Grant and Dawson 2006, Grant et al. 2015), and the National Survey on Drug Use and Health (NSDUH) (Substance Abuse and Mental Health Services Administration 2018).

Variations among Alcohol Use Disorders

Although all who have alcohol use disorders encounter problems resulting from their drinking, the range and intensity of these adverse outcomes differ widely among individuals.

The terms *alcoholism* and *alcoholic* are in wide use in both professional entities (e.g., National Institute of Alcohol Abuse and Alcoholism) and nonprofessional organizations (Alcoholics Anonymous). However, the scientific value of these terms is limited by their frequent use in referring to widely varying disorders and individuals (Kranzler and Li 2008). The DSM and other diagnostic protocols do not use the terms *alcoholism* and *alcoholic* (partly due to the persistent negative connotations associated with these labels), and the terms are not used often in this text. *Alcoholism* may imply a unitary disorder rather than a group of related but not identical alcohol use disorders. In a similar manner *alcoholic* implies an unwarranted close similarity (if not identity) among the many individuals who use alcohol to their detriment. The label *alcoholic* also promotes an "either–or" distinction and essentially ignores the great number of less severe, borderline cases of alcohol use disorder.

The question – of whether there is one, or several (different) alcohol use disorders – is far from settled (Jackson et al. 2014). Some scholars emphasize the differences among disorders and individuals (e.g., Heilig et al. 2011, Hesselbrock and Hesselbrock 2006). Others, notably Vaillant (1995), argued that even with the definite heterogeneity, the concept of a single basic disorder (alcoholism) is defensible.

The concept of a single disorder is basic to the principles of Alcoholics Anonymous. For many members, a sense of unity ("we all have the same problem") relieves the feeling of isolation that commonly occurs in those with severe alcohol use problems. Certainly, many that benefit from twelve-step meetings find much comfort in the similarity between their own problems with alcohol and the accounts they hear from others in AA meetings. For this reason, the commonly used terms (alcoholic, alcoholism) are often useful for individuals in recovery from alcohol use disorders. However, they are less appropriate for accurate description or satisfactory explanation of problematic alcohol use.

The currently most used diagnostic system (DSM-5) attempts to accommodate the variability among the characteristics of alcohol use disorders by listing eleven criteria indicative of an alcohol use disorder (Chapter 2). With the DSM-5 system, the presence of two criteria (symptoms or signs) can identify a mild disorder, with the occurrence of additional criteria indicating more severe levels of the disorder. Therefore, two individuals could have the same diagnosis but share none of the same symptoms – a disadvantage of this diagnostic system. Different types of alcohol use disorders are discussed further in subsequent sections of the current chapter.

Measuring Severity: DSM-IV and DSM-5
The consequences of alcohol use can be ordered on a continuum that varies from an absence of problems resulting from drinking through increasingly frequent, numerous and severe effects (Jackson et al. 2014, Saha et al. 2006). The wide

range of severity is one major source of variation among alcohol use disorders. Although extreme cases are easy to identify, less severe cases of alcohol use disorder are more difficult to differentiate from nonproblematic use (Karriker-Jaffe 2015). The widespread social use of alcohol – including tolerance of some intoxication in many locations (e.g., bars, sports events) – often obscures the transition point between moderate use and a low-level use disorder. Another difficulty for identifying a less severe disorder is that some problems in a drinking individual's life – domestic, work related, interpersonal – may not be due to alcohol use. Although amount of use per se is not a diagnostic criterion, the risk of developing an alcohol use disorder rises as drinking increases, and at high levels of alcohol consumption, addiction and other adverse consequences are much more frequent (Greenfield et al. 2014).

In 2013, DSM-5 replaced DSM-IV, providing a revised system for identifying alcohol use disorders, with the level of severity indicated by the number of diagnostic criteria present in an individual. A severe SUD is now often referred to by the unofficial term *addiction*. The DSM-IV terms *abuse* and *dependence* (which primarily indicated differences in disorder severity) are rarely used in current scientific investigations or clinical diagnosis. However, the many investigations of SUD conducted prior to the adoption of DSM-5 use the earlier terminology in describing important findings. The large-scale NESARC study, a multiyear project started in 2001 and continued through 2013, is an example of an investigation using DSM-IV terminology that provides very useful information about alcohol use disorders and related conditions (Grant and Dawson 2006, Grant et al. 2015).

Incidence of Alcohol Use Disorders

Alcohol use disorders are among the most **prevalent psychiatric syndromes** in the United States (Hasin and Grant 2015, Substance Abuse and Mental Health Services Administration 2018). A large majority of those who suffer from an alcohol use disorder have never been in treatment, so their behavioral and health problems are rarely diagnosed by mental health professionals as related to excessive drinking. Therefore, the prevalence of the disorder in the overall population is best determined by epidemiological surveys. These surveys provide representative information about use patterns, demographic correlates, and problems resulting from consumption of alcohol as well as use of other drugs.

A population survey of 68,032 respondents, the National Survey on Drug Use and Health (Substance Abuse and Mental Health Services Administration 2018), indicated that in the United States, 5.6 percent of adults (age eighteen or older) – about 10.1 percent of those who currently consume alcohol – suffer from an alcohol use disorder (Figure 10.2). The survey indicated the presence of an alcohol use

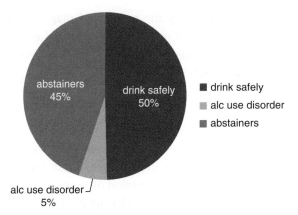

drink safely
50%

abstainers
45%

alc use disorder
5%

■ drink safely
■ alc use disorder
■ abstainers

Figure 10.2 NSDUH estimates for the prevalence of alcohol use and use disorders. Alcohol use and abstention values are for consumption during the month previous to the survey. Abstention is less prevalent for less frequent alcohol use, such as "a few times a year." "Drink safely" indicates no self-report of diagnosable alcohol use problems. Alcohol use disorder prevalence indicates occurrence during the previous year. All values are rounded to whole percentages (Substance Abuse and Mental Health Services Administration 2018).

disorder in 10 percent of all young adults ages eighteen to twenty-five – approximately 18 percent of the current drinkers of this age group. A gradual decline in the prevalence of alcohol use disorders among young adults as indicated by the annual NSDUH commenced in 2008 and has continued in the ensuing years.

Because there is no distinct boundary between a mild form of the disorder and heavy use that does not meet clinically identifiable criteria, there is little doubt that many additional individuals experience much difficulty resulting from their alcohol consumption although these problems do not qualify as an alcohol use disorder.

The National Institute on Alcohol Abuse and Alcoholism conducted three waves of the National Epidemiologic Survey on Alcohol and Related Conditions (NESARC) (Dawson et al. 2004, Grant et al. 2004, 2015). The initial survey included 43,093 respondents carefully chosen to represent all ages (eighteen or older), ethnic groups and living conditions (including group housing such as dormitories, and individual homes and apartments). A diagnostic interview with each respondent was guided by DSM-IV criteria for the initial surveys, and DSM-5 criteria for the third survey.

The NESARC surveys determined the prevalence of alcohol use disorders of different levels of severity, and all indicated that more severe disorders were less prevalent than the milder forms. The 2002 survey indicated that 4.65 percent of respondents suffered from alcohol abuse – the less severe disorder – and 3.81 percent were alcohol dependent (Grant et al. 2004). The third wave NESARC survey, conducted in 2012–2013, assessed severity of alcohol use disorders according to

DSM-5 definitions as determined by the number of diagnostic criteria exhibited by respondents (Grant et al. 2015). Consistent with the earlier NESARC survey, the 2013 survey also indicated a higher prevalence of the less severe – relative to the more severe – alcohol use disorders. A mild alcohol use disorder (2–3 criteria) was more than twice as prevalent as moderate (four to five criteria) or severe disorders (six or more criteria).

The 2002 NESARC survey interviewers also inquired about alcohol dependence (but not alcohol abuse) prior to the previous year, so this part of the survey assessed the incidence of lifetime dependence. These results indicate that the occurrence of alcohol dependence over a period of years of the lives of individuals is of higher incidence (10 percent) than is that of the state of dependence at the time the survey was taken (3.81 percent). The difference in current versus lifetime dependence, similar to that found in other epidemiological studies and long-term clinical investigations, indicates the erratic course of alcohol dependence when measured over a period of years (Finney et al. 1999, Vaillant 1995).

The NESARC surveys provide a large amount of information on persistence of the disorder, and on recovery and treatment effectiveness, discussed later in this chapter and in Chapter 16.

Development of Alcohol Use Disorders

Alcohol use disorders develop in a minority of the very large population of those who drink. Identification of risk factors, seen more often in this vulnerable subset of those who drink alcohol, is of great importance. Some of these conditions and behaviors are probable causes of the disorder, others may predict its development, and yet others may be a result of heavy alcohol use.

Risk Factors

As discussed in previous chapters, most risk factors known to be associated with the development of alcohol use disorders are also related to harmful use of other addictive drugs. No single factor is a certain predictor, and a greater number of risk factors increases the incidence and severity of problematic alcohol use and lowers the age of onset of the disorder. These risk factors include genetic predisposition/ family history, certain psychiatric disorders and personality characteristics, and use of other addictive drugs (Grant et al. 2015, Saha et al. 2018). Additional factors are childhood experiences (trauma, some parenting styles) and behavior (conduct disorder, ADHD), frequent drug use (including nicotine or alcohol) during early adolescence, and social or cultural factors that encourage alcohol use and intoxication. Combinations of these risk factors differ among individuals who develop problems with alcohol use, a finding thought to be related to the different types of the disorder. Essentially, anyone who consumes alcohol is somewhat vulnerable to the occurrence of alcohol abuse or addiction. Although a greater number of risk factors increases the probability of an alcohol use disorder, some individuals develop drinking problems in the absence of known risk factors.

The NESARC survey of 2013 identified demographic variables associated with the severity of alcohol use disorders. Severe disorders tend to emerge at younger ages – a mean of age 23.9, relative to mean age 30.1 for a mild disorder – and more often in respondents with only high school or a lower educational level (Grant et al. 2015).

Transition from Benign Use into Use Disorder

Chapter 7 describes the transition of alcohol or other drug use from a rewarding activity into the compulsive and damaging behavior of addiction. Initially pleasant or useful consequences are gradually replaced by increasingly harmful outcomes of drinking. The aversive effects of drinking diminish other sources of pleasure, comfort, and resources for coping. Paradoxically, drinking becomes a primary, if ineffective, solution for the problems caused or worsened by alcohol use.

The rewarding nature of alcohol intoxication differs among individuals. Some report feeling less anxious, whereas others feel more powerful or experience a more complex desirable effect (Chapter 7). Caroline Knapp describes one such subjective experience in *Drinking: A Love Story*, the account of her alcohol addiction and recovery:

> For a long time, when it's working, the drink feels like a path to a kind of self-enlightenment, something that turns us into the person we think we really are. In some ways, the dynamic is this simple: alcohol makes everything better until it makes everything worse. And when drinking makes things better, it does so with such easy perfection, lifting you, shifting you – just like that – into another self.

> And it does, at least for a little while. It melts down the pieces of us that hurt or feel distress; it makes room for some other self to emerge, a version that's new and improved and decidedly less conflicted. (Knapp 1996, pp. 65–66)

Although the subjective nature of intoxication varies, for many drinkers the pleasurable effects of alcohol promote more frequent drinking, and in larger amounts.

All who develop problems with alcohol use do not progress to addiction, with many showing changes of both increasing and decreasing severity of the disorder over a period of years (Dawson et al. 2005, Lee and Sher 2018, Vaillant 1995). Human lives are complex and differ markedly among individuals. Alcohol use disorders cause various types of problems that are imposed on different personalities and lifestyles. Although not all cases of problematic alcohol use are identical, some common features occur, both in the **progression** and in the eventual full expression of the disorder.

Some who suffer from alcohol use disorders maintain that they were "born an alcoholic" or that the malady appeared full-blown with their first drink. However, clinicians and investigators agree that the disorders develop fully only after repeated exposure to alcohol, typically over a period of months or years (Kinney 2009). In George Vaillant's long-term study of alcohol problems, the transition from asymptomatic social use through harmful use to alcohol addiction for most men occurred gradually over a span of three to fifteen years (Vaillant 1995). Some of Vaillant's subjects drank socially for twenty years before their use of alcohol could be identified as abuse or addiction.

Development and progression of the disorders vary widely among individuals. The personality traits of poor impulse control and negative emotionality, and the disorders of antisocial and borderline personality – risk factors for SUD – often accelerate progression of problematic alcohol use. For many individuals with these difficult behavioral and emotional characteristics, early stages of alcohol use disorder may not be very different from their life without alcohol. Arguments and fights, other interpersonal problems, emotional upheavals, reckless and antisocial behavior in general may be common even when sober, but increased by alcohol use. These individuals are apparently those most likely to profess "instant alcoholism."

In the early stages of progression (especially the less rapid "slow-track" transitions), some negative consequences of drinking may not be recognized as clearly connected to alcohol use. Even those who abstain or drink safely sometimes have "bad days" – or evenings – when they feel lethargic, ill, depressed, or anxious; act irresponsibly; or fail to meet an obligation. Of course, individuals who drink too much, or at the wrong place or time, must quite often explain (at least to themselves, and sometimes to others) the reason for some unpleasant outcome of their drinking.

Making excuses that do not involve drinking is sometimes convenient and easy. Drinking-related incidents can often be explained in a manner that does not implicate intoxication: "I didn't forget my credit card because I had three martinis – it was hidden by the napkin that the bartender carelessly laid over it." Another example: "Yeah, I fell and hurt my knee, but not because I drank wine at the reception. There was a loose brick on the steps." Placing the blame for a bad outcome on drinking might threaten an important source of pleasure and comfort and would call into question the wisdom of the decision to drink.

As drinking-related problems become more frequent and severe, simple excuses become inadequate to justify continued drinking. Denial, rationalization, and other **defense mechanisms** can distort reality to prevent recognition of the destructive role of drinking. Individuals without substance use problems sometimes use these defense mechanisms to deal with self-destructive behavior or other difficulties of life. However, the reality distortions often become quite prevalent and of increasing importance as the abusive drinker attempts to understand what is happening in her life, while protecting her use of alcohol. An obsessive relationship with alcohol emerges and drives the compulsive drinking. This pathological connection to alcohol is typically hidden from self-awareness – or justified – at least most of the time. The obsession with drinking may be briefly acknowledged, but reasons for alcohol use are emphasized, even if they are of doubtful validity.

Caroline Knapp describes thinking that often accompanies excessive and harmful drinking:

> The mind's capacity to play with the facts becomes limitless. *I have my reasons.... I know I am obsessing and I know it's crazy, but I have my reasons.*
>
> And yes, we all have our reasons. We're bored or we're restless or we're depressed. We're worried or anxious or stressed. We're celebrating, or we're grieving. Tomorrow. We'll deal with it tomorrow. We'll deal with it *when things get better.* (Knapp 1996, p. 155)

Advanced Stages of Alcohol Addiction

Unfortunately, for many with an alcohol use disorder things do not get better, at least not for long, and they improve only after becoming much worse. In this advanced stage of problematic drinking alcohol causes many difficulties and much pain. However, the early parts of a drinking session can still be quite comforting, giving an illusion of emotional authenticity and access to true feelings (Knapp 1996, p. 116). An emotional relationship with alcohol often underlies the inability to consistently control the frequency and amount of drinking, and paradoxically produces even more disturbing consequences.

As an individual's control over drinking declines, actions become unpredictable. Work demands and family obligations are often unmet. Unreliability, plus the tendency to blame others for erratic behavior, damages relationships with other people. There are attempts to conceal alcohol use by avoiding many social interactions and withdrawing from close personal contacts. As isolation from friends, family and work associates grows, so does the use of alcohol as an emotional solace.

Eventually even defense mechanisms cannot prevent the realization that alcohol use is a serious problem. Three DSM-5 diagnostic criteria for alcohol use disorder (Chapter 2) are based on unsuccessful attempts to control drinking, and the persistence of behavior that is clearly self-destructive. Except for the most antisocial, narcissistic, or insensitive (well-defended?) individuals, the damage to self-esteem is severe. It is quite difficult for the alcohol-addicted person to avoid feelings of guilt, shame, and an overall sense of inadequacy and negative self-image. Intoxication eventually only worsens the emotional distress. The emotional costs of addiction, as well as the short-lived relief gained from drinking, are portrayed in many autobiographical accounts, works of fiction, poems and songs of many cultures.

The incidence of suicide is greater in alcohol-dependent individuals, and is sharply increased in those with a concurrent depressive disorder (Chapter 8).

At least three factors contribute to the anxiety, anger, and depression typical of alcohol addiction. The first is the emotional impact (isolation, shame, and guilt) resulting from the erratic behavior and failed responsibilities that accompany an addictive lifestyle. Second, neurological changes in the brain's reward system resulting from heavy alcohol use can produce a lingering dysphoric state. Finally, both affective disorders (bipolar and unipolar depression) and anxiety disorders such as PTSD are risk factors for alcohol use disorder. These psychiatric syndromes often co-occur with – and are worsened by – heavy alcohol use.

Many who persist in heavy drinking experience adverse consequences, such as amnesic episodes (blackouts) and a multitude of other crises or chronic difficulties. Some develop physiological dependence, as evidenced by a characteristic withdrawal syndrome.

Life-span Course of Alcohol Use Disorders

A basic principle of the classic disease theory of alcoholism is that early death or severe life disruption occurs unless the alcoholic stops drinking. This description of an inevitable life course of alcohol use disorder resulted from Jellinek's early and influential study based on subjective and retrospective accounts of a select group of AA members (Jellinek 1946). Jellinek's findings were inappropriately generalized and used to create a chart describing the supposed typical course of the disorder. The "Jellinek Chart" projects a worsening sequence of events, including increasingly destructive drinking and the harmful outcomes described in this text. The Jellinek Chart is often presented in treatment programs as an evidence-based description of the natural course of alcoholism rather than as the result of a small and biased sample of individuals. Research that is more recent – conducted with larger and more representative groups of individuals – shows clearly that the disorder is extremely variable, both among individual cases and over the course of a lifetime (Vaillant 1995, Yalisove 2004).

Premature death is more likely in those with alcohol use disorders than in a healthy population. Estimates of the odds ratio of earlier death vary from 3.64 for men during a twenty-year period (Marshall et al. 1994) to 9.5 for both genders during a ten-year period (Finney and Moos 1991). Although a disproportionate number of heavy drinkers die younger, many live for decades with an alcohol use disorder.

The life-span course of the disorder is of much interest, with several relevant studies conducted during the past half-century. In some long-term studies, individuals were interviewed periodically during a span of years after completion of treatment for alcohol use disorders (e.g., Skog and Duckert 1993, Taylor et al. 1985). Most of these extended studies of clinical populations were conducted in order to determine treatment effectiveness and the incidence of relapse, discussed further in Chapter 16.

In other investigations, groups of selected participants (not patients in treatment) underwent long-term observation of their drinking behavior and related conditions and events (e.g., McCord and McCord 1960, Schulenberg et al. 1996). George Vaillant's fifty-year study is the longest, and perhaps the best known, of such investigations (Vaillant 1995). These studies are more representative of the overall population than are the clinical follow-up studies. Such investigations provide information about the many individuals who develop drinking problems but never seek professional help for an alcohol use disorder.

Yet another source of information about the course of alcohol use disorders are epidemiological surveys, such as the NESARC studies. The surveys are not primarily longitudinal observations, but are subjective retrospective accounts, as were stories summarized in the original Jellinek report. However, the more recent surveys are carefully designed to represent the general adult population, and include a large number of respondents in order to maximize their statistical reliability.

The longitudinal studies encounter challenges as their respondents are tracked over a number of years. Attrition occurs as the investigators lose contact with some of their subjects. Such investigations are also expensive and require continued effort and attention during the entire observation period. Other matters – including changes in definitions of the disorders with revisions of the DSM system – make meaningful comparison among investigations difficult. Other relevant cultural changes include the availability of treatment programs and popularity of other addictive "recreational" drugs, such as marijuana (starting in the 1960s), Quaaludes (in the 1970s), cocaine (starting in the 1980s), and the increased use of pharmaceutical opioids in the second decade of the twenty-first century. These long-term cultural changes cause the results of longitudinal studies to be to some extent cohort-specific (Vaillant 1995).

Even with these limitations, studies of the long-term course of harmful drinking and its consequences provide valuable insights into the natural history of the disorders. All of these investigations show that as alcohol use problems develop, the disorders worsen progressively in only some individuals. The classic ("Jellinek-like") progression is just one of several different lifetime trajectories of alcohol use and life disruption. Some recover from the disorder (with or without treatment) and become securely abstinent. Others have periods of variable levels of alcohol use and consequent problems, often interspersed with periods of abstinence. Yet others continue to drink, but at apparently safe levels (Dawson et al. 2005, Grant et al. 2015).

The percentage of individuals drinking (or abstaining) in each of these long-term use patterns varies among the different investigations, but all studies reveal a complex array of results (Fillmore et al. 1991, Johnstone et al. 1996). The variability, in conjunction with the multivariate nature of risk factors, implies that alcohol use disorders are best described as a class of related, but not identical types of problematic drinking.

Patterns of disordered drinking can vary dramatically over a life-span. For many individuals, especially men, heavy drinking is most likely in the early adult years but alcohol consumption often lessens during midlife. The presence of two DSM-5 criteria – resulting in a diagnosis of a mild use disorder – at age twenty-five does not reliably predict the same diagnosis at age fifty. As noted previously, differentiating between periodic heavy drinking and a low-level use disorder is often difficult (Karriker-Jafe et al. 2015). Vaillant also maintains that an observation period of many years may be required to identify some patterns of progression (Vaillant 1995).

The long-term variation among use patterns is greater in less severe disorders. A greater proportion of persistently increasing use and worsening consequences occur in the more severe cases (Yalisove 2004). This difference is reflected in the somewhat greater heterogeneity in the community samples, the majority of which does not receive treatment for the disorder. The more homogeneous clinical follow-up studies include more extreme cases of the disorders.

Heavy drinking occurs in some adolescents, and several investigations have tracked the continuity of alcohol abuse from the teen years into early adulthood. These studies in general reveal a variety of drinking trajectories, with at least as many differences as in the longer-term course of alcohol use disorders of adults (D'Amico et al. 2002, Lee and Sher 2018, Maggs and Schulenberg 2004/2005, Windle 2016). Whereas some teen-aged individuals mature out of binge drinking within months or a few years, others maintain abusive drinking patterns, and still others who rarely drank as adolescents start heavy drinking as young adults.

Two specific examples of alcohol use disorder over a period of many years illustrate the wide range of differences in alcohol abuse and addiction. One "life story" is George Vaillant's account of an attorney who drank heavily throughout his adult life, with – as compared to many other cases – few harmful consequences. This individual was one of Vaillant's college sample of well-educated men, whose long-term drinking patterns were monitored for fifty years (Vaillant 1995, p. 181). The other is Donald Newlove's description of the alcoholism of a Nobel Prize–winning novelist (Newlove 1981, p. 142). Although achieving success and acclaim early in his career, the writer drank heavily for many years with many extremely harmful and disturbing consequences, culminating in death.

Types of Alcohol Use Disorder

The variability among alcohol use disorders motivates investigators to search for **homogeneous groups** of afflicted individuals with similar risk factors, use patterns and consequences of alcohol use. Identifying distinct, more homogeneous groups could facilitate understanding of the etiology of the disorders, guide diagnosis and enable better use of treatment methods, including medication. Appropriate matching of clients with specific treatment approaches (based on identification of valid subtypes) should improve treatment effectiveness (Leggio et al. 2009, Tam et al. 2014).

The attempt to determine types or subtypes of alcohol use disorders has a long history (Babor 1996). Early schemes of classification resembled those developed for subtypes of other psychiatric disorders, such as schizophrenia. These subtypes were based primarily on clinical observation of patterns of similarities and differences among patients with the disorder. These judgments were usually subjective and nonquantitative.

Jellinek's Gamma-Delta Classification

Jellinek (1960) described five types of alcohol use disorders, although he considered only two of these as representing true disease entities. Jellinek hypothesized several differences (including reasons for excessive drinking) between his gamma and delta types of alcoholism. There is little consistent evidence for many of these supposed differences, but these types did differentiate two well-recognized patterns of alcoholic drinking. Gamma alcoholics sometimes abstained from drinking for extensive periods, but once a "binge" was initiated, exerted little control and drank very heavily. Delta alcoholics drank frequently on most days and although somewhat intoxicated throughout much of the day, typically avoided extreme drunkenness. Jellinek's book *The Disease Concept of Alcoholism* was very popular and greatly influenced views of alcohol use disorders. Despite the wide acceptance of his gamma-delta typology, little empirical research was conducted to validate Jellinek's classification system, such as by means of diagnostic measurements. There were few attempts to match treatments with the different types (Babor and Dolinsky 1988).

Binary Classification Systems

Beginning in the 1970s theorists developed use disorder types based on multiple defining characteristics and empirical data (Babor 1996). Two of the most influential of these more recent typologies are those of Cloninger (Cloninger et al. 1981) and Babor (Babor et al. 1992). Cloninger's Type I–Type II system was based on personality characteristics, but included several other features including family history of alcohol use disorders. Cloninger's personality theory is summarized in Chapter 8. Babor's Type A/B system was developed by means of statistical cluster analysis, in which the groupings of seventeen features of the disorder were considered.

The two basic types identified by both Cloninger and Babor are quite similar. These groups are differentiated by vulnerability (number of risk factors), and the severity of the disorder (e.g., persistence of the disorder, adverse consequences of drinking) (Babor and Cateano 2006). Box 10.1 summarizes these two basic types. Several investigators have made use of and provided validation for binary systems, in particular the A/B types of Babor (e.g., Hesselbrock et al. 2000, Schuckit et al. 1995).

BOX 10.1 Two types of alcohol use disorder

Both Cloninger's and Babor's systems of alcohol use disorder types identify two groups of individuals with similar characteristics.

Lower Vulnerability and Less Severe: Cloninger Type I, Babor Type A

Late (after age twenty-five) onset of problem drinking
Few childhood risk factors (relatively trouble-free)
Little or no alcohol use disorder in family history (parents, grandparents)
Minimal preexisting and emergent psychopathology
Relatively lower level of alcohol consumption (than Type II)
Compared to Type II, lower incidence of disturbing consequences from drinking and fewer serious social, psychological, and physical difficulties resulting from alcohol use

Greater Vulnerability and More Severe: Cloninger Type II, Babor Type B

Early onset (before age twenty-five) of problem drinking (Figure 10.3)
Several childhood risk factors (conduct disorder, attention deficit hyperactive disorder)
Family history of alcohol use disorder
Preexisting and concurrent psychopathology (e.g., antisocial or borderline personality disorder)
Heavier and more persistent alcohol consumption (than Type I)
Frequent serious consequences from alcohol use (arrests, drunken fights)

Although Cloninger's and Babor's types are similar, there are some differences. For example, Cloninger's Type II included only men, but Babor's Type B included both genders. Cloninger's types were also differentiated by personality characteristics that are not listed here.

Tam and colleagues determined that the **binary classification** had predictive validity for respondents in the NESARC survey, demonstrating the usefulness of Type A/B typology in the general population of individuals with alcohol use disorders – as well as for patients in treatment (Tam et al. 2014). About one-third of dependent drinkers of the NESARC survey could be classified as the more severe Type B, a proportion similar to that previously reported for patients in treatment (e.g., Epstein et al. 2002).

Figure 10.3 Type II alcohol use disorder. Type II alcohol use disorder often emerges in adolescent boys or young men with several risk factors who drink to extreme levels of intoxication that can result in dangerous consequences. Photo: Paul Mansfield photography / Moment / Getty Images.

Type A individuals start drinking heavily only after years of socially acceptable alcohol use. This more benign form of the disorder progresses slowly with fewer complications, less disturbing behavior, and the prognosis is generally better. Conversely, Type B individuals start problem drinking earlier, they have more severe symptoms and adverse consequences from drinking, and their prognosis is worse than for those of Type A (Carpenter and Hasin 2001).

Each individual classified as Type A or B may not exhibit all the characteristics attributed to that type of alcohol use disorder. However, the risk factors, drinking patterns and consequences do tend to appear in clusters, so the occurrence of any one (e.g., early onset of heavy drinking) makes the presence of the other characteristics (such as severe consequences) more likely.

Evidence of genetic predisposition and underlying neurological abnormalities is more convincing for the more severe form of the disorders, which in many instances could be classified as Type B (Chapter 5).

The binary typology shows some promise for more effective pharmacological treatment of alcohol use disorders. For example, alcohol intake was significantly reduced in Type B subjects treated with the drug ondansetron/Zofran, an antagonist for serotonin at the $5HT_3$ receptor (e.g., Johnson 2010, Roache et al. 2008). Most studies with ondansetron show no effect or a much smaller reduction of drinking in subjects with the Type A disorder. The therapeutic drug may reduce drinking by decreasing the rewarding effect of alcohol-produced dopamine release, which depends partially on alcohol's agonist effect at this serotonin receptor. The differences in alcohol effects on brain function between Types A and B are as of yet undetermined.

In the Roache study the age-of-onset variable was a better predictor of a positive response to ondansetron treatment than was the classification of Type A/B disorder (based on the complete set of Babor's characteristics of the types). This finding suggests that age of onset may be the most robust and clinically useful differentiating feature of the binary classification system (Leggio et al. 2009).

Limitations of Binary Classification

Division of individuals with alcohol use disorder into two types does decrease within-group (type) differences. However, the binary classification may be too simple, and inadequate to account for the heterogeneity of alcohol use disorders (Epstein et al. 2002). Other investigators have developed systems of alcohol use disorder subtypes that are more complex than the two-group classification (e.g., Moss et al. 2007, Windle and Scheidt 2004). Most of these type systems include the basic types of the binary classifications, but further subdivide individuals into three, four, or even five groups. These subtypes are based primarily on gender differences, the presence and nature of co-occurring psychiatric disorders, and misuse of other addictive drugs concurrent with problematic alcohol consumption.

Accurate description of the heterogeneity of alcohol use disorders may require the creation of more than two subtypes. However, most treatment facilities cannot devote the time and effort required to diagnose and classify individuals in such a multiple-type system. Consequently, the clinical utility of the more complex type systems may be limited, even if they are more theoretically valid than a simpler two-type system that might require fewer diagnostic indicators (Hesselbrock and Hesselbrock 2006, Tam et al. 2014).

Some investigators place less importance on the typology of alcohol use disorders. Epstein (2001) suggests that the various types and subtypes reflect a continuum of severity, rather than distinct categories of the disorder. George Vaillant maintained that the single factor of antisocial personality disorder (ASPD) under-lies most of the differences used to establish types. ASPD promotes heavy drinking at an early age, with the more disturbing consequences and rapid progression of a more severe disorder. Vaillant defended the position that although problematic alcohol use patterns are quite heterogeneous, they are variations on essentially the same disorder (Vaillant 1995).

Alcohol Use Disorders in Women

Women are less likely to drink than men, and women who drink consume less alcohol than men (Substance Abuse and Mental Health Services Administration 2008). Women also have a lower incidence of alcohol use disorders than men (Grant et al. 2015). The NESARC epidemiological survey revealed an incidence ratio between men and women of 2.72:1 for alcohol abuse, and 2.32:1 for alcohol dependence. The ratio of men to women in treatment for alcohol use problems is about 3:1. The somewhat smaller difference between male-female ratios from epidemiological versus clinical studies reflects the lower probability of afflicted women to enter treatment (Greenfield et al. 2007).

The differences in both the amount of social drinking and the incidence of alcohol use disorders between genders are becoming smaller – partly due to the changed role of women during the last thirty years of the twentieth century (Hasin and Grant 2015). Drinking by women became more accepted, and women gained entry into occupations and activities (e.g., sports, law enforcement, military ser-vice) dominated by men (Brady and Randall 1999). Much of the earlier societal expectation that women should not drink has lessened, but many of the culturally determined special problems for women who drink excessively remain (Figure 10.4) (Blume and Zilberman 2005, Erol and Karpyak 2015). The gender-related differences in alcohol use and incidence of use disorders are much smaller in younger, compared to older women (Grant et al. 2015). An increased number of younger women also exhibit the Type II/B pattern of problematic drinking, previ-ously seen primarily in young men (Zilberman 2009).

Special Features of Use Disorders in Women
For much of the twentieth century – from Jellinek's promotion of the disease con-cept in the 1950s through Cloninger's adoption studies in the 1970s to Vaillant's description of the natural history of alcoholism in the 1980s – almost all research on alcohol use disorders dealt with men only. Following the increased prevalence of drinking and drug use by women, research on alcohol use disorders and other SUD of women has greatly increased since the 1990s (Greenfield et al. 2007). For women, many of the risk factors and consequences of heavy, destructive drinking

Figure 10.4 Women with alcohol use disorders face many of the same risks, vulnerabilities, and challenges as do men, and others that are unique to their gender. Photo: Image Source / Photodisc / Getty Images.

are very similar to those seen in men. However, some risk factors, vulnerabilities and consequences are either unique to or are more important for women. Box 10.2 summarizes some of the main clinical features of alcohol use disorders that are more prevalent in women than in men.

BOX 10.2 Gender-specific differences in alcohol use disorders

Relative to men, women with alcohol use disorder have the following characteristics:

Start problem drinking at a later age
Disorder progresses more rapidly

Consume significantly less alcohol
Husband (or significant other) more likely to be a substance abuser
More likely to be divorced, separated, or single
Have higher rates of co-occurring psychiatric disorder
Are more likely to have had previous psychiatric treatment
Have higher rates of concurrent prescription drug dependence
Are more likely to attempt suicide
Are more likely to have a history of physical and sexual abuse
Are more likely to attribute the onset of pathological drinking to a specific stressful event
Have a higher mortality rate

After Blume and Zilberman (2005)

Cultural Influences and Vulnerabilities

Several risk factors and consequences unique to women are determined by the prevalent **cultural judgment** of heavy drinking in women – or by relationships of an individual woman with the men in her life.

In regard to the pervasive and general cultural effects, heavy drinking is sometimes considered daring and "macho" in men – perhaps even given guarded admiration and approval. In women, however, similar drinking behavior is rarely condoned. Even for those with progressive and liberal attitudes, a hard-drinking woman is often seen as promiscuous or at least of questionable character. An intoxicated woman may appear more sexually available. In certain occupations (e.g., entertainment, some types of sales, and writing) some drinking in the workplace is accepted or at least tolerated – for men. The primary parenting role is still most often the mother's responsibility, and drinking is (appropriately) seen as incompatible with competent and responsible child-care. The stereotype or assumption of promiscuity and irresponsible parenting increase the shame and guilt of women with an alcohol use disorder. The ensuing secrecy and denial result in reluctance to seek assistance for problematic drinking (Erol and Karpyak 2015).

A husband without a substance use problem is much more likely to divorce or abandon his alcohol-dependent wife than is a healthy woman to detach from and leave an alcoholic husband (Kinney 2009). As a result, women with alcohol use disorders are more likely to be divorced than are men. When a husband and wife both have an alcohol use disorder, separation is less likely than if only the woman has a drinking problem (Blume and Zilberman 2005).

Sexual trauma, especially in female children or adolescents, greatly increases (approximately triples) the likelihood of later SUD – including alcohol use disorder. Because sexual assaults on girls are most often committed by men, this risk factor is another example of how behavior of men can contribute to the occurrence of alcohol use disorders in women. Early sexual trauma also increases risk of SUD in men, but is apparently more prevalent and the effect is greater in women. Incestuous relationships are especially severe risk factors, possibly due to their longer duration and the increased level of shame and guilt (Blume and Zilberman 2005).

Women in traditionally male occupations (e.g., law enforcement, military) are at higher risk of developing alcohol use disorders. Women who are "underemployed" in low-demand occupations may also be at risk due to boredom and the possible increased opportunity of clandestine drinking in the workplace. Yet another risk factor is the absence of young children, either because of never having been a mother, or after adult children have left the home (Greenfield et al. 2007).

Other Gender-Related Risk Factors

Women report drinking to control specific emotional states (reduce anxiety, gain confidence) or for increased sociability more often than men (Zilberman 2009). Some controlled investigations indicate that alcohol is more rewarding during the luteal (premenstrual) phase of the menstrual cycle (e.g., Evans and Levin 2011) although other studies have failed to detect similar effects. Emotional-behavioral motivation for drinking does not indicate the presence of an alcohol use disorder, but could easily lead to heavier alcohol use, and eventually to addiction as described in Chapter 8. Women, more than men, also identify external causes (personal difficulties or traumatic incidents) as triggering their progression from social drinking into problematic alcohol use (Greenfield et al. 2010).

Women are much more likely than men to suffer co-occurring psychiatric disorders (COD), especially those of depression and anxiety (Zilberman et al. 2003). Heavy drinking can cause or worsen depression and anxiety, so self-medication of a preexisting disorder is not always involved when a COD is present. However, the case for an alcohol use disorder being at least partially due to attempts to control anxiety by drinking is especially strong for women. In women, there is a greater probability that the concurrent psychopathology predates the harmful drinking and so may be the primary disorder (Greenfield et al. 2007). Whether a cause or a result of abusive drinking, CODs are clearly associated with alcohol use disorders in women. Eating disorders, more prevalent in women, are also a risk factor, especially for younger women (Blume and Zilberman 2005).

The genetic transmission of vulnerability to alcohol use disorders appears to be somewhat different between women and men (Prescott 2002). It is likely that environmental factors (including sexual trauma and cultural influences as mentioned previously) are relatively more important for women. If so, the proportion of total risk factors for disordered alcohol use contributed by genetic differences in women would be less than for men.

Patterns and Consequences of Disordered Alcohol Use in Women

Although women generally start heavy drinking later in life than men and even with a use disorder drink less, the disorder progresses more rapidly, and some consequences are more severe (Erol and Kapyak 2015). A significant gender difference was found in elapsed time between the start of regular intoxication and first seeking treatment, which was 15.8 years for men versus 11.6 years for women (Randall et al. 1999).

Most women fit better into the Type A category, mainly because their drinking starts later in life and is less likely to have socially disturbing consequences such as overt intoxication, fights and criminal activity. As with men, many women do not completely match all characteristics of either type of alcohol use disorder. Some use patterns more similar to those of men occur in younger women, probably reflecting both an age difference and recent cultural changes (Erol and Kapyak 2015, Schulte et al. 2009, Zilberman 2009).

Like men, women are often reluctant to seek professional help for problems with alcohol use. Those with alcohol-related problems are, however, more likely than men to request medical attention (and drugs) from a primary care physician for depression, anxiety, headache, insomnia, and other problems not necessarily related to drinking. The greater guilt and shame often felt by women about a drinking problem no doubt contribute to their attempts to conceal their alcohol use or even to realize that their drinking might cause the distressing symptoms (Greenfield et al. 2010, 2007).

Women with children may avoid seeking treatment that directly addresses an alcohol use disorder. One likely reason for this reluctance is that problematic alcohol use (and especially concurrent use of illicit drugs) can result in loss of custody of children. However, in some cases the threat of this consequence can motivate entry into a treatment program.

Women generally suffer more severely than men do from the harmful effects of heavy alcohol consumption on the liver, heart and other organs and biological functions such as maintenance of bone density (Sampson 2002) and the immune response (Kovacs and Messingham 2002). This toxicity occurs even with the relatively lower alcohol consumption of women with use disorders. Heavy alcohol use can also disrupt the normal menstrual cycle and counteract some protective effects of estrogen (Emanuale et al. 2002). The greater vulnerability of women to these toxic actions of alcohol results in a higher mortality rate for alcohol-dependent women relative to men. The risk of suicide is also greater in alcohol-addicted women than in men (Blume and Zilberman 2005).

The teratogenic effect of alcohol on the developing fetus is a risk of drinking for women. Fetal alcohol effects are discussed later in this chapter under the general topic of biological toxicity.

Medical Problems from Chronic Alcohol Consumption

When alcohol is consumed in large amounts for extended periods, the drug disrupts essential bodily functions and has toxic effects on several organs and tissues. With long-term high-dose use, the toxicity of alcohol may be greater than that of any other addictive drug (Kanny et al. 2015). Death can result from acute effects (lethal overdose), chronic effects (organ damage), or severe withdrawal after stopping heavy use.

Alcohol Withdrawal

The **alcohol withdrawal syndrome** has been recognized and described since ancient times. For centuries the characteristic signs and symptoms were thought to result from intoxication per se, rather than to the aftereffects of chronic, heavy alcohol use. During the nineteenth century, physicians began to suspect that the delirium, hallucinations and extreme emotional arousal were a result of stopping drinking after heavy alcohol consumption (Raistrick 2001). In the twentieth century the connection between stopping drinking and the emergence of the withdrawal syndrome was determined by clinical observation of 286 alcoholic patients (Victor and Adams 1953). The critical role of abstinence after prolonged drinking was later confirmed by a controlled study. Ten patients previously addicted to morphine were administered high doses of alcohol for twelve weeks. At this point alcohol intake was terminated and subsequently the signs and symptoms of withdrawal developed (Isbell et al. 1955). An investigation of this type would not be permitted under current ethical guidelines for conduct of research.

Many studies with animal subjects have shown conclusively that the withdrawal syndrome is a consequence of rebound of central nervous system activity after neuroadaptation to chronic alcohol administration (Koob and Le Moal 2006). Two neurotransmitter systems are implicated in this state of hyperarousal. Alcohol is an agonist for GABA activity, so the function of this inhibitory neurotransmitter is down-regulated during chronic alcohol consumption. The opposite actions occur with glutamic acid, as the function of this excitatory neurotransmitter is up-regulated in response to the antagonist effect of alcohol on glutamatergic activity.

Although patients are no longer administered (and then denied) alcohol in deliberate efforts to produce the withdrawal syndrome, clinicians have had many opportunities to observe and describe withdrawal in those with alcohol use disorders. The syndrome varies in intensity, depending in part on the amount of alcohol consumption before drinking is interrupted. At low levels withdrawal produces autonomic arousal and discomfort. As described previously, the delayed alcohol effect of hangover is considered as a very mild and short-lived form of withdrawal. At its most extreme, the withdrawal syndrome is a dramatic, harrowing and life-threatening combination of hyperarousal, convulsions, hallucinations, delirium and failed organ (mainly cardiac) function (Mayo-Smith 2003). Withdrawal is one of eleven criteria for alcohol use disorder in the DSM-5, and is neither necessary nor sufficient for a diagnosis of the disorder.

Goldstein (1983) describes the sequence of events that often occur when drinking is abruptly stopped (or markedly reduced) after consumption of ten to fifteen standard drinks each day over a period of ten days. The first symptoms may develop within a few hours after the last drink, but might be delayed as long as forty-eight hours. The individual is anxious, insomniac, and has muscular tremors (shakiness) which can be mild or moderate. Sympathetic nervous system activity (sweating, blood pressure, heart rate, body temperature) is increased, and convulsions may occur.

Perceptual disturbances, primarily increased sensitivity to sounds or light, may be experienced. Visual, auditory and tactile hallucinations also can occur during this first forty-eight-hour period of withdrawal (Mayo-Smith 2003). In withdrawal of moderate intensity, the patient may realize that the hallucinations are not "real," but in more severe cases, they are often seen as actual threats. In either case, the hallucinations are very frightening and cause much distress.

In about 10 percent of patients that do not receive medical attention, withdrawal becomes more intense, developing into the state of **delirium tremens** approximately two to four days after the last drink. The "DT's" are the extreme form of withdrawal, and include more pronounced expressions of the previously mentioned symptoms (hyperarousal, tremor). Marked delirium (loss of contact with reality), agitation and paranoia also characterize this advanced stage. Even with medical intervention, 1 or 2 percent of patients die in this state, usually due to extreme hyperthermia, hypoglycemia or cardiac failure. These fatal outcomes are most likely in patients who have concurrent medical problems in addition to alcohol dependence (Goldstein 1983).

Medical care, primarily administration of benzodiazepine drugs, is effective for controlling the severity of symptoms of most patients who undergo withdrawal from alcohol. These drugs typically prevent the progression of withdrawal into the most severe, delirium tremens stage, and their use has greatly reduced the occurrence of death that can otherwise result from alcohol withdrawal. Reassurance and supportive nursing care is helpful for the 90 percent of patients for whom pharmacological treatment is not necessary. Even in the severe cases of withdrawal, most symptoms abate within seven days, and in milder episodes within three days (Mayo-Smith 2003).

The withdrawal syndrome varies greatly in intensity among individuals. The severity is partly determined by the extent and amount of alcohol consumption that precedes the interruption of drinking. Another factor that apparently increases withdrawal severity is a previous history of withdrawals – especially if seizures (convulsions) occurred during these earlier withdrawals (Booth and Blow 1993).

Avoidance of alcohol withdrawal was considered by some to be a major incentive for continued drinking in those with alcohol dependence (Edwards 1990). However, the threat of acute withdrawal does not appear to be a motivating factor in most cases of alcohol dependence. Some abusive drinking patterns (e.g., periodic binge drinking) do not result in withdrawal, or at least no more than a mild withdrawal experienced as a hangover. Many individuals with alcohol use disorder do not experience the withdrawal syndrome.

In those that do undergo a harrowing withdrawal and resume drinking, avoidance of the aversive, potentially life-threatening experience can be a strong incentive to continue consuming alcohol. Duncan Raistrick reports two instances of alcohol-dependent patients that, after admission to a hospital for conditions not related to their drinking, stopped drinking and so underwent painful and frightening alcohol withdrawal. After recovery from withdrawal, one patient commented "I must never start drinking again!." The other patient remarked "I must never *stop* drinking again!" (Raistrick 2001, p. 536). Unfortunately, recovery from alcohol dependence requires much more than merely surviving withdrawal. Many who undergo withdrawal resume addictive use of alcohol, often to experience subsequent repeated bouts of withdrawal.

Brain Damage

Detectable cognitive or motor impairments are present in 33–50 percent of individuals with alcohol use disorders (Arciniegas and Beresford 2001). The impairments persist long after alcohol is metabolized, so they are not acute effects of intoxication, but evidence of injury to the central nervous system. These effects of brain damage are seen most frequently in those with definite alcohol dependence, but more subtle impairments can occur in individuals with long-term patterns of heavy "social drinking" (Chapter 9) (Parsons and Nixon 1998). Some of these problems improve with abstinence, but others do not (Sullivan et al. 2010, Zahr and Pfefferbaum 2017).

Behavioral and Cognitive Impairment

In some cases, the brain injury from alcohol and related conditions (such as malnutrition) results in the extreme impairments of the **Wernicke–Korsakoff syndrome**. Wernicke's and Korsakoff's syndromes have very different clinical presentations, but the underlying brain pathology of the two disorders is quite similar (Harper 2009). Wernicke's syndrome is the acute phase of the disorder, characterized by severe problems with gait, control of eye-movements, and global confusion. With abstinence from alcohol and high doses of thiamine, most symptoms of the acute phase disappear. However, about 25 percent of those with Wernicke's syndrome then develop the severe memory disorders of Korsakoff's syndrome. The most debilitating feature of this more persistent (typically irreversible) phase is anterograde amnesia, the inability to form new memories (Fadda and Rossetti 1998).

Another severe disorder, alcoholic dementia, shares features with other types of dementia, and includes a wide range of disrupted cognitive capacities and an over-all loss of contact with reality (Schmidt et al. 2005, Vetreno et al. 2011). Alcoholic dementia has a more variable clinical presentation than does the Wernicke–Korsakoff syndrome, and may be misdiagnosed as Alzheimer's or another form of dementia (Gupta and Warner 2008). A history of heavy drinking is the main criterion for a diagnosis of alcoholic dementia. Malnutrition, important in the etiology of the Wernicke–Korsakoff syndrome, occurs less consistently in cases of alcoholic dementia.

Lesser degrees of brain damage related to alcohol use may produce impairment of visual-spatial coordination, postural stability, working memory and executive function (planning, problem solving, response inhibition) (Sullivan et al. 2010). These impairments vary in severity. In some cases, the deficits are obvious to an untrained observer. More subtle impairment may be detected only by means of specialized tests (Green et al. 2010, Rosenbloom et al. 2005). Some effects, especially those related to poor impulse control and other deficiencies of executive function, can contribute to ongoing heavy alcohol use. In such cases, the alcohol use disorder might be seen as a result, as well as a cause of the brain injury (Crews et al. 2005).

Type and Location of Alcohol-Produced Brain Injury

The brain damage associated with the heavy drinking of alcohol has long been evident in autopsies of deceased individuals who suffered from the severe disorders of Wernicke–Korsakoff's syndrome or alcoholic dementia (Harper 2009). These postmortem examinations revealed gross lesions in specific brain structures, enlarged ventricles and smaller volumes of brain tissue. Alcoholics have reduced brain weight compared to controls and the degree of brain atrophy has been shown to correlate with the rate and amount of alcohol consumed over a lifetime (Harding et al. 1996).

Since the advent of brain-imaging techniques, more precise assessment of lesser degrees of brain damage is possible in living patients (e.g., Zucolli et al. 2010). Magnetic resonance imaging (MRI) studies can detect and measure abnormalities in brain size, shape and tissue composition. Changes over time, including recovery from damage that may follow abstinence from alcohol, can be monitored. Diffusion tensor imaging (DTI) reveals the integrity of white matter tracts that link regions of the brain to each other (Zahr and Pfefferbaum 2017). Other imaging techniques (positron emission tomography – PET scans, and functional MRI's) can assess metabolism and other functions of specific brain structures When brain tissue is available for analysis, differences in gene expression associated with alcohol intake can be determined. All these techniques are used in clinical studies of humans as well as in controlled experiments with animal subjects.

Heavy alcohol consumption, sometimes in combination with other conditions common in alcohol use disorders, causes injury to both gray matter and white matter of the brain. The cell bodies, dendrites and some axons of neurons are located in gray matter, and white matter contains myelinated axons and glial cells that make up the myelin sheaths. Neuron loss and dendritic shrinkage occurs most often in parts of the frontal cerebral cortex, the hypothalamus, the hippocampus and parts of the cerebellum (Fadda and Rossetti 1998, Harper 2009). Damage to the myelinated axons that interconnect brain structures is more widespread throughout the brain than is the gray matter damage, but is especially evident in the connections between the frontal cortex and the cerebellum. The corpus callosum, connecting the left and right brain hemispheres, is also frequently damaged. Much of the brain shrinkage related to heavy alcohol consumption is due to loss of white matter in these areas (Sullivan and Pfefferbaum 2005).

Functional MRI studies indicate that individuals with alcohol use disorders use less efficient neural pathways for execution of cognitive tasks. Alcohol-produced degradation of interconnections among brain areas reduces the functional reserve of the brain. Performance of cognitive and sensory-motor tasks that require function of several brain areas may still be possible, but there is less ability to carry out multiple activities in parallel (Sullivan et al. 2010).

The cerebellum is involved in executive functions as well as in control of posture and coordination of complex movement. The extensive connections between the frontal areas and the cerebellum enable efficient performance of planning, problem solving, and control of attention. Alcohol-produced damage to the cerebellum or its connections with the frontal cortex interrupts information processing and degrades the speed and accuracy of these behaviors (Sullivan and Pfefferbaum 2005).

PET scans of alcohol-addicted individuals reveal reduced blood flow and diminished metabolism throughout the cortex, especially in the frontal lobe. These results indicate functional impairment of brain activity that in many cases accompanies the well-documented structural damage (Zahr and Pfefferbaum 2017).

Mechanisms of Neurotoxicity

In addition to heavy alcohol consumption, many people who suffer from an alcohol use disorder are also exposed to other conditions or traumatic events that can harm the brain. These indirectly brain-injuring actions of alcohol or causes related to an addictive lifestyle include liver disease or damage, meningitis, hypoglycemia, malnutrition, head trauma and use of other addictive drugs (Brust 2010). HIV-1 infection also produces neurotoxic effects similar to those resulting from alcohol

(Persidsky et al. 2011). In many clinical cases, the role of alcohol consumption in producing brain damage is not certain, due to the other events or conditions that are confounded with alcohol intake.

Controlled studies with animal subjects have shown definitively that alcohol is a neurotoxin even in the absence of other possible causes. Clinical studies also indicate that cognitive impairment occurs with alcohol abuse in humans when indirect causes seem unlikely (Brust 2010). Animal studies demonstrate that some effects such as malnutrition can exacerbate the neurotoxic effects of alcohol (e.g., He et al. 2007, Vetreno et al. 2011).

A large amount of research has been directed toward understanding how alcohol causes brain damage. Animal subjects are used in many of these investigations. Alcohol probably causes brain damage by means of more than one mechanism (Box 10.3). Neurotoxic effects can result from alcohol's immediate actions on brain and liver metabolism, from adaptation of the body and brain to alcohol effects, and from the withdrawal syndrome. Several processes are involved, including **inflammatory responses, oxidative stress** caused by free radical molecules, increased levels of stress hormones, diminished production of new neurons, alterations in gene expression, and overactivity of the neurotransmitter glutamate. Most of these processes are interactive, occurring in a cascading sequence in which one reaction triggers the subsequent response. All the processes mentioned are promoted by alcohol, but it is not established that any one process is the primary mediator of neurotoxicity (Brust 2010, Crews et al. 2005).

Oxidative stress results from the action of highly reactive molecules that damage neurons and glial cells in the brain, as well as interfering with metabolic functions throughout the body. The highly reactive free radical molecules are normal products of energy utilization necessary for the function and survival of most cells of the body, and especially of neurons. The brain uses energy at a very high rate, and is thought to be particularly susceptible to damage from oxidative stress (Hovatta et al. 2010). In normal metabolic function, these reactive molecules are neutralized by antioxidants. Alcohol alters brain metabolism and results in an excess of these reactive molecules that then cause the damaging oxidative stress. Alcohol increases inflammatory responses in the liver and brain, an action that also promotes oxidative stress (de la Monte et al. 2009).

Oxidative stress inhibits the production of new neurons (neurogenesis), possibly by means of its suppression of brain-derived neurotrophic growth factors. The hippocampus, a brain structure vulnerable to alcohol-produced damage, is a site for the formation of new neurons. The interference with neurogenesis is considered to be a major mechanism of alcohol's neurotoxicity in the hippocampus that results in deficient memory formation (Crews et al. 2005, van Holst et al. 2012).

BOX 10.3   Mechanisms of alcohol-related brain injury

Chronic consumption of large amounts of alcohol can injure the brain by influencing several physiological processes.

Direct Effects of Alcohol or Alcohol Withdrawal

Oxidative stress (caused by the action of highly reactive molecules)
Inflammatory responses
Excitotoxicity (including glutamate overactivity)
Diminished neurogenesis
Stress hormones (chronic high levels)
Changes in genetic expression (including in genes for neurotransmitters)
Suppression of brain-derived neurotrophic factors (required for neuron maintenance)

Indirect Effects Resulting from Alcohol Use

Thiamine deficiency
Liver damage/changes in liver function

Lifestyle Factors Associated with Alcohol Use Disorders

HIV infection
Other diseases
Use of other addictive drugs, including nicotine
Head trauma

Alcohol is toxic to both the liver and the brain, and some mechanisms of damage are common to both these vital organs. Some alcohol-produced neurotoxicity is secondary to toxic alcohol effects on liver function. Chronic alcohol consumption promotes the production of ceramides (toxic lipids) by the liver. These lipids penetrate the blood–brain barrier, causing oxidative stress and neuron damage (de la Monte et al. 2009).

Alcohol withdrawal also produces major neurotoxic effects. Investigations with animal subjects demonstrate that repeated bouts of intermittent alcohol administration cause much more cognitive impairment and brain damage than does a similar amount of continuous alcohol treatment. Hippocampal function and learning ability in particular are degraded by repeated withdrawals after chronic alcohol administration (Vetreno et al. 2011).

Alcohol is an antagonist for glutamate, an excitatory neurotransmitter that is up-regulated in response to chronic drinking, resulting in excessive excitation during withdrawal. The excessive amounts of glutamate cause neuron damage and death (Lovinger 1993). Glutamate toxicity also produces brain damage in humans who undergo cerebral ischemia (stroke) and other types of brain trauma (Fadda and Rossetti 1998).

Hormonal stress responses are produced by the acute effects of alcohol consumption (Chapter 5), but are even more pronounced during withdrawal (Rose et al. 2010). High levels of glucocorticoids (secreted by the adrenal glands) during withdrawal in alcohol-addicted patients are associated with greater cognitive deficits (Errico et al. 2002). Suppression of neurotrophic growth factors by glucocorticoids is thought to result in shrinkage or loss of neurons in the hippocampus and other brain areas (Erickson et al. 2003, Sapolsky 2000).

Malnutrition, and in particular thiamine deficiency, is often implicated in the more severe cases of cognitive dysfunction associated with alcohol use disorders, including the Wernicke–Korsakoff syndrome (Victor et al. 1989). Alcohol-dependent individuals often have unhealthy eating habits and some are malnourished. Even if their diet is adequate, their alcohol consumption can interfere with thiamine-dependent functions. Some components of the Wernicke–Korsakoff syndrome improve with abstinence from alcohol and treatment with thiamine (Martin et al. 2003).

Age-Related Vulnerability to Neurological Damage
The extent of brain injury that results from alcohol consumption is influenced by age. White matter fibers are negatively affected in a similar manner by both aging and alcohol abuse. The similarity of damage from chronic heavy alcohol consumption and advanced age is revealed by postmortem evidence (Harper et al. 2003) and by DTI imaging studies (Sullivan and Pfefferbaum 2006, Colrain et al. 2011). Older brains are also more vulnerable to the neurotoxic actions of alcohol. "Depending on age, the brain of a detoxified alcoholic can appear as ravaged as that of a patient with Alzheimer's disease, although the behavioral and neuropsychological consequences are typically far less severe and the brain dysmorphology is at least partially reversible" (Sullivan and Pfefferbaum 2005, p. 583). The brains of alcohol-dependent individuals older than age fifty show greater loss of volume than do healthy age-matched controls or younger alcoholics. Some studies indicate that the differences are not completely due to the greater amounts of alcohol consumed during many years of heavy drinking, but also because the neurotoxic effects are greater in older individuals (Sullivan and Pfefferbaum 2005).

The developing brains of adolescents are also more vulnerable to the damaging effects of alcohol than are those of mature adults (De Bellis et al. 2005). Some of the cognitive deficits characteristic of alcohol-abusing adults are also seen in youths who drank heavily during adolescence (Tapert et al. 2002). Binge drinking, a style of alcohol use for some adolescents, results in high concentrations of alcohol in the blood and brain, a major determinant of alcohol-produced brain damage.

Most of the evidence of greater injury from alcohol in developing brains comes from research with animal subjects in which alcohol administration resembles patterns of human binge drinking (Coleman et al. 2011, Crews et al. 2005). Neurogenesis occurs at high rates during adolescence. Adolescent rats are twice as sensitive as adult rats to inhibition of neurogenesis caused by repeated high doses of alcohol (Crews et al. 2006). This effect may underlie the reduced number of neurons in the hippocampus and cortical areas of adult animals previously exposed to alcohol at an age analogous to adolescence in humans.

Clinical studies show differences in brain structure and behavior of human adolescents with alcohol use disorders. These abnormalities, thought to result from alcohol intake, could promote further heavy use of alcohol and other addictive drugs, most likely by impairment of learning, inhibition, problem solving and other executive functions. However, because these anatomical and cognitive differences occur early in life, after relatively limited exposure to alcohol, it is also possible that they preceded (and facilitated) the initial development of the alcohol use disorders.

Recovery from Cognitive Impairment

It has been known for many years that with abstinence from alcohol, much improvement can occur in the cognitive impairment associated with heavy drinking (Brandt et al. 1983). More recently, imaging techniques have also shown concomitant reversal in brain structure abnormalities (Rosenbloom et al. 2008, Zahr and Pfefferbaum 2017). Longitudinal studies of alcohol-dependent individuals have found that after about one month of abstinence cortical gray matter, overall brain tissue, and hippocampal tissue increase in volume. With longer-term follow-up, those who maintain sobriety can show further increases in brain volume notable in these and other areas. Cortical white matter seems to be particularly amenable to structural recovery with prolonged sobriety. Improvement and stabilization of brain tissue volume has been documented over a five-year period of abstinence (Pfefferbaum et al. 1998).

Some alcohol-related impairment, in particular the anterograde amnesia of Korsakoff's syndrome, shows little recovery over time. Even the impairments that often diminish with extended abstinence from alcohol show only limited improvement in some cases. Factors that limit recovery of function include older age, heavier alcohol consumption before cessation of drinking, history of withdrawal seizures, liver disease, malnutrition and concurrent smoking (Yeh et al. 2007).

Other Toxic Effects from Chronic Heavy Alcohol Use

Frequent exposure to high doses of alcohol produces dose-related injury to tissues and impairs normal function throughout the body. The widespread damage to several organ systems is caused partially by inflammation and oxidative stress, alcohol effects that also promote brain damage. Alcohol interferes with several steps in the complex sequence of the immune response. With a weakened immune system, bacterial and viral infections in heavy-drinking individuals are more frequent and severe and are more often fatal. The immune system compromise is especially problematic for chronic infections such as hepatitis C and HIV (Molina et al. 2010).

Liver Damage

Alcoholic liver disease – and particularly **cirrhosis** – has long been one of the most prevalent and devastating conditions caused by alcohol consumption and is a major cause of alcohol-related death (Osana et al. 2017). The toxic actions of alcohol on the liver produce a spectrum of pathological conditions. The least severe is fatty liver, which is reversible with abstinence. A more serious problem is alcoholic hepatitis and fibrosis, which sometimes improves with abstinence. The most severe conditions are cirrhosis and end-stage liver disease, which are irreversible and have a poor prognosis. Cirrhosis is the twelfth leading cause of death in the United States. The liver pathology in about 35–40 percent of alcoholic patients with fatty liver advances to hepatitis, and approximately 10–20 percent of those with hepatitis develop cirrhosis (O'Shea et al. 2010). Given similar amounts of drinking, women are more susceptible to liver damage than are men.

Alcohol and its toxic metabolites have direct toxic effects on the liver, primarily by producing inflammation and free radical molecules. Indirect effects occur because alcohol allows harmful bacteria to pass from the intestines into the bloodstream. The liver responds to the invading pathogens with inflammatory responses that can injure the liver (Lieber 2004).

Cardiovascular Problems

The cardiovascular system suffers damage from alcohol, as evidenced by hypertension and problems with the heart often seen in individuals with alcohol use disorders. Hypertension may result in part from increased resistance to blood flow through the liver caused by fatty liver or fibrosis. Hypertension increases the risk of damage throughout the body, including the kidneys, heart, and brain.

Cardiomyopathy (damage to the heart muscle) can result from continued use of large amounts of alcohol. Cardiomyopathy can lead to an enlarged heart, weakened ventricular contraction, inadequate blood circulation and heart failure. Dangerous cardiac arrhythmia can accompany the high blood alcohol concentrations resulting from binge drinking (Freiberg and Kraemer 2010, Piano 2017).

Light to moderate drinking (less than two standard drinks a day) is beneficial to coronary artery function. Small amounts of alcohol increase the levels of high-density cholesterol and lessen the incidence of myocardial infarction (Mochly-Rosen and Zakhari 2010). However, the higher levels of alcohol consumption typical of alcohol dependence are associated with increased risk of heart attack. Nine drinks a day in men increases the relative risk of a major cardiac event by a factor of 2.4, compared to those who do not drink (Freiberg and Kraemer 2010).

Fetal Alcohol Spectrum Disorders

Alcohol is a **teratogen,** the term for an agent that can disrupt the development of a fetus. The teratogenic effects of alcohol are dose related, in that babies with the most severe fetal alcohol effects are born to women with alcohol use disorders (Abel 1998, May et al. 2013, Riley et al. 2011). Because alcohol readily penetrates the placental barrier and is toxic to several organ systems, tissues and functions of the body, its teratogenic effect is not surprising. Although the abnormalities often seen in the babies born to alcoholic women had been apparent for many years, other factors confounded with heavy drinking were suspected to be the actual cause of the birth defects. The fetal alcohol syndrome, a triad consisting of brain dysfunction, prenatal growth deficiency, and distinctive head and facial features first appeared in clinical reports in 1973 (Figure 10.5). Controlled investigations

Figure 10.5 Babies born to women who drink alcohol while pregnant can have characteristic physical and behavioral abnormalities (the fetal alcohol spectrum disorder), which are more frequent with higher levels of alcohol consumption. Photo: Jupiterimages / Photolibrary / Getty Images Plus.

with animal subjects soon demonstrated that alcohol exposure (in the absence of other factors, such as malnutrition) could produce birth defects, including abnormalities in the central nervous system. Since the early 1970s a large research effort by many investigators has yielded much information about the deleterious effects of alcohol on the developing fetus (Streissguth and O'Malley 2000).

Both clinical studies and investigations with animal subjects have shown that prenatal alcohol exposure can produce a range of harmful effects, especially in the brain. Alcohol use during pregnancy is associated with increased incidence of miscarriage, premature birth and stillbirth. The originally reported fetal alcohol syndrome is the most severe teratogenic effect in live births, but less noticeable differences may also be associated with alcohol use by the mother. In the more subtle cases, imaging studies can reveal brain abnormalities. Some behavioral effects, such as deficits in attention, learning and memory, emotional regulation and executive function are not detectable in neonates, and are fully expressed only in older children. The term *fetal alcohol spectrum disorders* (FASD) now includes the full range of adverse outcomes (Hoyme et al. 2016).

Abnormalities of the brain and subsequent behavioral effects are often the most debilitating consequences of prenatal alcohol exposure. Alcohol disrupts numerous developmental processes in the embryonic and fetal brain, including neurogenesis, cell migration and axon growth (critical to establishing connections among neurons), synapse formation and neuron survival. Some of the neurotoxic mechanisms described previously (oxidative stress, inflammation) also prevent normal brain development (Riley et al. 2011).

Detection of the full syndrome at birth can be difficult, and diagnosis of the less severe cases of the FASD is even more problematic. The estimated incidence of the full fetal alcohol syndrome in the United States is between 0.5 and 2.0 cases per 1,000 live births (Thomas et al. 2010). The actual incidence varies with socioeconomic status, but in general may be higher than estimated because identifying the problem faces major challenges. These births are not frequent events, and most obstetricians have little experience in recognizing the consequences of maternal alcohol use. The behavioral problems, often appearing only months or years after birth, are sometimes diagnosed as other syndromes such as attention-deficit disorder or conduct disorder. In many cases, there is no acknowledgment of the probable role of prenatal alcohol exposure. Another challenge is determining the drinking habits of the mother during pregnancy, an important consideration for a valid diagnosis. Women may give unreliable reports of their drinking, and in some cases (adoption or abandonment) no information is available.

Although many women avoid alcohol after they become pregnant, pregnancy may not be recognized or confirmed until weeks after conception. Some of the most damaging teratogenic effects of alcohol are caused by exposure during the early stage of embryonic development (Goodlett et al. 2005). In a study conducted in Ireland, 61,000 women were interviewed shortly after confirmation of pregnancy, and 81 percent reported drinking after conception (Mullally et al. 2011). Most of these women reported drinking very low or moderate amounts of alcohol. A study of Australian women found that only 41 percent completely abstained from alcohol throughout their pregnancy (O'Leary et al. 2009). The incidence of fetal alcohol effects appears to be much lower than the prevalence of occasional drinking during pregnancy.

There is much interest in whether a safe level of drinking during pregnancy can be established (Charness et al. 2016). It is difficult to prove conclusively the absence of an effect, including that of the teratogenicity of low amounts of alcohol. First, the effects can be quite subtle – so it could be argued that some harmful consequences were present, but not detected. Although some animal studies show abnormalities from rather small amounts of prenatal alcohol exposure, there is doubt about the relevance of these low-dose effects for human birth defects (Abel 2009, Gray et al. 2009). Second, in clinical studies the influence of other factors cannot be excluded. The behavioral differences previously mentioned can also occur in children whose mothers drank no alcohol.

Henderson and colleagues (Henderson et al. 2007) reviewed the results of forty-six clinical studies of pregnancy outcomes of women who drank no more than about six standard drinks per week. These investigations revealed no consistently significant adverse effects (miscarriage, stillbirth, low birth weight, fetal alcohol syndrome) associated with this low level of alcohol consumption. The Mullally study of many pregnant women also found no significant occurrence of fetal alcohol syndrome associated with light (three or fewer drinks per week) to moderate (four to twelve drinks per week) drinking (Mullally et al. 2011). These investigators did find increased incidence of premature birth and low birth weight in the high-drinking (more than twelve drinks per week) group. Although these studies found no fetal alcohol syndrome associated with low levels of drinking, the babies were not carefully evaluated for the more subtle fetal alcohol effects.

The teratogenic effect of alcohol exposure seems to be worsened by several other factors. FASD is much more common and severe in low socioeconomic (SES) populations. The incidence estimate of full fetal alcohol syndrome in middle-income groups in the United States was 0.26/1,000, and the estimate for low SES groups was 2.29 (Abel 1995). This difference is not completely due to increased alcohol use – which is only one of the many harmful prenatal influences including inadequate medical care, malnutrition, disease, smoking and other drug use that are more common in poverty-stricken populations (May et al. 2013).

Medications for Treatment of Alcohol Use Disorder

In most respects, treatment of alcohol use disorders by mental health professionals is similar or identical to that for other forms of SUD (Chapter 16). However, certain medications are unique to pharmacotherapy for alcohol addiction. Three medications (**naltrexone, acamprosate, and disulfram**) are currently approved by The US Food and Drug Administration for treatment of alcohol use disorder (Zindel and Kranzler 2014). Additional drugs are undergoing clinical tests, and others – approved for treatment of symptoms such as nausea – are prescribed "off label" for alcohol use problems.

The two most recently approved medications (naltrexone and acamprosate) are effective for only some individuals and do not promote abstinence or a reduction in drinking for most cases of alcohol use disorder. The limited efficacy of these medications is thought to result from genetic differences among individuals that predispose toward alcohol use disorder (Jones et al. 2015). Much research is under way to identify the genotypes (or other individual physical differences) that may determine the most effective pharmacotherapy for alcohol addiction (Seneviratne and Johnson 2015).

The tablet form of naltrexone (ReVia) was approved for treatment of alcohol addiction in 1994, and the extended-release injectable form (Vivatrol) in 2006. Naltrexone is an opioid neurotransmitter antagonist at the *mu* receptor. The drug appears to decrease the rewarding effects of alcohol and perhaps reduce alcohol craving by means of interrupting the critical opioid link in alcohol's indirect effect on dopamine activity.

Acamprosate (Campral) was developed and first used in European countries, and was approved for use in the United States in 2004. Acamprosate has agonist effects at GABA receptors and weak antagonist action at NMDA (glutamate) receptors, apparently balancing the activity of the two amino acid neurotransmitters and reducing hyperexcitability of the nervous system. These actions may facilitate abstinence from alcohol use by decreasing craving.

The results of a meta-analysis suggest that both naltrexone and acamprosate have small but significant effects to improve treatment outcome. Based on the effect size determined by the analysis, one of nine patients prescribed naltrexone would not return to heavy drinking after resuming limited alcohol use. For patients treated with acamprosate, one of eight patients would maintain stable abstinence. Effect sizes for both drugs were derived by comparison with placebo treatment (Maisel et al. 2013). The drug effects appear to depend to some extent on the treatment goal – total abstinence or a reduction in alcohol consumption.

Disulfram (Antabuse) became available for alcoholism treatment in the 1940s, and is still widely used in some countries. Disulfram inhibits a liver enzyme from metabolizing acetaldehyde, resulting in increased levels of the initial alcohol metabolite. If alcohol is consumed, acetaldehyde quickly causes severe headache, nausea and other very aversive symptoms. Disulfram effectively prevents drinking, but patient compliance is a major problem. Because of poor compliance and potentially serious side effects, disulfram is now rarely prescribed in the United States (Seneviratne and Johnson 2015).

Use of medications specifically intended for treatment of addiction is absent or limited in many SUD treatment programs in the United States (Aletraris et al. 2015). Reasons for the relatively rare use of medications include perceived or actual lack of drug efficacy, drug side effects, limited access to medical professionals, expense of drugs, and in some cases strict compliance with twelve-step principles often seen as incompatible with "treatment of addiction by use of drugs" (Oser and Roman 2008).

Chapter Summary

In the United States, about 5 percent of the adolescent and adult population suffers from an alcohol use disorder, with the highest prevalence (about 10 percent) occurring in young adults ages eighteen to twenty-five. Problematic alcohol use varies in severity on a continuum, ranging from heavy "social drinking" to a diagnosable alcohol use disorder. With a severe disorder (often referred to as dependence or addiction), control of drinking is impaired, and compulsive alcohol consumption disrupts life in many ways.

Risk factors for alcohol use disorders – which also increase vulnerability for SUD of other addictive drugs – include genetic predisposition, difficult experiences in childhood, regular drug use (including alcohol or nicotine) during early adolescence, and certain psychiatric syndromes. The widespread social acceptance and popularity of alcohol promote drinking in vulnerable individuals even as a use disorder develops.

As problematic drinking escalates, an emotional connection with alcohol develops, based on the immediate but transient rewarding effects. Erratic behavior, failed responsibilities, and interpersonal difficulties emerge – often resulting in isolation, which in turn can promote even heavier drinking.

Two main types of harmful alcohol use are differentiated by severity of the disorder and a greater number of risk factors. The more severe and persistent type usually emerges before age twenty-five and often results in much dangerous intoxicated behavior. In comparison, the less severe type of disorder has a later onset, relatively fewer disturbing and harmful consequences, and a more favorable prognosis.

The course of alcohol use disorders over decades is quite variable among those who continue to drink. Some experience ever-increasing life disruption and early death. Other alcohol-addicted individuals exhibit erratic patterns of drinking, interspersed with periods of abstinence. For less severe cases, and especially in young men, heavy drinking often subsides later in life, although some alcohol use continues.

Certain features of alcohol use disorders are relatively unique to women. Some gender-related hazards and vulnerabilities are culture dependent, and others result from biological factors. Trauma, emotional issues, and psychiatric disorders are more important risk factors for women. Use disorders typically emerge at a later age in women, but the problems escalate more rapidly. Women are more vulnerable to many of the toxic effects of chronic alcohol use.

Mild alcohol withdrawal produces insomnia, tremors, autonomic arousal, and extreme discomfort. Severe withdrawal can result in convulsions, agitation, paranoia, hallucinations, and death due to heart failure.

Prolonged heavy use of alcohol damages several organ systems. The liver, cardiovascular system, and immune response are especially vulnerable. Injury to these or other organs causes or contributes to death in many with alcohol addiction.

The central nervous system is also quite vulnerable to alcohol's toxicity, which causes impaired behavioral and cognitive function. Disruption of several neurological and metabolic functions is responsible for the alcohol-produced brain damage. The damage is worsened by factors such as the malnutrition, head trauma, or disease (including hepatitis, HIV, and other infections) that often accompany heavy alcohol use. At least partial recovery from lesser degrees of brain injury can occur with prolonged abstinence from alcohol.

Some babies born to women who drink heavily during pregnancy exhibit the fetal alcohol syndrome – which includes low birth weight, distinctive head and facial abnormalities, and neurological/behavioral problems. Partial or less severe manifestations of these features are designated as fetal alcohol spectrum disorders. The incidence and severity of adverse effects are related to the amount of prenatal alcohol exposure. Fetal alcohol syndrome and spectrum disorders are more prevalent and severe in low-income populations, suggesting that other conditions, such as poor prenatal care, disease, and malnutrition, worsen the teratogenic effects of alcohol.

Alcohol's pleasures are well known, and its hazards are often accepted. Low doses produce desirable effects, but these good feelings encourage heavier use, which has an array of damaging consequences, including harmful behavior, many toxic effects, and possible death from high doses and from withdrawal. The drug is addictive, and about 10 percent of those who consume alcohol are in serious trouble from drinking. Because the majority of users do not suffer from the most harmful results, alcohol use is generally accepted. Other, more addictive drugs (such as methamphetamine and opioids) are more easily seen as dangerous, but due to its widespread use, alcohol causes much greater damage and is a greater threat to public health than these and other illicit drugs.

Treatment of and recovery from alcohol use disorders are discussed in Chapter 16.

Review Exercises

1. What is a major limitation of the use of the terms *alcoholic* and *alcoholism*?
2. "The consequences of alcohol use can be measured on a continuum." Explain the meaning of this quote from the text. How does DSM-5 attempt to measure the severity of an SUD involving alcohol?
3. Using the survey results on incidence of alcohol use disorders, make an argument that either alcohol is or is not a dangerous drug.
4. What are the risk factors for the development of an alcohol SUD?
5. How do defense mechanisms make it more difficult for an individual to recognize that he or she is developing and/or has an alcohol SUD?
6. The text states that "alcohol use disorders are best described as a class of related, but not identical, types of problematic drinking." Provide an in-depth explanation.
7. Describe the two basic types of alcohol use disorder and their limitations.
8. How are alcohol use disorders different in women as compared to men?
9. Describe the alcohol withdrawal syndrome and its biological substrates.
10. Describe the cognitive dysfunctions produced by alcohol's toxic effects on the brain.
11. Identify the types of brain damage produced by high levels of alcohol consumption.
12. What are the biological mechanisms by which alcohol produces neurotoxicity?
13. Identify the age groups that are most vulnerable to neurotoxicity from heavy alcohol consumption, and describe the research evidence that supports your answer.
14. What are the teratogenic effects of alcohol?
15. What medications are used to reduce or eliminate problematic use of alcohol?

Key Terms

alcohol withdrawal syn-
    drome (362)

binary classification (355)
cirrhosis (371)

cultural judgment (359)
defense mechanisms (348)

delirium tremens (363)

homogeneous groups (353)

inflammatory responses (367)

naltrexone, acamprosate, and disulfram (375)

National Epidemiologic Survey on Alcohol and Related Conditions (NESARC) (342)

oxidative stress (367)

prevalent psychiatric syndromes (344)

progression (347)

sexual trauma (359)

teratogen (372)

Wernicke–Korsakoff syndrome (364)

LEARNING OBJECTIVES

1. Explain the differences between nicotine and alcohol SUD.
2. Describe the history of tobacco use in the United States, including prevalence of use and attempts by the tobacco industry to deny the addictive nature of nicotine.
3. Describe how the behavioral principles of reinforcement and classical conditioning promote nicotine use and addiction.
4. Understand estimates of the prevalence of nicotine addiction among tobacco smokers in the United States and Germany.
5. Describe the routes by which nicotine can enter the body and how it is metabolized and eliminated.
6. Describe the biological actions of nicotine in the brain.
7. Describe the behavioral and cognitive effects of nicotine.
8. Describe the nicotine withdrawal syndrome in humans and in animals and explain how it is measured.
9. Explain why psychological disorders and personality factors are risk factors for nicotine use disorders.

10. Describe adolescent patterns of nicotine use, risk factors, and associations between nicotine use and development for SUD for other drugs.

11. Understand the empirical evidence of a genetic predisposition for nicotine addiction.

12. Describe the negative health consequences of chronic tobacco use.

13. Provide an overview of psychological and drug-based approaches to smoking cessation.

Introductory Vignette: Thinking about Stopping Smoking

Abby is a registered nurse who quit a good position with a prestigious hospital mainly because she could not smoke at work. Taking a "smoke break" was no longer permitted, and Abby is a heavy smoker.

Currently she works from her home as an online nurse advisor for a medical insurance company. She has just finished advising a client with lung cancer – who could not get coverage for a new type of chemotherapy. Abby could not provide much reassurance or support. She steps out onto her back porch, lights an American Spirit cigarette, inhales, and feels relief from the tension that came from the discussion. She is outside, so she can smoke without making the house smell. It is cold, and she should have put on a jacket.

She thinks about how much smoking is ingrained in her daily life and again considers how she might stop. She has tried to quit many times – but here she is, on the back porch on a cold November day, breathing in carcinogens that she knows can kill her.

She has tried nicotine gum and nicotine patches taped to her skin. They helped some – but not much – to relieve the withdrawal anxiety and discomfort. However, even with the gum or the patch, without smoking, she was still impatient and irritable with her patients, and especially with her daughter. Quitting is also hard because smoking is so closely connected with most of her routine activities – driving, talking on the phone, socializing with friends, drinking coffee or wine, and frequent breaks from work at the hospital. Now, as she works from home, she often needs a smoke after working with clients – especially when she has to give them disappointing news.

She avoids smoking when she is near her daughter, but Emily certainly knows that her mother smokes – and often. The thought of her daughter reminds her that another possible way to stop smoking – vaping – is not a good plan. She thinks that Emily has tried vaping, partly because of her comment that it is "safer than smoking." Abby knows that vaping probably is safer than smoking, but she also knows well the addictive power of nicotine. She is sure that if she starts vaping, any warning to Emily about the risks of inhaling nicotine vapor – even with an appealing flavor – will be ignored.

Abby attended one Nicotine Anonymous meeting. She didn't like all the talk about the "disease of nicotine addiction." She knew that smoking *caused* diseases but felt that she had an intractable and harmful habit rather than a disease. Most people at that meeting were apparently also alcoholics or cocaine addicts, with the other drug making smoking even harder to give up.

She recalls that the drug Chantix helps some smokers stop, or at least decrease, cigarette use. Maybe she will give it a try, she thinks, as she finishes her smoke and goes back to work.

Introduction

Several authoritative sources (e.g., the Centers for Disease Control and Prevention) state that the use of tobacco is the most preventable cause of disease and death in the United States, the United Kingdom, and several other countries. The chance that a lifelong smoker will die from a complication of smoking is approximately 50 percent, with about half of these deaths occurring between ages thirty-five and sixty-nine years (Benowitz 2010, Doll et al. 2004).

In the United States an estimated 22.4 percent of individuals twelve years of age and older are current (previous month) users of tobacco. This estimate includes 4.6 percent who smoke cigars, 0.9 percent pipe smokers, 3.2 percent using smokeless tobacco, and 17.9 percent who smoke cigarettes. About three-fifths of the adult and adolescent population that smoke cigarettes do so daily, and about two-fifths smoke at least a pack each day. Daily smoking is most prevalent in individuals age twenty-six or older (Figure 11.1) (Substance Abuse and Mental Health Services Administration 2018).

Many, perhaps most, individuals who consume tobacco on a regular basis are addicted to nicotine. Long-term cessation of use is often quite difficult. Risk factors for nicotine addiction are very similar to those for substance use disorders in general (Chapters 5 and 8). Contributors to vulnerability for nicotine dependence include regular drug use in adolescence, genetic predisposition, poor impulse control, psychiatric disorders, and subclinical levels of anxiety and depression.

Figure 11.1 In comparison to women and other age groups, tobacco smoking in the United States is most prevalent in men older than age twenty-six. Photo: AzmanL / E+ / Getty Images.

In addition to sharing risk factors and some behavioral features, smoking and nicotine dependence are subject to cultural influences similar to those that promote alcohol consumption and alcohol use disorders. The use of both tobacco and alcoholic beverages is legal and socially accepted in many cultures. Tobacco, like alcoholic beverages, is a major commodity, and powerful commercial interests promote its use. Tobacco use has become less accepted in the United States by certain demographic groups and is now restricted in many locations. Although the prevalence of smoking has decreased in recent decades, smoking is still a common activity.

Although similar in some respects, there are important differences between nicotine dependence and alcohol use disorders. In general, these differences promote the use of tobacco and facilitate the development of nicotine addiction. Unlike alcohol (and other addictive drugs), nicotine as normally used is not intoxicating. Smokers and consumers of tobacco in other forms rarely experience the myriad problems of behavioral **toxicity** (drunken behavior, overwhelming involvement with the drug) that accompany alcohol use disorders. Even individuals who are heavily dependent on nicotine can use tobacco frequently with little interruption of normal daily activities. Increasing social sanctions on tobacco use often causes some problems, but not to the extent often experienced with alcohol abuse and addiction.

Another difference from alcohol is that the multiple toxic consequences of tobacco use typically develop only after years of smoking or oral consumption. In contrast, high doses of alcohol can cause death within hours, and withdrawal from alcohol can also be lethal.

Nicotine is more addictive than alcohol, even though it initially appears to be less harmful and disruptive than heavy drinking. More people in the United States drink alcohol (approximately 65 percent of adults) than use tobacco (approximately 22 percent). About 10 percent of those who drink suffer from an alcohol use disorder, but nearly two-thirds of the nearly 28 million daily cigarette smokers are to some extent nicotine dependent. The **addictive potential** of nicotine, including comparisons with other addictive drugs (opiates such as heroin, stimulants such as cocaine) is discussed later in this chapter.

Tobacco Use in the United States

Tobacco use, production and export were economic and cultural factors in the British colonies even before they became the United States. During the eighteenth and nineteenth centuries, tobacco was a major exported agricultural product. The threat of tobacco use to public health was unknown or essentially disregarded. Consumption of tobacco as snuff or chewing tobacco – as well as by smoking – was common.

Twentieth Century

During the twentieth century, smoking, and, in particular, cigarette smoking, became the most common form of tobacco use in the United States and in most European countries. Cigarette smoke is milder than that of cigars and pipe tobacco, permitting more frequent smoking and easier inhalation of smoke. However, deeply inhaled cigarette smoke also has greater toxicity and addiction potential (Peto and Doll 2005). Cigarette use in the United States reached its peak in 1963 when about 40 percent of adults were regular smokers. Consumption was at the rate equivalent to 11.9 cigarettes per day for each adult in the United States (Brecher et al. 1972).

The first **Surgeon General's Report** on smoking, released in 1964, implicated smoking as a cause of several medical problems – primarily cancer and cardiovascular disease – and increased death rate in men (US Department of Health, Education and Welfare 1964). A 1988 Surgeon General's Report documented health risks of smoking in women, as well as the toxic effects of passive exposure to smoke ("secondhand smoke"). In addition, chronic cigarette use was described as addiction to nicotine (US Department of Health and Human Services 1988).

These reports received much attention, and during the following years, several government agencies acted to decrease the prevalence of smoking (Hanson et al.

2006). These actions included labels warning of toxicity on cigarette packages, prohibition of advertising on radio and TV and smoking on commercial airline flights and in many public places. Tobacco taxes were increased by the federal government as well as by some state governments.

The growing awareness of the dangers of tobacco use prompted many to quit smoking. Smoking prevalence and cigarette consumption decreased continuously during the following decades – and currently stands at less than half of the level of the 1960s.

As smoking rates declined, tobacco companies first attempted to deny the toxicity, and later the addictive potential of tobacco. The arguments that tobacco was not toxic were refuted by (1) animal studies, (2) clinical observations and autopsies, and (3) epidemiological surveys correlating cigarette smoking and shortened life-span.

In 2013, DSM-IV was replaced by DSM-5. The earlier diagnostic manual described severe SUD as **dependence**, a term essentially equivalent to the less formal term **addiction**, but no longer used in the DSM-5. *Addiction* often refers to behavior, and *dependence* to the occurrence of a physiological withdrawal syndrome (see Box 2.3 in Chapter 2). In this text, the terms are often used interchangeably.

An article in the scientific journal *Psychopharmacology,* written by scientists employed by the R. J. Reynolds Tobacco Company, criticized the 1988 Surgeon General's Report's description of nicotine as an addictive drug (Robinson and Pritchard 1992). Their case that habitual smoking was not addiction driven by nicotine dependence was refuted in 1995 by rebuttals published in the same journal (Stolerman and Jarvis 1995, Hennigfield and Heishman 1995). These and other prominent psychopharmacologists summarized the very large amount of clinical observations and controlled research that demonstrates the addictive potential of nicotine.

These scientists observed that Robinson and Pritchard used an outmoded definition of addiction that attempted to distinguish between habitual and addictive behavior. A problem with that distinction is that very persistent habitual behavior *is* a major component of addiction (Chapter 2). The case against the addictive potential of nicotine also relied heavily on the absence of intoxication from tobacco use. **Compulsive use**, rather than intoxication, is a critical feature of addiction. Robinson and Pritchard also argued that many former smokers had successfully stopped using tobacco, which in their view negated its addictive properties. However, many individuals dependent on heroin, cocaine, or alcohol have stopped use of these addictive drugs. Although difficult, achieving abstinence is clearly possible for many addicted people.

During the 1990s evidence was uncovered that the tobacco industry had long known of tobacco's toxicity but concealed this information from their customers. Knowledge of this deception changed the legal climate and made the tobacco companies more vulnerable to litigation. As a result, in 1997 the federal government reached a settlement with a group of tobacco companies, who paid $368 billion to state Medicaid programs. The companies also agreed to other concessions, including regulation of tobacco advertising, especially that intended to entice minors to try smoking. In return, a limit was placed on certain aspects of the companies' legal liability for health-related financial claims. Without this protection, the tobacco companies were threatened with bankruptcy (Highlights of the Tobacco Settlement 1997).

Early Twenty-First Century

Estimates from the Centers for Disease Control and Prevention (CDC) for the year 2017 were that 22.4 percent of adolescent and adult Americans were current tobacco users, with 10.2 percent smoking cigarettes daily (Substance Abuse and Mental Health Services Administration 2018). Incidence of smoking varies markedly across socioeconomic and educational levels. In 2008, for individuals who did not finish high school the rate was 28 percent; for college graduates, 10 percent; and for those with graduate degrees, 6 percent. Thirty-one percent of those living below the federal poverty level of income smoked, while for those above the poverty level the smoking rate was 19 percent (Centers for Disease Control and Prevention 2009).

Smoking prevalence continues to decline during the early years of the twenty-first century, and former smokers now outnumber current smokers. Among 94 million who have smoked at least 100 cigarettes, 51 percent were no longer smoking at the time of a 2008 Center for Disease Control survey (Centers for Disease Control and Prevention 2009). However, the rate of stopping smoking is much lower for those with less education and at lower income levels. Individuals in the demographic groups with the highest smoking and the lowest quitting rates may be less aware of the adverse health consequences of smoking, or more complex reasons might underlie continued tobacco use. The greater difficulty of stopping smoking for those with psychiatric disorders also contributes to the decreased rate of smoking cessation.

In 2007, a novel method for delivering nicotine without burning tobacco was introduced in the United States. With electronic cigarettes (and similar devices), heat converts a nicotine-containing liquid into an inhalable vapor. In 2018, 2.8 percent of the adult US population were current users of electronic cigarettes (EC), but use prevalence was much higher among young people, including high school students (Cullen et al. 2018). Most adult EC users are either current or former cigarette smokers. The long-term health consequences of EC use have not yet been determined.

Intensive, widespread efforts are under way to further reduce smoking in the United States. An internet search in 2019 for "smoking prevention" identified several thousand relevant websites. Government agencies, such as the Office on Smoking and Health (a part of the CDC), the National Institute on Drug Abuse, and the National Cancer Institute, collect information and sponsor research on tobacco use and ways to encourage individuals to stop smoking.

Much research is under way to better understand nicotine effects and dependence on the drug, and to improve the effectiveness of treatments to assist addicted smokers to stop using tobacco.

The Behavior of Addictive Tobacco Use

Addictive tobacco use is controlled by basic behavioral principles. Reinforcement (positive and negative) and classical conditioning are intimately involved in all substance use disorders. These factors, and especially conditioned stimuli, are particularly important in smoking and nicotine dependence.

Reinforcement

For most users, the initial rewards of tobacco are rather subtle, although the positive reinforcement is often sufficient to promote ongoing use of the substance. Some nicotine-dependent individuals describe their initial smoking experience as being pleasurable.

Others describe a combination of pharmacological effects and easing of social interactions that eventually became essential to many activities. Negative reinforcement – relief from the aversive withdrawal syndrome – is more important than positive reinforcement for the maintenance of nicotine addiction (Baker et al. 2004, Hughes 2007b).

Behavior is strengthened most effectively by positive or negative reinforcement that occurs very quickly. Nicotine enters the brain within seven or eight seconds after inhalation of tobacco smoke, with most smokers taking about ten puffs from each cigarette. During a one-day span of tobacco use by a smoker consuming twenty cigarettes, nicotine is delivered into the brain about 200 times. Each of these quick increments of nicotine level in the brain provides a reinforcement that maintains the act of smoking.

Nicotine has a relatively short half-life, in that it leaves the brain rapidly. In dependent individuals, unpleasant withdrawal effects develop as nicotine concentration falls below a moderate level. However, high levels of nicotine produce aversive effects even in frequent smokers who have developed tolerance to moderate doses. Frequent delivery of small amounts of the drug is required to maintain a desirable intermediate level of nicotine in the brain that prevents withdrawal, but does not result in high-dose toxicity. The inhalation route of administration (smoking) permits ongoing regulation of nicotine levels and good control of the resultant mood state (Koob and Le Moal 2006). The frequent and nearly immediate reinforcing effects of smoking readily promote the addictive use of tobacco.

Conditioning

The frequent pairing of nicotine effects with sensations and behavior of smoking (or oral use of tobacco) results in classical conditioning of these stimuli and actions. Through association with tobacco use, the stimuli take on some properties of nicotine including stimulation of similar neurological responses. The distinctive taste and odor of tobacco eventually produce some of the pleasure of smoking or oral tobacco consumption. The feeling of smoke in the mouth and throat (including, in many cases, the "bite" of an irritant substance!) also becomes pleasurable to addicted smokers, as do the specific and unique actions of smoking (lighting a cigarette, inhaling the smoke) (Dixon et al. 2003). These conditioned effects apparently provide some reward value even after much tolerance has developed to nicotine during the course of a day's frequent smoking.

Situations, places and activities related to smoking also become associated with nicotine effects (Figure 11.2). The conditioning occurs more frequently, and is associated with more common everyday events, than for any other addictive drug. These almost unavoidable parts of smokers' daily lives elicit craving for nicotine.

Figure 11.2 Smoking becomes associated with many routine situations and behavior, which become conditioned stimuli eliciting the urge to smoke. Photo: vasiliki / E+ / Getty Images.

The question of whether addiction is a disease or a behavioral disorder is of special relevance to nicotine dependence. Subsequent sections of the current chapter discuss the "disease-like" nature of nicotine dependence (genetic predisposition, changes in brain activity) and the high prevalence of tobacco addiction in psychiatric populations. However, many individuals who have difficulty in quitting cigarette use undoubtedly feel that smoking is an intractable habit that endangers their health, rather than a psychiatric disorder or a disease. The biopsychosocial view of addiction, a major premise of this text, maintains that addiction is a behavioral disorder with disease-like characteristics, partially caused by neurological abnormalities. Nicotine can definitely produce dependence, but to the public as well as to the chronic smoker, tobacco addiction may not fit the disease model as well as does alcohol, cocaine or heroin addiction.

Determining the Incidence of Nicotine Dependence/Addiction

Many individuals – but not all – who use tobacco are nicotine dependent. Cigarette smoking is the most addictive method of tobacco use, for reasons described in a later section. The NSDUH survey of 2017 indicated that in the United States 57.1 percent of those who smoke cigarettes do so daily, with about two out of five of these daily smokers using at least a pack of cigarettes each day (Substance Abuse and Mental Health Services Administration 2018). Daily smokers are the most likely to be dependent on nicotine. However, not even all daily smokers are addicted, and variations exist in the degree of addiction among those who are nicotine dependent. The term *chipper* (an extension of a term first applied to nonaddicted users of heroin) is often used to designate individuals who smoke no more than five cigarettes on at least four days per week (Shiffman 1989). These light smokers are much less likely to be nicotine dependent than are heavy smokers.

DSM Assessment of Nicotine Addiction

The critical features of substance use disorders are represented by the DSM diagnostic criteria, but are identified more succinctly by the "three C's": **compulsion**, **control** (problems with), and **consequences**. Although the consequences of nicotine dependence are neither certain nor immediate, the compulsion and control problems are quite apparent to many chronic tobacco users. The crux of addiction – persistent substance use despite the knowledge of significant adverse effects, coupled with the desire to stop use and great difficulty in doing so – certainly apply to compulsive smoking (Dodgen 2005, West 2005). Although some DSM criteria for SUD are not applicable to tobacco use, other criteria deal with control problems, compulsion to use, and difficulty of stopping use.

Disease and death are likely consequences of tobacco use, and especially for chronic cigarette smoking. However, these extremely harmful effects are long-delayed, uncertain, and cannot be attributed to any specific instance of tobacco use. Additionally, access to tobacco products is legal and convenient. Due to these factors, two DSM criteria are very unlikely to occur even in heavy smokers. These two criteria are "a great deal of time spent obtaining, using, or recovering from use," and "Important social, occupational, or recreational activities are given up or reduced because of substance use."

Hughes and colleagues reviewed several large-scale surveys that measured the incidence of nicotine dependence as defined by DSM-IV criteria (Hughes et al. 2006). One survey from the United States (the NESARC study; Grant et al. 2004), and two German surveys reported the proportion of nicotine-dependent individuals among current smokers. Current smokers were respondents who had used cigarettes recently, but included individuals who did not smoke every day. The German surveys indicated that 47 percent of currently smoking adults were dependent on nicotine (Hoch et al. 2004, Nelson and Wittchen 1998). The NESARC study indicated that 53 percent of current smokers were addicted to nicotine, based on DSM-IV standards of dependence.

Further analysis of the NESARC results determined the incidence of nicotine dependence in the 5,281 moderate to heavy daily smokers among the survey respondents. Mean values for these individuals are: age 41.4 years, 17.4 cigarettes smoked daily, duration of daily smoking twenty-three years. Of this subset of current smokers, 62.3 percent were nicotine dependent (Donny and Dierker 2007).

These epidemiological data indicate that approximately half of current smokers and nearly two-thirds of moderate to heavy daily cigarette smokers are nicotine dependent, as designated by DSM-IV criteria. While it is likely that some fraction of moderate daily smokers are not addicted to nicotine, several investigators suspect that the DSM-IV, which required the presence of three diagnostic criteria to identify dependence, failed to detect dependence in many addicted smokers (e.g., West 2005).

The Fagerström Test

The **Fagerström Test for Nicotine Dependence (FTND)** provides a measure of the strength of nicotine addiction (Heatherton et al. 1991). This test (Box 11.1) consists of six self-report questions about smoking behavior and subjective states related to smoking. Higher test scores (the sum of the individual test items) indicate more compulsive smoking behavior.

The test does not directly inquire about a withdrawal syndrome, but the questionnaire items concerning difficulty of not smoking in restricted locations, smoking when ill, and morning smoking likely indicate the presence of an uncomfortable state of withdrawal.

Two of the items in the FTND most clearly indicate the strength of nicotine dependence. These questions are (1) the elapsed time after awakening before the first cigarette is smoked and (2) the number of cigarettes consumed during a typical day (Baker et al. 2007, West 2005). A shorter instrument for assessing nicotine dependence is the Heaviness of Smoking Index (HSI) (Heatherton et al. 1991) consisting of only these two items taken from the FTND. Both the FTND and the HSI are valid predictors of relapse after attempts to stop smoking (Courvoiser and Etter 2010, Fidler et al. 2010).

Neither of these specific behavioral indicators of compulsive drug use is included in the DSM criteria for dependence or SUD. This omission may contribute to the inadequacies of the DSM-IV for detecting nicotine dependence.

The FTND is often employed in nicotine addiction research, and can have valuable clinical use. The test scores predict success in stopping smoking (West et al. 2001), and are also useful in determining the dose requirement for nicotine substitution therapy (via transdermal patches or chewing gum) (Heatherton et al. 1991). Higher scores predict less success in stopping, and requirement for higher nicotine substitution doses. Dodgen refers to the FTND as the "gold standard" for measuring nicotine addiction although a standard threshold (minimum score for addiction) has not been universally accepted (Dodgen 2005). For an incremental variable (nicotine addiction), a specific cutoff point may not be appropriate (Moolchan et al. 2002).

BOX 11.1 The Fagerström Test for Nicotine Dependence

Question	Scoring criteria	Score
1. How soon after you wake up do you smoke your first cigarette?	Within 5 min:	3
	6–30 min:	2
	More than 30 min:	0
2. How many cigarettes a day do you smoke?	10 or less:	0
	11 to 20:	1
	21 to 30:	2
	31 or more:	3
3. Do you find it difficult to stop smoking in no-smoking areas?	Yes:	1
	No:	0

Question	Scoring criteria	Score
4. Which cigarette would you most hate to give up?	The first in the morning:	1
	Any other cigarette:	0
5. Do you smoke more frequently in the first hours after waking than during the rest of the day?	Yes:	1
	No:	0
6. Do you smoke if you are so ill that you are in bed most of the day?	Yes:	1
	No:	0

Note. Total score (maximum value = 10) is a measure of strength of nicotine dependence.

From Heatherton et al. (1991)

As an example of FTND scores in a large-scale survey, the mean score of 15,740 smokers in the United Kingdom, was 3.20 (standard deviation = ± 2.39) (Fidler et al. 2010). In a study of 1,071 individuals recruited in the United States for participation in a smoking-cessation study, the mean FTND score was 5.41 (±2.25) (Piper et al. 2008). The difference in mean scores suggests that many individuals attempting to stop smoking are more heavily addicted to nicotine than are a larger general population of smokers.

Other Instruments for Investigating Nicotine Dependence

Other instruments based on smoker self-reports reveal more about the nature of nicotine dependence than the mere strength of the addiction as indicated by the Fagerström test. Compulsive smoking has several components that are assessed by these multidimensional tests, which are longer and more complex than the FTND (Piper et al. 2008). The Nicotine Dependence Syndrome Scale (NDSS) (Shiffman et al. 2004) estimates five dimensions of dependence, including principal components of craving, withdrawal and subjective feelings of compulsion. Other components involve priority (value of smoking over other activities), tolerance, rigidity of smoking patterns, and continuity or constancy of smoking. The NDSS is sensitive to differences among very light smokers, as well as variations in the dimensions among heavier smokers (Shiffman and Sayette 2005).

The Wisconsin Inventory of Smoking Dependence Motives (Piper et al. 2004) was designed to assess thirteen different motivational domains of smoking behavior.

In addition to questions about craving, other test items concern the influence of smoking-related cues, and the reward value (positive reinforcement and negative reinforcement) of smoking.

Nicotine in the Brain and Body

Tobacco and tobacco smoke contain at least 4,000 compounds, many of which are toxic (Wynder and Hoffman 1979). Nicotine is the primary component of tobacco that influences activity of the central and autonomic nervous systems, causing subjective and behavioral effects. The nicotine content of the tobacco plant is the result of evolution, due to the survival benefit (adaptive significance) gained from the chemical's toxicity for insects. The psychoactive chemical content of other plant materials such as coffee beans, coca leaves, and opium poppies, is also a result of the evolutionary process.

In earlier years, some insecticides for use with plants contained high concentrations of nicotine. Exposure to these products can be lethal to humans, so most were replaced with less toxic preparations.

Most individuals who experiment with smoking initially experience the toxic effects of low doses of nicotine. These mostly unpleasant effects were also observed in controlled studies by administering nicotine via injection to subjects who are nonsmokers. Nicotine produced a dose-related array of effects, including nausea, headache, dizziness, sweating and palpitations. Subjects who were smokers experienced none of these effects, having become tolerant to these actions of nicotine (Foulds et al. 1997). Transdermal application of nicotine causes similar, if less intense unpleasant effects in nonsmokers (Ashare et al. 2010).

Tobacco smoke also contains carbon monoxide and "tar" – a compound consisting largely of aromatic hydrocarbon plant resins. The tar particles give tobacco smoke its characteristic odor and flavor. Several types of carcinogenic nitrosamines are also components of tar.

Pharmacokinetics: Bioavailability

Nicotine is readily absorbed through the lungs, and the oral mucosa of the mouth and throat when tobacco is smoked or chewed, or when nicotine chewing gum, lozenges or spray are administered. The drug also penetrates the skin and enters the bloodstream (albeit more slowly) when nicotine patches are applied.

One cigarette contains between ten and twenty milligrams of nicotine. The acute lethal amount of nicotine for an adult human is approximately sixty milligrams, although individuals have ingested larger amounts and recovered (Koob and LeMoal 2006). Only about one milligram of nicotine from each cigarette enters the bloodstream, due to the loss of most of the drug in smoke that never enters the body, or is exhaled. Smokers can increase the amount absorbed by deeper inhalation and taking more puffs from a cigarette.

The half-life of nicotine is about two hours, and most dependent smokers attempt to maintain a relatively stable blood nicotine level during waking hours (Benowitz et al. 1984). Although there is variation, depending to some extent on the level of dependence, addicted cigarette smokers typically maintain nicotine plasma levels between twenty and fifty nanograms per milliliter. Oral routes of administration (chewing tobacco or nicotine gum) can result in nicotine plasma levels of ten to fifteen nanograms per milliliter (Benowitz et al. 1988).

In the liver, the enzyme CYP2A6 metabolizes about 90 percent of nicotine. The rate of nicotine metabolism varies among individuals, and some evidence indicates that addicted smokers with slower nicotine metabolism (and elimination) consume fewer cigarettes per day (Tyndall and Sellers 2001, Schoedel et al. 2004). Faster nicotine metabolism – and the associated higher rate of smoking during the day – also increases the probability that an experimental or regular smoker will progress into nicotine addiction (McGovern et al. 2006).

Pharmacodynamics: Effects on Brain Function

Extensive research, conducted primarily with animal subjects, provides a basic understanding of the neurological processes underlying the development of nicotine dependence (Benowitz 2010, Koob and Le Moal 2006, Prochaska and Benowitz 2016). Through its activation of a certain type of acetylcholine receptor, nicotine increases dopamine activity and promotes positive reinforcement (Wing et al. 2015). Adaptation to the initial agonist effect of nicotine then results in acute tolerance and eventually a withdrawal syndrome when nicotine levels subside. This process is a slight variation of the general sequence of events involved in the development of dependence by most other addictive drugs. The main differences from the general addictive process are the involvement of acetylcholine, and the very rapid production (and loss) of tolerance.

The neurotransmitter acetylcholine (Ach) has many functions in the brain and in other parts of the nervous system, including the autonomic nervous system and the nerve-muscle junction. Ach, like most neurotransmitters, activates several types of receptors. One type of Ach receptor is designated as nicotinic, so named because of this ionotropic receptor's sensitivity to nicotine. Nicotine causes the nAch ion channel to open, admitting Na^+ and Ca^{++} ions, exciting the neuron, thus facilitating its firing and release of neurotransmitter.

Many nAch receptors are located on dendrites or cell bodies of dopaminergic neurons in the mesolimbic tracts, including the ventral tegmental area and the nucleus accumbens. By activating these nAch receptors, nicotine increases dopamine release, indirectly contributing to positive reinforcement. By this action, nicotine initially increases the sensitivity of the mesolimbic system by lowering the threshold for the rewarding effects of electrical brain stimulation, a further indication that nicotine enhances positive reinforcement (Kenny and Markou 2006).

The nicotinic Ach receptors consist of five subunits that make up the ion channel. Receptors that are most sensitive to nicotine contain a certain combination of subunits. Nicotinic Ach receptors that include the $alpha_4$ and $beta_2$ subunits are the principal mediators of nicotine dependence (Benowitz 2010). The subunit combination can be altered in transgenic mice by means of selective mutations. These genetic manipulations of receptor configuration can either eliminate – or increase – nicotine's effects on behavior (including the reward value of nicotine) (Mineur and Picciotta 2008, Tuesta et al. 2011). Evidence of the nAch receptors' role in nicotine-produced reward is also demonstrated by infusion of a nicotine-antagonist drug directly into the ventral tegmental area, a procedure that decreases nicotine self-administration in rats (Corrigal et al. 1994).

With continued exposure to the drug, the initial response to nicotine stops, as the nAch receptors become saturated and desensitized (Wang and Sun 2005). At this point nicotine has an antagonist effect as it blocks the nAch receptors. Adaptation to the sustained blocking effect of nicotine promotes an increase in the number of nAch receptors (up-regulation) (Govid et al. 2009). Autopsy of heavy-smoking humans (Breese et al. 1997) and nicotine-treated experimental animals (Gentry and Lucas 2002) indicate the increased receptor density. Brain imaging of recently abstinent human smokers reveals increased density of nAch receptors containing the $beta_2$ subunit in comparison to nonsmokers (Staley et al. 2006).

When brain concentration of nicotine falls to a low level, the receptors regain their original sensitivity to nicotine. The resensitization (in the absence of nicotine stimulation), along with the increased number of nAch receptors, is thought to be the neurological substrate of the nicotine withdrawal syndrome, further described below. These processes cause the nicotine craving and the increased reward value of cigarettes typically experienced by addicted smokers when they awaken in the morning after several hours of abstinence from tobacco (Figure 11.3) (Benowitz 2010).

Nicotine withdrawal also decreases the hedonic tone of the reward-sensing areas of the brain as indicated by heightened thresholds for reinforcing electrical brain stimulation (Johnson et al. 2008). The decreased sensitivity of the mesolimbic dopaminergic tracts contributes to the aversive effects of withdrawal, which often include **irritability** and depressed mood. Koob and Le Moal comment that "the remarkable aspect of nicotine withdrawal is the pronounced and prolonged elevation in brain reward thresholds compared to its efficacy as a reinforcer" (Koob and

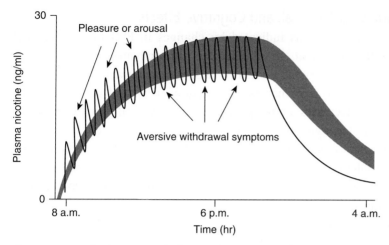

Figure 11.3 Levels of nicotine in the brain and psychoactive effects of smoking. The rapid fluctuations in brain levels of nicotine result from the use of each cigarette during a day of frequent smoking. The shaded area represents nicotine levels that produce neither pleasurable arousal nor aversive withdrawal. The first cigarette of the day produces a substantial euphoric arousal effect. Nicotine accumulates and tolerance develops as more cigarettes are consumed. With successive cigarettes, the pleasurable effect gradually becomes weaker, and withdrawal effects become more pronounced as nicotine concentration first rises above and then falls below the shaded area with each cigarette. Reprinted and adapted from *The New England Journal of Medicine*, Neal L. Benowitz, Nicotine Addiction (2010) vol. 362. © 2010. Massachusetts Medical Society. Reprinted with permission from Massachusetts Medical Society.

Le Moal 2006, p. 265). In other words, nicotine withdrawal can be persistent and intensely aversive, even though its reward value is rather subtle in nondependent humans.

Nicotine also alters the activity of other receptors, neurotransmitters and neurons, including those of the serotonin, opioid, GABA and glutamate systems. Many of these effects are secondary to the primary agonist action on nAch receptors. However, the indirect dopaminergic agonist effects and the subsequent adaptation are the pharmacological actions most directly involved with reinforcing and dependence-producing effects of nicotine (Koob and Le Moal 2006).

Brain-imaging investigations show that smokers have lower levels of monoamine oxidase (MAO) A and B, enzymes that metabolize dopamine and other monoamine neurotransmitters (Fowler et al. 2003). This inhibition of MAO does not result from nicotine, but from other alkaloids contained in tobacco smoke (Herraiz and Chaparro 2005). Lower levels of MAO result in prolonged action of dopamine, noradrenaline and serotonin, neurotransmitters involved in positive reinforcement, arousal, and mood. These effects of smoking would likely also promote use of tobacco.

Other Physiological, Behavioral, and Cognitive Effects

Nicotine is a CNS stimulant, as indicated by changes in EEG (brain electrical activity) patterns (Kadoya et al. 1994). Nicotine also activates the sympathetic branch of the autonomic nervous system to raise heart rate and blood pressure (Wignall and de Wit 2011) and increase production of cortisol and adrenaline. These actions cause decreases in peripheral blood flow and skin temperature (Karan et al. 2003). The sympathetic arousal action of nicotine can cause or worsen certain medical conditions, including cardiac dysfunction, hypertension and circulation problems. The calming effect often reported by addicted smokers (seemingly paradoxical to a stimulant action) is due to relief of the discomfort and anxiety of withdrawal.

Activity of acetylcholine receptors facilitates a variety of cognitive functions, including learning and memory, attention, concentration and vigilance (Changeux et al. 1998). Nicotine, a potent agonist for a subtype of Ach receptors, has well-documented effects of facilitating some cognitive functions in smokers (Heishman et al. 1994), and also in individuals suffering from Alzheimer's disease, schizophrenia, and attention deficit hyperactivity disorder (Levin et al. 2006). Early research was conducted primarily with nicotine-dependent subjects, and in many studies, these smokers were required to abstain from tobacco use and so were in some degree of withdrawal at the time of cognitive testing. Improved performance with nicotine could then be due to relief from cognitive impairment seen during withdrawal from the drug.

Nicotine can improve performance of animal subjects on several standard tests of learning and memory, including water- and radial-arm mazes for rats and mice and delayed match-to-sample tests for primates. In most cases, nicotine was administered acutely, the subjects were not nicotine dependent, and the drug improved performance in normal animals (Levin et al. 2006). Nicotine can also attenuate or reverse the impairing effects of brain lesions or toxins such as lead.

Nicotine improves cognition in healthy nonsmoking human subjects when administered by transdermal patches (Levin et al. 2000, Wignall and de Wit 2011) or nasal spray (Kalman 2002). The transdermal method of administration gives a longer period of relatively stable nicotine blood levels, allowing for more extended sessions of behavioral testing. Heishman and colleagues performed a meta-analysis to interpret the combined results of forty-one studies of nicotine administration in nonsmoking subjects or subjects who did smoke but were not nicotine deprived (Heishman et al. 2010). This analysis indicated that nicotine has positive effects on attention, reaction time, and some aspects of working memory.

Although these positive effects on concentration and vigilance are probably more pronounced in smokers who are withdrawing from nicotine, they also occur in nonsmokers, so are not completely due to relief of withdrawal syndrome.

Alleviation of cognitive impairment may motivate continued smoking in addicted individuals. However, because the effects are rather subtle, they seem less likely to be a primary reinforcement for initiation of smoking (Wignall and de Wit 2011).

The Nicotine Withdrawal Syndrome

The withdrawal syndrome that often follows cessation of tobacco use is a primary indication of nicotine dependence. Personal accounts of the aversive nature of withdrawal abound. Some stories are of a temporary state of annoying discomfort, while others recount dysphoria or more severe symptoms that often result in a resumption of smoking.

Michael Collins described his experience of early withdrawal after quitting smoking while a test pilot for the US Air Force. Later in his career, Collins was command module pilot of Apollo 11, the first moon-landing mission. Collins decided to stop his heavy cigarette use when he became aware of the cancer risk:

> Quitting was a most difficult but satisfying milestone for me. One morning I said to my wife, "All right goddamn it, when this pack of cigarettes runs out, that's it!" By evening, I was empty-handed, fidgety, angry, and determined. The next morning, nervous beyond description, I had to be co-pilot for a routine test of a B-52 with new engines. My duties were to throw a few switches the pilot could not reach from the left seat. We were to keep the lumbering beast up for four hours – an eternity for one who expects the imminent onset of *delirium tremens* as a symptom of nicotine withdrawal. For four of the most miserable hours I have ever spent – I chewed my fingertips, my pencils. I blew imaginary smoke rings, inhaled mightily and exhaled in staccato little puffs. Ted (the pilot) was motioning to one of my switches. I threw it and three or four more like it. I screwed up everything I touched, and Ted was as happy as I was to get back on the ground.

> Things slowly got better as the weeks went by, and finally I could make it through an entire day without thinking once of cigarettes. (Collins 1974, p. 153)

In most investigations, individuals attempting to quit smoking cigarettes describe subjective effects of abstinence from tobacco. In addition to these clinical studies, some reports have come from smokers not intending to stop tobacco use permanently, but who were paid to abstain temporarily during their time as research subjects.

The DSM-5 lists seven nicotine withdrawal symptoms, which can cause clinically significant distress or impairment after stopping tobacco use. The list of nicotine withdrawal symptoms is based on the results of many investigations, summarized by John Hughes and colleagues (Hughes 2007a, Hughes et al. 1990).

Anger, irritability, impatience, anxiety, depression (or dysphoria), difficulty in concentrating, insomnia and restlessness are commonly experienced after termination of chronic tobacco use (Figure 11.4). The time courses of the various symptoms differ slightly, but the overall syndrome (the presence of at least some of the components) begins within one or two days, peaks in the first week and lasts three to four weeks. The symptoms gradually dissipate and are much less intense during the latter days of this period.

Figure 11.4 Nicotine withdrawal symptoms include irritability and anxiety, which are quickly relieved by smoking. Photo: Seb Oliver / Cultura / Getty Images.

Some changes that emerge during nicotine withdrawal (e.g., increased hunger and weight gain, decreased heart rate) are better described as nicotine offset effects in that they are not transient (as are withdrawal symptoms), but may endure indefinitely. These physiological functions are altered by nicotine, and then change toward normal upon abstinence.

For many that stop smoking, the most noticeable results of tobacco abstinence are the subjective experiences of nicotine withdrawal. Impaired performance on various cognitive tasks is also typical, indicating difficulty in concentration (Heishman 2002). Michael Collins's account of the problems he encountered while working as a test pilot during nicotine withdrawal illustrates the performance decrement.

Craving, the sometimes-intense urge to smoke, is also a typical consequence of tobacco abstinence, but is not a DSM-5 nicotine withdrawal symptom. Withdrawal symptoms, as classically defined, emerge and increase as drug levels in the blood decrease after drug intake stops. If the drug use resumes, the symptoms abate. Craving is not included as a criterion of withdrawal primarily because many smokers experience craving even as they smoke, or very shortly after smoking at a time when nicotine blood levels are high (Jarvik et al. 2000). Craving also often persists much longer than nicotine withdrawal symptoms, and is more readily and persistently triggered by smoking-related stimuli (Piasecki 2006, Durcan et al. 2002). Some investigators disagree with the exclusion of craving as a withdrawal symptom in the DSM (Etter 2005). Craving is included in the ICD-10 description of nicotine withdrawal.

Withdrawal Syndrome in Nonhuman Subjects

Animal models provide information about the neurological basis of nicotine withdrawal and are used for preclinical tests of therapeutic drugs for alleviation of the syndrome (Malin and Goyarzu 2009). Behavioral effects and somatic signs indicate nicotine withdrawal in animal research subjects (most often, rats or mice). To produce withdrawal, nicotine is administered frequently (by injection), or continuously (by implanted mini-pumps) for several days. Cessation of nicotine administration or injection of a nicotine-antagonist drug then results in characteristic somatic signs of withdrawal: teeth-chattering, chewing, gasping, writhing, head shakes, body tremors (Le Foll and Goldberg 2009, Malin 2001).

Behavioral effects in rodents indicate the aversive nature of nicotine withdrawal. These behaviors are probably more relevant to the condition of recently abstinent nicotine-dependent humans than the somatic withdrawal signs (Koob and Le Moal 2006). In the conditioned place-avoidance paradigm animals spend less time in locations where they experienced nicotine withdrawal. The startle response, an indicator of anxiety, is potentiated. Operant behavior and interaction with other animals is also disrupted (Emmet-Ogelsby et al. 1990). The previously mentioned decreased sensitivity to electrical stimulation of brain reward circuits also indicates the dysphoric effects of nicotine withdrawal. These behavioral-motivational effects occur during withdrawal from relatively lower doses of chronic nicotine administration as compared to the doses required to produce the characteristic somatic effects of head shakes and body tremors (Le Foll and Goldberg 2009).

Withdrawal Relief and Nicotine Dependence

Although the withdrawal syndrome is a prominent feature of nicotine dependence, not all individuals who stop smoking experience these unpleasant effects. These differences are consistent with the results of the epidemiological surveys indicating that some smokers are not nicotine dependent. Large-scale retrospective surveys of the consequences of tobacco abstinence indicate that approximately half of smokers who try to quit experience four or more withdrawal symptoms (Hughes 2007b).

These population studies are influenced by several factors, including differences among the surveys in the specific symptoms assessed and failure by some investigators to report the respondents' rates of cigarette consumption. Additionally, the results of retrospective studies may be influenced by rationalization (especially for the respondents that attempted but failed to maintain abstinence), poor memory, and the natural occurrence of many of the symptoms unrelated to smoking history (anxiety, irritability, insomnia, depression, etc.).

Prospective studies assess withdrawal symptoms in fewer individuals than in the retrospective epidemiological surveys, and are less affected by uncontrolled factors. Preabstinence rates of smoking and symptoms expected during withdrawal are often measured. These studies show that most smokers report at least some withdrawal symptoms after stopping smoking (Hughes 2007a).

The retrospective epidemiological studies and the better-controlled prospective studies are in general agreement in that both find that irritability and restlessness are the most frequent withdrawal symptoms, followed closely by anxiety, depression, and **concentration difficulty** (Hughes 2007b).

Several self-report instruments specifically assess nicotine withdrawal. These tests have proven useful in both research and clinical settings and are much more efficient than therapist interviews. The Cigarette Withdrawal Scale (Box 11.2) is an example of an instrument for self-report of nicotine withdrawal symptoms (Etter 2005). At least eight of these nicotine withdrawal scales indicate the intensity of most of the DSM-5 withdrawal symptoms and have adequate psychometric properties. All these instruments yield scores that increase with tobacco abstinence, and some are used to measure the effectiveness of nicotine-replacement medications in smoking-cessation programs (e.g., West and Shiffman 2001).

BOX 11.2 The Cigarette Withdrawal Scale (CWS-21)

(Subscale Titles) and Some Questionnaire Items
(Depression-Anxiety)

   I feel depressed
   I feel worried
   I feel anxious

(Craving)

   The only thing I can think about is smoking a cigarette
   I miss cigarettes terribly
   I feel an irresistible need to smoke

(Irritability–Impatience)

I am irritable
I get angry easily
I have no patience

(Difficulty Concentrating)

I find it difficult to think clearly
I find it hard to focus on the task at hand

(Appetite–Weight Gain)

My appetite has increased
I have put on weight recently

(Insomnia)

I wake up often during the night
I have trouble falling asleep at night

An investigator in Switzerland surveyed 3,050 smokers and ex-smokers via the Internet during the development of this scale. For each item, possible responses ranged from "totally disagree" to "totally agree." The subscales assessed DSM-IV withdrawal symptoms but were not shown on the survey. All withdrawal ratings, except insomnia and appetite, predicted relapse to smoking, and all, except appetite, were higher in recent as compared to long-term ex-smokers (Etter 2005).

Abstinence from compulsive tobacco use, and in particular cigarette smoking, is remarkably difficult to maintain. In 2015, the large-scale National Health Interview Survey indicated that about two-thirds of cigarette smokers were interested in quitting and one-half attempted to do so. However, less than one in ten were successful (Babb et al. 2017). Despite the well-known risks of smoking, most quit attempts fail within a few days, when aversive consequences of abstinence are most intense (Brown et al. 2005).

Aggregate data reveal a predictable rate of occurrence and time course for the withdrawal syndrome. However, the specific symptoms of withdrawal vary markedly among individuals, and wax and wane daily during the weeks following abstinence. Naturalistic studies that include daily or hourly reports of mood from subjects attempting to remain abstinent have shown that negative affect (dysphoric feelings) or restlessness often immediately precede lapses (resumption of smoking) (Chandra et al. 2011, Piasecki 2006).

Anxiety or depressive disorders, as well as subclinical levels of negative affect make abstinence more difficult – in part because they closely resemble the nicotine withdrawal syndrome (Piasecki et al. 2003, Pomerleau et al. 2005). The dysphoric feelings, even if unrelated to tobacco abstinence, potentiate the discomfort of nicotine withdrawal, so withdrawal symptoms are often felt more intensely in individuals who suffer from these disorders (Lerman and Audrian-McGovern 2011).

Some individuals have a low tolerance for distress, including the aversive effects of nicotine withdrawal. Individual differences in distress tolerance decrease the relapse to smoking predictive validity of withdrawal symptom intensity (Brown et al. 2006). Intense withdrawal symptoms (particularly dysphoria and anxiety), coupled with a lower tolerance for distress, result in greater vulnerability for resumption of smoking (Abrantes et al. 2008). Conversely, other individuals may experience intense anxiety or depression during the initial days of abstinence, but for reasons unknown, endure the discomfort and remain abstinent. The **distress tolerance factor** is one of several conditions (personal characteristics as well as environmental influences) other than withdrawal intensity that determine whether an individual fails to maintain abstinence from smoking (Etter 2005, Piasecki et al. 2002).

Additional factors that encourage abstinence from smoking include presence of a dangerous medical condition related to tobacco use, and strong disapproval of smoking by family or friends. The intent to provide a positive example for children and the no-smoking requirement of a highly desired job also facilitate abstinence from tobacco (Babb et al. 2017).

Craving

The sometimes-intense desire or urge to smoke is often considered a core feature of nicotine addiction (DiFranza 2010, Goedeker and Tiffany 2008). Drug craving is an area of investigation for most addictions, and is of special interest for the study of nicotine dependence (Piasecki 2006). The intense distress of craving is described in this subjective account of nicotine withdrawal:

> The first three days I couldn't focus my mind and had no control over my body. I craved a cigarette so badly. I ached and cried. I was irritable and emotional. It seemed that every cell in my body hurt. For weeks, I was ready to burst into tears at the drop of a hat.... I was fighting incessantly with my very supportive boyfriend. I tossed and turned throughout the night, getting up every two or three hours, unable to sleep. I could do nothing but dedicate every waking moment to not taking that first drag. (Nicotine Anonymous 1998, p. 39)

This story of withdrawal and craving illustrates the intimate relationship between preoccupation with the desire to smoke and other aspects of withdrawal including irritability, insomnia, anxiety, dysphoria and the disruption of normal activity.

Most withdrawal symptoms gradually abate as nicotinic acetylcholine receptors return to normal, usually within six to twelve weeks of tobacco abstinence (Cosgrove et al. 2009). However, the urge to smoke may persist much longer, as surveys indicate that for some former smokers craving still occurs – at least occasionally – for years after quitting (Herd et al. 2009, Hughes 2010).

Craving is most likely and strongest during the time when the overall withdrawal syndrome is most intense. Craving – at a lesser intensity – can also occur in the absence of other withdrawal symptoms because the withdrawal syndrome has dissipated with time, or because it has not yet developed (Fidler et al. 2010). Similar to usage patterns and the effects of cocaine (another stimulant drug) an almost immediate consequence of nicotine intake is the urge for more nicotine – few, if any smokers inhale only once after lighting a cigarette. "Chain-smoking" appears to be an extreme example of frequent, nearly continuous nicotine intake, driven by ongoing craving.

In nicotine-dependent individuals, smoking accompanies many common daily activities, all of which can become cues that produce a strong desire to smoke. Eating, drinking coffee or alcohol, sexual activity, and other pleasurable activities, as well as stress and negative mood states can bring on the urge to use tobacco. These events and conditions that often trigger craving are apparently responsible for many instances of long-term persistent urges to smoke (Tiffany et al. 2009).

Craving can be either a desire for relief from an aversive withdrawal state, or essentially "appetitive" in nature when it is experienced as anticipation (or memory of) a pleasurable activity (smoking). Pleasurable craving states – or urges – often occur when the aversive withdrawal symptoms are no longer present, and especially during or after pleasurable activities that previously accompanied smoking. Craving that is appetitive, rather than aversive, may also be experienced by light smokers (who may not be nicotine dependent) when exposed to smoking-related cues or situations in which cigarettes are available (Goedeker and Tiffany 2008). Perhaps the feeling in that situation would be described as "I would really enjoy a cigarette now," whereas for a more nicotine-dependent person the feeling would be "I am uncomfortable now, and a cigarette would make me feel better."

Although craving states can be experienced as pleasurable anticipation, they are more often experienced as aversive, uncomfortable, and disruptive. Both types of craving (appetitive, and relief-seeking) increase the incentive value of smoking and present a risk of relapse (Robinson et al. 2011).

Several brain structures and neural circuits are involved in the overall behavior of addiction. Most brain structures and circuits that are activated by nicotine also become more active during states of craving (Chapter 7). The **insula** is an area of the cerebral cortex involved in processing information about bodily states, especially those related to emotion and motivation (Paulus et al. 2009). This brain area is thought to play a role in determining the incentive value of food and other reinforcers, and regulation of conscious urges, including craving for drugs (Lin et al. 2009, Naqvi and Bechara 2010). Craving for drugs in addicted individuals is often described as feeling like a physical need that is experienced throughout the body. The insula's role in sensing states within the body might then be critical in producing the subjective urges to smoke.

A clinical finding further implicates the insula in craving for nicotine (Naqvi et al. 2007). The smoking behavior of a group of patients who suffered brain damage (due to stroke) was determined in relation to the location of the stroke-produced damage. The smoking patients whose insula area was damaged were much more likely to quit smoking easily and immediately after the stroke than were those whose brain damage was in other areas. The patients with insula damage also remained abstinent and did not experience craving or urges to resume smoking, although hunger and eating were unaffected. These results could not be attributed to nonspecific effects of brain injury.

No specific brain area is solely responsible for compulsive drug use. However, the intent and action of drug consumption is (at least in many cases) driven by the conscious experience of craving. Craving for nicotine was eliminated in the insula-damaged patients, a consequence that interrupted addictive smoking. The importance of this information for the development of more effective treatments of nicotine or other addictions is not clear. However, the neuropeptide orexin seems to have a role in nicotine dependence, and neural circuits containing orexin are located in the insula (Kenny 2011). Inhibiting orexin activity in the insula area of rats disrupts nicotine self-administration, a preclinical research finding that could eventually have significant implications for clinical applications (Hollander et al. 2008, Paulus et al. 2009).

The role of craving in addictive behavior is discussed further in Chapters 5 and 7.

Psychiatric Disorders and Personality Factors

Smoking is more prevalent among those with psychiatric disorders or certain personality traits than in healthier individuals without these conditions or behavioral tendencies. These factors greatly increase the risk of dependence for all addictive drugs (Chapter 8), and their frequent co-occurrence with smoking is well established. Although addictive tobacco use is prevalent among those who use other addictive drugs, most information about the relation between SUD and psychiatric disorders presented in Chapter 8 does not specifically refer to nicotine dependence.

The rate of long-term stopping of cigarette use for nicotine-addicted individuals with co-occurring disorders is about half that of the general population of smokers, indicating a greater severity of nicotine addiction (Dodgen 2005, Ziedonis et al. 2008). The dramatic decrease in smoking incidence during the latter decades of the twentieth century did not occur in those with psychiatric disorders (Zeidonis and Williams 2003).

Most who suffer from a psychiatric disorder experience much negative affect such as anxiety, irritability/anger, and depressed mood, aversive states that are also characteristic of nicotine withdrawal. The similarity between symptoms of withdrawal and those of the co-occurring disorder is thought to contribute to the many failed attempts to stop smoking by psychiatric patients with disorders of depression (Leventhal et al. 2009) or anxiety (Morissette et al. 2007, Pomerleau et al. 2005). Based on subjective reports, nicotine withdrawal symptoms are felt with greater intensity in individuals with coincident psychiatric disorders than in healthier populations (e.g., Weinberger et al. 2009).

Anxiety Disorders and Depression

Many who suffer from chronic anxiety or depressed mood claim that they smoke to relieve (self-medicate) these unpleasant feelings (Figure 11.5). However, there is also evidence that for some, smoking increases the dysphoric states and may worsen a mood or anxiety disorder. The causal relationship is probably bidirectional and varies among specific individuals. Most investigations are cross-sectional and retrospective, providing little definite information about the direction of causality (Morissette et al. 2007, Ziedonis et al. 2008).

Figure 11.5 Smoking is associated with clinical mood disorders, including depression. Photo: Mixmike / E+ / Getty Images.

Nicotine-dependent smokers are twice as likely as nonsmokers to have a history of depression (Breslau and Johnson 2000) and lifetime depression rates among smokers in clinic-based smoking-cessation programs were found to be as high as 64 percent (Hitsman et al. 2003).

Smokers with a history of major depressive disorder more strongly endorsed beliefs that smoking has a variety of positive effects, including reducing boredom and negative affect, and increasing stimulation and social interaction. These individuals also reported a more enjoyable taste of cigarette smoke than did smokers without a history of, or not currently suffering from, major depression (Weinberger et al. 2011). Depressed adolescents may also be more vulnerable to social influences (peer pressure) that encourage smoking (Patton et al. 1998).

Although smoking temporarily relieves the emotional discomfort of nicotine withdrawal, there is also considerable evidence that smoking causes or increases depression. Several longitudinal studies indicate that daily smoking is a risk factor for depression (e.g., Klungsoyr et al. 2006, Steuber and Danner 2006). Other studies indicate that depression lifts after an extended period of abstinence from smoking (e.g., Leventhal et al. 2009).

Disorders of anxiety are the most common type of psychiatric syndrome, with about 25 percent of the general population experiencing at least one of the several varieties of this disorder during a lifetime. Some estimates indicate that 54 percent of individuals with generalized anxiety disorder are smokers (Lasser et al. 2000). Prevalence rates of smoking are very high in individuals with panic-spectrum disorder (Breslau et al. 2004).

Not only is smoking more prevalent in those with anxiety disorders, the emotional distress is more intense in smokers than in nonsmokers with anxiety disorders (Zvolensky et al. 2003). For instance, smokers with panic disorder tend to have more fear of anxiety and bodily indicators of anxiety as compared to nonsmokers with this anxiety disorder (Morissette et al. 2006).

As with the relationship between smoking and depression, there is evidence – or at least suggestion – of causality in both directions between anxiety disorders and addictive smoking. Some longitudinal studies indicate that social anxiety often precedes, and so could facilitate smoking and nicotine addiction (Dierker et al. 2001). However, much research implicates heavy smoking as a cause of **panic attacks** (Breslau et al. 2004). Women may be particularly vulnerable to smoking-induced panic disorder (Morissette et al. 2007). Although some types of anxiety disorders are worsened by smoking, smokers commonly relate that stress (and the resultant anxiety) often triggers the urge to smoke (Kassel et al. 2003).

Victims of posttraumatic stress disorder (PTSD) often use smoking in an attempt to regulate anxiety. However, nicotine dependence increases the risk of PTSD and withdrawal symptoms are more intense in smokers with this anxiety disorder (Koenen et al. 2005).

Several longitudinal studies (e.g., Pedersen and von Soest 2009) demonstrate that increases in anxiety, depression and suicidal thinking are more prevalent in individuals who became addicted to nicotine well before these symptoms appeared. These results suggest that daily smoking contributes to the development of emotional problems, although other factors (e.g., genetic predisposition, stressful conditions or experiences) could also increase both the probability of addictive tobacco use and vulnerability to psychiatric disorders.

Bipolar Disorder and Schizophrenia

About 1 percent of the general population suffers from bipolar disorder, and a similar proportion is schizophrenic. Heavy smoking and nicotine dependence are especially prevalent in individuals with these psychiatric disorders. Unique features of schizophrenia and bipolar disorder cause even greater vulnerability to nicotine addiction than for other mental and emotional disorders.

The estimated lifetime prevalence of daily smoking among individuals with bipolar disorder is 82 percent, which is higher than for unipolar disorder (Lasser et al. 2000). During the depressed phase of bipolar disorder, rates of smoking are similar to that of individuals with unipolar depression. Smoking, as well as alcohol consumption and the use of illicit drugs increase even further during the manic phase of the disorder when impulse control is impaired and risky behavior is more likely. Smoking among patients with bipolar disorder is associated with greater severity of the illness as indicated by increased psychosis, suicidal thoughts and actions (Ostacher et al. 2006).

Approximately 75–80 percent of individuals with schizophrenia use tobacco and half are heavy smokers (Workgroup on Substance Use Disorders 2006). Schizophrenics have higher FTND scores and take in more nicotine (more puffs from each cigarette) than controls who smoke the same number of cigarettes (Steinberg et al. 2005). Lo and colleagues found that fifteen minutes after smoking, schizophrenic subjects had significantly higher craving scores for tobacco than control subjects (Lo et al. 2011). The heavy smoking of many with schizophrenia is a major factor contributing to the increased incidence of other serious medical problems and the shorter life-spans of individuals who suffer from this disorder (Zeidonis et al. 2008).

Psychosocial factors are important contributors to the vulnerability to smoking and tobacco dependence of schizophrenic individuals. Such factors include limited education, poverty, unemployment, peer influence, and lack of support for quitting smoking. For many years, smoking was accepted and condoned in the mental health treatment system with hospitalized patients receiving no encouragement to abstain. Many patients with schizophrenia have less motivation in general for self-improvement. Some have reported that smoking satisfies a "core need" that provides meaning in their lives, even helping prevent a relapse to a deeper level of mental illness (Forchuk et al. 2002).

Individuals with schizophrenia often have impairments of attention, working memory and other cognitive functions. Inability to filter out unnecessary information may underlie deficits in sensory processing, which are also accompanied by abnormalities in brain electrical activity (EEG) (Kumara and Sharma 2002). These cognitive deficits and EEG irregularities are reduced by smoking or by administration of nicotine (by means of patches or chewing gum) to schizophrenic patients (George et al. 2002, Wing et al. 2011). Abnormalities of eye-movements during visual target tracking are characteristic of schizophrenia that tend to be normalized by nicotine. These improvements of behavior, cognition and brain activity are mediated by nicotine's agonist effect on cholinergic activity (Zeidonis et al. 2008). Whether this effect of nicotine improves other clinical symptoms of schizophrenia is not clear (Kalman et al. 2005). However, this action of nicotine is a likely incentive (self-medication) to smoke for schizophrenic individuals.

Tobacco smoking affects the metabolism of some antipsychotic medications (and other psychiatric drugs) by stimulating the production of liver enzymes. Consequently, the drugs are removed from the body more rapidly and their concentration in the brain is lower (Desai et al. 2001). Components of tobacco smoke other than nicotine cause this change in drug metabolism. The lower levels of drug in the blood are thought to bring about the lessened intensity of antipsychotic medication side effects seen in schizophrenic patients who are heavy smokers (Yang et al. 2002). Because these drug side effects (primarily the involuntary movements of extrapyramidal symptoms) are unpleasant, their attenuation is another incentive for smoking in patients who are administered antipsychotic medication. Smoking does not appear to cause schizophrenia or worsen its symptoms (Kalman et al. 2005).

Smoking and Use of Other Addictive Drugs

Users of alcohol and/or illicit drugs are more likely to smoke cigarettes than individuals who abstain from alcohol and addictive drugs other than tobacco. Concurrent use of tobacco is especially high in those with a use disorder for an additional addictive substance. The NESARC survey, a large-scale population study of alcohol use and related substance use disorders (Chapter 9) indicated that 3.4 percent of lifetime abstainers from alcohol smoked cigarettes. Of light drinkers, 12 percent were smokers as were 46 percent of those who were alcohol dependent.

Cigarette smoking in young adults is also associated with cannabis use. NSDUH results averaged over seven years indicate that 54.7 percent of current young adult cannabis users also smoked cigarettes. Prevalence of cigarette use among all individuals of this eighteen to twenty-five age group has declined steadily since the 1970s and in 2017 was 22.3 percent. Cigarette smokers tended to start cannabis use at an earlier age, and reported significantly more symptoms of cannabis use disorder (Dierker et al. 2018).

Further evidence of concurrent use of tobacco and cannabis comes from a survey of 2,000 college students in which 46 percent of cigarette smokers also reported using cannabis (Berg et al. 2015). Nicotine dependence is four times more likely in those who have used cannabis relative to those who have never used cannabis (Agrawal et al. 2012).

Clinical surveys of individuals addicted to cocaine or heroin show that 75–80 percent are heavy smokers. Nicotine-dependent individuals with additional drug use problems tend to be more severely addicted and to encounter more severe drug-related medical consequences (Kalman et al. 2005, Parker et al. 2018). Nicotine dependence in those with an additional drug use disorder has not decreased since the 1970s, unlike the prevalence of tobacco addiction in the general population.

Although the causal nature, if any, responsible for the association between use of tobacco and other drugs has not been established, a few reasons for causes have been suggested. Concurrent use of tobacco and other drugs may be motivated by attempts to increase the pleasurable effects, or decrease the aversive effects of either drug. For example, smoking reportedly relieves the anxiety caused by cocaine use, and the aftereffects of heroin or alcohol use. Conversely, marijuana use sometimes enhances the reward value of tobacco (Agrawal et al. 2012, Amos et al. 2004). Goodwin and colleagues found that addiction to opioids or antianxiety drugs was strongly associated with persistent, treatment-resistant nicotine dependence (Goodwin et al. 2014).

Much of the genetic predisposition for drug dependence is not drug-specific, but increases the vulnerability for addiction to several types of drugs (Chapter 6). As a result, the biologically inherited tendency for an individual to become nicotine dependent also makes the development of addiction to alcohol, cocaine, opioids, and cannabis more likely.

Personality Traits and Nicotine Dependence

Chapter 8 summarizes some of the extensive research literature concerning the association between personality (characteristic ways of thinking and acting) and use of several types of addictive drugs, including nicotine.

For the conduct of surveys intended to determine the personality profiles of drug users, investigators typically have more success recruiting cigarette smokers (most of whom are nicotine dependent) than individuals with problematic use of alcohol or illicit drugs. Consequently, there are many studies of personality factors and nicotine dependence in community samples in addition to the clinical studies of individuals in treatment for drug or other psychiatric disorders (Munafo et al. 2007).

In a large-scale study, the personality profiles of smokers were found to be similar to those of respondents who used cocaine or heroin, although the tobacco users showed less extreme differences from those who neither smoked nor used illicit drugs (Terracciano et al. 2008).

Many investigators have found associations between smoking and personality traits closely related to negative affect and lack of behavioral restraint. For example, Munafo and Black found that smokers had higher levels of neuroticism and extroversion. Negative affect, including anxiety and depression, often underlies neuroticism. Extroversion, which includes components of impulsivity and sensation seeking, is related to the factor of lessened behavioral restraint (Munafo and Black 2007). Kahler and colleagues found that even in respondents who did not suffer from concurrent psychiatric disorders, those who smoked were more likely to be impulsive, irritable, nervous and prone to worry and guilt (Kahler et al. 2009). FTND scores indicated that a general vulnerability to depression and negative emotions was strongest in those most heavily addicted to nicotine (Kahler et al. 2010).

Smoking in Women

Smoking is somewhat less prevalent in women than in men, although the difference is much smaller now than in the mid-twentieth century. Women often become nicotine dependent sooner than men after initial use of tobacco (Ridenour et al. 2006) and women also have more difficulty in stopping smoking. Women had lower success rates than men in smoking-cessation programs in the United States (Scharf and Shiffman 2004) and in France (Bohadana et al. 2003). The shorter periods of abstinence occur even though women typically have lower levels of nicotine intake and are often less nicotine dependent than men as indicated by FTND scores (Zeman et al. 2002). Laboratory studies of tobacco abstinence and withdrawal discomfort also indicate women's greater difficulty in avoiding relapse to smoking (Pomerlau et al. 2005).

Several reasons have been suggested for women's lower success rate in stopping smoking, including greater use of cigarettes for coping with stress, less tolerance of negative affect, and less confidence about quitting than men (Greaves 2015, Perkins 2001). However, the following four reasons for the difference have received the most empirical support are (1) the higher incidence of depressive and anxiety disorders in women, (2) the effect of hormone-level fluctuations related to the menstrual cycle, (3) concern about weight gain, and (4) gender-related differences in the efficacy of nicotine-replacement therapy.

The greater vulnerability of women to the coincident psychiatric disorders that increase the persistence of nicotine dependence is thought to account for much of the difficulty of women in abstaining from tobacco use (Husky et al. 2008, Pomerlau et al. 2005).

Weinberger and colleagues found that women with depression, posttraumatic stress disorder, or alcohol dependence had longer duration and more intense withdrawal symptoms, and more difficulty with smoking cessation than did male smokers with the same disorders (Weinberger et al. 2009).

Progesterone and estrogen (female reproductive hormones) influence smoking and nicotine dependence in women (Lynch and Sofuoglu 2010, McVay and Copeland 2011). Estrogen and progesterone levels generally follow opposite patterns during the menstrual cycle in humans and the estrous cycle in animals. Higher estrogen levels are associated with greater reward from nicotine (as well as from another stimulant, cocaine), as demonstrated from studies with both animal and human subjects. Conversely, progesterone reduces the reward value of nicotine and other addictive drugs, a hormonal effect also seen in both human and animal subjects. These effects on the reinforcing properties of nicotine are thought to be a result of the hormonal modulation of dopaminergic activity in brain reward systems (Mello 2010).

Women who stop smoking during the high-progesterone luteal phase experience more intense withdrawal symptoms, including irritability and other types of negative affect. The greater discomfort at this time apparently results from the combination of nicotine withdrawal symptoms and premenstrual symptoms that are in some respects similar. However, women have greater success at abstinence when they stop smoking during the high-progesterone (and lower-estrogen) premenstrual luteal phase than attempting to stop during the higher-estrogen follicular phase of the menstrual cycle (Allen et al. 2008, 2010). This somewhat surprising finding may be due to the decreased reward value of smoking, even in the presence of greater withdrawal-like symptoms during the premenstrual phase. Urges to smoke tend to be stronger when estrogen levels are higher, during the follicular phase.

A potential barrier to smoking cessation among women is concern about gaining weight upon quitting smoking (Copeland et al. 2006). Two-thirds of women smokers in the United States report being apprehensive about postcessation weight gain (Pomerlau et al. 2001). Concern about weight gain after quitting smoking was shown to be predictive of smoking relapse within one year (Jeffrey et al. 2000).

At least some of the overall lower quit rates of women smokers might be due to the lesser benefits for females of nicotine-replacement products, which are widely available as nonprescription aids for smoking cessation. Some of the evidence that women have more difficulty in stopping smoking has come from studies that employ nicotine-replacement therapy (NRT) (primarily nicotine patches, inhalers or chewing gum). These studies have shown that women tend to relapse sooner with NRT therapy, which is less effective in suppressing some nicotine withdrawal symptoms in women than men (Cepeda-Benito et al. 2004, Prochaska and Benowitz 2016).

Smoking in Adolescents

Approximately 95 percent of nicotine-addicted adults started smoking during adolescence (Falco 2005). Since tobacco is relatively accessible to many adolescents, is easy to conceal, and its use does not cause noticeable disruption of behavior, it is not surprising that at least half of adolescents or younger children experiment with smoking (Figure 11.6). Some become nicotine dependent, maintaining their addiction into adulthood. Adolescents perceive the severe health consequences of smoking as distant threats, and consistently underestimate the difficulty of quitting. The most blatant commercial messages intended for adolescents or children (e.g., the "Joe Camel" cartoon-like character) are no longer seen. However, in television and motion pictures smoking is often depicted as an edgy, daring activity, with appeal for many young people (Donaldson et al. 2017, Greydanus and Patel 2005). Delaying, preventing or stopping cigarette use by adolescents is critical for further reduction of smoking prevalence in adults. Intensive research efforts are under way to identify the factors that promote the start of smoking by adolescents, and to determine the most effective treatments for helping nicotine-addicted young people stop using tobacco.

Figure 11.6 Although prevalence of regular smoking among adolescents is declining, many experiment with cigarettes, and some become nicotine dependent. Nicotine addiction in adolescents is a risk factor for eventual development of other SUD. Photo: Flying Colours Ltd / Photodisc / Getty Images.

Prevalence and Consequences of Adolescent Smoking

In 2017, 787,000 adolescents (3.2 percent of individuals age twelve to seventeen) in the United States had smoked at least one cigarette within the past month, a decrease to about one-fourth of the smoking prevalence in 2002. Of these current users, 96,000 (12.2 percent) smoked cigarettes daily (Substance Abuse and Mental Health Services Administration 2018).

Although smoking among adolescents has declined in recent years, use of electronic nicotine delivery systems (primarily electronic cigarettes – "vaping" – described in a subsequent section) is increasing among teen-aged individuals. In 2018, 26.7 percent of high school seniors had used electronic cigarettes within the past month (National Institute of Drug Abuse 2018). Prevalence of electronic cigarette use by high school students has tripled since 2011.

Smoking during adolescence has serious consequences. As with most drug use, the adverse consequences of smoking are probabilistic rather than certain, but their likelihood increases with greater frequency and amounts of tobacco use or inhalation of nicotine-containing vapor. Most young people who try cigarettes or other types of tobacco or vaping do not become addicted – but some do, and nicotine dependence is a possible consequence of experimental use during adolescence. In a prospective study of the development of nicotine addiction, more than half of a group of 353 new adolescent smokers met at least one DSM-IV criterion and 25 percent satisfied the full criteria of nicotine dependence within a period of two years (Kandel et al. 2007).

Adolescent smoking is often limited by time spent in school or in the presence of parents. Although adolescent smokers consume fewer cigarettes and are less likely to smoke daily than most adult tobacco users, several prospective studies reveal that many teenage smokers experience nicotine withdrawal symptoms (e.g., Bailey et al. 2009, Smith et al. 2008). These investigations indicate that craving is the symptom most often reported by adolescent smokers who refrain from tobacco use. Other abstinence-related symptoms, including anxiety and anger, are less clearly related to nicotine withdrawal and may be partly due to emotional volatility of adolescents (Smith et al. 2008). Although comparisons are difficult, adolescents may suffer less discomfort than adults from smoking cessation, with relapse driven largely by desire for the social aspects and the pleasure of smoking.

Individuals who started smoking in **early adolescence** consume cigarettes at higher rates, are less likely to quit as adults, and are presumably more nicotine dependent than those who began smoking later (Breslau and Peterson 1996). Addicted adult smokers who started regular tobacco use during their adolescent years have little practical experience in living without the emotional comfort of smoking (Piasecki 2006).

Tobacco smoking, especially when combined with alcohol use, has long been implicated as an early and important step on the pathway to more serious drug use. Adolescents who smoke are quite likely to drink alcohol, and frequent smoking during early adolescence is a strong predictor of subsequent alcohol use disorders (Biederman et al. 2005). Multivariate analysis indicates that smoking, rather than the level of accompanying alcohol consumption, is more closely associated with development of alcohol use disorder (Grucza and Bierut 2006). Regular smoking before age fifteen is also associated with a **fourfold increase** in the probability of addiction to other drugs, including alcohol (Chapter 8).

The greater vulnerability of young smokers to use disorders of other addictive drugs could be due to risk factors common to most forms of SUD. Considering this commonality of risk factors, early use of nicotine might not contribute to further SUD occurrence, but merely be an early indicator of addictive vulnerability.

Evidence from animal studies indicates that nicotine exposure produces enduring changes in the adolescent brain, resulting in persistently increased sensitivity to the reinforcing effects of addictive drugs (McMillen et al. 2005). These changes, including effects on gene expression, are greater in the developing than in the mature brain and may be unique to adolescence (Trauth et al. 2001). These well-established effects of nicotine exposure on the development of the adolescent brain have not been studied in humans because ethical and practical limitations prevent such controlled research. However, their presence in experimental animals suggests an important effect – specific to nicotine – that could increase the general vulnerability to substance use disorders in humans.

Smoking during adolescence is associated with emotional instability and an increased vulnerability to psychiatric disorders. As discussed previously regarding adult smokers, the relationship between smoking and these risk factors in adolescents is often bidirectional. Some tobacco use by adolescents is an attempt to self-medicate negative affect, but conversely, smoking can also worsen emotional and behavioral difficulties of this age group (Griesler et al. 2011).

The most serious consequences of regular tobacco use are the myriad toxic effects. Individuals who start smoking early in life have more years for these toxic actions to accrue. Most tobacco-related medical problems emerge after years of smoking, but some (lung and respiratory problems) can occur in adolescent smokers (Arday et al. 1995). As noted above, early-starting smokers tend to smoke more heavily as adults, thereby further increasing the multiple medical consequences of tobacco use.

Risk Factors for Adolescent Smoking

Most risk factors for adolescent smoking are also associated with greater vulnerability for harmful use of alcohol and illicit addictive drugs (Chapter 8). These factors include positive attitudes toward smoking, peers who smoke and tolerate deviance, conduct disorder, poor academic performance, a family history of SUD, impulsiveness and risk taking, parental permissiveness, and ready availability of cigarettes.

Risk factors are more closely associated with the deviant practice of regular smoking than with the more common activity of merely experimenting with tobacco (Dodgen 2005, White et al. 2007). Some factors can decrease the probability of smoking when their status is opposite to the risk-prone condition. An example of such a protective factor is good academic performance.

Genetically determined biological differences account entirely for two factors that influence regular smoking and the transition to nicotine dependence. The first factor is the nature of the initial smoking experience. The second, discussed in the following section, is the variability among individuals in the rate of nicotine metabolism.

Individuals differ widely in their response to initial inhalation of tobacco smoke, which for most people occurs during adolescence (Chen et al. 2011, Pomerleau et al. 2005). Some experimental smokers feel relaxation, others pleasurable arousal, and yet others describe dizziness or nausea. Several investigators have found that more intense subjective reactions to initial smoking predict recurrent smoking and eventual nicotine dependence (Audriane-McGovern et al. 2007, Hu et al. 2008). Even dizziness and nausea, as well as more obviously pleasurable effects, are associated with subsequent heavier smoking. Perhaps the thrill-seeking or risk-taking motivation of many adolescents (who may be attracted to altered states of consciousness) results in the repeated use of a substance that at first produces what might be considered an unpleasant experience.

Genetics of Smoking and Nicotine Dependence

Smoking and nicotine dependence are heavily influenced by genetic predisposition. The strength and nature of these biologically inherited effects are similar to the genetic predisposition for use disorders of alcohol and other addictive drugs (Chapter 6). Although some genetic effects increase vulnerability to SUD in general, others are unique to disorders of tobacco use.

Many investigators in several countries conduct research to determine the nature of the genetics of tobacco use. These efforts include those of the Tobacco and Genetics Consortium (TAG), the European Network of Genetic and Genomic Epidemiology (ENGAGE) and the Oxford-GlaxoSmithKline (Ox-GSK) consortia. Very large numbers of subjects are required for use of certain techniques for genomic research such as genome-wide association studies (Bierut 2011, Tobacco and Genetics Consortium 2010).

Twin studies consistently indicate that genetic predisposition contributes 50–70 percent of the vulnerability to smoking and nicotine dependence (Maes and Neale

2009, Munafo and Johnstone 2008). The genetic influence is stronger for regular smoking and nicotine dependence than for initiation of smoking. Intensity of nicotine withdrawal is also partially genetically determined, with heritability of some symptoms estimated at 47 percent (Pergadia et al. 2006).

Several nicotine-specific biological functions are probable mechanisms for the genetic transmission of predisposition to smoking and nicotine addiction (Box 11.3). Small differences (alleles) in many genes influence the neurological functioning that underlies complex behaviors such as tobacco use and nicotine dependence. Each allele contributes a small part of the total genetic predisposition, and complex pattern of alleles probably differ even among individuals who carry similar vulnerability for addictive tobacco use.

Differences in several genes or specific areas within genes correlate significantly with frequency of smoking or degree of nicotine dependence. Most of the molecular differences detected between nicotine-addicted and nonaddicted smokers are located in or near genes relevant to the biological actions of nicotine. Three locations are on chromosome 15, within areas that control the production of nicotinic acetylcholine receptors. Other locations are on chromosome 19 in the *CPY2A6* gene that controls production of a nicotine-metabolic enzyme (Tobacco and Genetics Consortium 2010). All these alleles are implicated in some aspect of smoking behavior. However, the size of their combined effects is small, relative to the major genetic influence on smoking as indicated by the twin studies. Much of the molecular basis of vulnerability to nicotine addiction has yet to be determined.

BOX 11.3 Genetic transmission of vulnerability to nicotine addiction

Greater initial sensitivity to nicotine
  Pleasurable arousal, altered state of consciousness (including "dizziness")
Rate of nicotine metabolism
  Faster rate promotes heavier smoking
Vulnerability to withdrawal symptoms relatively specific to nicotine
  Anger and irritability
  Concentration difficulty

The functional significance – how the effects influence smoking and nicotine addiction – of most of these allelic differences has not been identified. One exception to this lack of knowledge is the effect of the *CPY2A6* gene on the rate of nicotine metabolism. Nicotine is metabolized (converted to cotinine) by a liver enzyme whose production is controlled by the *CPY2A6* gene (Messina et al. 1997). Variations of this gene occur frequently, and individuals with these alleles metabolize nicotine more slowly, extending the half-life of nicotine in the bloodstream (Bloom et al. 2011). Adults with slow-metabolizing alleles of the *CPY2A6* gene are half as likely to be smokers as fast-metabolizers, and those that do smoke consume fewer cigarettes (Schoedel et al. 2004).

In adolescent smokers, the differences in the rate of nicotine metabolism influence the amount of smoking and the development of nicotine dependence. Twelfth-grade students with the slow nicotine-metabolizing variants of the *CPY2A6* gene progressed into nicotine dependence more slowly than did students with the normal (faster) metabolizing genes. The slow nicotine-metabolizers smoked a mean of thirty-two cigarettes a week compared to the mean of seventy-three per week for students with the normal-metabolizing genes (Audrain-McGovern et al. 2007). Since regular smokers often attempt to maintain blood levels of nicotine by frequent smoking, those who metabolize nicotine faster consume more cigarettes each day. The more frequent smoking provides more reinforcement from and conditioning of nicotine effects, further ingraining the habit of smoking and the development of nicotine dependence.

Genetic effects can influence complex behavior such as drug use and abuse only by interacting with environmental conditions. Twin studies and genomic investigations have shown that low parental monitoring of adolescents, combined with inherited genetic risk, results in greater incidence of smoking. With closer and more consistent monitoring, even adolescents with genetic predisposition for nicotine dependence did not have greater incidence of tobacco use (Chen et al. 2011, Dick et al. 2007).

Another developmental factor, **childhood adversity**, can influence the effect of genomic differences on nicotine dependence. A variation in the *CHRNA5* gene (the same allele studied in the parental monitoring investigations) was associated with a greater level of nicotine dependence in subjects who had undergone childhood neglect or trauma. Both the childhood adversity and the *CHRNA5* allele increased nicotine dependence in men and women, but the adversity effect on heavy smoking was much greater in women (Xie et al. 2012).

Toxic Consequences of Tobacco Use

The use of tobacco causes or contributes to a host of deleterious effects on the body. These toxic effects range from premature wrinkling of the skin, through cataracts of the eye and macular degeneration, to death – from cancer, cardiovascular problems (strokes and heart attacks) and lung diseases such as emphysema. Although the fatal consequences of smoking are often delayed for many years, the practice kills more people each year than alcohol, cocaine, opioids, homicide, suicide and AIDS combined (US Department of Health and Human Services 2014, Vivolo-Kantor et al. 2018).

Heavy smoking reduces mean life-span by 13.2 years in men and 14.5 years in women (Centers for Disease Control and Prevention 2002, 2009). Death rates of smokers are at least twice as high in smokers during mid-life, and remain higher than nonsmokers well into old age. At age thirty, 13 of 1,000 nonsmoking men will die (from any cause) within ten years, but 30 of 1,000 men who smoke will die within this time interval. The probability of death in men from any cause within ten years at age forty-five is 0.039 for nonsmokers and 0.091 for smokers. These probabilities at age fifty-five are 0.066 and 0.125, and at age eighty, 0.65 and 0.95. Similar differences occur between smoking and nonsmoking women (Woloshin et al. 2002). In the United States, approximately 480,000 people die each year from smoking-related causes, and the estimate of worldwide premature deaths due to tobacco use is 6 million per year (www.cdc.gov/tobacco).

Growing recognition of the toxicity of tobacco use has markedly reduced its use in the United States and in some other countries. However, a substantial number of individuals continue to smoke or use tobacco via the oral route (snuff or chewing tobacco). The adverse health consequences of smoking are often long-delayed and their occurrence – for a specific individual – is uncertain (*all* smokers don't die sooner than all nonsmokers), counteracting the threat of illness or death as a fully effective deterrent to smoking. Such disregard of probable harm is especially common among adolescents, at ages when most adult smokers initiate tobacco use.

Medical problems become more prevalent as the amount of exposure to tobacco or tobacco smoke increases. Individuals who start smoking at younger ages and/or smoke more cigarettes per day are more likely to suffer the health consequences, and develop these problems sooner than those who smoked less often and for fewer years (Karan et al. 2003). Toxicity is partially determined by the tar and nicotine content of tobacco smoke. In most brands of cigarettes the concentration of these toxins has decreased from levels common in the mid-twentieth century. However, addicted smokers typically compensate for the reduced nicotine content by inhaling more deeply and smoking more often. Consequently, cigarettes with lower tar and nicotine content are still quite toxic.

Most pipe or cigar smokers inhale less smoke into the lungs than do cigarette smokers. However, nicotine and other toxic components of tobacco smoke are also absorbed from the mouth and throat. As with "smokeless" use of tobacco (chewing tobacco and snuff), these other forms of smoking are less toxic than deeply inhaled cigarette smoke, but many adverse health consequences still occur (Karan et al. 2003).

The public health hazard of smoking is not limited to those who choose to smoke. The toxic consequences of passive exposure are now well established and this knowledge promoted the legal restrictions on smoking in many public places. The estimate of annual deaths in the United States due to environmental tobacco smoke is approximately 53,000, making passive exposure a major preventable cause of death. These deaths are primarily due to cardiovascular disease and to a lesser extent, lung cancer (American Cancer Society 2011, US Department of Health and Human Services 2010). Passive exposure is a special hazard for the children of parents who smoke. Tobacco use is more prevalent among those of lower income and the health hazards of passive smoke exposure in children often add to other child health problems associated with poverty.

Mechanisms of Toxicity

Tobacco smoke contains thousands of chemicals, many of which are carcinogenic or have other toxic actions. Damage to the body comes from the particulate components (the "tar" content), and various gases, including carbon monoxide, hydrogen cyanide, ammonia and oxidant gases (Zevin and Benowitz 1998).

The tar content contains many carcinogenic chemicals, such as the N-nitrosamines, aromatic amines, 1,3-butadiene, benzene, and ethylene oxide (US Department of Health and Human Services 2010). Carbon monoxide reduces oxygen delivery to all organs, including the heart and brain. Oxidant gases cause widespread harm and dysfunction, including damage to the heart and cardiovascular system. The damaging effects of **oxidative stress** are described in Chapter 10.

Most toxic effects of tobacco use come from the tar and gases of tobacco smoke. Although nicotine is the main addictive component of tobacco, the drug is not the primary cause of damage to the body. Consequently, nicotine-replacement therapy (e.g., nicotine patches and chewing gum) to assist in smoking cessation is relatively safe. Nicotine use (even without the more toxic components of tobacco) is not entirely risk-free. High doses can be lethal, and nicotine is implicated in some deleterious fetal effects from smoking by pregnant women. Nicotine is a vasoconstrictor, raising blood pressure and worsening circulatory problems such as Burger's disease.

Diseases Caused by or Related to Tobacco Use

Tobacco use accounts for 87 percent of lung cancer deaths and at least 30 percent of all cancer deaths (American Cancer Society 2011). The risk of cancers of the mouth, larynx, esophagus, lung, stomach, pancreas, kidney, urinary bladder, and uterine cervix are directly related to the intensity and duration of exposure to tobacco smoke (Karan et al. 2003). Genetic predisposition increases vulnerability to these carcinogenic effects, a biologically inherited tendency that is different from the predisposition for nicotine dependence (Bierut 2011).

Smoking is a major cause of coronary heart disease, stroke, aortic aneurysm, and peripheral arterial disease, and is responsible for about 30 percent of deaths due to these conditions. These effects are primarily the result of inflammation, oxidative stress, and changes in lipid metabolism caused by constituents of tobacco smoke. Smoking also produces insulin resistance and chronic inflammation, which can accelerate neuropathy and microvascular complications (US Department of Health and Human Services 2010).

In addition to the increased occurrence of cancer and cardiovascular problems, smoking also causes chronic obstructive pulmonary disease (COPD), including emphysema. About 90 percent of deaths from COPD are attributed to smoking (Anczak and Nogler 2003). As with cancer, smoking-related COPD vulnerability is partly due to genetic predisposition (US Department of Health and Human Services 2010).

Women who smoke throughout pregnancy have babies that weigh a mean of one-half pound less than those of nonsmoking women. There is also an increased probability of miscarriage or preterm delivery (Walsh 1994). These effects are dose related in that they are greater in heavier-smoking women. Carbon monoxide displaces oxygen in the blood supply to the fetus, impairing growth and development. Nicotine and other toxic components of tobacco smoke are also implicated in prenatal harm, which includes subtle neurological and cognitive deficits (US Department of Health and Human Services 2010).

The health consequences of tobacco use are synergistic with the risks from the use of other drugs in that toxic effects from both tobacco and the additional drug are increased. Heavy use of alcohol, combined with smoking, results in higher incidence of most of the adverse effects discussed here for tobacco, and in previous chapters for alcohol (Karan et al. 2003). Women smokers who use oral contraceptives are at increased risk for cardiac failure and strokes due to blood clot formation (McClave et al. 2010). This risk is especially great for women older than age 35.

Is Tobacco the Most Addictive Substance?

Nicotine is sometimes described as the most addictive of drugs – with greater dependence potential than even cocaine or heroin. A meaningful comparison of the addictive potential of drugs must include consideration of cultural-societal influences and restraints on drug use as well as the pharmacological properties of the drugs. A drug's availability, convenience and expense are cultural determinants of its use, which in turn affect the probability of dependence. Prevalence of tobacco use (and nicotine addiction) is much higher in less educated and lower-income populations, a difference illustrating social-cultural factors in nicotine dependence.

Two observations indicate the high addiction potential of nicotine relative to other drugs of abuse: (1) the proportion of users who become dependent and (2) many individuals suffering from multiple addictions report greater difficulty of maintaining abstinence from tobacco compared to stopping use of other addictive drugs.

Addiction to a drug or a substance is often not an "either–or" (binary) condition, in that heavy use merges into dependence without a clear separation point in many borderline cases. However, it is still useful to consider the proportion of frequent users of a drug who become addicted. Only a small fraction of individuals who drink alcohol become dependent on the drug, but most regular smokers are to some degree nicotine dependent. Because in many cultures neither alcohol nor tobacco use is illicit (for adults), and both are generally socially accepted, the greater proportion of dependent tobacco users (mostly cigarette smokers) indicates that nicotine is more addictive than alcohol.

A similar comparison of tobacco against cannabis, stimulants (cocaine and amphetamine), and opiate drugs is more difficult and less informative because with the exception of cannabis in eleven US states, nonmedical (recreational) use is illicit. The legal restriction limits access to these drugs and results in greater expense and the risk of greater social consequences of use (criminal charges). If cocaine and heroin were legally available in convenience stores at a price comparable to that of cigarettes, the use of these drugs would increase greatly. Not all users would become dependent, but addiction rates would also certainly increase.

In twelve-step groups as well as in drug treatment programs, some nicotine-dependent individuals who are also addicted to alcohol or another drug maintain that smoking is harder to quit than alcohol, cocaine or heroin (Karan and Rosecrans 2000). In a survey of 1,000 tobacco-smoking individuals seeking treatment for alcohol or drug dependence, 57 percent said cigarettes would be more difficult to quit than the other drug upon which they were dependent. Respondents who were severely nicotine dependent were those most likely to make this prediction. Alcohol-dependent individuals were about four times more likely than those who were addicted to an illicit drug to say that urges for cigarettes were at least as strong as the desire for their primary problem drug (Kozlowski et al. 1989). Those addicted to both an illicit drug and nicotine are only a small fraction of the overall population of nicotine-dependent smokers. The far greater number of alcohol-dependent heavy smokers are apparently more representative of the overall population of tobacco users.

The positive reinforcement value of a drug is a major factor in determining its addictive potential, and especially for continued use that can lead to dependence. Research paradigms used with animal subjects – conditioned place preference or drug self-administration – allow assessment of reward value of drugs based solely on pharmacological effects. Even with the obvious species differences, these studies with animals usually yield results quite similar to the relative reward value of drugs as typically reported by humans. Intravenous injection of nicotine is positively reinforcing to several types of animals (rodents, primates, dogs). However, nicotine is less rewarding to animal subjects than stimulants (cocaine, amphetamine) or opiates (e.g., heroin). Animals will not "work as hard" (as determined by operant schedules of reinforcement) for nicotine as for the other addictive drugs, especially cocaine (e.g., Risner and Goldberg 1983).

Additionally, for both operant reinforcement and conditioned place preference, the reward value of nicotine is quite dependent on dose and other factors, including species and strain differences (Le Foll and Goldberg 2009). The conditions under which nicotine is positively reinforcing to animals are much more specific and limited than for stimulant or opiate drugs. Inhalation of tobacco smoke, the route of administration most addictive for humans, cannot be used in most animal studies of nicotine reinforcement. However, the overall indication from animal-based research is that nicotine is less rewarding than most other drugs with abuse potential for humans.

Informal and anecdotal reports by humans generally support the implications of animal studies that tobacco use (even including smoking) is less pleasurable than the use of other addictive substances. Few systematic surveys have addressed the relative hedonic value of addictive drugs, but most respondents (addicts in treatment) in the survey conducted by Kozlowski and colleagues rated cocaine, heroin or alcohol as more pleasurable than cigarettes (Kozlowski et al. 1989).

Although for most users the initial pharmacological reward value of nicotine is subtle, other factors mentioned previously (social facilitation, convenience, absence of intoxication and compatibility with normal activities) facilitate smoking. Subjective pleasure often, but not always, accompanies positive reinforcement (Chapter 7). Continued use of tobacco can occur even in the absence of strong pleasurable effects.

So, why is quitting cigarettes so difficult? Continuing to use a drug, or stopping drug use, usually depends on the relative immediate consequences – **benefits versus adversity** – of either action, as well as events or conditions that motivate use. For a nicotine-dependent smoker, a major benefit (negative reinforcement) of continued use is the immediate (if temporary) relief from aversive withdrawal. Nicotine withdrawal symptoms are much less intense, disturbing and life-threatening than withdrawal from alcohol, and for most individuals much less aversive than withdrawal from cocaine or heroin. However, even withdrawal effects that are "only" annoying and uncomfortable can maintain drug use if the symptoms persist and are hard to ignore.

For all addictive substances, conditioned stimuli associated with drug effects are major triggers for craving and resumption of drug use. These conditioned stimuli are probably more pervasive with nicotine dependence than in most cases of addiction to other drugs whose reward value may be greater than that of tobacco (Le Foll and Goldberg 2009). In heavy smokers, cues conditioned to tobacco use and nicotine intake are intimately intertwined with daily activities, producing craving and withdrawal symptoms throughout waking hours. As described previously, these conditioned cravings may be quite persistent and are very difficult to avoid.

Smoking, including resumption after a period of abstinence, is unlikely to result in immediate and serious adverse consequences. Few tobacco-dependent individuals lose family or employment because they continue to smoke. Heavy smokers do not go to prison because of their tobacco use. Smoking seldom "takes over a life" in that nicotine dependence almost never results in overwhelming involvement with tobacco use. The grave medical consequences are long-delayed and uncertain. As a result, for many individuals in most cultures nicotine dependence is indeed the addiction that is the most difficult to overcome (Karan and Rosecrans 2000).

Electronic Nicotine Delivery Systems

Devices that produce an **inhalable nicotine aerosol** – rather than smoke from burning tobacco – were introduced in the European market in 2006, and became available in the United States in 2007. Electronic cigarettes (EC) are the most widely used of these devices (Figure 11.7). The extent of EC use in the United States and several other countries has risen rapidly in the decade since their introduction. Devices that produce vapor for inhalation can also deliver other addictive drugs, and use of these devices is commonly referred to as "vaping."

Figure 11.7 Electronic cigarettes deliver addictive nicotine vapor that, although less toxic than tobacco smoke, can have adverse effects on the respiratory system and the brain. Photo: Daniel Griffith / EyeEm / Getty Images.

Prevalence of EC use is greatest among young people. For young adults (age eighteen to twenty-four), prevalence of current EC use in 2018 was 13.6 percent, twice as great as in 2011. For all adults EC use rate in 2018 was 2.8 percent (Cullen et al. 2018, US Department of Health and Human Services 2016). Adolescents of high school age show even higher rates of vaping than do young adults. In 2018 20.8 percent of high school students in the United States were current (previous month) EC users, as were 5 percent of middle school students, use rates much higher than in 2011 – 1.5 percent and 0.6 percent, respectively. Although the prevalence of smoking in high school seniors has decreased steadily for several years, use rates of vaping now surpass those of tobacco and have increased in recent years, as illustrated in Figure 11.8.

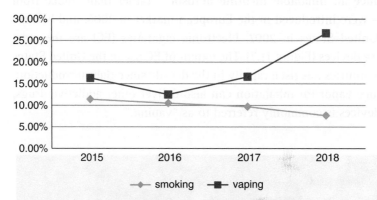

Figure 11.8 Prevalence of smoking and vaping in twelfth-grade students. Estimates provided by the Monitoring the Future survey for 2018 are for smoking or vaping during the month preceding the survey. Vaping percentages are for "any vaping" and so include some electronic cigarette use of THC. Nicotine is the drug vaped most often, but some respondents were unsure of the components of the vaporized drug inhaled (Cullen et al. 2018, National Institute of Drug Abuse 2019a).

Many adult EC users also use tobacco. In 2015, 55 percent of individuals age eighteen to twenty-four who were primarily EC users also smoked cigarettes. Nicotine vapor is less toxic than tobacco smoke, so some smokers also use EC and reduce cigarette consumption in an attempt to avoid medical problems (Green et al. 2018, Pasquereau et al. 2017, Prochaska and Benowitz 2016). Some cigarette smokers who also use EC do so in certain environments because the exhaled nicotine vapor appears to be less offensive to nonsmokers than is tobacco smoke (King et al. 2015).

The vapor delivered by EC contains nicotine, but not most of the other toxic components of tobacco smoke (primarily the aromatic tar content), so EC use is presumably safer than smoking (Glasser et al. 2017). However, high levels of nicotine can produce adverse effects, and other components of the vapor may be toxic

(Schier et al. 2019). The harmful effects of long-term EC use have not been determined (Huang et al. 2018). Accidental ingestion of the nicotine-containing liquid (EC refill cartridges) can be severely toxic, especially to children.

A potential use of EC is to assist addicted cigarette smokers in stopping tobacco use, although in 2013 only 1.3 percent of EC users were former smokers. Personal accounts of successful abstinence from addictive smoking, aided by EC use, appear on social media and other internet sources (van der Tempel et al. 2016). However, the few available controlled outcome studies reveal primarily inconsistent or marginal results of EC as facilitating smoking cessation (Prochaska and Benowitz 2016, Glasser et al. 2017). For example, in a study by Bullard and colleagues, 7 percent of nicotine-addicted subjects using EC became abstinent, as did 6 percent who used nicotine patches, and 5 percent using a placebo EC containing no nicotine (Bullard et al. 2013). Some studies report a reduction in tobacco use, although not long-term abstinence from smoking (e.g., Pasquereau et al. 2017).

Most addicted smokers report that vaping nicotine is less rewarding – and less effective in relieving withdrawal symptoms – than is inhaling tobacco smoke. With EC use, there are fewer conditioned stimuli associated with smoking, including the taste, odor, and other sensations of smoke exposure as well as behavior characteristic of tobacco use. Because of these and other differences between smoking and EC use, inhalation of vaporized nicotine appears to be somewhat less addictive than cigarette smoking (Etter and Eissenberg 2015, Glasser et al. 2017). Controlled studies of EC reduction of nicotine withdrawal symptoms in addicted cigarette smokers produce mixed results. Symptom reduction is greater with a higher nicotine content of the EC aerosol (Browne and Todd 2018, Breland et al. 2014).

Although in the United States, smoking prevalence among adolescents has decreased in recent years, vaping by middle and high school students has markedly increased. Many adolescent EC users have never smoked cigarettes (Singh 2016). Survey results from the United States in 2015 indicated than an estimated 10.4 percent of high school seniors used EC only (did not also smoke cigarettes), 5.8 percent used both electronic and tobacco cigarettes and 5.3 percent smoked tobacco but did not use EC (US Department of Health and Human Services 2016). Estimates for vaping and smoking prevalence for 2018 (Figure 11.8) indicate that an even smaller proportion of seniors who vape are also smoking tobacco.

EC use among adolescents is a major public health concern. Many young adolescents perceive vaping as safer and less addictive than smoking tobacco, and nicotine-containing liquids in EC devices are often produced with enticing flavors (e.g., cherry, bubble gum) (Chaffee et al. 2015). Advertisements for tobacco cigarettes attractive to children are now illegal, but EC commercials are less restricted (Singh et al. 2016). In 2018 the US Food and Drug Administration announced a program intended to reduce the availability and appeal of EC products to children and adolescents (FDA 2018).

EC use can enable reduction of smoking in nicotine-dependent individuals, but vaping also introduces many nonsmoking adolescents to the use of very addictive nicotine. Morean and colleagues assessed nicotine dependence symptoms in 520 adolescent past-month EC users. Respondents who started vaping at an earlier age, vaped more frequently, and inhaled vapor of liquids with higher concentrations of nicotine reported higher levels of dependence (Morean et al. 2018).

Two large-scale prospective studies assessed both EC use and cigarette smoking in adolescents or young adults. Both surveys indicate that EC use often precedes initiation of cigarette smoking. Leventhal and colleagues found that over a one-year period, ninth and tenth graders who used EC were 4.27 times more likely (odds ratio) to start smoking cigarettes than those who did not use an electronic nicotine delivery device (Leventhal et al. 2015). Primack and colleagues reported an odds ratio of 8.3 for initiation of cigarette use in EC-using respondents ages 16–26, relative to individuals who did not use EC during a one-year period (Primack et al. 2015). These results do not establish cause–effect between EC use and cigarette smoking, but do identify inhalation of nicotine vapor as a risk factor for the more toxic and very addictive smoking of tobacco. The recent increase in nicotine vaping among adolescents might attenuate or even reverse the years-long steady decline of smoking in young people.

In addition to the risk of nicotine dependence, vaping of nicotine by adolescents also exposes the developing brain to long-term effects of the drug, including increased vulnerability to other addictions (Grucza and Bierut 2006; see also Chapter 8).

A third hazard of vaping is the risk of severe pulmonary disease, as described by a warning from the Centers for Disease Control and Prevention (Schier et al. 2019). Although representing a small fraction of EC users, by 2019, 200 cases of lung damage associated with vaping had been reported to the CDCP. Preliminary analysis indicates that these toxic effects result from chemical components of the vaporized liquid, rather than from nicotine. Production and distribution of "pods" for use in EC devices is essentially unregulated by the Food and Drug Administration, and most cases of acute vaping toxicity apparently come from vaping liquid preparations containing extracts of THC (the primary psychoactive component of cannabis). The THC, as well as toxic ingredients, are often added to these "bootleg" preparations that are clandestinely produced and distributed.

Stopping Smoking

Most smokers have attempted to stop tobacco use at least once, and a return to smoking after failed attempts at abstinence is common. However, many nicotine-dependent individuals eventually succeed in permanently halting the addictive behavior. Smoking prevalence in the United States and other countries has decreased sharply since the 1960s, and there is now a larger population of former smokers than of current smokers (Babb et al. 2017).

Most regular smokers are addicted to nicotine, and stopping compulsive tobacco use shares many features with successful termination and effective treatment of dependence on other addictive drugs (Chapter 16). A basic similarity is the fact that most individuals who recover from addictions do so without professional assistance. For those who cannot terminate their drug use without additional assistance, treatment programs typically include counseling or group therapy, and for some addictions, access to therapeutic drugs as prescribed by physicians. Encouragement from and cooperation of family and friends is very important. No one type of treatment works for all individuals, and even with treatment, many addicts soon relapse to active drug use. **Relapse prevention** is the critical test of treatment effectiveness, because almost any intervention treatment effort can briefly interrupt drug use.

Some aspects of nicotine dependence and its treatment are unique. The smaller role of twelve-step programs in recovery from compulsive smoking is an important difference from most treatments for addiction to other substances. Active participation in Alcoholics Anonymous or Narcotics Anonymous and the assumption that addiction is a disease is heavily emphasized in most drug treatment programs. Twelve-step programs are also the sole source of guidance and support for many recovering addicts who do not receive professional treatment. For many years, counselors in drug treatment programs (and twelve-step program sponsors) were not likely to encourage or support smoking-cessation attempts in individuals addicted to both nicotine and another drug (Kalman et al. 2005). Many of these helping individuals smoked, and the use of tobacco was seen as benign, or at least a less serious problem than disordered use of an intoxicating drug.

The tendency to ignore nicotine dependence in those with an additional drug use disorder became less prevalent as the general disapproval of smoking increased. Many patients as well as clinicians have found that the tactics used to remain drug and alcohol-free (twelve-step programs, cognitive behavioral therapy) are also effective for stopping smoking and avoiding relapse. However, addicted smokers who have no additional drug use problems are very unlikely to attend AA or NA meetings, and these twelve-step programs are not an important support for such individuals.

Nicotine Anonymous is a twelve-step movement that originated in 1980, decades later than AA and NA(Narcotics Anonymous). The late arrival of Nicotine Anonymous on the recovery scene was apparently due to the long-delayed recognition of tobacco use as an addictive disorder. For many years, the rooms of AA and NA meetings were often heavy with tobacco smoke. Many twelve-step meetings are now smoke-free, but smoking is still prevalent among members of these groups. There are relatively few Nicotine Anonymous meetings, compared to the very large numbers of AA and NA groups located throughout the United States and in other countries. The Nicotine Anonymous website lists only one such meeting group in the tobacco-growing state of Kentucky. California, a state in which smoking in public places is heavily restricted, has seventy-five twelve-step meetings for addicted smokers. Numbers of such meetings in other representative states include five in Missouri, and thirty-six in New York. Nicotine Anonymous support is also offered by means of internet meetings, but in many parts of the United States there are no twelve-step meetings accessible to those who are dependent on only nicotine, rather than on nicotine in addition to other addictive drugs.

Many drug treatment programs are residential, in that participants move temporarily from their homes to live in a controlled environment. However, residential programs for nicotine dependence only are quite rare.

There are many nonresidential treatment programs for stopping smoking. These vary greatly in the activities offered and supported. Nicotine-dependent smokers are typically not as ashamed of their behavior and are less isolated from others than are those addicted to other drugs. Addicted smokers are also less likely to accept the premise that their compulsive tobacco use is the result of a disease. Because of these (and other) differences from other substance use disorders, most smoking-cessation programs are not based on twelve-step concepts of addictive disease and emphasis on spiritual growth as the basis of recovery. Programs often promote specific ways to stop smoking and avoid relapse, and these tactics typically include some form of cognitive behavioral therapy. With their emphasis on empowerment by changing specific behavior and finding ways to reduce temptation, these programs are somewhat similar to weight loss programs. Learning to avoid stimuli that produce craving and situations likely to trigger resumption of smoking are important components of these programs (Babb et al. 2017). Counseling and group support may also involve finding solutions to more general problems such as boredom, anxiety and depression, but treatment of psychopathology is not often emphasized (Dodgen 2005).

Many smokers who intend to stop using tobacco prefer to do so without counseling or other professional assistance. Advice and assistance in stopping smoking are available from several organizations or agencies, including the American Cancer Society, the American Lung Association, the Foundation for a Smokefree America, and many others. These sources of information can be quite useful, and most are available on the Internet at no cost.

Medications for Smoking Cessation

Three medications are available to help with smoking cessation (Prochaska and Benowitz 2016). Zyban (generic name is buprorion) is an indirect agonist (blocking reuptake) of the neurotransmitters noradrenaline and dopamine. The drug is also sold as an antidepressant medication under the name Wellbutrin. Zyban reduces craving and the intensity of the nicotine withdrawal syndrome. **Chantix** (generic name is varenicline) is a partial agonist at nicotine receptors. This drug's action lessens the intensity of nicotine withdrawal, and as it occupies the nicotine receptors it also attenuates the initial reinforcing effects of nicotine. Zyban and Chantix are available only by prescription.

Nicotine-replacement preparations are the third type of medication for treatment of compulsive smoking. Nicotine chewing gum, lozenges, and transdermal patches are available without prescription. Access to medications for nicotine dependence without supervision of a physician is another major difference between treatment options for smoking, compared to treatment for dependence on other drugs, including alcohol. A prescription is required for the use of nicotine inhalers and nasal spray. These replacement medications ease the transition from smoking to nicotine abstinence by suppressing withdrawal symptoms and allowing the patient to focus on stopping the habitual behavior of smoking. Instructions for use direct a gradual decrease in nicotine dose, with an intended outcome of complete abstinence from the drug.

All these drug therapies have proven effective for improving the success rate of smoking cessation. They are most effective when used in combination with counseling or cognitive behavioral tactics (Cahill et al. 2013). A large-scale study conducted in the United Kingdom determined long-term abstinence in addicted smokers who were given various combinations of treatments (West et al. 2000). In a comparison group that received no treatment (the "willpower alone" condition), 3 percent achieved long-term abstinence. For those receiving advice from a physician plus nicotine-replacement therapy, abstinence rate was 10 percent. For those receiving nicotine replacement plus intensive support from a specialist, the abstinence rate was 18 percent. Murphy and colleagues found that treatment with varenicline produced reduction in smoking that was not different from that resulting from transdermal nicotine treatment (Murphy et al. 2017). Even the best therapies do not result in long-term tobacco abstinence for all who attempt to stop smoking.

Chapter Summary

In the 1960s, about 40 percent of adults in the United States used tobacco. In 1964, it became evident that smoking is a major cause of lung cancer, heart disease, and premature death. In 2017, 22.4 percent of adults and adolescents used tobacco, with 17.9 percent smoking cigarettes – and 10.2 percent smoking daily. Smoking prevalence continues to decrease, but more slowly than in previous years.

About two-thirds of daily smokers are addicted to nicotine. About half of those who use tobacco less often are also to some extent nicotine dependent.

Nicotine is an agonist for a type of acetylcholine receptor, indirectly increasing dopamine release and resulting in a low to moderate degree of positive reinforcement. After initial stimulation, nicotine blocks and desensitizes acetylcholine receptors, resulting in rapid development of tolerance to the positive reinforcement effect.

Nicotine effects become conditioned to the distinctive actions and stimuli of smoking, including the taste, odor, and tactile sensations, adding to the reward value of smoking. Situations and activities associated with smoking also become potent triggers for tobacco craving, especially during nicotine withdrawal.

The nicotine withdrawal syndrome includes irritability, anxiety, anger, and depression as well as insomnia and difficulty concentrating. These effects can be quite intense, seemingly discordant with the small amount of pleasure produced by initial nicotine use. The supposed relaxing effects of smoking are mainly due to relief of withdrawal symptoms and are a major incentive for continued smoking. Craving for nicotine can recur long after other withdrawal symptoms have dissipated. Emotional states that resemble the transient withdrawal symptoms can also elicit craving and a resumption of smoking.

Addictive smoking rarely immediately interrupts a person's life – the adverse consequences (severe medical problems) are usually long delayed. However, the critical features of addiction – continued use even with the knowledge of adverse consequences, coupled with a desire, but difficulty or inability, to stop or reduce use – identify nicotine dependence in most daily users of tobacco. Instruments such as the Fagerström Test for Nicotine Dependence assess the strength of addiction.

Risk factors for addictive tobacco use are similar to those associated with SUD for other addictive drugs: genetic predisposition, trauma or neglect during childhood and adolescence, regular drug use (especially smoking) prior to age fifteen, certain personality traits, and most psychiatric disorders.

Prevalence of smoking and nicotine dependence is high among individuals with psychiatric conditions, who often find quitting tobacco use to be quite difficult. Attempts to self-medicate anxiety or depression may drive smoking in these individuals, but heavy smoking can also trigger or worsen some emotional disorders (e.g., panic attacks).

The greater difficulty of stopping smoking for women (relative to men) may be due to their higher incidence of depression and anxiety disorders. Other probable reasons for the gender-related difference include hormonal changes related to the menstrual cycle, concern about weight gain, and lessened effectiveness of nicotine-replacement medications in relieving withdrawal symptoms in women.

Those who began regular tobacco use at a young age become more heavily addicted and are less likely to quit smoking as adults. The adolescent brain is more susceptible than the mature brain to long-term changes resulting from nicotine exposure. Such changes could contribute to the fourfold increase of use disorders for alcohol and other addictive drugs in individuals who become regular smokers younger than age fifteen. Risk factors for adolescent smoking include relations with deviant peers, poor academic performance, parental permissiveness, availability of cigarettes, and other conditions that also increase smoking rates in adults.

Genetic predisposition accounts for at least half of the vulnerability to nicotine addiction. Much of the genetic effect also increases the probability of other SUD, but some of the predisposition is specific for nicotine dependence. Abnormalities in DNA structure often occur in addicted smokers. At least three of these alleles are located in genes that control the production of nicotinic acetylcholine receptors.

Tobacco use shortens life-span by an average of thirteen to fourteen years. Half of all heavy smokers will die from a tobacco-related disease or condition. Tobacco use also contributes to the occurrence of a wide range of additional medical problems, including adverse prenatal effects.

Inhalation of nicotine vapor via electronic delivery devices (EC) is increasing in prevalence, especially among young adolescents. Although nicotine vapor is less toxic than tobacco smoke, EC users are more likely to become smokers, so the behavior is a growing threat to public health.

Some addicted individuals maintain that nicotine dependence is the hardest SUD to overcome. Smoking is socially accepted (or at least tolerated), convenient, and produces neither intoxication nor immediate adverse consequences. These features, coupled with the frequent withdrawal discomfort and craving triggered by daily activities and stimuli that become associated with tobacco use, contribute to the generally low success rates of smoking cessation.

Many smokers eventually become securely abstinent, typically after several unsuccessful attempts at quitting. Most addicted individuals who stop tobacco use do so without professional assistance. Few smokers without other drug use disorders view their tobacco use as a disease or participate in twelve-step programs. However, much help is available from internet sites, support groups, and physician-prescribed drugs as well as nicotine-replacement products not requiring a prescription for purchase. In the United States, former smokers now outnumber current users of tobacco.

Review Exercises

1. How is nicotine use different from the use of other addictive drugs?
2. State the arguments used by the tobacco industry that tobacco was not toxic or addictive and the scientific evidence used to refute these claims.

3. Explain why some of the DSM-IV criteria for SUD are of very limited use for diagnosing nicotine SUD.

4. Explain how the effects of positive and negative reinforcement are particularly strong for the behavior of smoking tobacco cigarettes.

5. Describe how the Fagerström Test for Nicotine Dependence measures addiction to nicotine. What are some of its limitations?

6. What neurotransmitters are affected by nicotine, and what is the result (e.g., positive reinforcement, effects on memory) of the action of nicotine?

7. Describe some of the methods used to measure the nicotine withdrawal syndrome.

8. How is the nicotine withdrawal syndrome in humans similar to and different from that seen in laboratory animals?

9. Explain how craving is experienced as either "appetitive" in nature or a desire for relief from an aversive state.

10. Explain why certain personality characteristics are risk factors for nicotine use disorders.

11. What characteristics of depression, anxiety, schizophrenia, and bipolar disorder increase the likelihood of using nicotine?

12. Explain why women have less success in stopping smoking than do men.

13. Describe adolescent patterns of nicotine use, risk factors, and associations between nicotine use and development of SUD for other drugs.

14. How does cigarette smoking compare with nicotine vaping in regard to health risks?

15. The text states that "nicotine is sometimes described as the most addictive of drugs." What evidence supports this statement?

16. If a friend asked you for advice on an effective method to use to stop smoking, what advice, based on empirical evidence, would you give?

Key Terms

addiction (386)

addictive potential (385)

benefits versus adversity (424)

Chantix (431)

childhood adversity (419)

compulsion (390)

compulsive use (386)

concentration difficulty (402)

consequences (390)

control (390)

dependence (386)

distress tolerance factor (404)

early adolescence (415)

Fagerström Test for Nicotine Dependence (FTND) (391)

fourfold increase (416)

inhalable nicotine aerosol (425)

insula (405)

irritability (396)

Nicotine Anonymous
(429)
nicotine replacement
(431)

oxidative stress (421)
panic attacks (408)
relapse prevention
(429)

Surgeon General's
Report (385)
toxicity (384)
Zyban (430)

12

Cannabis Use Disorders

LEARNING OBJECTIVES

1. Understand the role of THC in determining the potency of cannabis.
2. Be able to summarize the history and prevalence of cannabis use in the United States.
3. Describe the pharmacokinetics of THC, the functions of the endogenous cannabinoid system, and effects of cannabis on brain function.
4. Describe the acute biological, behavioral, and cognitive effects of cannabis.
5. Describe the essential features of cannabis use disorders.
6. Describe the symptoms of cannabis withdrawal in humans and laboratory animals.
7. Describe the relationship between cannabis use by adolescents and mental health problems.
8. Be able to explain the theory that cannabis is a gateway drug and give the actual risk factors for adolescent development of SUD.
9. Understand the evidence for the biological and neurological toxicity of cannabis as well as cognitive impairment associated with cannabis use.
10. Be able to describe the medical uses for cannabis and the evidence for the efficacy of those treatments.

Introductory Vignette: Getting High and Getting Down to Work?

Sam sits at his computer, looking over the many photographs he has taken in recent weeks. He intends to edit and assemble the images into a sequence of scenes – a requirement for his visual arts class. He was high on marijuana when he took most of the photos, and while shooting a variety of objects and scenes, he felt that the images were creative and artistic. However, he now sees that they were mundane and not very interesting.

He has tried several times, on previous days, to work with these images. Each time he took a few tokes to get the creative juices flowing, but then the time was not well spent, and he made no progress as he diverted into web surfing, Twitter reading, and watching YouTube videos. He told himself he was researching novel ways to present his pictures – but he also suspects he was just wasting time, and that maybe he should try to work straight rather than stoned.

He considers stopping marijuana use until he finishes the art class project – but he gets high almost every day (okay – every day), and the last few times he had decided to cut back on smoking weed, he felt really down, anxious, and restless – and his sleep was disturbed by intense, bizarre dreams. That condition would not be good for finishing up this project, and probably worse than doing it high. So, he puts a small bud of potent cannabis into his pipe. Maybe this time he will keep on-task and actually accomplish something.

Introduction

Millions of people in many countries consume cannabis to attain a unique altered state of consciousness. After tobacco, alcohol, and caffeine (in coffee and tea), cannabis is the most widely used psychoactive substance in the world (United Nations Office of Drug Control 2012).

In the United States, two-thirds of individuals who used any illicit drug use only cannabis. In 2017, 9.6 percent of the adolescent and adult population (26 million individuals) were current (previous month) cannabis users, and 44 percent reported having at least some experience (lifetime use) with the substance (Substance Abuse and Mental Health Services Administration 2018).

As most often used, cannabis is less dangerous than alcohol, tobacco, cocaine, or heroin. Although cannabis has a reputation among users as a harmless substance, heavy use can cause adverse behavioral effects and biological toxicity. Frequent use in adolescence is of particular concern. Cannabis can produce drug dependence, although its addictive potential is much lower than that of nicotine, cocaine, or heroin, and somewhat less than that of alcohol (Lopez-Quintero et al. 2011).

Cannabis and THC

There are several varieties of the plant *Cannabis sativa*, some of which contain psychoactive chemicals. In the psychoactive varieties of cannabis, leaves, flowering tops, and especially the resin contain delta-9-tetrahydrocannabinol (THC) as well as other chemicals that affect biological functions, including that of the central nervous system. The potency of cannabis preparations is determined primarily by the concentration of THC. The relationship between the plant material (*C. sativa*) and the drug (THC) is similar to that between tobacco and nicotine, although cannabis contains psychoactive chemicals in addition to THC.

The cannabis product most often used for psychoactive effects is a combination of dried leaves and flowering tops of the plant. This substance is known as marijuana in the United States, as herbal cannabis in the United Kingdom and Western Europe, and by various names in other parts of the world. Cannabis also has many other "street names," a few of the most common in the English language being: pot, weed, grass, herb, and reefer (an older name). The potency of this product varies considerably, but has increased during recent years (Burgdorf et al. 2011). For the years from 2000 through 2009 the mean THC concentration in samples seized by the US Drug Enforcement Administration (DEA) ranged from 4.5 to 12.5 percent (Slade et al. 2012). As some state laws in the United States now permit recreational use of cannabis and the product has become an openly distributed commodity, potency has increased further in certain varieties of the plant (Figures 12.1

Figure 12.1 A cannabis dispensary in Oregon. According to federal laws in the United States, recreational use of cannabis is illegal. However, several states permit sale of cannabis to adults by commercial vendors. Photo: Heath Korvola / DigitalVision / Getty Images.

Figure 12.2 Buds of potent cannabis for sale by a commercial vendor. Photo: Stuart Dee / Stockbyte / Getty Images.

and 12.2). "Skunk" is an unofficial name associated with many strains of high-potency cannabis, some of which have a THC content of 20 percent (Freeman and Winstock 2015, Greydanus et al. 2013).

The most resinous parts of the cannabis plant are used to prepare hashish, a substance composed primarily of cannabis resin. Hashish was once the most potent cannabis-derived substance available. However even more potent products – cannabis oils – are now available, containing THC concentrations of 50–80 percent (Raber et al. 2015). Higher-potency cannabis products are considered to be more toxic and addictive than the leaves and flowering tops of the cannabis plant (Freeman and Winstock 2015).

Some History of Cannabis Use

Five thousand years ago, cannabis was used as medicine in central Asia. Although not nearly as effective as opium (introduced later) as an analgesic, cannabis provided some relief from many symptoms ranging from poor appetite and nausea, through rheumatism, premenstrual discomfort and menstrual cramps. From China, cannabis use eventually spread to India, where the substance served a religious function in Hinduism (Li 1975). The Scythians, an aggressive and mobile middle-eastern tribe, spread cannabis use to many areas, including Africa, Russia and Europe during the second century BCE. *Cannabis* is a Scythian word (Benet 1975).

In European countries, cannabis use for pleasurable intoxication was introduced during the middle years of the nineteenth century. The medical uses of cannabis included treatment for psychiatric conditions such as depression, and neurological disorders such as epilepsy. Mitch Earleywine (Earleywine 2002) and Leslie Iversen (Iversen 2008) provide extensive accounts of the history of cannabis use in European countries.

Early and Middle Twentieth Century
In the early years of the twentieth century Mexican laborers introduced cannabis smoking (and the term *marijuana*) into the United States. Use of the substance spread slowly among racial minorities, and was especially popular with jazz musicians. Alarmist stories appeared in newspapers, attributing much crime and violence to marijuana use. With almost no real evidence about the effects of cannabis, these racially charged and often-fabricated accounts of a dangerous substance went essentially unchallenged. The 1936 film *Reefer Madness* was an absurd portrayal of cannabis as producing insanity and violence. The movie however did represent (and promote) a typical view of cannabis use. Concern about the supposed threat to public health and safety led to the passage of the Marijuana Tax Act in 1937. This legislation imposed heavy fines and prison terms for use or possession of cannabis.

Through the 1950s cannabis use persisted among a small minority of the population. The substance was popular with jazz musicians and socially unconventional "bohemian" artists and poets.

From the 1960s to the Twenty-First Century
In the mid-1960s, cannabis use became closely connected to rapid cultural change in the United States and Europe. Its use was associated with youthful rebellion against authority, and protest against the Viet Nam war. In the United States, the media made much of the emergence of a so-called counterculture that encouraged abandonment of traditional values and ambitions. Interest grew for new types of rock music, Eastern religions, and hallucinogenic drugs. Cannabis use was also a prominent aspect of this movement. Many young people who otherwise made only token concessions to the alternative lifestyle used cannabis, and some became regular users. Prevalence of cannabis use by adolescents and young adults increased dramatically during the late 1960s and throughout the 1970s.

Many young people (as well as others with liberal political views) ignored "establishment" claims of the hazards of cannabis use. Such warnings were seen as exaggerated or patently false. The movie *Reefer Madness*, mentioned previously as a 1930s depiction of cannabis use as dangerous, became a camp hit in the late 1960s – producing much laughter from audiences, many of whom were under the influence of cannabis as they viewed the film.

In 1970, the federal government approved the Controlled Substances Act, in which cannabis was classified as a Schedule I drug, placed in the same strictly controlled category as heroin and labeled as a drug with high potential for abuse and no accepted medical use.

In 1972, the Shafer Commission (appointed by president Richard Nixon) reported that cannabis use did not appear to be very dangerous, and that its classification as a Schedule I drug was probably not justified (National Commission on Marihuana and Drug Abuse 1972). President Nixon repudiated the commission's conclusion, demonstrating the heavy political aspects of the "marijuana issue." Nixon eventually declared the nation's "war on drugs," which over the ensuing decades has been an extremely expensive law enforcement effort to suppress traffic in and use of cannabis and other illicit drugs.

In 1979 cannabis use in the United States peaked, with prevalence of previous-month use among eighteen- to twenty-five-year-olds at 35 percent, and lifetime use by adults of all ages at 28 percent. Prevalence of use declined in later years, sometimes rising but not reaching the 1979 level.

By the 1980s the Viet Nam war was over, and no longer an issue that encouraged resistance to government regulations, including those concerning drug use. The counterculture lifestyle was also of little interest to most young people. The public seemed less alarmed by ongoing cannabis use, perhaps because of a general recognition of the absence of immediate and certain harmful consequences. By 1981, eleven states had decriminalized possession of small amounts of cannabis.

Even with greater cultural acceptance of cannabis use, the federal government under the Reagan administration continued and increased vigorous pursuit of the war on drugs that had started a decade earlier. Cocaine distribution and use were of major concern, but many cannabis users were also prosecuted and imprisoned. The ongoing attempt to control drug use by imposing criminal penalties resulted in an enormous increase in the jail and prison population in the United States. Federal laws remained essentially unchanged, or became even more restrictive. The Reagan administration also opposed efforts to increase approval of medical uses for cannabis.

During the 1980s First Lady Nancy Reagan promoted her "just say no" campaign, emphasizing the dangers of cannabis and other illicit drugs. An ally of Ms. Reagan was Dr. Gabriel Nahas, a physician-scientist at Columbia University who was renowned for his strident opposition to cannabis use. Dr. Nahas published many articles and books, including *Marijuana – Deceptive Weed* (Nahas 1973), in which he made claims regarding cannabis effects that were widely criticized as exaggerated and unrealistic (Hollister 1986). In one of his most extreme assertions about cannabis, he stated that the plant was the original "forbidden fruit" with which the serpent tempted Eve in the Garden of Eden.

Such obviously invalid warnings about cannabis encouraged a persistent "stoner culture," among many young people who used and enjoyed the substance.

Individuals with this cultural attitude ignored or rejected even objective and realistic concerns about cannabis, and often read such publications as *High-Times* magazine, an enthusiastic and uncritical advocate of cannabis use.

During the 1990s California was the first state to relax restrictions on medical uses of the substance – a lessening of cannabis restrictions eventually followed by many other states. Several additional states also decriminalized personal use of cannabis during this decade.

Prevalence and Methods of Cannabis Use

As of 2019, eleven states and the District of Columbia do not prohibit recreational cannabis use – although sales are controlled and use by individuals under age twenty-one is illegal. Medical use of cannabis is permitted in thirty-three states, with restrictions that differ among individual states. Although possession or use of cannabis still violates federal law, such laws are not often enforced in these states.

As previously described, the potency of cannabis has increased during the four to five decades since use of the substance first became more prevalent in North America, Europe and other parts of the world. The greater potency is a result of increased use of indoor locations for growing cannabis plants, along with other methods of improved cultivation and selection of seeds (Figure 12.3)

Figure 12.3 Indoor locations, artificial illumination, improved cultivation, and selection of seeds have greatly increased the potency of cannabis products. Photo: Ian Philip Miller / Moment / Getty Images.

(Cascini et al. 2012, Sachs et al. 2015). The scientific and medical research communities monitor use and assess the consequences of use of highly potent cannabis products.

The prevalence of current cannabis use in the adolescent and adult population of the United States in 2017 was 9.6 percent (26 million individuals), a slight but statistically significant increase from the generally stable use levels during the years 2002–2016. Age is an important factor in use prevalence. Of respondents of ages twelve to seventeen in the National Survey of Drug Use and Health (NSDUH), 6.5 percent used cannabis during the previous month. For ages eighteen to twenty-five, use prevalence was 22.1 percent, and for ages twenty-six and older, it was 7.9 percent (Substance Abuse and Mental Health Services Administration 2018). The increase in current cannabis use was due to greater use prevalence in young and older adults. Adolescent use did not increase in 2017.

Inhaling the smoke of dried plant material is the most common method of using cannabis, but other methods – eating, or inhalation of aerosols containing THC – are also used. A survey of 1,548 currently using individuals age eighteen or older indicated that 92 percent smoked cannabis, using cigarettes ("joints"), pipes, hookahs, or "blunts" (cannabis packed into hollowed-out tobacco cigars). Sixteen percent consumed edibles or beverages containing cannabis, and 7.6 percent used a vaporizer or electronic cigarettes. More than one method of use was reported by 41.2 percent of previous-month users. In regard to reasons for cannabis use, 53.4 percent reported only recreational use, 10.5 percent used only for medical purposes (symptom relief), and 36.1 percent used the substance for both purposes (Schauer et al. 2016).

Inhalation of aerosols of cannabis or cannabis-derived material is a relatively new method of using the substance. The use of aerosols was increased by the emergence of electronic delivery systems – primarily e-cigarettes originally intended for nicotine delivery but also usable with cannabis products – and by the production of extremely potent cannabis oils (Giroud et al. 2015, Morean et al. 2015). Cannabis extracts containing high concentrations of THC are also vaporized by means of "dab rigs" – special pipes so named because with use of these devices a very small amount of the oil can provide a strong psychoactive effect (Raber et al. 2015).

Inhalation of THC by inhaling vapor avoids intake of toxic products of burned cannabis, so is potentially safer than "smoking" the dried plant. THC delivery via aerosol may be useful for medical purposes (Van Dam and Earleywine 2010). However, the prevalence of e-cigarette use is increasing among adolescents (Chapter 11). There is concern that this newer method of cannabis intake will encourage use by individuals in this vulnerable age group.

THC in the Brain and Body

Research on the psychopharmacology of cannabis eventually resulted in the discovery of a previously unknown system of receptors and naturally occurring brain chemicals. Thirty years earlier, in the investigation of opioid drug effects, a similar sequence of scientific advances led to the discovery of the endogenous opioid system (Chapter 14).

Pharmacokinetics: Bioavailability

Unlike many drugs of abuse that can be taken into the body by several methods of administration, THC in cannabis is usually administered by only two methods: inhalation of smoke or vapor, or eating. Smoking is currently the most popular method of recreational cannabis use, but oral ingestion has a longer history, including for medical use. Cannabis effects are felt very soon (within seconds) after deep inhalation of smoke or vapor, and the level of intoxication can be better controlled than with oral ingestion (Heishman et al. 1989). Synthetic cannabinoid drugs, with effects similar to that of THC, can be injected. The injection route of administration is used in scientific research, but not in recreational or addictive use.

Oral administration of cannabis results in a much slower onset of effects, which emerge gradually sixty to ninety minutes after consumption. As compared to smoking cannabis or inhaling vapor, the amount of THC entering the bloodstream (and eventually the brain) is greatly diminished. Only about 6–7 percent of ingested THC survives degradation by digestive processes and first-pass metabolism in the liver. As a result, subjective and physiological effects of a given amount of cannabis are much less intense (Grotenhermen 2003). As with alcohol, the amount of food in the digestive tract when cannabis is consumed alters the time of onset and strength of the drug effect.

In India and middle-eastern countries preparation of cannabis-containing confections and other food and beverages is a long-standing tradition (Abel 1980). Consumption of cannabis in foods has not been a common practice in the United States and Western Europe – with the possible exception of cookies or "brownies" containing cannabis. However, there are now few legal restraints on the recreational use of cannabis in eleven of the United States, so edible cannabis-containing products have become a commodity and their consumption has increased (Figure 12.4).

Duration of the subjective effects (the "high") from cannabis use depends on the dose, but for smoking typically endures for one to two hours. After eating cannabis, the effects can endure for four to five hours. THC is more fat-soluble than most other psychoactive drugs, a characteristic that influences the time course of its action, producing its rapid onset of effects, and especially its long elimination time (Agurell et al. 1986).

Figure 12.4 When cannabis products became a commodity, many edible items containing cannabis then became available. Photo: CasarsaGuru / E+ / Getty Images.

THC half-life in the blood is about thirty minutes, with only 10 percent of the highest concentration remaining after one hour. THC is eventually metabolized by the liver and excreted in the feces and urine, but the initial rapid removal from the bloodstream after smoking or eating is mainly due to absorption by fat deposits throughout the body. Elimination of THC and its metabolites is a complex process, and these compounds remain in the body far longer than the duration of the psychoactive effects (McGilveray 2005).

After THC leaves the bloodstream and enters fatty tissues, it is slowly released back into the bloodstream at levels too low to cause noticeable psychoactive effects. The liver converts THC into many metabolites that are excreted even more slowly than is the parent compound (THC). Half-life of the metabolites is five to six days, and these compounds can be detected in the urine of a chronic cannabis user for thirty days after last use of the substance (Smith-Kielland et al. 1999). Time required for elimination varies with amount of body fat – and may be shorter in leaner individuals.

The Endogenous Cannabinoid System

In 1964 delta-9 tetrahydrocannabinol (THC) was identified as the primary psychoactive compound in cannabis sativa (Gaoni and Mecholaum 1964). The plant also contains many other chemicals, including cannabidiol and cannabinol. The latter two compounds have some effects on neurological activity, but primarily interact with the immune system. In most strains of cannabis sativa their concentration is about one-tenth that of THC (ElSohly et al. 2000). THC also acts on the immune system and has anti-inflammatory effects in some parts of the body (Rizzo et al. 2019).

Identification of THC enabled the development of synthetic cannabinoid-like compounds that facilitated investigation of the pharmacology of **cannabinoids** (chemicals that are physically similar to THC). Radioactive tagging of agonists that were water-soluble and less readily absorbed by fat made possible the identification of cannabinoid receptors (Devane et al. 1988).

Two receptors, CB1 and CB2, mediate cannabinoid physiological effects, and there is evidence that additional receptors are also activated by cannabinoids. CB1 receptors are found primarily in the central nervous system and most CB2 receptors are located in white blood cells and other parts of the immune system (Mackie and Stella 2006).

CB1 receptors are located on presynaptic axon terminals, rather than on dendrites and neuron cell bodies – the more common postsynaptic location of receptors for most neurotransmitters. In rats, primates and humans, high densities of CB1 receptors are located in the cerebral cortex, basal ganglia, cerebellum, hippocampus, hypothalamus and cingulate cortex (Herkenham et al. 1991). The relative absence of cannabinoid receptors in brain stem areas that control respiration may explain why a fatal overdose of THC is quite unlikely (Freund et al. 2003).

The discovery of cannabinoid receptors triggered the search for endogenous neurotransmitter-like brain chemicals that activated these receptors. The first such chemical, **anandamide** (arachidonyl ethanol-amide) was discovered in 1992 (Devane et al. 1992). The shorter name is taken from the Indian Sanskrit word *ananda*, meaning "bringer of inner bliss and tranquility." A second endocannabinoid, **2-AG** (2-arachidonyl glycerol), was discovered in 1995 (Sugiura et al. 1995). Relative to anandamide, 2-AG is present at much higher levels in the brain and is thought to be the primary neurotransmitter for both subtypes of cannabinoid receptor. Additional cannabinoid-like chemicals are also found in the brain, although much less is known about their function.

The endocannabinoid system (ECS) consists of cannabinoid receptors and the naturally occurring neurotransmitters that bind to and activate these receptors. The ECS modulates the activity of other neurotransmitters, rather than directly exciting or inhibiting neurons. Bidirectional control occurs between the ECS and the endogenous opioid system (Cascio and Pertwee 2012).

The ECS is involved in regulation of food consumption, energy metabolism and body weight. It also influences pain sensitivity, inflammatory processes, control of cardiovascular function, the immune system, stress responses and reproductive processes (Acharya et al. 2017). Cannabinoids also have a role in memory function, including removal or dampening the long-term effects (fear) of painful experiences. Some of these actions can be seen in the effects of cannabinoid agonists such as THC (Cascio and Pertwee 2012, Iversen 2008). Drugs with agonist or antagonist action at specific cannabinoid receptors have potential medical use, such as for treatment of chronic pain, eating disorders, obesity and other conditions.

Pharmacodynamics: Effects on Brain Function

Endocannabinoids (2-AG and anandamide) fine-tune neurological activity by modulating excitatory and inhibitory input into neurons in the hippocampus, the cerebellum and other parts of the brain. Neural input is regulated by a **retrograde action** in which the endocannabinoids are released from dendrites of the postsynaptic neuron to bind with CB1 receptors on the axon terminals of the presynaptic neuron (Figure 12.5). This information flow between neurons is opposite in direction to that seen with most neurotransmitters.

The endocannabinoids are not stored in vesicles for eventual use, but are released from the postsynaptic neuron immediately after synthesis. Their synthesis and

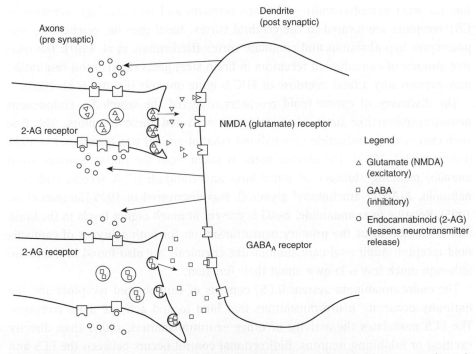

Figure 12.5 Retrograde regulation of neurotransmission by endocannabinoids. When receptors located on dendrites are activated, neurons may release endocannabinoid neurotransmitters (anandamide or 2-AG). These neurotransmitters diffuse back to the presynaptic axon to bind with endocannabinoid receptors. Activation of these receptors decreases that entry of calcium ions into the axon and reduces neurotransmitter release. Reduction of GABA release decreases inhibition, and reduction of glutamate release decreases excitation, of the postsynaptic neuron.

release is initiated by excitatory or inhibitory input to the neuron (Iversen 2012). Activation of the metabotropic CB1 receptors reduces release of neurotransmitter from the presynaptic neuron (Wilson and Nicoll 2001).

The retrograde feedback to presynaptic neurons decreases the release of either excitatory (e.g., glutamate) or inhibitory (e.g., GABA) neurotransmitters, so the overall effect on the postsynaptic neuron can be inhibition or disinhibition (Figure 12.5). The **modulating** effect can persist for several seconds, and may influence the activity of other nearby synapses.

The effects of THC and other exogenous cannabinoid compounds are mediated by the actions of CB receptors – for psychoactive effects, primarily the CB1 receptor subtype. THC is a partial CB agonist – it is less effective in activating the receptors than are the endogenous cannabinoids 2-AG and anandamide. Synthetic full-agonist compounds (WIN55 212-2) have been developed, as have cannabinoid antagonists such as rimonabant that block the actions of THC or other agonists at CB receptors.

THC and other cannabinoid agonists inhibit the release of several neurotransmitters (Schlicker and Kathemann 2001). Although these drugs exert their effects via CB1 receptors, their actions are different from the precise fine-tuning of neural function by the ECS system that supports complex cognitive processes, motor activity and other behavioral and physiological functions. When THC is administered, the localized and time-limited modulation actions of the ECS are not duplicated. In most cases, the drug administration produces very high (nonbiological) levels of cannabinoids and for hours activates CB receptors throughout the body. At high doses cognition, memory formation and coordinated motor activity are disrupted. These acute drug effects, including the reward value of THC, are discussed further in a later section of this chapter.

Tolerance to some effects of THC develops rapidly in humans and animals. The diminished effects are seen most clearly in experimental animal subjects repeatedly administered large doses of cannabinoids. In similar controlled studies, human subjects show some tolerance to cannabis effects on cognition and behavior and a decrease in pleasurable subjective effects (Haney et al. 1999b). Tolerance is much less evident in recreational users who infrequently smoke moderate amounts of cannabis that produce less intense subjective and behavioral effects (Iversen 2008, Earleywine 2002).

Acute Effects of Cannabis

In 1937, possession and use of cannabis became illegal in the United States. For the next thirty years, objective and reliable knowledge about cannabis effects was essentially nonexistent. Information was based only on subjective accounts by some individuals from the small population of illicit users, and a few rudimentary studies conducted with prisoners or soldiers. Cannabis was considered a dangerous substance, unsuitable for research with most human subjects. In 1968 Andrew Weil and colleagues at Harvard University conducted the first well-designed controlled studies of cannabis effects on human behavior (Weil et al. 1968).

In subsequent years, many properly controlled investigations of cannabis effects on humans were conducted. Cannabis research with human subjects was permitted by the federal Drug Enforcement Administration (DEA) for investigators licensed for use of a Schedule I substance – the controlled drug class with the most stringent restrictions. Although properly controlled experiments ideally produce objective information, even these results can be subject to different interpretations. Discussions about the relevance of toxic or other harmful effects are often politically charged, with bias undoubtedly influencing some investigations (Iversen 2008). Such bias is less evident in determining immediate, acute effects and their importance. The consequences of long-term use seem to be more subject to varying interpretations.

Drug dose is a critical factor in psychopharmacology studies, and dose-control for cannabis experiments presents special problems. The amount of THC absorbed from inhaled cannabis smoke (the route of administration typical of recreational use, and used in many controlled studies) is determined by the depth and duration of inhalation, as well as by the potency of cannabis. Most experimenters give subjects specific instructions for smoke inhalation (e.g., puff duration) in an attempt to standardize THC dose for all subjects. Placebo control conditions are provided by use of cannabis from which all THC has been extracted.

Other factors which can influence drug effects are the user's expectations (e.g., based on previous experience with the drug), and the environment for testing of behavior, cognition or subjective states. These factors are relevant for all psychopharmacology research, but are of special importance for investigating the sometimes subtle effects of cannabis.

Research with Nonhuman Subjects

Investigation of cannabinoid effects in animal subjects became possible after THC was identified and extracted from the cannabis plant, and was facilitated when water-soluble cannabinoid compounds were synthesized. Research with rodents and primates has revealed much about the pharmacology of cannabinoids, including their mechanisms of action and the development of tolerance. Some physiological and behavioral effects of cannabinoids, such as analgesia, memory impairment, increased food intake, and positive reinforcement occur in both human subjects and nonhuman animals.

The results of some animal studies of cannabis effects are of limited relevance to human use of the substance. With animal subjects, THC or other cannabinoids are administered by injection, a method not used for recreational purposes or in addiction by humans. Animal subjects often receive very high doses of cannabinoid drugs, much higher than doses self-administered by even heavy cannabis users (Iversen 2008). Because metabolic rates are higher in small animals than in humans, higher drug doses are required to produce analogous effects. However, cannabinoid doses in many studies are much higher than required to account for metabolic differences. Such doses are sometimes used in order to clearly demonstrate a drug effect.

High doses of cannabinoid-agonist drugs administered to mice produce a characteristic array of physiological and behavioral responses – reduced body temperature, analgesia, decreased motor activity and tonic immobility (Abood and Martin 2002). These responses are often used to rapidly screen novel drugs for cannabinoid receptor activation.

Subjective emotional and cognitive effects, often complex and sometimes subtle, may be the most interesting actions of cannabis in humans. Although animals can be trained to recognize the cannabinoid-produced drug state by means of the drug-discrimination paradigm (e.g., Jarbe 2011), the investigation of most subjective effects and many behavioral effects of cannabis is limited to studies of human subjects.

Physiological Effects

Pulse rate reliably increases after THC administration (Huestis et al. 1992). Absorption of THC varies, especially with inhalation of cannabis smoke. Heart rate increase is an easily measured response sometimes used in research with human subjects to indicate that the THC was absorbed and entered the bloodstream.

Vasodilation of blood vessels after cannabis use is indicated by enlargement of blood vessels in the sclera that produces a "bloodshot eye" appearance. Dryness of the mouth and throat results from decreased secretion of saliva (Weller and Halikas 1982).

Hunger and food consumption increase, a response that occurs somewhat later than the immediate effects on the cardiovascular system. The appetitive effects arise from both interaction with hormonal control of hunger and satiety, and increased appreciation of food (Kirkham 2009). The increased hedonic value (better taste) of food is further discussed in subsequent section on the rewarding effects of cannabis.

Sensitivity to pain is reduced (analgesia) – an effect sometimes reported by recreational users and well established by controlled studies of humans and animals (Sagar et al. 2009). Both the analgesic and the appetite-increasing effects are important in the medical applications of cannabinoids.

Regarding the probability of a fatal overdose, THC is a very safe drug. Rodents, dogs and monkeys can tolerate doses of 1,000 milligrams per kilogram, a dose five thousand times greater than that required to produce intoxication in humans (Iversen 2008). Extreme overdoses of cannabis are also very unlikely to produce death in humans.

Behavioral and Cognitive Effects

During the initial stages of cannabis intoxication – the state of being "high" or "stoned" – general activity often increases, along with animated conversation and laughter (Figure 12.6). The early arousal phase later merges into a more contemplative, quiescent state. These activity changes are less dramatic and reliable than those of alcohol, cocaine or other depressant and stimulant drugs. As with subjective effects, overt behavioral changes seen after cannabis use are partly determined by the social situation and expectations of the drug effect. At a lively party with music and dancing, drug-produced stimulation may predominate. For a solitary individual, the quieter introspective effect of cannabis is a more probable consequence.

Figure 12.6 The initial effects of cannabis often include laughter and animated conversation. Photo: JennaWagner / E+ / Getty Images.

Several types of mental processes are clearly different when an individual is high on cannabis. These actions of cannabis have been intensively studied since the late 1960s. The effects of cannabis on cognitive functions are more consistent than the general behavioral effects, and somewhat less influenced by the nonpharmacological factors of setting and expectation. When the important variables of dose and tolerance are controlled, reliable effects on **time perception, memory,** and **complex information processing** are evident. These actions of cannabis are familiar to recreational users and confirmed by controlled investigations.

Cannabis users consistently experience a subjective slowing of time during the intoxicated state, an effect reported by early investigators (e.g., Weil et al. 1968, Tinklenberg et al. 1972) as well as in many subsequent studies. The time distortion contributes to unique subjective effects of the cannabis intoxication. Duration of time intervals (usually measured in intervals ranging from several seconds to a few minutes) is overestimated – and when asked to produce a specific time interval (such as thirty seconds) intoxicated subjects generate intervals of shorter duration. The internal sense of passing time speeds up, resulting in slowing of perceived time as indicated by external measures. Recreational users often perceive the time required to walk across a room, or the apparent duration of a conversation, to be much longer than indicated by a clock. THC administration causes a similar altered **perception** of time in rats and primates (Han and Robinson 2001, Schulze et al. 1988), as well as in human subjects.

Impairment of learning and memory is another very reliable effect of cannabis intoxication. Memory for material learned prior to smoking or eating cannabis generally remains intact, but memory of events that occur during the intoxicated state often declines dramatically (Earleywine 2002). The most obvious immediate effect is disruption of working (short-term) memory, although establishment of long-term memory can also be impaired. The amnesic effect of cannabis is different from that of alcohol-produced "blackout," in which episodic memory is entirely obliterated, but is a more specific inability to recall certain types of information. Recall of words presented during the intoxicated state becomes more impaired at higher doses and with more demanding tasks (Ranganathan and D'Souza 2006).

At higher levels of intoxication (not unusual in some recreational users of cannabis), the impairment of working memory interferes with a complex train of thought, or even in maintaining a coherent conversation (Riedel and Davies 2005).

Individuals who are high after smoking or eating cannabis have difficulty with sustained vigilance and concentration, performing two actions simultaneously, and inhibiting responses in some situations. Research results on this effect are less consistent than those on the impairment of memory and timing, mainly due to the many ways of testing for these deficits, dose-dependent effects, and variability of tolerance among subjects (Solowij and Pesa 2012). However, there is little doubt that the immediate effects of cannabis are likely to impair any activity that requires elaborate, precise or quick thinking. Executive cognitive functions – planning, organizing, and decision-making – are often degraded (Crean et al. 2011).

Subjective Effects and Reward Value

Cannabis intoxication is often described as emotionally pleasing and cognitively interesting – incentives that promote the widespread popularity of the substance. Cannabis is neither a central nervous system stimulant nor a depressant, and its effects are less intense than the rush of pleasurable arousal from cocaine or the surge of euphoria from heroin. Much of the pleasing drug effects come from subtle changes in thinking, emotional feeling, and perception. However, with the possible exception of extremely high doses, cannabis is not a hallucinogen. The following passage from *A Child's Garden of Grass* (an unabashedly favorable treatise on cannabis from the late 1960s) alludes to perceptual effects (Margolis and Clorfene 1969).

> "One thing to remember when you are stoned is that grass heightens, but subtly changes your awareness of both the outside world and your own psyche. Suddenly you're through the looking glass. It's your living room all right, and everything is the same, but everything is also different than it ever was before you were stoned. (Margolis and Clorfene 1969, p. 26)

Cannabis or THC administration is rewarding to rodent and primate subjects, although the experimental procedures that produce positive reinforcement in animals are more restricted than for stimulants or opioids (Mechoulam and Parker 2013). Positive reinforcement as indicated by conditioned place preference and operant self-administration of cannabinoid agonists is counteracted by pretreatment with the cannabinoid antagonist rimonabant. As with other addictive drugs, THC sensitizes the ventral tegmental area to positive reinforcement from electrical stimulation, indicating that the drug enhances dopamine transmission (Serrano and Parsons 2011).

In controlled laboratory studies, human subjects often report pleasurable subjective states after smoking cannabis or ingesting THC (e.g., Cooper and Haney 2009, Hart et al. 2002). However, these positive effects, as determined by the Profile of Mood States (POMS) test or other standard self-report instruments, are inconsistent and in some cases, negative states are reported (e.g., Chait and Zacny 1992).

Some investigators find that individuals who regularly use cannabis scored higher than nonusers on a test of creativity (Jones et al. 2009), and on openness to experience (Bleim et al. 2013). Cannabis may produce rewarding effects more reliably in individuals with these traits, although several other factors could also promote their cannabis use.

The environment of drug use and the expectation of drug action influence the subjective consequences of cannabis administration. Quite different (and much more positive) experiences are likely to result from using cannabis in comfortable, familiar or interesting surroundings, relative to a grim, threatening environment –

such as a prison, where in fact some very early drug effect investigations were conducted (Iversen 2008). Expectations of drug effects, either pleasing or frightening, also color the experience. As described below, cannabis seems to enhance the emotional content of pleasant experiences – and may increase negative emotional responses as well.

Subjective accounts, providing insight into the experience of cannabis intoxication, are based on a combination of thoughts, feelings, sensations and perceptions – and depend to some extent on an individual's facility with language. Some first-person literary accounts of cannabis intoxication, such as those by Gautier, Baudelaire, Ludlow and other nineteenth-century authors, are extensive and lurid descriptions of high-dose hashish effects (Ludlow 1857). The dramatic nature of these accounts may be partially due to the literary style of the time in which they were written.

Subjective descriptions of the cannabis-produced high state differ widely among individuals (Green et al. 2003). For example, some users feel that the high state increases their focus on the "here and now," although others maintain that they have better access to old memories (Earleywine 2002). Some self-reported effects, such as that of perceived time distortion, have been scientifically confirmed. However, for most subjective effects (such as "a sense of childlike wonder" or "better orgasms"), scientists are limited to collecting and categorizing the varied accounts of cannabis users.

In the latter decades of the twentieth century, investigators surveyed many cannabis users who described their personal experiences with the substance, often answering specific questions about the drug effects (e.g., Berke and Hernton 1974, Tart 1971, Weller and Halikas 1982). These subjective accounts were of the respondents' recreational use of cannabis, not of controlled tests in laboratories. Although the accounts varied considerably, several effects were reported by most users. All the respondents were familiar with and in general liked the effects of cannabis. The substance sometimes produces unpleasant effects (described below), but individuals who disliked the immediate results of cannabis use were unlikely to be included in these surveys of experienced users.

Most respondents consistently reported improved mood and feelings of relaxed euphoria (Green et al. 2003). The following quotes are from respondents interviewed by Berke and Hinton (1974).

In the absence of external distraction, one's own thought processes often become a source of fascination and entertainment:

> Fantasies, your thoughts seem to run along on their own to the extent that you can relax and "watch" them (rather like an intense day-dream) ... images come to mind that may be funny, curious, interesting in a story-telling sort of way.

During the early stages of the high state, the sense of humor is sharpened and laughter comes more easily:

> I often feel very giggly, jokes become even funnier, people's faces become funny and I can laugh with someone else who's stoned just by looking at them.

Much of the pleasurable effect comes from increased appreciation of things that are inherently enjoyable in the nondrugged condition – including visual beauty and music. A degree of emotional loading, usually positive, is also added to even commonplace experiences.

> It was like the pagoda had been painted a bright red since I had last seen it – about an hour before. The colour was not just bright, but more than bright, it was a different hue altogether, a deep red that was redder than red. It was like my eyes had opened to colour for the first time.

Hunger, the pleasure of eating and the taste of food are enhanced, effects that may contribute to increased eating in animals administered cannabis. The sensuality of sexual activity is heightened, although cannabis (or THC) is not an aphrodisiac in humans and does not increase sexual behavior in animals.

Painting and other artistic efforts are reportedly more enjoyable while high, as is playing music. In the mid-twentieth century, many jazz musicians used cannabis while playing, as did rock musicians a decade later. Performers may feel more competent and confident during cannabis intoxication. Such an effect on a musician seems to be expressed in Paul Simon's *Late in the evening*, as he describes playing guitar for an audience after smoking cannabis – "I stepped outside and smoked myself a J, then I came back in the room, began to play, and *I blew that room away!*"

Over half of 2,760 cannabis users reported feelings of increased creativity while high (Green et al. 2003). Beyond such anecdotal accounts, the link between cannabis intoxication and creativity has not been studied extensively. Creativity can take many forms and is difficult to measure objectively. Some, but not all, subjects' divergent thinking (an indicator of creativity) increased during cannabis intoxication (Schafer et al. 2012).

Although cannabis may improve some types of creativity, intoxication also promotes unrealistic judgment of the significance of thought and ideas. Many users describe thinking of a clever solution to a problem, or arriving at a seemingly important insight while high. As the intoxicated state wanes, the actual significance (usually very limited) of the "brilliant and creative" thinking becomes apparent.

Controlled studies demonstrate tolerance to the positive subjective effects of smoking of cannabis or oral THC administration (Haney et al. 1999a, 1999b). In these investigations, moderately high doses of THC or high-potency cannabis were administered four times daily at four-hour intervals for four consecutive days. Subjects' ratings of "drug liking" decreased significantly over the four days. The frequency of drug administration in these studies was much higher than in most recreational users of cannabis. When cannabis is used occasionally at low to moderate doses, the pleasurable effects often continue during months or years of use without escalation of the amount taken. The low degree of tolerance apparently contributes to the lower addictive potential of cannabis, as compared to heroin, cocaine, nicotine and (for many users) alcohol. Positive subjective effects are apparently less diminished by tolerance than are performance impairments, although quantitative comparison of the two types of cannabis effects is difficult.

Unpleasant subjective effects occur, most frequently in individuals with little or no previous experience with cannabis, and especially if they are apprehensive about the nature of an altered state of consciousness. The most common aversive effects include nausea, anxiety, paranoia, unsettling confusion, and fear of "losing control." High-dose effects may cause great anxiety. Oral consumption of hashish can produce very frightening experiences, as described by Ludlow and other nineteenth-century writers (Ludlow 1857).

Unpleasant effects also sometimes reported by experienced recreational users. Nearly all of 464 male cannabis users surveyed by Scherrer and colleagues described a combination of pleasant and unpleasant effects (Scherrer et al. 2009). Pleasant effects included feeling very good, sociable, creative and insightful, relaxed and mellow. Unpleasant subjective effects included depression, paranoia, confusion and inability to concentrate. A majority of respondents (67 percent) reported predominately positive (pleasant) effects, but also some negative (unpleasant) effects. Twenty-two percent reported mostly negative effects, but also positive effects.

Immediate Hazardous Effects

Even very large doses of cannabis do not produce coma, death or other immediate toxic effects.

Extremely disinhibited or aggressive behavior, as often occurs with high doses of alcohol or cocaine, is an unlikely consequence of cannabis use. However, the impairment of timing, memory, concentration and vigilance produced by THC, degrades the performance of most tasks that require careful judgment and complex information processing.

Air-traffic controllers, trial attorneys, and surgeons, as well as individuals engaged in other tasks that require a high level of cognition and quick decision-making are not likely to undertake these duties after smoking cannabis. However, more common activities that also require vigilance and concentration – such as the operation of an automobile – can be impaired by cannabis intoxication. Many people who smoke or eat cannabis drive while under the influence of THC.

In a road-side survey, almost 14 percent of teenage drivers who consented to blood or saliva tests showed positive THC results. These volunteers were not tested for driving performance, and the elapsed time since cannabis use was not determined (Pressley et al. 2019).

Controlled studies of target tracking and other cognitive functions required in driving show small but statistically significant impairments after smoking amounts of cannabis typical of recreational use (Battistella et al. 2013). Impairments are dose related, and complex tasks that require divided attention are particularly susceptible to the drug effect (Berghaus and Gau 1995).

Cannabis produces a dose-related impairment of driving performance (Bondallaz et al. 2016). However, controlled investigations of these cannabis effects, both in simulators and in automobiles, generally show less impairment than would be expected from the results of target tracking studies and other tasks involved in driving. Even when subjects are not informed as to whether they have smoked placebo or active cannabis ("blind" protocols), drivers recognize their state of intoxication and attempt to compensate for the effects on driving. At low to moderate doses, some effects of cannabis are effectively counteracted by such deliberate effort. Subjects tend to drive more slowly, pass more carefully, and follow other vehicles less closely. These results have been found in several studies of actual and simulated driving (Sewell et al. 2009).

However, in the natural situation (when not under observation by an experimenter) some drivers high on cannabis may be less likely to compensate for drug impairment.

Epidemiological studies examine the relationship between traffic accidents and cannabis intoxication. In their assessment of how drug use might influence driving, investigators allow for the long duration of THC metabolites in bodily fluids that far exceeds the time course of detectable behavioral impairment. These investigations show inconsistent results. Some studies indicate that drivers with high levels of THC or its metabolites (but no alcohol) in their blood or urine are more likely to be involved in automobile crashes than drug-free drivers, but other investigators do not find such differences (Asbridge 2005). Some differences among results of these naturalistic surveys may be due to interaction of THC effects with other factors that also contribute to traffic accidents. Such factors include weather conditions, fatigue, and distractions such as cell-phone usage.

Although the evidence of effects of cannabis intoxication on traffic accidents is inconsistent, there is no doubt about the consequences of alcohol use on driving – and the two intoxicants are very frequently used together (Moskowitz 2006, Shults et al. 2019). Combination of alcohol and cannabis results in greater driving impairment and probability of accidents than the use of either drug alone (Sewell et al. 2009).

Cannabis intoxication can degrade some aspects of executive function – especially decision-making (Crean et al. 2011). However, in controlled studies these effects are often minimal and inconsistent, seen most reliably at higher doses and with inexperienced users (Ramaekers et al. 2009, Vadhan et al. 2007). Cannabis intoxication had an opposite effect on delay discounting (an indicator of impulse control) to that typical of alcohol and other addictive drugs in that subjects were less likely to prefer an immediate rather than a delayed reward (Metrik et al. 2012).

Metrik and colleagues also found that in other tests of executive function, subjects who expected THC effects controlled impulsive responding better than those who did not expect a drug effect. The deliberate compensation for drug-produced impairment of response inhibition appears to be similar to the attenuation of cannabis effects on driving performance – and again, perhaps more probable in the laboratory than in a natural environment.

As cannabis becomes a more widely available commodity, products that are more potent and provide higher doses of THC are likely to become available and more widely used. If so, the resultant increase in behavioral and cognitive impairments will present a greater public health hazard than with recent and current levels of cannabis use. A special hazard is consumption of edible cannabis-containing products. High doses of THC can be quickly consumed by the oral route, and the greater time lag (relative to smoking or vaping) between intake and subjective effects can result in extreme and possibly dangerous levels of intoxication.

Cannabis Use Disorders

For several years after the upsurge of popularity and use of cannabis in the 1960s, the substance was generally thought to be nonaddicting. Most who used cannabis did so many times without harmful consequences and did not escalate frequency or amount of use. Few had difficulty abstaining when use was inappropriate or hazardous.

Even those that did use heavily and often seldom encountered immediate severe consequences – such as paranoia from cocaine, dangerous drunken behavior from alcohol, or painful "hangovers" as from use of either of these drugs – effects that discourage excessive use in nonaddicts, and reveal the compulsive nature of use in those with an SUD.

Heavy cannabis use, especially when started during adolescence, does increase the probability of eventual adverse outcomes – but, as with tobacco, harmful consequences that typically come only after years of usage provide little incentive to reduce or stop use.

However, some harmful effects appear sooner. Important activities, including work, family responsibilities and academic performance, are often impaired by frequent long periods of cannabis intoxication – consequences that can motivate attempts to stop use. Many heavy users find stopping or even reducing use to be quite difficult – revealing the compulsive nature of their cannabis addiction. Addiction to cannabis, although less probable and life-disruptive than dependence on other addictive drugs, is nevertheless a possible adverse outcome (Figure 12.7). In recent years the potency of cannabis has increased, with a greater severity of dependence and other harmful outcomes of cannabis use (Freeman and Hines 2015).

Figure 12.7 About 8–10 percent of persistent cannabis users eventually become addicted. Mayara Photo: Klinger / EyeEm / Getty Images.

Addictive Potential

Large-scale epidemiological studies indicate that about 8 percent of cannabis-using individuals become addicted within ten years after their initial use of the substance (Wagner and Anthony 2002). About 4 percent become addicted during their first two years of use, and by age fifty-four, the estimated probability of addiction during the lifetime of ever-users is 10 percent (Chen et al. 2005). Other investigators report similar rates of addiction (8–10 percent) in users of cannabis (Copeland and Swift 2009, Hoch et al. 2015, Lopez-Quintero et al. 2011).

Heavy users (larger amounts and greater frequency), and especially those who began use during adolescence are at higher risk of addiction. German investigators, after a review of many recent studies, concluded that 17 percent of adolescent users, and at least 25 percent of daily users (of all ages) are addicted to cannabis (Hoch et al. 2015).

In 2017, approximately 4 million residents (1.5 percent of the population) of the United States age twelve and older had a cannabis use disorder, as indicated by the National Survey on Drug Use and Health (NSDUH) (Substance Abuse and Mental Health Services Administration 2018). The number of individuals with a cannabis use disorder has remained relatively stable between the years 2005 and 2017. However, there is concern that problematic use will increase as legitimate access to potent cannabis becomes more available.

In the United States, those in treatment for cannabis use disorder represent the largest number of individuals receiving treatment for problematic use of an illicit drug – twice as many as for opioid addiction, and exceeded only by number in treatment for alcoholism (Substance Abuse and Mental Health Services Administration 2018). Only a small percentage of individuals with an SUD for any addictive drug – including cannabis – seeks or receives treatment (Wu et al. 2017). However, the treatment-seeking indicators for cannabis-related problems may be increased by the illicit status (in many locations) of cannabis possession. In the United States, Canada, and some additional countries, entry into a treatment program is often offered as an alternative to criminal punishment for minor offenses of possession of the substance. Treatment entry may also be an alternative to job loss when a workplace urine screen shows evidence of cannabis use. Parents who discover cannabis use by adolescent children may also insist on SUD treatment. It is quite likely than many individuals coerced into treatment in these situations use the substance but do not have a cannabis use disorder.

Addictive Use of Cannabis

The NESARC epidemiological survey (described in previous chapters) inquired about the nature of the disorder in 530 respondents who reported either current or previous excessive and problematic cannabis use. Table 12.1 shows the percentage of these individuals endorsing each of five DSM-IV diagnostic criteria (symptoms of addiction). The feature most often reported was the unsuccessful effort to control use of cannabis. The excessive cannabis use led to the second-ranked diagnostic criterion – too much time spent in obtaining, using and recovering from use. The self-defined excessive use continued despite physical or psychological problems – the third-ranked criterion of cannabis dependence.

A similar pattern of symptoms was indicated in a study of 450 treatment-seeking cannabis users in which 96 percent reported inability to quit or decrease use, 95 percent experienced recurrent psychological or physical problems, and 83 percent spent large amounts of time using the substance. All of the symptoms listed

Table 12.1 Symptoms of cannabis SUD

Diagnostic criterion (symptom)	Percentage of respondents fulfilling criterion	
	Currently dependent	Lifetime dependent
Unsuccessful efforts to decrease or control use	88.2	86.7
Too much time spent obtaining, using, recovering	70.1	79.9
Use despite physical or psychological problems	65.8	72.6
Taken in larger amounts or longer time than intended	59.3	59.8
Important activities given up due to drug use	24.3	52.0

Note. Percentages are based on 530 respondents indicating cannabis dependence at some point during their lifetime and 133 indicating dependence during the previous year.
Source. Based on information from NESARC survey of 2001–2002 and Blanco et al. (2008).

in Table 12.1 were experienced by 69 percent of these individuals with a cannabis use disorder (Stephens et al. 2002).

Most individuals with cannabis use problems do not seek or enter treatment programs, but attempt to decrease or quit use by means of their own efforts, without professional assistance or self-help groups (Blanco et al. 2015, Hughes et al. 2016, Wu et al. 2017). Reasons for quitting given by non-treatment-seeking heavy cannabis users are related to some of the criteria for clinical diagnosis of use disorders. Adults most often gave internal incentives for controlling use, including improving self-image: "to show myself that I can quit," "to feel in control of my life," "to have more energy and get things accomplished," in addition to concern about potential health problems from heavy cannabis use. Some incentives were more external: "seeking approval (or avoiding disapproval) of my family and friends," "not being a bad example for my children," and concern about workplace testing for drug use (Chauchard et al. 2013, Hughes et al. 2008). External (often coerced) motivations for quitting were more common in adolescents, whereas internal motivations were more common in adults (Copersino et al. 2006). The cannabis use problems of many of these individuals may be less severe than the SUD of those in treatment, but all were heavy daily smokers – and most did not quit use after their current or most recent attempt at abstinence from cannabis.

Less is known about the natural history of cannabis use disorder than that of the more addictive drugs – nicotine, stimulants, opioids and alcohol. However, typical patterns of problematic use have been identified (Hughes et al. 2014,

Rosenberg and Anthony 2001). As previously mentioned, dependence can emerge within months, especially in younger individuals. For almost half of all users who eventually become cannabis dependent, the disorder appears within two years of initial use. The rewarding effects of cannabis intoxication promote an increase from occasional recreational use into more frequent use in less appropriate situations. Problems with control (use of larger amounts and more frequent use than intended) may at first seem to be mere overindulgence in a pleasurable activity – unlike the later-appearing unmistakable compulsion to use. The progression of dependence, similar to that seen with other addictive drugs, was further described in Chapter 7.

As use increases, activities narrow down to those compatible with being high or stoned – that is, not impaired by the acute cognitive effects of cannabis. Work, care and supervision of children, and interaction with family and friends who are not using cannabis often decrease. Since cannabis increases the pleasure of mundane activities that are ordinarily enjoyable and require little effort, time spent watching television, listening to music, engaged with social media or other internet sites often expands greatly. These mostly passive activities may be harmless, but when high on cannabis they are typically preferred to more demanding endeavors, including academic study. Obviously the appeal of relaxation and pleasure is not limited to cannabis intoxication, but being high seems to further encourage procrastination (or outright avoidance) of productive activity. This immediate effect of cannabis is probably responsible for the supposed "amotivational syndrome," further discussed below.

As addiction progresses, cannabis use dominates the life of some individuals who spend most waking hours intoxicated (Hughes et al. 2014). At this point, the harmful consequences increase. When such heavy use stops, an uncomfortable withdrawal syndrome often develops, making abstinence difficult.

Cannabis dependence is often concurrent with heavy use or addiction to other drugs with more dangerous acute effects (opioids, stimulants) and/or withdrawal syndrome (alcohol). Such co-occurrence of another SUD complicates and worsens cannabis dependence and makes recovery more difficult.

The losses incurred during years of heavy use may be fully realized only in retrospect. In the NESARC survey (Table 12.1), the biggest difference between respondents currently dependent and those indicating lifetime dependence was for the "important activities given up due to drug use" diagnostic criterion. Only 24.3 percent of currently dependent individuals endorsed this criterion, compared to 52.0 percent of those with dependence at some time during their life.

The eventual recognition of the consequences of long-term excessive cannabis use is conveyed in the words of poet-songwriter Shel Silverstein: "when my earthly race is over and they ask me how my life has been I guess I'll have to say – I was stoned and I missed it."

Cannabis Withdrawal

During the latter decades of the twentieth century, the existence of a cannabis withdrawal syndrome was in doubt. After stopping frequent cannabis use most individuals felt (at worst) only moderate, transient discomfort. The DSM-TR-IV (American Psychiatric Association 2000) mentioned the possibility of a cannabis withdrawal syndrome, but stated that the clinical significance of the symptoms was uncertain.

Intense withdrawal symptoms occur after stopping heavy use of drugs that are rapidly eliminated from the body, such as alcohol and heroin. When cannabis use is discontinued, THC is slowly released from fat deposits, greatly extending the time course of its elimination. The brain and body adapt to gradual decrease of THC levels, decreasing the intensity of withdrawal.

The slow rate of THC elimination prevented the reliable demonstration of withdrawal effects in animal subjects until the introduction of the cannabinoid antagonist rimonabant. Rimonabant occupies cannabinoid receptors, blocking the agonist action of THC and producing almost immediate "precipitated withdrawal" when administered to animal subjects after dosage regimens similar to heavy cannabis use in humans (Lichtman and Martin 2006). Precipitated withdrawal signs in rats include tremors, "wet-dog shakes," excessive grooming behavior, ataxia and hunched posture (Gonzalez et al. 2005).

As long-term heavy users of cannabis sought treatment for substance use disorders, reports of an apparent withdrawal syndrome accumulated (Budney and Hughes 2006). Many individuals in treatment for cannabis use disorder had multiple addictions, and underwent simultaneous withdrawal from alcohol, nicotine, and other illicit drugs as well as from cannabis (e.g., Chung et al. 2008). The specific effects of cannabis withdrawal were often obscured in these accounts of negative affect and drug craving.

Laboratory studies of human subjects, not in treatment for cannabis addiction but in a controlled environment, established the occurrence of a significant cannabis withdrawal syndrome (Haney et al. 1999a, 1999b). After four days of cannabis smoking or oral consumption of THC capsules, drug administration was stopped. Subjects reported significant dose-related increases in irritability, anxiety, depression and other symptoms such as stomach pain and decreased appetite. These subjects did not use alcohol or drugs other than nicotine during this study, demonstrating that abstinence from cannabis or THC produced the withdrawal symptoms.

Budney and colleagues conducted a more naturalistic study of heavy cannabis users who were not seeking treatment, but agreed to abstinence (monitored by frequent urine tests) for forty-five days. Withdrawal symptoms (similar to those of the Haney studies) emerged within three days of abstinence and were strongest between days two and six. Most symptoms had dissipated within fourteen days (Budney et al. 2003). A more recent study of cannabis abstinence in heavy users, conducted in a closed residential environment, also indicated a similar pattern of withdrawal symptoms (Lee et al. 2014).

The cannabis withdrawal symptoms indicated by these and other studies are presented in Box 12.1. The DSM-5 revision now includes a cannabis withdrawal syndrome (Hasin et al. 2013).

Clinically significant withdrawal symptoms impair normal daily function and make abstinence from the drug difficult. Allsop and colleagues monitored these effects in Australian cannabis users who were paid to abstain from cannabis for a two-week period (Allsop et al. 2012). These participants had used cannabis for at least five days a week for the previous three months, with a mean amount of about eight grams (0.28 ounces) used each week. During abstinence, participants in the Allsop study reported feeling depressed, anxious, trouble sleeping, no appetite, and that "life felt like an uphill struggle." These symptoms were rated for intensity, and stronger symptoms were associated with impaired daily activities and relapse to cannabis use. Other studies have also shown that stressful and dysphoric effects of withdrawal predict resumption of cannabis use (e.g., Davis et al. 2016).

BOX 12.1 Cannabis withdrawal symptoms

Irritability, anger, or depression
Nervousness or anxiety
Sleep difficulty (insomnia and strange, vivid dreams)
Decreased appetite or weight loss
Restlessness
Depressed mood
Physical symptoms causing significant discomfort from stomach pain, shakiness/tremors, sweating, fever, chills, or headache

After Gorelick et al. (2012) and Lee et al. (2014)

Withdrawal from cannabis has been described as similar to that of nicotine addiction by several investigators (e.g., Vandrey et al. 2008). Although the symptoms are typically less intense than those occurring after abstinence from other addictive drugs, the cannabis withdrawal syndrome contributes to ongoing substance use and relapse during attempts at prolonged abstinence.

Risk Factors

Risk factors for cannabis dependence are essentially the same as those associated with greater vulnerability to use disorders of alcohol, tobacco, and other illicit drugs (Palmer et al. 2013, Mulligan 2019, Schlossarek et al. 2016, Sartor et al.

2010). These conditions, behaviors or personal characteristics are summarized in previous chapters (Chapters 6–8) and include family history of SUD, access to the addictive substance, early-childhood trauma, additional psychiatric syndromes as well as certain personality traits (negative emotionality, poor impulse control). Regular use of any addictive substance (including tobacco, alcohol or cannabis) during early adolescence is a major risk factor for eventual development of addiction to cannabis or other substances (Toumbourou et al. 2007, Volkow et al. 2014, Wu et al. 2017).

The risk factor of **adolescent use** is particularly important for cannabis dependence. Many individuals first experience the effects of cannabis during this developmental period, and are more likely to develop a use disorder than are those who commence use later in life. Young adolescents (ages eleven to fifteen) appear to be especially vulnerable to developing a cannabis use disorder (Chen et al. 2005, Haberstick et al. 2014, Hines et al. 2016). The greater prevalence of rapid progression to cannabis dependence in these young individuals could be due to a general vulnerability to all addictive drugs, a specific age-related effect of cannabis, or to social consequences of early cannabis use (e.g., expulsion from school, closer association with deviant peers).

The higher estimates of addiction prevalence in very young cannabis users may be partially due to an age-associated factors that influence answers to questions about clinical features of addiction (such as inability to control use). Prevalence of addiction among cannabis users is estimated by the results of self-report surveys rather than by clinical interviews. Young adolescents may interpret questions about control and craving differently than do older individuals, and more readily give answers that imply addiction even in the absence of heavy and compulsive cannabis use. For example, endorsement of the statement "It is hard for me to stop using marijuana" might reflect a general inability to decline an opportunity for any pleasurable activity – rather than a specific problem with cannabis use. Although some misleading responses are likely, use at this early developmental stage is a definite risk factor for rapid development of cannabis dependence (Chen and Anthony 2003).

Cannabis Use by Adolescents

Monitoring the Future, the annual large-scale survey of drug use and related information concerning adolescents in the United States, indicated that in 2018, 22 percent of high school seniors reported using cannabis during the previous month. Although much use is experimental and irregular, 5.8 percent of seniors were using cannabis daily. These self-reported use rates in adolescents have remained relatively stable between 2011 and 2018 (National Institute of Drug Abuse 2018).

Adolescents' perceived hazard of cannabis use declined markedly during the early years of the twenty-first century. In the year 2000 approximately 58 percent of twelfth-grade students judged regular cannabis use as a risky activity, but in 2018 only 27 percent expressed a similar level of concern. The increased cultural acceptance of cannabis, including commercial availability and use for recreational and medical purposes, is implicated in the decreased perception of risk associated with the substance (National Institute of Drug Abuse 2018, Schuermeyer et al. 2014). Although the perception of danger has declined, in 2018, 67 percent of seniors expressed disapproval of regular cannabis use.

As with other addictive drugs, use of cannabis by adolescents is more hazardous than for adults. In addition to the greater vulnerability to addiction, cannabis use is also associated with many problems in adolescence, including poor school performance, deviant behavior, retarded emotional maturation, and exacerbation of mental health problems (Copeland et al. 2013, Hines et al. 2016, MacLeod et al. 2004, Volkow et al. 2014). Most of these behaviors and problems are also associated with moderate to heavy use of tobacco, alcohol, and other illicit drugs by adolescents (Chapters 8 and 11).

A definite causal link between cannabis use and the many associated problems is difficult to establish – primarily due to the confounded factors (e.g., use of other recreational drugs, stressful home life, association with deviant peers) that contribute to both the substance use and correlated problems. Even though there is little firm evidence that cannabis use alone can cause difficulties during adolescence, the sequence of occurrence often indicates that use of the substance facilitates the development of problems. Cannabis use by adolescents often predates (and predicts) such mental health problems as anxiety disorders, depression, suicidal ideation, interpersonal violence and certain personality disorders. These associations with cannabis use are stronger in adolescents relative to adults, and younger age of starting use increases the risk of developing mental health disorders. In many studies, confounding factors were statistically controlled, strengthening the case for an exacerbating effect from cannabis use (Copeland et al. 2013).

In adults, demands of work, child-care and other family duties often limit cannabis use, especially in individuals not addicted to the substance. The primary required activity of most adolescents is school attendance and involvement in study and learning. Unfortunately, a student can use cannabis frequently and still attend school (be present in the classroom), although cannabis use is associated with poor grades and lack of interest and effort in schoolwork. The absence of adult responsibilities can enable heavy use of cannabis by adolescents. Adult monitors probably fail to detect adolescent cannabis dependence more often than they miss the signs of addiction to other drugs, such as alcohol.

Is Cannabis a "Gateway Substance"?

In North America, Australia and several European countries a common sequence of drug use begins with alcohol and tobacco, followed by cannabis use, and then in a small proportion of substance-using individuals, use of more dangerous illicit drugs, including heroin or cocaine.

In the early years after the increased use of cannabis in the United States, a "Gateway theory" was proposed: that the use of each drug predicted progression to the next step in the sequence (Kandel and Faust 1975). Anticannabis crusaders popularized a simple version of the gateway concept – maintaining that cannabis use not only predicted, but also caused progression to use of heroin or other dangerous and addictive drugs (Nahas 1973). In subsequent years, the gateway explanation of drug use progression was widely publicized.

Many individuals suffering from an SUD started using the supposed gateway drugs as adolescents. Although alcohol and tobacco use typically precede cannabis use by adolescents, experimentation with the more familiar and widely used substances was often viewed as a relatively harmless "rite of passage," a common experience of becoming an adult. Cannabis use is less immediately dangerous than other illicit drugs, but a common warning in the early years of its increased popularity was that cannabis use was likely to lead to the use of "harder" drugs. The gateway theory of cannabis use had considerable face validity and was accepted by many individuals, although with little supporting evidence. We now know that although some who use cannabis progress to use of other illicit drugs, the large majority of adult and older adolescent cannabis users do not exhibit this pattern of progressive drug use (e.g., Earleywine 2002, Wu et al. 2017).

Results of a World Health Organization mental health survey of drug use in seventeen countries throughout the world also casts doubt on the unique role of cannabis (or other specific drugs) as a gateway substance that causes subsequent use of additional dangerous and addictive drugs (Degenhardt et al. 2010). Easy access to drugs, high prevalence of drug use, and pervasive cultural attitudes about substance use were factors most likely to shape the order of initiation of various addictive drugs. For example, in Nigeria and Japan, countries with lower levels of cannabis use, other illicit drugs (opioids, stimulants) were often used before first use of cannabis. In several different cultures, the risk of eventually developing an SUD appeared to depend more on the age of onset of use and the extent of prior use of any drug, rather than on a particular sequence of substance use.

Other investigators (e.g., Iacono 2008, Vanyukov et al. 2012) have also found an association between early use of any addictive substance and the later development of an SUD. Both the early drug use as well as the eventual SUD may be caused by common factors, such as family history, personality characteristics, or unknown environmental or developmental conditions. However, the early drug use is obviously a possible contributor to the later-emerging use disorder. Implications for public health policy are that rather than attempting to prevent use of a specific drug such as cannabis, prevention efforts should be directed toward use of all psychoactive substances (including tobacco, nicotine and alcohol) by adolescents.

Long-Term Consequences of Heavy Cannabis Use

Long-term consequences of chronic cannabis consumption are less easily identified than are the immediate effects. As the substance became more widely used in the late 1960s, concerns were expressed that continued use of cannabis would eventually result in biological toxicity and other adverse effects – perhaps becoming evident only after years of consumption. The most extreme predictions of harmful effects were not supported by evidence from controlled experiments with animal subjects, clinical studies and epidemiological surveys. However, some concerns remain about physical and psychological health risks of prolonged heavy use – especially given the lessened legal sanctions, greater availability and increased cultural acceptance of cannabis and derived products. Cause–effect relations between cannabis use and adverse consequences are difficult to establish with certainty. Many confounding factors accompany heavy and prolonged cannabis use and make it difficult to demonstrate that the substance is a primary cause of problems such as lung cancer, lower adult IQ scores, and schizophrenia.

Biological Toxicity

The National Institute of Mental Health conducted extensive long-term tests of THC toxicity on rats and monkeys (Braude 1972). High doses of THC were administered daily for ninety days, after which autopsies assessed organ damage and blood abnormalities. These studies were similar in design to those required for approval of new drugs for medical use. The drug treatment caused reduced eating and weight loss, but no significant organ damage. In the 1990s similar tests found no evidence of carcinogenic effects or genetic damage in rats (Chan et al. 1996).

Some studies have shown a temporary reduction in fertility of female animals, spontaneous abortions and low birth weight after treatment with very high doses of THC, but implications for human cannabis use are doubtful (Paria and Dey 2000). Several large-scale studies indicate that many women who use cannabis during pregnancy give birth to smaller (lower birth weight) babies. However, most of these women also smoked tobacco, and when tobacco use is taken into account the effect of cannabis use is no longer statistically significant (Zuckerman et al. 1989). A syndrome of characteristic birth defects (as caused by alcohol use during pregnancy) is not associated with cannabis use (Fergusson et al. 2002).

The gaseous and particulate content of cannabis smoke is similar to that of tobacco smoke, with the exception of the primary psychoactive chemicals (THC and nicotine) (British Medical Association 1997). Inhalation of cannabis smoke deposits more toxic particulates per puff than does tobacco smoke, and cannabis smoke contains a higher concentration of certain carcinogens (Wu et al. 1988). Although moderate to heavy tobacco smokers often consume many more cigarettes each day than do heavy cannabis users, cannabis smoke is typically drawn more deeply into the lungs and held there for a longer time than is tobacco smoke. The characteristic topography of cannabis smoking increases the exposure to inhaled toxins.

Tobacco smoke is quite toxic to the respiratory system. Two of the most serious effects are cancer and chronic obstructive pulmonary disorder (e.g., emphysema). Many users of cannabis also smoke tobacco, and for these individuals toxic effects of the two substances are combined and difficult to separate. Some investigators have compared respiratory tract abnormalities in individuals who smoke only cannabis with those who smoke only tobacco (Tashkin 2005). Both groups exhibited inflammation of the respiratory tract and evidence of immune response impairment in the lungs. These effects were similar in both groups at an initial examination, but after ten years had increased in severity only in the tobacco smokers. Like tobacco smokers, cannabis-only smokers also have a greater incidence of coughing and other indicators of lung and throat irritation than nonsmokers (Howden and Naughton 2011). These effects are thought to be caused by the particulate toxins in cannabis smoke, rather than by THC.

Premalignant changes have been found in the lungs of cannabis smokers (Mehra et al. 2006) but a large-scale epidemiological study found no evidence of higher frequency of cancer of the lung or respiratory tract related to cannabis use (Hashibe et al. 2006). Although as of yet there is no firm evidence of actual cancer occurrence caused by cannabis use, it should be remembered that only after several decades of widespread tobacco use did it become undeniably evident that smoking is a major cause of cancer and premature death. Heavy use of cannabis by smoking presents definite risks of respiratory system damage, and future studies may reveal an increased incidence of lung cancer.

Neurological Toxicity and Cognitive Impairment

Heavy and frequent cannabis use is associated with lower educational and occupational achievement, especially in individuals whose regular use starts before age fifteen (Arria et al. 2015, Curran et al. 2016, Horwood et al. 2010). These consequences could be partially due to the impaired cognition and decreased motivation that occur during cannabis intoxication. The acute effects of THC persist for hours after drug intake, and withdrawal symptoms from extensive cannabis use can endure for several days, so a frequent user may be intoxicated, or withdrawing, during most waking hours. An often-expressed concern about heavy cannabis use is the possibility that some detrimental effects endure far beyond the time of acute intoxication and withdrawal, and perhaps are permanent. Such enduring consequences might result from neurological abnormalities – cannabis-produced brain damage. Of particular concern is the possibility of detrimental effects on the immature brain of young adolescents (Hurd et al. 2013, Volkow et al. 2014).

Some MRI studies reveal significantly smaller hippocampal sizes in long-term heavy cannabis users (e.g., Ashtari et al. 2011). All investigators do not consistently find brain abnormalities in cannabis users (Lorenzetti et al. 2010). Although gross brain damage does not occur, improved imaging techniques indicate subtle neurological differences in some users, including abnormalities in interconnections among brain areas. Such differences are most reliably detected in individuals with extensive cumulative exposure to cannabis, often those who started heavy use at an early age (Batalla et al. 2013, Wetherill et al. 2015).

As with most investigations of long-term drug effects in humans, other possible sources of observed differences must be considered for interpretation of results. The accuracy of drug use history based on retrospective accounts is often in doubt. Differences present before drug exposure are typically unknown. Investigators attempt to minimize the effects of alcohol or other brain toxins by careful screening of subjects, or use of statistical control. However, the actual cause of any differences found in brain structure or function is often uncertain.

Studies with animal subjects are better controlled than are investigations of humans, with confounded variables eliminated and differences prior to drug exposure minimized. Additionally, the brains of experimental animals can be directly examined for subtle drug-produced differences in structure, metabolism, or gene expression. In adult animals, THC sometimes produces neurological damage – only when administered at doses considerably higher than those resulting from cannabis use by humans. Immature rats are much more vulnerable than full-grown animals to enduring THC effects (Iversen 2008).

Rats administered THC or a synthetic cannabinoid agonist (WIN 55 212 2) during puberty displayed cognitive impairments that persisted into maturity (e.g., Schneider and Koch 2003). Similar studies revealed enduring neurological differences in the hippocampus after prolonged administration of these drugs to immature animals (Schneider 2008, 2012). After adjusting for the higher metabolic rates of small animals, the THC doses used in most of these investigations were similar to those sometimes used by humans. These lower doses have minimal or no long-term effects when administered to mature rats.

In both rats and humans, the brain's endocannabinoid system develops during puberty. Cannabinoid receptors are overexpressed (are at their greatest density) during this developmental period, and eventually become less dense through the normal neuronal pruning that occurs as the brain matures (Bossong and Niesink 2010). These maturational changes during puberty or adolescence are thought to contribute to the greater vulnerability to enduring THC effects during this period

(Schneider 2012). The results of these animal studies suggest a neurological basis for the increased risk of long-term adverse consequences in cannabis-using adolescent humans.

Long-term heavy cannabis users show impaired cognitive function that persists for at least days or weeks, far longer than subjective effects of intoxication – feeling high or stoned. Deficits of attention and concentration, working memory, executive function and decision-making are residual effects of such cannabis use (Crean et al. 2011, Solowij and Pesa 2012, Sagar et al. 2015, Schreiner and Dunn 2012). These effects could result from the slow elimination of THC and metabolites from the body, withdrawal from cannabinoids, or from enduring drug-produced neurological damage.

Early studies of long-term cognitive effects had mixed results, with inconsistent findings of impairment in abstinent former users. A major difference among investigations was variation in the duration of cannabis abstinence. Schreiner and Dunn conducted meta-analyses combining the results of thirty-three studies. The initial analysis indicated a small but significant impairment of general cognitive function in currently abstinent cannabis users, as well as the specific impairments previously mentioned. A second analysis including only studies of users abstinent for at least twenty-five days, found no significant impairment related to previous cannabis use (Schreiner and Dunn 2012). Other investigators also find that most (in some cases, all) cognitive deficits seen in cannabis users eventually abate with extended abstinence (Crean et al. 2011, Solowij and Pesa 2012). Although cognitive deficits often occur in long-term cannabis users, the impairment in many individuals may not cause much difficulty in daily life. Small cognitive impairments, although statistically significant, often have negligible consequences for everyday function.

Many of the studies of long-term cannabis effects on human cognition suffer from the problems described previously regarding investigations of neurological abnormalities. Preexisting differences or other factors could contribute to the differences detected. However, cannabis use is implicated as a cause or contributor to the impairment because recovery of function (sometimes only partial, but often complete) eventually follows abstention from cannabis – concentration and memory improve after cannabis use stops. The diminution or disappearance of cognitive differences suggests that the impairment of neurological function is not permanent, although the recovery might involve use of compensatory processes to overcome persisting, if subtle, brain damage (Solwij and Pesta 2012).

In a large-scale study of long-term cannabis effects on cognition conducted in New Zealand, Meier and colleagues determined the **intelligence quotient (IQ)** of 1,037 thirteen-year-old individuals who had never used cannabis. Cannabis effects were indicated in this prospective investigation by within-subject changes in IQ scores, eliminating a major limitation of previous retrospective studies that did not determine the level of cognitive function before cannabis use started. The participants reported their cannabis use again at age eighteen and at four additional times during the subsequent twenty years. IQ was measured a second time at age thirty-eight. The cognitive performance of participants who started regular cannabis use before age eighteen had decreased significantly at age thirty-eight, but no such decline occurred in participants whose cannabis use commenced after age eighteen, or in those who never used the substance (Meier et al. 2012).

In the Meier study cognitive ability was tested by means of the Wechsler Intelligence Scale for Children-Revised, and the Wechsler Adult Intelligence Scale-IV. At age thirteen, IQ scores were similar for participants that never used, and those who later became users of cannabis. Tests of processing speed and executive function revealed the largest deficits, but significant differences were also detected in global intellectual function. The largest declines in IQ scores (mean of six points) occurred in participants whose use started in adolescence and who were diagnosed as cannabis dependent or identified as persistent regular users three or more times during the twenty-year period. IQ decline in adolescent-onset cannabis users was still significant after controlling for the effects of known confounding factors, including differences among participants in years of schooling, persistent abuse of alcohol, tobacco and other addictive drugs, as well as the occurrence of schizophrenia.

No significant declines (mean of one point) were detected in individuals whose use started in adolescence, but who never used cannabis regularly over the ensuing years. Regular use was defined as use at least four times per week. The IQ scores of subjects who never used cannabis also remained the same over the twenty-year period. These investigators also state that the IQ declines associated with early and frequent cannabis use persisted in participants who had stopped cannabis use for a short time prior to testing, and maintain such decline indicates an enduring cognitive impairment and a possible neurotoxic effect. All participants who had previously used cannabis were abstinent during the week before testing, although the time of last cannabis use prior to cognitive testing was not specified. Previous research demonstrates that cognitive deficits can persist for nearly a month before eventually disappearing, so the lower test scores could be the result of either permanent deficits in brain function or temporary ones that would dissipate after a longer period of abstinence.

Participants in the Meier investigation were not assigned to groups by random or matching procedures (as would occur in a more completely controlled study), but by their cannabis use during adolescence. Consequently, factors related to their cannabis use – such as traits of impulsiveness or emotional instability – might have also influenced IQ score changes, although not because of pharmacological effects of THC (Daly 2013). Cannabis use can also promote environmental influences that may have long-term effects on intelligence test performance – such as encouraging interaction with peers who have little interest in schoolwork or traditional achievement (Rogeburg 2013).

These nonpharmacological environmental factors could have contributed to the long-term IQ decline, and the impairment might resolve with continued abstinence from cannabis. However, the Meier study is an important addition to the increasing evidence indicating that adolescents are especially vulnerable to harmful consequences of persistent cannabis use, including the possibility of neurotoxic effects.

Amotivational Syndrome?

The concept of an "amotivational syndrome," and its association with cannabis use, was first expressed in the mid-twentieth century when use of the substance increased – initially among adolescents and young adults. Many parents, teachers, and other authority figures became alarmed as they observed young people, many who used cannabis, whose priorities did not reflect ambition and pursuit of long-term goals (Smith 1968). Cannabis intoxication often results in reluctance to engage in productive work and academic study, and encourages indulgence in enjoyable, low-demand activities. A desire to spend time listening to music, socializing with friends, and in general having a good time at the expense of working hard is hardly unique to cannabis users. Cannabis use does often promote such hedonistic pursuits during the state of intoxication. However, proponents of the amotivational syndrome concept maintained that the tendency toward passivity and avoidance of work indicated an enduring erosion of a desirable **work ethic** resulting from use of cannabis (e.g., Nahas 1973).

Cannabis-induced diversion from less pleasurable pursuits (including academic study and onerous work) is apparently to some extent culture bound (Earleywine 2002). Caffeine and nicotine are often used as "work drugs" in most Western countries, a role seldom given to the use of cannabis. In technologically advanced cultures, cannabis is a substance most often used for relaxation and pleasure. However, in less developed countries cannabis is sometimes used by laborers as they perform menial tasks. A study conducted in the 1970s indicated that Jamaican field workers felt that use of *ganja* provided energy (Comitas 1976).

The lifestyle of some, if not all, frequent heavy cannabis users indicates general apathy and a diminished willingness to carry out complex long-term plans, follow difficult routines, and endure frustration. Such characteristics are incompatible with academic achievement and impede work in all but the least demanding of occupations. However, it is far from certain that cannabis use alone reliably causes less motivation for achievement, as traditionally defined. Commitment to work is influenced by many factors. The most obvious alternative explanation for the association between heavy cannabis use and lower educational and occupational achievement is that individuals with less work ethic and lower motivation are more likely to use cannabis frequently. Many people have less opportunity to receive rewards for hard work and persistent effort because of genetically determined limitations, childhood living conditions (e.g., poverty, inadequate parental support), personality traits, or other factors. Recognition of these limitations can discourage ambition and promote use of cannabis and other recreational but addictive substances.

Occasional recreational use of cannabis is unlikely to result in a generalized loss of motivation. Many individuals who used cannabis as adolescents or young adults have achieved success in a variety of professions and occupations. As a result, concern about an amotivational syndrome resulting from cannabis use is of much less current interest than it was in the 1960s. However, research conducted in Norway indicates a correlational relationship between a lower commitment to work and heavy cannabis use that starts early in life and persists into adulthood (Hyggen 2012). Some decreased work commitment may result from acceptance of cannabis use along with rejection of a traditional work ethic, a combination of attitudes not dependent on the pharmacological effects of the drug (Hammersley et al. 2001). As Hyggen stated, "we do not know whether individuals disenchanted with work turn to cannabis – or vice versa." There appears to be little definite evidence to resolve this interesting question.

Psychosis

Persistent cannabis use is associated with increased incidence of several types of mental health problems (Copeland et al. 2013, Patton et al. 2002). The association could be due to attempts to self-medicate a disturbing mental or emotional state, or the psychiatric syndrome could be a result of heavy cannabis use. In a third possible connection, a factor like ongoing stress might promote both drug use and the concurrent mental or emotional disorder (Ksir and Hart 2016). The greater risk of depressive, anxiety, and psychotic disorders for heavy users of cannabis is similar to that of individuals suffering from other types of SUD (Chapters 8 and 11). The mental health risk is greater for adolescent relative to adult users of addictive drugs.

In rare cases, individuals experience transient psychotic states during cannabis intoxication (Casadio et al. 2011). In a controlled investigation, intravenous administration of THC produced a temporary psychotic state (D'Souza et al. 2004). Such a consequence from using cannabis is unusual, but some intoxicated individuals seen in hospital emergency rooms report hallucinations and other symptoms of psychosis. The symptoms typically subside as the acute intoxication fades. Subclinical psychotic experiences and schizotypical thought processes are also associated with cannabis use in a minority of individuals (Barkus and Lewis 2008).

Pooled evidence from thirty-five population-based studies conducted in several countries shows that cannabis use is a modest risk factor for psychosis, primarily schizophrenia (Moore et al. 2007). These studies indicated an odds ratio of 1.41 for a psychotic outcome with any use of cannabis. The odds ratio increased to 2.09 for those using the substance most heavily. Confounded factors influenced the results of many of these studies. Though still significant, the odds ratios diminished after adjustments for the occurrence of conditions also correlated with schizophrenia, such as childhood trauma and heavy use of stimulant drugs.

In a prospective study, Bechtold and colleagues monitored cannabis use and evaluated the physical and mental health of 506 men annually for a period of thirty years – from adolescence through their mid-forties (Bechtold et al. 2015). After statistical control for several correlated factors, including socioeconomic status, alcohol, and other drug use, cannabis users were not different from nonusers. These results from a recent long-term prospective investigation indicate the variability in findings regarding an association between cannabis use and mental health problems.

Although epidemiological studies consistently reveal an association between cannabis use and schizophrenia, any causal connection is poorly understood. Cannabis is neither necessary nor sufficient to cause a persistent psychotic disorder. A large majority of cannabis users never experience any type of psychosis, but there appears to be a small subset of individuals for whom the substance contributes to development of the serious mental disorder (Ksir and Hart 2016). Adolescents are thought to be more vulnerable, but few young individuals – even those who use heavily – become psychotic (Wilkinson et al. 2014). The additional factor (or factors) that cause the vulnerability is not known, although genetic influence is thought to be an important variable (Di Forti et al. 2012). Interaction of THC with the **developing endocannabinoid system** in adolescent users is a suspected contributor to the association between cannabis use and schizophrenia (Bossong and Niesink 2010, Casadio et al. 2011).

The risk for developing schizophrenia is very low in the general population. If, as population studies suggest, heavy use of cannabis doubles the risk of schizophrenia, the probability of experiencing the disorder rises to about 1.5 percent (Zammit et al. 2012). In the very large worldwide population of cannabis users, many cases of schizophrenia appear to be related to use of the substance. However, although cannabis use has increased greatly during the past forty years, especially in developed countries, there has been no corresponding increase in the incidence of schizophrenia (Gage et al. 2013). This observation complicates the interpretation of the many investigations that show an association between cannabis use and psychotic disorders.

Illicit Use of Synthetic Cannabinoids

Early in the twenty-first century, products advertised as a mixture of natural herbs that produced a cannabis-like state of intoxication – but were not illegal – became available. These products were sold via the Internet, in convenience stores, and at service stations under various names like Spice, K2, and Purple Haze. Analysis of the substances revealed the presence of **synthetic cannabinoids**, most often a chemical designated as JWH-018 (Huffman et al. 1994). This drug or other synthetic cannabinoids were identified in similar products marketed in several European countries, Japan, Australia and New Zealand as well as in North America (Grabenauer et al. 2012, Uchiyama et al. 2010). Spice and similar products consist of nonpsychoactive plant materials sprayed with JWH-018 or similar synthetic cannabinoids.

Anecdotal reports and individual case studies suggest that cannabis-like effects, including a subjective high state, occur after smoking Spice or a similar product (Gunderson et al. 2012). The full effects of the drugs are unknown, due to an absence of systematic studies. Generalizations about the drug effects are also limited in that the specific chemical composition varies among the several products available. Some case histories indicate that Spice-type products produce more intense intoxication than natural cannabis, a result consistent with studies showing that JWH-018 activates cannabinoid receptors more strongly than does THC (Atwood et al. 2010). Reports from hospital emergency departments and poison control centers also suggest that Spice and similar products can cause agitation, suicidality, or exacerbation of preexisting psychosis (e.g., Every-Palmer 2011). The occurrence of serious outcomes and medical emergencies demonstrate the possible hazards of using the preparations containing synthetic cannabinoids.

The psychoactive ingredients in Spice and similar products are classified as designer drugs, meaning that the chemical composition can be altered slightly – to evade criminal penalties based on specific molecular configuration – while retaining the primary psychoactive effects. To overcome this legal difficulty in restricting access to these products, the Synthetic Drug Abuse Prevention Act of 2012 placed "synthetic compounds commonly found in synthetic marijuana" into Schedule I of the Controlled Substances Act.

Medical Use of Cannabis and Cannabinoids

Cannabis or cannabinoid drugs are often administered for relief of **neuropathic pain**, muscle spasms, nausea, vomiting, loss of appetite, and other painful or aversive conditions. Patients suffering from multiple sclerosis or AIDS and those undergoing chemotherapy for cancer are among those most likely to receive a prescription from a physician for an approved cannabinoid drug, purchase high-potency cannabis from a legitimate dispensary, or obtain cannabis of unknown purity and potency from an illicit source. Cannabis or cannabinoid drugs often provide some degree of relief for all these maladies, although such use of cannabis is controversial (Sachs et al. 2015).

Dronabinol (Marinol), a preparation of synthetic THC, was approved in the United States in 1985 as a Schedule III drug for treatment of chemotherapy-induced nausea and AIDS-related anorexia and wasting. Nabilone (Cesamet), a synthetic THC analog, is also approved for similar use. There is little controversy concerning these medications, which have minimal abuse potential. These synthetic drugs are not used for pleasure and have no "street value." However, the use of natural ("botanical") cannabis as medicine has resulted in warnings from the National Institute of Drug Abuse and objections from professional medical organizations, including the American Society of Addiction Medicine.

Cannabis has a long history of medical use to treat many afflictions. The substance was not very effective for most problems, but its use continued because for centuries few effective medicines were available. For some ailments, much of the relief associated with cannabis use apparently came from a placebo effect – desperate patients' fervent hope that the medication would help them. During the twentieth century, better medicines were discovered or developed, and cannabis was administered less often by physicians. In the United States, cannabis was classified as a Schedule I drug in 1970, marking the substance as dangerous and as having no approved medical usage. This classification was the result of public opinion and political pressure rather than scientific and medical evidence. Federal laws resulted in severe punishment for dispensing or unauthorized possession of Schedule I drugs.

Recreational use of cannabis increased dramatically in America and Europe in the latter decades of the twentieth century. Recreational users of cannabis who suffered from neuropathic pain (as from multiple sclerosis or diabetes), nausea concurrent with cancer chemotherapy, or anorexia and weight loss (as from AIDS) found that the substance, most often taken by smoking, relieved these painful or unpleasant symptoms. Most of these individuals discovered the beneficial effects as they used cannabis for relaxation and pleasure, so the boundary between cannabis use for pleasure and for health care became blurred (Bostwick 2012, Schauer et al. 2016). Some relief from disease symptoms probably came from cannabis-produced euphoria and temporary lifting of depressed mood. However, scientific studies indicate that with appropriate dosage, smoked cannabis can have analgesic, anti-emetic, and antispasmodic effects and promote appetite even without producing a subjective high state (Grant et al. 2012).

Many anecdotal reports of medical benefits of cannabis, combined with evidence that cannabis had no immediate toxic effects, resulted in the state of California in 1996 legalizing possession, use, and sale of cannabis for loosely defined medical purposes. Since that time, thirty-two additional states, Guam, Puerto Rico, the US Virgin Islands, and the District of Columbia have enacted similar laws. Control of marijuana "dispensaries" varies among states, but most require a physician's approval or recommendation (rather than a traditional prescription) for purchase of self-administered cannabis. Cannabis retains its classification by the US federal government as a closely controlled Schedule I drug. In most cases law enforcement officials do not enforce federal laws against sale or possession of cannabis obtained from state-approved dispensaries. Some communities enact and enforce regulations concerning the growth of cannabis plants, and California monitors the potency and content of cannabis plant products sold in state-approved dispensaries.

Individuals with conservative political ideology, including some officials of the National Institute of Drug Abuse and the federal Drug Enforcement Agency, often oppose the use of cannabis as medicine (Clark et al. 2011). Physicians and pharmacologists are divided on the issue, with some individuals and organizations opposing but others advocating medical use of cannabis (Mechoulam 2012). Opponents emphasize adverse effects, including the addictive potential of cannabis. Many also maintain that approval would "send the wrong message" to the public from the medical establishment, increasing the general cultural acceptance of cannabis.

Proponents of medical cannabis use point out that some symptoms, especially neuropathic pain, are often intractable and for many patients not relieved much by currently approved medications. For some patients, suffering is relieved more completely and with fewer side effects by inhaling cannabis smoke or vapor than by using other medications (Sachs et al. 2015). Although bringing relief to many patients, the most effective analgesics are also addictive (opioids) or have dangerous side effects (aspirin and similar drugs). No drug is completely safe and effective for all users, so the question becomes one of weighing benefits against dangers, rather than summary disapproval of a particular drug.

Well-controlled studies show that the dose-related effects of cannabis can be titrated (closely controlled) better by means of smoke or vapor inhalation than by oral consumption of approved synthetic cannabinoids. Analgesia and nausea relief also occur much more quickly with inhalation of natural cannabinoids (Grant et al. 2012).

Botanical cannabis, as opposed to synthetic cannabinoids, contains another ingredient in addition to THC with beneficial properties. **Cannabidiol (CBD)** is a nonpsychoactive anti-inflammatory and neuroprotective component of cannabis (Sarne et al. 2011). CBD is a ligand for (activates) CB2 receptors, found primarily in the immune system. CBD has much therapeutic potential for treatment of epilepsy and other neuropsychiatric disorders (Devinsky et al. 2014). Unlike THC, CBD does not produce the subjective effects (the "high" state) characteristic of cannabis intoxication.

Greater use of medical cannabis has apparently increased general acceptance of cannabis for recreation and pleasure, which could increase prevalence of cannabis use disorders (Schuermeyer et al. 2014). Careful screening of patients, similar to that done for opioid treatment, is expected to minimize abuse and addiction resulting from medical use of cannabis and cannabinoids (Grant et al. 2012). Opioids, stimulants and benzodiazepines are important and useful medications that, like cannabis, have abuse potential. Access to these approved drugs is closely controlled, limiting to some extent harm resulting from their use. Medical practitioners and regulatory agencies view the trade-off between benefit and harm from the use of these drugs as acceptable. Eventually a similar general acceptance of medical use of cannabis seems likely.

Treatment of Cannabis Use Disorders

For adults, the primary incentives for stopping disordered cannabis use are often internal (personal dissatisfaction with drug use), rather than forced by external coercion due to disastrous consequences. The relatively lower severity of the disorder can make brief intervention and guided self-change an appropriate treatment approach for many with cannabis addiction (Sobell et al. 2006). These less intensive interventions (described further in Chapter 16) promote "natural recovery," in which many addicted individuals eventually recover from the disorder without extensive professional treatment. Family involvement increases the effectiveness of brief interventions for adolescents (Danovitch and Gorelick 2012). No effective drug treatments specifically intended for cannabis dependence are currently available, although several are under development (Copeland and Pokorski 2016).

Many individuals with a cannabis use disorder are also addicted to another substance: tobacco, alcohol, or an illicit drug. Treatment procedures are typically quite similar for use disorders of any addictive drug, with the exception of nicotine (Chapter 16).

Chapter Summary

Cannabis use can be addictive, and heavy use has harmful consequences, although the substance is neither as addictive nor as dangerous as other, less restricted substances – tobacco and alcohol.

In the United States, cannabis became a focal point of controversial cultural change in the late 1960s, as use increased dramatically among young people. Research conducted since the mid-1980s has greatly increased knowledge of cannabis's actions both as a recreational intoxicant and as medicine.

As government restriction of medical and recreational use in the United States decreased, cannabis became a commercial product. Improvements in cultivation and strain selection resulted in the availability of very potent cannabis – containing a higher percentage of THC.

In the endogenous cannabinoid system, natural brain chemicals anandamide and 2-AG stimulate cannabinoid receptors in the brain and the immune system to assist in regulation of hunger and food intake, pain perception, inflammation, and stress responses. THC and other components of cannabis activate cannabinoid receptors, producing the characteristic drug effects.

The high state produced by cannabis is emotionally pleasing and cognitively interesting to many individuals, although THC can also produce unpleasant and frightening effects. The euphoria of cannabis intoxication is reportedly less intense than that produced by cocaine or heroin.

Intoxication also produces impairment in some cognitive processes, including time perception, memory formation, concentration, and vigilance. Complex information-processing tasks, such as those used in automobile driving, are degraded. Some users can overcome the performance impairment by means of deliberate effort as they attend to and compensate for the drug's effects.

Cannabis has no immediately dangerous toxic effects in healthy individuals. In many long-term users, chronic toxicity is often difficult to distinguish from effects of other drugs, including tobacco, alcohol, and cocaine/amphetamine.

Eight to 10 percent of cannabis users become addicted. For most users, cannabis is much less addictive than tobacco, cocaine/amphetamine, or opioids, and somewhat less than alcohol. Addiction is much more prevalent (approximately 25 percent) among daily or near-daily users. Young adolescents who are regular users are also more vulnerable – showing greater prevalence of cannabis addiction than adult users.

Adverse outcomes most likely with cannabis addiction are not as severe as with dependence on other drugs. Too much time spent intoxicated and important activities given up because of drug use are frequently reported diagnostic symptoms. Excessive use despite efforts to stop and worsening of physical and psychological problems are also common complaints.

The cannabis withdrawal syndrome consists primarily of irritability, anxiety, depression, and sleep difficulties. Withdrawal from cannabis is somewhat similar to the nicotine withdrawal syndrome.

Long-term heavy use of cannabis is associated with poor grades and failure to complete school, decreased motivation for most types of work, subtle but significant cognitive impairment, and greater prevalence of mental health problems. The associations are strongest when heavy and persistent use commences early in adolescence. Cognitive deficits persist after weeks of abstinence, although they often eventually diminish or disappear.

A small but significant drop in IQ scores occurred over a twenty-year period in individuals who started persistent cannabis use before age eighteen. The scores of users and nonusers were not different at age thirteen, prior to any cannabis use. Test scores of nonusers increased slightly over the next two decades.

Adverse consequences of cannabis use for adolescents could be due to enduring neurological impairment caused by THC effects on the immature brain. Deficits in academic and occupational achievement could also come from missed opportunities and other (nonpharmacological) results of frequent intoxication during a critical developmental period.

In past years, the notion that cannabis fostered an enduring "amotivational syndrome" was advanced. However, there is very little evidence of a drug-produced decrease in ambition or work ethic that persists beyond the intoxicated state. Many factors influence motivation to work. Cannabis use may be one such factor, but many recreational users of cannabis are productive workers.

The "gateway concept" implicated cannabis use in promoting involvement with other, more dangerous addictive drugs. A more accepted theory postulates that common factors drive use of all recreational (and addictive) drugs, and the sequence of specific drugs used depends mainly on drug availability and cultural acceptance. Most individuals start drug use with tobacco and alcohol before using cannabis, and a large majority of users do not progress to other addictive drugs.

Greater cultural acceptance of cannabis is indicated by lessened governmental restrictions and increased use in medicine. Cannabis can relieve nausea, improve appetite, and lessen neuropathic pain. Medical uses for cannabis are somewhat controversial, partially because for some users the difference between symptom relief and pleasant intoxication is indistinct. Medical use may increase cannabis addiction, a risk somewhat similar to that of other, more traditional medications for pain, anxiety, and attention disorders.

Review Exercises

1. What chemical determines the potency of cannabis?
2. Describe the cultural changes in the twentieth century that led to increased legal restrictions for cannabis use and the more recent cultural changes and scientific findings that led to decriminalization of cannabis in many states.
3. Describe the various methods of using *cannabis sativa*. How have the methods of use changed in the past decade?
4. Explain why, given the same amount and potency of cannabis, there is a different time course and intensity of the experienced effect for smoking (or vaping) and for ingesting the drug.
5. What are the two types of receptors for cannabis, their location in the body, and the differences in their function?
6. Describe the endocannabinoid system (ECS), and summarize its many functions.
7. What are the acute (immediate or short-latency) effects of cannabis on emotion, perception, memory, and cognition?

8. How do the acute effects of cannabis affect driving performance? Include in your answer the effects of higher doses and of expectation.
9. In what way(s) are currently dependent and lifetime-dependent individuals similar and different in the self-reported symptoms of a cannabis use disorder?
10. What is the nature of the cannabis withdrawal syndrome?
11. What is the relationship between cannabis use by adolescents and mental health problems?
12. Explain the theory that cannabis is a gateway substance, and give the actual risk factors for adolescent use of dangerous and addictive drugs.
13. After reviewing the research evidence on the effect of prolonged use of cannabis on human cognitive functioning, provide an argument that such use does or does not negatively affect cognition.
14. Describe the evidence for a link between persistent cannabis use and psychosis.
15. What are the medical problems for which cannabis has been shown to be effective?
16. Assume you are on a committee charged with making a recommendation to Congress regarding the legalization of cannabis at the national level. What would you recommend? Justify your answer using information from the text.

Key Terms

2-AG (447)
adolescent use (466)
anandamide (447)
cannabidiol (CBD) (479)
cannabinoids (447)
complex information processing (453)

developing endocannabinoid system (476)
intelligence quotient (IQ) (472)
memory (453)
modulating (449)

neuropathic pain (477)
perception (453)
retrograde action (448)
synthetic cannabinoids (477)
time perception (453)
work ethic (474)

13 Use Disorders of Cocaine and Methamphetamine

CHAPTER OUTLINE

LEARNING OBJECTIVES

1. Describe the similarities and differences between cocaine and amphetamine.
2. Know the utilitarian as well as the medical uses of stimulant drugs.
3. Summarize the use prevalence of pharmaceutical and illicit stimulants in the general population and in young adults.
4. Describe how cocaine and amphetamine affect neurotransmitter function.
5. Describe the behavioral and subjective effects of stimulant drugs.
6. Describe the addictive potential of the pharmaceutical and the illicit stimulants, including the percentage of users with an SUD.
7. Summarize the distressing and dangerous consequences of chronic heavy use of cocaine or methamphetamine.
8. Describe the nature of stimulant withdrawal.
9. Describe the use prevalence and the dangerous and distressing effects of MDMA.

Introductory Vignette: The Pharmacist Dispenses Drugs

John is a pharmacist. He does not suffer from attention-deficit disorder, but five hours ago, he took four Adderall tablets – as he does every day – and later he went into the restroom and insufflated the methamphetamine he bought from a street dealer last night.

At first, the stimulant drugs brightened his mood and energized his working through the daily requirements of managing the pharmacy. But now he feels agitated and is out of the pharmacy area – compulsively rearranging the shelf displays of aspirin, laxatives, and hemorrhoid medications. He is tense, feels feverish, and suspects that his blood pressure is elevated. This disturbing sequence of drug effects occurs every day, and he knows that a couple of Xanax tablets will relieve his anxiety, and then he can take even more amphetamine. Before John can take the tranquilizer, a customer approaches. Could this well-dressed man with a briefcase be from the state pharmacy board? Or a DEA inspector? Is John being paranoid? Maybe – the amphetamine does make him extremely vigilant – but he knows his falsified records of Adderall sales would not pass a close examination.

John understands that the discovery of his illicit use of pharmaceutical amphetamine would cause the loss of his job and his pharmacist's license. He also realizes that he is addicted to the drug. Every night, as he takes Ambien to counteract the long-lasting stimulant effects so he can sleep, he vows to stop using amphetamine, risking his career, and tolerating the distressing drug effects. However, the next morning, as he enters his workplace, these fears seem unrealistic, and taking Adderall or methamphetamine seems like a really good plan for the day.

Introduction

Cocaine and amphetamine have dramatic effects on feelings, motivation, and behavior. The pleasures as well as the harm that can come from use of these drugs are celebrated and lamented in many popular songs, such as "Cocaine" (written by Gary Davis, sung by Jackson Brown) and "Cocaine Blues" (written and sung by Johnny Cash). The central nervous system stimulants can facilitate tedious and demanding work and produce extremely rewarding effects but can also cause dangerous behavior and biological toxicity. Cocaine and amphetamine have much abuse and addiction potential, especially when injected or inhaled. These drugs also have limited medical applications.

Stimulant Drugs

Cocaine and amphetamine (including methamphetamine) are indirect agonists for monoamine neurotransmitters dopamine, norepinephrine, and serotonin. These drugs also activate the **sympathetic nervous system**. Other stimulant drugs with similar pharmacological actions include methylphenidate (Ritalin), phenmetrazine and cathinone. The stimulant drugs caffeine, nicotine and modafinil, also activate the sympathetic nervous system to some extent but have less effect on monoamine neurotransmitter function.

Cocaine and amphetamine have very similar effects on physiological responses, subjective feelings and behavior. Their overall effect on neurotransmitter function is also similar, although their specific mechanisms of action are somewhat different. Their addiction potential is also similar, especially when administered by insufflation, intravenous injection or by inhalation of drug vapor. The two drugs are different regarding their duration of action, in that amphetamine effects persist much longer than cocaine effects. In the current chapter, the term *CNS stimulants* refers to cocaine, amphetamine and methamphetamine unless an exception is noted.

Methamphetamine penetrates the blood–brain barrier (Chapter 4) more rapidly than does amphetamine, producing stronger central effects (e.g., increased arousal and euphoria) with less autonomic activation (increased blood pressure and heart rate) than does an equal dose of amphetamine. The central effects of the two drugs are quite similar, but the methamphetamine salt (methamphetamine hydrochloride) can be vaporized and inhaled whereas the amphetamine salt (d-amphetamine sulfate) cannot be "smoked." This difference in possible routes of administration makes methamphetamine a much more addictive drug. In much of the following text, the term *amphetamine*, especially regarding effects on the brain and body, also refers to methamphetamine.

MDMA (3,4-methylenedioxy-methamphetamine), a drug with some properties of cocaine and amphetamine is discussed in a subsequent section of this chapter.

Cocaine and Amphetamine Use: A Brief History

Since their introduction in the nineteenth century, these sympathomimetic drugs have been used for medical, utilitarian, and "recreational" purposes. Among other effects, cocaine, and especially amphetamine, can delay the onset of fatigue and enable sustained physical and mental effort. This work-facilitation action is quite attractive to many, especially in a demanding, fast-paced modern culture. The drugs are also used often in cultures that require much manual labor, as in rural areas of Latin American countries.

In the years since these drugs became available, the useful and pleasurable effects of CNS stimulants resulted in their frequent nonmedical use by many individuals. However, neither cocaine nor amphetamine has ever achieved enduring widespread social acceptance as a recreational or utilitarian drug. A typical sequence of use of these drugs has been repeated cyclically in several different cultures and countries, including the United States, the United Kingdom, Japan, Thailand, and Sweden (Rutkowski and Maxwell 2009). Initial enthusiasm and acceptance of use are followed by disapproval, government restriction of drug availability, and some decrease of use upon recognition of harmful effects, including high addiction potential. This recurrent sequence has been described as "episodic collective amnesia through history about the behavioral toxicity associated with excessive use of these drugs" (Koob and Le Moal 2006, p. 108).

Several authors have compiled extensive histories of stimulant use in various cultures and countries. Accounts of cocaine use and misuse include that of Erickson et al. (1994) and for methamphetamine Halkitis (2009), Iversen (2006), and Weisheit and White (2009). Many concurrent cultural forces influence use and use disorders of recreational drugs. The following summary of events since 1900 outlines the prevalence of cocaine and amphetamine use in the United States.

Twentieth Century

In the early 1900s, many widely used patent medicines contained cocaine. The oral route of administration for these preparations was less addictive and produced few harmful effects. In 1914, following fabricated or exaggerated accounts of aggression after cocaine use by African Americans, laws were passed making cocaine use illicit. Clandestine recreational use – mainly by disenfranchised elements of society – continued during the following half-century.

From 1931 until 1951, Benzedrine (amphetamine sulfate) was available without prescription for treatment of nasal congestion, for weight loss, and to increase endurance for such activities as long-haul truck-driving and academic study. Amphetamine effects are quite useful for military purposes, which often require constant vigilance and effort for long periods with little food or rest. The armed forces of all nations that fought in World War II used the drug extensively.

For about twenty-five years following the Second World War, amphetamine use increased greatly, including for treatment of certain medical problems (see Box 13.1). Amphetamine use for medical purposes required a prescription, provided readily by many physicians. Large amounts of the drug, diverted from manufacturers or distributors, were easily available for use without medical supervision for recreational or utilitarian purposes. Production of amphetamine by pharmaceutical companies increased tenfold between 1949 and 1968. Use of amphetamine and methamphetamine was known to be "habit-forming," but in general was not considered addictive.

BOX 13.1 Medical uses for stimulant drugs

Amphetamine or similar drugs are useful for treatment of a few medical conditions. Side effects, mostly resulting from sympathetic nervous system stimulation, may cause problems. Although the risk of abuse is only moderate for oral ingestion, some individuals treated for medical problems seek to increase the euphoric effect by progressing to more direct (and addictive) routes of administration.

Obesity. Amphetamine decreases appetite and food intake and increases metabolic rate, resulting in moderate weight loss during the initial few weeks of treatment. Tolerance to the anorectic effect soon develops, requiring larger drug doses to maintain weight loss but also increasing undesirable or dangerous side effects and the risk of addiction. During the years prior to 1970, when amphetamine was less strictly controlled, many individuals used amphetamine to manage body weight, including many who did so without medical supervision. The relatively easy access to the drug resulted in many cases of at least moderate-level degrees of amphetamine abuse and dependence. Currently most physicians are very unlikely to prescribe stimulants for weight reduction.

Narcolepsy. Amphetamine is an effective treatment for narcolepsy, a rare sleep disorder. Narcoleptic individuals treated with amphetamine are at little risk of abuse but may experience some uncomfortable side effects. A newer drug, modafinil (Provigil), is not a dopamine agonist and appears to be as effective as amphetamine for treatment of this sleep disorder.

Attention-deficit hyperactive disorder (ADHD). Amphetamine and methylphenidate (an amphetamine-like drug) are often quite effective in increasing the attention span of both children and adults (Iversen 2006). This cognitive effect of dopamine-stimulant drugs is one of the actions that promote nonmedical (utilitarian) use of amphetamine and cocaine. Treatment of attention disorders is currently the principal medical use of amphetamine and similar drugs.

Attentional disorders (mainly ADHD) affect about 5 percent of school-age children, and an estimated 1.5 million adults also receive medication for this condition (Matthews et al. 2014). Amphetamine (Vyvanse, Adderall) and methylphenidate (Ritalin, Concerta, Focalin) are approved medications for these disorders and are effective and reasonably safe if used under medical supervision. The drugs can produce marked behavioral improvement in children with ADHD (Brown et al. 2005). ADHD in children and adolescents is a risk factor for eventual development of substance use disorders (Chapter 8). However, treatment with stimulant drugs reduces the risk of SUD associated with ADHD, possibly due to the beneficial effect of relief from the symptoms of ADHD (Wilens et al. 2003, Zulauf et al. 2014).

By the late 1960s it became apparent that recreational and utilitarian use of amphetamine was dangerous and addictive. In 1970, a federal law placed the amphetamines (as well as cocaine) in a category (Schedule II) of drugs approved for medical use, but that also had high potential for abuse and dependence. Access to the drug became more difficult and most physicians prescribed less amphetamine for fewer patients. However, individuals who sought the effects of stimulants often turned to the use of cocaine – a "new" and supposedly safer alternative.

During the late 1970s and the early 1980s, the use of cocaine increased, reaching its peak in 1985, when 11.5 percent of those older than age twelve and 17.9 percent of those of ages eighteen to twenty-five reported using cocaine at least once (Anthony 1992). Initially, cocaine use was seen as benign, in part because most use was infrequent, and most users took the drug by the less addictive intranasal route of administration (Figure 13.1). Cocaine was expensive, and for many the high cost limited the amount of use. The acknowledged use of cocaine by many celebrities added glamour to the drug – cocaine was often described as the "champagne of drugs."

Figure 13.1 Cocaine use prevalence in the United States was highest in the 1980s. Most users insufflated the drug. Photo: hiphunter / E+ / Getty Images.

However, even insufflation of cocaine can become addictive. During the early 1980s, drug abuse treatment facilities began receiving requests for assistance from many individuals with cocaine use problems. Most of these heavy cocaine users were quite different from heroin or alcohol addicts. Many were high-functioning individuals in business or professions, and others who could afford the high price of frequent cocaine use. The emergence of cocaine addiction was an important event that promoted a revision of medical diagnosis of substance use disorders.

In the mid-1980s inhalation of cocaine vapor, via the use of "crack" cocaine became more prevalent, driven partly by the emerging AIDS epidemic that presented a serious risk of infection by the use of shared injection needles. However, crack-"smoking" is very addictive, and the appearance of the new form of cocaine increased the number of cocaine addicts as well as a change in their demographic characteristics. Small amounts of crack were sold for a few dollars, making its initial use more accessible to many with less disposable income.

Cocaine addiction increased in low-income inner city residents, although these individuals were not the only consumers of crack cocaine. Heavy crack use had significant negative effects on many minority neighborhoods.

Media coverage, especially related to concerns about crack use by minorities and others of the "underclass," was extensive. In most cases the extent and danger of the "crack epidemic" was exaggerated. In 1986 one-thousand stories about cocaine appeared in the national media. Five cover stories of Time and Newsweek magazines featured cocaine. Penalties of much greater severity were established for trafficking in and possession of crack than for the powder form of cocaine.

Throughout the 1990s and the early years of the twenty-first century, methamphetamine use increased and spread from the West Coast to the Midwest and, eventually, the eastern United States (Gruenwald et al. 2010). Initially, methamphetamine use was most prevalent in rural areas, but in later years the difference between urban and rural use became smaller. Most users were Caucasian or Hispanic, with a much smaller proportion of African Americans producing or consuming methamphetamine. In 1999, an estimated 4.7 percent of twelfth-grade students had used methamphetamine at least once during the past year (Johnston et al. 2009). Amphetamine-related admissions to treatment facilities for SUD increased by sevenfold between the years 1993 and 2003 (Office of Applied Statistics 2006).

In the mid-1990s the use of "ice" became more prevalent. Ice is a street name for a very addictive form of methamphetamine that is similar to crack cocaine in that it can be vaporized and inhaled. However, inhaled methamphetamine produces a longer-lasting high state and often causes more dangerous behavioral and toxic effects than inhaled cocaine.

During the years of increasing methamphetamine use, the drug was produced by many small-scale "meth labs," most of which were located in isolated rural areas. Methamphetamine can be produced by several methods, all requiring the use of toxic and inflammable chemicals. The public health hazard from the toxic by-products of methamphetamine production added to the growing public concern about the addiction and disturbing behavior associated with methamphetamine use.

Early Twenty-First Century

Methamphetamine use peaked early in the first decade of the twenty-first century, but use of both cocaine – especially of crack – and amphetamine has decreased considerably from the higher levels seen in previous years (Table 13.1). Some investigators maintain that use prevalence of the more addictive forms of cocaine and methamphetamine are self-limiting, due partly to the obviously destructive consequences of such practice (Erickson et al. 1994). Only a small percentage of the general US population uses these drugs frequently. However, the estimates of current use prevalence indicate that nearly 5 million individuals consume stimulant drugs – including misuse of pharmaceutical stimulants – although a much smaller number use crack cocaine or methamphetamine (Substance Abuse and Mental Health Services Administration 2018).

Table 13.1 Prevalence of stimulant use and use disorders

	Age 12 or older	Age 18–25
Previous month use		
Cocaine (including crack)	0.8%	1.9%
Crack cocaine	0.2%	0.1%
Pharmaceutical stimulants	0.7%	2.1%
Methamphetamine	0.3%	0.4%
Previous year use disorder		
Cocaine	0.4%	0.7%
Pharmaceutical stimulants	0.2%	0.5%
Methamphetamine	0.4%	0.5%

Note. Estimates of stimulant use and use disorders as indicated by the National Survey on Drug Use and Health (NSDUH). Entries for cocaine and methamphetamine indicate the percentage of the population of the designated age group using the drug within the previous month. Cocaine use estimates include crack use. Entries for pharmaceutical drugs are for previous month misuse (nonmedical use) of amphetamine (Adderall) and methylphenidate (Ritalin, Concerta). Use disorder values are for SUD during the year previous to the survey. Some respondents with use disorder reported no drug use during the previous month (Substance Abuse and Mental Health Services Administration 2018).

Although the anonymity of the respondents is carefully maintained, the self-report surveys may underestimate the actual extent of stimulant use (Rutkowski and Maxwell 2009). One possible limitation is that some parts of the population most likely to use illicit drugs may not be adequately sampled. Nonetheless, these sources of information, based on the responses of many thousands of individuals, are considered valid indicators of drug use, and especially useful for monitoring changes in this behavior over a period of years.

Cocaine, methamphetamine, and pharmaceutical stimulants are dangerous drugs whose use presents a high risk of addiction. Although their use is not common in the overall population, the NSDUH survey indicates that about 2 million individuals are in some degree of trouble from using these drugs. Prevalence of use and the associated risk of addiction are much higher among certain demographic groups. These more vulnerable groups are discussed in subsequent sections.

Methamphetamine use and abuse is also a public health concern in other countries and regions of the world, including the United Kingdom and Australia, the Czech and Slovak Republics, Russia, Thailand, Malaysia, the Philippines, Indonesia, and the Republic of South Africa (Degenhart and Hall 2012, Rawson and Condon 2007).

Stimulant Drugs in the Brain and Body

Amphetamine and cocaine can be administered by insufflating the drug (in powder or granular form), by inhaling the vapor when the drug is heated (crack cocaine, or ice methamphetamine), or administered by intravenous or other methods of injection. Amphetamine can also be taken orally as pills or capsules. Although the patent medicines that contained cocaine in past years were taken by mouth, cocaine is not often taken orally because the drug is less readily absorbed from the GI tract.

Oral administration of amphetamine and similar drugs such as methylphenidate (Ritalin, Concerta) produces slower absorption into the bloodstream and a gradual onset of longer-lasting subjective and behavioral effects, a time course most favored for medical purposes. Extended-release preparations (e.g., amphetamine as Adderall) further prolong the drug action. When cocaine or amphetamine are self-administered without medical supervision (often to produce pleasurable arousal) the drugs are typically insufflated, inhaled, or injected, greatly enhancing their effects. These routes of administration, especially inhalation or injection, present greater risks of addiction.

Pharmacokinetics: Bioavailability

Subjective and behavioral effects commence within ten to thirty minutes after oral ingestion of amphetamine. Effects begin within two or three minutes after insufflation of amphetamine or cocaine, thirty to forty-five seconds after intravenous injection, and within eight to ten seconds after inhalation (Verebey and Gold 1988). Amphetamine effects last much longer than do the effects of cocaine, a major difference between the two drugs. Subjective effects indicate the difference in duration, as do studies of blood levels of the drugs (Newton et al. 2005). Plasma half-life of cocaine ranges from forty-eight to seventy-five minutes (Wilkinson et al. 1989), and half-life for amphetamine and methamphetamine is about twelve hours (Cook et al. 1993). The half-life for the amphetamines is influenced by the pH of the urine, in that this value with alkaline urine may be extended to sixteen hours, or reduced to eight hours with acid urine (Davis et al. 1971). The effects peak sooner and more sharply when the drugs are inhaled or injected. Duration of effects depends to some extent on the dose, but at moderate doses the cocaine high may last fifteen to thirty minutes, and the subjective effects of amphetamine can endure for several hours. The physiological and behavioral effects abate before the drug levels in the brain decrease markedly, indicating the development of acute tolerance. The drugs are metabolized in the liver, with the metabolites excreted in the urine. At normal pH about 30 percent of amphetamine is excreted unchanged in the urine, but a much smaller amount of cocaine is excreted without being metabolized.

Pharmacodynamics: Effects on Brain Function

Amphetamine and cocaine enhance the actions of the **monoamine neurotransmitters** dopamine, noradrenaline, and serotonin. Peripheral effects (on the autonomic nervous system) result from the increased noradrenaline activity, whereas the primary central nervous system effects on cognition, emotion and behavioral activation come mainly from the increased activity in dopamine circuits (Koob and Le Moal 2006). The agonist effect on monoamine receptors is indirect in that the drugs do not bind with and activate these receptors. Both cocaine and amphetamine increase the amount of neurotransmitter available in the synapse, although by different mechanisms of action.

After release into the synaptic space, dopamine and the other monoamine neurotransmitters are removed from the synapse by transporters (complex protein molecules) located in the membrane of the presynaptic neuron. Cocaine blocks this reuptake from the synapse, allowing more binding and activation of dopamine receptors in the postsynaptic neuron and resulting in the subsequent increase in effect on neurons downstream from the site of drug action (Figure 13.2) (Izenwasser 1998). Cocaine exerts this indirect agonist effect on serotonin as well as on the function of dopamine and noradrenaline.

Amphetamine (and methamphetamine) also act at the membrane transporters whose function is to recapture and move dopamine and noradrenaline from the synapse into the presynaptic neuron. However, the action of these drugs is more complex than the relatively simple reuptake-blocking action of cocaine. The molecular structure of amphetamine is similar to that of the neurotransmitters, so the membrane reuptake transporters transfer the drug into the presynaptic

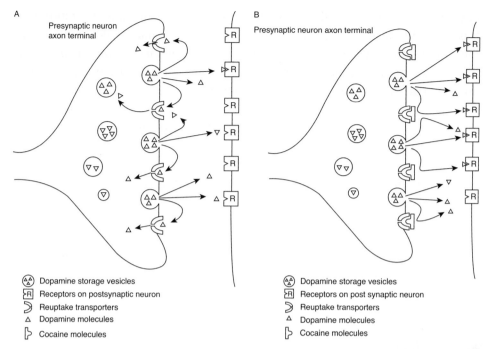

Figure 13.2 Cocaine mechanism of action on dopamine function at the synapse. (A) Release of dopamine molecules into the synapse and their reuptake into the presynaptic neuron. The reuptake limits dopamine binding to postsynaptic receptors. (B) Cocaine blocks the reuptake transporters, increasing the amount of dopamine in the synapse and dopaminergic transmission.

neuron. Additionally, amphetamine enters the neuron by directly penetrating the neuron membrane. Inside the neuron, amphetamine interferes with storage of the neurotransmitter in protected vesicles. After the drug causes premature release of dopamine from these storage sites, the neurotransmitter is pumped back into the synapse by a reverse action of the membrane transporter mechanism. Through these alterations of neuronal processes, greater amounts of dopamine and noradrenaline are released into the synapse, increasing activation of receptors in the postsynaptic neuron (Fleckenstein et al. 2007, Sulzer et al. 2005).

The CNS stimulant drugs indirectly cause increased activation of all five types of dopamine receptors. Dopamine function produces or supports several aspects of behavior, emotion and cognition, and the role of dopaminergic activity varies among the specific receptor types and different brain areas. Positive reinforcement, the directing of attention and the initiation of movement are the dopaminergic functions most involved in drug-seeking and the development of addictive behavior (Chapter 5). Research with antagonist drugs that block specific dopamine receptors demonstrates how activation of these receptors mediates the effects of cocaine and amphetamine. Positive reinforcement in animal subjects and feelings of pleasure in humans produced by amphetamine or cocaine administration is at least partially dependent on activation of the D1, D2, and D3 dopamine receptors. These three receptors have slightly different functions, as indicated by animal studies of conditioned place preference and operant self-administration of drugs, but all three contribute to the reinforcement produced by the CNS stimulant drugs. Drugs that block these receptors also reduce the motor-activating effects of cocaine and amphetamine in animal subjects (Hanson and Fleckenstein 2009, Koob and Le Moal 2006).

Amphetamine also has complex influences on neuron function in addition to the primary action of increasing dopamine release into the synaptic space. The drug inhibits the neurotransmitter-metabolizing action of monoamine oxidase (MAO), providing an indirect agonist effect on all the monoamine neurotransmitters and probably increasing the acute effects of the drug. However, the heavy chronic use typical of addiction also depletes the monoamine neurotransmitters. Addictive use of methamphetamine can be neurotoxic, as described later in this chapter (Hanson and Fleckenstein 2009, Kitanaka et al. 2003).

Acute Effects

At low to moderate doses, all CNS sympathomimetic stimulant drugs have similar acute effects. The initial effects include **increased energy**, alertness and sociability, elation or euphoria, and decreased fatigue, need for sleep, and appetite. These effects typically occur after administration of 5–20 milligrams of oral amphetamine, methamphetamine, or methylphenidate; 100–200 milligrams of oral cocaine, 40–100 milligrams of insufflated cocaine, or 15–25 milligrams of intravenously injected or smoked cocaine or methamphetamine (Harris et al. 2003, Mendelson et al. 2006). Higher doses may produce more intensely pleasurable effects, but also present a risk of aversive, dangerous consequences.

Behavioral and Physiological Effects

Many controlled studies have confirmed the performance-enhancing effects of amphetamine in both human and animal subjects (Iversen 2006). The effects are most general and reliable when the subjects are fatigued or sleep-deprived. Methamphetamine improved performance of human subjects on tests of attention, reasoning ability, and various computerized cognitive tasks (e.g., Johnson et al. 2000). These effects are dose dependent in that a high dose of amphetamines increases arousal level to a degree that often impairs complex cognition.

Amphetamine reliably prolongs high states of vigilance, an effect valued in military operations. The drug was used by armed forces in the Second World War, and in many subsequent conflicts. In most cases, this use was not clandestine, but approved of and encouraged by military commanders (Iversen 2006). Because of current knowledge of the addictive potential and other hazards of amphetamine, its widespread use among military personnel has diminished considerably. However, use of amphetamine on extended combat flights and in other situations requiring prolonged effort and vigilance continued during relatively recent years (Bower 2003, Kenagy et al. 2004).

Amphetamine can counteract fatigue, increasing stamina and endurance. Professional athletes made use of this effect in the years before the practice was prohibited and illicit drug use was detected by compulsory urine testing. Perhaps the most pervasive use of stimulants was in the sport of long-distance bicycle racing, such as the Tour de France (Figure 13.3). The death of amphetamine-using cyclists due to accidents, extreme exertion, dehydration, and overheating prompted eventual reforms that reduced the use of performance-enhancing drugs in cycling and other sports (Voet 2002).

Figure 13.3 In the years before urine screens for detection of drug use were introduced, many bicycle racers and other athletes often used amphetamine to increase endurance. Photo: GibsonPictures / E+ / Getty Images.

Cocaine and amphetamine also stimulate activity in the sympathetic branch of the autonomic nervous system, causing increased body temperature and sweating, blood pressure and heart rate. Metabolic rate is increased, and appetite decreased. At low doses, these effects are seldom harmful in a healthy person.

Chronic use results in a modest decrease in body weight, an effect further described in Box 13.1.

The CNS stimulant drugs have complex effects on sexual arousal, interest, and performance, depending heavily on the context or situation as well as the drug dose. An aphrodisiac effect can encourage dangerous sexual behavior, further described in the subsequent section on adverse effects of stimulant use.

Self-Administration of Stimulants in Nonhuman Subjects

Studies with animal subjects dramatically demonstrate the powerful positive reinforcement effect of stimulant drugs. Rats and primates readily perform operant responses to self-administer cocaine or amphetamine via implanted intravenous catheters. Behavior of animal subjects in these operant paradigms indicates that the positive reinforcement produced by stimulants is stronger than for other types of addictive drugs. In early studies, animals were given unlimited access to the drugs. Some animals persistently self-administered increasing amounts of cocaine or amphetamine, eventually ignoring other basic needs (food and water) until they became debilitated and died (Dworkin et al. 1986, Johanson et al. 1976). Lethal patterns and amounts of drug self-administration were more likely with cocaine than with heroin (Bozarth and Wise 1985). In later studies, rats' access to cocaine was restricted to limited periods. Under the conditions of limited access, operant self-administration also increased in a behavioral pattern similar to that of human cocaine addicts, although drug intake did not cause death (Ahmed and Koob 1998, Paterson and Markou 2003).

The reward value of drugs is also tested in the conditioned place preference paradigm (Figure 13.4). After rats are administered a stimulant drug in a distinctive location, and no drug in a different distinctive place, they are later tested for their place preference as they choose between the two places. A greater amount of time spent in the drugged location indicates preference for the drugged state, and the positive reinforcement of the drug-conditioned stimuli. Cocaine, amphetamine and methylphenidate (Ritalin) readily produce place preference in laboratory rats and mice.

Animal self-administration paradigms differ markedly from the situations or behavior of humans with substance use disorders. However, compulsive drug use is a critical feature of drug addiction in humans, and a rat paradigm demonstrates an analog of **compulsive cocaine self-administration**. After extensive experience with cocaine-reinforced operant behavior, rats continued to work for cocaine injections even though the drug-rewarded responses also produced an aversive conditioned stimulus (Vanderschuren and Everitt 2004) or footshock (Pelloux et al. 2007). Operant responses of rats with more limited histories of cocaine reward were suppressed by the aversive stimuli.

Figure 13.4 This laboratory rat prefers the distinctive location where it was administered amphetamine, relative to the place where it was injected with water. The conditioned place preference paradigm tests the reward value of drug treatments.

The behavioral and neurological effects of cocaine and amphetamine in animal subjects provided much evidence for the development of current theories of addiction as presented in Chapter 5. Important components of these theories, including the behavioral functions of dopamine and glutamate, changes in hedonic setpoint, incentive sensitization, and the effects of stress, were initially conceived as a result of research on the actions of stimulant drugs. Studies of the effects of other addictive drugs also helped to validate these theories.

Subjective Effects

The positive feelings of initial low-dose effects have often been described in literature and accounts intended for the general public, as well as in clinical or scientific reports. In a study conducted in 1955, the account of a subject after amphetamine administration describes the powerful euphoriant effects:

I began to feel a deep sense of well-being come over me and a feeling of confidence and power. I feel similar when I'm playing the piano at my best ... a feeling of exhilaration and satisfaction, not unlike the feeling that accompanies sexual satisfaction. All feelings of inadequacy or depression that I've felt at other times seem remote and trivial. (Lasagna et al. 1955, p. 156)

In a more recent autobiographical account, Maia Szalavitz describes the subjective effects of insufflating cocaine:

On coke, I felt a smug sense of superiority, of being in on something, of being powerful and utterly desirable. I felt intellectual clarity, sophistication and strength.... My heart rate elevated, and I felt a quickening, a sense that everything was moving faster and becoming more exciting.... Cocaine made it seem like you were able to conquer the world. (Szalavitz 2016, p. 107)

Descriptions of the feelings produced by drugs vary in details among individuals, but these accounts reflect a common element of stimulant effects at low to moderate doses. Rather than producing an unnatural "high" state, the subjective states are often familiar and much like the natural good feelings that accompany pleasant, rewarding experiences or activities. Another user describes his initial experience with methamphetamine:

The odd thing about methamphetamine is that it doesn't get you that stoned, at least not in the conventional sense of the word.... I actually felt more sober after taking the drug than I did before, as if I had awoken from a long slumber. Unlike other drugs that I had tried before, meth didn't blur the senses, but sharpened them to a machinelike focus.... Most drugs are about losing control or escaping to some distant region of the mind. Meth was exactly the opposite: I felt ultrasharp. Edgy and exhilarated. (Owen 2007, p. 31)

Many scientific studies have also assessed the subjective effects of methamphetamine (summarized by Rush et al. 2009) and cocaine (e.g., Collins et al. 2006, Rush et al. 1999). These studies are representative of many that employ standardized rating scales. Subjects in these experiments typically indicate effects such as "like drug," "good mood," "excited-elated," "talkative-friendly," and "euphoric" after receiving CNS stimulant drugs.

Concurrent with the positive, enjoyable feelings these drugs often increase the motivation for enthusiastic performance of tasks that might be onerous, boring, or fatiguing. A subject who had received amphetamine describes these feelings:

Increased energy ... I have done things today I usually dislike but which I rather enjoyed doing today. The last hour and a half of work is usually an effort, today I felt fine – did not have my usual lethargic period after lunch ... nothing seemed impossible of accomplishment ... I was able to organize my work quickly and efficiently. My mind felt clear all day. (Grinspoon and Hedblom 1975, p. 78)

Differences among Individuals in Response to Stimulant Drugs

An array of pleasurable and useful effects makes the use of cocaine and amphetamine very attractive to many people. Controlled laboratory studies confirm that most individuals who are administered cocaine or amphetamine like the drug effects and want to receive more of the drug (Iversen 2006).

However, the use of these drugs is not as pleasurable for some individuals who either respond less positively or find the effects of even low doses to be uncomfortable or aversive. De Wit and colleagues administered a low dose of amphetamine to thirty-one subjects, among whom twenty described the drug effect as an increase in friendliness and elation, but eleven reported depression and anxiety (de Wit et al. 1986). Similar variations in response to amphetamine are reported in many other studies of the subjective effect of the drug. A better understanding of these differences might provide useful information concerning the vulnerability to addiction.

Generalizations about the relationship between personality factors and drug effects are limited, in part because of the differences among instruments used to assess personality (Chapter 8). However, evidence from several investigations suggests that positive responses to stimulants are more likely in individuals with higher levels of sensation seeking and extraversion, and negative responses may predominate in those with more negative affect and neuroticism (de Wit 2005).

Genetic factors partially account for variations in dopamine function thought to play a major role in the response to addictive drugs. The intensity of feelings of elation after amphetamine administration was related to the presence of specific genetic variations (single-nucleotide polymorphisms) in the dopamine transporter gene (Lott et al. 2005). Similar studies have found correlations between the response to amphetamine and the presence of alleles of other genes, including those controlling the production of noradrenaline transporters (e.g., Dlugos et al. 2009).

Several studies indicate that progesterone, a hormone whose levels are higher during the luteal (premenstrual) phase of the menstrual cycle, attenuates the positive response to stimulant drugs in women. Orally administered amphetamine produced stronger positive responses in women during the follicular phase (lower progesterone and higher estrogen levels) of their menstrual cycle than during the luteal phase (White et al. 2002). Sofuoglo and colleagues found that administration of progesterone to women during the early follicular phase diminished positive responses to inhaled cocaine (Sofuoglo et al. 2002). Another study found a similar attenuation of positive drug effects in both men and women who received progesterone prior to intravenous administration of cocaine (Sofuoglo et al. 2004). As described in Chapter 11, progesterone also decreases pleasurable effects of smoking tobacco in nicotine-dependent women.

Some investigations reveal a positive correlation between pleasant feelings after amphetamine administration and the level of hormonal stress responses to a challenging social situation (Wand et al. 2007, Hamidovic et al. 2010). In the stress conditions, subjects were required to prepare for an employment interview in one experiment, and to solve a difficult arithmetic problem within a limited time in the second investigation. Cortisol secretion, cardiovascular indicators of arousal, and negative mood states induced by the social stress tests predicted the degree of pleasurable response to acute amphetamine administration. The social stress tests were conducted separately (on different days) from the amphetamine administration sessions.

These results indicated that individuals who react more intensely to stress also respond more positively to the dopamine-agonist stimulant drug. The positive correlation might also imply that higher stress responses sensitize the reward system to certain drug effects. As described in Chapter 5, the effects of stress promote the development of substance use disorders. A large amount of evidence supporting the role of stress in SUD has come from research with animal subjects as well as from clinical studies with cocaine addiction in humans (e.g., Sinha et al. 2006).

Most of the controlled experiments with human subjects were conducted with individuals who did not have stimulant use disorders. It is not known whether differences in "drug liking" of these subjects predict the development of stimulant abuse or **dependence**. However, an individual who is more rewarded (positively reinforced) by initial experimentation with amphetamine or cocaine is more likely to continue use of the drug, and repeated use of stimulants is a definite risk for the development of **addiction**.

Injecting or Inhaling Cocaine and Methamphetamine

When concentration of stimulants in the brain rapidly rises to high levels, as with inhalation or intravenous injection of the drug, humans report intensely pleasurable effects. The experience is often said to be similar to sexual orgasm – except that the feeling is stronger and of longer duration. The rapid onset of this euphoria gives rise to its description as a "rush." Rather than the natural good feeling typical of low to moderate doses taken orally or by insufflation, accounts of the initial reactions to more direct routes of administration often describe a decidedly different experience. A methamphetamine addict's description: "he feels as if he is ascending into the cosmos, every fiber of his body trembling with happiness" (Rylander 1969, p. 49). Not surprisingly, there is a strong motivation to prolong and repeat the experience. However, acute tolerance develops rapidly, limiting the duration of the intensely pleasurable effects (Breiter et al. 1997). Not only does the euphoric effect soon fade, feelings of depression and dysphoria then follow the initial pleasurable feeling. In early use, the intensity of both the initial rush and the delayed aversive effect is related to the drug dose – larger doses produce stronger emotional changes. With chronic use the pleasurable effects diminish and the aversive dysphoria emerges sooner and eventually dominates the experience. High doses of the drug – especially methamphetamine – can also lead to periods of unproductive frenzied activity, stereotyped behavior and other disturbing consequences. These aversive effects are intensified by largely futile attempts to recreate and extend the initial positive effects by taking more of the drug.

A description of the euphoria of initial crack cocaine use, followed by the reactive dysphoria, comes from Bill Clegg's *The Portrait of the Addict as a Young Man*:

> He feels the high at first as a flutter, then a roar. A surge of new energy pounds through
> every inch of him.... It spreads down from his temples into his chest, to his hands and
> everywhere. It storms through him – kinetic, sexual, and euphoric – like a magnificent
> hurricane. Then, as it recedes, a bleak and cold feeling arises and he misses the first
> rush even before it's left him and not only does he want more, he needs it. (Clegg 2010,
> p. 84)

The dysphoric state that follows the initial pleasurable feeling occurs sooner with cocaine than with amphetamine. With amphetamine (including methamphetamine), a period of energetic positive feeling that may endure for hours follows the brief, intense pleasure of the rush. This longer period of less intense rewarding effects is also subject to tolerance, and with chronic use becomes shorter and soon replaced by aversive agitation, anxiety and depression. However, both the early euphoric effects and the limited relief from the emergent dysphoria – gained from taking more of the drug – contribute to the repetitive, compulsive drug use characteristic of addiction to stimulants.

Stimulant Use Disorders

The strong positive reinforcement produced by cocaine or amphetamine promotes repeated use, often leading to higher doses and deeper involvement with the drug. Richard Pryor, an entertainer popular in the 1980s, sometimes included grim references to his cocaine addiction in his stand-up comedy performances: "When you take a hit of cocaine, it makes you a *new man* – and the first thing the new man wants is a hit of cocaine!" The incentive to escalate drug intake is especially great with inhaled (crack or ice) and injected (cocaine or methamphetamine) routes of administration. Sidney Cohen, a prominent investigator of addictive drugs, described cocaine as "the ultimate reinforcer" (Cohen 1985, p. 3). Dr. Cohen's comment was made at the time when cocaine use was at its highest prevalence in the United States.

Prevalence of Addiction in Users of Stimulant Drugs

Before the increased prevalence of cocaine use in the late 1970s, the drug was thought to be not very addictive. This erroneous belief was largely due to the prevailing view of addiction at that time, which emphasized the overt, easily recognizable withdrawal syndromes that occur with heroin or alcohol dependence. Compulsive, seemingly uncontrollable drug use, coupled with a withdrawal syndrome unlike that seen with opiates or depressants, is characteristic of stimulant dependence.

By the early 1980s, cocaine use had become widespread, especially in urban areas. Many middle-class, gainfully employed people (a quite different population compared to most heroin addicts of that time) found that their use of cocaine had become a disturbing problem and sought help from medical and mental health professionals. These individuals reported an inability to stop or limit cocaine use, even though the drug caused depression, insomnia, panic attacks and many other adverse effects. Based primarily on the overwhelming clinical evidence of cocaine abuse and dependence, the criteria for substance use disorders were modified in the DSM-IV revision of 1994. These changes in diagnostic criteria resulted in a greater reliance on behavioral indicators of SUD, and less requirement for overt physiological signs (tolerance, withdrawal) for identification of drug dependence (Washton and Zweben 2009).

A reminder: two terms – *dependence* and *addiction* – are often used to designate a severe SUD. *Dependence* is a DSM-IV term, designating a severe SUD. In the DSM-5 revision of 2013, *dependence* refers primarily to the presence of drug tolerance and withdrawal – which can occur in nonaddicted individuals as well as in those who are addicted and use drugs compulsively. However, the two terms are often used interchangeably – with dependence equaling addiction, especially in pre-2013 investigations.

Given the (now obvious) conclusion that users of stimulants can become addicted, what is the addictive potential of these drugs? Many people use a stimulant drug only once or a few times. Most of these individuals who experiment with the drug do not advance to regular use or dependence, as shown by the large-scale epidemiological surveys such as the National Survey on Drug Use and Health (NSDUH). These surveys reliably indicate that the number of respondents using stimulants at least once is larger than that of the previous-year users, which is larger than the number of more frequent or regular users.

The number of individuals in treatment for SUD related to stimulants is not an accurate indicator of the degree of addictive potential. Only a small proportion (approximately 10 percent) of those with a drug use disorder seek professional help (Courtney and Ray 2014, Substance Abuse and Mental Health Services Administration 2018).

A realistic estimate of addiction potential requires a determination of its prevalence among those who use the drug frequently. During the years 1991 through

1993, NHSDA (a national survey forerunner to the NSDUH) respondents provided extensive information about cocaine use and its consequences. These self-reports of cocaine use were compared to DSM-IV dependence criteria to determine the prevalence of cocaine addiction (Chen and Kandel 2002). Of nearly 88,000 respondents age twelve or older, 2.5 percent (2,349 individuals) reported using cocaine at least once during the previous year. Of these cocaine users, 35 percent (822) had used the drug during the previous month, and about 5 percent (117) used daily or almost every day. Approximately 14 percent of previous-year users satisfied the criteria for cocaine dependence.

Chen and Kandel found a close relationship between frequency of cocaine use and the likelihood of dependence. Whereas 17 percent of those who used cocaine once or twice a month were dependent, 32.7 percent of once- or twice-weekly users and 73.8 percent of daily users were classified as dependent. The results show clearly that regular use of cocaine is a definite risk factor for addiction to the drug, and the risk increases with greater frequency of use. Approximately three out of four daily users are dependent on the drug, and a smaller proportion of less frequent users are also addicted.

The results indicate that the addiction potential of cocaine is greater than that of alcohol, and is similar to that of tobacco. Most individuals who drink alcohol every day are not addicted (Chapter 10), but a majority of daily smokers are to some extent nicotine dependent (Chapter 11). As with alcohol and most other psychoactive drugs, harmful consequences can occur in the absence of addiction or even frequent use of cocaine.

The NHSDA surveyed cocaine usage in the early 1990s, shortly after the time of peak levels of cocaine use in the United States. The survey also provides information about cocaine use by intravenous injection and inhalation (use of crack). The results concerning amounts of use and addiction to cocaine given above include these more intense and addictive routes of administration. Eighty-eight percent of cocaine-using respondents took cocaine by insufflation, with 12.1 percent of these users becoming addicted. Eleven percent injected the drug, with 32.2 percent of the IV users becoming addicted. Nineteen percent smoked crack, with addiction prevalence of 37.8 percent. Since the sum of percentage-of-use values for the three methods of use is greater than 100 percent, some respondents used more than one route of administration. The analysis of survey results did not give the correlation between frequency of use and dependence for IV injection and inhalation, but it is apparent that these routes of administration are more addictive than insufflation.

Comparison of SUD indicators between the NHSDA survey of the late 1990s and the NSDUH 2018 survey (Table 13.1) is limited in that the later survey assessed all cocaine use disorders rather than addiction/dependence. The 2018 estimate indicates that almost half of previous-month cocaine users suffer from SUD, but that proportion includes users who have a less severe use disorder, some of whom are not addicted. Additionally, "previous month use" (2018 survey) also includes more frequent cocaine users, whose use patterns were separately assessed in the earlier survey.

The 2018 NSDUH survey also indicated that nearly one-third of all current misusers of pharmaceutical stimulants (amphetamine and methylphenidate) had a use disorder for these drugs. About one-fourth of young adult age (eighteen to twenty-five) misusers were identified as having an SUD.

Large-scale epidemiological studies of methamphetamine use that include detailed information on drug dependence, similar to the NHSDA survey of cocaine use in the early 1990s, have not been conducted. Although cocaine and methamphetamine have similar pharmacological properties, patterns of use are somewhat different. Studies directly comparing the use and effects of the two stimulants are rare (Wu et al. 2009). Simon and colleagues compared methamphetamine and cocaine use patterns in 183 individuals. Methamphetamine users took the drug on most days, and did so throughout the day. Cocaine users were more likely to use the drug in the evening, and their use was more sporadic (on fewer days than the methamphetamine users). Cocaine appeared to be used more often in a recreational manner than was methamphetamine. Typical methamphetamine use patterns were more often identifiable as addiction (Simon et al. 2002).

The 2018 NSDUH survey (Table 13.1) indicates a much lower use prevalence of methamphetamine than cocaine, but a higher proportion of SUD in methamphetamine users. Gonzales and colleagues found that individuals seeking treatment for methamphetamine addiction progressed more rapidly from first use to regular use and then to treatment entry than those dependent on cocaine (Gonzalez et al. 2000). Methamphetamine thus appears to have even greater addictive potential than cocaine, and some adverse consequences of heavy use (e.g., behavioral effects and neurotoxicity) are greater for methamphetamine than for cocaine, as further described in a subsequent section.

Risk Factors

The factors predicting problematic use of cocaine and amphetamine are similar to risk factors for use disorders with other addictive drugs. These risk factors include a family history of SUD (with both genetic predisposition and childhood experiences), early use of psychoactive substances, certain personality traits and psychiatric disorders. However, frequent and regular use of cocaine or amphetamine leads many individuals into a use disorder even without the presence of additional risk factors. The high reward value of the stimulants for most individuals apparently makes mere **exposure to and availability of** these drugs a greater risk factor than for other addictive drugs (Washton and Zweben 2009). The highly reinforcing actions of stimulants for experimental animals also indicates a relatively greater importance of their pharmacological effects for addiction, compared to other risk factors (Koob and Le Moal 2006). In other words, these drugs have high addiction potential largely because for most individuals their use is so rewarding – and addiction to stimulants is less dependent on other risk factors than is the case for other addictive drugs.

Cocaine, and especially methamphetamine, are associated with better (more enjoyable), longer, and more varied sexual activity. Initial use of stimulants increases energy, stamina, confidence and libido, as well as delayed and more intense orgasms (Halkitis 2009, Rawson et al. 2002, Washton and Zweben 2009). In addition to direct enhancement of sexual responses, drug effects on sexual desire and function can also be subtle and indirect. A participant in a methamphetamine users' focus group describes how the drug influences his sexual feelings:

> I'm kind of sexually inhibited, so it allows me to access part of myself that I normally can't.... It kind of allows me to get past those fears of rejection, or fears of not being good enough for somebody or not being sexy enough for somebody, because it makes you feel sexy. (Hunter et al. 2012, p. 113)

Stimulants are not aphrodisiacs for everyone, but about 50 percent of men and 20 percent of women seeking treatment for cocaine abuse reported positive sexual effects from their initial use of cocaine (Washton 1989). Methamphetamine produces similar effects in 60–70 percent of treatment-seeking men and women (Rawson et al. 2002). Clinicians who treat stimulant addiction find that the **aphrodisiac effect** is an important risk factor for use disorders of cocaine and methamphetamine. Individuals whose sexual activity is enhanced by stimulants are at increased risk of addiction due to the intense reinforcement value of the drug-sex combination (Washton and Zweben 2009).

Nonmedical Use of Pharmaceutical Stimulants

Physicians often treat the symptoms of ADHD with stimulant medications (Adderall, Ritalin and similar drugs). These drugs, most often prescribed for children, adolescents and young adults, promote increased concentration and can improve academic performance. Individuals treated for ADHD sometimes illicitly sell or give the drugs to friends for use without medical supervision (Singh et al. 2014, Veliz et al. 2013). The situation of relatively easy access to stimulant drugs is somewhat reminiscent of that of the mid-twentieth century when such access to these drugs resulted in their widespread use for utilitarian and recreational purposes.

The possibility of adverse effects from use of stimulants is much greater without medical supervision. Addiction is a possible consequence of nonmedical use, especially when the tablets or contents of capsules are crushed and insufflated or injected. Elizabeth Wurtzel gives an autobiographical account of Ritalin addiction, in which she progressed from taking several tablets each day to frequent insufflation. Her heavy use of methylphenidate eventually led her to cocaine addiction (Wurtzel 2002).

Table 13.1 indicates that the misuse prevalence of pharmaceutical stimulants is similar to that of cocaine. However, the proportion of current users of Adderall or Ritalin who develop SUD appears to be less than the proportion of users of cocaine and much less than the proportion of methamphetamine users.

Development and Progression of Stimulant Addiction

Infrequent low-dose use of cocaine or amphetamine/methamphetamine produces pleasurable and useful effects. These drugs do not produce "instant addiction," even in individuals who start their use with the most addictive forms, IV injection or inhalation. Compulsive use can however, start to emerge in some users after only a few exposures to the highly reinforcing drug effects. Rapid progression from initial drug exposure into abuse and addiction occurs more often with cocaine than with alcohol or marijuana (Wagner and Anthony 2002, Florez-Salamanca et al. 2013). A similar relatively rapid development also occurs with methamphetamine addiction.

As with entry into alcohol dependence, there are various pathways leading from casual "social" cocaine or methamphetamine use into the overwhelming involvement of addiction (Erickson et al. 1994, Halkitis 2009). Several biographical or autobiographical accounts of stimulant addiction portray some of these different routes into stimulant use disorders (e.g., Carr 2008, Sheff 2008, Woodward 1984). Although these stories are not objective findings of scientific investigations, they convey the subjective experiences of addiction as well as accounts of addictive behavior as seen by friends, family, and associates of the addicts. These accounts describe use patterns and consequences of stimulant dependence often heard by clinicians who treat individuals with such use disorders.

For most users in early stages of addiction, frequent stimulant use at low doses does not disrupt ongoing activities but increases work performance, elevates mood and improves social interactions (at least at a superficial level). Workers in retail sales occupations may be at special risk for frequent use of stimulants, and development of dependence due to the drug's facilitation of work performance. Maintaining enthusiasm for extended periods while selling automobiles or describing the chef's daily special in a high-end restaurant seem easier with a boost to self-confidence and energy from cocaine or amphetamine. Individuals in journalism, entertainment, and many other occupations may also use stimulants to maintain high levels of performance. These same effects can also increase the pleasure and excitement of a lifestyle that includes frequent parties, drinking and use of other recreational drugs. As mentioned previously, sexual attraction and interest are often heightened and some aspects of sexual performance are enhanced. Many other examples could illustrate the positive stimulant effects that promote frequent use, and most of these effects still occur at early stages of excessive use.

Prolonged use of stimulants produces tolerance, especially for the desired pleasurable effects. As amounts and frequency of use increase, several adverse consequences emerge, interfering with activities previously enhanced by cocaine or methamphetamine. Increased enthusiasm for work often merges into states of agitated excitement that impair performance, especially if the work requires careful deliberation. Problems often arise in personal interactions as sensitivity to subtle social cues suffers. Anxiety, irritability, and early hints of paranoia (that become more disruptive as use escalates) replace the increased self-confidence of initial stimulant use. Increased sexual performance gives way to frequent impotence in men. Fatigue and insomnia are common, but rest and sleep are compromised, especially with longer-lasting methamphetamine. Even when the user recognizes that his discomfort and maladaptive behavior are caused by the stimulant, attempts to stop or decrease use are very difficult. Craving for the drug continues, and as the compulsion to use progresses, the individual experiences "wanting, even though not liking" the drug.

Concurrent Use of Other Drugs
Most stimulant-dependent individuals soon discover that the more disturbing effects of chronic high-dose methamphetamine or cocaine use can be managed by concurrent use of other drugs. Alcohol, benzodiazepines (such as Xanax), cannabis, and opiates (such as Vicodin or OxyContin) relieve much of the **anxiety and agitation** of heavy stimulant use. The relief from the aversive effects allows the heavy stimulant use to continue and greatly facilitates further progression into addiction. Much cocaine and methamphetamine use occurs in locations and among people who often use these other drugs freely. All the drugs, and in particular alcohol, may be available in these social situations, and their concurrent use is condoned and encouraged.

Stimulants can also counteract some of the depressant effects of alcohol and heavy cannabis use. Individuals who use methamphetamine or cocaine concurrently with high doses of these other drugs (especially alcohol) can reach higher levels of intoxication without falling asleep or otherwise losing consciousness. Not surprisingly, dependence on alcohol or an opiate drug is not unusual in individuals also addicted to stimulants. As many as 60–80 percent of treatment-seeking cocaine addicts meet diagnostic criteria for alcohol use disorder, and the alcohol problems often developed subsequent to the heavy use of cocaine (Carroll et al. 1993). First-person accounts of stimulant abuse typically describe dual or multiple addictions (e.g., Carr 2008, Sheff 2008).

Stimulant Use Binges
A characteristic pattern of stimulant use is additional drug intake soon after the initial euphoric effect fades. Although the pleasurable effects are decreased and

shortened due to tolerance, the drive to continue use is powerful, and often results in extended "runs" of compulsive drug-taking. Runs or binges may continue for many hours or several days, until the drug supply is exhausted. This pattern of use is quite different from those of other addictive drugs. When smoking marijuana or injecting heroin, even addicted users typically reach a desired level of intoxication and stop drug intake for several hours (depending in part on the degree of dependence). Some alcohol-addicted individuals drink in extended binges, but at some point, they sleep or become too intoxicated to continue drinking (unless they are also using cocaine or methamphetamine!).

During the extended binges of stimulant use, the arousal, agitation, and other aversive effects persist and worsen. Alcohol or other drugs taken to ease these stimulant effects also produce discomfort and dysphoria. The heavy stimulant use of addicted individuals, even if they are "only" insufflating cocaine or methamphetamine, incurs a definite toll. The damaging consequences come not only from the direct effects (and aftereffects) of the drugs but also from the addictive lifestyle. David Carr comments on the hard life of a cocaine addict relative to individuals dependent on heroin:

> Cokeheads, well, that's a different story. All that ripping and running sparks a kind of corrosion – no sleep, lots of booze to take the edge off – that wears even the hardiest souls down to a nub. It is a lifestyle that leaves marks. (Carr 2008, p. 108)

Because binges are so debilitating, a stimulant user may rest and take no cocaine or methamphetamine for a day or two following an intense and extended run. The intermittent pattern of drug use often allows the addicted individual to deny (to herself) the presence of a drug use disorder. "I don't use every day – sometimes I go for a week or longer without doing any coke – so how could I be an addict?" (Washton and Zweben 2009).

Inhalation and Intravenous Injection of Stimulants

The NHSDA epidemiological survey indicated that in the early 1990s, about 10 percent of cocaine users injected the drug intravenously, and about 20 percent smoked crack cocaine. Individuals using these routes of administration were three or four times more likely to be addicted than were those who took cocaine by insufflation. Advancing from insufflation into the more addictive methods of cocaine use is a major step in the progression of cocaine or methamphetamine dependence (Kiluk et al. 2013). Many who use cocaine or methamphetamine stop short of taking this step, often because they see the grim results in the lives of those who do start "smoking or shooting" the drugs. With inhalation or IV use of stimulants, the aversive and dangerous consequences become more intense and disruptive (Figure 13.5). The drug effects of lighter use seen as beneficial – improved work performance, increased sociability, more intense and pleasurable sexual activity – are mostly gone. What remains is an intense focus on continued stimulant use – all other activity diminishes or disappears. Binges are usually longer and harder to interrupt – often stopping only when no more drug is available or the individual is completely exhausted to a degree that even the stimulant cannot overcome. Descriptions of injecting or smoking cocaine or methamphetamine are reminiscent of early studies of rats and monkeys self-administering the drug until death – with one difference being that the experimental animals had unlimited supplies of the stimulant.

Box 13.2 includes an excerpt from David Carr's account of cocaine addiction and crack smoking, illustrating some of these features of stimulant dependence.

BOX 13.2 Smoking crack cocaine

David Carr, a reporter for the *New York Times*, eventually recovered after years of drug abuse and addiction. In his book *Night of the Gun*, he recounts his extensive use of cocaine and alcohol as well as his experiences in treatment and recovery. Chapter 18, entitled "Crack: A Brief Tutorial," describes how despite the warnings of cocaine-using friends, he started using the more addictive form of the drug. Within a short time, the pleasures of insufflating cocaine were replaced with compulsive binges of crack smoking:

> I ended up with a whole new crop of running buddies, people who lived and breathed coke life with little regard for other pursuits....
>
> There is no such thing as a social crack user. There is only this *one thing* until all the crack is gone. The drinking, the chatting, dancing that goes with snorting coke is not really part of the crack experience. Smoking crack is less of a party and more of a religious ceremony, with a group of people gathered around a central icon – in this case the crack pipe....
>
> After two minutes, or two hours, or two days, supply dwindles and desperation sets in. People fall to their knees and claw the carpet for a crumb that might have been dropped. But smoking crack was a completely unmanageable activity from the beginning, the vehicle for my trip from party boy to junkie.

David Carr died of natural causes in 2015.

From NIGHT OF THE GUN by David Carr. Copyright © 2008 by David Carr. Reprinted with the permission of Simon and Schuster, Inc. All rights reserved.

Figure 13.5 Inhalation of stimulant drug (crack cocaine or crystal methamphetamine) vapor typically results in the compulsive use of severe addiction. Photo: Apolinar B. Fonseca / Moment / Getty Images.

Intravenous injection of stimulants is even more dangerous than inhaling the vapor from crack or ice. The risk of fatal overdose is greater, especially when an opiate drug such as heroin is combined with the stimulant for a "speedball" injection – increasing the euphoric effect of both drugs and reducing the unpleasant agitation from the stimulant. A high dose of heroin can stop respiration and cause death as it counteracts the arousing stimulant effect. Injection also presents the risk of infection with HIV, hepatitis, and other diseases (Domier et al. 2000).

Intravenous drug injection is more likely in methamphetamine users than in users of cocaine, partially because the longer time course of methamphetamine results in a less frequent need for injections to maintain the desired drug effect (Washton and Zweben 2009). Many addicted IV methamphetamine users are more cognitively impaired, have more intense craving, and are less engaged in treatment than are individuals who use smoking or other routes of administration (Galloway et al. 2010, Rawson et al. 2007).

Consequences of Heavy Cocaine or Methamphetamine Use

Chronic high-dose use of cocaine or methamphetamine results in several very aversive and dangerous consequences. Most of these behavioral, cognitive, and psychiatric changes typically emerge after extensive heavy use of the stimulant, but some can occur soon after initial use in vulnerable individuals.

Effects on Sexual Activity

The previously described aphrodisiac effect is often an alluring, desirable consequence of stimulant use. However, the increased sexual activity associated with cocaine or methamphetamine use is often hazardous to both heterosexual and homosexual populations (Corsi and Booth 2008, Chen et al. 2012, Vosburgh et al. 2012). The primary sex-related risks associated with stimulant use are increased amounts of unprotected and more hazardous types of sex with multiple, often anonymous partners. These sexual practices increase the risk of infection with syphilis, HIV, and other sexually transmitted diseases.

Individuals with higher levels of impulsivity are more likely to use illicit drugs and to suffer from drug and alcohol use disorders (Chapter 8). Poor impulse control contributes to hazardous sexual activity as well as to heavy drug use, so the characteristic sexual behavior often seen in stimulant users may partially be a result of this preexisting behavioral tendency. As with many correlates of heavy drug use, the cause–effect direction is difficult to establish.

The use of methamphetamine among homosexual men has received much attention. The concern is due to the greater sex-related risks for gay and bisexual men and the more prevalent use of this drug among men who have sex with men (MSM) (Rutkowski and Maxwell 2009, Hoenigl et al. 2016). Box 13.3 describes methamphetamine-driven sexual activity of some gay men in New York City. The actual incidence of such behavior was not documented.

BOX 13.3 Methamphetamine abuse in a New York City bathhouse

Excerpt from a *New York Times* article, January 2004, by Andrew Jacobs:

Bob looked haggard but was feeling fabulous. Chewing gum at a manic clip, circling the labyrinthine halls of the West Side Club on a recent Sunday afternoon, he had been awake since Friday, thanks to a glassine pouch of crystalline powder he had tucked beneath the mattress of a room he had rented in this Chelsea bathhouse.

The powder, methamphetamine (crystal meth), had helped Bob conquer a half-dozen sex partners during a thirty-five-hour binge. Like many of the men cruising the two-level club lined with closet-sized cubicles, Bob, a thirty-seven-year-old advertising copywriter, was "tweaking," high on a wildly addictive stimulant that has been sweeping through Manhattan's gay ghettos.

"The stuff is a wonder," he said, taking a pause from his prowling. Asked about condoms, Bob shrugged. "Whatever," he said, turning away.

BOX 13.3 Continued

There were plenty of condoms for the taking, courtesy of the management, but, in conversations with a dozen patrons who acknowledged using crystal, only two men said they were following the rules of engagement in the age of AIDS. "Some guys just throw you out of the room if you pull one out," said one of the men. "To them, rubbers are a killjoy."

The incidence of methamphetamine use in the urban gay population rose in the late 1990s, and the increase persisted into the second decade of the twenty-first century. The illicit status of the drug appealed to many gay men who felt that their sexual preference and lifestyle were also illicit and disapproved of by mainstream culture. The increased energy and stamina from methamphetamine use fit well with some aspects of urban gay life, such as long-duration dance parties. The drug-produced disinhibition and increase of sexual endurance also facilitated anonymous sex with multiple partners and anal sex without use of condoms (Reback et al. 2018). In MSM populations, with greater incidence of HIV infection, these practices were especially dangerous. Efforts to educate younger men were intended to reduce complacency about the threat of AIDS and the risks of methamphetamine-driven sex. These efforts apparently promoted safer sexual behavior that eventually became more common among urban gay men (Halkitis 2009, Washton and Zweben 2009).

In addition to the risks of infection from sexually transmitted disease, stimulant use often degrades the quality of sexual interaction. Although sexual pleasure may be increased, the delayed orgasm and prolonged endurance can result in "marathon" hours-long bouts of intercourse that often become mechanical and compulsive. Sexually aroused users of cocaine or methamphetamine often focus almost completely on their own pleasure, ignoring the feelings and even the presence of their partner. While stimulants may work well for the user seeking anonymous sex, this effect can be quite damaging to long-term romantic relationships. Many gay men maintain that social and sexual relations in their subculture became harder and more predatory, largely due to the widespread use of methamphetamine (Halkitis 2009).

Some heavy users of methamphetamine eventually turn to masturbation while viewing pornography, finding this activity preferable to the "nuisance" of dealing with a sexual partner (Weisheit and White 2009). These negative effects on sexual activity occur in both straight and gay stimulant users.

With high doses of stimulants, and especially with chronic heavy use, the increased level of sympathetic nervous system arousal often causes an inability to attain or maintain erection. The drug still increases sexual desire, so the impotence is quite frustrating and stressful. The erectile dysfunction is sometimes counteracted by medications like sildenafil (Viagra) or similar drugs (Halkitis 2009).

Stereotyped Behavior

Low doses of amphetamine, methamphetamine, or cocaine increase physical activity, an effect that can facilitate productive work output and athletic performance. With high doses the effects on motor activity change as compulsive stereotyped behavior emerges. As the dose increases, behavior becomes progressively more constricted and repetitive. Stimulant-produced stereotyped behavior has been investigated in several animal species and frequently occurs in humans addicted to methamphetamine (Iversen 2006) or cocaine (Fasano et al. 2008). After injection of a high dose of methamphetamine, laboratory rats make repetitive head movements for extended periods. Primates and other animals lick or bite themselves compulsively. Humans exhibiting stereotyped behavior may spend hours sorting objects (jewelry, coins, tools, etc.) or disassembling electronic equipment, engines, or other machinery (Weisheit and White 2009). The repetitive behavior sometimes takes the form of excessive cleaning or household activities, as in repeatedly vacuuming floors or rearranging furniture. Other stereotyped behavior is either odd or bizarre – such as extended periods of lining up rocks according to size or counting the flakes in a box of cereal. Humans, as well as animals, also often obsessively groom and pick at their skin. With continued high-dose drug use, normal activity decreases, as the stereotyped behavior becomes pervasive and resistant to interruption.

A Swedish investigator originated the term *punding* to designate stimulant-induced stereotyped behavior in humans (Rylander 1971). The term *tweaking* is sometimes used (informally) to describe the repetitive behavior, although this term also refers to methamphetamine use in general.

The dopamine-agonist effect of the stimulant drugs underlies punding (Kelley et al. 1988). Dopamine activity in the brain promotes movement, in addition to having an important role in positive reinforcement and directing attention. Parkinson's disease is a movement disorder resulting from dysfunction of dopaminergic circuitry, and dopamine-replacement drugs (such as L-dopa) used for treatment of Parkinson's disease can also cause punding (Fasano and Petrovic 2010).

Extreme forms of punding drastically alter normal activity, and for the duration of the drug effect greatly impair social interaction. Injuries can result from compulsive scratching and picking as the drug user attempts to remove "bugs" felt to be crawling under the skin. The sensations that cause the self-injurious behavior are tactile hallucinations (Snyder 1972). The neurological changes that produce obsessive behavior may also cause abnormal patterns of cognition that eventually develop into dangerous states of paranoia (Iversen 2006, Koob and Le Moal 2006).

Psychiatric Syndromes

Stimulant-dependent individuals, and in particular those seeking treatment for their heavy drug use, commonly suffer from a considerable amount of distress. A study of 1,016 methamphetamine users seeking treatment revealed a high prevalence of psychiatric symptoms. Depression and anxiety were the most frequent complaints that approximated DSM-defined psychiatric disorders. These methamphetamine users also scored high on scales indicating psychotic-like symptoms and paranoid ideation. Twenty-seven percent reported attempting suicide and 43 percent reported problems with controlling violent behavior (Zweben et al. 2004). Similar proportions of psychiatric symptoms or syndromes occur in other large populations of individuals seeking treatment for methamphetamine abuse (e.g., Shoptaw et al. 2003). Common effects of chronic high-dose cocaine and methamphetamine use are sometimes early signs of serious psychiatric conditions or dangerous antisocial behavior. Depression may indicate a risk for suicide. Increased arousal level and vigilance can merge into extreme anxiety. Irritability may predict physical violence. Suspicion can intensify and become paranoia.

The elevated rate of psychiatric symptoms can be due to immediate or delayed drug effects, genetic predispositions for psychopathology, or a combination of these factors. Regardless of etiology, co-occurring psychopathology is frequently seen in drug treatment facilities and is characteristic of cocaine (Carroll and Ball 2005) and methamphetamine abuse (Rawson et al. 2005). Methamphetamine use is more closely associated with a variety of adverse effects, including psychiatric problems, than is use of cocaine, MDMA (ecstasy), nicotine, alcohol, or cannabis (Kono et al. 2001, Mahoney et al. 2008).

Paranoid psychosis is not an unusual occurrence in heavy users of methamphetamine and – to a lesser extent – in cocaine users (Erickson et al. 1994, Iversen 2006, Rush et al. 2009). Paranoid psychosis presents special hazards to afflicted individuals as well as those they may encounter. Paranoid individuals often mistakenly perceive threats in entirely innocuous situations and sometimes respond with violent aggression (Figure 13.6). Even when the delusions do not cause aggression, intense fear is typical (Angrist 1994).

Nick Reding's nonfiction book *Methland* portrays methamphetamine use and its effects in a small Iowa town. The following excerpt describes a psychotic episode

Figure 13.6 Heavy and prolonged use of cocaine, amphetamine, or methamphetamine often causes severe paranoia, including delusions that people or situations present imminent threats. Photo: RapidEye / E+ / Getty Images.

of a methamphetamine "cook" (a manufacturer of "homebrew" methamphetamine) who was also a heavy user of the drug:

> On a cold winter night in 2001, Roland Jarvis looked out the window of his mother's house and saw that the police had hung live human heads in the trees of the yard. Jarvis knew the police did this when they meant to spy on people suspected of being meth cooks. The heads were informants, placed like demonic ornaments to look in the windows and through the walls. As Jarvis studied them, they mumbled and squinted hard to see what was inside the house. Then the heads, satisfied that Jarvis was in fact cooking meth in the basement, conveyed the message to a black helicopter hovering over the house.... Jarvis knew he had to hurry: Once the helicopter sent coordinates to the police, it would be only moments before they raided the house. (Reding 2009, p. 40)

In his paranoid frenzy, the meth cook attempted to dispose of the chemicals he had stockpiled for making the drug. After accidentally igniting these caustic and inflammable chemicals, he suffered severe burns on most of his body. This example of paranoia is exceptionally lurid, but such psychotic states occur and can lead to disastrous outcomes.

Paranoia, often a component of psychosis, has been observed in stimulant addicts since the use of these drugs became widespread. For many years the paranoia was thought to be caused primarily by a drug-induced increase in concern about the quite real threats and dangers experienced by the typical "street addict." These individuals risk arrest and incarceration due to their frequent involvement in illegal activities, including, of course, their drug use. Added dangers came from encounters with drug dealers, other criminals or violence-prone people. Early research demonstrated that amphetamine treatment produced psychosis in experimental subjects who were not drug addicts and who were maintained in a controlled and protected laboratory environment (Angrist and Gershon 1970, Griffith et al. 1968). Such experiments would be prohibited under current ethical standards of research. However, in a more recent laboratory investigation less severe degrees of suspicion and paranoia were produced in human subjects who smoked crack cocaine under controlled conditions (Mooney et al. 2006). These controlled studies demonstrate that dopamine-agonist stimulants can produce paranoid psychosis, and the psychiatric syndrome is not a result solely of a dangerous lifestyle.

Risk factors for methamphetamine-induced psychosis include first drug use at a younger age, larger amounts of drug use, having more premorbid schizoid characteristics, and a certain type of allele in the gene that produces the dopamine transporter. Alcohol dependence, major depression or other psychiatric disorders as well as antisocial personality are also risk factors for development of psychosis after methamphetamine use (Chen et al. 2003, Ujike et al. 2003).

The occurrence of paranoid psychosis becomes more likely with repeated stimulant use, even if the dose is not increased. Potentiation of effects resulting from repeated drug administration is termed sensitization – a process in some respects opposite to that of tolerance. Sensitization resulting from chronic stimulant treatment has been demonstrated in animal experiments, primarily with stereotyped behavior. Controlled studies with human subjects have also demonstrated sensitization to amphetamine effects on several types of behavior (Strakowski et al. 1996). The physiological changes responsible for sensitization are not well understood, but the process is thought to be involved in stimulant-produced psychosis (Iversen 2006).

Stimulant-induced paranoid psychosis is often indistinguishable from psychosis not related to drug use (Shaner et al. 1998), although certain features unique to methamphetamine psychosis can aid in differentiating the similar disorders (Iversen 2006). Visual hallucinations are rare in nondrug psychosis, but hallucinations involving faces often occur with the amphetamine-produced disorder. The tactile hallucinations (feelings of insects under the skin) occur only in stimulant users. Antipsychotic medications, many of which are dopamine antagonists, relieve the most disturbing symptoms of paranoid psychosis, whether induced by stimulant use or due to other unknown causes (Misra et al. 2000).

Duration of psychosis after termination of stimulant use is quite variable. In most cases symptoms abate within hours or days but sometimes persist for months

(Rawson et al. 2005). Such enduring effects, including lingering anhedonia, greatly decrease the probability of secure abstinence and successful recovery from stimulant use disorders.

Antisocial Behavior: Violence and Child Abuse

Individuals who use methamphetamine are often involved in antisocial behavior, including child abuse, interpersonal violence, and various types of crime (Cartier et al. 2006). As with other drug effects on behavior (including that of alcohol), pharmacological actions are intermingled with cultural, situational, mental health, and personality factors. The specific causes of much antisocial behavior cannot be easily identified. The high prevalence of stimulant use in individuals seen by law enforcement and emergency medical personnel does not prove that the drugs cause the criminal behavior or injuries (Farabee and Hawken 2009). However, the close association of stimulant use with a variety of harmful consequences is well established. In many cases, paranoid thinking, emotional lability, panic, and lowered impulse control are instrumental factors (Logan et al. 1998). Most investigators who study the problem are convinced that the drugs, and especially methamphetamine, are major threats to public health and safety (Shoptaw et al. 2009).

The occurrence of domestic violence and child abuse is high among methamphetamine users (Baskin-Sommers and Sommers 2006, Brown and Hohman 2006). The association is greatest among methamphetamine users for whom domestic life is often chaotic, and the abusive behavior is frequent even without the disruption of substance abuse (Haight et al. 2005).

In *Methland*, Reding relates how methamphetamine use and production were associated with the deterioration of the quality of life in a small Iowa town (Reding 2010). The drug's availability and consequences of its use seemed to be a cause as well as a result of the community's widespread problems. Reding's account is representative of economic and cultural changes that occurred throughout the rural Midwest during the 1990s and early years of the twenty-first century (Weisheit and White 2009). Industrialization of agriculture played an essential role in loss of jobs and the severe economic decline of many small towns. Small-scale production of methamphetamine provided income for many "meth cooks." As the drug became easily available, its energizing antifatigue effects facilitated work in one or more demanding, low-paying jobs for many individuals, and methamphetamine addiction increased greatly. The drug also provided temporary euphoria for those whose lives were bleak and discouraging. Mental health and substance abuse treatment is inadequate in most rural communities, so methamphetamine addicts had little access to professional assistance. Many public health and safety problems followed the introduction of methamphetamine into these communities. Crime (including illegal activities not involving methamphetamine production, sale, and use) increased greatly, as did domestic violence, child neglect, and abuse. High demands were placed on fire departments, emergency medical personnel, and law enforcement facilities in communities as methamphetamine use increased.

Stimulants do not cause violence or dangerous behavior in all users of these drugs, but they increase such behavior in a subset of individuals, probably those who already had a tendency for aggression or antisocial behavior. Even these limited effects result in the widespread use of stimulants presenting a danger to society in general as well as to the drug users.

Cognitive Impairment

Many individuals with a history of heavy stimulant use are impaired in some aspects of memory, attention, and executive functioning. These and other **cognitive deficits** are revealed by performance on neuropsychological tests and are implicated in the ongoing difficulties of stimulant abusers in management of daily living and in finding and maintaining employment (Proebstl et al. 2018, Weber et al. 2012). Cognitive impairment has been detected in 40 percent of some populations of methamphetamine users (Rippeth et al. 2004).

Scott and colleagues conducted a meta-analysis of cognitive function in methamphetamine users, and Jovanovski and colleagues did a similar analysis with cocaine users (Jovanovski et al. 2005, Scott et al. 2007). In the statistical procedure of meta-analysis, the results of many different studies are combined, confirming the generality of the findings as well as providing estimates of the size of drug effects.

Jovanovksi and colleagues' meta-analysis combined the results of fifteen studies of cognitive function that included 481 individuals with cocaine dependence and 586 healthy comparison subjects. The largest differences (deficits) found in the drug-using subjects were in measures of attention, visual memory and working memory. Attentional deficits were revealed by performance on tasks that required sustained and focused attention. Executive function was impaired for complex decision-making tasks, but not for simpler requirements for information processing. The impairments were specific and subtle rather than generalized, a finding consistent with earlier studies of cognitive deficits in cocaine users (Bolla et al. 1998).

Scott and colleagues' meta-analysis was based on the results of eighteen studies that tested 487 individuals with methamphetamine use disorder and 464 healthy comparison participants. The drug users showed moderate deficits in episodic memory, executive function (e.g., response inhibition, novel problem solving) and complex information-processing speed. Somewhat smaller effects were evident in attention/working memory, and language. These cognitive impairments appeared to be somewhat greater than those found by Jovanski in cocaine-dependent individuals. Other investigators also conclude that methamphetamine use is associated with more general and severe impairments than is cocaine use (Meredith et al. 2005).

The extent and degree of cognitive impairment is thought to be related to the duration and intensity of stimulant use (Simon et al. 2002). However, evidence to confirm the effect of amount of drug use is inconsistent, possibly due to inaccurate self-reports of drug use history (e.g., Scott et al. 2007).

As with most other problems often seen in stimulant users (e.g., psychiatric symptoms, antisocial behavior) the drug effects are confounded with many other possible causes for the cognitive deficits. Most stimulant-abusing individuals consume much alcohol and many use other addictive drugs. Simon and colleagues found that 20–35 percent of individuals with methamphetamine use disorder were also alcohol dependent (Simons et al. 2005). Several psychiatric disorders are risk factors for all substance use disorders, and some of these conditions (e.g., ADHD) include definite cognitive deficits (Jaffe et al. 2005, Sim et al. 2002). Infection with HIV, more prevalent in methamphetamine abusers, is another condition that can result in impaired cognition (Carey et al. 2006).

These and other factors, especially in methamphetamine users, may precede drug use and contribute to differences revealed by neuropsychological tests. Simon and colleagues assessed cognitive performance in methamphetamine-addicted subjects who were screened to ensure that none were alcohol dependent, and did not suffer from a medical condition or another psychiatric disorder (Simon et al. 2010). These drug-using subjects exhibited mild degrees of cognitive impairment as compared to healthy comparison subjects. When years of education were included as a co-factor in the analysis, the group differences were no longer significant. These results suggest that subject differences other than drug use were responsible for lower scores on the cognitive tests. Careful screening of subjects to eliminate identifiable confounds (such as amount of education) might clarify the effects of stimulant use on cognitive function. However, subject pools resulting from such screening would not represent the typical stimulant-abusing population and so might limit the generality of findings about cognitive deficits in these heavy users of cocaine or methamphetamine.

Research with animal subjects provides convincing evidence that administration of cocaine or amphetamine can cause a variety of persistent cognitive impairments in rodents and primates (Iversen 2006). Studies with animal subjects are better controlled than are investigations of humans, and confounded factors can be essentially eliminated. However, the dose and patterns of drug administration in animal studies are often not representative of human drug abuse, even after adjustment for the higher metabolic rates in small animals. Some stimulant effects on cognition in humans cannot be satisfactorily modeled in animal subjects. However, Reichel and colleagues investigated methamphetamine effects in a rat analog of episodic memory. Rats exhibited deficient memory of contact with a novel object seven days after methamphetamine treatment. Methamphetamine was self-administered by the animals in a procedure intended to emulate drug doses and use patterns of human addicts (Reichel et al. 2012).

Cognitive impairment is often greatest in withdrawal, during early abstinence from stimulant use. The emotional distress of withdrawal can influence performance on neuropsychological tests. Some improvement may gradually occur as abstinent time accrues, but it is not clear whether cognitive function changes substantially (Scott 2007). Some long-term studies show that deficits in episodic memory and other cognitive functions – although of decreased severity – remain for at least several months after abstinence from use of methamphetamine (e.g., Johanson et al. 2006) or cocaine (Strickland et al. 1993).

Deficits of working and episodic memory, attentional processes and executive functions are likely to cause problems in daily life. Memory lapses, difficulty in focusing and staying on task, and poor impulse control are often more apparent in the lives of stimulant-abusing individuals, even after a period of drug abstinence. In at least one study, the impact of these cognitive impairments was confirmed by means of systematic recording and analysis of daily activities (Sadek et al. 2007).

Appropriate social interactions require a relatively high level of cognitive function, including recognition of subtle behavioral cues in other individuals. Some methamphetamine addicts are deficient in social skills, possibly due to drug-impaired social-cognitive function (Homer et al. 2008). Deficits in social awareness could lead to problems for the methamphetamine user in dealing with family, friends, or other individuals.

The deficits also limit the effectiveness of treatment for drug addiction, especially when cognitive behavioral tactics are used to maintain abstinence. Cognitively based interventions involve developing and using new strategies to avoid relapse. Adequate memory and attention abilities are required to prevent resumption of drug use. Stimulant-addicted individuals with neuropsychological deficits are more likely to violate treatment program rules and drop out of treatment prematurely (Ahoronavich et al. 2003, Simon et al. 2004).

Deficits in decision-making and impulse control often seen in stimulant-dependent individuals are similar to (although less severe than) impairments resulting from damage caused by strokes or wounds to areas of the prefrontal cerebral cortex, and in particular the orbitofrontal cortex (Gold et al. 2009).

Neurotoxicity

The neurological consequences of chronic stimulant use include persistent alterations in monoamine neurotransmitter function, changes in glucose utilization and blood circulation, and damage to the microstructure of neurons. In some cases, neuron death and atrophy of brain tissue occur. These changes contribute to the long-term emotional, cognitive and behavioral effects of the drugs.

Studies with rodent and primate subjects demonstrate the neurological effects of repeated high-dose administration of stimulants (Meredith et al. 2005, Scott et al. 2007). Some neurological changes are adaptations to the prolonged hyperstimulation of neural circuits by methamphetamine or cocaine. These adaptations include a decreased number of dopamine receptors, dopamine transporters, and reduced activity of enzymes involved in the synthesis of dopamine and other monoamine neurotransmitters.

Neurotoxic effects as indicated by early studies with animal subjects used drug administration regimens that exceeded the stimulant intake of most human addicts, but investigations that are more recent have indicated similar effects with lower doses. Persistent neurological changes are more evident from methamphetamine than from cocaine treatment (Iversen 2006).

Brain-imaging studies conducted with stimulant-using humans provide results consistent with much of the evidence from animal studies (Payer and London 2009). PET scans and functional MRI studies show that chronic users of methamphetamine exhibit altered neurological activity, including decreases in markers of dopamine and serotonin function that persist during months of drug abstinence. The differences in dopamine activity are found in the orbitofrontal cortex, the dorsolateral frontal cortex, and in the subcortical caudate-putamen areas (Volkow et al. 2001b). In many studies, the degree of neurological abnormalities correlate positively with the severity of cognitive deficits.

Magnetic resonance stereoscopic studies reveal differences in metabolic function of the brain related to methamphetamine use. Most of these investigations indicate a lower level of N-acetylaspartate (a marker of neuronal integrity) in brain structures most affected by methamphetamine (e.g., Sung et al. 2006). These and other indicators of neuronal health suggest that chronic methamphetamine use is associated with injury or death of neurons.

In some cases, MRI scans reveal frontal lobe atrophy in heavy methamphetamine users (Halkitis 2009).

The mechanisms by which methamphetamine produces persistent brain abnormalities, including injury or death of neurons are complex, but partially understood. Methamphetamine releases dopamine from protected vesicular storage locations inside the neuron. High levels of dopamine, either within or outside the neuron are then metabolized to form reactive molecules that cause oxidative stress and inflammation, damaging the neuron terminals. The drug also appears to initiate apoptosis, a natural process that culminates in the death of neurons. Other toxic actions include damage of DNA and alteration of gene expression (Cadet and Krasnova 2009).

The brain eventually recovers, at least partially, from the effects of heavy stimulant use. The decreased density of dopamine receptors and other adaptive changes recover (normalize) sooner and more completely than does the damaged neuron microstructure. Some neurological abnormalities are still detected after several months of drug abstinence (Volkow et al. 2001a). Investigations with addicted human subjects are by necessity conducted only after extensive drug use, so information about neurological structure and function prior to drug use is not available. It is possible that stimulant-abusing individuals had low levels of dopamine receptors or reuptake transporters prior to drug use, predisposing them to develop a use disorder (Meredith et al. 2005).

Other Toxic Effects

In addition to damaging effects on the brain, methamphetamine or cocaine use is associated with **medical problems of multiple organ systems** (Mooney et al. 2009). Chronic methamphetamine use produces the greatest damage, but toxic effects, including death, can occur after a single dose of any of the catecholamine-agonist stimulants. As with most SUD, other factors common to stimulant abuse can contribute to the medical problems. Infections (including AIDS and hepatitis), toxic impurities in drug preparations, lack of sleep and adequate nutrition, and other drug use (primarily alcohol) can cause or worsen many of the medical problems frequently seen in cocaine-or methamphetamine-addicted patients. However, controlled studies with animal subjects demonstrate that chronic high-dose stimulant administration can cause the medical problems similar to those often seen in human users of the drugs (Meredith et al. 2005).

Most of the drug-produced harm to organ systems and biological function is a result of the release of catecholamine neurotransmitters (dopamine and noradrenaline) in the brain and the sustained extreme activation of the sympathetic nervous system. These actions increase the demands on the cardiovascular system and cause hypertension and elevated body temperature. Cerebral hemorrhage and myocardial infarction (heart attack) can be acute effects of large stimulant doses (Davidson et al. 2001). Coma and death can result from hyperthermia after a single administration of cocaine or methamphetamine (Numachi et al. 2007). With chronic stimulant use, the sustained high blood pressure and greater body temperature eventually damage the kidneys, liver, and other organ systems (Karch 2002).

Many studies document effects of cocaine and methamphetamine on the cardiovascular system (Kaye et al. 2007, Maceira et al. 2014). Damage to the heart, cardiac arrhythmia and other irregularities occur often in stimulant users. Younger, otherwise healthy stimulant users may not experience the most serious cardiac problems, but those with preexisting cardiac conditions are susceptible to these drug effects (Weisheit and White 2009).

A toxic effect with often-dramatic visual impact is "meth mouth." Media accounts of the harm of methamphetamine use often feature photographs of severely decayed and abscessed teeth. Although the anti-methamphetamine campaign literature may exaggerate the prevalence of the worst problems, many chronic users of the drug have poor dental health unrelated to stimulant use but seen more often when dental care is unaffordable or unavailable. The specific problems seen frequently in methamphetamine users include (1) rampant dental caries, (2) fractured teeth, and (3) periodontal disease (Curtis 2006).

Prenatal Exposure to Stimulants

The emergence of crack cocaine as a recreational drug in the mid-1980s triggered general public alarm, a reaction driven in part by sensationalistic media coverage. Demands were made for increased government intervention to suppress the use of cocaine. Of particular concern was the possibility that cocaine-using pregnant women inflicted severe damage to their unborn children. Public expectations of harm to children fueled implementation of controversial legal sanctions directed toward addicted mothers. The "**crack baby**" scare resulted in hundreds of women in thirty states undergoing criminal prosecution for child abuse because of their cocaine use during pregnancy. Scholars and professional organizations condemned efforts to sterilize or criminally prosecute addicted mothers as ethically and legally flawed, racially discriminatory, and an impediment to providing appropriate medical care to these women and their children (Haack et al. 1997, Paltrow et al. 2000).

Many of the initial reports of the catastrophic effects of prenatal cocaine exposure were exaggerated and influenced by the evaluators' preconceived attitudes toward the mothers' drug use (identification as a drug addict), ethnicity and socioeconomic status. The teratogenic action of many confounded factors, including use of other legal or illicit drugs, malnutrition, poor prenatal care and lack of medical attention were seldom considered (Held et al. 1999).

Frank and colleagues conducted a systematic review of thirty-six scientifically rigorous studies that avoided the shortcomings of previous investigations (Frank et al. 2001). This review indicated that the effects of prenatal cocaine exposure could not be differentiated from those of the other confounded factors, especially tobacco use. In most cases, cocaine use was not specifically associated with lower scores on tests of development from birth to age six. These authors pointed out that cocaine use during pregnancy was often a marker for poor health and impaired care giving due to factors ranging from infectious diseases to domestic violence – all risks to the mother and child.

Studies with rodents and primates, not influenced by the confounded factors mentioned above, show subtle abnormalities in brain development in offspring of female animals treated with stimulants during pregnancy (Dow-Edwards 2011, Glatt et al. 2000, Harvey 2004). The primary differences in the brain are in cortical and mesolimbic dopaminergic systems, and in the hippocampus. Behavioral impairments are seen mainly in executive function, memory, inhibitory control and reversal learning. Impairment is absent or minimal in performance of simple tasks, but becomes more apparent with more demanding behavioral requirements.

Most of these cognitive impairments resulting from prenatal cocaine exposure diminish if the animals are reared from birth in an enriched environment.

Most investigations of physical, behavioral and cognitive effects of prenatal stimulant exposure in humans reported since 2000 feature extensive attempts to account for the influence of confounded variables. In these studies, typically conducted prospectively (rather than retrospectively), cocaine or methamphetamine use by the mothers is determined by means of interviews and urine testing, and analysis of meconium (neonatal feces) for the presence of drug metabolites. Subjects (mothers) in exposed and nonexposed groups are matched for socioeconomic status, tobacco and other substance use, and additional relevant factors that might influence the children's physical characteristics, cognition and behavior. The effects of these correlated variables are also controlled statistically by multivariate analysis of results. Observers who are unaware of the subjects' exposure condition provide objective behavioral assessments. The Infant Development, Environment and Lifestyle study (IDEAL) is an example of an improved, large-scale study of prenatal drug effects (Arria et al. 2006).

No distinguishing physical features can identify a baby as cocaine or methamphetamine exposed. Cocaine or methamphetamine use during pregnancy does not cause detectable characteristic birth defects, but the use of either drug is associated with slower gestational growth and lower birth weight (Bada et al. 2002, Smith et al. 2006). The decreased fetal growth is thought to result partially from the vasoconstrictive effects of stimulant drugs, which reduces the flow of blood and the supply of oxygen and nutrients to the developing fetus. Inadequate food intake by stimulant-using mothers could also contribute to the lower mean birth weight.

Behavioral – and to a lesser extent cognitive – differences associated with prenatal stimulant exposure are detectable even after accounting for the influence of known confounded variables. These differences are much less dramatic and extensive than those described by early, inaccurate reports that triggered the alarmist "crack baby" warnings of the late 1980s. It appears that differences seen in the motor activity of neonates and very young babies disappear within a few months (Smith et al. 2011). However, increased emotional reactivity may persist at some level, sometimes predicting the emergence of externalizing behavior and ADHD characteristics (LaGasse et al. 2012). As children mature and enter the more challenging social environment of school, the stimulant-exposed children appear to lag behind, exhibiting less mature behavioral patterns (Richardson et al. 2011). Some subtle deficits in language function appear to persist into early adolescence (Bandstra et al. 2011, Lewis et al. 2004). There is much variability in both exposed and nonexposed children. Some children without a history of prenatal stimulant exposure will exhibit behavior similar to those whose mothers did use cocaine or methamphetamine during pregnancy.

In general, effects of prenatal exposure to cocaine or methamphetamine appear to be similar. The similarity occurs although the populations studied typically differed for cocaine, compared to methamphetamine-exposure investigations. Caucasian or Hispanic women and babies, often from rural areas, were most often the subjects of the methamphetamine studies, whereas urban African Americans were typical subjects of the cocaine studies.

Research teams attempt to control for the many known factors that might cause or contribute to differences associated with prenatal stimulant exposure. However, especially for behavioral differences observed in older children and adolescents, control of some relevant and confounded variables is difficult or impossible. Conduct disorder and other externalizing behaviors in children are attributed in part to neurobehavioral disinhibition, a condition influenced by genetic predisposition and early environment (mainly parenting practices; Chapter 8). These factors are risks for substance use disorder and are often correlated with prenatal stimulant exposure. As a child whose mother used cocaine or methamphetamine matures, the increase in externalizing behavior might be due to any, or a combination of these factors – family environment, genetic background, or prenatal stimulant exposure.

The protection against the effects of prenatal stimulant exposure provided by rearing of experimental animals in an enriched environment can be used as evidence to promote programs to provide experiences intended to reduce the similar impairments in human babies.

Withdrawal from Heavy Stimulant Use

DSM-5 criteria for withdrawal from prolonged cocaine, amphetamine or methamphetamine use include dysphoric mood, emotional lability, fatigue, vivid unpleasant dreams and insomnia or hypersomnia (American Psychiatric Association 2013). Many clinical observations and a few systematic studies have confirmed the occurrence of most of these symptoms in individuals who have stopped long-term heavy stimulant use. Craving for the drug is also a common feature that is strongest during early abstinence. The dysphoria wanes within a few weeks in most cases. The craving is more persistent, but also diminishes with the passage of time.

A female patient vividly describes the depression, dysphoria and agitation of methamphetamine withdrawal:

> After every methamphetamine binge I was bouncing off the walls experiencing crazy shifting moods. It was ten times worse than the most intense PMS I've ever experienced. One minute I felt fine and the next minute I was either crying hysterically or boiling over with anger. At other times I felt just plain numb. I was out of my mind. I got mad easily and flew off the handle. Everything annoyed me, even the stupidest little

problem. My boyfriend said that he just could not stand being with me like this. I got scared, thinking that maybe meth had damaged my brain and that this horrible condition would never go away. I couldn't imagine tolerating such a depressing, unhappy existence. But eventually, within a week or so it passed, just as my therapist said it would. The idea that this misery was just temporary is what allowed me to keep going each day. Otherwise I probably would have given up and just gotten high all over again. (Washton and Zweben 2009, p. 149)

The aftereffects of stimulant use differ from the withdrawal syndrome seen with alcohol or opiates, but are somewhat similar (although much more intense) to withdrawal from nicotine. Stimulant withdrawal produces no distinctive and objective physiological signs, such as the tremor or seizures of alcohol withdrawal, or the vomiting and diarrhea of opiate withdrawal. The essentially subjective (cognitive and emotional) and behavioral effects are not medically dangerous although suicide is a definite risk in severe cases. No satisfactory drug is available, and decreasing doses of the addictive drug is not an effective treatment for alleviation of withdrawal distress. Although stimulant withdrawal produces few overt signs, use of these drugs alters brain function, resulting in a neurological basis for the mostly subjective withdrawal syndrome. Box 2.3 in Chapter 2 of this text further describes the relationship between "physiological" and "psychological" withdrawal symptoms. Obviously, the stimulant-withdrawal syndrome is a powerful incentive to resume drug use.

Prospective studies of subjects in early stages of abstinence after chronic use of cocaine (e.g., Coffey et al. 2000) and methamphetamine (e.g., Zorick et al. 2010) confirm that **dysphoria and depression** are characteristic psychological stimulant-withdrawal symptoms. Standardized instruments, including the Profile of Mood States and the Beck Depression Inventory assessed mood and other subjective states. Other tests, specifically created to measure characteristics of stimulant withdrawal also determined the presence of DSM-IV withdrawal symptoms. Examples of these drug-specific instruments are the Methamphetamine Withdrawal Questionnaire (Srisurapapanont et al. 1999) and the Cocaine Selective Severity Assessment (Kampan et al. 1998). Depression, anxiety, anger, concentration difficulty, irritability, and loss of pleasure and interest were highest during the first few days of abstinence and gradually decreased during the following four or five weeks. Depression was largely resolved within a week in many subjects, although drug craving often persisted throughout the monitoring period.

Inhalation (smoking) and especially injection of stimulants usually produce more severe withdrawal effects than does insufflation (Rawson et al. 2007), as does greater frequency and a longer duration of addictive drug use (Zweben et al. 2004). Methamphetamine dependence often results in a more intense and longer-duration period of withdrawal than cocaine dependence (Meredith et al. 2005, Zweben et al. 2004).

Early descriptions of cocaine withdrawal included a "crash" during which individuals that had stopped chronic drug use slept excessively for several days (e.g.,
Gawain and Kleber 1986). Subsequent reports of withdrawal described insomnia,
disrupted and poor-quality sleep (e.g., Lago and Kosten 1994). Methamphetamine
withdrawal is more likely to produce lethargy and increased sleep than abstinence
from heavy cocaine use (McGregor et al. 2005). Some of the initial distress of
withdrawal from heavy stimulant use – including sleep disturbances – may result
from the disrupted life and personal losses of an addictive lifestyle as well as from
the pharmacological effects on the nervous system.

Chronic cocaine or methamphetamine use alters the function of neurotransmitters critical to normal states of motivation, mood, and feelings of pleasure. Assays
of brain tissue from animal subjects show decreased levels of the neurotransmitters and fewer receptors and reuptake transporters after chronic administration
of cocaine or methamphetamine (Koob and Le Moal 2006). PET scans of cocaine-
dependent humans indicate similar effects on dopamine receptors (Volkow et al.
1990). Most of these changes in neurotransmitter function are a result of compensatory processes as the nervous system adapts to the drug agonist effect. These
adaptations shift the hedonic set-point, decreasing the tone of the dopaminergic
reward system and resulting in anhedonia – the reduced ability to experience
pleasure that is a typical stimulant-withdrawal symptom. Ahmed and colleagues
observed decreased sensitivity to rewarding electrical brain stimulation in rats
after chronic cocaine administration, evidence for the drug-altered hedonic set-
point (Ahmed et al. 2002).

These neurological changes are at least partially reversible, in that they become
smaller with extended drug-free time in both experimental animals and in recovering human stimulant addicts (Harvey et al. 2000, Volkow et al. 1990). Mood states
also become more normal and emotional stability improves with drug abstinence.

Craving for the drug is a prominent feature of stimulant withdrawal. The strong
desire to take cocaine or methamphetamine typically endures longer than other
withdrawal symptoms, but eventually wanes in most individuals. Craving is likely
to recur during periods of stress, or when drug-related stimuli are encountered.
Galloway and colleagues conducted an assessment of craving in 865 outpatients
in treatment for methamphetamine dependence. Periodic urine screens during this
test period confirmed that the subjects did not use methamphetamine during the
sixteen-week assessment period. Craving was assessed weekly and was defined
as "an urgent desire, longing, yearning, not just a passing thought," and was
measured on a 100-point scale. Endpoint anchors were "no craving" (0) and "most
craving ever experienced" (100).

In the Galloway study 61 percent of the subjects took methamphetamine primarily by smoking, 23 percent insufflated the drug, and 13 percent used the intravenous injection route of administration. The remaining 3 percent of subjects took

the drug orally. The mean craving score during the first week of abstinence was 30.2 for IV users (significantly different from all other groups), 24.2 for smoking, 21.0 for insufflation, and 13.2 for the oral route of administration. Weekly tests of all groups showed a progressive decrease in craving, and by the tenth week mean craving scores were near zero. These results were similar to those of previous investigations in demonstrating that craving does decrease steadily with continued abstinence from stimulant use. In the absence of stress and contact with the drug or drug-related stimuli the craving can be expected to dissipate within three months after stimulant use is terminated (Galloway et al. 2010).

MDMA (Ecstasy, Molly)

"Ecstasy," and "Molly" are common "street" names for 3,4-methylenedioxy-methamphetamine (MDMA), an amphetamine-derivative drug with euphoric, energizing, and mildly psychedelic properties. Some MDMA effects are similar to those of amphetamine and cocaine. The drug has abuse potential, but although a dopamine agonist, is less addictive than cocaine and amphetamine.

Within an hour of orally ingesting 100–120 milligrams of MDMA users typically report extremely pleasant feelings of mental stimulation, **emotional warmth**, empathy toward others, and a general sense of well-being. Accompanying the feelings of euphoria is increased pleasure from physical contact with others – ecstasy has been called "the hug drug." Social interaction seems more intimate and satisfying, emotional barriers to close contact break down. Tactile sensations, sounds (e.g., music), smells and tastes are more vivid – these perceptual changes are the psychedelic aspect of the MDMA experience. The effects are sensual, but not distinctively pro-sexual. The feelings of emotional warmth and closeness can promote sexual activity, but the drug is not primarily an aphrodisiac. The increased energy is often expressed in prolonged sessions of dancing, an effect consistent with ecstasy's reputation as a **club drug**. Peak effects occur sixty to ninety minutes after ingestion, and the primary effects can last three to five hours. Women are more sensitive to the drug, so their optimal dose proportional to body weight is often smaller than for men (Iversen 2006).

During the late 1970s some psychiatrists in the United States began using MDMA as an **adjunct to therapy** for various emotional disorders. MDMA was not a controlled drug at that time, and the purported therapeutic benefits came from increased empathy and emotional openness in psychiatric patients (Holland 2001). In 1985, the writer of an article in Newsweek described his MDMA experience as "a year of therapy in two hours." Not surprisingly, use of MDMA soon spread from the psychiatrist's office to the wider world, as it became a popular recreational drug. By the late 1980s the drug was used widely in the United Kingdom, with its use contributing to the "rave scene" of England, Australia and European countries. "Raves" were huge gatherings of young people, often in remote locations, who danced to a new type of music for many hours. Similar events were held in California and eventually MDMA became a club drug (along with other illicit drugs), used at dance parties held in more traditional locations.

In the United States in 1985, MDMA was designated as a Schedule I drug. This classification, indicating high abuse potential and no approved medical use, curtailed most therapeutic use of ecstasy. Many psychiatrists and some scientific investigators felt that supervised medical use of the drug was safe and beneficial, and that its severe restriction was not justified (Iversen 2006). The Food and Drug Administration has approved tests of MDMA for treatment of posttraumatic stress disorder, but the Schedule I classification still prohibits its standard use in psychiatry. However, there is still interest in the potential use of MDMA in psychiatry, including for treatment of alcohol use disorders (Sessa 2018, Yazar-Klosinski and Mithoefer 2017).

The NSDUH survey indicated that in the United States 0.2 percent of individuals age twelve and older used MDMA within the past month (current use). For ages eighteen to twenty-five, estimated prevalence of current use was 0.7 percent. These use rates indicated a slight decrease from the previous two years in use rates for young adults, but no change for the wider-age-range respondents (Substance Abuse and Mental Health Services Administration 2018).

In the brain, MDMA releases serotonin, dopamine and noradrenaline from axon terminals into the synapse (Liechti et al. 2001). These effects on neurotransmitters are somewhat similar to those of cocaine and methamphetamine, but for MDMA the release of serotonin is much greater, and that of dopamine and noradrenaline much smaller. Much of the temporary elevation of mood states is thought to result from the indirect agonist effect on serotonin function. Activation of the 5-HT$_{2A}$ serotonin receptor by MDMA may bring about the subtle perceptual alterations (Iversen 2006). LSD and other hallucinogenic drugs are agonists for this serotonin receptor. Some of the positive reinforcement effect comes from the stimulation of dopamine and noradrenaline receptors, actions that also mediate the increased arousal and energizing effects of MDMA.

Although quite pleasurable to most users, MDMA has less addictive potential than methamphetamine and cocaine. Tolerance develops readily to the primary rewarding effect – the feelings of emotional warmth and connection to others. This rapid loss of pleasurable reaction to MDMA (apparently due to temporary depletion of serotonin) is an important factor that limits the development of dependence. With frequently repeated use, the primary euphoric effect of MDMA diminishes greatly – although much of the pleasurable effect is regained after a few days' abstinence from the drug (Parrot 2005). So, although some individuals may take the drug once or even twice a week, most are unlikely to get into the extended bouts of more frequent or constant use that characterize stimulant addiction. The weaker activation of dopamine function may also contribute to this drug's relatively lower addiction potential.

Addiction to MDMA does occur in some individuals (Cottler et al. 2001, Leung and Cottler 2008). Some of these addicted users ingest the drug daily or even more frequently. The dopamine and noradrenaline agonist effects that are less subject to tolerance are thought to promote the escalation of MDMA use. With heavy use, the emotional warmth and gentle euphoria of the earlier and less frequent drug intake are absent – jittery tension and anxiety predominate (Reynolds 1998). The pattern of drug use that persists even after much of the original rewarding effects have diminished is, of course, similar to that often seen with addiction to other addictive drugs. These heavy and frequent users typically also use other addictive drugs, including alcohol and other stimulants, so it is often difficult to determine that MDMA is the primary addictive agent.

MDMA has moderate abuse potential even in the absence of addiction. MDMA effects are not always pleasurable, and can include anxiety, confusion, and depression (Cottler et al. 2001). Aftereffects of lethargy and depression may persist for days after use. These delayed aversive effects, probably resulting from temporary depletion of serotonin, might be compared to an alcohol hangover in that they are uncomfortable, but temporary (Parrot 2002). Perhaps the most dangerous acute effect is hyperthermia. Elevated body temperature, which is worsened by strenuous activity (dancing) in an overheated environment, can cause coma, organ damage and death (Kalant 2001).

Neurotoxicity, enduring cognitive deficits and emotional disorders (depression) resulting from MDMA use are matters of much concern. Animal studies show that high doses of MDMA deplete brain serotonin levels and damage nerve terminals. Some investigators find slow recovery, with near-normal levels evident a year after drug administration (e.g., Green et al. 2003). Brain-imaging studies show decreased serotonin function in human users of ecstasy that also recovers to some extent after drug abstinence (Buchert et al. 2004). Whether complete recovery occurs has not yet been determined. Much evidence indicates that neurological abnormalities persist for months or longer (Di Lorio et al. 2012).

Many investigations have determined that MDMA treatment can cause memory impairment in animals (e.g., Vinals et al. 2013). Research with animal subjects can establish drug effects with certainty, but are of uncertain relevance to human drug use, in part because of the high drug doses administered in these preclinical studies.

Cognitive deficits, predominantly in memory function, have been observed in both current and abstinent human users of MDMA. In some cases the extent of memory impairment is correlated with detectable alterations in serotonin function (Reneman et al. 2000). Some users of MDMA exhibit deficits in several aspects of memory, including visuospatial (Murphy et al. 2012) and prospective memory

(Weinborn et al. 2011). However, although statistically significant, the deficits are typically rather small and unlikely to impair the daily activities of most MDMA users (Rogers et al. 2009).

Heavy use of the drug is also associated with sleep disorders, depressed mood, elevated anxiety and impulsiveness (Morgan 2000, Matthews and Bruno 2010).

As with all investigations of chronic drug effects in humans, differences seen in MDMA users can be influenced by the use of alcohol and other recreational drugs and by the level of cognitive and psychological function prior to drug use. Subject screening and statistical control procedures can sometimes account for the effects of these confounded factors.

Little research has been conducted on the effects of prenatal exposure to MDMA in human babies. A prospective investigation by Singer and colleagues indicated that prenatal exposure to MDMA was associated with poorer motor quality and lower developmental milestone attainment at four months of age (Singer et al. 2012).

Treatment of Stimulant Addiction

While there are probably more similarities than differences among addictions to different drugs, the differences do exist and must be addressed by clinicians if they are to provide effective treatment (Washton and Zweben 2009). When cocaine use disorders became widespread during the mid-1980s, treatment programs for addiction were at first unprepared for the large increase in the number of patients. As mentioned previously, these patients were not only addicted to a drug quite different from alcohol or heroin but they were also of a different demographic – including more young upper-and middle-class individuals employed in business or in professional occupations.

Most treatment programs eventually made changes to meet these new demands. One major change was the greater use of cognitive behavioral therapy, based largely on learning theory and reinforcement principles. Cognitive behavioral therapy (CBT) is described more fully in Chapter 16. The Matrix Model approach was developed at UCLA specifically to treat cocaine addiction (Shoptaw et al. 1994). The Matrix Model and similar programs are based primarily on CBT strategies and also feature conventional treatment procedures such as individual psychotherapy and participation in twelve-step activities. The emphasis on CBT is now integral to many contemporary treatment programs for all types of SUD.

When methamphetamine abuse became more prevalent a decade after the years of highest levels of cocaine use, the demographic characteristics of those seeking treatment for stimulant addiction changed again (Reback et al. 2018). Many methamphetamine addicts live in rural areas in which treatment facilities and after-care support groups are inaccessible. Women who abuse methamphetamine may be concerned with the gain in body weight that typically follows stopping long-term stimulant use. Some aspects of gay culture may be especially troublesome for homosexual clients attempting to abstain from methamphetamine use. Individuals with HIV have special health problems and concerns that both promote methamphetamine use and increase the harmful medical consequences. The Matrix Model was revised slightly to improve treatment engagement of these methamphetamine-abusing individuals (Rawson et al. 2004).

In addition to the treatment-relevant characteristics of many stimulant addicts, the unique behavioral, emotional, and cognitive effects of cocaine and methamphetamine also present special issues that threaten recovery (Courtney and Ray 2014). Although heavy stimulant use eventually decreases sexual pleasure and performance, memory of enhanced sexual pleasure combined with the euphoria of drug intoxication lingers as a powerful attraction that can easily trigger relapse. Sexual arousal can also stimulate craving for resumption of drug use. These issues must be addressed in the treatment of both heterosexual clients and MSM.

Heavy stimulant use often causes long-term cognitive deficits and emotional vulnerability. Both of these effects make engagement with a treatment program and maintaining abstinence more difficult. The emotional aftermath of stimulant addiction includes tendencies for anhedonia and depression that can facilitate a return to drug use.

For most SUD, drug therapy is often a valuable part of treatment (Chapter 16). In contrast to treatment for addiction to other types of drugs (nicotine, opiates, alcohol) there is currently no FDA-approved pharmacotherapy for stimulant use disorders. Many drugs have been tested as treatment adjuncts for stimulant addiction, but none have proven safe and effective for cocaine- or methamphetamine-dependent individuals (Brackins et al. 2011, Marsden 2009, Morley et al. 2017).

Methylphenidate (Ritalin) treatment has shown some success in facilitating abstinence in cocaine addicts. However, most investigators maintain that methylphenidate elicits and prolongs craving for cocaine or methamphetamine in individuals with a history of stimulant abuse, so the drug is not accepted as a safe adjunctive treatment. Similar results have come from tests of bupropion (Wellbutrin) (Brensilver et al. 2012), modafinil (Provigil) (Shearer et al. 2009), and varenicline (Chantix – effective for treatment of nicotine dependence) (Plebani et al. 2012). These drugs are unlikely to cause craving for stimulants, but were not proven reliably effective for management of stimulant use disorder.

Research is in progress toward the development of vaccines to block the pharmacological effects of stimulants, thereby preventing or stopping abuse and addiction (Evans et al. 2016, Kosten et al. 2014, Orson et al. 2014). These medications stimulate the production of drug-specific antibodies that attach to drug molecules in the bloodstream, producing a compound molecule that cannot cross the blood–brain barrier – and so do not influence brain function. If effective vaccines are developed they may be useful for addiction treatment, but their use could face ethical, legal, and regulatory barriers.

Cocaine (and especially crack) addiction was initially thought to produce such strong attraction and compulsion for drug use as to be essentially untreatable. Similar pessimism accompanied the early years of extensive methamphetamine use. However, the improved treatment programs show effectiveness (recovery rates) for stimulant use disorders similar to that for problematic use of other addictive drugs (Washton and Zweben 2009, Halkitis 2009). Treatment effectiveness is discussed in Chapter 16.

Chapter Summary

Cocaine and methamphetamine produce a quick, intense high state that makes most users feel elated, confident, focused, and sexy. The drugs also give increased energy and the ability to work at physical or mental tasks for extended periods. These stimulants are highly addictive and can produce unpleasant or dangerous behavioral and physiological effects.

In the United States, use of stimulant drugs has declined considerably in recent years, but more than 2 million adolescents and adults are current users of cocaine, nearly 2 million misuse pharmaceutical stimulants, and hundreds of thousands use methamphetamine.

The positive reinforcement effect of stimulants is mostly due to an increase in dopamine activity, and much of the autonomic arousal is a result of increased noradrenaline function.

Adaptation to the abnormal activation causes reactive dysphoria (depression, anxiety) that emerges soon after the initial euphoria of methamphetamine use. Attempts to counteract the dysphoria by means of additional drug intake eventually cause the anxiety and agitation characteristic of stimulant abuse and addiction.

A use disorder is present in about half of current cocaine users and in about one-third of those who misuse pharmaceutical stimulants, although not all of these individuals are addicted. Addiction is most likely in daily users and those who intravenously inject cocaine or inhale cocaine vapor. Methamphetamine users are somewhat more likely than those who use cocaine to become addicted. Cocaine and methamphetamine are more addictive than alcohol, with an addictive potential similar to nicotine's. When addiction develops, the progression is more rapid than with other substances, such as alcohol or cannabis.

Stimulant addiction often results in extended binges of drug use that can persist uninterrupted for days. Alcohol, cannabis, antianxiety medications, or opioids are commonly taken to alleviate the aversive effects of such binges. Consequently, many stimulant addicts have multiple SUD.

Antisocial behavior, including domestic violence, child neglect and abuse, and criminal activity, are prevalent in many stimulant addicts. Extreme irritability, suspicion, and social withdrawal are common. Obsessive thought patterns can emerge and sometimes culminate in full-blown psychotic paranoia. Clinical depression and suicide are also definite risks.

Withdrawal from extended stimulant use is not life-threatening but is strong motivation to maintain or resume drug use. Common effects are depression and loss of pleasure from and interest in most activities, irritability, and emotional lability. Craving for the drug persists longer than other aftereffects.

Heavy stimulant use damages the cardiovascular system, the kidneys, and the brain – with some of the problems secondary to prolonged hypertension. Impairment of memory and executive function can persist for weeks or months after cessation of drug use. Gum disease and loss of teeth are common.

Harmful effects of stimulants on the developing fetus are not as dramatic as portrayed in the "crack baby" coverage by the media in the mid-1980s. Smaller babies result from prenatal exposure to stimulants. Differences in motor activity and increased emotional reactivity can occur, but most disappear by age three.

The stimulant drug MDMA produces pleasant feelings of emotional warmth, greater empathy with others, and a general sense of well-being. The drug is less addictive, and its use has fewer dangerous consequences than heavy use of other stimulant drugs. However, chronic use can cause emotional and cognitive problems, mainly depression and memory impairment. Dangerous levels of hyperthermia can result from a high dose of MDMA.

In the 1990s the diagnostic criteria for identifying drug addiction changed, based on clinical experience with cocaine and methamphetamine addicts. The earlier emphasis on objectively identifiable (physiological) withdrawal syndromes shifted toward the behavioral indicators of compulsive drug use, including difficulty in stopping the destructive behavior.

In the United States and other parts of the world, the use of cocaine and methamphetamine is a definite problem for public health and safety, although less harmful than alcohol use, and causing fewer deaths than opioid or tobacco use. However, the stimulant drugs are generally more closely controlled and less widely accepted than are alcohol and tobacco. If the dopamine-agonist stimulants were easily and legally available to the general population, prevalence of use, abuse, and addiction would be much greater, as would the resulting damage.

Review Exercises

1. What are the primary effects of amphetamine and cocaine that are of utilitarian value?
2. What medical problems were treated with amphetamine in earlier years, and which are currently approved for treatment with stimulants?
3. How do cocaine and amphetamine (including methamphetamine) differ in their overall effects on feelings and behavior?
4. Describe the effects on neurotransmitters for which there is good evidence of involvement in the addiction potential of stimulant drugs.
5. In relation to other addictive drugs (e.g., alcohol, nicotine), how much do traditional risk factors for SUD influence use disorders of stimulants?
6. Compare self-administration of stimulants in laboratory animals to recreational use of and addiction to stimulants in humans.
7. How do the subjective effects of oral ingestion of a low dose of amphetamine differ from IV injection of methamphetamine or inhalation of crack cocaine?
8. What factors are thought to influence whether an individual enjoys, or dislikes, a moderate dose of orally ingested amphetamine or methylphenidate?
9. How did the sharp increase in cocaine use and addiction in the 1980s influence changes for the diagnostic criteria for SUD in the DSM-IV for all addictive drugs?
10. Explain how features of stimulant addiction make this SUD different in use patterns from that seen with addiction to alcohol or opioids.
11. How does the concurrent use of other recreational/addictive drugs facilitate addictive use of stimulants?
12. How do stimulant drugs affect sexual behavior?
13. How is the compulsive and repetitive behavior produced by high doses of amphetamine similar to certain features of a psychiatric syndrome that often results from heavy stimulant use?
14. What evidence shows that heavy stimulant use results in cognitive impairment? What is the nature of that impairment?
15. Was the "crack baby scare" of the mid-1980s a valid public health threat? Defend your answer by describing the effects of prenatal exposure to cocaine.
16. How is the stimulant-withdrawal syndrome different from the withdrawal from alcohol or opioids?
17. Based on the evidence presented in the text, present an argument that MDMA use is dangerous and a threat to public health.

Key Terms

addiction (502)

adjunct to therapy (530)

anxiety and agitation (509)

aphrodisiac effect (507)

club drug (530)

cognitive deficits (520)

compulsive cocaine self-administration (498)

crack baby (525)

dependence (502)

DSM-5 criteria for withdrawal (527)

dysphoria and depression (528)

emotional warmth (530)

exposure to and availability of (506)

increased energy (496)

medical problems of multiple organ systems (524)

monoamine neurotransmitters (494)

paranoid psychosis (516)

sympathetic nervous system (487)

14 Opioid Use Disorders

CHAPTER OUTLINE

LEARNING OBJECTIVES

1. Provide definitions of key opioid terminology.
2. Summarize the history of opioid use and misuse from the twentieth century until the present.
3. Describe the endogenous opioid system, including subtypes of opioid receptors, the types of opioid peptides, and the functions with which both are involved.
4. Identify the opioid drugs that are full agonists, partial agonists, and antagonists.
5. Identify the neurological structures and pathways involved in opioid-produced analgesia, negative reinforcement, and positive reinforcement.
6. Describe the effects of opioids on pain perception, emotion, cognition, and physiological functions.
7. Describe opioid tolerance, withdrawal, and conditioned withdrawal.
8. Describe the general features of opioid use disorders.
9. Explain the four types of opioid use disorders and give the incidence and demographics of each.
10. Describe the neonatal abstinence syndrome.
11. Describe the options for drug treatment of opioid SUD.

Introductory Vignette: Anticipation

James worked as an Uber driver until he was let go because a urine screen test revealed his drug use. He lied to his family about the reason he was fired and now does even more drugs – including heroin. His parents give him money while he "looks for a new job," but they are becoming impatient with his lack of employment. He worries about keeping this up – at least until he does heroin. Then, nothing bothers him for hours.

James feels the first hints of nausea and is tense and anxious, dreading the bad shape he well knows he will soon be in unless he gets some china girl – or goodfella, or whatever they were calling fentanyl and heroin today. He tells himself he should have known better than to get into this situation – but here he is, in the early stages of being really sick. At a party four months ago, Sally gave him a Vicodin pill that, along with some beer, made him slightly high – more than just from the beer – for a couple of hours. No big thing, but when he was offered the pills again some days later, he took them. Eventually he tried some OxyContin and found that if he crushed the pills and then snorted the powder, he got a nice floaty feeling that he really liked. After a few weeks of doing oxy pretty often, it had less effect, and he missed how good it had felt at first. A guy he met in a bar said James should try some "china girl." It was easy to score, and injecting it would give him the best high. James knew that china girl was heroin, or probably a combination of heroin and fentanyl. Taking that stuff was scary, and he didn't like the idea of using a needle. However, the oxy wasn't doing much for him – and he figured he could risk taking something stronger at least once.

Wow! This stuff was something else – so much better than the oxy. So now, he shoots up almost every day. It is winter, so he wears a jacket and a shirt with long sleeves to hide the injection marks. He doesn't have a job, so he can be high or on the nod and nobody gives him any trouble. The only downside is that if he doesn't get a hit every day, he gets the sick feeling of withdrawal, vomiting and with cramping and aches all over his body – *really* ill. He can feel it coming on now, and when he finds some heroin or fentanyl, he will take it without a second thought of a possible bad outcome.

Introduction

Opioid drugs can effectively reduce pain and so are very important in medical practice. These drugs can also produce intense euphoric pleasure, as well as temporary relief from anxiety, depression, and boredom. Drug misuse and the development of substance use disorders sometimes accompany opioid use, especially when use is not supervised by medical professionals.

Box 14.1 explains the sometimes confusing terminology used in reference to morphine, heroin, and similar drugs and endogenous hormones and neurotransmitters.

For many years, public concern about drug abuse was primarily about addiction to heroin, seen as the prototypical form of drug addiction. Although the worldwide prevalence of nonmedical heroin and fentanyl use has varied over the years, individuals addicted to these drugs have consistently composed a very small percentage of the overall population (United Nations Office for Drug Control 2012).

Misuse and abuse of opioid drugs other than heroin or heroin–fentanyl combinations has increased markedly in recent decades. These drugs are legally available for medical use, but in the United States, the extent of their nonmedical use is second only to that of marijuana in prevalence of illicit substance use, and is at least six times greater than that of heroin (Substance Abuse and Mental Health Services Administration 2018).

Misuse of pharmaceutical opioids and use of illicit opioids have resulted in an alarming increase in deaths caused by these drugs in recent years. In 2017, 47,600 individuals in the United States died from opioid overdose (National Institute of Drug Abuse 2019b).

BOX 14.1 Opioid drug terminology

The term **opiate** refers to drugs derived from opium (morphine, heroin, and codeine). The broader term **opioid** refers to compounds that bind with opioid receptors and produce similar pharmacological effects, including opiates, and synthetic drugs not derived from opium (e.g., methadone, oxycodone, fentanyl, and others). **Endogenous opioids** are certain peptides found in the nervous system and other parts of the body that have actions and effects similar to the synthetic and plant-derived opioid drugs (Meyer and Quenzer 2013). The designation of a drug as a *narcotic* indicates sleep-producing and analgesic properties. However, the term *narcotic* is most often used for legal or regulatory purposes. These two systems refer to several substances or drug types with quite different pharmacological properties as narcotics (e.g., cannabis, cocaine, the opioid drugs). The term *narcotic* is rarely used in scientific discourse.

Some History of Opioid Use and Misuse

Thousands of years ago (approximately 3400 BCE), opium was used in the Sumerian culture to relieve pain (Booth 1986). In the ensuing years, compounds derived from the sap of the opium poppy (*Papaver somniverifum*) found important use in the medical practice of many cultures (Figure 14.1). The pleasure-producing and addictive properties of opium have also been apparent for millennia. When opium smoking was introduced in the sixteenth century, its use for pleasure – and its abuse potential – increased. Morphine was first extracted from opium in 1803, and with the mid-nineteenth-century advent of the hypodermic needle, opiate addiction became even more prevalent. Near the end of that century, heroin – a more potent opiate drug produced by a chemical transformation of morphine – became available. Fentanyl, a synthetic drug similar to but even much more potent than heroin, was introduced in the 1960s.

Figure 14.1 Poppy flowers and opium-producing seed pods. Morphine, heroin, and other opiate drugs are derived from opium. Several other opioid drugs, including fentanyl, are produced synthetically. Photo: kenansavas / E+ / Getty Images.

Opioid Use in the Twentieth Century

Commerce, government regulation and taxation, exploration, wars, innovations in transportation and medicine, organized criminal activity, and other events have affected the use of opium and its derivatives during most of recorded history. Some of these events that occurred in the United States during the twentieth century and more recently are briefly described here.

In the early 1900s, opium, morphine, and heroin were in wide use, both as administered or prescribed by physicians and as active ingredients in many patent medicines. The easy availability of opiate drugs was similar to that of cocaine during the first years of the twentieth century. Estimates of the prevalence of dependence varied greatly, in part because there was no standard definition of addiction, and reliable information about drug use was unavailable. One estimate indicated that half a million individuals were to some extent dependent on these drugs (Kolb and Du Mez 1924). This extensive habitual use did not cause much public concern in that opiate addicts were often seen as unfortunate individuals, deserving of pity but not vilified or feared.

The **Harrison Narcotics Act** of 1914 required the licensure of physicians, dentists, veterinarians, and pharmacists for dispensing opiate medications. Physicians were not allowed to administer morphine to addicted individuals for the sole purpose of relieving withdrawal symptoms. Eventually, heroin use was completely prohibited – although the effects of heroin and morphine (which remained legal for medical use) are quite similar. The government restriction of legal opiate use resulted in the extensive involvement of organized crime in importing (smuggling) and selling opiate drugs (mainly heroin), an enterprise that continues today. It also made criminals of addicts, resulting in the incarceration of many individuals for sale or possession of opiate drugs.

As legal access to opiates diminished, the addict population changed during the 1920s, becoming composed primarily of young, lower-class men who injected morphine or heroin. When supplied by illegal dealers, these drugs were expensive and many users turned to burglary and other crimes against property to finance their opiate dependence. The association with crime, plus the belief that most users were African American or Hispanic, resulted in scorn and condemnation of opiate users by society – attitudes encouraged by the popular press and law enforcement agencies (Lindesmith 1940).

The criminalization of drug addiction resulted in imprisonment of many opiate users. In the 1930s (as in the twenty-first century), incarceration of prisoners was quite expensive. With little knowledge of causes or treatment of drug addiction, an early attempt was made to find an alternative to simple imprisonment to address the threat to society. In 1935, a federal prison/hospital "for the confinement and treatment of persons addicted to the use of habit-forming narcotic drugs" was opened in Lexington, Kentucky (Musto 1999). At its peak capacity the facility housed 1,500 individuals. The facility included a farm and a dairy, because work was considered therapeutic for the patients/inmates. Some patients were volunteers, but two-thirds were either convicted of drug use crimes, or committed to the hospital as an alternative to imprisonment for drug-related offenses. The most common drug of abuse for those sent to the facility was heroin or morphine.

Research on the effects of addictive drugs was an important function of the facility until its closure as a hospital in 1974 (Kosten and Gorelick 2002). Many of the early studies involved administering drugs to prisoners, in some cases for extended periods, in order to observe withdrawal syndromes. Several well-known individuals were inmates at the Lexington prison, including jazz musicians Chet Baker and Zoot Sims. William Burroughs, a heroin addict who wrote about drug addiction in the lurid, controversial novel *Naked Lunch*, also spent time at this facility.

After some decrease in heroin use during the Second World War, use of the drug increased in many American cities in the postwar years. During the 1950s, many news stories and articles in popular magazines portrayed heroin addiction as an incurable affliction, and addicts as dangerous criminals. Heroin addiction also became linked to the threat of communism during this period, a time of extreme concern about influence of the Soviet Union and Communist China. The Narcotics Control Act of 1956 increased penalties for selling and possession of heroin and removed the possibility of probation or suspended sentences (Lattimer and Goldberg 1981). The concept of a drug supplier as a "pusher" – a predatory individual who aggressively recruited new heroin users – became popular during this period. Sale of heroin to a minor could result in the death penalty.

American military personnel serving in the Viet Nam conflict in the late 1960s and early 1970s had access to potent, inexpensive heroin. The ready availability of the drug, coupled with the rigors of military deployment and conflict, encouraged some to use heroin, at least experimentally. Traces of opiate drugs were found in 5.1 percent of 100,000 returning troops urine tested in 1971.

Heroin was seen as a highly addictive drug, with its casual, nonaddictive use unlikely. There was great concern that Viet Nam veterans who used the drug would continue addictive use upon returning to the United States and entering civilian life. However, only 1 or 2 percent of those who initially tested positive for heroin use were still using opioid drugs a year later (Robins 1974). Most of those who no longer used heroin had not received treatment for a substance use disorder.

Many (perhaps most) Viet Nam veterans who used the drug were probably never addicted, because although there is a definite risk of a severe SUD, heroin can be used without that consequence. For those who did become addicted, removal from the environment that fostered use and entry into a place where use was less convenient and more dangerous greatly facilitated abstinence from heroin. Some soldiers and marines that became addicted to heroin in Viet Nam did continue heavy use after leaving the service, but there was no great increase in cases of veteran addiction as was anticipated. Many who study addiction feel that the Viet Nam experience with heroin use removed some of the false mystique about the drug. The "heroin mystique" included unrealistic conceptions such as: all users are addicted, heroin dependence is an incurable condition, and heroin addicts are weak, immoral individuals (Fernandez and Libby 2011).

The late 1960s also brought an increase in the use of illicit drugs by rebellious youth of the counterculture. Marijuana and hallucinogens such as LSD were the drugs most favored by young people who sought a lifestyle different from that of the "straight" mainstream culture. However, the acceptance of illicit drug use by many middle-class young people increased experimentation with opioid drugs. Frequency of deaths from heroin overdose increased, including those of well-known entertainers Janis Joplin in 1970 and John Belushi in 1982. The heroin addict population was no longer seen as consisting solely of disenfranchised individuals. Many young people did not take seriously the 1950s "dope fiend" image of a heroin addict, but heroin was still feared and avoided by most individuals that used less dangerous drugs. However, some who enjoyed risk taking or wanted a more intense drug experience did try heroin. Some of these experimenters became addicted.

The early 1980s saw the emergence of Acquired Immune Deficiency Syndrome (AIDS), resulting in vulnerability to many often-fatal opportunistic infections. HIV, the virus that causes AIDS, is spread by intimate contact with bodily fluids, including blood of an infected person. Use of contaminated needles and syringes by intravenous drug users (who often share injection equipment) presents a great risk of HIV transmission, as well as infection with other blood-borne diseases including hepatitis. Although unprotected sexual activity is the greatest risk factor for HIV infection, intravenous drug injectors are also at high risk.

The threat of AIDS did not eliminate intravenous (IV) heroin use, but it is likely that concern about the risk of this deadly disease did deter some users from the dangerous practice. Although IV injection is the favored route of administration for most heroin addicts, the drug can also be taken by insufflation or by inhaling its vapor (smoking). Many nonaddicted individuals used these less dangerous methods, which can lead to addiction but present less risk of fatal overdose or AIDS transmission than IV injection.

In the 1990s, many physicians became aware of the frequent undertreatment of pain, resulting in their increased use of opioid drugs for pain management (American Pain Society 1997). Pharmaceutical companies conducted aggressive marketing campaigns aimed at physicians. Sales personnel for the drug companies promoted opioid use for acute as well as chronic pain, concomitant with minimizing the risk of dependence and addiction (Macy 2018). The more frequent use of the drugs for legitimate medical purposes was accompanied by a substantial increase in nonmedical use of prescription opioids – misuse, abuse, and addiction (Rosenblum et al. 2008, Zacny et al. 2003).

Twenty-First Century

The trend of growing use and abuse of opioid drugs continued throughout the first and second decades of the twenty-first century. The misuse of pharmaceutical opioids became a threat to public health rivaling or exceeding that of heroin addiction. In 2010, production and sale of opioid analgesic drugs had quadrupled since 1999. The amount of opioid drugs dispensed by medical professionals was sufficient to medicate every adult American with a typical dose (equivalent to five milligrams of hydrocodone) every four hours for one month (Centers for Disease Control and Prevention 2011). In 2011 the Centers for Disease Control and Prevention, in conjunction with the National Institute of Drug Abuse (NIDA) declared an "opioid use epidemic."

A primary reason for this warning of an epidemic was the alarming rise in fatal drug overdoses. The number of deaths due to drug overdose in the United States in 2017 (70,237) was more than four times greater than in 2000, with large increases also occurring in Canada. About 47,600 (68 percent) of these deaths involved opioid drugs (Figure 14.2). Since 1999, more than 399,000 Americans have died of an opioid overdose – sometimes in combination with another drug (King et al. 2014, Scholl et al. 2019, Volkow et al. 2017).

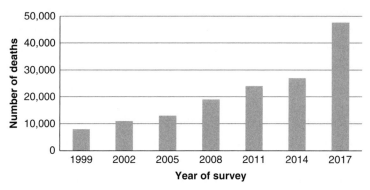

Figure 14.2 The annual number of deaths due to opioid overdose has risen greatly during the first two decades of the twenty-first century. These values indicate the total fatalities due to overdose of pharmaceutical and illicit opioids (National Institute of Drug Abuse 2019b).

For several years, a greater number of fatalities involved pharmaceutical opioids than those resulting from heroin use. In recent years, the rising overdose death rate has also been driven by the increased nonmedical use of fentanyl and fentanyl analogs (e.g., carfentanil), extremely potent synthetic opioids used in medicine that have become available from illicit sources (O'Donnell et al. 2017, Scholl et al. 2019).

During recent years, about one-third of the US population age twelve or older used pharmaceutical opioids. A large majority of these individuals used the medications only as directed by a medical professional, but about one in eight misused the drugs at some point during the year. The National Survey on Drug Use and Health (NSDUH) definition of misuse includes use by individuals other than those for which the prescription was written, as well as by those who took the medications in larger doses or for a longer period than as directed by their physician or dentist. As defined by the NSDUH, misuse could occur when the drugs are taken for any reason, including for relief of pain, "recreation," or for relief of withdrawal symptoms (Hughes et al. 2016).

Estimates from the NSDUH for heroin use and opioid misuse are presented in Table 14.1. Because heroin obtained from illicit sources is often combined with fentanyl, the values presented here for heroin use include use of fentanyl. In the United States, annual misuse of pharmaceutical opioids is at least ten times more prevalent than heroin/fentanyl use. Among all adolescents and adults, fewer than 1 million (886,000) used heroin/fentanyl, and 11.1 million misused the pharmaceutical drugs during the year of the survey. Use or misuse of both types of opioids is most prevalent in the age group eighteen to twenty-five (Substance Abuse and Mental Health Services Administration 2018).

About 5 percent of respondents that misused pharmaceutical opioids also used heroin/fentanyl. A majority of heroin users have also used pharmaceutical opioids (Hughes et al. 2016). Some individuals start use of illicit opioids after initial exposure to the drug effects during treatment of pain by a medical professional, and such exposure is a risk factor for heroin use (Lipari and Hughes 2015, National Institute of Drug Abuse 2018). However, the much greater prevalence of pharmaceutical analgesic misuse relative to the lower use rate of heroin indicates that most individuals who misuse the licit drugs do not progress to the use of illicit opioids.

In 2016, the Centers for Disease Control and Prevention issued guidelines for prescribing opioids, with the intent of improving communication between physicians and patients about the risks and benefits of opioid therapy (Rudd et al. 2016). These guidelines primarily address the treatment of chronic pain, and indicate an increased recognition of medical professionals regarding the risks of overuse of opioid analgesics for treatment of all types of pain. Initial evidence suggests that the rate of fatal opioid overdose decreased slightly in 2018 (Scholl et al. 2019).

Table 14.1 Opioid drug use in the United States

Pharmaceutical opioid drugs		
Age group	Misuse in previous year	Misuse in previous month
12+ years	4.1%	1.2%
18–25 years	7.2%	1.8%
	Heroin (or heroin–fentanyl combined)	
	Use in previous year	Use in previous month
12+ years	0.3%	2%
18–25 years	0.6%	0.3%

Note. Estimates provided by the National Survey of Drug Use and Health, indicating percentage of US population of the specified age group. See text for definition of opioid misuse. Pharmaceutical opioids include hydrocodone (Vicodin), oxycodone (OxyContin), and other drugs.

Source. Substance Abuse and Mental Health Services Administration (2018).

Opioid Drugs in the Brain and Body

Although the pain-relieving and pleasure-producing properties of opium and its derivatives were well known for millennia, the neurological basis of these effects was unknown until the latter half of the twentieth century. As understanding of brain function advanced, the critical role of neurotransmitters and receptors in neurological activity became evident. The molecular structure of most psychoactive drugs resembles that of neurotransmitters, enabling the drug to bind with receptors to produce their effects. **Opioid receptors** were identified and localized in 1973 (Pert and Snyder 1973).

It soon became apparent that there were at least three subtypes of opioid receptors – mu, delta, and kappa (Lord et al. 1977). Opioid receptors are found in many areas of the brain and spinal cord, and in other body organs such as the intestines. Brain and spinal cord structures related to pain perception and reward/positive reinforcement contain high concentrations of opioid receptors. The anatomical distribution of the different subtypes of opioid receptors suggests that the mu and delta receptors are critically involved in the production of pleasure and analgesia. Kappa receptors appear to regulate other functions such as eating, drinking and temperature control. All the opioid receptors activate metabotropic responses in neurons, initiating a complex sequence of chemical processes that eventually influence gene expression in the cell nucleus (Chapter 4). Opioids can also have an ionotropic effect at opioid receptors.

The Endogenous Opioid System

The discovery of opioid receptors triggered intense research efforts to identify naturally occurring (endogenous) chemicals that activated these receptors. Enkephalins (peptide neurotransmitters) were the first to be discovered (Waterfield et al. 1976). Soon thereafter the endorphins (opioid hormones secreted by the pituitary and adrenal glands) were discovered (Li et al. 1976). Eventually three distinct families of **opioid peptides** were identified: enkephalins, endorphins, and dynorphins (Koob and Le Moal 2006).

The neurons and glands that produce these peptides, and neurons and other cells containing opioid receptors, make up the endogenous opioid system (EOS). The EOS is involved in many bodily functions and aspects of behavior as indicated by a very large amount of research conducted since these initial discoveries (Bodnar 2011). The enkephalins and endorphins are the opioid peptides most clearly implicated in analgesia, reinforcement and addiction. These endogenous opioids, in addition to dynorphin, the third type of opioid peptide, also contribute to control of eating and drinking, sexual activity, stress responses, the immune system, and other body processes and actions.

All opioid drugs that relieve pain and have addictive potential influence bodily functions and behavior by means of their actions on the EOS. These drugs are primarily agonists for mu receptors (Kreek et al. 2009, Traynor 2012). Research with mutant mice and investigations using selective blocking agents (opioid antagonist drugs) have established these critical functions of the mu receptor (e.g., Gaveriaux-Ruff and Kieffer 2002, Sora et al. 2001). Extensive efforts by pharmacologists and other scientists to develop an effective opioid analgesic drug without addictive properties have not been successful (Corbett et al. 2006, Meyer and Quenzer 2013).

Agonists and Antagonists

Opium-derived drugs, as well as numerous synthetic drugs, interact with opioid receptors. Several of these drugs are **full agonists** in that they have strong effects at the opioid receptors similar to those of the endogenous opioids. Drugs that are **partial agonists** have similar effects but a lower level of activity at the receptors. The drugs differ in their potency, side effects, delay of onset and duration of effects, and effective routes of administration.

Opioid antagonists bind with the receptors but do not initiate activity in neurons. These antagonist drugs block the action of both endogenous opioids and opioid-agonist drugs.

The drugs described in Box 14.2 are those most relevant to opioid abuse and its treatment. This list does not include all synthetic opioid drugs. Among those not included are the mixed *agonist-antagonist* agents that block some, but not all, opioid receptors. Some of these drugs bind with and activate kappa receptors as well as having weak agonist action at mu receptors. Mixed agonist-antagonist drugs have little potential for abuse and currently have only limited clinical applications. These drugs are used primarily in research intended to clarify the functions of the EOS.

BOX 14.2 Opioid Drugs

Parentheses indicate a drug trade (brand) name used in the United States. Most drugs manufactured or distributed in countries other than the United States have different trade names, as do opioid preparations containing an additional drug.

See the pharmacokinetics section for additional comments on duration of action and potency of opioid drugs.

Full-Agonist Drugs

Morphine. The prototypical opioid analgesic, extracted from opium, has had important use in medicine for two centuries. The dose required for morphine-produced analgesia is a standard for expressing potency of other opioid drugs. Injection is the most frequent route of administration. Duration of analgesia after IV injection is five to six hours.

Heroin. Derived from morphine, and three times as potent as the prototypical drug primarily due to its increased lipid solubility that allows rapid entry into the central nervous system. Heroin is not available for medical use in the United States. For nonmedical (recreational/addictive) use, the drug is insufflated, inhaled, or injected. Heroin is converted to morphine in the body, resulting in duration of action similar to that of morphine. Diacetylmorphine is another name for heroin.

Codeine. Extracted from opium, about 1/3 as potent as morphine, often prescribed as a cough-suppressant medication. Codeine is most often taken by mouth and has moderate addiction potential. Medications containing codeine often also include nonopioid analgesic drugs (aspirin or acetaminophen). Duration of effect is four to six hours.

Meperidine (Demerol). A synthetic opioid less potent than morphine but with similar analgesic effect and addiction potential. Meperidine can be injected, or administered orally. Duration of action is two to four hours.

Oxycodone (Percodan, OxyContin). A semisynthetic opium derivative similar in effect and potency to morphine. The use of OxyContin, a slow-release preparation, is prevalent in nonmedical misuse and abuse of oxycodone.

The drug is administered orally in medical practice, and often insufflated or injected in addictive use. Duration of action is four to six hours.

Hydrocodone (Vicodin). Derived from opium but less potent than morphine. Preparations containing hydrocodone are those most often diverted for recreational/abusive use. Commercial preparations in the United States contain an additional nonopioid analgesic drug (such as acetaminophen). Administration in medical practice is by the oral route, or by insufflation when misused. Duration of effect is four to six hours.

Fentanyl (Sublimaze). A synthetic opioid many times more potent than morphine. This drug has a very short duration of action, often used in conjunction with anesthetic drugs for surgical procedures. Duration of effects after IV administration is thirty minutes to one hour, but the drug is available in a transdermal (skin patch) preparation for prolonged analgesia. Fentanyl is also available as a lozenge (lollipop) for transbuccal/sublingual oral

BOX 14.2 Continued

administration. When used without medical supervision the drug presents a high risk of addiction and fatal overdose.

Methadone (Dolophine). A synthetic opioid with a long duration of action. Since the 1960s the drug has been used to manage opioid dependence by preventing withdrawal syndrome. Relatively high doses, given once a day, are used for this purpose. Methadone is also an effective, long-acting analgesic agent for treatment of chronic pain syndromes. For pain control, relatively lower doses are administered and the analgesic effect lasts about twelve hours. The drug is administered orally for medical uses (including dependence management), but in nonmedical use is often injected, producing a euphoric effect similar to that of morphine or heroin.

Partial Agonists

Buprenorphine (Subutex, Suboxone). Binds with mu-opioid receptors but produces less analgesic and euphoric effect than full-agonist drugs. The drug prevents withdrawal syndrome in opioid-dependent individuals and has a long duration of action. Its main use is for management of opioid dependence, although it also has medical use as an analgesic drug. As an analgesic, the duration of effect is about six hours. The approved route of administration is sublingual. Suboxone, a combination of buprenorphine and the opioid antagonist naloxone, is often used for management of opioid dependence. This combination of drugs is intended to prevent euphoric effects if Suboxone is injected.

Opioid Antagonists

Naloxone (Narcan). Binds with opioid receptors to block the actions of agonist drugs, including the extreme respiratory depression of a fatal opioid overdose. Counteraction of opioid overdose is the primary clinical use for naloxone, which is typically administered by intravenous injection. Duration of effect is four to six hours.

Naltrexone (ReVia). A longer-acting (than Naloxone) opioid antagonist that is taken by mouth. Naltrexone prevents euphoric, analgesic, and other effects of morphine-like drugs. When taken daily the drug is effective in maintaining abstinence in individuals recovering from opioid dependence. Naltrexone is also used for a similar purpose in treatment of alcohol use disorders, although less effective for most patients. Duration of effect is twenty-four to seventy-two hours.

From Karch (2013)

Pharmacodynamics: Effects on Brain Function

Opioid drugs influence neural function because they mimic the actions of endogenous opioids as they bind with one or more types of opioid receptors. Their direct-agonist mechanism of action is different from that of indirect agonists like cocaine and amphetamine, which increase the availability of neurotransmitters (dopamine and noradrenaline) in the synapse.

The actions of endogenous opioids and opioid drugs at the cellular level and their effects on neural activity are very complex, with at least three types of receptors and three endogenous opioids involved in many physiological and behavioral functions. The following discussion is mostly limited to actions of opioids at **mu receptors**. Much evidence indicates that activation of these receptors is critical for positive reinforcement and analgesia produced by morphine-like drugs. The neurophysiological and pharmacological processes mentioned in the following paragraphs are discussed in more detail in Chapter 4.

Mu receptor activation inhibits neural activity and release of several types of neurotransmitters. The inhibition of neurotransmitter release is the initial step in producing the central nervous system effects of opioids (analgesia, euphoria). A similar action occurs in the peripheral nervous system – in the GI tract – and results in constipation, a major opioid side effect. Mu receptors are located on both presynaptic and postsynaptic areas of neurons. When opioid agonists bind with presynaptic receptors, entry of calcium ions critical for neurotransmitter release is decreased. Activation of postsynaptic mu receptors opens potassium ion channels, hyperpolarizing the neuron and inhibiting initiation of action potentials (Corbett et al. 2006).

The effects on ion movement occur very quickly, but all opioid receptors are also metabotropic, so longer-term effects mediated by G-protein linkage reduce neural excitation by altering internal signaling processes within the neuron. Long-term effects include changes in the expression of genes and production of RNA, and some underlie the development of tolerance to drug effects (Traynor 2012).

Opioid drugs differ in their affinity (strength of attraction) for receptors. Variations in the strength of attraction between the drug molecules and the receptors (protein molecules) contribute to differences in the actions of drugs. Morphine is a potent analgesic drug but has relatively low affinity for mu receptors (Goodman et al. 2011). Naloxone, an opioid antagonist, has greater receptor affinity than morphine and most other opioid agonists. The higher affinity of the antagonist drug results in naloxone displacing less tightly bound morphine molecules from the opioid receptor. Naloxone binds well to the receptor but has no agonist effect – does not initiate ion movements and internal changes in the neuron. Consequently, naloxone blocks morphine's effects on neural activity and counteracts dangerous effects of a morphine or heroin overdose, such as suppression of respiration.

Buprenorphine, which is sometimes misused, has even greater opioid receptor affinity than naloxone, making the antagonist (naloxone) much less effective for treating overdose of the partial agonist (Volpe et al. 2011).

Analgesia

Pain is a complex subjective experience resulting from incompletely understood neurological processes and psychological factors such as expectation and attention.

The suppression of pain by opioid agonists results from inhibition of neural activity at several locations in pain-signal pathways. The pain-suppression function of the endogenous opioid system modulates pain at three levels of the nervous system (Mansour et al. 1995). In the spinal cord, opioids block the transmission of sensory information related to some types of tissue injury. In the midbrain periaqueductal gray area, disinhibition by opioids increases neural activity that suppresses pain signals. Finally, opioid receptors in the amygdala inhibit the emotional aspect of pain (Figure 14.3).

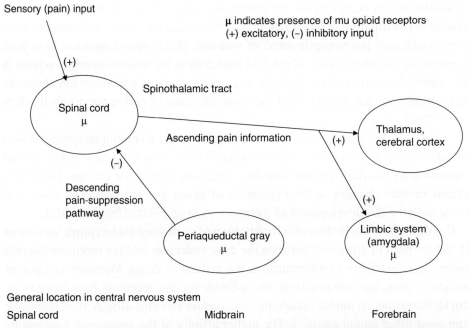

Figure 14.3 Circuits and structures of the central nervous system involved in pain and analgesia. Neural signals indicating bodily damage or noxious stimuli enter the spinal cord and are relayed to the brain via the spinothalamic tract. Opioid receptors (μ) are activated by endogenous opioids (endorphins or enkephalin) or opioid-agonist drugs. These receptors suppress components of pain due to action in at least three nervous system locations: (1) in the spinal cord, pain signals en route to the brain are attenuated; (2) in the amygdala and other limbic system structures, the emotional component of pain ("suffering") is decreased; (3) the periaqueductal gray sends pain-inhibition signals to the spinal cord.

Positive Reinforcement

The production of positive reinforcement by opioid drugs occurs via inhibitory effects in mesolimbic structures (Figure 14.4). Dense concentrations of mu receptors are located on inhibitory neurons in the ventral tegmental area. GABA released by neurons in this area inhibits dopaminergic neurons that project to the nucleus accumbens. Activation of mu receptors inhibits these inhibitory neurons and by this process of disinhibition increases the amount of dopamine released in the nucleus accumbens (Koob et al. 1998). This explanation of opioid-produced positive reinforcement is derived from research with animal subjects. Supporting evidence comes from research with genetically altered mice (with no mu receptors) and injection of opioid drugs directly into relevant brain structures of experimental animals (Koob and Le Moal 2006).

Components of the mesolimbic dopamine system

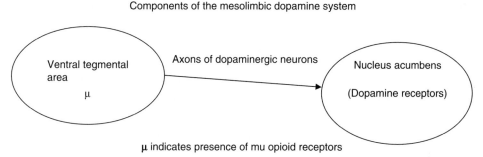

μ indicates presence of mu opioid receptors

Figure 14.4 Central **nervous system structures and pathways involved in opioid-produced positive reinforcement**. An important link in the production of positive reinforcement (which often includes feelings of pleasure) is the input of the neurotransmitter dopamine into the nucleus acumbens. The axons of dopaminergic neurons in the ventraltegmental area (VTA) extend into the nucleus acumbens. Activation of μ. receptors (by endogenous opioids or opioid-agonist drugs) decreases activity of neurons in the VTA that normally inhibit the dopaminergic neurons. The disinhibition of these neurons increases the dopamine input to the nucleus acumbens.

Positive reinforcement is often (but not always – see Chapter 7) accompanied by the experience of pleasure. Evidence suggests that pleasurable feelings ("liking") result from or are amplified by activation of opioid receptors located in small "hedonic hot spots" in subcortical areas of the rat brain. The functions of similar brain areas and circuits are thought to underlie subjective pleasure in humans (Berridge and Robinson 2016; see also Chapter 5).

The endogenous opioid system modulates the effects of other addictive drugs (alcohol, nicotine, cannabis, and possibly cocaine) in addition to playing a critical role in opioid drug reinforcement. This interaction with the actions of other drugs may involve enhancement of dopamine activity by endogenous opioids (Trigo et al. 2010). Naltrexone, an opioid antagonist often used for treatment of alcohol use disorders, reportedly reduces the pleasurable effect of alcohol intoxication in some patients (Krystal et al. 2001). In the limbic system reward circuitry, CB1 cannabinoid receptors are located in close proximity to mu-opioid receptors and bidirectional interactions between the two systems occur (Pickel et al. 2004).

Pharmacokinetics: Bioavailability

The opioid drugs listed in Box 14.2 vary considerably in duration of action as well as rapidity of onset and effective routes of administration. The shortest-acting drug is fentanyl, with an effect duration of less than one hour when injected. Duration of analgesia depends on the severity of pain and drug dose, as well as the half-life of the specific drug. The half-life of morphine, administered either orally or by IV injection, is about ninety minutes (Osborne et al. 1990). The effects of most of the analgesic opioids with abuse potential endure for two to six hours when administered by injection or by mouth. The effects of naltrexone, methadone, and buprenorphine endure much longer, requiring administration once a day or even less often.

Drugs with high lipid solubility (fentanyl, heroin) enter the brain rapidly, producing their effects sooner, and are more likely to cause a euphoric rush. Such drugs are also generally more potent because they act on the brain before metabolic processes substantially decrease blood and brain concentrations. The route of administration also determines the time delay before the drug effect commences. Individuals addicted to opioids generally prefer fast-onset routes, such as insufflation, inhalation (smoking), or intravenous injection.

Opioid drugs are metabolized primarily in the liver. The metabolites as well as small amounts of nonmetabolized drug are excreted in the urine and feces.

Routes of Administration

Opioid drugs can enter the bloodstream by all possible routes of administration, including oral, injection, insufflation, inhalation, mucous membranes of the mouth (transbuccal or sublingual), transdermal, or by suppository (through the rectum or vagina) (Figure 14.5). The oral route is less efficient and often ineffective for heroin, fentanyl, and other opioids. Digestive enzymes in the GI tract slow absorption from the intestine, and the first-pass effect (rapid metabolism by the liver) results in only a small percentage of ingested drug entering the central nervous system (Borg and Kreek 2003). The sublingual route of administration is an effective alternative for these drugs when injection is not feasible.

Several opioid drugs can be administered in forms that greatly extend the duration of effects. Fentanyl can be administered transdermally, by means of a drug-saturated gauze patch taped to the skin. Oxycodone is available in a slow-release formulation taken orally, as is a long-acting injectable form of naltrexone. Longer-duration effects, yielding constant levels of drug in the blood and brain, are beneficial for control of chronic pain and for medical management of opioid dependence (Borg and Kreek 2003).

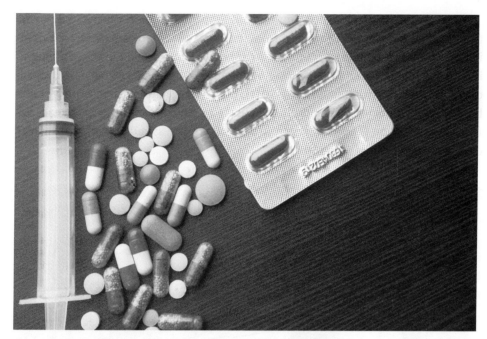

Figure 14.5 Opioid drugs can be administered by several routes of administration, including injection or swallowing pills or capsules. Fentanyl can also be administered by means of a transdermal patch (not shown here), and other less common routes of administration can be used for some opioids (see text). Photo: Towfiqu Photography / Moment / Getty Images.

Subjective, Physiological, and Behavioral Effects

Opioid drugs produce acute effects that relieve pain and emotional distress as well as producing pleasure and positive emotional states. Consequently, these drugs have great value for medical treatment but also can be highly addictive.

Analgesia and Negative Reinforcement

Pain results from injury or a noxious stimulus and has both sensory and emotional-motivational components. The sensation of pain can be sharp and immediate – sometimes referred to as the "first pain." A second sensory aspect of pain is a dull and prolonged ache, often emerging after the initial sharper sensation. Opioid drugs are most effective in counteracting the more persistent pain, although also reducing the awareness of some kinds of sharp, immediate pain (Cooper et al. 1986). At appropriate doses, the drugs can suppress the sensation of pain while having minimal effect on other aspects of consciousness and cognition. This relatively specific analgesic action is in contrast to the effects of general anesthetics or CNS depressants (barbiturates, alcohol) that at high doses eliminate pain by producing loss of consciousness.

The motivational and emotion-producing properties of pain cause anxiety, distress, and an urgent desire for relief from the aversive sensation (Figure 14.6). Pain insures awareness of injury, is critical for survival, and therefore is very difficult to ignore. An important analgesic action of opioids is elimination of the motivational component of pain (Goodman et al. 2011). In cases of sharp pain, as from a severe burn, a patient treated with morphine is likely to report that although he can still feel the pain, there is less distress – it does not "hurt" as much, and its presence does not dominate his attention.

Figure 14.6 Opioid drugs can suppress or eliminate pain and relieve the distressing emotional and motivational components of the pain experience. Photo: davidf / E+ / Getty Images.

Opioid drugs also very effectively alleviate emotional pain that is not caused by physical injury. Anxiety, sadness, anger, worry, loneliness, low self-esteem – essentially any negative emotion or cognition – is greatly diminished, a negative reinforcement effect that becomes a major factor in addiction to heroin, oxycodone, or any opioid drug.

Euphoria and Positive Reinforcement

Subjective descriptions of opioid-produced pleasure abound. Some accounts were written by famous authors who often used the drugs – ranging from Samuel Taylor Coleridge to William Burroughs. Other descriptions of the subjective effects come from interviews with a wide variety of individuals – many of whom were addicts familiar with the effects of heroin.

Many users report a brief, intense rush of pleasure, often described as sexual/ orgasmic in nature, after initial intravenous injections. Intake by mouth, insufflation, or inhalation often produces calm relaxation and indifference to any difficult or disturbing situation – serene pleasure that lasts for hours. This prolonged time of good feeling also follows the intense initial rush of intravenous injection.

Although many who use opioid drugs find the effects quite pleasurable, such positive accounts come from only a subset of individuals. Others report unpleasant as well as enjoyable feelings, and some describe predominately aversive feelings – often due to nausea, itching, or other drug side effects. Many factors influence the subjective effects of opioids (Comer and Zacny 2005). These factors include drug dose, route and rate of administration, and type of drug administered. Pleasurable effects are most likely from rapid intravenous injection of a moderate dose (avoiding the side effects of higher doses) of a full-agonist drug (e.g., morphine). Early scientific studies identifying some of these factors were conducted at Harvard University and at the Public Health Hospital in Lexington, Kentucky. The Kentucky research program utilized subjects incarcerated in the federal prison (mentioned previously) for drug-related crimes.

Patients experiencing pain are the most likely to receive opioid drugs under medical supervision, but most information collected from these individuals refers to the analgesic, rather than pleasurable, drug effects. The limited evidence available suggests that most of these patients rarely experience the positive euphoric effects often described by some subjects in controlled investigations or by individuals addicted to opioid drugs (Comer and Zacny 2005). Pain sometimes appears to act as a "natural antagonist" to euphoric effects of opioids (Conley et al. 1997).

The anticipated results of taking a drug and the situation in which a drug is taken often influence the drug effect – a basic principle of psychopharmacology that applies to the subjective experience of opioid drug use. An individual who injects (or inhales) heroin after a friend's assurance that the result will be pleasurable is different from a woman who receives an injection of Demerol for relief of labor pain during childbirth. One person is seeking a new, exciting, but risky experience, a situation and expectation very different from that of the patient in the obstetrics ward.

The drug use history of the individual is an important determinant of the subjective response to opioid drugs. Not surprisingly, several studies indicate that opioid addicts are more likely to describe their first exposure to the drug as pleasurable than are individuals who did not abuse opioids (e.g., Comer and Zacny 2005, MacAuliffe 1975). Additional factors thought to influence subjective opioid effects include genetic and other physiological differences (Kreek et al. 2009).

Primates, rodents, and other animal species readily learn to self-administer mu-agonist opioid drugs. However, response rates maintained by opioid injections are much lower, as are the amounts of drug received, than those that can occur with self-administration of stimulants (McKim and Hancock 2013). Self-administration response patterns are relatively stable and somewhat similar to drug intake in many opioid-dependent humans. The abuse potential of newly developed opioid drugs can be predicted by operant self-administration studies conducted with rhesus monkeys (Woods et al. 1993).

Other Physiological Effects

In addition to the production of analgesia and (for many users) some degree of pleasurable feeling, opioid drugs also have several other effects. Some of the secondary effects are medically useful; others are unpleasant and annoying, or fatal. Activation of the parasympathetic branch of the autonomic nervous system produces some of these actions – pupillary constriction, reduced blood pressure, decreased body temperature, and other responses. Release of histamine, caused by some opioids, produces intense itching and other allergic reactions. Decreased secretion of sex hormones may reduce sex drive in both genders and alter menstrual cycles in women (Brunton et al. 2008). Inhibition of peristalsis (smooth-muscle movement of the intestinal tract) controls extreme diarrhea, an effect of opioid drugs important in medical practice. The same effect also produces constipation. Codeine and other opioids suppress coughing (the antitussive effect).

Nausea and vomiting are side effects unpleasant to most users, but often tolerated by addicts. In many countries heroin is available only from illicit sources, and the product purchased "on the street" may be adulterated with an inert substance, containing very little of the opioid drug. If an addict vomits soon after injection, the drug's potency is confirmed.

Opioid drugs produce overall relaxation and some degree of sedation. Patients treated with morphine or similar drugs become drowsy and are likely to sleep, although they can be easily awakened. A similar state eventually occurs with non-medical use (after the immediate postinjection euphoric rush), and in addict terminology this state is described as being "on the nod." Some opioid users have an opposite reaction as they become moderately aroused with a feeling of increased energy (Bieber et al. 2008, Washton and Zweben 2006). This unusual and somewhat paradoxical arousal response occurs only at moderate doses, and higher doses reliably produce sedation.

Opioids depress respiration, and at high doses, breathing is completely suppressed. This effect is typically the cause of death by overdose in medically unsupervised addictive use. The risk is greatly increased by combining opioids with other drugs such as alcohol or other CNS depressants (Paulozzi et al. 2006).

Consequences of Long-Term Opioid Use

When opioids are taken repeatedly, tolerance develops, and a characteristic withdrawal syndrome emerges when chronic use is terminated. Both tolerance and withdrawal occur in both medical use and with opioid SUD.

Tolerance

Case studies of patients suffering from chronic pain, subjective accounts of addicted individuals, and research with animal subjects demonstrate that after continued drug use, a dose much greater than the original is required to reproduce most initial effects. Cross-tolerance occurs to some extent in that after chronic use of a specific drug, dose effects of all mu-agonist opioids are decreased (Koob and Le Moal 2006).

Tolerance for analgesic effects is an important problem in medical use, and tolerance for euphoric effects is typical in the development of opioid addiction. Increasing doses result in unwanted side effects in medical use, and risk of death in unsupervised addictive use. Although opioid-agonist drugs differ in the degree of tolerance produced, the effect occurs with use of all these drugs and the search for tolerance-free morphine-like drugs has proven to be futile (Kieffer and Evans 2002). Some opioid effects – including constriction of the pupil of the eye, and constipation – are resistant to tolerance.

Homeostatic responses that oppose the primary opioid effect are similar to those producing tolerance to other psychoactive drugs (Pasternak and Pan 2010). Another probable contributor to tolerance for analgesic effects in some cases is opioid-produced **hyperalgesia**, in which chronic opioid treatment has a paradoxical action of increasing pain responses. This difficult problem is of much concern to pain control physicians (Lee et al. 2011).

The intense rush and subsequent euphoria of injected or inhaled opioids become weaker and shorter-lived with repeated use. Tolerance also develops to the pleasurable effects of opioids taken orally. Addicts attempt to regain the original rewarding effects by increasing drug dose, but many accounts of individuals dependent on heroin, oxycodone, or Vicodin maintain that these efforts are usually futile.

Ethical considerations limit controlled studies of repeated heroin self-administration in humans, but one such investigation was conducted in the 1970s (Mirin et al. 1976). Adult male heroin addicts were detoxified and maintained in a controlled hospital environment. They were then allowed to self-administer increasing doses of heroin over a ten-day period, during which their response to the drug, mood states and social interactions were recorded. Euphoria and positive feelings of liking the drug effect occurred during the initial injection days, but these feelings decreased in intensity and duration with subsequent injections. Unpleasant mood states, belligerence and social isolation became more frequent, following only a brief period of relief after each drug injection.

Associative (learning) processes contribute to the development of tolerance to opioid effects, including the lethal effects of high drug doses. As described in Chapter 7, homeostatic responses to opioid effects can come under stimulus control. Stimuli that reliably predict the onset of drug effects become conditioned, eliciting compensatory responses that attenuate (provide tolerance to) the drug action. Some instances of death in addicted individuals who injected heroin in unfamiliar locations apparently resulted from the lack of conditioned tolerance – in the absence of drug-associated conditioned stimuli (Siegel et al. 1982).

Withdrawal Syndrome

When chronic use of opioid drugs is terminated, or upon administration of an opioid antagonist drug, withdrawal signs and symptoms emerge (Box 14.3). The withdrawal syndrome results from adaptation of the central nervous system to the drug (pharmacodynamic tolerance) and consists primarily of compensatory responses – opposite to the initial drug effects. A major component of withdrawal comes from activation of the sympathetic nervous system. As with the investigation of opioid tolerance, physiological and behavioral features of opioid withdrawal have been observed in many studies with animal subjects, reports of patients treated for chronic pain, and subjective accounts of addicts. Early controlled studies of withdrawal in opioid-dependent human subjects were conducted at the US Public Health Service Hospital in Lexington, Kentucky (Himmelsbach 1943).

BOX 14.3 The opioid withdrawal syndrome

The withdrawal syndrome commences with feelings of anxiety and craving for the addictive drug, followed by other symptoms and indicators of sympathetic nervous system arousal:

Anxiety, agitation, irritability, and restlessness
Dysphoria and depression
Drug craving
Insomnia
Perspiration, piloerection
Lacrimation (excessive tear production), nasal secretions, pupillary dilation
Yawning
Chills, hot flashes
Aching bones and muscles
Muscle cramps, twitches, and spasms
Increased blood pressure and body temperature
Nausea and vomiting
Diarrhea

From Goodman et al. (2011)

The signs and symptoms of withdrawal are similar for all opioids but differ in intensity, time of onset, and duration for specific drugs. A general principle is that drugs with more rapid onset and shorter duration of action have correspondingly shorter delays before the emergence of a relatively brief but intense withdrawal syndrome as compared to longer-acting drugs. The early stages of withdrawal from heroin, a fast-acting drug, emerge six to eight hours after the last drug injection, reach peak intensity in twenty-four to seventy-two hours, and diminish during the next few days. Methadone withdrawal symptoms first occur twenty-four to forty-eight hours after the last administration, increase to a moderate level of intensity over a period of several days, and persist for weeks (Goodman et al. 2011).

Anxiety, dysphoria, and drug craving are emotional-motivational components of withdrawal. These feelings are the first symptoms to appear, becoming more intense as the full withdrawal syndrome develops. Somatic and physiological signs (e.g., piloerection, vomiting) emerge later in the course of withdrawal (Koob and Le Moal 2006).

Given similar patterns of drug administration, the somatic component of withdrawal is similar whether drug intake terminates after medical treatment for pain or after nonmedical addictive use. However, the withdrawal experience is often interpreted differently for the pain patient compared to the addict. The difference in motivational-emotional aspects of withdrawal related to dependence versus addiction is further discussed in a subsequent section.

Additional Consequences of Long-Term Opioid Use

Opioid drugs have powerful effects on neurological functioning and other biological processes. However, if doses administered are nonfatal there are generally few direct toxic effects of even prolonged opioid use. Individuals acquiring and using drugs without medical supervision are at risk of harm from adulterated drugs, injection-related infections and the lifestyle of some addicts.

Even patients administered opioids under medical care sometimes suffer aversive consequences. In some cases of prolonged opioid treatment of chronic pain, patients become hypersensitive to the original pain or a different pain. This paradoxical effect, termed opioid-induced hyperalgesia, is a problematic possible consequence of long-term administration of high doses of opioids (Lee et al. 2011). Long-term increases in emotional sensitivity and lability also may develop. These persistent emotional effects may result from some of the same neurological effects thought to underlie opioid-induced hyperalgesia (Shurman et al. 2010).

Some investigators have described persistent aftereffects of opioid use as "protracted withdrawal syndrome" (Koob and Le Moal 2006). It is difficult to determine whether these effects, which include hyperthermia and metabolic abnormalities, are due to lingering withdrawal syndrome, or other consequences of drug use. The shift in hedonic set-point (described in Chapter 5) might contribute to the sometimes reported extended state of anhedonia and depression (Garland et al. 2013).

Opioid Misuse and Use Disorders

Opioids can produce powerful rewarding effects, promoting in some individuals misuse that progresses into dangerous use disorders and addictive dependence. Misuse of pharmaceutical opioid drugs is defined as use not prescribed by a medical professional – but for pleasure, relief of anxiety or depression or for some other purpose (Substance Abuse and Mental Health Services Administration 2018). Substance use disorders, as defined by the DSM-5, can be slight, moderate or severe – with severe SUD often unofficially designated as addiction.

Use disorders, including addiction to opioid drugs, can take several distinctively different forms. Differences are seen in the initial motivation for drug use, the specific drug used, how the drug is acquired, typical routes of administration, hazards of drug use, populations most likely to develop a use disorder, and the presence of an addictive lifestyle. Even with these differences, some general features are common among all varieties of opioid misuse and use disorders, and the similarities often become more evident as the disorder progresses.

General Features of Opioid Use Disorders

Tolerance to desirable effects is characteristic of all forms of extended opioid use. The development of tolerance promotes increasing drug doses, and in some cases of use disorders a shift from the oral route of administration to more direct methods of intake (insufflation, inhalation, injection). Classical conditioning of drug-linked stimuli can produce craving for the drug and subvert attempts to limit use.

As an opioid use disorder progresses, nondrug ways of enjoying life and coping with difficulties diminish, resulting in greater reliance on the drug. As a painful and debilitating withdrawal syndrome emerges, incentive for drug use changes from seeking pleasure to avoiding discomfort and illness.

Risk factors for opioid addiction resemble those related to substance use disorders for other addictive drugs (Chapters 6 and 8). Conditions or personal characteristics likely to precede or accompany the SUD include genetic predisposition, environmental and developmental factors, and several types of psychopathology and personality traits. Pleasurable feelings from initial use of opioids, which occur in only some individuals, increases the probability of further use and the development of SUD. The powerful tranquilizing action of opioids is often particularly appealing to those who are depressed or anxious.

Greater availability of the drugs is a definite risk factor. In contrast to generally accepted and widely available addictive substances (alcohol, tobacco) opportunity of access to opioids is limited in many social environments. Opioid drugs are more easily accessible in certain environments such as medical care facilities, and urban or rural locales with few economic opportunities and fewer options for nondrug pain management (National Institute of Drug Abuse 2017a).

Although most opioid use disorders eventually lead to adverse outcomes, even addictive use is often relatively stable and less disruptive compared to use disorders of alcohol and stimulant drugs (Hser et al. 2008). Opioid-addicted individuals are typically sedate for a few hours after taking the drug, not showing the disturbing intoxicated behavior of alcohol abuse or the sometimes frenzied or stereotyped activity of amphetamine or cocaine intoxication. Eventually, as the opioid effects wane, addicts crave more drug, but the bingeing (extended bouts of continuous high-dose drug use) typical of cocaine and some forms of alcohol addiction does not occur.

The behavior and outcomes of opioid use disorders resemble compulsive and harmful use of other addictive drugs in several ways. However, with the possible exception of barbiturates, addiction to opioids presents by far the greatest risk of fatal overdose, especially when administered via IV injection or when combined with alcohol or other CNS depressants.

Dependence in the Absence of a Use Disorder

Opioid drugs are a mainstay of medical management of pain. Although their use can become addictive, a majority of patients treated with morphine, fentanyl, hydrocodone or similar drugs do not develop a use disorder – especially when dose and duration of drug administration are limited. However, patients treated with opioids for chronic pain develop tolerance and often experience withdrawal syndrome if drug administration stops. These individuals are then **dependent** on the drug, but most do not show **addictive behavior**, characterized by compulsive use and other symptoms as described in Chapter 2. The important difference between dependence and addiction is further explained in a subsequent section. Most, if not all, opioid addicts are dependent, but many opioid-dependent individuals are not addicted.

Withdrawal in Addicts

Many addicts have repeatedly experienced the full range of the opioid withdrawal syndrome symptoms. The motivational symptoms of anxiety and drug craving are especially intense in these individuals as they anticipate the oncoming discomfort and illness (Figure 14.7).

Figure 14.7 Anxiety and dysphoria occur in the initial stages of severe opioid withdrawal. Vomiting, piloerection, and muscle cramps follow as the full withdrawal syndrome develops. Photo: By Matthew Heptinstall / Moment / Getty Images.

The withdrawal syndrome, summarized in Box 14.3, is uncomfortable, distressing and painful. Some symptoms resemble those of an intense bout of influenza, and addicts often refer to withdrawal as "being sick." Certain descriptions of opioid addiction are thought to have originated from and relate to withdrawal symptoms – "cold turkey" may refer to the "gooseflesh" of sympathetic arousal, "kicking the habit" might come from muscle cramps in the legs. Although an individual experiencing withdrawal may be miserable, the syndrome is not medically dangerous in an otherwise healthy person. Withdrawal syndrome varies in intensity, depending partially on the amount, duration and type of opioid drug use.

Administration of an opioid drug rapidly relieves the discomfort of withdrawal. Although the positive reinforcement of opioids decreases markedly as tolerance develops, the considerable negative reinforcement reward of withdrawal relief is less diminished by tolerance, and is an important factor in maintaining addictive use of the drugs.

Locations, odors, injection paraphernalia, or other stimuli associated with opioid use elicit classically conditioned compensatory responses that oppose the initial drug effects. When an opioid drug is taken in the presence of these conditioned stimuli, the drug effect is attenuated as previously described – **conditioned tolerance**. When the stimuli are encountered and no drug is taken, the **conditioned** withdrawal **responses** occur. Clinical case studies (Box 14.4) as well as controlled studies with detoxified addicts demonstrate that drug-associated stimuli can produce withdrawal symptoms even after the initial syndrome has dissipated (Childress et al. 1986).

BOX 14.4 Conditioned withdrawal syndrome in addicts

Stimuli associated with use of most psychoactive drugs elicit or influence the feelings and responses produced by the drug. Classical conditioning of heroin withdrawal can be especially dramatic because administration of opioid drugs triggers powerful compensatory responses that readily come under stimulus control. These compensatory responses are responsible for tolerance as well as withdrawal symptoms. When drug-linked stimuli are encountered, conditioned withdrawal responses occur. Case histories illustrate that withdrawal-like feelings and responses can be experienced long after the actual withdrawal has dissipated.

In a typical case, a heroin addict underwent withdrawal in prison but, after months of drug-free incarceration, no longer felt any withdrawal discomfort. Upon returning to his home environment, he felt nausea, started to perspire, and craved heroin. These feelings were quite severe, and he vomited in certain locations (public toilets) in which he had injected heroin during his drug-using days. The conditioning is most effective if the drug onset is rapid (as with IV injection) and the conditioned stimuli are distinct (such as the odor of a public toilet) (O'Brien et al. 1986).

Types of Opioid Misuse and Use Disorders

The various forms of problematic opioid use are not DSM-defined types nor as well differentiated as the subtypes of alcohol use disorders. However, relatively distinct groups of individuals who misuse opioids or exhibit an opioid use disorder include (1) those who misuse pharmaceutical opioids by taking the drugs without medical supervision, (2) users of heroin and other illicit opioids (primarily fentanyl), (3) patients who become opioid addicted during drug treatment for chronic pain, and (4) medical personnel who illicitly self-administer opioids.

Misuse and Use Disorders with Pharmaceutical Opioids

In the late 1990s a dramatic increase in opioid use in medical practice followed the easing of restrictions by state medical boards for the treatment of chronic noncancer pain (Kolodny et al. 2015, Manchikanti et al. 2012). Other factors, including the aging population and aggressive marketing by the pharmaceutical industry, also promoted a large rise in prescription of opioid medications, including the more potent drug oxycodone (Barrett et al. 2018, Compton and Volkow 2006, Volkow et al. 2017).

About one-third of the adolescent and adult population of the United States have used pharmaceutical opioids, primarily hydrocodone (Vicodin) and oxycodone (OxyContin), but also including other opioid drugs. A large majority of these individuals uses these drugs only as directed by a medical professional, but about one in eight misuse the drugs (Hughes et al. 2016). Misuse includes using legally prescribed drugs for self-medication for pain relief (in greater amounts or for different types of pain than directed by the physician or dentist) as well as use to relieve anxiety, change mood, or promote sleep. Misuse also occurs when legitimately prescribed pharmaceutical opioids are taken for pleasurable effects or some other purpose. Some of the unused medication may be sold, or shared with friends.

The prevalence of past-year misuse of these drugs in the general population was 4.1 percent (more than 11 million individuals), approximately twelve times greater than the use of heroin/fentanyl. Misuse prevalence was 7.2 percent for ages eighteen to twenty-five. In the United States, misuse of pharmaceutical drugs, primarily opioids, is second only to cannabis use as the nation's most prevalent illicit drug use issue. Use disorders for pharmaceutical opioid drugs occur in about one in seven past-year misusers of these drugs – 0.6 percent of the adolescent and adult population (Substance Abuse and Mental Health Services Administration 2018).

Those who misuse pharmaceutical opioid drugs are most likely to be young male adults, unmarried, with lower income than nonmisusing individuals. A greater proportion of nonmedical users also report nicotine, alcohol and illicit drug use, earlier onset of drug use, and more severe psychological distress than nonusers. Unlike heroin use, which is more prevalent in cities, misuse rates of pharmaceutical opioids are similar in rural and urban locations. Caucasians are overrepresented among urban users of pharmaceutical opioids, an ethnic difference not seen among rural users. Rural, but not urban, users are in general less educated than nonusers (Scholl et al. 2019, Wang et al. 2013).

Vicodin and OxyContin are the most widely prescribed, as well as the most misused, pharmaceutical opioid drugs (Butler et al. 2011, Substance Abuse and Mental Health Services Administration 2018). Vicodin is a formulation of hydrocodone combined with acetaminophen. OxyContin (more potent than Vicodin), in immediate or extended-release formulations, contains oxycodone, as do the older products Percocet and Percodan. Several other pharmaceutical opioid drugs are also used nonmedically (misused), including codeine, methadone, morphine, fentanyl (Sublimaze), hydromorphone (Dilaudid), and buprenorphine. Opportunistic misusers, who are likely to use the drug for recreation or experimentation and often have had little previous experience with opioids, are more likely to take Vicodin. These individuals typically take the drug by mouth, less often by insufflation and very rarely by injection. More experienced opioid misusers, including many who are addicted, typically prefer oxycodone or pharmaceutical fentanyl and often inject these drugs (Cicero et al. 2011).

The National Survey of Drug Use and Health indicated that among those who misused opioids, 38 percent were given the drugs free from a friend or relative, most of whom had received the opioid medication by means of a legitimate prescription from a physician or dentist. For 36 percent a personal physician or dentist had prescribed the drug (for the drug user), and 10 percent bought or stole the drug from a friend or relative. The remaining 16 percent obtained the drugs by theft from hospitals or pharmacies or purchase from an illegitimate dealer (Hughes et al. 2016, Substance Abuse and Mental Health Services Administration 2018).

Heavy users sometimes "doctor-shop" as they visit several physicians to acquire an excessive amount of medication. Quasi-legal sources are so-called pill mills, where opioids are distributed or prescribed by physicians who do not comply with established medical practice standards (Manchikanti et al. 2012). In a similar manner, some pain clinics rather freely distribute opioid analgesics for the treatment of real or feigned medical problems, although these practices are not in compliance with recent advice from the Centers for Disease Control and Prevention (Dowell et al. 2016).

The method of drug acquisition appears to be influenced by willingness to take risks. Younger individuals and those who inject opioids are more likely to procure drugs from dealers or by theft. Older people and those who take the drugs by mouth or insufflation more frequently obtain drugs from physicians (King et al. 2014).

The NSDUH survey indicated that for respondents age twelve or older who misused opioids, 63 percent used the drugs primarily for relief of physical pain; 17 percent to relax, manage emotions or sleep; 13 percent to feel good or get high; and 3 percent because they were curious about the drug's effect. Only 2 percent gave addiction as a reason for use (Substance Abuse and Mental Health Services Administration 2018).

Sean McCabe and colleagues assessed self-reported incentives for drug use among a large number of college and high school students, an age group of special interest in that misuse prevalence of opioid drugs is consistently higher among adolescents and young adults than in the general population. The McCabe surveys indicated that about 30 percent of these younger opioid users stated that they took the drugs only for pain relief, without approval or care of a physician. An additional 45 percent report using for both recreation and relief of pain. Recreational use only was reported by 25 percent, but only a miniscule number of students stated that they were addicted (McCabe and Cranford 2012).

Survey results indicate that a substantial proportion of both young and older individuals misuse opioids to control pain, although other incentives also promote the unsupervised drug use. Pain control appears to be relatively less important and other motivations more prevalent for younger, relative to older misusers of opioid medications.

These results, like those of most drug use surveys, might be influenced by social desirability. Stating that the drug was taken for pain relief is more socially acceptable than the incentives of pleasure or addiction. However, carefully designed and administered anonymous surveys have been shown to provide useful and reasonably valid information (Johnson 2012).

The surveys conducted by McCabe and colleagues indicate that for college and high school students there are distinct subtypes of nonmedical users of pharmaceutical opioid drugs. The recreational users are more likely than those who report use only for pain relief to insufflate opioids, use illicit addictive drugs, binge drink alcohol, and combine opioid use with alcohol or other drugs. Subtype differences were related to gender and ethnicity. The highest rates of self-treatment-only responses were from female and African American students. The recreation-only or mixed-motivation responses were more frequent from male and white students.

NSDUH results indicate that 1.57 million individuals – about one in seven of the 11.1 million who misused pharmaceutical opioids – suffered from a use disorder with these drugs (Substance Abuse and Mental Health Services Administration 2018). An earlier survey found that approximately one-third of respondents with opioid SUD were drug dependent, which in DSM-5 terms indicates severe SUD (addiction) (Wu et al. 2011). These surveys indicate that approximately 0.6 percent of adolescents and adults of the US population have a pharmaceutical opioid SUD, with 0.2 percent (566,000 individuals) addicted to these drugs (Figure 14.8). This

Misuse and use disorders of pharmaceutical opioids

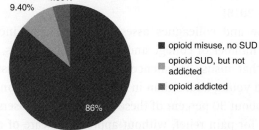

4.60%
9.40%

- opioid misuse, no SUD
- opioid SUD, but not addicted
- opioid addicted

86%

Figure 14.8 Misuse and use disorders of pharmaceutical opioids. NSDUH estimates that 11.1 million adolescents and adults misused pharmaceutical opioids during the year of the survey. Fourteen percent of these individuals suffered from an SUD, including 4.6 percent who were opioid addicted (Substance Abuse and Mental Health Services Administration 2018).

number does not include the patients, under medical care for treatment of chronic pain, who are opioid dependent – some of whom are addicted. Nonaddictive dependence is discussed in a subsequent section.

With some exceptions (fentanyl, oxycodone), pharmaceutical opioids are taken orally by most who misuse the drugs. As typically self-administered, these drugs are less addictive than heroin, which is effective only when administered by the more direct and addictive methods (insufflation, inhalation, injection). However, the much greater misuse prevalence of the pharmaceutical drugs results in a larger number of individuals (1.57 million) with a use disorder for these drugs than of those with a heroin/illicit fentanyl use disorder (652,000).

In 2017, 17,029 individuals in the United States died from drug overdoses that involved prescription opioids (National Institute of Drug Abuse 2019b). Many of these deaths involved the use of fentanyl, which although a pharmaceutical drug is also available from illicit sources and is commonly combined with heroin. Fentanyl is administered by injection or by means of a transdermal skin patch.

Individuals with a less severe use disorder, even though not addicted, sometimes use the pharmaceutical opioids in a dangerous or harmful manner. Opioid overdose is a definite hazard, causing deaths even in misusers who do not inject the drug (O'Donnell et al. 2017). Many fatal opioid-related overdoses also involve alcohol or another drug (Witkiewitz and Vowles 2018). Overdose is only one of the possible adverse outcomes of casual, nonmedical misuse of these powerful drugs.

With addiction – a more severe opioid use disorder – drug use becomes compulsive, even as drug-produced problems develop. The illness and dysphoria of withdrawal make stopping drug use very difficult. Most addicted persons never seek treatment, but the number who do ask for professional help indirectly indicates the prevalence of severe SUD. In 2015, 822,000 individuals received professional treatment for opioid use disorder, a large increase relative to earlier years of the twenty-first century (Hughes et al. 2016). Most (76 percent) of the treated individuals were older than twenty-five (the age range of highest misuse prevalence is eighteen to twenty-five). The age distribution of patients suggests that as with other SUD, disordered use of pharmaceutical opioids often develops or progresses during months or years of use until the consequences become intolerable, requiring assistance from treatment providers.

Use disorders for alcohol, nicotine and illicit drugs are common in people who seek treatment for problematic use of pharmaceutical opioids, and much more prevalent than in the general population (Morasco et al. 2013, Witkiewitz and Vowles 2018). As with other forms of SUD, individuals with opioid use disorders are also likely to suffer from additional psychiatric problems, especially depression or anxiety, as well as subclinical degrees of these distressing conditions. Chapter 8 includes a discussion of how these SUD risk factors can be either a cause, or a result of problematic drug use.

When individuals use opioids as directed by a medical professional, the euphoric effects are minimal and pain is relieved. Opioid preparations in the form of tablets, capsules, or transdermal patches are typically given to patients for self-administration. Many who misuse or are addicted to the opioids attempt to increase the pleasurable effects by tampering with the tablets or capsules so the drug can be taken by insufflation or injection. Euphoric effects can also be increased if the extended-release feature of some products is compromised by pulverizing or chewing the tablets or contents of capsules. These more direct routes of administration increase the risk of addiction and are more likely to result in a dangerous drug overdose. Box 14.5 summarizes measures taken by pharmaceutical companies to prevent or discourage nonmedical use of opioid drugs.

BOX 14.5 Drug manufacturing and formulation procedures intended to deter nonmedical opioid use

In attempts to prevent abuse of their products, pharmaceutical manufacturers have developed tamper-resistant formulations of opioid drugs. The formulations incorporate two main methods to deter abuse of the drugs – physical or pharmacological modifications of the tablet and its contents (Janoff et al. 2016). Oxycodone formulations that resist crushing or dissolution in water (Remoxy, CR OxyContin) are examples of physical modification to impede tampering and misuse.

A pharmacological approach to prevent misuse is the combination of a sequestered opioid antagonist (naltrexone) with morphine or oxycodone. The sequestered antagonist is released to counteract the desired drug effect only if the product is crushed for insufflation or injection. A similar result occurs if Suboxone, a formulation of buprenorphine combined with the antagonist naloxone, is injected rather than taken orally (Raffa et al. 2012). The effectiveness of these precautions has not been tested in large-scale studies. The reformulated products have no effect on a common form of abuse – that of taking the drug in larger amounts or more often than prescribed. The combination of an opioid-agonist and antagonist presents some risk of opioid withdrawal in compliant patients who may crush or chew tablets with no intent to misuse the drug – such as stroke victims who have difficulty in swallowing (Stanos et al. 2012).

Of special concern is that some who misuse pharmaceutical opioids eventually start using illicit opioids, primarily heroin – often combined with illicit fentanyl. A small minority of individuals switch to the illicit drugs after being introduced to the rewarding effects of pharmaceutical opioids during medical treatment for pain, or (more often) by misuse of these drugs (Lipari and Hughes 2015). Nonmedical use of opioids, especially by adolescents, predicts onset of heroin use in early adult-hood (Cerda et al. 2015).

Misuse of pharmaceutical opioids is a definite risk factor for illicit opioid use and addiction although escalation to use of heroin/fentanyl occurs in only a small subset of misusers. Annual misuse of pharmaceutical opioids is about ten times more prevalent than use of the illicit drugs. Although heroin/fentanyl use is nine-teen times more probable in pharmaceutical drug misusers than in nonmisusers, 95 percent of the misusers do not progress to the illicit drugs (Cicero et al. 2014, Muhuri et al. 2013, National Institute of Drug Abuse 2018, Substance Abuse and Mental Health Services Administration 2018).

Heroin/Fentanyl Users

During much of the twentieth century, a common public misconception of a heroin user was that of the "dope fiend." This mostly inaccurate view included predatory "pushers" introducing the illicit drug to naive young people who immediately became addicted, suffered agonizing withdrawal and committed grievous crimes to satisfy their insatiable drug hunger. Heroin is addictive, withdrawal can be very unpleasant, and the typical addict's life is often dangerous. However, many aspects of that pop-ular image of heroin addiction were exaggerations of actual conditions and events.

The majority – although certainly not all – of heroin addicts of the 1950s through the 1990s were young men, living in cities. In addition to the pleasurable effects of heroin, certain aspects of heroin use often promoted the hazardous behavior. Many heroin addicts identified with a deviant subculture characterized by (1) alienation from mainstream society; (2) strong social ties with other drug users; (3) anticipa-tion, excitement, and pleasure from the challenge of acquiring heroin; and (4) feel-ings of effectiveness and competence from coping with the associated risky activity (Moshier et al. 2012). Some users of cocaine or other illicit drugs also had these attitudes that were especially prevalent in heroin users. Many heroin addicts admit-ted to treatment programs were unemployed, and stigmatized by drug-free family members and health care providers (Ahern et al. 2007). For many, the life of a regular user offered something to look forward to each day, bringing more meaning, excite-ment, and opportunity than did a "straight" lifestyle (Mullen and Hammersley 2006).

The attraction of the **subculture of heroin addiction** was incomprehensible to most individuals who did not use the drug. However, for the heavily dependent individual each day presents a specific purpose (obtaining heroin), which has a nearly certain, immediately positive outcome. Some addicts maintained that they liked such a structured life, preferring it to the uncertainties and delayed rewards of a nonaddicted life. Daily use is driven by both need for relief from the early stage of withdrawal and anticipation of the pleasure of heroin use, even if that pleasure is much reduced due to tolerance (Moshier et al. 2012).

Use and use disorders of illicit opioids emerged in a different population during the first two decades of the twenty-first century. Of people entering treatment for heroin addiction who began misusing opioids in the 1960s through the 1980s, more than 80 percent started with heroin (Cicero et al. 2014). Surveys of the general population indicate that of those who started using heroin in the 2000s, 80 percent reported that their first opioid was a pharmaceutical drug (Jones 2013, Muhuri et al. 2013).

In the second decade of the twenty-first century, the extremely potent pharmaceutical opioid fentanyl became available from illicit dealers whose product was often a combination of heroin and fentanyl. Consequently, discussion of recent and current heroin use also refers to the use of heroin combined with fentanyl or fentanyl analogs (similar drugs). Postmortem evidence implicates fentanyl in many opioid overdose fatalities (O'Donnell et al. 2017).

Use of heroin and illicit fentanyl is now closely intertwined with the misuse of pharmaceutical opioids. Most individuals who move from misuse of legitimate opioids to heroin use do not identify with the deviant subculture described above that was apparently more prevalent in heroin addicts of earlier years. Some of these lifestyle features of heroin use may still facilitate heroin use and addiction, especially in young urban men. The demographics of heroin/fentanyl use have shifted toward users that are somewhat older (mean age of twenty-three years for first opioid use), with a greater proportion of white and fewer minorities, more rural and suburban, and an increased proportion of women users.

Estimates from the National Survey of Drug Use and Health (NSDUH) indicate that 886,000 individuals age twelve or older in the United States used heroin/fentanyl in the year before the survey – about 0.3 percent of the adolescent and adult population (Substance Abuse and Mental Health Services Administration 2018). Approximately 652,000 of these individuals had an opioid use disorder (Figure 14.9). About 85 percent of those with the SUD are addicted, so the estimated

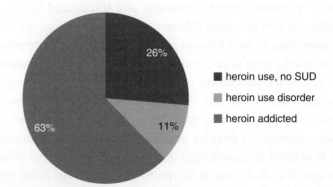

Figure 14.9 Prevalence of use disorders in users of heroin/fentanyl. NSDUH estimates that 886,000 adolescents and adults used heroin/fentanyl during the year of the survey. Seventy-four percent of these individuals suffered from an SUD, including 63 percent who were opioid addicted (Substance Abuse and Mental Health Services Administration 2018).

prevalence of heroin addiction in the adult population was about 0.18 percent (554,000) individuals (Lipari and Hughes 2015).

As previously described, misuse of pharmaceutical opioid drugs is a risk factor for the use of heroin/fentanyl. About 5 percent of misusers of pharmaceutical opioids develop use disorders for heroin/fentanyl – a small minority, but illicit opioid use in these individuals is at least ten times more prevalent than in the general population.

Factors associated with other SUD – genetic, developmental, environmental, and the presence of psychiatric disorders – also contribute to opioid addiction. The transition to the illicit drugs is more frequent in polydrug users – including alcohol binge drinkers and especially those who intravenously inject methamphetamine (Jones et al. 2015).

Socioeconomic factors – sometimes referred to as "upstream determinants" of SUD – are thought to be especially important for many cases of heroin/fentanyl addiction and overdose deaths (Hill and Jorgenson 2018, Thombs and Osborn 2019). These upstream factors are indirect influences such as unemployment and income inequality that are prevalent in states with the highest numbers of opioid-related fatalities.

Availability of heroin also promotes its use – mostly by individuals exposed to other risk factors. Some heavy misusers of pharmaceutical opioids soon become aware that heroin/fentanyl produces a more intense euphoric effect than most licit opioids, creating a market opportunity for dealers of the illicit drugs. When these drugs become easily available and less expensive, their use increases greatly as does the occurrence of fatal overdose (Macy 2018, National Institute of Drug Abuse 2018).

Heroin can be administered by insufflation, and some forms of the drug can be vaporized and inhaled ("smoked"). Heroin used by these methods can produce a moderate degree of addiction, and can also lead to intravenous (IV) injection of the drug. IV heroin injection can produce an intensely pleasurable rush and is more addictive than the less direct methods of drug intake. The words of Rafella Fletcher are a subjective account of a first-time intravenous heroin user:

> He hit the vein, and within seconds the smack hit me. It came from my belly like cream and spread everywhere – warm, calm, dreamy, filling me up with a sensation that was like nothing I had ever felt before. (Fletcher and Mayle 1990, p. 22)

Although some individuals (often referred to as "chippers") inject heroin occasionally without progressing to more frequent use, the start of IV drug use is often a major step toward heavy addiction (Figure 14.10) (Harding and Zinberg 1983).

IV use of an illicit drug presents an especially serious hazard – that of injecting a substance produced and distributed with no assurance of purity or control of potency. About 30,000 of the 47,000 opioid-involved overdose deaths in 2017

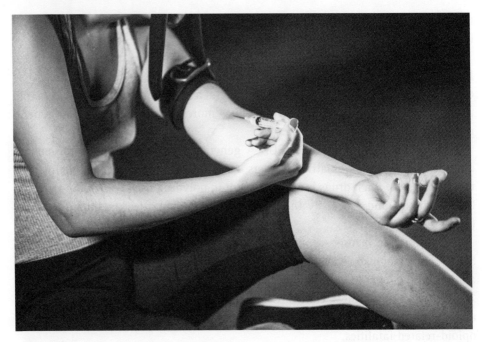

Figure 14.10 Intravenous injection of opioid drugs can result in an intense subjective effects but presents a risk of fatal overdose and is often a major step toward addiction. Photo: urbazon / E+ / Getty Images.

resulted from the use of heroin or a combination of heroin and fentanyl (National Institute of Drug Abuse 2019b). Heroin addicts often become accustomed to injecting large amounts of a low-potency product. When a mixture of unexpectedly greater potency – such as a heroin–fentanyl combination – is injected, a fatal overdose can occur. The probability of early death from opioid overdose in users of illicit opioids increased greatly in recent years, after the introduction of illicit fentanyl (Scholl et al. 2019). Death can also result from heroin injection when tolerance has decreased after a period of abstinence, such as relapse after treatment or upon release from incarceration.

Although death can result from unexpectedly high doses, moderate doses of heroin or heroin/fentanyl in combination with other nonopioid drugs (mainly alcohol or benzodiazepines) can also be fatal (Hakkinen et al. 2012, Jones et al. 2012). The highly publicized "overdose deaths" of certain music and entertainment celebrities – including Jim Morrison (The Doors), Hillel Slovak (The Red Hot Chili Peppers), River Phoenix and Phillip Seymour Hoffman (actors), and others – were apparently caused by combining heroin and alcohol.

Addicts sometimes inject a combination of cocaine or methamphetamine and heroin as a "speedball." The simultaneous effects of two addictive drugs can be extremely rewarding. The following account came from a recovered-addict friend of the author:

When you shoot up a speedball, the first thing that hits is the cocaine – an electric thrill, a lightning bolt of pleasure runs up your spinal cord ... then right behind that is the rush from the heroin – slower than the cocaine but a powerful, overwhelming surge of soothing ecstasy.

Heroin counteracts the aversive agitation of a high dose of the stimulant drug, but the mixture of two drugs of unknown potency or purity can result in a fatal overdose. Death from injecting the combination apparently results from heroin-produced respiratory depression. Cocaine, as well as fentanyl, has been identified in confiscated illicit drugs, apparently combined with heroin to increase pleasurable effects (O'Donnell et al. 2017).

Several long-term studies provide evidence of higher rates of earlier death from overdose as well as from other causes in long-term heroin users (e.g., Oppenheimer et al. 1994). Smyth and colleagues determined mortality rates and years of potential life lost in a thirty-three-year prospective study of 581 heroin addicts (Smyth et al. 2007). The study participants were Caucasian, Hispanic, and African American men, mean age twenty-five years, who were court-ordered into a drug treatment program. Years of potential life lost (an index of premature death used by the Centers for Disease Control and Prevention) was indicated by subtracting age at death from sixty-five. At year 33 of the study, 282 (49 percent) of the men had died; mean age of death was 46.9 years with a mean of 18 years of potential life lost.

Fatalities occurred for many reasons. The limited effectiveness of the treatment program was indicated by the high incidence of relapse of the study participants. The leading cause of death was heroin overdose – forty-nine deaths, with over half occurring within the first fifteen years of the observation period. Heavy use of alcohol, tobacco and other drugs by many of the men contributed to some early deaths. Other frequent causes of death were liver disease (primarily hepatitis B and C), accidents and injuries (from falls, assaults, traffic accidents, firearms), cardiovascular disease, homicide, and suicide.

For much of the observation period of the Smyth study (1960s through 1990s) HIV and AIDS were not causes of death in intravenous drug users or in the general population. HIV, along with other infectious diseases became a threat to the health of IV heroin users in the mid-1980s, a risk that persists (Fernandez and Libby 2011).

Criminal involvement is associated with more severe and persistent drug use (Hser et al. 2008). As a result, a history of addiction to or use of heroin or other illicit drugs is common among individuals in jails and prisons. Some drug use persists among prisoners although this behavior is limited by control and monitoring of visitors and staff members who have contact with incarcerated individuals. Heroin, with its tranquilizing and sedating effects is especially valued by prisoners who must endure loneliness, boredom and threatened or actual violence (Fernandez and Libby 2011). Even if a heroin user avoids arrest and incarceration for use of an illicit drug, he or she is likely to frequent unsafe places with increased probability of assault or robbery.

Dependence and Addiction in Chronic-Pain Patients

Opioids have been used to alleviate pain and suffering for thousands of years, and are still very important analgesic drugs in modern medicine. Their addiction potential is also well known, and physicians and dentists attempt to balance the benefits of pain control against risk of opioid misuse (Dowell et al. 2016). Short-term opioid use for treatment of acute pain presents a relatively low risk of addiction, although this practice does expose patients to rewarding drug effects, resulting in some misuse and use disorders.

Chronic pain is a common symptom sometimes treated with long-term opioid therapy. Such opioid treatment results in tolerance for the analgesic effect, and the **withdrawal syndrome** can occur when drug intake stops. These indicators of drug dependence are typical in patients after extended opioid use, but by themselves do not indicate addiction (Matteliano et al. 2014, Sehgal et al. 2012). Because tolerance and withdrawal are DSM criteria for SUD, patients treated with opioids for chronic pain are often mistakenly identified as drug addicts, a **stigmatizing and pejorative label.**

Many individuals, including some medical personnel, are not aware of the difference between opioid dependence and opioid addiction. In addition to the common presence of tolerance and withdrawal symptoms, patients treated with opioids for chronic pain may also "act like addicts" by aggressively demanding drugs or resisting attempts by the physician to reduce drug dosage (Box 14.6). These and other behaviors, similar to DSM criteria for SUD, are often driven by need for pain relief rather than by the compulsive drug-seeking of addiction. In the absence of genuine addiction, the syndrome is termed **pseudo-addiction** (Matteliano et al. 2014, Fishbain et al. 2008). Pseudo-addiction may be particularly prevalent in patients suffering from certain painful medical conditions such as sickle-cell disease, and probably results from inadequate treatment of pain (Elander et al. 2004). Anxiety about recurrent pain is difficult to distinguish from addictive craving and fear of withdrawal from opioids. When the pain is relieved for the pseudo-addict, the addict-like behavior stops.

Although most patients treated with opioids for an extended time are dependent (to some degree) but not addicted, long-term use of these drugs is a risk for addiction (Garland et al. 2013). Assessment of true addiction in patients with chronic pain is complex, in that several traditional diagnostic criteria are probably not appropriate. Three professional medical organizations (the American Society for Addiction Medicine, the American Pain Society, and the American Academy of Pain Medicine) concurrently proposed criteria to facilitate valid diagnosis of addiction in these patients (Savage et al. 2008). These criteria emphasize that in cases of true addiction, (1) important functions or valued activities are given up because of drug use and (2) drug use continues despite knowledge of physical or psychological harm. In short, opioids can make life better (improve general functioning) for a pain patient who is dependent but not addicted. Conversely, opioid addiction impairs normal function, usually due to sedation or intoxication. To indicate addiction, the drug-produced impairment of function would be greater than that caused by the painful condition for which the drug was administered.

Use of opioid drugs by chronic-pain patients varies from strict adherence to the physician's direction, through use to adjust mood (counteract depression) or promote sleep, to misuse and use disorders including addiction. Opioid use disorders are sometimes indicated by the presence of **aberrant drug-related behaviors** that include drug hoarding, unauthorized dose escalation, and in extreme cases injection of drugs intended for oral use (Gourlay and Heit 2008). Some of these behaviors may be due to pseudo-addiction, so their presence is not a sure sign of genuine addiction. However, "compulsive consumption of opioids to satisfy craving and allay withdrawal irrespective of the presence of actual injury or tissue damage may be seen as a hallmark of addiction among pain patients" (Garland et al. 2013, p. 2608). Use of additional (nonprescribed) opioid drugs is also an aberrant behavior, sometimes revealed by urine toxicology tests.

BOX 14.6 Aberrant drug-related behaviors

Behaviors Suggestive of Opioid Abuse or Addiction

Selling prescription drugs
Prescription forgery
Stealing drugs from others
Injecting oral formulations
Obtaining prescription drugs from nonmedical sources
Obtaining drugs from multiple medical sources without informing primary physician
Concurrent abuse of alcohol or illicit drugs
Multiple episodes of dose escalation, despite warnings not to do so
Multiple episodes of prescription "loss"
Evidence of functional deterioration not explained by pain or other illness
Resistance to lowering drug dose despite evidence of adverse effect from higher dose

---

BOX 14.6 Continued

Behaviors Less Suggestive of Abuse or Addiction – Possible Pseudo-addiction

Aggressive complaints about the need for more drug

Drug hoarding during periods of less intense pain

Requesting specific drugs

Occasional unsanctioned dose escalation

Unapproved use of opioid to treat another symptom (e.g., insomnia)

Expression of family concerns about drug use

From Portenoy et al. (2005)

Although diagnosis of opioid use disorders in chronic-pain patients can be difficult, reviews of a large number of published studies reveal that only a small percentage of these patients misuse the medications or become addicted. In the United States, Fishbain and colleagues found an abuse/addiction rate of 3.27 percent among 2,500 patients reported in sixty-seven studies (Fishbain et al. 2008). From Italy, Minozzi and colleagues determined a median 4.5 percent prevalence of addiction in seventeen studies that included 88,000 patients (Minozzi et al. 2012). These representative rates of use disorders were based on studies that did not include patients treated for cancer, but did include individuals with preexisting substance use disorders. In the Fishbain review, the prevalence of aberrant drug-related behaviors – suggesting, but not definitive evidence of SUD – was 11.5 percent.

A large-scale study of noncancer pain treatment with opioids determined the risk factor of extended opioid treatment (longer than ninety-one days) at three dose levels on the occurrence of opioid use disorder (Edlund et al. 2014). At the low dose range, 0.72 percent of the patients developed an SUD. At medium doses, opioid disorder prevalence was 1.28 percent, and 6.1 percent at the high doses. Expressed as morphine equivalence, low doses were 1–36 milligrams, medium doses 36–120 milligrams, and high doses 120+ milligrams. These investigators suggest that in the absence of a designation of dose administered, a single "use disorder rate" among patients receiving chronic opioid treatment is of little value.

The probability of fatal overdose in opioid treatment for chronic pain – an extreme adverse consequence of drug misuse – is also dose related. One in 550 patients in treatment for chronic noncancer pain died from opioid overdose at a median of 2.6 years after their first opioid prescription. In a higher-dose group (greater than 200 milligram morphine equivalents), one in thirty-two patients succumbed to a fatal overdose (Kaplovitch et al. 2015).

A critical issue in management of chronic pain is prediction of which patients are most likely to misuse, abuse or become addicted to opioids. Retrospective studies provide much information describing characteristics of high-risk patients (Morasco et al. 2013, Sehgal et al. 2012). Medical history, demographic factors, and genetic factors also predict opioid use disorders. Caucasian men are most likely to develop a use disorder, and other risk factors include tobacco and alcohol use, and psychopathology. Although older individuals more often experience chronic pain, patients over age sixty-five are much less likely than those younger than age thirty to misuse or become addicted to the drugs.

The factor most consistently associated with prescription opioid abuse is a history of substance use disorder. Most risk factors for opioids are also associated with substance use disorders for other addictive drugs. Patients with chronic pain are more likely to self-medicate with alcohol, tobacco or other psychoactive substances, thereby increasing the probability of abuse or addiction (Witkiewitz and Vowles 2018). Additionally, individuals with an SUD may be more sensitive to, or at least more distressed by pain, and the delayed effects of most addictive drugs are uncomfortable, dysphoric and sometimes painful.

Among patients suffering from chronic pain, addiction is more likely in those with intense pain – in part, because they require higher medication doses (Edlund et al. 2014). Depressed patients are also at increased risk, as are those who doubt their ability to cope with pain (Morasco et al. 2013). Even in patients with no history of substance abuse, depression increases misuse of opioids, including taking the drug for reasons less directly related to pain, such as improvement of mood (Grattan et al. 2012). Only a small percentage of chronic-pain patients report an aroused, euphoric response to initial opioid administration, but those who do are more likely to develop an opioid use disorder (Bieber et al. 2008).

Several opioid-specific screening instruments are available to assist pain physicians in identifying patients who are likely to misuse or become addicted to analgesic drugs (Sehgal et al. 2012). These questionnaires inquire about the primary risk factors such as age, personal and family history of substance use and disorders, sexual abuse victimization, and psychiatric conditions. Pain intensity and experience with opioid drugs are also assessed. An example of a brief screening instrument is the Opioid Risk Tool, shown to accurately predict misuse and addiction in chronic-pain patients (Webster and Webster 2005). However, many screening tools lack rigorous validation and have weak psychometric properties. Most are subject to deception by experienced individuals whose intent is to obtain opioids for real or feigned chronic pain.

Although pain patients with substance abuse problems are at higher risk for opioid abuse, not all such individuals will misuse the analgesic drugs (Morasco et al. 2013). A physician can prescribe opioids to these patients with relative safety, and can minimize the chance of drug misuse by more stringent monitoring of pain relief, limiting the amount of drug provided by each prescription, and scheduling regular urine tests. Safe and effective management of opioid treatment for all patients includes vigilance for aberrant drug-related behavior and a clear establishment of the physician's expectations of opioid use compliance (Dowell et al. 2016, Matteliano et al. 2014).

Opioid Misuse and Addiction by Medical Professionals

Overall prevalence of substance misuse and use disorders is similar in physicians, dentists, nurses, veterinarians and pharmacists as compared to others of similar status, education and income (Baldisseri 2007, Carinci and Christo 2009). However, these medical professionals are ordinarily highly trusted, and errors in their work can cause much harm to their patients. As a result, any substance misuse in medical personnel, and especially impairment caused by addiction or intoxication, can have more severe consequences than for most who suffer from a substance use disorder.

Problematic alcohol use is the most prevalent substance use disorder among physicians, with opioids the second most misused drug class. Physicians are more likely than other individuals to misuse opioids or benzodiazepines, but less likely to use and misuse illicit drugs (Galanter et al. 2007). Prevalence rates for pharmaceutical drug abuse differ among medical specialties. Anesthesiologists are among the most vulnerable, often showing a preference for the potent, short-duration drug fentanyl (Luck and Hendrick 2004). Psychiatrists are most likely to misuse benzodiazepines, and emergency room doctors have higher rates of cocaine use. Pediatricians, obstetricians and gynecologists have the lowest rates of substance abuse among physicians (Carinci and Christo 2009). Addiction prevalence among nurses appears to be similar to that of physicians, with corresponding differences among medical specialties (Storr et al. 2000).

Many risk factors for medical professionals and other health care workers are the same conditions and predispositions that increase the probability of substance use disorders for the general population. However, certain major risk factors for opioid use disorders are unique to this special population: access to the drugs and injection equipment, and familiarity with drug administration techniques and drug effects (Tischler 2015).

Drug abuse by individuals with easier access to drugs was probably much more common in earlier years when opioids were less closely controlled. Currently many safeguards are in place to limit drug diversion and misuse. Extensive record-keeping, effective physical security of drugs, and close surveillance of controlled drug use by the federal government (Drug Enforcement Administration) are examples of these safeguards. However, highly motivated, clever medical workers intent on obtaining opioids for their own unauthorized use can defeat these precautions, at least temporarily. Doctors and nurse-practitioners can prescribe drugs for themselves, although self-prescribing of addictive drugs is considered unadvisable and could arouse suspicion of misuse. Frequent unannounced urine screen tests are standard procedure in many medical facilities, although risk-taking addicts are likely to believe that they can avoid detection.

In addition to the important risk factor of access to and familiarity with opioids, the stressful nature and heavy responsibility of medical care work also promotes drug abuse (Merlo et al. 2013). Many nurses and physicians are required to work long, irregular hours. Time-management problems and heavy workloads can create stress, as can conflicts with patients. Critical, life-and-death decisions are inherent features of practicing medicine and caring for patients.

Additional risks include personal characteristics common among these highly trained, hard-working individuals. Most are very self-confident, enjoy challenges, and some have "pharmacological optimism" which means that they know well that opioids have useful and pleasing effects, believing that they can use drugs safely for purposes other than pain relief. They often assume that their medical knowledge and training will protect them from any adverse consequences, including addiction. Even if a doctor or nurse becomes aware of her developing drug use problem, she may be reluctant to seek help due to professional pride and fear of job loss. As with many other addicts who are not in medical care occupations, refusal to recognize or acknowledge the problem (denial) also decreases the probability of seeking help.

Individuals in the prestigious, high-status medical professions are less likely to be questioned by associates about suspicious behavior – such as unexplained absences or marginal work performance. Unfortunately, blatant incompetence or unmistakable intoxication often appear only late in the progression of the disorder, in many cases after harmful errors have occurred (Carinci and Christo 2009).

Nursing is apparently the medical profession most vulnerable to substance abuse. In addition to long working hours and demanding tasks, most nurses are women, subject to the unique gender-specific vulnerabilities discussed in Chapter 10. Nurses also compose the largest group of health care professionals and have extensive contact with patients, so their behavior impaired by substance abuse is often more noticeable. Nurses who develop a substance use disorder are often more stigmatized than other medical professionals and receive more severe sanctions than physicians (Shaw et al. 2004).

When substance abuse (most often with alcohol or opioids) is detected in physicians – often by colleagues – they are subject to loss of license to practice medicine by action of state's physician licensing board. Nearly all states in the United States have a **physician health program (PHP)**, operating under the authority of the state licensing board. The PHP attempts to protect the impaired physician from permanent loss of license and occupation while at the same time protecting the public. The PHP conducts an evaluation of a professional brought to their attention. If impairment (usually due to addiction or psychiatric disorder) is detected, the physician is required to suspend clinical practice and enter a treatment program. In most cases, a five-year contract is arranged, during which periodic unannounced urine tests are conducted. A designated colleague also monitors the recovering physician for appropriate behavior and compliance with an ongoing relapse prevention program. As long as the PHP contract is satisfied and sobriety maintained, the physician's license is safe – the PHP acts as intermediary between the physician and the state licensing board. Most physicians do well under the PHP contracts. A survey of 802 recovering physicians indicated that at a five-year after-treatment follow-up, 78.7 percent were still licensed and practicing medicine. This recovery rate is considerably higher than for substance use treatment in general (McClellan et al. 2008).

Most states have similar health programs for promoting intervention, treatment and ongoing recovery support for nurses and other medical professionals with substance abuse problems. The incentive of retaining a valued occupation, in conjunction with mandatory treatment and copious support by other recovering individuals who work in the medical field, results in high recovery rates similar to those of impaired physicians.

The Neonatal Abstinence Syndrome

Yet another expression of opioid dependence is that seen in some newborn infants exposed to the drugs during pregnancy. Women who take opioids for extended periods during pregnancy are likely to bear babies that exhibit withdrawal symptoms within forty-eight to seventy-two hours after birth (Wexelblatt et al. 2017). The neonatal abstinence syndrome (NAS) includes excessive crying, irritability, exaggerated motor reflexes, less sleep-time, tremors, rapid breathing, sweating and vomiting. Symptoms can sometimes persist for weeks or months after birth, and newborn babies with NAS are retained in the hospital three to four times longer than those without the syndrome (Tolia et al. 2015).

In 2012 the NAS occurred in 21,732 infants in the United States, an incidence of 5.8 of 1,000 hospital births. Incidence varied widely among states, with the highest rates reported in Kentucky, Tennessee, Mississippi and Alabama, states with high rates of prescriptions for opioid analgesic drugs. The rate of NAS occurrence increased nearly fivefold between 2000 and 2013, accompanied by the rise in prescriptions for opioid analgesics during these years (Patrick et al. 2015a). The probability of NAS occurrence increases with the duration of pharmaceutical opioid use, use of longer-acting opioid drugs, and the frequency of tobacco usage during pregnancy (Patrick et al. 2015b). Nationally, over 80 percent of infants with NAS were enrolled in state Medicaid programs.

Popular-media accounts often describe infants expressing the NAS as "born addicted." As previously mentioned, the presence of a withdrawal syndrome is not sufficient to identify addiction, for which compulsive drug use is a critical feature. Obviously, a newborn cannot seek drugs, so opioid-dependent babies are not addicted.

Opioid exposure during pregnancy can result from the mother's treatment with or misuse of pharmaceutical opioid drugs, as well as use of heroin. Maintenance on an opioid-agonist drug (methadone or buprenorphine) is a major component of many addiction treatment programs, including medical care for opioid-addicted pregnant women. Opioid-agonist maintenance prevents withdrawal, which is especially hazardous during pregnancy in that it may cause miscarriage. There are also other benefits of methadone maintenance for addicted pregnant women. Many conditions hazardous to fetal health are common in heroin addiction. Methadone maintenance programs often promote improved prenatal care, lower risk of HIV infection and other medical problems. The NAS that occurs in babies exposed *in utero* to methadone is less severe after methadone treatment than in many cases of heroin addiction (Martin et al. 2009).

Although methadone has been the standard treatment for opioid-addicted pregnant women for decades, the use of buprenorphine for this purpose is increasing. Buprenorphine causes less suppression of fetal heart rate and movement, and most importantly results in a less severe FAS (Jones et al. 2014).

NAS can be managed without drugs by means of supportive care, but about 60 percent of all babies withdrawing from opioids require drug treatment. For severe cases, opioids (morphine or buprenorphine) or sedative drugs (diazepam or phenobarbital) are administered in gradually decreasing doses (Osborn et al. 2010).

Children born to opioid-addicted mothers often have a variety of cognitive and behavioral abnormalities, some of which become less pronounced as the child matures (Logan et al. 2013, Oei 2018).

Management of Opioid Addiction via Drug Treatment

Since the early 1900s physicians in the United States have been unable to legally prescribe most opioid drugs to individuals addicted to heroin or pharmaceutical opioids for the purpose of treating or managing their addiction. However, since the mid-1960s opioid-replacement treatment has been legal and available. Opioid addiction can be effectively managed by replacing the abused drug with slower-acting, longer-duration opioid-agonist drugs: methadone (Dolophine) or buprenorphine (Subutex). With agonist-replacement management, the individual is still drug dependent, but much of the dangerous behavior of opioid addiction is reduced or eliminated – including risk of infection and overdose as well as prostitution or crimes against property undertaken to finance the illegal purchase of drugs.

Methadone Maintenance

In 1965, Dole and Nyswander introduced methadone for treatment of opioid addiction (Dole and Nyswander 1965). Replacement therapy with the opioid-agonist was soon widely adopted and is currently a major method of managing addiction to heroin and other opioid drugs (Connery 2015, National Institute of Drug Abuse 2019a).

When methadone, a full-agonist opioid, is administered orally to an opioid-dependent individual, the primary effect is elimination of withdrawal symptoms for about twenty-four hours (Brunton et al. 2008). To the extent that opioid craving results from seeking withdrawal symptom relief, methadone also reduces drug craving. Methadone is an effective analgesic drug, sometimes used in medical practice for relief of chronic pain. Unless injected IV, methadone produces little pleasurable effect, and no euphoria in dependent individuals. Methadone reduces or eliminates the pleasurable effects of heroin injection, although this reduction of euphoria can be counteracted by large heroin doses. The withdrawal symptoms of methadone dependence are less intense than those of other full-agonist opioids (e.g., heroin, morphine, oxycodone, fentanyl), but last much longer – in some cases for a period of weeks (Kreek 2000).

Many studies have shown that with daily methadone treatment there are significant reductions in use of other opioids, criminal behavior, drug injection and needle-sharing, and risky sexual behavior (e.g., Bertschy 1995). Methadone treatment programs are also inexpensive and very cost-effective. Most clients do well on methadone maintenance, with a greatly improved and more stable life compatible with gainful employment and care of children. Some methadone maintenance programs schedule stepwise reductions in methadone dose and provide counseling intended to assist the opioid-dependent individual in becoming drug-free. These efforts at promoting eventual abstinence from opioids are frequently unsuccessful, and many clients return to heroin use when methadone dose is reduced. Other maintenance programs allow methadone administration to continue for extended periods (Bart 2012).

Because methadone is addictive and can be abused, its use is regulated by strict federal and state guidelines. The drug can be administered for addiction management only through specially licensed treatment programs. Most clients receive the drug in a flavored solution that must be consumed at the treatment center, preventing injection, or sale to other individuals. Many clients are low-income minorities, typically individuals court-ordered into a methadone maintenance program. A considerable amount of stigma is attached to methadone programs, resulting in reluctance by many addicted individuals of moderate to high economic status to take advantage of this effective form of addiction management (Macy 2018, Washton and Zweben 2006).

Partial Agonist Treatment: Buprenorphine

In 2002 the Food and Drug Administration approved buprenorphine (Subutex) for treatment of opioid addiction. Buprenorphine is a partial agonist for opioid receptors, having typical agonist effects (including analgesia) at low to moderate doses. At higher doses, the receptors are occupied but not activated by the drug. This "ceiling effect" reduces, but does not eliminate, the abuse potential of buprenorphine (Smith et al. 2007). Buprenorphine has an even longer duration of effect than methadone, allowing less frequent dosing. For two to three days after administration, the drug prevents the emergence of withdrawal syndrome and blocks the effects of full-agonist opioids. Buprenorphine is safer than, and as effective as methadone in preventing relapse to heroin use (Donaher and Welsh 2006). The withdrawal syndrome is less severe than that of methadone, and many individuals have become drug-free after a period of buprenorphine treatment (Nielsen et al. 2015).

Unlike methadone, which for addiction treatment is ordinarily administered only in daily visits to a special clinic, fewer restrictions are placed on buprenorphine treatment. After receiving specific training on use of the drug, physicians can prescribe buprenorphine to patients during office visits. After assessment and a brief trial period, some patients may be given a thirty-day supply of the medication, so even the office visits are required less frequently. If injected, buprenorphine does have some abuse potential, so for take-home use, a formulation of the drug intended to prevent abuse is generally prescribed. Suboxone is a formulation of buprenorphine in combination with the opioid antagonist naloxone. If the drug combination is injected (for addictive misuse), the antagonist prevents a euphoric effect (Soyka 2015).

Resistance to Medication-Assisted Treatment (MAT)

Methadone maintenance programs and buprenorphine treatment have made possible a marked increase in quality of life for many thousands of opioid-addicted individuals, as well as reducing much addiction-driven crime and fatal opioid overdose. However, opioid-replacement treatment (MAT) is held in low regard by many addiction counselors and others in the drug abuse treatment field who often insist that for "true recovery" an individual must be drug-free – and not still dependent on methadone or buprenorphine. Some treatment programs are quite reluctant to allow MAT, often requiring that an applicant to their program withdraw from a maintenance drug before admission. Such an attitude is misguided and often harmful because for many opioid addicts the drug therapy offers a much more certain and favorable outcome than does a treatment program that disallows adjunct pharmacological therapy (Washton and Zweben 2006).

Beth Macy gives a journalistic account of inadequate treatment for opioid addiction in rural areas of the United States with a high prevalence of the often-deadly affliction. She reports that some local law enforcement and court systems prevent addicts from entering MAT programs in lieu of incarceration. A similar attitude is held by many fundamentalist ministers, who resist viewing opioid addiction as a disease. These spiritual leaders and authority figures often vehemently reject management of the disorder by means of MAT even though such treatment sharply reduces the rate of fatal overdose (Macy 2018).

Opioid Antagonists in Addiction Treatment

Opioid antagonist drugs (naloxone, naltrexone) block the reinforcing addictive effects of heroin and other opioid drugs. The antagonist drugs occupy receptors for the endogenous opioid neurotransmitters but do not produce the physiological and behavioral effects of agonist drugs. The antagonist drugs are generally safe, with few effects other than blocking the action of heroin and pharmaceutical opioids. Naloxone (Narcan), effective only when injected and with a short duration of action, is used primarily to counteract opioid overdose (Brunton et al. 2008). Naltrexone (Trexan, ReVia) can be taken orally and has a longer duration of action. Daily administration of naltrexone prevents euphoric (as well as analgesic) effects of heroin or pharmaceutical opioids. It does not, however, prevent drug craving, as does methadone or buprenorphine treatment for some individuals.

If naloxone or naltrexone are administered to an opioid-dependent individual prior to detoxification, counteraction of the opioid effect will result in a full-blown withdrawal syndrome. After the addictive drug and its metabolites are no longer in the body, there is no noticeable adverse effect of the antagonist drugs for most users.

Naltrexone is useful for maintenance of abstinence for only some opioid-addicted individuals – it does not have wide use in most recovery programs. A limiting factor is that the most used formulation of the drug must be taken daily to effectively block the rewarding effects of opioid drugs. Relapse can occur if naltrexone is not taken for a day or two (Connery 2015). Recovering addicts who are highly motivated to remain drug-free may readily accept the daily regimen of taking the preventive drug – seeing it as effective insurance against relapse. Opioid-addicted medical professionals participating in mandated recovery programs are often highly motivated to prevent loss of licensure. Naltrexone treatment is a valuable part of successful recovery for many physicians and other health care workers (DuPont et al. 2009).

Vivitrol is an extended-release formulation of naltrexone administered via intramuscular injection that provides opioid-blocking effects for at least one month (Kunoe et al. 2012). This long-acting form of the drug may overcome the problem of lack of compliance with daily oral use of naltrexone (Jackson et al. 2015).

Chapter Summary

In the United States and many other countries, heroin is one of the least used illicit drugs. The nonmedical use of pharmaceutical opioids is much more common, a type of illicit drug use second in prevalence only to that of cannabis. Users of opioids without medical supervision risk addiction and fatal overdose.

Opioid drugs are mainstays of pain management in medicine because they suppress pain and pain-related suffering. The drug-produced state of calm relaxation and contentment relieves all types of emotional distress. Intravenous injection of the drugs can produce brief, intense euphoria – a rush of pleasurable feeling.

Opioid drugs mimic the actions of endorphin neurotransmitters and hormones of the endogenous opioid system. This system modulates pain and activates brain areas that produce pleasurable sensations.

When chronic opioid use stops, a painful withdrawal often occurs – consisting of intense anxiety, irritability, nausea and vomiting, diarrhea, muscle pain, and cramping. Distinctive stimuli associated with opioid effects can become conditioned, eliciting withdrawal symptoms long after drug use has stopped – triggering craving and presenting a risk for relapse.

An upsurge in nonmedical use of pharmaceutical opioids occurred in the early years of the twenty-first century. In 2017, the rate of opioid overdose fatalities in the United States (including deaths from use of illicit opioids) had quadrupled. The alarming rise in opioid misuse and fatalities followed an increase in prescriptions written for the analgesic drugs for treatment of pain. Many who misuse opioids obtain the drugs from friends or relatives who were prescribed the analgesics for treatment of a temporary painful condition.

Motivations for opioid use without medical supervision include recreation (pleasure or experimentation), self-medication of pain or insomnia, improvement of mood, and addiction. Those who use these drugs for pleasure also have a high prevalence of tobacco use, binge drinking of alcohol, and use of illicit drugs.

An estimated one-seventh of the 11 million individuals misusing pharmaceutical opioids suffer from a use disorder and about 5 percent are addicted. Risk factors for addiction or a less severe use disorder include genetic predisposition, use of other addictive drugs, a stressful lifestyle, and ready access to opioid drugs.

Use of heroin or a heroin/fentanyl combination greatly increases the risk of addiction and fatal overdose. Many users of heroin/fentanyl started opioid use with pharmaceutical drugs, but a large majority – about 95 percent – of those who misuse medical analgesics do not progress to use of illicit opioids. About three-fourths of the 866,000 heroin/fentanyl users have a drug use disorder, and a majority of these individuals are addicted. Misuse of pharmaceutical opioids is a risk factor for use of the illicit opioids, as is heavy use of alcohol and other addictive drugs as well as the easy availability of heroin/fentanyl. The relatively recent availability of extremely potent illicit fentanyl has greatly increased the incidence of overdose deaths.

Most chronic-pain patients treated with opioid analgesics for extended periods are to some extent drug dependent in that they develop tolerance to opioids and experience withdrawal syndrome if drug treatment stops. However, only a small percentage of such patients become addicted. For most chronic-pain patients the sometimes-aggressive demands for opioid drugs are driven by a need for pain relief and are not the compulsive drug-seeking behavior of addiction. Opioids improve functioning for these drug-dependent individuals, as opposed to impairment of function for addicts.

Treatment of chronic pain with opioids does present a risk of addiction. However, with adequate surveillance and support by medical professionals, the risk can be minimized. Screening instruments are available for identifying patients who require special attention to prevent drug misuse.

Physicians, nurses, and other health care workers are at increased risk of opioid use disorders. These medical professionals have access to addictive analgesic drugs, they are trained in the use of these medications, and their work is often stressful and demanding.

State health programs and licensing boards protect the public from drug-impaired health care workers but also facilitate their treatment of and recovery from SUD. Most health care workers do well in treatment programs and, with stable recovery, can regain their suspended professional licenses.

With the neonatal abstinence syndrome (NAS), opioid withdrawal symptoms occur in babies born to opioid-using women. Infants with the NAS are drug dependent but cannot exhibit the characteristic drug-seeking behavior of addiction. In severe cases, the abstinence syndrome is treated with decreasing doses of sedatives, morphine, or another opioid drug. Some babies show persistent behavioral problems, possible results of other factors that often accompany the mothers' opioid use (e.g., tobacco or alcohol use, poor prenatal care).

Opioid addiction can be managed by replacing shorter-duration drugs (e.g., heroin, oxycodone) with longer-acting opioids (methadone, buprenorphine) that are less dangerous and not disruptive to a conventional lifestyle. When taken orally, these drugs delay withdrawal symptoms for one to three days and block or reduce the reward value of shorter-acting opioids. Many opioid addicts have gained more stable, safer, and productive lives by means of treatment with these drugs. Treatment of addiction by means of replacement drugs is somewhat controversial in part because some program managers insist that true recovery must be drug-free and so do not support medication-assisted treatment.

Review Exercises

1. Define *opiate, opioid,* and *endogenous opioid.*
2. Summarize the history of opioid use and misuse from the twentieth century until the present.
3. Describe the 2018 incidence of pharmaceutical opioid drug misuse compared to heroin use. Make a case that either the former or the latter is a much greater public health threat.
4. Identify the three subtypes of opioid receptors, their location in the brain or body, and their functions (e.g., pain perception, reinforcement).
5. Identify the three types of opioid peptides and their functions.
6. Define the terms *full-opioid agonist, partial agonist,* and *opioid antagonist* and give examples of each.
7. Describe the three ways that opioid agonists produce analgesia.
8. Describe how opioid drugs produce positive reinforcement and the neural pathways that are involved.
9. What is the most likely primary cause of long-term opioid use – positive or negative reinforcement? Justify your answer with evidence given in the text.
10. Describe the characteristics of opioid tolerance, withdrawal, and conditioned withdrawal.
11. Describe the risk factors for and general features of opioid use disorders.
12. Describe each of the four types of opioid use disorder.
13. Summarize the primary reason for the declaration of an "opioid crisis" in the United States. How did the illicit availability of a potent opioid prescription drug contribute to the public health threat?
14. Chronic pain patients who take opioids for years, under proper medical supervision, can develop both tolerance and withdrawal, yet are not considered addicted. Explain why.
15. What does comparing the incidence of SUD in misusers of pharmaceutical opioids (Figure 14.8) to the incidence in users of heroin combined with fentanyl (Figure 14.9) reveal about the degree of risk associated with each?
16. What are the risk factors for heroin use? What are the risk factors for death caused by heroin use (alone or in combination with other drugs)?
17. Describe the factors that increase the probability of addiction in those taking opioids for chronic pain.
18. Describe the treatment methods for pregnant women who are misusing opioids and the positive outcome(s) for the child.
19. State the advantages and disadvantages of the drugs that are employed to treat opioid SUD.

Key Terms

aberrant drug-related
  behaviors (579)
addictive behavior (565)
conditioned tolerance
  (566)
conditioned withdrawal
  responses (566)
dependent (565)
endogenous opioids
  (542)

full agonists (550)
Harrison Narcotics Act
  (544)
hyperalgesia (561)
mu receptors (553)
opiate (542
opioid (542)
opioid antagonists (550)
opioid peptides (549)
opioid receptors (549)

partial agonists (550)
physician health
  program (PHP) (583)
pseudo-addiction (578)
stigmatizing and
  pejorative label (578)
subculture of heroin
  addiction (573)
withdrawal syndrome
  (578)

<table>
<tr><td>15</td><td></td></tr>
</table>

15 | Tranquilizers and Sedative Use Disorders

CHAPTER OUTLINE

LEARNING OBJECTIVES

1. Provide a brief history of tranquilizers and sedative-hypnotic drugs as treatments for anxiety and sleep problems.
2. Describe the patterns of misuse of tranquilizers and sedative-hypnotic drugs in the United States and Europe.
3. Describe the psychopharmacology of barbiturates.
4. Describe the psychopharmacology of benzodiazepines and identify specific short-acting, intermediate-acting, and long-acting drugs.
5. Explain the mechanism of action of benzodiazepine drugs on the $GABA_A$ receptor complex of GABA neurons.
6. Describe the characteristics and incidence of benzodiazepine use disorder.
7. Describe the pharmacology of three popular benzodiazepine receptor agonists (BZRA drugs) used to promote sleep.
8. Describe the abuse potential, abuse rates for, and withdrawal from the BZRA drugs.

Introductory Vignette: Doctor-Shopping for Xanax

"No, I won't be using medical insurance," Wendy replied to the receptionist in the physician's office. Her facial expression and voice revealed her anxiety – which was not a problem, because she fervently hoped that this new doctor would prescribe Xanax so she could get the drug from the pharmacy today.

Wendy had started regular use of the tranquilizer after she broke up with her most recent boyfriend – who was also her cocaine connection. She did like cocaine's energy and mood uplift, but not the tense arousal that for her was also part of doing coke. She soon learned that Xanax could eliminate that unpleasant edginess, and then she found that the tranquilizer effects felt good even without the coke. When she and Tom parted ways months ago, she quit doing coke but kept using the Xanax – and now she felt wired and bad if she didn't take it every day.

She had persuaded her primary care doctor – who wanted to use Zoloft to manage her anxiety – that she needed a real tranquilizer, not an antidepressant. She concocted a story that her occupation as a sales rep required frequent air travel and that she had an intense fear of flying and trouble sleeping in hotels. He eventually wrote the scrip for Xanax but then balked at her too-frequent requests for refills.

She became proficient at finding new doctors, giving them the same story about phobia of flying and her need to get the drug before a flight later that day. It usually worked – at least for a while – especially with busy doctors who didn't question her too closely. She couldn't use medical insurance because her doctor-shopping would certainly be obvious.

"The doctor will see you now."

Introduction

Anxiety and insomnia are common conditions that are distressing, often disrupt normal activity, and, in extreme cases, threaten good health. Both problems can sometimes be managed by measures ranging from aerobic exercise to meditation or prayer. Most of these nondrug remedies require effort, persistence and in some cases assistance from other individuals – perhaps for therapy, advice, and cooperation to allow for a change in daily activity – assistance which is not readily available to all individuals. Anxiety and sleep difficulties are more quickly, if temporarily, relieved by drugs – primarily anxiolytics and sedative-hypnotics. **Anxiolytic drugs**, more commonly referred to as tranquilizers, reduce anxiety and agitation. **Sedative-hypnotics** are drugs designed to reduce anxiety or induce sleep and whose effect is to depress the activity of the central nervous system. Older sedative-hypnotic drugs decrease anxiety and, at higher doses, produce sleep. Newer sedative-hypnotic drugs are specifically designed to promote sleep. However, drug use for such relief, especially for the older type of sedative-hypnotics, presents risks of dangerous misuse and addiction along with the desirable benefits.

Several other types of drugs, including alcohol and the opiates, can reduce anxiety and promote sleep, although they are often used without medical supervision for other effects such as pleasurable intoxication. Alcohol is an unreliable agent for reducing anxiety, and like opiates is addictive and potentially fatal at high doses. Three types of drugs are used medically for more specific relief of anxiety and insomnia: **barbiturates**, benzodiazepines, and sleep-aid drugs with effects similar to those of benzodiazepines. Barbiturates, the oldest of these general drug types, are the most dangerous and addictive, although the newer drugs can also have adverse effects.

Drug Treatment of Anxiety since 1900

In 1912 phenobarbital was introduced to medical practitioners as a sedative drug, the first of a group of drugs designated as barbiturates. Many other barbiturate drugs were later developed for medical use. Barbiturates are effective sedatives and anxiolytics, and have other medical uses such as production of general anesthesia. However, they are also addictive and are lethal at high doses.

In 1960 chlordiazepoxide (Librium), a benzodiazepine, was introduced as an anxiolytic drug. Diazepam (Valium) and other **benzodiazepine (BZD)** drugs were soon developed and a new era in treatment of anxiety and insomnia began. BZDs were effective for reducing anxiety and promoting sleep and were very safe because unlike barbiturates, they did not depress respiration much, even at high doses. Fatal overdose was a very unlikely consequence of BZD treatment, and anxiety reduction did not often cause disinhibited intoxication. At appropriate dosage, fear, worry, and physical symptoms of anxiety were often decreased without excessive sedation. Insomnia and anxiety are very common problems, and during the mid-to-late 1970s, BZDs – typically referred to as "tranquilizers" – were the most frequently prescribed drugs (Wick 2013). These drugs were apparently the subject of the Rolling Stones song "Mother's Little Helper" – in which the calming effect of "little yellow pills" was touted.

Most physicians and their patients complaining of a variety of anxiety-related problems, enthusiastically accepted treatment with BZDs. For several years after their introduction, a "drug honeymoon" occurred with the BZD drugs, similar to initial widespread medical use of other psychoactive drugs before undesirable effects and other problems became apparent. During the 1980s, it became obvious that the BZD drugs had unwanted side effects, including memory impairment (anterograde amnesia) and some potential for misuse and addiction. Although less dangerous than barbiturates, BZD use in combination with alcohol also increased the risk of unsteady movement and falls, especially in older patients (Figure 15.1).

In the mid-1990s, the serotonin-specific reuptake inhibitor (SSRI) antidepressant drugs (e.g., sertraline/Zoloft) became the primary medication for several types of anxiety disorders. Unlike BZDs, these drugs do not relieve anxiety very quickly. After weeks of administration, SSRIs can be effective for treatment of panic disorder and generalized anxiety. For long-term use, the newer drugs have less abuse potential than BZDs, and can also relieve the depression that often accompanies anxiety disorders.

During the late 1980s and early 1990s drugs with sedative effects similar to the benzodiazepines, but with different molecular structures, were introduced to medical practice. Although these drugs are not BZDs, they share some of the same effects on neural receptors. Because of this action, the drugs are referred to as

Figure 15.1 The distress of anxiety, as well as some of the associated medical problems, can be relieved by various drugs. Management of anxiety with psychoactive drugs often includes risk of unwanted drug effects and addiction. Photo: aznd / E+ / Getty Images.

(atypical) **benzodiazepine–receptor agonists (BZRAs)**. Most of these drug names start with the letter Z, so they are sometimes referred to as the "Z-drugs." These drugs promote sleep, with rapid onset and little residual (next day) sedation. For treatment of most cases of insomnia, BZRAs have replaced BZDs (Buysse 2013). Although these drugs have less abuse potential than BZDs, unwanted effects, including dependence, can result from high doses or combination with alcohol or other drugs.

Misuse of Anxiolytic and Sedative-Hypnotic Drugs

Each of the three types of anxiolytic drugs (excluding the antidepressants) is approved for medical use for their sleep-producing, anxiolytic or anticonvulsant actions. However, as with the analgesic opioid drugs discussed in the previous chapter, problematic use can occur. Misuse occurs when the drug is used in a manner not instructed by a physician – either by the person for whom the drug was intended, or by another individual (Substance Abuse and Mental Health Services Administration 2018). Misuse of hypnotic and anxiolytic drugs includes recreational use, and chronic quasi-therapeutic use (Griffiths and Johnson 2005).

Recreational abuse is driven by a desire to experience the drug effect (get high, become intoxicated), rather than for relief of sleep or anxiety problems. In this form of misuse, large doses, often in combination with alcohol or another drug, are typical. The hypnotic or anxiolytic drug may be used to increase the high state produced by another drug, to reduce unpleasant agitation produced by a stimulant drug, or to relieve hangover or withdrawal. Individuals with this form of abuse are more likely to be young, male, and involved in a culture of illicit drug use (Hughes et al. 2016).

In a common form of quasi-therapeutic misuse, the self-administration of a hypnotic or anxiolytic drug (for relief of anxiety or insomnia) is continued for a longer duration and/or with larger doses than instructed by the prescribing physician. Such extended misuse of the medication occurs frequently in several European countries, the United Kingdom, and the United States (Manthey et al. 2011, Ohayon et al. 2002). The prolonged use is often accomplished by seeking treatment for the same problem from several physicians, or from illicit sources (Ibanez et al. 2013).

The appropriate duration of taking hypnotic and anxiolytic medications is a matter of some disagreement among medical professionals. Many physicians maintain that low doses of the newer drugs can be used safely for extended periods for management of chronic anxiety or insomnia – judging the benefits derived as outweighing the risks involved (O'Brien 2005).

Both types of misusers (recreational and quasi-therapeutic) are at risk for adverse drug effects, including memory impairment and risks of falls or traffic accidents. Frequent use of benzodiazepines – and especially barbiturates – presents a risk of SUD, including addiction.

Griffiths and Johnson (2005) ranked the relative recreational abuse potential of eighteen sedative drugs. Abuse potential was determined by the reward (positive reinforcement) value of each drug and the incidence of abuse as indicated by epidemiological studies and clinical case reports. The barbiturate drug pentobarbital was the highest-ranked for this type of abuse potential, benzodiazepines were given lower scores, and zolpidem (a widely used nonbenzodiazepine hypnotic drug) was ranked as presenting less risk of abuse than most of the benzodiazepines. The negative reinforcement value (primarily anxiety relief) that can promote and maintain abuse or quasi-therapeutic misuse was not evaluated in this ranking of abuse potential.

Barbiturates

Until the early 1960s barbiturates were widely used to treat excessive anxiety and insomnia. The drugs relieve these conditions, but also produce undesirable effects. Intoxication and unwanted sedation often accompany the anxiolytic effect, and the sleep produced by barbiturates is abnormal in that the REM phase is suppressed. Barbiturate treatment also presents a definite risk of addiction and fatal overdose.

Barbiturates in the Brain and Body

Several barbiturate drugs are available for medical use. These drugs have a common mechanism of action, but widely varying time courses of effect.

Pharmacodynamics: Effects on Brain Function

The neurotransmitter GABA is released by approximately 20–30 percent of all central nervous system neurons. GABA performs the important function of counterbalancing excitatory input to neurons – thereby controlling arousal level, emotional tone, memory formation and muscle tension. GABA receptors are widely distributed throughout the central nervous system, located in several different brain structures and neural circuits. GABA regulates the level of activity throughout the brain, including prevention of seizures.

The primary barbiturate mechanism of action that causes central nervous system depression is facilitation of the inhibitory effect of GABA. When $GABA_A$ (ionotropic) receptors in the postsynaptic neuron membrane are activated by the inhibitory neurotransmitter, chloride (Cl^-) channels are opened. Entry of Cl^- ions hyperpolarizes the neuron, opposing any depolarizing excitatory input and making the neuron less likely to initiate an action potential. Binding sites for barbiturates are located in the $GABA_A$ receptor complex – parts of the protein molecule that is the Cl^- channel. As the drug binds to these sites, the Cl^- channel opening is increased (Olsen and Li 2011). In addition to facilitating the action of GABA at the $GABA_A$ receptor, barbiturates can also open Cl^- channels independently of GABA activity (Brunton et al. 2008). This additional inhibitory action of barbiturates may be responsible for their greater – potentially fatal – depressant effects at higher doses.

Pharmacokinetics: Bioavailability

Several barbiturate drugs are available for medical use, with marked variations in lipid solubility that result in different courses of action. Drugs with higher lipid solubility penetrate the blood–brain barrier more quickly, giving an earlier, stronger but shorter effect. The sedation produced by phenobarbital (Luminal), a barbiturate with relatively low lipid solubility, starts about an hour after administration, enduring for ten to twelve hours. Pentobarbital (Nembutal) is more lipid-soluble and subjective effects are felt within thirty minutes after drug intake and endure for five to eight hours. The longer-acting drugs are most often used for seizure control in epileptic patients or for prolonged sedation. The faster-onset and shorter-duration drugs, including pentobarbital and a similar drug secobarbital

(Seconal) are typically preferred by recreational abusers to produce intoxication. Most barbiturates are administered orally, with some exceptions such as methohexital (Brevital), an extremely short-acting barbiturate administered intravenously to produce anesthesia.

Acute Effects

Barbiturate drugs are often considered as prototypical central nervous system (CNS) depressants in that they reduce the excitability of neurons and decrease metabolic and electrical activity of the brain (Dickinson et al. 2002). As dose is increased, these drugs reduce anxiety, control seizures, facilitate muscle relaxation, cause sedation, promote sleep and induce surgical anesthesia. High doses cause potentially fatal depression of respiration.

The dose-related subjective, behavioral, and physiological actions of barbiturate drugs are very similar to those of alcohol. However, death after a large dose of barbiturate is a much more likely consequence than with excessive intake of alcohol. The depressant effects of alcohol and barbiturates are additive, further increasing the risk of death when both drugs are consumed.

Barbiturates, especially the more lipid-soluble and faster acting drugs, produce subjective and behavioral effects similar to those of alcohol. As with alcohol, barbiturate intoxication is very rewarding for many individuals, partly due to relief from anxiety but also because of lessened behavioral inhibition. At higher levels of intoxication, cognition and motor coordination are severely impaired. **Anterograde amnesia** (loss of memory for events that occur during intoxication) is a frequent consequence of moderate to high barbiturate doses. The amnesia and impaired judgment sometimes lead to inadvertent and possibly fatal overdose when the earlier drug ingestion is not remembered and additional pills or capsules are taken.

Barbiturate Misuse and Use Disorder

There are obvious differences between social and cultural influences on use and misuse of alcohol, relative to barbiturates. Alcohol is a commodity and a widely used recreational drug, whereas barbiturates are sedative drugs, dispensed by medical professionals. However, the origins and course of barbiturate use disorders are quite similar to those of alcohol, as described in Chapters 9 and 10. As with alcohol, barbiturate overdose can be fatal, as can the withdrawal syndrome when prolonged heavy use of the drug is stopped abruptly.

During much of the twentieth century, after barbiturates were introduced and before the introduction of the safer benzodiazepines, medical treatment of insomnia and anxiety with barbiturates was commonplace in the United States and many other countries. Many individuals, prescribed barbiturates for self-administration, suffered from adverse effects including addiction and deaths from accidental overdose or by suicide. In a popular culture depiction of some of these damaged lives, a novel "Valley of the Dolls" by Jacqueline Susann was published in 1966. Although a work of fiction, several characters in the novel were apparently based upon celebrities with drug use disorders, some of whom died after barbiturate overdose. The deaths of Judy Garland, Marilyn Monroe and other film stars of the 1950s and 1960s were drug related, often involving a combination of excessive alcohol and barbiturate use.

Since the mid-1960s, medical use of barbiturates as sedatives has declined greatly, as has nonmedical use (misuse) of these drugs. The estimate of the National Survey of Drug Use and Health (NSDUH) for misuse of sedative drugs in the United States during the previous month by individuals age twelve and older in 2017 was 0.1 percent, and for ages eighteen to twenty-five, 0.2 percent of the population (Substance Abuse and Mental Health Services Administration 2018). These estimates indicated the misuse prevalence of all pharmaceutical sedatives, including barbiturates as well as the newer **Z-drugs** (e.g., zolpidem/Ambien, discussed below). Similar low incidence rates of nonmedical sedative use were indicated for the years 2000 through 2016. The more widely used and misused benzodiazepines are not included in these NSDUH estimates.

Tolerance and Withdrawal

With continued use, especially at high doses, tolerance develops rapidly for most barbiturate effects. A particularly dangerous feature of these drugs is that tolerance to respiratory depression develops more slowly than for other effects, a difference that increases the probability of a fatal overdose (Brunton et al. 2008).

The withdrawal syndrome that emerges after extended high-dose barbiturate use is very similar to that of the alcohol withdrawal syndrome. As described in Chapter 10, this syndrome includes extreme sympathetic nervous system arousal and other very distressing symptoms. If not medically managed, fatal convulsions can occur, making barbiturate withdrawal extremely dangerous (Sellers 1988).

Benzodiazepines

BZDs are now prescribed less often for anxiety disorders than in earlier years, but are sometimes used in combination with antidepressant drugs. Although medical practice guidelines do not recommend BZDs for most anxiety-related conditions, many physicians still often prescribe the specific anxiolytic drugs. Patients may request (or demand) BZDs because they desire reliable and rapid reduction of anxiety (Figure 15.2). In addition, the SSRI drugs have side effects that many patients find intolerable, including weight gain and sexual dysfunction.

Figure 15.2 Benzodiazepine drugs are most appropriately used to relieve anxiety in specific stressful situations. These anxiolytic drugs reduce anxiety much sooner than SSRI drugs, but the quick effects can also produce abuse, dependence, and withdrawal when extended use is terminated. Photo: Jose Luis Pelaez Inc. / DigitalVision / Getty Images.

The least controversial and most appropriate use of BZDs is for relief of acute anxiety in specific and time-limited situations, including air travel and preparation for surgery or painful medical procedures. Introduction of more recently introduced benzodiazepine-receptor agonist drugs has greatly reduced the use of BZD drugs for insomnia.

BOX 15.1 Benzodiazepine drugs

Thirteen benzodiazepine drugs are approved for medical use in the United States. Those most widely used are listed here. Additional benzodiazepines are in medical use in other countries.

Trade name	Generic name	Mean half-life in hours (range)
Long-acting agents		
Valium	diazepam	60 (50–100)
Librium	chordiazepoxide	60 (50–100)
Dalmane	flurazepam	80 (70–160)

Trade name	Generic name	Mean half-life in hours (range)
Intermediate-acting agents		
Klonopin	clonazepam	15 (10–24)
Ativan	lorazepam	30 (18–50)
Short-acting agents		
Xanax	alprazolam	12 (11–18)
Serax	oxazepam	8 (5–15)
Halcion	triazolam	3 (1.5–5)
Versed	midazolam	3 (1.5–5)

After ingestion, the long-acting agents are converted into active compounds that are slowly metabolized and excreted. The elimination times listed here are for these active metabolites.

The wide range for elimination times is partly due to slower metabolism and excretion by older individuals.

Midazolam, used to prepare patients for invasive medical procedures or as a preanesthetic agent, is administered intravenously. All other benzodiazepine drugs are administered only orally, except Valium and Ativan, which can also be administered intravenously.

Benzodiazepines in the Brain and Body

The term *benzodiazepine* indicates that a drug has a particular molecular structure. Several drugs are classified as BZDs, and some of the most widely used are listed in Box 15.1. As with barbiturates, the various BZD drugs have a common mechanism of action, but differing duration of effect, depending primarily on their **lipid solubility** and the production of psychoactive metabolites.

Pharmacodynamics: Effects on Brain Function

Benzodiazepine drugs facilitate the inhibitory action of GABA by means of a mechanism of action similar to that of barbiturates. Like barbiturate receptors, BZD receptors are also located in the $GABA_A$ receptor complex. When the drug binds to these receptors, the inhibitory neurotransmitter GABA opens Cl^- channels more frequently, suppressing the firing rate of the postsynaptic neuron (Figure 15.3). Benzodiazepines modulate the function of GABA, but do not inhibit neurons (by opening Cl^- channels) in the absence of GABA activity – making these drugs safer even at high doses than barbiturates, which can suppress neural activity independently of GABA.

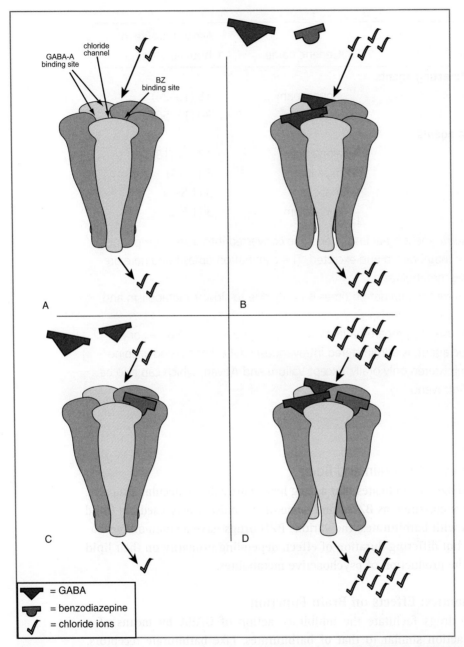

Figure 15.3 The GABA$_A$ receptor complex. The GABA$_A$ receptor complex consists of five subunits forming a conducting channel for chloride (Cl⁻) ions, through which the negative ions can enter and reduce the firing rate of the neuron. (A) Binding sites for GABA and for benzodiazepines are located in the receptor complex. (B) When GABA molecules bind to the receptor, the channel widens, so Cl⁻ ions enter and inhibit the neuron. (C) When benzodiazepines bind to the receptor in the absence of GABA, there is no effect on the chloride channel. (D) When benzodiazepines bind to the receptor in the presence of GABA, the channel opens even further, increasing inhibition of the neuron. The GABA receptor complex also contains binding sites for other drugs, not shown here. Reprinted from *Stahl's Essential Psychopharmacology*, Third Edition with permission from Cambridge University Press (Stahl 2008). © Stephen M. Stahl 2008. Reproduced with permission of the Licensor through PLSclear.

The GABA$_A$ receptor complex consists of five components or subunits that surround the Cl$^-$ ion channel. GABA receptors, as well as barbiturate and benzodiazepine receptors, are located on (or formed by junctions between) these components. Variations in molecular structure of the GABA$_A$ receptor complex result in different responses to BZD drugs (Engin et al. 2012).

The structure of GABA$_A$ receptors varies slightly among different brain circuits and areas.

Specific BZD effects occur as the drug binds with GABA$_A$ receptors in various brain areas.

When the drug facilitates GABA inhibition in the amygdala and other limbic system structures, emotional arousal is attenuated. Benzodiazepines produce anterograde amnesia by modulating GABA activity in hippocampal neurons. Additional specific BZD effects result from enhanced GABA inhibition at other central nervous system locations (Mohler et al. 2004).

Obviously, some BZD effects are useful and therapeutic, whereas others are undesirable, at least in some cases. Current knowledge of how these BZD effects result from enhanced GABA activity indicates the potential for development of drugs with greater selectivity of actions.

Research with mutant mice (with genetic modifications that result in subtle differences in structure of the receptor complex) demonstrates the role of GABA$_A$ receptor subtypes in producing various BZD effects (Atack 2011, Lalive et al. 2011). Depending on the specific structure of the receptors, the mutant mice are differently sensitive to BZD drug effects of anxiety reduction, sedation, muscle relaxation, and anterograde amnesia. These results suggest that anxiolytic drugs with more specific actions can be developed. Such drugs might reduce anxiety without causing sedation, or other unwanted effects such as memory deficits, impairment of motor coordination, and the potential for addiction (Tan et al. 2011).

An experimental drug reduced anxiety without causing sedation in rats and monkeys. Preliminary work conducted with humans appeared to be promising, but clinical tests were terminated when animal studies demonstrated toxic effects (Mohler et al. 2002).

Pharmacokinetics: Bioavailability

Marked differences among specific drugs in time of onset and duration and of action determine the type of medical use, and influence abuse potential. Most BZDs are taken orally, but a few can be administered intravenously, resulting in prompt onset of sedation.

With oral administration, BZD drugs with greatest lipid solubility penetrate the blood–brain barrier and enter the central nervous system most rapidly. Individuals seeking a pleasurable effect often prefer diazepam, a fast-acting and highly lipid-soluble drug. Lipid-soluble BZDs are soon absorbed into fat deposits and are also bound to protein molecules in the bloodstream. Both processes extend the metabolism and elimination times as BZD molecules are slowly released from these protected sites. The duration of action is also greatly prolonged as the older BZDs, including diazepam (Valium), chlordiazepoxide (Librium) and flurazepam (Dalmane) are converted into active metabolites that have long elimination times during which they continue to affect brain function (Brunton et al. 2008). The elimination times of all BZDs vary considerably among individuals, and are longer in older people as well as others with less efficient liver function.

Long-acting BZDs can be useful for treating chronic anxiety. However, with daily administration their slow elimination results in drug accumulation in the body, causing unwanted sedation that impairs activities such as driving. When chronic drug use is stopped, withdrawal symptoms emerge slowly and are less intense than with shorter-acting drugs.

Conversely, short-acting BZDs (e.g., alprozalam/Xanax) are less likely to cause drug accumulation and increasing degrees of sedation, but after extended use, more severe withdrawal symptoms emerge soon after termination of drug treatment.

Acute Effects

All BZD drugs currently approved for medical use share several common effects: Sedation, anxiety reduction, anterograde amnesia, muscle relaxation, and prevention of seizures (anticonvulsant effect).

Benzodiazepines, like most medications, sometimes cause undesirable effects even when used appropriately and in compliance with a physician's directions. Excessive sedation is a common side effect that can result in impaired driving (Bramness et al. 2002) and accidental injuries, such as from falls (Brandt and Leong 2017). Impaired cognition, and in particular memory deficits (Stewart 2005), are additional unwanted effects of prescribed BZD use. Physicians prescribe BZD medications when they judge that the adverse effects of acute or chronic anxiety justify the risk of these unwanted drug effects. When BZDs are used addictively – typically at higher doses and taken more often than as prescribed – the frequency of adverse effects increases greatly.

Flunitrazepam (Rohypnol), a BZD with high abuse potential, is also highly rated for pleasurable effects by some individuals who abuse anxiolytic drugs (Mintzer and Griffiths 2005). Rohypnol is also sometimes administered clandestinely to produce sedation and anterograde amnesia in order to facilitate sexual assault (Box 15.2).

BOX 15.2 Drug-facilitated sexual assault

Flunitrazepam (Rohypnol) is a potent benzodiazepine used medically in Mexico and many other countries. The drug is neither approved for medical use nor available from legitimate sources in the United States. Among the BZD drugs, flunitrazepam has relatively high abuse potential (Mintzer and Griffiths 2005) and is often used in combination with other drugs of abuse, especially "club drugs" like MDMA and GHB (gamma-hydroxybutyrate) (Wu et al. 2006).

"Roofies" is perhaps the most common of many street names for flunitrazepam.

In the mid-1990s, reports appeared of sexual assaults that were facilitated by surreptitious administration of flunitrazepam, often added to an alcoholic drink. Similar to other BZDs, flunitrazepam produces sedation and anterograde amnesia, which are especially severe when the drug is combined with alcohol (Treweek et al. 2010). After drinking the alcohol–drug combination, individuals become more vulnerable to persuasion or coercion to submit to sexual advances and are often unable to remember the event. Although other drugs were also used to cause intoxication and reduce resistance to forced sexual activity, flunitrazepam became known as the "date-rape drug."

Intoxication from any central nervous system depressant drugs (including alcohol) can render an individual less able to resist unwanted sexual advances and in some cases can impair memory (see alcohol blackout in Chapter 9). However, surreptitious administration of a potent, fast-acting BZD such as flunitrazepam – even without consumption of alcohol – can greatly increase the probability of sexual assault.

Benzodiazepine Misuse and Use Disorder

Although BZDs are safer and less addictive than barbiturates, misuse and use disorders occur with these anxiety-relieving drugs. Tolerance for the anxiolytic effect can develop with chronic use, resulting in a risk for the misuse of unauthorized dosage increase. Extended BZD treatment can result in dependence and addiction, including uncomfortable and sometimes dangerous withdrawal symptoms. However, the risk and consequences of BZDs as addictive drugs were likely exaggerated by highly publicized accounts of individual cases (Rosenbaum 2005). In 1979, Barbara Gordon published an autobiographical description of her difficulties with BZD treatment, including withdrawal – entitled *I'm dancing as fast as I can* (Gordon 1979). This book, a best-seller, was reissued with an updated preface in 2006 and 2011. A movie version of Ms. Gordon's harrowing story followed the initial publication. The public, and to some extent the medical community, became concerned about inappropriate and excessive prescription of BZDs, resulting in some decrease in treatment with these drugs.

The risks and benefits of long-term BZD use were assessed by national survey data from consumers, results of controlled studies of drug preferences in healthy subjects, and a controlled clinical study of diazepam treatment, dependence and withdrawal (Uhlenhuth et al. 1999). This assessment indicated that the risks of

BZD overuse, including dependence and addiction were relatively low. Although dependence often develops when the drugs are taken regularly for several months, many patients continue to derive benefits from long-term BZD treatment. These and other investigations of BZD abuse (O'Brien 2005, Hasin and Grant 2015) indicated that the risk of addiction to these drugs is much greater for patients with a history of problematic use of other addictive drugs.

The NSDUH estimated that 0.6 percent of adults and adolescents (1.7 million individuals) in the United States age twelve and older misused a BZD drug during the month prior to the survey. Misuse was reported by 0.5 percent (128,000) of individuals) ages twelve to seventeen, 1.6 percent (552,000) of individuals ages eighteen to twenty-five, and 0.5 percent (1 million) of individuals age twenty-six or older (Substance Abuse and Mental Health Services Administration 2018). The prevalence for misuse of tranquilizing drugs has not changed significantly during the last decade.

Estimates from the NSDUH survey also indicate the presence of an SUD for anxiolytic drugs in 0.3 percent of respondents age twelve or older. These results suggest that about half of all individuals misusing BZD medications have a use disorder for these drugs, with the use disorder most prevalent in adolescents and young adults.

Positive and negative reinforcement are key factors in current explanations of drug use disorders (Chapter 7). Both reward-seeking and anxiety reduction are described as incentives for BZD use by drug-dependent individuals (Vogel et al. 2013).

Benzodiazepines are less rewarding (positively reinforcing) to many individuals than most addictive drugs, including barbiturates, cannabis, alcohol, stimulants, and opioids. Experimental animals self-administer BZDs under certain conditions, although not as avidly as stimulant or opioid drugs (Griffiths and Weerts 1997). Controlled studies demonstrate that most healthy human subjects prefer certain BZDs to placebos, and indicate moderate degrees of "liking" on scales of subjective experience (de Wit and Griffiths 1991, Evans et al. 1996). It seems that among nonanxious individuals, those with a history of moderate or heavier use of alcohol or other recreational drugs – and so having familiarity with drug-produced altered states of consciousness – are most likely to describe BZD effects as pleasurable. Diazepam (Valium), a fast-acting BZD, is most likely to produce feelings of euphoria.

BZD drugs relieve anxiety, an effect important in their extensive medical use. Relief of anxiety can be powerful negative reinforcement, and many addicted individuals report that they crave and use BZDs and other drugs to relieve anxiety (Kassel and Veilleux 2010). The large-scale National Epidemiological Survey on Alcohol and Related Conditions (NESARC) indicates that about half of individuals with generalized anxiety disorder also suffer from a substance use disorder

(Alegria et al. 2010). The presence of an anxiety disorder approximately doubles the probability (and the odds ratio) of a substance use disorder (Grant et al. 2004, Hasin and Grant 2015).

Researchers and clinicians disagree about the direction of causality between anxiety and use of addictive drugs (McCarthy et al. 2010). Chronic anxiety often precedes problematic drug use, a sequence that supports the concept of self-medication of anxiety by drugs. However, heavy drug use eventually causes or worsens anxiety and other psychiatric disorders (Chapter 8), so the relationship could be bidirectional. Whatever the causal relation between chronic anxiety and problematic drug use, these two conditions very frequently occur together.

Concurrent Use of BZDs with Other Addictive Drugs

Benzodiazepine abuse and addiction can occur in the absence of other SUD, but a major nonmedical use of the anxiolytic agents is in combination with other addictive drugs (Woods and Wenger 1995, Grant et al. 2015). Physicians and researchers have studied the widespread concurrent use of opioids and BZDs since the 1970s. Many studies (reviewed by Jones et al. 2012) reveal that at least half of heroin addicts entering treatment also frequently use BZD drugs.

BZD use is associated with increased risk of death from illicit heroin injection (e.g., Bachhuber et al. 2016, Oliver and Keen 2003, McCowan et al. 2009).

In addition to BZD use by many individuals using heroin or other opioids illicitly, the tranquilizing drugs are sometimes prescribed for drug-dependent patients maintained on opioid-agonist therapy – including buprenorphine (Schuman-Olivier et al. 2013), methadone, and in some European countries, heroin (Vogel et al. 2013). Anxiety, a prominent feature of opioid withdrawal, is no doubt an incentive for concurrent BZD use – either medically approved, or illicit (Chen et al. 2011).

The concurrent administration of opioids and BZDs in opioid-replacement programs is controversial, in part due to concerns about drug misuse and patient safety, including possible overdose. The probability of an opioid overdose death is greater in individuals maintained on the full-opioid agonist methadone who also use BZDs (e.g., McCowan et al. 2009). Opioid-replacement programs using the partial opioid-agonist buprenorphine may be less dangerous than those administering methadone, at least in regard to concomitant BZD use. A study of 328 individuals maintained on buprenorphine who were also prescribed BZD indicated no overdose incidents, but an increased number of ER visits due to accidents (Schuman-Olivier et al. 2013).

In Finland and other European countries, illicit use of buprenorphine is common among opioid addicts. Postmortem examinations in 182 buprenorphine-overdose deaths in Finland indicated the presence of BZD drugs in 82 percent of these fatalities (Hakkinen et al. 2012). Apparently, the relative safety of buprenorphine as administered under medical supervision (as in an opioid-replacement program) diminishes for individuals using the drug illicitly, especially when combined with a BZD drug.

The combination of opioid and BZD drugs is a clear example of how the euphoric effect of one drug (the opioid) is increased by the secondary drug (the benzodiazepine). In response to questions about subjective effects of combining the two drug types, opioid-dependent patients described a "boosting" of opioid-produced reward by BZDs (Fatseas et al. 2009, Vogel et al. 2013). In a similar study, some BZD-using patients in a methadone maintenance program described the combination of drugs as producing "a more intense and exciting experience – more like heroin," although greater relief from tension and anxiety was a more frequent description (Chen et al. 2011). A controlled clinical study of combination of diazepam and buprenorphine or methadone in opioid-dependent patients also indicated that the BZD increased the intensity of the drugs' subjective effects (Lintzeris et al. 2007).

Benzodiazepines are also frequently a secondary drug of abuse by individuals with alcohol use disorders (Grant et al. 2015, O'Brien 2005, Rosenbaum 2005). Both alcohol and BZDs are GABA agonists, and share some common behavioral and subjective effects. Alcohol-dependent individuals often use BZDs to produce some alcohol effects (e.g., anxiety reduction) in locations or situations where drinking alcohol is unacceptable, such as the workplace. Aftereffects of alcohol (hangover and withdrawal) can be relieved with BZDs. The drugs are sometimes self-administered by alcohol addicts undergoing withdrawal, and physicians may administer BZDs to individuals during early phases of treatment for alcohol dependence. The anxiety component of opioid withdrawal can also be lessened by BZD treatment.

Stimulant drugs, primarily cocaine and the amphetamines, can produce intense positive reinforcement (euphoric arousal) and are highly addictive, especially when inhaled or injected. At high doses, these drugs also cause extreme agitation and anxiety, aversive effects that in some individuals limit problematic use. Many stimulant addicts soon discover that much of the unpleasant consequences of heavy stimulant use can be reduced or eliminated by BZDs (Martin et al. 2008, Vogel et al. 2013).

Lou Reed's song, *Walk on the wild side*, is a popular culture reference to use of a BZD to ease the effects of heavy stimulant use. The song describes how Valium might have helped a woman who "crashed" after a long run of amphetamine use. When the consequences of addiction become intolerable, stimulant-dependent individuals may seek professional help, or stop drug use without such help. Although the anxiolytic drugs relieve the anxiety that accompanies addictive stimulant use, the relief also enables ongoing compulsive use and prolongs the use disorder (Ghitza et al. 2008).

Addictive drugs produce an array of adverse effects, including death as well as many less severe consequences. Benzodiazepines are relatively safe drugs when used as directed under medical supervision. However, when used as a secondary drug of abuse, BZDs often increase the amount and intensity of harmful consequences of addiction to a more dangerous drug.

Although misuse of tranquilizing drugs is most often one part of a pattern of polydrug abuse, some individuals using only BZDs develop an SUD, including some who become addicted. Compulsive use of BZDs, even without heavy use of another drug of abuse, has harmful consequences. One such adverse effect is physiological dependence, revealed by the emergence of a characteristic withdrawal syndrome when BZD use is interrupted.

Benzodiazepine Withdrawal

A withdrawal syndrome emerges in many individuals within a few days after cessation of extended BZD use. The probability and intensity of the withdrawal symptoms are greater with higher doses and longer periods of chronic use. The syndrome is similar to, although typically less severe, than withdrawal from other CNS depressants such as alcohol and barbiturates.

Many individuals using BZDs as directed by a physician for extended periods become drug dependent, experiencing withdrawal symptoms if drug intake stops – although not addicted. The "dependent, but not addicted" condition was discussed in the previous chapter as **pseudo-addiction** – a consequence of drug use that is also prevalent in chronic-pain patients receiving long-term treatment with opioid analgesics. Addicts compulsively seek the subjective effect of the drug – getting high. In contrast, the incentive for drug use by nonaddicted (but physiologically dependent) individuals is relief from anxiety – often the original problem relieved by the drug, but also prominent in the withdrawal syndrome. This difference is often made less distinct in that for addicts, drug-produced euphoria usually wanes (due to tolerance), and eventually addicts also seek relief from the anxiety of withdrawal. However, most addicted individuals are impaired by their compulsive behavior, whereas most that are dependent (but not addicted) function better with therapeutic drug use – even though they are likely to suffer from withdrawal when drug use is stopped (LaLive et al. 2011, O'Brien 2005). Older patients and those suffering from chronic pain are most likely to use these drugs for extended periods (Hughes et al. 2016).

For several years after the introduction of BZDs to medical practice, it was thought that significant withdrawal symptoms occurred only in individuals who used the drugs without medical supervision, typically at high doses. Clinical observations eventually identified a characteristic withdrawal syndrome in many patients under medical care. In an early study, patients who had taken diazepam or a similar BZD for at least one year were observed as their drug dose was first decreased, then stopped completely as the drug was replaced with placebos (Petursson and Lader 1981). Within three to seven days all patients reported anxiety, agitation, restlessness and sleep disturbance. Most patients were irritable, tremulous and shaky, with aversion to bright lights. Some reported feelings of depersonalization. The dysphoria of withdrawal, described as a combination of malaise, depression and anxiety, persisted for two to four weeks, but gradually diminished. During the subsequent decades, many similar studies have identified this syndrome of **BZD withdrawal symptoms** in at least one-third of patients administered BZDs at therapeutic doses for longer than six months (Lader 2014).

In patients treated for chronic anxiety with BZDs, the previous state of anxiety often recurs after drug use stops. Although anxiety is one component of the withdrawal syndrome, withdrawal also includes other features (such as sensitivity to light) which fade with abstinence from the drug. Time-limited withdrawal-related anxiety is also typically more severe than that experienced prior to drug treatment. Physicians have developed procedures for managing BZD withdrawal (Lader et al. 2009). The effectiveness of these withdrawal management procedures varies among patients.

BZD withdrawal consists of an array of obviously aversive symptoms. However, books and websites intended for the general public seem to exaggerate the difficulty of terminating BZD therapy. As an example, Robert Mercer's *Worse than heroin: The world's most difficult addiction problem* describes the "agony" of BZD withdrawal – greatly overgeneralizing the probability of addiction and minimizing the time-limited nature of withdrawal (Mercer 2008). Book-vendor websites display several books on BZD addiction and withdrawal. Readers' reviews suggest that these books are well received by many individuals.

Benzodiazepine doses taken by addicted recreational abusers are often much higher than therapeutic doses. The more severe withdrawal syndrome that can occur after a month of use at the higher doses may be similar to barbiturate withdrawal and can include delirium and possible convulsions (Griffiths and Sannerud 1987, Lader 2011). Shorter-duration drugs, such as alprazolam/Xanax are more likely to produce more intense withdrawal symptoms that also emerge sooner and dissipate within ten days.

Benzodiazepine-Receptor Agonists (BZRA)

Relative to BZDs, benzodiazepine-receptor agonists (BZRA – the Z-drugs), the third class of drugs, have effects that are similar but more specific, providing sedation with less concurrent anxiolytic, anticonvulsant and muscle-relaxant actions (Brunton et al. 2008). Due to their rapid onset and brief duration of action with little residual (next day) sedation, these drugs are very useful for treatment of insomnia. Z-drugs have little effect on stages of sleep (REM and slow-wave sleep patterns), and the sleep-promoting action is maintained over extended periods (Figure 15.4).

Figure 15.4 The benzodiazepine-receptor agonist drugs (such as zolpidem/Ambien) are effective for the management of insomnia. The drugs' short duration of action promotes sleep with little sedation on the following day. Photo: jhorrocks / E+ / Getty Images.

BZRA Drugs in the Brain and Body

Three Z-drugs are approved for medical use in the United States. All have mechanisms of action similar to that of benzodiazepines and relatively short durations of action (Mendelson 2011). The duration of effects is somewhat longer in older individuals.

Pharmacokinetics: Bioavailability

Zolpidem is the generic name for Ambien, the most widely prescribed sleep-promoting drug in the United States. Its half-life is 1.4 to 4.5 hours. Ambien CR is an extended-release formulation of zolpidem, with a longer duration of action. Zolpidem is also available as an oral spray and as a sublingual formulation.

Eszopiclone is the generic name for Lunesta, a drug with effects similar to that of zolpidem but with a half-life of five to eight hours, resulting in a longer duration of action. **Zopiclone** (generic name for Immovane) is a different formulation of the same drug (a racemic mixture of steroisomers), not available in the United States.

Zaleplon is the generic name for Sonata, the shortest-acting of the Z-drugs, with a half-life of 1 to 1.5 hours. Its brief duration of action may permit an individual who awakens during the night to take the drug and still have no residual sedation the following morning.

Pharmacodynamics: Effects on Brain Function

BZRA drugs are GABA agonists by means of a mechanism of action similar to that of benzodiazepine drugs. However, zolpidem and zaleplon bind more selectively to the alpha-1 subtype of the benzodiazepine receptor than do most benzodiazepines (Sanna et al. 2002). The selective binding action is thought to produce the more specific sedation effect of these BZRA drugs (Mendelson 2011). Zopiclone and eszopiclone are less selective in their binding to specific benzodiazepine receptors (Doble 1999).

Abuse Potential

In 2012, according to the NSDUH estimate, 0.2 percent of individuals in the United States age twelve and older used zolpidem for a nonmedical purpose during the month before the survey (Substance Abuse and Mental Health Services Administration 2013). This prevalence of use without medical direction or supervision was considerably less than (about one-fourth of) such use of benzodiazepines in 2012. Z-drug misuse prevalence was not reported separately in more recent NSDUH surveys but was included in the general category of sedatives. In 2017, the estimate for prevalence of current sedative misuse in adolescents and adults was 0.1 percent of the population, again much less (about 17 percent) of the misuse rate of benzodiazepine tranquilizers. In Griffiths and Johnson's ranking of abuse potential of hypnotic drugs, all the Z-drugs were rated as safer than diazepam and most other benzodiazepines. Zolpidem was ranked as having slightly less abuse potential than eszopiclone and zaleplon (Griffiths and Johnson 2005).

The Z-drugs apparently have only limited appeal as recreational intoxicants. Controlled studies with healthy subjects (screened for psychiatric problems and histories of drug abuse) indicate that zolpidem produces only modest abuse-related subjective effects (pleasurable feelings) (e.g., Licata et al. 2011). In the Licata study, the drug was administered over a range of doses, including those higher than prescribed for insomnia. Some subjects reported liking the effect of higher doses, but most also indicated that they would prefer not to take the drug again. Many subjects also reported negative effects, such as feelings of confusion. Subjects in this study were not attempting to sleep during the time of the drug effects.

Although safer than benzodiazepines, undesirable effects including dependence can occur in individuals treated with Z-drugs – which are often prescribed for relief of insomnia (Brandt and Leong 2017). Epidemiological studies and extensive surveys of case histories from the United States, several European countries and Japan indicate that dependence occurs in a small fraction of those treated with these drugs (Hajak et al. 2003, Soyka et al. 2000). Most of these cases involved supra-therapeutic doses of the drugs, taken by individuals with histories of substance use disorders or other psychiatric syndromes. Considering their wide use, these Z-drugs were judged to be relatively safe, with much less abuse potential than benzodiazepines.

A French survey of pharmaceutical records of zolpidem and zopiclone prescriptions for 107,000 individuals also found a low rate of problematic use of these drugs (Victorri-Vigneau et al. 2013). One percent of 25,000 regular zolpidem users showed use patterns that indicated misuse or dependence – consulting more than one doctor, obtaining the drug from multiple pharmacies, and excessive levels of drug use. Although some of nearly 22,000 regular zopiclone users showed use patterns suggesting misuse, the investigators concluded that dependence was less likely with this drug than with regular zolpidem use.

Withdrawal from Z-Drugs

The rapid elimination of BSRA drugs results in a short-duration of receptor occupation and less time for activation of regulatory processes that produce tolerance and withdrawal effects.

Controlled experiments with animal subjects demonstrate withdrawal-related anxiety after chronic high-dose administration of zolpidem (e.g., Wright et al. 2014). In this experiment, mice were injected with zolpidem twice daily for seven days before testing for withdrawal effects.

Insomnia is the primary symptom for which the Z-drugs are prescribed. Therefore, rebound insomnia seems a likely withdrawal symptom that might be expected upon termination of drug use. However, a controlled study with insomniac patients treated with zolpidem for twelve months indicated no significant withdrawal symptoms, including rebound insomnia, during repeated placebo probe trials (Roehrs et al. 2012). These patients, ages thirty-two to sixty-five years and with no drug abuse or psychiatric disorders, received a therapeutic ten milligram zolpidem dose. Other controlled studies have also reported an absence of withdrawal insomnia in healthy subjects after extended use of Z-drugs (e.g., Voderholzer et al. 2002).

Reports based on surveys of physicians (primarily general practitioners) and patients indicate that withdrawal symptoms can occur in a minority of Z-drug users. In response to a questionnaire, 28 percent of 458 German physicians replied that withdrawal symptoms often occur when extended use of zolpidem or zopiclone stops (Hoffman 2013). The responding physicians did not describe these symptoms, and the patients were not screened for other medical conditions or problematic use of other drugs. In a study from the United Kingdom, 700 patients who had taken Z-drugs for at least four weeks reported their experience with these drugs. Of 370 patients who had stopped, or attempted to stop taking the drug, 20 percent reported withdrawal effects, consisting primarily of feelings of anxiety and panic (Siriwardena et al. 2008). As with the German study, these respondents may have included individuals with a history of substance abuse or psychiatric conditions.

A small number of case reports describe seizures following sudden termination of extended Z-drug use. Individuals described in these reports invariably suffer from other disorders, including addiction to alcohol or other drugs, and used the BZRAs at doses greatly exceeding therapeutic levels (e.g., Cubula and Landowski 2007). There is some evidence that at very high doses, zolpidem's mechanism of action becomes less selective for the alpha-1 subtype of benzodiazepine receptor, taking on a more general $GABA_A$ agonist action similar to that of BZD drugs (Huang et al. 2007). Such a dose-related effect would likely produce a benzodiazepine-like withdrawal syndrome upon termination of high-dose drug administration.

Other Adverse Effects

Zolpidem and zopiclone (and eszopiclone) impair cognitive and complex motor function, as do other central nervous system depressants. Anterograde amnesia is another reliable consequence of use of these hypnotic drugs. Kleykamp and colleagues conducted a controlled study to determine the effects of zolpidem on performance and memory in healthy males (Kleykamp et al. 2012). These subjects were administered a therapeutic dose (12.5 milligrams) of extended-release zolpidem at bedtime for twenty-two to thirty days, and tested with a battery of cognitive tasks during forced nighttime awakening. Attention, working memory, and performance on psychomotor tasks were significantly impaired. Episodic memory of the nighttime tests was impaired when assessed on the following day. These results were similar to those of previous demonstrations of zolpidem-impaired performance and memory, but in addition indicated that tolerance to these effects did not develop with chronic drug treatment.

When Z-drugs are taken at bedtime these time-limited effects on performance and memory rarely cause problems. If taken at other times, or during nighttime awakening, an individual may eat, drive, send emails, or perform other activities with no recollection of this behavior on the following day (Gustavsen et al. 2008, Siddigui et al. 2008). Descriptions of these episodes of amnesia are typically retrospective accounts, with no reliable estimate of their frequency of occurrence (Gunja 2013).

Much evidence implicates impaired driving resulting from Z-drug usage (Brandt and Leong 2017, Verster et al. 2002, 2007). In a controlled test of driving performance eight hours after administration of 7.5 milligrams of zopiclone on the previous night, stability of vehicle control was significantly degraded, as were reaction time and other tests of cognitive ability (Mets et al. 2011).

Zopiclone or zolpidem was detected in the blood of some Norwegian drivers judged as impaired by law enforcement officers (Gustavsen et al. 2009). A similar association between drug use and driving impairment was found in other European countries (Denis and Bocca 2003) and Florida (Reidy et al. 2008). A Norwegian study indicated that traffic accidents increased in some drivers during the month after they were prescribed zopiclone or zolpidem, relative to the month before receiving the prescription (Gustavsen et al. 2008). Impaired drivers found to have a BZRA drug in their blood typically have (1) blood levels exceeding therapeutic doses, (2) failed to take their medication at the correct time or to remain in bed for a sufficient time, or (3) combined the Z-drug with alcohol or another central nervous system depressant (Pressman 2011).

As with benzodiazepines, adverse effects of Z-drug use can occur in individuals taking the drug in compliance with medical directions. However, the dangerous consequences occur most frequently in drug-abusing individuals who may take high doses in inappropriate situations, and in combination with other addictive drugs.

Treatment of Sedative Use Disorders

For many cases of barbiturate or benzodiazepine misuse, the sedative drug is part of a pattern of **polydrug abuse**, and the general problem of compulsive substance use is addressed in the treatment program. When the sedative is the sole drug of abuse, the treatment plan often closely resembles that used for an alcohol use disorder. Several nondrug treatment tactics can be used to manage recurrent anxiety that may have been present before drug use commenced, and which commonly occurs during early recovery from drug dependence.

Chapter Summary

Three types of drugs – barbiturates, benzodiazepines, and benzodiazepine-receptor agonists – have been developed for medical treatment of high levels of anxiety and insomnia.

The first of these drugs to be used were barbiturates, which effectively reduce anxiety and promote sleep but are addictive and, at high doses, can be fatal. Barbiturates were used in many suicides during the years when these drugs were freely prescribed. Medical use of barbiturates to treat anxiety and insomnia decreased greatly in the 1970s after the much safer benzodiazepine drugs (BZDs) became available.

BZDs facilitate the neural inhibitory action of the neurotransmitter GABA. These drugs do not depress respiration and are less likely than barbiturates to produce pleasurable intoxication. With careful dose adjustment, BZDs can reduce anxiety without producing much sedation.

BZD drugs can impair driving and other activities that require complex information processing. The sedative effect also increases the probability of accidental falls, especially in older individuals. Impaired episodic memory (anterograde amnesia) is another adverse consequence of BZD use. These undesirable effects are much more prevalent when alcohol is used concurrently with BZDs.

Stopping extended intake of BZDs without gradual dose reduction results in a withdrawal syndrome characterized by anxiety, insomnia, and a general feeling of malaise. Withdrawal symptoms indicate BZD dependence, but not necessarily addiction. An addict's motivation for drug use typically persists much longer than do the withdrawal symptoms.

Addiction to hypnotic or anxiolytic drugs can follow recreational misuse by individuals deliberately seeking pleasurable drug effects. Misuse or addiction can also occur in patients under medical care – most often when they use the drugs at higher doses and for longer periods than as directed by a physician.

Addiction to BZD drugs occurs most often in individuals with a history of a use disorder of another addictive drug. As a secondary drug of abuse, BZDs can potentiate the effects of opioid drugs, produce effects similar to those of alcohol, and relieve the anxiety and agitation of addictive stimulant use. The probability of a fatal overdose is increased when the sedative drug is used concurrently with alcohol or opioids.

In the late 1980s, the SSRI drugs, originally intended for treatment of the mood disorder of depression, became the approved medication for chronic anxiety. The anxiolytic effects of SSRI drugs emerge only after weeks of treatment. Although the treatment of anxiety problems with BZDs has decreased somewhat, physicians continue to prescribe these drugs, partly in response to patient demands for quick and reliable relief of anxiety.

The prevalence of BZD misuse is much lower than that of other addictive drugs. About half of individuals misusing BZDs have a use disorder for the anxiolytic drugs, although not all with a BZD use disorder are addicted.

In the early 1990s the Z-drugs, with a more specific and shorter-acting hypnotic effect than that of BZDs became available. These drugs are widely prescribed for insomnia primarily because of their shorter duration of effect, with little residual sedation on the following day. The treatment of insomnia by BZD drugs has been largely replaced by these benzodiazepine-receptor agonists.

Z-drugs are unlikely to produce pleasurable intoxication and so have less abuse potential than BZDs. These drugs can produce amnesia and impaired cognition, similar to the effects of alcohol and BZD drugs. When used to promote sleep – taken shortly before bedtime – these temporary effects are unlikely to cause problems. Occurrences of nighttime activities while under the influence of a Z-drug (such as driving or eating) that cannot be recalled later upon awakening have been reported. However, the prevalence of such occurrences in patients prescribed the drug is not known.

Review Exercises

1. Define, and state the intended medical use of, anxiolytic, sedative-hypnotic, and BZRA drugs.
2. What classes of drugs for treatment of anxiety and insomnia have been developed since 1900, and what are the advantages and disadvantages of each?
3. What are the functions of the GABA neurotransmitter system?
4. Describe the effects of barbiturates on the GABA$_A$ receptor complex. What effects are produced (e.g., sedation) on the individual?
5. What are the effects of barbiturates that make them so dangerous?
6. What are the current medically approved uses of benzodiazepines (BZDs)?
7. Describe the effects of BZDs the GABA$_A$ receptor complex. What subjective and behavioral effects are produced by this action on GABA activity?
8. Describe how certain BZD drugs can facilitate sexual assault.
9. What is a prominent feature of the BZD withdrawal syndrome?
10. What risk factors increase the probability of BZD misuse and addiction?
11. Summarize the proportion of BZD misuse among the general population and the proportion of individuals with a BZD use disorder among those who misuse the drugs.
12. What is the relationship between BZD misuse and concurrent use disorders of other recreational drugs?
13. What are the relative advantages of BZRA drugs as compared to BZDs?
14. What are possible adverse effects of BZRA drugs?

Key Terms

anterograde amnesia (600)

anxiolytic drugs (595)

barbiturates (595)

benzodiazepine (BZD) (596)

benzodiazepine-receptor agonists (BZRAs) (597)

BZD withdrawal symptoms (612)

eszopiclone (613)

lipid solubility (603)

polydrug abuse (617)

pseudo-addiction (611)

sedative-hypnotics (595)

zaleplon (614)

Z-drugs (601)

zolpidem (613)

zopiclone (613)

PART V
Treatment of Substance Use Disorders

16 | Treatment of Substance Use Disorders

LEARNING OBJECTIVES

1. Provide a brief history of treatment for SUD in the twentieth century, including the disease concept, the Minnesota Model of treatment, and evidence-based treatment methods.
2. Describe internet-based treatment resources for SUD and the status of addiction treatment in the twenty-first century.

3. Describe the features of SUD that are important considerations for treatment.

4. Provide both the incidence of untreated remission from SUD and reasons given for not seeking treatment.

5. Describe the factors that promote remission in untreated individuals.

6. Provide, with a focus on Alcoholics Anonymous, the tenets of mutual-assistance groups as well as other possible reasons why mutual-assistance groups can be effective.

7. Provide an overview of the types of SUD treatments provided by mental health professionals, including individual and group therapy as well as residential and nonresidential treatment programs.

8. Summarize some of the different types of psychotherapies used to treat those with a substance use disorder.

9. Describe the circumstances under which nonabstinent remission and recovery are most appropriate.

10. Review the research on outcomes of SUD treatment and describe proposed treatment improvements designed to increase positive outcomes.

Introductory Vignette: The Almost-Intervention

Lester likes to party, mostly drinking and smoking weed, and sometimes doing a bit of meth. He has just been released from a weekend in jail that followed his third DUI offense. He is ashamed and angry with himself, the police, and the judge. His driving is restricted for a year, and his car insurance expense will go up a lot. He very much wants to avoid getting into more trouble – but recently bad things seem to happen often. He intends to be smarter and more careful, but not to stop drinking – or smoking weed and snorting meth. Drinking and drugging is too much fun to stop – or at least it was for a long time.

When he arrives home, he is surprised to see Jimmy and Susan, as well as Mark, who shares the apartment with Lester. Jimmy is a friend from his construction job, and Lester is dating Susan.

MARK: Welcome home, Lester. We need to talk to you about your DUI arrests, and some other things.

LESTER: Don't tell me this is an intervention!

MARK: Not an intervention like on TV. We have no ultimatums for you, but we have serious concerns about your drinking and drugging. Please hear us out.

JIMMY: Most guys at work don't want to work with you because you are usually hung over, or probably high on something. I'm surprised that you haven't failed a urine screen yet. You are close to being fired.

SUSAN, *with tears in her eyes*: Lester, I won't ride with you any more if you are stoned or drunk. I will probably stop seeing you.

MARK: I won't go with you to football or basketball games. You embarrass me when you get loaded. We are your friends, but if you don't straighten up we will distance ourselves from you. We think you should consider professional treatment.

LESTER: Okay, I hear you. But I can do better by myself. I will be careful and drink less. I don't think treatment works anyway. I see people going into rehab, coming out, and going right back into drinking and using.

Introduction

Addiction is a treatable condition – and treatment does "work," with effectiveness similar to that of intervention for several other chronic medical or psychological problems (Arria and McLellan 2012). Based on research (controlled studies, epidemiological surveys, and clinical observations), much is now understood about the causes and course of SUD, as discussed in previous chapters of this book. Some of this knowledge is applicable to treatment of addiction, although many treatment providers are reluctant to implement changes shown by evidence to be beneficial (Denning and Little 2017, Willenbring 2010).

Estimates from the National Survey on Drug Use and Health (NSDUH) indicate that in the United States in 2017, 20.7 million adolescent and adult individuals had SUD. Approximately 2.5 million (12 percent) of these individuals were treated in a facility or by a professional specializing in substance use disorders. About 1.5 million with SUD did not receive specific treatment for the disorder but participated in a mutual-help group (mostly AA or NA) or received assistance from a nonspecialized source such as a hospital emergency room, a physician's office, or in a prison or jail. Of the 18.2 million individuals with SUD who did not receive specialized treatment, only 1 million felt a need for such treatment. Seventeen million individuals with SUD expressed feeling no need for treatment (Substance Abuse and Mental Health Services Administration 2018).

Addiction (severe SUD) is designated as a psychiatric disorder in the DSM and ICD systems. Most individuals suffering from mental health problems, such as clinical depression or anxiety disorder, ask for help and are grateful for offers of assistance with their problem. In marked contrast, many addicted individuals dismiss offers of help for (and especially advice and warnings about) their self-destructive behavior with replies such as "leave me alone – I am okay, so please don't bother me!"

Previous chapters of this text describe the many difficulties caused by heavy drug use. Some people with a substance use disorder die young – and those who avoid premature death typically experience greatly degraded lives. However, during most of their time of active addiction, many addicts are extremely reluctant to stop drug use. The lyrics of Amy Winehouse's song "Rehab" ("no, no, no – I won't go!") express her defiant refusal to stop destructive drinking and use of other drugs. Ms. Winehouse died from alcohol overdose at age twenty-seven, five years after recording that song.

Many individuals with a severe SUD do eventually stop harmful drug use and in most cases experience a greatly improved quality of life. Some seek assistance from various sources, including health care professionals specializing in substance use problems – that is, they enter treatment programs for addictive disorders. Others become involved in mutual-assistance groups (most often AA, NA, or other twelve-step programs). However, most who manage to stop harmful drug use do so without the assistance of either medical professionals or mutual-assistance groups (natural recovery).

Theories of the basic nature of SUD can influence treatment philosophy and methods. Disease theory and cognitive behavioral theory are two prominent explanations of drug addiction (Chapters 3 and 7). Even though these theories emphasize different causes for SUD, the influence of both viewpoints is apparent in most contemporary treatment programs. The increased public awareness of the disease concept of SUD was important in diminishing the once-prevalent assumption that addiction is essentially immoral behavior – a change in attitude that greatly facilitated public acceptance of medical and psychological treatment of the disorder. Treatments based on cognitive behavioral theory are directed toward changing the processes and factors that promote drug use – such as altering maladaptive thinking, and increasing the reward value of abstaining from drugs. These behavioral approaches are widely applied, even though most treatment programs are based on disease theory principles. The default advice of Alcoholics Anonymous for avoiding relapse: "Call your sponsor, or go to a meeting" is essentially a behavioral tactic. The compatibility of treatment methods based on these two somewhat different concepts of addiction is discussed further in this chapter.

Some History of Addiction Treatment

The harm resulting from misuse of psychoactive drugs has long been recognized, and the history of attempts to deal with this problem is varied and convoluted. In the United States, excessive alcohol use was the major concern for many years, and is still a bigger threat to public health than is use of illicit drugs – including opioids. Attempts to deal with alcohol-related problems largely determined society's response to addiction in general and to other destructive consequences of drug use. Societal attitudes, theories of addiction and treatment philosophies developed during the twentieth century in response to alcohol use problems still have much influence on current treatment of SUD. The emergence and general acceptance of the disease theory of addiction, as described in Chapter 3, was an important factor in the evolution of SUD treatment.

In the eighteenth and nineteenth centuries, the medical profession could do little to alleviate drug or alcohol addiction. Heavy users of alcohol were often ignored, or tolerated. Those who caused serious trouble were confined in prisons, or asylums for the insane. Currently, response to drug use problems is often more humane than in earlier times. Unfortunately, many addicts are still incarcerated in our prisons or committed to the few remaining inpatient mental health facilities – and receive essentially no treatment for their SUD.

Addiction Treatment in the Twentieth Century

Starting in the 1920s, psychoanalysis became very popular in the United States, as well as in many other Western countries. Those who could afford the expense sought help from this popular approach to mental health. Since that time, psychoanalysis, especially in its original form, has proven to be largely ineffective for relieving addiction.

The treatment of substance abuse and addictions evolved separately from treatment for other types of psychiatric disorders or therapy for unhappy and distressed individuals. The differentiation occurred for several reasons, including the assumption that addiction was different from other mental health problems, and required specialized treatment (Glidden-Tracy 2005).

Alcoholics Anonymous

In the late 1930s and early 1940s, many hospitals would not admit patients for treatment of addiction. Individuals with SUD were generally seen as hopeless cases for which there was no effective treatment. Additionally, many with addiction problems were (or were assumed to be) dishonest and defiant, characteristics that made their care difficult and unrewarding. As a result, nonprofessional approaches – developed outside the field of medicine, became important. Alcoholics Anonymous (AA) was founded in 1935, based on the premise that those addicted to alcohol could help each other overcome their compulsion to drink and the related problems. AA inspired the creation of many other "twelve-step" programs, such as Narcotics Anonymous (NA).

The Minnesota Model

In the 1950s a state hospital in Minnesota developed a residential treatment program for alcoholism that in later years was widely promulgated by the Hazelden Foundation. The Minnesota Model of addiction rehabilitation is based on the disease concept of alcoholism and the twelve-step principles of AA. Although relying heavily on the disease concept of addiction, the Minnesota Model is different from standard medical treatment of diseases or psychological therapy for psychiatric disorders. The Minnesota Model had, and continues to have, enormous influence on SUD treatment (Straussner 2014). Residential treatment of addiction is very expensive, but from the late 1970s until the emergence of managed care in the early 1990s, medical insurance coverage for such treatment was easily accessible. During these years residential (inpatient) treatment programs flourished and most programs were based closely on Minnesota Model philosophy and treatment methods (O'Dwyer 2014). In the last decade of the twentieth century, 90 percent of treatment programs followed the Minnesota Model, offering lectures, group counseling, referral to AA, and little else (McClellan and Meyers 2004).

Approximately half of individuals with SUD also exhibit a psychiatric disorder (Chapter 8). Life stress and psychological problems can cause or contribute to SUD, and heavy drug use can cause or intensify depression, anxiety, and even temporary states of psychosis. Although the co-occurrence is common, treatment programs based on the Minnesota Model rarely provide the psychiatric care and treatment needed by many addicted individuals. Box 16.1 summarizes the primary differences between the Minnesota Model version of SUD treatment, and that provided by professionals in clinical psychology, counseling and social work.

Many addicted individuals have recovered after treatment in a Minnesota Model program, usually followed by active involvement in a twelve-step program. However, these treatment programs are typically quite inflexible, and are often ineffective – especially for those with less severe substance abuse problems or co-occurring psychiatric conditions (Fletcher 2013, CASA Columbia 2012, Szalavitz 2016).

Unfortunately, after receiving treatment from either a specialized addiction treatment facility, or another type of mental health practitioner, the compulsive drug use and consequent problems persist or recur in more than half of individuals with an SUD (see Figure 16.2). Treatment effectiveness in promoting stable sobriety is discussed later in this chapter.

BOX 16.1 Treatment for SUD based on the Minnesota Model

compared to those of other mental health treatment facilities

The Minnesota Model dominated the specialized treatment of SUD for several decades, although its influence has decreased to some degree in recent years. Some features that characterize treatment philosophy and practices of the many specialized treatment programs based on the Minnesota Model include the following:

Assume that all cases of SUD are an indication of an underlying disease, with heavy emphasis on genetic factors as causing addiction – and little attention given to other probable causes

Assume that all persons who enter SUD treatment are addicted (designated as dependence [DSM-IV] or severe SUD [DSM-5]) and that most clients deny and minimize problems of alcohol or other drug use

Insist that clients self-identify as **addicts** or **alcoholics**, as part of the treatment

Attribute the cause of most of a client's distress and difficulties to drug use, rather than seeing preexisting stress or mental illness as promoting the SUD – and show little concern regarding problems not directly related to drug use

Tend to minimize or ignore the presence or importance of co-occurring disorders

View most forms of individual therapy as inappropriate for clients with SUD

Rely heavily on group meetings for sharing of consequences of drug use and ways to overcome compulsion to use

Primary emphasis for treatment on spirituality, surrender, and the twelve steps of AA and similar organizations – assuming that this approach is best for *all* individuals with SUD

Tend to doubt the effectiveness of counselors or therapists not in recovery; therefore heavy reliance on counselors who are recovering addicts/ alcoholics, with little requirement for professional training of these mental health workers

Reluctance to use pharmacological treatments for SUD or, in some cases, for treatment of other accompanying psychiatric disorders (e.g., clinical depression)

Typically attribute relapse or early termination of treatment to "denial"

Total abstinence from drug use is the only acceptable treatment goal; harm reduction (controlled drug use) attempts considered as inappropriate and futile

Reluctance to consider changes in treatment based on evidence from research

In contrast, therapists or counselors treating SUD but following standard methods of clinical psychology, counseling, and social work are characterized by the following:

View excessive and compulsive drug use as a variation of, and in many ways similar to, other mental/emotional/behavioral disorders, treatable with standard therapeutic techniques including individual therapy and cognitive behavioral procedures

Are less likely to accept a simple disease concept of SUD for all clients

Realize that drug misuse does not always indicate severe SUD (addiction)

Are unlikely to insist on self-identification as addict or alcoholic

Often approve use of therapeutic drugs for treatment of addiction or accompanying psychological problems or conditions

Typical strategy is an attempt to identify basic causes of distress that led to excessive drug use, with emphasis on reward value and apparent benefits of early drug use

Identify developmental, family, and environmental factors that promote drug use

Emphasis on spirituality, admission of powerlessness, and twelve-step participation is not a critical component of treatment

Promote a sense of empowerment in dealing with emotional and behavioral problems as well as with harmful drug use

In some cases will accept significant nonabstinent reduction of drug use as a successful treatment outcome

Are likely to have graduate degrees in medicine (psychiatry), clinical psychology, social work, or counseling and been trained in accredited and supervised internship programs

Will change and improve treatment methods based on evidence from research

Sources for these characteristics of treatment programs, therapy, and counseling are CASA Columbia (2012), Fletcher (2013), Glidden-Tracy (2005), Miller et al. (2019), O'Dwyer (2014), Straussner (2014), Szalavitz (2016), Willenbring (2010)

Addiction Treatment in the Twenty-First Century

Many in recovery from addiction make the transition with assistance from friends, family members, significant others, spiritual guides, twelve-step sponsors, and a variety of medical or mental health professionals. Primary care physicians, psychiatrists, addictionologist MDs, clinical psychologists, social workers, and counselors are among the professionals who can help addicted individuals. Counselors or therapists may specialize in substance use disorders, working with families or couples, or pastoral counseling. These health care providers may work together as a team in a treatment program. They can also work alone as they assist the afflicted individual, or in the case of AA or NA sponsors (who are not treatment professionals), in conjunction with other recovering individuals.

Addiction, Treatment, and Popular Culture

Treatment for addiction is now quite visible in the popular culture. Many films have dealt with addiction, and among them two films from the 1990s – *Clean and Sober* (1998) and *When a Man Loves a Woman* (1994) – were stories of residential treatment for addiction. These fictional accounts are realistic depictions of treatment and early recovery, which in some respects have not changed much since that time. More recently, so-called reality programs, such as *Celebrity Rehab*, may attract many viewers, but hardly present a typical picture of addiction treatment. Other reality programs, including *Intervention*, may give a somewhat more representative look at how some addicts are persuaded to enter treatment. In short, popular media has increased general awareness of addiction treatment, but the portrayals are often incomplete or inaccurate (Fletcher 2013). The expense involved, the general inflexibility of many treatment programs, and the dishearteningly low probability of long-term remission after an initial treatment period are unlikely to be accurately conveyed in popular culture accounts of addiction treatment.

The Internet

The Internet has become a major source of information about treatment for SUD. Thousands of websites offer advice for individuals concerned about drug use, either their own or that of friends or family members. A large number of treatment programs are advertised, including many that make unrealistic promises of certain recovery. The perceived anonymity of internet users encourages searches for information about SUD and treatment services by those who are reluctant to make personal inquiries about these topics. Because internet-based information is essentially unregulated, the quality and validity of material about SUD varies greatly. Government-sponsored agencies, such as NIDA and NIAAA, present summaries of recent research findings from prominent investigators, as well as excellent educational material and advice intended for individuals seeking help for addiction. However, for-profit treatment programs also aggressively market their services, and much information presented is of questionable value (Cunningham 2009).

Some aspects of treatment can be accessed online as chat rooms offer opportunities to share stories of addiction, and mutual support groups such as SMART Recovery and twelve-step groups provide online meetings for recovering individuals. Social networks devoted to people in recovery are now easily found on Facebook,

Twitter, and on stand-alone websites, such as www.addictionrecoveryguide.org and www.intherooms.com. These sites feature discussion boards, blogs, links to news articles about addiction and recovery, and listings of treatment providers. These websites are also accessible on mobile phones for use in many locations, including while traveling (Figure 16.1). The use of **social networking** for recovery is growing rapidly.

Figure 16.1 Internet sites offer support for individuals with or in recovery from SUD. Online twelve-step or other meetings as well as other treatment or recovery-oriented social media sites can be accessed from any location. Photo: 10'000 Hours / DigitalVision / Getty Images.

A primary benefit of social networking for recovering individuals is the availability of support at almost any time or location, when meeting a therapist, a sponsor or attending a meeting is not possible. A possible drawback is that some individuals may prefer online communication to the detriment of face-to-face interaction with friends and family that can be critical for recovery. Personal contact with others in healthy recovery is especially important. Excessive involvement with social media may also become part of an addiction-like obsession with the Internet. Yet another hazard is the possibility of inappropriate advice, and victimization of troubled, lonely and vulnerable addicts by predatory individuals. On social media, one cannot be certain if they are receiving advice from a person with years of healthy recovery, or from an unreliable source – with a possibly harmful intent (Reardon 2010).

Current State of Addiction Treatment

In the second decade of the twenty-first century, most addiction treatment occurs in **intensive outpatient** settings – with clients typically attending several hours of treatment each week. The greater expense of living in a residential treatment center, not often covered by medical insurance, has reduced the prevalence of such treatment, although many of these programs are still in operation.

About 77 percent of both residential and nonresidential treatment programs have treatment philosophies and procedures quite similar to those of the Minnesota Model presented in the first part of Box 16.1 (Denning and Little 2017). In these programs, treatment consists largely of promoting twelve-step principles and practices by means of lectures and group meetings, although some programs do offer a limited amount of individual therapy. However, an increasing number of specialized addiction programs are becoming available that are less bound by the original twelve-step ideology and inflexible treatment plans.

Although the treatment philosophy and procedures of the Minnesota Model are still very influential in many treatment programs, other options are available. Some practitioners, usually clinical psychologists, licensed professional counselors or social workers, offer *office-based treatment* that consists primarily of individual counseling or therapy sessions, and encouragement for engagement with a mutual-assistance group. Some office-based mental health professionals are closely associated with primary care physicians, allowing convenient referrals to them when a physician detects indication of drug-related problems (Rubin 2012). Their treatment methods are likely to resemble those listed in the second part of Box 16.1. For example, these psychologists or counselors are unlikely to insist that the client accepts the label of addict, will conduct individual therapy (not relying solely on group work), and will support the use of mutual-help groups other than AA or NA. These professionals also realize that not every client with drug-related problems is addicted – knowing that less severe forms of SUD (especially for alcohol and cannabis) are quite common (Willenbring 2010). An increasing number of addiction treatment providers will work with certain clients toward reducing drug use, rather than maintaining an inflexible requirement of total abstinence as a treatment goal (Davis and Rosenberg 2013, Hingson 2010, Willenbring 2013).

Evidence-Based Treatments

Controlled research on treatment effectiveness for individuals suffering from SUD presents special challenges (Chapter 1). However, evidence from such research has accumulated in recent years, and there is increasing demand from government agencies, insurance companies and other funding sources that treatment practices be proven effective by the results of scientific studies (Sorensen et al. 2009). Reliance on evidence-based research to guide treatment practice has been emphasized by the American Psychological Association for more than two decades.

The managers of many treatment programs and, in particular those not bound by twelve-step ideology, incorporate treatments shown to be effective by scientific evidence. Some examples of these innovations are cognitive behavioral therapy, motivational interviewing, and brief interventions. The increased amount of clinical research on SUD treatment and the growing requirement for use of evidence-based practices are important recent developments in the field of addiction treatment.

The use of medication as an **adjunct treatment** for addiction is now prevalent, as new drugs with proven effectiveness for some individuals have become available. For alcohol use disorder, Campral (acamprosate) or naltrexone may be prescribed, or the older medication Antabuse (disulfram). Naltrexone can also be effective for treatment of opioid dependence, and nicotine dependence is often treated with Chantix (varenicline). Use of these drugs is described in the previous drug-specific chapters.

Many Pathways out of SUD

No single pathway leads everyone with addiction away from compulsive substance use and into healthier behavior and a better life. The various routes into remission and recovery are not mutually exclusive, and none is universally effective – meaning that no method "works" for all individuals with substance use problems. The continuum of options for stopping addictive behavior ranges from unassisted change, through participation in mutual-assistance groups, individual counseling or therapy, to an extended stay in the controlled environment of a residential treatment program.

Remission and Recovery

Remission of an SUD occurs when destructive alcohol or other drug use stops, or is reduced to a nonharmful level. Some who have made this major change refer to themselves as being in recovery from the disorder, meaning that in addition to stopping or reducing drug use they have also examined and improved their psychosocial functioning, relationships, and quality of life in general, including the spiritual aspects (Kelly and Greene 2013). As defined by a panel of substance abuse experts, recovery is "A voluntarily maintained lifestyle comprised of sobriety, personal health and citizenship" (McLellan 2010, p. 109).

Treatment-Relevant Features of SUD

Most addicts are ambivalent about drug use. Although they want to avoid the trouble caused by drug use, the emotional attachment to the drug makes long-term abstinence very difficult. Motivation for drug use is very strong, as well as, in some cases, for stopping use. The NSDUH survey indicated that two out of five respondents who felt a need for professional assistance did not seek treatment because they were not ready to stop using drugs or alcohol (Substance Abuse and Mental Health Services Administration 2018). Recognition of both incentives is important in treatment.

When the consequences of an addictive lifestyle become intolerable (sometimes referred to as "bottoming out"), individuals often temporarily reduce or stop heavy drug use even without treatment. Unfortunately, if the distress lessens with a period of abstinence, many addicted individuals resume the self-destructive behavior. As a result, harmful drug use is often intermittent. Relapse prevention is an essential, perhaps the most important, part of treatment and recovery.

Disorders of substance use share some common features, but there are also differences among the individual drug users and the causes and consequences of their compulsive or harmful use. The opposing motivations for stopping versus continuing drug use, and the risk of relapse after stopping use are common elements of SUD. Both the similarities, as well as the differences, among individuals with SUD are relevant to treatment.

Similarities among Addiction Treatments

Persistent compulsion to use drugs and the resulting harm are basic features of substance use disorders that occur in most addicted individuals – regardless of the specific drug. In many treatment programs, some clients have use problems with alcohol, but for others the primary addictive drug is cannabis or cocaine. Box 16.1 summarizes some differences among treatment programs. However, for most treatment programs, the same treatment philosophy guides, and similar tactics are commonly used for, treatment of all substance use disorders regardless of the specific "drug of choice." Many clients will have use problems with more than one drug, and a generic all-SUD program of treatment is especially beneficial for such individuals.

Differences among Addicted Individuals

Although much behavior, ways of thinking and emotional responses are common among most individuals with substance use disorders, important differences also occur, and some of these differences are relevant to treatment.

The intensity of substance use disorders varies considerably among afflicted individuals. The DSM-IV system differentiated *substance abuse* (less severe) from *substance dependence* (more severe). The newer DSM-5 system designates mild, moderate, or severe levels of use disorder, based on the number of diagnostic criteria occurring in an individual. The treatment method *brief intervention* (discussed later in this chapter) is often used for less extreme indications of dangerous drug use, such as some cases of binge drinking of alcohol, or an initial occurrence of driving while intoxicated. A more extensive SUD treatment program intended for helping addicts is usually not appropriate for nor acceptable to individuals with less severe drug use problems.

Adolescents with SUD also often require treatment different from that of programs or counseling most often offered for adults with similar problems. In many treatment programs, the assumption is made that all clients are addicted to cannabis, alcohol, or other drugs – and considerable pressure exerted for all individuals to refer to themselves as addicts. It is not unusual for adolescents to be entered into treatment even when their drug use is not extensive and is accompanied by other behavioral and emotional problems. Many addiction treatment programs do not adequately address these other problems. Although many programs are advertised as specialized for adolescents, their treatments are often quite similar to those of programs for adults (Fletcher 2013, McLellan and Meyers 2004, Szalavitz 2016).

The frequent presence of an additional psychological disorder, concurrent with an SUD, is another important difference among addicted individuals that has major relevance to treatment. Individuals with anxiety, mood, or psychotic disorders are at increased risk for drug use difficulties, as are those with antisocial or borderline personality disorders (Chapter 8). Heavy drug use, including attempts to self-medicate anxiety or depression, exacerbates psychiatric syndromes, worsens the prognosis and presents a greater challenge for treatment of both addiction and the co-occurring disorder. Medical treatment for addiction is typically quite different from that for psychological problems not related to drug use. A special treatment approach is needed for dual-diagnosed clients, who often cannot be engaged with and helped by the procedures of most SUD treatment programs.

Clients with a less severe use disorder, adolescents, or individuals with a co-occurring psychological disorder may not be well served by a treatment program that does not recognize the importance of these common variations among those with SUD. In the United States, the orientation of most SUD treatment programs and many individual addiction counselors is based on disease theory and the Minnesota Model/twelve-step program of treatment and recovery (Box 16.1). Most addiction treatment professionals justify their reluctance to modify treatment much to accommodate client differences by citing the common features of addiction. Program philosophy typically downplays differences among addicted individuals – as in the often-heard slogan "we all suffer from the same disease." Many treatment programs and counselors typically exhibit marked inflexibility in their concepts and treatment tactics (Denning and Little 2017, Fletcher 2013, Szalavitz 2016).

Most treatment programs rely heavily on group discussions – usually *in lieu* of individual therapy sessions. Some clients with special and sensitive addiction-related issues may be uncomfortable or unable to speak freely in general group discussions. Victims of sexual abuse, and gay or lesbian clients are prime examples of individuals who often can speak openly only in special selected groups. Therefore, most programs, even those essentially bound by twelve-step philosophy, will arrange for group therapy sessions limited to participants who share a common background related to these sensitive issues.

Medical Management of Withdrawal

Medical support and nursing care may be required for management of initial stages of withdrawal, during which intense distress or life-threatening conditions can occur. Treatment procedures that address the addictive drug use cannot commence at this time. The acute withdrawal syndrome from extended heavy use of CNS depressant drugs (alcohol, barbiturates) can be life-threatening, requiring supervision and care by medical professionals. Withdrawal from opioids often produces intense physical distress – vomiting, diarrhea, and muscle cramps. Initial stages of withdrawal from stimulants often include marked depression and exhaustion.

Unfortunately, many addicts leave a hospital or otherwise terminate medical care when the immediate distress of early withdrawal subsides, never entering actual treatment for their heavy drug use. Stopping extended use of any addictive drug typically results in lingering dysphoria and depression. However, treatment for addiction can proceed during these persistent states of less intense distress.

Medical Treatment for SUD

Drugs may be necessary to manage acute detoxification and early stages of withdrawal. Drug treatment has an additional, if limited, role in recovery for some cases of SUD, especially for those addicted to alcohol, opioid drugs, or nicotine.

Administration of medication specifically intended to interrupt one or more phases of the addictive cycle (including reduction of craving for or attenuating the rewarding effects of nicotine, alcohol, and opioids) is most often considered as adjunctive to treatment methods that require more active effort and participation by the afflicted individual (Swift and Leggio 2009).

Treatment programs differ in their reliance on the use of adjunctive medication. However, many individuals recovering from an addictive disorder do not require medication – at least not for treatment of the addiction *per se*. Pharmaceutical agents are in wide use in general psychiatry for the co-occurring disorders that often accompany SUD. Some treatment programs allow concurrent drug treatment of such additional psychiatric syndromes.

The medications used to treat compulsive drug use are described in the previous drug-specific chapters of this text. Unfortunately, at the present time treatment with these medications – in the absence of nondrug treatment methods – does not interrupt or decrease the compulsive and destructive drug use in many or even most individuals with SUD.

Most of the treatment methods described in this chapter do not involve medication. Effective treatments for SUD require effort and active engagement by the recovering individual – rather than the easier and more passive act of swallowing a capsule or tablet. Such engagement is encouraged by counseling, therapy, and interaction with recovering and healthy individuals. Motivation for change is critical. The twelve-step program of recovery, basic to many treatment programs, emphasizes spiritual growth – a term whose meaning varies widely among recovering individuals.

Many with nicotine or opioid dependence can avoid the destructive aspects of addictive behavior by long-term use of agonist-replacement drugs. The use of such replacement drugs, and in particular the opioid replacements (methadone, buprenorphine), is not accepted in many treatment programs – and in particular, programs based on twelve-step principles of recovery.

Box 16.2 summarizes characteristics of addiction and hazardous drug use that are relevant to treatment of SUD.

BOX 16.2 Treatment-relevant features of substance use disorders

Most addicted individuals are ambivalent about drug use – compulsively taking drugs, but fearing the adverse consequences – so drug use is often intermittent but persistent. Motivation for both using and for stopping use should be recognized in treatment.

After periods of abstinence, return to drug use is common – either with or without treatment. Prevention of relapse is a primary goal of treatment.

Common patterns of behavior and thinking occur in most with severe SUD, so there is much similarity among treatment programs – especially among the many programs based on a disease concept of addiction and twelve-step principles.

Most treatments for use disorders of nearly all addictive drugs (including alcohol) are similar.

Although addiction has common features, effective treatment requires special consideration for those with less severe cases of the disorder, co-occurring psychiatric conditions, and adolescents.

Some addicts, including victims of sexual abuse and other traumas, require special therapy groups not open to all patients.

Detoxification is not treatment, and treatment cannot start during intense stages of withdrawal.

Medications are available that reduce craving and help prevent relapse in some individuals. However, many patients will not receive therapeutic drugs.

> ### BOX 16.2 Continued
>
> Controlled administration of the addictive or similar drugs can effectively manage nicotine or opioid dependence. However, such addiction management is neither accepted nor considered treatment by treatment programs following the Minnesota Model.

Untreated Remission of SUD

A majority of individuals with a substance use disorder do not seek specific treatment or assistance for their problematic use of drugs or alcohol. Epidemiological evidence (NESARC, NSDUH surveys) indicates that only about 25 percent of alcohol-dependent and 38 percent of drug-dependent individuals (dependence based on satisfaction of DSM-IV criteria) ever receive treatment during their lifetimes (Compton et al. 2007, Hasin et al. 2007). Even fewer (12 percent) received treatment for an SUD during the year previous to the 2017 NSDUH survey (Substance Abuse and Mental Health Services Administration 2018).

Although many SUD treatment programs are based on AA principles, participation in twelve-step groups is not classified as treatment. Many who seek assistance from AA or similar organizations have never received addiction-specific treatment from mental health professionals. When the number of individuals who participated in twelve-step groups is added to those who received treatment, the percentage of help-seekers is about 20 percent of those with SUD.

There are several reasons for not seeking specialized assistance for treatment of SUD. One reason is a common perception that treatment is not very effective – yielding a low rate of success and not likely to be helpful (Mojtabai and Crum 2013). Other reasons include dislike for the strong religious orientation of twelve-step programs and their emphasis on the concept of powerlessness, coupled with resistance to self-labeling as an alcoholic or addict (Klingemann and Klingemann 2009). Reluctance to give up drug or alcohol use completely (the intended outcome of most treatment programs), is another important reason that many with SUD avoid addiction-specific treatment for their drug use problems. Other reasons mentioned in epidemiological surveys include financial expense of treatment (and lack of insurance coverage), concern about negative effects on employment, or judgment of neighbors or community (Substance Abuse and Mental Health Services Administration 2018).

Many who never receive treatment or addiction-specific assistance eventually stop or greatly reduce their drug use. The **NESARC epidemiological survey** of

43,093 individuals identified 4,422 as currently or previously DSM-IV dependent on alcohol (Dawson et al. 2005). A majority (3,217) of these respondents with a history of alcohol dependence had never sought treatment or participated in AA (Figure 16.2).

The NESARC results show that a sizable fraction (about one-third) of these untreated people eventually stop drinking entirely or consume alcohol at reduced and safe levels (Figure 16.2A). Both active SUD and remission from this condition are often intermittent, waxing and waning over periods of months or years. The primary NESARC study was a one-time assessment, but did provide much useful information, especially concerning the persistence of the disorder in untreated individuals who were at one time addicted to alcohol. The results of a second-wave survey of NESARC respondents conducted three years later provided additional information, with results similar to those gained from the initial interviews (Grella and Stein 2013).

The Centers for Disease Control and Prevention indicate that a level of **safe alcohol consumption** for men under age sixty-five is no more than two standard drinks on any one day, and one drink per day for women and for individuals over

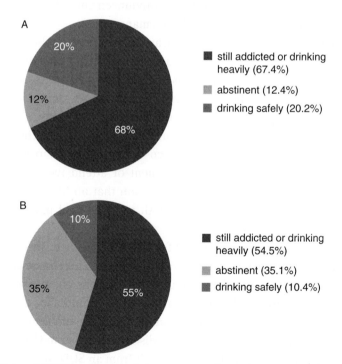

Figure 16.2 Status of NESARC epidemiological survey respondents who were currently or previously alcohol dependent as defined by DSM-IV diagnostic criteria. (A) Current status of respondents who had neither received professional treatment for alcohol use disorder nor attended AA meetings. (B) Current status of respondents who had received SUD treatment and/or attended AA meetings (Dawson et al. 2005). Safe drinking is defined by the Centers for Disease Control and Prevention.

age sixty-five (www.cdc.gov). For most individuals these levels of safe drinking are unlikely to be harmful. Reports of "safe drinking" generally refer to these patterns of alcohol consumption.

Most research-based evidence concerning remission of SUD comes from studies of treatment effectiveness – so is based on individuals who underwent some form of addiction-specific intervention. Twelve-step program participants (many of whom were never in a treatment program) are not easily recruited for detailed longitudinal studies, but dedicated investigators have conducted some research on these individuals (Miller et al. 2011). Less information is available about remission in untreated individuals, mainly because this population is largely unidentified – rather than conveniently accessible while under treatment, or in AA or NA meetings.

Interviews with respondents in epidemiological studies such as NESARC yield some information about untreated individuals and their methods of reducing or stopping compulsive drug use (Dawson et al. 2005, Grella and Stein 2013). Additional methods can identify and obtain information from individuals who overcame SUD without addiction-specific treatment or twelve-step participation. These nontreated individuals include drop-outs from treatment waiting lists, and media-recruited individuals responding to announcements of self-change studies (Carballo et al. 2007, Klingemann and Klingemann 2009).

In general (as a group), SUD is less severe and causes fewer problems in untreated individuals than in those who enter treatment or seek help from mutual-assistance organizations. Under DSM-IV definitions of SUD, many members of the untreated population would be considered as drug abusers, rather than drug dependent. However, as shown by the NESARC survey, there are also many with severe SUD (addiction/drug dependence) among the untreated individuals. Those treated for an SUD are also more likely to suffer from co-occurring psychiatric disorders than are those who never enter addiction treatment or attend twelve-step meetings. This difference is consistent with the observation that an SUD is generally more severe and life-disruptive in individuals with an additional psychiatric disorder (Chapter 8).

Women are less likely to seek treatment for SUD than are men. This difference may come partially from the greater vulnerability of women to the shame and stigma still associated with addictive disorders. Cultural expectations about women – mainly involving care of children and assumptions about the immorality of addicts, cause many women to be especially reluctant to admit a drug use problem and enter treatment. These special problems of women are discussed further in Chapter 10.

A majority of untreated individuals that remit from an SUD continue to use drugs or alcohol, but at reduced levels and without harmful consequences (Figure 16.2A). Such "nonabstinent recovery" is more likely for problematic use of alcohol than for such use of other addictive drugs (Dawson et al. 2005). A smaller proportion of untreated individuals become completely abstinent in their recovery from SUD.

Addiction treatment professionals – and especially those with firm belief in the disease concept of SUD – are often skeptical that untreated remission from addiction is rather common, or at least not unusual (based on the NESARC survey, about one-third of individuals dependent on alcohol). Some of this doubt about **natural recovery** may result from the greater severity of SUD of those in treatment. Each day these health care workers see and interact with severely addicted, damaged individuals. They may rarely see the many people who have real but lesser problems with alcohol or other drugs, resulting in an unrealistic view of the overall population of those with some form of SUD. The less obvious distress and less dramatic remission of SUD in many untreated individuals may contribute to the ignorance about untreated recovery.

Factors Promoting Untreated Remission

Untreated individuals who stop destructive and compulsive use of drugs make this change by means of various methods. Some consult physicians, clinical psychologists, or family or couples counselors, but for assistance with problems not directly related to drug use. Excessive drug use might be addressed as a part of an overall pattern of unhealthy behavior, but not as the primary problem. In a similar manner, religious guidance might fulfill a spiritual need, resulting in emotional well-being as well as abstinence or reduced drug use. Remission of harmful drug use by means of these less specific methods is sometimes referred to as "natural recovery."

Motivation to stop drug use is important for stable remission either with or without treatment by medical professionals. Incentive to stop addictive behavior can come from an abrupt emergence of serious medical, personal, or legal consequences of drug use – such as liver disease, abandonment by family members, loss of employment, or repeated convictions for driving while intoxicated. Such "bottoming out" can drive an addicted individual into treatment, or motivate a decrease in destructive behavior in the absence of treatment.

Individuals with sufficient **recovery capital** are most likely to succeed in stopping drug use. Recovery capital refers to sources of support and self-esteem that have survived the addiction – such as financial resources, family and friends, employment, and relatively intact physical, emotional and mental health. In short, those whose history of SUD is less extensive, who have fewer losses and more resources are more likely to succeed in maintaining a drug-free life. As with the factor of motivation, the amount of recovery capital influences remission for untreated individuals as well as those who do receive addiction-specific assistance (Klingemann and Klingemann 2009, Grella and Stein 2013).

Some methods used by untreated individuals to stop compulsive drug use are the same or similar to tactics useful for controlling harmful behaviors unrelated to drug use. Such methods include a realistic consideration of the benefits and losses of drug use, recognition of the inability to use drugs without adverse consequences, and learning to avoid people, locations and activities that trigger drug use. Recognition of faulty assumptions, habitual patterns of thinking, and maladaptive responses to emotional states that lead to drug use are also often helpful. These tactics are essentially those promoted by cognitive behavioral therapy, and are very similar to some basic twelve-step techniques used to avoid resumption of drug use. Many untreated individuals with drug use problems learn to use these methods, sometimes by reading self-help literature or consulting recovery-oriented internet sites.

Other, rather common types of compulsive behavior are often arrested without treatment. Some examples include overeating, gambling, excessive internet use, and the use of the addictive drug nicotine. All these compulsive behaviors can be very difficult to stop, but many, perhaps most, individuals who have overcome these compulsions have done so without professional assistance or participation in mutual-assistance support groups.

Substance use disorders vary greatly in severity. Most treatment programs are intended for those suffering from severe addiction. Twelve-step programs also are best suited for individuals with extreme and compulsive drug or alcohol use problems. During meeting testimonials enthusiastic AA members sometimes identify themselves as having been "low-bottom drunks" – an informal term indicating that the alcoholic persisted in heavy drinking until the consequent losses and damage became quite severe. Many with untreated SUD have a mild or moderate drug use disorder, and perceive treatment or twelve-step programs as unneeded or inappropriate.

Even those suffering from severe SUD often refuse to acknowledge the true nature of the problem. Because of this denial or for other reasons, these individuals tend to avoid treatment programs and twelve-step participation. Many untreated addicts will die from heavy drug use if the disorder is not recognized and overcome. Some with a moderate disorder will progress to a more severe condition. Others will eventually recover without treatment, and although treatment is not a certain path into remission, it does increase the chance of achieving stable abstinence (Figure 16.2B).

Mutual-Assistance Groups

Although some individuals manage to halt life-disruptive drug use with no assistance from others for the specific problem, many find that the support of people who have overcome similar difficulties is essential for recovery. The term *mutual assistance* is more accurate than *self-help* for describing the rich network of support groups for SUD, because a basic feature of these groups is reciprocal help and reaching outside one's self for guidance.

The best-known and largest support networks are the twelve-step programs, but there are other groups with similar purpose but somewhat different methods and principles. These groups do not offer actual treatment or therapy, and with some exceptions – SMART Recovery and Women for Sobriety – activities are not directed by trained health care providers. Many members of these groups never enter a treatment program or consult a counselor, but many other members have received treatment for SUD. These programs can be extremely valuable for ongoing maintenance of sobriety either with or without treatment. Treatment programs or therapy can be very expensive and insurance coverage is limited. Mutual-assistance groups are free, an important benefit. These groups have a growing presence on the Internet, expanding their convenient and continuous accessibility.

Alcoholics Anonymous and Other Twelve-Step Programs

Alcoholics Anonymous (AA) is by far the largest and most popular mutual-assistance group. AA has a worldwide presence, claiming 116,000 groups and approximately 2.1 million members (Alcoholics Anonymous 2010). The movement originated in the 1930s, and in subsequent years inspired the creation of several other groups (e.g., Narcotics Anonymous, Cocaine Anonymous) based closely on AA philosophy and principles. Although some addiction professionals are skeptical of AA's value for everyone with alcohol use problems, a large majority of SUD treatment providers enthusiastically encourage clients to become active AA participants. As previously described, the highly influential Minnesota Model treatment programs incorporated AA principles into their methods for management of addiction and promoting recovery – and a majority of treatment programs in the United States continue to rely heavily on AA philosophy and methods. The following discussion concerns AA, but most comments also apply to twelve-step programs intended for other addictions, or those close to addicted individuals (Al-Anon, Alateen).

Basic Principles

The basic principles of AA are listed in the twelve steps (Box 16.3) and in writings of the founders, Bill Wilson and Robert Silkworth. The *Big Book* (Alcoholics Anonymous) also contains much program philosophy. Two primary AA principles are **acceptance** (Step 1), and **surrender** (Steps 2 and 3). Acceptance is recognition that drinking cannot be controlled – and admission of powerlessness over alcohol. Surrender is turning over one's life and will to God – and the AA principles and the wisdom of the AA group. Abstinence from alcohol and addictive drugs is essential. Moral self-inventory is also important, as is making amends for harm done to others and reaching out to other alcohol-addicted individuals (Wallace 2012, Miller et al. 2011).

The spirituality so evident in AA philosophy is welcomed by most AA members, but is a problem for many with alcohol use problems – especially those who are not religious in the traditional sense. Defenders of AA maintain that the spiritual emphasis need not be religious, and that the God mentioned in five of the twelve steps (and implied in the second step) can be a higher power that is not necessarily the Judeo-Christian deity. However, the influence of the program's origin in traditional American protestant and catholic theology is obvious, given the emphasis on sin (harmful behavior), confession, repentance, humility and salvation through grace rather than on one's own merit (Miller et al. 2011).

The basic suggestions for improving a life: admitting powerlessness (Step 1), acknowledging insanity (Step 2), and giving up control and turning one's life and will over to God (Step 3) often seem extreme and unattractive to those who dislike religion and/or have not progressed to real trouble from drinking – such as many college-age binge drinkers. The program's emphasis on surrender and powerlessness also contradict dominant Western cultural norms of self-reliance (Laudet 2003). However, for those in extreme distress, having repeatedly failed to improve, the "surrender" plan is often acceptable. Studies have indicated that individuals most likely to affiliate with AA are those with greater loss of control of drinking, greater amounts of daily alcohol consumption, physical dependence on alcohol, more concern about drinking, and a stronger commitment to abstinence (Emrick et al. 1993, Tonigan et al. 1996).

In contrast to some religions, judgment and shaming are absent from the AA approach to a better life. The application of program principles provides sound guidance that can be helpful to many, even those not recovering from addiction. The AA program might be considered as a folk-wisdom combination of some parts of Christianity (forgive those against whom you have grievances), and Zen Buddhism (some things cannot be controlled – some battles cannot be won and effort expended in fighting them is wasted). The serenity prayer, written by Reinhold Niebuhr and adopted by AA in 1941, is often recited in some AA meetings: "God, grant me the serenity to accept the things I cannot change, the courage to change the things I can, and the wisdom to know the difference."

BOX 16.3 The twelve steps of Alcoholics Anonymous

1. We admitted we were powerless over alcohol – that our lives had become unmanageable.
2. Came to believe that a Power greater than ourselves could restore us to sanity.

3. Made a decision to turn our will and our lives over to the care of *God, as we understood Him.*

4. Made a searching and fearless moral inventory of ourselves.

5. Admitted to God, to ourselves and to another human being the exact nature of our wrongs.

6. Were entirely ready to have God remove all these defects of character.

7. Humbly asked Him to remove our shortcomings.

8. Made a list of all persons we had harmed, and became willing to make amends to them all.

9. Made direct amends to such people wherever possible, except when to do so would injure them or others.

10. Continued to take personal inventory and when we were wrong promptly admitted it.

11. Sought through prayer and meditation to improve our conscious contact with God, as we understood him, praying only for knowledge of His will for us and the power to carry that out.

12. Having had a spiritual awakening as a result of these steps, we tried to carry this message to alcoholics, and to practice these principles in all our affairs.

Beneficial Features

Many beneficial effects of the AA fellowship result from the interactions that occur in the meetings (Figure 16.3). There are several types of meetings, including discussion meetings, which may be of the greatest value. Members talk about their recovery, and to a lesser extent the misery and pain caused by heavy drinking. Speakers are strongly encouraged to identify themselves as alcoholics as they recount their experiences, which are essentially testimonial monologues. Questioning or confronting a speaker – or other types of "cross-talk" – are not acceptable. AA meetings are not group therapy, although the candor and honesty of interactions may be similar to that of a therapy group led by a trained professional. Any member who is uncomfortable with sharing is not required to speak, although the warm, nonjudgmental atmosphere encourages even reluctant individuals to unburden themselves and express their feelings. Open sharing in AA discussion meetings does much to reduce the corrosive shame of alcohol addiction.

AA provides a welcoming, inclusive culture of sobriety – which can be very helpful to those who have become isolated because of their addictive behavior or whose only friends and acquaintances are heavy drinkers. Members in stable recovery, with healthy and happy lives provide excellent role models for the

Figure 16.3 AA meetings provide warm acceptance and encouragement to individuals whose lives have been damaged by an alcohol use disorder. Although serious problems are shared, meetings are typically upbeat and positive. Photo: SolStock / E+ / Getty Images.

recently abstinent alcohol addict. New members are encouraged to find a sponsor, who becomes a mentor providing personal support and guidance for the newcomer in "working" the twelve steps of recovery. Some who study AA culture suggest that the fellowship and camaraderie – and the overall and unconditional support – provided are at least as important as the spirituality of the program (Nealon-Woods et al. 1995, Kelly et al. 2009).

AA literature, as well as advice given (when requested) in AA meetings, suggests very effective methods for maintaining abstinence from alcohol – tactics that are similar or identical to basic cognitive behavioral methods intended for the same purpose (Nowinski 2012). Cognitive behavioral tactics, discussed in a subsequent section, facilitate thoughts and behaviors incompatible with drinking. When tempted to relapse, members are advised to call their sponsor, attend a meeting, or engage in some activity (perhaps physical exercise) that makes drinking less likely. Similar tactics encourage interrupting negative emotional states and patterns of thinking that lead to alcohol use. The warmth and support of an AA meeting or the pleasure of other activities can eventually become more rewarding than drinking. *Living Sober* (Alcoholics Anonymous World Services 1975) is an AA publication that suggests cognitive behavioral approaches to prevention of drinking – and employment of these tactics does not require acceptance of the AA philosophy or principles.

Although all AA groups follow the basic twelve-step program principles, groups in various parts of the country and in other cultures differ in some ways. For example, versions of spirituality commonly expressed in meetings may depend on the dominant religious culture of the geographical location. In mid-western and southern areas of the United States, where fundamentalist religions are more prominent, the higher power that helps a member stay sober is usually referred to as God, and prayer may be quite similar to that heard in a church service. In more religiously liberal areas – including the Northeast and much of the West Coast area, the higher power may be more vaguely defined and prayer more meditative.

Objections and Limitations

Many individuals with SUD, as well as some addiction treatment professionals, have difficulty accepting the philosophy, common beliefs and practices of AA and other twelve-step groups (Mendola and Gibson 2016, Rodriguez 2016). William Miller and colleagues suggest that some objections to twelve-step programs are actually "myths," which upon close examination have little credibility (Miller et al. 2011). Examples of these problematic "myths" are (1) absolute acceptance of the disease concept of SUD, (2) claims that AA methods are uniquely and universally effective for addiction recovery, (3) assigning a critical role to spirituality – closely linked to Christian religion – for recovery, (4) pressure to stop taking psychiatric medication, and (5) insistence that only therapists/counselors in recovery can be effective for addiction treatment. Miller maintains that careful examination of AA philosophy and principles reveals that these criticisms are invalid. However, there are differences between official program philosophy as contrasted to advice given and opinions expressed in AA meetings and in many twelve-step-based treatment programs. The "rank and file" of AA members often adhere to some version of these problematic views about addiction and recovery. The extreme and inflexible views are also widely held by administrators and counselors in many treatment programs (Davis and Rosenberg 2013).

The pervasive influence of twelve-step concepts on many treatment programs can be a definite barrier for many individuals seeking help for their drug use problems. In *Unbroken Brain*, Maia Szalavitz maintains that "the 12-step programs and the medical system are a terrible mix. These groups were never intended to be a medical treatment. They were designed as mutual-help organizations, not professional therapy. No psychiatric hospital would dream of forcing depressed patients to write 'moral inventories' – and yet many rehab programs require it. No mainstream treatment for bipolar disorder or OCD demands submission to a Higher Power ... consequently, indoctrination into 12-step ideology should not be the core component of rehab – it should not be a part of professional care at all" (Szalavitz 2016, p. 221). Szalavitz also points out that in many treatment programs, insurance companies or individuals pay very high prices for what can be had free in church basements – at AA meetings.

Evidence of Effectiveness

For many years the effectiveness of twelve-step programs was indicated only by the enthusiastic testimonials of dedicated members of these groups. Conduct of controlled research, with subjects randomly assigned to treatment and comparison groups, is difficult for outcome studies of all forms of addiction treatment. Such research is especially difficult for the study of groups of individuals who prefer anonymity and are often resistant to and sometimes skeptical of efforts to carefully scrutinize their abstinence from alcohol and other addictive drugs.

Several relatively recent studies consistently indicate that AA involvement correlates positively with abstinence from alcohol in both treated as well as untreated individuals, and in adolescents as well as adults (e.g., Chi et al. 2009, Gossop et al. 2007, Moos and Moos 2006a). These studies show that many individuals actively engaged in AA activities were abstinent over a period of years – and the more active the involvement (meeting attendance, working with a sponsor, following the twelve steps), the higher the frequency of maintaining abstinence. The positive correlation implies, but does not prove, that AA involvement results in abstinence because the more abstinent individuals may have been more motivated to change and ready to engage with AA. However, the correlations are consistent with the widely held belief that AA participation does promote abstinence and recovery. Many who attend some meetings do not stop drinking, or resume drinking after a period of abstinence. A smaller amount of objective information is available about the effectiveness of NA participation in promoting abstinence and recovery. Although these programs are not effective for all, there is good reason to expect that many individuals with SUD can improve their chances for stable sobriety by attending twelve-step meetings.

Secular Mutual-Assistance Groups

In the 1980s and subsequent years several mutual-assistance movements were formed as alternatives to AA and other twelve-step groups. Similarities to AA include provision of social support for abstinence and recovery, suggestions for self-analysis and improvement, explicit advice for avoiding drinking or using addictive drugs, and little or no involvement of treatment professionals in group leadership. As with AA, these groups encourage total abstinence from addictive drugs. Meeting attendance and program participation are free.

These secular groups do not emphasize powerlessness and surrender, or heavy reliance on a higher power to maintain sobriety. Although some groups include a version of spirituality in their basic principles for recovery from addiction, there are no overtly religious "steps," such as praying for knowledge of God's will.

Rather than powerlessness, **personal empowerment** as facilitated by group support and other methods is encouraged. Some groups attempt to incorporate current scientific findings on addiction and recovery into their programs. Concepts based on rational-emotive therapy and cognitive behavioral methods may be presented in meetings or in program literature.

Many individuals with addiction problems come to these groups after unsatisfactory attempts to engage with twelve-step principles or practices. Some members continue to attend AA or similar meetings, and such dual involvement is quite acceptable in the secular programs. Secular groups are generally more attractive to well-educated and intellectual individuals who are less interested in reliance on a higher power to stop compulsive drug use (Szalavitz 2006).

The secular groups have a shorter history than do twelve-step groups, and fewer or none of the newer meetings are available in many areas – especially outside large cities or where fundamentalist religions are predominant. All these movements have websites that offer online meetings as well as recovery-related books and other resources.

Most secular groups do not encourage lifelong involvement as do twelve-step groups. All groups except Moderation Management teach skills promoting abstinence and recovery during early sobriety without the expectation of ongoing program involvement. After learning these methods of recovery, most members move on with their life and stop attending meetings. As a result, active membership grows less rapidly – with few "veterans" who have years of program participation. The relative absence of long-term members may limit the growth of a robust culture of recovery that is a positive aspect of twelve-step programs.

The Secular Organization for Sobriety (SOS) (www.secularsobriety.org) was founded in 1986. Although SOS may be the largest secular group, its total membership is about 1 percent as large as that of AA. This group was formed as a secular humanist alternative to AA, specifically separating spirituality from sobriety (Humphreys et al. 2004).

Another recovery support network is LifeRing Secular Recovery (www.lifering .org). This website provides a national meeting list, daily online meetings, and extensive links to other recovery resources.

SMART Recovery (self-management and recovery training) (www.smartrecovery .org) features evidence-based methods for facilitating recovery (Horvath 2000). The meetings, led by trained volunteers, often feature cognitive behavioral methods for interrupting thoughts and actions that lead to recurrence of drug or alcohol use. This group avoids the labels "addict" and "alcoholic" and does not emphasize the disease concept of addiction. SMART Recovery originated as a part of Rational Recovery (a for-profit organization offering recovery services and information), but is now a separate mutual-assistance group.

Women for Sobriety (WFS) (www.womenforsobriety.org) was founded in 1976, primarily because at that time AA did not provide much support for problems often encountered by women with alcohol use disorders – such as issues with parenting and spousal abuse. WFS retains the spirituality of AA to some extent, but has replaced the twelve steps with thirteen statements that encourage spiritual and emotional growth. A newsletter, *Sobering Thoughts*, provides information of special value to women.

Moderation Management (www.moderation.org) is also a mutual-assistance group, but differs from the other groups in that support is offered for reducing drinking, rather than only for abstinence from alcohol. Participants are encouraged to attempt a thirty-day abstinence period before returning to drinking moderately. Advice on careful self-monitoring of alcohol use and methods for avoiding heavy drinking are presented in meetings, literature and the website.

Treatment of SUD by Professionals

Professional treatment of SUD is administered in various modes or types of facilities. Office-based treatment requires less time commitment and interruption of a client's personal life, but may be inadequate for severe cases of the disorder. Treatment programs typically provide a more comprehensive plan for promoting abstinence and recovery (Box 16.4). Treatment when an additional psychiatric disorder co-occurs with the SUD presents a special challenge.

Office-Based Treatment

Many individuals realize that they need professional help to deal with certain problems in their lives, including possibly excessive drug or alcohol use. Some may have a relatively low level of SUD, and are uncertain whether the drug use is a significant problem. Others may be addicted, but high-functioning (Chapter 2) in that their compulsive drug use has not yet become very disruptive. Yet others may consult a primary care physician for insomnia, anxiety or another health problem and receive advice to seek help from a mental health professional for reducing their alcohol or drug use. Such individuals are typically unwilling to enter an addiction treatment program, although they are often agreeable to working with a counselor or therapist for "office-based treatment" (OBT).

OBT is more private than is participation in a larger addiction treatment program, provides a more flexible and personalized approach to changing heavy drug use, and offers individual counseling or psychotherapy that is often unavailable in programs that rely exclusively on group therapy (Washton and Zweben 2006). Privacy is maintained because many individuals see therapists for reasons unrelated to drug use, but entry into "rehab" (an addiction treatment program) indicates the unmistakable presence of a drug use problem.

In most addiction treatment programs, it is assumed that entering individuals are severely addicted, and that the drug use is responsible for difficulties and problems encountered. However, many individuals using addictive drugs and or drinking heavily do not have a diagnosable use disorder. A large number of those who actually do have an SUD suffer from a less intense form of the disorder. Practitioners providing effective OBT have training and experience in SUD treatment, but can also discuss and provide support concerning other sources of anxiety, depression, and interpersonal difficulties. They are also likely to use motivational interviewing procedures (further described in a subsequent section) to guide the client in understanding the role of drug use in her life. Many clients in OBT may not be addicted, but drug use is detrimental to their health and well-being, and the OBT practitioner recognizes these gradations in the severity of drug-related problems. In a less flexible Minnesota Model–type program, a client who doubts that he is actually addicted will almost certainly be labeled as being "in denial."

The individual psychotherapy of OBT is an important advantage of this form of treatment. Many clients need and appreciate the personal attention of the counselor or therapist who can respond to their specific concerns, including those not directly related to drug use. A therapeutic alliance, so important for effective therapy, is difficult to establish without extended one-on-one contact. Most addiction treatment programs rely heavily on group work, dealing exclusively with the common problems faced by many with an SUD. Psychotherapy offered by OBT may be specific for addiction (as in twelve-step facilitation therapy), or a more general form of therapy that can be applied to drug use issues (e.g., cognitive behavioral therapy, dialectical behavior therapy).

Anxiety and other emotional, behavioral or interpersonal problems often accompany heavy use of alcohol or other drugs. Distressed, drug-using individuals often seek help from therapists or counselors not specializing in addiction treatment. These mental health professionals can provide emotional support and therapy for clients with substance use problems, encouraging them and assisting with their reduction of – or stopping – harmful drug use. However, some clients do not fully disclose the extent, persistence and consequences of their drug use. In that case, the therapist may not recognize the importance and harmful result of the drug use, and perhaps fail to detect an SUD (O'Dwyer 2014).

Variations in Diagnostic Procedures

Because clients often do not present to practitioners as having a substance use disorder, office-based treatment often commences without a formal structured evaluation for or diagnosis of a possible substance use disorder. Initial OBT sessions typically explore the client's drug use, and the consequences of that use, by means of less structured diagnostic interviews. In contrast, entry into a comprehensive treatment program for SUD ordinarily starts with, or is preceded by, the structured and standardized diagnostic procedures discussed in Chapter 2. A professional diagnosis of an SUD is ordinarily required for compensation by medical insurance for admission to an SUD treatment program, or in some cases for legal purposes.

The evaluation and diagnosis provide information used to plan the treatment, and can also be therapeutic. The therapeutic benefit comes as the client hears an objective evaluation of his drug use from a treatment professional – perhaps giving much-needed insight to the potential or actual harm resulting from his behavior. Ideally, the initial diagnostic interview will also start to create a therapeutic alliance with an empathic clinician.

Residential Treatment Programs

Treatment in a residential facility is the most intensive form of intervention intended to stop and prevent the resumption of compulsive and harmful drug use. Currently, this mode of treatment is used much less frequently than in the latter decades of the twentieth century when medical insurance often paid for the considerable expense of a twenty-eight-day stay in a residential facility. When managed care sharply reduced such generous insurance coverage in the late 1990s, many of these "rehabilitation" facilities closed. Currently most treatment for SUD occurs in nonresidential settings. Residential (mostly private, for-profit) facilities still exist, and their patients are primarily those with severe addiction, additional psychiatric disorders, or other individuals who choose to pay for this expensive form of treatment. Less expensive publicly funded residential facilities are also available, but typically have long waiting lists for admission.

Residential treatment facilities provide a controlled environment that reduces or eliminates the opportunity to use drugs and shields the patients from the distraction and demands of normal daily life. The protected mode of living allows them to focus on drug-related problems and learning how to avoid returning to drug use after discharge from treatment. Periodic urine screens or breath tests monitor for clandestine drug use. Residential programs provide extensive involvement in treatment procedures and therapeutic activities throughout the day. Another benefit of these live-in programs is the fostering of close relationships with others in early recovery, reducing the isolation that is so often a part of an addictive lifestyle.

Many residential programs are very similar to the original Minnesota Model, and as such emphasize AA philosophy and promote engagement with twelve-step groups. Education about addiction as a disease is also a primary focus. Lectures and discussions promote these themes, and most counseling and therapy occurs in groups. Families or others with close ties to patients are sometimes included in these educational and therapeutic sessions.

Most facilities promote a complete program of healthy living, including proper diet, exercise, and regular hours for sleep and therapeutic activities. Some education and counseling deals with issues such as anxiety, loneliness, anger, and other problems that result from or are made worse by heavy drug use. However, the primary emphasis of this education and counseling is on stopping drug use.

Some more expensive programs provide spa-like services such as massage and yoga instruction, as well as extensive recreational and athletic facilities. These, as well as other for-profit treatment programs are heavily marketed – both on the Internet and by means of advertisements in professional journals or magazines intended for medical practitioners.

Entry into residential programs may occur as a result of a formal intervention, in which the family, friends or work-mates confront an individual with their observations of erratic behavior and obvious heavy drinking or drug use. These interventions typically conclude with a demand that the addicted person seek professional help to stop the problematic behavior. The consequences of refusal to take action to stop drug use are typically withdrawal of contact with and support from family and friends. When an employer is involved in the intervention, treatment entry may be required to avoid job loss. In such cases, entry into a residential treatment facility – "going to rehab" – is often seen as a more definitive action toward stopping the unacceptable drug or alcohol use than is starting a less intensive form of treatment.

A primary advantage of residential treatment – the protected environment – can also present difficulties when the individual returns to the outside world where drugs are accessible and relapse to active addiction is a definite threat. This transition is sometimes made in steps by first moving to a halfway house that offers no structured treatment, but provides a drug-free environment and less temptation for relapse. Such a gradual entry into the natural world after intensive residential treatment is most important for individuals who have less recovery capital, including no relatively safe place to live.

Nonresidential Treatment Programs

It is often not possible for people with substance use problems to suspend their normal lives for weeks to enter residential treatment. In addition to the greater expense, the most common barriers to intensive, full-time treatment are demands of work, and family responsibilities – including care of young children. Currently most SUD treatment is conducted in intensive outpatient settings, in which clients come to treatment sessions, often scheduled during evening hours. Treatment sessions may be conducted several times each week, but clients continue to live at home.

Nonresidential programs are similar to residential treatment in that they (1) educate about addiction – usually emphasizing the disease concept, (2) provide group therapy, (3) teach clients methods for preventing relapse to drug use, (4) encourage (often require) involvement in twelve-step groups (or other mutual-assistance groups), and (5) foster development of friendships with other recovering individuals.

These less intensive programs cannot provide the control and protection of residential treatment for preventing continuing drug use during treatment, and against the distractions of daily life. However, the frequent contact with others and periodic urine screens make it unlikely that clandestine drug use goes undetected. The group meetings, including educational discussions and group therapy, counteract the unhealthy isolation of an addictive lifestyle.

An advantage of nonresidential treatment is that because clients are not separated from their normal life activities, there is no difficult transition from a protected environment when treatment is ended. Individuals can practice maintaining a drug-free life in a natural environment as their treatment progresses.

BOX 16.4 Features typical of substance use disorder treatment programs

Education of patients, and families – on disease theory of addiction and situations that increase risk of drug use

Counseling and therapy in group settings

Engagement in twelve-step groups; indoctrination into AA philosophy

Introduction into the culture of recovery – promoting supportive social interactions

Encouragement of healthy lifestyle – diet, fitness, and exercise

Periodic urine screens or breath tests to detect clandestine drug or alcohol use

Residential treatment programs provide these services more intensively and frequently than nonresidential programs or office-based treatment. Residential programs also provide a controlled and protected environment that reduces the opportunity for drug use and allows for greater focus on treatment activities.

Treatment with Co-occurring Psychiatric Disorders

About 45 percent of those with SUD have another diagnosable mental or emotional disorder (Substance Abuse and Mental Health Services Administration 2018). As discussed in Chapter 8, such co-occurrence typically increases the severity of both disorders and presents a special challenge for treatment. Treatments for addiction developed in isolation from mainstream medical treatment for psychiatric disorders and the separation is partly responsible for the differences summarized in Box 16.1. Most SUD treatment programs are not intended to deal with psychiatric disorders unrelated to drug use, and general mental health facilities offer little help to addicted clients. Often a dually afflicted individual must choose which disorder is to be treated first, and the dilemma may discourage entry into either type of treatment. Office-based treatment providers can sometimes effectively treat such clients whose disorders are not severe, but many with both disorders need the more intensive care of a treatment program.

A much-needed innovation in treatment is integrated dual-disorder treatment (IDDT) programs. These programs, which are becoming more available, are designed to address both disorders simultaneously, in the same clinic, and with the same treatment providers. A multidisciplinary team meets regularly to discuss the client's progress in all aspects of recovery (Miller et al. 2019).

Agonist Drug Maintenance

The opioid full-agonist methadone and the partial opioid-agonist buprenorphine are widely used to manage drug dependence in individuals addicted to opioid drugs (Chapter 14). Most clients in these programs reduce or stop their use of illegal opioids, and for many the destructive features of addictive behavior are eliminated. Obviously these individuals are not drug-free, and many twelve-step advocates would argue that those in an agonist-replacement program are not really in recovery. Some of these programs provide counseling – including in some cases support for eventually stopping methadone or buprenorphine maintenance. Some programs also encourage or require patients to reduce drug maintenance dose or limit the time in which the drugs can be administered.

For most drug treatment programs, the intended result is abstinence from addictive drugs, markedly different from the intent of agonist maintenance programs. Consequently comparison of the two types of programs is difficult, especially in regard to treatment effectiveness.

Psychotherapy and Counseling

Maladaptive drug use, and especially the most severe form of SUD – addiction – is typically quite difficult to stop. Achieving stable sobriety may require (1) realization that drug use is destructive and life degrading, (2) sufficient motivation to stop the harmful behavior, (3) learning specific ways to stop drug use, (4) understanding the nature of addiction – the emotional connection to drug effects that often underlie the excessive use, (5) reduction of isolation and shame, (6) increased feelings of self-worth and confidence in the ability to change, (7) identifying and dealing with feelings and situations that promote drug use, and (8) learning how to have a satisfying life without using drugs. Complete achievement of all these goals may not be necessary. The most important objectives are the first three, but accomplishing the other objectives will also facilitate the recovery process.

Some of these objectives can be met by education – from lectures or group discussions about the effects of drugs, addiction, and ways to stay drug-free. Useful information can also be gained from twelve-step participation, by reading self-help literature, or from relevant internet sources. However, some of the important steps are most effectively accomplished by counseling or therapy administered by health care professionals trained to facilitate these desired outcomes. These therapeutic interactions can occur in a group setting, or more privately between a counselor and one individual.

Much of the important information about addiction becomes more compelling when clearly connected to the individual's personal situation (destructive drug effects, irrational and maladaptive addictive behavior), and such a connection can come from the objective view provided by a counselor or therapist. A skillful counselor tries to reduce the defensive denial that so often prevents a realistic self-assessment of addiction. Encouragement, support, and specific advice for the difficult work of stopping destructive drug use are also provided by effective therapy and counseling. Psychotherapy and counseling are the most used methods for treatment of SUD (National Institute of Drug Abuse 2009).

Several different specific types of counseling and therapy are used for treatment of SUD. However, certain nonspecific factors are important for the effectiveness of all types of therapeutic interactions (Wild and Wolfe 2009). A therapist must provide a safe place so the patient feels free to take risks, revealing sensitive information about his fears, vulnerabilities, and drug use. A warm, accepting and non-judgmental attitude of the counselor is critical for engagement of the client with the treatment process. Early establishment of a therapeutic alliance is of special importance (Norcross and Lambert 2011).

The terms **counseling** and **therapy** (psychotherapy) have slightly different meanings, although often used interchangeably and sharing many features. Counseling is typically considered to be more short-term and focused on a specific problem. In psychotherapy a longer-term approach is often taken, with more emphasis on the individual's response to difficult situations in general and improving overall quality of life. Therapy addresses the whole of an individual's problems, including those related to interpersonal relationships, employment, anxiety or depression – issues often ignored or minimized in twelve-step program treatment.

Some clinicians maintain that counseling (specific ways to stop drug use, dealing with craving) is needed to initially achieve sobriety. Eventually psychotherapy may be more beneficial to maintain a secure recovery by deeper consideration of such issues as self-esteem and emotional stability (Straussner 2014).

Psychotherapy for drug use problems is similar in several ways to psychotherapy for more general problems not necessarily related to drug use, such as anxiety and depression. However, a counselor or therapist working with a drug-abusing client must be somewhat more directive in keeping the therapeutic focus primarily on the problem of excessive drug use. In twelve-step meetings, some individuals testify that they underwent months or years of therapy, with no improvement in their addictive behavior – often because the addict managed to avoid discussing her compulsive drug use. A therapist should be aware that a therapeutic interaction can relieve shame, anxiety and depression related to drug use in a motivationally conflicted client who has little intention of stopping drug use, and may not even recognize (or admit) that much of her distress comes from such use. In such cases, if the client is permitted to control the topic of conversation, the counselor essentially enables the SUD – which can then continue unabated.

An effective counselor must maintain a balance between concentrating on the client's drug use and other sources of distress that may also promote the drug use (Washton and Zweben 2006). Many clients in treatment programs would rather keep the topic of therapy away from drug use in preference to discussion of other problems. A skilled therapist will acknowledge other difficulties, but place primary importance on the SUD.

Group Therapy

Although individuals with SUD differ in age, gender, occupation or socioeconomic status, and use a variety of addictive drugs, most experience common problems related to drug use. They are often quite secretive about their drug use and the harmful consequences, feeling isolated and ashamed. Under the direction of a skilled leader, therapeutic discussions conducted in a group can be a very effective aid in stopping and recovering from addiction (Figure 16.4). As a result, group

Figure 16.4 Group therapy provides a safe place to practice open and honest communication. Support and acceptance by individuals with similar problems reduce the shame and isolation that are so often a part of SUD. Photo: FatCamera / E+ / Getty Images.

therapy is the most used mode of SUD treatment, and in many programs is the sole form of treatment. In addition to the similar difficulties encountered by addicted individuals, another justification for use of group treatment is the increased efficiency, allowing for more frequent therapeutic sessions and decreasing the expense of providing treatment.

Group therapy can be quite powerful, given a competent leader and with appropriate selection of participants. "When people in trouble join together in the pursuit of shared goals, a variety of potent forces are mobilized that motivate and inspire them to confront the problem and resolve it successfully" (Washton and Zweben 2006, p. 242). Acceptance by peers, social support, and role modeling of others who dealt successfully with similar problems can relieve the intense feelings of shame, self-recrimination and despair related to addiction. Interaction with group members provides a safe place to practice open and honest communication – so often unfamiliar to those attempting to change an addictive lifestyle.

Although some interactions in a therapy group resemble those that occur in twelve-step meetings, there are definite differences between the two venues. In therapy groups, responses to self-disclosures ("cross-talk") are encouraged, and are part of the therapeutic process. Therapy group members are carefully selected, all members are expected to actively participate, and the discussion is monitored and guided by a trained counselor or therapist. In contrast, in twelve-step groups individuals' testimonies are not challenged or questioned, an attendee can choose not to speak, no trained leader directs the discussion, and for most meetings group members are not screened or selected.

Group therapy has benefits, but also some limitations. The interaction among individuals with similar problems is helpful, but the benefit comes with a loss of privacy. For some with an SUD the trade-off is entirely worthwhile, but for others is unacceptable. Although confidentiality is emphasized, it is never a certainty, so reputations, relationships, or employment could be damaged by disclosure – especially of illegal or antisocial activity. Another undesirable feature of the group mode of treatment is that only a limited amount of time and attention can be given to the unique problems of individual members. Those with SUD do have similar difficulties, but other group members do not share all problems, which are sometimes serious and quite complex. In such cases, a combination of group and individual therapy may be optimal.

Individual Counseling and Therapy

Group therapy, the preferred treatment method in most addiction treatment programs, can be a powerful aid to recovery. However, some individuals feel threatened by discussing details of their private lives in the presence of others – even those with a similar problem. A reluctance to be open and share personal experiences and feelings impairs the therapeutic benefits of group work even when fears of disclosure outside the group are not a major concern.

Individual counseling or psychotherapy provides greater privacy as well as more specific attention to each client. Problems unique to an individual can be addressed, including some topics that might not be suitable for group discussion. Addiction-relevant issues such as sexual abuse or co-occurring psychiatric disorders may not be of concern to most members of a group, but can be of vital importance to an individual. Individual therapy allows giving sufficient time and attention to such issues. The flexibility of individual counseling also accommodates differences in rates of progress that vary among clients.

The relationship between the client and counselor is a major factor in the effectiveness of therapy (Washton and Zweben 2006). The more private and intimate interactions that occur in individual therapy often promote a closer connection and a strong **therapeutic alliance**. As mentioned previously, individual therapy is not an option for clients in many addiction treatment programs, but is often the primary mode of office-based treatment.

Motivating Abstinence

Unfortunately, many who enter treatment for an SUD fail to engage with the therapeutic efforts, withdraw from treatment prematurely and return to maladaptive drug use. Motivation – the desire and determination to keep working toward stopping addictive behavior – is an obvious and important factor in achieving stable recovery. Motivation comes from internal as well as external sources – an intrinsic desire to improve, but also threats of legal consequences, loss of employment and damaged relationships. Motivation is not a stable trait, but a complex and dynamic process influenced by interpersonal interaction (Miller et al. 2011).

Individuals who use drugs compulsively often fail to acknowledge or fully appreciate the real or potential damage of their addictive behavior. Until the early 1990s direct confrontation – and typically, assigning the "addict" label – was a standard treatment procedure intended to "break denial," and motivate the patient/client to stop drug use. Although confrontation can be useful at certain times, it often hardens resistance to change and decreases intrinsic motivation (Washton and Zweben 2006). Few individuals like to be told directly that they are wrong, and must change their behavior.

Therapy and counseling during treatment for SUD can strengthen motivation to stop drug use. Group therapy can provide encouragement from others who are seeking recovery, but for many with much ambivalence about their drug use individual therapy is more effective for increasing intrinsic motivation. The collaborative therapeutic alliance that can develop in the course of individual therapy can do much to decrease ambivalence and strengthen desire and determination to stop drug use.

Many with addiction problems realize that they are in some degree of trouble but their ambivalence – the desire for the short-term comfort of drugs conflicts with the need to avoid the ensuing problems – prevents taking action to stop drug use. **Motivational interviewing (MI)** is a therapeutic technique for increasing intrinsic motivation, and is often effective for helping individuals to change their addictive behavior (Miller and Rollnick 2002, Glynn and Moyers 2009).

In motivational interviewing, a therapist works with a client's ambivalence to help her see stopping drug use as a desirable, internally motivated goal rather than as yielding to externally imposed change. Extrinsic motivation can force change, but intrinsic motivation is often more effective. To achieve this shift in motivation the therapist becomes an empathic and supportive ally, rather than an accusing, controlling adversary. The therapist respects the client's opinions by asking for her view of drug use – her "side of the story." The immediate rewards and comfort of drug use are acknowledged, and the therapist avoids triggering resistance by not arguing, lecturing or acting as an expert on addiction. Highly collaborative therapists may encourage "power sharing" in therapeutic sessions by allowing the client's comments and experiences to influence the direction of discussion (Tooley and Moyers 2012).

As a collaborative partner, the therapist carefully points out the discrepancy between the client's values and goals – and the consequences of drug use. The clinician nonjudgmentally emphasizes that giving up drug use is in the client's best interest – increasing the awareness and consideration of reasons to stop, while acknowledging her autonomy and stating that the choice is hers alone. The therapist deliberately encourages any "change talk" by the client, in which she considers the benefits of stopping drug use. Comments expressing intention to maintain drug use (not change) are usually not directly challenged, but neither are they discussed.

In addition to strengthening intrinsic motivation to change, a therapist using an MI approach also expresses confidence in the client's ability to stop drug use, once the decision is made. A client who doubts that he is capable of change is less likely to attempt the daunting task. Such encouragement is more effective when given by a friendly collaborator.

Motivational interviewing can be used as the main focus of therapy. It may be especially useful in the brief intervention mode of counseling. The techniques can also be integrated into most of the other specific therapeutic approaches often used in addiction treatment.

Therapies Used in SUD Treatment

Several types of therapy are useful to facilitate abstinence and recovery from disordered drug use. Some are suitable for working with individual clients or groups. Others are used with couples or families. Some are intended for individuals still using but considering stopping drug use, while others support ongoing abstinence and avoiding relapse. One method relies heavily on twelve-step principles and others emphasize techniques useful for many types of behavioral or psychological problems.

Brief Intervention

Many that use drugs or drink heavily, with risk of dangerous consequences, have no intention to stop or reduce their substance use because they do not see this behavior as a problem. Such risky drinkers – with no immediate harmful effects of alcohol use – far outnumber those with diagnosable SUD, although some are in the early stages of an alcohol use disorder (CASA 2012). These individuals may come to the attention of physicians who detect signs of alcohol misuse, or emergency department personnel who suspect that intoxication caused injuries from falls or other accidents. In a similar manner, university counselors or disciplinary committees may suspect heavy drinking or drug use by students exhibiting unacceptable behavior or who are experiencing academic difficulties.

Primary care physicians and emergency department personnel are those most likely to see evidence of such heavy drug or alcohol use, but these busy medical professionals have little time or training for more than a brief counseling session. College counselors may have opportunity and training for more extended discussions, but often students who misuse alcohol or drugs are reluctant to attend more than one or two counseling sessions.

Brief intervention is a counseling method that can include simple structured advice, written or internet-based information, and motivational counseling (National Institute on Alcohol Abuse and Alcoholism 2005, Miller 2000). Although many hard-drinking or drug-using individuals are very unlikely to seek or accept SUD treatment intended to bring about complete abstinence, they may consider reduction of dangerous substance use if the medical or other risks are clearly described by a credible source. Some of the tactics of motivational interviewing are useful in brief interventions, such as warmth, empathy, and not scolding or lecturing while imparting accurate information about heavy drinking (Kaner et al. 2009). One such tactic is the emphasis that any reduction of drinking or drug use is entirely the patient's choice – and not compliance to a demand from the authority figure.

A considerable amount of evidence demonstrates that brief intervention can reduce risky drinking (Kaner et al. 2009). Brief Intervention can assist smokers in reducing tobacco use (Richmond et al. 1990), and might help decrease use of other addictive recreational drugs including cannabis, stimulants, and opioids. Brief Intervention is in some respects primarily a tactic for prevention of SUD, but is also similar to treatment in that the purpose is to reduce harm from drinking or drug use.

Cognitive Behavioral Therapy

Cognitive behavioral therapy (CBT) is based on the premise that compulsive drug use is learned behavior that can be modified or replaced with new behavior and thinking incompatible with drug use (Rotgers 2012). Genetic factors and neurological abnormalities contribute to the complex causes of addiction in many cases of SUD. However, the environments, cognitions and emotions of addiction are the only components of the disorder subject to long-term change by treatment. Pharmaceutical agents may alleviate some neurological sources of compulsive drug use, but as of yet drug treatment is not a certain or adequate sole treatment for most cases of addiction.

In CBT therapy sessions, new behaviors and ways of thinking are learned – including identification of situations likely to result in drug use, social skills such as ways to gracefully decline an invitation to drink alcohol, finding rewarding activities other than drug use, and other methods promoting confidence in remaining abstinent. Erroneous thought-sequences and assumptions are also challenged – for example, "if I want to enjoy myself I need a drink," or "the only way I can finish this work assignment is by using amphetamine." Participants are taught that unpleasant emotions or mental states (boredom, anxiety, depression) are not irresistible reasons for drug use and can often be relieved without taking a drug. Encouragement of self-efficacy, empowerment and problem solving are critical components of CBT (Marinchak and Morgan 2012). These methods may appear to be obvious and simplistic, but they are intended to correct cognitions, emotions and behaviors that are common in individuals with SUD.

Individuals in CBT groups do not merely listen passively to directions for new ways to think, deal with feelings, and act. These new skills are practiced under the guidance of the therapist, and clients report on their progress in subsequent sessions. A collaborative therapeutic alliance with the therapist is very important for the effectiveness of CBT.

CBT can be conducted in either group or individual formats. However, a major benefit of CBT is flexibility for accommodating differences among clients, a feature usually requiring individual therapy sessions (Finney et al. 2007). CBT can promote a reduction in harmful drug use as well as the treatment goal of total abstinence. CBT is especially useful for dealing with and preventing relapse to compulsive drug use (Barry and Petry 2009).

CBT concepts of addiction, as well as methods to treat the disorder, are often seen as opposed to twelve-step philosophy and treatments for addiction. The antagonism between those that favor either of the two approaches apparently comes primarily from the following differences: (1) an emphasis on empowerment (CBT) versus powerlessness (AA), (2) the flexibility of CBT (in particular the willingness to consider nonabstinent reduction of drug use as a treatment goal), (3) the importance of spirituality for AA but not for CBT, and (4) the strong belief of many addiction counselors in recovery from an SUD that twelve-step methods are uniquely and universally effective.

The rivalry between practitioners of behavioral methods and adherents to twelve-step principles is less intense than in previous years. The decrease in animosity may be due to the recognition that many CBT tactics are quite similar to those of AA. Modeling (of a drug-free life) is important in both CBT (avoid heavy-drinking or drugging people) and AA (attend meetings, get a sponsor). Identifying nondrug sources of pleasure and methods of coping with stress are basic to both approaches to maintaining a sober life. The AA book *Living Sober* (Alcoholics Anonymous World Service 1975) gives many examples of behavioral tactics (although not labeled as such) for avoiding relapse to drinking.

Twelve-Step Facilitation

AA or NA are effective in supporting abstinence and recovery for many, but some individuals have difficulty accepting twelve-step concepts and do not become actively engaged in the program. Mere passive attendance at group meetings is typically insufficient, and such less involved people often return to use of alcohol or other addictive drugs. An experienced AA or NA sponsor can encourage and facilitate better program engagement. However, some individuals require professional assistance in becoming a willing and active group member. *Twelve-step facilitation therapy* (TSF) is conducted by a professional counselor who explains and advocates for the basic program principles and supports the client's involvement in AA or NA (Humphreys 2003).

TSF therapy focuses on the AA principles of **abstinence** (acceptance of the inability to drink responsibly) and surrender (to a higher power, or the AA group's guidance for recovery). A basic premise of TSF is that the counselor/therapist cannot directly promote recovery – which can come only from the AA group. Counselors encourage regular AA or NA meeting attendance, speaking in meetings, finding a sponsor, and involvement in the recovery culture of AA. Counselors also prevent the conversation from drifting to other issues or life problems, and ensure that abstinence and twelve-step involvement are the primary topics of discussion (Nowinski 2012).

TSF therapy can be conducted individually or in a group format. Counselors need not be recovering from an SUD and active in AA or NA, but they must be very familiar with twelve-step program principles and practices.

TSF therapy has some features in common with motivational interviewing and cognitive behavioral therapy. As therapists advocate for the twelve-step program they emphasize that program involvement is in the client's best interest – attempting to increase the intrinsic appeal of AA or NA. Although spirituality is identified as important to recovery, some attention is also given to dealing with emotional states, places and situations that are risks for relapse – which is a basic tactic of cognitive behavioral approaches to staying sober.

Mindfulness Training

Mindfulness therapy was originally developed for management of chronic pain, stress, and depressive states, but has also been used in treatment of SUD (Zgierska et al. 2009). Mindfulness promotes the intentional acceptance and nonjudgmental focus of attention on the emotions, thoughts and sensations occurring in the present moment (Kabat-Zinn 1990). Individuals suffering from an SUD often experience stress from drug craving, drug withdrawal, or the anxiety of the addictive lifestyle. For addicted individuals drug use is the typical reflexive, automatic response to stress or other unpleasant emotional states. In contrast, a mindful response to stress or pain allows for observation and acceptance of the situation, but not preoccupation by the experience. "Being in the present moment" may attenuate anticipation of a drug effect – thinking of the "next fix." The addicted individual is unwilling to experience the unpleasant subjective state and attempts to change the experience by taking a drug. Mindfulness training fosters recognition that the experience occurs, but can be tolerated and need not be immediately escaped.

Mindfulness, based on Buddhist concepts, is learned by means of training in meditation techniques. The method of alteration of thought processes and response to discomfort has been incorporated into several types of cognitive behavioral therapies used to treat SUD. Mindfulness techniques are especially appropriate for relapse prevention (Witkiewitz and Bowen 2010, Bowen et al. 2014).

Dialectical Behavior Therapy

Dialectical behavior therapy (DBT) was initially developed for suicidal patients but has been used most extensively to treat individuals with borderline personality disorder (Linehan 1993). The characteristic features of borderline personality disorder include inadequate emotional regulation (frequent and intense anger and mood swings) and impulse-control problems resulting in self-harm behavior and heavy use of alcohol and other addictive drugs. These individuals are also exquisitely sensitive to criticism, and have much difficulty with interpersonal relations. These behavioral and emotional characteristics are associated with the high prevalence of SUD, actual or attempted suicide, and generally chaotic lives of individuals with borderline personality disorder.

Some of these characteristics are also common to many individuals with SUD, but are especially intense in those suffering from both addiction and borderline personality disorder. The two disorders quite often co-occur, and such individuals present a difficult challenge for SUD treatment. They are reluctant to engage with treatment, tend to miss therapy appointments and often leave treatment prematurely. Establishing a collaborative therapeutic alliance is very difficult. Suggestions for change may be taken as criticism and provoke defensive anger.

Dialectical behavior therapy for SUD is a comprehensive and extensive form of treatment that combines cognitive behavior therapy, mindfulness, and some elements of twelve-step philosophy – with the overall goal of improving emotional regulation. DBT attempts to promote a balance between acceptance (of negative emotions) and **change** (of harmful behavior). Behavioral tactics include stopping contact with drug users, destroying drug use paraphernalia, and learning better ways to relate to others. Mindfulness meditation promotes acceptance of negative emotions without extreme response. Twelve-step concepts include abstinence from drugs, and the serenity prayer's recognition that although some things must be accepted, others can be changed (Dimeff and Linehan 2008). Improved emotional control was correlated with less drug use in patients undergoing DBT, suggesting that the beneficial effect on SUD was mediated by the better regulation of emotion (Axelrod et al. 2011).

Couples Therapy

Close interpersonal relationships are quite often damaged by addictive substance use. *Couples therapy* is intended to improve relations between partners in a way that facilitates recovery. The therapist helps clients identify types of interaction that promote destructive drug use. In behavioral couples therapy both partners are instructed on how to perform daily activities that improve communication, rebuild trust and support abstinence. The emphasis is on actions and situations that minimize the probability of drinking rather than on emotional state or background problems of either partner that might have contributed to the heavy drug use. Couples are encouraged to find enjoyable activities that can be shared but do not involve drinking or drug use. When successful, behavioral couples therapy can promote abstinence and recovery as well as improve the relationship. Couples therapy often requires more therapeutic training and skill than individual counseling – more complex interactions occur among the two clients and the therapist – but can be very effective (Lam et al. 2012, McCrady and Epstein 2008).

Family Therapy

Although addicts may eventually become isolated, many – especially adolescents – still live in a family that is a network of close social interactions. These interactions can influence drug use as well as promote and maintain remission and recovery (McCrady 2006). Family therapy is often a very important component of treatment, with some similarity to couples therapy. Education about SUD as well as guidance on how to promote sobriety and to respond to relapse are included in family counseling and therapy. Training in coping and parenting skills and in effective communication may also be a part of family therapy. Appropriate roles and responsibilities are clarified, and parents or other family members without substance use problems are engaged in a specific plan to reduce or eliminate drug and alcohol use in the individual with SUD. Family therapy is most often used in cases of alcohol use problems but has also proven to be effective for use disorders with illicit drugs (Rowe 2012).

Relapse Prevention

Mark Twain commented that stopping smoking was very easy – he had done it hundreds of times! Saul Shiffman and colleagues give a more recent and objective discussion of the difficulty of remaining abstinent from tobacco use in those addicted to nicotine (Shiffman et al. 2005). Recurrence after a temporary halt is quite likely for all types of habitual compulsive behavior – including gambling, internet use, overeating, risky sexual activity, as well as drug use (Brandon et al. 2007). In a representative example of the frequency of relapse, 61 percent of 350 patients returned to stimulant use within one year after treatment for methamphetamine addiction (Brecht and Herbeck 2014).

Relapse is defined as a setback that occurs during a process of behavioral change, such that progress toward stable abstinence is interrupted by a return to drug use (Hendershot et al. 2011). Marlatt and colleagues developed a cognitive behavioral concept of relapse and its prevention (Marlatt and Gordon 1985, Witkiewitz and Marlatt 2004). Relapse prevention treatment is intended to limit the occurrence and severity of a return to drug use.

In the cognitive behavioral view, a brief return to drug use is referred to as a lapse, which does not necessarily lead to a relapse to full-blown addictive behavior. A lapse, although a definite warning sign of possible relapse, is considered a normal part of the process of eventual permanent cessation of the compulsive behavior. A lapse can be a learning opportunity for the recovering individual, demonstrating how drug use is triggered by situations, thoughts, and mood states. Sometimes decisions that initially appeared not directly related to the drug use (e.g., taking on an unreasonably heavy, stress-producing workload) can be identified as a part of a sequence of thoughts or behaviors that led to the lapse.

The **abstinence violation effect** occurs when an initial return to drinking, smoking or other drug use elicits anxiety, guilt and depression – negative feelings about a failure to remain abstinent. These feelings of self-recrimination can promote further drug use, and cause a lapse to escalate into a relapse to more severe and persistent addictive behavior. Relapse prevention treatment warns against the abstinence violation effect and encourages the individual to learn from the event in order to prevent further lapses and especially to avoid thinking "I have failed in my recovery – I might as well get loaded to feel better" (briefly relieving the frustration and shame). A lapse is more likely to trigger a full-blown relapse if the recovering individual feels that the incident resulted from uncontrollable internal forces (such as a disease state), rather than being produced by factors that can be changed. Ideally, cognitive behavioral therapy can protect against lapses, and especially relapses, by increasing awareness of behaviors, thoughts, and situations that can lead to resumed drug use.

Ongoing participation in mutual-assistance groups helps to prevent relapse by maintaining awareness of lingering vulnerability to a return of active addiction. Twelve-step programs, with their encouragement of lifetime involvement, can be especially effective. AA and NA groups reward periods of continuous abstinence with tokens – plastic chips of various colors indicating the duration of sobriety. The initial chip given when drug use stops is white, indicating an intent to remain sober. If a lapse or a relapse does occur, the acceptance of another white chip indicates a renewed commitment to abstinence. Mutual-assistance groups invariably provide warm acceptance and support to their members, who sometimes lose the struggle to avoid relapse but persist in their attempt to remain sober. Relapse prevention is a primary goal of all forms of treatment for SUD (Marlatt and Witkiewitz 2005).

Nonabstinent Remission and Recovery

In the United States, most treatment programs for alcohol use disorders have, for decades, focused on the most severely addicted individuals (Willenbring 2010). Their treatment philosophy and practices are heavily influenced by a traditional version of the disease theory of addiction (Chapter 3) and the principles of Alcoholics Anonymous in which SUD is seen as a progressive disease that can be arrested only by complete abstinence. As a result, there is little support or even tolerance for a treatment goal of **controlled drinking** that would reduce or eliminate the harmful effects of compulsive alcohol use. A more flexible approach to treatment and recovery, with acceptance of controlled drinking for some patients, is prevalent in Canada, the United Kingdom, and several European countries (Larimer et al. 2012).

Both clinical and epidemiological studies have consistently shown that many individuals with alcohol use disorder moderate their drinking to asymptomatic levels, meaning that although not abstinent, they suffer no discernible harm from their continued but reduced alcohol use. Such nonabstinent remission of alcohol use disorder occurs in both untreated individuals as well as those who have undergone treatment – which in the great majority of cases, was intended to promote complete abstinence.

The NESARC epidemiological survey indicated that of 4,422 individuals (currently or previously) dependent on alcohol, about 20 percent of never-treated respondents, and 10 percent who had received treatment were drinking alcohol without harmful consequences (Figure 16.2) (Dawson et al. 2005). About three-fourths of these respondents had never been active in AA or received treatment for their alcohol addiction.

Clinical studies also provide information about posttreatment alcohol consumption. A meta-analysis of several clinical studies indicated that about 11 percent of individuals treated for alcohol dependence drank at safe levels during the year after treatment – while 24 percent were abstinent during this time (Miller et al. 2001).

These clinical and epidemiological results are typical of those indicating that moderated drinking occurs in a substantial proportion of DSM-IV alcohol-dependent individuals whose alcohol use problems remit – especially in those never in treatment or participating in AA. Outcome studies focus on alcohol addiction, so much less is known about remission of less severe alcohol use problems (DSM-IV alcohol abuse). However, most investigators have found that moderated or controlled drinking is a more probable outcome for alcohol-abusing individuals than for more severe cases of the disorder (Larimer et al. 2012, Yalisove 2004).

Treatment intended to assist some individuals with alcohol use disorders to drink responsibly was advocated in the 1970s (e.g., Sobell and Sobell 1973), and by several investigators in intervening years (e.g., Marlatt 1996). Clinical reports and scientific studies of controlled drinking invariably elicit controversy and disagreement from individuals and interest groups avidly opposed to consideration of an alternative to abstinent recovery. The disease theory of SUD is a primary basis for criticism of controlled drinking. The value, as well as the limitations of classical disease theory of addiction is discussed in Chapter 3.

Most active participants in AA programs assume that successful recovery cannot include moderated drinking. This mistaken belief comes at least partly from the reluctance of individuals who at one time suffered from problematic alcohol use – but eventually reduced their drinking to a safe level – to attend an AA group and describe their experience. Such accounts would not be well received, whereas the testimonials of failed attempts at controlled drinking, followed by successful abstinent recovery, are common in twelve-step meetings and are enthusiastically welcomed. As a result, AA groups essentially self-select for individuals strongly committed to total abstinence as the pathway to recovery.

The AA members and disease theory advocates are correct in their opinion that for most individuals with a severe alcohol use disorder (dependence/addiction) controlled drinking is not a safe option. Many (but certainly not all) alcohol addicts would prefer to control their drinking rather than attempt complete abstinence. Given this reluctance to give up alcohol use completely, provision of a treatment option for controlled drinking could be dangerous for many who are alcohol dependent. Even for those who might succeed at moderating their drinking, total abstinence provides a more distinct marker for ongoing recovery. For many with a history of alcohol problems identification with the AA community is very attractive – and not using alcohol is a defining feature of that culture of recovery. Abstaining individuals have access to group recognition and approval while those who continue to drink – at any level – do not (Nowinski 2012).

However, the reluctance to give up alcohol use prevents many from seeking help if the only apparent treatment option is total abstinence – even for those who with professional assistance might be able to moderate their drinking (Heather 2006). In the United States and many other countries, alcoholic beverage use is culturally accepted and although many do not drink, total abstinence is somewhat deviant, especially among young adults. A more flexible approach to treatment would attract more individuals with a wider range of alcohol use disorders. Young adults who consume dangerous amounts of alcohol but are not yet addicted nor harmed by drinking are often good candidates for controlled drinking advice, as in a brief intervention (previously described). Successful moderation of alcohol use in such cases prevents progression into a severe SUD (Ambrogne 2002).

For some (perhaps most) with an alcohol use disorder moderate drinking may be a more difficult recovery path than complete abstinence. However, even those who attempt to consume no alcohol sometimes briefly lapse (or "slip"), and are then vulnerable to the abstinence violation effect, which may contribute to further relapse into heavy drinking. Individuals pursuing a course of light or moderate drinking are unlikely to feel remorse about limited alcohol consumption, so long as it remains at a safe level.

Given that some with an alcohol use disorder can reduce their drinking to a safe level, which individuals are good candidates for this option? Many studies show that: less severe disorder (not DSM-IV dependent), low incidence of family alcohol problems (implying less genetic loading), no additional psychiatric disorder, emotional stability, family support, and female gender are characteristics predicting greater success in moderating drinking (Davis and Rosenberg 2013, Yalisove 2004).

Controlled drinking as a treatment option has become somewhat more acceptable than in earlier years as an intended treatment outcome for alcohol-abusing individuals. A few treatment programs are not constrained by disease theory and twelve-step principles, and many independent office-based treatment providers condone controlled drinking for some clients (Larimer et al. 2012). In response to a web-based survey by Davis and Rosenberg, more than half of 913 addiction professionals rated nonabstinence as a somewhat or completely acceptable intermediate (58 percent) or final (51 percent) treatment outcome for alcohol abusers. Most respondents did not endorse controlled use as an acceptable treatment option for alcohol-dependent clients (84 percent) or for clients dependent on an illicit drug (85 percent). Only 21 percent of these addiction professional respondents worked in residential treatment settings, but all were asked to rate acceptability of controlled drinking (for any patient) in various treatment settings. Seventy-four percent rated nonabstinence as unacceptable in residential treatment, 57 percent for intensive outpatient programs, and 28 percent for clients treated in independent private practice (Davis and Rosenberg 2013). The difference among treatment locations in perceived acceptance of nonabstinence treatment outcomes may result from the greater severity of SUD in residential patients, and the greater flexibility of private practitioners for selecting treatment plans.

Most treatments intended to promote controlled drinking employ some version of cognitive behavioral therapy, or other therapies mentioned above (with the exception of twelve-step facilitation) (Larimer et al. 2012). Treatments are also available for controlled use of tobacco/nicotine (Phillips et al. 2012) and cannabis (Roffman and Stephens 2012), but less evidence exists for stable moderate use of these drugs by addicted individuals. There is also little support for or evidence of controlled nonmedical use by individuals dependent on stimulants (amphetamine and cocaine) or opioids (heroin and fentanyl) (Davis et al. 2017).

Controlled or moderate drinking as a treatment outcome is part of a much wider range of **harm reduction** efforts intended to reduce the effects of risky behavior. These other harm reduction actions include distribution of clean injection needles to users of opioids or stimulants, providing condoms to certain populations of sexually active young people, and offering shelter to homeless people with no requirement for abstinence from drinking or drug use (Collins et al. 2012, Hawk et al. 2017). As with controlled drinking, other forms of harm reduction are a source of controversy. However, "Unlike the disease and moral models of substance use, harm reduction ... allows for complexity and nuance in our understanding of human behavior. It empowers affected individuals to take control of their own behavior on their terms. It focuses on the reduction of harm *and* improvement in quality of life" (Collins and Marlatt 2012, p. xiv).

Treatment Effectiveness

Public perceptions of how well SUD treatment "works" vary greatly. Testimonials of successful treatment are common in AA and NA meetings as members describe years of abstinent recovery following addiction treatment – which in most cases was also the start of prolonged participation in a twelve-step program. However, many people witness a return to compulsive drug or alcohol use by a friend or relative after treatment for the disorder and/or participation in AA. A common reason stated by untreated NESARC respondents dependent on alcohol for not seeking assistance was a belief that treatment is not effective (Grella and Stein 2013).

Substance use disorders are a major public health problem, but professional treatment (and especially inpatient programs) is expensive and time-consuming. Consequently, objective evaluation of treatment effectiveness is very important – but several problems challenge the design, conduct and interpretation of outcome studies. These problems include definition of treatment success, difficulty of long-term monitoring of treated individuals, and valid comparisons to untreated remission and recovery.

Most treatment programs, based on twelve-step concepts of recovery, emphasize abstinence as the intended outcome of treatment. However, a substantial reduction in drug or alcohol use is also at least a partial success. A NIDA panel designated a decrease in the amount of drug use to half of pretreatment levels as a clinically meaningful outcome (Donovan et al. 2012). An improvement in quality of life is also an important positive outcome of treatment, but one that is more difficult, although possible, to measure (Kelly et al. 2009).

The duration of abstinence or significantly reduced drug use is an important treatment outcome. George Vaillant's forty-year naturalistic study of alcohol-dependent men revealed the intermittent nature of SUD over a lifetime in both treated and untreated individuals (Vaillant 1995). More recent long-term studies have also shown that alcohol use disorders can recur during a sixteen-year posttreatment period (e.g., Moos and Moos 2006b). Because of the often-intermittent nature of remission, the most valuable studies of treatment outcomes monitor patients for one or more years after treatment, a challenging and expensive requirement.

Because many with SUD recover or remit without specific treatment or assistance for managing the disorder, comparisons of treatment outcomes with untreated remission rates are very important for firmly establishing treatment effectiveness. Satisfactory control groups with random assignment to treatment versus nontreatment conditions are in most cases neither possible nor ethical. Some studies use comparison groups to determine relative rates of SUD remission between treated and untreated individuals. Untreated individuals with drug or alcohol problems often have less severe SUD than those who enter treatment, so may be less motivated to decrease their use of addictive intoxicants. These and other uncontrolled differences between treated and untreated groups typically limit the unequivocal interpretation of treatment outcome studies. Successful outcomes are often described as being *associated* with treatment, and positive results as *suggesting* that treatment is effective.

Most treatment outcome studies have focused on alcohol use disorders, with fewer studies conducted on treatment of addiction to illicit drugs. Because twelve-step participation is typically encouraged or required by treatment programs, the effects of AA or NA in combination with professional treatment are combined in many studies of treatment effectiveness.

Remission rates indicated by outcome studies of treatment for alcohol use disorders vary widely, ranging from approximately 30 percent to somewhat greater than 50 percent of individuals stopping or reducing drinking – depending partly on severity of the disorder and definition of improvement (Miller et al. 2001, Yalisove 2004). Many who commence treatment do not complete a specified treatment program, and such early departure (treatment drop-outs) is an important factor in the large proportion of unsuccessful treatment outcomes (Brorson et al. 2013). Treated individuals are more likely to stop alcohol use than are those who do not seek treatment. The results of several representative studies were combined in a meta-analysis indicating that 43 percent of alcohol-dependent patients became abstinent from alcohol after treatment, versus 21 percent of individuals in untreated comparison groups (Moyer and Finney 2002).

A study of less severe alcohol use disorders indicated an abstinence rate of 62 percent in treated, compared to 43 percent in untreated individuals (Moos and Moos 2006b). Some individuals reduce their drinking to safe levels after treatment but do not remain abstinent, although as indicated by the NESARC survey, this outcome is more likely in those who neither enter treatment nor become engaged in an AA program. If nonabstinent remission is included in the comparison, differences between treated and untreated respondents are smaller. Based on percentages shown in Figure 16.2, 35.1 percent of treated and 12.4 percent of untreated respondents were abstinent. When safe drinking was combined with abstinence, the percentage for treated respondents was 45.5 percent, and for untreated 32.6 percent.

A very large number of outcome studies for SUD treatment are available from several professional journals and government sources (e.g., Houge et al. 2014, Wild and Wolfe 2009).

Proposed Improvements in SUD Treatment

SUD treatment promotes remission and recovery in many individuals. However, a majority of those afflicted do not seek treatment, and the interventions are largely ineffective in about half who do enter treatment. Professional treatment of SUD is in obvious need of improvement in effectiveness.

Most individuals with drug or alcohol use problems do not have a severe disorder, but most treatments are intended to deal with cases of full-blown dependence/addiction. These treatment programs (characteristics listed in the first part of Box 16.2) are typically the only option offered and are most often inappropriate and unacceptable to a great number of those who could benefit from a more flexible and less intrusive form of treatment. The increase in the use of brief interventions, acceptance of treatments intended to promote nonabstinent recovery, and the emergence of office-based treatment are steps in the right direction that may improve treatment by widening the range of services offered (Willenbring 2013).

The concept of severe SUD as a disease is generally accepted by the medical community and is a basic tenet of most addiction treatment. However, SUD treatment originated and evolved separately from mainstream medical thought and practice – due in part to its close and long-standing association with Alcoholics Anonymous. Currently most treatment programs are still segregated and isolated from traditional medical and psychological concepts and care, including medication administered by psychiatrists and psychotherapy as provided by clinical psychologists. Addiction treatment would be improved by considering the affliction as a psychological disorder – as designated by the DSM system (Arria and McClellan 2012, Kellogg and Tatarsky 2012, Szalavitz 2016, Thombs and Osborn 2019).

Yet a third improvement in SUD treatment would be recognizing that severe cases of the disorder are a chronic condition. Other chronic medical problems – such as bipolar disorder, diabetes, and multiple sclerosis – require ongoing management rather than a brief single course of treatment, as is most often offered initially to addicted individuals. Continuing participation in a mutual-assistance group (either twelve-step or a secular organization) provides some long-term support for management of a chronic addiction problem, but sustained medical and psychological care would also contribute to ongoing relapse-free recovery (Arria and McClellan 2012, Kellogg and Tatarsky 2012, Willenbring 2013).

Chapter Summary

Most who suffer from substance use disorders are resistant to change, with much ambivalence about their self-destructive drug behavior.

There are several pathways out of destructive drug use. A majority of afflicted persons improve without assistance specifically intended to address the SUD. Most of these individuals apparently have a less severe disorder, and many reduce, rather than completely stopping, use of alcohol or cannabis. Others, often those with a more severe disorder, need help from health care professionals or mutual-assistance groups.

Many who have stopped addictive drug use attribute their sobriety to active participation in Alcoholics Anonymous or similar twelve-step groups. These mutual-assistance groups offer support for avoiding drinking or drug use and provide a welcoming community and culture based on complete abstinence. Their principles are based on spirituality and emphasize powerlessness, surrender, lessening of character faults, and assistance to others.

Several secular mutual-assistance groups (e.g., SMART Recovery, Secular Organization for Sobriety) offer less spiritually focused support. Mutual-assistance groups do not provide treatment for SUD but are often used after treatment for ongoing support of continued recovery. Others with drug use problems join these groups without receiving professional help.

The Minnesota Model of treatment, developed in the 1970s and based on a disease theory concept of addiction, continues to be a dominant form of professional

SUD treatment in the United States. This treatment approach relies heavily on the principles of Alcoholics Anonymous, which are incorporated into lectures and group therapy.

Most SUD treatment is currently offered via intensive outpatient programs in which clients live at home and attend several treatment sessions each week.

Residential treatment programs provide a protected environment to support early abstinence and offer more therapeutic activities than nonresidential treatment.

Counseling and psychotherapy are the primary treatments for SUD and, in treatment programs, are most often conducted in groups. Sharing common experiences and consequences of drug use can relieve feelings of shame and isolation that impede recovery.

Office-based treatment provides individual psychotherapy or counseling that can be modified to meet the specific needs of each client. With this more flexible form of treatment, other issues, including co-occurring disorders, can be addressed in addition to the primary problem of alcohol or drug use. Some office-based treatment providers also offer group therapy.

Treatment is most effective when the helping professional forms an alliance with the client, promoting intrinsic motivation and strengthening the resolve to become securely abstinent.

Therapies frequently used for treatment of SUD include cognitive behavioral, twelve-step facilitation, mindfulness, dialectical behavior change, and couples or family therapy. Brief interventions are conducted in short, informative counseling sessions that are most appropriate for individuals with indications of early-stage substance abuse – as often found on college campuses.

Medications specifically intended to decrease craving and other aspects of compulsive drug use are sometimes used as adjuncts to the counseling and therapy that are the mainstay of treatment programs and office-based treatment. Agonist-replacement drugs (for nicotine and opioid dependence) are rarely part of SUD treatment intended to promote abstinence from addictive drugs.

Nonabstinent recovery (controlled drinking) from alcohol use disorders is a subject of long-standing controversy. Alcoholics Anonymous and Minnesota Model–based treatment programs do not accept this harm-reduction approach to recovery. However, a substantial proportion of individuals with alcohol use problems do not become abstinent but reduce their drinking to safe levels – either with, or in the absence of, treatment for the disorder. Nonabstinent recovery has become more acceptable for those with less severe alcohol use problems, especially by independent practitioners not affiliated with an SUD treatment program.

Alcohol or other drug use often recurs after treatment – and the prevention and management of such relapse is a primary goal of SUD treatment. Ongoing support of mutual-assistance groups is associated with lower rates of relapse.

SUD treatment results in stable remission for about 30 to 50 or 60 percent of individuals who commence treatment. Treatment effectiveness varies with the proportion of clients who complete a full course of treatment, the severity of the disorder, and the definition of treatment success – abstinence or significant reduction of drug use. Because many with SUD improve without treatment, comparisons between treated and untreated groups are required to measure treatment effectiveness. Most comparisons show that treated individuals have a greater probability of decreased use of alcohol or other addictive drugs, and especially of abstinent recovery.

Review Exercises

1. State the reasons that peer-based treatment for addiction became prevalent and well accepted.
2. State both the strengths and weaknesses of the Minnesota Model of treatment for addiction.
3. Box 16.1 lists general characteristics of the SUD treatments used by psychologists and other mental health professionals. State both the strengths and weaknesses of such approaches to treatment.
4. Describe differences among addicted individuals that require flexibility in SUD treatments for different populations of misusers.
5. State the treatment-relevant features of SUD. Which ones do you think are the most important, and why?
6. One of the reasons given, by those misusing drugs, for not seeking treatment is the belief that treatment does not work. State an argument that treatment does or does not work using the information in Figure 16.2.
7. Describe the factors that promote remission in untreated individuals.
8. Describe, with a focus on Alcohol Anonymous, the tenets of as well as other possible reasons that such mutual-assistance groups can be effective.
9. In what ways are faith-based twelve-step and secular mutual-assistance groups similar? What are their major differences?
10. What are the ways in which office-based and residential SUD treatment programs differ?
11. What are the advantages of office-based treatment for SUD (especially treatment related to the type of psychotherapy and counseling offered in OBT)?
12. What are critical limitations of residential treatment programs, including their handling of co-occurring mental illness?
13. Compare and contrast group therapy to twelve-step group meetings.
14. Describe the purpose and procedures of motivational interviewing.
15. Describe the procedures and advantages of brief intervention.

16. What are the features of mindfulness that could, and perhaps already are, part of both CBT and twelve-step facilitation?

17. What approaches do CBT and mutual-assistance groups use to try to prevent relapse?

18. What are the advantages, as well as the disadvantages, of accepting nonabstinent recovery as a treatment goal?

19. Based on information presented here, make a case for the statement that "SUD treatment is effective" or, alternatively, "SUD treatment does not work very well."

Key Terms

abstinence (665)

abstinence violation effect (668)

acceptance (645)

adjunct treatment (635)

change (667)

cognitive behavioral therapy (664)

controlled drinking (669)

counseling (658)

harm reduction (672)

intensive outpatient (634)

motivational interviewing (MI) (662)

natural recovery (643)

NESARC epidemiological survey (640)

personal empowerment (651)

recovery capital (643)

safe alcohol consumption (641)

social networking (633)

surrender (645)

therapeutic alliance (661)

therapy (658)

References

Abbey A, Zawacki T, McAuslan P (2000) Alcohol's effects on sexual perception. Journal of Studies on Alcohol **61**: 688–697.

Abel E (1980) Marijuana: The First Twelve Thousand Years. New York: Plenum.

Abel EL (1995) An update on incidence of FAS: FAS is not an equal opportunity birth defect. Neurotoxicology and Teratology **17**: 437–443.

Abel EL (1998) Fetal alcohol syndrome: The "American paradox." Alcohol and Alcoholism **33**: 195–201.

Abel EL (2009) Fetal alcohol syndrome: Same old, same old. Addiction **104**: 1274–1275.

Abood ME, Martin BR (2002) Neurobiology of marijuana abuse. Trends in Pharmacological Science **13**: 201–206.

Abrams DB, Niaura RS (1987) Social learning theory. In Blane HT, Leonard KE (eds.) Psychological Theories of Drinking and Alcoholism. New York: Guilford Press.

Abrantes AM, Strong DR, Lejuez CW, et al. (2008) The role of negative affect in risk for early lapse among low distress tolerance smokers. Addictive Behaviors **33**: 1394–1401.

Acharya N, Penukonda S, Shcheglova T, et al. (2017) Endocannabinoid system acts as a regulator of immune homeostasis in the gut. Proceedings of the National Academy of Sciences of the USA **114**: 5005–5010.

Agrawal A, Bierut LJ (2012) Identifying genetic variation for alcohol dependence. Alcohol Research: Current Reviews **34**: 274–281.

Agrawal A, Budney AJ, Lynskey MT (2012) The co-occurring use and misuse of cannabis and tobacco: A review. Addiction **107**: 1221–1233.

Agrawal A, Edenberg HJ, Foroud T, et al. (2006) Association of GABRA2 with drug dependence in the colloborative study of the genetics of alcoholism sample. Behavior Genetics **36**: 640–650.

Agrawal A, Lynskey MT, Hinrichs A, et al. (2011) A genome-wide association study of DSM-IV cannabis dependence. Addiction Biology **16**: 514–518.

Agrawal A, Neale MC, Jacobson KC, et al. (2005) Illicit drug use and abuse/dependence: Modeling of two-stage variables using the CCC approach. Addictive Behavior **30**: 1043–1048.

Agrawal A, Wetherill L, Bucholz KK, et al. (2013) Genetic influences on craving for alcohol. Addictive Behavior **38**: 1501–1508.

Agurell S, Halldin M, Lindgren J-E (1986) Pharmacokinetics and metabolism of delta-9 tetrahydrocannabinol and other cannabinoids with emphasis on man. Pharmacological Review **38**: 21–38.

Aharonovich E, Nunes E, Hasin D (2003) Cognitive impairment, retention and abstinence among cocaine abusers in cognitive-behavioral treatment. Drug and Alcohol Dependence 71: 207–211.

Ahern J, Stuber J, Galea S (2007) Stigma, discrimination and the health of illicit drug users. Drug and Alcohol Dependence 88: 188–196.

Ahmed SH, Kenny PJ, Koob GF, et al. (2002) Neurobiological evidence for hedonic allostasis associated with escalating cocaine use. Nature Neuroscience 5: 625–626.

Ahmed SH, Koob GF (1998) Transition from moderate to excessive drug intake: Change in hedonic set point. Science 282: 298–300.

Albertson DN, Schmidt CJ, Kapatos G, et al. (2006) Distinctive profiles of gene expression in the human nucleus accumbens associated with cocaine and heroin abuse. Neuropsychopharmacology 31: 2304–2312.

Alcoholics Anonymous (1975) Living Sober. New York: Alcoholics Anonymous World Services Inc.

Alcoholics Anonymous (2010) AA Fact File. New York: Alcoholics Anonymous World Services Inc.

Aletraris L, Edmond MB, Roman PM (2015) Adoption of injectable naltrexone in US substance use disorder programs. Journal of Studies on Alcohol and Drugs 76: 143–151.

Alexander BK, Beyerstein BL, Hadaway PF, et al. (1981) Effects of early and later colony housing on oral ingestion of morphine in rats. Pharmacology, Biochemistry, and Behavior 15: 571–576.

Algeria AA, Hasin DS, Nunes EV, et al. (2010) Comorbidity of generalized anxiety disorder and substance use disorders: Results from the National Epidemiological Survey on Alcohol and Related Conditions. Journal of Clinical Psychiatry 71: 1187–1195.

Allen AM, Allen SS, Lunos S, et al. (2010) Severity of withdrawal symptomology in follicular versus luteal quitters: The combined effects of menstrual phase and withdrawal on smoking cessation outcome. Addictive Behaviors 35: 549–552.

Allen SS, Bade T, Center B, et al. (2008) Menstrual phase effects on smoking relapse. Addiction 103: 809–821.

Allsop DJ, Copeland J, Norberg MM, et al. (2012) Quantifying the clinical significance of cannabis withdrawal. PLoS ONE 7: e44864.

Alvarez VA, Emory E (2006) Executive function and the frontal lobes: A meta-analytic review. Neuropsychological Review 16: 17–42.

Alvarez VA, Sabatini BL (2007) Anatomical and physiological plasticity of dendritic spines. Annual Review of Neuroscience 30: 79–97.

Ambrogne JA (2002) Reduced-risk drinking as a treatment goal: What clinicians need to know. Journal of Substance Abuse Treatment 22: 45–53.

American Cancer Society (2011) Cancer facts and Figures 2011. www.cancer.org/Cancer/CancerCauses/TobaccoCancer

American Heritage (2004) Disease. In The American Heritage Stedman's Medical Dictionary. New York: Houghton Mifflin.

American Pain Society (1997) The use of opioids for the treatment of chronic pain. A consensus statement from the American Society of Pain Medicine and the American Pain Society. Clinical Journal of Pain 13: 6–8.

American Psychiatric Association (2000) Diagnostic and Statistical Manual of Mental Disorders. 4th ed., Text Revision. Washington, DC: American Psychiatric Association.

American Psychiatric Association (2013) Diagnostic and Statistical Manual of Mental Disorders. 5th ed. Washington, DC: American Psychiatric Association.

Amos A, Wiltshire S, Bostock Y, et al. (2004) "You can't go without a fag ... you need it for your hash" – a qualitative exploration of smoking, cannabis and young people. Addiction 99: 77–81.

Anczak JD, Nogler RA (2003) Tobacco cessation in primary care: Maximizing intervention strategies. Clinical Medicine and Research 1: 201–216.

Anderson D (1942) Alcohol and public opinion. Quarterly Journal of Studies on Alcohol 3: 376–392.

Andrews JA, Hampson SE, Barckley M, et al. (2008) The effect of early cognitions on cigarette and alcohol use during adolescence. Psychology of Addictive Behaviors 22: 96–106.

Angrist B (1994) Amphetamine psychosis: Clinical variations of the syndrome. In Cho AK, Segal DS (eds.) Amphetamine and Its Analogs: Neuropharmacology, Toxicology and Abuse. New York: Academic Press.

Angrist B, Gershon S (1970) The phenomenology of experimentally induced amphetamine psychosis. Biological Psychiatry 2: 95–207.

Anokhin AP, Vedeniapin AB, Sirevaag EJ, et al. (2000) The P300 brain potential is reduced in smokers. Psychopharmacology 149: 409–413.

Anslie G (2001) Breakdown of will. Cambridge, England: Cambridge University Press.

Anthenelli RM, Schuckit MA (1991) Genetic influences in addiction. International Journal of Addiction 125: 81–90.

Anthony JC (1992) Epidemiological research on cocaine use in the USA. In Bock GR (ed.) Cocaine: Scientific and Social Dimensions. CIBA Foundation Symposium 166. Chichester, UK: John Wiley.

Anthony JC (2006) The epidemiology of cannabis dependence. In Roffman RA, Stephens RS (eds.) Cannabis Dependence: Its Nature, Consequences, and Treatment. Cambridge: Cambridge University Press.

Anthony JC, Chen CY (2004) Epidemiology of drug dependence. In M Galanter, HD Kleber (eds.) Texbook of Substance Abuse Treatment. Washington, DC: American Psychiatric Association.

Anthony JC, Warner LA, Kessler RC (1994) Comparative epidemiology of dependence on tobacco, alcohol, controlled substances, and inhalants: Basic findings from the national comorbidity survey. Experimental and Clinical Psychopharmacology 2: 244–268.

Anton RF (1999) What is craving? Models and implications for treatment. Alcohol Research and Health 23: 165–173.

Arciniegas DB, Beresford TP (2001) Neuropsychiatry: An Introductory Approach. Cambridge: Cambridge University Press.

Arday DR, Giovino GA, Schulman J, et al. (1995) Cigarette smoking and self-reported health problems among high-school seniors 1982–1989. American Journal of Health Promotion 10: 111–116.

Arrazola RA, Neff LJ, Kennedy SM, et al. (2014) Tobacco use among middle and high school students – United States 2013. Morbidity and Mortality Weekly Report **63**: 1021–1026.

Arria A, Caldeira KM, O'Grady KE, et al. (2015) The academic consequences of marijuana use during college. Psychology of Addictive Behaviors **29**: 564–575.

Arria AM, Derauf C, Lagasse LL (2006) Methamphetamine and other substance use during pregnancy: Preliminary estimates from the Infant Development Environment and Lifestyle (IDEAL) study. Maternal and Child Health Journal **10**: 293–302.

Arria AM, McClellan AT (2012) Evolution of concept – but not action – in addiction treatment. Substance Use and Misuse **47**: 1041–1048.

Asbridge M (2005) Letter to the editor and reply on: "Drugs and driving." Traffic Injury Prevention **5**: 241–253.

Ashare RL, Baschangel JS, Hawk LW Jr. (2010) Subjective effects of transdermal nicotine among nonsmokers. Experimental and Clinical Psychopharmacology **18**: 167–174.

Ashtari M, Avants B, Cyckowski L, et al. (2011) Medial temporal structures and memory functions in adolescents with heavy cannabis use. Journal of Psychiatric Research **45**: 1055–1066.

Atack JR (2011) GABA-A receptor subtype-selective modulators I. alpha2/alpha3-selective agonists as non-sedating anxiolytics. Current Topics in Medicinal Chemistry **11**: 1176–1202.

Atwood BK, Huffman J, Straiker A, et al. (2010) JWH018, a common constituent of "Spice" herbal blends, is a potent and efficacious cannabinoid CB receptor agonist. British Journal of Pharmacology **160**: 585–593.

Audrain-McGovern J, Koudsi NA, Rodriguez D, et al. (2007) The role of *CYP2A6* in the emergence of nicotine dependence in adolescents. Pediatrics **119**: e264.

Axelrod SR, Perepletchikova F, Holtzman K, et al. (2011) Emotion regulation and substance use frequency in women with substance dependence and borderline personality disorder receiving dialectical behavior therapy. American Journal of Drug and Alcohol Abuse **37**: 37–42.

Babb S, Malarcher A, Schauer G, et al. (2017) Quitting smoking among adults – United States 2000–2015. Morbidity and Mortality Weekly Reports **65**: 1457–1464.

Babor TF (1996) The classification of alcoholics: Typology theories from the 19th century to the present. Alcohol Health and Research World **20**: 6–14.

Babor TF (2007) We shape our tools, and thereafter our tools shape us: Psychiatry, epidemiology, and the alcohol dependence syndrome concept. Addiction **102**: 1534–1535.

Babor TF, Caetano R (2006) Subtypes of substance dependence and abuse: Implications for diagnostic classification and empirical research. Addiction **101**(Suppl. 1): 104–110.

Babor TF, Caetano R (2008) The trouble with alcohol abuse: What are we trying to measure, diagnose, count and prevent? Addiction **103**: 1057–1059.

Babor TF, Dolinsky ZS (1988) Alcoholic typologies: Historical evolution and empirical evaluation of some common classification schemes. In Rose RM,

Barret J (eds.) Alcoholism: Origins and Outcome. New York: Raven Press.

Babor TF, Hoffmann MI, Del Boca FK, et al. (1992) Types of alcoholics I. Evidence for an empirically derived typology based on indicator of vulnerability and severity. Archives of General Psychiatry **49**: 599–608.

Bachhuber MA, Hennessy S, Cunningham CO, et al. (2016) Increasing benzodiazepine prescriptions and overdose mortality in the United States, 1996–2013. American Journal of Public Health **106**: 686–688.

Bachman JG, O'Malley PM, Schulenberg JE (2002) The Decline of Substance Abuse in Young Adulthood: Changes in Social Activities, Roles, and Beliefs. Mahwah, NJ: Lawrence Erlbaum.

Bada HS, Das A, Bauer CR (2002) Gestational cocaine exposure and intrauterine growth: Maternal Lifestyle Study. Obstetrics and Gynecology **100**: 916–924.

Badiani A, Robinson TE (2004) Drug-induced neurobehavioral plasticity: The role of environmental context. Behavioural Pharmacology **15**: 327–339.

Bagge CL, Sher KJ (2008) Adolescent alcohol involvement and suicide attempts: Toward the development of a conceptual framework. Clinical Psychology Review **28**: 1283–1296.

Bailey CP, Andrews N, McKnight AT, et al. (2000) Prolonged changes in neurochemistry of dopamine neurons after chronic ethanol consumption. Pharmacology, Biochemistry, and Behavior **66**: 153–161.

Bailey SR, Harrison CT, Jeffery CJ, et al. (2009) Withdrawal symptoms over time among adolescents in a smoking cessation intervention: Do symptoms

vary by levels of nicotine dependence? Addictive Behaviors **34**: 1017–1022.

Baker TB, Piper ME, McCarthy DE, et al. (2004) Addiction motivation reformulated: An affective processing model of negative reinforcement. Psychological Review **111**: 33–51.

Baker TB, Piper ME, McCarthy DE, et al. (2007) Time to first cigarette in the morning as an index of ability to quit smoking: Implications for nicotine dependence. Nicotine and Tobacco Research **9**: S555–570.

Baldisseri MR (2007) Impaired healthcare professional. Critical Care Medicine **35**: S106–1116.

Ball D, Pembrey, SD (2007) Genomics. In Nutt D, Robbins TW, Stimson GV, et al. (eds.) Drugs and the Future: Brain Science, Addiction, and Society. London: Academic Press.

Ball SA, Carroll KM, Babor TF, et al. (1995) Subtypes of cocaine abusers: Support for a type A–type B distinction. Journal of Consulting and Clinical Psychology **63**: 115–124.

Bandstra ES, Morrow CE, Accornero VH, et al. (2011) Estimated effects of *in utero* cocaine exposure on language development through early adolescence. Neurotoxicology and Teratology **33**: 25–35.

Bandura A (1977) Social Learning Theory. Englewood Cliffs, NJ: Prentice Hall.

Banich MT, Compton RJ (2018) Cognitive Neuroscience. Cambridge: Cambridge University Press.

Barkley-Levenson AM, Crabbe JC (2012) Bridging animal and human models: Translating from (and to) animal genetics. Alcohol Research: Current Reviews **34**: 325–335.

Barkus E, Lewis S (2008) Schizotypy and psychosis-like experiences from recreational cannabis in a non-clinical sample. Psychological Medicine **38**: 1267–1276.

Barrett ML, Olenski AR, Jenna AB (2018) Opioid-prescribing practices of emergency physicians and risk of long-term use. New England Journal of Medicine **376**: 663–673.

Barry D, Petry NM (2009) Cognitive behavioral treatments for substance use disorders. In Miller PM (ed.) Evidence-Based Addiction Treatment. Burlington, MA: Academic Press.

Bart G (2012) Maintenance medication for opiate addiction: The foundation of recovery. Journal of Addictive Disorders **31**: 207–225.

Barta WD, Portnoy DB, Kliene SM, et al. (2008) A daily process investigation of alcohol-involved sexual risk behavior among economically disadvantaged problem drinkers living with HIV/AIDS. AIDS Behavior **12**: 729–740.

Baskin-Sommers D, Sommers I (2006) Methamphetamine use and violence among young adults. Journal of Criminal Justice **34**: 661–674.

Basu D, Ball SA, Feinn R, et al. (2004) Typologies of drug dependence: comparative validity of a multivariate and four univariate models. Drug and Alcohol Dependence **73**: 289–300.

Batalla A, Bhattacharyya S, Yucel M, et al. (2013) Structural and functional imaging studies in chronic cannabis users: A systematic review of adolescent and adult findings. PLoS ONE **8**: e55821.

Battistella G, Fornari E, Thomas A, et al. (2013) Weed or wheel! fMRI, behavioural, and toxicological investigations of how cannabis smoking affects skills necessary for driving. PLoS ONE **8**: e52545m.

Bauer LO (2001) CNS recovery from cocaine, cocaine and alcohol, or opioid dependence: A P300 study. Neurophysiology **112**: 1508–1515.

Bauer LO, Hesselbrock VM (2003) Brain maturation and sub-types of conduct disorder: Interactive effects on P300 amplitude and topography in male adolescents. Journal of the American Academy of Child and Adolescent Psychiatry **42**: 106–115.

Beaver KM, Wright JP, Delisi M, et al. (2008) Genetic influences on the stability of low self-control: Results from a longitudinal sample of twins. Journal of Criminal Justice **36**: 478–485.

Bechara A (2005) Decision making, impulse control and loss of willpower to resist drugs: a neurocognitive perspective. Nature Neuroscience **8**: 1458–1463.

Bechara A, Dolan S, Denburg N, et al. (2001) Decision-making deficits, linked to a dysfunctional ventromedial prefrontal cortex, revealed in alcohol and stimulant abusers. Neuropsychologia **39**: 376–389.

Bechara A, Van Der Linden M (2005) Decision-making and impulse control after frontal lobe injuries. Current Opinions in Neurology **18**: 734–739.

Bechtold J, Simpson T, White HR, et al. (2015) Chronic adolescent marijuana use as a risk factor for physical and mental health problems in young adult men. Psychology of Addictive Behaviors **29**: 552–562.

Beck M, Dietrich S, Matschinger H, et al. (2003) Alcoholism: Low standing with the public? Attitudes towards spending financial resources on medical care and research on alcoholism. Alcohol **38:** 602–605.

Begleiter H, Porjesz B, (1999) What is inherited in the predisposition toward alcoholism? A proposed model. Alcoholism: Clinical and Experimental Research **23:** 1125–1135.

Begleiter H, Porjesz B, Bihari B, et al. (1984) Event-related potentials in boys at risk for alcoholism. Science **225:** 1493–1496.

Begleiter H, Reich T, Hesselbrock V, et al. (1995) The collaborative study on the genetics of alcoholism. Alcohol Health and Research World **19:** 228–236.

Belin D, Belin-Rauscent A, Murray JE, et al. (2013) Addiction: Failure of control over maladaptive incentive habits. Current Opinions in Neurobiology **23:** 564–572.

Belin D, Belin-Rauscent A, Everitt BJ, et al. (2016) In search of predictive endophenotypes in addiction: Insights from preclinical research. Genes, Brain, and Behavior **15:** 74–88.

Belin D, Mar AC, Dalley JW, et al. (2008) High impulsivity predicts the switch to compulsive cocaine-seeking. Science **320:** 1352–1355.

Belujon P, Grace A (2015) Regulation of dopamine system responsivity and its adaptive and pathological response to stress. Proceedings in Biological Science **282:** 20142516.

Benegal V, Antony G, Venkatasubramanian G, et al. (2007) Gray matter volume abnormalities and externalizing symptoms in subjects at high risk for alcohol dependence. Addiction Biology **12:** 122–132.

Benet S (1975) Early diffusion and folk uses of hemp. In Rubin V (ed.) Cannabis and Culture. The Hague: Mouton.

Benowitz NL (2010) Nicotine addiction. New England Journal of Medicine **362:** 2295–2303.

Benowitz NL, Kuyt F, Jacob P (1984) Influence of nicotine on cardiovascular and hormonal effects of cigarette smoking. Clinical Pharmacology and Therapeutics **36:** 74–81.

Benowitz NL, Porchet H, Sheiner L, et al. (1988) Nicotine absorption and cardiovascular effects with smokeless tobacco use: Comparison with cigarettes and nicotine gum. Clinical Pharmacology and Therapeutics **44:** 23–28.

Berg CJ, Stratton E, Schauer G, et al. (2015) Perceived harm, addictiveness, and social acceptability of tobacco products and marijuana among young adults: Marijuana, hookah, and electronic cigarettes win. Substance Use and Misuse **50:** 79–89.

Berghaus G, Guo B (1995) Medicines and driver fitness – findings from a meta-analysis of experimental studies as basic information to patients, physicians and experts. In Kloeden C, McLean A (eds.) Alcohol, Drugs and Traffic Safety – T95: Proceedings of the 13th International Conference on Alcohol, Drugs and Traffic Safety: 1995. Adelaide, Australia: NHMRC Road Accident Research Unit, University of Adelaide.

Berke J, Hernton C (1974) The Cannabis Experience. Aylesbury, UK: Hazell Watson and Viney.

Berridge KC (2007) The debate over dopamine's role in reward: The case for incentive salience. Psychopharmacology **191**: 391–431.

Berridge KC (2017) Is addiction a brain disease? Neuroethics **10**: 24–28.

Berridge KC, Kringelbach ML (2013) Neuroscience of affect: Brain mechanisms of pleasure and displeasure. Current Opinions in Neurobiology **23**: 294–303.

Berridge KC, Robinson TE (2016) Liking, wanting, and the incentive-sensitization theory of addiction. American Psychologist **71**: 670–679.

Berridge KC, Robinson TE, Aldridge JW (2009) Dissecting components of reward: "Liking," "wanting," and learning. Current Opinions in Pharmacology **9**: 65–73.

Bertschy G (1995) Methadone maintenance treatment: An update. European Archives of Psychiatry Clinical Neuroscience **245**: 114–124.

Bieber CM, Fernandez K, Borsook D, et al. (2008) Retrospective accounts of initial subjective effects of opioids in patients treated for pain who do or do not develop opioid addiction: A pilot case-control study. Experimental and Clinical Psychopharmacology **16**: 429–434.

Biederman J, Monuteaux MC, Mick E, et al. (2005) Is cigarette smoking a gateway to alcohol and illicit drug use disorders? A study of youths with and without attention deficit hyperactivity disorder. Biological Psychiatry **59**: 258–264.

Bierut LJ (2009) Nicotine dependence and genetic variation in the nicotinic receptors. Drug and Alcohol Dependence **104**(Suppl. 1): S64–S69.

Bierut LJ (2011) Genetic vulnerability and susceptibility to substance dependence. Neuron **69**: 618–627.

Bierut LJ, Agrawal A, Bucholz KK, et al. (2010) A genome-wide study of alcohol dependence. PNAS **107**: 5082–5087.

Bierut LJ, Dinwiddie SH, Begleiter H, et al. (1998) Familial transmission of substance dependence: Alcohol, marijuana, cocaine, and habitual smoking. Archives of General Psychiatry **55**: 982–988.

Bierut LJ, Madden PAF, Breslau N, et al. (2007) Novel genes identified in a high-density genome wide association study for nicotine dependence. Human Molecular Genetics **16**: 24–35.

Birkley EL, Smith GT (2011) Recent advances in understanding the personality underpinnings of impulsive behavior and their role in risk for addictive behaviors. Current Drug Abuse Reviews **4**: 215–227.

Blanco C, Iza M, Fernandez-Roderigues JM, et al. (2015) Probability and predictors of treatment-seeking for substance use disorders in the US. Drug and Alcohol Dependence **149**: 136–144.

Blanco C, Ogburn E, do los Cobos JP, et al. (2008) DSM-IV criteria-based clinical subtypes of cannabis use disorders: Results from the National Epidemiological Survey on Alcohol and Related Conditions (NESARC). Drug and Alcohol Dependence **96**: 136–144.

Bleim B, Unterrainer HF, Papousek I, et al. (2013) Creativity in cannabis users and in drug addicts in maintenance treatment and in rehabilitation. Neuropsychiatry **27**: 2–10.

Block RI, Farinpour R, Braverman K (1992) Acute effects of marijuana on cognition: Relationships to chronic effects and smoking techniques. Pharmacology, Biochemistry, and Behavior **43**: 907–917.

Bloom J, Hinrichs AL, Wang JC, et al. (2011) The contribution of common CYP2A6 alleles to variation in nicotine metabolism among European-Americans. Pharmacogenetic Genomics **21**: 403–416.

Blum K, Febo M, Badgaiyan R, et al. (2017) Common neurogenetic diagnosis and meso-limbic manipulation of hypodopaminergic function in reward deficiency syndrome (RDS): Changing the recovery landscape. Current Neuropsychopharmacology **15**: 184–194.

Blum K, Febo M, McLaughlin T, et al. (2014) Hatching the behavioral addiction egg: Reward deficiency solution syndrome (RDSS) as a function of a dopaminergic neurogenetics and brain functional connectivity linking all addictions under a common rubric. Journal of Behavioral Addictions **3**: 149–156.

Blum K, Febo M, Smith DE, et al. (2015) Neurogenetic and epigenetic correlates of adolescent predisposition to and risk for addictive behaviors as a function of prefrontal cortex dysregulation. Journal of Child and Adolescent Psychopharmacology **25**: 286–292.

Blum K, Thanos P, Oscar-Berman M, et al. (2015) Dopamine in the brain: Hypothesizing surfeit or deficit links to reward and addiction. Journal of Reward Deficit Syndrome **1**: 95–104.

Blum K, Noble EP, Sheridan A, et al. (1990) Allelic association of human dopamine D2 receptor gene in alcoholism. Journal of the American Medical Association **263**: 2055–2060.

Blum K, Oscar-Berman M, Demetrovics Z, et al. (2014) Genetic addiction risk score (GARS): Molecular neurogenetic evidence for predisposition to reward deficiency syndrome (RDS). Molecular Neurobiology **50**: 765–796.

Blume S, Zilberman M (2004) Addiction in women. In Galanter M, Kleber H (eds.) Textbook of Substance Abuse Treatment. Arlington, VA: American Psychiatric Association.

Blume SB, Zilberman ML (2005) Addictive disorders in women. In Frances RJ, Miller SI, Mack AH (eds.) Clinical Textbook of Addictive Disorders. New York: Guilford Press.

Boardman JD, Finch BK, Ellison CG, et al. (2001) Neighborhood disadvantage, stress, and drug use among adults. Journal of Health and Social Behavior **42**: 151–165.

Bobova L, Finn PR, Rickert ME, et al. (2009) Disinhibitory psychopathology and delay discounting in alcohol dependence: Personality and cognitive correlates. Experimental and Clinical Psychopharmacology **17**: 51–61.

Bodnar RJ (2011) Endogenous opiates and behavior: 2010. Peptides **32**: 2522–2552.

Bogdanowicz KM, Stewart R, Broadbent M, et al. (2015) Double trouble: Psychiatric comorbidity and opioid addiction-all-cause and cause-specific mortality. Drug and Alcohol Dependence **148**: 85–92.

Bohadana A, Nilsson F, Rasmussen T, et al. (2003) Gender differences in quit rates following smoking cessation with combination nicotine therapy: Influence of baseline smoking behavior. Nicotine and Tobacco Research **5**: 111–116.

Bohn MJ, Krahn DD, Staehler BA (1995) Development and initial validation of a measure of drinking urges in abstinent alcoholics. Alcoholism: Clinical and Experimental Research **19**: 600–606.

Boileau I, Assad JM, Pihl RO, et al. (2003) Alcohol promotes dopamine release in the human nucleus accumbens. Synapse **49**: 226–231.

Boileau I, Dagher A, Leyton M, et al. (2007) Conditioned dopamine release in humans: A positron emission tomography [^{11}C]raclopride study with amphetamine. Journal of Neuroscience **27**: 3998–4003.

Bolla K, Eldreth D, London E, et al. (2003) Orbitofrontal cortex dysfunction in abstinent cocaine abusers performing a decision-making task. Neuroimage **19**: 1085–1094.

Bolla KI, Cadet JL, London ED (1998) The neuropsychiatry of chronic cocaine abuse. Journal of Neuropsychiatry and Clinical Neurosciences **10**: 280–289.

Bolla R, Eldreth D, Matochik J, et al. (2005) Neural substrates of faulty decision-making in abstinent marijuana users. Neuroimage **26**: 480–492.

Bolles RC (1972) Reinforcement, expectancy and learning. Psychological Review **79**: 394–409.

Bondallaz P, Favrat B, Haithem C, et al. (2016) Cannabis and its effects on driving skills. Forensic Science International **268**: 92–102.

Booth BM, Blow FC (1993) The kindling hypothesis: Further evidence from a US national study of alcoholic men. Alcohol and Alcoholism **28**: 593–596.

Booth M (1986) Opium: A History. New York: St. Martin's Press.

Borg L, Kreek MJ (2003) The pharmacology of opioids. In Graham AW, Schultz TK, Mayo-Smith MF, et al. (eds.) Principles of Addiction Medicine. 3rd ed. Chevy Chase, MD: American Society of Addiction Medicine.

Bornovalova MA, Lejuez CW, Daughters SB, et al. (2005) Impulsivity as a common process across borderline personality and substance abuse disorders. Clinical Psychology Review **25**: 790–812.

Bossong MG, Niesink RJ (2010) Adolescent brain maturation, the endogenous cannabinoid system and the neurobiology of cannabis-induced schizophrenia. Progress in Neurobiology **92**: 370–385.

Bostwick JM (2012) Blurred boundaries: The therapeutics and politics of medical marijuana. Mayo Clinic Proceedings **87**: 172–186.

Bot SM, Engels RC, Knibbe RA (2005) The effects of alcohol expectancies on drinking behaviour in peer groups: Observations in a naturalistic setting. Addiction **100**: 1270–1279.

Boudreau AC, Wolf ME (2005) Behavioral sensitization to cocaine is associated with increased AMPA receptor surface expression in the nucleus accumbens. Journal of Neuroscience **25**: 9144–9151.

Bowen S, Witkiewitz K, Clifasefi SL, et al. (2014) Relative efficacy of mindfulness-based relapse prevention, standard relapse prevention, and treatment as usual for substance use disorders: A randomized clinical trial. JAMA Psychiatry 71: 547–556.

Bower EA (2003) Use of amphetamines in the military environment. Lancet 362(Suppl.): 18–19.

Bowers BJ (2000) Applications of transgenic and knockout mice in alcohol research. Alcohol Research and Health 24: 175–184.

Boyd CJ, McCabe SE, Morales M (2005) College students' alcohol use: A critical review. In Fitzpatrick JJ, Stevenson JS, Sommers MS (eds.) Annual Review of Nursing Research. Vol. 23. New York: Springer.

Bozarth MA, Wise RA (1985) Toxicity associated with long-term intravenous heroin and cocaine self-administration. Journal of the American Medical Association 254: 81–83.

Brackins T, Brahm NC, Kissack JC (2011) Treatments for methamphetamine abuse: A literature review for the clinician. Journal of Pharmacology Practice 24: 541–550.

Bradberry CW (2002) Dose-dependent effect of ethanol on extracellular dopamine in mesolimbic striatum of awake rhesus monkeys: Comparison with cocaine across individuals. Psychopharmacology 165: 67–76.

Brady KT, Randall CL (1999) Gender differences in substance use disorders. Psychiatric Clinics of North America 22: 241–252.

Bramham CR, Messaoudi E (2005) BDNF function in adult synaptic plasticity: The synaptic consolidation hypothesis. Progress in Neurobiology 76: 99–125.

Bramness JG, Skurtveit S, Morland J (2002) Clinical impairment of benzodiazepines – relation between benzodiazepine concentrations and impairment in apprehended drivers. Drug and Alcohol Dependence 68: 131–141.

Brandon TH, Vidrine J, Litvin EB (2007) Relapse and relapse prevention. Annual Review of Clinical Psychology 3: 257–284.

Brandt J, Butters N, Rayan C, et al. (1983) Cognitive loss and recovery in long-term alcohol abusers. Archives of General Psychiatry 40: 435–442.

Brandt J, Leong C (2017) Benzodiazepines and Z-drugs: An updated review of major adverse outcomes reported on in epidemiologic research. Drugs Research and Development 17: 493–507.

Braude MC (1972) Toxicology of cannabinoids. In Paton WM, Crown J (eds.) Cannabis and Its Derivatives. Oxford: Oxford University Press.

Bray JH, Adams GJ, Getz JG, et al. (2003) Individuation, peers, and adolescent alcohol use: A latent growth analysis. Journal of Consulting and Clinical Psychology 71: 553–564.

Brecher EM (1972) Cigarettes – and the 1964 Report of the Surgeon General's Advisory Committee. In Consumers Union Report on Licit and Illicit Drugs. New York: Consumer Reports.

Brecht ML, Herbeck D (2014) Time to relapse following treatment for methamphetamine use: A long-term perspective on patterns and predictors. Drug and Alcohol Dependence 139: 18–25.

Breese CR, Marks MJ, Logel J, et al. (1997) Effect of smoking history on [^{3}H] nicotine binding in human postmortem brain. Journal of Pharmacology and Experimental Therapeutics 282: 7–13.

Breiter HC, Gollub RL, Weisskoff RM, et al. (1997) Acute effects of cocaine on human brain activity and emotion. Neuron **19**: 591–611.

Breland A, Spindle T, Weaver M, et al. (2014) Science and electronic cigarettes: current data, future needs. Journal of Addiction Medicine **8**: 223–233.

Brensilver M, Heinzerling KG, Swanson AN, et al. (2012) A retrospective analysis of two randomized trials of bupropion for methamphetamine dependence: Suggested guidelines for treatment discontinuation/augmentation. Drug and Alcohol Dependence **125**: 169–172.

Breslau N, Johnson EO (2000) Predicting smoking cessation and major depression in nicotine-dependent smokers. American Journal of Public Health **90**: 1122–1127.

Breslau N, Novak SP, Kessler RC (2004) Daily smoking and the subsequent onset of psychiatric disorders. Psychological Medicine **34**: 323–333.

Breslau N, Peterson EL (1996) Smoking cessation in young adults: Age at initiation of cigarette smoking and other suspected influences. American Journal of Public Health **86**: 214–220.

Briddell DW, Wilson G (1976) Effects of alcohol and expectancy set on male sexual arousal. Journal of Abnormal Psychology **87**: 418–430.

British Medical Association (1997) Therapeutic Uses of Cannabis. Amsterdam: Harwood Academic.

Brodie MS, Pesold C, Appel SB (1999) Ethanol directly excites dopaminergic ventral tegmental area reward neurons. Alcoholism: Clinical and Experimental Research **23**: 1848–1852.

Brody AL, Mandelkern MA, Olmstead RE, et al. (2007) Neural substrates of resisting craving during cigarette cue exposure. Biological Psychiatry **62**: 642–651.

Brorson HH, Arnevik E, Rand-Henderson K, et al. (2013) Drop-out from addiction treatment: A systematic review of risk factors. Clinical Psychology Review **33**: 1010–1024.

Brown JA, Hohman M (2006) The impact of methamphetamine on parenting. Journal of Social Work Practice in the Addictions **6**: 63–88.

Brown RA, Lejuez CW, Kahler CW, et al. (2005) Distress and early smoking lapse. Clinical Psychology Review **6**: 734–760.

Brown RT, Amler RW, Freeman WS, et al. (2005) Treatment of attention-deficit disorder: Overview of the evidence. Pediatrics **115**: 749–757.

Brown SA, Christiansen BA, Goldman MS (1987) The Alcohol Expectancy Questionnaire: An instrument for the assessment of adolescent and adult alcohol expectancies. Journal of Studies on Alcohol **48**: 483–491.

Browne M, Todd DG (2018) Then and now: Consumption and dependence in e-cigarette users who formerly smoked cigarettes. Addictive Behavior **76**: 113–121.

Brunton L, Parker K, Blumenthal D, et al. (2008) Goodman and Gilman's Manual of Pharmacology and Therapeutics. New York: McGraw-Hill Medical.

Brust JC (2010) Ethanol and cognition: Indirect effects, neurotoxicity and neuroprotection – a review. International Journal of Environmental Research and Public Health **7**: 1540–1547.

Budney AJ, Hughes JR (2006) The cannabis withdrawal syndrome. Current Opinions in Psychiatry **19**: 233–238.

Budney AJ, Moore BA, Vandrey RG, et al. (2003) The time course and significance of cannabis withdrawal. Journal of Abnormal Psychology **112**: 393–402.

Budney AJ, Roffman R, Stephens RS, et al. (2007) Marijuana dependence and its treatment. Addiction Science and Clinical Practice **4**: 4–15.

Bulik CM, Prescott CA, Kendler KS (2001) Features of childhood sexual abuse and the development of psychiatric and substance abuse disorders. British Journal of Psychiatry **179**: 444–449.

Bullen C, Williman J, Howe C, et al. (2013) Study protocol for a randomized controlled trial of electronic cigarettes versus nicotine patch for smoking cessation. BMC Public Health **13**: 210.

Burgdorf JR, Kilmer B, Pacula RL (2011) Heterogeneity in the composition of marijuana seized in California. Drug and Alcohol Dependence **117**: 59–61.

Busch AB, Weiss RD, Najavits LM (2005) Co-occurring substance use disorders and other psychiatric disorders. In Frances RJ, Miller SI, Mack AH (eds.) Clinical Textbook of Addictive Disorders. 3rd ed. New York: Guilford Press.

Butchert R, Thomasius R, Wilke F (2004) A voxel-based PET investigation of the long term effects of "ecstasy" consumption on brain serotonin transporters. American Journal of Psychiatry **161**: 1181–1189.

Butler SF, Black RA, Cassidy TA, et al. (2011) Abuse risks and routes of administration of different prescription opioid compounds and formulations. Harm Reduction Journal **8**: 1–17.

Buysse DJ (2013) Insomnia. JAMA **309**: 706–716.

Cadet JL, Krasnova IN (2009) Molecular bases of methamphetamine-induced neurodegeneration. International Review of Neurobiology **88**: 101–119.

Cadoret RJ, O'Gorman T, Troughton E, et al. (1985) Alcoholism and antisocial personality: Interrelationships, genetic and environmental factors. Archives of General Psychiatry **42**: 161–167.

Cadoret RJ, Troughton C, O'Gorman TW (1987) Genetic and environmental factors in alcohol abuse and antisocial personality. Journal of Studies on Alcohol **48**: 1–8.

Cahill K, Stevens S, Perera R, et al. (2013) Pharmacological interventions for smoking cessation: An overview and network meta-analysis. Cochrane Database Systematic Reviews 5: CD009329.

Caille S, Alvarez-Jaimes L, Polis I, et al. (2007) Specific alternations of extracellular endocannabinoid levels in the nucleus acumbens by ethanol, heroin, and cocaine self-administration. Journal of Neuroscience **27**: 3695–3702.

Caine ED (2013) Forging an agenda for suicide prevention in the United States. American Journal of Public Health **105**: 822–829.

Calhoun VD, Pekar JJ, Pearlson GD (2004) Alcohol intoxication effects on simulated driving: Exploring alcohol dose-effects on brain activation using functional MSRI. Neuropsychopharmacology **29**: 2097–3017.

Campbell AD, McBride WJ (1995) Serotonin-3 receptor and ethanol-stimulated dopamine release in the nucleus accumbens. Pharmacology Biochemistry and Behavior **51**: 835–842.

Carballo JL, Fernandez-Hermida JR, Secades-Villa R, et al. (2007) Natural recovery from alcohol and drug problems: A methodological review of the literature from 1999 through 2005. In Klingemann H, Sobell LC (eds.) Promoting Self-Change from Addictive Behaviors: Practical Implications for Policy, Prevention, and Treatment. New York: Kluwer.

Carey CL, Woods SP, Rippeth JD, et al. (2006) Additive deleterious effects of methamphetamine dependence and immunosuppression on neuropsychological functioning in HIV infection. AIDS and Behavior **10**: 185–190.

Carinci AJ, Christo PJ (2009) Physician impairment: Is recovery feasible? Pain Physician **12**: 487–491.

Carlson NR (2014) Foundations of Behavioral Neuroscience. 9th ed. Upper Saddle River, NJ: Pearson Education.

Carlson RG (2006) Ethnography and applied substance misuse research: Anthropological and cross-cultural factors. In Miller WR, Carroll KM (eds.) Rethinking Substance Abuse: What the Science Shows and What We Should Do about It. New York: Guilford Press.

Carpenter KM, Hasin DS (2001) Reliability and discriminant validity of the type I/II and type A/B alcoholic subtype classifications in untreated problem drinkers: A test of the Apollonian–Dionysian hypothesis. Drug and Alcohol Dependence **63**: 51–67.

Carr D (2008) *The Night of the Gun: A Reporter Investigates the Darkest Story of His Life: His Own.* New York: Simon and Schuster.

Carrigan MH, Ham LS, Thomas SE, et al. (2008) Alcohol outcome expectancies and drinking to cope with social situations. Addictive Behavior **33**: 1162–1166.

Carroll KM, Ball SA (2005) Assessment of cocaine dependence. In Donovan DM, Marlatt GA (eds.) Assessment of Addictive Behaviors. 2nd ed. New York: Guilford Press.

Carroll KM, Rounsaville BJ (2006) Behavioral therapies: The glass would be half full if only we had a glass. In Miller WR, Carroll KM (eds.) Rethinking Substance Abuse. New York: Guilford Press.

Carroll KM, Rounsaville BJ, Bryant KJ (1993) Alcoholism in treatment-seeking cocaine abusers: Clinical and prognostic significance. Journal of Studies on Alcohol **54**: 199–208.

Carter BL, Bordnick P, Traylor A, et al, (2008) Location and longing: The nicotine craving experience in virtual reality. Drug and Alcohol Dependence **95**: 73–80.

Carter BL, Tiffany ST (1999) Meta-analysis of cue-reactivity in addiction research. Addiction **94**: 327–340.

Cartier J, Farabee D, Pendergast ML (2006) Methamphetamine use, self-reported violent crime, and recidivism among offenders in California who abuse substances. Journal of Interpersonal Violence **21**: 435–445.

CASA Columbia (2012) Addiction Medicine: Closing the gap between science and practice. National Center on Addiction and Substance Abuse at Columbia University. www.casacolumbia.org.

Casadio P, Fernandes C, Murray RM, et al. (2011) Cannabis use in young people: The risk for schizophrenia. Neuroscience and Biobehavioral Reviews 35: 1779–1787.

Cascini F, Aiello C, Di Tanna G (2012) Increasing delta-9-tetrahydrocannabinol content in herbal cannabis over time: Systematic review and meta-analysis. Current Drug Abuse Reviews 5: 32–40.

Cascio MG, Pertwee R (2013) The function of the endocannabinoid system. In Castle D, Murray RM, D'Souza DC (eds.) Marijuana and Madness. 2nd ed. Cambridge: Cambridge University Press.

Caspi A, Moffitt TE, Newman DL, et al. (1996) Behavioral observations at age 3 years predict adult psychiatric disorders: Longitudinal evidence from a birth cohort. Archives of General Psychiatry 53: 1033–1039.

Cecil CA, Walton E, Viding E (2016) Epigenetics of addiction: Current knowledge, challenges, and future directions. Journal of Studies on Alcohol and Drugs 77: 688–691.

Center for Behavioral Health Statistics and Quality (2015) Behavioral Health Trends in the United States: Results from the 2014 National Survey on Drug Use and Health. HHS Publication SMA 15-4927, NSDUH Series H-50. Rockville, MD: Substance Abuse and Mental Health Services Administration.

Center for Behavioral Health Statistics and Quality (2016) Key Substance Use and Mental Health Indicators in the United States: Results from the 2015 National Survey on Drug Use and Health. HHS Publication SMA 16-4984, NSDUH Series H-51. Rockville, MD: Substance Abuse and Mental Health Services Administration.

Centers for Disease Control and Prevention (2002) Annual smoking-attributable mortality, years of potential life lost, and economic costs – United States 1995–1999. Morbidity and Mortality Weekly Reports 51: 300–303.

Centers for Disease Control and Prevention (2009) Cigarette smoking among adults and trends in smoking cessation – United States 2008. Morbidity and Mortality Weekly Reports 58: 1227–1232.

Centers for Disease Control and Prevention (2009) State-specific smoking-attributable mortality and years of potential life lost – United States 2000–2004. Morbidity and Mortality Weekly Reports 58: 1–5.

Centers for Disease Control and Prevention (2010) National Vital Statistics Reports 58(19): 21–24. www.cdc.gov/nchs/products/nvsr.htm.

Centers for Disease Control and Prevention (2011) Vital Signs: Overdoses of prescription opioid pain relievers – United States 1999–2008. Morbidity and Mortality Weekly Reports 60: 1487–1492.

Centers for Disease Control and Prevention (2014) Cigarette smoking among adults – United States 2005–2013. Morbidity and Mortality Weekly Reports 63: 1108–1112.

Centers for Disease Control and Prevention (2015) Vital signs: Alcohol poisoning deaths – United States, 2010–2012.

Morbidity and Mortality Weekly Reports 63: 1238–1242.

Cepeda-Benito A, Reynoso JT, Erath S (2004) Meta-analysis of the efficacy of nicotine replacement therapy for smoking cessation: Differences between men and women. Journal of Consulting and Clinical Psychology 72: 712–722.

Cerda M, Santaella J, Marshall BD, et al. (2015) Nonmedical prescription opioid use in childhood and early adolescence predicts transitions to heroin use in young adulthood: A national study. Journal of Pediatrics 167: 605–612.

Chaffee BW, Gansky SA, Halpern-Feisher B, et al. (2015) Conditional risk assessment of adolescents' electronic cigarette perceptions. American Journal of Health 39: 421–432.

Chait LD, Zacny JP (1992) Reinforcing and subjective effects of oral delta 9-THC and smoked marijuana in humans. Psychopharmacology 107: 255–262.

Chambers CD, Garavan H, Bellgrove MA (2009) Insights into the neural basis of response inhibition from cognitive and clinical neuroscience. Neuroscience and Biobehavioral Reviews 33: 631–646.

Chambers A, Krystal JH, Self DA (2001) A neurobiological basis for substance abuse comorbidity in schizophrenia. Biological Psychiatry 50: 71–83.

Chambers RA, Taylor JR, Potenza MN (2003) Developmental neurocircuitry of motivation during adolescence: A critical period of addiction vulnerability. American Journal of Psychiatry 160: 1041–1052.

Chan PC, Sills RC, Braun AG, et al. (1996) Toxicity and carcinogenicity of delta-9-tetrahydrocannabinol in Fischer rats and B6C3F1 mice. Fundamentals of Applied Toxicology 30: 109–117.

Chandra S, Scharf D, Shiffman S (2011) Within-day temporal patterns of smoking, withdrawal symptoms, and craving. Drug and Alcohol Dependence 117: 118–125.

Changeux JP, Bertrand D, Corringer PJ, et al. (1998) Brain nicotinic receptors: Structure and regulation, role in learning and reinforcement. Brain Research Review 26: 198–216.

Charness ME, Riley EP, Sowell ER (2016) Drinking during pregnancy and the developing brain: Is any amount safe? Trends in Cognitive Science 20: 80–82.

Chassin L, Presson CC, Rose J, et al. (2007) What is addiction? Age-related differences in the meaning of addiction. Drug and Alcohol Dependence 87: 30–38.

Chauchard E, Levin KH, Copersino ML, et al. (2013) Motivations to quit cannabis use in adult non-treatment sample: are they related to relapse? Addictive Behaviors 38: 2422–2427.

Cheer JF, Wassum KM, Sombers LA, et al. (2007) Phasic dopamine release evoked by abused substances requires cannabinoid receptor activation. Journal of Neuroscience 27: 791–795.

Chen CK, Lin SK, Sham PC (2003) Pre-morbid characteristics and co-morbidity of methamphetamine users with and without psychosis. Psychological Medicine 33: 1407–1414.

Chen C-Y, Anthony JC (2003) Possible age-associated bias in reporting of clinical features of drug dependence: Epidemiological evidence on adolescent-onset marijuana use. Addiction 98: 71–82.

Chen C-Y, O'Brien MS, Anthony JC (2005) Who becomes cannabis dependent soon after onset of use? Epidemiological evidence from the United States: 2000–2001. Drug and Alcohol Dependence **79**: 11–25.

Chen K, Kandel D (2002) Relationship between extent of cocaine use and dependence among adolescents and adults in the United States. Drug and Alcohol Dependence **68**: 65–85.

Chen KW, Berger CC, Forde DP, et al. (2011) Benzodiazepine use and misuse among patients in a methadone program. BMC Psychiatry **11**: 90–95.

Chen L-S, Johnson EO, Breslau N, et al. (2011) Interplay of risk factors and parent monitoring in risk for nicotine dependence. Addiction **104**: 1731–1740.

Chen YH, Raymond HF, Grasso M, et al. (2012) Prevalence and predictors of conscious risk behavior among San Franciscan men who have sex with men. AIDS Behavior. Advance online publication.

Cherpital CJ (2000) A brief screening instrument for problem drinking in the emergency room: The RAPS4. Journal of Studies on Alcohol **61**: 447–449.

Cherpitel CJ (1995) Screening for alcohol problems in the emergency room: A rapid alcohol problems screen. Drug and Alcohol Dependence **40**: 133–137.

Chi FW, Kaskutas LA, Sterling S, et al. (2009) Twelve-step affiliation and 3-year substance use outcomes among adolescents: Social support services and religious service attendance as potential mediators. Addiction **104**: 927–939.

Childress AR (2006) What can human brain imaging tell us about vulnerability to addiction and to relapse? In Miller WR, Carroll KM (eds.) Rethinking Substance Abuse: What the Science Shows, and What We Should Do about It. New York: Guilford Press.

Childress AR, Ehrman RN, Wang Z, et al. (2008) Prelude to passion: Limbic activation by "unseen" drug and sexual cues. PLoS ONE **3**: e1506.

Childress AR, Franklin TR, Listerud J, et al. (2002) Neuroimaging of cocaine craving states: Cessation, stimulant administration, and drug cue paradigms. In David KL, Charney D, Coyle JT, et al. (eds.) Neuropsychopharmacology: The Fifth Generation of Progress. Philadelphia: Lippincot Williams and Wilkins.

Childress AR, McLellan T, O'Brien CP (1986) Abstinent opiate abusers exhibit conditioned craving, conditioned withdrawal, and reductions in both through extinction. British Journal of Addiction **81**: 655–660.

Childress AR, Mozley PD, McElgin W, et al. (1999) Limbic activation during cue-induced cocaine craving. American Journal of Psychiatry **156**: 11–18.

Chung T, Creswell K, Bachrach R, et al. (2018) Adolescent binge drinking: Developmental context and opportunities for prevention. Alcohol Research: Current Reviews **39**: 5–15.

Chung T, Martin CS (2005) What were they thinking? Adolescents' interpretations of DSM-IV alcohol symptom queries and implications for diagnostic validity. Drug and Alcohol Dependence **80**: 191–200.

Chung T, Martin CS, Cornelius JR, et al. (2008) Cannabis withdrawal predicts severity of cannabis involvement at 1-year follow-up among treated adolescents. Addiction 103: 787–799.

Cicero TJ, Surratt HL, Kurtz SP (2014) The changing face of heroin use in the United States: A retrospective analysis of the past 50 years. JAMA Psychiatry 71: 821–826.

Cicero TJ, Kurtz SP, Surratt HL, et al. (2011) Multiple determinants of specific modes of prescription diversion. Journal of Drug Issues 41: 283–304.

Cicero TJ, Surratt HL, Inciardi JA, et al. (2007) Relationship between therapeutic use and abuse of opioid analgesics in rural, suburban, and urban locations in the United States. Pharmacoepidemiology and Drug Safety 16: 827–840.

Clark DB, Cornelius JR, Kirisci L, et al. (2005) Childhood risk categories for adolescent substance involvement: A general liability typology. Drug and Alcohol Dependence 77: 13–21.

Clark PA, Capuzzi K, Fick C (2011) Medical marijuana: Medical necessity versus political agenda. Medical Science Monitor 17: RA249-261.

Clegg B (2010) Portrait of the Addict as a Young Man. New York: Little, Brown.

Cloninger CR (1987a) A systematic method for clinical description and classification of personality variants: A proposal. Archives of General Psychiatry 44: 573–588.

Cloninger CR (2004) Genetics of substance abuse. In Galanter M, Kleber HD (eds.) Textbook of Substance Abuse Treatment. Washington, DC: American Psychiatric.

Cloninger CR, Bohman M, Sigvardsson S (1981) Inheritance of alcohol abuse: Cross-fostering analysis of adopted men. Archives of General Psychiatry 38: 861–868.

Cloninger CR, Svrakic DM, Pryzbeck TR (1993) A psychobiological model of temperament and character. Archives of General Psychiatry 50: 975–990.

Coffey SF, Dansky BS, Carrigan MH, et al. (2000) Acute and protracted cocaine abstinence in an outpatient population: A prospective study of mood, sleep and withdrawal symptoms. Drug and Alcohol Dependence 59: 277–286.

Cohen P, Chen H, Crawford TN, et al. (2007) Personality disorders in early adolescence and development of later substance use disorders in the general population. Drug and Alcohol Dependence 88: S71–S84.

Cohen S (1985) The Substance Abuse Problems: Vol. 2. New Issues for the 1980s. New York: Haworth Press.

Coleman LG, He J, Lee J, et al. (2011) Adolescent binge drinking alters adult brain neurotransmitter gene expression, behavior, brain regional volumes, and neurochemistry in mice. Alcoholism: Clinical and Experimental Research 35: 671–688.

Collins FS, Lander ES, Rogers J, et al. (2004) Finishing the euchromatic sequence of the human genome. Nature 431: 931–945.

Collins M (1974) Carrying the Fire: An Astronaut's Journeys. New York: Ballantine Books.

Collins SE (2016) Associations between socioeconomic factors and alcohol outcomes. Alcohol Research: Current Reviews 38: 83–94.

Collins SE, Clifasefi SL, Logan DE, et al. (2012) Eating Disorders. In Marlatt GA, Larimer ME, Witkiewitz K (eds.) Harm Reduction: Pragmatic Strategies for Managing High-Risk Behaviors. 2nd ed. New York: Guilford Press.

Collins SE, Marlatt GA (2012) Seeing the writing on the wall: A lesson in harm reduction. In Marlatt GA, Larimer ME, Witkiewitz K (eds.) Harm Reduction: Pragmatic Strategies for Managing High-Risk Behaviors. 2nd ed. New York: Guilford Press.

Collins SL, Levin FR, Foltin RW, et al. (2006) Response to cocaine, alone and in combination with methylphenidate in cocaine abusers with ADHD. Drug and Alcohol Dependence 82: 158–167.

Colombo G, Agabio R, Fa M, et al. (1998) Reduction of voluntary ethanol intake in ethanol-preferring SP rats by the cannabinoid antagonist SR-141716. Alcohol and Alcoholism 33: 126–130.

Colrain IM, Sullivan EV, Ford JM, et al. (2011) Frontally mediated inhibitory processing and white matter microstructure: age and alcoholism effects. Psychopharmacology 213: 669–679.

Comer SM, Zacny JP (2005) Subjective effects of opioids. In Earleywine M (ed.) Mind-Altering Drugs: The Science of Subjective Experience. Oxford: Oxford University Press.

Comitas L (1976) Cannabis and work in Jamaica: A refutation of the amotivational syndrome. Annals of the New York Academy of Science 282: 24–32.

Compton WM, Conway KP, Stinson FS, et al. (2005) Prevalence, correlates, and comorbidity of DSM-IV antisocial personality syndromes and alcohol and specific drug use disorders in the United States: Results from the national epidemiological survey on alcohol and related conditions. Journal of Clinical Psychiatry 66: 677–685.

Compton WM, Dawson DA, Goldstein RB, et al. (2013) Crosswalk between DSM-IV dependence and DSM-5 substance use disorders for opioids, cannabis and alcohol. Drug and Alcohol Dependence 132: 387–390.

Compton WM, Thomas YF, Stinson FS, et al. (2007) Prevalence, correlates, disability, and comorbidity of DSM-IV drug abuse and dependence in the United States. Archives of General Psychiatry 64: 566–576.

Compton WM, Volkow ND (2006) Abuse of prescription drugs and the risk of addiction. Drug and Alcohol Dependence 83(Suppl. 1): S4–S7.

Conklin CA, Robin N, Perkins KA, et al. (2008) Proximal vs. distal cues to smoke: The effects on smokers' cue reactivity. Experimental and Clinical Psychopharmacology 16: 207–214.

Conley KM, Toledano AY, Apfelbaum JI, et al. (1997) The modulating effects of a cold water stimulus on opioid effects in volunteers. Psychopharmacology 131: 313–320.

Connery HS (2015) Medication-assisted treatment of opioid use disorder: Review of the evidence and future directions. Harvard Review of Psychiatry 23: 63–75.

Conway KP, Compton WM, Stinson FS, et al. (2006) Lifetime comorbidity of DSM-IV mood and anxiety disorders: Results from the national epidemiological survey on alcohol and related conditions. Journal of Clinical Psychiatry **67**: 247–257.

Conway KP, Kane RJ, Ball SA, et al. (2003) Personality, substance of choice, and polysubstance involvement among substance dependent patients. Drug and Alcohol Dependence **71**: 65–75.

Cook CE, Jeffcoat AR, Hill JM, et al. (1993) Pharmacokinetics of methamphetamine self-administered to human subjects by smoking S-(+)-methamphetamine hydrochloride. Drug Metabolism and Disposition **21**: 717–732.

Cooney NL, Kadden RM, Steinberg HR (2005) Assessment of alcohol problems. In Donovan DM, Marlatt GA (eds.) Assessment of Addictive Behaviors. 2nd ed. New York: Guilford Press.

Cooper BY, Vierck CJ Jr., Yeomans DC (1986) Selective reduction of second pain sensations by systemic morphine in humans. Pain **24**: 93–116.

Cooper ZD, Haney M (2009) Actions of delta-9-tetrahydrocannabinol in cannabis: relations to use, abuse, dependence. International Review of Psychiatry **21**: 104–112.

Copeland AL, Martin PD, Rash C, et al. (2006) Predictors of attrition from smoking cessation treatment among pre- and postmenopausal weight-concerned women. Eating Behaviors **7**: 243–251.

Copeland J, Pokorski I (2016) Progress toward pharmacotherapies for cannabis-use disorder: an evidence-based review. Substance Abuse and Rehabilitation **7**: 41–53.

Copeland J, Rooke S, Swift W (2013) Changes in cannabis use among young people: Impact on mental health.

Current Opinion in Psychiatry **26**: 325–329.

Copeland J, Swift W (2009) Cannabis use disorder: Epidemiology and management. International Review of Psychiatry **21**: 96–103.

Copeland NG, Jenkins NA, Gilbert DJ (1993) A genetic linkage map of the mouse: Current applications and future prospects. Science **262**: 57–66.

Copeland WE, Keeler G, Angold A, et al. (2007) Traumatic events and posttraumatic stress in childhood. Archives of General Psychiatry **64**: 577–584.

Copersino ML, Boyd SJ, Taskin DP, et al. (2006) Quitting among non-treatment-seeking marijuana users: Reasons and changes in other substance use. American Journal on Addictions **15**: 297–302.

Corbett AD, Hendeson G, McKnight AT, et al. (2006) 75 years of opioid research: The exciting but vain quest for the holy grail. British Journal of Pharmacology **147**: S153–S162.

Cornelius JR, Clark DB, Reynolds M (2007) Early age of first sexual intercourse and affiliation with deviant peers predict development of SUD: A prospective longitudinal study. Addictive Behaviors **32**: 850–854.

Correia CJ (2005) Behavioral theories of choice. In Earleywine M (ed.) Mind-Altering Drugs. New York: Oxford University Press.

Corrigal WA, Coen KM, Adamson KL (1994) Self-administered nicotine activates the mesolimbic dopamine system through the ventral tegmental area. Brain Research **653**: 278–284.

Corrigall WA, Franklin KB, Coen KM, et al. (1992) The mesolimbic dopaminergic system is implicated in the reinforcing effects of nicotine. Psychopharmacology **107**: 285–289.

Corsi KF, Booth RE (2008) HIV sex risk behaviors among heterosexual methamphetamine users: Literature review from 2000 to present. Current Drug Abuse Reviews **1**: 292–296.

Cosgrove K, Batis J, Bois F, et al. (2009) B$_2$-nicotinic acetylcholine receptor availability during acute and prolonged abstinence from tobacco. Archives of General Psychiatry **66**: 666–676.

Costa PT, McCrae RR (1992) Revised NEO Personality Inventory (NEO-PI-R) and NEO Five-Factor Inventory (NEO-FFI) Professional Manual. Odessa, FL: Psychological Assessment Resources.

Costello EJ (2007) Psychiatric predictors of adolescent and young adult drug use and abuse. Drug and Alcohol Dependence **88**(Suppl.): S1–S3.

Costello EJ, Mustillo S, Erkanli A, et al. (2003) Prevalence and development of psychiatric disorders in childhood and adolescence. Archives of General Psychiatry **60**: 837–844.

Cottler LB, Womack SB, Compton WM, et al. (2001) Ecstasy abuse and dependence among adolescents and young adults: Applicability and reliability of DSM-IV criteria. Psychopharmacology **16**: 599–606.

Courtney KE, Ray LA (2014) Methamphetamine: An update on epidemiology, pharmacology, clinical phenomenology, and treatment literature. Drug and Alcohol Dependence **115**: 11–21.

Courvoisier DS, Etter JF (2010) Comparing the predictive validity of five cigarette dependence questionnaires. Drug and Alcohol Dependence **107**: 128–133.

Cox LS, Tiffany ST, Christen AG (2001) Evaluation of the Brief Questionnaire of Smoking Urges (QSU-Brief) in laboratory and clinical settings. Nicotine and Tobacco Research **3**: 7–16.

Crabb DW, Edenberg HJ, Bosron WF, et al. (1989) Genotypes for aldehyde dehydrogenase deficiency and alcohol sensitivity: The inactive *ALDH2(2)* allele is dominant. Journal of Clinical Investigation **83**: 314–316.

Crabbe JC (2002) Alcohol and genetics: New models. American Journal of Medical Genetics (Neuropsychiatric Genetics) **114**: 969–974.

Crabbe JC, Kendler KS, Hitzemann RJ (2013) Modeling the diagnostic criteria for alcohol dependence with genetic animal models. Current Topics in Behavioral Neuroscience **13**: 187–221.

Crabbe JC, Phillips TJ, Harris RA, et al. (2006) Alcohol-related genes: Contributions from studies with genetically engineered mice. Addiction Biology **11**: 195–269.

Craig AD (2009) How do you feel – now? The anterior insula and human awareness. Nature Reviews: Neuroscience **10**: 59–70.

Crean RD, Crane NA, Mason BJ (2011) An evidence-based review of acute and long-term effects of cannabis use on executive cognitive functions. Journal of Addictive Medicine **5**: 1–8.

Crews FT, Buckley T, Dodd PR, et al. (2005) Alcoholic neurobiology: Changes in dependence and recovery. Alcoholism:

Clinical and Experimental Research 29: 1504–1513.

Crews FT, Mdzinarishvili A, Kim D, et al. (2006) Neurogenesis in adolescent brain is potently inhibited by ethanol. Neuroscience 137: 437–435.

Crisp A, Gelder M, Rix S, et al. (2000) Stigmatization of people with mental illnesses. British Journal of Psychiatry 177: 4–7.

Criswell HE, Breese GR (2005) The effect of ethanol on ion channels in the brain: A new look. In Preedy VR, Watson RR (eds.) Comprehensive Handbook of Alcohol Related Pathology. Vol. 2. London: Elsevier.

Cubela WJ, Landowski J (2007) Seizure following sudden zolpidem withdrawal. Progress in Neuropsychopharmacology: Biological Psychiatry 31: 539–540.

Cullen KA, Ambrose BK, Gentzke AS (2018) Notes from the field: Use of electronic cigarettes and any tobacco product among middle and high school students – United States, 2011–2018. Morbidity and Mortality Weekly Reports 67: 1276–1277.

Cunningham JA (2000) Remission from drug dependence: Is treatment a prerequisite? Drug and Alcohol Dependence 59: 211–213.

Cunningham JA (2009) Internet-based treatments. In Miller PM (ed.) Evidence-Based Addiction Treatment. Burlington, MA: Academic Press.

Curran HV, Brignell C, Fletcher S, et al. (2002) Cognitive and subjective and dose-response effects of acute oral delta-9-tetrahydrocannabinol (THC) in infrequent cannabis users. Psychopharmacology 164: 61–70.

Curran HV, Freeman TP, Mokrysz C, et al. (2016) Keep off the grass? Cannabis, cognition and addiction. Nature Reviews: Neuroscience 17: 293–306.

Curtis EK (2006) Meth mouth: A review of methamphetamine abuse and its oral manifestations. General Dentistry 54: 125–129.

Czoty PW, Morgan D, Shannon EE, et al. (2004) Characterization of dopamine D1 and D2 receptor function in socially housed cynomolgus monkeys self-administering cocaine. Psychopharmacology 174: 381–388.

Darvishi N, Farhadi M, Haghtalab T, et al. (2015) Alcohol-related risk of suicidal ideation, suicide attempt, and completed suicide: A meta-analysis. PLoS ONE 10: e0126870.

D'Amico EJ, Metrik J, McCarthy DM, et al. (2002) Progression into and out of binge drinking among high school students. Psychology of Addictive Behaviors 15: 341–349.

D'Onofrio G, Degutis LC (2002) Screening and brief intervention for alcohol problems in the emergency department: A systematic review. Academic Emergency Medicine 9: 627–638.

D'Souza DC, Perry E, MacDougall L, et al. (2004) The psychomimetic effects of delta-9-tetrahydrocannabinol in healthy individuals: Implications for psychosis. Neuropsychopharmacology 29: 1558–1572.

Daigre C, Rodriguez-Cintas L, Tarifa N, et al. (2015) History of sexual, emotional or physical abuse and psychiatric comorbidity in substance-dependent patients. Psychiatry Research 229: 743–749.

Dalley JW, Everitt BJ, Robbins TW (2011) Impulsivity, compulsivity, and top-down cognitive control. Neuron **69**: 680–691.

Dalley JW, Fryer TD, Brichard L, et al. (2007) Nucleus accumbens D2/D3 receptors predict trait impulsivity and cocaine reinforcement. Science **315**: 1267–1270.

Daly M (2013) Personality may explain the association between cannabis use and neuropsychological impairment. Proceedings of the National Academy of Sciences of the USA **110**: E979.

Danovitch I, Gorelick DA (2012) State of the art treatments for cannabis dependence. Psychiatric Clinics of North America **35**: 309–326.

Darke S, Zador D (1996) Fatal heroin "overdose": A review. Addiction **91**: 1765–1772.

Darkes J, Greenbaum PE, Goldman MS (2004) Alcohol expectancy mediation of biopsychosocial risk: Complex patterns of mediation. Experimental and Clinical Psychopharmacology **12**: 27–38.

Davidson C, Gow AJ, Lee TH (2001) Methamphetamine neurotoxicity: Necrotic and apoptotic mechanisms and relevance to human abuse and treatment. Brain Research Reviews **36**: 1–22.

Davidson D, Amit Z (1997) Naltrexone blocks acquisition of voluntary ethanol intake in rats. Alcoholism: Clinical and Experimental Research **21**: 677–683.

Davis AK, Rosenberg H (2013) Acceptance of non-abstinence goals by addiction professionals in the United States. Psychology of Addictive Behaviors **27**: 1102–1109.

Davis AK, Rosenberg H, Rosansky JA (2017) American counselors' acceptance of non-abstinence outcome goals for clients diagnosed with co-occurring substance use and other psychiatric disorders. Journal of Substance Abuse Treatment **82**: 29–33.

Davis JM, Kopin IJ, Lemberger L, et al. (1971) Effects of urinary pH on amphetamine metabolism. Annals of the New York Academy of Sciences **179**: 493–501.

Davis JP, Smith DC, Morphew JW, et al. (2016) Cannabis withdrawal, post-treatment abstinence, and days to first cannabis use among emerging adults in substance use treatment: A prospective study. Journal of Drug Issues **46**: 64–83.

Dawe S, Loxton NJ (2004) The role of impulsivity in the development of substance use and eating disorders. Neuroscience and Biobehavioral Reviews **28**: 343–351.

Dawson D, Grant B, Stinson F, et al. (2006) Recovery from DSM-IV alcohol dependence. Alcohol Research and Health **29**: 131–142.

Dawson DA (2000) Alcohol consumption, alcohol dependence, and all-cause mortality. Alcoholism: Clinical and Experimental Research **24**: 72–81.

Dawson DA (2003) Methodological issues in measuring alcohol use. Alcohol Research and Health **27**: 18–29.

Dawson DA, Grant BF, Ruan WJ (2005) The association between stress and drinking: Modifying effects of gender and vulnerability. Alcohol and Alcoholism **40**: 453–460.

Dawson DA, Grant BF, Stinson FS, et al. (2005) Recovery from DSM-IV alcohol dependence: United States, 2001–2002. Addiction **100**: 281–292.

Dawson DA, Grant BF, Stinson FS, et al. (2005) Recovery from DSM-IV alcohol dependence: United States, 2001–2002. Addiction **100**: 281–292.

Dawson DA, Grant BF, Stinson FS, et al. (2006) Recovery from DSM-IV alcohol dependence. Alcohol Research and Health **29**: 131–142.

De Bellis MD, Clark DB, Beers SR (2000) Hippocampal volume in adolescent-onset alcohol use disorders. American Journal of Psychiatry **157**: 737–744.

De Bellis MD, Narasimhan A, Thatcher DL, et al. (2005) Prefrontal cortex, thalamus, and cerebellar volumes in adolescent-onset alcohol use disorders and comorbid mental disorders. Alcoholism: Clinical and Experimental Research **29**: 1590–1600.

De la Monte SM, Longato L, Tong M, et al. (2009) The liver-brain axis of alcohol-mediated neurodegeneration: Role of toxic lipids. International Journal of Research in Public Health **7**: 2055–2075.

de Wit H (2005) Relationships between personality and acute subjective responses to stimulant drugs. In Earleywine M (ed.) Mind-Altering Drugs. New York: Oxford University Press.

de Wit H (2009) Impulsivity as a determinant and consequences of drug use: A review of underlying processes. Addiction Biology **14**: 22–31.

de Wit H, Griffiths RR (1991) Testing the abuse liability of anxiolytic and hypnotic drugs in humans. Drug and Alcohol Dependence **28**: 83–111.

de Wit H, Richards JB (2004) Dual determinants of drug use in humans: Reward and impulsivity. Nebraska Symposium on Motivation **50**: 19–55.

de Wit H, Uhlenhuth EH, Johanson CE (1986) Individual differences in the behavioral and subjective effects of amphetamine and diazepam. Drug and Alcohol Dependence **16**: 341–360.

Deas D, Thomas S (2002) Comorbid psychiatric factors contributing to adolescent alcohol and other drug use. Alcohol Research and Health **26**: 116–121.

Degenhardt L, Hall W (2012) Extent of illicit drug use and dependence, and their contribution to the global burden of disease. The Lancet **379**: 55–70.

Del Boca FK, Darkes J (2003) The validity of self-reports of alcohol consumption: State of the science and challenges for research. Addiction **98**(Suppl 2): 1–12.

Denis P, Bocca ML (2003) Effects of zolpidem 10 mg, zopiclone 7.5 mg and flunitrazepam 1 mg on nighttime motor activity. European Neuropsychopharmacology **13**: 111–115.

Denisco RA, Chandler RK, Compton WM (2008) Addressing the intersecting problems of opioid misuse and chronic pain treatment. Experimental and Clinical Psychopharmacology **16**: 417–428.

Denning P, Little J, Glickman A (2004) Over the Influence: The Harm Reduction Guide for Managing Drugs and Alcohol. New York: Guilford Press.

Denning P, Little J (2017) Over the Influence: The Harm Reduction Guide to Controlling Your Drug and Alcohol Use. 2nd ed. New York: Guilford Press.

Desai HD, Seabolt J, Jann MW (2001) Smoking in patients receiving psychotropic medications: A pharmacokinetic perspective. CNS Drugs **15**: 469–494.

Devane WA, Dysarz FA, Johnson MR, et al. (1988) Determination and characterization of a cannabinoid receptor in rat brain. Molecular Pharmacology **34**: 605–613.

Devane WA, Hanus L, Breuer A, et al. (1992) Isolation and structure of a brain constituent that binds to the cannabinoid receptor. Science **258**: 1946–1949.

Devinsky O, Cilio MR, Cross H, et al. (2014) Cannabidiol: Pharmacology and potential therapeutic role in epilepsy and other neuropsychiatric disorders. Epilepsia **55**: 791–802.

Di Chiara G (1999). Drug addiction as dopamine-dependent associative learning disorder. European Journal of Pharmacology **375**: 13–30.

Di Forti M, Henquet C, Verdoux H, et al. (2012) Which cannabis users develop psychosis? In Castle D, Murray RM, D'Souza DC (eds.) Marijuana and Madness. 2nd ed. Cambridge: Cambridge University Press.

Di Iorio CR, Watkins TJ, Dietrich MS, et al. (2012) Evidence for chronically altered serotonin function in the cerebral cortex of female 3,4-methylenedioxymethamphetamine polydrug users. Archives of General Psychiatry **69**: 399–409.

Diamond I, Gordon A (1997) Cellular and molecular neuroscience of alcoholism. Physiology Review **77**: 1–20.

Diana M, Brodie M, Muntoni A, et al. (2003) Enduring effects of chronic ethanol in the CNS: Basis for alcoholism. Alcoholism: Clinical and Experimental Research **27**: 354–361.

Dick DM (2016) The genetics of addiction: Where do we go from here? Journal of Studies on Alcohol and Drugs **77**: 673–675.

Dick DM, Agrawal A (2008) The genetics of alcohol and other drug dependence. Alcohol Research and Health **31**: 111–118.

Dick DM, Agrawal A, Wang JC, et al. (2007) Alcohol dependence with comorbid drug dependence: Genetic and phenotypic associations suggest a more severe form of the disorder with stronger genetic contribution to risk. Addiction **102**: 1131–1139.

Dick DM, Bierut LJ (2006) The genetics of alcohol dependence. Current Psychiatry Reports **8**: 151–157.

Dick DM, Foroud T (2002) Genetic strategies to detect genes involved in alcoholism and alcohol-related traits. Alcohol Research and Health **26**: 172–180.

Dick DM, Foroud T (2003) Candidate genes for alcohol dependence: A review of genetic evidence from human studies. Alcoholism: Clinical and Experimental Research **27**: 868–879.

Dick DM, Jones K, Saccone N, et al. (2006a) Endophenotypes successfully lead to gene identification: Results from the collaborative study on the genetics of alcoholism. Behavior Genetics **36**: 112–126.

Dick DM, Kendler KS (2012) The impact of gene–environmental interaction on alcohol use disorders. Alcohol Research: Current Reviews **34**: 318–324.

Dick DM, Rose RJ, Kaprio J (2006b) The next challenges for psychiatric genetics: Characterizing the risk associated with identified genes. Annals of Clinical Psychiatry **18**: 223–231.

Dick DM, Smith G, Olausson P, et al. (2010) Understanding the construct of impulsivity and its relationship to alcohol use disorders. Addiction Biology 15: 217–226.

Dick DM, Viken R, Purcell S, et al. (2007) Parental monitoring moderates the importance of genetic and environmental influences on adolescent smoking. Journal of Abnormal Psychology 116: 213–218.

DiClemente CC (2003) Addiction and Change: How Addictions Develop and Addicted People Recover. New York: Guilford Press.

Dierker LC, Avenovoli S, Merikangas KR, et al. (2001) Association between psychiatric disorders and the progression of tobacco use behaviors. Journal of the American Academy of Child and Adolescent Psychiatry 40: 1159–1167.

Dierker LC, Braymiller J, Rose J, et al. (2018) Nicotine dependence predicts cannabis use disorder symptoms among adolescents and young adults. Drug and Alcohol Dependence 187: 212–220.

DiFranza JR (2010) A new approach to the diagnosis of tobacco addiction. Addiction 105: 381–382.

Dimeff LA, Linehan MM (2008) Dialectical behavior therapy for substance abusers. Addiction Science and Clinical Practice 4: 39–47.

Dixon M, Kochlar N, Prasad K, et al. (2003) The influence of changing nicotine to tar ratios on human puffing behavior and perceived sensory response. Psychopharmacology 170: 434–442.

Dlugos AM, Hamidovic A, Palmer AA, et al. (2009) Further evidence of association between amphetamine response and SLC6A2 gene variants. Psychopharmacology 206: 501–511.

Doble A (1999) New insights into the mechanism of action of hypnotics. Journal of Psychopharmacology 13(Suppl. 1): S11-S20.

Dodgen CE (2005) Nicotine Dependence. Washington, DC: American Psychological Association.

Dole VP, Nyswander MA (1965) Medical treatment for diacetylmorphine (heroin) addiction. Journal of the American Medical Association 193: 645–656.

Doll R, Peto R, Boreham J, et al. (2004) Mortality in relation to smoking: 50 years' observations on male British doctors. BMJ 328: 1519.

Domier CP, Simon SL, Rawson RA, et al. (2000) A comparison of injecting and non-injecting methamphetamine users. Journal of Psychoactive drugs 32: 229–232.

Donaher PA, Welsh C (2006) Managing opioid addiction with buprenorphine. American Family Physician 73: 1573–1578.

Donaldson EA, Hoffman AC, Zandberg I, et al. (2017) Media exposure and tobacco product addiction beliefs: Findings from the 2015 Health Information National Trends Survey (HINTS-FDA 2015). Addictive Behavior 72: 106–113.

Donny EC, Dierker LC (2007) The absence of DSM-IV nicotine dependence in moderate-to-heavy daily smokers. Drug and Alcohol Dependence 89: 93–96.

Donovan DM (2005) Assessment of addictive behaviors for relapse prevention. In Donovan DM, Marlatt GA (eds.) Assessment of Addictive Behaviors. 2nd ed. New York: Guilford Press.

Donovan DW, Bigelow GE, Brigham GS, et al. (2012) Primary outcome indices in illicit drug dependence treatment research: Systematic approach to selection and measurement of drug use end-points in clinical trials. Addiction 107: 694–708.

Doty P, de Wit H (1995) Effect of setting on the reinforcing and subjective effects of ethanol in social drinkers. Psychopharmacology 118: 19–27.

Dougherty DM, Marsh-Richard DM, Hatzis ES, et al. (2008) A test of alcohol dose effects on multiple behavioral measures of impulsivity. Drug and Alcohol Dependence 96: 111–120.

Dougherty DM, Mullen J, Hill-Kapturczak N, et al. (2015) Effects of tryptophan depletion and a simulated alcohol binge on impulsivity. Experimental and Clinical Psychopharmacology 23: 109–121.

Dow-Edwards D (2011) Translational issues for prenatal cocaine studies and the role of environment. Neurotoxicology and Teratology 33: 9–16.

Doweiko H (2006) Concepts of Chemical Dependency. 6th ed. Belmont, CA: Thompson Brooks/Cole.

Dowell D, Haegerich TM, Chou R (2016) CDC guideline for prescribing opioids for chronic pain – United States 2016. Morbidity and Mortality Weekly Reports 65: 2016.

Driessen M, Schulte S, Luedecke C, et al. (2008) Trauma and PTSD in patients with alcohol, drug, or dual dependence: A multi-center study. Alcoholism: Clinical and Experimental Research 32: 481–488.

Drummond DC (2001) Theories of drug craving, ancient and modern. Addiction 96: 33–46.

Dube SR, Anda RF, Felitti VJ, et al. (2002) Adverse childhood experiences and personal alcohol abuse as an adult. Addictive Behaviors 27: 713–725.

Duke AA, Begue L, Bell R, et al. (2013) Revisiting the serotonin–agression relation in humans: A meta-analysis. Psychological Bulletin 139: 1148–1172.

Dumont E, Mark G, Mader S, et al. (2005) Self-administration enhances excitatory synaptic transmission in the bed nucleus of the stria terminalis. Nature Neuroscience 8: 413–414.

Duncan PM, Alici T, Woodward JD (2000) Conditioned compensatory response to ethanol as indicated by locomotor activity in rats. Behavioural Pharmacology 11: 395–402.

Dunn M, Tarter R, Mezzich A, et al. (2002) Origins and consequences of child neglect in substance abuse families. Clinical Psychology Review 22: 1063–1090.

DuPont RL, McLellan AT, Carr G, et al. (2009) How are addicted physicians treated? A national survey of physician health programs. Journal of Substance Abuse Treatment 37: 1–7.

Durcan MJ, Deener G, White J, et al. (2002) The effect of buproprion sustained-release on cigarette craving after smoking cessation. Clinical Therapeutics 24: 540–551.

Dworkin S, Goeders NE, Grabowski J, et al. (1986) The effects of 12-hour limited access to cocaine: Reduction in drug intake and mortality. In Harris LS (ed.) Problems of Drug Dependence. DHHS Publication ADM 85-1414. Washington, DC: US Government Printing Office.

Earleywine M (2002) Understanding Marijuana. Oxford: Oxford University Press.

Edenberg HJ (2007) The genetics of alcohol metabolism: Role of alcohol dehydrogenase and aldehyde dehydrogenase variants. Alcohol Research and Health 30: 5–13.

Edenberg HJ, Dick DM, Xialong X, et al. (2004) Variations in GABRA2, encoding the alpha2 subunit of the GABA$_A$ receptor, are associated with alcohol dependence and with brain oscillations. American Journal of Human Genetics 74: 705–714.

Edenberg HJ, Xuei S, Chen H-J, et al. (2006) Association of alcohol dehydrogenase genes with alcohol dependence: A comprehensive analysis. Human Molecular Genetics 15: 1539–1549.

Edlund MJ, Forman-Hoffman VL, Winder CR, et al. (2015) Opioid abuse and depression in adolescents: Results from the National Survey on Drug Use and Health. Drug and Alcohol Dependence 152: 131–138.

Edlund MJ, Martin BC, Russo JE, et al. (2014) The role of opioid prescription in incident opioid abuse and dependence among individuals with chronic non-cancer pain: The role of opioid prescription. Clinical Journal of Pain 30: 557–564.

Edwards G (1990) Withdrawal symptoms and alcohol dependence: Fruitful mysteries. British Journal of Addictions 85: 447–461.

Ehrlich ME, Sommer J, Canas E, et al. (2002) Preadolescent mice show enhanced Delta FosB upregulation in response to cocaine and amphetamine. Journal of Neuroscience 22: 9155–9159.

Ehrman RN, Robbins SJ, Childress AR, et al. (1992) Conditioned responses to cocaine-related stimuli in cocaine abuse patients. Psychopharmacology 107: 523–529.

Eisenberg DT, Mackillop J, Modi M, et al. (2007) Examining impulsivity as an endophenotypes using a behavioral approach: A DRD2 Taql A and DRD4 48-bp VNTR association study. Behavioral and Brain Functions 3: 2–10.

Elander J, Lusher J, Bevan D, et al. (2004) Understanding the causes of problematic pain management in sickle-cell disease: Evidence that pseudoaddiction plays a more important role than genuine analgesic dependence. Journal of Pain and Symptom Management 27: 156–169.

Elkins IJ, King SM, McGue M, et al. (2006) Personality traits and the development of nicotine, alcohol, and illicit drug disorders: Prospective links from adolescence to young adulthood. Journal of Abnormal Psychology 115: 29–39.

Elkins IJ, McGue M, Malone S, et al. (2004) The effect of parental alcohol and drug disorders on adolescent personality. American Journal of Psychiatry 161: 670–676.

ElSohly MA, Ross SA, Mehmedic Z, et al. (2000) Potency trends of delta-9 THC and other cannabinoids in confiscated marijuana from 1980–1997. Journal of Forensic Sciences 45: 24–30.

Elster J (1999) Introduction. In Elster J (ed.) Addiction: Entries and Exits. New York: Russell Sage Foundation.

Emanuele MA, Wezman F, Emanuele NV (2002) Alcohol's effects on female reproductive function. Alcohol Research and Health 26: 274–281.

Emmett-Oglesby MW, Mathis DA, Moon RTY, et al. (1990) Animal models of drug withdrawal symptoms. Psychopharmacology **101**: 292–309.

Emrick CD, Tonigan JS, Montgomery H, et al. (1993) Alcoholics Anonymous: What is currently known? In McCrady BS, Miller WR (eds.) Research on Alcoholics Anonymous: Opportunities and Alternatives. New Brunswick, NJ: Rutgers Center on Alcohol Studies.

Engin E, Liu J, Rudolph U (2012) Alpha-2-containing GABA-A receptors: A target for the development of novel treatment strategies for CNS disorders. Pharmacological Therapeutics **136**: 142–152.

Epstein DH, Preston KL (2003) The reinstatement model and relapse prevention: A clinical perspective. Psychopharmacology **168**: 31–41.

Epstein DH, Preston KL, Stewart J, et al. (2006) Toward a model of drug relapse: An assessment of the validity of the reinstatement procedure. Psychopharmacology **189**: 1–16.

Epstein EE (2001) Classification of alcohol-related problems and dependence. In Heather N, Peters TJ, Stockwell T (eds.) International Handbook of Alcohol Dependence and Problems. Chichester, UK: John Wiley.

Epstein EE, Labouvie E, McCrady BS, et al. (2002) A multi-site study of alcohol subtypes: Classification and overlap of unidimensional and multi-dimensional typologies. Addiction **97**: 1041–1053.

Erickson CK (2007) The Science of Addiction: From Neurobiology to Treatment. New York: WW Norton.

Erickson K, Drevets W, Schulkin J (2003) Glucocorticoid regulation of diverse cognitive functions in normal and pathological states. Neuroscience and Biobehavioral Reviews **27**: 233–246.

Erickson PG, Adalf EM, Smart RG, et al. (1994) The Steel Drug: Cocaine and Crack in Perspective. New York: Lexington Books.

Erol A, Karpyak V (2015) Sex and gender-related differences in alcohol use and its consequences: Contemporary knowledge and future research considerations. Drug and Alcohol Dependence **156**: 1–13.

Errico AL, King AC, Lovallo WR, et al. (2002) Cortisol dysregulation and cognitive impairment in abstinent male alcoholics. Alcoholism: Clinical and Experimental Research **26**: 1198–1204.

Etter JF (2005) A self-administered questionnaire to measure cigarette withdrawal symptoms: The cigarette withdrawal scale. Nicotine and Tobacco Research **7**: 47–57.

Etter JF. Eissenberg T (2015) Dependence levels in users of electronic cigarettes, nicotine gums and tobacco cigarettes. Drug and Alcohol Dependence **147**: 68–75.

Evans AH, Pavese N, Lawrence AD, et al. (2006) Compulsive drug use linked to sensitized ventral striatal dopamine transmission. Annals of Neurology **59**: 852–858.

Evans SM, Griffiths RR, de Wit H (1996) Preference for diazepam, but not buspirone, in moderate drinkers. Psychopharmacology **123**: 154–163.

Evans SM, Levin FR (2011) Response to alcohol in women: Role of the menstrual cycle and a family history of alcoholism. Drug and Alcohol Dependence **114**: 18–30.

Evans SM, Foltin RW, Hicks MJ, et al. (2016) Efficacy of an adenovirus-based anti-cocaine vaccine to reduce cocaine self-administration and reacquisition using a choice procedure in rhesus macaques. Pharmacology, Biochemistry, and Behavior **150–151**: 76–86.

Evenden JL (1999) Varieties of impulsivity. Psychopharmacology **146**: 348–361.

Evenden JL, Ryan CN (1999) The pharmacology of impulsive behavior in rats VI: The effects of ethanol and selective serotonergic drugs on response choice with varying delays of reinforcement. Psychopharmacology **146**: 413–421.

Every-Palmer S (2011) Synthetic cannabinoid JWH-018 and psychosis: An explorative study. Drug and Alcohol Dependence **117**: 152–157.

Ewing JA (1983) Alcoholism- another biopsychosocial disease. Psychosomatics **21**: 371–372.

Eysenck HJ (1993) The nature of impulsivity. In McCown WG, Johnson JL, Shure MB (eds.) The Impulsive Client: Theory, Research and Treatment. Washington, DC: American Psychological Association.

Fadda F, Rossetti ZL (1998) Chronic ethanol consumption: From neuroadaptation to neurodegeneration. Progress in Neurobiology **56**: 385–431.

Faden VB, Goldman MS (2004) The scope of the problem. Alcohol Research and Health **28**: 111–120.

Fagerstrom KO, Furberg H (2008) A comparison of the Fagerstrom test for nicotine dependence and smoking prevalence across countries. Addiction **103**: 841–845.

Falco M (2005) US federal drug policy. In Lowinson JH, Ruiz P, Millman RB, et al. (eds.) Substance Abuse: A Comprehensive Textbook. 4th ed. New York: Lippincott Williams and Wilkins.

Falk DE, Yi H, Hiller-Sturmhofel S (2006) An epidemiological analysis of co-occurring alcohol and tobacco use and disorders. Alcohol Research and Health **29**: 162–171.

Falk DE, Yi H, Hiller-Sturmhofel S (2008) An epidemiological analysis of co-occurring alcohol and drug use and disorders. Alcohol Research and Health **31**: 100–110.

Fals-Stewart W (2005) Substance use disorders. In Maddux JE, Winstead, BA (eds.) Psychopathology: Foundations for a Contemporary Understanding. Mahwah, NJ: Lawrence Erlbaum.

Farabee D, Hawken A (2009) Methamphetamine and crime. In Roll JM, Rawson RA, Ling W, Shoptaw S (eds.) Methamphetamine Addiction: From Basic Science to Treatment. New York: Guilford Press.

Fasano A, Barra A, Nicosia P, et al. (2008) Cocaine addiction: From habits to stereotypical-repetitive behaviors and punding. Drug and Alcohol Dependence **96**: 178–182.

Fatseas M, Lavie E, Denis C, et al. (2009) Self-perceived motivation for benzodiazepine use and behavior related to benzodiazepine use among opiate-dependent patients. Journal of Substance Abuse Treatment **37**: 407–411.

Federenko IS, Nagamine M, Hellhammer DH, et al. (2004) The heritability of hypothalamus pituitary adrenal axis responses to psychosocial stress is context dependent. Journal of Clinical Endocrinological Metabolism **89**: 6244–6250.

Feldstein SW, Miller WR (2007) Does subtle screening for substance abuse work? A review of the Substance Abuse Subtle Screening Inventory (SASSI). Addiction **102**: 41–50.

Fenton T, Wiers RW (2017) Free will, black swans and addiction. Neuroethics **10**: 44–52.

Fergusson DM, Horwood J, Ridder EM (2007) Conduct and attentional problems in childhood and adolescence and later substance use, abuse and dependence: Results of a 25-year longitudinal study. Drug and Alcohol Dependence **88**(Suppl.): S14–S26.

Fergusson DM, Horwood LJ, Northstone K (2002) Maternal use of cannabis and pregnancy outcome. BJOG: An International Journal of Obstetrics and Gynecology **109**: 21–27.

Fergusson DM, Swain-Campbell N, Harwood L (2002) Deviant peer affiliations, crime and substance use: A fixed-effects regression analysis. Journal of Abnormal Child Psychology **30**: 419–430.

Fernandez H, Libby TA (2011) Heroin: Its History, Pharmacology and Treatment. 2nd ed. Center City, MN: Hazelden.

Ferren M (2010) Speed-Speed-Speedfreak. Port Townsend, WA: Feral House.

Fidler JA, Shahab L, West R (2010) Strength of urges to smoke as a measure of severity of cigarette dependence: Comparison with the Fagerstrom Test for Nicotine Dependence and its components. Addiction **106**: 631–638.

Field M, Christiansen P, Cole J, et al. (2007) Delay discounting and the alcohol Stroop in heavy drinking adolescents. Addiction **102**: 579–586.

Fields H, Hjelmstad G, Margolis E, et al. (2007) Ventral tegmental area neurons in learned appetitive behavior and positive reinforcement. Annual Review of Neuroscience **30**: 289–316.

Filbey FM (2019) The Neuroscience of Addiction. Cambridge: Cambridge University Press.

Fillmore KM (2003) Drug abuse as a problem of impaired control: Current approaches and findings. Behavioral and Cognitive Neuroscience Reviews **2**: 179–197.

Fillmore KM, Harta E, Johnstone BM, et al. (1991) A meta-analysis of life-course variation in drinking. Journal of Addiction **86**: 1221–1268.

Fillmore M, Rush C (2002) Impaired inhibitory control of behavior in chronic cocaine users. Drug and Alcohol Dependence **66**: 265–273.

Fink DS, Hu R, Cerda M, et al. (2015) Patterns of major depression and nonmedical use of prescription opioids in the United States. Drug and Alcohol Dependence **153**: 258–264.

Finn PR, Sharkansky EJ, Brandt KM, et al. (2000) The effects of familial risk, personality, and expectancies on alcohol use and abuse. Journal of Abnormal Psychology **109**: 122–133.

Finn PR, Zeitouni RG, Pihl RO (1990) Effects of alcohol on psychophysiological hyperreactivity to nonaversive and aversive stimuli in men at high risk for alcoholism. Journal of Abnormal Psychology **99**: 79–85.

Finney JW, Moos RH (1991) Long-term course of treated alcoholism I: Mortality, relapse and remission rates and comparisons with community controls. Journal of Studies on Alcohol **52**: 44–54.

Finney JW, Moos RH, Timko C (1999) The course of treated and untreated substance use disorders: Remission and resolution, relapse and mortality. In McCrady BS, Epstein EE (eds.) Addictions: A Comprehensive Guidebook. New York: Oxford University Press.

Finney JW, Wilbourne PL, Moos RH (2007) Psychosocial treatments for substance use disorders. In Nathan PE, Gorman JM (eds.) A Guide to Treatments That Work. New York: Oxford University Press.

Fishbain DA, Cole B, Lewis J, et al. (2008) What percentage of chronic nonmalignant pain patients exposed to chronic opioid analgesic therapy develop abuse/addiction and/or aberrant drug-related behaviors? A structured evidence-based review. Pain Medicine **9**: 444–459.

Fleckenstein AE, Volz TJ, Riddle EL, et al. (2007) New insights into the mechanism of action of amphetamines. Annual Review of Pharmacology and Toxicology **47**: 681–698.

Fletcher AM (2013) Inside Rehab: The Surprising Truth about Addiction Treatment – and How to Get Help That Works. New York: Viking Penguin.

Fletcher R, Mayle P (1990) Dangerous Candy. London: Sinclair-Stevenson.

Florez-Salamanca L, Secades-Villa R, Hasin DS, et al. (2013) Probability and predictors of transition from abuse to dependence on alcohol, cannabis, and cocaine: Results from the National Epidemiological Survey on Alcohol and Related Conditions. American Journal of Alcohol Abuse **39**: 168–179.

Food and Drug Administration (2018). Statement from FDA commissioner on new e-cigarette enforcement actions. www.fda/gov/.

Forchuk C, Norman R, Malla A, et al. (2002) Schizophrenia and the motivation for smoking. Perspectives in Psychiatric Care **38**: 41–49.

Foulds J, Stapleton JA, Bell N, et al. (1997) Mood and physiological effects of subcutaneous nicotine in smokers and never-smokers. Drug and Alcohol Dependence **44**: 105–115.

Fowler J, Volkow N, Kassed C, et al. (2007) Imaging the addicted human brain. Science and Practice Perspectives, pp. 4–16.

Fowler JS, Longan J, Wang G-J, et al. (2003) Monoamine oxidase and cigarette smoking. Neurotoxicology **24**: 75–82.

Fox HC, Hong KI, Siedlarz K, et al. (2008) Enhanced sensitivity to stress and drug/alcohol craving in abstinent cocaine-dependent individuals compared to social drinkers. Neuropsychopharmacology **33**: 796–805.

Frank DA, Augustyn M, Knight WG, et al. (2001) Growth, development and behavior in early childhood following prenatal cocaine exposure: A systematic review. JAMA **285**: 1613–1625.

Franken IH, Hendricks VM, van den Brink W (2002) Initial validation of two opiate craving questionnaires: The Obsessive Compulsive Drug Use Scale and the Desires for Drug Questionnaire. Addictive Behaviors **27**: 675–685.

Franklin TR, Wang Z, Wang J, et al. (2007) Limbic activation to cigarette smoking cues independent of nicotine withdrawal: A perfusion fMRI study. Neuropsychopharmacology 32: 2301–2309.

Freeman TP, Winstock AR (2015) Examining the profile of high-potency cannabis and its association with severity of cannabis dependence. Psychological Medicine 45: 3181–3189.

Freiberg MS, Kraemer KL (2010) Focus on the heart: Alcohol consumption, HIV infection, and cardiovascular disease. Alcohol Research and Health 33: 237–245.

Freund TF, Katona I, Piomelli D (2003) Role of endogenous cannabinoids in synaptic signaling. Physiological Reviews 83: 1017–1066.

Froelich JC (1997) Opioid peptides. Alcohol Health and Research World 21: 132–143.

Fromme K, D'Amico EJ (1999) Neurobiological bases of alcohol's psychological effects. In Leonard KE, Blane HT (eds.) Psychological Theories of Drinking and Alcoholism. 2nd ed. New York: Guilford Press.

Fu A, Heath AC, Bucholz KK, et al. (2002) Shared genetic risk of major depression, alcohol dependence, and marijuana dependence. Archives of General Psychiatry 59: 1125–1132.

Gage SH, Zammit S, Hickman M (2013) Stronger evidence is needed before accepting that cannabis plays an important role in the aetiology of schizophrenia in the population. F1000 Medicine Reports 5(2).

Galanter M, Dermatis H, Mansky P, et al. (2007) Substance-abusing physicians: Monitoring and twelve-step-based treatment. American Journal on Addictions 16: 117–123.

Gallagher KE, Parrott DJ (2011) Does distraction reduce the alcohol-aggression relation? A cognitive and behavioral test of the attention-allocation model. Journal of Consulting and Clinical Psychology 79: 319–329.

Galloway GP, Singleton EG, Buscemi R, et al. (2010) An examination of drug craving over time in abstinent methamphetamine users. American Journal on Addictions 19: 510–514.

Gaoni Y, Mechoulam R (1964) Isolation, structure, and partial synthesis of an active constituent of hashish. Journal of the American Chemical Society 86: 1646–1647.

Garavan H, Hester R (2007) The role of cognitive control in cocaine dependence. Neuropsychology Review 17: 337–345.

Garavan H, Lingford-Hughes A, Jones T, et al. (2007). Neuroimaging. In Nutt D, Robbins TW, Stimson GV, et al. (eds.) Drugs and the Future: Brain Science, Addiction and Society. London: Academic Press.

Gardner EL (1999) The neurobiology and genetics of addiction: Implications for the "reward deficiency syndrome" for therapeutic strategies in chemical dependency. In Elster J (ed.) Addiction: Entries and Exits. New York: Russell Sage Foundation.

Garland EL, Froeliger B, Zeidan F, et al. (2013) The downward spiral of chronic pain, prescription opioid misuse, and addiction: Cognitive, affective, and neuropsychopharmacologic pathways. Neuroscience and Biobehavioral Reviews 37: 2597–2607.

Gauvin DV, Baird TJ, Briscoe RJ (2000) Differential development of behavioral tolerance and the subsequent hedonic effects of alcohol in AA and NA rats. Psychopharmacology 15: 335–343.

Gavieraux-Ruff C, Kieffer BL (2002) Opioid receptor genes inactivated in mice: The highlights. Neuropeptides 36: 62–71.

Gawain FH, Kleber HD (1986) Abstinence symptomatology and psychiatric diagnosis in cocaine abusers: Clinical observations. Archives of General Psychiatry 43: 107–113.

Gelernter J, Panhuysen C, Wilcox M, et al. (2007) Genome-wide scan for opioid dependence and related traits. American Journal of Human Genetics 78: 759–769.

Gendel MH (2006) Substance misuse and substance-related disorders in forensic psychiatry. Psychiatric Clinics of North America 29: 649–673.

Gentry CL, Lukas RJ (2002) Regulation of nicotinic acetylcholine receptor numbers and function by chronic nicotine exposure. Current Drug Targets: CNS Neurological Disorders 1: 359–385.

George WH, Davis KC, Heiman JR, et al. (2011) Women's sexual arousal: Effects of high alcohol dosages and self-control instructions. Hormones and Behavior 59: 730–738.

George WH, Davis KC, Norris J, et al. (2009) Indirect effects of acute alcohol intoxication on sexual risk-taking. Archives of Sexual Behavior 38: 498–513.

George WH, Davis KC, Norris J, et al. (2006) Alcohol and erectile response: The effects of high dosage in the context of demands to maximize sexual arousal. Experimental and Clinical Psychopharmacology 14: 461–470.

George WH, Stoner SA, Norris J, et al. (2000) Alcohol expectancies and sexuality: A self-fulfilling prophecy analysis of dyadic perceptions and behavior. Journal of Studies on Alcohol 61: 168–176.

Gessa GL, Muntoni F, Collu M, et al. (1985) Low doses of ethanol activate dopaminergic neurons in the ventral tegmental area. Brain Research 348: 201–203.

Ghitza UE, Epstein DH, Preston KL (2008) Self-report of illicit benzodiazepine use on the addiction severity index predicts treatment outcome. Drug and Alcohol Dependence 97: 150–157.

Giancola P, Tarter R (1999) Executive cognitive functioning and risk for substance abuse. Psychological Science 10: 203–205.

Giancola PR, Josephs RA, Parrott DJ, et al. (2010) Alcohol myopia revisited: Clarifying aggression and other acts of disinhibition through a distorted lens. Perspectives on Psychological Science 5: 265–278.

Gifford-Smith M, Dodge KA, Dision TJ, et al. (2005) Peer influence in children and adolescents: Crossing the bridge from developmental to intervention science. Journal of Abnormal Child Psychology 33: 255–265.

Giroud C, de Cesare M, Berthet A, et al. (2015) E-cigarettes: A review of new trends in cannabis use. International Journal of Environmental Research and Public Health 12: 9988–10008.

Gitlow S (2007) Substance Use Disorders. 2nd ed. Philadelphia: Lippincott Williams and Wilkins.

Glasser AM, Katz L, Pearson JL, et al. (2017) Overview of electronic nicotine delivery systems: A systematic review. American Journal of Preventive Medicine **52**: e33.

Glatt SJ, Bolanos CA, Trksak GH, et al. (2000) Effects of prenatal cocaine exposure on dopamine system development: A meta-analysis. Neurotoxicology and Teratology **22**: 617–629.

Glidden-Tracey CE (2005) Counseling and Therapy with Clients Who Abuse Alcohol or Other Drugs: An Integrative Approach. Mahwah, NJ: Lawrence Erlbaum.

Glynn LH, Moyers TB (2009) Motivational interviewing for addictions. In Miller PM (ed.) Evidence-Based Addiction Treatment. Burlington, MA: Academic Press.

Gmel G, Rehm J (2003) Harmful alcohol use. Alcohol Research and Health **27**: 52–62.

Goedeker KC, Tiffany ST (2008) On the nature of nicotine addiction: A taxometric analysis. Journal of Abnormal Psychology **117**: 896–909.

Gold MS, Kobeissy FH, Wang KW, et al. (2009) Methamphetamine- and trauma-induced brain injuries: Comparative cellular and molecular neurobiological substrates. Biological Psychiatry **66**: 118–127.

Goldenson NI, Leventhal AM, Stone MD, et al. (2017) Associations of e-cigarette nicotine concentrations and subsequent cigarette smoking and vaping levels in adolescents. JAMA Pediatrics **171**: 1192–1199.

Goldman MS (2002) Expectancy and risk for alcoholism: The unfortunate exploitation of a fundamental characteristic of neurobehavioral adaptation. Alcoholism: Clinical and Experimental Research **26**: 737–746.

Goldstein DB (1983) Pharmacology of Alcohol. New York: Oxford University Press.

Goldstein R, Volkow N (2002) Drug addiction and its underlying neurobiologcal basis: Neuroimaging evidence for involvement of the frontal cortex. American Journal of Psychiatry **159**: 1642–1652.

Goldstein RZ, Craig AD, Bechara A, et al. (2009) The neurocircuitry of impaired insight in drug addiction. Trends in Cognitive Science **13**: 372–380.

Gonzalez R, Castro F, Barrington EH, et al. (2000) Cocaine and methamphetamine: differential addiction rates. Psychology of Addictive Behavior **14**: 390–396.

Gonzalez S, Cebeira M, Fernandez-Ruiz J (2005) Cannabinoid tolerance and dependence: A review of studies in laboratory animals. Pharmacology, Biochemistry, and Behavior **81**: 300–318.

Goodlett CR, Horn KH, Zhou FC (2005) Alcohol teratogenesis: Mechanisms of damage and strategies for intervention. Experimental Biology and Medicine (Maywood) **230**: 394–406.

Goodman A (1990) Addiction: Definition and implications. British Journal of Addiction **85**: 1403–1408.

Goodman LS, Brunton LL, Chabner B, et al. (2011) Goodman and Gilman's Pharmacological Basis of Therapeutics. New York: McGraw-Hill.

Goodwin DW (1995) Alcohol amnesia. Addiction **90**: 315–317.

Goodwin DW, Crane JB, Guze SB (1969) Alcoholic "blackouts": A review and clinical study of 100 alcoholics. American Journal of Psychiatry **126**: 191–198.

Goodwin DW, Schulsinger F, Hermansen L, et al. (1973) Alcohol problems in adoptees raised apart from alcoholic parents. Archives of General Psychiatry **28**: 238–243.

Goodwin DW, Schulsinger F, Knopf J, et al. (1977) Alcoholism and depression in adopted-out daughters of alcoholics. Archives of General Psychiatry **34**: 751–755.

Goodwin RD, Sheffer CE, Chartrand H, et al. (2014) Drug use, abuse, dependence and the persistence of nicotine dependence. Nicotine and Tobacco Research **16**: 1601–1612.

Gordon B (1979) I'm Dancing as Fast as I Can. New York: Beaufort Books.

Gorelick DA, Levin KH, Copersino ML, et al. (2012) Diagnostic criteria for cannabis withdrawal syndrome. Drug and Alcohol Dependence **123**: 141–147.

Gossop M, Stewart D, Marsden J (2007) Attendance at Narcotics Anonymous and Alcoholics Anonymous meetings, frequency of attendance and substance use outcomes after residential treatment for drug dependence: A 5-year follow-up study. Addiction **103**: 119–125.

Gourlay DL, Heit HA (2008) Pain and addiction: Managing risk through comprehensive care. Journal of Addictive Disorders **27**: 23–30.

Govid AP, Vezina P, Green WN (2009) Nicotine-induced upregulation of nicotinic receptors: Underlying mechanisms and relevance to nicotine addiction. Biochemical Pharmacology **78**: 756–765.

Grabenauer M, Krol WL, Wiley JL, et al. (2012) Analysis of synthetic cannabinoids using high-resolution mass spectrometry and mass defect filtering: Implications for non-targeted screening of designer drugs. Analytical Chemistry **84**: 5574–5581.

Graham K, West P (2001) Alcohol and crime: Exploring the link. In Heather N, Peters TJ, Stockwell T (eds.) International Handbook of Alcohol Dependence and Problems. Chichester, UK: John Wiley.

Graham NJ (2000) Selected lines and inbred strains: Tools in the hunt for the genes involved in alcoholism. Alcohol Research and Health **24**: 159–163.

Grant BF, Chou SP, Goldstein RB, et al. (2008) Prevalence, correlates, disability, and comorbidity of DSM-IV borderline personality disorder: Results from the Wave 2 National Epidemiological Survey on Alcohol and Related Conditions. Journal of Clinical Psychiatry **69**: 533–545.

Grant BF, Dawson DA (1997) Age at onset of alcohol use and its association with DSM-IV alcohol abuse and dependence: Results from the National Longitudinal Alcohol Epidemiological Survey. Journal of Substance Abuse **9**: 103–110.

Grant BF, Dawson DA (2006) Introduction to the national epidemiologic survey on alcohol and related conditions. Alcohol Research and Health **29**: 74–78.

Grant BF, Dawson DA, Stinson FS, et al. (2004) The 12-month prevalence and trends in DSM-IV alcohol abuse and dependence: United States, 1991–1992 and 2001–2002. Drug and Alcohol Dependence **74**: 223–234.

Grant BF, Goldstein RB, Saha TD, et al. (2015) Epidemiology of DSM-5 alcohol use disorder. JAMA Psychiatry 72: 757–766.

Grant BF, Hasin DH, Chou SP, et al. (2004) Nicotine dependence and psychiatric disorders in the United States: Results from the National Epidemiological Survey on Alcohol and Related Conditions. Archives of General Psychiatry 61: 1107–1115.

Grant BF, Stinson FS, Dawson DA, et al. (2004a) Prevalence and co-occurrence of substance use disorders and independent mood and anxiety disorders. Archives of General Psychiatry 61: 807–816.

Grant BF, Stinson FS, Dawson DA, et al. (2004b) Co-occurrence of 12-month alcohol and drug use disorders and personality disorders in the United States. Archives of General Psychiatry 61: 361–368.

Grant I, Atkinson JH, Bouaux B, et al. (2012) Medical marijuana: Clearing away the smoke. Open Neurology Journal 6: 18–25.

Grattan A, Sullivan MD, Saunders KW, et al. (2012) Depression and prescription opioid misuse among chronic opioid therapy recipients with no history of substance abuse. Annals of Family Medicine 10: 304–311.

Grau LE, Dasgupta N, Harvey AP, et al. (2007) Illicit use of opioids: Is Oxy-Contin a "gateway drug"? American Journal on Addictions 16: 166–173.

Gray R, Mukherjee RA, Rutter M (2009) Alcohol consumption during pregnancy and its effects on neurodevelopment: What is known and what remains uncertain. Addiction 104: 1270–1273.

Greaves L (2015) The meanings of smoking to women and their implications for cessation. International Journal of Research on Public Health 12: 1449–1465.

Green LW, Fielding JE, Brownson RC (2018) The debate about electronic cigarettes: Harm minimization or the precautionary principle. Annual Review of Public Health 39: 189–191.

Green A, Garrick T, Sheedy D, et al. (2010) The effect of moderate to heavy alcohol consumption on neuropsychological performance as measured by the repeatable battery for the assessment of neuropsychological status. Alcoholism: Clinical and Experimental Research 34: 443–450.

Green AR, Mechan AO, Elliott JM, et al. (2003) The pharmacology and clinical pharmacology of 3,3-methylenedioxymethamphetamine (MDMA, "ecstasy"). Pharmacological Review 55: 463–508.

Green B, Kavanagh D, Young R (2003) Being stoned: A review of self-reported cannabis effects. Drug and Alcohol Review 22: 453–460.

Greenfeld LA (1998) Alcohol and Crime: An Analysis of National Data on the Prevalence of Alcohol Involvement in Crime. Washington, DC: Bureau of Justice Statistics.

Greenfield SF, Back SE, Lawson K, et al. (2010) Substance abuse in women. Psychiatric Clinics of North America 33: 339–355.

Greenfield SF, Brooks AJ, Gordon SM, et al. (2007) Substance abuse treatment entry, retention, and outcome in women: A review of the literature. Drug and Alcohol Dependence 86: 1–21.

Greenfield SF, Hennessy G (2004) Assessment of the patient. In Galanter M, Kleber HD (eds.) Textbook of Substance Abuse Treatment. 3rd ed. Arlington, VA: American Psychiatric.

Greenfield SF, Ye Y, Bond J, et al. (2014) Risks of alcohol use disorders related to drinking patterns in the US general population. Journal of Studies on Alcohol and Drugs 75: 319–327.

Greenfield TK (2001) Individual risk of alcohol-related disease and problems. In Heather N, Peters TJ, Stockwell T (eds.) International Handbook of Alcohol Dependence and Problems. Chichester, UK: John Wiley.

Greenfield TK, Rogers JD (1999) Who drinks most of the alcohol in the US? The policy implications. Journal of Studies on Alcohol 60: 78–89.

Grekin ER, Sher KJ, Wood PK (2006) Pesonality and substance dependence symptoms: Modeling substance-specific traits. Psychology of Addictive Behaviors 20: 415–424.

Grella CE, Stein JA (2013) Remission from substance dependence: Differences between individuals in a general population survey who do and do not seek help. Drug and Alcohol Dependence 133: 146–153.

Greydanus DE, Hawver EK, Greydanus MM, et al. (2013) Marijuana: Current concepts. Frontiers in Public Health 1: Article 42.

Greydanus DE, Patel DR (2005) The adolescent and substance abuse: Current concepts. Disease a Month 51: 392–431.

Griesler PC, Hu MC, Schaffran C, et al. (2011) Comorbid psychiatric disorders and nicotine dependence in adolescence. Addiction 106: 1010–1020.

Griffith J, Oates JA, Cavanaugh JH (1968) Paranoid episodes induced by drug. JAMA 205: 39–42.

Griffiths RR, Johnson MW (2005) Relative abuse liability of hypnotic drugs: A conceptual framework and algorithm for differentiating among compounds. Journal of Clinical Psychiatry 66(Suppl. 9): 31–41.

Griffiths RR, Sannerud CA (1987) Abuse and dependence on benzodiazepines and other anxiolytic/sedative drugs. In Meltzer HY (ed.) Psychopharmacology: The Third Generation of Progress. New York: Raven Press.

Griffiths RR, Weerts EM (1997) Benzodiazepine self-administration in humans and laboratory animals – implications for problems of long-term use and abuse. Psychopharmacology 134: 1–37.

Grinspoon L, Hedblom P (1975) The Speed Culture: Amphetamine Use and Abuse in America. Cambridge, MA: Harvard University Press.

Groman SM, James AS, Jentsch JD (2009) Poor response inhibition: At the nexus between substance abuse and attention deficit/hyperactivity disorder. Neuroscience and Biobehavioral Reviews 33: 690–698.

Grotenhermen F (2003) Pharmacokinetics and pharmacodynamics of cannabinoids. Clinical Pharmacokinetics 42: 327–330.

Gruber SA, Silveri MM, Dahlgren MK, et al. (2011) Why so impulsive? White matter alterations are associated with impulsivity in chronic marijuana smokers. Experimental and Clinical Psychopharmacology 19: 231–241.

Grucza RA, Bierut LJ (2006) Cigarette smoking and the risk for alcohol use disorders among adolescent drinkers. Alcoholism: Clinical and Experimental Research 30: 2046–2054.

Gruenwald PJ, Johnson FW, Ponicki WR, et al. (2010) Assessing correlates of the growth and extent of methamphetamine abuse and dependence in California. Substance Use and Misuse 45: 1948–1970.

Gullo MJ, Dawe S (2008) Impulsivity and adolescent substance use: Rashly dismissed as "all bad"? Neuroscience and Biobehavioral Reviews 32: 1507–1518.

Gullo MJ, Potenza MN (2014) Impulsivity: Mechanisms, moderators and implications for addictive behaviors. Addictive Behaviors 39: 1543–1546.

Gunderson EW, Haughey HM, Ait-Daoud N, et al. (2012) "Spice" and "K2" herbal highs: A case series and systematic review of the clinical effects and biopsychosocial implications of synthetic cannabinoid use in humans. American Journal on Addictions 21: 320–326.

Gunderson JG, Zanarini MC, Choi-Kain LW, et al. (2011) Family study of borderline personality disorder and its sectors of psychopathology. Archives of General Psychiatry 68: 753–762.

Ginja N (2013) In the zzz zone: The effects of Z-drugs on human performance and driving. Journal of Medical Toxicology 9: 163–171.

Gupta S, Warner J (2008) Alcohol-related dementia: A 21st-century silent epidemic? British Journal of Psychiatry 19: 351–353.

Gurling HMD, Oppenheim BE, Murray RM (1984) Depression, criminality and psychopathology associated with alcoholism associated with alcoholism: Evidence from a twin study. Acta Geneticae Medicae et Gemollologiae 33: 333–339.

Gustavsen I, Al-Sammurraie M, Morland J, et al. (2009) Impairment related to blood drug concentrations of zopiclone and zolpidem compared to alcohol in apprehended drivers. Accident Analysis Prevention 41: 462–466.

Gustavsen I, Bramness JG, Skurtveit S, et al. (2008) Road traffic accident risk related to prescriptions of the hypnotics zopiclone, zolpidem, flunitrazepam and nitrazepam. Sleep Medicine 9: 818–822.

Gutierrez-Cebollada J, del la Torre R, Ortuno J, et al. (1994) Psychotropic drug consumption and other factors associated with heroin overdose. Drug and Alcohol Dependence 35: 169–174.

Haacke R (1997) Drug-Dependent Mothers and Their Children: Issues in Public Policy and Public Health. New York: Springer.

Haber S, Knutson B (2010) The reward circuit: Linking primate anatomy and human imaging. Neuropsychopharmacology Reviews 35: 4–26.

Haberstick BC, Young SE, Zeiger JS, et al. (2014) Prevalence and correlates of alcohol and cannabis disorders in the United States: Results from the National Longitudinal Study of Adolescent Health. Drug and Alcohol Dependence 136: 158–161.

Haggard H, Jellinek E (1942) Alcohol Explored. New York: Doubleday.

Haight W, Jacobsen T, Black J, et al. (2005) "In these bleak days": Parent methamphetamine abuse and child welfare in the rural Midwest. Children and Youth Services Review 27: 949–971.

Hajak G, Muller WE, Wittchen HU, et al. (2003) Abuse and dependence potential for the non-benzodiazepine hypnotics zolpidem and zopiclone: A review of case reports and epidemiological data. Addiction 98: 1371–1378.

Hakkinen M, Launiainen T, Vuori E, et al. (2012) Benzodiazepines and alcohol are associated with cases of fatal buprenorphine poisoning. European Journal of Clinical Pharmacology 68: 301–309.

Halkitis PN (2009) Methamphetamine Addiction: Biological Foundations, Psychological Factors and Social Consequences. Washington, DC: American Psychological Association.

Halkitis PN, Homer BD, Moeller RW, et al. (2007) Methamphetamine and social cognition: Findings from project MASC. Paper presented at the New York University Developmental Psychology Colloquium.

Hall KM, Irwin MM, Bowman KA, et al. (2005) Illicit use of prescribed stimulant medication among college students. Journal of American College Health 53: 167–174.

Hamidovic A, Childs E, Conrad M, et al. (2010) Stress-induced changes in mood and cortisol release predict mood effects of amphetamine. Drug and Alcohol Dependence 109: 175–180.

Hamill P (2003) Foreword. In Shannonhouse R (ed.) Under the Influence. New York: Modern Library.

Hamilton KR, Polenza MN (2012) Relations among delay discounting, addictions, and money mismanagement: Implications and future directions. American Journal of Drug and Alcohol Abuse 38: 30–42.

Hammer R, Dingel M, Ostergren J, et al. (2013) Addiction: Current criticism of the brain disease paradigm. AJOB Neuroscience 4: 27–32.

Hammersley R, Jenkins R, Reid M (2001) Cannabis use and social identity. Addiction Research and Theory 9: 133–150.

Han CJ, Robinson JK (2001) Cannabinoid modulation of time estimation in the rat. Behavioral Neuroscience 115: 243–246.

Hancock DB, Markunas CA, Bierut MD, et al. (2019) Human genetics of addiction: New insights and future directions. Current Psychiatry Reports 20: 120–130.

Haney M, Ward AS, Comer SD, et al. (1999A) Abstinence symptoms following oral THC administration in humans. Psychopharmacology 141: 385–394.

Haney M, Ward AS, Comer SD, et al. (1999B) Abstinence symptoms following smoked marijuana in humans. Psychopharmacology 141: 395–404.

Hanninen V, Koski-James A (1999) Narratives of recovery from addictive behaviours. Addiction 94: 1837–1848.

Hanson GR, Fleckenstein AE (2009) Basic neuropharmacological mechanisms of methamphetamine. In Roll JM, Rawson RA, Ling W, et al. (eds.) Methamphetamine Addiction: From Basic Science to Treatment. New York: Guilford Press.

Hanson GR, Venturelli PJ, Fleckenstein AE (2006) Drugs and Society. 9th ed. Sudbury, MA: Jones and Bartlett.

Hanson MD, Chen E (2007) Socioeconomic status and health behaviors in adolescence: A review of the literature. Journal of Behavioral Medicine **30**: 263–285.

Harding AJ, Halliday GM, Ng JLF (1996) Loss of vasopressin-immunoreactive neurons in alcoholics is dose-related and time-dependent. Neuroscience **72**: 699–708.

Harding WM, Zinberg NE (1983) Occasional opiate use. Advances in Substance Abuse **3**: 27–61.

Harper C (2009) The neuropathology of alcohol-related brain damage. Alcohol and Alcoholism **44**: 136–140.

Harper C, Dixon G, Sheedy D, et al. (2003) Neuropathological alterations in alcoholic brains: Studies arising from the New South Wales Tissue Resource Center. Progress in Neuropsychopharmacological Biological Psychiatry **27**: 951–961.

Harris DS, Boxenbaum H, Everhart ET (2003) The bioavailability of intranasal and smoked methamphetamine. Clinical and Pharmacological Therapeutics **74**: 475–486.

Harrison ELR, McKee SA (2008) Young adult non-daily smokers: Patterns of alcohol and cigarette use. Addictive Behavior **33**: 668–674.

Hart CL, Ward AS, Haney M, et al. (2002) Comparison of smoked marijuana and oral Delta(9)-tetrahydrocannabinol in humans. Psychopharmacology **164**: 407–415.

Hartzler B, Fromme K (2003) Cognitive-behavioral profiles of college risk-takers with type II and psychopathic personality traits. Addictive Behavior **28**: 315–326.

Hartzler B, Fromme K (2003) Fragmentary and en bloc blackouts: Similarity and distinction among episodes of alcohol-induced memory loss. Journal of Studies on Alcohol **64**: 547–550.

Harvey JA (2004) Cocaine effects on the developing brain: current status. Neuroscience and Biobehavioral Reviews **27**: 751–764.

Hashibe M, Morgenstern H, Cui Y (2006) Marijuana use and the risk of lung and upper aerodigestive tract cancers: Results of a population based case-control study. Cancer Epidemiology Biomarkers Prevention **15**: 1829–1834.

Hasin D, Fenton MD, Skodol A, et al. (2011) Personality disorders and the 3-year course of alcohol, drug, and nicotine use disorders. Archives of General Psychiatry **68**: 1158–1167.

Hasin DH (2003) Classification of alcohol use disorders. Alcohol Research and Health **27**: 5–17.

Hasin DH, Beseler CL (2009) Dimensionality of lifetime alcohol abuse, dependence and binge drinking. Drug and Alcohol Dependence **101**: 53–61.

Hasin DS, Grant BF (2015) The national epidemiological survey on alcohol and related conditions (NESARC) waves 1 and 2: Review and summary of findings. Social Psychiatry and Psychiatric Epidemiology **50**: 1609–1640.

Hasin DH, Stinson FS, Ogburn E, et al. (2007) Prevalence, correlates, disability, and comorbidity of DSM-IV alcohol abuse and dependence in the United States: Results from the National

Epidemiological Survey on Alcohol and Related Conditions. Archives of General Psychiatry **64**: 830–842.

Hasin DS, O'Brien CP, Auriacombe M, et al. (2013) DSM-5 criteria for substance use disorders: Recommendations and rationale. American Journal of Psychiatry **170**: 834–851.

Hasin DS, Stinson FS, Ogburn E, et al. (2007) Prevalence, correlates, disability, and comorbidity of DSM-IV alcohol abuse and dependence in the United States. Archives of General Psychiatry **64**: 830–842.

Haughwout SP, LaValee RA, Castle IP (2016) Apparent Per Capita Alcohol Consumption: National, State and Regional Trends, 1977–2014. Surveillance Report 104. Bethesda, MD: National Institute on Alcohol Abuse and Alcoholism.

Hawk M, Coulter RWS, Egan JE, et al. (2017) Harm reduction principles for healthcare settings. Harm Reduction Journal **14**: 70–85.

He S-Q, Zhang A-N, Guan J-S, et al. (2011) Facilitation of mu-opioid receptor activity by preventing delta-opioid co-degradation. Neuron **69**: 120–131.

He X, Sullivan EV, Stankovic RK (2007) Interaction of thiamine deficiency and voluntary alcohol consumption disrupts rat corpus callosum ultrastructure. Neuropsychopharmacology **32**: 2207–2216.

Heath AC, Bucholz KK, Madden PAF, et al. (1997) Genetic and environmental contributions to alcohol dependence risk in a national twin sample: Consistency of findings in women and men. Psychological Medicine **27**: 1381–1389.

Heath AC, Eaves LJ, Martin NG (1998) Interaction of marital status and genetic risk for symptoms of depression. Twin Research **1**: 119–122.

Heath AC, Madden PA, Bucholz KK, et al. (1999) Genetic differences in alcohol sensitivity and the inheritance of alcoholism risk. Psychological Medicine **29**: 1069–1081.

Heather N (2001) Editor's introduction to Treatment and Recovery Section. In Heather N, Peters TJ, Stockwell T (eds.) International Handbook of Alcohol Dependence and Problems. Chichester, UK: John Wiley.

Heather N (2001) Pleasures and pains of our favorite drug. In Heather N, Peters TJ, Stockwell T (eds.) International Handbook of Alcohol Dependence and Problems. Chichester, UK: John Wiley.

Heather N (2006) Controlled drinking, harm reduction and their roles in the response to alcohol-related problems. Addiction Research and Theory **14**: 7–18.

Heather N (2017) Q: Is addiction a brain disease or a moral failing? A: Neither. Neuroethics **10**: 115–123.

Heatherton TF, Kozlowski LT, Frecker RC, et al. (1991) The Fagerstrom Test for Nicotine Dependence: A revision of the Fagerstrom Tolerance Questionnaire. British Journal of Addiction **86**: 1119–1127.

Heil SH, Johnson MW, Higgins ST, et al. (2006) Delay discounting in currently using and currently abstinent cocaine-dependent outpatients and non-drug using matched controls. Addictive Behavior **31**: 1290–1294.

Heilig M, Epstein D, Nader M, et al. (2016) Time to connect: Bringing social context into addiction neuroscience. Nature Reviews: Neuroscience **17**: 592–599.

Heilig M, Goldman D, Berrettini W, et al. (2011) Pharmacogenetic approaches to the treatment of alcohol addiction. Nature Reviews: Neuroscience **12**: 670–684.

Heilig M, Koob GF (2007) A key role for corticotropin-releasing factor in alcohol dependence. Trends in Neurosciences **8**: 399–406.

Heinz A (2006) Neurobiological correlates of the disposition and maintenance of alcoholism. Pharmacopsychiatry **36**(Suppl. 3): S255–S258.

Heinz A, Lober S, Georgi A, et al. (2003) Reward craving and withdrawal relief craving: Assessment of different motivational pathways to alcohol intake. Alcohol **38**: 35–39.

Heinz A, Seissmeier T, Wrase J, et al. (2004) Correlation between dopamine D2 receptors in the ventral striatum and central processing of alcohol cues and craving. American Journal of Psychiatry **161**: 1783–1789.

Heinz A, Siessmeier T, Wrase J, et al. (2005) Correlation of alcohol craving with striatal dopamine synthesis capacity and D2/D3 receptor availability: A combined [^{18}F]DOPA and [^{18}F]DMFP PET study in detoxified alcoholic patients. American Journal of Psychiatry **162**: 1515–1520.

Heishman SJ (2002) What aspects of human performance are truly enhanced by nicotine? Addiction **93**: 317–320.

Heishman SJ, Kleykamp BA, Singleton EG (2010) Meta-analysis of the acute effects of nicotine and smoking on human performance. Psychopharmacology **210**: 453–469.

Heishman SJ, Lee DC, Taylor RC, et al. (2010) Prolonged duration of craving, mood, and autonomic responses elicited by cues and imagery in smokers: Effects of tobacco deprivation and sex. Experimental and Clinical Psychopharmacology **18**: 245–256.

Heishman SJ, Singleton EG, Ligouri A (2001) Marijuana craving questionnaire: Development and initial validation of a self-report instrument. Addiction **96**: 1023–1034.

Heishman SJ, Stitzer ML, Yingling JE (1989) Effects of tetrahydrocannabinol content on marijuana smoking behavior, subjective reports, and performance. Pharmacology, Biochemistry and Behavior **34**: 173–179.

Heishman SJ, Taylor RC, Henningfield JE (1994) Nicotine and smoking: A review of effects on human performance. Experimental and Clinical Psychopharmacology **2**: 1–51.

Held JR, Riggs ML, Dorman C (1999) The effect of prenatal cocaine exposure on neurobehavioral outcome. Neurotoxicology and Teratology **21**: 619–625.

Hendershot CS, Witkiewitz K, George WH, et al. (2011) Relapse prevention for addictive behaviors. Substance Abuse Treatment, Prevention, and Policy **6**: 1–17.

Henderson J, Gray R, Brocklehurst P (2007) Systematic review of effects of low-moderate prenatal alcohol exposure on pregnancy outcomes. British Journal of Obstetrics and Gynaecology **114**: 243–252.

Hennigfield JE, Heishman SJ (1995) The addictive role of nicotine in tobacco use. Psychopharmacology 117: 11–13.

Herd N, Borland R, Hyland A (2009) Predictors of smoking relapse by duration of abstinence: Findings from the International Tobacco Control (ITC) Four Country Survey. Addiction 104: 2088–2099.

Herkenham M, Lynn AB, Johnson MR, et al. (1991) Characterization and localization of cannabinoid receptors in rat brain: A quantitative and *in vitro* autoradiographic study. Journal of Neuroscience 11: 563–583.

Herraiz T, Chaparro C (2005) Human monoamine oxidase is inhibited by tobacco smoke: beta-carboline alkaloids act as potent and reversible inhibitors. Biochemical and Biophysical Research Communications 5: 378–386.

Hesselbrock V, Hesselbrock M, Segal B (2000) Multivariate phenotypes of alcohol dependence among Alaskan natives – type A/type B. Alcoholism: Clinical and Experimental Research 24(Suppl.): 107A.

Hesselbrock VM, Hesselbrock MN (2006) Are there empirically supported and clinically useful subtypes of alcohol dependence? Addiction 101(Suppl. 1): 97–103.

Hesselbrock VM, Hesselbrock MN (2006) Developmental perspectives on the risk for developing substance abuse problems. In: Rethinking Substance Abuse: What the Science Shows, and What We Should Do About It. New York: The Guilford Press.

Hester R, Dixon V, Garavan H (2006) A consistent attentional bias for drug-related material in active cocaine users across word and picture versions of the emotional Stroop test. Drug and Alcohol Dependence 81: 251–257.

Hester R, Garavan H (2004) Executive dysfunction in cocaine addiction: Evidence for discordant frontal, cingulate, and cerebellar activity. Journal of Neuroscience 24: 11017–11022.

Hester R, Garavan H (2009) Neural mechanisms underlying drug-related cue distraction in active cocaine users. Pharmacology, Biochemistry, and Behavior 93: 270–277.

Heyman GM (2009) Addiction: A Disorder of Choice. Cambridge, MA: Harvard University Press.

Heyman GM (2011) Received wisdom regarding the roles of craving and dopamine in addiction: A response to Lewis's critique of addiction – a disorder of choice. Perspectives on Psychological Science 6: 156–160.

Hibell B, Andersson B, Bjarnasson B (2004) The 2003 ESPAD Report: Alcohol and Other Drug Use among Students in 35 European Countries. Stockholm: Swedish Council for Information on Alcohol and Other Drugs.

Hickman M, Lingford-Hughes A, Bailey C, et al. (2008) Does alcohol increase the risk of overdose death: The need for a translational approach? Addiction 103: 1060–1062.

Hicks BM, Bernat E, Malone SM, et al. (2007) Genes mediate the association between P300 amplitude and externalizing disorders. Psychophysiology 44: 98–105.

Hicks BM, Krueger RF, Iacono WG, et al. (2004) Family transmission and heritability of externalizing disorders.

Archives of General Psychiatry **61**: 922–928.

Hicks MJ, Kaminsky SM, De BP, et al. (2014) Fate of systemically administered cocaine in nonhuman primates treated with the dAd5GNE anticocaine vaccine. Human Gene Therapy Clinical Development **25**: 40–49.

Higgins ST, Heil SH, Lussier JP (2004) Clinical implications of reinforcement as a determinant of substance use disorders. Annual Review of Psychology **55**: 431–461.

Hill TD, Jorgenson A (2018) Bring out your dead! A study of income inequality and life expectancy in the United States 2000–2010. Health and Place **49**: 1–6.

Hill SY (1998) Alternative strategies for uncovering genes contributing to alcoholism risk: Unpredictable findings in a genetic wonderland. Alcohol **16**: 53–59.

Hill SY, DeBellis MD, Keshavan MS, et al. (2001) Right amygdala volume in adolescent and young adult offspring from families at high risk for developing alcoholism. Biological Psychiatry **49**: 894–905.

Himmelsbach CK (1943) Can the euphoric, analgesic, and physical dependence effects of drugs be separated? Federation Proceedings **2**: 201–203.

Hines LM, Ray L, Hutchison K, et al. (2005) Alcoholism: The dissection for endophenotypes. Dialogues in Clinical Neuroscience **7**: 153–163.

Hines LA, Morley KI, Strang J, et al. (2016) Onset of opportunity to use cannabis and progression from opportunity to dependence: Are the influences consistent across transitions? Drug and Alcohol Dependence **160**: 57–64.

Hingson RW (2010) Magnitude and prevention of college drinking and related problems. Alcohol Research and Health **33**: 45–54.

Hingson RW, Heeren T, Winter MR (2006) Age of drinking onset and alcohol dependence: Age at onset, duration, and severity. Archives of Pediatric Adolescent Medicine **160**: 739–746.

Hingson RW, Klendel D (2004) Social, health, and economic consequences of underage drinking. In Bonnie RJ, O'Connell ME, National Research Council and Institute of Medicine (eds.) Reducing Underage Drinking: A Collective Responsibility. Washington, DC: National Academies Press.

Hitsman B, Borrelli B, McChargue DE, et al. (2003) History of depression and smoking cessation outcome: A meta-analysis. Journal of Consulting and Clinical Psychology **71**: 657–663.

Hoch E, Bonnet U, Thomasius R, et al. (2015) Risks associated with the non-medical use of cannabis. Deutsches Arzteblatt International **112**: 271–278.

Hoch E, Muehlig M, Lieb R, et al. (2004) How prevalent is smoking and nicotine dependence in primary care in Germany? Addiction **99**: 1586–1598.

Hoffman F (2013) Benefits and risks of benzodiazepines and Z-drugs: Comparison of perceptions of GPs and community pharmacists in Germany. German Medical Science **11**: 1–7.

Hoffman PL, Miles M, Edenberg HJ, et al. (2003) Gene expression in the brain: A window on ethanol dependence, neuroadaptation, and preference. Alcoholism: Clinical and Experimental Research **27**: 155–168.

Hoffman PL, Rabe CS, Moses F, et al. (1989) NMDA receptors and ethanol: Inhibition of calcium flux and cyclic GMP production. Journal of Neurochemistry 52: 1937–1940.

Holahan CJ, Schutte KK, Brennan PL, et al. (2012) Wine consumption and 20-year mortality among late-life moderate drinkers. Journal of Studies on Alcohol and Drugs 73: 80–88.

Holdcraft LC, Iacono WG, McGue MK (1998) Antisocial personality disorder and depression in relation to alcoholism. Journal of Studies on Alcohol 59: 222–226.

Holdstock L, de Wit H (1998) Individual differences in the biphasic effects of ethanol. Alcoholism: Clinical and Experimental Research 22: 1903–1911.

Holland J (2001) The history of MDMA. In Holland J (ed.) Ecstasy: The Complete Guide. Rochester, VT: Park Street Press.

Hollander JA, Lu Q, Cameron MD, et al. (2008) Insular hypcretin transmission regulates nicotine reward. Proceedings of the National Academy of Sciences of the USA 105: 480–485.

Hollister LE (1986) Health aspects of cannabis. Pharmacological Review 38: 1–20.

Homer BD, Solomon TM, Moeller RW, et al. (2008) Methamphetamine use and impairment of social functioning: A review of the underlying neurophysiological causes and behavioral implications. Psychological Bulletin 134: 301–310.

Horvath AT (2000) SMART recovery: Addiction recovery support from a cognitive-behavioral perspective. Journal of Rational-Emotive and Cognitive Behavior Therapy 18: 181–191.

Hoenigl M, et al. (2016) Clear links between starting methamphetamine and increasing sexual risk behavior: A cohort study among men who have sex with men. Journal of Acquired Immune Deficiency Syndrome 71: 551–557.

Horwood LJ, Fergusson DM, Hayatbakhsh MR, et al. (2010) Cannabis use and educational achievement: Findings from three Australasian cohort studies. Drug and Alcohol Dependence 110: 247–253.

Hovatta L, Juhila J, Donner J (2010) Oxidative stress in anxiety and comorbid disorders. Neuroscience Research 68: 261–275.

Howard DE, Griffin MA, Boekeloo LO (2008) Prevalence and psychosocial correlates of alcohol-related sexual assault among university students. Adolescence 43: 733–750.

Howard MO, Kivlahan D, Walker RD (1997) Cloninger's tridimensional theory of personality and psychopathology: Applications to substance use disorders. Journal of Studies on Alcohol 58: 48–66.

Howden ML, Naughten MT (2011) Pulmonary effects of marijuana inhalation. Expert Reviews of Respiratory Medicine 5: 87–92.

Hoyme HE, Kalberg WO, Elliot AJ, et al. (2016) Updated clinical guidelines for diagnosing fetal alcohol spectrum disorders. Pediatrics 138: e20154256.

Hser Y, Huang D, Brecht M-L, et al. (2008) Contrasting trajectories of heroin, cocaine, and methamphetamine use. Journal of Addictive Disorders 27: 13–21.

Hu SS, Neff L, Agaku IT et al. (2016) Tobacco product use among adults –

United States, 2013–2014. Morbidity and Mortality Weekly Reports **65**: 685–691.

Huang MC, Lin HY, Chen CH (2007) Dependence on zolpidem. Psychiatry Clinical Neuroscience **61**: 207–208.

Huang SJ, Xu YM, Lau ATY (2018) Electronic cigarette: A recent update on its toxic effects on humans. Journal of Cell Physiology **233**: 4466–4478.

Huestis MA, Sampson AH, Holicky BJ, et al. (1992) Characterization of the absorption phase of marijuana smoking. Clinical and Pharmacological Therapeutics **52**: 31–41.

Huffman JW, Dai D, Martin BR, et al. (1994) Design, synthesis and pharmacology of cannabimemetic indoles. Bioorganic and Medicinal Chemistry Letters **4**: 563–566.

Hufford MR (2001) Alcohol and suicidal behavior. Clinical Psychology Review **21**: 797–811.

Hughes A, Williams MR, Lipari RN, et al. (2016) Prescription drug use and misuse in the United States: Results from the 2015 National Survey on Drug Use and Health. NSDUH Data Review. www .samhsa.gov/data/.

Hughes JR (2006) Should criteria for drug dependence differ across drugs? Addiction **101**(Suppl. 1): 134–141.

Hughes JR (2007a) Effects of abstinence from tobacco: Valid symptoms and time course. Nicotine and Tobacco Research **9**: 315–327.

Hughes JR (2007b) Effects of abstinence from tobacco: Etiology, animal models, epidemiology, and significance: A subjective review. Nicotine and Tobacco Research **9**: 329–339.

Hughes JR (2010) Craving among long-abstinent smokers: An internet survey. Nicotine and Tobacco Research **12**: 459–462.

Hughes JR, Finger JR, Budney AJ, et al. (2014) Marijuana use and intoxication among daily users: An intensive longitudinal study. Addictive Behavior **39**: 1464–1470.

Hughes JR, Higgins ST, Hatsukami DK (1990) Effects of abstinence from tobacco: A critical review. Research Advances in Alcohol and Drug Problems **10**: 317–398.

Hughes JR, Naud S, Budney AJ, et al. (2016) Attempts to stop or reduce daily cannabis use: An intensive natural history study. Psychology of Addictive Behavior **30**: 389–397.

Hughes JR, Peters EN, Callas PW, et al. (2008) Attempts to stop or reduce marijuana use in non-treatment seekers. Drug and Alcohol Dependence **97**: 180–184.

Humeniuk R, Ali R, Babor TF, et al. (2008) Validation of the alcohol, smoking, and substance involvement screening test (ASSIST). Addiction **103**: 1039–1047.

Humphreys K (2003) Alcoholics Anonymous and 12-step alcoholism treatment programs. In Galanter M (series ed.) Recent Developments in Alcoholism: Vol. 16. Methodology, Psychosocial Treatment, Selected Treatment Topics, Research Priorities. New York: Springer.

Humphreys K, Wing S, McCarty D, et al. (2004) Self-help organizations for alcohol and drug problems: Toward evidence-based practice and policy. Journal of Substance Abuse Treatment **26**: 151–158.

Hunter C, Strike C, Barnaby L, et al. (2012) Reducing widespread pipe sharing and risky sex among crystal methamphetamine smokers in Toronto: Do safer smoking kits have a potential role to play? Harm Reduction Journal 9: 9–18.

Hurd YL, Michaelides M, Miller ML, et al. (2013) Trajectory of adolescent cannabis use on addiction vulnerability. Neuropharmacology. Advance online publication.

Husky MM, Mazure CM, Paliwal P, et al. (2008) Gender difference in comorbidity of smoking behavior and major depression. Drug and Alcohol Dependence 93: 176–179.

Hyggen C (2012) Does smoking cannabis affect work commitment? Addiction 107: 1309–1315.

Hyman S, Malenka R, Nestler E (2006) Neural mechanisms of addiction: The role of reward-related learning and memory. Annual Review of Neuroscience 29: 565–598.

Hyman SM, Sinha R (2009) Stress-related factors in cannabis use and misuse: Implications for prevention and treatment. Journal of Substance Abuse Treatment 36: 400–413.

Iacono W, Malone S, McGue M (2008) Behavioral disinhibition and the development of early-onset addiction: Common and specific influences. Annual Review of Clinical Psychology 4: 325–348.

Iacono WG, Carlson SR, Malone SM, et al. (2002) P3 event-related potential amplitude and risk for disinhibitory disorders in adolescent boys. Archives of General Psychiatry 59: 750–757.

Iacono WG, Malone SM, McGue M (2008) Behavioral disinhibition and the development of early-onset addiction: Common and specific influences. Annual Review of Clinical Psychology 4: 325–348.

Ibanez GE, Levi-Minzi MA, Rigg KK, et al. (2013) Diversion of benzodiazepines through healthcare sources. Journal of Psychoactive Drugs 45: 48–56.

International HapMap Consortium (2005). A haplotype map of the human genome. Nature 437: 1299–1320.

Isbell H, Fraser HF, Wikler A (1955) An experimental study of the etiology of "rum fits" and delirium tremens. Quarterly Journal of Studies of Alcohol 16: 1–33.

Iversen L (2006) Speed, Ecstasy, Ritalin: The Science of Amphetamines. New York: Oxford University Press.

Iversen L (2008) The Science of Marijuana. Oxford: Oxford University Press.

Iversen L (2012) How cannabis works in the brain. In Castle D, Murray RM, D'Souza DC (eds.) Marijuana and Madness. 2nd ed. Cambridge: Cambridge University Press.

Izenwasser S (1998) Basic pharmacological mechanisms of cocaine. In Higgins ST, Katz JL (eds.) Cocaine Abuse: Behavior, Pharmacology, and Clinical Applications. San Diego, CA: Academic Press.

Jackson H, Mandell K, Johnson K, et al. (2015) Cost effectiveness of injectable extended release naltrexone compared to methadone maintenance and buprenorphine maintenance treatment for opioid dependence. Substance Abuse 36: 226–231.

Jackson KM, Bucholz KK, Wood PK, et al. (2014) Towards the characterization and validation of alcohol use disorder subtypes: Integrating consumption and symptom data. Psychological Medicine **44**: 143–159.

Jacob T, Waterman MPH, Heath A, et al. (2003) Genetic and environmental effects of offspring alcoholism. Archives of General Psychiatry **60**: 1265–1272.

Jaffe C, Bush KR, Straits-Troster K, et al. (2005) A comparison of methamphetamine-dependent inpatients' childhood attention deficit hyperactivity disorder symptomology. Journal on Addictive Disorders **24**: 133–152.

Jang KL, Livesley WJ, Angleitner A (2002) Genetic and environmental influences on the covariance of facets defining the domains of the five-factor model of personality. Personality and Individual Differences **33**: 83–101.

Janoff SL, Perrin NA, Coplan PM, et al. (2016) Protocol: Changes in rates of opioid overdose and poisoning events in an integrated health system following the introduction of a formulation of OxyContin with abuse-deterrent properties. BMC Pharmacology and Toxicology **17**: Article 21.

Jarbe TUC (2011) Perceptual drug discriminative aspects of the endocannabinoid signaling system in animals and man. In Glennon RA, Young R (eds.) Drug Discrimination: Applications to Medicinal Chemistry and Drug Studies. Hoboken, NJ: John Wiley.

Jarjour S, Bai L, Gianoulakis C (2009) Effect of acute ethanol administration on the release of opioid peptides from the midbrain including the ventral tegmental area. Alcoholism: Clinical and Experimental Research **33**: 1033–1043.

Jarvik ME, Madsen JL, Olmstead RE, et al. (2000) Nicotine blood levels and subjective craving for cigarettes. Pharmacology, Biochemistry, and Behavior **66**: 553–558.

Jasinska AJ, Stein EA, Kaiser J, et al. (2014) Factors modulating neural reactivity to drug cues in addiction: A survey of human neuroimaging studies. Neuroscience and Biobehavioral Reviews **38**: 1–16.

Jeffery R, Hennrikus D, Lando H, et al. (2000) Reconciling conflicting findings regarding post-cessation weight concerns and success in smoking cessation. Health Psychology **19**: 242–246.

Jellinek EM (1946) Phases in the drinking history of alcoholics: Analysis of a survey conducted by the official organ of Alcoholics Anonymous. Journal of Studies on Alcohol **7**: 1–88.

Jellinek EM (1960) The Disease Concept of Alcoholism. New Haven, CT: Hillhouse Press.

Johanson CE, Balster RL, Bonese K (1976) Self-administration of stimulant drugs: The effects of unlimited access. Pharmacology, Biochemistry, and Behavior **4**: 45–51.

Johanson CE, Frey KA, Lundahl LH, et al. (2006) Cognitive function and nigrostriatal markers in abstinent methamphetamine abusers. Psychopharmacology **185**: 327–338.

Johnson BA (2010) Medication treatment of different types of alcoholism. American Journal of Psychiatry **167**: 630–639.

Johnson BA, Ait-Daoud N, Seneviratne C, et al. (2011) Pharmacogenetic approach at the serotonin receptor transporter gene as a method of reducing the severity of alcohol drinking. American Journal of Psychiatry **168**: 265–275.

Johnson BA, Ait-Daoud N, Wells T (2000) Effects of Isradipine, a dihydropyridine-class calcium-channel antagonist, on d-methamphetamine-induced cognitive and physiological changes in humans. Neuropsychopharmacology **22**: 504–512.

Johnson EO, Breslau N (2006) Is the association of smoking and depression a recent phenomenon? Nicotine and Tobacco Research **8**: 257–262.

Johnson PM, Hollander JA, Kenny PJ (2008) Decreased reward function during nicotine withdrawal in C57BL6 mice: Evidence from intracranial self-stimulation (ICSS). Pharmacology, Biochemistry, and Behavior **90**: 409–415.

Johnson TP (2012) Failures in substance use surveys. Substance Use and Misuse **47**: 1676–1682.

Johnston JH, Linden DEJ, van den Bree MBM (2016) Combining stress and dopamine based models of addiction: Towards a psycho-neuro-endocrinological theory of addiction. Current Drug Abuse Reviews **9**: 61–74.

Johnston LD, O'Malley PM, Bachman JG, et al. (2009) Monitoring the Future National Results on Adolescent Drug Use: Overview of Key Findings 2008. Bethesda, MD: National Institute on Drug Abuse.

Johnston LD, O'Malley PM, Bachman JG, et al. (2013) Monitoring the Future National Results on Drug Use: 2012 – Overview, Key Findings on Adolescent Drug Use. Ann Arbor: Institute for Social Research, University of Michigan.

Johnston LD, O'Malley PM, Miech RA, et al. (2016) Monitoring the Future National Results on Drug Use: 1975–2016 – Overview, Key Findings on Adolescent Drug Use. Ann Arbor: Institute for Social Research, University of Michigan.

Johnston LD, O'Malley PM, Miech RA, et al. (2015) Monitoring the Future National Survey Results on Drug Use: 1975–2014 – Overview, Key Findings on Adolescent Drug use. Ann Arbor: Institute for Social Research, University of Michigan.

Johnstone BM, Leino IV, Ager C, et al. (1996) Determinants of life-course variation in the frequency of alcohol consumption: Meta-analysis of studies from the Collaborative Alcohol-Related Longitudinal Project. Journal of Studies on Alcohol **57**: 494–506.

Jones AW (1993) Disappearance rate of ethanol from the blood of human subjects: Implications in forensic toxicology. Journal of Forensic Science **38**: 104–118.

Jones CM (2013) Heroin use and heroin use risk behaviors among nonmedical users of prescription opioid pain relievers – United States 2002–2004 and 2008–2010. Drug and Alcohol Dependence **132**: 95–100.

Jones CM, Logan J, Gladden RM, et al. (2015) Vital signs: Demographic and substance use trends among heroin users – United States, 2002–2013.

Morbidity and Mortality Weekly Reports **66**: 697–704.

Jones HE, Dengler E, Garrison A, et al. (2014) Neonatal outcomes and their relationship to maternal buprenorphine dose during pregnancy. Drug and Alcohol Dependence **134**: 414–417.

Jones JD, Comer SD, Kranzler HR (2015) The pharmacogenetics of alcohol use disorder. Alcoholism: Clinical and Experimental Research **39**: 391–402.

Jones JD, Mogali S, Comer SD (2012) Polydrug abuse: A review of opioid and benzodiazepine combination use. Drug and Alcohol Dependence **125**: 8–18.

Jones KA, Blagrove M, Parrot AC (2009) Cannabis and ecstasy/MDMA: Empirical measures of creativity in recreational users. Journal of Psychoactive Drugs **41**: 323–329.

Jones SA, Lueras JM, Nagel BJ (2018) Effects of binge drinking on the developing brain: Studies in humans. Alcohol Research: Current Reviews **39**: 87–96.

Jonsson EG, Nothen MM, Gruhage F, et al. (1999) Polymorphisms in the dopamine D2 receptor gene and their relationships to striatal dopamine receptor density of healthy volunteers. Molecular Psychiatry **4**: 290–296.

Joseph M, Datala K, Young A (2003) The interpretation of the measurement of nucleus accumbens dopamine by in vivo dialysis: The kick, the craving or the cognition? Addiction **102**: 1131–1139.

Jovanovski D, Erb S, Zakzanis KK (2005) Neurocognitive deficits in cocaine users: A quantitative review of the evidence. Journal of Clinical and Experimental Neuropsychology **27**: 189–204.

Julien RM. Advokat CD, Comaty JE (2008) A Primer of Drug Action. 11th ed. New York: Worth.

Kabat-Zinn J (1990) Full Catastrophe Living: Using the Wisdom of Your Body and Mind to Face Stress, Pain, and Illness. New York: Delta.

Kachadourian LK, Pilver CE, Potenza MN (2014) Trauma, PTSD, and binge and hazardous drinking among women and men: findings from a national study. Journal of Psychiatric Research **55**: 35–43.

Kadoya C, Domino EF, Matsuoka S (1994) Relationship of electroencephalographic and cardiovascular changes to plasma nicotine levels in tobacco smokers. Clinical Pharmacology and Therapeutics **55**: 370–377.

Kahler CW, Daughters SB, Leventhal AM, et al. (2009) Personality, psychiatric disorders, and smoking in middle-aged adults. Nicotine and Tobacco Research **11**: 833–841.

Kahler CW, Leventhal AM, Daughters SB, et al. (2010) Relationships of personality and psychiatric disorders to multiple domains of smoking motives and dependence in middle-aged adults. Nicotine and Tobacco Research **12**: 381–389.

Kalant H (2001) The pharmacology and toxicology of "ecstasy" (MDMA) and related drugs. Canadian Medical Association Journal **165**: 917–928.

Kalivas P, O'Brien C (2008) Drug addiction as a pathology of staged neuroplasticity. Neuropsychopharmacology Reviews **33**: 166–180.

Kalivas PW (2009) The glutamate homeostasis hypothesis of addiction. Nature
Reviews: Neuroscience **10**: 561–572.

Kalman D (2002) The subjective effects
of nicotine: Methodological issues, a
review of experimental studies, and recommendations for future research. Nicotine and Tobacco Research **4**: 25–70.

Kalman D, Morissette SB, George TP (2005)
Co-morbidity of smoking in patients
with psychiatric and substance use disorders. American Journal of Addiction
14: 106–123.

Kaminer Y, Bukstein OG, Tarter RE (1991)
The Teen Addiction Severity Index:
Rationale and reliability. International
Journal of the Addictions **26**: 219–226.

Kampman KM, Volpicelli JR, McGinnis DE,
et al. (1998) Reliability and validity of the Cocaine Selective Severity
Assessment. Addictive Behaviors **23**:
449–461.

Kandel D, Chen K (2000) Types of marijuana
users by longitudinal course. Journal of
Studies on Alcohol **61**: 367–378.

Kandel D, Faust R (1975) Sequence and
stages in patterns of adolescent drug
use. Archives of General Psychiatry **32**:
923–932.

Kandel DB (2002) Stages and Pathways
of Drug Involvement: Examining the
Gateway Hypothesis. Cambridge: Cambridge University Press.

Kandel DB, Hu M-C, Griesler PC, et al.
(2007) On the development of nicotine
dependence in adolescence. Drug and
Alcohol Dependence **91**: 26–39.

Kaner E, Newbury-Birch D, Heather N
(2009) Brief intervention. In Miller PM
(ed.) Evidence-Based Addiction Treatment. Burlington, MA: Academic Press.

Kanny D, Brewer RD, Mesnick JB, et al.
(2015) Vital signs: Alcohol poisoning
deaths – United States, 2010–2012.
Morbidity and Mortality Weekly Reports
63: 1238–1242.

Kapoor M, Wang J-C, Wetherill L, et al.
(2013) A meta-analysis of two genome-
wide association studies to identify
novel loci for maximum number of
alcoholic drinks. Human Genetics **132**:
1141–1151.

Karan LD, Dani JA, Benowitz N (2003) The
pharmacology of nicotine and tobacco.
In Graham AW, Schultz TK, Mayo-Smith
MF, et al. (eds.) Principles of Addiction
Medicine. 3rd ed. Chevy Chase, MD:
American Society of Addiction Medicine.

Karan LD, Rosecrans JA (2000) Addictive
capacity of nicotine. In Piasecki M,
Newhouse PA (eds.) Nicotine in Psychiatry: Psychopathology and Emerging
Therapeutics. Washington, DC: American Psychiatric Press.

Karch AM (2013) Lippincott's Nursing
Drug Guide. Philadelphia: Lippincott
Williams and Wilkins.

Karch SB (2002) Synthetic stimulants. In
Karch SB (ed.) Karch's Pathology of
Drug Abuse. 3rd ed. Boca Raton, FL:
CRC Press.

Karkoski LM, Prescott CA, Kendler KS
(2000) Multivariate assessment of
factors influencing illicit substance
use in twins from female-female pairs.
American Journal of Medical Genetic
Neuropsychiatry **96**: 665–670.

Karriker-Jaffe KJ, Witbrodt J, Greenfield
TK (2015) Refining measures of alcohol
problems for general population surveys. Alcoholism: Clinical and Experimental Research **39**: 363–370.

Kassel JD (2010) Substance Abuse and Emotion. Washington, DC: American Psychological Association.

Kassel JD, Stroud LR, Paronis CA (2003) Smoking, stress and negative affect: Correlation, causation and context across stages of smoking. Psychological Bulletin **129**: 270–304.

Kassel JD, Vielleux JC (2010) Introduction: The complex interplay between substance abuse and emotion. In Kassel JD (ed.) Substance Abuse and Emotion. Washington, DC: American Psychological Association.

Kassel JD, Wardle MC, Heinz AJ, et al. (2010) Cognitive theories of drug effects on emotion. In Kassel JD (ed.) Substance Abuse and Emotion. Washington, DC: American Psychological Association.

Kauer J, Malenka R (2007) Synaptic plasticity and addiction. Nature Reviews: Neuroscience **8**: 844–858.

Kaufman J, Yang B-Z, Douglas-Palumberi H, et al. (2007) Genetic and environmental predictors of early alcohol use. Biological Psychiatry **61**: 1228–1234.

Kaufman JN, Ross TJ, Stein EA, et al. (2003) Cingulate hypoactivity in cocaine users during a GO-NOGO task as revealed by event-related functional magnetic resonance imaging. Journal of Neuroscience **23**: 7839–7843.

Kaye S. McKetin R, Duflou J (2007) Methamphetamine and cardiovascular pathology: A review of the evidence. Addiction **102**: 1204–1211.

Keller M (1976) The disease concept of alcoholism revisited. Journal of Studies on Alcohol **37**: 1694–1717.

Kelley AE, Christopher GL, Gauthier AM (1988) Induction of oral stereotypy following amphetamine microinjection into a discrete subregion of the striatum. Psychopharmacology **95**: 556–559.

Kellogg SH, Tatarsky A (2012) Re-envisioning addiction treatment: A six-point plan. Alcoholism Treatment Quarterly **30**: 109–128.

Kelly JF, Greene CM (2013) The twelve promises of Alcoholics Anonymous: Psychometric measure validation and meditational testing as a 12-step specific mechanism of behavior change. Drug and Alcohol Dependence **133**: 633–640.

Kelly JF, Magill M, Stout RL (2009) How do people recover from alcohol dependence? A systematic review of the research on the mechanisms of behavior change in Alcoholics Anonymous. Addiction Research and Theory **17**: 236–259.

Keltner N (2003) Psychiatric Nursing (4th edition). St. Louis: Elsevier-Mosby.

Kenagy DN, Bird CT, Webber CM, et al. (2004) Dextroamphetamine use during B-2 combat missions. Aviation and Space Environmental Medicine **75**: 381–386.

Kendler KS (2005) "A gene for ...": The nature of gene action in psychiatric disorders. American Journal of Psychiatry **162**: 1243–1252.

Kendler KS, Aggen SH, Patrick CJ (2012) A multivariate twin study of the DSM-IV criteria for antisocial personality disorder. Biological Psychiatry **7**: 247–253.

Kendler KS, Heath AS, Neale MC, et al. (1992) A population based twin study of alcoholism in women. Journal of the American Medical Association **268**: 1877–1882.

Kendler KS, Jacobson KC, Prescott CA, et al. (2003a) Specificity of genetic and environmental risk factors for use and abuse/dependence of cannabis, cocaine, hallucinogens, sedatives, stimulants, and opiates in male twins. American Journal of Psychiatry 160: 687–697.

Kendler KS, Prescott CA (2006) Genes, Environment, and Psychopathology. New York: Guilford Press.

Kendler KS, Prescott CA, Myers J, et al. (2003b) The structure of genetic and environmental risk factors for common psychiatric and substance use disorders in men and women. Archives of General Psychiatry 60: 929–937.

Kendler KS, Prescott CA, Neale MC, et al. (1997) Temperance board registration for alcohol abuse in a national sample of Swedish male twins, born 1902 to 1949. Archives of General Psychiatry 54: 178–184.

Kendler KS, Xiangning C, Dick D, et al. (2012) Recent advances in the genetic epidemiology and molecular genetics of substance use disorder. Nature Neuroscience 15: 181–189.

Kenny PJ (2011) Tobacco dependence, the insular cortex and the hypocretin connection. Pharmacology, Biochemistry, and Behavior 97: 700–707.

Kenny PJ, Markou A (2006) Nicotine self-administration acutely activates brain reward systems and induces a long-lasting increase in reward sensitivity. Neuropsychopharmacology 31: 1203–1211.

Kertesz SG, Madan A, Wallace D, et al. (2006) Substance abuse treatment and psychiatric comorbidity: do benefits spill over? Analysis of data from a pro-

spective trial among cocaine-dependent homeless persons. Substance Abuse Treatment, Prevention, and Policy 1: 27–35.

Kessler RC, Chiu WT, Demler O, et al. (2005) Prevalence, severity and comorbidity of 12-month DSM-IV disorders in the National Comorbidity Survey Replication. Archives of General Psychiatry 62: 617–627.

Kessler RC, Crum RM, Warner LA, et al. (1997) Lifetime co-occurrence of DSM-III-R alcohol abuse and dependence with other psychiatric disorders in the National Comorbidity Survey. Archives of General Psychiatry 54: 313–321.

Ketcham K, Asbury W (2000) Beyond the Influence: Understanding and Defeating Alcoholism. New York: Bantam Books.

Keyes KM, Hatzenbuehler ML, Grant BF, et al. (2012) Stress and alcohol: Epidemiological evidence. Alcohol Research: Current Reviews 34: 391–400.

Keyes MA, Iacono WG, McGue M (2007) Early onset problem behavior, young adult psychopathology, and contextual risk. Twin Research and Human Genetics 10: 45–53.

Keyser-Marcus L, Alvanzo A, Rieckmann T, et al. (2015) Trauma, gender, and mental health symptoms in individuals with substance use disorders. Journal of Interpersonal Violence 30: 3024.

Khantzian EJ (1997) The self-medication hypothesis of addictive disorders: A reconsideration and recent applications. Harvard Review of Psychiatry 4: 231–234.

Khantzian EJ (2003) The self-medication hypothesis revisited: The dually diagnosed patient. Primary Psychiatry 10: 47–54.

Khuder SA (2001) Effect of cigarette smoking on major histological types of lung cancer: A metanalysis. Lung Cancer 31: 139–148.

Kieffer BL, Evans CJ (2002) Opioid tolerance – in search of the holy grail. Cell 108: 587–590.

Kiluk BD, Babuscio TA, Nich C, et al. (2013) Smokers versus snorters: Do treatment outcomes differ according to routes of cocaine administration? Experimental and Clinical Psychopharmacology 21: 490–498.

King BA, Patel R, Nguyen KH, et al. (2015) Trends in awareness and use of electronic cigarettes among US adults, 2010–2013. Nicotine and Tobacco Research 17: 219–227.

King NB, Fraser V, Boikos C, et al. (2014) Determinants of increased opioid-related mortality in the United States and Canada, 1990–2013: A systematic review. American Journal of Public Health 104: e32.

Kinney J (2009) Loosening the Grip: A Handbook of Alcohol Information. 9th ed. New York: McGraw-Hill.

Kirby KN, Petry NM (2004) Heroin and cocaine abusers have higher discount rates for delayed rewards than alcoholics or non-drug-using controls. Addiction 99: 461–471.

Kirisci L, Mezzich AC, Reynolds M, et al. (2009) Prospective study of the association between neurobehavior disinhibition and peer environment on illegal drug use in boys and girls. American Journal of Drug and Alcohol Abuse 35: 145–150.

Kirisci L, Tarter R, Mezzich A, et al. (2007) Developmental trajectory in substance use disorder etiology. Psychology of Addictive Behaviors 21: 287–296.

Kirisci L, Tarter R, Vanyukov M, et al. (2004) Relation between cognitive distortions and neurobehavioral disinhibition on the development of substance abuse during adolescence and substance use disorder by young adulthood: A prospective study. Drug and Alcohol Dependence 76: 125–133.

Kirkham TC (2009) Cannabinoids and appetite: Food craving and food pleasure. International Review of Psychiatry 21: 163–171.

Kitanaka N, Kitanaka J, Takemura M (2003) Behavioral sensitization and alteration in monoamine metabolism in mice after single versus repeated methamphetamine administration. European Journal of Pharmacology 474: 63–70.

Kleykamp BA, Griffiths RA, McCann UD, et al. (2012) Acute effects of zolpidem extended-release on cognitive performance and sleep in healthy males after repeated nightly use. Experimental and Clinical Psychopharmacology 20: 28–39.

Klingemann H, Klingemann J (2009) How much treatment does a person need? Self-change and the treatment system. In Miller PM (ed.) Evidence-Based Addiction Treatment. Burlington, MA: Academic Press.

Klungsoyr O, Nygard JF, Sorensen T, et al. (2006) Cigarette smoking and incidence of first depressive episode: An 11-year, population-based follow-up study. American Journal of Epidemiology 163: 421–432.

Knapp C (1996) Drinking: A Love Story. New York: Dell.

Knight JR, Palacios JN, Shannon M (1999) Prevalence of alcohol problems among pediatric residents. Archives of Pediatrics and Adolescent Medicine 153: 1181–1183.

Koenen KC, Hitsman B, Lyons MJ, et al. (2005) A twin registry study of the relationship between posttraumatic stress disorder and nicotine dependence in men. Archives of General Psychiatry 62: 1258–1265.

Kolb L, DuMez AG (1924) The prevalence and trend of drug addiction in the United States and factors influencing it. Public Health Reports 39: 1179–1204.

Kollins SH (2003) Delay discounting is associated with substance use in college students. Addictive Behavior 28: 1167–1173.

Kolodny A, Courtwright DT, Hwang CS, et al. (2015) The prescription opioid and heroin crisis: a public health approach to an epidemic of addiction. Annual Review of Public Health 36: 559–574.

Kono J, Miyata H, Ushijima S, et al. (2001) Nicotine, alcohol, methamphetamine, and inhalant dependence: A comparison of clinical features with the use of a new clinical evaluation form. Alcohol 24: 99–106.

Koob G, Le Moal M (2006) Neurobiology of Addiction. London: Academic Press.

Koob G, Sanna PP, Bloom FE (1998) Neuroscience of addiction. Neuron 21: 467–476.

Koob GF (2006) The neurobiology of addiction: A hedonic Calvinist view. In Miller W, Carroll K (eds.) Rethinking Substance Abuse. New York: Guilford Press.

Koob GF (2009) Neurological substrates for the dark side of compulsivity in addiction. Neuropharmacology 56: 18–31.

Koob GF (2013) Neurobiological mechanisms of drug addiction: An introduction. In Milner P (ed.) Biological Research on Addiction. Vol. 2. New York: Academic Press.

Koob GF, Le Moal M (1997) Drug abuse: Hedonichomeostatic dysregulation. Science 278: 52–58.

Koob GF, Ahmed SH, Boutrel B, et al. (2004) Neurobiological mechanisms in the transition from drug use to drug dependence. Neuroscience and Biobehavioral Reviews 27: 739–749.

Koob GF, Arends MA, Le Moal M (2014) Drugs, Addiction, and the Brain. Waltham, MA: Academic Press.

Koob GF, Le Moal M (2001) Drug addiction, dysregulation of reward, and allostasis. Neuropsychopharmacology 24: 97–129.

Koob GF, Le Moal M (2006) Neurobiology of Addiction. New York: Academic Press.

Koob GF, Volkow ND (2010) Neurocircuitry of addiction. Neuropsychopharmacology 35: 217–238.

Koopmans JR, Slutske WS, van Baal GCM, et al. (1999) The influence of religion on alcohol use initiation: Evidence for genetic X environment interaction. Behavior Genetics 29: 445–453.

Kopetz CE, Lejuez CW, Wiers RW, et al. (2013) Motivation and self-regulation in addiction: A call for convergence. Perspectives in Psychological Science 8: 3024.

Kosten TR, Domingo CB, Shorter SP, et al. (2014) Vaccine for cocaine dependence:

A randomized double-blind placebo-controlled efficacy trial. Drug and Alcohol Dependence **140**: 42–47.

Kosten TR, Gorelick DA (2002) The Lexington narcotic farm. American Journal of Psychiatry **159**: 1–11.

Kovacs EJ, Messingham KA (2002) Influence of alcohol and gender on immune response. Alcohol Research and Health **26**: 257–260.

Kozlowski LT, Wilkinson DA, Skinner W, et al. (1989) Comparing tobacco cigarette dependence with other drug dependencies: Greater or equal "difficulty of quitting" and "urges to use," but less "pleasure" from cigarettes. Journal of the American Medical Association **261**: 898–901.

Kranzler HR, Li T-K (2008) What is addiction? Alcohol Research and Health **31**: 93–95.

Kreek MJ (1987) Multiple drug abuse patterns and medical consequences. In Meltzer HY (ed.) Psychopharmacology: The Third Generation of Progress. New York: Raven Press.

Kreek MJ (2000) Methadone-related opioid agonist pharmacotherapy for heroin addiction. In Glick SD, Maisonneuve IB (eds.) New Medications for Drug Abuse. New York: New York Academy of Sciences.

Kreek MJ, Koob GF (1998) Drug dependence: Stress and dysregulation of brain reward pathways. Drug and Alcohol Dependence **51**: 23–47.

Kreek MJ, Nielsen DA, Butelman ER, et al. (2005) Genetic influences on impulsivity, risk-taking, stress responsivity and vulnerability to drug abuse and addiction. Nature Neuroscience **11**: 1450–1457.

Kreek MJ, Zhou Y, Butelman ER, et al. (2009) Opiate and cocaine addiction: From bench to clinic and back to the bench. Current Opinions in Pharmacology **9**: 74–80.

Kring AM, Davison GC, Neale JM, et al. (2007) Abnormal Psychology. 10th ed. Hoboken, NJ: John Wiley.

Kringelbach ML, Rolls ET (2004) The functional neuroanatomy of the human orbitofrontal cortex: Evidence from neuroimaging and neurophysiology. Progress in Neurobiology **72**: 341–372.

Krueger RF, Hicks BM, Patrick CJ, et al. (2002) Etiologic connections among substance dependence, antisocial behavior, and personality: Modeling the externalizing spectrum. Journal of Abnormal Psychology **111**: 411–412.

Krystal JH, Cramer JA, Krol WF, et al. (2001) Naltrexone in the treatment of alcohol dependence. Veterans Affairs Naltrexone Cooperative Study 425 Group. New England Journal of Medicine **345**: 1734–1739.

Ksir C, Hart CL (2016) Cannabis and psychosis: A critical overview of the relationship. Current Psychiatry Reports **18**: 11–18.

Kumari V, Sharma T (2002) Effects of typical and atypical antipsychotics on prepulse inhibition in schizophrenia: A critical evaluation of current evidence and directions for future research. Psychopharmacology **162**: 97–101.

Kunoe N, Lobmaier P, Ngo H, et al. (2012) Injectable and implantable sustained release naltrexone in the treatment of opioid addiction. British Journal of Clinical Pharmacology **77**: 264–271.

Kushner HI (2010) Toward a cultural biology of addiction. Biosocieties **5**: 8–24.

Lachman HM (2006) An overview of the genetics of substance use disorders. Current Psychiatry Reports **8**: 133–143.

Lader M (2011) Benzodiazepines revisited – will we ever learn? Addiction **106**: 2086–2109.

Lader M (2014) Benzodiazepine harm: How can it be reduced? British Journal of Clinical Pharmacology **77**: 295–301.

Lader M, Tylee A, Donoghue J (2009) Withdrawing benzodiazepines in primary care. CNS Drugs **23**: 19–34.

LaGasse LL, Derauf C, Smith LM, et al. (2012) Prenatal methamphetamine exposure and childhood behavior patterns at 3 and 5 years of age. Pediatrics **129**: 681–688.

Lago JA, Kosten TR (1994) Stimulant withdrawal. Addiction **89**: 1477–1481.

Lai HMX, Cleary M, Sitharthan T, et al. (2015) Prevalence of comorbid substance use, anxiety and mood disorders in epidemiological surveys, 1990–2014: A systematic review and meta-analysis. Drug and Alcohol Dependence **154**: 1–13.

Lalive AL, Rudolph U, Luscher C, et al. (2011) Is there a way to curb benzodiazepine addiction? Swiss Medical Weekly **141**: w13277.

Lam WKK, O'Farrell TJ, Birchler GR (2012) Family therapy techniques for substance abuse treatment. In Walters ST, Rotgers F (eds.) Treating Substance Abuse: Theory and Technique. New York: Guilford Press.

Lang AR, Patrick CJ, Stritzke WG (1999) Alcohol and emotional response: A multidimensional-multilevel analysis. In Leonard K, Blane H (eds.) Psychological Theories of Drinking and Alcoholism. 2nd ed. New York: Guilford Press.

Lange JE, Devos-Comby L, Moore RS, et al. (2011) Collegiate drinking groups: Characteristics, structure, and processes. Addiction Research and Theory **19**: 312–322.

Langelben DD, Ruparel K, Elman I, et al. (2008) Acute effect of methadone maintenance dose on brain fMRI response to heroin-related cues. American Journal of Psychiatry **165**: 390–394.

Larimer ME, Cronce JM, Lee CM, et al. (2004) Brief intervention in college settings. Alcohol Research and Health **28**: 94–104.

Larimer ME, Dillworth TM, Neighbors C, et al. (2012) Harm reduction for alcohol problems. In Marlatt GA, Larimer ME, Witkiewitz K (eds.) Harm Reduction: Pragmatic Strategies for Managing High-Risk Behaviors. 2nd ed. New York: Guilford Press.

Lasagna L, von Felsinger JM, Beecher HK (1955) Drug-induced mood changes in man: Observations on healthy subjects, chronically ill patients and "postaddicts." JAMA **157**: 1006–1020.

Lasser K, Boyd JW, Woolhandler S, et al. (2000) Smoking and mental illnes: A population-based prevalence study. JAMA **284**: 2606–2610.

Lattimer D, Goldberg J (1981) Flowers in the Blood: The Story of Opium. New York: Franklin Watts.

Laudet AB (2003) Attitudes and beliefs about 12-step groups among addiction treatment clients and clinicians:

Toward identifying obstacles to participation. Substance Use and Abuse **38**: 2017–2047.

Lawford CK (2009) Moments of Clarity: Voices from the Front Lines of Addiction and Recovery. New York: HarperCollins.

Lazareck S, Robinson J, Crum RM et al. (2012) A longitudinal investigation of the role of self-medication in the development of comorbid mood and drug use disorders. Journal of Clinical Psychiatry **73**: 588–593.

Le Foll B, Goldberg SR (2009) Effects of nicotine in experimental animals and humans: An update on addictive properties. Handbook of Experimental Pharmacology **192**: 335–367.

Lee D, Schroeder JR, Karschner EL, et al. (2014) Cannabis withdrawal in chronic, frequent cannabis smokers during sustained abstinence within a closed residential environment. American Journal of Addiction **23**: 234–242.

Lee H, Roh S, Kim DJ (2009) Alcohol-induced blackout. International Journal of Environmental Research and Public Health **6**: 2783–2792.

Lee MR, Sher KJ (2018) "Maturing out" of binge and problem drinking. Alcohol Research: Current Reviews **39**: 31–42.

Lee M, Silverman S, Hansen H, et al. (2011) A comprehensive review of opioid-induced hyperalgesia. Pain Physician **14**: 145–161.

Leeds J, Morgenstern J (1996) Psychoanalytic theories of substance abuse. In Rotgers F, Keller D, Morgenstern J (eds.) Treating Substance Abuse: Theory and Technique. New York: Guilford Press.

Leeds J, Morgenstern J (2003) Psychoanalytic theories of substance abuse. In Rotgers F, Morgenstern J, Walters ST (eds.) Treating Substance Abuse: Theory and Technique. 2nd ed. New York: Guilford Press.

Leeman RF, Grant JD, Potenza MN (2009) Behavioral and neurological foundations for the moral and legal implications of intoxication, addictive behaviors and disinhibition. Behavioral Sciences and the Law **27**: 237–259.

Leggio L, Kenna GA, Fenton M, et al. (2009) Typologies of alcohol dependence: From Jellinek to genetics and beyond. Neuropsychology Review **19**: 115–129.

Leiber CS (2004) Alcoholic fatty liver: Its pathogenesis and mechanism of progression to inflammation and fibrosis. Alcohol **34**: 9–19.

Leigh BC, Stacy AW (2004) Alcohol expectancies and drinking in different age groups. Addiction **99**: 215–227.

Leonard K (1989) The impact of explicit and implicit nonagressive cues on aggression in sober and intoxicated males. Personality and Social Psychology Bulletin **15**: 390–400.

Lerman C, Audrain-McGovern J (2011) Reinforcing effects of smoking: More than a feeling. Biological Psychiatry **67**: 699–701.

Leshner A (2003) Understanding drug addiction: Insights from the research. In Graham A, Schultz T, Mayo-Smith M, et al. (eds.) Principles of Addiction Medicine. 3rd ed. Chevy Chase, MD: American Society of Addiction Medicine.

Leung KS, Cottler LB (2008) Ecstasy and other club drugs: A review of recent epidemiological studies. Current Opinions in Psychiatry **21**: 234–241.

Leventhal AM, Kahler CS, Ray LA, et al. (2009) Refining the depression–nicotine dependence link: Patterns of depressive symptoms in psychiatric outpatients with current, past, and no history of nicotine dependence. Addictive Behaviors **34**: 297–303.

Leventhal AM, Strong DR, Kirkpatrick MG, et al. (2015) Association of electronic cigarette use with initiation of combustible tobacco product smoking in early adolescence. JAMA **314**: 700–707.

Levey DF, Le-Niculescu H, Frank J, et al. (2014) Genetic risk prediction and the neurobiological understanding of alcoholism. Translational Psychiatry **4**: e391.

Levin ED, McClernon FJ, Rezvani AH (2006) Nicotinic effects on cognitive function: Behavioral characterization, pharmacological specification, and anatomic localization. Psychopharmacology **184**: 523–539.

Levin ED, Simon BB, Conners CK (2000) Nicotine effects and attention deficit disorder. In Newhouse P, Piasecki M (eds.) Nicotine in Psychiatry: Psychopathology and Emerging Therapeutics. Washington, DC: American Psychiatric Press.

Levine A, Huang Y, Drisaldi B (2011) Molecular mechanism for a gateway drug: Epigenetic changes initiated by nicotine prime gene expression by cocaine. Science Translational Medicine **3**: 107–109.

Lewis BA, Singer LT, Short EJ, et al. (2004) Four-year language outcomes of children exposed to cocaine *in utero*.

Neurotoxicology and Teratology **26**: 617–627.

Lewis MD (2011) Dopamine and the neural "now": Essay and review of Addiction – a disorder of choice. Perspectives on Psychological Science **6**: 150–155.

Lewis MD (2015) The Biology of Desire: Why Addiction Is Not a Disease. New York: Public Affairs.

Lewis MD (2017) Addiction and the brain: Development, not disease. Neuroethics **10**: 7–18.

Li CH, Lemaire S, Yamishiro D, et al. (1976) The synthesis and opiate activity of beta-endorphin. Biochemical and Biophysical Research Communications **71**: 19–25.

Li CR, Sinha R (2008) Inhibitory control and emotional stress regulation: Neuroimaging evidence for frontal-limbic dysfunction in psycho-stimulant addiction. Neuroscience and Biobehavioral Reviews **32**: 581–597.

Li D, Sham PC, Owen MJ, et al. (2006) Meta-analysis shows significant association between dopamine system genes and attention deficit hyperactivity disorder (ADHD). Human Molecular Genetics **15**: 2276–2284.

Li HL (1975) The origin and use of cannabis in Eastern Asia: Their linguistic-cultural implications. In Rubin V (ed.) Cannabis and Culture. The Hague: Mouton.

Li MD (2006) The genetics of nicotine dependence. Current Psychiatry Reports **8**: 158–164.

Li MD, Cheng R, Ma JZ, et al. (2003) A meta-analysis of estimated genetic and environmental effects on smoking behavior in male and female adult twins. Addiction **98**: 23–31.

Li MD, Ma JZ, Beuten J (2004) Progress in searching for susceptibility loci and genes for smoking-related behavior. Clinical Genetics **66**: 382–392.

Licata SC, Mashhoon Y, MacLean RR, et al. (2011) Modest abuse-related subjective effects of zolpidem in drug-naïve volunteers. Behavioral Pharmacology **22**: 160–166.

Lichtman AH, Martin BR (2006) Understanding the pharmacology and physiology of cannabis dependence. In Roffman RA, Stephens RS (eds.) Cannabis Dependence: Its Nature, Consequences and Treatment. Cambridge: Cambridge University Press.

Lieber CS (1997) Ethanol metabolism, cirrhosis and alcoholism. Clinica Chimica Acta **257**: 59–84.

Lieber CS (2004) Alcoholic fatty liver: Its pathogenesis and mechanism of progression to inflammation and fibrosis. Alcohol **34**: 9–19.

Liechti ME, Vollenweider FX (2001) Which neuroreceptors mediate the subjective effects of MDMA in humans? A summary of mechanistic studies. Human Psychopharmacology **16**: 589–598.

Lin JY, Roman C, Reilly S (2009) Insular cortex and consummatory successive negative contrast in the rat. Behavioral Neuroscience **123**: 810–814.

Lindesmith AR (1940) Dope fiend mythology. Journal of Criminal Law and Criminology **33**: 199–208.

Linehan MM (1993) Cognitive-Behavioral Treatment of Borderline Personality Disorder. New York: Guilford Press.

Lingford-Hughes A, Acton P, Gacinovic S, et al. (1998) Reduced levels of GABA-A benzodiazepine receptor in alcohol dependency in the absence of grey matter atrophy. British Journal of Psychiatry **173**: 116–122.

Lingford-Hughes A, Nutt DJ (2001) Neuropharmacology of ethanol and alcohol dependence. In Heather N, Peters TJ, Stockwell T (eds.) International Handbook of Alcohol Dependence and Problems. Chichester, UK: John Wiley.

Link B, Phelan J, Bresnahan M, et al. (1999) Public conceptions of mental illness: Labels, causes, dangerousness, and social distance. American Journal of Public Health **89**: 1328–1333.

Lintzeris N, Mitchell TB, Bond AJ, et al. (2007) Pharmacodynamics of diazepam co-administered with buprenorphine or methadone under high dose conditions in opioid dependent patients. Drug and Alcohol Dependence **9**: 187–194.

Lipari RN, Hughes A (2015) *The NSDUH Report: Trends in Heroin Use in the United States – 2002 to 2013.* Rockville, MD: Substance Abuse and Mental Health Services Administration, Center for Behavioral Health Statistics and Quality.

Lister JJ, Milosevic A, Ledgerwood DM (2015) Personality traits of problem gamblers with and without alcohol dependence. Addictive Behavior **47**: 48–54.

Lister RG, Gorenstein C, Fisher-Flowers D (1991) Dissociation of the acute effects of alcohol on implicit and explicit memory processes. Neuropsychologia **29**: 1205–1212.

Litt MD, Cooney NL, Morse P (2000) Reactivity to alcohol-related stimuli in the laboratory and in the field: Predictors of craving in alcoholics. Addiction **95**: 889–900.

Liu J, Schulteis G (2004) Brain reward deficits accompany naloxone-precipitated withdrawal from acute opioid dependence. Pharmacology, Biochemistry, and Behavior **79**: 101–108.

Lo S, Heishman SJ, Raley H, et al. (2011) Tobacco craving in smokers with and without schizophrenia. Schizophrenia Research **127**: 241–245.

Logan BA, Brown MS, Hayes MJ (2013) Neonatal abstinence syndrome: Treatment and pediatric outcomes. Clinical Obstetrics and Gynecology **56**: 186–192.

Logan BK, Fligner CL, Haddix T (1998) Cause and manner of death in fatalities involving methamphetamine. American Journal of Psychiatry **43**: 28–34.

Logrip ML, Zorrilla EP, Koob GF (2012) Stress modulation of drug self-administration: Implications for addiction comorbidity with post-traumatic stress disorder. Neuropharmacology **62**: 552–564.

Loiselle M, Fuqua WR (2007) Alcohol's effects on women's risk detection in a date-rape vignette. Journal of American Collegiate Health **55**: 261–266.

Lopez-Quintero C, Perez de los Cobos J, Hasin DS, et al. (2011) Probability and predictors of transition from first-use to dependence on nicotine, alcohol, cannabis and cocaine: Results of the National Epidemiological Survey on Alcohol and Related Conditions (NESARC). Drug and Alcohol Dependence **115**: 120–130.

Lord JA, Waterfield AA, Hughes J, et al. (1977) Endogenous opioid peptides: Multiple agonists and receptors. Nature **267**: 495–499.

Lorenzetti V, Lubman DI, Whittle S (2010) Structural MRI findings in cannabis users: What do we know? Substance Use and Misuse **45**: 1787–1808.

Lott DC, Kim SJ, Cook EH, et al. (2005) Dopamine transporter gene associated with diminished subjective response to amphetamine. Neuropsychopharmacology **30**: 602–609.

Lovinger DM (1993) Excitotoxicity and alcohol-related brain damage. Alcoholism: Clinical and Experimental Research **17**: 19–27.

Lovinger DM, White G (1991) Ethanol potentiation of 5-hydroxytryptamine-3 receptor-mediated ion current in neuroblastoma cells and isolated adult mammalian neurons. Molecular Pharmacology **40**: 263–270.

Lowman C, Hunt WA, Litten RZ, et al. (2000) Research perspectives on alcohol craving: An overview. Addiction **95**(Suppl. 2): S45–S54.

Luck S, Hendrik J (2004) The alarming trend of substance abuse in anesthesia providers. Journal of PeriAnesthesia Nursing **19**: 308–311.

Ludlow FH (1857) The Hasheesh Eater: Being Passages from the Life of a Pythagorean. New York: Harper.

Luo X, Kranzler HR, Zuo L, et al. (2005) *CHRM2* gene predisposes to alcohol dependence, drug dependence and affective disorders: results from an extended case-control structured association study. Human Molecular Genetics **14**: 2421–2434.

Lynch WJ, Sofuoglu M (2010) Role of progesterone in nicotine addiction: Evidence from initiation to relapse. Experimental and Clinical Psychopharmacology 18: 451–461.

Lyvers M (2000) "Loss of control" in alcoholism and drug addiction: A neuroscientific interpretation. Experimental and Clinical Psychopharmacology 8: 225–249.

MacDonald T, MacDonald G, Zanna M, et al. (2000) Alcohol, sexual arousal, and intentions to use condoms in young men: Applying alcohol myopia theory to risky sexual behavior. Health Psychology 19: 290–298.

MacDonald T, Zanna M, Fong G (1995) Decision-making in altered states: Effects of alcohol on attitudes toward drinking and driving. Journal of Personality and Social Psychology 68: 973–985.

Maceira AM, Ripoli C, Cosin-Sales J, et al. (2014) Long-term effects of cocaine on the heart assessed by cardiovascular magnetic resonance at 3T. Journal of Cardiovascular Magnetic Resonance 16: 26–34.

Mackie K, Stella N (2006) Cannabinoid receptors and endocannabinoids: Evidence for new players. AAPS Journal 8: E298.

MacKillop J, Menges DP, McGeary JE, et al. (2007) Effects of craving and DRD4 VNTR genotype on the relative value of alcohol: An initial human laboratory study. Behavioral and Brain Functions 3: 11–17.

Macleod J, Oakes R, Copello A, et al. (2004) Psychological and social sequelae of cannabis and other illicit drug use by young people: A systematic review of longitudinal, general population studies. Lancet 363: 1579–1588.

Macy B (2018) Dopesick: Dealers, Doctors, and the Drug Company That Addicted America. New York: Little, Brown.

Maddux JE, Winstead BA (2005) Psychopathology: Foundations for a Contemporary Understanding. Mahwah, NJ: Lawrence Erlbaum.

Maes HH, Neale MC (2009) Genetic modeling of tobacco use behavior and trajectories. In Swain GE, Baker TB, Chassin L, et al. (eds.) Phenotypes and Endophenotypes: Foundations for Genetic Studies of Nicotine Use and Dependence. NCI Tobacco Control Monograph Series 20. Bethesda, MD: US Department of Health and Human Services, National Institutes of Health.

Maes HH, Sullivan PF, Bulik CM, et al. (2004) A twin study of genetic and environmental influences on tobacco initiation, regular tobacco use and nicotine dependence. Psychological Medicine 34: 1251–1261.

Maggs JL, Schulenberg JE (2004/2005) Trajectories of alcohol use during the transition to adulthood. Alcohol Research and Health 28: 195–204.

Mahoney JJ, Kalechstein AD, De La Garza R, et al. (2008) Presence and persistence of psychotic symptoms in cocaine- versus methamphetamine-dependent participants. American Journal of Addiction 17: 83–98.

Maisel NC, Blodgett JC, Wilbourne PL, et al. (2013) Meta-analysis of naltrexone and acamprosate for treating alcohol use disorders: When are these medications most helpful? Addiction 108: 275–293.

Maisto SA, Krenek M (2009) History and current substance use. In Miller PM (ed.) Evidence-Based Addiction Treatment. New York: Academic Press.

Maldonado R, Valverde O, Berrendero F (2006) Involvement of the endocannabinoid system in drug addiction. Trends in Neuroscience **29**: 225–232.

Malin DH (2001) Nicotine dependence: Studies with a laboratory model. Pharmacology, Biochemistry, and Behavior **70**: 551–559.

Malin DH, Goyarzu P (2009) Rodent models of the nicotine withdrawal syndrome. Handbook of Experimental Pharmacology **192**: 401–434.

Malinen H, Hyytia P (2008) Ethanol self-administration is regulated by CB1 receptors in the nucleus accumbens and ventral tegmental area in alcohol-preferring AA rats. Alcoholism: Clinical and Experimental Research **32**: 1976–1983.

Manchikanti L, Helm S, Fellows B, et al. (2012) Opioid epidemic in the United States. Pain Physician **15**: ES9.

Mansour A, Fox CA, Akil H, et al. (1995) Opioid-receptor mRNA expression in the rat CNS: Anatomical and functional implications. Trends in Neuroscience **18**: 22–29.

Manthey L, van Veen T, Giltay EJ, et al. (2011) Correlates of (inappropriate) benzodiazepine use: the Netherlands study of Depression and Anxiety (NESDA). British Journal of Clinical Pharmacology **71**: 263–272.

Margolis J, Clorfene R (1969) A Child's Garden of Grass. New York: Pocket Books.

Marinchak JS, Morgan TJ (2012) Behavioral treatments techniques for psychoactive substance use disorders. In Walters ST, Rotgers F (eds.) Treating Substance Abuse: Theory and Technique. New York: Guilford Press.

Marlatt GA (1996) Harm reduction: Come as you are. Addictive Behaviors **21**: 779–788.

Marlatt GA, Gordon JR (1985) Relapse Prevention: Maintenance Strategies in the Treatment of Addictive Behaviors. New York: Guilford Press.

Marlatt GA, Witkiewitz K (2005) Relapse prevention for alcohol and drug problems. In Marlatt GA, Donovan DM (eds.) Relapse Prevention: Maintenance Strategies in the Treatment of Addictive Behaviors. 2nd ed. New York: Guilford Press.

Marsden J (2009) The long road to pharmacotherapies for stimulant dependence. Addiction **104**: 234–240.

Marshall EJ, Edwards G, Taylor C (1994) Mortality in men with drinking problems: A 20-year follow-up. Addiction **89**: 1293–1298.

Martin CS (2008) Timing of alcohol and other drug use. Alcohol Research and Health **31**: 96–98.

Martin CS, Chung T, Langenbucher JW (2008) How should we revise diagnostic criteria for substance use disorders in the DSM-V? Journal of Abnormal Psychology **117**: 561–575.

Martin CS, Earleywine M, Musty RE, et al. (1993) Development and validation of the Biphasic Alcohol Effects Scale. Alcoholism: Clinical and Experimental Research **17**: 140–146.

Martin CS, Fillmore MT, Chung T, et al. (2006) Multidisciplinary perspectives on impaired control over substance use.

Alcoholism: Clincal and Experimental Research **30**: 265–271.

Martin ED, Sher KJ (1994) Family history of alcoholism, alcohol use disorders and the five-factor model of personality. Journal of Studies on Alcohol **55**: 81–90.

Martin PR, Arria AM, Fischer G, et al. (2009) Psychopharmacologic management of opioid-dependent women during pregnancy. American Journal of Addiction **18**: 148–156.

Martin PR, Singleton CK, Hiller-Sturmhofel S (2003) The role of thiamine deficiency in alcoholic brain diseases. Alcohol Research and Health **27**: 134–142.

Martin S (2009) Improving diagnosis worldwide. Monitor on Psychology **40**: 62–63.

Martinez D, Broft A, Foltin RW, et al. (2004) Cocaine dependence and D2 receptor availability in the functional subdivisions of the striatum: Relationship with cocaine-seeking behavior. Neuropsychopharmacology **29**: 1190–1202.

Martins SS, Keyes KM, Storr CL, et al. (2009) Pathways between nonmedical opioid use/dependence and psychiatric disorders: Results from the National Epidemiological Survey on Alcohol and Related Conditions. Drug and Alcohol Dependence **103**: 16–24.

Masten AS, Faden VB, Zucker RA, et al. (2009) A developmental perspective on underage alcohol use. Alcohol Research and Health **32**: 3–15.

Matochik J, London E, Eldreth D, et al. (2003) Frontal cortical tissue composition in abstinent cocaine abusers: A magnetic resonance imaging study. Neuroimage **19**: 1095–1102.

Matteliano D, St. Marie BJ, Oliver J (2014) Adherence monitoring with chronic opioid therapy for persistent pain: A biopsychosocial-spiritual approach to mitigate risk. Pain Management Nursing **15**: 391–405.

Matthews AJ, Bruno R (2010) An investigation of factors associated with depressive symptoms among a sample of regular ecstasy consumers. Neuropsychobiology **61**: 215–222.

Matthews M, Nigg JT, Fair DA (2014) Attention deficit hyperactivity disorder. Current Topics in Behavioral Neuroscience **16**: 235–266.

May PA, Tabachnick BG, Gossage JP, et al. (2013) Maternal factors predicting cognitive and behavioral characteristics of children with fetal alcohol spectrum disorders. Journal of Developmental and Behavioral Pediatrics **34**: 314–325.

Mayo-Smith MF (2003) Management of alcohol intoxication and withdrawal. In Graham AW, Schultz TK, Mayo-Smith MF, et al. (eds.) Principles of Addiction Medicine. 3rd ed. Chevy Chase, MD: American Society of Addiction Medicine.

McAuliffe WE (1975) A second look at first effects: The subjective effects of opiates on non-addicts. Journal of Drug Issues **5**: 369–399.

McBride WJ, Li TK (1998) Animal models of alcoholism: Neurobiology of high alcohol-drinking behavior. Critical Reviews in Neurobiology **12**: 339–369.

McCabe SE, Boyd CJ, Teter CJ (2009) Subtypes of nonmedical prescription drug misuse. Drug and Alcohol Dependence **102**: 63–70.

McCabe SE, Cranford JA (2012) Motivational subtypes of nonmedical use of prescription medications: Results from a national study. Journal of Adolescent Health 51: 445–452.

McCabe SE, Cranford JA, Morales M, et al. (2006) Simultaneous and concurrent polydrug use of alcohol and prescription drugs: Prevalence, correlates, and consequences. Journal of Studies on Alcohol 67: 529–537.

McCarthy DE, Curtin JJ, Piper ME, et al. (2010) Negative reinforcement: Possible clinical implications of an integrative model. In Kassel JD (ed.) Substance Abuse and Emotion. Washington, DC: American Psychological Association.

McClave AK, Hogue CJ, Brunner LR, et al. (2010) Cigarette smoking women of reproductive age who use oral contraceptives: Results from the 2002 and 2004 behavioral risk factor surveillance systems. Women's Health Issues 20: 380–385.

McCord W, McCord J (1960) Origins of Alcoholism. Stanford, CA: Stanford University Press.

McCowan C, Kidd B, Fahey T (2009) Factors associated with mortality in Scottish patients receiving methadone in primary care: Retrospective cohort study. British Medical Journal 338: b2225.

McCrady B (2006) Family and other close relationships. In Miller WR, Carroll KM (eds.) Rethinking Substance Abuse. New York: Guilford Press.

McCrady B, Epstein E (2008) Overcoming Alcohol Problems: A Couples-Focused Program Therapist Guide. New York: Oxford University Press.

McCrae RR, Costa PT (1990) Personality in Adulthood. New York: Guilford Press.

McDonald J, Schleifer L, Richards JB, et al. (2003) Effects of THC on behavioral measures of impulsivity in humans. Neuropsychopharmacology 28: 1356–1365.

McGilveray IJ (2005) Pharmacokinetics of cannabinoids. Pain Research and Management 10(Suppl. A): 15A–22A.

McGregor C, Srisurapanont M, Jittiwutkarn J, et al. (2005) The nature, time course and severity of methamphetamine withdrawal. Addiction 100: 1320–1329.

McGue M (1999) Behavioral genetic models of alcoholism and drinking. In Leonard KE, Blane HT (eds.) Psychological Theories of Drinking and Alcoholism. 2nd ed. New York: Guilford Press.

McGue M, Iacono WG (2005) The association of early adolescent problem behavior with adult psychopathology. American Journal of Psychiatry 162: 1118–1124.

McGue M, Iacono WG (2008) The adolescent origins of substance abuse disorders. International Journal of Methods of Psychiatric Research 17(Suppl. 1): S30–S38.

McGue M, Pickens RW, Svikis DS (1992) Sex and age effects on the inheritance of alcohol problems: A twin study. Journal of Abnormal Psychology 101: 3–17.

McGue M, Slutske WS, Iacono WG (1999) Personality and substance use disorders: II. Alcoholism vs. drug use disorders. Journal of Consulting and Clinical Psychology **67**: 394–404.

McKeganey N, Neale J, Lloyd C, et al. (2007) Sociology and substance use. In Nutt D, Robbins TW, Stimson GV, et al. (eds.) Drugs and the Future: Brain Science, Addiction and Society. New York: Academic Press.

McKim WA, Hancock SD (2013) Drugs and Behavior: An Introduction to Behavioral Pharmacology. 7th ed. Upper Saddle River, NJ: Prentice Hall.

McLellan AT (2010) What is recovery? Revisiting the Betty Ford Institute consensus panel definition. Journal of Social Work Practice in the Addictions **10**: 109–113.

McLellan AT, Kushner H, Metzger D (1992) The fifth edition of the Addiction Severity Index. Journal of Substance Abuse Treatment **9**: 199–213.

McLellan AT, Meyers K (2004) Contemporary addiction treatment: A review of systems problems for adults and adolescents. Biological Psychiatry **56**: 764–770.

McLellan AT, Skipper GS, Campbell M, et al. (2008) Five year outcomes in a cohort study of physicians treated for substance use disorders in the United States. British Medical Journal **337**: a2038.

McMillen BA, Davis BJ, Williams HL, et al. (2005) Periadolescent nicotine exposure causes heterologous sensitization to cocaine reinforcement. European Journal of Pharmacology **509**: 161–164.

McNair D, Lorr M, Droppleman L (1992) EITS Manual for Profile of Mood States. San Diego, CA: Educational and Industrial Testing Service.

McNair DM, Lorr M, Droppleman LF (1971) Manual: Profile of Mood States (POMS). San Diego, CA: Educational and Industrial Testing Service.

McVay M, Copeland AL (2011) Smoking cessation in peri- and post-menopausal women: A review. Experimental and Clinical Psychopharmacology **19**: 192–202.

Mechoulam R (2012) Cannabis – a valuable drug that deserves better treatment. Mayo Clinic Proceedings **87**: 107–109.

Mechoulam R, Parker LA (2013) The endocannabinoid system and the brain. Annual Review of Psychology **64**: 21–47.

Mehlenbeck R, Spirito A, Barnett N, et al. (2003) Behavioral factors: Substance use. In Spirito A, Overholser JC (eds.) Evaluating and Treating Adolescent Suicide Attempters: From Research to Practice. San Diego, CA: Academic Press.

Mehra R, Moore BA, Crothers K, et al. (2006) The association between marijuana and lung cancer. Archives of Internal Medicine **166**: 1359–1367.

Mehta AK, Ticku MK (1988) Ethanol potentiation of GABAergic transmission in cultured spinal cord neurons involves gamma-aminobutyric acidA-gated chloride channels. Journal of Pharmacology and Experimental Therapeutics **246**: 558–564.

Meier MH, Avshalom C, Ambler A, et al. (2012) Persistent cannabis users show neuropsychological decline from childhood to midlife. Proceedings of the National Academy of Sciences of the USA **109**: E2657.

Melchoir CL (1990) Conditioned tolerance provides protection against ethanol lethality. Pharmacology Biochemistry and Behavior 37: 205–206.

Melkonian AJ, Hunt LS (2018) The effects of alcohol intoxication on young adult women's identification of risk for sexual assault: A systematic review. Psychology of Addictive Behaviors 32: 162–172.

Mello NK (2010) Hormones, nicotine, and cocaine: Clinical studies. Hormones and Behavior 58: 57–71.

Mendelson J, Uemura N, Harris D (2006) Human pharmacology of the meth-amphetamine stereoisomers. Clinical Pharmacology and Therapeutics 80: 402–420.

Mendola A, Gibson RL (2016) Addiction, 12-step programs, and evidentiary standards for ethically and clinically sound treatment recommendations: What should clinicians do? AMA Journal of Ethics 18: 646–655.

Mendelson W (2011) Hypnotic medications: Mechanisms of action and pharma-cologic effects. In Kryger MH, Roth T, Dement WC (eds.) Principles and Practices of Sleep Medicine. 5th ed. St. Louis, MO: Elsevier.

Mercer RE (2008) Worse than Heroin. New York: Lulu Press.

Meredith CW, Jaffe C, Ang-Lee K, et al. (2005) Implications of chronic meth-amphetamine use: A literature review. Harvard Review of Psychiatry 13: 141–154.

Merikangas KR, Risch N (2003) Will the genomics revolution revolutionize psy-chiatry? American Journal of Psychiatry 160: 625–635.

Merikangas KR, Stolar M, Stevens DE, et al. (1998) Familial transmission of substance use disorders. Archives of General Psychiatry 55: 973–979.

Merlo LJ, Singhakant S, Cummings SM, et al. (2013) Reasons for misuse of pre-scription medication among physicians undergoing monitoring by a physician health program. Journal of Addictive Medicine 7: 3459–3465.

Merrill JE, Carey KB (2016) Drinking over the lifespan: Focus on college ages. Alcohol Research: Current Reviews 38: 103–114.

Messina ES, Tyndale FR, Sellers EM (1997) A major role for CYP2A6 in nicotine C-oxidation by human liver micro-somes. Journal of Pharmacology and Experimental Theraperutics 282: 1608–1614.

Metrik J, Kahler CW, Reynolds B, et al. (2012) Balanced placebo design with marijuana: Pharmacological and expectancy effects on impulsivity and risk-taking. Psychopharmacology 223: 489–499.

Mets MA, de Vries JM, de Senerpont Domis LM, et al. (2011) Next-day effects of ramelteon (8 mg), zopiclone (7.5 mg), and placebo on highway driving performance, and mood in healthy adults subjects. Sleep 34: 1327–1334.

Metzner R (2005) Psychedelic, psychoac-tive, and addictive drugs and states of consciousness. In Earleywine M (ed.) Mind-Altering Drugs. New York: Oxford University Press.

Meyer JS, Quenzer LF (2013) Psycho-pharmacology: Drugs, the Brain, and Behavior. 2nd ed. Sunderland, MA: Sinauer.

Meyer JS, Quenzer LF (2018) Psychopharmacology: Drugs, the Brain, and Behavior. 3rd ed. Sunderland, MA: Sinauer.

Midanik LT, Tam TW, Welsner C (2007) Concurrent and simultaneous drug and alcohol use: Results of the 2000 national alcohol survey. Drug and Alcohol Dependence **90**: 72–80.

Miller B, Windle M (1990) Alcoholism, Problem Drinking, and Driving While Impaired. In Wilson RJ, Mann RE (eds.) Drinking and Driving: Advances in Research and Prevention. New York: Guilford Press.

Miller FG, Lazowiski LE (1999) The Adult SASSI-3 Manual. Springville, IN: SASSI Institute.

Miller FG, Lazowiski LE (2001) The Adolescent SASSI-2 Manual: Identifying Substance Use Disorders. Springville, IN: SASSI Institute.

Miller PM (2009) Evidence-Based Addiction Treatment. Burlington, MA: Academic Press.

Miller WR (1976) Alcoholism scales and objective assessment methods: A review. Psychological Bulletin **83**: 649–674.

Miller WR (2000) Rediscovering fire: Small interventions, large effects. Psychology of Addictive Behaviors **14**: 6–18.

Miller WR, Carroll KM (2006) Rethinking Substance Abuse: What the Science Shows, and What We Should Do about It. New York: Guilford Press.

Miller WR, Forcehimes AA, Zweben A (2011) Enhancing motivation for change. In Treating Addiction: A Guide for Professionals. New York: Guilford Press.

Miller WR, Forcehimes AA, Zweben A (2019) Treating Addiction: A Guide for Professionals. 2nd ed. New York: Guilford Press.

Miller WR, Rollnick (2002) Motivational Interviewing: Preparing People for Change. 2nd ed. New York: Guilford Press.

Miller WR, Walters ST, Bennet ME (2001) How effective is alcoholism treatment in the United States? Journal of Studies on Alcohol **62**: 211–220.

Miller WR, Westerbery VS, Waldron HB (1995) Evaluating alcohol problems in adults and adolescents. In Hester RK, Miller WR (eds.) Handbook of Alcoholism Treatment Approaches: Effective Alternatives. 2nd ed. Boston: Allyn and Bacon.

Mills KI, Tesson M, Ross J, et al. (2006) Trauma, PTSD, and substance use disorders: Findings from the Australian National Survey of Mental Health and Well-Being. American Journal of Psychiatry **163**: 652–658.

Mineur YS, Picciotto MR (2008) Genetics of nicotinic acetylcholine receptors: Relevance to nicotine addiction. Biochemical Pharmacology **75**: 323–333.

Minozzi S, Amato L, Davoli M (2012) Development of dependence following treatment with opioid analgesics for pain relief: A systematic review. Addiction **108**: 688–698.

Mintzer MZ, Griffiths RR (2005) An abuse liability comparison of flunitrazepam and triazolam in sedative drug abusers. Behavioral Pharmacology **16**: 579–584.

Mirin SM, Meyer RE, McNamee B (1976) Psychopathology and mood during heroin use. Archives of General Psychiatry **33**: 1503–1508.

Misra LK, Kofoed L, Oesterheld JR, et al. (2000) Olanzapine treatment of methamphetamine psychosis. Journal of Clinical Psychopharmacology **20**: 393–394.

Missale C, Nash SR, Robinson SW, et al. (1998) Dopamine receptors: From structure to function. Physiological Review **78**: 189–225.

Mistry CJ, Bawor M, Desai D, et al. (2014) Genetics of opioid dependence: A review of the genetic contribution to opioid dependence. Current Psychiatry Reviews **10**: 156–167.

Mitchell JM, Fields HL, D'Esposito M, et al. (2005) Impulsive responding in alcoholics. Alcoholism: Clinical and Experimental Research **29**: 2158–2169.

Moallem NR, Ray LA (2012) Dimensions of impulsivity among heavy drinkers, smokers, and heavy drinking smokers: Singular and combined effects. Addictive Behavior **37**: 871–874.

Mochly-Rosen D, Zakhari S (2010) Focus on: The cardiovascular system. What did we learn from the French (paradox)? Alcohol Research and Health **33**: 76–86.

Moeller FG, Dougherty DM (2001) Antisocial personality disorder, alcohol, and aggression. Alcohol Research and Health **25**: 5–11.

Mohler H, Fritschy JM, Crestani F, et al. (2004) Specific GABA(A) circuits in brain development and therapy. Biochemical Pharmacology **68**: 1685–1690.

Mohler H, Fritschy JM, Rudolph U (2002) A new benzodiazepine pharmacology. Journal of Pharmacology and Experimental Therapeutics **300**: 2–8.

Mojtabai R, Crum RM (2013) Perceived unmet need for alcohol and drug use

treatments and future use of services: Results from a longitudinal study. Drug and Alcohol Dependence **127**: 59–64.

Molina PE, Happel KI, Zhang P, et al. (2010) Focus on: Alcohol and the immune system. Alcohol Research and Health **33**: 97–108.

Montes KS, Witkiewitz K, Andersson C, et al. (2017) Trajectories of positive alcohol expectancies and drinking: An examination of young adults in the US and Sweden. Addictive Behavior **73**: 74–80.

Moolchan ET, Radzius A, Epstein DH, et al. (2002) The Fagerstrom Test for Nicotine Dependence and the Diagnostic Interview Schedule: Do they diagnose the same smokers? Addictive Behaviors **27**: 101–113.

Mooney M, Sofuoglu M, Dudish-Poulsen S, et al. (2006) Preliminary observations of paranoia in a human laboratory study of cocaine. Addictive Behavior **31**: 1245–1251.

Moore BA, Budney AJ (2001) Tobacco smoking in marijuana dependent outpatients. Journal of Substance Abuse **13**: 585–598.

Moore TH, Zammit S, Lingford-Hughes A, et al. (2007) Cannabis use and risk of psychotic or affective mental health outcomes: A systematic review. Lancet **370**: 319–328.

Moos RH, Moos BS (2006a) Participation in treatment and Alcoholics Anonymous: A 16-year follow-up of initially untreated individuals. Journal of Clinical Psychology **62**: 735–750.

Moos RH, Moos BS (2006b) Rates and predictors of relapse after natural and treated remission from alcohol use disorders. Addiction **101**: 212–222.

Moran PB, Vuchinich S, Hall NK (2004) Associations between types of maltreatment and substance use during adolescence. Child Abuse and Neglect **28**: 565–574.

Morasco BJ, Turk DC, Donovan DM, et al. (2013) Risk for prescription opioid misuse among patients with a history of substance use disorder. Drug and Alcohol Dependence **127**: 193–199.

Morean ME, Kong G, Camenga DR, et al. (2015) High school students' use of electronic cigarettes to vaporize cannabis. Pediatrics **136**: 611–616.

Morean ME, Krishnan-Sarin S, O'Malley S (2018) Assessing nicotine dependence in adolescent E-cigarette users: The 4-item patient-reported outcomes measurement information system (PROMIS) nicotine dependence item bank for electronic cigarettes. Drug and Alcohol Dependence **188**: 60–63.

Morgan D, Grant KA, Gage HD, et al. (2002) Social dominance in monkeys: Dopamine D2 receptors and cocaine self-administration. Nature Neuroscience **5**: 169–174.

Morgan MJ (2000) Ecstasy (MDMA): A review of its possible persistent effects. Psychopharmacology **152**: 230–248.

Morgenstern J, Langenbucher EL, Labouvie E, et al. (1997) The comorbidity of alcoholism and personality disorders in a clinical population: Prevalence rates and relation to alcohol typology variables. Journal of Abnormal Psychology **106**: 74–84.

Morissette SB, Brown TA, Kamholz B, et al. (2006) Differences between smokers and nonsmokers with anxiety disorders. Journal of Anxiety Disorders **20**: 597–613.

Morissette SB, Tull MT, Gulliver SB, et al. (2007) Anxiety, anxiety disorders, tobacco use, and nicotine: A critical review of interrelationships. Psychological Bulletin **133**: 245–272.

Morley KC, Cornish JL, Faingold A, et al. (2017) Pharmacotherapeutic agents in the treatment of methamphetamine dependence. Expert Opinion in Investigating Drugs **26**: 563–578.

Morse SJ (2007) The non-problem of free will in forensic psychiatry and psychology. Behavioral Sciences and the Law **25**: 203–220.

Moshier SJ, McHugh K, Calkins AW, et al. (2012) The role of perceived belongingness to a drug subculture among opioid-dependent patients. Psychology of Addictive Behaviors **26**: 812–820.

Moskowitz H (2006) Commentary on variability among epidemiological studies of drugs and driving. Transportation Research Center Circular E-C096, pp. 36–40.

Moss HB, Chen CM, Yi HY (2007) Subtypes of alcohol dependence in a nationally representative sample. Drug and Alcohol Dependence **91**: 149–158.

Moss HB, Chen CM, Yi HY (2012) Measures of substance consumption among substance users, DSM-IV abusers, and those with DSM-IV dependence disorders in a nationally representative sample. Journal of Studies on Alcohol and Drugs **73**: 820–828.

Moyer A, Finney JW (2002) Outcomes for untreated individuals involved in randomized trials of alcohol treatment. Journal of Substance Abuse Treatment 23: 247–252.

Mueser KT, Drake RE, Turner W, et al. (2006) Comorbid substance use disorders and psychiatric disorders. In Miller WR, Carroll KM (eds.) Rethinking Substance Abuse: What the Science Shows, and What We Should Do about It. New York: Guilford Press.

Mueser KT, Noordsky DL, Drake RE, et al. (2003) Integrated Treatment for Dual Disorders. New York: Guilford Press.

Muhuri PK, Gfroerer JC, Davis C (2013) Associations of nonmedical pain reliever use and initiation of heroin use in the United States. CBHSQ Data Review, August.

Mulder RT (2002) Alcoholism and personality. Australian and New Zealand Journal of Psychiatry 36: 44–52.

Mulholland PJ, Chandler LJ (2007) The thorny side of addiction: Adaptive plasticity and dendritic spines. Scientific World Journal 7(S2): 9–21.

Mulia N, Ye Y, Zemore SE, et al. (2008) Social disadvantage, stress, and alcohol use among black, Hispanic, and white Americans: Findings from the 2005 US National Alcohol Survey. Journal of Studies on Alcohol and Drugs 69: 824–833.

Mullally A, Cleary BJ, Barry J, et al. (2011) Prevalence, predictors and perinatal outcomes of peri-conceptional alcohol exposure-retrospective cohort study in an urban obstetric population in Ireland. BMC Pregnancy and Childbirth 11: 27–34.

Mullen K, Hammersley R (2006) Attempted cessation of heroin use among men approaching mid-life. Drugs: Education, Prevention and Policy 13: 77–92.

Müller KW, Dreier M, Duven E, et al. (2017) Adding clinical validity to the statistical power of large-scale epidemiological surveys on internet addiction in adolescence: A combined approach to investigate psychopathology and development-specific personality traits associated with internet addiction. Journal of Clinical Psychiatry 78: 244–251.

Mulligan MK (2019) Genetic factors in cannabinoid use and dependence. Advances in Experimental Medical Biology 1162: 129–150.

Munafo MR, Black S (2007) Personality and smoking status: A longitudinal analysis. Nicotine and Tobacco Research 9: 397–404.

Munafo MR, Clark TG, Johnstone EC, et al. (2004) The genetic basis for smoking behavior: A review and meta-analysis. Nicotine and Tobacco Research 6: 583–598.

Munafo MR, Johnstone EC (2008) Genes and cigarette smoking. Addiction 103: 893–904.

Munafo MR, Zetteler JI, Clark TG (2007) Personality and smoking status: A meta-analysis. Nicotine and Tobacco Research 9: 405–413.

Murphy PN, Bruno R, Ryland I, et al. (2012) The effects of "ecstasy" (MDMA) on visuospatial memory performance: Findings from a systematic review with meta-analysis. Human Psychopharmacology 27: 113–138.

Murphy CN, MacKillop J, Martin RA, et al. (2017) Effects of Varenicline versus transdermal nicotine replacement therapy on cigarette demand on quit day in individuals with substance use disorders. Psychopharmacology **234**: 2443–2452.

Musgrave-Marquart D, Bromley SP, Dalley MB (1997) Personality, academic attribution, and substance abuse as predictors of academic achievement in college students. Journal of Social Behavior and Personality **12**: 501–511.

Musto D (1999) The American Disease: Origins of Narcotic Control. 3rd ed. New York: Oxford University Press.

Myers MG, Kelly JF (2006) Cigarette smoking among adolescents with alcohol and other drug use problems. Alcohol Research and Health **29**: 221–227.

Nader MA, Czoty PW (2005) PET imaging of dopamine D2 receptors in monkey models of cocaine abuse: Genetic predisposition versus environmental modulation. American Journal of Psychiatry **162**: 1473–1482.

Nader MA, Morgan D, Gage HD, et al. (2006) PET imaging of dopamine D2 receptors during chronic cocaine self-administration in monkeys. Nature Neuroscience **9**: 1050–1056.

Nahas GG (1973) Marijuana – Deceptive Weed. New York: Raven Press.

Naqvi NH, Bechara A (2010) The insula and drug addiction: An interoceptive view of pleasure, urges, and decision-making. Brain Structure and Function **214**: 435–450.

Naqvi NH, Bechara A (2009) The hidden island of addiction: The insula. Trends in Neuroscience 32: 56–67.

Naqvi NH, Rudrauf, DH, Bechara A (2007) Damage to the insula disrupts addiction to cigarette smoking. Science **315**: 531–534.

National Commission on Marihuana and Drug Abuse (1972) Marihuana: A Signal of Misunderstanding. Washington, DC: US Government Printing Office.

National Highway Traffic Safety Administration (2018) Traffic safety facts: 2017 traffic safety assessments – alcohol-impaired driving fatalities. Report DOT HS 811 016.

National Institute of Drug Abuse (2009) Principles of Drug Addiction Treatment: A Research-Based Guide. 2nd ed. Bethesda, MD: US Department of Health and Human Services.

National Institute of Drug Abuse (2016) NIDA Strategic Plan 2016–2020. http://drugabuse.gov.

National Institute of Drug Abuse (2017a) Addressing the opioid crisis means confronting socioeconomic disparities. www.drugabuse.gov.

National Institute of Drug Abuse (2017b) Monitoring the Future 2016 survey results. www.drugabuse.gov/related-topics/trends-statistics.

National Institute of Drug Abuse (2018) Prescription opioid use is a risk factor for heroin use. www.drugabuse.gov.

National Institute of Drug Abuse (2019a) Everything you need to know about methadone maintenance clinics. www.drugabuse.gov.

National Institute of Drug Abuse (2019b) Overdose death rates. www.drugabuse.gov.

National Institute of Drug Abuse (2020) Monitoring the Future survey. www.drugabuse.gov/related-topics/trends-statistics/monitoring-future.

National Institute on Alcohol Abuse and Alcoholism (2000) 10th Special Report to the U.S. Congress on Alcohol and Health. Rockville, MD: US Department of Health and Human Services.

National Institute on Alcohol Abuse and Alcoholism (2004) Task Force Report on Binge Drinking. Rockville, MD: US Department of Health and Human Services.

National Institute on Alcohol Abuse and Alcoholism (2005) Helping Patients Who Drink Too Much: A Clinician's Guide. Rockville, MD: National Institute on Alcohol Abuse and Alcoholism.

National Institute on Alcohol Abuse and Alcoholism (2010) Prevalence of Alcohol Use Disorders. www.niaaa.nih.gov/publications/brochures-and-fact-sheets.

Nauta W (1971) The problem of the frontal lobe: A reinterpretation. Journal of Psychiatric Research 8: 167–187.

Neale MC, Kendler KS (1995) Models of comorbidity for multifactorial disorders. American Journal of Human Genetics 57: 935–953.

Nealon-Woods MA, Ferrari JR, Jason LA (1995) Twelve-step program use among Oxford House residents: Spirituality or social support in sobriety? Journal of Substance Abuse 7: 311–318.

Neavyn MJ, Blohm E, Babu KM, et al. (2014) Medical marijuana and driving: A review. Journal of Medical Toxicology 10: 269–279.

Nelson CB, Wittchen HU (1998) Smoking and nicotine dependence: Results from a sample of 14- to 24-year-olds in Germany. European Addiction Research 2: S103–S112.

Nestler EJ (2002) Common molecular and cellular substrates of addiction and

memory. Neurobiology of Learning and Memory 78: 637–647.

Nestler EJ (2011) Hidden switches in the mind. Scientific American 305: 76–83.

Nestler EJ (2013) Cellular basis of memory for addiction. Dialogues in Clinical Neuroscience 15: 431–443.

Newlin DB, Thomson JB (1990) Alcohol challenge with sons of alcoholics: A critical review and analysis. Psychological Bulletin 108: 383–402.

Newlove D (1981) Those Drinking Days: Myself and Other Writers. New York: Horizon Press.

Newton TF, De La Garza R, Kalechstein AD, et al. (2005) Cocaine and methamphetamine produce different patterns of subjective and cardiovascular effects. Pharmacology Biochemistry and Behavior 82: 90–97.

NIAAA (2004) National Institute on Alcohol Abuse and Alcoholism council approves definition of binge drinking. NIAAA Newsletter, winter, p. 3.

Niaura R (2000) Cognitive social learning and related perspectives on drug craving. Addiction 95(Suppl. 2): S155–S163.

Nicotine Anonymous (1998) Our Path to Freedom: Twelve Stories of Recovery. Huntington Beach, CA: Nicotine Anonymous World Services.

Nielsen DA, Kreek MJ (2012) Common and specific liability to addiction: Approaches to association studies of opioid addiction. Drug and Alcohol Dependence 123: S33–S41.

Nielsen DA, Nielsen EM, Dasari T, et al. (2014) Pharmacogenetics of addiction therapy. Methods in Molecular Biology 1175: 589–624.

Nielsen S, Hillhouse M, Mooney L, et al. (2015) Buprenorphine pharmacotherapy and behavioral treatment: Comparison of outcomes among prescription opioid users, heroin users and combination users. Journal of Substance Abuse **48**: 70–76.

Noble EP (2000) Addiction its reward process through polymorphisms of the D2 receptor gene: A review. European Psychiatry **15**: 79–89.

Noble EP (2003) D2 dopamine receptor gene in psychiatric and neurologic disorders and its phenotypes. American Journal of Medical Genetics **116B**: 103–125.

Norcross JC, Lambert MJ (2011) Psychotherapy relationships that work: II. Psychotherapy **48**: 4–8.

Nowinski J (2012) Facilitating 12-step recovery from substance abuse. In Walters ST, Rotgers F (eds.) Treating Substance Abuse: Theory and Technique. New York: Guilford Press.

Numachi Y, Ohara A, Yamashita M (2007) Methamphetamine-induced hyperthermia and lethal toxicity: Role of dopamine and serotonin transporters. European Journal of Pharmacology **572**: 120–128.

Nurnberger JI, Bierut LJ (2007) Seeking the connections: Alcoholism and our genes. Scientific American, April, pp. 46–53.

Nutt DJ, Lingford-Hughes A, Erritzoe D, et al. (2015) The dopamine theory of addiction: 40 years of highs and lows. Nature Reviews: Neuroscience **16**: 305–312.

O'Brien CP (2005) Benzodiazepine use, abuse, and dependence. Journal of Clinical Psychiatry **66**(Suppl. 2): 28–33.

O'Brien CP, Ehrman RN, Ternes JM (1986) Classical conditioning in human opioid dependence. In Goldberg SR, Stolerman IP (eds.) Behavioral Analysis of Drug Dependence. New York: Academic Press.

O'Donnell JK, Halpin J, Mattson CL, et al. (2017) Deaths involving fentanyl, fentanyl analogs, and U-47700. Morbidity and Mortality Weekly Reports **66**: 697–704.

O'Dwyer P (2014) Assessment and treatment of individuals dependent on alcohol and other central nervous system depressants. In Straussner SLA (ed.) Clinical Work with Substance-Abusing Clients. New York: Guilford Press.

Oehmichen M, Auer RN, Konig HG (2005) Forensic Neuropathology and Associated Neurology. New York: Springer.

Oei JL (2018) Adult consequences of prenatal drug exposure. Internal Medicine Journal **48**: 25–31.

Office of Applied Statistics (2006) Trends in Methamphetamine/Amphetamine Admissions to Treatment: 1993–2003. DASIS Report 9. Rockville MD: Substance Abuse and Mental Health Services Administration.

Ohayon MM, Lader MH (2002) Use of psychotropic medication in the general population of France, Germany, Italy, and the United Kingdom. Journal of Clinical Psychiatry **63**: 817–825.

Olds J, Milner P (1954) Positive reinforcement produced by electrical stimulation of septal area and other regions of rat brain. Journal of Comparative and Physiological Psychology **47**: 419–427.

O'Leary CM, Nassar N, Kurinczuk JJ, et al. (2009) The effect of maternal alcohol consumption on fetal growth and preterm birth. British Journal of Obstetrics and Gynaecology 116: 390–400.

Olfson E, Bierut LJ (2012) Convergence of GWA and candidate gene studies for alcoholism. Alcoholism: Clinical and Experimental Research 36: 2086–2094.

Oliver P, Keen J (2003) Concomitant drugs of misuse and drug using behaviors associated with fatal opiate-related poisonings in Sheffield, UK, 1997–2000. Addiction 98: 191–197.

Olsen RW, Li G-D (2011) GABA$_A$ receptors as molecular targets of general anesthetics: Identification of binding sites provides clues to allosteric modulation. Canadian Journal of Anesthesiology 58: 206–215.

O'Malley PM (2004) Maturing out of problematic alcohol use. Alcohol Research and Health 28: 202–203.

O'Malley PM, Johnston LD (2002) Epidemiology of alcohol and other drug use among American college students. Journal of Studies on Alcohol 14(Suppl.): 22–39.

O'Malley SS, Krishnan-Sarrin S, Farren C, et al. (2002) Naltrexone decreases craving and alcohol self-administration in alcohol-dependent subjects and activates the hypothalamo-pituitary axis. Psychopharmacology 160: 19–29.

Oppenheimer E, Tobutt C, Taylor C, et al. (1994) Death and survival in a cohort of heroin addicts from London clinics: A 22-year follow-up study. Addiction 89: 1299–1308.

Orlando M, Tucker JS, Ellickson PL (2005) Concurrent use of alcohol and cigarettes from adolescence to young adulthood: An examination of developmental trajectories and outcomes. Substance Use and Misuse 40: 1051–1069.

Orson FM, Wang R, Brimijoin S, et al. (2014) The future potential for cocaine vaccines. Expert Opinion in Biological Therapeutics 14: 1271–1283.

Osana NA, Donohue TM, Kharbanda KK (2017) Alcoholic liver disease: Pathogenesis and current management. Alcohol Research: Current Reviews 38: 147–161.

Osborn DA, Jeffery HE, Cole MJ (2010) Opiate treatment for opiate withdrawal in newborn infants. Cochrane Database of Systematic Reviews 6: CD002059.

Osborne R, Joel S, Drew D (1990) Morphine and metabolite behavior after different routes of morphine administration: Demonstration of the importance of the active metabolite morphine-6-glucoronide. Clinical Pharmacology and Therapeutics 47: 12–19.

Oser CB, Roman PM (2008) A categorical typology of naltrexone-adopting private substance abuse treatment centers. Journal of Substance Abuse Treatment 34: 433–442.

O'Shea RS, Dasarthy S, McCullough AJ (2010) Alcoholic liver disease. American Journal of Gastroenterology 105: 14–32.

Ostacher MJ, Nierenberg AA, Perlis RH (2006) The relationship between smoking and suicidal behavior, comorbidity, and course of illness in bipolar disorder. Journal of Clinical Psychiatry 67: 1907–1911.

Oswald LM, Wong LM, Wong DF, et al. (2005) Relationships among ventral striatal dopamine release, cortisol secretion, and subjective responses to amphetamine. Neuropsychopharmacology 30: 821–832.

Owen F (2007) No Speed Limit: The Highs and Lows of Meth. New York: St. Martins Press.

Ozburn AR, Janowsky AJ, Crabbe JC (2015) Commonalities and distinctions among mechanisms of addiction to alcohol and other drugs. Alcoholism: Clinical and Experimental Research 39: 1863–1877.

Palmer RH, Brick L, Nugent NR, et al. (2014) Examining the role of common genetic variants on alcohol, tobacco, cannabis, and illicit drug dependence. Addiction 110: 530–537.

Palmer RH, Young SE, Corely RP, et al. (2013) Stability and change of genetic and environmental effects on the common liability to alcohol, tobacco, and cannabis DSM-IV dependence symptoms. Behavioral Genetics 43: 374–385.

Paltrow LM, Cohen D, Carey CA (2000) Year 2000 Overview: Governmental Responses to Pregnant Women Who Use Alcohol or Other Drugs. Philadelphia: National Advocates for Pregnant Women of the Women's Law Project.

Paria BC, Dey SK (2000) Ligand-receptor signaling with endocannabinoids in pre-implantation embryo development and implantation. Chemistry of Physiological Lipids 108: 211–220.

Parker MA, Streck JM, Sigmond SC (2018) Associations between opioid dependence in nationally representative samples of United States adult daily smokers. Drug and Alcohol Dependence 186: 167–170.

Parrot AC (2002) Recreational ecstasy/MDMA, the serotonin syndrome, and serotonergic neurotoxicity. Pharmacology, Biochemistry, and Behavior 71: 837–844.

Parrot AC (2005) Chronic tolerance to recreational MDMA (3,4-methylenedioxymethamphetamine) or ecstasy. Journal of Psychopharmacology 19: 71–93.

Parsons OA (1998) Neurocognitive deficits in alcoholics and social drinkers: A continuum? Alcoholism: Clinical and Experimental Research 22: 954–961.

Parsons OA, Nixon SJ (1998) Cognitive functioning in sober social drinkers: A review of the research since 1986. Journal of Studies on Alcohol 59: 180–190.

Parvaz M, Alia-Klein N, Woicik PA, et al. (2011) Neuroimaging for drug addiction and related behaviors. Reviews in Neuroscience 22: 609–624.

Pasquereau A, Guignard R, Andler R, et al. (2017) Electronic cigarettes, quit attempts and smoking cessation: A 6-month follow-up. Addiction 112: 1620–1628.

Pasternak GW, Pan Y-X (2010) Mix and match: Heterodimers and opioid tolerance. Neuron 69: 6–8.

Paterson NE, Markou A (2003) Increased motivation for self-administered cocaine after escalated cocaine intake. Neuroreport 14: 2229–2232.

Patrick ME, Azar B (2018) High-intensity drinking. Alcohol Research: Current Reviews 39: 49–55.

Patrick CJ, Bernat E, Malone SM, et al. (2006) P300 amplitude as an indicator of externalizing in adolescent males. Psychophysiology 43: 84–92.

Patrick SW, Davis MM, Lehman CU, et al. (2015a) Increasing incidence and geographic distribution of neonatal abstinence syndrome: United States 2009–2012. Journal of Perinatology 35: 650–655.

Patrick SW, Dudley J, Martin PR, et al. (2015b) Prescription opioid epidemic and infant outcomes. Pediatrics 135: 20–26.

Patton GC, Carlin JB, Coffey C, et al. (1998) Depression, anxiety and smoking initiation: A prospective study over 3 years. American Journal of Public Health 88: 1518–1522.

Patton GC, Carlin JB, Degenhardt L, et al. (2002) Cannabis use and mental health in young people: Cohort study. BMJ 325: 1195–1198.

Patton JH, Stanford MS, Barratt ES (1995) Factor structure of the Barratt Impulsiveness Scale. Journal of Clinical Psychology 61: 768–774.

Paulozzi LJ, Budnitz DS, Xi Y (2006) Increasing deaths from opioid analgesics in the United States. Pharmacoepidemiology and Drug Safety 15: 618–627.

Paulus MP, Tapert SF, Schulteis G (2009) The role of interoception and alliesthesia in addiction. Pharmacology, Biochemistry, and Behavior 94: 1–7.

Payer D, London ED (2009) Methamphetamine and the brain. In Roll JM, Rawson RA, Ling W, et al. (eds.) Methamphetamine Addiction. New York: Guilford Press.

Peavy KM, Banta-Green CJ, Kingston S, et al. (2012) "Hooked on" prescription-type opiates prior to using heroin: Results from a survey of syringe exchange clients. Journal of Psychoactive Drugs 44: 259–265.

Pedersen W, van Soest T (2009) Smoking, nicotine dependence and mental health among young adults: A 13-year population-based study. Addiction 104: 129–137.

Peele S (2000) What addiction is and is not: The impact of mistaken notions about addiction. Addictive Behaviors 8: 599–607.

Peele S, Brodsky A, Arnold M (1992) The Truth about Addiction and Recovery. New York: Fireside Press.

Peer K, Rennart LK, Lynch KG, et al. (2013) Prevalence of DSM-IV and DSM-5 alcohol, cocaine, opioid, and cannabis use disorders in a largely substance dependent sample. Drug and Alcohol Dependence 127: 215–217.

Pelloux Y, Everitt BJ, Dickinson A (2007) Compulsive drug seeking by rats under punishment: Effects of drug taking history. Psychopharmacology 194: 127–137.

Pergadia ML, Heath AC, Agrawal A, et al. (2006) The implications of simultaneous smoking initiation for inferences about the genetics of smoking behavior from twin data. Behavior Genetics 36: 567–576.

Pergadia ML, Heath AC, Martin NG, et al. (2006) Genetic analysis of DSM-IV nicotine withdrawal in adult twins. Psychological Medicine 36: 963–972.

Perkins KA (2001) Smoking cessation in women: Special considerations. CNS Drugs 15: 391–411.

Perry JL, Carroll ME (2008) The role of impulsive behavior in drug abuse. Psychopharmacology 200: 1–26.

Persidsky Y, Ho W, Ramirez SH, et al. (2011) HIV-1 infection and alcohol abuse: Neurocognitive impairment, mechanisms of neurodegeneration and therapeutic interventions. Brain and Behavioral Immunology 25(Suppl. 1): S61–70.

Pert CB, Snyder SH (1973) Opiate receptor: Demonstration in nervous tissue. Science 179: 1011–1014.

Peto R, Doll R (2005) The hazards of smoking and the benefits of stopping. In Bock G, Goode J (eds.) Understanding Nicotine and Tobacco Addiction. Chichester, UK: John Wiley.

Petry NM (2001) Delay discounting of money and alcohol in actively using alcoholics, currently abstinent alcoholics, and controls. Psychopharmacology 154: 243–250.

Petursson H, Lader MH (1981) Withdrawal from long-term benzodiazepine treatment. British Medical Journal 283: 643–645.

Peugh J, Belenko S (2001) Alcohol, drugs and sexual function: A review. Journal of Psychoactive Drugs 33: 223–232.

Pfefferbaum A, Sullivan EV, Mathalon DH, et al. (1998) A controlled study of cortical gray matter and ventricular changes in alcoholic men over a five year interval. Archives of General Psychiatry 55: 905–912.

Phillips CV, Heavner MC, Bergen PL (2012) Tobacco: Untapped potential for harm reduction. In Marlatt GA, Larimer ME, Witkiewitz K (eds.) Harm Reduction: Pragmatic Strategies for Managing High-Risk Behaviors. 2nd ed. New York: Guilford Press.

Piano MR (2017) Alcohol's effects on the cardiovascular system. Alcohol Research: Current Reviews 38: 219–242.

Piasecki TM (2006) Relapse to smoking. Clincal Psychology Review 26: 196–215.

Piasecki TM, Jorenby DE, Smith SS, et al. (2003) Smoking withdrawal dynamics: III. Correlates of withdrawal heterogeneity. Experimental and Clinical Psychopharmacology 11: 276–285.

Piasecki TM, Niaura R, Shadel WG, et al. (2000) Smoking withdrawal dynamics in unaided quitters. Journal of Abnormal Psychology 109: 74–86.

Piasecki TM, Niaura R, Shadel WG, et al. (2002) Have we lost our way? The need for dynamic formulations of smoking relapse proneness. Addiction 97: 1093–1108.

Piasecki TM, Robertson BM, Epler AJ (2010) Hangover and risk for alcohol use disorders: Existing evidence and potential mechanisms. Current Drug Abuse Reviews 3: 92–102.

Piasecki TM, Sher KJ, Slutske WS, et al. (2005) Hangover frequency and risk for alcohol use disorders: Evidence from a longitudinal high-risk study. Journal of Abnormal Psychology 114: 223–234.

Pickel VM, Chan J, Kash TL, et al. (2004) Compartment-specific localization of cannabinoid 1 (CB1) and mu opioid receptors in rat nucleus accumbens. Neuroscience 127: 101–112.

Pierce R, Kumaresan V (2006) The mesolimbic dopamine system: The final common pathway for the reinforcing effect of drugs of abuse? Neuroscience and Biobehavioral Reviews 30: 215–238.

Piontek D, Kraus L, Klempova D (2008) Short scales to assess cannabis-related problems: a review of psychometric properties. Substance Abuse Treatment, Prevention, and Policy **3**: 25–41.

Piper ME, McCarthy DE, Bolt DM, et al. (2008) Assessing dimensions of nicotine dependence. Nicotine and Tobacco Research **10**: 1009–1020.

Piper ME, Piasecki TM, Federman EB, et al. (2004) A multiple motives approach to assessing tobacco dependence: The Wisconsin Inventory of Smoking Dependence Motives (WISDM-68). Journal of Consulting and Clinical Psychology **72**: 139–154.

Pizzimenti CL, Lattal KM (2015) Epigenetics and memory: Causes, consequences and treatments for post-traumatic stress disorder and addiction. Genes, Brain, and Behavior **14**: 73–84.

Plebani JG, Lynch KG, Yu Q, et al. (2012) Results of an initial clinical trial of varenicline for the treatment of cocaine dependence. Drug and Alcohol Dependence **121**: 163–166.

Plomin R, DeFries JC, McClearn GE, et al. (2008) Behavioral Genetics. 5th ed. New York: Worth.

Plomin R, Schalkwyk LC (2007) Microarrays. Developmental Science **10**: 19–23.

Polich J, Pollock VE, Bloom FE (1994) Meta-analysis of P300 amplitude from males at risk for alcoholism. Psychological Bulletin **115**: 55–73.

Pomerlau CS, Zucker A, Stewart A (2001) Characterizing concerns about post-cessation weight gain: Results from a national survey of women smokers. Nicotine and Tobacco Research **3**: 51–60.

Pomerleau OF, Pomerleau CS, Mehringer AM, et al. (2005) Nicotine dependence, depression, and gender: Characterizing phenotypes based on withdrawal discomfort, response to smoking, and ability to abstain. Nicotine and Tobacco Research **7**: 91–102.

Pomplili M, Gianluca S, Innamorati M, et al. (2010) Suicidal behavior and alcohol abuse. International Journal of Environmental Research and Public Health **7**: 1392–1431.

Ponomarev I (2013) Epigenetic control of gene expression in the alcoholic brain. Alcohol Research: Current Reviews **35**: 69–76.

Porjesz B, Begleiter H. (2003) Alcoholism and human electrophysiology. Alcohol Research and Health **27**: 153–160.

Porjesz B, Rangaswamy M, Kamarajan C, et al. (2005) The utility of neurophysiological markers in the study of alcoholism. Clinical Neurophysiology **116**: 993–1018.

Portenoy RK, Lussier D, Kirsh KL, et al. (2005) Pain and addiction. In Frances RJ, Miller SI, Mack AH (eds.) Clinical Textbook of Addictive Disorders. New York: Guilford Press.

Potter JS, Prather K, Weiss RD (2008) Physical pain and associated clinical characteristics in treatment-seeking patients in four substance use disorder treatment modalities. American Journal of Addiction **17**: 121–125.

Poulos CX, Cappell H (1991) Homeostatic theory of drug tolerance: A general model of physiological adaptation. Psychological Review **98**: 390–408.

Prescott CA (2002) Sex differences in the genetic risk for alcoholism. Alcohol Research and Health **26**: 264–273.

Prescott CA, Madden PAF, Stallings MC (2006) Challenges in genetic studies of the etiology of substance use and substance use disorders: Introduction to the special issue. Behavior Genetics **36**: 473–482.

Pressley JC, Arora A, Sarmah R (2019) Marijuana use in teen drivers: A comparison of road-side survey of reported use and fluid tests for tetrahydrocannabinol (THC). Injury Epidemiology **6**: 25–31.

Pressman MR (2011) Sleep driving: Sleepwalking variant or misuse of Z-drugs? Sleep Medicine Review **15**: 285–292.

Primack BA, Soneji S, Stoolmiller M, et al. (2015) Progression to traditional cigarette smoking after electronic cigarette use among US adolescents and young adults. JAMA Pediatrics **169**: 1018–1023.

Prochaska JJ, Benowitz NL (2016) The past, present, and future of nicotine addiction therapy. Annual Review of Medicine **67**: 467–486.

Proebstl L, Kamp F, Koller G, et al. (2018) Cognitive deficits in methamphetamine users: How strong is the evidence? Pharmacopsychiatry **51**: 243–250.

Raber JC, Elzinga S, Kaplan C (2015) Understanding dabs: contamination concerns of cannabis concentrates and cannabinoid transfer during the act of dabbing. Toxicological Science **40**: 797–803.

Raffa RB, Pergolizzi JV, Muniz E, Taylor RT, Pergolizzi J (2012) Designing opioids that deter abuse. Pain Research and Treatment **2012**: 1–10.

Raganathan M, D'Souza DC (2006) The acute effects of cannabinoids on memory in humans: A review. Psychopharmacology **188**: 425–444.

Raistrick D (2001) Alcohol withdrawal and detoxification. In Heather N, Peters TJ, Stockwell T (eds.) International Handbook of Alcohol Dependence and Problems. Chichester, UK: John Wiley.

Ramaekers JG, Kauert G, Theunissen EL, et al. (2009) High-potency marijuana impairs executive function and inhibitory motor control. Neuropsychopharmacology **31**: 2296–2303.

Randall CL, Roberts JS, Del Boca FK, et al. (1999) Telescoping of landmark events associated with drinking: A gender comparison. Journal of Studies on Alcohol **60**: 252–260.

Randolph C, Tierney CM, Mohr E, et al. (1998) Repeatable Battery for the Assessment of Neuropsychological Status as a screening test (RBANS): Preliminary clinical validity. Journal of Clinical and Experimental Neuropsychology **20**: 310–319.

Randrup A, Munkvard I (1974) Pharmacology and physiology of stereotyped behavior. Journal of Psychiatric Research **11**: 1–10.

Rangaswamy M, Jones KA, Porjesz B, et al. (2007) Delta and theta oscillations as risk markers in adolescent offspring of alcoholics. International Journal of Psychophysiology **63**: 3–25.

Rangaswamy M, Porjesz B, Chorlian DB (2004) Resting EEG in offspring of male alcoholics: Beta frequencies.

International Journal of Psychophysiology **51**: 239–251.

Rather BC, Goldman MS, Roehrich L, et al. (1992) Empirical modeling of an alcohol expectancy memory network using multidimensional scaling. Journal of Abnormal Psychology **101**: 174–183.

Ratsma JE, Van Der Stelt O, Gunning WB (2002) Neurochemical markers of alcoholism vulnerability in humans. Alcohol and Alcoholism **37**: 522–533.

Rawson RA, Condon TP (2007) Why do we need an *Addiction* supplement focused on methamphetamine? Addiction **102**(Suppl. 1): 1–4.

Rawson RA, Gonzales R, Marinelli-Casey P, et al. (2007) Methamphetamine dependence: A closer look at treatment response and clinical characteristics associated with route of administration in outpatient treatment. American Journal on Addiction **16**: 291–299.

Rawson RA, Gonzales R, Pearce V, et al. (2008) Methamphetamine dependence and HIV risk behavior. Journal of Substance Abuse Treatment **35**: 279–284.

Rawson RA, Marinelli-Casey P, Anglin MD, et al. (2004) A multi-site comparison of psychosocial approaches for the treatment of methamphetamine dependence. Addiction **99**: 708–717.

Rawson RA, Sodano R, Hillhouse M (2005) Assessment of amphetamine use disorders. In Donovan DM, Marlatt GA (eds.) Assessment of Addictive Behaviors. 2nd ed. New York: Guilford Press.

Rawson RA, Washton AM, Domier CP, et al. (2002) Drugs and sexual effects: Role of drug type and gender. Journal of Substance Abuse Treatment **22**: 103–108.

Read JP, O'Connor RM (2006) High- and low-dose expectancies as mediators of personality dimensions and alcohol involvement. Journal of Studies on Alcohol **67**: 204–214.

Reardon C (2010) Social networking in addiction recovery – raising hopes, concerns. Social Work Today **10**: 8–9.

Reback CJ, Fletcher JB, et al. (2018) Associations between sociodemographic characteristics and sexual risk behaviors among methamphetamine-using men who have sex with men. Substance Use and Misuse **53**: 1826–1833.

Reding N (2009) Methland: The Death and Life of an American Small Town. New York: Bloomsbury.

Reed SC, Evans SM, Bedi G, et al. (2011) The effects of oral micronized progesterone on smoked cocaine self-administration in women. Hormones and Behavior **59**: 227–235.

Regier DA, Farmer ME, Rae DS, et al. (1990) Comorbidity of mental disorders with alcohol and other drug abuse: Results from the epidemiological catchment area (ECA) study. JAMA **264**: 2511–2518.

Reichel CM, Ramsey LA, Schwendt M, et al. (2012) Methamphetamine-induced changes in the object recognition memory circuit. Neuropharmacology **62**: 1119–1126.

Reidy L, Gennaro W, Steele BW, et al. (2008) The incidence of zolpidem use in suspected DUI drivers in Miami-Dade, Florida: A comparative study using immunalysis zolpidem ELISA KIT and gas chromatography-mass spectrometry screening. Journal of Analytical Toxicology **32**: 688–694.

Reinarman C (2005) Addiction as accomplishment: The discursive construction of disease. Addiction Research and Theory **13**: 307–320.

Reis RK, Fiellin DA, Miller SC, et al. (2014) Principles of Addiction Medicine. 5th ed. Chevy Chase, MD: American Society of Addiction Medicine.

Reneman L, Booij J, Schmand B, et al. (2000) Memory disturbances in "ecstasy" users are correlated with an altered brain serotonin neurotransmission. Psychopharmacology **148**: 322–324.

Rescorla RA (1987) A Pavlovian analysis of goal-directed behavior. American Psychologist **42**: 119–129.

Reynolds B (2006) A review of delay-discounting research with humans: Relations to drug use and gambling. Behavioural Pharmacology **17**: 651–667.

Reynolds B, Patak M, Shroff P, et al. (2007) Laboratory and self-report assessments of impulsive behavior in adolescent smokers and nonsmokers. Experimental and Clinical Psychopharmacology **15**: 264–271.

Reynolds B, Richards JB, de Wit H (2006) Acute-alcohol effects on the Experiential Discounting Task (EDT) and a question-based measure of delay discounting. Pharmacology, Biochemistry, and Behavior **83**: 194–202.

Reynolds S (1998) Energy Flash: A Journey through Rave Music and Dance Culture. London: Picador.

Rhee SH, Hewitt JK, Young SE, et al. (2006) Comorbidity between alcohol dependence and illicit drug dependence in adolescents with antisocial behavior and matched controls. Drug and Alcohol Dependence **84**: 85–92.

Richardson GA, Goldschmidt L, Leech S, et al. (2011) Prenatal cocaine exposure: Effects on mother- and teacher-related behavior problems and growth in school-age children. Neurotoxicology and Teratology **33**: 69–77.

Richmond R, Heather N, Holt P, et al. (1990) Workplace Policies and Programmes for Tobacco, Alcohol and Other Drugs in Australia. Canberra: Australian Government Printing Service.

Ridenour TA, Lanza ST, Donny EC, et al. (2006) Different lengths of time for progression in adolescent substance involvement. Addictive Behaviors **31**: 962–983.

Riedel G, Davies SN (2005) Cannabinoid function in learning, memory and plasticity. Handbook of Experimental Pharmacology **168**: 445–477.

Riley EP, Infante MA, Warren KR (2011) Fetal alcohol spectrum disorders: An overview. Neuropsychology Review **21**: 73–80.

Rippeth JD, Heaton RK, Carey CL, et al. (2004) Methamphetamine dependence increases risk of neuropsychological impairment in HIV infected persons. Journal of the International Neuropsychological Society **10**: 1–14.

Risinger RC, Salmeron BJ, Ross TJ, et al. (2005) Neural correlates of high and craving during cocaine self-administration using BOLD fMRI. NeuroImage **26**: 1097–1108.

Risner ME, Goldberg SR (1983) A comparison of nicotine and cocaine self-administration in the dog: Fixed-ratio and progressive schedules of intravenous drug infusion. Journal of

Pharmacology and Experimental Therapeutics **224**: 319–326.

Rizzo MD, Crawford RB, Bach A, et al. (2019) Tetrahydrocannabinol suppresses monocyte-mediated astrocyte production of monocyte chemoattractant protein 1 and interleukin-6 in a human coculture. Journal of Pharmacology and Experimental Therapeutics **371**: 191–201.

Roache JD, Wang Y, Ait-Daoud N, et al. (2008) Prediction of serotonergic treatment efficacy using age of onset and type A/B typologies of alcoholism. Alcoholism: Clinical and Experimental Research **32**: 1502–1512.

Robbins SJ, Ehrman RN, Childress AR, et al. (2000) Mood state and recent cocaine use are not associated with levels of cocaine cue reactivity. Drug and Alcohol Dependence **59**: 33–42.

Robbins SJ, Ehrman RN, Childress AR, et al. (1997) Relationships among physiological and self-report responses produced by cocaine-related cues. Addictive Behaviors **22**: 157–167.

Robbins T, Cardinal R, DiCiano P, et al. (2007) Neuroscience of drugs and addiction. In Nutt D, Robbins T, Stimson G, et al. (eds.) Drugs and the Future: Brain Science, Addiction and Society. Burlington, MA: Academic Press.

Roberto M, Schweitzer P, Madamba SG, et al. (2004) Acute and chronic ethanol after glutamatergic transmission in rat central amygdala: An in vitro and in vivo analysis. Journal of Neuroscience **24**: 1594–1603.

Roberts RE, Roberts CR, Xing Y (2007) Comorbidity of substance use disorders and other psychiatric disorders among adolescents: Evidence from an epidemiologic survey. Drug and Alcohol Dependence **88**: S4–S13.

Robinson JD, Lam Cy, Carter BL, et al. (2011) A multimodal approach to assessing the impact of nicotine dependence, nicotine abstinence, and craving on negative affect in smokers. Experimental and Clinical Psychopharmacology **19**: 40–52.

Robinson JH, Pritchard WS (1992) The role of nicotine in tobacco use. Psychopharmacology **108**: 397–407.

Robinson TE, Berridge KC (2000) The psychology and neurobiology of addiction: an incentive-sensitization view. Addiction **95**(Suppl. 2): S91–S117.

Robinson TE, Berridge KC (2003) Addiction. Annual Review of Psychology **54**: 25–53.

Robinson TE, Berridge KC (2008) The incentive sensitization theory of addiction: some current issues. Philosophical Transactions of the Royal Society **363**: 3137–3146.

Robison AJ, Vilou V, Mazei-Robison M, et al. (2013) Behavioral and structural responses to chronic cocaine require a feed-forward loop involving delta FosB and CaMKII in the nucleus accumbens shell. Journal of Neuroscience **33**: 4295–4307.

Roderiguez LA, Wilson JR, Nagoshi CT (1993) Does psychomotor sensitivity to alcohol predict subsequent alcohol use? Alcoholism: Clinical and Experimental Research **17**: 161–166.

Rodriguez T (2016) Criticism of 12-step groups: Is it warranted? Psychiatry Advisor October 5.

Roehrs TA, Randall S, Harris E, et al. (2012) Twelve months of nightly zolpidem does not lead to rebound insomnia or withdrawal symptoms: A prospective placebo-controlled study. Journal of Psychopharmacology **26**: 1088–1095.

Roffman RA, Stephens RS (2012) Harm reduction and cannabis. In Marlatt GA, Larimer ME, Witkiewitz K (eds.) Harm Reduction: Pragmatic Strategies for Managing High-Risk Behaviors. 2nd ed. New York: Guilford Press.

Rogeberg O (2013) Reply to Moffit et al.: Causal inference from observational data remains difficult. Proceedings of the National Academy of Sciences of the USA **110**: E983.

Rogers G, Elston J, Garside R, et al. (2009) The harmful health effects of recreational ecstasy: a systematic view of observational evidence. Health Technology Assessment **13**: 1–315.

Rojas NL, Killen JD, Haydel KF, et al. (1998) Nicotine dependence among adolescent smokers. Archives of Pediatric and Adolescent Medicine **152**: 151–156.

Rolls E (2000) The orbitofrontal cortex and reward. Cerebral Cortex **10**: 284–294.

Room R (2004) The cultural framing of addiction. Janus Head **6**: 221–234.

Room R (2014) Legalizing a market for cannabis for pleasure: Colorado, Washington, Uruguay and beyond. Addiction **109**: 345–351.

Rose AK, Shaw SG, Prendergast MA, et al. (2010) The importance of glucocorticoids in alcohol dependence and neurotoxicity. Alcoholism: Clinical and Experimental Research **34**: 2011–2018.

Rosenbaum JF (2005) Attitudes toward benzodiazepines over the years. Journal of Clinical Psychiatry **66**(Suppl. 2): 4–8.

Rosenberg MF, Anthony JC (2001) Early clinical manifestations of cannabis dependence in a community sample. Drug and Alcohol Dependence **64**: 123–131.

Rosenbloom MJ, O'Reilly A, Sassoon SA, et al. (2005) Persistent cognitive deficits in community-treated alcoholic men and women volunteering for research: Limited contribution from psychiatric comorbidity. Journal of Studies on Alcohol **66**: 254–265.

Rosenbloom MJ, Pfefferbaum A (2008) Magnetic resonance imaging of the living brain: Evidence for brain degeneration among alcoholics and recovery with abstinence. Alcohol Research and Health **31**: 362–376.

Rosenblum A, Marsch LA, Portenoy RK, et al. (2008) Opioids and the treatment of chronic pain: Controversies, current status, and future directions. Experimental and Clinical Psychopharmacology **16**: 405–416.

Rotgers F (2003) Cognitive-behavioral theories of substance abuse. In Rotgers F, Morgenstern J, Walters ST (eds.) Treating Substance Abuse: Theory and Technique. 2nd ed. New York: Guilford Press.

Rowe CL (2012) Family therapy for drug abuse: Review and updates 2003–2010. Journal of Marital Therapy **38**: 59–81.

Rubin EM (2012) Integrating theory, research, and practice: A clinician's perspective. In Walters ST, Rotgers F (eds.) Treating Substance Abuse:

Theory and Technique. New York: Guilford Press.

Rudd RA, Seth P, David F, et al. (2016) Increases in drug and opioid-involved overdose deaths – United States, 2010–2015. Morbidity and Mortality Weekly Reports 65: 1445–1452.

Rush CR, Baker RW, Wright K (1999) Acute physiological and behavioral effects of oral cocaine in humans: A dose-response analysis. Drug and Alcohol Dependence 55: 1–12.

Rush CR, Stoops WW, Ling W (2009) Behavioral pharmacology and psychiatric consequences of methamphetamine. In Roll JM, Rawson RA, Ling W, et al. (eds.) Methamphetamine Addiction. New York: Guilford Press.

Rutkowski BA, Maxwell JC (2009) Epidemiology of methamphetamine use: A global perspective. In Roll JM, Rawson RA, Ling W, et al. (eds.) Methamphetamine Addiction. New York: Guilford Press.

Ryan F (2002) Detected, selected, and sometimes neglected: Cognitive processing of cues in addiction. Experimental and Clinical Psychopharmacology 10: 67–76.

Ryback RS (1971) The continuum and specificity of the effects of alcohol on memory. Quarterly Journal of Studies on Alcohol 32: 995–1016.

Rylander G (1969) Clinical and medico-criminological aspects of addiction to central stimulating drugs. In Sjoqvist F, Tottie M (eds.) Abuse of Control Stimulants. Stockholm: Almqvist and Wiksell.

Rylander G (1971) Stereotype behavior in man following amphetamine abuse.

In Baker SB (ed) The Correlation of Adverse Effects in Man with Observations in Animals. Amsterdam: Excerpta Medica.

Sachs J, McGlade E, Yurgelun-Todd D (2015) Safety and toxicology of cannabinoids. Neurotherapeutics 12: 735–746.

Sacks JJ, Gonzales KR, Bouchery EE, et al. (2015) National and state costs of excessive alcohol consumption. American Journal of Preventive Medicine 49: e73.

Sadek JR, Vigil O, Grant I, et al. (2007) The impact of neuropsychological functioning and depressed mood on functional complaints in HIV-1 infection and methamphetamine dependence. Journal of Experimental Neuropsychology 29: 266–276.

Sagar DR, Gaw AG, Okine BN, et al. (2009) Dynamic regulation of the endocannabinoid system: Implications for analgesia. Molecular Pain 5: Article 59.

Sagar KA, Dahlgren MK, Gonenc A, et al. (2015) The impact of initiation: Early onset marijuana smokers demonstrate altered Stroop performance and brain activation. Developmental Cognitive Neuroscience 16: 84–92.

Saha TD, Chou SP, Grant BF (2006) Toward an alcohol use disorder continuum using item response theory: Results from the National Epidemiological Survey on Alcohol Related Conditions. Psychological Medicine 36: 931–941.

Saha TD, Grant BF, Chou PS, et al. (2018) Concurrent use of alcohol with other drugs and DSM-5 alcohol use disorder comorbid with other drug use disorders: Sociodemographic characteristics, severity, and psychopathology. Drug and Alcohol Dependence **187**: 261–269.

Saha TD, Stinson FS, Grant BF (2007) The role of alcohol consumption in future classifications of alcohol use disorders. Drug and Alcohol Dependence **89**: 82–92.

Saitz R (2005) Clinical practice: Unhealthy alcohol use. New England Journal of Medicine **352**: 596–607.

Sampson HW (2002) Alcohol and other factors affecting osteoporosis risk in women. Alcohol Research and Health **26**: 292–298.

Sanna E, Busonero F, Talani G, et al. (2002) Comparison of the effects of zaleplon, zolpidem, and triazolam at various GABA(A) receptor subtypes. European Journal of Pharmacology **451**: 103–110.

Sapolsky RM (2000) Glucocorticoids and hippocampal atrophy in neuropsychiatric disorders. Archives of General Psychiatry **57**: 925–935.

Sarne Y, Asaf F, Fishbein M, et al. (2011) The dual protective-neurotoxic profile of cannabinoid drugs. British Journal of Pharmacology **163**: 1391–1401.

Sartor CE, Grant JD, Bucholz KK, et al. (2010) Common genetic contributions to alcohol and cannabis use and dependence symptomatology. Alcoholism: Clinical and Experimental Research **34**: 545–554.

Saunders JB, Aasland OG, Babor TF, et al. (1993) Development of the Alcohol Use Disorders Identification Test (AUDIT): WHO collaborative development project on early detection of persons with harmful alcohol consumption – II. Addiction **88**: 791–804.

Savage SR, Kirsh KL, Passik SD (2008) Challenges in using opioids to treat pain in persons with substance use disorders. Addiction Science and Clinical Practice **4**: 4–25.

Sayette MA (1999) Does drinking reduce stress? Alcohol Research and Health **23**: 250–255.

Sayette MA (2016) The role of craving in substance use disorders: Theoretical and methodological issues. Annual Review of Clinical Psychology **12**: 407–433.

Sayette MA, Shiffman S, Tiffany ST, et al. (2000) The measurement of drug craving. Addiction **95**(Suppl. 2): S189–S210.

Schafer G, Fielding A, Morgan CJA, et al. (2012) Investigating the interaction between schizotypy, divergent thinking and cannabis use. Consciousness and Cognition **21**: 292–298.

Scharf D, Shiffman S (2004) Are there gender differences in smoking cessation, with and without Bupropion? Pooled and meta-analyses of clinical trials of Bupropion SR. Addiction **99**: 1462–1469.

Schauer GL, King BA, Bunnell RE, et al. (2016) Toking, vaping, and eating for health or fun. Marijuana use patterns in adults, US 2014. American Journal of Preventive Medicine **50**: 1–8.

Scherrer JF, Grant JD, Duncan AE, et al. (2009) Subjective effects to cannabis are associated with use, abuse and dependence after adjusting for genetic and environmental influences. Drug and Alcohol Dependence **105**: 76–82.

Schier JG, Meiman JG, Layden J (2019) Severe pulmonary disease associated with electronic-cigarette-product use – interim guidance. Morbidity and Mortality Weekly Report **68**: 787–790.

Schlaepfer T (2006) Decreased white-matter volume in chronic substance abuse. International Journal of Neuropsychopharmacology **9**: 147–153.

Schlicker E, Kathmann M (2001) Modulation of transmitter release via presynaptic cannabinoid receptors. Trends in Pharmacological Science **22**: 565–572.

Schlossarek S, Kempkensteffen J, Reimer J, et al. (2016) Psychosocial determinants of cannabis dependence: A systematic review of the literature. European Addiction Research **22**: 131–144.

Schmidt KS, Gallo JL, Ferri C, et al. (2005) The neuropsychological profile of alcohol-related dementia suggests cortical and sub-cortical pathology. Dementia and Geriatric Cognitive Disorders **20**: 286–291.

Schneider J (2003) Deviant drinking as disease: Alcoholism as a social accomplishment. In Orcutt JD, Rudy DR (eds.) Drugs, Alcohol and Social Problems. Lanham, MD: Rowan and Littlefield.

Schneider M (2012) The impact of pubertal exposure of cannabis on the brain: A focus on animal studies. In Castle D, Murray RM, D'Souza C (eds.) Marijuana and Madness. 2nd ed. Cambridge: Cambridge University Press.

Schneider M, Koch M (2003) Chronic pubertal, but not adult chronic cannabinoid treatment impairs sensorimotor gating, recognition memory and the performance of in a progressive ratio task in adult rats. Neuropsychopharmacology **28**: 1760–1769.

Schoedel KA, Hoffman EB, Rao Y, et al. (2004) Ethnic variation in CYP2A6 and association of genetically slow nicotine metabolism and smoking in adult Caucasians. Pharmacogenetics **14**: 615–626.

Scholl L, Seth P, Karlisa M, et al. (2019) Drug and opioid-involved deaths – United States, 2013–2017. Morbidity and Mortality Weekly Report **67**: 1419–1427.

Schomerus G, Matschinger H, Angermeyer MC (2006) Alcoholism: Illness beliefs and resource allocation preferences of the public. Drug and Alcohol Dependence **82**: 204–210.

Schreiner AM, Dunn ME (2012) Residual effects of cannabis use on neurocognitive performance after prolonged abstinence: A meta-analysis. Experimental and Clinical Psychopharmacology **20**: 420–429.

Schrieks IC, Stafleu A, Kalien VL, et al. (2014) The biphasic effects of moderate alcohol consumption with a meal on ambiance-induced mood and autonomic nervous system balance: A randomized crossover trial. PLoS ONE **9**: e86199.

Schuckit MA (1980) Self-rating of alcohol intoxication by young men with and without family histories of alcoholism. Journal of Studies on Alcoholism **41**: 242–249.

Schuckit MA (1994) Introduction to section I: Substance-related disorders. In Widiger TA, Frances AJ, Pincus HA, et al. (eds.) DSM-IV Sourcebook. Vol. 1. Washington, DC: American Psychiatric Association.

Schuckit MA (1996) Alcohol, anxiety, and depressive disorders. Alcohol Health and Research World **20**: 81–85.

Schuckit MA (2002) Vulnerability factors for alcoholism. In Davis KL, Charney D, Coyle JT, et al. (eds.) Neuropsychopharmacology: The Fifth Generation of Progress. Baltimore, MD: Lippincott Williams and Wilkins.

Schuckit MA, Edenberg HJ, Kalmijn J (2001) A genome-wide search for genes that relate to a low level of response to alcohol. Alcoholism: Clinical and Experimental Research 25: 323–329.

Schuckit MA, Smith TL (2000) The relationships of a family history of alcohol dependence, a low level of response to alcohol and six domains of life functioning to the development of alcohol use disorders. Journal of Studies on Alcohol 61: 827–835.

Schuckit MA, Smith TL (2006) An evaluation of the level of response to alcohol, externalizing symptoms, and depressive symptoms as predictors of alcoholism. Journal of Studies on Alcoholism 67: 215–227.

Schuckit MA, Smith TL (2006a) The relationship of behavioural undercontrol to alcoholism in higher-functioning adults. Drug and Alcohol Review 25: 393–402.

Schuckit MA, Smith TL, Kalmijn J (2004) The search for genes contributing to the low level of response to alcohol: Patterns of findings across studies. Alcoholism: Clinical and Experimental Research 28: 1449–1458.

Schuckit MA, Tipp JE, Smith TL, et al. (1995) An evaluation of Type A and B alcoholics. Addiction 90: 1189–1203.

Schuckit MA, Windle M, Smith TL, et al. (2006b) Searching for the full picture: Structural equations modeling in alcohol research. Alcoholism: Clinical and Experimental Research 30: 194–202.

Schuermeyer J, Salomonsen-Sautel S, Price RK, et al. (2014) Temporal trends in marijuana attitudes, availability and use in Colorado compared to non-medical marijuana use states: 2003–2011. Drug and Alcohol Dependence 140: 145–155.

Schulkin J (2003) Addiction to drugs. In Rethinking Homeostatis: Allostatic Regulation in Physiology and Pathophysiology. Cambridge, MA: MIT Press.

Schulte MT, Ramo D, Brown SA (2009) Gender differences in factors influencing alcohol use and drinking progression among adolescents. Clinical Psychology Review 29: 535–547.

Schulteis G, Liu J (2006) Brain reward deficits accompany withdrawal (hangover) from acute ethanol in rats. Alcohol 39: 21–28.

Schulze GE, McMillan DE, Bailey JR, et al. (1988) Acute effects of delta-9-tetrahydrocannabinol in rhesus monkeys as measured by performance in a battery of complex operant tests. Journal of Pharmacological and Experimental Therapeutics 245: 178–186.

Schuman-Olivier Z, Hoeppner BB, Weiss RD, et al. (2013) Benzodiazepine use during buprenorphine treatment for opioid dependence: Clinical and safety outcomes. Drug and Alcohol Dependence 132: 580–586.

Scofield MD, Heinsbrock CD, Gipson YM, et al. (2016) The nucleus accumbens: Mechanisms of addiction across drug classes reflect the importance of glutamate homeostasis. Pharmacological Reviews 68: 816–871.

Scott JC, Woods SP, Matt GE, et al. (2007) Neurocognitive effects of methamphetamine: A critical review and meta-analysis. Neuropsychology Review 17: 275–297.

Sehgal N, Manchikanti L, Smith HD (2012) Prescription opioid abuse in chronic pain: A review of opioid abuse predictors and strategies to curb opioid abuse. Pain Physician 15: ES67-ES92.

Sellers E (1988) Alcohol, barbiturate and benzodiazepine withdrawal syndromes: Clinical management. CMAJ 139: 113–121.

Seneviratne C, Johnson BA (2015) Advances in medications and tailoring treatment for alcohol use disorder. Alcohol Research: Current Reviews 37: 15–28.

Serrano A, Parsons LH (2011) Endocannabinoid influence in drug reinforcement, dependence and addiction-related behaviors. Pharmacology and Therapeutics 132: 215–241.

Sessa B (2018) Why MDMA therapy for alcohol use disorder? And why now? Neuropharmacology 142: 83–88.

Sewell RA, Poling J, Sofuoglu M (2009) The effect of cannabis compared with alcohol on driving. American Journal of Addiction 18: 185–193.

Sewell RA, Schnakenberg A, Elander J, et al. (2013) Acute effects of THC on time perception in frequent and infrequent cannabis users. Psychopharmacology 226: 401–413.

Shaham Y, Erb S, Stewart J (2000) Stress-induced relapse to heroin and cocaine-seeking in rats: A review. Brain Research Reviews 33: 13–33.

Shaham Y, Shalev U, Lu L, et al. (2003) The reinstatement model of drug relapse: History, methodology and major findings. Psychopharmacology 168: 3–20.

Shalev U, Grimm J, Shaham Y (2002) Neurobiology of relapse to heroin and cocaine: A review. Pharmacological Review 150: 337–346.

Shaner A, Roberts LJ, Eckman TA (1998) Sources of diagnostic uncertainty for chronically psychotic cocaine abusers. Psychiatric Services 49: 684–690.

Shankman SA, Klein DN, Lewisohn PM, et al. (2008) Family study of subthreshold psychopathology in a community sample. Psychological Medicine 38: 187–198.

Shaw MF, McGovern MP, Angres DH, et al. (2004) Physicians and nurses with substance use disorders. Nursing and Health Care Management and Policy 47: 561–571.

Shearer J, Darke S, Rodgers C, et al. (2009) A double-blind, placebo-controlled trial of modafinil (200 mg/day) for methamphetamine dependence. Addiction 104: 224–233.

Sheff N (2008) Tweak: Growing Up on Methamphetamines. New York: Atheneum Books.

Sher KJ (1985) Subjective effects of alcohol: The influence of setting and individual differences in alcohol expectancies. Journal of Studies on Alcohol 46: 137–146.

Sher KJ, Bartholow BD, Wood MD (2000) Personality and substance use disorders: A prospective study. Journal of Consulting and Clinical Psychology 68: 818–829.

Sher KJ, Gotham H (1999) Pathological alcohol involvement: A developmental disorder of young adulthood. Development and Psychopathology 11: 933–956.

Sher KJ, Greken ER, Williams NA (2005) The development of alcohol use disorders. Annual Review of Clinical Psychology 1: 493–523.

Sher KJ, Wood MD (2005) Subjective effects of alcohol II: Individual differences. In Earleywine M (ed.) Mind-Altering Drugs: The Science of Subjective Experience. New York: Oxford University Press.

Sher KJ, Wood MD, Richardson AE, et al. (2005) Subjective effects of alcohol I: Effects of the drink and drinking context. In Earleywine M (ed.) Mind-Altering Drugs: The Science of Subjective Experience. New York: Oxford University Press.

Sher KJ, Wood MD, Wood PK, et al. (1996) Alcohol outcome expectancies and alcohol use: A latent variable cross-lagged panel study. Journal of Abnormal Psychology 105: 561–574.

Shiffman S (1989) Tobacco "chippers" – individual differences in tobacco dependence. Psychopharmacology 97: 539–547.

Shiffman S, Kassel J, Gwaltney C, et al. (2005) Relapse prevention for smoking. In Marlatt GA, Donovan DM (eds.) Relapse Prevention: Maintenance Strategies in the Treatment of Addictive Behaviors. 2nd ed. New York: Guilford Press.

Shiffman S, Sayette MA (2005) Validation of the Nicotine Dependence Syndrome Scale (NDSS): A criterion-group design contrasting chippers and regular smokers. Drug and Alcohol Dependence 79: 45–52.

Shiffman S, Waters A, Hickcox M (2004) The Nicotine Dependence Syndrome Scale: A multidimensional measure of nicotine dependence. Nicotine and Tobacco Research 6: 327–348.

Shnitko TA, Spear LP, Robinson DL (2016) Adolescent binge-like alcohol alters sensitivity to acute alcohol effects on dopamine release in the nucleus accumbens of adult rats. Psychopharmacology 233: 361–371.

Shoptaw S, King WD, Landstrom E, et al. (2009) Public health issues surrounding methamphetamine dependence. In Roll JM, Rawson RA, Ling W, et al. (eds.) Methamphetamine Addiction: From Basic Science to Treatment. New York: Guilford Press.

Shoptaw S, Peck J, Reback C, et al. (2003) Psychiatric and substance-dependence comorbidities, sexually transmitted diseases, and risk behaviors among methamphetamine-dependent gay and bisexual men seeking outpatient drug abuse treatment. Journal of Psychoactive Drugs 35: 161–168.

Shoptaw S, Rawson RA, McCann MJ, et al. (1994) The Matrix Model of outpatient stimulant abuse treatment: Evidence of clinical efficacy. Journal of Addictive Diseases 13: 129–141.

Shults RA, Jones JM, Komatsu KK, et al. (2019) Alcohol and marijuana use among young injured drivers in Arizona, 2998–2014. Traffic Injury Prevention 20: 9–14.

Shurman J, Koob GF, Gutstein HB (2010) Opioids, pain, the brain, and hyperkatifeia: A framework for the rational use of opioids for pain. Pain Medicine 11: 1092–1098.

Shurtleff D, Liu R, Sasek C (2009) Sponsor's foreword. Neuropharmacology 56: 1–2.

Siddiqui F, Osuna E, Chokroverty S (2009) Writing e-mails as part of sleepwalking after increase in zolpidem. Sleep Medicine 10: 262–264.

Siegel S (1975) Evidence from rats that morphine tolerance is a learned response. Journal of Comparative and Physiological Psychology 89: 498–506.

Siegel S (2001) Pavlovian conditioning and drug overdose: When tolerance fails. Addiction Research and Theory 9: 503–513.

Siegel S, Baptista MAS, Kim JA, et al. (2000) Pavlovian psychopharmacology: The associative basis of tolerance. Experimental and Clinical Psychopharmacology 8: 276–293.

Siegel S, Hinson RE, Krank MD, et al. (1982) Heroin "overdose" death: Contribution of drug-associated environmental cues. Science 216: 436–437.

Siegel S, Ramos BMC (2002) Applying laboratory research: Drug anticipation and the treatment of drug addiction. Experimental and Clinical Psychopharmacology 10: 162–183.

Sigmon SC (2007) Investigating the pharmacological and nonpharmacological factors that modulate drug reinforcement. Experimental and Clinical Psychopharmacology 15: 1–20.

Sigvardsson S, Bohman M, Cloninger CR (1996) Replication of the Stockholm adoption study of alcoholism: Confirmatory cross-fostering analysis. Archives of General Psychiatry 53: 681–687.

Silvers JM, Tokunaga S, Berry RB (2003) Impairments in spatial learning and memory: Ethanol, allopregnanolone and the hippocampus. Brain Research Reviews 43: 275–284.

Sim T, Simon SL, Richardson K, et al. (2002) Cognitive deficits among methamphetamine users with attention deficit hyperactivity disorder symptomology. Journal of Addictive Disorders 21: 35–44.

Simon SL, Domier CP, Sim T, et al. (2002) Cognitive performance of current methamphetamine and cocaine abusers. Journal of Addictive Disorders 21: 61–74.

Simon TL, Dacey J, Glynn S, et al. (2004) The effect of relapse on cognition in abstinent methamphetamine abusers. Journal of Substance Abuse Treatment 27: 59–66.

Simons JS, Oliver MN, Gaher RM, et al. (2005) Methamphetamine and alcohol abuse and dependence symptoms: Association with affect lability and impulsivity in a rural treatment population. Addictive Behaviors 30: 1370–1381.

Singer LT, Moore DG, Fulton S, et al. (2012) Neurobehavioral outcomes of infants exposed to MDMA (ecstasy) and other recreational drugs during pregnancy. Neurotoxicology and Teratology 34: 303–310.

Singh I, Bard I, Jackson J (2014) Robust resilience and substantial interest: A survey of pharmacological cognitive enhancement among university students in the UK and Ireland. PLoS ONE 9(10): e105969.

Singh T, Marynak K, Arrazola RA, et al. (2016) Vital signs: Exposure to electronic cigarette advertising among middle school and high school students – United States 2014. Morbidity and Mortality Weekly Reports **64**: 1403–1408.

Sinha R (2001) How does stress increase risk of drug abuse and relapse? Psychopharmacology **158**: 343–359.

Sinha R (2007) The role of stress in addiction relapse. Current Psychiatry Reports **9**: 388–395.

Sinha R, Garcia M, Paliwal P, et al. (2006) Stress-induced cocaine craving and hypothalamic-pituitary-adrenal responses are predictive of cocaine relapse outcomes. Archives of General Psychiatry **63**: 324–331.

Sinha R, Li CS (2007) Imaging stress and cue-induced drug and alcohol craving: Association with relapse and clinical implications. Drug and Alcohol Review **26**: 25–31.

Siriwardena AN, Qureshi MZ, Dyas JV, et al. (2008) Magic bullets for insomnia? Patients' use and experiences of newer (Z drugs) versus older (benzodiazepine) hypnotics for sleep problems in primary care. British Journal of General Practice **58**: 417–422.

Skenderian JJ, Siegel JT, Crano WD, et al. (2008) Expectancy change and adolescents' intent to use marijuana. Psychology of Addictive Behaviors **22**: 563–569.

Skog O (2000) Addicts' choice. Addiction **95**: 1309–1314.

Skog OJ, Duckert F (1993) The development of alcoholics' and heavy drinkers' consumption: A longitudinal study. Journal of Studies on Alcoholism **54**: 178–188.

Slade D, Mehmedic Z, Chandra S, et al. (2012) Is cannabis becoming more potent? In Castle D, Murray RM, D'Souza C (eds.) Marijuana and Madness. 2nd ed. Cambridge: Cambridge University Press.

Slutske WS, Piasecki TM, Hunt-Carver EE (2003) Development and initial validation of the Hangover Symptoms Scale: Prevalence and correlates of hangover symptoms in college students. Alcoholism: Clinical and Experimental Research **27**: 1442–1450.

Smith AE, Cavallo DA, Dahl T, et al. (2008) Effects of acute tobacco abstinence in adolescent smokers as compared with nonsmokers. Journal of Adolescent Health **43**: 46–54.

Smith DE (1968) The acute and chronic toxicity of marijuana. Journal of Psychedelic Drugs **2**: 37–48.

Smith GT, Goldman MS, Greenbaum PE, et al. (1995) Expectancy for social facilitation from drinking: The divergent paths of high-expectancy and low-expectancy adolescents. Journal of Abnormal Psychology **104**: 32–40.

Smith LM, LaGasse LL, Derauf C, et al. (2006) The infant development, environment and lifestyle study: Effects of prenatal methamphetamine exposure, polydrug exposure, and poverty on intrauterine growth. Pediatrics **118**: 1149–1157.

Smith LM, LaGasse LL, Derauf C, et al. (2011) Motor and cognitive outcomes through three years of age in children exposed to prenatal methamphetamine. Neurotoxicology and Teratology **33**: 176–184.

Smith MY, Bailey JE, Woody GE, et al. (2007) Abuse of buprenorphine in the United States: 2003–2005. Journal of Addictive Disorders **26**: 107–111.

Smith-Kielland A, Skuterud B, Morland J (1999) Urinary excretion of 11-nor-9-carboxy-delta 9 tetrahydrocannabinol and cannabinoids in frequent and infrequent users. Journal of Analytical Toxicology **23**: 323–332.

Smoller JW, Finn C, White C (2000) The genetics of anxiety disorders: An overview. Psychiatry Annals **30**: 745–753.

Smyth B, Hoffman V, Fan J, et al. (2007) Years of potential life lost among heroin addicts 33 years after treatment. Preventive Medicine **44**: 369–374.

Snoek A, Mattews S (2017) Introduction: Testing and refining Marc Lewis' critique of the brain disease model of addiction. Neuroethics **10**: 1–6.

Snyder SH (1972) Catecholamines in the brain as mediators of amphetamine psychosis. Archives of General Psychiatry **27**: 169–179.

Sobell LC, Sobell MB, Wagner EF, et al. (2006) Guided self-change: A brief motivational intervention for cannabis abuse. In Roffman RA, Stephens RS (eds.) Cannabis Dependence: Its Nature, Consequences and Treatment. Cambridge: Cambridge University Press.

Sobell MB, Sobell LC (1973) Individualized behavior therapy for alcoholics. Behavior Therapy **4**: 49–72.

Sofuoglu M, Babb DA, Hatsukami DK (2002) Effects of progesterone treatment on smoked cocaine response in women. Pharmacology, Biochemistry, and Behavior **72**: 431–435.

Sofuoglu M, Mitchell E, Kosten TR (2004) Effects of progesterone treatment on cocaine responses in male and female cocaine users. Pharmacology, Biochemistry, and Behavior **78**: 699–705.

Soka M, Bottlender R, Moller HJ (2000) Epidemiological evidence for a low abuse potential of zolpidem. Pharmacopsychiatry **33**: 138–141.

Solomon RL, Corbit JD (1974) An opponent-process theory of motivation: 1. Temporal dynamics of affect. Psychological Review **81**: 119–145.

Solowij N, Pesa N (2012) Cannabis and cognition: Short-term and long-term effects. In Castle D, Murray RM, D'Souza C (eds.) Marijuana and Madness. 2nd ed. Cambridge: Cambridge University Press.

Sommers CH, Satel S (2005) One Nation under Therapy. New York: St. Martin's Press.

Sora I, Elmer G, Funada M, et al. (2001) Mu opiate receptor gene dose effects on different morphine actions: Evidence for differential in vivo mu receptor reserve. Neuropsychopharmacology **79**: 278–283.

Sorensen JL, Hettema JE, Larios S (2009) What is evidence-based treatment? In Miller PM (ed.) Evidence-Based Addiction Treatment. Burlington MA: Academic Press.

Spear LP (2018) Effects of adolescent alcohol consumption on the brain and behavior. Nature Reviews: Neuroscience **19**: 197–214.

Spear LP, Swartzwelder HS (2014) Adolescent alcohol exposure and persistence of adolescent-typical phenotypes into adulthood: A mini-review. Neuroscience and Biobehavioral Reviews **45**: 1–8.

Spencer S, Scofield M, Kalivas PW (2016) The good and bad news about glutamate in drug addiction. Journal of Psychopharmacology **30**: 1095–1098.

Spitzer RL, Williams JBW, Gibbon M, et al. (1992) The structured clinical interview for DSM-III-R (SCID). Archives of General Psychiatry **49**: 624–636.

Srisurapanont M, Jarusuraisin N, Jittiwutkarn J (1999) Amphetamine withdrawal: I. Reliability, validity and factor structure of a measure. Australian and New Zealand Journal of Psychiatry **33**: 89–93.

Stacy AW, Newcomb MD, Bentler PM (1991) Cognitive motivation and drug use: A 9-year longitudinal study. Journal of Abnormal Psychology **100**: 502–515.

Stahl S (2008) Stahl's Essential Psychopharmacology: Neuroscientific Basis and Practical Applications. 3rd ed. New York: Cambridge University Press.

Staley JK, Krishnan-Sarin S, Cosgrove KP, et al. (2006) Human tobacco smokers in early abstinence have higher levels of beta2 nicotinic acetylcholine receptors than nonsmokers. Journal of Neuroscience **26**: 8708–8714.

Stanos SP, Bruckenthal P, Barkin RL (2012) Strategies to reduce the tampering and subsequent abuse of long-acting opioids: Potential risks and benefits of formulations with physical or pharmacological deterrents to tampering. Mayo Clinic Proceedings **87**: 683–694.

Starkman BG, Sakharkar AJ, Pandey SC (2014) Epigenetics – beyond the genome in alcoholism. Alcohol Research: Current Reviews **34**: 293–305.

Steele CM, Josephs RA (1990) Alcohol myopia: Its prized and dangerous effects. American Psychologist **45**: 921–933.

Steinberg ML, Williams JM, Steinberg HR, et al. (2005) Applicability of the Fagerstrom Test for Nicotine Dependence in smokers with schizophrenia. Addictive Behaviors **30**: 49–59.

Steketee JD, Kalivas PW (2011) Drug wanting: Behavioral sensitization and relapse to drug-seeking behavior. Pharmacological Reviews **63**: 348–365.

Stephens RS, Babor TF, Kadden R, et al. (2002) The Marijuana Treatment Project: Rationale, design and participant characteristics. Addiction **97**(Suppl. 1): 109–124.

Steuber TL, Danner F (2006) Adolescent smoking and depression: Which comes first? Addictive Behaviors **31**: 133–136.

Stewart SA (2005) The effects of benzodiazepines on cognition. Journal of Clinical Psychiatry **66**(Suppl. 2): 9–13.

Stewart SH (1996) Alcohol abuse in individuals exposed to trauma: A critical review. Psychological Bulletin **120**: 83–112.

Stewart SH (2009) Dependence and diagnosis. In Miller PM (ed.) Evidence-Based Addiction Treatment. Burlington, MA: Academic Press.

Stewart SH, Conners GJ (2004) Screening for alcohol problems: What makes a test effective? Alcohol Research and Health **28**: 5–16.

Stolerman IP, Jarvis MJ (1995) The scientific case that nicotine is addictive. Psychopharmaocology **117**: 2–10.

Strakowski SM, Sax KW (1998) Progressive behavioral response to repeated d-amphetamine challenge: Further evidence for sensitization in humans. Biological Psychiatry **44**: 1171–1177.

Strakowski SM, Sax KW, Setters MJ, et al. (1996) Enhanced response to repeated d-amphetamine challenge: Evidence for behavioral sensitization in humans. Biological Psychiatry **40**: 872–880.

Straussner SLA (2014) Assessment and treatment of clients with substance use disorders: An overview. In Straussner SLA (ed.) Clinical Work with Substance-Abusing Clients. New York: Guilford Press.

Streissguth AP, O'Malley K (2000) Neuropsychiatric implications and long-term consequences of fetal alcohol spectrum disorders. Seminars in Clinical Neuropsychiatry **5**: 177–190.

Strickland TL, Mena I, Villaneuva-Meyer J, et al. (1993) Cerebral perfusion and neuropsychological consequences of chronic cocaine use. Journal of Neuropsychiatry and Clinical Neurosciences **5**: 419–427.

Substance Abuse and Mental Health Services Administration (2008) Results from the 2007 National Survey on Drug Use and Health: National Findings. SDUH Series H-34, DHHS Publication SMA 08-4343. Rockville, MD: Substance Abuse and Mental Health Services Administration

Substance Abuse and Mental Health Services Administration (2012) Results from the 2011 National Survey on Drug Use and Health: Summary of National Findings. HHS Publication SMA 12-4713, NSDUH Series H-44.

Rockville, MD: Substance Abuse and Mental Health Services Administration.

Substance Abuse and Mental Health Services Administration (2013) Results from the 2012 National Survey on Drug Use and Health: Summary of National Findings. HHS Publication SMA 13-4795, NSDUH Series H-46. Rockville, MD: Substance Abuse and Mental Health Services Administration.

Substance Abuse and Mental Health Services Administration (2017) Key Substance Use and Mental Health Indicators in the United States: Results from the 2016 National Survey on Drug Use and Health. HHS Publication SMA 17-5044, NSDUH Series H-52. Rockville, MD: Substance Abuse and Mental Health Services Administration.

Substance Abuse and Mental Health Services Administration (2018) Key Substance Use and Mental Health Indicators in the United States: Results from the 2017 National Survey on Drug Use and Health. HHS Publication SMA 18-5068, NSDUH Series H-53. Rockville, MD: Substance Abuse and Mental Health Services Administration.

Sugiura T, Kondo S, Sukagawa A, et al. (1995) 2-Arachidonoylglycerol: A possible endogenous cannabinoid receptor ligand in brain. Biochemical and Biophysical Research Communications **215**: 89–97.

Sullivan EV, Harris RA, Pfefferbaum A (2010) Alcohol's effects on brain and behavior. Alcohol Research and Health **33**: 127–143.

Sullivan EV, Pfefferbaum A (2005) Neurocircuitry in alcoholism: A substrate of disruption and repair. Psychopharmacology **180**: 583–594.

Sullivan EV, Pfefferbaum A (2006) Diffusion tensor imaging and aging. Neuroscience and Biobehavioral Reviews **30**: 749–761.

Sullivan PF, Kendler KS (1999) The genetic epidemiology of smoking. Nicotine and Tobacco Research **1**: 851–857.

Sullivan PF, Neale MC, Kendler KS (2000) Genetic epidemiology of major depression: review and meta-analysis. American Journal of Psychiatry **157**: 1552–1562.

Sulzer D, Sonders MS, Poulsen NW, et al. (2005) Mechanism of neurotransmitter release by amphetamines: A review. Progress in Neurobiology **75**: 406–433.

Sumner SA, Mercy JA, Dahlberg LL, et al. (2015) Violence in the United States: Status, challenges, and opportunities. Journal of the American Medical Association **314**: 478–488.

Sung YH, Cho S, Hwang J, et al. (2006) Relationship between N-acetyl-aspartate in gray and white matter of abstinent methamphetamine users and their history of drug abuse: A proton magnetic resonance spectroscopy study. Drug and Alcohol Dependence **88**: 28–35.

Sutin AR, Evans MK, Zonderman AB (2013) Personality traits and illicit substances: The moderating role of poverty. Drug and Alcohol Dependence **131**: 247–251.

Swartzwelder HS, Wilson WA, Tayyeb MI (1995) Differential sensitivity of NMDA receptor-mediated synaptic potentials to ethanol in immature vs. mature hippocampus. Alcoholism: Clinical and Experimental Research **19**: 320–323.

Swendsen J, Conway KP, Degenhardt L, et al. (2009) Socio-demographic risk factors for alcohol and drug dependence: The 10-year follow-up of the National Comorbidity Survey. Addiction **104**: 1346–1355.

Swendsen J, Conway KP, Degenhardt L, et al. (2010) Mental disorders as risk factors for substance use, abuse and dependence: Results from the 10-year follow-up of the National Comorbidity Survey. Addiction **105**: 1117–1128.

Swift R, Leggio L (2009) Adjunctive pharmacotherapy in the treatment of alcohol and drug dependence. In Miller PM (ed.) Evidence-Based Addiction Treatment. Burlington, MA: Academic Press.

Szalavitz M (2006) Help at Any Cost. New York: Riverhead Books.

Szalavitz M (2016) Unbroken Brain.New York: Picador St. Martins Press.

Tam TW, Mulia N, Schmidt LA (2014) Applicability of type A/B alcohol dependence in the general population. Drug and Alcohol Dependence **138**: 169–176.

Tan KR, Rudolph U, Luscher C (2011) Hooked on benzodiazepines: GABA-A receptor subtypes and addiction. Trends in Neuroscience **34**: 188–197.

Tapert SF, Granholm E, Leedy N, et al. (2002) Substance use and withdrawal: Neuropsychological functioning over 8 years in youth. Journal of the International Neuropsychological Society **5**: 481–493.

Tapert SF, Theilmann RJ, Schweinsburg AD (2003) Reduced fractional anistropy in the splenium of adolescents with alcohol use disorder. Proceedings of the International Society of Magnetic Resonance Medicine 11: 8217.

Tart CT (1971) On Being Stoned. Palo Alto, CA: Science and Behavior Books.

Tarter RE (1983) The causes of alcoholism: A biopsychosocial analysis. In Gottheil K, Druley K, Skolada T, et al. (eds.) Etiological Aspects of Alcohol and Drug Abuse. Springfield, IL: Thompson.

Tarter RE (2005) Psychological evaluation of substance use disorder in adolescents and adults. In Frances RJ, Miller SI, Mack AH (eds.) Clinical Textbook of Addictive Disorders. New York: Guilford Press.

Tarter RE, Kirisci L, Habeych M, et al. (2004) Neurobehavior disinhibition in childhood predisposes boys to substance use disorder by young adulthood: Direct and mediated etiologic pathways. Drug and Alcohol Dependence 73: 121–132.

Tarter RE, Kirisci L, Mezzich A, et al. (2003) Neurobehavior disinhibition in childhood predicts early age onset of substance disorder. American Journal of Psychiatry 160: 1078–1085.

Tashkin DP (2005) Smoked marijuana as a cause of lung injury. Monalid Archives of Chest Disorders 63: 93–100.

Taylor C, Brown D, Duckitt A, et al. (1985) Patterns of outcome: Drinking histories over ten years among a group of alcoholics. British Journal of Addictions 80: 45–50.

Taylor SP (1993) Experimental investigation of alcohol-induced aggression in humans. Alcohol Health and Research World 17: 108–112.

Tellegen A (1985) Structures of mood and personality and their relevance to assessing anxiety, with an emphasis on self-report. In Tuma AH, Maser JD (eds.) Anxiety and Anxiety Disorders. Hillsdale, NJ: Lawrence Erlbaum.

Tellegen A, Waller NG (2001) Exploring Personality through Test Construction: Development of the Multidimensional Personality Questionnaire. Minneapolis: University of Minnesota Press.

Terracciano A, Lockenhoff CE, Crum RM, et al. (2008) Five-factor model personality profiles of drug users. BMC Psychiatry 8: 22–30.

Tevyaw TO, Monti PM (2004) Motivational enhancement and other brief interventions for adolescent substance abuse: Foundations, applications, evaluations. Addiction 99(Suppl. 2): 63–75.

Thanos PK, Volkow ND, Freimuth P, et al. (2001) Overexpression of dopamine D2 receptors reduces alcohol self-administration. Journal of Neurochemistry 78: 1094–1103.

Thatcher DL, Clark DB (2008) Adolescents at risk for substance use disorders: Role of psychological dysregulation, endophenotypes, and environmental influences. Alcohol Research and Health 31: 168–176.

Thom B (2001) A social and political history of alcohol. In Heather N, Peters T, Stockwell T (eds.) International Handbook of Alcohol Dependence and Problems. Chichester, UK: John Wiley.

Thomas JD, Warren KR, Hewitt BG (2010) Fetal alcohol disorders: From research to policy. Alcohol Research and Health 33: 118–126.

Thombs DL (1993) The differentially discriminating properties of alcohol expectancies for female and male drinkers. Journal of Counseling and Development **71**: 321–325.

Thombs DL, Osborn CJ (2013) Introduction to Addictive Behaviors. 4th ed. New York: Guilford Press.

Thombs DL, Osborn CJ (2019) Introduction to Addictive Behaviors. 5th ed. New York: Guilford Press.

Tiffany S, Warthen M, Goedecker K (2009) The functional significance of craving in nicotine dependence. Nebraska Symposium on Motivation **55**: 171–191.

Tiffany ST (1990) A cognitive model of drug urges and drug-use behavior: Role of automatic and nonautomatic processes. Psychological Review **97**: 147–168.

Tiffany ST, Conklin CA (2000) A cognitive processing model of alcohol craving and compulsive alcohol use. Addiction **95**(Suppl. 2): S145–S153.

Tiffany ST, Singleton E, Haertzen CA, et al. (1993) The development of a cocaine craving questionnaire. Drug and Alcohol Dependence **34**: 19–28.

Tiffany ST, Warthen MW, Goedeker KC (2009) The functional significance of craving in nicotine dependence. Nebraska Symposium on Motivation **55**: 171–197.

Tinklenberg JR, Kopell BS, Melges FT, et al. (1972) Marihuana and alcohol, time production and memory functions. Archives of General Psychiatry **27**: 812–815.

Tischler V (2015) Dr. Junkie. The doctor addict in Bulgakov's *Morphine*: What are the lessons for contemporary medical practice? Journal of Medical Humanities **36**: 359–368.

Tobacco and Genetics Consortium (2010) Genome-wide meta-analyses identify multiple loci associated with smoking behavior. Nature Genetics **42**: 441–447.

Toila VN, Patrick SW, Bennett MM, et al. (2015) Increasing incidence of the neonatal abstinence syndrome in US neonatal ICUs. New England Journal of Medicine **372**: 2118–2126.

Tonigan JS, Toscova R, Miller WR (1996) Meta-analysis of the literature on Alcoholics Anonymous: Sample study characteristics moderate findings. Journal of Studies on Alcohol **57**: 65–72.

Tooley EM, Moyers TB (2012) Motivational interviewing in practice. In Walters ST, Rotgers F (eds.) Treating Substance Abuse: Theory and Technique. New York: Guilford Press.

Toumbourou J, Stockwell T, Neighbors C, et al. (2007) Interventions to reduce harm associated with adolescent substance use. Lancet **396**: 1391–1401.

Towe SL, Hobkirk AL, Ye DG, et al. (2015) Adaptation of the Monetary Choice Questionaire to accommodate extreme monetary discounting in cocaine users. Psychology of Addictive Behavior **20**: 22–29.

Tracy S (2005) Alcoholism in America: From Reconstruction to Prohibition. Baltimore, MD: Johns Hopkins University Press.

Trauth JA, Seidler FJ, Ali SF, et al. (2001) Adolescent nicotine exposure produces immediate and long-term changes in CNS noradrenergic and dopaminergic function. Brain Research **892**: 269–280.

Traynor J (2012) mu-Opioid receptors and regulators of G protein signaling (RGS) proteins: From a symposium on new concepts in mu-opioid pharmacology. Drug and Alcohol Dependence **121**: 173–180.

Treloar H, Piasecki TM, McCarthy CM, et al. (2015) Ecological evidence that affect and perceptions of drink effects depend on alcohol expectancies. Addiction **110**: 1432–1442.

Treweek JB, Roberts AJ, Janda KD (2010) Superadditive effects of ethanol and flunitrazepam: implications of using immunopharmacotherapy as a therapeutic. Molecular Pharmacology **7**: 2056–2068.

Trigo JM, Martin-Garcia E, Berrendero F, et al. (2010) The endogenous opioid system: A common substrate in drug addiction. Drug and Alcohol Dependence **108**: 183–194.

Trull TJ, Sher KJ, Minks-Brown C, et al. (2000) Borderline personality disorder and substance use disorders: A review and integration. Clinical Psychology Review **20**: 235–253.

Tsuang MT, Lyons MJ, Harley RM, et al. (1999) Genetic and environmental influences on transitions in drug use. Behavior Genetics **29**: 473–479.

Tuesta L, Fowler CD, Kenny PJ (2011) Recent advances in understanding nicotinic receptor signalling mechanisms that regulate self-administration behavior. Biochemical Pharmacology. **82**: 984–985.

Tyacki RJ, Lingford-Hughes A, Reed LJ, et al. (2010) GABA-B receptors in addiction and its treatment. Advances in Pharmacology **58**: 373–396.

Tyndale RF, Sellers EM (2001) Variable CYP2A6-mediated nicotine metabolism alters smoking behavior and risk. Drug Metabolism and Disposition **29**: 548–552.

Uchiyama N, Kikura-Hanajiri R, Ogata J, et al. (2010) Chemical analysis of synthetic cannabinoids as designer drugs in herbal products. Forensic Science International **198**: 31–38.

Uhart M, Oswald L, McCaul ME, et al. (2006) Hormonal responses to psychological stress and family history of alcoholism. Neuropsychopharmacology **31**: 2255–2263.

Uhart M, Wand GS (2009) Stress, alcohol and drug interaction: An update of human research. Addiction Biology **14**: 43–64.

Uhl GR, Drgon T, Johnson C, et al. (2008) Molecular genetics of addiction and related heritable phenotypes: genome-wide association approaches identify "connectivity constellation" and drug target genes with pleiotropic effects. Annals of the New York Academy of Science **1141**: 318–381.

Uhlenhuth E, Balter M, Ban T, et al. (1999) International study of expert judgement on therapeutic use of benzodiazepines and other psychotherapeutic medications: IV. Therapeutic dose, dependence and abuse liability of the benzodiazepines in the long-term treatment of anxiety disorders. Journal of Clinical Psychopharmacology **19**(Suppl. 2): 23S–29S.

Ujike H, Harano M, Inada T (2003) Nine- or fewer repeat alleles in VNTR polymorphism of the dopamine transporter gene is a strong risk factor for prolonged methamphetamine psychosis. Pharmacogenomics Journal 3: 242–247.

United Nations Office of Drug Control (2012) World Drug Report 2012 (United Nations publication, Sales No. E.12. XI.1).

Urban NB, Kegeles LS, Slifstein M, et al. (2010) Sex differences in striatal dopamine release in young adults after oral alcohol challenge: A positron emission tomography imaging study with [llC] raclopride. Biological Psychiatry **68**: 689–696.

US Department of Health and Human Services (1988) The Health Consequences of Smoking: Nicotine Addiction – a Report of the Surgeon General. DHHS Publication (CDC)88-8406. Washington, DC: US Government Printing Office.

US Department of Health and Human Services (2010) How Tobacco Smoke Causes Disease: The Biology and Behavioral Basis for Smoking-Attributable Disease: A Report of the Surgeon General. Atlanta, GA: Centers for Disease Control and Prevention, National Center for Chronic Disease Prevention and Health Promotion, Office on Smoking and Health.

US Department of Health and Human Services (2012) National Survey on Drug Use and Health, 2012. Ann Arbor, MI: Inter-university Consortium for Political and Social Research.

US Department of Health and Human Services (2014) The Health Consequences of Smoking – 50 Years of Progress. Report of the Surgeon General. Atlanta, GA: Centers for Disease Control and Prevention, National Center for Chronic Disease Prevention and Health Promotion, Office on Smoking and Health.

US Department of Health and Human Services (2016) E-Cigarette Use among Youth and Young Adults. A Report of the Surgeon General. Atlanta, GA: Centers for Disease Control and Prevention, National Center for Chronic Disease Prevention and Health Promotion, Office on Smoking and Health.

US Department of Health, Education and Welfare (1964) Smoking and Health: Report of the Advisory Committee to the Surgeon General of the Public Health Service. DHEW Publication PHS 64-1103. Washington, DC: US Government Printing Office.

Vadhan NP, Hart CL, Van Gorp WG, et al. (2007) Acute effects of smoked marijuana on decision making, as assessed by a modified gambling task, in experienced marijuana users. Journal of Clinical and Experimental Neuropsychology **29**: 357–364.

Vaillant G (2003) Natural history of addiction and pathways to recovery. In Graham AW, Schultz TK, Mayo-Smith MF, et al. (eds.) Principles of Addiction Medicine. 3rd ed. Chevy Chase, MD: American Society of Addiction Medicine.

Vaillant GE (1995) The Natural History of Alcoholism Revisited. New York: Cambridge University Press.

Vaillant GE (2003) A 60-year follow-up of alcoholic men. Addiction **98**: 1043–1051.

van Dam NT, Earleywine ME (2010) Pulmonary function in cannabis users: Support for a clinical trial of the vaporizer. International Journal on Drug Policy 21: 511–513.

van der Tempel J, Noormohamed A, Schwartz R, et al. (2016) Vape, quit, tweet? Electronic cigarettes and smoking cessation on Twitter. International Journal of Public Health 61: 249–256.

Van Holst RJ, de Ruiter MB, von den Brink W, et al. (2012) A voxel-based morphometry study comparing problem gamblers, alcohol abusers, and healthy controls. Drug and Alcohol Dependence 124: 142–148.

Vanderschuren LJ, Everitt BJ (2004) Drug seeking becomes compulsive after prolonged cocaine self-administration. Science 305: 1017–1019.

Vandrey RG, Budney AJ, Hughes JR, et al. (2008) A within-subject comparison of withdrawal symptoms during abstinence from cannabis, tobacco, and both substances. Drug and Alcohol Dependence 92: 48–54.

Vann BB, Wolfgang LA (1999) Animal models of craving: A roundtable discussion. Alcohol Research and Health 23: 233–236.

Vanukov MM, Tarter RE, Kirillova GP, et al. (2012) Common liability to addiction and "gateway hypothesis": Theoretical, empirical and evolutionary perspective. Drug and Alcohol Dependence 123(Suppl. 1): S3–S17.

Vega WA, Gil AG (2005) Revisiting drug progression: Long-range effects of early tobacco use. Addiction 100: 1358–1369.

Veliz P, Boyd C, McCabe SE (2013) Adolescent athletic participation and non-medical Adderall use: An exploratory analysis of a performance-enhancing drug. Journal of Studies on Alcohol and Drugs 74: 714–719.

Vengeliene V, Bilbao A, Molander A, et al. (2008) Neuropharmacology of alcohol addiction. British Journal of Pharmacology 154: 299–315.

Venter JC, Celera Genomics (2001) The sequence of the human genome. Science 291: 1304–1351.

Verdejo-Garcia A, Bechara A (2009) A somatic marker theory of addiction. Neuropharmacology 56: 48–62.

Verdejo-Garcia A, Lawrence AJ, Clark L (2008) Impulsivity as a vulnerability marker for substance-use disorders: Review of findings from high-risk research, problem gamblers and genetic association studies. Neuroscience and Biobehavioral Reviews 32: 777–810.

Verdejo-Garcia A, Perez-Garcia M (2007) Profile of executive deficits in cocaine and heroin polysubstance users: common and differential effects on separate executive components. Psychopharmacology 190: 517–530.

Verebey K, Gold MS (1988) From coca leaves to crack: The effects of dose and routes of administration in abuse liability. Psychiatric Annals 18: 513–520.

Verheul R, Kranzler HR, Poling J, et al. (2000) Axis I and axis II disorders in alcoholics and drug addicts: Fact or artifact. Journal of Studies on Alcohol 61: 101–110.

Verster JC, Volkerts ER, Olivier B, et al. (2007) Zolpidem and traffic safety – the importance of treatment compliance. Current Drug Safety 2: 220–226.

Verster JC, Volkerts ER, Schreuder AH, et al. (2002) Residual effects of middle of the night administration of zaleplon and zolpidem on driving ability, memory functions and psychomotor performance. Journal of Clinical Psychopharmacology 22: 576–583.

Vetreno RP, Hall HM, Savage LM (2011) Alcohol-related amnesia and dementia: Animal models have revealed the contributions of different etiological factors on neuropathology, neurochemical dysfunction and cognitive impairment. Neurobiology of Learning and Memory 96: 596–608.

Victor M, Adams RD (1953) Effect of alcohol on the nervous system. Research Publication of the Association for Research in Nervous and Mental Diseases 32: 526–523.

Victor M, Adams RD, Collins GH (1989) The Wernick–Korsakoff Syndrome and Related Disorders due to Alcoholism and Malnutrition. 2nd ed. Philadelphia: FA Davis.

Victorri-Vigneau C, Feuillet F, Wainstein L, et al. (2013) Pharmacoepidemiological characterization of zolpidem and zopiclone usage. European Journal of Pharmacology 69: 1965–1972.

Viken RJ, Rose RJ, Morzorati SL, et al. (2003) Subjective intoxication in response to alcohol challenge: Heritability and covariation with personality, breath alcohol level, and drinking history. Alcoholism: Clinical and Experimental Research 27: 795–803.

Vinals X, Maldonado R, Robledo P (2013) Effects of repeated treatment with MDMA on working memory and behavioural flexibility in mice. Addiction Biology 18: 263–273.

Vink JM, Willemsen G, Boomsma DI (2005) Heritability of smoking initiation and nicotine dependence. Behavior Genetics 35: 397–406.

Vivolo-Kantor AM, Seth P, Gladden RM, et al. (2018) Trends in emergency department visits for suspected opioid overdoses – United States, July 2016–September 2017. Morbidity and Mortality Weekly Reports. Advance online publication.

Voderholzer U, Reimann D, Hornyak M, et al. (2002) A double-blind, randomized and placebo-controlled study on the polysomnographic withdrawal effects of zopiclone, zolpidem and triazolam in healthy subjects. European Archives of Psychiatry, Clinical Neuroscience 25: 117–123.

Voet W (2002) Breaking the Chain. Fotheringham W (trans.). London: Yellow Jersey Press.

Vogel M, Knopfli B, Schmid O, et al. (2013) Treatment or "high": Benzodiazepine use in patients on injectable heroin or oral opioids. Addictive Behaviors 38: 2477–2484.

Vogel-Sprott M (1997) Is behavioral tolerance learned? Alcohol Health and Research World 21: 161–168.

Vogel-Sprott M, Fillmore MT (1999) Learning theory and research. In Leonard KE, Blane HT (eds.) Psychological Theories of Drinking and Alcoholism. 2nd ed. New York: Guilford Press.

Volavka J, Czobor P, Goodwin D (1996) The electroencephalogram after alcohol administration in high-risk men and the development of alcohol use disorders 10 years later. Archives of General Psychiatry 53: 258–263.

Volkow N, Doherty N, Gottlieb S (2017) Federal efforts to combat the opioid crisis: A status update on CARA and other initiatives. www.drugabuse.gov/about-nida/legislative-activities.

Volkow N, Fowler J, Wang G (2002a) Role of dopamine in drug reinforcement and addiction in humans: results from imaging studies. Behavioural Pharmacology 13: 355–366.

Volkow N, Fowler J, Wang G (2003) The addicted human brain: Insights from imaging studies. Journal of Clinical Investigation 111: 1444–1451.

Volkow ND, Baler RD, Compton WM, et al. (2014) Adverse health effects of marijuana use. New England Journal of Medicine 370: 2219–2227.

Volkow ND, Chang L, Wang GJ, et al. (2001) Low level of brain dopamine D2 receptors in methamphetamine abusers: Association with metabolism in the orbitofrontal cortex. American Journal of Psychiatry 158: 2015–2021.

Volkow ND, Chang L, Wang GJ, et al. (2001a) Loss of dopamine transporters in methamphetamine abusers recovers with protracted abstinence. Journal of Neuroscience 21: 9414–9418.

Volkow ND, Chang L, Wang GJ, et al. (2001b) Association of dopamine transporter reduction with psychomotor impairment in methamphetamine abusers. American Journal of Psychiatry 158: 377–382.

Volkow ND, Fowler JS (2000) Addiction, a disease of compulsion and drive: Involvement of the orbitofrontal cortex. Cerebral Cortex 10: 318–325.

Volkow ND, Fowler JS, Wang GJ (2003) The addicted human brain: Insights from imaging studies. Journal of Clinical Investigation 111: 1444–1451.

Volkow ND, Fowler JS, Wang GJ (2004) The addicted human brain viewed in the light of imaging studies: Brain circuits and treatment strategies. Neuropharmacology 47: 3–13.

Volkow ND, Fowler JS, Wang GJ, et al. (2009) Imaging dopamine's role in drug abuse and addiction. Neuropharmacology 56(Suppl. 1): 3–8.

Volkow ND, Fowler JS, Wang GJ, et al. (2004) Dopamine in drug abuse and addiction: Results from imaging studies and treatment implications. Molecular Psychiatry 9: 557–569.

Volkow ND, Fowler JS, Wolf AP, et al. (1990) Effects of chronic cocaine abuse on postsynaptic dopamine receptors. American Journal of Psychiatry 147: 719–724.

Volkow ND, Swanson JM (2003) Variables that affect the clinical use and abuse of methylphenidate in the treatment of ADHD. American Journal of Psychiatry 160: 1908–1919.

Volkow ND, Wang GJ, Begleiter H, et al. (2006) High levels of dopamine D2 receptors in unaffected members of alcoholic families: Possible protective factors. Archives of General Psychiatry 63: 999–1008.

Volkow ND, Wang G-J, Fowler JS, et al. (2012) Addiction circuitry in the human brain. Annual Review of Pharmacology and Toxicology 52: 321–336.

Volkow ND, Wang GJ, Fowler JS, et al. (2002) Brain DA D2 receptors predict reinforcing effects of stimulants in humans: Replication study. Synapse 46: 79–82.

Volkow ND, Wang GJ, Fowler JS, et al. (2002b) Brain DA D2 receptors predict reinforcing effects of stimulants in humans: Replication study. Synapse 46: 79–82.

Volkow ND, Wang GJ, Telang F, et al. (2006) Cocaine cues and dopamine in dorsal striatum: Mechanism of craving in cocaine addiction. Journal of Neuroscience 26: 6583–6588.

Volkow ND, Wang GJ, Telang F, et al. (2014) Decreased dopamine brain reactivity in marijuana abusers is associated with negative emotionality and addiction severity. *PNAS*, Article E3149. Advance online publication.

Volpe DA, McMahon GA, Mellon RD, et al. (2011) Uniform assessment and ranking of opioid mu receptor binding constants for selected opioid drugs. Regulatory Toxicology and Pharmacology 59: 385–390.

Vosburgh HW, Mansergh G, Sullivan PS, et al. (2012) A review of the literature on event-level substance abuse and sexual risk behavior among men who have sex with men. AIDS Behavior 6: 1394–1410.

Vrecko S (2010) "Civilizing technologies" and the control of deviance. Biosocieties 5: 36–61.

Wagner FA, Anthony JC (2002) From first drug use to drug dependence: Developmental periods for risk of dependence upon marijuana, cocaine and alco-hol. Neuropsychopharmacology 26: 479–488.

Wagner FA, Anthony JC (2002) Into the world of illegal drug use: exposure opportunity and other mechanisms linking the use of alcohol, tobacco, marijuana, and cocaine. American Journal of Epidemiology 155: 918–925.

Wakefield JC (1999) Evolutionary versus prototype analyses of the concept of disorder. Journal of Abnormal Psychology 108: 374–399.

Wakefield JC, First MB (2003) Clarifying the distinction between disorder and nondisorder: Confronting the overdiagnosis problem in DSM-IV. In Phillips KA, First MB, Pincus HA (eds.) Advancing DSM: Dilemmas in Psychiatric Diagnosis. Washington, DC: American Psychiatric Association.

Walker JL, Carey PD, Mohr N, et al. (2004) Gender differences in prevalence of childhood sexual abuse and in the development of pediatric PTSD. Archives of Women's Mental Health 7: 111–121.

Wallace J (1993) Modern disease models of alcoholism and other chemical dependencies: The new biopsychosocial models. Drugs and Society 8: 69–87.

Wallace J (2012) Theory of 12-step oriented treatment. In Walters ST, Rotgers F (eds.) Treating Substance Abuse: Theory and Technique. New York: Guilford Press.

Walsh RA (1994) Effects of maternal smoking on adverse pregnancy outcomes: Examination of the criteria of causation. Human Biology 66: 1059–1092.

Walter M, Gunderson JG, Zanarini MC, et al. (2009) New onsets of substance use disorders in borderline personality disorder over 7 years of follow-ups: Findings from the Collaborative Longitudinal Personality Disorders Study. Addiction **104**: 97–103.

Walters G (1999) The Addiction Concept: Working Hypothesis or Self-Fulfilling Prophesy? Boston: Allyn and Bacon.

Walters GD (2002) The heritability of alcohol use and dependence: A meta-analysis of behavior genetic research. American Journal of Drug and Alcohol Abuse **28**: 557–584.

Wand GS, McCaul ME, Gotjen D, et al. (2001) Confirmation that offspring from families with alcohol-dependent individuals have greater hypothalamic-pituitary-adrenal axis activation induced by naloxone compared with offspring without a family history of alcohol dependence. Alcoholism: Clinical and Experimental Research **25**: 1134–1139.

Wand GS, Oswald LM, McCaul ME, et al. (2007) Association of amphetamine-induced striatal dopamine release and cortisol responses to psychological stress. Neuropsychopharmacology **32**: 2310–2320.

Wang B (2005) Cocaine experience establishes control of midbrain glutamate and dopamine by corticotropin releasing factor: A role in stress-induced relapse to drug seeking. Journal of Neuroscience **25**: 5389–5396.

Wang GJ, Volkow ND, Logan J, et al. (1997) Dopamine D2 receptor availability in opiate-dependent subjects before and after naloxone-precipitated withdrawal. Neuropsychopharmacology **16**: 174–182.

Wang H, Sun X (2005) Desensitized nicotinic receptors in brain. Brain Research Review **48**: 420–437.

Wang JC, Hinrichs AL, Stock H, et al. (2004) Evidence of common and specific genetic effects: association of the muscarinic acetylcholine receptor M2 (*CHRM2*) gene with alcohol dependence and major depressive syndrome. Human Molecular Genetics **13**: 1903–1911.

Wang KH, Becker WC, Fiellin DA (2013) Prevalence and correlates for nonmedical use of prescription opioids among urban and rural residents. Drug and Alcohol Dependence **127**: 156–162.

Warner EA (2003) Laboratory diagnosis. In Graham AW, Schultz TK, Mayo-Smith MF, et al. (eds.) Principles of Addiction Medicine. 3rd ed. Chevy Chase, MD: American Society of Addiction Medicine.

Warren KR, Hewitt BG (2010) NIAAA: Advancing alcohol research for 40 years. Alcohol Research and Health **33**: 5–17.

Washton A, Zweben J (2009) Cocaine and Methamphetamine Addiction: Treatment, Recovery, and Relapse Prevention. New York: WW Norton.

Washton AM (1989) Cocaine and compulsive sexuality. Medical Aspects of Human Sexuality **13**: 32–39.

Washton AM, Zweben JE (2006) Treating alcohol and drug problems in psychotherapy practice. In Doing What Works. New York: Guilford Press.

Waterfield AA, Hughes J, Kosterlitz HW (1976) Cross tolerance between morphine and methionine-enkephalin. Nature **260**: 624–625.

Weafer J, Fillmore MT (2015) Alcohol-related cues potentiate alcohol impairment of behavioral control in drinkers. Psychology of Addictive Behaviors **29**: 290–299.

Weber E, Blackstone K, Iudicello JE, et al. (2012) Neurocognitive deficits are associated with unemployment in chronic methamphetamine users. Drug and Alcohol Dependence **125**: 149–153.

Webster LR, Webster RM (2005) Predicting aberrant behaviors in opioid-treated patients.: Preliminary validation of an opioid risk tool. Pain Medicine **6**: 432–442.

Weil AT, Zinberg NE, Nelsen JM (1968) Clinical and psychological effects of marihuana in man. Science **162**: 1234–1242.

Weinberger AH, George TP, McKee SA (2011) Difference in smoking expectancies in smokers with and without a history of major depression. Addictive Behavior **36**: 434–437.

Weinberger AH, Maciejewski PK, McKee SA, et al. (2009) Gender differences in associations between lifetime alcohol, depression, panic disorder, and posttraumatic stress disorder and tobacco withdrawal. American Journal on Addictions **18**: 140–147.

Weinborn M, Woods SP, Nulsen C, et al. (2011) Prospective memory deficits in ecstasy users: Effects of longer ongoing task delay interval. Journal of Clinical and Experimental Neuropsychology **33**: 1119–1128.

Weisheit R, White WL (2009) Methamphetamine: Its History, Pharmacology, and Treatment. Center City, MN: Hazelden.

Weiss RD, Griffin ML, Mazurick C, et al. (2003) The relationship between cocaine craving, psychosocial treatment, and subsequent cocaine use. American Journal of Psychiatry **160**: 1320–1325.

Weller RA, Halikas JA (1982) Change in effects from marijuana: A five- to six-year follow-up. Journal of Clinical Psychiatry **43**: 362–365.

Wertz JM, Sayette MA (2001) A review of the effects of perceived drug use opportunity on self-reported urge. Experimental and Clinical Psychopharmacology **9**: 3–13.

West R (2005) Defining and assessing nicotine dependence in humans. In Bock G, Goode J (eds.) Understanding Nicotine and Tobacco Addiction. Chichester, UK: John Wiley.

West R (2006) Theory of Addiction. Oxford: Blackwell.

West R, McNeill A, Raw M (2000) Smoking cessation guidelines for health professionals: An update. Thorax **55**: 987–999.

West R, McEwen A, Bolling K, et al. (2001) Smoking cessation and smoking patterns in the general population: A 1-year follow-up. Addiction **96**: 891–902.

Westermeyer J (2004) Cross-cultural aspects of substance abuse. In Galanter M, Kleber HD (eds.) Textbook of Substance Abuse Treatment. 3rd ed. Washington, DC: American Psychiatric.

Wetherill RR, Childress AR, Jagannathan K, et al. (2014) Neural responses to subliminally presented cannabis and other emotionally evocative cues in cannabis-dependent individuals. Psychopharmacology 231: 1397–1407.

Wetherill RR, Jaganathan K, Hager N, et al. (2015) Cannabis, cigarettes, and their co-occurring use: Disentangling differences in gray matter volume. International Journal of Neuropsychopharmacology 1: 1–8.

Wexelblatt SL, McAllister JM, Hall ES (2018) Opioid neonatal abstinence syndrome: An overview. Clinical and Pharmacological Therapeutics 103: 979–981.

White A, Hingson R (2014) The burden of alcohol use: Excessive alcohol consumption and related consequences among college students. Alcohol Research: Current Reviews 35: 201–218.

White AM (2003) What happened? Alcohol, memory blackouts, and the brain. Alcohol Research and Health 27: 186–196.

White AM, Jamieson-Drake DW, Swartzwelder HS (2002) Prevalence and correlates of alcohol-induced blackouts among college students: Results of an e-mail survey. Journal of American College Health 51: 117–131.

White AM, Matthews DB, Best PJ (2000) Ethanol, memory and hippocampal function: A review of recent findings. Hippocampus 10: 88–93.

White HR, Metzger L, Stouthamer-Loeber S, et al. (2007) Developmental and protective factors for cigarette smoking among African-American and white adolescent males. In Jeffries TC (ed.) Progress in Smoking and Health Research. New York: Nova Science.

White TL, Justice AJH, de Wit H (2002) Differential subjective effects of d-amphetamine by gender, hormone levels and menstrual cycle phase. Pharmacology, Biochemistry, and Behavior 73: 729–741.

White W (1998) Slaying the Dragon: The History of Addiction Treatment and Recovery in America. New York: Chestnut Health Systems.

White W (2000) The rebirth of the disease concept of alcoholism in the 20th century. Counselor 1: 62–66.

White W (2001) A disease concept for the 21st century. Counselor 2: 314–320.

Whiteside SP, Lynam DR (2001) The five factor model of impulsivity: Using a structural model of personality to understand impulsivity. Personality and Individual Differences 30: 669–689.

Whitfield JB (2002) Alcohol dehydrogenase and alcohol dependence: variation in genotype-associated risk between populations. American Journal of Human Genetics 71: 1247–1250.

Wick JY (2013) The history of benzodiazepines. Consulting Pharmacology 28: 538–548.

Widiger TA (2005) Classification and diagnosis: Historical development and contemporary issues. In Maddux JE, Winstead BA (eds.) Psychopathology: Foundations for a Contemporary Understanding. Mahwah, NJ: Lawrence Erlbaum.

Wignall ND, de Wit H (2011) Effects of nicotine on attention and inhibitory control in healthy nonsmokers. Experimental and Clinical Psychopharmacology 19: 183–191.

Wilbanks W (1989) Drug addiction should be treated as a lack of self-discipline. In Leone B (ed.) Chemical Dependency:

Opposing Viewpoints. San Diego, CA: Greenhaven.

Wild TC, Wolfe J (2009) The clinical course of addiction treatment: The role of nonspecific therapeutic factors. In Miller PM (ed.) Evidence-Based Addiction Treatment. Burlington, MA: Academic Press.

Wilens TE, Faraone SV, Biederman J, et al. (2003) Does stimulant therapy of attention-deficit disorder beget later substance abuse? A meta-analytic review of the literature. Pediatrics 111: 179–185.

Wiley JL, Burston JJ, Leggett DC, et al. (2005) CB1 cannabinoid receptor-mediated modulation of food intake in mice. British Journal of Pharmacology 145: 293–300.

Wilhite E, Mallard T, Fromme K (2018) A longitudinal event-level investigation of alcohol intoxication, alcohol-related blackouts, childhood sexual abuse, and sexual victimization among college students. Psychology of Addictive Behaviors 32: 289–300.

Wilkinson P, Van Dyke C, Jatlow P, et al. (1980) Intranasal and oral cocaine kinetics. Clinical Pharmacology and Therapeutics 27: 386–394.

Wilkinson ST, Radhakrishnan R, D'Souza DC (2014) Inpact of cannabis use on the development of psychotic disorders. Current Addiction Reports 1: 115–128.

Willenbring ML (2010) The past and future of research on treatment of alcohol dependence. Alcohol Research and Health 33: 55–63.

Willenbring ML (2013) Gaps in clinical prevention and treatment for alcohol use

disorders. Alcohol Research: Current Reviews 35: 238–243.

Willis TA, Walker C, Mendoza D, et al. (2006) Behavioral and emotional self-control: Relations to substance use in samples of middle and high school students. Psychology of Addictive Behaviors 20: 265–278.

Wilson G, Lawson DM (1976) Effects of alcohol on sexual arousal in women. Journal of Abnormal Psychology 85: 489–497.

Wilson RI, Nicoll RA (2001) Endogenous cannabinoids mediate retrograde signaling at hippocampal synapses. Nature 410: 558–592.

Wilson SJ, Creswell KG, Sayette MA, et al. (2013) Ambivalence about smoking and cue-elicited neural activity in quitting-motivated smokers faced with an opportunity to smoke. Addictive Behaviors 38: 1541–1549.

Wilson SJ, Sayette MA (2014) Neuroimaging craving: urge intensity matters. Addiction 110: 195–203.

Windle M (2016) Drinking over the lifespan: Focus on early adolescents and youth. Alcohol Research: Current Reviews 38: 95–101.

Windle M, Scheidt D (2004) Alcoholic subtypes: Are two sufficient? Addiction 99: 1508–1519.

Wing VC, Bacher I, Sacco KA, et al. (2011) Neuropsychological performance in patients with schizophrenia and controls as a function of cigarette smoking status. Psychiatry Research 188: 320–326.

Wing VC, Payer DE, Houle S, et al. (2015) Measuring cigarette smoking-induced cortical dopamine release: A [11 C]

FLB-457 PET study. Neuropsychopharmacology **40**: 1417–1427.

Winstanley C, Dalley J, Theobald D, et al. (2004) Fractionating impulsivity: Contrasting effects of central 5-HT depletion on different measures of impulsive behavior. Neuropsychopharmacology **29**: 1331–1343.

Wise R (1998) Drug-activation of brain reward pathways. Drug and Alcohol Dependence **51**: 13–22.

Witkiewitz K, Bowen S (2010) Depression, craving and substance use following a randomized trial of mindfulness-based relapse prevention. Journal of Consulting and Clinical Psychology **78**: 362–374.

Witkiewitz K, Marlatt GA (2004) Relapse prevention for alcohol and drug problems: That was Zen, this is Tao. American Psychologist **59**: 224–235.

Witkiewitz K, Vowles KE (2018) Alcohol and opioid use, co-use, and chronic pain in the context of the opioid epidemic: A critical review. *Alcoholism Clinical and Experimental Research.* Advance online publication.

Woloshin S, Schwartz LM, Welch HG (2002) Risk charts: Putting cancer in context. Journal of the National Cancer Institute **94**: 799–804.

Woods JH, France CP, Winger G, et al. (1993) Opioid abuse liability assessment in rhesus monkeys. In Herz A (ed.) Opioids II: Handbook of Experimental Pharmacology. New York: Springer.

Woods JH, Winger G (1995) Current benzodiazepine issues. Psychopharmacology **118**: 107–115.

Woodward B (1984) Wired: The Short Life and Fast Times of John Belushi. New York: Simon and Schuster.

Workgroup on Substance Use Disorders, American Psychiatric Association Steering Committee on Practice Guidelines (2006) Treatment of patients with substance use disorders, second edition. American Journal of Psychiatry **163**(Suppl. 8): 5–82.

World Health Organization (1992) The ICD-10 Classification of Mental and Behavioral Disorders: Clinical and Diagnostic Guidelines. Geneva: World Health Organization.

World Health Organization (2008) The Global Burden of Disease: 2004 Update. Geneva: World Health Organization.

World Health Organization (2014) WHO Global Status Report on Alcohol and Health 2014. Geneva: World Health Organization.

Wright BT, Gluszek CF, Heldt SA (2014) The effects of repeated zolpidem treatment on tolerance, withdrawal-like symptoms and GABA-A receptor mRNAs profile of expression in mice: Comparison with diazepam. Psychopharmacology **231**: 2967–2971.

Wu L-T, Blazer DT, Patkar AA, et al. (2009) Heterogeneity of stimulant dependence: A national drug abuse treatment clinical trials network study. American Journal of Addiction **18**: 206–218.

Wu L-T, Schlenger WE, Galvin DM (2006) Concurrent use of methamphetamine, MDMA, LSD, ketamine, GHB, and flunitrazepam among American youths. Drug and Alcohol Dependence **84**: 102–113.

Wu L-T, Woody GE, Yang C, et al. (2011) How do prescription opioid users differ from users of heroin or other drugs in psychopathology. Journal of Addiction Medicine **5**: 28–35.

Wu TC, Tashkin DP, Djaheb B, et al. (1988) Pulmonary hazards of smoking marijuana as compared with tobacco. New England Journal of Medicine **31**: 347–351.

Wu L-T, Zhu H, Mannelli P, et al. (2017) Prevalence and correlates of treatment utilization among adults with cannabis use disorder in the United States. Drug and Alcohol Dependence **17**: 153–162.

Wurtzel E (2002) More, Now, Again: A Memoir of Addiction. New York: Simon and Schuster.

Wynder EL, Hoffman D (1979) Tobacco and health: A societal challenge. New England Journal of Medicine **300**: 894–903.

Xie P, Kranzler HR, Zhang H, et al. (2012) Childhood adversity increases risk for nicotine dependence and interacts with a5 nicotinic acetylcholine receptor genotype specifically in males. Neuropsychopharmacology **37**: 669–676.

Yalisove D (2004) Introduction to Alcohol Research: Implications for Treatment, Prevention, and Policy. Boston: Pearson Education.

Yancy JR, Venables NC, Hicks BM, et al. (2013) Evidence for a heritable brain basis to deviance-promoting deficits in self-control. Journal of Criminal Justice **41**: 1–13.

Yang YK, Nelson L, Kamaraju L, et al. (2002) Nicotine decreases bradykinesia-rigidity in haloperidol-treated patients with schizophrenia. Neuropsychopharmacology **27**: 684–686.

Yazar-Klosinski BB, Mithoefer MC (2017) Potential psychiatric uses for MDMA. Clinical Pharmacological Therapeutics **101**: 194–196.

Yeh PH, Gzdzinski S, Durazzo TC (2007) Hierarchical linear modeling (HLM) of longitudinal brain structural and cognitive changes in alcohol-dependent individuals during sobriety. Drug and Alcohol Dependence **91**: 195–204.

Yoder KK, Albrecht DA, Dzemidzic M, et al. (2016) Differences in IV alcohol-induced dopamine release in the ventral striatum of social drinkers and non-treatment-seeking alcoholics. Drug and Alcohol Dependence **160**: 163–169.

Yoder KK, Kareken DA, Seyoum RA, et al. (2005) Dopamine D2 receptor availability is associated with subjective responses to alcohol. Alcholism: Clinical and Experimental Research **29**: 965–970.

Yoon JH, Higgins ST, Heil SH, et al. (2007) Delay discounting predicts postpartum relapse to cigarette smoking among pregnant women. Experimental and Clincal Psychopharmacology **15**: 176–186.

Young KA, Franklin TR, Roberts DCS, et al. (2014) Nipping cue reactivity in the bud: Baclofen prevents limbic activation elicited by subliminal drug cues. Journal of Neuroscience **34**: 5038–5043.

Young RM, Lawford BR, Nutting A, et al. (2004) Advances in molecular genetics and the prevention and treatment of substance misuse: Implications of association studies of the A1 allele of the D2 dopamine receptor gene. Addictive Behavior **29**: 1275–1294.

Young-Wolff KC, Kendler KS, Ericson ML, et al. (2011) Accounting for the association between childhood maltreatment and alcohol-use disorders in males: A twin study. Psychological Medicine **41**: 59–70.

Yucel M, Lubman D (2007) Neurocognitive and neuroimaging evidence of behavioural dysregulation in human drug addiction: Implications for diagnosis, treatment and prevention. Drug and Alcohol Reviews **26**: 33–39.

Yucel M, Lubman D, Solowij N, et al. (2007) Understanding drug addiction: A neuropsychological perspective. Australian and New Zealand Journal of Psychiatry **41**: 957–968.

Zacny J, Bigelow G, Compton P, et al. (2003) College on problems of drug dependence taskforce on prescription opioid non-medical use and abuse: Position statement. Drug and Alcohol Dependence **69**: 215–232.

Zahr NM, Pfefferbaum A (2017) Alcohol's effect on the brain: Neuroimaging results in humans and animal models. Alcohol Research: Current Reviews **38**: 183–206.

Zammit S, Arseneault L, Cannon M, et al. (2012) Does cannabis use cause schizophrenia? The epidemiological evidence. In Castle D, Murray RM, D'Souza DC (eds.) Marijuana and Madness. 2nd ed. Cambridge: Cambridge University Press.

Zanarini MC, Frankenburg FR, Hennen J, et al. (2004) Axis I comorbidity in patients with borderline personality disorder: 6-year follow-up and prediction of time to remission. American Journal of Psychiatry **161**: 2108–2114.

Zeidonis D, Hitsman B, Beckham JC, et al. (2008) Tobacco use and cessation in psychiatric disorders: National Institute of Mental Health Report. Nicotine and Tobacco Research **10**: 1691–1715.

Zeidonis DM, Williams JM (2003) Management of smoking in people with psychiatric disorders. Current Opinion in Psychiatry **16**: 305–315.

Zeman MV, Hiraki L, Sellers EM (2002) Gender differences in tobacco smoking: Higher relative exposure to smoke than nicotine in women. Journal of Women's Health Gender Based Medicine **11**: 147–153.

Zerhouni O, Begue L, Brousse G, et al. (2013) Alcohol and violence in the emergency room: A review and perspectives from psychological and social sciences. International Journal of Environmental and Public Health **10**: 4584–4606.

Zevin S, Benowitz NL (1998) Pharmacokinetics and pharmacodynamics of nicotine. In Piasecki M, Newhause P (eds.) Nicotine: Neurotropic and Neurotoxic Effects. Washington, DC: American Psychiatric Press.

Zgierska A, Rabago D, Chawla N, et al. (2009) Mindfulness meditation for substance use disorders: A systematic review. Substance Abuse **30**: 266–294.

Ziedonis DM, Hitsman B, Beckham JC, et al. (2008) Tobacco use and cessation in psychiatric disorders: National Institute of Mental Health report. Nicotine and Tobacco Research **10**: 1691–1715.

Zilberman ML (2009) Substance abuse across the lifespan in women. In Brady KT, Back SE, Greenfield SF (eds.) Women and Addiction: A Comprehensive Handbook. New York: Guilford Press.

Zilberman ML, Tavares H, Blume SB, et al. (2003) Substance use disorders: Sex differences in psychiatric comorbidities. Canadian Journal of Psychiatry **48**: 5–5.

Zimmerman P, Wittchen H, Hofler M, et al. (2003) Primary anxiety disorders and the development of subsequent alcohol use disorders: A 4-year community study of adolescents and young adults. Psychological Medicine **33**: 1211–1222.

Zimmerman U, Spring K, Kunz-Ebrecht SR, et al. (2004) Effect of ethanol on hypothalamic-pituitary-adrenal system response to psychosocial stress in sons of alcohol-dependent fathers. Neuropsychopharmacology **29**: 1156–1165.

Zindel LR, Kranzler HR (2014) Pharmacotherapy of alcohol use disorders: Seventy-five years of progress. Journal of Studies on Alcohol and Drugs **75**: 79–88.

Zorick T, Nestor L, Miotto K, et al. (2010) Withdrawal symptoms in abstinent methamphetamine-dependent subjects. Addiction **105**: 1809–1818.

Zuccoli G, Siddiqui N, Cravo I, et al. (2010) Neuroimaging findings in alcohol-related encephalopathies. American Journal of Roentgenology **195**: 1378–1384.

Zuckerman B, Frank DA, Hingson R (1989) Effects of maternal marijuana and cocaine use on fetal growth. New England Journal of Medicine **320**: 762–768.

Zuckerman M (1994) Behavioral Expressions and Biosocial Bases of Sensation Seeking. New York: Cambridge University Press.

Zulauf CA, Sprich SE, Safaren SA, et al. (2014) The complicated relationship between attention/deficit hyperactivity disorder and substance use disorders. Current Psychiatry Reports **16**: 436–442.

Zvolensky MJ, Schmidt NB, McCreary BT (2003) The impact of smoking on panic disorder: An initial investigation of a pathoplastic relatiohship. Journal of Anxiety Disorders **17**: 447–460.

Zweben JE, Cohen JB, Christian D, et al. (2004) Psychiatric symptoms in methamphetamine users. American Journal on Addictions **13**: 181–190.

Index